Ultimate
Sacrifice

Ultimate Sacrifice

John and Robert Kennedy, the Plan for a Coup in Cuba, and the Murder of JFK

LAMAR WALDRON
WITH THOM HARTMANN

CARROLL & GRAF PUBLISHERS

NEW YORK

To my wonderful parents.

To Bill, Mary, Paul, Gary,
and the many others whose
decades of hard work paved the way.

ULTIMATE SACRIFICE:
John and Robert Kennedy, the Plan for a Coup in Cuba, and the Murder of JFK

Carroll & Graf Publishers
An Imprint of Avalon Publishing Group Inc.
245 West 17th Street
11th Floor
New York, NY 10011

AVALON
publishing group incorporated

Copyright © 2005 by Lamar Waldron

First Carroll & Graf edition 2005

ISBN-10: 0-7867-1441-7
ISBN-13: 987-0-78671-441-4

9 8 7 6 5 4 3 2 1

Interior design by Maria E. Torres
Index by Melody Englund, Songbird Indexing Services
Printed in the United States of America
Distributed by Publishers Group West

contents

PART TWO

PART THREE

Introduction

FOR MORE THAN FOUR DECADES since his death in 1963, John F. Kennedy has captured the imagination of the American people. Myth and conjecture have swirled around JFK, his political legacy, his family, and its multiple tragedies. Admirers and critics have examined every detail of his life and work, gradually lifting one veil after another to shed new light on his presidency, from his maneuvering behind the scenes during the Cuban Missile Crisis to his personal weaknesses. Nonetheless, the secret with the most profound and catastrophic effect on America has remained hidden. *Ultimate Sacrifice* reveals this secret for the first time, transforming the history of the Kennedy years and providing the missing piece to one of the great puzzles of post-war America: the true circumstances behind JFK's assassination on November 22, 1963.

Seventeen years ago, Thom Hartmann and I began writing a book about the battles of President Kennedy and his brother, Attorney General Robert F. Kennedy, against the Mafia and Fidel Castro. Drawing on new information and exclusive interviews with those who worked with the Kennedys, in addition to thousands of recently declassified files, we discovered that John and Robert Kennedy had devised and were executing a secret plan to overthrow Fidel Castro on December 1, 1963. "The Plan for a Coup in Cuba" (as it was titled in a memo for the Joint Chiefs of Staff) would include a "palace coup" to eliminate Castro, allowing a new Cuban "Provisional Government" to step into the power vacuum, and would be supported by a "full-scale invasion" of Cuba by the US military, if necessary.[1]

The "Plan for a Coup in Cuba" was fully authorized by JFK and personally run by Robert Kennedy. Only about a dozen people in the US government knew the full scope of the plan, all of whom worked for either the military, the CIA, or reported directly to Robert. The Kennedys' plan was prepared primarily by the US military, with the CIA playing a major supporting role. Input was also obtained from key officials in a few other agencies, but most of those who worked on the plan knew only about carefully compartmentalized aspects, believing it to be a theoretical exercise in case a Cuban official volunteered to depose Fidel.

Unique and different from any previously disclosed operation, the Kennedys' "Plan for a Coup in Cuba" is revealed in this book for the first time. The CIA's code name for their part of the coup plan has never surfaced in any book, article, or government investigation. Officially declassified in 1999, "AMWORLD" is the cryptonym the CIA used for the plan in its classified internal documents. Since the overall coup plan was under the personal control of Attorney General Kennedy, who did not use a code-name for it, we call it "C-Day" in this book, a name entirely of our own invention. Its evocation of D-Day is intentional, since the Kennedys' plan included the possibility of a US military invasion.

C-Day was undoubtedly one of the most secret covert operations in United States history. In its secrecy, however, lay tragedy. Even though the Kennedys' coup plan never came to fruition, three powerful Mafia dons—Carlos Marcello, Santo Trafficante, and Johnny Rosselli—learned of the plan and realized that the government would go to any lengths to avoid revealing it to the public. With that knowledge, the three mob bosses were able to assassinate JFK in a way that forced the truth to be buried for over forty years.

Marcello, Trafficante, and Rosselli undertook this extraordinary act of vengeance in order to halt the Kennedy administration's unrelenting prosecution of them and their allies. The Kennedy Justice Department had vigorously pursued Marcello, even subjecting him to a brief, nightmarish deportation. Once he returned, Marcello hated the Kennedy brothers with a deep and vengeful passion. The two other Mafia bosses suffered similar pursuit, and eventually Marcello, Trafficante, and Rosselli decided that their only way to avoid prison or deportation was to kill JFK. Our investigation has produced clear evidence that the crime bosses arranged the assassination so that any thorough investigation would expose the Kennedys' C-Day coup plan. They were confident that any such exposure could push America to the brink of war with Cuba and the Soviet Union, meaning that they could assassinate JFK with relative impunity.

They did not carry out the act themselves, but used trusted associates and unwitting proxies. The most widely known are Jack Ruby and Lee Harvey

Oswald, who were both in contact with associates of Marcello, Trafficante, and Rosselli in the months before the assassination. Reports in government files show that Oswald and Ruby knew about parts of the Kennedys' plan and even discussed it with others.

Robert Kennedy told several close associates that Carlos Marcello was behind JFK's death, but he couldn't reveal what he knew to the public or to the Warren Commission without C-Day being uncovered. As this book shows, RFK and other key government officials worried that exposure of the plan could trigger another nuclear confrontation with the Soviets, just a year after the Cuban Missile Crisis.

None of the seven governmental committees that investigated aspects of the assassination, including the Warren Commission, were officially told about the Kennedys' C-Day plan.[2] However, over the decades, each successive committee came increasingly close to discovering both the plan and the associates of Marcello who assassinated JFK. We were able to piece together the underlying story by building on the work of those committees, former government investigators, and revelations in four million documents that were declassified in the 1990s. Key to our efforts were new and often exclusive interviews with many Kennedy insiders who worked on the coup plan or dealt with its consequences, some of whom revealed aspects of JFK's assassination and the coup plan for the first time. They include Secretary of State Dean Rusk, Press Secretary Pierre Salinger, and the Kennedys' top Cuban-exile aide, Enrique "Harry" Ruiz-Williams. Their inside information allows us to tell the story, even though a 1998 report about the JFK Assassinations Records Review Board confirms that "well over a million CIA records" related to JFK's murder have not yet been released.[3] NBC News' Tom Brokaw confirmed on his September 29, 1998 broadcast that "millions" of pages remain secret and won't be released until the year 2017.[4]

By necessity, *Ultimate Sacrifice* examines this complex story from several angles. Part One documents every aspect of the Kennedys' C-Day plan and how it developed, beginning with the Cuban Missile Crisis. Though it is widely believed that JFK agreed not to invade Cuba in order to end the Cuban Missile Crisis in the fall of 1962, Secretary of State Rusk told us that the "no-invasion" pledge was conditional upon Castro's agreement to on-site UN inspections for nuclear weapons of mass destruction (a term that JFK first used). Historians at the National Security Archive confirmed that because Castro refused such inspections, the pledge against invasion never went into effect.[5] Consequently, in the spring of 1963, John and Robert Kennedy started laying the groundwork for a coup against Fidel Castro that would eventually be set for December 1, 1963.

Robert Kennedy put the invasion under the control of the Defense Department because of the CIA's handling of 1961's Bay of Pigs disaster. The "Plan for a Coup in Cuba," as written by JFK's Secretary of the Army Cyrus Vance with the help of the State Department and the CIA, called for the coup leader to "neutralize" Cuban leader "Fidel Castro and . . . [his brother] Raul" in a "palace coup." Then, the coup leader would "declare martial law" and "proclaim a Provisional Government" that would include previously "selected Cuban exile leaders" who would enter from their bases in Latin America.[6] Then, at the invitation of the new government, after "publicly announcing US intent to support the Provisional Government, the US would initiate overt logistical and air support to the insurgents" including destroying "those air defenses which might endanger the air movement of US troops into the area." After the "initial air attacks" would come "the rapid, incremental introduction of balanced forces, to include full-scale invasion" if necessary. The first US military forces into Cuba would be a multiracial group of "US military-trained free Cubans," all veterans of the Bay of Pigs.[7] Upon presidential authorization, the US would "recognize [the] Provisional Government . . . warn [the] Soviets not to intervene" and "assist the Provisional Government in preparing for . . . free elections."[8]

This "palace coup" would be led by one of Castro's inner circle, himself a well-known revolutionary hero.[9] This man, the coup leader, would cause Castro's death, but without taking the credit or blame for doing so. The coup leader would be part of the new Provisional Government in Cuba, along with a select group of Cuban exiles—approved by the Kennedys—who ranged from conservative to progressive.[10] The identity of the coup leader is known to the authors, and has been confirmed by Kennedy associates and declassified documents. However, US national security laws may prevent the direct disclosure of past US intelligence assets even long after their deaths, so we will not directly name the coup leader in this book. Since we have no desire to violate national security laws or endanger US intelligence assets, we will only disclose official information that has been declassified or is available in the historical record.

We have uncovered historical accounts of Cuban leaders that have been long overlooked by the public or are in newly released government files. For example, a formerly secret cable sent to the CIA director on December 10, 1963—just nine days after the original date for the C-Day coup—reports "Che Guevara was alleged to be under house arrest for plotting to overthrow Castro," according to "a Western diplomat."[11] Newly declassified documents and other research cast Che's growing disenchantment with Fidel Castro in a new light. These revelations include Che's secret meetings with three people close to the Kennedys, followed by yet another house arrest after a C-Day exile leader was captured in Cuba.

The Kennedys did not see C-Day as an assassination operation, but rather as an effort to help Cubans overthrow a Cuban dictator. A June 1963 CIA memo from one of Robert Kennedy's Cuban subcommittees of the National Security Council explains the Kennedy policy as "Cubans inside Cuba and outside Cuba, working" together to free their own country.[12] Nor was C-Day an attempt to install another US-backed dictator in Cuba, like the corrupt Batista regime that had been overthrown by Castro and many others on January 1, 1959. The Kennedys' goal in 1963 was simply a free and democratic Cuba.

As several Kennedy associates told us, the only man who knew everything about C-Day was Robert Kennedy, the plan's guiding force.[13] Secretary of the Army Cyrus Vance was one of the few military leaders who knew the full scope of C-Day while the plan was active. The others were generals the Kennedys especially trusted, including Chairman of the Joint Chiefs of Staff Maxwell Taylor and General Joseph Carroll, head of the Defense Intelligence Agency (DIA). High CIA officials involved in C-Day included CIA Director John McCone, Deputy Director for Plans Richard Helms, Desmond FitzGerald, and key field operatives like David Morales and David Atlee Phillips. Most high US officials didn't know about C-Day prior to JFK's assassination. There is no evidence that Lyndon Johnson was told anything about C-Day prior to JFK's death. Likewise, no evidence exists showing that Secretary of Defense Robert McNamara knew about C-Day before JFK's assassination. Dean Rusk told us he did not learn about the actual C-Day plan until soon after JFK's death.[14] There is no evidence that Edward Kennedy was told about the plan. Documents and sources indicate that FBI Director J. Edgar Hoover had no active role in C-Day, although he may have learned a great deal about it from field reports. The Secret Service was even less informed about C-Day, which no doubt hindered their actions when serious threats seemingly related to Cuba surfaced against JFK in the weeks before C-Day.

However, officials ranging from Dean Rusk to hawkish Air Force Chief of Staff General Curtis LeMay were needed for the planning of C-Day, so the Kennedys used a shrewd technique that let those officials participate in planning for C-Day while keeping them in the dark about the plan itself. Rusk, LeMay, and others were simply told that all the planning was needed "just in case" a coup happened in Cuba. Officials like Rusk and LeMay were generally aware of other CIA efforts against Castro in the fall of 1963, such as the CIA's AMTRUNK operation, which looked for disaffected Cuban military officers. Some US officials also knew about a CIA asset named Rolando Cubela, a disgruntled mid-level Cuban official who the CIA code-named AMLASH. However, unlike AMWORLD—the CIA's portion of C-Day—neither of those operations reached high in the Cuban government or was close to producing results in the fall of 1963. The Kennedys' "just in case" technique allowed extensive planning to be done for all facets of the military invasion and the post-coup Provisional Government without revealing C-Day or the coup leader's identity to most of those doing the planning. If the C-Day coup had actually occurred, Rusk and the other officials not privy to the full plan would nonetheless have been fully prepared for its aftermath, with plans they had already approved and helped create.[15]

While such tightly compartmentalized secrecy kept C-Day from becoming widely known within the government and protected C-Day from public exposure, it also contributed to JFK's death. In 1963, the public would have been shocked to learn that two months before JFK was shot in Dallas, US officials under the direction of Robert Kennedy began making contingency plans to deal with the "assassination of American officials."[16] In the event of an assassination (expected to happen only outside the US), these contingency plans would have mandated certain security measures, and, as this book documents, such principles would be applied to and responsible for much of the secrecy surrounding the JFK assassination.

Robert Kennedy and the others making the contingency plans were concerned only about possible retaliation by Castro for C-Day. They failed to consider the threat from others the Attorney General had targeted, especially Mafia bosses Carlos Marcello, Santo Trafficante, and Johnny Rosselli. The Kennedys and key aides had gone to great lengths to keep the Mafia out of C-Day. The CIA's earlier efforts with the Mafia to assassinate Castro—which began in 1959 under Vice President Richard Nixon—had complicated the Kennedys' intense prosecution of the Mafia. Without telling the Kennedys, the CIA was continuing to work with the Mafia on plots against Castro in the fall of 1963, which helped to allow associates of Marcello, Trafficante, and Rosselli to infiltrate the plans for C-Day.

In Part II, we will show how—and why—mob bosses Carlos Marcello, Santo Trafficante, and Johnny Rosselli worked together to penetrate the Kennedys' C-Day plan and assassinate JFK. In 1963, Carlos Marcello was America's most ruthless and secretive Mafia boss, completely free of FBI wiretaps. From his New Orleans headquarters, he ruled a territory that included Louisiana, Mississippi, and parts of Texas and Alabama.[17] Marcello's Mafia family was the oldest in North America, able to stage major "hits" without needing the approval of the national Mafia organization, and his associates had a long history of targeting government officials who got in their way.[18] The Kennedys had pursued Marcello since 1959, even before JFK was elected president. Recently declassified FBI documents confirm that just a few years before his own death, Carlos Marcello confessed on three occasions to informants that he had had JFK killed.[19]

Tampa godfather Santo Trafficante was Marcello's closest Mafia ally. Trafficante's territory included much of Florida, as well as parts of Alabama, and his organization provided a major conduit for the French Connection heroin trade, whose primary routes included New York City, Texas, New Orleans, Georgia's Fort Benning, Montreal, Chicago, and Mexico City. The Internet magazine *Salon* noted that Trafficante "had been driven out of the lucrative Havana casino business by Castro and" that he "had been recruited in the CIA" plots with the Mafia to kill Castro months before JFK became president.[20] Like Marcello, Trafficante later confessed his involvement in JFK's assassination.[21]

Johnny Rosselli, according to his biographers, also claimed to know what had really happened in Dallas, and he sometimes worked with both Trafficante and Marcello. Rosselli was the Chicago Mafia's point man in Hollywood and Las Vegas, and his close friends included Frank Sinatra and Marilyn Monroe. Internal CIA reports admit that they recruited Rosselli and Trafficante for their own plots to assassinate Castro prior to JFK's election in 1960. Unknown to the Kennedys, Rosselli was continuing in that role in the fall of 1963.[22]

Jack Ruby met with Rosselli just weeks before JFK's assassination, had met much earlier with Santo Trafficante, and had numerous ties to Carlos Marcello, according to government investigators.[23] *Ultimate Sacrifice* reveals new information from Pierre Salinger—a member of the Kennedys' first organized crime investigation team—that just weeks before Jack Ruby shot Oswald, Ruby received a large payoff in Chicago from someone working for a close ally of Marcello and Trafficante.[24] Ruby also made surprising comments that wound in up the Warren Commission's files but not in their report. Just weeks after Ruby's arrest for shooting Oswald in 1963, an FBI document quotes Ruby as talking about "an invasion of Cuba" that "was being sponsored by the United States Government."[25]

Ultimate Sacrifice shows how Carlos Marcello, Santo Trafficante, and Johnny Rosselli were able to keep their roles in JFK's death from being exposed because they had infiltrated C-Day. Long-secret government files confirm that ten men who worked for the mob bosses had learned about C-Day. Five of those ten actually worked on C-Day, giving the Mafia chieftains a pipeline directly into C-Day and the plans for keeping it secret. Less than a dozen trusted associates of the mob bosses were knowingly involved in the hit on JFK.

Though Mafia hits against officials are rare, the Mafia families of Carlos Marcello, Santo Trafficante, and Johnny Rosselli had killed officials who threatened their survival. Nine years earlier, Santo Trafficante's organization had helped to assassinate the newly elected Attorney General of Alabama because he was preparing to shut down Trafficante's operations in notoriously corrupt Phenix City.[26] In 1957, associates of Marcello and Rosselli assassinated the president of Guatemala, a murder that was quickly blamed on a seemingly lone Communist patsy who, like Lee Harvey Oswald, was then killed before he could stand trial. Just nine months before JFK's murder in November 1963, Rosselli's Chicago Mafia family had successfully assassinated a Chicago city official, using an associate of Jack Ruby.[27]

The House Select Committee on Assassinations (HSCA) found in 1979 that Marcello and Trafficante had had the means and the motive to assassinate JFK. Before the HSCA could question Rosselli, he "was kidnapped, murdered, dismembered, and sunk" in the ocean in an oil drum that later surfaced.[28] But the CIA didn't tell the HSCA about AMWORLD or other aspects of C-Day, so the HSCA couldn't uncover exactly how Marcello and Trafficante did it or Rosselli's role in working with them. Newly declassified files, many unavailable to the HSCA, show that Marcello, Trafficante, and Rosselli penetrated C-Day and used parts of it as cover to assassinate JFK.

By using the secrecy surrounding C-Day, the mob bosses could target JFK not only in Dallas, but also in two earlier attempts, one of which is revealed in this book for the first time. They first attempted to kill JFK in Chicago on November 2, 1963, and then in Tampa on November 18, before succeeding in Dallas on November 22. Since Chicago was home to Rosselli's Mafia family, Tampa was Trafficante's headquarters, and Dallas was in Marcello's territory, the risk was shared between the three bosses. While the Chicago attempt—thwarted when JFK canceled his motorcade at the last minute— was briefly noted by Congressional investigators in the 1970s, the attempt to assassinate JFK during his long Tampa motorcade has never been disclosed in any book or government report. It was withheld from the Warren Commission and all later investigations, even though the Tampa plot was uncovered by authorities and revealed to JFK before he began his motorcade —which he continued, despite the danger.

With C-Day set to begin the following week, JFK planned to give a speech in Miami just hours after his trip to Tampa, a speech that included a message written to the C-Day coup leader in Cuba that promised him JFK's personal support.[29] Canceling the Tampa motorcade simply wasn't an option for JFK or Bobby, even though the motorcade would reportedly be the longest of JFK's presidency, slowly making its way past teeming crowds and many unsecured buildings. Our interviews with officials from Florida law enforcement and the Secret Service, supported by newspaper files and declassified CIA and FBI documents, reveal that the Tampa attempt to kill JFK shares a dozen striking parallels to what happened in Dallas four days later. They include a young male suspect who was a former defector with links to both the Fair Play for Cuba Committee and Russia, just like Lee Harvey Oswald. As in Dallas, JFK's Tampa motorcade also included a hard left turn in front of a tall red-brick building with many unguarded windows—a key site that officials feared might be used by snipers to target JFK.

John and Robert Kennedy kept the Tampa assassination attempt secret at the time, and Robert Kennedy kept it secret until his death in 1968. The Secret Service, FBI, CIA, and other agencies have similarly maintained silence about it, as well as keeping secret other information about the assassination that might have exposed the Kennedys' C-Day coup plan. In November 1994, the authors first informed the JFK Assassination Review Board about the Tampa assassination attempt. The Review Board had been created by Congress in 1992 and appointed by President Clinton soon after, to release all the JFK records. But just weeks after we told the Board about the Tampa attempt, the Secret Service destroyed their records for that time period. That does not implicate the Secret Service or the FBI or the CIA (as an organization) in JFK's assassination. As the book shows, officials were forced into such cover-ups because the Mafia bosses had tied the potentially destabilizing C-Day plan to their attempts to assassinate JFK in Chicago, Tampa, and finally Dallas.

Within hours of JFK's assassination, Robert Kennedy suspected that someone linked to Marcello and Trafficante, and to C-Day, was involved in his brother's death. The afternoon of JFK's death, Robert Kennedy revealed his suspicion to Pulitzer Prize–winning reporter Haynes Johnson, who was meeting with C-Day exile leader Enrique "Harry" Ruiz-Williams.[30] Evan Thomas, author of a biography of Robert Kennedy and a *Newsweek* editor, said "Robert Kennedy had a fear that he had somehow gotten his own brother killed" and that his "attempts to prosecute the mob and to kill Castro had backfired in some terrible way."[31] It has been publicly known only since 1992 that Robert Kennedy told a few close advisers that New Orleans mob boss Marcello was behind JFK's assassination, as we confirmed with Kennedy aide Richard Goodwin. *Salon* received additional confirmation of Mafia involvement from Robert Kennedy's former press secretary, Frank Mankiewicz, who conducted a secret investigation of JFK's death for Robert.[32]

Goodwin and Mankiewicz are just two of over a dozen associates of Robert Kennedy who either heard his belief in a conspiracy in his brother's death or who believe in a conspiracy themselves. Among them are Justice Department prosecutors Ronald Goldfarb, Robert Blakey, and Walter Sheridan, as well as Robert's first biographer, Jack Newfield. Others include JFK's CIA Director John McCone, the President's personal physician at his autopsy Admiral George Burkley, and JFK aides Dave Powers, Kenneth O'Donnell, and Arthur Schlesinger, Jr.[33] This book adds to that list Pierre Salinger and Robert's top Cuban exile aide "Harry" Ruiz-Williams, plus another Kennedy aide who worked on C-Day. Most of those associates of Robert Kennedy point to a conspiracy involving Carlos Marcello or his close allies.

In suspecting that C-Day was such a powerful weapon, history has proven the Mafia bosses correct. JFK's death threw the whole US government into turmoil, but the intelligence agencies were especially frantic: Their numerous and extensive anti-Castro plots were so secret that they needed to be kept not only from the Congress and the public, but also from the Warren Commission.

Although many Warren Commission findings were discredited by later government investigators, Evan Thomas recently told ABC News that the commission achieved its real purpose. He said that after JFK's assassination, "the most important thing the United States government wanted to do was reassure the public that there was not some plot, not some Russian attack, not some Cuban attack." As a result, Thomas concluded, "the number one goal throughout the upper levels of the government was to calm that fear, and bring a sense of reassurance that this really was the work of a lone gunman."[34]

President Lyndon Johnson and the Warren Commission were also under tremendous time pressure: With Johnson facing an election in less than a year, the Commission had to assemble a staff, review and take testimony, and issue their final report just ten months after JFK's death. "There was a cover-up," Evan Thomas confirmed to ABC News, explaining that in the Warren Commission's "haste to reassure everybody, they created an environment that was sure to come around and bite them." He emphasized that Earl Warren, Lyndon B. Johnson, J. Edgar Hoover, and others were not covering up a plot to kill JFK, as some have speculated. Instead, they covered up "for their own internal bureaucratic reasons—because Hoover wanted to keep his job, and because Bobby Kennedy didn't want to be embarrassed, or the CIA didn't want to have the public know they were trying to kill somebody," like Fidel Castro.[35]

It was not until 2004 that Joseph Califano, assistant to Secretary of the Army Cyrus Vance in 1963, briefly hinted at the sensitive operation that Robert Kennedy had managed and had withheld from the Warren Commission. Califano wrote: "No one on the Warren Commission . . . talked to me or (so far as I know) anyone else involved in the covert attacks on Castro. . . . The Commission was not informed of any of the efforts of Desmond FitzGerald, the CIA and Robert Kennedy to eliminate Castro and stage a coup" in the fall of 1963.[36]

Since Robert Kennedy knew more about C-Day than anyone else, his death in 1968 helped to ensure that C-Day stayed secret from all later government investigations into the assassination. The anti-Castro operations of the 1960s that were hidden from the Warren Commission only started to be uncovered by the investigations spawned by Watergate in the 1970s: the Senate Watergate Committee (which took secret testimony from Johnny Rosselli), the Rockefeller Commission, the Pike Committee, and the Church Committee.[37] More details about those CIA plots were uncovered by the House Select Committee on Assassinations in the late 1970s, though many of their discoveries weren't declassified until the late 1990s by the Assassination Records Review Board (ARRB). C-Day, far more sensitive and secret than any of those anti-Castro plots, was never officially disclosed to any of those seven government committees.

The military nature of C-Day also helps to explain why it has escaped the efforts of historians and Congressional investigators for forty years. The C-Day coup plan approved by Joint Chiefs Chairman General Maxwell Taylor was understandably classified TOP SECRET when it was created in 1963. But twenty-six years later, the Joint Chiefs reviewed the coup plan documents and decided that they should still remain TOP SECRET.[38] The documents might have remained officially secret for additional decades, or forever, if not for the JFK Assassination Records Review Board, created by Congress in the wake of the furor surrounding the film *JFK*. After efforts by the authors and others, the Review Board finally located and declassified some of the C-Day files just a few years ago. However, someone who worked with the Review Board confirmed to a highly respected Congressional watchdog group, OMB Watch, that "well over one million CIA records" related to JFK's assassination have not yet been released.[39] The C-Day documents that have been released show just the tip of the iceberg, often filled with the names of CIA assets and operations whose files have never been released, even to Congressional investigators.

Part Three of *Ultimate Sacrifice* shows how C-Day affected history and continues to impact American lives. It provides a new perspective on LBJ's operations against Cuba, and how they impacted the war in Vietnam. *Ultimate Sacrifice* casts Watergate in a whole new light since it involved a dozen people linked to various aspects of C-Day.

On a more personal level, *Ultimate Sacrifice* also solves the tragedy of Abraham Bolden, the first black Presidential Secret Service agent, who was framed by the Mafia and sent to prison when he tried to tell the Warren Commission about the Chicago and Tampa assassination attempts against JFK. His career and life ruined, Bolden has spent the last forty years seeking a pardon.[40] Now, new information from the CIA and other sources shows that the man behind Bolden's framing was an associate of Rosselli and Trafficante, someone linked to JFK's assassination who had penetrated C-Day while working for the Mafia.

JFK made the ultimate sacrifice in his quest to bring democracy to Cuba using C-Day. Instead of staying safely in the White House, he put his own life on the line, first in Tampa and finally in Dallas. It has long been known that

JFK talked about his own assassination the morning before he was shot. He commented to an aide about how easy it would be for someone to shoot him from a building with a high-powered rifle. Just hours earlier, JFK had demonstrated to his wife Jackie how easily someone could have shot him with a pistol.[41] We now know the reason for JFK's comments, since he knew that assailants from Chicago and Tampa were still at large, and that he himself was getting ready to stage a coup against Castro the following week.

John Kennedy once said: "A man does what he must—in spite of personal consequences, in spite of obstacles and dangers." He didn't just mouth the slogan that Americans should be willing to "pay any price" and "bear any burden"—he paid the highest price, making the ultimate sacrifice a leader can make for his country. JFK had always been obsessed with courage, from PT-109 to *Profiles in Courage* to his steely resolve during the Cuban Missile Crisis.[42] So it's not surprising that he died as he had lived, demonstrating the courage that had obsessed him all his life, and making the ultimate sacrifice for his country.

Until 1988, we had no more interest in the JFK assassination than the average person—but the twenty-fifth anniversary of the JFK assassination spawned numerous books and articles, many of which focused on evidence that a conspiracy was involved in JFK's death. The only question seemed to be: Which conspiracy? Conspirators included anti-Castro forces, elements of the CIA, and the Mafia. We started to look more closely at what had already been published about the assassination. We felt that a book focused solely on Bobby Kennedy's battles against the Mafia and against Castro in 1963 might also yield some interesting perspectives on the JFK assassination. We expected the research to require reading a dozen books, looking at a few hundred documents, and trying to interview some Kennedy associates—something that might take a year at most. That was seventeen years, dozens of sources, hundreds of books, and hundreds of thousands of documents ago.

We started by looking at the work of the six government commissions (the Review Board had not yet been created) and focused on areas that previous writers hadn't been able to fully explore. When we compiled all that data into a massive database, we realized that their findings weren't mutually exclusive at all—in fact, when their data was grouped together, it filled in gaps and told a coherent story. Putting all their data together didn't make the conspiracy bigger, as one might have expected. It actually made it smaller, since it became clear—for example—that one conspirator could be a Cuban exile, a CIA asset, and also work for the Mafia. However, we were stymied because much key information was still classified, much of it involving anti-Castro operations and associates of godfathers such as Carlos Marcello. We needed to find someone who knew the information and would talk, or some type of document the government couldn't classify top secret—a newspaper, for instance.

Our first break came the day we discovered an article in the *Washington Post* dated October 17, 1989 about the tragic death of Pepe San Roman, the Cuban exile who had led the Kennedys' ill-fated Bay of Pigs invasion. One sentence caught our attention: It said that in 1963, Pepe's brother had been "sent by Robert Kennedy to Central American countries to seek aid for a second invasion" of Cuba.[43] We were puzzled. A "second invasion" of Cuba in 1963? Surely it must be wrong. None of the history books or government committees had ever mentioned a US invasion of Cuba planned for 1963. But a check of newspaper files from the summer and fall of 1963 uncovered a few articles confirming that there had been activity by Kennedy-backed Cuban exiles in Central America at that time.

In January 1990, we arranged to interview JFK's Secretary of State, Dean Rusk. When we asked him about the "second invasion" of Cuba in 1963, he confirmed that indeed there were such plans. They weren't the same as the CIA-Mafia plots, which he only learned about later. Nor were they the CIA's assassination plot with a mid-level Cuban official named Rolando Cubela. Rusk described the "second invasion" as a "coup" and said that it wasn't going to be just some Cuban exiles in boats like the Bay of Pigs, but would involve the US military. Rusk indicated that the "second invasion" plans were active at the time JFK died in November 1963 and that the plan was personally controlled by Bobby Kennedy, but that he, Rusk, hadn't learned about it until just after JFK's death.

We theorized that there might be some connection between JFK's assassination and the second invasion of Cuba. We asked ourselves why Bobby would cover up crucial information about his own brother's murder—especially if he thought Marcello was behind it. What could be more important than exposing his brother's killers? Well, during the Cold War, one thing that would be more important than the death of a president would be the deaths of millions of Americans in a nuclear exchange with the Soviets. Revealing such a plan after JFK's death, just a year after the tense nuclear standoff of the Cuban Missile Crisis, could have easily sparked a serious and dangerous confrontation with the Soviets. That fear could explain why so much about JFK's assassination had been covered up for so long. At the time, this was a very novel hypothesis, but we agreed that it made sense in light of what we had uncovered so far.

Slowly, over the next few years, we found scattered pieces of evidence. For example, at the National Security Archive in Washington, we found a partially censored memo from one of Bobby Kennedy's secretive subcommittees of the National Security Council that discussed "Contingency Plans" in case Fidel Castro retaliated against the US by attempting the "assassination of American officials." The memo was written just ten days before JFK's assassination, and talked about "the likelihood of a step-up in Castro-incited subversion and violence" in response to some US action.[44] The document had been declassified a year after the HSCA had finished its work, and had never been seen by any of the government commissions that had investigated the assassination.

We were shocked when Dave Powers, head of the John F. Kennedy Presidential Library in Boston and a close aide to JFK, vividly described seeing the shots from the "grassy knoll." Powers said he and fellow JFK aide Kenneth O'Donnell clearly saw the shots, since they were in the limo right behind JFK. Powers said they felt they were "riding into an ambush"—explaining for the first time why the driver of JFK's limo slowed after the first shot. Powers also described how he was pressured to change his story for the Warren Commission.[45] We quickly found confirmation of Power's account of the shots in the autobiography of former House Speaker Tip O'Neill (and later, from the testimony of two Secret Service agents in the motorcade with Powers and O'Donnell).[46]

Months after talking with Powers, we made another startling discovery: a planned attempt to kill JFK during his Tampa motorcade on November 18, 1963. It was mentioned in only two small Florida newspaper articles, each in just one edition of the newspaper and then only after JFK was killed in Dallas. Nothing appeared at the time of the threat, even though authorities had uncovered the plot prior to JFK's motorcade. It was clear that someone had suppressed the story.

We decided to pursue Cuban exile and Bay of Pigs veteran Enrique Ruiz-Williams, who had been interviewed by former FBI agent William Turner in 1973. Williams had told Turner that he had been working on the plan with high CIA officials in Washington—something rare for Cuban exiles—on November 22, 1963. The timing was right, since Rusk had told us that the coup/invasion plan was active when JFK died. A former Kennedy aide confirmed Williams's connection to Bobby and the CIA to William Turner. We eventually found Harry Williams, and in a most unlikely place: the snowy mountains of Colorado, about as far from the tropical climate of his native Cuba as one could imagine. Thoughtful and highly intelligent, he quickly grasped that we had done our homework and already knew many of the pieces of the puzzle—just not how they all fit together. Then in the twilight of his life, he wanted to see the truth come out, as long as the spotlight was kept away from him.

By the end of our second interview on that first trip, Harry had given us a detailed overview of the Kennedys' secret plan to overthrow Castro on December 1, 1963 and how it was connected to JFK's assassination. We finally understood how associates of Marcello, Trafficante, and Rosselli had learned of the plan and used parts of it against JFK—forcing Bobby Kennedy and key government officials into a much larger cover-up, to protect national security. After getting the overview of C-Day from Harry—and more details from the Kennedy associates he led us to—we were able to make sense of previously released documents that had baffled investigators for decades. In 1993 we gave a short presentation of our discoveries at a historical conference in Dallas that included top historians, journalists, and former government investigators. Some of those experts were able not only to get additional documents released by the Review Board, but also to provide us with additional information that they had previously uncovered. In 1994, a brief summary of our findings was featured on the History Channel and in *Vanity Fair*. In November 1994, we gave the Review Board written testimony about our discovery of the Tampa assassination attempt and the Kennedys' C-Day "Plan for a Coup in Cuba in the Fall of 1963" (the quote is from our actual submission). Three years later, in 1997, the Review Board located and released a trove of documents confirming what Harry had told us about C-Day, including the first declassified documents from fall 1963 entitled "Plan for a Coup in Cuba." It was only in 1998, after the Review Board had finished its work and submitted its final report to the president and Congress, that we learned that the Secret Service had destroyed records covering the Tampa attempt just weeks after we first revealed it to the Review Board.

It took us fifteen years to uncover the full story, bringing together all these files and obscure articles in one place—and that was only because we were able to build on decades of work by dedicated historians, journalists, and government investigators. We also had the help of almost two dozen people who had worked with John or Robert Kennedy, who told us what files to look for and gave us the framework for C-Day, especially Harry Williams. Now we can tell the full story in much more detail, quoting directly from hundreds of government documents from the National Archives. These files, many quoted for the first time, verify everything Kennedy insiders had told us, long before most of those files were released. The files support what we said publicly over ten years ago, to the Review Board, to the History Channel, and in *Vanity Fair*. Some of the very records that prove C-Day's existence also show connections between C-Day and JFK's assassination, and how C-Day was penetrated by the associates of Mafia bosses Carlos Marcello, Santo Trafficante, and Johnny Rosselli.

The secrecy surrounding the Kennedys' fall 1963 coup plan—and the Mafia's penetration of it—created most of the continuing controversies about the JFK assassination. Was Lee Harvey Oswald an innocent patsy, an active participant in the conspiracy to kill JFK, or a participant in a US intelligence operation that went awry? As we lay out the evidence about C-Day, and how the Mafia used it to kill JFK, it will answer that and other questions that have long baffled historians, investigators, and the public.

All the secrecy that shrouded C-Day in 1963, and in the decades since, has had a tremendous impact on American life and politics. While much of the ensuing cover-up of C-Day and its links to JFK's assassination had a legitimate basis in national security, we also document which agencies covered up critical intelligence failures that allowed JFK's assassination to happen. Since C-Day was never exposed, and its lessons never learned, its legacy has continued to harm US relations and intelligence. *Ultimate Sacrifice* shows how the ongoing secrecy surrounding C-Day and the JFK assassination has continued to cost American lives.

PART ONE

The Cuban Missile Crisis and C-Day

ALTHOUGH THE CUBAN MISSILE CRISIS is largely remembered as a stunning success for the United States, the little-known reality is that it left President John F. Kennedy and his brother Robert with a sense of unfinished business and the need for a permanent solution to the problem of Cuba. In fact, the Missile Crisis was never fully resolved, because of Fidel Castro's refusal to allow UN inspections for nuclear weapons, to ensure that all the Soviet missiles had been removed. However, decades of misinformation about JFK's supposed pledge not to invade Cuba to end the Crisis is so pervasive that it is important to finally put it to rest. This chapter not only documents that JFK made no such pledge, but shows how the failure to fully resolve the crisis led to the creation of the C-Day coup plan the following year.

JFK's Secretary of State, Dean Rusk, explained to us in 1990 that JFK never agreed not to invade Cuba, the reason being that Castro refused to allow UN weapons inspectors into Cuba in the fall of 1962.[1] Those inspections had been part of JFK's deal with Russia's Nikita Khrushchev to end the tense nuclear standoff of the Cuban Missile Crisis. At the time, we were surprised to hear this from Rusk, because almost every history book or media report about the Cuban Missile Crisis cited JFK's so-called no-invasion pledge as a key reason for ending the Crisis. However, we quickly found confirmation of what Rusk had told us.

A transcript of President Kennedy's November 20, 1962 prime-time TV news conference provided the first confirmation. That night, JFK declared that he would "give assurances against an invasion of Cuba" only when "adequate arrangements for [UN] verification had been established." JFK emphasized that "the Cuban Government has not yet permitted the United Nations to verify whether all offensive weapons have been removed" and that "serious problems remain."[2] (While researching JFK's comments, we also found that he had been the first president to use the term "weapons of mass destruction," as well as the concept of "UN inspections" for them, and he used both phrases during the Missile Crisis.[3])

A year after we talked to Dean Rusk, presidential historian Michael Bechloss discussed the supposed "no-invasion pledge" in his 1991 book, *The Crisis Years*. Making use of the new documents about the Missile Crisis that were being declassified, Bechloss was one of the first major historians to question the existence of the pledge. He said JFK "may have deliberately avoided such an unambiguous commitment," and that JFK "watered down the pledge" by adding conditions that "had the effect of neutralizing" it. Bechloss concluded that JFK did not "rule out further American efforts to topple the Castro regime, including invasion."[4]

More documents about the Missile Crisis and the so-called no-invasion pledge continued to be declassified, and by 1992 it was clear that the pledge had never gone into effect, as Rusk had said. The National Security Archive, located at George Washington University and the world's largest nongovernmental library of declassified documents, was a major force in getting the new files released.[5] The Archive published the documents in a massive volume called *The Cuban Missile Crisis, 1962* that included an analysis by historians Laurence Chang and Peter Kornbluh.[6]

Chang and Kornbluh confirm that "for almost thirty years after the Cuban Missile Crisis, the myth persisted that Kennedy had struck a secret deal with Khrushchev binding the US to a commitment not to invade Cuba. But the recent declassification of the remaining correspondence between Kennedy and Khrushchev, and of internal State Department memoranda, reveals that no such deal was ever made." They explain that "President Kennedy's pledge not to invade Cuba . . . was conditioned on the implementation of adequate inspection and verification procedures." They quote JFK's letter to Khrushchev on October 27, 1962, in which JFK said that "upon the establishment of adequate arrangements through the United Nations to ensure . . . these commitments . . . [the US would] give assurances against an invasion of Cuba." But as Chang and Kornbluh document, "Cuba did not allow on-site inspection" to verify that all the Russian missiles had been removed, so the pledge never took effect."[7]

The National Security Archive historians present many pages of declassified documents confirming what Dean Rusk told us in 1990. The documents are especially interesting in light of the recent events in Iraq: The actions of

George W. Bush, Saddam Hussein, and UN Secretary General Kofi Anan in the fall of 2002 regarding weapons of mass destruction parallel very closely the actions—and even the words—of JFK, Fidel Castro, and UN Secretary General U Thant in the fall of 1962.

The documents show that Dean Rusk was one of the US officials who encouraged JFK not to make a firm no-invasion pledge in 1962, in order to allow the US more flexibility in getting rid of Castro. As the book states, "Internal State Department memoranda declassified in April 1992 reveal that US officials who saw the Missile Crisis as a great opportunity to overthrow Castro lobbied hard against any pledge that would inhibit future US policy toward Cuba." A strategy paper from Rusk's State Department dated November 7, 1962 called for "maximal US strategy . . . directed at the elimination . . . of the Castro regime," even as the Missile Crisis was winding down. Chang and Kornbluh say that Rusk's position was that "the latitude to overthrow Castro . . . was more important than a concrete resolution to the most dangerous international crisis of the twentieth century." During the crisis, Rusk wrote to JFK adviser John McCloy—appointed to the Warren Commission a year later—saying "Our interest lies in . . . avoiding the kind of commitment that unduly ties our hands in dealing with the Castro regime while it lasts."[8]

As the days passed in November 1962, neither JFK nor Khrushchev wanted to return to the tense standoff of October, but neither man was able to find a solution to the problem. JFK complained in a letter to Khrushchev on November 15, 1962 that "There has been no United Nations verification that other missiles were not left behind and, in fact, there have been many reports of their being concealed in caves and elsewhere, and we have no way of satisfying those who are concerned about these reports."[9]

At his November 20, 1962 prime-time press conference, JFK was asked: "Is it your position, sir, that you will issue a formal no-invasion pledge only after satisfactory arrangements have been made for [UN] verification?"[10] After JFK made it clear that that was indeed the case, he was asked by a reporter "If we [the US] wanted to invade Cuba . . . could we do so without the approval of the United Nations?" JFK essentially said yes, replying that the US "has the means as a sovereign power to defend itself . . . in a way consistent with our treaty obligations, including the United Nations Charter." JFK said that while he hoped "to always move in concert with our allies," he reserved the right to act "on our own if that situation was necessary to protect our survival or integrity or other vital interests."[11]

But Khrushchev was unable to get Fidel Castro to allow the UN inspections. A leading Cuban journalist at the time, Carlos Franqui, said that Castro "could never accept the idea of an inspection of any kind by any agency . . . because that would have finished him off" by making him look weak.[12] So, on November 21, 1962, JFK notified Khrushchev that the Missile Crisis was over—but with the issues of UN inspections and a no-invasion pledge still unresolved. JFK wrote Khrushchev that "I am now instructing our negotiators [at the UN] in New York to move ahead promptly with proposals for a solution of the remaining elements in the Cuban problem," meaning the UN inspections in Cuba. JFK said: "I regret that you have been unable to persuade Mr. Castro to accept a suitable form of [UN] inspection or verification in Cuba . . . but, as I said yesterday, there need be no fear of any invasion of Cuba while matters take their present favorable course." As *The Cuban Missile Crisis, 1962* notes, "in the end there was no formal resolution of the Missile Crisis."[13]

Since there never were any UN inspections in Cuba, JFK and his cabinet made it clear, both in their private meetings and to a Congressional committee, that there wasn't a no-invasion pledge.[14] As Dean Rusk told us, without the UN inspections, the Cuban Missile Crisis never really ended. JFK and members of his administration felt that they had to do something to make sure all the missiles were gone and wouldn't be reintroduced, since their efforts at the UN had proven fruitless. By the spring of 1963, JFK and his key advisers were looking at new ways to topple Castro. However, Rusk agreed that the American public—and possibly the Soviets—had assumed that there was such a pledge, which made the Kennedys' efforts in 1963 all the more risky. That's why they needed a legitimate—or seemingly legitimate—"coup," not just an assassination or a full-out US invasion while Castro was still in power. They didn't want to risk a nuclear confrontation with the Soviets, so any US military action against Cuba would have to take place under very special circumstances. It would have to appear to be a peace-keeping mission, in response to a "palace coup" against Castro, to quote a recently declassified memo.[15] As Dean Rusk explained to us, Castro's refusal to allow the UN inspections led directly to what became the Kennedys' C-Day plan for a coup.

The problem of Cuba remained a growing thorn in the side of JFK into the spring and summer of 1963. The *New York Times* reported on May 10, 1963 that a Senate subcommittee said that at least 17,000 Soviet troops remained in Cuba, including 5,000 combat troops. Worse, the report said that concealed missile sites were "quite possible," a charge that JFK couldn't completely refute without the UN inspections that Castro wouldn't allow. Hawkish sub-committee chairman John Stennis was demanding that JFK take "positive" steps to make getting the Communists out of Cuba his highest priority.[16]

A few weeks later, the *Times* reported that CIA Director John McCone had testified to Congress that "only onsite [UN] inspection can completely con-firm" the "end of the [Cuban] missile threat."[17] A June 14, 1963 secret National Intelligence Estimate said that while it was "unlikely that the USSR" would "reintroduce strategic [nuclear] missiles into Cuba . . . we cannot, however, rule out such an attempt." Moreover, the US might not be able to find the missiles if they were reintroduced, since the report said it would be "possible" for the Soviets "to adopt improved measures of concealment and deception . . . to avoid providing many of the indicators that US intelligence would be relying on" to detect any new missiles.[18] We could not always depend on U-2 spy planes to do the job, since they were now sometimes being approached by Soviet MiG jets. This forced the U-2s to abort, since procedures "call for aborts when Cuban aircraft [come] within 40 miles of U-2 and at altitude in excess of 40,000 feet."[19] Finally, U-2s were useless if new Soviet missiles were put in caves or underground sites.

However, JFK had already been planning to take some type of action to prevent the reintroduction of Soviet missiles into Cuba and to resolve the problems with Castro once and for all. White House memos declassified just a few years ago show that in late April 1963, the Kennedy administration was beginning a major push to eliminate Castro, setting the stage for C-Day. The April 23, 1963 notes from a National Security Council subcommittee on Cuba say that Defense "Secretary McNamara . . . made clear his belief that the elimination of the Castro regime was a requirement." McNamara sug-gested a program that would create "such a situation of dissidence within Cuba as to allow the US to use force in support of anti-Castro forces without leading to retaliation by the USSR on the West." Then "the Attorney General proposed . . . a list of measures we would take following . . . the death of Castro" and "a program with the objective of overthrowing Castro in eighteen months." JFK adviser Ted Sorenson listed one of the "objectives raised at the meeting" as being to "develop a program to get rid of Castro." Another objective was to provide "support for dissident elements in Cuba."[20] This was the second meeting of the "Standing Group of the National Secu-rity Council," a subcommittee recently formed to focus solely on Cuba.[21] It was just one of several such groups, all under the control of Bobby Kennedy.

The notes from a different Cuba subcommittee two days later develop the plans further. These April 25, 1963 notes say that CIA Director McCone talked about creating "a feasible climate for a successful attempt to fragment the Castro organization." The CIA's point man on Cuba, Desmond FitzGerald, said at the meeting that "we will have to be able to assure" high Cuban officials who might be willing to overthrow Castro for the US "that the US will be sympathetic to possible successors" to Castro "even though such people maybe have been former Castro supporters." FitzGerald also discussed "support to selected Cuban exile groups . . . as being one of the key points of the possible new program."[22]

The third of the seven government committees that investigated aspects of the JFK assassination was the Rockefeller Commission, which found that "McCone once stated one ultimate objective of our policy toward Cuba should be 'to encourage dissident elements in the . . . power centers of the regime to bring about the <u>eventual liquidation of the Castro/Communist entourage</u> and the elimination of the Soviet presence from Cuba'" [emphasis in original].[23]

In directing the Cuban subcommittees in these actions to topple Castro, Bobby Kennedy was not acting on his own. Investigative journalist Gus Russo, who has numerous CIA sources, documented that "although Robert Kennedy assumed the task of dealing with the nuts and bolts of policy implementation, this by no means implies that the younger brother was operating without JFK's implicit agreement. When Robert Kennedy issued his April 23, 1963 directive seeking studies aimed at overthrowing Castro in 1964, he was merely echoing the President's own words."[24]

A "Memorandum for the President" from that time period foreshadows many of the key elements of the C-Day coup plan. Though addressed to President Kennedy, the memo also had a section where the Defense Department, the CIA, and Bobby Kennedy's Justice Department could all check their "concurrences" with the policy. This 1963 memo—finally declassified in 1997, due to our efforts and those of other researchers—makes it clear that the administration's "ultimate objective with respect to Cuba remains the overthrow of the Castro/Communist regime and its replacement by one compatible with the objectives of the US." The memo foreshadowed C-Day, saying "We should <u>seek to create conditions conducive to incipient rebellion to which we could then respond</u>" [emphasis in original].[25]

The memo makes it clear that after a "rebellion," the US should "respond with open military support . . . and Special Forces, up to the full range of military forces." This would come in response "to a request for assistance from any anti-Castro . . . group . . . in Cuba which demonstrates an ability to survive, [and] which seriously threatens the present [Castro] regime." The memo notes that "US military forces employed against Cuba should be accompanied by US military-trained free Cubans."[26] Cuban exiles trained by the US military would soon be a key part of C-Day.

These April 1963 meetings were not the first time the Kennedys had targeted Castro with a broad plan of covert action. The previous year, President Kennedy and the National Security Council had approved "OPERATION MONGOOSE," a large program involving the US military and other agencies including the CIA. Robert Kennedy was actively involved, though he did not dominate it to the extent he would dominate C-Day the following year. For decades, OPERATION MONGOOSE has been described as primarily a relentless and escalating campaign of sabotage and small Cuban exile raids that would somehow cause the overthrow of Castro. Only in recent years have newly released documents and accounts shown that MONGOOSE also included plans for an invasion of Cuba in the fall of 1962. The military was heavily involved with MONGOOSE, and suggested a variety of often outrageous plans to justify the military invasion, such as blaming the sinking of a ship or the crash of an airliner—or a US space capsule—on the Cubans, or staging a phony attack on Guantanamo. In recent years, historians have begun to focus on the Soviet and Cuban response to MONGOOSE, and whether it actually helped to trigger the Cuban Missile Crisis. MONGOOSE was quietly terminated in early 1963 after a demonstrable lack of results.

The April 1963 meetings and memos were in response to a lack of progress in efforts against Castro that had followed in the wake of MONGOOSE. Some of those programs were known to the Kennedys and their Cuban subcommittees. One was AMTRUNK, a CIA program conceived three months earlier by *New York Times* journalist Tad Szulc, a close friend of JFK. It was an attempt to find disgruntled military officials in Cuba who might be willing to recruit higher military officials in a plot to overthrow Castro. Detailed in a later chapter, AMTRUNK was making little progress. In addition, the CIA had been supporting dozens of Cuban exile groups for years, but most were ineffective, and the Kennedys were starting to scale back their support and shut down the groups' raids on Cuba.

The CIA had two other major operations against Cuba that were being hidden from the Kennedys in April 1963. One was CIA backing for the violent Cuban exile group Alpha 66, which even attacked Soviet ships in Cuban waters, a dangerous act during the Cold War. Even as JFK denounced Alpha 66 and tried to clamp down on its leadership, he didn't realize that the CIA was actually directing the group's activities. The other major operation was the CIA's ongoing plots with Mafia boss Johnny Rosselli to assassinate Castro. The CIA-Mafia plots began in 1959, had been ramped up in the summer of 1960 prior to JFK's election, and continued even after the CIA had assured Bobby Kennedy in May 1961 that they had been stopped. These plots were still active in the spring of 1963, with two well-documented attempts. The CIA-Mafia plots with Rosselli were part of the CIA's ZRRIFLE "Executive Action" program, which employed a European assassin recruiter codenamed QJWIN, whose real name is still classified by the CIA. This program was first uncovered by the Senate Church Committee in the mid-1970s.

CIA Director John McCone, a recent JFK appointee, was kept in the dark about the unsanctioned CIA operations as much as JFK was. CIA officials who were aware of them, the highest of whom appears to have been Deputy Director for Plans Richard Helms, had far different ideas on overthrowing Castro by 1963 than did the Kennedys. Historian Arthur Schlesinger, Jr., a JFK aide at the time, wrote that "the CIA wished to organize Castro's overthrow from outside Cuba, as against the White House, the Attorney General's office and State who wished to support an anti-Castro movement inside Cuba. The CIA's idea was to fight a war; the others hoped to promote a revolution." Although our sources and documents indicate that Schlesinger did not know about C-Day, he worked closely enough with the Kennedys to accurately describe their feelings about Cuba.[27] The Kennedys wanted a change in Cuba to be part of a political solution, whether by a genuine coup or (by the fall of 1963) a negotiated agreement with Castro, whereas Helms and other CIA officials acted as if assassination of Castro by any means at any time was justified.

Since none of the CIA's sanctioned or unsanctioned actions were having much effect by April 1963, the Kennedys were very receptive just a few weeks later when one of the highest officials in Cuba contacted a Kennedy ally and offered to stage a coup against Castro, if the Kennedys would back him.[28] The offer fit perfectly with what the Kennedys were already looking for—a way to "get rid of Castro" by supporting "dissident elements in Cuba," which would "allow the US to use force . . . without leading to retaliation by the USSR."

Harry Williams

IN THE SPRING OF 1963, the Kennedys faced political pressure to take action to overthrow Castro from both hawks in Congress and potential rivals in the 1964 election. But JFK and Bobby had their own reasons to take an extraordinary risk to do something about Cuba. Pulitzer Prize–winning journalist Haynes Johnson wrote of a conversation years after JFK's death, in which "[Bobby] Kennedy, then a Senator, became so emotional about what had happened to the men his brother had sent ashore at the Bay of Pigs that he cried when speaking of the personal commitment he felt toward them."[1] A former Kennedy aide told us in 1992 that "JFK and Bobby acted in unison [in relation to Cuba]. But Bobby felt the plight of the [Bay of Pigs] Brigade more clearly."[2]

While JFK admired courage in general and saw the Bay of Pigs as a blot on his record as president, for Bobby Kennedy the matter of the Cuban exiles was more personal. *Newsweek* editor Evan Thomas wrote that "bitter CIA men" called Bobby's "Cuban friends . . . his 'pet Cubans,'" because "to the despair of their CIA handlers, [Bobby] Kennedy formed a private bond with" Cuban exiles like Harry "Williams and [Roberto] San Roman." Haynes Johnson told Evan Thomas that "Bobby trusted Harry. He loved it that Harry was full of shrapnel from the Bay of Pigs."[3] San Roman told the *Washington Post* that he "believes the Kennedys had a sense of guilt" over the failure of the Bay of Pigs "and wanted to help" in 1963.[4] Harry Williams (Enrique Ruiz-Williams)[*] was

---

[*]US documents in the 1960s often use different spellings and formats for Cuban names. For example, Harry Williams's name in a Department of the Army document was "Enrique Jose Ruiz William Alfert." Harry said Bobby Kennedy initially called him "Enrique," but had trouble pronouncing it properly, so Bobby nicknamed him the easier-to-pronounce "Enrico." His name as listed on the business card he gave us is "Enrique (Harry) Ruiz-Williams," and he was generally known as "Harry Williams." He asked us to call him "Harry," which is why we refer to him by that name in this book.

an especially charismatic figure, and he played a crucial role in the development of C-Day.

In 1964, Bobby talked about Harry Williams for an Oral History now at the John F. Kennedy Presidential Library. Bobby said that "Williams . . . was a very bright fellow" who was "very brave and had very good judgment." Bobby hinted at C-Day when he said that in 1963 Harry "wanted to go to the Dominican Republic and do something [about Cuba] from there" and admitted that he and Harry had "talked about" these plans.[5] As documented later, the Dominican Republic was to be the base for one of the Kennedys' five C-Day Cuban exile leaders. Though Harry was a very private man who shunned the limelight, many government files cited in Part 1 confirm Harry's role in C-Day and how close he was to Bobby. For example, a formerly secret August 1963 State Department memo says "the Attorney General had been talking to Enrique Ruiz [Harry] Williams, and as a result" a certain Cuban exile doctor would meet with a State Department official.[6]

Haynes Johnson coauthored a book with leaders of the Bay of Pigs, documenting that Harry had proved his heroism under fire during that ill-fated invasion and after. Haynes Johnson's description of Williams—"Harry was bluff, candid, blunt, and Catholic to the core"—sounds very much like Bobby himself, another reason the Attorney General would place his trust in Harry.[7] Former FBI agent William Turner wrote that "Harry Williams was a Kennedy kind of man, tough and liberal and ferociously anticommunist. He is burly, round-faced, and handsome; he combines the geniality of a Lions Club toastmaster with a tough-minded singleness of purpose."[8] Turner described the affable Harry as having "charisma," and the Kennedy associates we interviewed described Harry being a man of great integrity.[9]

Haynes Johnson, who described Harry as "willing to die at any moment," said that Harry told him "I was a hundred percent for the elimination of Castro. My plan was the physical elimination of Castro. My own feeling is that Kennedy was ready to eliminate Castro."[10] A Kennedy aide confirmed to William Turner that in 1963, "the CIA was 'running a kind of program' against Castro" and that "Harry Williams would drop by whenever he was in Washington to meet with CIA agents."[11] A Kennedy associate told Evan Thomas that Williams was "reliable . . . which is more than you could say about most of the other Cubans." Consequently, Thomas wrote, "increasingly through 1963, RFK relied on [Harry] Williams, organizing and motivating the others to keep the pressure on Castro."[12] Haynes Johnson wrote in the *Washington Post* that of all "the

Cuban leaders of the Bay of Pigs invasion," Harry "was the closest such person to the [JFK] administration."[13]

Harry's life prior to 1963 shows how he became so closely involved with the Kennedys and the fight against Castro. Harry told William Turner that his father was "very highly involved" in a much earlier fight to topple a Cuban dictator, "the revolution against Machado" in the early 1930s. After that, Harry's father was "one of the leaders" of the new Cuban government for a time, serving as the "Minister for Public Works."[14] Bobby Kennedy says in his Oral History that Harry himself "was the head engineer and general manager of the biggest mining company in Cuba."[15] Harry was educated at the Colorado School of Mines, which left him with an affinity for the American people and a good command of English.[16] Very friendly and easy-going, Harry speaks English with a discernible accent.

By 1958, Harry was successful in business and a family man, but, like many others in Cuba, he chafed under the repressive dictatorship of Batista. So, like his father, Harry began working to overthrow the dictator and, in the process, came into contact with two men he'd later deal with in 1963. Harry told Turner that he "was in contact with the group of Che Guevara" and because of his mining work, Harry was able to give Che's revolutionaries "food, dynamite, trucks, tractors, a lot of things." Harry also "gave money to . . . Eloy Menoyo," a future C-Day exile leader who "was in charge of that area before Che Guevara came in." Harry continued the aid "later, when Che Guevara was in charge" of the revolution in that region of Cuba.[17] However, Harry said that "because I helped them [I]" became "a little hot" with the authorities and had to leave "Cuba early in December 1958."[18] Harry was able to return to Cuba after Castro and Che took over in January 1959. Harry told us that "Che Guevara was more of a . . . thinker" than Fidel or Raul Castro, and that he "got along with Che a lot of" the time.[19]

Regarding the man who would later work with Harry on a coup for the Kennedys, Harry said "I think he was very bright . . . he did a lot of things in the [revolution] that made him outstanding." However, Harry soon became disillusioned with the violence and repression of Castro. After briefly running across the 1959 CIA-Mafia plots to kill Castro, Harry left Cuba once more and came to the US, returning only when he landed on the beach at the Bay of Pigs.[20]

Harry was almost forty, far older than the mostly young recruits in the CIA-trained Bay of Pigs invasion force. While Harry was not one of the top commanders, his maturity and bravery quickly made him one of the most

admired members of the brigade.[21] Cuban exile historian Nestor T. Carbonell wrote that at the Bay of Pigs, Harry "fought bravely" and was "blown
into the air by an enemy shell . . . and hit by more than seventy pieces of
shrapnel. Both of his feet were smashed and he had a hole near his heart and
a large one in his neck."[22] The man standing next to Harry soon died of his
wounds, and Harry was near death when Castro's army brought him to a
makeshift field hospital. What happened next became the stuff of legend
among Cuban exiles, but was the kind of daring act that JFK and Bobby
probably found irresistible: As Haynes Johnson wrote in *The Bay of Pigs*,
Harry and the other wounded men in a makeshift field hospital "were suddenly confronted by the person of Fidel Castro." The badly wounded
"Williams . . . recognized him at once. He groped under his thin mattress and
tried to reach a .45 pistol he had concealed there earlier in the afternoon."[23]
As Harry told us, he managed enough strength to point the weapon at Castro
and—at almost point-blank range—pull the trigger.[24]

But there was only a "click"—the gun was empty. Earlier, Harry's compatriots had been worried that Harry might be in such pain from his wounds
and so depressed over the failure of the invasion and their capture that he
might use the gun on himself. So they removed the bullets from his pistol
while Harry was unconscious.[25] Castro's men quickly set upon Harry, but
Fidel ordered them not to harm the gravely injured man. Haynes Johnson
wrote that Castro asked Harry: "'What are you trying to do, kill me?' and
Williams replied, 'That's what I came here for. We've been trying to do that
for three days.' Castro was not angry." According to Haynes Johnson, "Castro
gave orders" to take Harry and the other wounded men to a nearby city and
"put them in the hospital."[26]

Attempts by the Kennedys to arrange a "tractors for peace" deal to ransom
all the Bay of Pigs prisoners were scuttled by Richard Nixon and his hawkish
allies in Congress. For a year, the prisoners languished in harsh conditions,
until Castro released sixty of the most seriously wounded men, among them
Harry Williams. They were told to pressure JFK to cut a deal to ransom the
rest of the prisoners by the end of the year.[27] If not, the wounded men were
told they had to return, and their Cuban captors implied that one remaining
prisoner would be shot for every wounded man who didn't return.[28] Evan
Thomas confirms that "wounded while fighting valiantly at the Bay of Pigs,
[Harry] Williams was released by Castro in mid-April 1962 to negotiate a
ransom for the other prisoners."

Exile historian Carbonell wrote: "One of the most moving scenes I have ever witnessed was the arrival in Miami on April 14, 1962, of the sixty scarred warriors of the Bay of Pigs . . . one by one they came . . . this man with a leg off, and that one with an arm gone, the other with a patch over an injured eye." And "the leader of the wounded prisoners was Enrique 'Harry' Ruiz-Williams."[29] Historian Richard D. Mahoney, whose father was part of JFK's administration, wrote: "Throughout the summer [of 1962], amid Republican flak for attempting a trade with the enemy," Robert "Kennedy worked . . . with [Harry] Williams . . . to get the talks with Castro going again."[30] Carbonell says that in an effort to free the remaining prisoners, "Robert Kennedy . . . was in touch with Harry Ruiz-Williams almost on a daily basis."[31]

Bobby and Harry grew close over that time, and they were making progress until the Cuban Missile Crisis. For a time, it looked like the US was going to attack Cuba to take out the missiles, and it was felt that Castro would surely retaliate against the Bay of Pigs prisoners. According to Carbonell, "the Attorney General, who was in frequent contact with Harry Ruiz-Williams on the fate of the Bay of Pigs prisoners, asked him to remain on standby and told him, 'If we invade, I would like you . . . to join our 82nd Airborne Division to rescue the prisoners.'"[32] It would be a suicide mission, since the prisoners had been told that the prison was laced with explosives, to be detonated if the Americans ever attempted a rescue attempt. Harry was still recovering from his wounds, but he agreed to the mission—no doubt increasing his stature in the eyes of the Kennedys even more.[33]

After the Missile Crisis ended with Khrushchev's agreement to allow UN weapons inspectors into Cuba, Castro was furious, and a deal to free the Bay of Pigs prisoners seemed less likely than ever. Harry made preparations to return to prison in Cuba, as he'd promised, but Bobby Kennedy was shocked at the thought of his friend returning to Castro's prison. Haynes Johnson wrote in his *Bay of Pigs* that as the end of 1962 approached, Bobby moved heaven and earth to put a deal together, with Harry's constant encouragement.[34]

They were successful, and after the return of the 1,113 prisoners on Christmas Eve, "JFK invited the" Bay of Pigs "brigade chiefs to his villa in Palm Beach," wrote Carbonell. "There, flanked by . . . Jacqueline Kennedy and her sister, Princess Lee Radziwill," JFK "greeted Manuel Artime" and the others, including "Harry Ruiz-Williams. It was a friendly and informal meeting without presidential assistants, save the Press Secretary, Pierre Salinger, who was present part of the time. Harry served as translator." JFK apologized to the men and "explained to them why he did not provide" air support to the brigade: "the Soviet government had threatened to attack West Berlin if the United States" had openly "backed the invasion." There was also a big ceremony for all the freed prisoners and their families at the Orange Bowl, where JFK made an impromptu pledge to return the Brigade's flag to them "in a free Havana."[35] In the coming year, both JFK and Harry would risk their lives to do that.

In 1963, the Kennedys needed someone they could trust like Harry, to help them deal with the often-fractious Cuban exile leaders. The *New York Times* noted on May 23, 1963 that Cuban "exile political leaders jockeying for position against [the] day of Castro's overthrow complicates anti-Castro efforts." The same issue also noted that in a news conference, President "Kennedy . . . denies any US aid is now going to exile groups."[36] To maintain that public facade, JFK had to use someone outside his administration to handle what Haynes Johnson called the Kennedys' "complex relationship with the Cubans." Haynes Johnson explained that "there was genuine feeling and affection" toward the Cuban exiles on the part of Bobby. However, Bobby "Kennedy wanted to control the Cubans . . . he wanted to make them personally loyal to him. He didn't want them out there talking about betrayal" at the Bay of Pigs.[37] Already subject to criticism over Cuba from the Republicans, Democratic hawks, and his potential rivals in the 1964 elections, JFK made sure key Bay of Pigs leaders weren't part of that chorus by including them in C-Day.

Many of the Cuban exile leaders sought power, publicity, and money, but historian Evan Thomas wrote that "RFK . . . preferred more self-effacing types, quiet warriors . . . particularly a Bay of Pigs veteran named [Harry] Ruiz-Williams." Evan Thomas says that "to the despair of . . . the CIA, [Bobby] Kennedy formed a private bond with Williams" and that Harry was even "embraced by [Bobby] Kennedy's own family."[38] Harry was invited for visits to Bobby's Hickory Hill estate in Virginia, and when Harry traveled to New York City to see Bobby, he stayed at Bobby's lavish Manhattan townhouse. One CIA document confirms that "RFK . . . had gone [to] New York to interview" Harry.[39] (Bobby's New York townhouse was the location of one of three confrontations Harry would have with the Mafia in 1963, as they attempted to penetrate the C-Day plan. The fact that Harry survived those confrontations—one of which involved a shootout in a restaurant—probably only served to increase the Kennedys' regard for Harry and their willingness to trust with him with a risky and dangerous plan like C-Day.)

At times, it must have seemed to the CIA that when it came to Cuba,

Harry had more influence over Bobby than the CIA. Evan Thomas cites an incident when "a CIA official tried to explain to RFK that" one of his Cuban subcommittees "had decided not to use Guantanamo as a base for covert actions. 'We'll see about that,' Kennedy snapped" in reply.[40] Bobby must have done so, since Guantanamo would be Harry's destination on November 22, 1963, as the final countdown to C-Day began. Harry told us that he had "a lot of respect for" Bobby, who was "a tremendous, exceptional guy. He was good. And at that time [1963] it is my interpretation that he was running the CIA." Harry felt "that was one of the things the CIA didn't like" about him, because Harry "could sit down with Bobby and tell him what the hell I thought and . . . I think he trusted me."[41]

Harry's CIA file has never been declassified, but it must be voluminous, because CIA files for even minor Cuban exile leaders that have been released are often quite large. In Harry's case, even CIA records about his noncovert activities, such as his well-documented work in the release of the Bay of Pigs prisoners, haven't been declassified, apparently because that work gradually blended into his covert work with the Kennedys. However, some CIA documents about Harry have slipped through and been declassified because copies were contained in the files of other exiles. These files provide clues as to why most CIA documents about Harry remain classified.

First, some of the declassified files about Harry are from the CIA's official files about C-Day, code-named AMWORLD. A handful of AMWORLD documents was first declassified in 1992, when President George H. W. Bush was trying to forestall more drastic JFK assassination declassification efforts by Congress, and a few dozen more were released in the late 1990s. Second, most of the files for other Cuban exiles were declassified because they were originally given to Congressional investigations, but those investigations were never told about C-Day. We assume that most of the CIA documents about Harry and C-Day are among the "well over a million CIA records" relating to JFK's assassination that a former official with the JFK Assassination Records Review Board says have not yet been released.[42]

Among those that have been declassified, a CIA document from July 24, 1963, sent to the "Chief, Contact Division" from the "Chief, New York Field Office," gives Harry's Miami address and phone number. The document is an interview with an exile who had developed plans for an unmanned bomber to use against Cuba. The exile had been referred to Harry, and had given the plans to him. That was typical of one of Harry's roles in the summer and fall of 1963, being what he called a "bridge of communication" between exiles and "the Kennedy administration."[43] For most exiles, that involved Harry being friendly and making the exiles feel appreciated, while avoiding any promises of support. Only a few exiles saw the other side of Harry's work, the covert operation we call C-Day, and we'll quote extensively from several CIA documents about Harry and C-Day in upcoming chapters.

A former Kennedy C-Day aide told us that "I don't know any American who really cared about Cuba" by the fall of 1963.[44] There were occasional news stories in 1963 sparked by hawks in Congress and a few far-right tycoons about rumors of Soviet missiles still in Cuba, but they didn't gain any traction with the general public. Aside from the large newspapers in New York City and Miami, most articles were small ones about minor attacks on Cuba or its shipping by Cuban exiles, and stories about the Kennedys cracking down on most exile groups.

However, there were a few news stories—by reporters with sources close to C-Day—that hinted at big things to come. But those were rare, and were quickly cut off by the Kennedys or the CIA. In the summer and fall of 1963, Cuba was far from most peoples' minds. The handful of news stories quoted here generally didn't make a ripple among the American public. However, one of several newspaper articles at a crucial time started a chain of events that led directly to C-Day.

On May 10, 1963, the Associated Press released a story saying the following:

A new all-out drive to unify Cuban refugees into a single, powerful organization to topple the Fidel Castro regime was disclosed today by exile sources. The plan calls for formation of a junta in exile to mount a three-pronged thrust consisting of sabotage, infiltration, and ultimate invasion. The exile sources said the plan had been discussed with Cuban leaders by US Central Intelligence agents. Seeking to put together the junta was Enrique Ruiz Williams, a Bay of Pigs invasion veteran and friend of US Attorney General Robert F. Kennedy. Cuban leaders said intensive sabotage and guerrilla activities inside Cuba might start in a month to spark a possible uprising. Hundreds of exiles, reported itching for action and resentful of US-imposed curbs against the anti-Castro raids will be recruited to infiltrate Cuba, the sources said.[45]

Though the article appeared in several newspapers across the country, it created little stir at the time. This was one of three articles around that time that named Harry as Bobby's new coordinator for Cuban exiles, but Harry knew the importance of keeping a low profile when it came to covert Cuban operations. He told us he "didn't want publicity," and that's one reason he "never took any (US government) position" or payment for his actions.[46] Harry confronted the author of the other two articles to put a stop to them.

Harry told the reporter he didn't like to be called "Bobby's boy" and he tried to play down his close relationship to the Kennedys. "I know him [Bobby] and he knows me and we've worked together in the liberation of the [Bay of Pigs] brigade, but now I'm trying to help the brigade become useful." When the reporter protested that all her sources confirmed that Harry did "whatever Bobby says," Harry said that was "wrong." Technically, it was, since Harry saw his relationship with Bobby as one of equals and not taking orders. In fact, Harry was not afraid to confront Bobby or disagree with him, which is one reason Bobby respected Harry. Harry told the reporter Bobby "knows what I'm doing because you guys publish everything in the paper. You see me in the airport and you publish in the paper that Harry Williams is going to the CIA or the Pentagon or whatever."[47]

Harry's meeting with the reporter worked, because the articles about him stopped—but one had already been spotted by an old acquaintance of Harry's in Cuba, someone Harry had known during the Cuban Revolution who was now very high in the Cuban government. This very high Cuban official worked closely with Fidel and Raul Castro, so he had the access needed to "neutralize" them. He also had his own security apparatus and enough status throughout Cuba that his orders wouldn't be questioned. The high Cuban official told Harry that he was willing to lead a coup to replace Castro.

We will need to discuss Harry's contact in Cuba carefully, to reveal as much as possible without running afoul of current national security laws, which may prohibit directly naming a US intelligence asset even long after his or her death. So we will usually refer to Harry's contact as the C-Day "coup leader." Other times, we will cite on-the-record historical information about various Cuban leaders by name. However, we want to make it clear that we know who the coup leader was: Harry Williams told us the coup leader's name in April 1992, and it was later confirmed by two Defense Department sources, including one who had worked with the Kennedys.[48] A few US government documents related to C-Day have been declassified that contain the coup leader's name. We are confident that over time, the judgment of history will show that we made the right decision regarding the C-Day coup leader, and that we acted in accordance with National Security law.

Harry told us the high Cuban official's motivation for offering to lead the

coup at that particular time. The coup leader had been a hero of the Revolution that toppled Batista in 1959. But by 1963, the man felt that Castro had
betrayed the Revolution and was becoming nothing more than a dictator. To
make matters worse, the coup leader felt that his own high position in the
government had been weakening ever since the Bay of Pigs. Many other revolutionary heroes had been marginalized, exiled, or killed, and he feared the
same thing would happen to him.[49] As Cuba historian Daniel James said,
"Fidel has earned himself a reputation for perfidy in his dealings with his
earliest and closest associates," and he cites several examples of those allies
whom Castro had killed, imprisoned, or exiled.[50] Castro had emerged from
the Bay of Pigs with even more power and prestige for defeating the US,
leaving the other Cuban leaders in his shadow. Even though the coup leader
was one of the most powerful men in Cuba next to Castro, he realized that
it was only a matter of time until he met the same fate as his former comrades. Finally, Harry said that another key motivation for the coup leader was
that he didn't like the Soviet presence in Cuba, and he worried that Soviet
influence would only grow.[51] To the coup leader, C-Day was actually a continuation of the real Revolution.[52] If it meant cooperating with the Americans, he saw that as better than having to obey the Soviets.

It's well documented from historical records and news reports that a
number of Cuban leaders, including Che Guevara, deeply resented the
growing Russian influence in Cuba.[53] News reports of tension between Che
and the Soviets were common by the spring of 1963—so much so that just
weeks before the May Associated Press article naming Harry appeared, a
reporter for *Look* magazine felt compelled to tell Che about "rumors . . . that
he [Che] had been downgraded in power and was leaving the country for a
year's 'vacation.'"[54] An earlier issue of *Look* featured Che's boast that Cuba
would "resist to the last drop of blood any Soviet attempt to establish a Communist satellite in Cuba."[55] Both comments foreshadow events to come, like
the declassified December 10, 1963 cable to the CIA Director saying "that
Che Guevara was alleged to be under house arrest for plotting to overthrow
Castro" and Che's later exile from Cuba.[56]

It's ironic that a Cuban revolutionary would share a concern over the
Soviets with the Kennedy administration. But Castro had not been the only
Cuban leader to feel betrayed by the Soviets over the Cuban Missile Crisis.
Though Castro had been mollified somewhat by the Soviets since then, the
coup leader had not. Moreover, a former Kennedy administration official
told us that "it was well-known that the Soviet-Cuba relationship was at a

low ebb during late 1963. The Russians were . . . pressuring Cuba to shape up economically, so they wouldn't have to provide so much support."[57]

Some may question why the Kennedys would cooperate with a powerful member of a Communist government, but declassified files provide the answer. A formerly TOP SECRET memo to JFK's assistant for National Security Affairs from May 10, 1963 shows how dissatisfaction with the Soviet bloc could help "effect the removal of the Castro regime." In talking about "a revolt within the structure of the existing regime," it says it's "most likely" to "draw its inspiration and support from nationalistic elements who had become disenchanted by the abject dependence of the regime on the [Soviet] Communist Bloc." The memo also notes that factors in such a "revolt" would be a "deepening of the economic crisis" and, of course, "the death of Castro."[58]

A formerly secret National Intelligence Estimate from June 14, 1963 notes that any new Cuban "leadership . . . would have to be revolutionary and reformist to appeal to a majority of Cubans."[59] Even with the presence of progressive Cuban exiles in a new Provisional Government, the Kennedys knew it would still take a "revolutionary hero" to win over the "majority of Cubans." The coup leader's stature, combined with his access to Castro, offered the Kennedys an opportunity so rare that they were willing to risk their administration's political legacy on it, and the C-Day plan was born.

At the same time, the coup leader needed the Kennedys just as badly. A formerly TOP SECRET May 13, 1963 memo from the CIA was titled "Developments in Cuba and Possible US Actions in the Event of Castro's Death." It said "upon Castro's death, his brother Raul or some other figure in the regime would, with Soviet backing and help, take over control." However, it said, there is a "chance that such a struggle would" develop into a "conflict . . . with the Moscow-oriented Communists lined up on one side and those who are essentially Cuban nationalists on the other." It then noted that "anti-Moscow Cuban nationalists would require extensive US help in order to win, and probably US military intervention."[60] Based on everything Harry told us about the C-Day coup leader, and other information we'll present later, it's clear that he considered himself an "anti-Moscow Cuban nationalist" and not a "Moscow-oriented Communist." Whatever earlier feelings or statements he might have made, by the late spring of 1963 the C-Day coup leader harbored only ill feelings toward the Soviets and a growing frustrating with Castro.[61]

The May 10 memo says that "a palace coup . . . might start with the assassination of Castro and a plea to the US to fend off intervention by Soviet forces," which is very close to the actual C-Day plan that developed.[62] It discusses a "palace coup by the members of the 26th of July Movement" and indicates they might be receptive to staging a coup if they were worried about "Communist accession to complete control of the [Cuban] regime at the expense of the remaining members of the 26th of July Movement."[63] Harry confirmed that the coup leader had been "outstanding with the 26th of July Movement."[64]

The 26th of July Movement was the original revolutionary organization of Fidel and Raul Castro and Che Guevara. It was separate from the Cuban Communist Party, and relations between the two were often difficult, especially for Che, who "treated the Communist leaders personally with some scorn," according to historian Hugh Thomas.[65] Look magazine said in April 1963 that "when old-line Communists grabbed for power in the revolutionary apparatus, maverick 'Che' was a chief target and sheltered many victims of the 'purge.'"[66]

These analyses, along with the April 25, 1963 notes quoted earlier and the Kennedys' later secret negotiations with Castro, show that JFK was willing to accept a socialist regime in Cuba as long as it met certain criteria, which included being free of Soviet influence and not exporting revolution to the rest of Latin America.[67] As long as those criteria were met, the Kennedys were willing to deal with Fidel Castro or any other top Cuban official.

By June 1963, the man we call the C-Day coup leader was working with Harry and the Kennedys on the C-Day plan.[68] At the same time, the Kennedys were pursuing a peaceful solution to the problem of Cuba, one that was foreshadowed in the same May 1963 issue of the New York Times that carried the AP article mentioning Harry. The Times noted that in an interview with pioneering TV journalist Lisa Howard, "Castro lauds US ban on raids as a step toward peace," referring to the recent crackdown on Cuban exile raids by JFK.[69] The Kennedys were trying to walk a fine line—publicly appearing to suppress Cuban exile raids, while privately getting ready to support a few exile groups in a plan to topple Castro. Lisa Howard's interview with Castro soon led to another Kennedy initiative: She would be the catalyst for secret, back-channel negotiations between the Kennedys and Castro. With the Kennedys having so many seemingly contradictory irons in the fire, in retrospect it seems almost inevitable that tragedy would result. However, at the time, the Kennedys were simply trying different solutions to the very difficult problem of Cuba.

CHAPTER THREE

The C-Day
"Plan for a Coup in Cuba"

ONCE THE CUBAN OFFICIAL HAD secretly agreed to be the coup leader for the overthrow of Cuba, the Kennedys and Harry quickly refocused their plans. Instead of trying to unite all the Cuban exile groups, they now focused on using just a small, trusted handful in the C-Day plan, which included elements the administration had already been secretly discussing. The C-Day plan started to develop when the coup leader contacted Harry in mid-May 1963, and evolved over the summer and fall of 1963. However, it's important to look concisely at what the plan was supposed to achieve and entail, since the final reality was tragically different from what was originally planned. In essence, declassified files and sources confirm that C-Day called for a coup against Cuba, on a date eventually fixed as December 1, 1963. The coup leader would "eliminate" Fidel Castro (and probably his brother Raul) on that date, but their deaths would be blamed on someone else. If the coup leader were to put the blame on someone with ties to Russia, that would help to neutralize the Soviets still in Cuba. Just before the coup, Harry Williams would secretly go into Cuba from the US base at Guantanamo, and would meet face to face with the coup leader. After Castro's death, Harry would be quickly joined by several Cuban exile leaders previously selected by Harry and approved by the Kennedys. The exiles would have been operating from bases outside the continental US. Ranging from conservative to liberal, the exile leaders, Harry, and the coup leader would immediately form and announce a new Provisional Government.

The new Cuban Provisional Government would call for US military intervention, to help calm the situation and deter the Soviets. If all went well, that would initially involve a few hundred specially trained Cuban exile US military troops. If there were a few trouble spots, it could also involve US Special

Forces—the Green Berets—but it could also rise to the level of a "full-scale invasion" by US forces if necessary. The Provisional Government would rule Cuba until free and democratic elections could be held.

There were two supporting operations for C-Day, and they shared some of the same personnel. The Cuba Contingency Plans were developed to protect the secrecy of C-Day and give JFK time to plan a response if it appeared that Castro had found out about C-Day and retaliated by—for example—assassinating a US official. The other supporting operation was getting US intelligence assets into Cuba prior to C-Day. This was primarily a CIA operation, though Naval Intelligence was also involved. With no US embassy in Cuba to provide cover, the US assets had to either be slipped in at night by boat, or have carefully constructed cover stories so they could travel to Havana openly via Mexico City.

C-Day was primarily a military operation, supported by the CIA but directed by Bobby Kennedy with the full approval of JFK. However, the public wasn't supposed to know that, even if C-Day was a success, which accounts for so much of the secrecy that surrounded the plan then and for decades to follow. The goal was "plausible deniability" for the US government and for President Kennedy in particular. If the plan failed, JFK couldn't afford to take the blame, as he had for the Bay of Pigs. The complex way in which C-Day was delegated and planned not only kept it from becoming an open secret, like the disastrous Bay of Pigs; it also protected the reputation of JFK. Ironically, even though C-Day failed, and parts of it were used by the Mafia in JFK's assassination, the Kennedys' secrecy plans worked so effectively that C-Day remained secret for decades.

Though the C-Day plans clearly called for the elimination of Fidel Castro, the Kennedys saw it as a coup, not an assassination. This may seem like semantics or rationalization, but it's important for several reasons. First, evidence indicates that the distinction was significant to JFK and Bobby and shaped how C-Day developed. Second, the concept of a coup was very different from the Castro assassination schemes with the Mafia that the CIA had been pursuing since 1959. Finally, the Kennedys' distinction between a coup and an assassination caused controversy and division among historians and journalists that has indirectly helped to keep C-Day secret.

Forty years after JFK's death, debate continues as to whether John and Robert Kennedy knew about or directed assassination plots against Castro. The controversy began in the 1970s after the first press revelations of US assassination attempts against Castro. Former LBJ aide Bill Moyers and former JFK aide Arthur Schlesinger, Jr. feuded publicly in the press over the issue.[1] As late as 2001, the *Nation* magazine was still treating the issue cautiously, and the controversy generated by statements on either side of the issue has no doubt caused many historians and journalists to handle the issue with extreme caution or avoid it altogether. Part of the problem was always the use of the term "assassination," since the Kennedys didn't view C-Day as an assassination plan.

From our earliest interviews, Dean Rusk, Harry Williams, and other Kennedy associates made it clear that John and Robert Kennedy not only knew about the effort to "eliminate" Castro with C-Day, but were actively directing it. However, the Kennedys saw C-Day not as assassination, but as Cubans outside Cuba working with Cubans inside Cuba to overthrow Castro's brutal dictatorship. Bobby's own words confirm this. He addresses the issue in his Oral History, soon after praising Harry Williams. The interviewer—David Martin, who had just stepped down from a two-year stint as US Ambassador to the Dominican Republic—then asks Bobby if he had ever attempted any "direct assassination attempts on Castro." Although Bobby has just finished confirming his work with Harry Williams to the interviewer, Bobby replies "no" to the interviewer's question.[2] This shows Bobby's mindset, as well as careful wording—notice that the question included the term "direct assassination attempts." To Bobby, his work with Harry on C-Day wasn't a "direct assassination attempt." Bobby had encountered numerous problems with the CIA's efforts with the Mafia to assassinate Castro starting in 1959, when Bobby's attempt to question a gangster was blocked by the CIA, which was using the gangster to try to kill Castro.[3] To Bobby, that was a "direct assassination attempt"—hiring a hit man to shoot someone. Bobby and JFK saw C-Day far differently, according to those who worked with the Kennedy brothers.

Some officials in the CIA didn't see any difference between a coup and an assassination plot. Richard Helms, the CIA's Deputy Director for Plans in 1963—and CIA Director under Nixon during Watergate—later testified to the House Select Committee on Assassinations (HSCA) about the Kennedys and plans for a Cuban coup in 1963. In 1977, Helms was convicted of misleading Congress regarding Nixon's plan for a coup in Chile (which utilized several C-Day veterans). Helms received a slap-on-the-wrist fine, which his CIA colleagues promptly paid for him.[4] But when Helms was subpoenaed soon after that by the HSCA, he must have been aware that another conviction for misleading Congress would bring calls for harsher penalties. Though it received almost no attention in the press at the time, his testimony about the actions of the Kennedys and the CIA during 1963 is surprisingly forthcoming.

Under oath, Helms told the Committee that "All I am trying to say is the US Government had a policy for many months of trying to mount a coup against Fidel Castro" in 1963. Helms said that "these operations against Cuba were known to the Attorney General of the United States . . . the President of the United States . . . all kinds of people high up in the government." Helms stressed that "those operations went on nonstop during 1963." Pressed as to whether the operation he was talking about was a coup or an assassination, Helms replied: "When one government is trying to upset another government and the operation is successful, people get killed. I don't know whether they are assassinated or whether they are killed in a coup." But Helms emphasized that the coup he was talking about wasn't some small rogue CIA attempt to kill Castro, telling the committee "if you go through the records of those years, you will find the whole US government was behind this one."[5] Unfortunately, the HSCA was unable to obtain most of the relevant records from the military and intelligence agencies, and their limited budget and life-span made a long search impossible.

Helms was known as "the man who kept the secrets" (the title of his biography by Thomas Powers), but the few comments he made about the Kennedys' 1963 Cuba operations are consistent with what our Kennedy C-Day sources told us and what declassified documents confirm. Regarding the Kennedys' plans for getting rid of Castro in 1963, Helms told Kennedy biographer Richard Reeves that "Robert Kennedy ran with it, ran those operations, and I dealt with him almost every day."[6] But it wasn't Bobby alone—shortly before his death, Helms said on Jim Lehrer's *Newshour* on PBS that JFK had "organized his entire administration to get rid of Castro."[7] Helms told noted presidential historian Michael Bechloss in 1988 that "There are two things you have to understand: Kennedy wanted to get rid of Castro, and the Agency [CIA] was not about to undertake anything like that on its own."[8] That's consistent with what Helms had told another Congressional committee in the 1970s, when he said "If President Kennedy had not been the motivating force," then the 1963 Cuban effort "wouldn't have taken on the size and character it did."[9] Helms even said on the Discovery Channel in 1997 that "There isn't any doubt as to who was running that effort. It was Bobby Kennedy on behalf of his brother. It wasn't anybody else!"[10] Regarding the pressure Helms felt from Bobby Kennedy over Cuba in 1963,

Helms told Evan Thomas "I was also getting my ass beat. You should have enjoyed the experience of Bobby Kennedy rampant on your back."[11]

While all of Helms's statements are accurate, he left out a great deal, including the CIA-Mafia plots to assassinate Castro that began in 1959 and continued through the fall of 1963, other CIA attempts to kill Castro in 1963 that didn't have the backing of the Kennedys, and the attempts that the CIA continued after JFK's death. Helms also failed to mention the CIA's intelligence failures in 1963 that allowed mob bosses Marcello, Trafficante, and Rosselli to infiltrate C-Day and use parts of it against JFK. Helms showed remarkable candor when he told historian Bechloss that "A lot of people probably lied about what had happened in the effort to get rid of Castro."[12]

Helms was a career CIA man who had risen through the ranks, unlike John McCone, CIA Director in 1963. McCone, who had formerly headed the Atomic Energy Commission, was a political appointee with little intelligence experience. While he may seem an odd choice for CIA Director, JFK felt burned by the previous CIA head, Allen Dulles, over the Bay of Pigs. Dulles had been a career intelligence officer, and JFK may have hoped that someone like McCone would be more loyal to him than to the CIA. While that may have been true, Helms and other CIA officials didn't tell McCone about some operations—such as the CIA-Mafia plots—until they were pressed. Even then, Helms usually didn't give the CIA director the whole story.[13]

While Helms knew and dealt with the CIA case officers involved with C-Day, McCone's role in the operation was much smaller, although McCone did receive several of the key C-Day CIA documents that have since been declassified.

Another document confirms that CIA Director McCone was acting on the orders of JFK in regard to his actions on C-Day. A Department of the Army document from September 26, 1963—kept secret for thirty-four years—says that the "CIA would, as appropriate and with Presidential approval, deal with the potential leaders of a coup in Cuba."[14] We will soon detail two specific instances where the CIA did "deal with" the C-Day coup leader in Cuba. However, for C-Day, the CIA had only a supporting role, to the US military.

From C-Day's inception in May 1963, the US military officially had the lead role in the operation, having been assigned responsibility for covert invasions after the CIA's mismanagement of the Bay of Pigs fiasco. Documents from that month show that Joint Chiefs Chairman General Maxwell Taylor was focused on trying to "foment a revolt within Cuba which would call for US military intervention."[15] Taylor was the kind of Kennedy intimate who could be trusted with all the information about C-Day, unlike some members of the Joint Chiefs who were holdovers from the Bay of Pigs days. These included men like Air Force General Curtis LeMay—famous later for his "bomb 'em back to the Stone Age" remark about the North Vietnamese—who had ties to far-right Congressmen highly critical of JFK. Many of the nation's military leaders had been pressing for an invasion of Cuba since the Bay of Pigs failure. But, as historian Richard Reeves noted, JFK "distrusted the military, at least its commanders." JFK "felt . . . the Joint Chiefs of Staff . . . had misled him, even betrayed him, in the weeks leading up to the Bay of Pigs." However, by the spring of 1963, JFK finally had a Chairman of the Joint Chiefs he could trust, Maxwell Taylor. Reeves wrote that Taylor "was the only active or former senior officer with regular access to the Oval Office."[16]

That the US military got what it wanted when the opportunity for C-Day presented itself is clear in a military document that was first drafted on May 1, 1963, just before C-Day became an option. The document was then revised on May 13, right after the Cuban official first contacted Harry about staging a coup. This document was classified TOP SECRET, and the Joint Chiefs had taken action to keep it secret as recently as October 18, 1989, until its release by the JFK Assassination Records Review Board in 1997. It is a report to the Joint Chiefs of Staff that basically debates the pros and cons of two different approaches to overthrowing Castro. One approach is to "foment a revolt in Cuba," while the other would be to "engineer provocative incidents ostensibly perpetrated by the Castro regime" to provide "a pretext for overt US military intervention in Cuba."

The "provocative incidents" that the US could "engineer" had been the subject of extensive military planning the previous year. Codenamed OPERATION NORTHWOODS, these plans were also declassified in 1997, and they received a brief burst of attention in the news media because they were so shocking. Several C-Day documents were released at the same time, but the news media and even historians overlooked them because the NORTHWOODS documents were so bizarre. As ABC News reported, the NORTHWOODS documents show that in 1962, the US Joint Chiefs drafted plans "to kill innocent people and commit acts of terrorism in US cities to create public support for a war against Cuba." Specifically,

the plans reportedly included the possible assassination of Cuban émigrés, sinking boats of Cuban refugees on the high seas, hijacking planes, blowing up a US ship, and even orchestrating violent terrorism in US cities. The plans were developed as ways to trick the American public and the international community into supporting a war to oust Cuba's then new leader, Communist Fidel Castro. America's top military brass even contemplated causing US military casualties, writing: "We could blow up a US ship in Guantanamo Bay and blame Cuba," and, "casualty lists in US newspapers would cause a helpful wave of national indignation."[17]

Why would the Joint Chiefs have suggested such things in 1962? Because they had actually tried to use one of the ideas in 1961 to force JFK to commit US forces at the Bay of Pigs. ABC News reported that one of the Joint Chiefs' ideas from 1962 "was to pay someone in the Castro government to attack US forces at the Guantanamo naval base." That's close to what the US military and CIA had actually done just before the Bay of Pigs, without JFK's knowledge. FBI veteran William Turner discovered that the CIA intended "to mount a fake attack on Guantanamo that would make Castro look like the aggressor and justify direct American [military] intervention." However, the Cuban exiles who were supposed to stage the fake attack on Guantanamo refused.[18] Turner's discovery was confirmed by a former CIA employee.[19] Because JFK never learned about this deception planned during the Bay of Pigs, the Joint Chiefs felt safe in proposing similar provocations to JFK and his Secretary of Defense a year later. However, both men declined to pursue the bizarre schemes and JFK replaced the Chairman of the Joint Chiefs with his own man, Maxwell Taylor, a few months later.[20]

The May 1963 Joint Chiefs document provides extensive detail about plans for C-Day in its earliest stages. General Taylor's request for information about engineering a pretext for invasion may only have been a cover for his real goal, which was "using US military intervention" to support a "revolt within Cuba." At this early stage, the military role for C-Day was projected to be far smaller than the size it would grow to by the fall of 1963. The May estimates suggest that supporting a coup would require 1,123 officers and enlisted men, plus five civilians, a "SEAL team," a "Special Forces . . . headquarters and two companies," two "submarines," "Air Commandos" including "twenty aircraft," and "CIA forces."[21]

The Joint Chiefs felt that US military support for a revolt was needed because "any uprising without US overt [military] support is likely to be short-lived because of the improved Cuban/Soviet military capabilities presently in Cuba and Castro's increasingly efficient internal security operations." While the military had their own plans for "inciting a revolt in Cuba, followed by overt, large-scale US military operations," they figured it would take "15–18 months." That meant that the earliest the military thought they could get a revolt together was August 1964, possibly as late as November— which would be during the presidential elections. It's not hard to see why General Maxwell Taylor quickly got behind C-Day, because it promised dramatic results in just six months.[22]

The Joint Chiefs' recommendation in May 1963 was that "The US should . . . at a propitious time, launch appropriate military action to remove the Castro Communist government." Such "military action in Cuba" should be "in accordance with . . . plans . . . directed by the President." They felt that "one governmental organization [should] be given the primary responsibility for developing a national plan." Though they believed that "the Joint Chiefs of Staff should participate in the development of this national plan," they were aware of the political realities, so they said "the views of the joint Chiefs of Staff should be forwarded to" one of the Cuba subcommittees headed by Bobby Kennedy.[23]

The high degree of secrecy and sensitivity about this early C-Day planning is evident from its distribution. While part of it was to be forwarded to Secretary of the Army Cyrus Vance because he was the "Executive Agent of the Department of Defense for Policy toward Cuba," the document was so secret that it was *not* to be "forwarded to US officers assigned to NATO activities" or "to the Chairman, US Delegation, United Nations Military Staff Committee." It was distributed only to eighteen generals and admirals and one colonel. Among those getting the memo was General Joseph Carroll, the head of the DIA, who would be heavily involved with C-Day.[24]

The US military did see roles for other agencies, saying that "supporting operations by CIA, State, and USIA [the US Information Agency] will be required." One of those "supporting operations" was "the introduction by CIA as soon as practicable of assets into Cuba for the development of intelligence . . . and the development of a suitable cover plan."[25] This attempt to get "assets into Cuba" by the CIA would accelerate into the fall, and would include at least three men linked to JFK's assassination.

At this early stage, the Joint Chiefs were proposing procedures that would be radically shortened in the months to come. For example, they suggested that a new provisional "Cuban Government would be required to exist for at least 18 days" before the US sent in the troops. However, having a high-profile figure like the C-Day coup leader in position to take over immediately after Castro was eliminated meant that that time could be shortened greatly. By November 1963, the plan would talk of having people in place to make a decision within "twenty-four hours."[26]

Despite this extensive planning, C-Day remained secret for so long because knowledge of it was carefully limited and compartmentalized. Other than Generals Taylor and Carroll, it's unclear how much the other Joint Chiefs knew about the actual C-Day plan. Most, like General LeMay, were probably only told that the planning was necessary "just in case" the conditions for a coup developed, and that attempts were under way to find someone to stage a coup. Second, the US military doesn't like to reveal its covert failures: For almost five decades, the military covered up the true cause of the death of 749 Americans in one secret operation in World War II, the one-night practice run for D-Day called OPERATION TIGER.

The Joint Chiefs made several recommendations about using Cuban exiles in their plans, and they got some of what they wanted. While they said the creation of a Cuban exile "Expeditionary Force" was "a risk which cannot be justified and should not be undertaken," they suggested that "Cubans could . . . be formed into small teams for use in UW [unconventional warfare] activities." They "estimated that from two to four hundred carefully selected Cubans could be used in this role" and that "the CIA" could have a "supporting role to select and train the individuals."[27]

JFK and Bobby felt that the Cuban exiles deserved a more prominent role. More important, the Kennedys were aware of how much better it would look to the world if the first US troops into Cuba were a multiracial Cuban exile group. Consequently, several hundred Cuban exiles were selected and sent to Fort Benning, Georgia, where they were trained to be the first US force into Cuba after the C-Day coup.[28] Other exiles were sent for training to Fort Stewart, South Carolina, and two other bases.[29]

While the military handled the exile troops, the CIA was responsible for dealing with the exile groups that the Kennedys and Harry were choosing for C-Day. Bobby Kennedy told Harry that "you will direct the elements, direct the operation." But Harry was well aware of past problems between Cuban exiles and their often heavy-handed and patronizing CIA masters. So Harry bluntly told Bobby that he would only agree "if I don't deal with the CIA [bureaucracy]. I deal with you and you tell me which one of the CIA [men] comes to me and he works for me. I don't work for him. I'm going to call the shots if you want me to do it." Harry said Bobby agreed, and that was "the way that lasted until November [22, 1963] when President Kennedy was assassinated."[30]

Two CIA memos confirm that in June 1963, guidelines spawned by members of one of Bobby's Cuban committees "were approved" for the Cuban exile groups that would become part of the C-Day planning. The exile groups were supposed to appear "autonomous," although, as Bobby himself would explain to them shortly, they only had the appearance of being autonomous and really answered to him. To receive major funding from the US, "all operations had to be mounted outside the territory of the United States," were "to be executed exclusively by Cuban Nationals dedicated to the idea that the overthrow of" Castro was necessary, and "must be accomplished by Cubans inside and outside Cuba working in concert." This guideline mirrors closely the rationale that several Kennedy associates told us about C-Day: The Kennedys viewed C-Day as the US aiding "Cubans helping other Cubans," not as an assassination plan.[31] The June 1963 guidelines also say that "an experienced [CIA] liaison officer would be assigned to each group to provide general advice, funds and material support."[32] The June 1963 CIA memo says that "if ever charged with complicity, the US Government would publicly deny any participation in the groups' activities."[33]

A second, much longer CIA memo about the guidelines was finally declassified in 1997. This formerly SECRET, EYES ONLY memo was prepared by the CIA for one of Bobby Kennedy's Cuba subcommittee meetings on June 8, 1963. It bluntly says that "the ultimate objective" for the plan "would be to encourage dissident elements in the . . . power centers of the [Cuban] regime to bring about the eventual liquidation of . . . Castro" as well as "the elimination of the Soviet presence from Cuba."[34] The memo makes it clear that the exile guidelines and the "liquidation of . . . Castro" by a powerful dissident in the Cuban government are all part of the same plan. The memo stresses that all parts of its "covert program for Cuba" are "closely interrelated" and that "the total cumulative impact of the courses of action" are "dependent upon the simultaneous coordinated execution of the individual courses of action." In other words, it's not a list of separate plans, but a list of different parts of one coordinated plan. It says the guidelines for "autonomous anti-Castro Cuban groups" are meant "to supplement and assist" the other parts of the plan, including the "exploitation and stimulation of disaffection in the Cuban . . . power centers."[35]

Other parts of the plan to bring about the "liquidation of . . . Castro" include a focus on "covert collection of intelligence." This involves "increasing the volume and quality of intelligence needed . . . particularly for defections and penetrations." It notes that "assets trained and controlled by CIA will be used."[36] Later chapters show how some of those CIA assets were unknowingly manipulated by the Mafia in their plot to assassinate JFK.

Not everyone involved in the meeting knew about the C-Day plan, so the memo also talks about things like "propaganda actions" and "economic denial." But it makes it clear that the US is "undertaking an intensive . . . effort to . . . establish channels of communication with disaffected . . . elements in the power centers of the [Cuban] regime." The purpose is "to promote the fragmentation of the regime and . . . lead to an internal coup which would dislodge Castro . . . and force the withdrawal of the Soviet military presence." It hints that "several promising operations are already underway."[37] Since the CIA was just getting ready to reestablish contact with disgruntled mid-level Cuban official Rolando Cubela, and their AMTRUNK operation hadn't produced results of any significance, it's clear from our sources that the only "promising" plan at that point was the coup leader and C-Day.[38]

The June 8, 1963 memo repeats the same exile guidelines from the previous memo, but adds more detail.[39] Regarding the US government's plan to "deny publicly any participation in" the acts of the chosen exile groups, the memo says that will be done "no matter . . . how accurate may be the reports of US complicity."[40] The memo also notes that while "an experienced CIA officer would be assigned to work with" each "group in a liaison capacity," the CIA officer would "be expected to influence but not control the conduct of operations."[41] This confirms what we were told by Harry Williams, that he didn't work for the CIA officers assigned to him; instead, they were there to assist him.[42]

In the 1970s, the Senate Church Committee would note that after "the June 1963 decision" of Bobby's subcommittee, the "files of the intelligence agencies . . . document a series of meetings among major leaders of the anti-Castro movement." They also found that "some of these leaders claimed the support of the United States Government." For example, they cite an October 18, 1963 FBI report of such meetings.[43]

On June 22, 1963, "Bobby met with Harry Williams" and some of the other trusted Cuban exile leaders, according to two CIA memos uncovered by author Gus Russo. That was two days after JFK had personally approved the operations described in the exile guideline memos. Bobby Kennedy told them not to "get the idea you will be working independently" because "all [your] forces, though outside the country, will be coordinated." In other words, their supposedly "autonomous" operations were not autonomous at all. Bobby also wanted them to quit phoning him directly so much "because of the frequency of rumors linking him with certain operations against Cuba."[44] Bobby's Justice Department phone logs confirm the high volume of calls that he was talking about. They document twenty-five calls by Harry Williams to Bobby's office in 1963, most in the first half of the year before Harry switched to a less direct approach. That total doesn't count the calls Bobby made to Harry, or the calls Harry made to Bobby's home, or Harry's many meetings with Bobby (and Harry's occasional meetings with JFK).[45] Historian Richard Mahoney, whose father was part of the Kennedy administration, wrote that Harry Williams "spoke to Bobby at least once a week."[46] But to help preserve the secrecy of the Kennedys' support for C-Day, Harry started making greater use of Bobby's secretary to arrange meetings. Harry himself was often the conduit for other C-Day exile leaders to communicate with Bobby.[47]

The CIA's point man on Cuba, Desmond FitzGerald, flew "into a towering rage upon learning that Kennedy had been meeting privately with Cuban exiles," according to FitzGerald's daughter. She said that her father was enraged that "Bobby Kennedy was entertaining Cuban exiles at his house at Hickory Hill [Virginia] and calling them at their apartments at the Ebbitt Hotel." Evan Thomas wrote that Desmond FitzGerald viewed Bobby's Cuban exile leaders with "disgust and contempt." FitzGerald was from a wealthy "Eastern establishment family," his first wife's family had founded Radcliffe and Groton, and FitzGerald had been a Wall Street lawyer who lived on Park Avenue before joining the CIA. Thomas notes that FitzGerald's "elitism, by modern standards, was offensive."[48]

Harry Williams gave us his impression of the CIA's Desmond FitzGerald. He said that Bobby "introduced me to him in those days" and that FitzGerald "was very high up in the CIA." In terms of C-Day, Harry said that FitzGerald "was the representative of Bobby . . . he was really handling the scene" for the CIA. Harry told us that "I don't know [exactly] how much, [but] he knew a lot" about C-Day. For the CIA, Bobby "Kennedy had him in charge of this. Bobby was really handling the thing [C-Day], but" FitzGerald "was just next to Bobby." Several historians, including Evan Thomas and Gus Russo, have confirmed FitzGerald's work on Cuban operations with Bobby in 1963.[49]

Desmond FitzGerald wasn't the only career CIA official who couldn't stand the idea of Bobby dealing directly with Cuban exiles like Harry Williams and the other exile leaders; another was Ted Shackley, chief of the massive Miami CIA Station in the early 1960s. The Miami CIA Station, code-named JMWAVE, was the largest CIA base outside of Washington, larger than any CIA station in any foreign country. According to a Congressional report, at that time the Miami Station had "1,571 acres," ran "54 front corporations," and had "a staff of more than 300 Americans, mostly case officers." And "each case officer employed from 4 to 10 Cuban [exile] 'principal agents' who in turn, would each be responsible for between 10 and 30 regular agents."[50] Ted Shackley was responsible for that huge—and largely ineffective—effort. Shackley's deputy told *Nation* writer David Corn that Shackley "hated the idea that the Cubans had gotten to the Kennedys and convinced them that they could operate on their own."[51]

The "hatred" of Shackley and the "disgust and contempt" FitzGerald felt toward Bobby's exiles were probably mirrored by some other high CIA officials, and would impact both C-Day's planning and the tragic fallout from its failure. It's probably one reason that in June 1963, the CIA's Richard Helms began reviving and renewing his own Castro assassination plots, such as the ZRRIFLE "Executive Action" program with the CIA-Mafia plots and European assassin recruiter QJWIN, and renewing contact with mid-level Cuban official Rolando Cubela. These were programs controlled by the CIA, not Bobby Kennedy or Harry Williams or the US military, and Helms didn't even fully inform CIA Director McCone about them. After JFK's death, the CIA covered up huge amounts of information about the assassination, ostensibly to protect C-Day. Officials like FitzGerald and Helms may have rationalized that C-Day had somehow "blown-back" against JFK, but that was Bobby's program, not theirs, and thus dealing with that blowback was his responsibility. However, as we document in later chapters, the CIA's own Castro assassination plots and intelligence failures primarily allowed three Mafia bosses to infiltrate C-Day and use parts of it against JFK.

In June 1963, Harry Williams and the Kennedys targeted five Cuban exile leaders and some of their groups for recruitment into C-Day. If Harry was Bobby Kennedy's right arm for C-Day, then Harry saw these five as being the fingers of his right hand. Harry demonstrated how the C-Day plan was supposed to work when he opened his hand, and said to imagine Cuba in the palm of his hand. His five fingers represented the other exile leaders and groups, based at various places around the Caribbean and Central America, except for the exile troops at Ft. Benning, Georgia. On C-Day, with Harry already in Cuba, the coup leader in Cuba would kill Fidel (or have him killed). A signal would be given, and Harry's exile leaders would rush into Cuba—which Harry demonstrated by closing his five fingers into a fist. Five fingers, operating in perfect coordination, to help Harry and the C-Day coup leader set up the new Provisional Government. That's how it was supposed to work—although, as later chapters on each of the leaders and groups detail, trying to put that into effect was often a struggle. The five targeted were Manuel Artime (and his exile group, the MRR), Manolo Ray (and his group JURE), Eloy Menoyo (and his SNFE), Tony Varona (whose Cuban Revolutionary Council was almost moribund, so he was targeted primarily as an individual), and the Cuban exile officers training at Fort Benning (whose leadership was a traditional military command structure). Harry saw himself as a coordinator and liaison with Bobby, and he didn't have (or want) an exile organization of his own; that was one way he stayed above the politics and bickering that plagued most of the exile groups. That way, he could simply focus on persuading the "five fingers" to join the C-Day plan, using his own charisma and money authorized by the Kennedys. Bobby Kennedy ensured that the Fort Benning officers would be part of C-Day, and the first of the others to sign on to C-Day was Manuel Artime, in June 1963, with Tony Varona following in July. While the military was reponsible for the Fort Benning troops, the CIA was responsible for handling the exile groups and providing them with a wide range of support.

CHAPTER FOUR

AMWORLD:
The CIA's Portion of C-Day

ON "JUNE 28, 1963," THE CIA officially christened their portion of C-Day "AMWORLD" in a secret memo sent to a select group of CIA officials.[1] This initial AMWORLD MEMO was only declassifed in 1999, and was never seen by the Warren Commission or any of the Congressional investigating committees, none of whom were ever told about C-Day. This document appears here for the first time; it has never been cited in any previous book or article. It was only declassified in 1999 because of the efforts of the JFK Assassination Records Review Board, who had first been alerted to the existence of C-Day and AMWORLD by the authors in their 1994 written testimony to the Board. Even after documents are declassified, it can sometimes take months or years for them to show up in the National Archives, and this document was one of several AMWORLD documents discovered there in 2004 (a few others had been released in the early 1990s).[2] This initial AMWORLD memo confirms many things the authors had stated in their written testimony to the Review Board, on the History Channel, and to *Vanity Fair* years before this document was released.

Even in June 1963, C-Day and AMWORLD were the subject of intense secrecy by the CIA, even more than regular CIA operations. Also, AMWORLD documents are filled with CIA code words, which we will translate in our quotes for greater clarity. Some of the code words themselves—for instance, PBRUMEN, which meant Cuba—were still being kept secret by the CIA as late as 1995, which was yet another reason most historians had trouble making sense of the few C-Day documents that had slipped through and been declassified. Other code words we'll translate in the AMWORLD document quotes are: AMBIDDY (Manuel Artime), KUBARK (CIA), JMWAVE (Miami CIA station), ODYOKE (US government, in this case the Kennedy administration), AMYUM (Artime's exile group, the MRR), and PBPRIME (the US).

The first AMWORLD document was a SECRET, EYES ONLY five-page memo pre-
pared on June 28, 1963. It was sent by J. C. King, "Chief [of the CIA's]
Western Hemisphere Division," to the "Chiefs of Certain [CIA] Stations."
King, who effectively ranked just below Richard Helms and just above
Desmond FitzGerald, used his official code-name on the document, "Oliver
G. Galbond." The memo is titled "AMWORLD—Background of Program, Operational Support Requirements and Procedural Rules." It begins: "This will
serve to alert you to the inception of AMWORLD, a new CIA program targeted
against Cuba. Some manifestations of activity resulting from this program
may come to your notice before long." Echoing the exile guidelines cited earlier, the memo says:

> activities involved in this program are to be based outside the US and . . .
> any manifestations of CIA participation in the planning and execution of
> the program will be kept to a minimum. The CIA will . . . confine itself
> to supporting Artime's effort financially and logistically, and to giving gen-
> eral advice where appropriate. The Kennedy Administration, it should be
> emphasized, is willing to accept the risks involved in utilizing
> autonomous Cuban exile groups and individuals who are not necessarily
> responsive to CIA guidance and to face up to the consequences which are
> unavoidable in lowering professional standards adhered to by
> autonomous groups (as compared with fully controlled and disciplined
> agent assets) is bound to entail.

As documented in later chapters, the CIA is being somewhat disingen-
uous here, since Artime had actually been working for the CIA since the fall
of 1959, when he attempted his first CIA-backed coup against Castro. It's not
as if Artime was being forced on the CIA by the Kennedys, and Artime would
remain very close to CIA officers from this era until his death. But what was
different about AMWORLD was that Artime—and the others—were now taking
orders not from the CIA, but from Bobby Kennedy.[3]

The memo says that supporting groups like Artime's "is the price the
Kennedy Administration is willing to pay to enable it to deny publicly any
participation in the activities of autonomous groups, no matter how loud or
even how accurate reports of US complicity may turn out to be." Such
reports would occasionally surface in the press, to the great concern of Bobby
Kennedy and others.[4] By November 1963, however, the Kennedys and the
CIA would be so adept at controlling press reports that they would be able

to keep two assassination attempts against JFK out of the press, in Chicago and Tampa.

The AMWORLD memo lays out some details of the operation, saying that "Artime will be in touch with a senior CIA officer, operating under a fully documented alias, who is to serve as his advisor and hopefully as his sole direct link with the Kennedy Administration." The "hopefully" suggests that the CIA probably knew this would not be the case, since Artime would be able to get to Bobby through Harry Williams and, increasingly, by going to Bobby directly. However, Artime's CIA officer "and his staff will be based at the Miami CIA Station, and that office will be known by the code-name LORK." It will have a "separate communications net linking the Miami CIA Station/AMWORLD operations center with Artime's headquarters in Nicaragua." Miami CIA Chief of Operations David Morales would have assisted with the AMWORLD office there, at the same time that Morales was working closely with mob boss Johnny Rosselli on the CIA-Mafia plots to kill Castro.

The memo said that "meetings between the CIA officer (and assistants) and Artime will take place outside the US, in frequently shifting locations in order to obviate setting any pattern of contact arousing the interest of hostile, e.g., Cuban [intelligence] services." CIA Station chiefs "will . . . be given early warning of any planned meetings, their location and of the aliases being used by Artime and the CIA officer in charge of the project." CIA officer David Atlee Phillips shows up in later AMWORLD files as one of the CIA officers arranging meetings with Artime in Mexico City, using exactly the same procedure outlined in the first AMWORLD document.[5] Phillips worked closely with David Morales, and both men play key roles in the story of C-Day. It's important to notice a distinction here between Harry Williams and Artime. While Harry would travel to other countries to visit various C-Day bases, such as Artime's, most of Harry's meetings with his CIA support officers took place in America.

CIA Station Chiefs receiving the memo are cautioned to generally "keep aloof" from involvement in Artime's activities. It says that if their "host government" queries them "about Artime's activities . . . nothing should be said or hinted at which could in any manner be construed as implying Kennedy Administration official condonement let alone sponsorship of his activities. You should, on the other hand, feel free to convey in a subtle manner that the Kennedy Administration sympathizes with Artime's aspirations to see Cuba liberated from a foreign yoke and that his reputation as a leader of an important segment . . . dedicated to toppling the [Castro] regime continues to be very high." The CIA Station Chiefs were being asked to walk a fine line.

AMWORLD's sensitive nature, even within the CIA, is indicated by the directives to CIA Station Chiefs in case one of their local "sources" picks up any "information on Artime" or AMWORLD. The memo stresses that such information should not be forwarded "to [CIA] Headquarters as an intelligence report," as was usually the case; instead, they're told to "send all material on Artime or AMWORLD as an <u>operations report</u>, using this channel" [emphasis in original]. Reports were to be "addressed to Headquarters, info LORK (the AMWORLD base at the CIA Miami Station) and classified RYBAT SECRET TYPIC YOBITE AMWORLD." (Those additional code words have proven useful in identifying some older CIA AMWORLD documents where the term "AMWORLD" had been censored.) In addition, the memo talks about other ways to keep AMWORLD secret, like "briefing personnel assigned to your Station about the AMWORLD project" only on a "strict Need-to-Know" basis.

The first AMWORLD memo was sent to CIA Station Chiefs in Mexico City, Guatemala City, Nicaragua, the Dominican Republic, and, of course, Miami, among others. As primarily a "heads up" memo, it didn't detail sensitive operational aspects of AMWORLD and C-Day. The operation was listed under Desmond FitzGerald's Special Affairs Staff (SAS), and research by Dr. John Newman and *Washington Post* editor Jefferson Morley proves that CIA officers at some CIA stations—including Mexico City—had lines of communication to FitzGerald and Richard Helms that even the local CIA Station Chief didn't have access to. This would lead to much confusion and secrecy in the fall of 1963, when the number 3 man in Mexico City, David Atlee Phillips, was privy to information about Lee Harvey Oswald's visit there that even the Mexico City Station Chief didn't know about. This reflects the levels of knowledge various CIA officials had about AMWORLD and C-Day. The Mexico City CIA Chief would know generally about AMWORLD, and the Kennedy and CIA support for Artime, from this memo. But only someone like David Atlee Phillips would know sensitive operation details about AMWORLD, and how it fit into the C-Day coup plan.

One of the CIA officers who signed the first AMWORLD document, John Whitten (codename SCELSO), initially headed the CIA's secret internal investigation into JFK's assassination. According to Jefferson Morley, Whitten was removed from that duty by Richard Helms when he asked Helms for "files on Oswald's Cuba-related activities." Whitten later testified to the House Select Committee on Assassinations that he had been "appalled" to learn later that

Helms had been organizing other assassination attempts against Castro at the time of JFK's death, and hadn't informed Whitten.[6] While Whitten knew about C-Day and Artime, he didn't know about Helms's other plots—or that CIA files confirm that Artime and Varona had been part of the CIA-Mafia plots to kill Castro. The mob bosses who the CIA admits worked with Artime and Varona in these plots—Johnny Rosselli and Santo Trafficante—were among the mobsters blamed for JFK's assassination by the House Select Committee and other investigators.[*]

In addition to Washington-based officials like Richard Helms and Desmond FitzGerald, several other CIA officers and agents have been linked to C-Day by various documents and sources. There was a reason these particular people were chosen for an operation like C-Day: Many had worked together on similar operations before, operations that involved coups and assassinations. Several got their start working together in the CIA's 1954 Guatemala coup, which recent documents reveal also had an extensive assassination component. Their experiences there and in later CIA coup operations helped to shape their actions in regard to C-Day. Some of the CIA men worked with Harry Williams, some with Manuel Artime and other C-Day exile leaders, while others provided general support for the CIA's AMWORLD portion of C-Day.

As the Miami CIA's Chief of Operations, David Morales would have been responsible for the AMWORLD office there, code-named LORK in the CIA's initial memo about their part of C-Day. Morales was a veteran of the CIA's 1959 plots to assassinate Castro, as were CIA agent David Atlee Phillips and future C-Day exile leaders Manuel Artime and Tony Varona. Information about Morales was withheld from the Warren Commission and the next four government commissions to investigate aspects of JFK's assassination. The House Select Committee on Assassinations finally came across his name, but Morales died of a heart attack shortly after being told he would have to testify. Even then, the CIA withheld information from the Committee about Morales's key role in anti-Castro operations in 1963. It was only in 1990 that the Archivist for Miami-Dade County got former Miami CIA Chief Ted

---

[*]We do not believe the CIA as an organization killed JFK, or that it was the work of a large clique inside the CIA. More than anything, the CIA's decades-long, organizational cover-up was designed to hide intelligence failures and protect reputations, under the guise of protecting those involved in C-Day.

Shackley to admit that "Dave Morales . . . was my Chief of Operations" in 1963.[7]

The reason for the CIA's reticence with regard to Morales can be found in a recent comment by Shackley's deputy, who said that David Morales "would do anything, even work with the Mafia."[8] In fact, at the same time AMWORLD had a base at the Miami CIA Station, Morales was also helping to run the CIA-Mafia plots with mob kingpin Johnny Rosselli, a frequent visitor to Miami. The CIA-Mafia plots were one of the key ways the Mafia penetrated C-Day, and they are covered extensively in later chapters.

Partly because David Atlee Phillips had a high profile after leaving the CIA in the mid-1970s, and partly because so much information about Morales was—and is still—withheld by the CIA, for years it was assumed that Morales had been subordinate to Phillips in 1963, merely an operative for him. It's now clear that Morales, Chief of Operations at the CIA's largest station outside of Washington, was at least equal—if not superior—to David Phillips, the number-three man at the smaller Mexico City station. Nonetheless, they worked closely together in 1963.

To CIA officials like Richard Helms, Morales was the perfect choice for CIA coups and assassinations because "within the CIA, Morales was considered a dangerous but effective agent, a trained assassin who honed his skills in the bloody repression of the Tupemaro guerillas in Montevideo, Uruguay."[9] Prior to that, Morales had begun his work with David Atlee Phillips and other future C-Day figures in 1954, when the CIA staged a coup against the democratically elected president of Guatemala.[10] David Morales was one of seven people involved in the 1954 Guatemala coup who would later be linked to C-Day, by documents or participants. Many of these seven people, and the techniques first used in Guatemala in 1954, would keep resurfacing not just in C-Day, but also in the CIA-Mafia plots to kill Castro, the Bay of Pigs, and the C-Day–inspired plot against Chile that Nixon was pursuing at the time of Watergate.

The official CIA secrecy that still surrounds the 1954 Guatemala coup, after more than fifty years, helps to explain why only a few dozen CIA C-Day and AMWORLD documents have been declassified out of the thousands that should still exist. Most history books consider the 1954 CIA Guatemala coup as a bloodless affair, in which the propaganda of Phillips and E. Howard Hunt caused the elected president to flee. CIA documents finally declassified in 1997, because of a lawsuit filed in 1979, reveal that extensive assassination plans were also part of the coup. However, the National Security

Archive, the same group that pursued the Cuban Missile Crisis documents, notes that the CIA only "declassified some 1400 pages of over 100,000 estimated to be in its secret archives."[11] And almost all of the names of CIA agents—like Morales, Phillips, and Hunt—have been censored from those documents that have been released, as were the names of dozens of CIA assassination targets, making it hard to tell how many might have been killed.

David Atlee Phillips shows up in AMWORLD files as one of the CIA officers arranging meetings with Artime, using exactly the same procedure outlined in the first AMWORLD document.[12] Phillips had at least several roles for the CIA in the summer and fall of 1963, in addition to helping with C-Day. Phillips was based in Mexico City, but also worked in Miami and Washington, D.C. He also used at least three CIA code names in 1963: Michael C. Choaden (the name he used in AMWORLD), Lawrence F. Barker (a name he'd used for several years prior to C-Day), and Maurice Bishop (according to Congressional investigator Gaeton Fonzi).

Phillips's different CIA roles in 1963 all had an impact on C-Day and its tragic aftermath. In addition to his experience with coups and assassinations, Phillips was also a propaganda and media expert. He ran operations against the small pro-Castro group called the Fair Play for Cuba Committee. According to the testimony of E. Howard Hunt—a longtime friend of Phillips and Manuel Artime—Phillips also ran a non-C-Day exile group called the DRE for the CIA. The DRE is remembered today only because Lee Harvey Oswald had a highly publicized confrontation with it three months before JFK's assassination, which resulted in Oswald getting even more radio, TV, and newspaper publicity in the days that followed. Congressional investigator Fonzi concluded that shortly after Oswald's publicity bonanza, there was a meeting in public between Phillips, Oswald, and exile Antonio Veciana (the partner of C-Day exile leader Eloy Menoyo). Phillips's role in that—and in Oswald's unusual trip to Mexico City a few weeks later—and how they relate to C-Day is explained in later chapters, along with new information from Veciana.

Phillips was no doubt assigned to work on C-Day because of his previous experience with coups and assassinations. In addition to his work on the Bay of Pigs, in his own autobiography Phillips boasts about organizing the CIA's first coup attempt against Fidel Castro in 1959, around the time Phillips first met Che Guevara. Phillips also claims to have caused the CIA to open their first file on Che right after the 1954 Guatemala coup. Over twenty years later, Phillips and other C-Day veterans like Morales and Helms would try to stage a coup in Chile for Richard Nixon, resulting in tragedies like those depicted in the acclaimed film *Missing*.

James McCord, E. Howard Hunt, and Hunt's assistant Bernard Barker have all been linked to C-Day.[*]William Turner wrote that in 1963, "the CIA agents finally assigned to [Harry] Williams on a permanent basis were Howard Hunt and James McCord, the future Watergaters. Williams had dozens of meetings and countless telephone discussions with Hunt and McCord. The meetings were usually in Washington or New York, away from the rumors of Miami."[13] At the time, James McCord was a "Senior Security Officer" for the CIA's Security Office.[14] Harry told Turner that McCord "was a professional man" and implied they had a good "business"-like relationship.[15] A CIA document confirms that James McCord had once worked with Phillips on a CIA operation targeting the Fair Play for Cuba Committee, a small organization Oswald later joined.[16]

Gus Russo, an investigative journalist with numerous CIA sources, confirms that "E. Howard Hunt" was one of Harry's "CIA case officers," and Russo adds another name as well, also connected to Watergate, "Bernard 'Macho' Barker."[17] Barker was Cuban, and he had helped Manuel Artime flee the island after a failed CIA-backed assassination and coup attempt against Castro in the fall of 1959. Barker became a CIA agent and was very close to Hunt in the 1960s when they worked together on Cuban operations and, later, when Barker worked for Hunt as one of the Watergate burglars. Barker told Bill Moyers in a TV interview that "I would have followed Howard Hunt to hell and back."[18] In another TV interview, Barker gave a surprisingly accurate description of the status of the Kennedys' efforts to topple Castro in 1963. Barker said on TV that "at the time" of "the Kennedy assassination . . . President Kennedy's government had reached its 'peak' in its efforts to overthrow Castro. The Kennedys had given the green light and had gone ahead on camps in Nicaragua and Costa Rica. There was tremendous activity involved in those days." Barker said that "anyone who belonged to the intelligence community of the Cuban . . . liberation forces at that time could tell you the death of Kennedy was the destruction of the cause of liberation of Cuba at that time."

---

[*]Just because certain names have been linked to C-Day by documents or sources, it does not mean those individuals acknowledge being involved with AMWORLD or the broader effort we call C-Day. It also does not meant that any particular CIA officials were knowingly involved in JFK's assassination.

Former CIA agent Bernard Barker once described Hunt's feelings about Castro in words very similar to those Haynes Johnson ascribed to Harry. A book edited by former Senate Investigator Bernard Fensterwald says that "Barker recalled, in an NBC interview in April, 1974, that 'Mr. Hunt personally always had the theory that the physical elimination of Fidel Castro was the proper way for the liberation of Cuba.'"[19] Even though Hunt was far more conservative than Harry Williams, they shared the common goal of eliminating Castro. Harry, however, told Turner that Hunt "never opened up to me. . . . I never trusted him and he never trusted me."[20]

CIA documents and testimony all confirm that Bernard Barker, E. Howard Hunt, and James McCord were all working for the CIA in 1963. Barker's CIA file shows that he was working primarily on Cuban matters in 1963, and one document from his file even references C-Day. However, it's important to note that none of those men have ever acknowledged working on C-Day or on AMWORLD (whose name was still classified at the time of the Watergate, Church, and HSCA investigations).

Pulitzer Prize–winning journalist Tad Szulc has also written about the roles of Barker, Hunt, and McCord. Szulc writes that Hunt was "the political coordinator of the Bay of Pigs under the nom de guerre of 'Eduardo.'"[21] Later, Szulc says that "Hunt was secretly involved in" an "operation . . . intended to coordinate a second attempt to invade Cuba . . . with a plot to assassinate Castro."[22] Szulc wrote that, like Hunt, McCord was also "associated with the 1961 [Bay of Pigs] invasion" and "the second [Cuban] landing operation."[23]

"As part of the 'second invasion' scheme, Hunt is also believed to have spent time in San Jose, the Costa Rican capital, checking on preparations in the camps in Central America," Szulc writes. "Some CIA sources say that he and Artime shared a 'mansion' in downtown San Jose for a while." Szulc notes that E. Howard "Hunt was known to only a very few people outside the Agency [the CIA] under his real name. Throughout the Bay of Pigs period, Cubans knew him only as 'Eduardo.'"[24] Szulc wrote that in 1974, but Harry Williams had revealed Hunt's "Eduardo" alias to William Turner in 1973.

Harry said that Hunt and McCord both asked him to use the same CIA code name in his dealings with them: "both . . . said to call me Don Eduardo. Both Hunt and McCord. I was confused."[25] Bernard Barker told Bill Moyers on a CBS television special in 1977 that "I was one of the very, very few who knew that Howard Hunt was 'Eduardo.' Eduardo was a mythical name to the Cuban people. Eduardo was the man that was in charge of the CIA in this area. When you said 'Eduardo,' you said the final word in everything relating to Cuba."[26]

As for McCord also using the "Eduardo" code name, journalist Jim Hougan wrote that Harry Williams "is right on the money when he confesses that he was confused by the reliance of Hunt and McCord upon the same alias, Don Eduardo." Hougan points out that "Don Eduardo" is Spanish for "Mr. Edward" and points out another time both McCord and Hunt used an identical "Edward" alias during Watergate.[27]

With AMWORLD agents like Phillips and Morales often traveling and in the field, higher CIA officials like Desmond FitzGerald handled things in Washington. With the CIA's AMWORLD procedures and case officers in place, planning on C-Day continued in July by Bobby Kennedy and his secretive Cuban subcommittees. On July 14, 1963, a journalistic breach of security caused alarm all the way to the National Security Council when the *Miami Herald* published an article with the revealing title "Backstage with Bobby." Historian Richard Mahoney describes the article as detailing Bobby "Kennedy's role as the architect of the Nicaragua-based front against Castro."[28] The article focused on the activities there of Manuel Artime, one of the five Cuban exile C-Day leaders.

The concern in Washington is evident in the notes of the July 16, 1963 meeting of one of the Cuba subcommittees of the National Security Council, which were classified SECRET until 1997. Even then—and still today—five lines of the notes were deemed so sensitive they were not declassified. At the meeting, the CIA's Desmond FitzGerald discussed "press reports that the US was backing Cuban exiles who are planning raids against Cuba from Central American States." The notes say that "one news article shown the Attorney General was headed 'Backstage with Bobby' and referred to his conversations with persons involved in planning the Cuban raids." As for "how to deal with the press reports, the Attorney General suggested that we could float other rumors so that in the welter of press reports no one would know the true facts." CIA Director "McCone agreed that it would be possible to confuse the situation in this manner."[29]

The reporter who had written the article, Hal Hendrix, had won a Pulitzer Prize earlier that year. But he also had connections to the CIA and, years later, he would plead guilty to charges of lying to Congress about his CIA connections in regard to Nixon's coup against Chile's Salvador Allende.[30] Hendrix's article about Bobby Kennedy had been accurate. The CIA's Miami Station Chief in 1963, Ted Shackley, told Gus Russo that "The training camps in Central America were funded by Washington." Sam Halpern, who worked at the CIA for Desmond FitzGerald, told Russo that "we provided the dough . . . Bobby [Kennedy] knew everything we were doing. We were doing it under his orders. The Cubans got all the money they needed." And one of C-Day leader Manuel Artime's deputies, Raphael Quintero, said, in 1997, "Bobby Kennedy was the creator of this operation . . . it was much like Oliver North's [Iran-Contra] operation—autonomous of the CIA, and run by the White House."[31] Russo notes that Quintero was well qualified to make the comparison between Artime and North, since Quintero "would become a major player in North's . . . Iran-Contra . . .scheme of the 1980's," an operation that involved several C-Day veterans.[32] Shortly before his death in 1977, Artime told a reporter for the Orlando *Sentinel-Star* that "I was protected by Bob [Kennedy] until his brother was assassinated. He met with me personally in the offices of the Attorney General. He kept in touch with the entire operation."[33]

But it wasn't just Bobby Kennedy acting on his own. A declassified CIA memo says that on July 19, 1963, Harry Williams delivered a message to Manuel Artime at his Nicaraguan base, telling Artime that "you are now being supported by the offices of GPIDEAL"—and GPIDEAL was the CIA's official code name for President John F. Kennedy.[34] (For contrast, the official CIA code name for Fidel Castro was AMTHUG.)

On July 17, 1963, the *Times* reported that "Artime, leader of [the] April '61 invasion, says he is leaving [the] US to set up Central American headquarters to direct new military operations by exiles."[35] On July 22, 1963, the *Times* carried a US government statement that "US State Department denies published reports that US officers help build new Cuban army in exile in Nicaragua or elsewhere."[36] This was not only in response to the *Times*'s Artime article, but also to the *Miami Herald*'s article from a few days earlier, "Backstage with Bobby."[37]

In mid-August 1963, the *Washington Post* ran a brief mention of the JFK administration's new Cuba plans. Written by Dan Kurzman, the *Post*'s Latin America expert, the article said the US "is apparently trying to prevent independent exile organizations from engaging in parallel activities that might jeopardize its own" activities, since US "policy is to centralize the underground's control under the CIA. This agency is reportedly recruiting particularly trusted and competent members of individual exile groups in its service." The article said the CIA "is believed to be financing and cooperating with at least some independent organizations."[38] In the 1989 article we cited in our Introduction, the *Post* verified the Kennedys' support for the C-Day Cuban exile leaders. It said that in 1963, one of Artime's deputies, Roberto San Roman, "was sent by Robert Kennedy to Central American countries to seek aid for a second invasion [of Cuba]."[39]

CHAPTER FIVE

The Kennedy Men:
Vance, Haig, and Califano

BOBBY'S STRUGGLE TO KEEP A lid on press accounts about his operations pointed to broader issues he and JFK had to face. How could the Kennedys make sure that the military and other agencies planning C-Day didn't get bogged down in the bureaucracy and involve so many people that C-Day was no longer secret? How could the Kennedys maintain complete control over C-Day while also making sure some members of the military didn't go overboard or jump the gun?

The Kennedys used an old technique—divide and conquer. There would be three small groups involved with planning Cuban actions in the summer and fall of 1963. All were essentially run by Bobby Kennedy, even though as Attorney General he would ordinarily have little to do with covert Cuban actions. By using three groups, each could be small enough to actually get something accomplished in the time needed to make C-Day a reality. At the same time, only Bobby Kennedy and a few others would have the big picture of what all the groups were doing. However, the Kennedys' organization was also, apparently, confusing. The President's Special Assistant for National Security Affairs sent a memo to some members of the National Security Council, trying to clarify who was doing what.

It said there were basically three groups: One was the "Interdepartmental Committee on Cuba," chaired by a "Coordinator of Cuban Affairs." "On covert matters," that group's coordinator reported to another group, called "the Special Group." "The Special Group" was part of the National Security Council ("NSC 5412"), and was "responsible for covert activities." It liaised with another committee called "the Standing Group," which was "responsible for the development of contingency plans and the assessment of long-range policy objectives and [the] means for meeting them."[1] Regardless of their name, the bottom line was that all three groups were controlled by Bobby Kennedy throughout the summer and fall of 1963.

All three groups shared more than Bobby Kennedy—they also had the same strengths and weaknesses. The three-group structure proved excellent for keeping C-Day secret, both at the time and in later years. There were few leaks about C-Day to the press and none to Congress, which was a major accomplishment at the time. Even years later, the Church Committee was confused when it first came across a reference to one of Bobby's Cuba planning groups.[2] And when several C-Day documents were finally released in 1997, the various committees and personnel made the documents hard to understand for all but a handful of scholars and specialists.

Having small working groups away from the big meetings of the National Security Council chaired by JFK helped to "preserve the principle of deniability," according to a memo from one of the groups. This "plausible deniability" is used to insulate presidents from actions that could damage them politically if exposed. The memo, written by JFK's National Security Adviser, McGeorge Bundy, also stressed "the desirability of not spreading knowledge of covert operations any wider than absolutely necessary."[3] By having several small groups, Bobby could get input from a wider variety of advisers—who knew only part of the plan—while telling the whole plan to only a trusted few.

But the Kennedys' three-group approach also shared two problems, including a flaw that may have proved fatal to JFK. Each of the groups included representatives from some agencies—for instance, the State Department—that weren't told about C-Day. They had to participate in planning while knowing only generally about CIA operations involving Cuba or proposed efforts to try to find someone to stage a coup against Castro. While that kept C-Day secret, it also prevented all the members from having full, frank, and critical discussions among themselves about potential problems with C-Day. Worse, none of the three groups included representatives from the Secret Service or the FBI, or Justice Department Mafia experts (aside from Bobby Kennedy). This would have tragic consequences when the planning, in the fall of 1963, turned to how to protect "American officials" from "assassination" in retaliation for C-Day.

The Kennedys had one more way to make sure that none of America's top military officers could take control of C-Day: They made their military point man for covert Cuban operations not a career officer, but a civilian appointee. The National Archives confirms that "Secretary of the Army . . . [Cyrus] Vance was the" Defense Department's "Executive Agent for all meetings of the . . . Interdepartmental Coordinating Committee on Cuban Affairs" (ICCCA, sometimes abbreviated ICCC).[4] Alexander Haig said that JFK "designated . . . Vance, as the executive agent for the entire federal government in dealing with Cuba," including "responsibility for coordinating a secret war against Cuba."[5] And the National Archives adds that "Vance's special assistant, [Joseph] Califano, often represented him at meetings of the ICCCA, and was part of all ICCCA policy deliberations."[6]

Joseph Califano writes that the ICCCA was "nominally chaired by [a] State Department representative," but "the Committee was in reality run by Robert Kennedy. Its mission: to plan the future of the liberated Cuban [Bay of Pigs] Brigade and design a covert program to overthrow the Castro regime." JFK "charged the Army with responsibility for assimilating Cuban (Bay of Pigs) brigade members into American life and making available, on short notice, a military unit of Cubans to participate with US troops in any future action against Castro. Vance gave me this task and designated me his alternate as the Defense Department member of" the ICCCA.[7]

Bobby made sure that his role on the ICCCA and other subcommittees was hard to trace. In 1998, author Gus Russo showed Al Haig an "organizational chart of the numerous Cuban committees at various government agencies. At the top was the President; nowhere on it did the Attorney General, Robert Kennedy, appear. Viewing the chart, Haig chuckled and exclaimed, 'Bobby was the President!'" as far as Cuban operations were concerned. For emphasis, Haig repeated to the interviewer "He was the President. Let me repeat, as a reasonably close observer, HE WAS THE PRESIDENT!" [capitals for emphasis in original]. Haig said his time on one of those Cuba committees involved the "impatient prodding of Robert Kennedy and the frequent invocation of the President's name." Russo notes that, according to Haig, he and the others only "reluctantly followed Bobby Kennedy's imperative." Haig claimed that "Cy Vance was very unhappy with it. He's a decent human being—not a fellow who would ever be comfortable with operations that were covert. Califano the same."[8] On the other hand, there's no evidence so far that Vance, Haig, or Califano ever tried to resign or ask for a transfer or reassignment away from their Cuban duties. For an example of the fact that at least one of these men would have considered such a move, Vance later resigned as Secretary of State under Jimmy Carter due to a disagreement over the Iran hostage issue.[9]

While he was alive, Vance avoided speaking about C-Day or any of his other covert Cuban actions. He told journalists that he was saving stories about his work with the Kennedys on Cuba for his memoirs, which he would write after he retired. But Vance's long and distinguished career in public service lasted through the Clinton administration, and he passed away never having written his memoirs. Fortunately, we were able to interview five Kennedy insiders who worked with Vance on C-Day and its aftermath, including Dean Rusk and Harry Williams. Also, with the help of several others, we were able to get many key Vance C-Day documents declassified and released. Al Haig's 1992 autobiography revealed some of his work for the Kennedys, while Joseph Califano's 2004 autobiography detailed more about Vance and the coup plans. All this information allows us to give a detailed view of Vance's work on C-Day.

According to Al Haig's biographer, in 1963 "the Army Secretary's Office" was "a virtual hatchery of the famous-to-be," since "all starting there at once" were Cyrus "Vance, [Joseph] Califano, and [Al] Haig . . . two future White House advisers and three cabinet members, including two Secretaries of State."[10] As the many years of public service on the part of Vance and the others showed, the careers of some who worked on various aspects of C-Day could be long and distinguished—especially while the failure of the C-Day plan remained secret. In addition to their other considerable abilities, these men had shown future presidents that they were capable of the utmost discretion. Harry Williams summed it up when he told the authors in 1992 that "one reason why people like Vance and Haig and Califano . . . rose high in the government eventually [was] because they could be trusted not to talk."[11]

Harry Williams told William Turner that in 1963, he "had a tremendous amount of discussion with [Cyrus] Vance . . . we had at least three or four big meetings at Bobby's office, with" Cuban exile leaders "and Vance and myself and . . . Califano was there, too, a lot of times."[12] Califano's role in Cuban affairs is confirmed by many documents, like the minutes of an April 3, 1963 meeting where "the President met with a number of advisers for a 'meeting on Cuba' [and] attending were RFK, Vance, Califano, Fitzgerald, Helms."[13] Califano wrote that during the meeting, "as Robert Kennedy pressed for tougher actions, I thought: he is obsessed with Castro; he is pursuing a total war with Castro."[14]

Califano wrote that he can't "harbor pride" or "moral certainty . . . about my personal involvement in the nation's Cuba policy, aiding and abetting the obsession of the Kennedy brothers to get Castro." However, Califano's focus on a Kennedy "obsession" seems to overlook the fact that top US generals—especially hawks like General Curtis LeMay—were also anxious to get rid of

Castro. Many of the Joint Chiefs had been trying to find an excuse for a US military invasion of Cuba since the Bay of Pigs, even at the height of the Cuban Missile Crisis. Before Califano's tenure, some of the generals had even proposed a series of actions (OPERATION NORTHWOODS, cited earlier) "to kill innocent people and commit acts of terrorism in US cities to create public support for a war against Cuba."[15] And during Califano's work with the Kennedys, his own assistant, Colonel Alexander Haig, wrote a July 19, 1963 memo suggesting "a concerted effort to create circumstances leading to US . . . action to reestablish a non-Communist Cuba and expel the Soviet presence, including [US] military action and invasion if necessary."[16]

Califano does write about the political pressure JFK faced, saying that "President Kennedy had to do something about Cuba and Castro," because even though the Soviet missiles had been removed, thousands of "Russian troops remained on the island." Califano points out that after a press conference where JFK announced "that 1,000 Soviet troops had left Cuba," the President was still subject to "Republican attacks that he was unable to rid our hemisphere of the entire Soviet presence in Castro's Cuba." That is why "the *Washington Post* reported the next day that that 'Kennedy Administration is caught in a sliding squeeze,' since each 'announcement of how many Russian personnel have been withdrawn inevitably focuses new attention on the remaining number.'"[17]

Al Haig writes that his role in Cuban matters had begun earlier in 1963 when "I was appointed military assistant to Secretary of the Army Cyrus R. Vance. The job included the duty of acting in loco parentis to the rescued Cubans"—referring to the Bay of Pigs veterans, whose release had been engineered by Bobby and Harry two months earlier.[18] Haig says that "Vance's hard-driving and gifted right-hand man, Joe Califano, let me know early that the President himself, and even more to the point, his brother Robert were taking a close personal interest in the rescued Cubans. Apparently, one Kennedy or the other called Califano nearly every day to inquire about their welfare."[19] Califano confirms that, saying that "Brigade members often took their complaints to the Attorney General about restrictions I placed on their activities; more than once he overruled me, even when it meant backing off his own prior orders."

Califano explains one reason for Bobby's concern for the Cuban exiles, saying some of "the Bay of Pigs Brigade members . . . knew how to use the media" and "Robert Kennedy did not want them agitating in Miami's Cuban community, noisily demanding actions . . . such outbursts from Brigade members, he feared, could provide ammunition to Republicans in the 1964 election."

Haig also confirms that "I later played a role in a second campaign of secret military action against Cuba" because the Kennedy "administration appeared to believe that covert action was the only sort of action open to it in regard to Cuba."[20] He writes that "with the authorization of Vance . . . I processed the decisions, handing them on to representatives of the CIA for execution by their operatives in the field." However, Haig cautions: "By no means did I know everything; I was too junior to be included among those who attended the planning sessions in Robert Kennedy's office."[21] In his autobiography, Califano likewise indicates that he was not privy to everything Vance was involved in for the Kennedys. Both men keep the focus on the Kennedys as the driving force in the plans against Cuba.

Al Haig says "this clandestine operation against Cuba was . . . indistinguishable from" a traditional "war except that all knowledge that it was being fought was kept from . . . the American people."[22] Haig told ABC's *Nightline* that "Bobby Kennedy was running" the covert Cuban operations "hour by hour. I was part of it, as deputy to Joe Califano and military assistant to General Vance . . . people were being killed . . . and the United States Army was supporting and training these forces . . . Cy Vance, the Secretary of the Army, was [presiding] over the State Department, the CIA, and the National Security Council. I was intimately involved." Haig says that "weekly reports were rendered to Bobby Kennedy—he had a very tight hand on the operation."[23] A former Kennedy official who worked on C-Day and saw those reports confirms Haig's comment.[24] Haig also dealt with CIA officials regarding some of the Cuban exile C-Day leaders. For example, a CIA memo from November 1963 signed by Desmond FitzGerald discusses C-Day exile leader Manuel Artime's base in Nicaragua. The memo says that the information was obtained "through Lt. Col. Haig," who had given it to FitzGerald's deputy.[25]

Harry Williams told us that "Califano was a young guy, full of bullshit," although the blunt-spoken, jovial Williams meant that in an appreciative way. In contrast, Williams said that "Haig was very pragmatic."[26] A Kennedy associate from the defense establishment who worked on C-Day said that "Califano was just going through the motions" but "Haig was different." He said that he could count on Haig to give him "straightforward opinions and counsel" and he "believed that Haig really wanted to free Cuba" from Castro.[27]

Another Kennedy administration official, who wishes to remain confidential because of his long and distinguished government career, said he saw Vance, Califano, and Haig as being "sensible" and "not hard line" at all. He confirmed that in the summer and fall of 1963, "Haig and Califano worked on keeping the Bay of Pigs veterans happy and occupied." Key leaders of the Bay of Pigs were involved with C-Day, like Manuel Artime. This source also confirmed that "any covert action of significance against Cuba had to be approved by Bobby," whom he described as "hard-nosed" and "determined," but also "rash and arrogant and frequently wrong." He felt that Bobby's "Cuba policy wasn't dictated by concern for democracy as much as realism and resentment toward Castro over the Bay of Pigs defeat."[28]

Haig wrote that "on June 19, 1963, President Kennedy approved a new covert-action program designed 'to nourish a spirit of resistance and disaffection which could lead to significant defections and other byproducts of unrest in Cuba.'" Haig may not have known it, but JFK's program wasn't really intended to encourage "defections," but was actually meant to take advantage of the coup leader's offer to overthrow Castro. Califano says that earlier, JFK had "approved use of Defense facilities and personnel to support and train Cuban CIA agents . . . for CIA operations inside Cuba." Califano wrote a memo saying that "These personnel [along with those given parachute jump training on a military reservation] . . . would also be used in advance of the introduction of Special Forces, should there be a decision to invade Cuba."[29]

In his 2004 memoir, Califano said that as 1963 progressed, "Presidential demands for a covert program" to eliminate "the Soviet military presence in Cuba . . . intensified. Helping develop this covert program and direct the Defense Department's role in it occupied much of my time in 1963." Among uniformed officers, "Marine Corps General Victor Krulak—whose nickname 'Brute' was well deserved—became the ranking military officer for covert Cuban operations."[30] General Krulak will surface again later in the book; in the summer and fall of 1963, Krulak oversaw a program whereby Army officers were assigned to the CIA to help train Cuban exiles in southern Florida. According to one of Krulak's officers, also working with those exiles was a "Col. Rosselli"—actually mob boss Johnny Rosselli, who was working on the CIA-Mafia Castro assassination plots at the time for Miami CIA Operations Chief David Morales. Krulak wasn't involved with JFK's assassination, but it shows how the Mafia was infiltrating the Kennedys' plans.

Califano stressed that "at Robert Kennedy's insistence, covert actions were stepped up all that summer and fall" of 1963. Califano says he "felt overwhelmed with endless meetings in the Pentagon" and with "an increased number of sessions of the Cuban Coordinating Committee." Califano adds that "In the fall of 1963, pressed by Robert Kennedy and operating out of a secret base in Costa Rica, the CIA carried out sabotage raids in Cuba."[31]

Of course, Bobby Kennedy knew those raids were just a sideshow, to keep the pot boiling before the C-Day coup. Califano says that "at the direction of the Cuban Committee I compiled all the data we had in the Pentagon on key Cuban military personalities to help the CIA find a 'mole' in Castro's inner circle. Desmond FitzGerald said the CIA needed this to enhance its intelligence on Castro and his government. I took FitzGerald at his word, though I doubted he was revealing all his motives."[32] Califano was certainly right to be suspicious about FitzGerald. In addition to being one of the committee members who knew about C-Day, FitzGerald was in the process of secretly renewing contact with disgruntled mid-level Cuban official Rolando Cubela, in an effort to get him to assassinate Castro. Califano's list would have been to help FitzGerald find someone for Cubela to work with, or for the CIA's AMTRUNK operation, which Bobby Kennedy knew about, unlike the Cubela operation.

Califano goes on to say that "as I had suspected and later learned, FitzGerald was also operating on another, entirely separate track." When "the Joint Chiefs of Staff were concerned that the CIA program" of sabotage was not effective, this "led to a secret briefing of the Chiefs by FitzGerald on September 25, 1963. I repeatedly asked to attend that meeting, but the Joint Chiefs refused to invite me. The JCS memorandum for the record—which I pressed the Pentagon to declassify and first read in doing research for this memoir—revealed that the CIA was studying . . . a way to organize high-ranking Cuban" officials "to kill Castro." The JCS memo stated: "the plot to kill Hitler . . . is being studied in detail to develop an approach" to kill Castro. FitzGerald also talked in the meeting about "great success in getting closer to . . . personnel who might break with Castro."[33]

In this way, FitzGerald could prepare the Joint Chiefs and their staffs for C-Day without revealing that they already had one of the highest officials in Cuba ready to stage a coup against Castro. How much Califano and Haig actually knew about C-Day is hard to tell from their memoirs. On the one hand, they try to distance themselves from the meetings Vance had with Bobby, and from the CIA's actions. On the other hand, both seem anxious to indicate that Bobby Kennedy was actively trying to assassinate Castro. Further, because both worked on highly classified activities at the time, they would still be very constrained about anything they could say today. In Califano's recent autobiography, he seems to indicate that he had information about Cuban operations that could have been valuable to the Warren Commission in 1964, but he was never asked:

> No one on the Warren Commission . . . talked to me or (so far as I know) anyone else involved in the covert attacks on Castro and Cuba about those attacks. The Commission was not informed of any of the efforts of Desmond FitzGerald, the CIA and Robert Kennedy to eliminate Castro and stage a coup.[34]

In his book, Califano makes it clear that he's talking about the efforts against Castro in the late summer and fall of 1963.[35] Califano says in his autobiography that "I did not gain full knowledge of" the CIA's Castro assassination plot with mid-level Cuban official Rolando Cubela "until the mid-1970s," so it leaves unclear what Califano would have told the Warren Commission in 1964. Or what constitutes "full knowledge" of that assassination plot.

Califano says he first began to suspect that Castro assassination plots were under way on April 3, 1963, at a committee meeting that included Bobby Kennedy and Cyrus Vance, as well as the CIA's Richard Helms and Desmond FitzGerald. Califano wrote that he "left the meeting deeply troubled—and sensing that there was some other track upon which Cuban policy was running—involving the Kennedy brothers and the CIA, but not the Defense Department." Califano "suspected" that "Bobby Kennedy and his brother wanted Castro assassinated. I guessed that Desmond FitzGerald, head of CIA's Special Affairs Staff, was involved in the assassination plots, since he was the point man for covert raids and other dirty tricks to disrupt Cuba."[36]

While the CIA was indeed pursuing assassination plots at the time and their internal reports admit that they were still in touch with Johnny Roselli, those same internal CIA reports show that the Kennedys were not told about that. In fact, as a former Kennedy official who worked on C-Day told us, the Kennedys' personal emissary, James Donovan, was in Cuba at that time, negotiating the release of several prisoners, including several CIA agents. A major reason the Kennedys weren't being told about the CIA plots to assassinate Castro at the time was because the CIA was planning to endanger the life of Donovan. The emissary went skin-diving with Castro while negotiating with him, and the CIA considered having Donovan give Castro a poison diving suit as a gift, without realizing it. Luckily, that scheme—as well as one to booby-trap a seashell to explode when Castro swam near it—was abandoned, according to the Senate Church Committee Report. So the historical record actually shows that in 1963, it was CIA officials like Helms and FitzGerald who were interested in simply assassinating Castro at any cost, not the Kennedys.

However, Al Haig wrote in his autobiography that "under the personal leadership of Robert Kennedy, at least eight efforts were made to eliminate Castro." It's unclear how he would know this, since the CIA's own files indicate that Bobby Kennedy didn't know about them while they were going on, and the CIA admits that it continued them long after they told Bobby they had stopped. Haig doesn't mention that the CIA's efforts with the Mafia to assassinate Castro had begun in 1959, long before Bobby Kennedy or JFK took office in early 1961. Nonetheless, Haig goes on to say that "these attempts [to kill Castro] continued until the day President Kennedy was himself assassinated in Dallas." However, Haig claims, "I had no inkling of this at the time, [that] US action against Cuba had included plans to assassinate Fidel Castro."[37] Haig also says that "there was never any suggestion or intention of assassination in our planning of these operations." However, Haig later told Gus Russo that there was "No question but that Bobby Kennedy knew of the plots. It was John Kennedy and Bobby, not the CIA."[38] One has to wonder how Haig knew all that, if he "had no inkling . . . at the time" of any assassination plots. Also, there's no indication if Haig considers a coup involving the death of Castro to be different from an assassination, as did the Kennedys.

Califano is equally adamant about tying Bobby Kennedy to the CIA's Castro assassination plot with Rolando Cubela. Califano writes that "It is inconceivable to me that FitzGerald might have" discussed assassination with Cubela "without the approval of both Kennedys—or an explicit communication from Robert Kennedy." However, even the CIA's own internal report on the Cubela plot makes it clear from FitzGerald himself that Bobby Kennedy was not even informed of the Cubela assassination plot. The CIA's Cubela plot is discussed in an upcoming chapter, but Califano makes an odd comment about Cubela in his autobiography. Califano erroneously calls "Rolando Cubela . . . a disillusioned member of Castro's inner circle."[39] As other government reports and historians make clear, Cubela was not part of

Castro's inner circle. CIA reports show that Cubela was relatively powerless inside Cuba, aside from his friendship with a few people who did know Castro, but even they weren't part of Castro's small inner circle. If Califano were not fully informed about C-Day, it may be that someone exaggerated Cubela's role to him to make a coup staged by a relatively minor official seem possible. As we document later, the CIA's Desmond FitzGerald appears to have done that to at least one other Kennedy official involved with Cuban operations in the fall of 1963.

An article by Joseph A. Trento, Jr. for the January 10, 1981 issue of the *Wilmington News-Journal* casts the roles of Haig and Califano in a different light. At the time, Alexander Haig had been asked to serve as Secretary of State for the newly elected Ronald Reagan, and Joseph Califano was representing Haig in his confirmation hearings.[40] Trento is a veteran journalist with twenty years' experience with CNN, ABC, CBS, *60 Minutes*, *20/20*, *Nightline*, and the *New York Times*.[41] In those days, he was known for having excellent sources in the CIA. Trento wrote:

> Haig kept exile leaders informed of the continuing efforts to assassinate Castro and coordinated information about the progress of the plots between the Defense Department, White House, and CIA. A Marine officer who worked with Haig and currently is a top official of the Defense Intelligence Agency told the *News-Journal*: "Califano and Haig worked hand-in-hand in keeping the nationalists from the Cuban Brigade happy. They even checked out potential members for the hit teams with older members of the Cuban Brigade." Haig tried to dissuade the exiles from carrying out unauthorized raids by telling them Castro was as good as dead.

Trento went on to write that "this was confirmed by Ricardo Canette, a founder of the violent Cuban Nationalist Movement who turned government witness. 'Haig kept promising us things. We kept pressing the government,' Canette said. 'One of the ways they satisfied us was by giving us a role in the support teams to hit Castro.'"[42] However, it's possible that what one or more of Trento's sources might have assumed was that a traditional assassination attempt was actually part of the secret C-Day coup plan.

Califano talked about Bobby Kennedy and Castro's assassination to Evan

Thomas for his 2000 biography of Bobby. Evan Thomas was unable to uncover C-Day; consequently, Thomas was forced to conclude that Bobby's "own views on assassination" regarding Castro during 1963 "have remained difficult to ascertain." Unlike the authors, who were able to eventually talk to key sources like Dean Rusk and Harry Williams and many others, Evan Thomas says that he was unable to get sources to talk about it—"with one prominent exception." He writes that Joseph Califano admitted that at one of the Cuban subcommittee meetings in the summer of 1963, Bobby Kennedy "talked about knocking off Castro." Califano said that at the time, "I was stunned. . . . He was talking so openly, and there were other people in the room." Thomas asked Califano if he was sure that "knock off" meant "kill." Califano said yes, "no ifs, ands, or buts. No doubt."[43] Evan Thomas asked Haig about Califano's revelation, and Haig responded, "I have no doubt everything he told you is true."[44]

However, Califano wasn't quite so clear in his own autobiography, published four years later. He wrote:

> I felt I was working directly for the Attorney General and through him, for the President, and with one exception I enthusiastically joined the administration's effort to topple Castro. That exception erupted at a meeting where someone suggested mounting an effort to assassinate or encourage the assassination of Castro. . . . An assistant deputy attorney general and I argued against such a policy . . . the CIA representatives sat silent.[45]

It's unclear if this is the meeting that Califano told Evan Thomas about, regarding Bobby Kennedy; if it is, it's odd that Califano wouldn't name Bobby Kennedy if Bobby is the one who made the assassination comment.

In a later chapter, we document the roles of Haig and Califano in drafting the Cuba Contingency Plans, to deal with the possible "assassination of American officials" in the fall of 1963, in case Castro retaliated against the US covert operations against him. Neither man mentions those plans in his own autobiography. However, Haig told an interviewer in 1998 that "We were getting warnings. During the covert operation program" and that the warnings continued "right up until the day Kennedy was killed."[46] Of course, Haig thought the threat to JFK was from Castro, since he wasn't privy to all the information from the CIA, FBI, and other agencies showing that the real threat to JFK was from godfathers like Marcello, Trafficante, and Rosselli.

As with Bobby and JFK, Cyrus Vance's role in C-Day—and the roles of his assistants Califano and Haig in the operations surrounding it—remained secret for decades. The secret was almost made public twenty-seven years ago, before Califano and Vance joined Jimmy Carter's cabinet and before Haig became secretary of state for Reagan. But when the Church Committee published a few sentences from Haig's 1963 Cuba Contingency Plan memo in 1976, it didn't mention Haig's name, or that of Joseph Califano, which also appeared in the memo.[47] It was probably just an example of powerful Republicans and Democrats on the Senate Committee each protecting the reputations of their rising stars. As a result, the names of Haig and Califano didn't officially surface until the full document was finally declassified in 1994.[48]

Around the same time their names were being kept out of the Church Committee Report, another government memo about Bobby and assassinations was also suppressed. *Newsweek* editor Evan Thomas wrote that in a long-secret "memo of a conversation on January 4, 1975, Kissinger warns [President] Ford that . . . if more information comes out, 'blood will flow,' says Kissinger. 'For example, Robert Kennedy personally managed the operation on the assassination of Castro.'" This one sentence was considered so sensitive and explosive that the entire memo was kept secret for twenty-three years after it was written.[49] Of course, Kissinger and Ford weren't just interested in protecting the reputation of the Kennedys, Vance, or Califano. At that time, Ford, Kissinger, and CIA Director George H. W. Bush were all trying to suppress information about events surrounding CIA operations related to C-Day and JFK's assassination that could have been damaging to Republicans as well.

Harry Williams, RFK, and the Coup Leader

WHILE C-DAY PLANNING CONTINUED IN Washington by Vance and key CIA officials, Harry Williams traveled extensively while working with exile leaders and the coup leader. As the summer progressed, the US build-up for C-Day—which included small hit-and-run raids by some of the C-Day exile groups—made the Soviet presence in Cuba more intrusive. This caused even more resentment of the Soviets on behalf of some Cuban officials. On August 30, 1963, the *New York Times* carried a small story on its inside pages about "reports of a possible new invasion" of Cuba "from Central American bases," where "exiles in Costa Rica and Nicaragua reportedly train for invasion." It said that in response, the Cuban government issued alerts and "strategic points around Havana were taken over by USSR troops."[1]

A few days later, Kennedy friend Tad Szulc wrote a major article for the *Times* that laid out the political strains, in the Cuban leadership, over the Soviets. Headlined "Castro Reported Quarreling Again with Red Backers," the subhead was Cuban "Leadership is Shifting." Szulc said "Castro appears to be in serious political difficulties" and "reports of the split have been obtained from authoritative Cuban sources." He claimed that "the tense political situation within Cuba is the real reason Havana ordered military and militia units on the alert last week" and "the current alert is related primarily to the internal political situation" in Cuba. He noted that "the current problems . . . may present a political opportunity for the United States." Szulc says "the crux of the dispute is said to be that each faction holds the other responsible for the deepening chaos in the Cuban economy."[2]

In his *Times* article, Szulc reflects the feelings of the C-Day coup leader perfectly when he says that "Havana informants declare that many of the old Castro . . . associates have begun to feel that they are being used by the Premier for his own aims, instead of those of Cuba's real interests. Many are said to be deeply disenchanted."[3] Indeed, Szulc's article reflected aspects of the C-Day coup leader so closely that his article was the subject of much concern at the CIA and in high US government circles, though it attracted little public notice at the time.

The stakes were rising higher and higher for the coup leader and for the Kennedys. In spite of the coup leader's high position and reputation, if his plotting with the Kennedys was discovered by Castro, he faced at least imprisonment and—more likely—death. On the other hand, if the Kennedys were being deceived by the coup leader and if their plotting was exposed, the Kennedys would face international disgrace and certain defeat in next year's election. So each side came up with something to reassure themselves that the other side was sincere.

The reassurance for the Kennedys, and no doubt the CIA, was like something out of medieval Europe, when a king might ask another monarch for one of his family members to hold as a hostage to ensure compliance with a treaty or agreement. That's essentially what was done in the case of the C-Day coup leader. When we asked Harry how he and the Kennedys could be sure they weren't being deceived by the coup leader, Harry said that the coup leader had agreed to put one of his family members, someone in another country he was known to be close to, under the watchful eye of the CIA until after the coup.

To most Americans in 1963, entrusting a family member to the CIA might not have seemed like a big deal. We were still a decade away from widespread US news reports of CIA assassination plots and complicity in coups. However, for Latin Americans in 1963, the CIA was a daily reality; it was viewed by many as brutal and repressive. They were all too aware of governments the CIA had overthrown, brutal dictatorships it supported, and death squads the CIA tolerated if not actually assisted. For one of the leaders of a Communist country to entrust a family member in Latin America to the CIA was a very big deal.

The C-Day coup leader also needed reassurance that the Kennedys were serious and wouldn't abandon him, as the US and Eisenhower had done with the Hungarian revolt in the 1950s. In addition, if the coup leader had to flee Cuba, leaving behind everything he owned, he would need funds to start a new life; and if he were killed in the coup, he wanted to be sure his family could live comfortably.

When the coup leader told Harry that he wanted money, for himself or his family in the case of his death, Harry discussed it with Bobby Kennedy. Bobby said he could provide whatever funds were needed, but he didn't want to set the figure. He said that that should be between the two Cubans, and he left it up to Harry. So Harry came up with the figure of $500,000, almost $3 million in today's dollars. That was agreeable to both Bobby Kennedy and the coup leader in Cuba. A down payment of $50,000 ($289,000 in today's dollars) was actually made to the coup leader, using complex arrangements made by the CIA. The balance of the money was to be paid to the coup leader after C-Day, or to his family in the event of his death.

C-Day was the most secret US operation since World War II, but the "family hostage" and "payoff" plans were some of the most secret parts of C-Day. They were known only to JFK, Bobby, Harry, and a handful of people in the CIA. Since it took over thirty years for a few documents about C-Day to first be declassified, you can imagine how much longer— if ever—it will be before documents about the "hostage" and "payoff" plans are released. Yet two CIA documents about a payoff involving Harry and another Cuban close to Castro have been declassified, and they show many parallels to the Kennedy-authorized payoff Harry arranged for the C-Day coup leader.

One of the two 1963 documents about a huge payoff arranged by Harry for a Cuban official is an AMWORLD memo sent to CIA Director John McCone; the other is from the CIA file of Bernard Barker, aide to alleged C-Day Case Officer E. Howard Hunt. The Cuban official in this case was Carlos Franqui, Cuba's leading journalist after the Revolution. The AMWORLD memo says that Harry Williams helped Franqui defect to Paris, and the other CIA memo says that as part of that defection, Harry arranged a payment to Franqui of between $200,000 and $300,000. In addition to dealing with Harry, in the summer of 1963 Franqui met in Paris with C-Day exile leader Manolo Ray and with Che Guevara.

The AMWORLD CIA memo documents a discussion among Cuban exiles of "Plan Judas," the name some exiles on the fringe of the operation used for C-Day. This fall 1963 memo talks about "Enrique Ruiz (Harry) Williams" working with "RFK," and which exiles would have cabinet posts in the new Cuban Provisional Government. In another part, Harry says "he had arranged exit from Cuba of Carlos Franqui with his accumulated wealth."[4] Franqui had been one of the most prominent journalists in Cuba, and he had been close to Castro and others high in the Cuban government. Franqui had recently defected from Cuba to Paris, but without publicly announcing his defection, so to the world—and Castro—it looked at the time as if Franqui were simply on an extended trip to Paris.

The CIA document from Bernard Barker's file makes it clear that Kennedy aide Harry Williams engineered a huge payoff to Franqui in conjunction with his defection. This document is also a memo to the CIA Director, and it says that "during past two weeks" there have been "persistent rumors [name censored in original] produced defection [of] Carlos Franqui." It notes that "Franqui now living like [a] 'Pasha'" in "France," because "Franqui received either $200,000, $250,000, or 300,000" from the US for his defection.[5] Another reference in the document makes it clear that the person who arranged Franqui's defection and the big payoff was involved with C-Day. When paired with the earlier CIA memo, they show that Harry arranged both Franqui's defection and his huge payoff, probably using the same procedures and the same pool of funds provided by the Kennedys for the C-Day coup leader. In light of what Harry told us about the payment to the coup leader—two years before this document was declassified—the payment to Franqui makes sense. If the coup leader was worth $500,000, then one of the most prominent journalists in Cuba would be worth between $200,000 and $300,000, as the document says. It's not hard to speculate on the important role Franqui could have played after the C-Day coup, since his reputation and contacts would have allowed him to influence public opinion about the coup and the new Provisional Government both in Cuba and in Europe.

Also, it is ironic that Franqui should be mentioned in the same document that uses the name "Plan Judas" for C-Day. Franqui wrote a book named *Los Doce (The Twelve)* about the twelve disciples of Castro—including Raul and Che—who survived a major attack and became the leaders of the Revolution.[6] Franqui wrote that "Fidel was fond of biblical parables and always spoke of the Twelve. . . . Twelve men and a Christ-like Fidel."[7] Exiles believed the coup leader was one of those twelve disciples, who was now going to betray Castro, hence the origin of the name "Plan Judas" for C-Day.

Franqui was less important and was later called "a small Judas" by one Cuban writer.[8] As we detail in an upcoming chapter, around the time of Franqui's defection and huge payoff from Kennedy aide Harry Williams, Franqui had a dramatic meeting with Che Guevara in Paris. Also, the AMWORLD CIA document about Harry and Franqui bears the hand-signed initials "HH," which could stand for CIA agent and Watergate figure E. Howard

Hunt. The other document is from one of the CIA files of Watergate burglar
Bernard Barker, Hunt's assistant.

Harry Williams's contact with the C-Day coup leader continued through
the summer of 1963, and he used the CIA to deliver the first $50,000
installment of the $500,000 payoff to the coup leader via a third country. As
part of the CIA's work on the payment and the coup leader's family member
in a foreign country, a more secure line of communication was also established with the coup leader. After May 1963, the coup leader simply talked
to Harry Williams on the telephone, from Cuba. This may seem extremely
insecure, but keep in mind the coup leader's very high position in the Cuban
government—he would know which calls and lines were monitored by
Cuban intelligence and which were not. But as C-Day progressed, documents
indicate that some type of "secure radio" communication channel was established between the coup leader and the US.[9]

By September 1963, Manuel Artime, Tony Varona, and the Fort Benning
Cuban exiles were on board with C-Day, while Harry was still pursuing exile
leaders Manolo Ray and Eloy Menoyo. All five groups, along with Harry himself, were targeted for penetration by mob bosses Santo Trafficante, Carlos
Marcello, and Johnny Rosselli. The Kennedys and Harry Williams tried to
ensure that the Mafia was kept away from C-Day. The Kennedys had experienced problems since 1959, when JFK was a senator, in pursuing and prosecuting Mafia figures the CIA was using in its Castro assassination plots.
However, the Kennedys didn't realize that the CIA-Mafia plots were continuing in the summer and fall of 1963. This gave mob bosses like Johnny
Rosselli, who was working closely with CIA officer David Morales at the time,
a window into operations like C-Day.[10] The mob bosses would succeed to
varying degrees in infiltrating and compromising C-Day and other CIA operations, as detailed in the later chapters of Part I and much of Part II.

One of Harry's three Mafia confrontations happened while he was staying
at Bobby Kennedy's townhouse in New York City. While there, Harry was
confronted by notorious Cuban gangster and death-squad leader Rolando
Masferrer, an associate of Tampa godfather Santo Trafficante. Though Masferrer showed up with two thugs, Harry told us that he rebuffed Masferrer's
attempt to join C-Day, because he, Harry, wanted to exclude Cuban exiles

with ties to organized crime. This was a dangerous thing to do because, as another C-Day exile leader told us, Masferrer "was a Mafioso" and "it was known that he killed his enemies."[11] CIA documents confirm that Masferrer was secretly brought into C-Day after Tony Varona got a huge payoff from Johnny Rosselli's Chicago Mafia.[12] FBI files show that Masferrer was then linked to an attempt to tie Lee Harvey Oswald to progressive C-Day leader Manolo Ray.[13]

Later in 1963, Harry confronted Tampa godfather Santo Trafficante himself, turning down his large offer of money. Harry had been taken to the meeting in Miami by a CIA official who later figured prominently in Watergate. Harry's most dangerous confrontation with the Mafia over C-Day in 1963 was an attempt on Harry's life. C-Day exile leader Manuel Artime had several bases in Central America; on one trip there at Bobby's request, Harry was attacked by two pistol-wielding thugs in a restaurant in Guatemala City. Harry was only able to escape after a fierce gun battle in which he killed one of his assailants. The other assailant fled the scene and was never captured. Unknown to Harry, Mafia bosses Carlos Marcello and Johnny Rosselli had extensive ties to Guatemala. We also document, from the *New York Times* and other sources, an almost identical assassination in a Guatemala City restaurant by two pistol-wielding gunmen that was also linked to Manuel Artime.[14]

The "Plan for a Coup in Cuba": December 1, 1963

ON SEPTEMBER 26, 1963, CYRUS VANCE submitted to the Joint Chiefs the thirteenth draft of the "Plan for a Coup in Cuba," which had been developed with input from several agencies, including the CIA and the DIA. This draft contains a significant clue that indicates that most of the Joint Chiefs and their staffs still didn't know about the real C-Day plan. In a memo sent to "the Chairman, Joint Chiefs of Staff," Maxwell Taylor—but intended to be circulated to all the Joint Chiefs and their staffs—Vance makes a telling comment: He says that previous efforts have looked at making plans for several "possible variants of revolt" in Cuba, including long-shot possibilities like a spontaneous "mass uprising." However, Vance says, "this draft plan, in contrast to earlier drafts," is more "narrow" and focuses on just one type of "coup in Cuba which meets certain fixed criteria." Vance says that an "analysis of the situation in Cuba and of current US plans and programs indicates that" a plan like C-Day "is one of the most promising variants of revolt in Cuba for the foreseeable future." Vance then describes the one type of coup now being planned, and it matches C-Day. Vance claims that "draft plans for other types of revolt will follow," but of course they never did.[1]

C-Day was the only active plan for a coup at that time, since AMTRUNK was still in the recruiting stage and the CIA had resumed contact with Cubela only a short time earlier. Nonetheless, mentioning other possible types of revolt helped C-Day remain secret, while allowing detailed coup planning to go forward. That way, JFK wouldn't have to tell the rest of the Joint Chiefs about the full C-Day plan and the real identity of the coup leader until it was absolutely necessary.

The C-Day coup described by Vance in this formerly TOP SECRET document declassified in October 1997 was first described to us by Harry Williams and other Kennedy associates in early 1992. We even gave a general description of the plan on the History Channel in 1994, mentioning Vance's assistants Joseph Califano and Al Haig. Declassified documents like this confirmed, and added detail to, what several Kennedy associates had already told us.

Vance's September 26, 1963 document actually has several parts, a brief "Summary" of the "thirteenth draft" of "A State-Defense . . . Plan for a Coup in Cuba," and a much longer version labeled "Draft 13A," which includes a cover letter from Vance to General Maxwell Taylor. In the cover letter, Vance asks for "comments" on the Coup Plan from the Joint Chiefs of Staff "by 21 October 1963."[2] While not giving away C-Day completely, Vance makes it clear what the real plan is. When listing two or three alternative actions, he gets his point across by listing the ones that apply to the real C-Day plan first. Items that aren't part of the C-Day plan are listed last and called something like "less acceptable" options.[3] The document shows how much planning at the highest levels of government had gone into C-Day. However, keep in mind that most of those reading Vance's Coup Plan document didn't know the identity of the C-Day coup leader in Cuba, one of the most closely guarded secrets of the twentieth century. (In contrast, the secret plans for D-Day or the A-bomb's Manhattan Project were known by many times the dozen or so officials who knew the C-Day coup leader's identity.)

Vance says that the plan "represents an attempt . . . to encompass the views of State, CIA, and the JCS [Joint Chiefs of Staff]" and that "both State and CIA concur" in this draft. It says the coup would need to "establish a Provisional Government" and "hold a significant piece of territory long enough for [the] US to extend support." The coup would also need to "have some power base in the Cuban" government and "neutralize the top echelon of Cuban leadership." In blunt terms, that means the coup would need to kill Fidel Castro. This draft of the Coup Plan talks several times about that and in one part explicitly says that US support can begin only after "Fidel Castro . . . has been neutralized" in the coup.[4] Clearly, killing Fidel was the key to the entire plan.[5]

The Provisional Government would soon include the leaders of the Cuban exile C-Day groups, whose leaders would enter Cuba from points outside the US.[6] Further confirming what Harry Williams and our other Kennedy C-Day sources told us, the Coup Plan says these "selected Cuban exile leaders" would have "aims [that] are compatible with those of the" C-Day coup leader "within Cuba."[7] Of course, some of those working on the coup—like Vance—knew that five Cuban exile leaders had already been selected by Harry Williams and approved by the Kennedys. (A later CIA document will show that the Cuban exiles were already deciding among themselves what positions they would hold in the new Provisional Government.) Vance makes it clear that "a Presidential decision to intervene" after the coup "would require a request from the [new Cuban] Provisional Government . . . or intervention by local Soviet forces."[8] The new Cuban Provisional Government would make "a pre-arranged call for help" to "the US for recognition and support, particularly for air cover and a naval blockade."[9] As the Joint Chiefs noted, this could involve "US forces" in a "full-scale invasion if such becomes necessary."[10]

It says that "when the decision is made to support the Provisional Government, the President would send a message to [Soviet Chairman] Khrushchev . . . expressing the expectation that he will not intervene . . . and specifically requesting the Chairman to comply with the sea and air blockade . . . and to order Soviet troops to specified concentration points to minimize Soviet loss of life."[11]

The US might know exactly when the coup was going to start, but there was also a chance that "the coup might" have to happen ahead of schedule, in which case the US would find out about it after it had already begun. In either event, "on receiving word of [the] coup," several things would happen in sequence, including "President initiates blockade" of Cuba as in the Cuban Missile Crisis and "position US forces for intervention." That could include using "all or portions" of the military's detailed Cuban invasion plans, "OPLANS 312 and 316 as required to insure success."[12]

These coup plans also include "Political Actions," like "recognize Provisional Government" and "warn Soviets not to intervene." To show that the US is not acting unilaterally, it says the US should also "proceed through OAS [Organization of American States]" and "initiate consultation with Allies" and "initiate UN action." Finally, the plan calls for establishing "US civilian and OAS control when military operations are completed."[13]

In hindsight, it may seem hard to imagine that the UN, the OAS, and the rest of the world wouldn't immediately recognize that the coup had been staged by the US. But that was the reason the Kennedys placed so much reliance on Harry Williams and the supposedly "autonomous" Cuban exile leaders like Manuel Artime based in Central America. US and world newspapers were full of articles about a US crackdown on most Cuban exile groups, strains within Cuba over the economy, and bickering political factions in Cuba's ruling elite.[14] In that context, if a Cuban leader assumed control after Castro's death with the aid of a few exile leaders, it might be seen as free of US influence—if it occurred under certain conditions.

That leads to another reason the Kennedys felt the US wouldn't be blamed for C-Day: When the coup happened and Castro was killed, the C-Day coup leader in Cuba wouldn't step up and claim credit for killing Castro. Neither would Harry Williams, or any of the other C-Day Cuban exile leaders. As Harry Williams explained to us, that blame would go to someone else. Instead, the coup leader would use his stature from the Revolution and his power base to take control and appeal to the US to help prevent a Soviet takeover.[15]

We were initially surprised when Harry Williams indicated that the coup leader wasn't going to take the blame for Castro's death. However, given Castro's popularity with much of the Cuban populace in 1963, it makes sense. A Kennedy official who worked on C-Day told us that in 1963, they realized there was "much popular support for Castro" in Cuba.[16] Even the thirteenth draft of Vance's Coup Plan admits that "an important minority of the Cuban people now apparently gives positive support to Castro, and the majority passively accepts his regime."[17] So, much of the Cuban populace— including key bureaucrats and the military—would hardly support the coup leader if he proudly proclaimed that he had killed their beloved Fidel. The coup leader probably also knew that his own life would be in jeopardy, both at the time and for the rest of his life, if he took credit for killing Castro.

The solution to that problem would also help to address the thorny issue of how to contain the Soviets in Cuba after Fidel and Raul were killed. The Soviets might support some lower Cuban official and help him "take over control" of the government. That could lead to a civil war with the C-Day coup leader's new US-backed Provisional Government and perhaps a pro-tracted conflict just ninety miles from the US. Since it would essentially be a proxy fight between the Soviets and the US, it could easily have spiraled out of control in those tense Cold War times, even going nuclear. Those in Washington were well aware of the possibilities, as confirmed by a National Intelligence Estimate from June 14, 1963, which says that Castro's "death could result in . . . disorder . . . ranging from power struggles within the regime's leadership to open civil war." And it notes that "even under the most favorable circumstances," the US "would have to take account of the presence of Soviet troops."[18]

The only answer seems to be if Castro appeared to have been killed not as part of the coup itself, but by someone else. What if the public thought that

Castro (and Raul) had been killed by, for example, a Russian or Russian sympathizer? Then the coup leader wouldn't be seen as staging a coup, but merely picking up the reins of government. In that case, he would have the support and "sympathy of the Cuban people." They would even see him as justified in calling on the US military and exile help to prevent more hostile action on the part of the Soviets. Vance's memo says that "the insurgents . . . would have appealed to the US for . . . air cover and a naval blockade, ostensibly to make certain that the Soviets do not intervene." The summary also says "the insurgents simultaneously would have declared that Soviet nationals will not be harmed if they remain in their compounds while awaiting repatriation to the Soviet Union."[19] If the Cuban people were told by the coup leader that Fidel had been murdered by a Russian or a Russian sympathizer—for example, someone who had spent a couple of years in Russia and had recently met with a KGB agent at the Russian Embassy in Mexico City—the Soviet troops would have to "remain in their compounds" to keep from being attacked by the Cuban people.

Vance's plan of September 1963 says that "while fighting was going on, the insurgents would have announced via radio . . . the overthrow of the Castro/Communist regime and the establishment of a Provisional Government. They would have appealed to the US for recognition and support, particularly for air cover and a naval blockade, ostensibly to make certain that the Soviets do not intervene but actually, by pre-arrangement, to immobilize the Cuban Air Force and Navy."[20]

Still, Vance and the other C-Day planners knew that "from a political viewpoint, it is important . . . that the revolt appear genuine and not open to the charge of being a facade for a forcible US overthrow of Castro," which is, of course, what it actually was. However, the Coup Plan shows that Vance, the Kennedys, and others rationalized that they were merely providing "support to the insurgents"—meaning the coup leader and the C-Day Cuban exile leaders—"and of helping them to liberate Cuba themselves."[21] That line from Vance's Coup Plan is the same rationale that Harry Williams and other Kennedy sources told us, years before Vance's document was finally released.[22] That's also why Bobby Kennedy and the others didn't see C-Day as simply an assassination plan, like the earlier CIA-Mafia plots.

Vance noted in his cover letter to Maxwell Taylor that "there is a political requirement that US intervention on behalf of the coup be made as palatable to the world as is consistent with the military requirement." In words that echo the debate over Iraq in early 2003, Vance's Coup Plan says that "the support of our European allies for forceful US action in Cuba is highly desirable" and could help deter the Soviets. So "the US should make every effort to seek allied support for a decision to assist overtly the insurgents with military means." Toward that end, the September 1963 Coup Plan suggested using a special CIA-State–Defense Department team to go into Cuba within twenty-four hours of the coup, to see if the coup met all the criteria for US military intervention.[23] In retrospect, that may seem highly unrealistic, given that a coup might only have a critical window of a few hours in which US military intervention could make a crucial difference. But the State Department was helping with these plans, and it didn't know about C-Day or the powerful coup leader in Cuba. For agencies like State, the coup planning was more of an exercise for a long-shot possibility. Only Vance and a few others knew that these were life-or-death decisions for a real deadline that was rapidly approaching. In this plan, Vance acknowledges that "it might not be possible for the US to make a decision to support the coup in time to commit forces needed to sustain it" if they have to wait on a special team of US officials to go into Cuba after the coup.[24] (That's why Bobby made sure that someone he personally trusted more than the CIA, State, or Defense—his close friend Harry Williams—would go into Cuba in advance of the coup, to monitor the situation as it developed.[25])

The preferred way for the coup to start would be for the coup leader "in secure radio contact with CIA [to] implement" the coup "plan with US concurrence and establish a Provisional Government in full expectation of forthcoming US support." This "Provisional Government" can be "rudimentary," but it must have "some sort of public claim to political viability to provide an adequate political basis . . . for overt US action" to support it.[26] That's why Bobby Kennedy and Harry had worked hard to put together a group of C-Day Cuban exile leaders with good credentials from the Revolution, including some considered "socialist" by the CIA. When coupled with the coup leader in Cuba—widely admired by much of the Cuban populace—the Kennedys felt sure that the Provisional Government they had approved would be accepted by most Cubans once Castro was out of the way.

Vance's Coup Plan states that its goal is "to provide for sufficient US assistance to an anti-communist coup in Cuba to assure the replacement of the Communist government with one acceptable to the United States." In addition to killing Castro, the Coup Plan says the coup leader must "seize and hold a significant piece of territory, preferably including Havana" along "with a number of key government buildings and a major radio station."[27] It would take one of Cuba's most powerful men, after Castro, to do what the US required. That was far beyond the capability of someone like CIA asset Rolando Cubela (AMLASH) or anyone connected with AMTRUNK.

Vance says that the coup leader "may . . . be aware, from previous contact . . . that if" he can "agree to and appear capable of meeting certain specified conditions," his "revolt will be supported by the US." The plan says that "upon receipt of word that the" coup leader has "agreed to . . . the criteria for US support, approval would be given to [him to] commence the coup at the earliest practicable time."[28] In return, the Coup Plan says that "as soon as the request for help is received" from the new Provisional Government, "the president would announce publicly that the US will isolate Cuba by means of an air and sea blockade." Vance even provides the international legal "justification for this unilateral, interim action," saying it "would be based on Paragraph 3 of Resolution 2 of the Punta del Esta meeting of Foreign Ministers." The plan says that JFK's "announcement would be designed to immobilize the Cuban Navy and Air Force, encourage indigenous support for the insurgents, and reinforce a warning to the Soviet Union not to intervene."[29] Also, following JFK's announcement, "the US would initiate overt logistical and air support to the insurgents." The plan notes that "air strikes could make the difference of life or death to a revolt," something JFK was all too aware of after the Bay of Pigs disaster.[30] In addition, these "air strikes" made JFK want to complete the coup operation before the December 7 anniversary of Pearl Harbor.

According to the Coup Plan, US ground forces, in addition to the Cuban-American troops and Special Forces, would also be involved. The plan says "it is probable that the US would have to introduce conventional forces incrementally as required to sustain the uprising." This would involve "portions or all of" the military's Cuban invasion plans "OPLANS 312 and 316 as required." Vance notes that the Joint Chiefs "have pointed out that the 'best military response to the revolt would be the orderly implementation of' those plans." However, Vance says that unless the Soviets intervene militarily, "a full-scale US invasion would be the least desirable course of action from a political point of view. Such an invasion would raise the specter of US interventionism in Latin America, [and] could poison our future relations with Cuba and Latin America." Vance also points out that a massive invasion "would be difficult to justify in light of previous Presidential pronouncements. However, a well-planned and successful 'rescue' of a revolt could be made politically acceptable." Showing the diplomatic skill that would later serve him well under Presidents Carter and Clinton, Vance argues for a "measured execution" of the military's invasion plans, focusing on things like "air strikes." He seems hopeful that those—coupled with "unconventional forces" like the Cuban-American troops and US Special Forces—would be enough support for the coup leader to succeed. However, Vance does admit that "possibly as much as all the forces required" in the military's full Cuban invasion plans "may be required."[31]

The Coup Plan makes the high stakes involved very clear. The Soviets were a big factor to consider, since this was less than a year after the tense nuclear standoff of the Cuban Missile Crisis. Vance stresses that once JFK had decided to "intervene" militarily in Cuba to support the Coup Plan, that "would be the critical decision because, once made . . . the US would be committed to the ultimate success of the coup." But the plan notes that "at least twelve to thirteen thousand Soviet military personnel of all kinds remain" in Cuba. And if "Soviet troops" try "to suppress" the coup, "a military response by the US . . . could immediately bring about a direct, local US-Soviet confrontation." Of course, any such confrontation between the two nuclear superpowers could quickly go from "local" to something more. Vance says that "the greatest potential danger lies in those regions where the USSR may consider itself to possess a local advantage, e.g., Berlin."[32]

Though a nuclear exchange is not explicitly mentioned in the Coup Plan, Vance implies it when he asks "are we prepared to accept this risk, what do we estimate to be its probable consequences, and how would we propose to contain and minimize the degree of Soviet involvement?" Vance's question comes after he has already listed several things the US intends to try, like "a private warning to" the Soviets "not to intervene" and avoiding "attacks on Soviet personnel and installations in Cuba, unless there is an indication of a clear Soviet intention to intervene." Perhaps realizing that those steps aren't enough, Vance says that "an especially important objective would be to" find a way to "deter the Soviets from acting" while "avoiding, if possible, a direct challenge to the USSR."[33] "However," Vance says, "US planning should include plans, for implementation as circumstances warrant at the time, for the possible neutralization or elimination of Soviet forces in Cuba." Those words are chilling, when you realize their implication, and the nuclear war that could result. And while Vance signed the Coup Plan, we should realize that that view wasn't just his, but represented the views of the CIA, the State Department, and the Defense Department.

Vance's concerns show why JFK and Bobby would pursue secret back-channel negotiations with Castro, in the hopes of avoiding any chance of a deadly confrontation with the Soviets. Also, we will show that at the very moment Vance was posing his concerns, Bobby Kennedy, the CIA, and the DIA may have found a way to contain the Soviets in Cuba—while at the same time providing the coup leader with someone to take the blame for Castro's death.

Vance makes it clear that a "coup" is the Kennedy administration's primary focus for toppling Castro in the fall of 1963. He says that "the US does not contemplate . . . a premeditated full-scale invasion of Cuba" that is not in support of a coup, "except in the case of Soviet intervention or the reintroduction of offensive weapons." Nor was the US considering a "contrivance or a provocation which could be used as a pretext for" an invasion any longer. Also, Vance says "it is not US policy to encourage unorganized and uncoordinated mass uprisings since these would be too easily crushed" by the "Cuban military." Instead, the focus is on "a planned and coordinated revolt led by a significant element of the" Cuban government.[34]

Vance's September 1963 Coup Plan talks about integrating earlier comments from the Joint Chiefs of Staff. Although the document containing those comments hasn't been declassified, "their views" were "paraphrased" by Vance, which allowing us to see what the Joint Chiefs had contributed. They warned against "the commitment of forces blindly to support" the coup leader, but said that "a rapid incremental commitment of US forces might be desirable" and that it could include "full-scale invasion if such becomes necessary." They saw the Coup Plan as having the "promise of success if US aid can be provided rapidly" and that the coup "has a large measure of support among the . . . [Cuban] people." They also stressed that the coup leader in Cuba must be "identifiable and dependable." The coup leader in Cuba certainly fit that criterion, since he was known to everyone in Cuba and, as one of the main leaders of the Cuban Revolution, had proven experience in toppling a dictator.[35]

Vance's Coup Plan includes extensive details about what would happen in the hours, days, weeks, and even months after the coup had been launched. JFK will "convoke a joint session of Congress . . . to announce . . . in the form of a Joint Resolution, US determination to commit all necessary resources in support of the new [Cuban] government." The US would then announce "that the OAS will send representatives to the island to assist the Provisional Government in preparing for and [the] conduct of free elections." The US would also "appeal to all Cubans to avoid the inevitable bloodshed of invasion by cooperating with the Provisional Government in effecting the removal of the remnants of the Castro dictatorship and the Soviet presence."[36]

The Coup Plan optimistically notes that if the coup "gained rapid success with only unconventional US military forces" like the Cuban-American troops and US Special Forces, then the "US should accredit an Ambassador to the Provisional Government who, when so directed by the President, would become the senior US Representative in Cuba." The Coup Plans state that the ultimate US goal would be "the organization of national elections at the earliest suitable date."[37] The eventual goal was "free elections."[38] For the Kennedys, for Vance and other officials who worked on the coup plans, for Harry Williams and most of the other C-Day Cuban exile leaders, the goal would be a free and democratic Cuba.

Finally, the Coup Plan notes some follow-up actions. It says that the military's plans should be "revised to reflect the . . . military operations described" in the Coup Plan, "including budgetary considerations" and other "measures to reduce drastically the response time for both incremental introduction of forces and for full-scale invasion." It also says that "the series of papers developing policy recommendations on the host of problems connected with a post-Castro regime would be revised, in light of this plan, and subjected to continuing review."[39] That "series of papers" is among what must be hundreds, if not thousands, of military C-Day documents that have never been declassified. (Given that Castro is still in power, it's likely that the papers dealing with a post-Castro regime have been continually updated over the ensuing decades.)

Vance's Coup Plan says that the "CIA would, as appropriate and with Presidential approval, deal with the" leader of "a coup in Cuba."[40] This fits with what our Kennedy C-Day sources told us. Harry Williams had initially been the only Kennedy representative in secure contact with the C-Day coup leader in Cuba. However, when arrangements had to be made to pay the first installment of the $500,000 payoff to the coup leader, the CIA became involved, since that transaction required complex foreign bank transactions. Also, the CIA was involved in the special operation, mentioned earlier, involving a member of the coup leader's family in a foreign country.[41]

On September 26, 1963, Vance's thirteenth draft of the Coup Plan was about twenty-five pages long; within a couple of months, the file would grow to eighty pages with various additions and attachments, not counting the additional US military invasion plans and the "series of papers" on "a post-Castro" regime. For those reading the Coup Plan who didn't know about C-

Day, Vance explained this substantial amount of work by saying that "even though a coup in this environment seems unlikely at this time," a coup "appears to be the most probable variant of insurgent action as well as the type most likely to succeed."[42] Many of those reading the Coup Plan knew in at least general terms that the US was trying to find someone in Cuba to stage a coup, so those people probably thought all the coup planning was "just in case" one of those options came through.

An AMWORLD memo from CIA Director John McCone—sent on the morning of JFK's assassination, the day the countdown to C-Day would begin—confirms that the C-Day coup was "scheduled for 1 Dec [1963]."[43] This date matches what our Kennedy sources, including Harry Williams, had told us in 1992, even before this memo was released in 1993. Several crucial factors determined why that date was chosen.

The Kennedys and their C-Day coup leader in Cuba were facing a deadline partly imposed by Castro. As we said earlier, many Cuban leaders who had helped to free Cuba during the Revolution had been pushed aside by Castro, and some were now the Kennedys' C-Day Cuban exile leaders. As for the revolutionary leaders left in Cuba, it's well documented that Che Guevara was one of the few who still had a loyal following and power-base of his own, aside from Fidel and Raul Castro. But to help Fidel further solidify his own hold on power, Castro planned to institute a military draft for Cuban males. In this way, Castro could make sure that certain conscripts loyal to him, or agents appearing to be conscripts, were placed in all units of the Cuban armed forces and security services. This would make it difficult for anyone—even someone as powerful as Che Guevara, for example—to plan or carry out a coup effectively. Confirmation that Castro was concerned about some type of "internal uprising" is contained in another CIA message also sent on November 22, 1963, just prior to JFK's death. This message, from an AMTRUNK infiltrator into Cuba, said that "Castro recently expressed fear of the possibility of" an insurrection by some of his men and "so as to negate this possibility Castro was undertaking an intensive propaganda campaign to give confidence to his troops and to limit the occurrence of any internal uprising."[44]

Although the Cuban military draft had been in the works for a while, the Military Service Act, for "men aged 17–45 . . . for 3-year tours" was officially announced on Cuban radio, according to a November 13, 1963 dispatch in the *New York Times*.[45] Harry Williams told us that the draft was to start being implemented in early December, and that's why the C-Day coup leader felt pressure to act by December 1.[46]

The C-Day memo by CIA Director McCone confirms that the "uprising scheduled for 1 Dec" 1963 was "planned as [a] result of [the] Mil[itary] Service Act" because "in [the] opinion of" the C-Day "Leaders [it] would tremendously" impact the "clandestine movement in Cuba."[47] Although McCone's memo with the C-Day date wasn't declassified until 1993, and Harry didn't reveal the C-Day schedule to us until 1992, there was a published hint of the general timing for C-Day as early as 1981. In CIA veteran Joseph B. Smith's memoir, *Portrait of a Cold Warrior*, he mentioned that Desmond FitzGerald told him in 1964 that if JFK had lived, "we would have gotten rid of Castro by last Christmas [of 1963]."[48]

A Kennedy official who worked on C-Day confirmed that the 1963 Christmas holidays were one of two factors limiting how far into December C-Day could be launched. The Kennedy official said that Bobby and JFK didn't want US troops fighting in Cuba over the Christmas holidays. The C-Day coup needed to happen on or about December 1, 1963, so the US invasion would be completed well before Christmas.[49] Cuban exile leader Roberto San Roman knew Harry Williams and worked for C-Day exile leader Manuel Artime, and he told journalist Anthony Summers that "We were never closer to [the] liberation [of Cuba] than we were in November 1963."[50]

But another December date weighed on the mind of JFK in deciding when to launch C-Day, according to the same Kennedy official. JFK and Bobby were worried about how it might look if US planes staged a sudden attack on Cuba on or around December 7, the anniversary of the surprise Japanese attack on Pearl Harbor. Even though the US forces would have been "invited in" by the new Cuban Provisional Government, the Kennedys worried about world reaction to a powerful country like the US staging a sudden air attack against a much smaller country on the Pearl Harbor anniversary.

JFK and Bobby had another, more personal, reason to be concerned about any connection between C-Day and Pearl Harbor, as verified by Secretary of State Dean Rusk. Young Ensign John F. Kennedy had been assigned to Naval Intelligence Headquarters in Washington when that office had, in Rusk's word, "lost" the half of the Japanese fleet that ended up attacking Pearl Harbor. Rusk said that Naval Intelligence subsequently destroyed key documents and transferred personnel to remote posts to stymie any investigation of the mistake and its cover-up. Rusk told us in 1990 that those actions were at the root of the controversies that still linger over Pearl Harbor. We learned later that the same Naval Intelligence office carried out similar document destruction in 1963, when they destroyed files about their ongoing "tight surveillance" of Lee Harvey Oswald in the two days after JFK's assassination.[51] As *New York Post* investigative reporter Tony Sciacca noted, JFK's small role in the Pearl Harbor intelligence failure was "so potentially embarrassing to the later politician that all of his biographers, official or not" usually "pass over" JFK's Naval Intelligence assignment "with a single sentence" that doesn't mention the intelligence failure.[52]

The Kennedy official quoted earlier told us about JFK's sensitivity to the Pearl Harbor date in 1992, and in 1997 documents were finally declassified confirming that US air strikes were to be part of C-Day. These documents, part of the Vance Coup Plan memos, are filled with references to "air strikes" by the US military, US "air attacks," "air support," and "air cover."[53] Documents like those clearly show the important role that air attacks would have had in the C-Day plan and why it was necessary to avoid the Pearl Harbor anniversary date. With lack of air cover often being blamed for the failure of the Bay of Pigs, the Kennedys and the US military were determined to provide all the air strikes necessary to ensure C-Day's success.

JFK and the military knew they had to launch C-Day just as soon as they were ready, something echoed in a memo written by Colonel Alexander Haig, which states that "with the passage of time, the Communist regime in Cuba is likely to become more strongly entrenched and more difficult to root out." Haig pointed out that "US policy toward Cuba is time-sensitive" and "the prospects for a satisfactory outcome diminish as time goes on."[54]

The Kennedys also realized that C-Day could play a decisive role in the upcoming 1964 presidential election. Polls showed that by the fall of 1963, just over half of the American public approved of the way JFK was handling Cuba. Right after the Cuban Missile Crisis, the percentage of Americans who disapproved of JFK's Cuba actions stood at almost zero, but by the spring of 1963 it had grown to 33 percent.[55] A Kennedy C-Day official told us that both JFK and Bobby were determined to complete action on Cuba by the end of 1963 so Cuba wouldn't become a "political football" during the 1964 presidential race, which would kick off in January.[56] Such worry about Cuba and elections was not new, and went back to JFK's 1960 race with Nixon.

(In later years, Nixon and his supporters garnered sympathy by claiming that in the 1960 debates, JFK was able to press hard on the issue of Cuba while Nixon had to remain silent about plans for the Bay of Pigs invasion. What Nixon always left out—although it is amply documented in official documents—was that the main operation the CIA had to topple Castro in the fall of 1960 was not the 1,500-man amphibious exile invasion force that was eventually used at the Bay of Pigs. Before the election, the CIA exile force numbered only 300.[57] In fact, Nixon was counting on a successful outcome to the CIA-Mafia plots to assassinate Castro before the election, as we shall detail in the second part of this book.)

Political problems with Cuba had cropped up again for the Kennedys in the 1962 Congressional elections. Nixon had lobbied hard against any attempt to free the nearly 1,200 Bay of Pigs prisoners suffering in Castro's prisons.[58] A CIA document released thirty-four years later shows that while Bobby Kennedy was trying to find a politically acceptable solution, Bobby confided to CIA Director McCone his worry that trying to ransom the Bay of Pigs prisoners might be used against the Democrats by the Republicans in the 1962 Congressional elections.[59] The Cuban Missile Crisis interrupted the negotiations in October, and the prisoners weren't ransomed until Christmas, preventing any political fallout.

The political heat over Castro and Cuba was already building by the fall of 1963. A long-secret memo from JFK's UN adviser, William Attwood, stated there was a need in the fall of 1963 to "remove the Cuban issue from the 1964 campaign" for president.[60] Attwood's memo says that he worried that JFK's "policy of isolating Cuba economically and politically will not overthrow the Castro regime in time to keep Cuba out of the 1964 campaign."[61] Attwood had not been told about C-Day, so in September 1963 he started pressing for JFK to pursue secret back-channel negotiations with Castro, which we will detail shortly. Just a week after Attwood's memo, the *New York Times* ran a story headlined "Nixon calls Cuba situation important issue in US '64 Presidential election."[62]

Nixon's comments in the *New York Times* were part of a rising tide of Republican criticism of JFK over Cuba that had been growing in intensity since May 1963. A review of articles in the *Times* from May to November 1963 shows a constant stream of charges that JFK was soft on Cuba, from presidential hopefuls Richard Nixon, Nelson Rockefeller, and Barry Goldwater, as well as from the Republican National Chairman. JFK or his supporters would respond to their charges, only to see new charges made.[63] Barry Goldwater was especially vocal, accusing JFK of "doing everything in his power" to keep the flag of Cuban exiles "from ever flying over Cuba again."[64]

If C-Day succeeded, JFK and Bobby would reduce Goldwater's taunts to partisan bleating. After Bobby and Harry Williams had engineered the Bay of Pigs prisoners' release, JFK welcomed the former prisoners and their families at a huge ceremony at the Orange Bowl in Miami.[65] In an emotional ceremony, Artime and the other Bay of Pigs leaders presented JFK with the flag of the Bay of Pigs brigade. Cuban exile Nestor Carbonell wrote that JFK told the crowd "I want to express my great appreciation to the brigade for making the United States the custodian of this flag." Carbonell says that JFK "paused, and then his voice soared with emotion" as JFK proclaimed "I can assure you that this flag will be returned to this brigade in a free Havana."[66] The stadium erupted in cheers at JFK's spur-of-the-moment remark.

Imagine the political impact if JFK had been able to return the flag to Harry Williams, Artime, and the other heroes of the Bay of Pigs "in a free Havana" just one year after his promise. C-Day would give JFK a chance to make good on his pledge. The Brigade flag was kept at Fort Benning, Georgia, where the multiracial Cuban-American troops were getting ready to be the first US forces into Cuba after the C-Day coup.[67] NBC News was planning a prime-time TV special on the Bay of Pigs for December 1963. But if C-Day succeeded, instead of opening old wounds that JFK's rivals could use against him in the '64 election, the TV special could end with the ultimate success of JFK and the Cuban exiles. JFK risked his own life to give his Cuban drama a successful conclusion. Instead, the TV special was postponed after JFK's murder—and NBC news anchor Chet Huntley would wind up playing a small role in the tragedy of C-Day.[68]

Still there was always the chance that C-Day would fail, and what was supposed to seem like an internal coup would be exposed as a US government plan. In that case, Bobby Kennedy would do what he had offered to do for his brother after the Bay of Pigs—resign, taking full responsibility for the disaster. (That's why the "plausible deniability" for JFK in planning C-Day was so important.) That was yet another reason that C-Day was set for December 1, 1963: In order for JFK and the Democrats to have time to recover from the political fallout from such a failure, C-Day had to be attempted before the 1964 campaign season got under way in January.

CHAPTER EIGHT

The Contingency Plans

MANY OF THE PEOPLE WORKING on Cyrus Vance's coup plans were also working on Cuba Contingency Plans to protect C-Day, and on the lower-level CIA plots. The fear was that if Castro found out about C-Day (or the other plots), or perhaps only suspected that something big was brewing, he might stage a preemptive strike against US officials or other targets. In that case, it was important not only to protect the American targets, but also to keep C-Day secret so the coup against Castro could still be launched. JFK and other officials would need time to prepare a reasoned response to any seeming Cuban attack and not be rushed into actions that could lead to nuclear war or even prematurely reveal their coup plans. However, as with the coup plans, one of the problems was that some of those working on the Cuba Contingency Plans knew about C-Day, and some of them didn't. For some it was mainly an exercise, while others knew that it was deadly serious. The Senate Church Committee—which didn't know about C-Day—noted a similar issue when they observed that the CIA's Desmond FitzGerald and his staff were "both plotting with AMLASH [Cubela] and at the very same time participating in this interagency review of contingency plans for possible Cuban retaliation."[1] The planning began in September 1963 and continued well into November 1963, even after the assassination plot against JFK in Chicago was a factor in forcing him to cancel his motorcade there.

Only three documents about the Cuba Contingency Plans have been declassified, though it's clear from them that many more—from a variety of agencies—were generated at the time. However, we were also able to find two sources with firsthand knowledge of the plans. One was a Kennedy administration official who knew about the Cuba Contingency Plans but didn't know about C-Day.[2] The other was a Kennedy C-Day official who at

the time was familiar with the Contingency Plans and with C-Day.[3] Both
sources wish to remain confidential, though their positions and information
were confirmed by numerous government documents and other sources.

Our sources told us that one of the functions of the Cuba Contingency
Plans was to give JFK, the National Security Council, and the Joint Chiefs
time to make a careful, reasoned response before retaliating against Castro, if
it appeared that the Cuban leader had attacked a US official or target. To cite
two examples from the Cuba Contingency Plan documents, "Sabotage of a
US commercial . . . aircraft" or "assassination of American officials" might
simply turn out to be mechanical malfunction or a shooting by common
criminals.[4] With so many Soviets still in Cuba, any quick retaliation could
go nuclear, hence the need for time to gather information so JFK could make
a prudent decision. Such time had been crucial during the Cuban Missile
Crisis, when, for over a week, JFK resisted the pressure for an immediate
strike against the Soviet missiles in Cuba until he could find a peaceful solution. Years later, the US learned that tactical nuclear missiles in Cuba had
been under local Soviet control, so a quick US strike would indeed have
brought nuclear retaliation against the US, leading to the nuclear
armageddon so prevalent in popular books and movies of the time.[5]

One of Vance's declassified Coup Plan documents confirms this thinking
when it talks about "the essentiality of" having certain types of "information
. . . in order to enable the President to make a decision whether to intervene
in support of a coup." Otherwise, "it is very likely that the Government
would lack essential, evaluated information . . . but would, at the same time,
be under heavy pressure to respond quickly."[6] The same point was made by
our sources regarding the Cuba Contingency Plans.[7] As we document in
later chapters, one of the ways to make sure "the President" avoided "heavy
pressure to respond quickly" was to cover up the November 1963 assassination attempts in Chicago and Tampa with seeming links to Cubans, when
their exposure in the press at the time might have revealed C-Day or brought
calls for a quick invasion of Cuba. So the basic principle behind the Cuba
Contingency Plans—to ensure that the President had "essential, evaluated
information" before he was put under "heavy pressure to respond quickly"—
was sound and may have prevented a war with Cuba in November 1963—
though at the cost of JFK's life.

The three declassified Cuba Contingency Plan documents lack any mention of the Secret Service. That's because while "assassination of American
officials" was considered "likely," it was considered "unlikely in the US." The

planners' concerns about assassination and most of the other terrorist acts were mainly focused on Latin America, and since JFK wasn't scheduled to travel outside the country prior to C-Day, he wasn't considered a "likely" target. But later, we'll show how the thinking behind the Cuba Contingency Plans affected government behavior after the JFK assassination, resulting in years of controversy over things like JFK's autopsy.[8]

The first memo about Cuba Contingency Plans from September 1963 was kept TOP SECRET until discovered by the Senate Church Committee in 1976. Even then, they only quoted a few lines—and left out the names of rising Democrat Joseph Califano (who would join Jimmy Carter's cabinet the following year, along with his old boss Cyrus Vance) and Republican Alexander Haig (Nixon's last White House Chief of Staff), whose signature appears on the notes.[9] The memo itself listing the names of Califano and Haig wasn't fully declassified until 1994, as part of the massive releases due to the furor created by the Oliver Stone film *JFK*.

This "Memorandum for the Record" of September 12, 1963, written by "A. M. Haig, Lt Col, USA," consists of notes from the first meeting about the Cuba Contingency Plans, held by the Interdepartmental Cuban Coordinating Committee, one of the three Cuban subcommittees that Bobby controlled. While not all the participants at the meeting are listed, those that are include "Mr. Gordon Chase of the White House" and "Mr. Califano." There were also representatives from the State Department and from the CIA, either Desmond FitzGerald or someone from his staff.[10] Haig wrote that the purpose of the meeting was "the possible development of new contingency plans to meet the changing Cuban situation." The main thing "changing" about the "Cuban situation" at that time was the extensive planning for C-Day that involved Haig and Califano's boss, Cyrus Vance, as well as the CIA's Desmond FitzGerald. Haig's memo said that "there was a strong likelihood that Castro would retaliate in some way against the rash of covert activity in Cuba."[11] However, the coordinator of the meeting "emphasized that it was his view that any Castro retaliation will be at a low level and not along a track which would precipitate a direct confrontation with the United States." The coordinator for this particular meeting wasn't identified; it usually would have been Vance, but if he wasn't there, it could have been his deputy, Califano. If Bobby Kennedy were present, he would have been calling the shots.

Haig's memo then lists a long "series of possible Castro actions for which the US should be prepared," and each was noted as to whether "the Committee agreed" it was "likely" or "unlikely." When they discussed "action against targets in the US," they felt that "sabotage or terrorist bombings" were "unlikely," as were "attacks against US officials." However, when discussing "action against US targets in Latin America," the Committee felt that "sabotage on US . . . aircraft or ships" was "likely." Also in Latin America, they felt that "increased attempts at kidnapping" and "attempts at assassination of American officials or citizens" were "likely."[12] This is important to remember in looking at later events following JFK's assassination: Where assassination was concerned, the focus by US officials prior to JFK's death was on ways to deal with Castro assassinating someone like a US ambassador to a country like Panama.

Reflecting the coordinator's view, there was a long list of relatively minor items that the committee felt were "likely," including "demonstrations or attacks against US Embassies or cultural centers in one or more Latin American countries," "Cuban harassment of US shipping," "jamming of US radio stations," and various diplomatic moves by Cuba. So it's important to remember that "assassination" of "US officials," even in Latin America, was just one of many things the committee felt was "likely" and needed to be planned for. State was asked to "provide the principals with a list of the most significant Castro actions on Friday the 13th," and "the next meeting was set for 18 September 1963."[13]

The next set of declassified Cuba Contingency Plan notes is from their meeting on September 24, 1963. It's unclear whether the September 18 meeting was delayed, the notes for it no longer exist, or they simply haven't been declassified. As an indication of how secret these plans were at the time and even decades later, the notes from the September 24 meeting say the participants were asked to prepare "ten copies" of their assignment for the next meeting—yet none of those copies were uncovered by the Church Committee or the JFK Assassination Records Review Board.[14] And only one copy of the notes for the September 24 and 12 meetings was uncovered, even though many agencies were present and no doubt had all had memos about the meetings. It shows how sensitive this whole operation was, since those at the highest levels (like Bobby and Cyrus Vance) knew that it was designed to protect C-Day.

The notes for the September 24 meeting are addressed to the committee from the "Coordinator of Cuban Affairs." These are not signed, but Cyrus Vance usually acted as coordinator. The coordinator says he has "prepared a list of assignments for contingency papers relating to possible retaliatory actions by the Castro regime" and that "draft contingency papers, in ten copies, should be transmitted to" him by "October 1 [1963]." He says they should be prepared "in the form of scenarios wherever the subject matter readily lends itself to this treatment." It then lists the possible actions by Castro they're studying—but there's one glaring omission: In the list of potential actions by Castro, "attacks against US officials . . . in the US" had been dropped completely from the list, because in the earlier meeting it had been considered "unlikely."[15] Although the real threat JFK faced in the fall of 1963 was from the Mafia and not Castro, it's still possible that steps taken to protect JFK from Castro would have also protected him from the Mafia plot to kill him.

Actions considered "likely" were assigned for further study, for example, to the "State [Department] with advice of USIA [the US Information Agency]." More extensive plans are made for other actions. Regarding possible "Harassment of Guantanamo," it says an "inter-agency team will visit [Guantanamo] Base next week to review plans with Base Commander. Following trip DOD [Department of Defense], State and USIA will" consider other actions. (Califano's trip to Guantanamo is discussed in a later chapter.) For "Actions against Cuban exiles," it says "a working group with representatives from State, CIA, and DOD will review existing plans."[16]

Regarding "attempts at assassination of American officials" occurring "in Latin America," it says the ICCCA "Subcommittee on Cuban Subversion will prepare these," and they are due "October 4." So this planning was basically assigned to a subcommittee (on Cuban Subversion) of a subcommittee (the ICCCA), which was a subcommittee of the National Security Council.[17] While such compartmentalization was good for maintaining security, it made it difficult to make effective, broad-based plans, especially since some subcommittee members knew about C-Day and some didn't.

Among "Actions against Targets in the US," the most serious item being studied was "sabotage or terroristic bombings against US territory." The committee's "Justice [Department] representative" was to "bring" the "Committee's views to the attention of FBI." It's unfortunate that "assassination of American officials" occurring "in the US" wasn't given the same treatment. Instead, the notes make it clear that the main focus was on "protection of installations in US possessions" like "Swan Island," a small US-controlled island near Cuba used for radio broadcasts.[18]

The next memo about the Cuba Contingency Plans is from November 12, 1963, and it again talks about "assassination of American officials." This was two weeks after the Chicago attempt to kill JFK, only six days before the

Mafia's second attempt in Tampa, and ten days before Dallas. From this memo and the previous ones, it's clear that Cuba contingency planning continued through October, but none of those memos has ever been declassified, if they indeed still exist. The November 12, 1963 memo was not found by the Church Committee or the House Select Committee on Assassinations (the HSCA) which followed it; instead, it was released in 1980 by the JFK Presidential Library, which was headed by close JFK aide and longtime friend David Powers. (Powers was a key witness to the assassination, one of several people in the limo right behind JFK who talked about seeing shots from the "grassy knoll." Powers was later one of our key sources, when he told us not only about the shots, but also about the intense pressure to get him to change his testimony "for the good of the country."[19]) However, all of the Congressional committees investigating the JFK assassination had finished their work when Powers released this memo, so it received no attention in the press at the time. As far as we can tell, this is the first time it has been quoted in any book or article.[20]

The formerly SECRET November 12, 1963 memo is to "The Chairman of the Interdepartmental Coordinating Committee on Cuban Affairs" (ICCCA), and is from the "Subcommittee on Cuban Subversion."[21] The "Chairman" is not named, and although Vance was ostensibly the head of the ICCCA, as we noted earlier, Al Haig stressed that Bobby Kennedy was the one calling the shots on all the Cuba committees, even if Bobby appeared on none of the organizational charts.[22]

The two-page memo is a "Status Report on Assigned Contingency Papers" regarding "plans to counter . . . possible actions by Castro." Some of the document is censored, with words and even whole lines missing. Among the "possible actions by Castro" it lists are "sabotage of US . . . ships and aircraft" and "assassination of American officials."[23]

However, the memo says, "the subcommittee has concluded that these particular lines of attack by Castro do not readily lend themselves to the usual contingency planning providing for a direct United States response to Cuban actions." Keep in mind that their focus is still on these actions occurring in Latin America, not in the US. So the memo notes that "protection against attacks occurring within the jurisdiction of another country must be provided by the police and security forces of that country." Although the committee was still focused on attacks outside the US, this thinking would soon affect the actions of Bobby and others after JFK's assassination. After several censored lines, the memo goes on to talk about sending a warning "message to all Latin American posts to alert them to the likelihood of a step-up in Castro-incited subversion and violence" and asks them to "review and revise their . . . plans accordingly."[24] That line also indicates that C-Day was drawing near, since that's what might provoke a "step-up in Castro-incited subversion and violence." (It's hard to ignore the parallel with the 9/11 tragedy, when many pre-9/11 warnings were interpreted by officials to apply only to overseas targets, and so attention was only focused there.[25])

One of our sources was a Kennedy administration official who actually saw the November 12, 1963 memo shortly after it was written. This official hadn't been told about C-Day, but Desmond FitzGerald of the CIA had told him about the Cubela operation, presenting it as a sort of long-shot chance for a coup against Castro. The administration official assumed that that was the reason for all the Cuba contingency planning, in case Castro found out about the Cubela operation and retaliated against the US. Back in the 1970s, the Senate Church Committee had suggested another explanation for all the planning, since the committee didn't know about C-Day. The Church Committee speculated that it was possible that the Cuba Contingency Plans were begun in response to a September 1963 newspaper article in which Castro seemed to threaten US officials. However, our administration official was able to put that to rest once and for all, saying that the Castro article had nothing to do with the Cuba Contingency Plans and wasn't taken seriously.[26]

The Kennedy administration official told us that the US response to any Castro sabotage or terrorist attack would have been "increased economic sanctions, increased covert actions," and "military intervention only as a last resort." He also said that "the FBI felt like they had Cuban subversion in the US under control," which, he implied, was one reason the planners hadn't focused their attention on actions Castro might take in the US. However, this administration official says that he had not been informed of the assassination threat to JFK in Chicago two weeks before the November 12, 1963 memo.[27] Likewise, he was not told about the Tampa assassination attempt on November 18, 1963, even though both attempts initially appeared to be linked to Cubans. Both attempts were kept secret at the time, and there was simply no mechanism for the Cuba Contingency Committee to be informed, unless they learned about them through their own agency or from Bobby Kennedy.

Another of our sources was a Kennedy official who worked on parts of C-Day. While he didn't help draft the official Cuba Contingency Plans we've quoted, he had seen them. He was familiar with the thinking behind them, including additional plans to keep C-Day secret—and viable—if Castro appeared to strike out at the US. In that case, it would be important to ensure that C-Day wasn't exposed while any apparent attack by Castro was thoroughly investigated. It was important that any possible Castro involvement in such an attack be kept from the press in the early stages of any investigation; otherwise, the hawks in Congress would be clamoring for a quick strike on Cuba before the US could be sure that Castro was definitely involved.[28]

The irony is that the Cuba Contingency Plans were supposed to buy time for JFK to react to something like the "assassination" of an "American official" in "Latin America"—and instead, some of the planning wound up being applied to JFK's own murder. Keeping in mind the original purpose of the Cuba Contingency plans, the Kennedy official helped us understand why certain things were done after JFK's assassination.

For example, imagine that on the eve of C-Day, JFK had been informed that the US Ambassador to Panama had been shot to death. It would be important to get accurate medical information, to confirm that the official had died of foul play (as opposed to suicide or an accident) and how it happened (how many gunmen, direction of the shots, etc.). So, instead of doing the autopsy at a local Panamanian hospital, it would be best to do the autopsy at a secure US military facility, which would also keep possibly explosive medical details about the wounds from leaking to the press. In general, information about the shooting would need to be tightly controlled, so that press reports didn't lead to immediate calls for strikes against Castro before the investigation was complete. C-Day would need to be put temporarily on hold, while still being kept tightly secure.[29] As few officials as possible would be told about C-Day and the Cuba Contingency Plans, and usually only at the highest levels. That way, top officials could influence the actions of hundreds in the field, without having to tell the field agents about C-Day. (A real-life example of this in action: Once J. Edgar Hoover publicly announced that Oswald was the lone assassin, FBI agents in the field knew they risked their careers if they pushed too hard in other directions.)

The Kennedy official wasn't just speaking hypothetically—he had first-hand experience of how the thinking behind the Cuba Contingency Plans was applied to the JFK assassination. As he said, he was involved in helping Bobby Kennedy make sure JFK's autopsy didn't compromise national security.[30] His role is confirmed by a detailed written account of the autopsy, authorized by Bobby Kennedy.[31] The Kennedy official's information—when paired with testimony of others at the autopsy, like JFK's personal physician,

Dr. George Burkley—helps to explain many of the unusual aspects of the autopsy that have baffled historians for years, such as:

- Why JFK's body was forcibly removed from the Dallas hospital before the autopsy required by Texas law could be performed there.[32]
- Why the body was flown all the way to Washington, so the autopsy could be done at a secure military facility like the Bethesda Naval Hospital.
- Why the ambulance with JFK's body outran its official escort at Bethesda, so that the body was in the examination room well before the beginning of the "official" autopsy.[33]
- Why witnesses reported that wounds at Bethesda seemed enlarged from those observed by doctors in Dallas, as if there had been hasty exploratory examinations prior to the "official" autopsy.[34] (Some researchers call such a preliminary medical examination of JFK the "National Security autopsy.")
- Why Bobby Kennedy tightly controlled the autopsy—including examination of the wounds—from the tower suite on the 17th floor of the hospital, via JFK's personal physician who was in the autopsy room.[35]

JFK's autopsy room was packed with officials and officers from various agencies and branches of the military, almost none of whom knew about C-Day.[36] It's not as if Bobby could have gone down to the autopsy room and told them all about the impending C-Day coup against Castro, and asked for their cooperation, if he wanted to keep C-Day secret and viable. Plus, at that point, Oswald was still alive and expected to face trial, so his defense would have access to the official autopsy results. Also, at that point it wasn't clear what connection Oswald—or a second or third gunman—might have to Castro. So actions to protect national security had to be quickly improvised, based on the earlier thinking that had gone into the Cuba Contingency Plans.

Since the autopsy was controlled by two people who knew about C-Day, it should come as no surprise that JFK's body and funeral arrangements were handled by two aides to C-Day official Cyrus Vance. Alexander Haig wrote in his autobiography that he and Joseph Califano were assigned to "help with the preparations for the President's funeral," including "handling details concerning the burial."[37] When Vance, Haig, and Califano received information indicating a possible Castro link to Oswald, Haig wrote that he was ordered to destroy the information.[38] While such document destruction helped keep

C-Day secret, information not known to Haig or Califano showed that most of the information saying that Oswald killed JFK on the orders of Castro could be traced to associates of Marcello, Trafficante, or Rosselli.[39]

Agencies like the FBI were faced with trying to investigate the assassination while not endangering C-Day or national security. While the FBI was not formally part of the meetings about the Cuba Contingency Plans, the September 26 version confirms that the FBI was contacted about them. Plus, J. Edgar Hoover's extensive informant network had learned about the CIA's Cubela operation a month before JFK's death, so it's likely that Hoover had at least learned generally about C-Day prior to JFK's death. After JFK's death, new President Lyndon Johnson would have told Hoover more about C-Day. That explains why the FBI often refused to effectively follow up leads that were related to Castro, or that got too close to US operations against Cuba (like those involving mobster John Martino, the close associate of Trafficante and Rosselli who used hints about C-Day to get FBI agents to back off).

Two long-overlooked articles by Pulitzer Prize–winning journalist Tad Szulc provide additional insight into the Cuba Contingency Plans. Szulc was a friend of the Kennedys who worked on the CIA's AMTRUNK operation in 1963. He later found out about C-Day and the Cuba Contingency Plans when the CIA tried to combine the remnants of C-Day with the AMTRUNK operation after JFK's death. Much later, near the end of his life, Szulc curtly admitted to an interviewer that he got the information about the Cuba Contingency Plans "from sources close to Bobby. It was as close as possible, fair enough?"[40]

That Szulc even wrote the articles—one in the *Boston Globe* on May 28, 1976, and a slightly different version in the *New Republic* on June 5, 1976— is remarkable. During most of his distinguished life and journalistic career, the public knew nothing of Szulc's involvement in covert operations like AMTRUNK. However, when he wrote the articles in 1976, numerous revelations were coming out about all sorts of covert operations, including ties between the CIA-Mafia plots and JFK's assassination. It was front-page news in much of the country, especially when potential Senate witnesses like Sam Giancana were the victims of mob hits before they could testify. Szulc himself had been interviewed in secret by the Church Committee about AMTRUNK, and perhaps even about the Cuba Contingency Plans. He may have figured that the information would come out anyway. However, both articles appeared when Senator Frank Church was locked in a heated primary race with Jimmy Carter that was dominating the headlines, so the articles

attracted little attention at the time. When former Church Committee witness Johnny Rosselli's body was found butchered in an oil drum off the coast
of Florida two months later, the Szulc articles were forgotten in the push by
the press and public for a new Congressional JFK assassination investigation
(which became the House Select Committee on Assassinations).

Szulc's articles began by saying: "The Federal Bureau of Investigation and
the Central Intelligence Agency engaged in a cover-up of highly relevant
information when the Warren Commission was investigating President John
Kennedy's assassination. . . . President Lyndon Johnson and Attorney General Robert F. Kennedy became party to the effort which consisted of withholding key facts from the Warren Commission." Szulc then revealed the
Cuba Contingency Plans: "The Warren Commission was never told that
Attorney General Kennedy secretly formed—*before* [emphasis in original]
his brother was killed—a special intergovernmental committee, which
included FBI and CIA representatives, to look into the possibility that Cuba's
Premier Fidel Castro might organize attempts on the lives of high United
States government officials."[41]

Szulc says: "that this committee existed has been kept secret although
information about it reposes in FBI files."[42] That is interesting, because the
FBI has never made public any information about the Cuba Contingency
Plans. The FBI told the Church Committee that they couldn't find anything
about the Cuba Contingency Plans, even though one of the September
memos says they were to be contacted about it.[43]

Szulc reveals that "the top-secret committee was created by Robert
Kennedy presumably out of concern that Castro might retaliate against CIA
attempts on his life, carried out directly by the agency's operatives and with
help from the Mafia." This was written just after the Cubela and CIA-Mafia
plots had received a great deal of press attention, which is why Szulc focused
on those. Szulc's AMTRUNK operation with the CIA was known to the Church
Committee, but wouldn't be publicly revealed for almost twenty years. And
while Szulc had earlier written another article and a book that hinted at C-
Day, that operation hadn't been uncovered by the Church Committee.[44]

The Contingency Plans had been withheld from the Warren Commission,
Szulc explains, because "Robert Kennedy, the CIA and the FBI decided to
keep from the Warren Commission the fact that a special group had been set
up to protect American leaders from possible *Cuban* [emphasis in original]
assassination plots. To justify its existence, it would have been necessary to
expose the CIA's own conspiracies against Castro. These were among the

most closely held secrets of the Kennedy-Johnson period." Szulc says "all the indications are that the existence of this committee was known to very few people: Robert Kennedy himself, probably Dulles and McCone, FBI Director J. Edgar Hoover, and a few selected associates. Several aides of Robert Kennedy, including a former assistant director of the FBI, said in interviews last week that they had not known of the committee."[45]

Unlike an earlier article and a book he wrote, Szulc doesn't hint at C-Day in this article. To do so might have led to the exposure of his own role in the CIA's AMTRUNK plan, risking his career. Still, it's amazing that Szulc wrote as much about the Cuba Contingency Plan as he did—and that it received so little attention at the time. After these two articles, Szulc never again wrote about the Cuba Contingency Plans or hinted of C-Day.

CHAPTER NINE

"Playing with Fire"

THERE WAS ONE PLAN TO deal with Castro in the fall of 1963 that wasn't a military or CIA plan, though several officials of both groups were aware of it.[1] It was the Kennedys' secret, back-channel negotiations with Castro. Starting in September 1963—and continuing even as the countdown for C-Day began on November 22, 1963—the Kennedys were still trying a last-ditch effort to find a peaceful solution to the Cuba problem.

There were two catalysts for the secret negotiations: ABC-TV journalist Lisa Howard and C-Day. Howard was known for landing historic interviews, including some with Fidel, and she initially pushed for the negotiations. However, before this book and the revelation of C-Day, it was never clear why the secret negotiations assumed such intensity and urgency as the fall of 1963 progressed. It's now clear that the looming deadline of C-Day gave JFK and Bobby an incentive to try to find a peaceful solution before risking so many American lives.

In the political climate of 1963, JFK's secret negotiations had their own risk. If JFK's rivals had been able to show that he had dared to negotiate with Castro, it would have spelled disaster for JFK in the 1964 election. As Bobby himself said in a secret memo from September 1963, they had to be extremely careful or they would risk "the accusation that we were trying to make a deal with Castro."[2] It was a sign of JFK's determination that as C-Day drew nearer, he actually accelerated the secret negotiations and added a second back channel to Castro. In late October 1963, JFK asked French journalist Jean Daniel to speak with Castro on Kennedy's behalf. However, it took Daniel weeks to finally get to speak with Castro, and they would actually be meeting when the news came of JFK's assassination.

JFK's Secretary of State Dean Rusk confirmed the Kennedys' C-Day coup plan to the authors in 1990.[3] Three years later, at the authors' suggestion, *Vanity Fair* contacted Rusk about the coup plan. Rusk confirmed the existence of the plan to the magazine, but provided no details. However, *Vanity Fair* received a surprising answer when they asked Rusk about the Kennedys' attempts to negotiate with Castro at the same time they were also planning a coup against Castro. In pursuing the two strategies at the same time, "Rusk admits that the Kennedys were 'playing with fire.'" Rusk told *Vanity Fair*, "Oh, there's no particular contradiction there . . . it was just an either/or situation. That went on frequently."[4]

This dual strategy is reflected in Bobby Kennedy's Oral History at the John F. Kennedy Presidential Library. Bobby says that "There were some tentative [peace] feelers that were put out by [Castro] which were accepted by us." But in the very next sentence, Bobby adds that at the same time "we were also making more of an effort [against Castro] through espionage . . . in . . . August, September, October [1963]. It was better organized than it had been before and was having quite an effect." In an oblique reference to C-Day, Bobby says that one of his goals was "internal uprisings" and that "we were more [than just] assisting" because of his "contact with some of those people."[5] Pursuing peace and war at the same time reflected the indecisiveness of the American public about Cuba. JFK biographer Richard Reeves noted that 60 percent of Americans in 1963 thought that Castro "was a serious threat to world peace," yet a slightly higher percentage "were against sending United States troops to invade Castro's island."[6]

The Kennedys probably felt that they had no choice but to proceed with C-Day while the secret negotiations continued, since the negotiations were going slowly and not producing tangible results. The Kennedys' main negotiator, Special UN Envoy William Attwood, said in a TOP SECRET; EYES ONLY memo from October 21, 1963 that "he is not hopeful" about the negotiations. The Kennedys also felt pressure from some of their advisers. Formerly SECRET minutes of one of the Cuba subcommittees show that the CIA's Richard Helms didn't see the negotiations as an opportunity. Helms told Bobby and Vance that he felt that the peace negotiations were a "problem," and he urged caution before "making any contacts."[7] This raises yet another possible reason Helms pursued other Castro assassination plots that fall: He may have wanted to be sure something brought down Castro before JFK could make a peace deal with him.

Nevertheless, the Kennedys pressed forward with the Attwood negotiations and with Jean Daniel. Attwood continued his efforts with the help of

Lisa Howard, and memos confirm that there was a flurry of calls on November 11, 18, and 19. It's ironic that one of the people Castro "specifically" excluded from his side of the negotiations was Che "Guevara." Attwood sent a memo about his efforts to the National Security Council on November 22, 1963, apparently just prior to JFK's assassination.[8]

Long-secret memos from December 1963 confirm that Attwood tried to continue the negotiations with Castro after JFK's death. There had been speculation in the press that Oswald had been working for Castro, mostly because of reports fed to intelligence agencies and newspapers by sources later shown to be linked to Mafia bosses Marcello, Trafficante, or Rosselli. But a TOP SECRET, EYES ONLY memo from December 3, 1963 gave "assurances re Oswald" to the "National Security Council Staff" that Oswald hadn't been working for Castro. (Such assurances could be given because the DIA's Naval Intelligence had had Oswald under constant "tight" surveillance in the months prior to the assassination.) The way seemed clear to continue the negotiations. However, even after cutting "Lisa Howard . . . out of the picture," LBJ didn't want to proceed.[9] There would be no high-level contacts between a US official and a Cuban official for another year, when US Senator Eugene McCarthy had one of three private meetings with Che Guevara in New York City. Che's other private meetings at that time were with AMTRUNK journalist Tad Szulc and with Lisa Howard, just months before her tragic death and Che's disappearance.[10]

Even as the secret peace feelers continued, the Joint Chiefs prepared their response to Vance's Coup Plan, and another branch of the military—the Defense Intelligence Agency (DIA)—was also working on C-Day. The DIA, created in the first year of JFK's presidency, was headed by General Joseph F. Carroll.[11] While Carroll was not as close to the Kennedys as Joint Chiefs Chairman Maxwell Taylor, the Kennedys admired Carroll for his work in finding the Soviet missiles in Cuba before the Missile Crisis.[12] That is probably why General Carroll was one of the military people trusted to know about C-Day.[13] Not well known, the DIA is the umbrella agency of US military intelligence, responsible for groups like the Office of Naval Intelligence and Army Intelligence.

General Carroll was a low-profile figure, and much of what is known about him comes from a few declassified documents, several references, and a book about him by his son, award-winning novelist James Carroll.[14] Carroll had served in the FBI until the late 1940s, and, while in the FBI, Carroll shared at least one major case with an agent named Guy Banister. By 1963, Banister was a New Orleans private detective with ties to Naval Intelligence—and Carlos Marcello.[15]

The DIA's role in covert Cuban operations has received little attention over the years, and, in contrast to the CIA, almost no documents about DIA Cuban operations have been released. In some ways, that's not surprising, since Army Intelligence admitted in the 1970s that it destroyed its records about the JFK assassination. A Congressional committee found indications that Marine Intelligence destroyed documents about Oswald and JFK's assassination, while we uncovered extensive Naval Intelligence document destruction after the assassination.[16] However, we know that General Carroll and the DIA were involved with C-Day because of a CIA AMWORLD report about comments Carroll made regarding the CIA and C-Day to a CIA informant, and because of DIA notations on documents from other agencies.[17]

Even within the Pentagon, keeping secrets about C-Day was a huge concern, since most of America's highest officers and civilian officials didn't know about it. When General Carroll needed to meet with a Cuban exile about C-Day, he met with the exile away from his office and the Pentagon—in a car. The general's unusual car meeting was due to his concerns about secrecy, because he didn't want anyone to overhear his complaints about a CIA operation interfering with C-Day. In that particular case, General Carroll's precautions didn't work, because the Cuban exile he met with appears to have told someone connected with the CIA about Carroll's concerns, and the CIA recorded them in this memo. The CIA report of General Carroll's November 10, 1963 meeting duly noted that the Cuban exile "had meeting in automobile with Chief DIA who spoke against activities" of the CIA "because they [are] interfering with Plan Judas," a name a few exiles on the fringe of the operation used for C-Day.[18] The CIA operation General Carroll was complaining about could have been the CIA's Cubela operation, AMTRUNK, or the CIA-Mafia Castro assassination plots, since a CIA file admits that C-Day exile leader Manuel Artime was working on the Mafia plots when the CIA was supporting Artime.[19]

It's ironic that the November 10, 1963 AMWORLD CIA document we just quoted described DIA Chief General Carroll's concerns about CIA activities, because an earlier document reflects CIA concern about the DIA. Written on a "Central Intelligence Agency Official Routing Slip" is the handwritten notation "I have a sneaking suspicion that DIA has a hand in this. . . ." Then, approximately two lines are censored. The slip is undated, but was between two files from late September 1963 that were in the CIA's file on corrupt ex-Cuban President Carlos Prio. The slip appears to be signed by "JC," which might stand for J. C. King, the CIA's Western Hemisphere Chief in 1963, who issued the CIA's very first AMWORLD document, and a copy of the memo went to Desmond FitzGerald.[20] Taken together, this document and the earlier one indicate that the CIA and the DIA had problems coordinating with each other over C-Day.

One of the few relevant documents originated by the DIA that has been declassified is a formerly SECRET memo of October 8, 1963, from General Carroll to Secretary of Defense Robert McNamara. Carroll says he is responding to "an oral request from the Military Aide to the President," who apparently wanted to know about current Soviet military strength in Cuba. Carroll says that their "assessment . . . prepared in collaboration with the CIA, concludes that Soviet military personnel withdrawals are continuing." He says that "total Soviet military strength in Cuba is now estimated to be between 5,000 and 8,000—representing a reduction of at least two-thirds of the number . . . on the island during the [Cuban Missile] Crisis." General Carroll says that "Most of those remaining are advisors and technicians engaged in training Cuban personnel in the operation of Soviet weapons . . . and in operating the Soviet-controlled air defense system. No organized Soviet ground combat units remain in Cuba."[21] Note the careful use of the words "most" and "no *organized* . . . combat units"—it doesn't definitively say that no Soviet *combat forces* are in Cuba, because that would be difficult for the US to assess.

Given its timing, the memo was likely requested because JFK or one of his advisers read Vance's Coup Plan from a couple of weeks earlier. The Coup Plan had discussed "the possible neutralization or elimination of Soviet forces in Cuba" and a "US-Soviet confrontation" in Cuba, while trying "to minimize Soviet loss of life."[22] JFK and his advisers would have wanted to know exactly what the US would be up against, hence the request to General Carroll from the White House.

The memo also notes that "Soviet military . . . withdrawals are continuing" and that overall Soviet strength in Cuba was one third what it had been a year earlier. In other words, the Soviet situation in Cuba was improving, even as JFK's critics like Goldwater and Nixon were increasing their rhetoric suggesting just the opposite. Still, there was no way JFK could prove that no

Soviet missiles were left in Cuba to the satisfaction of his critics; so planning for C-Day continued, as a military document from two weeks later shows.

On October 21, 1963, "General Maxwell D. Taylor, Chairman of the Joint Chiefs of Staff" sent a memo to JFK's Secretary of Defense with the Joint Chiefs' formal response to Vance's September 26, 1963 "Plan for a Coup in Cuba." Classified TOP SECRET for thirty-four years, it was among the documents finally declassified in 1997 by the JFK Assassination Records Review Board in response to our efforts and those of other researchers. The Joint Chiefs "concluded that the [coup] plan envisaged in the State-Defense paper is militarily feasible."[23] Alexander Haig is noted as one of three people who handled the Joint Chiefs' memo.[24]

It appears that some, if not most, of the Joint Chiefs and their staffs still didn't know about C-Day. Taylor's memo, on behalf of all the Joint Chiefs, says they still feel as they did on June 15, that "although a coup may be one of the most promising types of revolt in Cuba, it is unlikely to occur." They had also noted that Vance's Coup Plan extensively detailed "US actions following a coup," and said they considered those "statements . . . as assumptions for the purpose of the paper, rather than as approved national policy."[25] Of course, they really were "approved national policy," as other documents and sources close to the Kennedys have confirmed. It's possible that General Taylor and General Carroll were the only members who knew that the Joint Chiefs were approving a plan actually scheduled to happen in little more than a month. The other Joint Chiefs would know only about the more general efforts to find someone to stage a coup, as described in the memo about their September 25, 1963 meeting with CIA officer Desmond FitzGerald.

The Joint Chiefs noted "serious reservations" about the proposal in the most recent version of Vance's Coup Plan to send a "special team" of CIA-State-Defense representatives into Cuba within twenty-four hours after the coup, to see if it met the requirements for massive US military support. They noted the "short time frame" the US would have in which to make a decision to support the coup. And "further, in the case of a coup initiated by [a] dissident" leader "who had agreed to meet the criteria for US support and to whom prior approval had been given to commence the coup at the earliest practicable time, the United States would have some obligation to intervene" regardless of what any "special team" said.[26] (The Kennedys were of a like mind, and by November 22, 1963, the trigger for sending in at least the

Cuban-American exile troops was going to be Castro's death, coupled with an announcement from the coup leader and whatever prearranged message or signal Harry Williams could send from inside Cuba.)[27]

The Joint Chiefs noted that a "broad, multiple-source intelligence assessment" would be "necessary for the critical decision which would commit the United States to the employment of portions or all of the military forces required by" the military's full Cuban invasion plans.[28] Multiple sources were important because Cuba was a large island, and it would be necessary to gauge the reaction of the Cuban people in Havana and other key cities to the coup. Likewise, it would be important to know how each of the major Soviet garrisons was reacting. In May 1963, the Joint Chiefs had wanted the CIA to develop "a suitable cover plan" and start getting "assets into Cuba for the development of intelligence . . . as soon as practicable."[29] Evidence later in Part I indicates that the CIA had been doing that since at least September 1963, when they established a "cover plan" that would let them get assets into Cuba who could move freely among the Cuban people, unlike the Cuban exiles who sneaked into Cuba from speedboats at night and had to stay hidden to avoid capture.

The Joint Chiefs also point out that "the early commitment of airborne or air-landed forces" for the coup "might entail less risk if the US Naval Base, Guantanamo, had been reinforced and a combat-loaded amphibious force were at sea."[30] In fact, one of the memos for the Cuba Contingency Plan to protect C-Day said that an "inter-agency team will visit [Guantanamo] Base . . . to review plans with Base Commander."[31] That "inter-agency team" was to focus on plans to deal with possible "Harassment of Guantanamo" by Castro, in retaliation for the US plans directed against him. But that could also provide the opportunity to have Guantanamo "reinforced," like the Joint Chiefs wanted. (As documented later, personnel changes were made at Guantanamo during the visit of one of Vance's assistants, while he was working on the Cuba Contingency Plans.) The military leaders would also get the "combat-loaded amphibious force" they wanted, since several documents refer to the use of Special Forces after the coup and a Defense source told us that C-Day plans called for the Cuban-American troops to be ready to go into Cuba at a moment's notice.[32]

Planning continued after the Joint Chiefs gave their response in October; the last draft of the plan we have was finalized by late November 1963 and has no draft number. There had been more than a dozen drafts of the Coup Plan, over the summer and into the fall of 1963. Not all of the drafts still exist—or, if they do, they haven't been declassified. From what has been released, we know that the fourth draft was completed on June 8, 1963. Paralleling the increase in activity of Harry Williams and other exile leaders for C-Day, by late September 1963 Vance was already up to his thirteenth draft. By the late November 1963 draft, the plan had grown to more than eighty pages with the addition of various memos, attachments, and additions. Separate from that were the "series of papers" on "a post-Castro" regime and the military's extensive plans for the actual invasion of Cuba, code-named CINCLANT OPLANS 312 and 316.[33] The November plan refines, and adds detail to, the plan from September, but is essentially the same.[34] As with the earlier version, this was classified TOP SECRET. The Joint Chiefs kept it that way when they reviewed it in 1989, and the JFK Assassinations Records Review Board finally declassified it in 1997. This version was sent (in 1963) to the Joint Chiefs and their staffs, seventeen top brass in all, including General Maxwell Taylor and General Carroll. However, since it also went to extreme hawks like General Curtis LeMay, who was close to JFK's adversaries in Congress, Vance continued to be careful about giving too much away about C-Day. Some hints slip through, nonetheless. For example, this Plan uses the term "palace coup," which makes it clear that the coup leader is someone who is very close to Castro, part of his inner circle.[35]

The late November 1963 "Plan for a Coup in Cuba" notes that it was the result of "several months" of effort by "interagency staff," including "State and Defense in coordination with the Central Intelligence Agency." Vance notes that the plan represents a "working-level consensus," meaning that "the plan . . . was developed by, and has the concurrence at the planners level." Now Vance says it's time to obtain the "formal approval of the Secretary of State and the Director of the Central Intelligence Agency." The submission cover letter is signed by "Cyrus R. Vance, Secretary of the Army."[36]

This version of the Coup Plan repeats all the key points of the earlier plan, like the need to "neutralize the top echelon of Cuban leadership" and a coup leader with "some power base in the Cuban" government who is ready to "establish a Provisional Government . . . with some sort of public claim to political viability." It also says that at some point, the US needs to consult "with our NATO allies (to alert them to possible Soviet action in Berlin or elsewhere)."[37]

Vance says that the preferred way for the coup to start is for the coup leader, "in secure radio contact with [the] CIA," to "implement" his "plan with US concurrence, in full expectation of forthcoming US support, barring an immediate crushing of the uprising." The "US intervention would be based on a prearranged call for help from" the new Cuban "Provisional Government." However, even without the prearranged call, "the US would immediately and overtly render necessary support to assure the success of the" coup "in the event of intervention by local Soviet forces." The plan says that "US . . . personnel" would "liais[e] with the coup leaders" even as the US military was "establishing a full air and sea blockade of Cuba."[38] Given the high-stakes tension surrounding the previous year's US naval blockade of Cuba during the Missile Crisis, this shows just how serious the Kennedys were about making sure that the C-Day coup succeeded.

The plans for C-Day were almost complete. FBI veteran William Turner wrote that in November 1963, the Kennedys' Cuba "program was just about at the go. The CIA's navy was operating in the Caribbean, Manuel Artime . . . was nearing readiness in Central America. And Harry Williams was shuttling between Miami and Washington, finalizing details."[39] Evan Thomas recently uncovered a piece of information linking JFK himself to a coup in Cuba. Thomas says that "in early November" 1963, a "senior CIA official . . . was sitting in Desmond FitzGerald's office at CIA headquarters in Langley, Virginia, while FitzGerald spoke on a secure phone directly to President Kennedy." Thomas writes that the CIA "official overheard FitzGerald tell the President about the possibility of an anti-Castro coup in Havana."[40]

Around that time, Soviet leader Khrushchev gave JFK a new reason to worry about the upcoming C-Day coup. The *New York Times* reported on November 7, 1963 that "Khrushchev warns US that attack on Cuba will lead to war."[41] More detail about the threat was added the following day, when the *Times* reported that "Khrushchev tells [group of US] industrialists at reception that if US attacks Cuba, USSR will attack US allies."[42] The Soviet leader may have been reacting to the small raids on Cuba from Artime and some of the other C-Day exile groups. While the stories weren't front-page news (they were buried on page 4 of the second section), it's certain that they caught the attention of avid news-reader JFK and those in the White House and CIA who closely monitored the Soviet Union. For example, a White House memo still exists about a later warning from Khrushchev that was reported in the *Times*.[43]

Khrushchev's warnings pointed out the high stakes involved as C-Day drew nearer. By the second week of November 1963, it was time for JFK himself to review the Cuban situation with several of his key officials and advisers. This would not be easy to do in a large meeting, since several of them still did not know about C-Day and some were only generally aware of US efforts to find a Cuban official willing to stage a coup.

The following three documents provide a rare "on the record" glimpse of John and Robert Kennedy presiding over a meeting where overthrowing Castro was the main topic of conversation. Most such meetings weren't well documented, and usually involved only Bobby instead of JFK.[44] That approach provided "plausible deniability" for JFK if the plans ever turned into a Bay of Pigs–style disaster.

The meeting took place on November 12, 1963, just ten days before the countdown to C-Day was to begin and less than three weeks before C-Day itself. With C-Day looming so close, it was apparently felt that JFK himself needed to be present at a key meeting of one of Bobby's Cuban committees— ordinarily the President wouldn't attend a meeting of what was just a subcommittee of the National Security Council. Luckily, three different records exist of the meeting, including one from a meeting participant who knew about C-Day and one from someone who didn't.

One document is a brief summary of the November 1963 meeting, prepared in 1975 for the Senate Church Committee investigation into CIA assassination plots against foreign leaders and their possible connection to the JFK assassination. The summary is very brief, and it's easy to see why the Church Committee couldn't uncover C-Day working from such abbreviated material. However, even this brief summary was kept secret not only at the time, but for another nineteen years. Among those the summary lists as present at the meeting were JFK, Bobby, Dean Rusk, CIA Director John McCone, CIA Deputy Director for Plans Richard Helms, and Desmond FitzGerald. The summary says that "FitzGerald reported to the President . . . on disaffections in the [leadership] in Cuba." He said that "some leaders might break with the regime" and that "the principal aim of the US is to 'get leaders who have become disenchanted with the Castro regime to dare to talk and plot Castro's downfall with each other.'" FitzGerald also noted that "25 [CIA] agents had been either captured or killed in the last year" in actions against Cuba, at a time when the general public assumed that the Kennedys were putting Cuba on the back burner.[45]

FitzGerald had to word things carefully, because Rusk and some others at the meeting didn't know about the existence of C-Day at that time, even though it had been in the works for over five months. This is borne out by what a "senior official" in the CIA at the time told Bobby's recent biographer Evan Thomas. At that meeting, the official said: "FitzGerald consciously played down" another assassination "operation" of the CIA's involving a mid-level Cuban official named Cubela, "because he [FitzGerald] knew most of the President's advisers opposed any action that would deepen US involvement" in Cuba.[46] Many of FitzGerald's comments in the meeting couldn't apply to the Cubela operation, but only to C-Day. Other documents will show that Rusk was considered at that time to be one of those against action to "eliminate" Castro, since he had softened his hard position of the previous year over the summer, when secret negotiations became an option. However, by dealing with the possible overthrow of Castro at the meeting, even in general terms, Rusk and other officials who didn't know about C-Day wouldn't be surprised when the C-Day coup occurred; they would just assume that a long-shot possibility had come through.

In 1997, a much longer record of the November 12, 1963 meeting prepared by JFK's CIA Director John McCone was finally declassified. It gives a more complete list of those present, adding officials like General Maxwell Taylor, Cyrus Vance, and the head of the CIA's huge Miami Station, Ted Shackley.[47] Indications are that Taylor and Vance were fully informed about C-Day. It's unclear if Ted Shackley knew fully about C-Day, or only had the general knowledge imparted by the initial AMWORLD memo quoted extensively earlier. Even though Shackley supervised Miami Operations Chief David Morales, there are a couple of indications in documents that Shackley was not fully informed about C-Day, in the same way that Morales's close associate David Atlee Phillips—the number-three man at the CIA's Mexico City station—was involved in CIA operations that his boss in Mexico City wasn't fully aware of.[48] (For that sensitive operation related to C-Day, detailed in later chapters, Phillips was reporting to FitzGerald in Washington even though the operation was being carried out in Mexico City.) Though Shackley surely knew that five Cuban exile groups were getting major support from the Kennedys, that is not the same as knowing about C-Day. Only a small number of officials knew about the impending coup and the US military's invasion plans, and an even smaller number (about a dozen) knew the identity of the coup leader, the very high Cuban official and Revolutionary hero who would "eliminate" Castro at the start of the coup. But as with Rusk, it was important for Shackley not to be surprised when Castro was hopefully toppled by the C-Day coup, hence his presence at the meeting. CIA Director McCone reviewed the situation in Cuba at the meeting by saying that powerful members of the Cuban government "remain essentially loyal to Castro," though there was "some evidence of dissension and dissidents which are being exploited by the CIA."[49]

In addition to C-Day, CIA Director McCone also knew very generally about the Cubela operation—though not about its assassination aspects, or FitzGerald's recent meeting in Paris with Cubela—and was fully aware of another CIA operation called AMTRUNK. Both the Cubela operation and AMTRUNK were like lower-level versions of C-Day which didn't reach nearly as high in the Cuban government and weren't nearly as far along; both operations and their relation to C-Day are explained in Chapter 18. Officials like Rusk knew generally about the Cubela operation and AMTRUNK, so CIA Director McCone was careful to say at the meeting that "the program which had been followed for the last several months, having been approved about the first of June, was integrated and interdependent one part of the other and therefore should be considered as a comprehensive program and not a number of independent actions."[50] In this way, US officials like Rusk who didn't know about C-Day wouldn't feel completely deceived after the coup, since they would assume that the operations they did know about had been part of C-Day.

After McCone spoke, the CIA's Desmond "FitzGerald then made a presentation." It included mention of the CIA's efforts at "covert collection of intelligence" about Cuba and "exploitation of disaffection with the Cuban [government's] power centers." Then FitzGerald updated the group on the progress of what JFK, Bobby, Vance, and other C-Day insiders knew was the largest of the five C-Day Cuban exile groups, "the Artime group." FitzGerald "forecast that once Artime was in business, we might expect some events to take place which were not exactly to our liking."[51] This comment appears intended for non-C-Day officials like Rusk, since documents and news accounts confirm that Artime had been "in business" and launching raids against Cuba for several months at that point. But again, this would help to prepare officials like Rusk for the coup that JFK, Bobby, Vance and others knew was scheduled to take place just a little over two weeks later.

Rusk—a brilliant man, an experienced diplomat, and the consummate team player—apparently got the drift of what was he was being primed for. Rusk had been viewed as soft on getting rid of Castro in recent months, ever since the back-channel negotiations with Castro had started. Now, though,

Rusk declared at the meeting that "we must replace Castro." Toward that end, Rusk even said he "had no problem with [the] infiltration of black teams" into Cuba.[52] Those were US intelligence operatives, part of the CIA's task of getting assets into Cuba before C-Day, which is discussed later. These highly-secret intelligence agents will be discussed in more detail, later in this section.[53]

The next view of this important November 12, 1963 meeting comes from notes prepared by Rusk's State Department. They show that JFK's presence at such a meeting was considered so sensitive and unusual that he wasn't referred to by name or even called "The President." Instead, he was only called the "Higher Authority." Everyone else who attended was listed by their last name, except for "Mr. Robert Kennedy." The notes themselves were classified SECRET; EYES ONLY, so it's remarkable that they were preserved at all, until they were finally declassified in 1997.[54]

These notes echo the other descriptions of "FitzGerald's report on Cuban operations" in several areas, including "Covert Collections [of intelligence]," "Disaffections in the" Cuban government, and "Support of Autonomous Anti-Castro Groups" (the official term for the C-Day exile groups). Regarding the collection of intelligence, FitzGerald explained the "25 [agents who] had been either captured or killed" was due to "the increasing effectiveness of Castro's internal security forces and discovery brought about when agents try to obtain food. No matter how good the documentation, an outsider in a community is viewed with suspicion."[55] Given those difficulties, getting good intelligence on the ground in Cuba before, during, and after C-Day could be a problem. But as we document later, US intelligence had recently come up with a way to get a different type of agent into Cuba via Mexico City, one who could move freely among the Cuban populace.

The State Department notes say that FitzGerald told the meeting that "there are indications that some [Cuban government] leaders would like to break with the regime." FitzGerald said that the "CIA is in touch with three persons . . . who have highly placed contacts in such circles" and that "the principal aim is to get . . . leaders who have become disenchanted with the Castro regime to dare to talk and plot Castro's downfall with each other."[56] These comments helped to prepare non-C-Day officials such as Rusk for the upcoming C-Day coup. Rusk knew that mid-level Cuban officials like Cubela and those in the CIA's AMTRUNK operation didn't have the power to stage a coup against Castro. But this way, when C-Day happened, Rusk would simply assume that the CIA had been successful in getting those mid-level officials to recruit the powerful C-Day coup leader.

The notes say that FitzGerald then discussed the "Autonomous Anti-Castro Groups," referring to the C-Day Cuban exile groups who were being backed by the Kennedys. He said that "much could be accomplished by the autonomous groups once they become operational"—leaving out the fact that most of the groups were already operational, as documented by the occasional newspaper stories that had been appearing for the past three months. FitzGerald said "they would operate from outside US territory," such as the "two bases of the [Manuel] Artime group, one in Costa Rica and the other in Nicaragua." FitzGerald mentioned another key C-Day Cuban exile Leader, "Manolo Ray."[57] Later, we show how the Kennedys and Harry Williams were getting the very liberal Ray to work with the extremely conservative Artime for C-Day.

CHAPTER TEN

The Countdown for C-Day Begins: November 22, 1963

THE BIG NOVEMBER 12, 1963 meeting, just ten days before JFK's trip to Dallas, was only the latest in a series of meetings that had been building in urgency and intensity since the spring of 1963. But in the last week of JFK's life, planning for C-Day would reach new heights, starting with a personal message to the coup leader in Cuba from JFK.

Pressure for JFK to make a statement of support for the coup had been building since October 1, 1963, when one of the Cuban subcommittees of the National Security Council discussed "recommending to the President that he comment on the future of Cuba in a forthcoming speech." This was after "Desmond FitzGerald of CIA reviewed the situation in Cuba, empha-sizing that a swing of the pendulum was taking place." As was usually the case, JFK was not at this meeting, which was chaired by Bobby Kennedy. However, as was also usually the case, some of the officials attending knew about C-Day and some didn't, so things had to be worded carefully. But even officials who didn't know about C-Day did know that US action toward Cuba was growing steadily throughout the summer and fall of 1963, and that extensive plans were being made just in case a coup happened in Cuba.[1] This meeting also shows that there were problems coordinating the efforts against Cuba. At one point, FitzGerald complained "that the CIA had never gotten the Joint Chiefs' suggestions" about two covert actions. Bobby then "expressed some concern about whether suggested Cuban actions were being followed up."[2] These problems would only grow, as C-Day drew nearer and the various agencies didn't share all of their pertinent information with each other.

By mid-November, after Khrushchev's threat and pressure from the coup leader for a personal message of support from JFK, it was decided that JFK would deliver a major speech about Cuba on November 18, 1963, and that it would include phrases of support directed to the coup leader in Cuba. The speech would be delivered in Miami, which would ensure plenty of coverage of it in Havana. To send an added message of US strength, JFK would watch, for the first time, the launch of a Polaris missile from a submarine, at a specially-arranged, heavily publicized event on November 16. It would receive wide press coverage and be front-page news in most Sunday newspapers in Florida on November 17. In addition to large photos of the "spectacular" launch and JFK, articles reported that the President "voiced his warm appreciation for the demonstration of [US] naval power." JFK was quoted as talking about "control of the seas," having "the most modern weapons system in the world."[3] On November 18, prior to delivering his speech with the lines for the coup leader, JFK met privately with top brass at the Army's Strike Force (Central Command) headquarters in Tampa. While the agenda of the meeting was secret, the fact that it was being held was leaked to the press in advance. Press reports of that meeting were one more signal to the coup leader that JFK was serious about supporting the upcoming C-Day.

Proof that parts of JFK's November 18, 1963 speech were intended for the leader of the coup in Cuba can be found in the reports of the Senate Church Committee, in particular the report of the subcommittee on the JFK assassination, which included Democrat Senator Gary Hart and Republican Richard Schweiker. The Senate report cited JFK's November 18, 1963 speech and said "the fact that the CIA intended President Kennedy's speech to serve as a signal to [a] dissident" leader "in Cuba that the US would support a coup is confirmed by a CIA paper, completed less than two weeks after Kennedy's assassination." The CIA paper talked about "statements" the President could make that would "stimulate anti-Castro action on the part of [a] dissident" leader "in the Cuban [government]." It also says that the "anti-Castro dissident . . . assert[s] that" he "must have solemn assurances from [a] high level US spokesman, especially the President, that the United States will exert its decisive influence during and immediately after the coup to prevent" his "personal liquidation." The CIA paper goes on to say that "the President . . . must instill a genuine sense of US commitment to our efforts," and it cites JFK's November 18, 1963 speech in Miami as an example.[4] According to a declassified memo, JFK's National Security Adviser—McGeorge Bundy— told LBJ after the assassination that the "November 18 [1963] speech" by "President Kennedy . . . was designed to encourage anti-Castro elements within Cuba to revolt."[5]

Journalist Gus Russo wrote that "according to CIA Officer Seymour Bolton, President Kennedy personally approved the secret-encoded message" for the Miami speech and "Bolton told a congressional investigator that he personally carried the key paragraph from CIA headquarters to the White House for Kennedy's approval."[6] However, the speech was crafted and fine-tuned at JFK's Palm Beach estate up until the day before it was delivered. We explain later why even as JFK worked on his crucial speech, two Cuban exiles had taken the house next to JFK—and one of the exiles would make an unusually early call to Harry Williams about Lee Harvey Oswald shortly after JFK's assassination.

According to JFK aide Arthur Schlesinger, Jr., he and several other Kennedy aides—including McGeorge Bundy—were involved in discussions about the speech. But Schlesinger says the "chief author" of the speech was JFK aide Richard Goodwin.[7] In some ways, Goodwin was an odd choice, since he hadn't been directly involved with Cuban affairs at that point for two years. Goodwin had had to leave his post dealing with Cuba after he had an extensive, well-documented discussion with Che Guevara that drew too much fire from conservatives in Congress.[8] In another unusual move—in an era when most people thought presidents wrote their own speeches— Goodwin's role in writing the November 18 speech was touted in Florida newspaper articles. The front page of the *St. Petersburg Times* featured a wire-service story saying "President Kennedy relaxed" in Palm Beach "and pre-pared a major Latin American policy address that will climax a busy day of speechmaking in Tampa and Miami." It noted that "two of his advisers on Latin American affairs flew here from Washington to help the President with his talk before the Inter-American Press Association in Miami." The news-paper noted that one of the two advisers was "Richard Goodwin, former State Department official who is now a Peace Corps consultant."[9] At that time, it was highly unusual for presidential speechwriters to be publicized; even today, many people assume presidents write their own speeches. We do not think it was a coincidence that Goodwin in particular was chosen to help on this speech or that his involvement with it was publicized, since Goodwin was the last JFK adviser to have had official, nonsecret contact with a high Cuban leader. Goodwin's cordial, informal talks with Che Guevara in 1961 had caused a firestorm of controversy among conservatives at the time, forcing JFK to reassign Goodwin away from Latin American affairs.

While Goodwin was not told about C-Day, or that several words of the speech had been carefully crafted by the CIA, linking Goodwin's name in the press to the speech would be a form of reassurance to those reading about it in Cuba. Goodwin told us that he recalled that the audience in Miami for the speech—the Inter-American Press Association—was not really JFK's kind of audience, since they were mostly fairly conservative publishers and editors. Goodwin said that JFK's speech really wasn't very well received by them.[10] However, JFK knew that the speech's real target was ninety miles away in Cuba.

C-Day was so important, and so far along, that JFK felt he had to deliver his message to the coup leader in Cuba just eleven days after Khrushchev's warning. JFK may have felt that he had no choice. The secret peace negotiations sparked by Lisa Howard and being pursued by William Attwood weren't producing results, so C-Day seemed the only option that could resolve the Cuban problem by the end of the year. In fact, Khrushchev's threat increased the need for the speech. The coup leader was also no doubt aware of Khrushchev's threat. If he were going to risk his life, and the life of one of his relatives, he had to be sure that Khrushchev's warning hadn't deterred the Kennedys from supporting C-Day.

As mentioned earlier—and documented in Chapter 18—there were two other CIA plans in the fall of 1963 that had only recruited a few mid-level Cuban officials. Still, the CIA felt that it could also use JFK's speech to encourage these lower-level operatives, in the hope that they would back the C-Day coup when it happened. One of these CIA plans was AMTRUNK, and a CIA document finally declassified in 1998 confirms that they were contacted about the speech. The day after JFK's speech, the CIA sent a secret "message to [AMTRUNK] agent on island [of Cuba], asking that he tune into Radio America . . . [which] would carry two major guarantees from US Government." It said that the radio "program was designed to inspire rebel army to unite and rise in coup against Fidel."[11] The CIA also had an ongoing plot with disgruntled mid-level official Rolando Cubela. According to the Senate Church Committee Report, Cubela met in Paris with his CIA "case officer . . . on November 22, 1963 [prior to JFK's assassination] . . . the case officer referred to the President's November 18 [1963] speech in Miami as an indication that the President supported a coup. The case officer" even told Cubela "that [the CIA's Desmond] FitzGerald had helped write the speech."[12]

On the day JFK and his advisers were finishing up work on his important speech, Bobby Kennedy was busy secretly meeting with Harry Williams,

Manuel Artime, and other C-Day leaders, according to a report sent to Cyrus Vance and Joe Califano.[13] This November 17, 1963 meeting was kept classified until 1997, when notes about it were finally released due to the efforts of the authors and others. These declassified notes involved a DIA report of a meeting on that date between "Mr. Robert Kennedy" and "Manuel Artime," two of Artime's lieutenants, and "Enrique Ruiz [Harry] Williams." The memo noted that these exiles "were also scheduled to meet with Mr. Robert Kennedy on either 21 or 22 November 1963." The same memo also talked about a meeting between "Mr. Robert Kennedy, the Attorney General" and a leader of the C-Day Cuban-American troops at Fort Benning, which had been scheduled for "18 Nov 63" in "Washington, DC." It was unusual to have so many meetings with Bobby Kennedy scheduled so close together, but they were necessary since C-Day was rapidly approaching. In the same document, the "CIA queried Mr. Califano's office" with a question regarding Artime's C-Day base for "training Cuban exiles in Nicaragua." Regarding the query, "Lt. Col. Haig" of "Califano's office requested" they "carefully explore" the question while "exercising great caution so as not to inadvertently get into a 'going operation.'"[14]

Following Harry's meeting with Bobby and Artime, Bobby went to a benefit movie premiere in New York City, while Harry went to Miami to help with security there for JFK's speech. Harry hadn't been told the real reason for Bobby's worry about security in Florida: Authorities had received credible reports of threats against JFK, and Tampa authorities had uncovered a plan to assassinate JFK during his long motorcade there. Bobby Kennedy would have known that a similar attempt had been a factor in JFK canceling his Chicago motorcade at the last minute, just fifteen days earlier.

Long-secret Congressional reports confirm that "the threat on Nov. 18, 1963 was posed by a mobile, unidentified rifleman shooting from a window in a tall building with a high power rifle fitted with a scope."[15] One Secret Service agent told Congressional investigators that "there was an active threat against the President of which the Secret Service was aware in November 1963 in the period immediately prior to JFK's trip to Miami made by 'a group of people.'"[16] Still another Secret Service agent eventually linked the threat to "organized crime," an assessment shared by a high Florida law-enforcement source. However, at the time, they also focused suspicion on the Tampa Fair Play for Cuba Committee and a young man with over a dozen parallels to Lee Harvey Oswald. There were even reports—later linked to David Morales—that a possible Cuban agent had recently been in Florida.

The Tampa threat was confirmed to us by Chief of Police Mullins, who also confirmed that it wasn't allowed to be publicized at the time. However, as with Chicago, JFK knew about the Tampa assassination threat. In the words of a high Florida law-enforcement official at the time, "JFK had been briefed he was in danger."[17] But less than three weeks after canceling his Chicago motorcade, JFK couldn't afford to cancel another one without raising suspicion or appearing weak. With C-Day set to start the following week, JFK was giving a speech later that day which included lines written specifically for the C-Day coup leader in Cuba, promising him JFK's personal support.[18] JFK's speech, his visit to Central Command headquarters in Tampa, and even his recent visit to Cape Canaveral to watch a test firing of a Polaris missile from a submarine—which made the front page of the *Miami Herald*—were all designed to send a clear signal of US strength and support to the C-Day coup leader in Cuba. Canceling the Tampa motorcade simply wasn't an option. Later, we'll detail exactly how JFK braved the assassination threat in Tampa.

How could such a serious assassination threat, with so many parallels to Dallas, be kept secret—not just at the time, but for another forty years? Keep in mind the national security implications of C-Day and the thinking behind the Cuba Contingency Plans. Even officials and Secret Service agents who didn't know about C-Day got the clear message that keeping the Tampa attempt secret was of the highest national importance.

After he arrived in Tampa on November 18, 1963, newspapers say that JFK was first "closeted" with "General Paul Adams, commanding officer of the Strike [Force] Command" for a "secret session at MacDill." Joining General Adams were the commander of the Tactical Air Command headquartered at Langley AFB, Virginia, and the commander of the Continental Army Command based at Fort Monroe, Virginia. One might wonder why JFK would go to Florida to meet with commanders stationed near Washington, D.C., but we feel that such a meeting was necessary as the date for the C-Day invasion drew near.[19]

The Strike Force Command is known as Central Command, or CentCom, today. It was described by newspapers at the time as "the nation's brushfire warfare force," designed for rapid deployment to trouble spots. While "the Army–Navy–Air Force Strike Command" had "responsibility for American defense activities in the Middle East, Southern Asia, and Africa," its proximity to Cuba would make it ideal to use as part of the US invasion for C-Day.[20] Keep in mind that the invasion would be designed to look not like a premeditated attack, but rather as the impromptu response to a seemingly unexpected, internal "palace coup."

Following his brief meeting with the military leaders, JFK continued a heavy schedule of speeches and public appearances. His main motorcade for the public lasted about forty minutes, which must have seemed like an eternity to JFK, knowing that potential assassins were at large. The reports were being kept out of the press, but there was no guarantee that they wouldn't surface after—or even during—JFK's scheduled appearances. Whether it was because of the tension, or to show the public (and the coup leader) that he wasn't afraid if reports of the attempt did surface, photos show that JFK spent several segments of his motorcade actually standing up in his limousine.

At one point, JFK passed a key security worry for local law enforcement: a tall red-brick building that overlooked a hard left turn on JFK's motorcade route, just before a bridge. The tallest building in Tampa at the time—it looks very much like a taller version of the Texas School Book Depository—the Grand Floridian Hotel had numerous unguarded windows where authorities worried that at-large snipers might be lurking. Their security precautions are detailed in Part III, but JFK managed to complete his motorcade without incident, and by 3:35 P.M. he was addressing the United Steelworkers Union at the International Inn.*

After leaving Tampa without incident, JFK headed for Miami to deliver his important speech. In reading it in hindsight, it's clear that the words were—as the documents have stated—intended for the leader of the coup in Cuba. Yet they were so carefully crafted that they also were viewed by some as supporting JFK's attempts at secret negotiations with Castro. As reported in the *New York Times*, JFK said:

> The genuine Cuban revolution, because it was against the tyranny and corruption of the past, had the support of many whose aims and concepts were democratic. But that hope for freedom was destroyed.
>
> The goals proclaimed in the Sierra Maestra were betrayed in Havana.
>
> It is important to restate what now divides Cuba from my country and from the other countries of this hemisphere. It is the fact that a small band

---

* Unknown to JFK, the Secret Service, or local authorities, Tampa godfather Santo Trafficante had been tipped off that his plot to kill JFK in Tampa had been uncovered, and the attempt had been called off. Just four days later, Trafficante would go to the site of JFK's last speech in Tampa, to publicly toast and celebrate JFK's death in Dallas, in a plot that used many of the elements from the Chicago and Tampa attempts.

of conspirators has stripped the Cuban people of their freedom and handed over the independence and sovereignty of the Cuban nation to forces beyond the hemisphere. They have made Cuba a victim of foreign imperialism, an instrument of the policy of others, a weapon an effort dictated by external powers to subvert the other American republics.

This, and this alone, divides us.

As long as this is true, nothing is possible. Without it everything is possible. Once this barrier is removed we will be ready and anxious to work with the Cuban people in pursuit of those progressive goals which a few short years ago stirred their hopes and the sympathy of many people throughout the hemisphere.[21]

A CIA report finally declassified ten years ago stated that "on 18 November 1963 President Kennedy . . . delivered a major policy address in Miami . . . at the time the press, reportedly on the basis of what 'White House sources' said about it, viewed it as a call for the Cuban people to overthrow the Castro regime."[22]Though most newspapers didn't particularly highlight those crucial lines of JFK's speech, a few did—including, ironically, the *Dallas Times Herald*. Just three days before JFK's Dallas visit, they trumpeted JFK's speech with a big front-page headline saying "Kennedy Virtually Invites Cuban Coup." They said that "President Kennedy all but invited the Cuban people today to overthrow Fidel Castro's Communist regime and promised prompt US aid if they do." The article says that JFK "also promised that this country would work to block any effort to replace Castro with a right-wing government reminiscent of the former Fulgencio Batista dictatorship." JFK was trying to send a clear signal that leftists could be included in the new Cuban government. The article made no mention of the attempt to assassinate JFK in Tampa, hours before the Miami speech, saying instead that "The chief executive was reported encourage[d] by the warm reception he received in Tampa." Foreshadowing JFK's imminent Dallas visit, the article went on to say that "Kennedy acted like a man running for the White House as he motorcaded past cheering crowds, shook hands with dozens of bystanders and flashed his familiar campaign smile."[23]

Hal Hendrix, the Pulitzer Prize–winning journalist with close CIA connections, got very close to the mark when he wrote in the *Miami Herald* that JFK's speech "may have been meant for potential dissident elements in Castro's" government.[24] However, it's important to remember that JFK's speech attracted little attention in most parts of America and in most newspapers.

But that was fine with JFK, since his target audience was in Havana, not the US. JFK's message found its intended target. The coup leader was satisfied with JFK's assurances, and probably communicated his approval through the "secure radio contact" discussed earlier. So Bobby Kennedy set up a final round of meetings about C-Day. After meeting with Harry Williams, Artime, and other C-Day exile leaders on November 17 and 18, a DIA document says that Bobby was set to meet with Harry Williams and Artime again on November 21, 1963.[25] The countdown to C-Day would begin the following day, when Bobby had arranged for Harry to meet with several key CIA officials in Washington.

NOVEMBER 22, 1963: THE COUNTDOWN FOR C-DAY BEGINS

The countdown to C-Day was essentially beginning on November 22, and by December 1, 1963—if everything went according to plan—Castro would be eliminated, the Russians in Cuba would be neutralized, and the new Cuban Provisional Government would invite in US troops to help restore order. That morning—prior to JFK's assassination—CIA Director John McCone sent a cable to the Miami CIA Chief saying that the coup was set for December 1, just nine days later. The memo from CIA Director McCone also says that C-Day groups were to "maintain passive status until 23 Nov [1963] in order [to] allow . . . Coordinator Artime . . . to provide instructions and supplies." McCone notes that some information in his memo had been passed along by the "Navy in Guantanamo Base" and that any reply should be "via Navy Channels." This shows the close coordination on C-Day between the CIA and the military, including the DIA's Naval Intelligence.[26]

Also in Washington on the morning of November 22, Harry Williams was having a final meeting with several high CIA officials. In an article long overlooked by most historians, the *Washington Post* confirms that Harry was the "Cuban leader" who was "closest . . . to the [Kennedy] administration" and that Harry's plan "had reached an important point." The *Post* says that on November 22, 1963, Harry "participated in the most crucial of a series of secret meetings with top-level CIA and governmental people about . . . 'the problem of Cuba.'"[27] The author of the *Washington Post* articles was Pulitzer Prize–winning journalist Haynes Johnson. Though Harry told us that his friend Haynes had not been told about C-Day, Haynes explained to an interviewer that "he knew RFK very well," and Haynes was working on a book at the time with C-Day leaders like Artime.[28] Haynes had clearly sensed that something very important was in the air. According to the handwritten notes

of an interview Haynes gave to journalist Dick Sprague in 1973, Harry's
meeting with the CIA officials was "to discuss plans for Cuban operation."
While Haynes Johnson didn't know about specific plans for C-Day, he did tell
the interviewer that "CIA-back[ed] plans for [a] second Cuban invasion
were going on in 1963."[29]

Haynes Johnson said the CIA officials meeting with Harry on "Nov. 22,
1963 in Wash, DC" included "Kirkpatrick, Helms" and "Hunt," according to
notes from his 1973 interview.[30] "Kirkpatrick" was Lyman Kirkpatrick, the
CIA's Inspector General at the time of the Bay of Pigs disaster. He was
included to ensure that this operation couldn't become another fiasco. In
terms of power within the CIA in 1963, Kirkpatrick and Helms were just
below the CIA Director and Deputy Director—and Helms would become
Director in 1966, a position he would hold through Watergate and into 1973
when Haynes gave his interview. "Hunt" refers to E. Howard Hunt, the CIA
veteran who was later convicted for his role in Watergate.

This wasn't the first time Harry had met with CIA officials. Haynes told
his interviewer that "Harry Williams . . . knew and met all of the CIA people
in Wash[ington] & Miami in . . . 1963." According to Haynes, this was
because Bobby "had the CIA reporting to him [Bobby] . . . in 1963" and "JFK
and RFK had been very sympathetic to Williams."[31] Harry confirmed to us
that Bobby had personally "introduced me to" one of the high CIA officials
at the meeting, earlier.[32]

At Harry's November 22, 1963 meeting with the CIA officials, Harry told us
they discussed "what would happen if Castro was out of the picture." They
talked about Harry's planned trip later that day to "Guantanamo . . . to get into
Cuba." There he would "contact" the person "close to Castro" about "killing
Castro," as part of the C-Day coup. Harry was "working on" a way "of
watching the . . . killing [of] Castro." This was apparently to ensure that
Castro's death really happened, and wasn't just staged—to double-cross Harry
and the Kennedys—or to make sure that Castro wasn't just wounded.[33] The
trigger for sending in at least the Cuban-American exile troops was going to
be Castro's death, followed by an announcement from the coup leader and
whatever prearranged message or signal Harry Williams could send from
inside Cuba. Massive US military support would depend on a variety of other
factors, including the reaction of the Cuban people and the Soviets to the
coup.[34] Bobby Kennedy had made sure that someone he personally trusted
more than the CIA, State, or Defense—his close friend Harry Williams—
would go into Cuba in advance of the coup, to monitor the situation as it

developed.[35] Harry would be putting his life on the line yet again—for the sixth time—in an attempt to bring democracy and freedom to Cuba.

Harry's meeting with the CIA officials broke for lunch; Harry dined apart from the CIA men. By the time the meeting resumed, everything was different, because the first reports were coming in saying that JFK had been shot in Dallas. One of the CIA men began eyeing Harry himself with suspicion. Harry had not been told about the Chicago assassination attempt or the Tampa attempt (Harry had been busy keeping several Cuban exiles away from JFK's Miami speech), and didn't realize that the CIA was probably aware that both attempts appeared linked to Cubans. When the meeting adjourned, Harry returned to his room at Washington's Ebbitt Hotel, and immediately put in a call to Bobby Kennedy. While waiting to hear back, Harry was met at the hotel by his friend Haynes Johnson, who was working on a book with Harry and Manuel Artime. Haynes Johnson wrote that his meeting with Harry on November 22 "was the most important meeting they had."[36]

The *Washington Post* and *Vanity Fair* both confirm that just two hours after JFK died, Bobby Kennedy called Harry Williams and made a startling revelation about his brother's murder.[37] In the uncertain hours after JFK was shot and before LBJ returned to Washington, Bobby Kennedy was in many ways the center of power in America. Though Bobby was officially just Attorney General, as the President's brother he wielded a much wider swath of power over the CIA and other agencies. Since Bobby was the second most powerful man in America while JFK was President, the official demands on Bobby in those early hours after the assassination must have been enormous. Yet C-Day was so critical that two hours after JFK's death, Bobby took the time to call Harry Williams, who was still meeting with Haynes Johnson.

Bobby told Harry that C-Day would have to be put on hold. Harry had planned on leaving that very night for Guantanamo, where he would slip into Cuba to meet the C-Day coup leader, but not now. When Harry told Bobby Kennedy that Haynes Johnson was in the hotel room, Bobby asked to speak with him.[38] As Haynes Johnson wrote: "Robert Kennedy was utterly in control of his emotions when he came on the line and sounded almost studiedly brisk as he said: 'One of your guys did it.'"

Harry Williams and the Cubans

IT IS IMPOSSIBLE TO FULLY understand C-Day, the Mafia penetration of it, and JFK's assassination without looking closely at the Cuban exiles who were actually going to stage the C-Day coup for the Kennedys. Their roles in C-Day help to explain why Bobby Kennedy said "one of your guys did it"—killed JFK—to Haynes Johnson and not to Harry Williams, as well as explaining who Bobby had in mind when he said that, and why. Though these exile leaders played key roles in C-Day, and some in events surrounding the JFK assassination, there is a great deal of information about them that isn't widely known today, even among most historians. As we detail each of the Cuban exile leaders of C-Day, a consistent pattern emerges: Associates of mob bosses Carlos Marcello, Santo Trafficante, and Johnny Rosselli try to get close to each of them as soon as they become the focus of Harry and the Kennedys. The more the mob bosses could infiltrate the Kennedys' C-Day plan, the more parts of it could be linked to JFK's assassination, to divert suspicion and prevent a thorough investigation to keep from compromising C-Day and related intelligence operations. The following chapters also cover the US intelligence assets who worked on or knew about C-Day, as well as operations supporting C-Day that were also utilized by the Mafia.

Getting even a handful of Cuban exile leaders from across the political spectrum to work together on C-Day was a huge, perhaps impossible, task. In fact, it was the Kennedys' struggle to deal with the Cuban exile groups in the spring of 1963 that led to Harry Williams's role in C-Day in the first place. As Bobby Kennedy said in his Oral History at the JFK Library, "there were all these conflicts between all the various Cuban groups" in the spring of 1963.[1] They often fought and bickered among themselves, leading to such bad blood that by the 1970s there would be open warfare between the groups, with numerous killings and bombings. Things were not yet that bad in 1963, but there were still problems, so Bobby called Harry Williams and said "I don't have time to talk with them and all they want is money, and I want you to take charge of the whole thing. I'm not going to see any more Cubans unless they come through you, because they make me crazy."[2]

The Kennedys and Harry Williams knew that for the post-coup Provisional Government to have the backing of the Cuban people, it had to be broad-based and include progressive Cuban exile leaders. Even the CIA acknowledged—in a long-secret report from July 1963—that Castro should be given "credit for reforms in such areas as health care, housing, education, lowering rents, honest administration, and racial equality," and the Cuban people would not want to lose those reforms.[3] At the same time, the new Provisional Government would also need more traditional and conservative Cuban exile leaders to encourage the many upper- and middle-class Cubans in the US to return to Cuba prior to the eventual free elections. However, the only conservative Cuban exile leaders considered by the Kennedys for C-Day were those who had fought against the Batista dictatorship. Numerous government documents confirm that in the summer and fall of 1963, a few exile groups from vastly different ends of the political spectrum began working together on a plan backed by the Kennedys.

Harry told us, and documents confirm, that he "divided the exiles into . . . groups."[4] Most weren't deemed worthy of support. Some Harry tried to placate by passing them off to the State Department, which didn't know about C-Day, but which could give them some attention.[5] A handful made the cut, to become part of the C-Day plan and the Provisional Government after the coup, and were approved by the Kennedys. Harry told us that the exile leaders chosen for C-Day were Antonio (Tony) "Varona, Gutierrez Menoyo, Manolo Ray, a good man, . . . and (Manuel) Artime was also under me. Those four represented the action," in addition to the Cuban-American troops training at Fort Benning, making a total of five key individuals and groups.[6]*

Manuel Artime was the most active of the C-Day exile leaders, with the largest organization. Viewed as very conservative, he was a medical doctor

---

*As noted, official Washington sometimes had difficulty with Cuban names. For example, "Manuel" is sometimes replaced with "Manolo," and vice versa. There are other variations: "Manuel Artime" is actually "Manuel Artime Buesa," but his last name is rarely used in documents. On the other hand, "Eloy Gutierrez Menoyo" is usually referred to by his last name. These issues with names were one reason C-Day was able to stay secret for so long. Since the following section quotes so many documents—which don't always use the same spellings and names for the same individuals—to avoid confusion, we're going to standardize their use in quotes as follows: Manuel Artime, Manolo Ray, Eloy Menoyo, Tony Varona.

who had fought with Harry at the Bay of Pigs. Artime was also close to ruthless Nicaraguan strongman Luis Somoza, the second most powerful man in that country, who allowed Artime to use his country as a base. Artime was the first exile leader Harry persuaded to join C-Day.

Manolo Ray was more low-key, but had a keen intellect and was regarded as a man of great integrity. Ray was viewed as one of the more liberal exile leaders. Because of that and Ray's leadership, his group JURE was seen one of the most effective reaching out to those inside Cuba. An FBI report from May 30, 1963 said that "JURE was considered one of the five major exile groups with clandestine assets."[7] Ray was always leery about joining with other exile groups, and he was cautious about joining C-Day.

Eloy Menoyo was seen as perhaps the most liberal exile leader, almost a socialist, and had been the last of the C-Day exile leaders to leave Castro's government, shortly before the Bay of Pigs. That, and his political views, caused him to be viewed with suspicion by some in the CIA. Menoyo's closest ally in the exile field, Antonio Veciana, had the opposite reputation— he was seen as one of the most violent and reactionary exile leaders. Yet Menoyo's group, the SNFE, and Veciana's, Alpha 66, were so close that the FBI viewed them as one organization. Still, only Menoyo was sought for C-Day, which may be why Menoyo was leery about joining the plan.

Tony Varona, a former Cuban senator, had been a political leader for the Bay of Pigs. His organization, the Cuban Revolutionary Council (CRC), was in great decline by the summer of 1963, so Harry and Bobby wanted Varona more as an individual than as the leader of a group. However, Varona's past associations would compromise C-Day. Varona was the protégé of former Cuban President Carlos Prio, noted for his corruption and involvement with mobsters. Varona himself knew Santo Trafficante and Johnny Rosselli, having worked with them on the CIA-Mafia plots since the summer of 1960—and those plots were continuing into the fall of 1963 without the knowledge of the Kennedys or Harry Williams. In fact, Varona only joined C-Day in August 1963 after after receiving a huge bribe from Rosselli's Chicago Mafia family, which is documented from CIA files in Chapter 15.

Ideally, Harry wanted these exile leaders, and the Cuban exile troops at Fort Benning, to function as the five fingers on his right hand, perfectly coordinated before, during, and after the coup. However, their hatred for Castro and their support of the Kennedys and Harry were really the only things the five C-Day groups had in common, so at times Harry's vision was more of a goal than a reality. Documents and published accounts show that the five exile C-Day leaders had various problems and alliances that made forming them into a cohesive group difficult. It's interesting that even with hundreds of Cuban exile groups active in the US in 1963, the Kennedy associates we interviewed remembered each of the "five fingers" very well—and all had very definite opinions about them that they shared with us.

Harry was still negotiating with Menoyo and Ray in mid-November of 1963, though C-Day would go ahead on December 1, 1963, with or without them. Harry was sure that once the coup happened, each man would readily agree to be part of the new Provisional Government. They were in agreement with the basic aims of the C-Day coup and Provisional Government, and both had been following all the requirements for the Cuban exile C-Day groups, such as basing their operations outside the continental US. They were receiving support from the Kennedys, both directly and through Harry. Harry had been encouraging the C-Day groups to work together, and documents confirm that that was starting to happen. Harry's efforts with Menoyo and Ray had also caught the attention of mob bosses Santo Trafficante and Johnny Rosselli, and their resulting actions are detailed later.

Since Varona and Artime joined C-Day quickly, Harry would have told them many of the details about C-Day. They would have been told the coup was set for December 1, 1963, and probably given the identity of the C-Day coup leader, at least as the date drew near. Ray and Menoyo would have been informed more generally about C-Day. For example, they may have been told only the approximate date for the coup (late November or early December), but not the exact date. They were probably told the coup leader's powerful position, but not his actual identity. In the case of all the C-Day exile leaders, their subordinates and close associates may have been told some, but not all, of what they knew, to keep the secrecy of the operation. For example, Menoyo never told his closest associate about Harry's plans for C-Day.

All of the C-Day exile leaders had worked for the Revolution, and most had served in the early post-Revolution government before Castro consolidated his power. This would let the exile leaders claim that C-Day was a continuation of the Revolution they had fought for. The coup leader would give the new Provisional Government even more Revolutionary legitimacy, as well as the backing of the Cuban people, the government bureaucracy, and the security apparatus.

Just because a Cuban exile leader had been chosen by Harry and the Kennedys for C-Day doesn't mean they were told in advance all the details about C-Day. The Bay of Pigs had shown how difficult it was to keep an operation secret in the exile community. Harry told the exile leaders only the minimum necessary, sometimes not even the true identity of the C-Day coup leader.[8] Also due to the tight secrecy surrounding C-Day, the exile leaders could not all meet together. Instead, Harry would meet with one or two at a time, sometimes with Bobby. This also cut down on potential problems, since the groups were so different politically.

The many Cuban exile groups excluded from C-Day suffered various fates. A few continued to receive some CIA funding, such as the DRE, an exile group that grew out of an organization Rolando Cubela had helped to start before the Revolution. According to E. Howard Hunt, David Atlee Phillips ran the DRE for the CIA.[9] (In the summer of 1963, the DRE was involved in a well-publicized incident with Lee Harvey Oswald.[10]) However, most Cuban exile groups not only lost their CIA funding, but were also subject to the massive US crackdown that began in the spring of 1963 on covert exile activities. With C-Day coming up, the US could not afford to have unauthorized exile raids bringing too much attention to Cuba or interfering with the timetable for C-Day. The House Select Committee on Assassinations wrote that in 1963, "Suddenly there was a crackdown on the very training camps and guerrilla bases which had been originally established and funded by the United States." They noted that "the exile raids, which once had the Government's 'green light,' were now promptly disavowed and condemned." The Kennedys wanted to give the impression they were backing away from the exiles, and even Castro was fooled for a while: On June 28, 1963, the *Times* reported that "Castro says US [has] 'abandoned' rebel forces fighting his regime."[11]

However, the crackdown did not apply to the five C-Day exile groups. Their activities were allowed to continue and grow, as long as they followed certain guidelines. A few of the groups, mainly Artime's, were still allowed to occasionally stage small raids on Cuba, if they were not launched from American bases. The raids weren't really intended to have any dramatic effect, but provided an excuse for the large buildup at the C-Day exile bases in Latin America. They also ensured that equipment and manpower for getting into Cuba were ready, since the Cuban exile leaders (except for the Cuban-American troops and Harry) would need to get into Cuba on their own for C-Day, to avoid the appearance that the US was simply staging the coup.[12]

A May 28, 1963 White House memo, declassified in 1997, provides a look at the formative days of selecting the five C-Day Cuban exile groups. The memo was sent from a National Security Council staffer to JFK's National Security special assistant, and was prepared by "the Cuban Coordinator" of one of Bobby's Cuba subcommittees—either Cyrus Vance or one of his subordinates.[13] At this early stage, only Bobby, JFK, Vance, Harry, and a few others knew about the contact with the coup leader in Cuba, so the language in the memo had to be circumspect. At this stage, "the Coordinator [Vance] recommends that the US follow a 'hands-off' policy toward exile efforts to achieve unity." On the memo itself, JFK's National Security assistant wrote that he agreed and had "cleared this in principle with the President." But then he added: "altho I would not exclude a shift if Bobby felt strongly the other way."[14] That's exactly what happened, since Bobby and Harry soon took a leading role in choosing the C-Day exile groups.

The memo accurately notes that a recent "still embryonic movement toward 'unity' . . . has taken place in the Cuban exile community." It then lists the main exile groups and alliances which seemed to be emerging. First, it notes that Menoyo's group—"the Second National Front of Escambray" (or SNFE)—has begun working with other groups, including "Alpha 66."[15] While Menoyo's SNFE was considered very progressive, Alpha 66 was considered very violent and hard to control. Two months earlier, Alpha 66 had claimed credit for firing on Russian ships in Cuban waters. That was bad enough, but it also happened while JFK's emissary was in Cuba negotiating the release of twenty-one American prisoners and around the time of a CIA-Mafia assassination attempt against Castro. Shortly after that, JFK had ordered Alpha 66 leader Antonio Veciana confined to Miami-Dade County in an effort to stop the raids.[16]

Not surprisingly, Vance's memo expresses the hope that Menoyo could work with a more progressive group like "Manolo Ray's Revolutionary Junta (JURE)." Having Menoyo work with Ray "would increase the influence of this grouping" since Ray's liberal JURE "has the most potential appeal to Castro's opponents within Cuba."[17] Bobby Kennedy and Harry Williams thought so too, which is why Harry pursued Menoyo and Ray for C-Day.[18] However, Vance's memo points out the political reality that Ray was considered so liberal that he "is an object of concern to more conservative exiles."[19] Menoyo and Ray were seen by some in the CIA as being so liberal that they were practically Communist. E. Howard Hunt had resigned from the Bay of Pigs rather than include someone as liberal as Ray in that operation.[20]

However, Ray and Menoyo were balanced on the right by conservatives like Tony Varona and Manuel Artime. Of course, labels like "liberal" and "conservative" can vary, depending on who is doing the labeling. Vance labeled Artime's group as being in the "center."[21] Many others, including

Harry Williams, saw Artime as being extremely right-wing, and this would be borne out years later when Artime supported the Watergate efforts of arch-conservatives like G. Gordon Liddy and E. Howard Hunt.[22] Vance's memo notes that as of May 28, 1963, Artime's group had "held aloof from attempts at unity" with other groups, though once Harry brought Artime into C-Day, Artime was soon willing to work with progressive leaders like Menoyo and Ray. In the middle of the political spectrum was the leadership of the Cuban-American troops at Fort Benning.

Vance's memo then discusses "Enrique Ruiz [Harry] Williams," who has "formed a unity committee" and who "claims the personal support of Attorney General Kennedy." Vance notes that Harry's "efforts have shown only limited results thus far," but it was still just weeks since Harry had been contacted by the high Cuban official who would become the coup leader. The goals of Harry's efforts are reflected in a formerly SECRET National Intelligence Estimate that spells out the need for a broad-based exile coalition to lead Cuba after C-Day. It points out that while the current Cuban regime's "dependence on . . . Castro is a major vulnerability" for it, the new post-coup leadership "would have to be revolutionary and reformist to appeal to a majority of Cubans."[23] So the post-coup government would need progressives like Menoyo and Ray to work with the coup leader, if it was to be accepted by the Cuban people.

Even as Harry's work with the five C-Day Cuban exile leaders and groups continued, the Kennedys were also pursuing their back-channel peace negotiations with Fidel Castro, without telling Harry. In September 1963, while the peace negotiations were being initiated, Harry apparently sensed a lull in Bobby's enthusiasm and support for C-Day. To Harry, it must have seemed as if the Kennedys were inexplicably dragging their feet for some reason. Although Harry knew about the small group of Cuban-American troops being trained for C-Day at Fort Benning, he didn't know about the far more extensive US military plans that Cyrus Vance and the Joint Chiefs were working on.[24] That's why Harry thought C-Day needed the backing of someone like Nicaraguan strongman General Luis Somoza, for a larger military force to supplement the Fort Benning Cuban-American troops. Harry knew that the Somoza family was strongly anti-Castro and had greatly aided the Bay of Pigs operation.[25] A September 14, 1963 "CIA Classified Message to Director" of the CIA John McCone from the Miami CIA Station discusses an airport meeting of several prominent Cuban exiles, including three of the C-Day leaders: "At the airport were Tony Varona," "Manuel Artime," and

General "Luis Somoza"—the second most powerful man in Nicaragua—who was "brought to the airport by Enrique [Harry] Ruiz Williams."[26]

A memo uncovered by the JFK Assassination Records Review Board provides a glimpse into Harry's plans and frustrations in early October 1963. The memo was sent to Bobby from one of his aides, saying that Harry wanted to talk to Bobby about getting a "green light" for the Somozas to help with a larger anti-Castro force. Harry said that he "has men and territory; needs weapons and money. Harry feels this is the best plan currently being considered." In analyzing the memo, *Newsweek* editor Evan Thomas wrote that "Williams was apparently becoming impatient," and Williams says in the memo that he doesn't know "whether to go back into mining or work in Cuban affairs."[27]

Bobby got the message, and the CIA money spigots were soon opened wide. Within a short time, "General Somoza was encouraged to announce that 'in November [1963] strong blows will begin against Cuban Prime Minister Fidel Castro by groups we are training,'" according to FBI veteran William Turner.[28] An AMWORLD MEMO TO the CIA Director from the Miami CIA Station discusses a November 18, 1963 report from a Cuban exile who "has no doubt [Harry] Ruiz [Williams is the] true personality in Cuban situation and all US plans [are] being coordinated through him."[29]

By November 10, 1963, the C-Day plan was in high gear, according to one of the most detailed CIA documents released so far about C-Day and Harry Williams. This AMWORLD memo was sent to the CIA Director from the Miami CIA Station, reporting what a Cuban exile CIA informant has learned about C-Day from an associate of Artime. The Cuban exile says he's talking about "Plan Judas," one of the names a few Cuban exiles used for C-Day. The exile says a C-Day exile leader is angry about recent comments hinting at C-Day made by corrupt ex-Cuban President Carlos Prio, since Prio wasn't even part of the coup plan. Next, the exile says that the Artime associate told him that "while in Washington DC, he met with Enrique [Harry] Ruiz Williams." Harry informed him that "he, Ruiz, was to lead" the Provisional Government after the coup. Harry said that "he had been so named [by] RFK who had gone [to] New York to interview him. RFK said Ruiz could work with any or every sector he wished" but that Ruiz was "to be [the] boss" of the operation. "Ruiz called [name censored from original] to Washington, DC, to name him future Health Minister," and "[different name censored from original] is also to be in the Cabinet" of the new Cuban Provisional Government.[30]

We should point out that the Artime associate's statement that Harry said "he, Ruiz, was to lead" the new Provisional Government doesn't quite jibe with what others have said. Harry told us he saw himself as a behind-the-scenes type, a coordinator who could get things done. Harry's statements were confirmed by another C-Day leader who indicated in a confidential interview that one of the other C-Day leaders would actually head the Provisional Government.[31]

Before documenting the roles of each of the five Cuban exile C-Day leaders working with Harry, here is another "on the record" comment from an exile, which documents part of C-Day. Eugenio Martinez was a Cuban exile who was not a major player in C-Day. However, Martinez made the following comments on television in May 1976, and they confirm the high level of activity going on to topple Castro on the day JFK died. Martinez said: "The day of the killing of Kennedy, I was coming from one of my trips to Cuba [for the CIA]. We have bases in Nicaragua at that time . . . the Cuban people who were willing to fight for democracy, they were all busy with Kennedy. They have a tremendous organization here. They have the biggest organization working against Castro. They knew that Kennedy would not rest until he defeated Castro."[32] Martinez later went on to become one of the Watergate burglars working for E. Howard Hunt, along with Bernard Barker and James McCord.[33]

Pulitzer Prize–winning journalist Haynes Johnson said in his 1973 interview that while "CIA-backed plans for [a] second Cuban invasion were going on in 1963" and "Harry Williams . . . had become the prime contact" for Cuban exiles, "there was not enough money" left for the other Cuban exile groups. So, he said, "other people were trying to raise money separate from [the] CIA."[34] Based on declassified documents and testimony, Haynes was right, and that's why some Cuban exile groups left out of C-Day turned to the Mafia for funding.[35] Also, some Cuban exile groups who weren't part of C-Day tried to align themselves with one or more of the C-Day exile groups. As we'll document, this was one of several methods the Mafia used to penetrate C-Day.

We want to avoid giving the wrong impression about Cuban exiles, most of whom were never involved with criminal activity. This is true for the C-Day exile leaders, as well as the many exile groups who had been excluded from C-Day. All too often, Cuban exiles have been stereotyped as criminals; for some people, even the term "Cuban exile" immediately brings to mind the JFK assassination. While numerous Cuban exile veterans of the Bay of Pigs had turned to criminal activity by the 1970s, the vast majority led perfectly normal and often exemplary lives. Both at the Bay of Pigs and after, many of them risked their lives fighting not just to bring democracy to Cuba, but also fighting a kind of proxy war against Castro for the US.

CHAPTER TWELVE

Manuel Artime

MANUEL ARTIME'S GOOD FRIEND E. HOWARD Hunt wrote that "Artime . . . fought first for Castro, then defected" to the US.[1] The fact that Artime had fought in the Cuban revolution was important, since even though he was considered very conservative, he still had revolutionary credentials. Artime was one of the leaders of the Bay of Pigs who was captured and released in December 1962—with the rest of the prisoners—thanks to the efforts of Bobby Kennedy and Harry Williams.

Artime's daughter quoted Bernard Barker when she wrote about her father in 1996. According to her, Barker said that "Artime was able to work with President Kennedy and not hate him [for the Bay of Pigs disaster], saying 'Well, he's human. The important thing is that he makes restitution for the mistake.' And it sure looked like he was going to."[2] A "CIA Internal Memo" titled "CIA Involvement with Cubans and Cuban Groups" says that Artime "was supported by both the CIA and the White House . . . [and] had direct access to President Kennedy and top Executive Branch aides."[3]

By September 1, 1963, Artime had bases operational in Nicaragua and Costa Rica that would house up to three hundred soldiers, and the *New York Times* reported that Cuba's UN Ambassador, Carlos Lechuga, was "in Cuba to confer on bringing before (the) UN charges that (the) US is behind exile raids staged from Caribbean and Central American bases."[4] On September 7, 1963, the *Times* reported that the Cuban "government blames US for raid" and pointed out that the "raid occurred [the] day after exile leader Manuel Artime, in Miami, announced plans to step up military action against Castro." The *Times* also noted Artime's "operations from an undisclosed Central American site" in the same article.[5]

The *Times*'s stories document the rapid progress Artime made, from leaving the US in mid-July to staging attacks from his Central American bases by early September. His support from the Kennedys and the CIA was crucial, but Artime also progressed so quickly due to an alliance with General Luis Somoza, the strongman of Nicaragua. This is confirmed by a CIA memo from August 9, 1963 from Desmond FitzGerald to "the President's Special Assistant for National Security Affairs," titled "Luis Somoza's Involvement in Cuban Exile Operations." It confirms "recent talks between ex-President Luis Somoza and Manuel Artime, prominent exile leader."[6]

FitzGerald notes that their plan is "essentially designed to rebuild an indigenous resistance movement inside Cuba," and speculates whether their plan "can be sufficiently refined to . . . keep" it "out of the limelight of public curiosity." FitzGerald then wonders "whether the Somozas could temperamentally adjust to . . . a program . . . that can only prosper in an atmosphere of conspiratorial tranquility."[7]

"Conspiratorial tranquility" is an elegant phrase for a messy reality. FitzGerald knew that the Somozas and Artime had big egos, and both wanted to be in control. But for the plan to succeed, they had to get along not only with each other, but also with the other C-Day exile leaders, as well as obeying the wishes of the CIA and the Kennedys. The difficulty of the last is shown by FitzGerald's next sentence, when he says "Artime to forego raids and externally based sabotage actions and to concentrate on resistance within Cuba."[8] Just over three weeks later, the *New York Times* was reporting on Artime's raids into Cuba. So much for the plan to have Artime "forego raids" and keep things "out of the limelight."

The case officer who began working with Cubela in 1963 was asked by the Church Committee: "Had the CIA been using Artime, or was the CIA using Artime at this period in covert actions in Cuba?" Replying under oath, the case officer stated: "I believe so."[9] A few years after this 1975 testimony, Congressional investigators for the House Select Committee on Assassinations wrote that "by October 1963," Artime "had established four bases, two in Costa Rica and two in Nicaragua. Artime's 300-man force consisted mainly of veterans of the [Bay of Pigs] brigade . . . his resources included two large ships, eight small vessels, two speed boats, three planes, and more than 200 tons of weapons and armaments and about $250,000 in electronic equipment." The Congressional investigators noted that after JFK and Bobby were dead, "Artime said publicly that both the President and his brother were responsible for his establishing the Latin American bases . . . that he had had direct contact with both President Kennedy and Robert Kennedy," and that "he felt the death of President Kennedy marked the end of the US Government's attempts to liberate Cuba." After speaking briefly with Congressional investigator Gaeton Fonzi, Artime "agreed to be interviewed by the committee" in more detail, "but, before that was possible, he died . . . after a very brief illness."[10]

Journalist Al Burt wrote the most extensive article about C-Day that would be written for the next three decades in the January 25, 1965 issue of the *Nation*. Burt may not have known about C-Day, but it's clear that his source did. It detailed Artime's operation in Central America, which began in 1963 "to ready a military force for response to any developments within Cuba." These "developments" were the hope that "a coup could be engendered inside Cuba" and "Castro might be assassinated." Burt says the "coup" could come about "by playing on the split between old-line Communists and Castro's July 26th disciples," a reference to the July 26 revolutionary group that included Raul Castro and Che Guevara.[11]

Burt was able to give stunning details of Artime's C-Day operation, such as Artime's receipt of a $167,784 check issued on November 19, 1963, less than two weeks before C-Day. Burt said that sometimes "an American would call the office, say that a certain amount of money had been deposited in a Miami bank under a certain name," and Artime's group "would then draw on it." But sometimes checks were sent directly to Costa Rica, site of one of Artime's bases for C-Day. "Checks would arrive in the mail, drawn on the accounts of legitimate American firms, usually from New York City banks," according to Burt's source. This included the check for $167,784, which arrived "in a plain white envelope bearing a US cancellation but no return address." Burt was even shown records that documented "the check number, the bank, and the American firm" that issued the check. And that wasn't even the largest check—Burt was told about "one for $450,000 used to purchase modern military equipment."[12] The Kennedys and the CIA used these American firms to allow them to claim that the C-Day groups were "autonomous" and not funded by the US government.[13]

Burt wrote in his article that in 1963, Artime "declared that he had commandos training in Costa Rica and Nicaragua, and had support from 'powerful groups' in the United States." Burt noted Artime's support by Nicaraguan strongman "Luis Somoza," who claimed US backing. Somoza got the Costa Rican president to allow "training camps" for Artime in his country, because "the Costa Ricans were convinced that a secret operation was being conducted by the Central Intelligence Agency." Burt notes that "US support, although denied, does seem evident. Veteran Latin America observers cannot believe that any Central American government would permit military preparations against Cuba without US approval."[14]

"One Artime man," Burt writes, "explained that the operation was initiated because the Kennedy administration felt an obligation to the invaders whom it had backed in the abortive 1961 [Bay of Pigs] invasion. A man close to President Kennedy is reported to have outlined the plan to Artime."[15] That's consistent with what Harry Williams and our other C-Day sources have told us. Further corroboration for Harry's account comes from another passage in Burt's article, when he notes that the Cuban exiles like Artime "were to work with the Central American governments and, unlike the Bay of Pigs venture, were to have control of the operation." Burt notes that Artime was called "the 'Golden Boy' of the CIA."[16]

Burt says that "Volunteers were recruited in Miami, their credentials arranged so that they could move on to Central America with no more difficulty than stepping aboard a plane in Miami or boarding a ship in New Orleans."[17] "The commandos received a salary scaled to their family status"; Burt says that a "social worker" from Artime's group "would hand over cash, and the wife would sign a receipt. The number of men sent to Central America has been estimated from a low of 200 to a high of 500." Burt notes that Artime's "officials concede their payroll ran more than $50,000 a month. It has been estimated that military equipment, boats, salaries and expenses have brought costs of the operation to between $3 million and $6 million."[18]

The *Nation* article says Artime's plan included "a coup . . . engendered inside Cuba by power factors" and a way "that Castro might be assassinated." Burt said that Artime's role was "to ready a military force" to respond to some dramatic development within Cuba, then "hope that what appeared to be a genuine fight for freedom on Cuban soil would merit support from the Organization of American States or from the United States itself."[19]

As Burt says, Artime's plan hinged on creating "an atmosphere conducive to revolt" and eliminating Castro, since "many believe that only Castro can keep his revolution cemented together. Without him, therefore, a revolt is possible. The United States has encouraged this supposition by its past policy statements"; and Burt accurately cites JFK's November 18, 1963 speech as an example.

One of Artime's deputies at his camps in Central America was an exile named Felix Rodriguez, whose name will be familiar to some because of his roles in the capture of Che Guevara and in the Iran-Contra scandal in the 1980s. In fact, Rodriguez's 1989 autobiography, *Shadow Warrior: The CIA Hero of a Hundred Unknown Battles*, says that "what we did in Nicaragua twenty-five years ago has some pretty close parallels to the Contra operation."

In 1961, Rodriguez was part of a special infiltration unit during the Bay of Pigs, and was one of the few men who escaped capture. He continued working for the CIA, and after all the prisoners were released, Rodriguez says that JFK gave the Bay of Pigs "Brigade officers the opportunity to become commissioned as regular US Army officers, even though we were not citizens." Rodriguez says he "accepted President Kennedy's offer, was commissioned as a second lieutenant, and in March 1963, I reported for my basic training at the infantry school in Fort Benning, Georgia." However, "even before the basic course was completed, I had a visit from Manuel Artime . . . which changed the direction of my life." Artime explained to Rodriguez that "the President of the United States himself was sponsoring a liberation movement. Even better, this force would be entirely Cuban-run and Cuban-led. Unlike our previous efforts we would not have to endure the whims of US advisers and bureaucrats that we'd had to endure prior to the Bay of Pigs." Rodriguez said that Artime "guaranteed the US Government was behind the plan; that it was sponsored by Robert Kennedy and the President himself."[20]

Artime insisted that Rodriguez would "have to resign my army commission," since "the operation was covert," but Rodriguez could become "a high-ranking officer in the endeavor," so Rodriguez accepted. Rodriguez writes that he "finished basic training . . . and on October 9, 1963, I received an honorable discharge from the US Army."[21] Rodriguez's autobiography says that he "left for Central America" to join Artime "around the time President Kennedy was assassinated," so there is probably much he didn't know about C-Day.[22] Still, his book provides a good firsthand account of Artime's huge Kennedy-backed operation. When Rodriguez arrived in Nicaragua, he realized that the operation "was considerable—more than three hundred people in all, based in Nicaragua, Costa Rica, and Miami. Our three main bases were in Nicaragua: the operational headquarters, my communications base, and the commandos' base. Artime was in Miami, and our arms cache was in Costa Rica." Rodriguez confirms that "the funding for the project came from the CIA, but the money's origin was hidden through the use of a cover corporation, a company called Maritima BAM, which are Artime's initials spelled backwards. Periodically, deposits of hundreds of thousands of dollars would be made in Maritima BAM's accounts, and disbursed by Cuban corporation officers. The US government had the deniability it wanted; we got the money we needed."[23]

Artime's armaments, Rodriguez writes, included "two mother ships, each 250 feet long; two 50-foot aluminum-frame Swift boats for our commando forces, plus assorted smaller craft for silent landings and special operations. There was one C-47 aircraft plus a couple of Cessnas and a small Beaver aircraft that was capable of water landings." Rodriguez confirms Al Burt's account written twenty-four years earlier: "there were more than 200 tons of arms—all American-made . . . in all, the operation ended up costing the Americans somewhere in the area of $6 million over two and a half years."[24] Rodriguez also mentions the covert side of Artime's operation, saying "up-to-date documents, everything from identity cards and drivers licenses to the sorts of detritus normally found in old coat and trouser pockets had to be designed and fabricated."[25] Rodriguez confirms that Artime's "operation had been conceived and planned by the Kennedys."[26]

A few months before his unexpected death in 1977, Artime himself went on the record about his work with the Kennedys, for the *Miami News*. In this interview published on July 2, 1977, the interviewer noted that "Manuel Artime—general practitioner, poet, meat importer, sometimes psychiatrist, and full-time revolutionary—can't afford to take chances," and Artime conducted the interview with a "gun" that was "tucked into his pants."[27] Given what an earlier article called the "mysterious shoot-outs and deaths among" Artime's associates—including the recent violent deaths of Trafficante associates Rolando Masferrer and Carlos Prio, it's easy to see why Artime wore a gun.[28]

The *Miami News* calls "Artime . . . the leader of the CIA-backed anti-Castro training camps in Central America" in 1963. They note that this was "after the 1961" Bay of Pigs invasion and Artime's release from Castro's prison in late December 1962, when "he and his men were ransomed from Cuba for $53 million in food and medicine (Artime's ransom alone was $500,000)." They say that back in 1963, Artime regularly had chats with "American Presidents and Attorney Generals." It started after Artime's release, when "(President) Kennedy invited" Artime "to talk with him" and "Artime . . . met Robert Kennedy in his office." Bobby told Artime that "if you are capable of getting . . . a Central American country—without mentioning the US—to lend you their territory, I guarantee you I'll make sure you get the aid." The *Miami News* says that "Costa Rica and Nicaragua agreed unofficially and two training camps were set up in each country."[29]

Artime told the interviewer that "the money was routed from Canada to banks in Switzerland to Costa Rican or Nicaraguan subsidiary companies. The weapons, 200 tons of armament and explosives, were brought to us in a flatbed ship and exchanged in the high seas." The *Miami News* says Artime's "camps operated from mid-1963 to 1964, at an estimated cost of more than $7 million." For the first time, this article mentions a specific type of sniper weapon Artime had: "Among the weapons the Artime commandos experimented with were the M-16 rifle, with infrared sniper sights—before they were in full use in Vietnam."[30]

Artime had to "handle the thousands of logistics details necessary to feed, clothe and train 300 guerillas spread throughout four camps in two countries." Artime requested—and received—trained personnel from 'The Company' (the CIA) to operate them. Artime's men were paid $275 to $300 a month."[31] Tying the program once again to RFK, the article concludes: "The overt anti-Castro campaign condoned by the US government ended, 'when Bobby Kennedy separated from the Johnson administration,' Artime says."[32] Four months after this article, one of the only interviews Artime gave about his work for the Kennedys in 1963, Artime was dead.

Evan Thomas was recently able to get some of Artime's CIA handlers to talk about him. Thomas wrote that in 1963, "RFK . . . pushed ahead with his idea to help create a private Cuban guerrilla army. With funds funneled through the CIA, Dr. Artime bought several tons of weapons and ammunition, some small boats and planes, and established bases in Guatemala, Costa Rica, and Nicaragua." But Thomas notes that "the CIA was very uneasy about a rebel force they could not control." He quotes "Sam Halpern, who helped run Cuban operations for the CIA from Langley headquarters," as saying: "We told them where to buy guns without getting rooked, but this was Bobby's deal."[33] Grayston Lynch, a paramilitary specialist for the CIA, told Thomas that "Their camps were horrible." Lynch said "There was no discipline, no nothing. I had spies in the organization. They went through $50 million in nothing flat, mostly on Managua R and R."[34]

The CIA sources who spoke to Evan Thomas now seem like they want to distance themselves from Artime, as if they only dealt with Artime because of the Kennedys. However, FBI veteran William Turner wrote that "the CIA had never trusted Harry Williams, who . . . bore the stigma of having been RFK's hand-picked leader." But the CIA "continued to take good care of its own golden boy, Manuel Artime," even after JFK's death, "providing him funds in exchange for a promise that he would clear all missions in advance."[35]

CIA agent E. Howard Hunt had a very close relationship with Artime, who helped raise money for Hunt's defense during Watergate, but it's clear that Artime's relationship with others in the CIA was more complex. Artime had begun working with the CIA in 1959, and it's possible that Artime was viewed more positively by the CIA in 1963 than he was many years later. The CIA thought enough of Artime in 1964 and 1965 to try to get him to work on their Cubela operation, at a time when Bobby Kennedy no longer held sway over the CIA.[36] Some insight into Artime's relationship with the CIA comes from a Kennedy administration official who had some contact with Artime in 1963. This official didn't work for the CIA, and he told us that Artime struck him as "unreliable and very slick" and that Artime "exploited the guilt the Kennedys felt over the Bay of Pigs. He also blackmailed—in a general way—the" CIA. The official explained that "once Artime, and other exile leaders, had done things for the CIA, they could then use that information to make sure the CIA had to keep supporting them."[37]

Harry Williams was adamant when he told us that "Artime was run 100% by the CIA. I mean if the CIA tell him to go on the street at midnight, then undress and make a speech, he'd do it. That is the [kind of] guy [Artime] is."[38] Also, Harry said there were times that Bobby Kennedy called Artime without going through Harry, though that didn't seem to bother Harry too much. However, Harry would get frustrated when Artime would contact Bobby directly and then boast about meeting with Bobby without Harry. After all, Harry was the one who had brought Artime into C-Day in the first place and had smoothed over things between Artime and Bobby. Plus, it was hard enough trying to coordinate all the C-Day exile leaders—and placate those left out of C-Day—without Artime going to Bobby behind Harry's back.[39] Based on our conversations with Harry, we got the impression that as the fall of 1963 progressed and C-Day drew nearer, Harry trusted Artime less and less. When Harry indicated that he had considered beginning C-Day a day earlier than the official starting date, to make sure that none of the C-Day exile leaders tried to get a jump on the others, we got the impression that it was Artime he was worried about.[40]

More confirmation of Artime's operation comes from a familiar name, journalist and Kennedy associate Tad Szulc, who detailed Artime's role in C-Day for *Esquire* magazine in February 1973. Unfortunately, the growing Watergate scandal at the time diverted press attention away from Szulc's revelations. Though Szulc wasn't involved in C-Day during 1963, some remnants of C-Day (like Artime) were combined with AMTRUNK and the Cubela operation the following year, giving Szulc access to the information he used. The article doesn't mention Szulc's work on AMTRUNK but does confirm that starting in 1963, there was "a new secret plan to combine Castro's assassination with a second invasion of the island by Cuban exiles from bases located this time in Costa Rica and Nicaragua. Some infiltrators were to be trained in the Dominican Republic" (a reference to Menoyo's camps there). Szulc says "the scenario was to bring ashore some 750 armed Cubans at the crucial moment when Castro would be dead and chaos had developed."[41]

In his 1973 *Esquire* article, Szulc cites "men who participated in this project" who told him that "the CIA disbursed $750,000 monthly for the operation" of Artime in Central America. But Szulc also points out that "some $2,000,000 in these funds remains unaccounted for." Szulc also says that "subsequently, there were mysterious shoot-outs and deaths among Miami Cubans involved in the still-born invasion."[42]

Szulc's *Esquire* article also said that after the Artime operation came to an end in the mid-1960s, "we find that the same cast of characters, ranging from gung-ho Florida CIA operatives to gullible or corruptible Miami Cubans and Cuban-Americans, reappeared on the scene in 1971 and 1972 as key personages in the Watergate affair." In this list Szulc includes Artime, "E. Howard Hunt" (calling him "the man who first recommended Castro's murder in 1960"), and "Bernard L. Barker . . . who was Hunt's aide." Szulc also notes "James W. McCord" and mentions that McCord "was associated with . . . the use of Cuban [exile] pilots in the Congo."[43]

In 1974, Szulc published a biography of E. Howard Hunt called *Compulsive Spy*. He says that "Hunt was involved" with Artime's operation, which was "directed by the CIA . . . camps were established in Nicaragua and Costa Rica to train some 700 Cuban exiles." Szulc also says that "involved in the new enterprise . . . is believed to have been James McCord, a CIA security specialist who had played an ancillary role in the Bay of Pigs. McCord reportedly accepted the assignment when he returned from Europe, where he was the CIA's senior security officer."[44]

Szulc described the operation involving McCord, Hunt, Barker, and Artime as follows: "The idea, according to a number of men involved in the operation, was that a force led by Artime would land in Cuba . . . after Castro was assassinated. Hunt, according to the version with which I am familiar, was coordinating or helping to coordinate the assassination plot."[45]

Hunt, Barker, and C-Day leader Artime seem to have been particularly close. Hunt himself wrote that Artime was "exfiltrated to the US" from Cuba in 1959 "by [the] CIA through Bernard L. Barker."[46] Hunt also says that after the Bay of Pigs and Artime's release from prison in Cuba in late 1962, "Artime . . . was given US money and equipment, a channel to [the] CIA and verbal encouragement."[47] When the *Miami News* interviewed Artime in 1977, it noted that Artime "keeps in touch with such old friends as Watergate burglars Bernard (Macho) Barker . . . and neighbor E. Howard Hunt (Artime is godfather to Hunt's youngest son, David)" [parentheses in original].[48]

A Cuban exile C-Day leader told us that the "CIA and [the] Joint Chiefs were the only ones supporting Artime. Not the military or the Cubans here in the USA. Keep in mind that they saw us Cubans as . . . mercenaries and no respect was afforded us by the 'American' guys. [They were] very paternalistic." This exile leader said that "Artime had $6 to 7 million from somewhere, but probably from CIA."[49]

How much of those CIA millions authorized by the Kennedys wound up in Artime's own pockets? Szulc suggested that $2,000,000 remained unaccounted for.[50] Later, we'll document other types of profiteering Artime engaged in, with a Trafficante associate. This may have been related to the tip received by Senate investigator Gaeton Fonzi that Artime had "guilty knowledge" of JFK's assassination.[51] Also troubling is Bobby's comment, just hours after JFK's death, to Haynes Johnson, who was writing a book about the Bay of Pigs, that "one of your guys did it."[52] Was Bobby referring to Artime? In the fall of 1963, Harry and Artime were among a handful of exiles collaborating with Johnson.[53] Of those exiles, only Artime was ever linked to criminal activity; all the others have sterling reputations. Also, both types of Artime's criminal associates—profiteering and drugs—were linked to mob boss Santo Trafficante, who later confessed to his attorney his role in JFK's assassination.

One route to the corruption of Artime was Nicaraguan General Luis Somoza. Somoza's brother was president, and their family had run—and would run—Nicaragua for years. Luis Somoza was the epitome of a banana-republic strongman, described by Haynes Johnson at one ceremony as "dressed like a musical comedy potentate (who) wore powder on his face and was surrounded by gunmen" and "sycophants."[54] Harry was unaware that the Somozas also had ties to New Orleans godfather Carlos Marcello. It would be 1979 before the FBI learned that Marcello and Luis Somoza had shared the same powerful Washington lobbyist for decades.[55] The Somozas had been trying to get into C-Day since July 1963, when they helped sponsor a sort of minor-league training camp for Cuban exiles just outside New Orleans. One report says that Carlos Marcello's pilot, David Ferrie, was involved with the camp.

However, having the camp on US soil violated one of the Kennedys' guidelines for acceptable Cuban exile activity, so it was shut down when the FBI raided an adjacent camp run by Mafia associates.[56] A CIA memo from Desmond FitzGerald to the White House sent shortly after the raid confirms that "Luis Somoza" had been involved with "Carlos Prio," the corrupt former president of Cuba who was linked to Jack Ruby and Santo Trafficante, and Prio would soon attempt to infiltrate Artime's operation.

After the raid, Somoza quickly grasped how the C-Day game had to be played. The highly detailed *Nation* article by Al Burt says that Somoza told "Costa Rican President Francisco J. Orlich . . . that the United States wanted to back a new anti-Castro operation—but this one must be organized completely outside US territory and with no US participation, except financial." This mirrors the wording of the Kennedys' June 1963 exile guidelines, which wouldn't be declassified until fourteen years later. When Al Burt asked the State Department to comment for his article, they "denied any US involvement," just as the exile guidelines said they would.[57]

CIA documents from October 31 and November 7, 1963 confirm that Somoza continued to secretly deal with Carlos Prio, an associate of Santo Trafficante and Jack Ruby, and the mentor of Tony Varona. Somoza and Prio—who is detailed in Chapter 15—even exchanged information about C-Day, using the code name "Plan Judas."[58] After JFK's assassination, the Somozas and Artime would be linked to many demonstrably false stories linking Oswald and Ruby to Castro.[59] A Warren Commission document says the false stories were designed to "cause the USA to take action against Castro."[60] Also, these stories raised the specter that Castro had killed JFK in retaliation for C-Day, and helped to prevent a thorough investigation of JFK's death.

Incredibly, none of the C-Day Cuban exile leaders were ever interviewed by the Warren Commission, in spite of the links (staged or real) between most of them and Lee Harvey Oswald.[61] This is especially tragic in the case of Artime, who had several associates linked to the Mafia, associations he continued after the CIA shut down his camps. For example, Luis Somoza and Carlos Prio were involved with Artime in an operation linked to a 1972 restaurant assassination in Guatemala City, which closely paralleled the 1963 restaurant assassination attempt on Harry Williams.[62] Artime had grown rich by the early 1970s, from being business partners with the Somozas.[63] By the mid- to late 1970s, many Americans—the authors included—wondered why US officials continued to support the increasingly corrupt and brutal Somoza dictatorship in Nicaragua. However, that was also the time of many Congressional investigations into the JFK assassination, like the Church Committee and the House Select Committee on Assassinations—and the Somozas knew secrets that could have embarrassed both political parties if they revealed what they knew about C-Day.

A CIA memo kept from law enforcement agencies by CIA Director George H. W. Bush in 1976, cited here for the first time in any book, shows one way Artime's part of C-Day could have been infiltrated and used by the Mafia. The memo says that at the same time Manuel "Artime and his group were supported by the CIA," Artime "was used by the Mafia in the Castro operation." That is a reference to the CIA-Mafia plots, which included Santo Trafficante and Johnny Rosselli, as well as Artime associate Tony Varona. Artime's role in the CIA-Mafia plots has not been detailed in any of the documents the CIA has previously released about the plots, which are detailed in Part II.[64]

CIA memos we quote extensively later show that in August 1963, Rosselli's Chicago Mafia bribed their way into Artime's "Nicaraguan matter" with a huge payoff to Tony Varona.[65] Coupled with Somoza's ties to associates of Marcello and Trafficante, the Mafia chiefs' plan to penetrate C-Day and use it against JFK worked all too well. Artime's operation expanded so rapidly in the buildup to C-Day that it was easy for the three mob bosses to take advantage of the confusion.

We do not believe Artime was an active participant in JFK's assassination. Instead, the Congressional investigator's "guilty knowledge" tip fits with the facts we will later present: that Artime had dealings with those behind the assassination, both before JFK's death (when Artime might not have known what was planned) and after. After all, the Kennedys and Harry were using certain exile leaders in C-Day without telling them critical information. So it's possible that just prior to—and shortly after—JFK's death, Artime was being directed to take certain actions that he felt would put him in a better position for C-Day, without realizing that those actions were part of the plot to kill JFK.

However, Artime's activities and associates in future years certainly put him in a position to learn or suspect who had killed JFK, yet he continued those associations. As detailed in later chapters, Artime was involved with associates of mob bosses Johnny Rosselli and Santo Trafficante, and a protégé of Artime became one of Florida's biggest drug kingpins shortly after Artime's death. In 1977, Artime talked briefly with Congressional investigator Gaeton Fonzi, who wanted Artime to testify about his work for the Kennedys and the JFK assassination.[66] However, Artime became ill and died before he could give his testimony, apparently going to his grave with his "guilty knowledge" about JFK's murder.[67]

CHAPTER THIRTEEN

Manolo Ray

MANOLO RAY HAD EXCEPTIONAL QUALITIES that made Bobby Kennedy and Harry Williams seek him out for C-Day. A CIA cable described Ray as having the "highest intellect, sincerity, and conviction" and being "soft-spoken and unassuming."[1] These descriptions mesh with those from our sources, who all saw Ray as a leader with charisma and integrity.[2] An FBI report noted "Ray's dynamic leadership" of the Cuban Revolutionary Junta, known by its acronym in Spanish, JURE.[3]

Congressional investigators wrote that Manolo Ray fought against Batista's dictatorship before joining Castro's government as "Minister of Public Works in February, 1959." But the relationship between Ray and Castro soon soured and "Ray was relieved of his [government] position" by Castro in November 1959. Ray then organized his first "resistance group" against Castro in "May 1960" and he came to "the United States on November 10, 1960." Once in America, Ray was seen as too socialist and liberal by some in the CIA. E. Howard Hunt wrote that Ray "defected late," seemingly implying that it took Ray far too long to grow disenchanted with Castro.[4] Tad Szulc wrote that in 1961, Hunt had resigned from the Bay of Pigs operation rather than accept Ray as part of the new Cuban government that would follow the invasion.[5]

In July 1962, more than a year after the Bay of Pigs, Ray formed JURE. Its "Declaration of Principles" for a new Cuba advocated "breaking relations with the Soviet bloc" and banning "the Communist Party." However, Ray also advocated "agrarian reform," along with "human rights and social justice" and "free elections," so some in the CIA and other agencies still saw him as a leftist.[6] On the other hand, that same month, a CIA cable confirms that "Ray began giving information to the US government regarding possible recruitment or defection of Castro officials." Congressional investigators wrote that "the degree of Ray's success in this area is not documented, but his efforts continued into the summer of 1963."[7] There are indications that Ray's attempts to find disaffected Castro officials were related to the CIA's AMTRUNK operation, which was going on at the same time.[8]

While Ray wasn't able to recruit anyone high in Castro's government, he didn't need to once Harry Williams was contacted by the C-Day coup leader. As Cyrus Vance noted in his May 28, 1963 memo, the Kennedys and Harry knew the value of having someone like Ray in the new Cuban Provisional Government after the C-Day coup. Ray was the type of progressive leader whom many people in Cuba people would be likely to accept.

At a high-level meeting of US officials on June 21, 1963, Secretary of State Dean Rusk, CIA Director John McCone, and CIA Cuba coordinator Desmond FitzGerald discussed the fact that "Manolo Ray and his JURE will be offered financial support within the next day." Consistent with the C-Day exile guidelines quoted earlier, the notes of this meeting say that "every trace of US involvement in the program possible would be concealed" and that "these operations would be based outside of the United States." McCone and FitzGerald knew about C-Day, but Rusk didn't, though Rusk was aware in general that efforts were being made to find a way to stage a "palace coup" against Castro. So, at the meeting, Ray's efforts were described in general terms, as "autonomous operations" designed "to develop resistance capabilities inside Cuba."[9]

As with Artime's C-Day exile group, "military operations were also initiated" by Ray's group, according to a CIA memo dated August 23, 1963.[10] Congressional investigators wrote that "by the fall of 1963, Ray was devoting his full time to JURE" and, like Artime, Ray was "traveling extensively in Latin American countries to gain support which would allow JURE to mount resistance operations inside Cuba."[11] Congressional investigators confirm that in the fall of 1963, Ray "was conferring with Attorney General [Robert] Kennedy about the Cuban situation."[12]

At a time when the FBI, the Coast Guard, and Customs were stopping most exile activities against Castro, Manolo Ray's JURE operated freely. Confirmation of this, surprisingly, comes from James P. Hosty, the FBI agent assigned to Oswald in Dallas. In 1993, Hosty talked to an interviewer about Ray's group, and said that "That was the group they were going to use when they were going to overthrow Castro . . . the Customs men were going after the ones that weren't part of that operation. [But] Customs was working with

JURE."[13] Ray was clearly given special consideration by the US government, and Congressional investigators noted "Ray's meeting with Attorney General Robert F. Kennedy in September 1963."[14]

The Warren Commission didn't interview any of the C-Day exile leaders, even when leads indicated that they might have relevant information. However, one Warren Commission document not published in their report but declassified several years later says that JURE's "leadership in exile consisted of the following: Manolo Ray—Puerto Rico" and "Rogelio Cisneros" in "Miami." It continues, "On October 21, 1963 Rogelio Cisneros stated JURE believes that the overthrow of the Fidel Castro regime by an internal uprising would be the final answer." It quotes another JURE coordinator as saying two weeks earlier that "JURE had no plans for military action against Cuba except from within Cuba."[15]

A Kennedy administration official who dealt with Ray said that "some in the Administration saw Ray as the possible leader of a new Cuban government . . . and some like [the] State [Department] wanted to encourage and support Ray, since he was seen as much more democratic than many [other exile leaders who were] ex-Batistas. But the other groups were more conservative and powerful and gave Ray a very hard time—so much so that eventually, Ray had to move his base to Puerto Rico."[16]

Perhaps that helps to explain Ray's attitude toward the CIA and others as discovered by Congressional investigators. They wrote that "Manolo Ray himself was personally critical of the CIA and told one JURE associate that he thought CIA agents 'were more dangerous than the Kennedy administration.' He maintained that 'The Kennedy administration would end but CIA agents always stayed and their memory was longer than the memory of elephants and they never forgot or forgave.'" As with DIA head General Joseph Carroll, Ray's comments critical of the CIA wound up in a CIA dispatch, this one dated July 22, 1963.[17] The CIA seemed outstanding at picking up a wide range of information, especially criticism of the CIA. But when it came to making use of vital information—like the Mafia payoff to Tony Varona to sell out C-Day—the CIA's intelligence failures led to tragic results.

If Ray was skeptical of the CIA, the CIA was skeptical of Ray. As C-Day neared, CIA memos say that "Ray acquired a 25-foot boat for infiltration and exfiltration purposes." The CIA notes that an operation "to deliver military equipment to JURE that would then be transported into Cuba" was "originally scheduled for November 23, 1963" but "was moved up two days" to November 21, 1963. However, the CIA said, "the JURE boat failed to make the scheduled pickup and Ray offered no satisfactory explanation for this failure to perform."[18] The CIA seemed to hold this against Ray. However, given the dates involved—ten days before C-Day—we feel it's likely that the real need for the boat might have been related to getting Ray into Cuba after the C-Day coup. If that's so, Ray wouldn't want to risk losing it several days early, since he didn't have backup boats and equipment like Artime. Most CIA officers didn't know about C-Day, and some knew only very generally about AMWORLD, so it's quite possible that the CIA agent dealing with Ray on this particular mission wasn't fully informed about C-Day. For that matter, it's also unclear how much precise information Ray himself had been given about C-Day, since he was still negotiating with Harry at the time.

Harry Williams told us that he "saw Ray in Puerto Rico" and that "Ray had a pretty good organization within Cuba, one of the few (exile leaders) that really had it," and Harry "wanted to use" that organization. Harry clearly admired Ray and said that "there is no question that Manolo Ray had a good name in Cuba" as being "against Fidel." As the date for C-Day approached, Harry was "trying to get everyone together," referring to all five of the C-Day exile leaders he and the Kennedys wanted in the new Provisional Government. But in spite of his contacts with Ray, Harry said that he still had "no definite commitment from Ray," as of November 22, 1963.[19] However, the contacts between Harry and Ray about C-Day had brought Ray to the attention of mob bosses Santo Trafficante and Johnny Rosselli.

Ray was cautious about joining with other exile groups, a pattern he had maintained since first leaving Cuba. Congressional investigators wrote that before the Bay of Pigs in 1961, Ray "resisted joining the newly formed Cuban Revolutionary Council (CRC)," which was the umbrella exile group the CIA was using. Ray had earlier "resisted inclusion into the FRD," a previous Cuban exile alliance. "However," the Congressional investigators note, shortly "before the Bay of Pigs invasion . . . Ray was persuaded to join the CRC as a show of unity."[20] Harry was well aware of Ray's past record, and seemed certain that Ray would officially commit to C-Day once he realized the coup was under way.[21]

Memos like the following CIA "Field Information Report" show that Artime, Ray, and Eloy Menoyo were eventually brought together. Declassified in 1993, the report confirms "direct contacts between Manuel Artime, Manolo Ray and Eloy Menoyo." The information in the report was obtained from an exile group which was not involved in C-Day, but which was observing the activities of Artime, Ray, and Menoyo with much interest. They said they had heard that the groups were working on "'Plan Omega' which supposedly would carry the war to Cuba in a combined operation by these organizations."[22]

While "Plan Omega" wasn't the official CIA name for C-Day, which was AMWORLD, documents show that it was used by some exiles, as was "Plan Judas." "Omega" is defined as "the ending," which was appropriate since C-Day was supposed to end Castro's reign once and for all.[23] It also evokes the quote from Revelations—"I am Alpha and Omega, the beginning and the ending."

Ray's good qualities were apparently evident to the Mafia bosses as well. If they tried to buy Ray off, as they attempted with Harry and did success-fully with at least Varona, they were not able to. So a blatant attempt was made to link Oswald to Ray's JURE group, and thus to C-Day, prior to JFK's assassination.

The attempt took place in late September 1963, when Ray was in the midst of C-Day negotiations with Harry and having a series of meetings with Robert Kennedy.[24] Detailed with new information in Part II, it involved a visit by three men—including someone who appeared to be Oswald—to Silvia Odio, the daughter of a major JURE figure, who lived in Dallas. According to Congressional investigators, during the awkward visit "the men identified themselves as members of JURE" and "spoke of both its founder, Manolo Ray, and her father, who had worked closely with Ray."[25] The men wanted letters of support from Ms. Odio, but she refused.[26] A couple of days later, one of the men called to say that Oswald "had been a Marine, that he was an expert marksman, and that he was 'kind of loco'" and that Oswald said JFK "should have been assassinated after the Bay of Pigs."

Two months later, when Ms. Odio saw Oswald on TV after JFK's assassi-nation, she fainted. As word of what she had seen and discussed with others in September 1963 filtered up to investigators, it caused consternation at the highest levels of the FBI and the Warren Commission.[27] That was exactly what the Mafia wanted, because the incident both made Oswald look guilty and cast suspicion on JURE. It also ensured that the government couldn't investigate Oswald's ties to apparent anti-Castro activists who were actually working for the Mafia, without risking exposing C-Day or other CIA plots against Castro. The Oswald-JURE "Odio incident" can be linked to four asso-ciates of Mafia godfather Santo Trafficante, including two who knew about C-Day prior to JFK's death.

Eloy Menoyo

ELOY MENOYO WAS SEEN AS even more liberal and progressive than Manolo Ray. Like Ray, Menoyo was also targeted by Trafficante and his associates, who tried to link Menoyo's group and close associate to Oswald and the bullets in his rifle. Unlike the other exile leaders for C-Day, Menoyo finally made it into Cuba on a covert mission—only to meet a tragic fate there.

By the fall of 1963, Menoyo was setting up his base in the Dominican Republic, in the Caribbean, in accordance with the C-Day exile guidelines. Bobby Kennedy's Oral History at the JFK Library has Bobby on tape, mentioning Harry's plan to "do something from" a base in the "Dominican Republic."[1] Menoyo's base had also gotten the attention of Castro, whose UN Ambassador was reported in the *New York Times* as considering "bringing before (the) UN charges that (the) US is behind exile raids staged from Caribbean . . . bases."[2]

E. Howard Hunt wrote that "Menoyo" was a pro-"Castro fanatic who defected shortly before the [Bay of Pigs] invasion."[3] FBI veteran William Turner notes that even after Menoyo came to the US, Menoyo "was detained for months because the CIA suspected his intentions" and worried that he might be a double agent. Their worries were based on Menoyo's murky role in the CIA's 1959 coup attempt against Castro, detailed in Part II. Turner writes that "Menoyo's defection from" Cuba "was more colorful than most. In January 1961," just three months before the Bay of Pigs invasion, "Castro assigned [Menoyo] to board the Portuguese luxury liner *Santa Maria*, which had been hijacked by revolutionaries, and proceed to Portuguese Angola to start an insurrection. Instead [Menoyo] took off from Florida in an open boat."[4]

That kind of personal daring, coupled with Menoyo's progressive political views, made Harry Williams seek out Menoyo for C-Day. Harry was also familiar with Menoyo's courageous exploits during the fight to overthrow the dictator Batista, and had given Menoyo money "before Che Guevara came in" to assume command.[5] Harry wanted exile leaders who, like himself, were willing to risk their lives: The exile leaders who would make up the new Provisional Government would have to get into Cuba right after the coup, from bases outside the US, while the situation in Cuba was still unstable and dangerous. Harry told us he "knew Eloy Menoyo was a man of action."[6]

Menoyo's exile group in 1963 usually went by its initials, SNFE, which stood for the Second National Front of the Escambray, a reference to Menoyo's original revolutionary group in Cuba's Escambray mountains.[7] In addition, Menoyo had a base in the Dominican Republic, which Harry visited and Bobby Kennedy mentioned in his Oral History at the JFK Library.[8] Its close proximity to Cuba (the Dominican capital is only about 300 miles from Guantanamo) would make it the perfect jumping-off point for Menoyo to get into Cuba after the coup, while complying with the Kennedys' exile guidelines which said that C-Day groups had to "operate from outside US territory."[9]

Finally, Harry hoped to make Menoyo a C-Day leader because he knew that Menoyo's socialist leanings would make him appealing to many in Cuba. The problem was that Menoyo's SNFE group was aligned very closely with the violent Alpha 66 group. In fact, a Miami FBI report states that as of "March 20, 1963," Menoyo's "SNFE and Operation Alpha 66 were one and the same organization."[10] However, the reputations of the SNFE's Menoyo and Antonio Veciana of Alpha 66 were as different as night and day. While Menoyo was seen as so progressive and socialist that the CIA worried that he might be a Communist, Veciana and Alpha 66 were seen as violent and beyond the control of the Kennedy administration, which is why JFK ordered Alpha 66's Veciana confined to Miami-Dade County in the spring of 1963 after Veciana's group claimed credit for raids on Russian ships in Cuban waters.[11]

A Kennedy administration official source contrasted Menoyo with Alpha 66. This official didn't know about C-Day, but did know about exile activity in the summer and fall of 1963. The official said that Menoyo struck him as "more intelligent and less doctrinaire in political terms than most [Cuban exile] leaders." The official summed up Alpha 66 in one word: "irresponsible."[12]

Several CIA documents confirm that in November 1963, Menoyo was meeting with Harry Williams about C-Day and preparing for major action against Cuba. One memo to the CIA Director from the Miami CIA Station, which detailed Menoyo's November 13, 1963 meeting with Harry, even has the official CIA code name for their part of C-Day, AMWORLD. The first part of the memo talks about a November 18, 1963 report from a Cuban exile who has been "insisting [for the] last two months that [Cuban exile] leaders" like Eloy Menoyo have "met with Enrique [Harry] Ruiz Williams." The second part of the memo details a November 13, 1963 meeting between Harry and Menoyo.[13] This meeting is confirmed by another CIA summary dated "11/23/63."

The CIA memo of the meeting confirms that "on 13 Nov [1963] . . . Eloy Menoyo" and three others "met at Ruiz's home." (This CIA memo refers to Harry Ruiz-Williams as "Ruiz.") The name of one of the three other men is censored, possibly because he was the CIA informant or agent who told the CIA about the meeting. The memo says that "During [the] meeting, Ruiz said Cubans must unite to produce action inside Cuba." Harry told them that "he [was] certain US will lend necessary aid for final fall." Harry "said he [was the] coordinator between 'offices of this country and Cuban groups.'" Then Harry stated that he "had dedicated himself [to] smoothing things over after RFK and (name censored in original, but probably Artime) had strong discussions following prisoner release . . . subsequent to this, Nicaragua matter emerged, followed by Costa Rica." Harry "said he believed he [was] instrumental [in] obtaining aide for (name censored in original) organization."[14]

The CIA memo concludes with a "comment" about a discussion Menoyo and one of the other exiles had, after they left Harry's house. The exile said that "neither he nor" Menoyo "can believe, under any circumstances, that Ruiz, no matter how friendly with RFK, could have any authority in Liberation plan."[15] Even after Harry's months of wooing, Menoyo still had doubts about Harry's C-Day plan. Apparently, Menoyo was reluctant to proceed without Alpha 66, possibly because its chief, Antonio Veciana, was the only mainstream exile leader who had stuck by Menoyo.[16]

The document shows the dilemma Harry faced. Could exile leaders like Ray and Menoyo be trusted with critical information—like the date for C-Day or the identity of the coup leader—before they had officially committed to Harry's plan? What if he told them and then they decided not to commit but leaked the information to other exiles? Yet without such knowledge, one could see why Ray and Menoyo would be hesitant to officially join C-Day. Even with the Kennedys' lavish support, without knowing the identity of the powerful C-Day coup leader close to Castro, Ray and Menoyo would think that staging a successful coup against Castro was a tremendous long shot. Nonetheless, Harry was confident that both would join the new Provisional

Government after the C-Day coup. CIA documents show that other exiles assumed that Ray and Menoyo were already leaders in Harry's plan, not realizing that Harry was still in final negotiations with them. Harry continued to pursue Menoyo, since C-Day was just over two weeks away. Harry told us that he was so anxious to have Menoyo officially join C-Day that he even agreed to meet Menoyo in his Miami home at 3:00 A.M.![17]

A CIA report from late November 1963 says that "Menoyo is military chief of Plan Omega." A later CIA summary makes that point clear, saying that Menoyo was "actively planning for military infiltration into Cuba as part of Plan Omega for overthrow of Castro government." That CIA summary also notes that "in late summer '63" Menoyo was "involved . . . with obtaining [a] plane, later reported to have been hidden in Cuba; Browning automatic rifles; and other provisions for massive assault from inside Cuba."[18] The last part shows that Menoyo was part of a coup "from inside Cuba," not an external invasion like the Bay of Pigs.[19]

Confirmation that Menoyo was preparing to take action against Cuba "by December 1963" comes from a different part of the Warren Commission document quoted earlier, which showed that Menoyo, Ray, and Artime were all working on the same plan by late 1963. This long document, "Warren Commission Document 1085," was not in their final report and was kept secret until it was declassified by the Justice Department in 1970 and finally released to the public on January 8, 1971. Though the Commission staff gave it a single document number, it's actually a massive compilation of FBI material, consisting of "46 memoranda and 15 reports."[20]

Warren Commission Document 1085 says that "during August 1963 SFNE leader"—Menoyo—"announced publicly that he and his men would be in Cuba by December 1963." It notes that by "October 1963 . . . the SNFE was then interested in purchasing arms for the proposed military action in Cuba . . . Eloy Menoyo came to Los Angeles October 11, 1963 and appeared at a public meeting of" an exile group and "announced that the organization would be in Cuba in less than six months." The document reported that a circular was printed in November 1963 announcing that Menoyo's group had joined forces with other groups and "all were working together in the 'Omega Plan.'" Another announcement a short time later said the plan involved "a revolutionary invasion of Cuba coordinated with [an] internal uprising" that would be led by "Eloy Menoyo."[21] A CIA summary says that "Menoyo commented on 21 November 63 that 'something very big would happen soon that would advance the Cuban cause.'"[22]

When FBI head J. Edgar Hoover heard about Menoyo's comment, he was concerned that Menoyo's "something very big" might have been referring to advance knowledge of JFK's assassination, since it happened the following day. On December 3, 1963, Hoover ordered the head of the Miami FBI office to look into the source for Menoyo's comment.[23] The Miami FBI Special Agent in Charge sent a report back to Hoover three days later, saying that "the source was interviewed on 12-6-63 by the CIA," and she stated that Menoyo's remark was "in no way related to the assassination of President Kennedy." Instead, she said "this information related to a plan of the group of Eloy Menoyo to carry out the military action against the communist Government of Cuba." The FBI report closes with a comment to Hoover, saying that "inasmuch as this matter related to the Cuban situation and obviously had no connection with the [JFK] assassination, no further action is contemplated by the Miami Division."[24] As was always the case for the FBI, when they got close to "the Cuban situation" involving one of the C-Day groups supported by Bobby Kennedy or a CIA operation, their investigation was dropped, swept under the rug, or left unresolved.[25] All the evidence shows that Menoyo had no knowing involvement with JFK's death. However, a thorough investigation would have exposed C-Day (and other CIA operations) to dozens if not hundreds of FBI agents, and probably to the press at some point—hence the dilemma for Hoover, LBJ, Bobby, and other high officials in deciding whether to pursue certain leads.

The Kennedys and Harry weren't the only ones wooing Menoyo in the fall of 1963. A CIA memo from October 31, 1963 confirms that that Artime's Nicaraguan ally, the Marcello-linked Luis Somoza, stated that "a mobilization of men in Nicaragua would begin for attacks against Cuba. According to the present schedule, such attacks would start taking place in early December 1963." The memo shows that Somoza was also talking about the plan with Carlos Prio, whom documents link to Jack Ruby and mob bosses like Santo Trafficante. The CIA memo says that "Prio" was trying to get four other exile leaders to deal with him, including "Eloy Menoyo," and all four of the exile leaders—including Menoyo—"have agreed to participate in Prio's plan by contributing men."[26] This document shows one reason why Harry was having trouble getting Menoyo to commit to C-Day: Harry was unknowingly having to compete with Trafficante's associate, Carlos Prio.

According to two reports, Menoyo had earlier had dealings with Santo Trafficante himself.

A CIA document in the National Archives says that on November 21,

1962, "the CIA received a report that Santo Trafficante Jr. had given Eloy Menoyo $250,000 worth of arms, which he had not yet paid for." As a result, the "informant reported that the Mafia planned to have Eloy Menoyo killed somewhere outside the US."[27] This report was a year prior to C-Day and JFK's assassination, so it's obvious that Trafficante didn't carry out his threat against Menoyo. Harry Williams told us that he assumed the arms came from the CIA, but he wasn't sure: "Menoyo had weapons because when we saw him in Santo Domingo, the Dominican Republic, in the camp there he had arms. But I thought that the CIA gave it to him, but I am not sure."[28]

Confirmation of Menoyo's arms dealings with Trafficante comes from one of Menoyo's closest associates, both in 1963 and decades later. He is Cuban exile Antonio Veciana, who in 1963 headed Alpha 66, the exile group very closely affiliated with Menoyo and the SNFE. When we interviewed Veciana in Miami in 1993 and asked him about Menoyo, he said "I was with him two hours ago." The on-the-record interview with Veciana took place in both English and Spanish, with the assistance of noted exile historian Gordon Winslow, archivist for Miami-Dade County and fluent in Spanish. Veciana told us that "I remember . . . when Menoyo was . . . having weapons business with Trafficante." Veciana was quick to add "of course, everybody knew who Trafficante was. I didn't know him personally and never met him."[29] Yet Trafficante knew Menoyo, which is why Menoyo's group would be linked to both Oswald and the bullets found in Oswald's rifle.

One of the few CIA documents with the official CIA cryptonym for C-Day, AMWORLD, also talks about Menoyo's SNFE and Alpha 66. As usual for CIA documents about C-Day, it was sent to the CIA Director, John McCone, with a copy to Desmond FitzGerald's office. Dated November 30, 1963, the day before C-Day was originally scheduled to start—but based on earlier information—it says that "SNFE-Alpha 66 . . . combine wishes to act before (name censored in original) starts anything."[30] The censored name could be Harry Williams, Manuel Artime, Carlos Prio, or the name of a group. But the document shows that Menoyo's group and Alpha 66 were acting in unison right before C-Day, and implies that they were hoping to get a head start on someone.

Harry Williams said about Menoyo, "I gave him money in cash," referring to the money the Kennedys had authorized him to distribute to C-Day exile groups.[31] (This is probably a good place to note that Harry says he never took any money for his services to the Kennedys, and government documents tend to back that up.) On the other hand, journalist Dick Russell interviewed a US intelligence operative who said that the notorious Cuban death squad leader "Rolando Masferrer was the key bagman . . . for Alpha 66" and their "funding came through the Syndicate because of Masferrer's connections with those people back in Cuba. He had ties with Santo Traffi- cante . . . he also had ties with Jimmy Hoffa."

Russell's intelligence source stressed that "Alpha 66 was the biggest recip- ient of the funding that was channeled through Rolando Masferrer." The source also said that Masferrer told him "not too long before the assassina- tion . . . that Kennedy was going to be hit."[32] If the intelligence operative is right, then Masferrer—the same man Harry had turned down during the confrontation at Bobby's New York townhouse—had found a way to get close to the C-Day operation. If Menoyo's SNFE and Alpha 66 were essentially one group, as Congressional investigators and documents indicate, that means that the same overall group that dealt with Trafficante was also getting money coming from the Kennedys for C-Day.[33]

It's important to note that just because Menoyo and Alpha 66 got money from Trafficante or Masferrer does not mean that they were involved know- ingly in the JFK assassination. Unless exile groups officially committed to C- Day, like Artime, funding was tight and getting tighter in 1963. Exile groups were constantly trying to raise funds, and the Mafia was always interested in making contributions that could buy influence if Castro were ever over- thrown. From reading all the available evidence, it's our opinion that Menoyo and Veciana were extremely focused on overthrowing Castro in November of 1963, and not involved in assassinating JFK.

Still, Menoyo's contacts with Harry Williams about the Kennedys' C-Day plan made Menoyo a target for Trafficante and the other mob bosses who were plotting JFK's assassination. The more links the Mafia chiefs could establish between Menoyo's group, its close affiliate Alpha 66, and JFK's assassination, the more federal authorities would have to compromise any thorough investigation into JFK's assassination, to avoid exposing C-Day to the public and risking a confrontation with the Soviets.

One attempt to link Menoyo's group to Lee Harvey Oswald occurred less than three months before JFK's assassination. Harry Williams started going after Menoyo for C-Day in the late summer and early fall of 1963—which is also when Menoyo's partner, Veciana, met Oswald in Dallas, according to his testimony. Congressional investigators checked Veciana's claims thoroughly, and one of them, Gaeton Fonzi, later wrote a book about Veciana's experi- ence and its ramifications. Veciana was asked to come to the meeting where he met Oswald by a man code-named "Maurice Bishop," whom Veciana said was his CIA handler. A Congressional report says that "Alpha 66 . . . according to Veciana, was Bishop's brainchild." Veciana told them that "the man behind all of Alpha 66's strategy"—even when it clashed with official Kennedy administration policy—"was Maurice Bishop."[34]

Who was "Maurice Bishop?" Former Congressional investigator Gaeton Fonzi makes a compelling case in his book *The Last Investigation* that the "Bishop" cover identity was used by CIA veteran David Atlee Phillips.[35] CIA agent Ron Crozier worked with Phillips and confirmed that Phillips used the alias of "Maurice Bishop."[36] We feel that the weight of the evidence supports Fonzi's conclusion, and that if more than one person used the "Bishop" identity —as was sometimes the case with CIA cover identities—then Phillips was a key person who did.

In the fall of 1963, David Atlee Phillips was "in charge of Cuban operations for the CIA" in Mexico, according to a Congressional report.[37] In our interview with Veciana, his description of how he named his group, Alpha 66, alludes to Philips: "I used the name 'Alpha' because it's the first letter of the alphabet and"—Veciana became quite emphatic as he talked—"I used the '66' because I was driving down the street and saw a Phillips 66 station and took that name." Congressional investigators say that "Veciana established himself as the civilian chief and principal fundraiser for Alpha 66 and recruited . . . Eloy Menoyo, as the military chief."[38]

A Congressional report described Veciana's meeting with Oswald: "At one meeting with Bishop in Dallas in late August or September 1963," Veciana saw with Bishop "a young man he later recognized as Lee Harvey Oswald."[39] This was "a few months before the assassination of John F. Kennedy"[40] and "took place in the lobby of a large office building in the downtown section" of Dallas.[41] "Veciana testified that he recognized the young man with Bishop as Lee Harvey Oswald after seeing photographs of him following the Kennedy assassination. There was absolutely no doubt in his mind that the man was Oswald, not just someone who resembled him."[42] Veciana told us his meeting with Bishop was about killing Castro, something Oswald discussed at the meeting as well.[43]

We will extensively document why the meeting between Menoyo's partner Veciana, Oswald, and Bishop/Phillips been engineered by associates of the Mafia bosses at that particular time, to link Oswald to C-Day. We show why the meeting occurred just weeks after Oswald's highly publicized activities in New Orleans with an exile group run by David Atlee Phillips, and only weeks before Oswald's trip to Mexico City, where Phillips ran Cuban operations for the CIA.[44] Phillips and the CIA had their own agenda for Oswald, an agenda that had nothing to do with JFK's assassination and everything to do with a US operation directed against Castro. However, the mob bosses knew that linking Oswald personally and publicly to Phillips would cause the CIA to go into cover-up mode when Oswald's name immediately surfaced as the prime suspect in the JFK assassination.

When Veciana first made his claims about meeting Oswald with Bishop/Phillips in the mid-1970s, the CIA had not yet admitted running any CIA assassination operations at the time of the meeting, let alone one involving Phillips or Veciana's close associates. Thirty years later, documents have been declassified showing that C-Day (AMWORLD to the CIA) was active at that time, and that it did involve Phillips and Veciana's close associate, Menoyo. Also, those documents and information from other C-Day sources allowed us to question Veciana in a way that was not possible for Congressional investigators, who had not been told about C-Day by the CIA. We do not see the meeting as implicating Phillips or Veciana as a knowing participant in JFK's assassination.

So, the mob bosses had linked Oswald to Menoyo's C-Day exile group, leaving a huge problem for Bobby Kennedy and US intelligence once Oswald's name arose in the JFK assassination. Like other C-Day leaders, Menoyo was not questioned by the Warren Commission and neither was his partner Veciana, even though Alpha 66 was viewed as one of the most anti-Kennedy exile groups and Alpha 66 kept surfacing in the JFK investigation. Congressional investigator Fonzi wrote that "Veciana never told Menoyo about Bishop." At the same time, Veciana told us that he didn't know about Harry Williams or C-Day. Apparently, Menoyo never told Veciana about the contact the CIA had documented between Harry Williams and Menoyo, which is what Harry would have wanted.

Fonzi got Veciana to pinpoint his meeting with Oswald to "early September, perhaps toward the end of the first week of" September 1963. Unknown to Veciana, Fonzi found "there is one span of time, between September 6th and 9th [1963], when Oswald's whereabouts are absolutely unknown."[45] As discussed in the last chapter, just a few weeks later four associates of Trafficante would similarly link Oswald to Manolo Ray's C-Day exile group JURE through Silvia Odio, also in Dallas. However, the Mafia had another connection to make between Menoyo's group and Oswald before the assassination, a ticking time bomb that would explode once Oswald's name surfaced in JFK's assassination: They would link the bullets in Oswald's rifle to C-Day.

Formerly secret CIA and FBI documents from fall 1963 tie Menoyo's group to an arms ring linked to mobster Jack Ruby—an involvement that left a remarkably accurate description of C-Day in government files. The bullets found in Oswald's rifle on November 22, 1963 were also linked to this incident, according to a report in the *Washington Post*. One can only imagine the chill that went through high government officials when they realized that the gun dealer who sold Oswald's bullets had also told a government informant about C-Day, using information FBI files say he obtained from one of Menoyo's men in SNFE.

"During October 1963," Menoyo's "SNFE was then interested in purchasing arms for their proposed military action in Cuba," according to the Warren Commission document quoted earlier.[46] A CIA document identifies a "Manuel Rodriguez . . . living in Dallas Texas" as an "SNFE member and organizer of the Dallas SNFE."[47] However, Menoyo's SNFE and Veciana's Alpha 66 were essentially one organization in the fall of 1963, so it should come as no surprise that a Warren Commission memo also identifies "Manuel Rodriguez" as the "Dallas Alpha 66 leader." That Warren Commission memo names a certain Dallas "gun dealer" as selling "stolen arms" to Rodriguez.[48]

The *Washington Post* says this same gun dealer "gave a sworn deposition" to Congressional investigators "acknowledging that the ammunition used in the [JFK] assassination probably came from his Dallas gun shop." The *Post* also says this gun dealer was selling "stolen arms" to Menoyo's organization.[49] Since Harry Williams said he "gave" Menoyo "money in cash"— money provided by the Kennedys for C-Day—the possibility exists that Kennedy money for C-Day could have gone to the very gun dealer who also sold the bullets found in Oswald's rifle.[50] It's clear why most of this information was kept secret until the 1990s.

The gun dealer in question—the source of Oswald's bullets, according to the *Post*—gave relatively accurate descriptions of C-Day to a government informant just weeks before JFK's assassination and the scheduled start of C-Day. FBI reports on this informant from late October and early November 1963 were sent directly to J. Edgar Hoover and kept secret for over thirty years. They say in "the last week of November 1963" that "a large scale amphibious operation would take place against the Cuba mainland." The FBI informant raised the possibility that "United States military forces or

Government agencies would possibly be involved in this operation."[51] The gun dealer said the "operation involved an attack by rebel Cuban forces centered against Cuba and that forces were presently staging at Caribbean bases." However, the gun dealer said that the exact locations of the "Caribbean bases" were "unknown to him," since he was getting the information secondhand. As we documented earlier, Menoyo's base—which Harry had visited and which Bobby Kennedy himself mentioned in his Oral History—was in the Caribbean.

The gun dealer told the FBI's informant that since the operation was going to be "big," he implied "that forehand knowledge of such information could result in considerable gain on the US Stock market." So the gun dealer wanted to know if the FBI informant knew "of anyone who would pay money for such information." As for how the gun dealer got his explosive information, he told the FBI informant it came from "a weapons buyer" named "Martinez." The FBI informant noted that he "believed" that Martinez was involved in "the Alpha 66 operation."[52]

The FBI's informant was listed in the documents as "Captain Nonte." He was actually US Army Captain George Nonte, the ordnance officer at Fort Hood, Texas—a base where the FBI had been investigating stolen arms.[53] According to a book-length study by the authors of the *Washington Post* article cited earlier, Nonte himself was part of an arms-theft and gunrunning operation that involved Jack Ruby. In fact, a Warren Commission witness— a former employee of Jack Ruby—discussed being at a meeting involving stolen arms destined for Cuba that "were being pilfered from the United States Army."[54] This wasn't the first time a group of Menoyo's had been involved in an arms deal with a ring involving Jack Ruby. As detailed in Part II, both Menoyo and Ruby had dealt with a gangster named "Dominick Bartone" back in 1959, when Senate Rackets Committee attorney Bobby Kennedy had grilled Bartone about his gunrunning partner known only by his alias of "Jack La Rue."[55]

Captain Nonte was never prosecuted for the arms he was stealing from Fort Hood, and instead seemed to be treated with much deference by the FBI. (In contrast, the gun dealer was arrested "on 11/21/63 for violation of the Federal Firearms Act," according to the FBI.[56]) Captain Nonte had a "top-secret clearance," according to the *Washington Post* authors, which raises the possibility that some federal authority was aware of—or even encouraging—Nonte's arms thefts, perhaps as a way to clandestinely provide arms to Cuban exiles the US couldn't overtly supply.[57] One is reminded of the comment that Desmond FitzGerald's assistant "who helped run Cuban operations for the CIA" made to *Newsweek's* Evan Thomas: "We told them where to buy guns without getting rooked, but this was Bobby's deal."[58] However, in a later AMWORLD document, it is the CIA that suggests using the Mafia as a cover for providing arms for Artime.[59] If Menoyo or Artime wound up inside Cuba with American arms, it would look much better for the US if the exiles appeared to be using weapons stolen from a National Guard Armory.

So, in the fall of 1963, Menoyo's group was apparently involved with the gun dealer who sold the bullets for Oswald's rifle, the same gun dealer who was describing C-Day to an FBI informant just a month before it was to begin. Menoyo's group was also evidently tied to an arms ring involving Jack Ruby. This does not mean that the gun dealer, Menoyo, or Manuel Rodriguez were knowingly involved in JFK's assassination. (Although the gun dealer's name is in all the documents and known to historians, he's sought to avoid publicity over the years, so we've chosen not to name him here.)

As in the cases cited previously, whenever there is a connection between Oswald and a Cuban exile C-Day group, one or more associates of mob bosses Marcello, Rosselli, or Trafficante is involved. Later chapters show how the same few mob associates—like Jack Ruby and Rolando Masferrer—were used, demonstrating how the Mafia bosses were able to penetrate C-Day and kill JFK using less than a dozen trusted professionals. With Menoyo, his partner Veciana, and Veciana's handler David Atlee Phillips focused so much on their upcoming Cuban operations, it was all too easy for the Mafia to penetrate their operations, by offering what they needed. In Menoyo's case it was weapons for C-Day; in David Atlee Phillips's case, it was an agent who could get into Cuba openly prior to C-Day. But in getting what they needed, they unknowingly linked themselves and their operations to Oswald, and thus to the JFK assassination.

Menoyo's case is especially tragic. Menoyo eventually proved that he was "a man of action," as Harry said, someone willing to risk his life to free Cuba. Unlike Artime, Menoyo didn't live comfortably in a mansion or grow rich. Instead, of all the C-Day exile leaders, Menoyo was the only one who finally got into Cuba, on a secret mission detailed in Part III. Menoyo's mission to Cuba took place just a couple of weeks after Che Guevara's December 1964 private meetings in New York City with three Kennedy associates. A CIA memo says that Menoyo was "reported captured by Cuban authorities January 4, 1965" and "later forced to go on Cuban television to publicly confess

[his] actions against Cuba."[60] Shortly after that, Che "Guevara dropped from sight altogether" and "rumors circulated at the time that" Che "had been executed by Fidel," according to Artime associate Felix Rodriguez. Che hadn't been executed, though he essentially received a death sentence: He was stripped of his high government position and property, and exiled to small poorly supplied and poorly supported guerrilla groups that faced overwhelming odds—first in Africa, then in Bolivia, where he was killed in the presence of Felix Rodriguez.[61] While Menoyo languished in a Cuban prison, Castro built and exploited the legend of Che. According to *Cuba: The Unfinished Revolution*, Menoyo "spent twenty-two years in Castro's concentration camps" and "lost all his hearing in one ear from a beating" and "had all his ribs broken," and was later "accused by the regime of having conspired to kill Castro."[62]

Menoyo's twenty-two years in captivity put him beyond the reach of all four Congressional and government investigations of the 1970s that looked into events surrounding the JFK assassination. Menoyo's imprisonment at that time may have also influenced the CIA and other intelligence agencies to withhold certain information from those committees—though aside from protecting Menoyo, it also served to hide the agencies' own intelligence failures. In 1987, Menoyo was finally released from prison. A few years later, knowing that his former associate was safely out of Cuba, Harry Williams began telling us about the story of C-Day. Menoyo spent most of the 1990s in the US, but returned to Cuba in 2004, where he continues to strive to bring change to Cuba, though he now advocates only peaceful means.[63]

CHAPTER FIFTEEN

Tony Varona

ON THE SURFACE, TONY VARONA (Manuel Antonio de Varona) was a logical choice for C-Day, as he had been for earlier US attempts to overthrow Castro. Varona had been part of the last legitimately elected government of Cuba, was a former president of the Cuban Senate, and had also worked to overthrow the dictator Fulgencio Batista. E. Howard Hunt, who worked on the Bay of Pigs at the same time as Varona, tersely wrote that Varona "Collaborated with Castro, fled" Cuba.[1] In 1961, Varona had been approved by the Kennedys to be a leader of the new Cuban government after the Bay of Pigs invasion because of his past credentials.[2] Physically imposing, Varona was described as being "bald, with broad shoulders and a barrel chest."[3]

Despite Varona's respectable surface, he had less savory associates—but even those made him valuable to the CIA. At the same time Varona was working for the Kennedys on the Bay of Pigs, he was also part of the expanded CIA-Mafia plots to kill Castro with Santo Trafficante and Johnny Rosselli.[4] However, because of a mix-up at the CIA, where only a handful of officials knew about the CIA-Mafia plots, Varona was unable to give the signal to assassinate Castro just prior to the Bay of Pigs. This was one of several largely overlooked missteps by the CIA that doomed the Bay of Pigs to failure.[5]

After that, Varona continued to deal with the Kennedys as a respected exile leader, but he also continued with the CIA-Mafia plots. The Church Committee reports that even after the Cuban Missile Crisis, Varona "was being used by the United States Government to aid in intelligence gathering and covert operations directed at Cuba." On one occasion, the Committee noted that Varona was "meeting with the Attorney General and waiting for an appointment from the White House." The source of the Church Committee's information about Varona and Bobby was godfather Johnny Rosselli, in his secret testimony to the Committee. Rosselli knew about Varona's meeting with Bobby because Rosselli had met Varona in Washington around the same time, while both men were working on the CIA-Mafia Castro assassination plots.[6]

When the US government decided to cut back on its support for most exile groups in the spring of 1963, Varona's Cuban Revolutionary Council (CRC) exile group was one that suffered. The CRC had been one of the largest US-backed exile groups, with offices in Miami and New Orleans. Its New Orleans branch originally shared a small office building with private detective Guy Banister and utilized David Ferrie, both of whom would be working for Carlos Marcello by 1963.[7] An April 25, 1963 memo from Dean Rusk to JFK outlines the funding cuts for the CRC, along with some candid comments about Varona. It noted that due to a recent political squabble, many of the CRC's "organizations and personalities" had withdrawn, turning Varona's group "into a rump organization of little attraction in the exile community." After the recent reorganization, the CRC "essentially constitutes 'Tony' Varona's effort to preserve his personal political machine, established through his control over the years of fifty per cent of the US-supplied CRC funds." Rusk accurately noted that since "Varona . . . lacks wide support," he "is actively seeking adhesion from a wide variety of exile leaders, including Batista elements." (Rusk didn't realize to what extremes Varona would soon go for more funds.) Rusk noted that Varona's group had been "receiving $137,000 monthly" and that "the next monthly installment of US financial assistance is due" to Varona's group "on May 1."[8]

A note at the top of Rusk's memo indicates that JFK's aide "called from the White House" to say that Rusk's plans to "call off aid" for Varona's group and others were "OK." However, JFK's aide noted that "something should be done for Varona." It also noted that "discontinuance of salaries would be accomplished gracefully, i.e., accompanied by notice and lump sum payments." Further, it said that "certain former and present" parts of Varona's group that were "essential to achieving our intelligence and other missions [will] continue to receive US financial assistance."[9] Several weeks later, as C-Day developed, guidelines for continued US financial assistance for certain exile leaders would be formalized in the Kennedys' guidelines, quoted earlier. Shortly after those guidelines were issued, the newly reorganized CRC elected Tony Varona to be president of the organization.[10]

The funding cutback, coupled with JFK's desire to do something for

Varona, probably helped motivate Varona to join the C-Day plan, but it also left him looking to others for funding. So while, on one hand, a "classified message" from the file of CIA agent (and future Watergate burglar) Bernard Barker notes "possible cooperation between Tony Varona and Manuel Artime," other reports show Varona renewing his old Mafia connections.[11] For example, an Army Intelligence report sent to "Mr. Joseph Califano" cites visits "to Nicaragua during July and August 1963" by "Varona" and "Manuel Artime." It notes that former Cuban President Carlos Prio—Varona's mentor—was also on the visits.[12]

However, Harry and the Kennedys had decided to make Tony Varona one of the main Cuban exile C-Day leaders. Varona's CRC organization was a shell of its former self, but Harry felt that Varona was attractive due to the respect many exiles held for him (notwithstanding Rusk's assessment), his former elected position, and his revolutionary credentials.

Harry confirmed to us that by the fall of 1963, Varona had agreed to join C-Day. Harry said he felt that "Varona was basically honest, [but] he didn't know how to deal with people."[13] A Kennedy administration official gave us his assessment of Varona: He said that "some liked Varona and thought he had a lot of influence" among Cubans, but others were less generous. This official said he was "in the middle" and "wasn't sure" which of the assessments was correct.[14] Documents released three decades later show that the official's uncertainty was more than justified.

CIA files show that Varona continued his dealings with the Mafia, even after he joined the Kennedys' C-Day plan. However, it's important to put this into perspective. Varona's ties to the Mafia predated the Bay of Pigs, when "Varona . . . met with Meyer Lansky to secure financing" for his exile group. Johnny Rosselli's biographers say that after that, Santo Trafficante "got wind of Varona's organizing activities, and initiated a series of meetings between himself, [Johnny Rosselli] . . . and Varona at the exile leader's home." The meetings were about Varona helping with the CIA-Mafia plots in 1960 and 1961, and included a representative of the CIA.[15]

Even after the failure of the CIA-Mafia plots during the Bay of Pigs, "Rosselli's primary contact among the Cuban exiles remained Tony Varona."[16] Rosselli continued the CIA-Mafia plots in the summer of 1963, and Varona found an additional source of funds.

In a shocking discovery, we uncovered two CIA documents showing that Rosselli's Chicago Mafia made a huge payoff to Tony Varona around the time he joined C-Day, in order to bring a dangerous killer secretly into the plan.

Taken together, these documents clearly show exactly how the mob bosses who later claimed credit for killing JFK were able to infiltrate and compromise C-Day. Both memos are from August 1963, the very time Varona was meeting with Harry Williams about joining C-Day. The first CIA memo says that "On Aug. 7, 1963" an "Informant" told the CIA that "while Varona was in Chicago recently [July 1963], four underworld figures made a contribution of $200,000 to him." That's over a million dollars in today's money, a considerable sum. The informant even identified one of the mobsters as Rosselli's boss, Sam "Giancana."[17]

The next CIA memo spells out at least one thing Varona did in return for the Mafia bribe. This "CIA Confidential Information Report" says that "between 12 and 27 Aug.," the notorious killer Rolando "Masferrer had met with Varona." Masferrer was an associate of Trafficante and Jack Ruby who had earlier confronted Harry Williams at Bobby's New York townhouse. Masferrer had been barred from C-Day by Harry and the Kennedys, who considered Masferrer a criminal. However, the CIA memo says "Varona . . . told Masferrer that things were going to change, and that Masferrer would take a large part in the Nicaraguan matter," referring to Artime's C-Day bases there. The memo says that "Varona also told him that there were certain obstacles in the way because Masferrer" had previously supported the Mafia-backed dictator Batista, "but that Varona would take charge of removing these obstacles."[18]

What "obstacles" did Varona plan on "removing"? Since the Kennedys and Harry were strongly opposed to Masferrer—JFK had once denounced Masferrer by name in a televised speech—the "obstacles" could have been a reference to "removing" JFK or Harry Williams. The CIA marked the "removing obstacles" memo as "routine," and there's no indication that it was shared with other agencies or the Kennedys. The memo has no indication that it was even shown to the CIA Director, John McCone.[19] Even if Varona's remark only referred to "removing" Harry or one of the other C-Day exile leaders like Manolo Ray, the CIA's not informing the Kennedys or Harry was still inexcusable. If the reference was to JFK, then the two CIA memos—and the lack of concern they raised at the time—constitute one of the most tragic US intelligence failures until the 9/11 attacks.

We believe the CIA's actions were an intelligence failure, not part of a CIA plot to kill JFK. Both Varona and Giancana were trusted veterans of the CIA's plot with the Mafia to assassinate Castro, so, to someone like Richard Helms or Desmond FitzGerald, it may not have seemed suspicious that Varona was dealing with Giancana. In addition, Helms was continuing the CIA-Mafia plots with Morales and Rosselli in the summer of 1963, without telling the CIA Director or the Kennedys. Also, several exile organizations solicited funds from the Mafia, or were sought out by the Mafia, so Varona's payoff may not have been seen as unusual. Finally, CIA files were full of meaningless deals and squabbles between Cuban exile leaders, which could have been what CIA officials thought Varona and Masferrer were talking about at the time.

Varona's comment about "removing obstacles" could also have referred to another C-Day exile leader. There are indications that Varona was one of four Trafficante associates who attempted to link Oswald to Manolo Ray's JURE by having someone claiming to be Oswald visit Silvia Odio. According to one document, Rolando Masferrer had a very close relative who lived in the same apartment complex as Ms. Odio.[20] In addition, Silvia Odio's uncle worked for Varona, in the small New Orleans chapter of Varona's group.[21] Her uncle just happened to be in the courtroom in the summer of 1963 on the very day when Oswald was fined for a scuffle over pro-Castro leaflets he was passing out. Tarnishing Manolo Ray's image—by linking Oswald to his group—could have cost Ray his role in C-Day, if it had continued full-bore after JFK's death, leaving an opening for Masferrer.

Varona's actions don't prove his knowing involvement in JFK's death. He could have simply been following the orders of Johnny Rosselli, unaware of what the final outcome would be. There is an indication that someone tried to link Varona himself to Oswald, just days before the assassination. Dallas reporter Earl Golz documented the unusual incident, which occurred in Abilene on November 17, 1963, the day before JFK's Tampa motorcade and his speech directed at the C-Day coup leader. Golz wrote that someone left a note signed "Lee Oswald" in plain sight on the door of a Cuban exile associate of Varona's, asking to be called at one of two Dallas phone numbers.[22] Such a link between a C-Day exile leader and Oswald prior to the assassination would fit the Mafia pattern discussed earlier, to compromise a thorough investigation of JFK's murder.

Harry Williams told us that he eventually "suspected Varona was getting money from Trafficante," partly as a result of something that happened after JFK's death, but by then it was too late.[23] Harry's suspicions were correct, because in addition to the payoff from Rosselli's Mafia family, Varona was also dealing with Carlos Prio, an associate of Trafficante. From the time when Varona was a Cuban senator, he had been considered a protégé of Prio. Prio, notorious for corruption, had been the last elected president of Cuba before he was overthrown by Batista.[24]

Prio appears frequently in our story, and never in a good light. Former Congressional investigator Gaeton Fonzi wrote that in the 1950s, "wealthy former [Cuban] President Carlos Prio . . . ensconced himself in an elegant home on Miami Beach and dispensed millions setting up arms and supply lines to the rebels while maintaining a close association with the American racketeers running the Havana gambling casinos."[25] That was during the time Prio was supporting Castro, who was trying to oust Batista. It is also when a Warren Commission document links Jack Ruby to Prio's gunrunning operations.[26] A confidential CIA report describes "Carlos Prio" as "an inveterate intriguer" who "has often demonstrated a complete lack of scruples in his actions." It says that in Cuba "during his administration, official corruption and gangsterism are known to have flourished, and he, like many of his colleagues, is reported to have profited considerably at public expense." A confidential CIA report notes that in 1955, Prio "became associated with" a political group whose "head, Tony Varona, was . . . described as a Prio henchman."[27]

When Cyrus Vance was listing possible exile leaders the US could support in May 1963, he called Prio a "rightist" who was an "old line . . . discredited politician" who was not likely to have much support within Cuba.[28] Vance's views reflect those of Bobby and Harry, who excluded Prio from C-Day. In August of 1963, Varona was dealing with Prio, even while Varona was joining the Kennedys' C-Day plan. An August 8, 1963 memo to CIA Director John McCone reports on a "UPI story datelined Managua 4 August headlined 'Enemies of Fidel Castro concentrating in Nicaragua.' Story reported presence in Nicaragua of Carlos Prio, [and] Tony Varona."[29] This was soon after the Chicago Mafia payoff to Varona, so it's possible that the Mafia first asked Varona to try to bring Prio into C-Day. If so, that attempt failed, resulting in Varona's secret deal with Masferrer.

Possibly at Varona's urging, Harry told us that he once "took Prio to Washington." Harry said he thought Prio "had a lot of appeal" to some Cubans, since he had been the last elected president of the country. However, Harry said he realized that Prio "was a dishonest man" and so Prio was not part of C-Day.[30]

Even the CIA was worried about Prio, apparently afraid that he would disrupt or corrupt one of the real C-Day exile leaders. So the CIA's Desmond FitzGerald sent a "CIA dispatch" to the Miami CIA Station on August 23,

1963. FitzGerald said that CIA headquarters "sees Prio's main role is one of creating a nuisance" and said that if Miami "can see a secure means of putting a spoke in Prio's wheels, its efforts along those lines would be appreciated." FitzGerald suggested they could "drop some hints to the effect that . . . observers view Prio as a has-been and refuse to take his leadership aspirations seriously." FitzGerald requested that Miami "air the above theme in a widely read column, making the following points . . . suggest that Prio could render one vital contribution . . . cough up some of the millions he stole from the Cuban people while President. As for the rest, he should lapse into silence and let respectable people do the job."[31] That's exactly what Miami did, using the power of the press—and the power of the CIA to influence the press—to get the following October 17, 1963 article in *Excelsior*, a Spanish-language newspaper. The wording is very close to what FitzGerald had suggested, including: "The only manner in which the multi-millionaire ex-president of Cuba can now help his people is by letting go of much of what he robbed when he occupied the presidency. He could also help the Cuban cause by discreetly staying behind the scenes so that respectable citizens with clean backgrounds are the ones to establish the movements organized to overthrow the present tyranny."[32]

Even when Harry turned Prio down, Prio continued his efforts to get into C-Day. Realizing that Artime was getting major backing from the Kennedys and Harry, Prio tried to get Artime to join him. However, a CIA "Telegram Information Report" sent on September 27, 1963 said that when Prio was "asked whether Manuel Artime would be working with him, Prio replied that Artime did not wish to join the forces" Prio was directing.[33] Undeterred, a later memo sent to CIA Director John McCone noted that "Prio has sent various men to join" Artime's group.[34] Still, Tony Varona remained Prio's closest source of information about C-Day.

Prio managed to learn some details about C-Day from Varona and Luis Somoza, the Artime supporter linked to godfather Carlos Marcello. In early November 1963, Prio made some public claims hinting at C-Day, which were reported only in the Hispanic community. Prio's public claims included exaggerated or erroneous information, perhaps to hide what he really knew. His private statements about C-Day, reported to CIA informants, were far more accurate.

The following CIA AMWORLD memo about C-Day contains information that the CIA gathered in mid-November 1963 and summarized a couple of weeks later—after JFK's assassination. This memo to CIA Director McCone quotes Prio talking about comments about upcoming plans of "US Gov . . . to replace" Fidel Castro "with "Tito-type government." Tito was the Yugoslavian ruler who ran his socialist government independent of Russia, and this was an apparent reference to a post-coup Provisional Government that would include leftists like Ray, Menoyo, and the C-Day coup leader. Prio also says that "he has verified" CIA "backing" of Artime's group and laments that aside from the selected groups like Artime's, "the other action groups [are] not permitted to operate, so they cannot gain prestige. Thus, [the] attitude of US Gov created disgust among persecuted groups who feel hurt when they see backing given" to groups like Artime's. Prio's worry is that he knows that within two years "after freedom" brought about by C-Day, a "General Election will have to take place" in Cuba. Prio says that for the elections, he "and [his] colleagues will have to present themselves as liberators to the Cuban people" to stand a chance in the elections. Prio's insistence on penetrating C-Day was driven by his desire to rush into Cuba after the coup as if he were a liberator. Prio notes that at least he and his cronies "have advantage of knowing how to organize political party better than other young[er] elements," an apparent reference to Artime and Ray, who had never run for public office.[35]

Prio also planned to disrupt the Kennedys' plans for a Provisional Government, and the document says that "at [the] right time Prio plans [to] denounce these plans so that Cuban people will know the truth and will not let themselves be directed." Prio then talks about two exiles who are part of his own plan "and have become associated [with] Richard Nixon in accordance with Republican Party plan [to] bring up the Cuban case before elections."[36] As explained in a later chapter, the link between Nixon and Prio (and others) helps to explain some lingering mysteries about Watergate. Prio himself even did some work for the Watergate operatives.[37]

The memo we've been quoting was released at two different times in the 1990s, and both versions are heavily censored, usually in the same places, but with one big exception: One version contains the CIA's official code-name for C-Day, AMWORLD.[38] In the other version, the word has been whited out.

A CIA "Telegram Information Report" from October 7, 1963 gives more insight into Prio's actions about C-Day. In regard to "operations" against Cuba that will "begin in November or December 1963," the report says that "Prio is trying to convince the wealthy Cubans in exile that, if they want to recoup their riches in Cuba in the future, they must contribute some of their wealth" to him. "If they do not, they will allow the United States to utilize a few Cubans to topple Castro and establish a government of their choosing, as was done in Japan after the Second World War. This government would then proceed to make economic and social changes which would cost them their wealth."[39]

Prio's concern that "a few Cubans" chosen by the Kennedys would "make economic and social changes" reflects Ray's and Menoyo's desire for land reform and other progressive policies. Another CIA "Information Report" from a couple of months later says that "Prio . . . has become convinced that the United States is giving" support to Artime's group and to "Manolo Ray" of JURE.[40] Since most exile groups were no longer getting US support, Prio would realize how unusual that was.

Another CIA document shows that Prio had a general idea of what was going to happen on C-Day, though he tended to see anyone with progressive or socialist leanings as a Communist. This memo to CIA Director John McCone says that on November 6, 1963, "Carlos Prio" said "that evidence exists" that "President Kennedy secretly plan[s to] replace Fidel Castro with more acceptable Cuban leader in . . . coup . . . replacement would puport[edly] be Tito-type thus paving [the] way for US recognition [of] Communist regime in Cuba." It also gives "Operation Judas" as the operation's name for "how President Kennedy . . . plan[s] to solve the Cuban problem."[41]

From the above documents, it might appear that Prio had learned everything about C-Day, from Varona. However, for length reasons and to avoid confusion, we left out some parts of the documents where Prio had details wrong or distorted. Some of that was probably due to his tendency to say one thing in public (putting the date for the coup after the 1964 elections) and another in private (where CIA documents show that he clearly knew the coup would happen in late November or early December 1963). But it's also possible that Varona wanted to keep some information to himself, or that he may have deliberately given Prio some erroneous information to see if it leaked. Plus, Harry didn't tell the C-Day leaders everything, so Prio may not have known details like the identity of the C-Day coup leader high in the Cuban government.

Despite Varona's numerous connections to Trafficante, Rosselli, and their associates like Masferrer and Prio, it does not mean that Varona was knowingly involved in the JFK assassination. While the evidence shows that

Varona's involvement probably went beyond the "guilty knowledge" of Artime, it does not prove that Varona was an active, knowing participant in JFK's assassination. After all, Trafficante, Rosselli, and Giancana had worked for the US government, specifically the CIA, and many exile groups took money from the Mafia. Varona had ties to Prio that predated the assassination by more than a decade. Finally, unlike most of those who were knowingly involved in JFK's assassination, Varona didn't prosper. Less than a year after JFK's murder, the former Cuban senator was selling cars in New Jersey.[42] Harry Williams told us which one of the C-Day participants he felt was knowingly involved in JFK's assassination (and it was not someone like E. Howard Hunt or James McCord), which led to corroborating documentary evidence, but such evidence does not currently exist for Varona's direct, knowing involvement in JFK's assassination. Varona may have been guilty of nothing more than bad judgment and trying to play both sides.

CHAPTER SIXTEEN

Cuban-American Troops on US Military Bases

THE LAST OF THE FIVE C-Day exile groups were the multiracial Cuban-American troops at Fort Benning, Georgia. Since they had a traditional military command structure, unlike the exile groups controlled by one man, we'll focus on the overall unit instead of a single individual. The vast majority of the Cuban-American troops were upstanding, even exemplary, soldiers and officers. However, the location of their main base provided a way for Carlos Marcello and Santo Trafficante to potentially monitor the exile troops' actions.

Former Congressional investigator Gaeton Fonzi summed up the origin of this unit when he said that the Bay of Pigs "Brigade veterans" were "offered a chance to receive an officer's commission in the US Army. Most of the Cubans were sent to Fort Knox, Kentucky, or Fort Jackson, South Carolina," but "a select few" were "sent to Fort Benning, Georgia."[1] Former FBI agent William Turner gives more precise figures, saying that "nearly half [of] the returned [Bay of Pigs] Brigade members joined the Army and were shipped to Fort Jackson, South Carolina. Three hundred who were considered officer material were sent to the command school at Fort Benning."[2]

At Fort Benning, Gaeton Fonzi says, "men in civilian suits gave advanced courses in covert operations, including clandestine communications and propaganda."[3] Obviously, these Cuban-Americans were being trained for a very special mission. Harry Williams told us that these multiracial troops would be the first US military force into Cuba after the C-Day coup. Instead of the Cuban populace seeing all-white, crew-cut American Marines as the first US troops after the coup, they would instead see a well-trained force of Cubans of all colors, men who could speak the language, many of whom were veterans of the Cuban military. These were troops who knew the country and the city where they would be deployed, and most of them still had family and friends in Cuba. They were an important part of the Kennedys' "Cubans helping Cubans" approach embodied in their exile guidelines for C-Day.[4]

Several of the Fort Benning officers went on to distinguished careers in the US military. Haynes Johnson wrote about one of the Fort Benning exile officers in the *Washington Post*, saying that "he graduated from virtually every school the Army offered—infantry, artillery and missiles, airborne, maintenance and language. He was assigned to the Office of the Secretary of the Army, and worked under Joseph Califano and Califano's young deputy of the time, Lt. Col. Alexander M. Haig."[5] In a distinguished career, this exile later achieved one of the highest ranks in the US military. Yet, because of the secrecy surrounding C-Day, accused terrorists like Luis Posada garner the headlines decade after decade, while the achievements of less-sensational exiles are overlooked by the media and historians.

JFK knew how important the multiracial Cuban-American troops at Fort Benning were to his plans for Cuba, and he talked about them at an April 3, 1963 press conference. JFK said that "between 400 and 500 members of the Brigade who were prisoners, who were at the Bay of Pigs, have joined the United States Army, 200 as officers and 250 as men who are now in training, and who, I think, will be very fine soldiers, and can serve the common cause." JFK singled out one of the exile officers as an example, saying that he "is a Cuban, a Negro" who "got all of his marks at 100% in joining the service. So I think there are a good many very determined, persistent Cubans who are determined that their island should be free, and we wish to assist them."[6]

At a public press conference, JFK didn't dare elaborate on what mission he envisioned for these men. But two weeks later, on April 19, 1963, during a question-and-answer session at the convention for the Society of Newspaper Editors, JFK spoke again about the Fort Benning exiles. He said that "We appreciate very much the fact that a good many Cubans have volunteered for the American Armed Forces. I think that they can be very valuable there. No one knows what the future is going to bring." One newspaper editor asked JFK if he thought that Castro would still be in power in five years. JFK replied "I don't accept the view that Mr. Castro is going to be in power in five years. I can't indicate the roads by which there will be a change, but I've seen enough . . . to make me feel that time will see Cuba free again. And I think when that happens, the record will show that the United States has played a significant role."[7] JFK was being far more revealing than any of the newspaper editors could have dreamed.

It's important to note that very few of the Fort Benning exile troops knew anything about C-Day, given the tight secrecy surrounding the operation. There was no need for them to know, since they were already getting the special training they needed and JFK had been clear in his speeches about his eventual goal for them. The flag that JFK had so emotionally waved at the Orange Bowl was kept at Fort Benning, a constant reminder to the men of JFK's promise to return it to them "in a free Havana."[8] The exile troops believed JFK's pledge and knew in general what they were being trained for, so there was no need for them to be told details about C-Day in advance. The strategy, the big picture, was for higher-level commanders and Defense Department officials.

One of those, a former Defense official, agreed to speak with us confidentially about the Fort Benning exile troops and C-Day. We easily verified his position from public sources, as well as from his numerous awards over the years. We also spoke to several people who had met or worked with this official, and they were all "impressed" with him and his ability. A former Secretary of State described him as being extremely honest and forthright. Harry Williams was typical of those we spoke with about this official, all of whom had only the highest regard for his honesty, ability, and integrity. In addition, a Pulitzer Prize–winning journalist vouched for the official's knowledge and involvement in Cuban matters in 1963.[9]

We asked the Defense official why any US forces—including the Cuban-American troops—were needed for C-Day. Why not just let the C-Day coup leader eliminate Castro (and his brother, Raul), and then have the US recognize the coup leader's new government, including the C-Day exile leaders? Even though the coup leader was a powerful official, with a significant following in Cuba, the Defense official said that he wasn't sure the coup leader had "the strength, political clout, or stature at that time to control Cuba" by himself, after the coup, without US military assistance.[10] After further research, and after more documents were declassified, we realized how right he was. With the large number of Soviets in Cuba, and the various political factions in the Cuban government—old-line Communists, socialists, various branches of the military and security services—all vying for control, it was clear that US forces would be needed after the coup. In addition, Mafia-backed exile leaders like Prio and Masferrer would also be trying to stake their own claims to legitimacy in Cuba. While Artime and the other C-Day exile leaders had enough forces to help them get into the country after the coup and join the Provisional Government, only US military might could ensure that Cuba wouldn't dissolve into civil war or that the Soviets wouldn't try to install their own regime.

The Defense official said that his "personal opinion was that a military operation was the way to take over Cuba." He said that he saw the operation as "purely military" and not as an "assassination plot against Castro." To him, it was a matter of "organizing and training . . . in the military." The goal, he said, "was to organize a professional fighting force, and to go back and invade Cuba" after the coup. He also emphasized that from his Defense perspective, he was referring to US military forces and not to Artime's exile forces.[11] He said that Artime went "many times to Fort Benning," something verified by documents and Felix Rodriguez's account of being recruited there by Artime.[12] However, the Defense official noted that Artime's funding—which he estimated at "six to seven million dollars"—was "from [the] CIA" and not from Defense. The Defense official also acknowledged being aware of Harry's activities and plans. He said that by November 22, 1963, the multi-racial Cuban-American forces were trained and ready to go.[13] We know from documents we've cited previously that the Cuban-American troops were to lead the way into Cuba after the coup, but would be backed up by "US military forces" ranging from "Special Forces, up to the full range of [US] military forces."

Unlike the other C-Day exile groups, you might think this part of the operation was immune from Mafia godfathers such as Santo Trafficante and Carlos Marcello. But a major French Connection heroin bust at Fort Benning linked to both godfathers—along with the assassination of Alabama's newly elected antimob Attorney General just across the river in a town run by Trafficante's men—shows that the reach of Marcello and Trafficante extended even there. Both events are detailed in Parts II and III.

It's important to remember that the vast majority of Cuban-American troops at Fort Benning and elsewhere were never involved with terrorism, with drugs, or with mobsters like Trafficante. None was involved in the JFK assassination. In the *Nation*, the former head of the Cuba branch of the DIA wrote that of the Cubans who had officer commissions arranged by "Joseph Califano" and "Col. Alexander Haig . . . sixty-three of them went on to serve with distinction in Vietnam."[14] Most of the Cuban-Americans at Fort Benning went on to lead normal—and in some cases exemplary—lives. They worked very hard, training for a mission that never came, because the Mafia bosses killed JFK before the C-Day coup could take place. The Cuban-American troops were willing to risk their lives to bring freedom to Cuba. While these Cubans trained in Georgia heat that reminded them of their subtropical homeland, another man willing to risk his life was back in Cuba. This was the very high Cuban official and hero of the Revolution, the man who would lead the C-Day Coup and "eliminate" Castro for the Kennedys—the man we call the "coup leader" in this book.

It's ironic that some of the Cuban exiles training at Fort Benning had been fighting for the Revolution with the coup leader just four years earlier. For a time after Castro assumed power, their goals had become very different, but by May 1963 their goals were the same and matched those of the Kennedy administration: to "foment a revolt within Cuba which would call for US military intervention," as the Joint Chiefs said in May 1963.[15] That memo was completed right after the coup leader high in the Cuban government first contacted the Kennedys' representative, Harry Williams. To use phrases from later memos, the coup leader was "identifiable" to all Cubans and "dependable" when it came to staging a coup. He was someone with "a large measure of support among the" Cuban "people."[16] Unlike lower-level Cuban officials like the CIA's Cubela, the coup leader had a "power base in the Cuban" government and he had enough clout and prestige "to establish a Provisional Government . . . with some sort of public claim to political viability."[17]

Che Guevara: A Reassessment

IN SOME WAYS, CHE GUEVARA had much in common with Artime, Menoyo, Ray, and Varona by the fall of 1963. The exiles had fought in the Revolution with Castro and helped him govern, before being forced out. Now Che's star was starting to wane, as he struggled to transform from revolutionary to bureaucrat and as he seethed over his resentment of the Soviets, who considered Che a "troublemaker."[1] As documented from news accounts, recent biographies, and declassified CIA documents, Che was having increasing problems with Fidel Castro. It culminated on December 10, 1963, when the CIA Director received a cable from his Miami CIA Station saying "a Western diplomat informed" them that "he had learned from" someone in the Cuban government "that Che Guevara was alleged to be under house arrest for plotting to overthrow Castro."[2]

For decades, it has not been easy to get objective, accurate information about Che Guevara, especially concerning key points in his life. Much written about Che since his puzzling death in the jungles of Bolivia has the aura of myth and legend. Many on the left have turned him into a heroic martyr, while those on the right have often demonized him. Meanwhile, the Cuban government has churned out reams of propaganda designed to turn Che into a potent symbol and revolutionary icon. Historian Andrew Sinclair wrote that "In death, Che has had more influence than when he was alive. Dead men may tell no tales, but they can make a legend."[3]

There have been some thoroughly documented accounts of Che's life in Cuba, notably Hugh Thomas's *Cuba: The Pursuit of Freedom*, but at almost 1,800 pages it is mainly of interest to academics. Even that book had only a few sentences about Che's mysterious break with Fidel, which has always been the subject of much speculation and controversy. In addition, Thomas, like most historians, reports only a few basic facts about Che's death, leaving many questions unanswered. The two most critical aspects of Che's life—his final rupture with Fidel that led to his exile from Cuba, and the reasons for his death—have often had to be glossed over by Che's fans, detractors, and historians. Today, most people are far more familiar with Che as a dramatic face on a poster—one of the most recognizable icons in the world—than with Che's actual life.

The problem of separating fact from legend has also served to obscure other aspects of Cuban history. For example, most people today believe there was only one main revolutionary leader and group—although, as we've documented, there were others who were gradually pushed out by Fidel Castro. In fact, after the Cuban dictator Batista fled to Miami, Fidel wasn't even the first president of the new revolutionary Cuba: that distinction belongs to Manuel Urrutia, long forgotten by all but a few historians.[4] In addition, popular belief holds that Castro closed the Mafia's casinos after he took over in 1959. However, that leaves out a crucial part of the story: The casinos were quickly reopened, under the supervision of Castro's "Minister for Games of Chance," future Watergate burglar Frank Fiorini (aka Frank Sturgis), who was also an associate of Santo Trafficante.[5] In fact, the New York Times reported that the last casino in Havana wasn't closed until September 30, 1961, five months after the failed Bay of Pigs invasion, and almost three years after Castro came to power.[6] And according to a Congressional report, some Havana nightclubs controlled by French associates of Trafficante's heroin supplier, Michel Mertz, may have still been open in 1963.[7]

However, in the case of Che, the historical record has become clearer as government documents were declassified and current scholars used those and fresh accounts from Che's associates, including those no longer in Cuba, to give a fuller, more accurate picture. Two of the most notable recent books are Jorge Castaneda's Companero: The Life and Death of Che Guevara and Che Guevara: A Revolutionary Life by Jon Lee Anderson.

Jorge Castaneda is a noted historian who has been a visiting professor at Harvard, Princeton, and Columbia. He's also written for the New York Times, Newsweek, and Time. His father was a Mexican foreign minister, and Castaneda himself served as Mexico's foreign secretary from late 2000 to early 2003. Castaneda writes that in July 1963, after a trip to Algeria, Che "stopped in Paris," where he "reflected upon his future in Cuba, in view of

Fidel's reconciliation with the USSR"—which Che still resented—"and the growing controversy surrounding [Che's] management of the economy."[8]

In Paris, Castaneda says that Che "met Carlos Franqui." Franqui had been Cuba's top journalist after the Revolution, but he was meeting the same fate Ray, Menoyo, and others had experienced earlier—he was being pushed out of Castro's inner circle. CIA documents cited earlier confirm that after C-Day developed in 1963, Harry Williams helped to arrange Franqui's defection to Europe along with a payment to Franqui authorized by the Kennedys of between $200,000 and $300,000.

According to Castaneda, prior to July 1963, "relations between" Che and Franqui "were strained . . . they had clashed several times in Cuba over a number of issues." However, they "had just celebrated a virtual reconciliation in Algeria" during a brief meeting there. Now, in Paris, "the two discovered many affinities." Franqui wrote later that at their meeting in Paris, Che "was seeking another path. He considered the Cuban situation very difficult . . . it was one of our best meetings." Castaneda evocatively writes that "Che put his arm around Franqui's shoulders and the two went walking along a deserted boulevard in the Paris summer, cooled by the chestnut trees and the last cobblestones paving the avenues of the French capital." Che mentioned "his own frictions with Castro. It was then, in the heart of the Latin Quarter, that Che gave vent to" a statement which has often been quoted: "With Fidel, I want neither marriage nor divorce."[9] Franqui himself later gave Che's wording as "with Fidel, there is neither marriage nor divorce."[10]

Che's July 1963 statement has been the subject of much speculation over the years. After all, Che was already in a very close political marriage with Fidel. If two people are trapped in a dysfunctional marriage that one of them doesn't want, and divorce isn't an option, what does that leave? Sometimes the solution is the death of one of the partners.

Two significant facts about Che Guevara's life in 1963 have not been noted in any previous books or articles about him. None of the accounts of Che's famous July 1963 statement to Franqui ever noted that Franqui was in Paris after having been helped to defect by Harry Williams. The CIA documents about that weren't declassified until 1993 and 1994, and have never been cited in any book until now. Similarly, no biography of Che has noted the CIA document previously quoted regarding reports of Che's "house arrest" in December 1963. These revelations show how much material is yet to be uncovered about such a seemingly well-known figure.

Franqui's situation in 1963 provides additional insight into what Che meant with his comment about Fidel. In the foreword to one of Franqui's memoirs, his friend Cabrera Infante wrote that 1959 had been Franqui's "heyday. Soon afterward, his fortunes began slowly to decline: from those of a politician in Castro's grace to those of a man who fell from grace with God into a sea of troubles."[11] Did Che see his fate going in the same direction as Franqui's? Franqui himself wrote that "Che Guevara . . . was beginning to make now, in 1963, a series of trips. . . . In Cuba, traveling meant disgrace, a kind of forward retreat." As Castaneda noted, Fidel had reconciled with "the Soviet Union in May 1963," but Che hadn't. Franqui writes that at their July 1963 meeting, he noticed that Che "was changing, taking on a more critical view" about "the Soviet Union" and that Che now "severely castigated the Soviets and their bureaucracy." As a result, Franqui—the defector being helped by the Kennedys—wrote that in July 1963, he "felt closer to Che than ever."[12]

Harry knew Che Guevara, according to an "on-the-record" statement Harry gave to FBI veteran William Turner in 1973, several years after Che's death. But Che had contact with other Kennedy associates as well, though only one of those is well known to historians. In all, we talked with four Kennedy officials or aides who had dealings with Che, plus another man who claimed to have been present when Che was executed.

Bobby Kennedy himself spoke admiringly of Che, at least after JFK's death. Arthur Schlesinger wrote that when one of Bobby's friends called Che a bandit, Bobby countered by saying "I think he is a revolutionary hero."[13] In November 1965—as the second anniversary of JFK's death and C-Day approached—Robert Kennedy was in South America with Richard Goodwin, a former JFK aide. Historian Evan Thomas quoted Goodwin as saying that on that trip, Bobby "never mentioned Cuba, except to express his admiration for Che Guevara . . . as a leader."[14] In 1968, after Che's death and shortly before Bobby's own assassination, Bobby said "You know, sometimes I envy the bastard [Che]. At least he was able to go out and fight for what he believed. All I ever do is go to chicken dinners."[15]

Goodwin himself had met Che in Uruguay at a conference in August 1961, when he worked on Cuban matters for JFK. Che had initiated the meeting with the JFK aide, sending Goodwin a gift of Cuban cigars and a note "extending my hand."[16] Goodwin got along well with Che, and Che later told an American journalist that he admired Goodwin. Later, Goodwin wrote, "following our meeting in 1961, Che Guevara's own career took a far more abrupt and fateful course than did my own . . . he became the target of mounting hostility from the Russians." Goodwin also noted that "as the Cuban economy lagged, Guevara was gradually relieved of his control. In addition, it is almost certain that Guevara's relations with Castro were marked by periods of violent strain . . . perhaps there was just not room enough in Cuba for both of them."[17]

This is the only contact between a Kennedy aide and Che known to most historians. Goodwin told us that he didn't know about C-Day, since he wasn't working on Cuban affairs in 1963, though he spoke candidly about earlier attempts of the Kennedys to eliminate Castro. Goodwin had been removed from Cuban matters in November 1961, after criticism from conservatives over what one Republican congressman denounced from the House floor as Goodwin's "so-called chance meeting" with Che.[18]

In our first interview with Harry Williams, we were discussing the plan to eliminate Fidel and Raul Castro during the coup. But when we asked "Che Guevara too?," Harry surprised us. Instead of saying that Che would have to be eliminated, too, Harry said "I got along with Che a lot of [the time]" and that "Che Guevara was . . . more of a thinker."[19] As we noted earlier, Harry told William Turner about giving supplies to Che and his group during the Revolution.[20]

One C-Day exile leader told us that he "had the opportunity to work with Che Guevara in Havana" after the Revolution.[21] In addition, we spoke with a Kennedy C-Day aide who had contact with Che in the year prior to JFK's death.[22] Another C-Day exile leader who had worked closely with Che was Manolo Ray. Franqui wrote that the Cuban revolutionary group called the "26th of July Movement" included not just its "creator . . . Fidel Castro," but also "Che" and "Manolo Ray."[23] It's also interesting to note that a "June 19, 1963" cable to CIA "Director" John McCone confirms that Manuel "Ray" had just met with Carlos "Franqui" in "Europe" and felt his trip was "very profitable."[24] That was just weeks before Che made his own visit to Franqui in Europe.

Franqui wrote that yet another figure from the 1963 plots, CIA asset Rolando Cubela (AMLASH), had also worked with Che in the Revolution. Franqui writes that a group "led by . . . Rolando Cubela" fought "alongside Che in" the "autumn [of] 1958."[25] Also, a document declassified in 1994 has a Senate investigator saying that "in reviewing the [Cubela] file at the" CIA, "I came across many references to . . . rumors that [Cubela] was intimate with Che Guevara."[26]

By 1963, the historical record shows that Che was beset by problems: with Castro, with the Communist Party in Cuba, and especially with the Soviet Union. With all the concern about the Soviets expressed by JFK and US officials in declassified documents from 1963, it's ironic how many of their concerns were shared by Che Guevara.

Historian Castaneda writes about "the increasing strain in Che's relations with the Communist parties of Latin America and the Soviet Union during 1963. Since Cuba was entering a period of creeping alignment with the Soviet Union, inevitably, Che's situation became more and more untenable." In the spring of 1963, Che told the Soviet Ambassador that he knew "he [Che] was perceived by Moscow as an 'ugly duckling' and a 'trouble-maker.'"[27] At the same time, Che's remaining power over his former revolutionary forces in Cuba also started to erode due to the Soviets, as "important segments of the Cuban militias began to be dismantled" and "military facilities . . . were placed under Soviet control. The Cuban air force commander of [one] base was arrested for refusing to transfer it to the Soviets. He was freed thanks only to Che's personal intervention."[28]

Che's problems with the Soviets had been developing even before what he saw as their betrayal over the UN weapons inspections issue to resolve the Cuban Missile Crisis. Historian Hugh Thomas wrote that months before the Crisis, Che had "angrily communicated . . . in the March 1962 issue of *Cuba Socialista*" unwelcome "news . .. . that henceforth Russian and East European raw materials would have to be paid for in foreign exchange earnings, not by Russian gifts or loans."[29] Since Che was increasingly involved in running the Cuban economy, this was a huge blow to him.

Carlos Franqui wrote that by "the first days of 1963," Cuba's "socialist romance with the USSR had lasted two years. It was born with the US economic blockade and ended with the [US] maritime blockade" during the Cuban Missile Crisis. "We had learned that ideals and realities are quite different things, like words and acts. The USSR had used us and then abandoned us."[30] Nonetheless, Franqui wrote that in spite of the Soviet actions, "Fidel never wanted to break with the Soviets because it was against his nature."[31] According to Franqui, "the communists . . . had guaranteed" Fidel's "power, and now there was no turning back" for Fidel.[32] And it wasn't just Fidel who remained loyal to the Soviets; Fidel's brother Raul Castro also championed the Soviets. Franqui wrote that "Che was not the same as Raul, who was Moscow's man."[33]

Che also had problems with the Communist Party in Cuba. Historian Hugh Thomas noted that by 1962, Che "Guevara . . . had no love for the sort of disciplined [Communist] party which seemed to be being built up" in Cuba. Che denounced it as a "party of administration, not pioneering, a new elite which sought an easy life with beautiful secretaries, Cadillacs, [and] air-conditioning."[34] Tad Szulc wrote in his portrait of Fidel Castro that "Che was losing his usefulness to Castro because the Communist community now regarded him [Che] with suspicion."[35]

Some historians have argued that Che's increasing difficulties with the Soviets in 1963 were because Che was aligning more with the Communist Chinese, but Che had problems with the Chinese as well. Castaneda writes that "The disagreement among China, the USSR, and [Che] Guevara was not just ideological . . . the underlying dispute involved economic policy."[36] And according to the *New York Times*, in June of 1963, Cuba's economy—Che's responsibility—was still in bad shape, although "Minister [Che] Guevara says Cuba has passed [the] worst of [its] economic crisis but conditions are still bad."[37] (When Che disappeared from sight in April 1965, the Cuban economy was doing much better, which rules out the economy as the reason for Che's final clash with Castro and his subsequent exile.) In 1963, Che's economic plans were having problems—which is not a surprise, since he prided himself on being an inspirational leader. As Carlos Franqui wrote, Che "could never be a bureaucrat," and by 1963 "I could see that Che was running into problems."[38]

Fidel's feud with Che in 1963 was nothing new. Franqui writes that as early as 1958, "Fidel's plan was simple . . . to downplay Che's importance."[39] He notes that "Che had always declared himself to be a Communist, but his brand of communism never convinced Fidel, who recognized Che's independence of character and his sense of morality." Che was aware of what was happening to Franqui and what had happened to others who had once been at Castro's side. One by one, they had been forced out of power, imprisoned, or killed. To Che and Franqui, it must have been clear that unless they could totally subjugate their ego and will to Fidel Castro, conflict was inevitable. This must have driven Franqui to risk defection, with the help of Harry Williams and the Kennedys.

Franqui wrote a book called *The Twelve*, about Castro and his "twelve disciples" who survived an early battle in the Revolution and went on to be the core of Cuba's early post-Revolution leadership. In 1956, Castro was bringing "eighty-one of his companions," including Che, from Mexico to invade Cuba "on the yacht *Granma*," according to Cuban exile author Nestor T. Carbonell. "Castro's plan had been to synchronize the landing with a revolt." However, "the operation was a debacle" and only Fidel and the twelve—including Che—survived. Just three years later, they were ready to take over Cuba.[40]

By 1963, things were very different for Che. Prior to the December 10, 1963 CIA report of his "house arrest" for plotting to overthrow Castro, Che had made only one major public appearance that year. That was not even in Cuba, but in Algiers on July 13, shortly before his visit to Franqui in Paris.[41] Franqui notes that as 1963 progressed, things seemed to be getting worse in Cuba and "in the early months of 1963 I sensed that a historical period was closing" and "the [Cuban] people were somber, silent, devoid of the humor they once had. I went to the movies; there were lots of seats for Russian films no one wanted to see and huge lines of people waiting to get in to see the Italian films. People went crazy if they had a chance to see an old Hollywood film." He says that "Che wondered if the people would ever be brought around, if they would ever get over the errors caused by party politics. In any case, Party pressure was coming back on, Security was back in action, and the Defense Committees were keeping their eyes peeled."[42]

Things were getting worse; so what was someone like Franqui—or Che—to do? As Franqui notes repeatedly in his book, "No one resigns under Fidel."[43] For Franqui, he was eventually driven to desperate and risky action, with the aid of Harry Williams.

What kind of action was Che considering in 1963, to deal with his many problems? Some indication comes from a memo a close Kennedy aide sent to a National Security Council staffer in early November 1963. It should be noted that this Kennedy aide did not know about C-Day, because he was helping JFK with the secret, back-channel negotiations with Castro. Nevertheless, this declassified memo contains information from well-connected sources in Cuba who talked with both Fidel and Che. It confirms "there was a rift between Castro" and Che Guevara "on the question of Cuba's future course." The well-connected source in Cuba "also said that [Che] Guevara . . . regarded Castro as dangerously unreliable; and would get rid of Castro if" he "could carry on without him and retain his popular support."[44] Another memo shows the level of mistrust between Fidel and Che when it says that Castro's representative "emphasized that only Castro and himself would be present at the talks and that no one else—he specifically mentioned [Che] Guevara—would be involved."[45]

Franqui himself grew disillusioned with Fidel by 1963, and sometimes argued with Fidel, who "would say that soon enough I would see Che arguing with and fighting against the Communists." Franqui cryptically adds "And that was a fact, but Che's enlightenment is another story."[46]

Che's feelings about Americans had been negative in the 1950s, because Che was in Guatemala during the CIA's 1954 coup, when the US overthrew the democratically elected government. Historian Hugh Thomas writes that "Guevara came out of his experience in Guatemala immensely hostile to the US." But by the early 1960s, Che's view of the US had shifted. Thomas wrote that Che "admitted" to a Venezuelan journalist "that 'the model whom we must cite as closest [to] the man most resembling man of the future society [is] the North American . . . the product of a developed economy, of modern technology, of abundance. . . . A revolutionary Cuban, Vietnamese, or Algerian of today [is] less like the man who is going to shape the Communist society than a Yankee . . . we men are children of the economic metier. But should this be told?'"[47] Apparently, by 1962 Che was aware of economic reality and the need for US assistance if the revolution was to prosper, but he wasn't sure that the Cuban public—or his fellow officials—could handle being told the truth. Because of Che's economic responsibilities, Che may have thought an accommodation with the US allowing socialism in Cuba would be preferable to Cuba simply becoming another Soviet (or Chinese) puppet state. Che's positive feelings about the US in 1962 would have only been more pronounced by 1963, since in the spring of 1963 Castaneda writes that Russia was pressuring Che and Cuba to focus only on being an agriculture economy and to grow sugar cane. Che, who wanted a more diversified economy with manufacturing, strongly resisted the Soviet pressure, making his relations with them even worse.[48]

Historian Jorge Castaneda provides clear evidence that Che planned to leave Cuba in December 1963 and had made extensive preparations prior to that. It took over thirty years for this information to surface because Che's planning was done in relative secrecy and the plans were never carried out.[49]

Apparently, Che wanted to have plans in place in case he needed to leave Cuba on short notice in December 1963.

Castaneda writes that "there are three indications that Ernesto Guevara intended to leave Cuba" and go to his native Argentina in late 1963. "First, the leaders of the Argentine expedition all belonged to his inner circle: two of his bodyguards, his best journalist friend, and his closest Cuban aide." Castaneda says that "Che summoned [Alberto] Castellanos," a close associate, and told him "I will go soon." It was more than "thirty years" before Castellanos revealed Che's plan to leave Cuba in late 1963, but "he never harbored any doubt that his boss fully intended" to go to Argentina at that time. He said that "Che was going to leave [Cuba] in 1963; he even sent me to wait for him. I had not said this before."[50]

But Che's plans were unusual. Until Che could join them, his men were told to just "wait for him" in Argentina and that they "should not recruit any peasants" there. Also, "combat was to begin only after Che's arrival."[51] In other words, don't do anything to start a revolution until Che got there. It was as if Che wanted to be able to quickly flee to Argentina in December 1963 if he needed to—but he didn't want to leave any sign of his plans, in the event he didn't have to go.

The story of Che continues in later chapters, where we shed new light on key incidents in Che's last years which have remain unexplained, or largely unknown, for decades. This includes an FBI report of Che's involvement in a 1959 coup plot against Castro and Che's meeting with CIA agent David Atlee Phillips that year. We detail Che's secret meetings with three Kennedy associates in New York City in December 1964, the capture of a C-Day exile leader in Cuba three weeks later, and Che's mysterious disappearance and reported house arrest when he returned to Cuba several weeks after that. We will document the first time Castro sent Che into exile on a doomed mission (to Africa) and how Castro betrayed Che when Che was at his lowest ebb. In addition, we explore Che's final doomed mission, to Bolivia, where Castro refused Che's pleas for help and C-Day veterans were involved in Che's execution. We also document that Castro was described as "frankly euphoric" over Che's death, according to his old friend Carlos Franqui.[52]

The Other Plots Against Castro

HARRY WILLIAMS TOLD THE AUTHORS that although he was Bobby's "closest partner" among the Cuban exiles, there were "a lot of people involved in" C-Day. Harry made it clear that he knew of almost a dozen people who knew major portions of the C-Day plan. But Harry also had the "feeling . . . that Bobby didn't tell me everything" and that Harry's role in C-Day "was just part of what" was being planned in November of 1963.[1] Declassified documents show that Harry was correct: While Harry knew about the multiracial Cuban exile troops who would be the first US military force into Cuba, he didn't know about the extensive plans of the Joint Chiefs for invading Cuba, code-named CINCLANT OPLANS 312 and 316. Harry knew about the Provisional Government planned for post-Castro Cuba, and CIA documents confirm that he had a lead role in shaping that Provisional Government;[2] but Harry wasn't privy to the extensive discussions in National Security Council subcommittees about a document called "Plan for a Coup in Cuba." Nor was Harry aware of the Kennedys' secret peace feelers to Castro or their earlier attempt with the CIA to find a Cuban official to stage a coup, code-named AMTRUNK.

While John and Robert Kennedy were devoting themselves to C-Day, there were other US government plans afoot in the fall of 1963 to deal with Castro. The fact that there were so many different plans active at the same time—some of which later overlapped with the remnants of C-Day—is yet another reason Congressional investigators were never able to uncover C-Day. Plus, the difficulty of maintaining adequate security for so many plots against Castro in the fall of 1963 also made it easier for the Mafia to penetrate C-Day.

The other plots to deal with Castro in the fall of 1963 fall into three categories:

- The CIA's own plots to assassinate Castro using the Mafia. Active since 1959, the plots had been ramped up in the summer of 1960 prior to JFK's election, and were continuing in the fall of 1963 without the knowledge of the Kennedys.
- The CIA's plot to assassinate Castro using mid-level Cuban official Rolando Cubela. The Kennedys' knowledge of this plot was murky, at best.
- Another Kennedy effort utilizing the CIA, an operation known as AMTRUNK. The Kennedys were fully aware of this operation.

THE CIA-MAFIA PLOTS

The CIA-Mafia plots to assassinate Castro in the fall of 1963 were hidden from the Kennedys. Much has been publicly documented about some of these CIA-Mafia plots over the years, beginning with the Church Committee investigations in the mid-1970s. The CIA has only reluctantly divulged and declassified information about them, usually trying to emphasize the sillier aspects of some of the plots: exploding cigars and seashells, poison pens, and trying to make Castro's hair fall out. The CIA has also tried to minimize the duration of the plotting, focusing on the period fall 1960 to fall 1962. However, CIA documents and other evidence show that the plots began much earlier, and lasted far longer, through the time of the JFK assassination and beyond. Many of the plots involved pistols and high-powered rifles with scopes.

Controversy still rages over how much the Kennedys knew about the CIA-Mafia plots and when they knew it, but we won't go into that here. What's important for C-Day is that the CIA-Mafia plots began in 1959, well before JFK's election, and they continued until after JFK's death.[3] Even JFK's most ardent detractors rarely contend that John or Bobby Kennedy knew about the ongoing CIA-Mafia plots in 1963, plots that even endangered a key Kennedy emissary.

According to a Kennedy official who worked on C-Day, during 1963 Bobby "got regular written reports" about the CIA's covert Cuban activity.[4] But Bobby wasn't being informed of everything by the CIA. For example, in the spring of 1963, the Kennedys sent their personal emissary, James Donovan, to Cuba to negotiate with Castro for the release of twenty-one American prisoners in Cuban jails, including three CIA agents. Castro sometimes invited Donovan to accompany him skin-diving, and the CIA later admitted considering having Donovan present Castro with a "diving suit" that was "contaminated" with poison. The CIA also looked at making a "seashell . . . rigged to explode" near Castro while he was diving.[5]

But that is only what the CIA was willing to admit to Congress. During the negotiations between Donovan and Castro, the CIA also tried to assassinate Castro more directly. On March 13, 1963, there was a plan to assassinate Castro in Havana during a meeting, using "a rifle with a telescopic sight," as well as "machine guns . . . grenades" and "an American bazooka." But Castro's agents captured the CIA's Cuban exile agents and their weapons. Undeterred, the CIA tried again to assassinate Castro on April 7, 1963, this time at a stadium, using "grenades and pistols," though again the men and their weapons were captured and, this time, photographed.[6] As with the earlier plotters and weapons, these photos became part of a detailed report put together by Castro years later—a report Richard Nixon wanted so desperately to obtain in 1972 that it resulted in three break-ins at the Watergate complex. What is also significant about the spring 1963 CIA-Mafia attempts is that Johnny Rosselli later admitted to columnist Jack Anderson that he was still actively working with the CIA at the time of these plots—something the CIA left out of its own internal report.[7]

A Kennedy official told us that the Kennedys had had "no inkling" of the CIA's attempts to assassinate Castro during the sensitive negotiations in March and April 1963, and that he, the Kennedy official, didn't learn about the attempts until the Church Committee hearings in the mid-1970s. He also confirmed that the Kennedys' emissary, James Donovan, was in Cuba around the time of the assassination attempts. The Kennedy official seemed appalled that the CIA would so callously risk the life of Donovan and the prisoners he was trying to free, who included three CIA men. In a supreme irony, the official told us that during the negotiations, Donovan actually talked with Castro about "his personal security and [earlier] attempts on Castro's life."[8]

Official CIA accounts date the end of their Castro assassination plots with Mafia chiefs like Santo Trafficante and Johnny Rosselli to early 1963 (although one CIA document admits that the plots lasted until at least June 1963).[9] However, the plots actually continued through the fall of 1963. For example, in the summer of 1963, Johnny Rosselli was seen by military trainer Capt. Bradley Ayers at a CIA training camp for Cuban exiles in upper Key Largo, where snipers were practicing with high-powered rifles.[10] At the same time, Miami CIA Operations Chief David Morales was supporting the CIA's AMWORLD portion of C-Day, but former Congressional investigator Gaeton Fonzi documented that "David Morales . . . worked closely with

Johnny Rosselli."[11] However, Morales's relationship with Rosselli went beyond just working together. An intelligence agent who met both men told Fonzi that "between the two men I witnessed a profound sense of camaraderie that transcended the operational situation." He said that Morales "and Rosselli had a very close relationship."[12] Fonzi documents that Morales was also prone to drinking heavily and, in relaxed social situations, to talking indiscreetly about top-secret operations. All at a time when Fonzi says Morales was working closely with David Atlee Phillips—who was also involved with C-Day and Artime.[13] This may explain the CIA document saying that Artime was involved in the Mafia plots at the same time the CIA was supporting him.[14]

The CIA probably chose Morales to work with Rosselli because Morales had extensive experience with CIA assassination operations, going back to the 1954 CIA Guatemala coup with David Atlee Phillips. Both men had also worked on coup and assassination plots in Cuba, including some of the earliest CIA attempts to eliminate Castro. From 1958 to 1960, Morales was listed as a "political attaché to the American consulate in Havana," according to Johnny Rosselli's biographers.[15] However, according to one expert, "David Morales was probably the highest CIA operations person in Havana in 1959."[16] We will document the roles of Morales and Phillips in the 1959 CIA plots to kill Castro, how those plots led to Jack Ruby's meetings with Santo Trafficante in Havana, and how all of that later impacted C-Day and JFK's assassination.

Another participant in the CIA-Mafia Castro assassination plots at the time of C-Day was a member of Rosselli's Chicago Mafia family, hit man Charles Nicoletti. According to a UPI report, Charles Nicoletti was involved in a Miami-based CIA-Mafia plot to kill Castro in October 1963.[17] Former FBI agent William Turner confirmed that an attorney for Carlos Marcello was also in Miami around that time, trying to recruit a hit man and pilot to kill Castro for a plan backed by "certain well-connected people in Washington."[18] Journalist Scott Malone uncovered FBI surveillance confirming that Johnny Rosselli met with Jack Ruby twice in Miami in October 1963, marking the second time that Ruby had crossed paths with the CIA-Mafia plots (the first time was in 1959).[19] Both Rosselli and Nicoletti were killed by brutal Mafia hits before they could be fully questioned by Congressional investigators about the plots.[20]

The Kennedys had mounted an intense and growing prosecution of the Mafia since taking office—and even before. In 1959 during their Senate rackets hearings, and in 1962, the Kennedys had faced problems going after mobsters because of earlier CIA-Mafia plots.[21] That's one reason the Kennedys were determined to keep the Mafia out of C-Day, and probably why CIA officials such as Richard Helms didn't dare tell the Kennedys that the CIA's plots with gangsters like Rosselli and others were continuing during planning for C-Day. Even the Director of the CIA, John McCone, wasn't told about the ongoing CIA-Mafia plots in the fall of 1963.[22] The evidence suggests that the only CIA officials who knew about the continuing CIA-Mafia plots in 1963 were Helms, Desmond FitzGerald, David Morales, and FitzGerald's predecessor, William Harvey. Part II presents the the CIA-Mafia plots in a whole new light. By revealing new facets of the CIA-Mafia plots from 1959 to the fall of 1963, it shows how the mob bosses used those connections to penetrate C-Day and assassinate JFK. It covers other aspects of the CIA-Mafia plots that would sound like something out of a James Bond movie if they hadn't been documented by the Church Committee: the CIA's "Executive Action" assassination program, codenamed ZRRIFLE, which included a European assassin recruiter codenamed QJWIN.[23]

AMLASH: THE CIA'S PLOT WITH ROLANDO CUBELA

The CIA's plot with mid-level Cuban official Rolando Cubela, codenamed AMLASH, has been known since 1976, but we have discovered new information about this plot, including how it was influenced by C-Day. As pried out of the CIA by the Senate Church Committee, the Cubela plot is disturbing enough, and it has been covered in many books. Briefly, it states that after some contact with Cubela in 1961, the CIA resumed active contact with Cubela in September 1963. According to the CIA account, Cubela wanted to assassinate Castro, and the CIA reluctantly agreed. The CIA's Desmond FitzGerald flew to Paris to meet with Cubela, posing as Bobby's personal representative. Richard Helms admitted that John and Bobby Kennedy, and even CIA Director John McCone, weren't told about the assassination planning with Cubela. On November 22, 1963, just as another CIA case officer was in Paris passing a CIA-constructed poison pen to Cubela to use against Castro, word came of JFK's assassination. The following year, the CIA tried to get Cubela and some of the C-Day Cuban exile leaders—including Manuel Artime—to work together. But Cubela was arrested soon after that, tried, and imprisoned in Cuba for almost twenty years, which should put to rest any thought that Cubela was a double agent for Castro, as some have claimed.

End of story, except for hints from CIA folks over the years that the Kennedys did somehow know about Cubela.[24]

The real story is far more complex. Without knowing about C-Day, the Church Committee could only conclude that "the exact purpose the CIA had for renewing contact" with Cubela "is unknown."[25] Our new information answers several key questions left unresolved by the Church Committee.

Cubela was one of many Cuban leaders who helped defeat Batista, but he was soon marginalized by Castro. Cubela was never very close to Castro, and by 1961 he no longer had much power. However, during the Revolution Cubela had led a small organization, the Revolutionary Directorate (abbreviated DR, forerunner of an exile organization called the DRE run for the CIA by David Atlee Phillips). Castro didn't want to alienate Cubela's former comrades in the DR, so Cubela was given a position with no power but many benefits, including a large travel budget that let him travel in style and relative privacy to Latin America and Europe.[26]

Part II documents Cubela's brief contact with Santo Trafficante in 1959 and Cubela's previously unknown role in the Bay of Pigs for the CIA. CIA testimony indicates that some time after the Bay of Pigs, Cubela wanted to defect. However, the CIA wanted him to stay in place and, in the summer of 1962, resumed contact with him.[27] During the same period, Bobby Kennedy was spearheading a program of sabotage and destabilization in Cuba, called OPERATION MONGOOSE. Recent disclosures from former Soviet officials at conferences about the Cuban Missile Crisis show that Soviet missiles were being placed into Cuba in the late summer of 1962 in response to this rising tide of American action against Cuba.

The CIA usually claims that Cubela surfaced again in September 1963. But one CIA document admits that the CIA resumed efforts to contact Cubela in June 1963, when C-Day was just getting under way. In addition to Cubela, at that time the CIA also renewed or reorganized the CIA-Mafia plots with Johnny Rosselli and their European assassin recruiter, QJWIN.[28] It was as if the CIA wanted to have plots against Castro that only they controlled, instead of being subject to the dictates of Bobby Kennedy or the military.

In the 1990s, Cuban officials revealed to US historians that David Morales had begun working with Cubela on the Castro assassination plots in September 1963.[29] That means that Morales was working on Cubela, the CIA-Mafia plots, and C-Day all at the same time (in addition to AMTRUNK, which we discuss shortly). To Morales, all those plots may have looked like simply different aspects of an overall CIA approach to killing Castro in

November 1963. If so, that was a fatal error for JFK. The involvement of a CIA assassination expert like Morales with Cubela also might explain why journalist Anthony Summers got a picture far different from official CIA accounts when he talked to Cubela in 1978. Cubela told Summers that it was the CIA who was pressuring him to take weapons like high-powered rifles with scopes and plan the assassination of Castro, but that he tried to rebuff them. Summers found Cubela to be "consistent and credible."[30] Official CIA reports show that their efforts with Cubela escalated greatly in October and November 1963.[31]

Among the questions that historians—and CIA officials—have had difficulty answering since the Cubela plot was exposed are: Why was the CIA suddenly trying so hard in the fall of 1963 to get Cubela to assassinate Castro? Why did the CIA's meetings with Cubela—and their pressure on him—increase as December 1, 1963 drew closer and closer? Why would a high CIA official like Desmond FitzGerald make a risky trip to Paris to meet with Cubela personally, even pretending to be the personal emissary of Bobby Kennedy? Why would FitzGerald's supervisor, Richard Helms, admit that he decided it was "unnecessary" to tell Bobby about Cubela? Why would Helms not even tell his own CIA Director about the assassination aspect of the Cubela operation?[32]

FitzGerald's assistant, Sam Halpern, offers one answer. Evan Thomas quotes Halpern as saying that FitzGerald "was really more interested in starting a coup, and he hoped that Cubela could organize other" disgruntled Cuban officials. "But in coups," FitzGerald "understood, people die. The way to start a coup is to knock off the top man." FitzGerald "felt it was a long shot, but it might work. We were desperate . . . willing to try anything."[33]

Why would the CIA's Helms and FitzGerald try so hard to get Cubela to do what the C-Day coup leader was already willing to do? The CIA knew that the coup leader had already been paid to stage the coup, because the CIA had arranged the payment. Harry Williams had been working closely with the two CIA officials assigned to assist him—so the CIA knew that the C-Day coup leader was ready to go, as soon as JFK signaled his personal support and Harry Williams slipped into Cuba for the final meeting. There's no evidence that FitzGerald's assistant knew about C-Day. But it is clear from the evidence that C-Day is the reason Helms and FitzGerald were so desperate regarding Cubela that they took foolish risks. If one were charitable, one could argue that perhaps they wanted Cubela as a backup for C-Day. Or they may have been trying to set up Cubela to take the fall for Castro's death on C-Day, since the coup leader didn't intend to take the blame himself.

If one were not charitable, one could argue that they simply wanted to beat C-Day to the punch with an operation that the CIA completely controlled.

Of course, the above options are not mutually exclusive. Long-overlooked CIA testimony, recently declassified documents, and exclusive new information show that Helms and FitzGerald saw Cubela as a way to support C-Day and obtain intelligence for it, as well as providing a type of cover story when dealing with US officials who didn't know about C-Day.

A Kennedy administration official who wishes to remain anonymous provides an example of the latter. This official didn't work for the CIA, but for another, nonintelligence, agency and was never told about C-Day. But in the fall of 1963, he was told about the Cubela operation.[34] Numerous documents released in 1997 confirm that this Kennedy administration official had contract with FitzGerald, both on various multiagency subcommittees of the National Security Council and individually. In the fall of 1963, he had had some input, both into the Cuba Contingency Plans to keep C-Day secret and into the thirteen drafts of Vance's "Plan for a Coup in Cuba"—all without being told about C-Day. Instead, this official was only told about the Cubela operation.

This marks the first time that any Kennedy administration official outside the CIA has ever admitted knowing about the Cubela operation at the time it was active. He knew about Cubela, was aware of Cubela's relatively low position, and saw any possibility of a coup as being something of a longshot. Yet plans still needed to be made just in case Cubela was able to do something or recruit someone higher in the government to help him. So the CIA was also using the Cubela operation as a cover story for C-Day, when dealing with this US official and probably others like him. It was the only way so much planning could go on for C-Day without making dozens of officials privy to it.

The Kennedy administration official told us that he and his agency "had doubts about some of the projects that Bobby wanted or supported," which is probably one reason he wasn't told about C-Day. Regarding the Cubela operation, the official said that "I don't believe the CIA was rogue during 1963. I thought Des [FitzGerald] was loyal and carried out Bobby's wishes." But the official went on to say that "Des was very bright, a charmer, and full of ideas—though some of them were a little far out" and "I didn't quite trust

Des." The official said that the CIA "often wouldn't fully answer a question unless you knew how to ask it in just the right way." He was certainly correct about that, in ways that he couldn't even imagine. Right after he made that comment, he told us how the CIA described Cubela to him—and the CIA's description clearly included elements of the coup leader that didn't apply to Cubela.

Regarding the Cubela operation, this Kennedy administration official said that "we only had a few discussions about him. In the office, we called him 'Cubela' and not any type of CIA code name, like AMLASH." The official said that the CIA "had presented Cubela to" him "as someone . . . with a position . . . who had influence . . . and could sound out" other government "leaders" who might also be interested in staging a coup against Castro. By presenting Cubela in this way, the CIA was also laying the groundwork for C-Day with this official and others like him. When the C-Day coup happened, this official would simply assume that Cubela had been involved somehow, and had managed to persuade the far more powerful coup leader to act.

However, because this official wasn't told about the C-Day coup leader, he was doubtful that there was actually going to be a coup, since "it was only Cubela." Instead, he saw a coup as "more a possibility than an actual plan, a hope that [other Cuban] leaders might be amenable to such a plan." The official confirmed that "this was in the late summer and early fall" of 1963. However, from what this official knew about the Cubela operation and plans for a coup, he didn't think the plans would succeed, because they didn't include: "1. People high enough [in the Cuban government]; 2. People dedicated to winning; 3. People willing to sacrifice themselves for the coup." This official was right in his doubts about Cubela—only he didn't realize that the Kennedys had a C-Day coup leader who met all those conditions.

When we told him briefly about the real C-Day coup plan, the official said "it wouldn't be the first time Bobby used a two-track approach" to a problem. The official knew only in very general terms that Bobby had other plans in the summer and fall of 1963 to overthrow Castro.

It's important to stress that the CIA "said nothing" to this official "about the assassination" aspect of the Cubela operation. That was something the official only learned years later, from the revelations of the Church Committee. The official said that "I don't know if Bobby knew about that aspect of Cubela or not." While he assumed that Bobby knew about the Cubela operation in general—since he had such a tight rein on covert Cuban operations—the official had no specific knowledge of whether he did or not.

Although Richard Helms said that Bobby, JFK, and CIA Director McCone were not told about Cubela, various CIA defenders and apologists have hinted that Bobby must have known.[35] Eventually, we found a source close to the Kennedys who could state with authority what Bobby knew. This Kennedy aide dealt with C-Day, so he was well aware of the differences between C-Day and the Cubela operation. He had many discussions with Bobby about Cuban operations, and he stated unequivocally that Bobby didn't know about the Cubela operation in the fall of 1963. However, he said that if Bobby had known about the Cubela operation, he was sure that Bobby wouldn't have minded.[36] Our source is a confirmed Kennedy loyalist who later viewed the CIA with some suspicion. Yet what he told us in 1992 matches closely with comments by Richard Helms that were first published three years later, in 1995. Regarding FitzGerald's personal meeting with Cubela in Paris, Evan Thomas quotes Helms as saying that "Bobby wouldn't have backed away" and that if he had informed Bobby about the meeting, Bobby "probably would have gone himself."[37] Nonetheless, Bobby wasn't informed. Nor is there any indication that Bobby was ever aware that the CIA's Cubela plan was "interfering with" C-Day by November 1963 (as the DIA's General Carroll said) or that the Cubela plan was penetrated by mob boss Trafficante.[38]

It's also interesting that Helms admitted that he and FitzGerald didn't bother telling CIA Director John McCone about the Cubela plot, just as they didn't tell McCone about the ongoing CIA-Mafia plots.[39] However, McCone did know about C-Day, and that knowledge helps to explain two matters that left unanswered questions for Senate Church Committee investigators back in 1976. One of those was a briefing that McCone gave to new President Lyndon Johnson on November 24, 1963 at 10:00 A.M. This was just two days after JFK's death, on the day of JFK's funeral. With Washington full of world leaders waiting to see LBJ, who was now the focus of world attention, it must been a very urgent matter. The briefing was about "CIA operational plans against Cuba." However, as the Church Committee report notes, "that briefing could not have included a discussion of" the Cubela plot, "since McCone testified that he was not aware of the" Cubela "assassination effort." Of course, the one Cuba plan the CIA was involved in that did demand immediate attention was C-Day. Harry Williams had postponed his trip to Cuba after JFK's death, but otherwise all the C-Day coup and invasion plans were ready to go.

Church Committee investigators also uncovered an unusual memo from about two weeks later, dated December 9, 1963. This memo to CIA Director

McCone "discusses US operations against Cuba" and although it "did mention a plot for a coup in Cuba, it does not refer to the" Cubela operation. It couldn't have referred to the Cubela operation, because McCone didn't know about it at the time. Although the Church Committee investigators didn't realize it, the memo must have been referring to C-Day. In fact, the memo they uncovered went on to ask McCone to encourage LBJ to give the same type of speech supporting the coup that JFK had given in Florida on November 18, 1963.[40]

The fact that the Cubela operation was a different operation from C-Day, and that C-Day was the big coup operation while Cubela was just a sideshow, is confirmed by a CIA memo, which says that "Rolando Cubela" was not the real leader or the major individual in the plot to eliminate Castro, although the CIA confirms that the actual name of the leader "is known to us."[41] The long-secret testimony of Cubela's CIA case officers to the Church Committee makes Cubela's role even clearer and indicates that at least one reason the CIA's Helms and FitzGerald were backing Cubela was to avoid what they feared would be a "bloody coup" on C-Day. When Cubela's two case officers testified, they said that they'd recently talked to people at the CIA about what they should say.[42] They didn't reveal C-Day, but they did come close, and they made it clear that the Cubela operation was in support of a separate US attempt to stage a coup against Castro.

The case officers realized that Cubela wasn't high enough in the government or powerful enough to stage a coup. As one said, Cubela had been "an important person at the time of the revolution and the overthrow of Batista" in 1959. But by 1963, "he certainly didn't figure prominently in Castro's cabinet. Obviously, he didn't hold much of a position" in the Cuban government.[43] One said that Cubela's "assignment" was "trying to screen and to look for Cubans whom we could use for a planned operation inside Cuba . . . a coup against Castro." The Church Committee attorney doing the questioning seems surprised to hear about a coup being planned against Castro in the fall of 1963, since the Cubela operation was understood to be basically a very small assassination operation. The attorney asks, "Were there papers on this coup?" The case officer responds that "I did not see the papers that were approved or were sent over to the higher authority for approval." Notes of a National Security Council subcommittee meeting indicate that "the higher authority" refers to JFK, so the case officer is saying that he didn't see the papers that were sent over to the White House for JFK's approval. The case officer stresses that "The objective, as I understood it, why we were doing all of this was in order to foment an . . . internal coup, against Castro. That was the objective."[44]

However, the case officer is careful to point out that in his talks with Cubela, the operation was "talked about in general terms as a . . . coup against Castro and not specifically in assassination terms."[45] Of course, the case officer points out, "The discussion of assassination as part of a . . . coup is evident by the description of the word 'coup,'" since assassination "could always happen." The case officer said he realized that in "planning" a "coup in Cuba, consideration would have to be given for the elimination or neutralization of the leadership." However, the case officer claims that the subject of "assassination" was "raised by" Cubela "as a way he foresaw of eliminating the coup." The case officer says that Cubela also suggested that assassination "could very easily be part of the . . . coup, that this could take place in a . . . coup."[46] The case officer says that Cubela "requested the high-powered rifles with the scopes and these were the center of the discussion," and that the CIA agreed to provide them in "late November [1963]."[47] In fairness to Cubela, it should be pointed out that he contended that it was the CIA who wanted him to assassinate Castro and wanted to give him rifles with scopes, not the other way around.

The case officer said that the CIA had another interest in Cubela as well. He said "the primary interest" in Cubela "was to [have him] develop intelligence in the . . . power around Castro," by which he meant "the power . . . which could overthrow Castro." He stressed that "we were looking for the information at the highest levels" of the Cuban government. In retrospect, it seems clear that the CIA wanted information about the C-Day coup leader, a high official who did have the power to overthrow Castro.[48]

This is confirmed by a CIA document from 1964. After JFK's death, LBJ shut down the C-Day operation, but in 1964 the CIA tried to revive the Cubela operation, this time attempting to combine it with three of the former C-Day Cuban exile leaders, most notably Manuel Artime. According to a November 1964 CIA memo, when Artime heard that the C-Day coup leader was no longer involved and that the relatively powerless Cubela was the highest Cuban official in the plan, he said "if [Cubela] is the chief of the dissident group we can all forget about the operation."[49]

One of the few ways in which the Cubela operation and C-Day were similar was that both had been penetrated by associates of godfather Santo Trafficante. The FBI picked up information in October 1963 that a Miami informant had learned about the Cubela plot, and similar information was reported in 1964 and 1965, including by a Trafficante associate. However, the FBI didn't bother to tell the CIA what their informant had heard.[50] It's ironic and tragic that a Mafia godfather like Trafficante not only knew about C-Day, but also knew about two plans—the CIA-Mafia plots and Cubela—that even JFK and Bobby didn't know about.

AMTRUNK

There was one more CIA plot to topple Castro that had begun before C-Day materialized, but this one the Kennedys knew about from the start. The CIA code name for this plan was AMTRUNK, and it was the brainchild of Pulitzer Prize–winning *New York Times* reporter Tad Szulc.

AMTRUNK, which began in February 1963, was in some ways a forerunner to C-Day. It also had some similarities to the Cubela operation, but AMTRUNK was a separate operation in 1963. This is confirmed by a CIA Inspector General's Report about CIA plots to kill Castro, which Helms had prepared for LBJ in 1967, when newspaper columnist Jack Anderson first hinted at the CIA-Mafia plots. The long-secret report discussed at length the CIA-Mafia and Cubela plots, and finally added that "two other plots were originated in 1963, but both were impracticable and nothing ever came of them."[51] Based on many other CIA documents, that must be a reference to AMTRUNK and C-Day (AMWORLD).

A CIA AMTRUNK document says "the proposal for this operation was presented to CIA by Tad SZULC, via Mr. Hurwitch, the State Department Cuban Coordinator, in February 1963." Also called the "Leonardo Plan," AMTRUNK's "objective was to overthrow the Cuban government by means of a conspiracy among high-level . . . leaders of the government culminating in a coup d'etat."[52] CIA notes say the first meeting about AMTRUNK "was held in (a) safehouse in Washington, between Hurwich" and "Tad Szulc, *New York Times* reporter," and five others: someone from the US Information Agency, a Cuban exile, and three people from the CIA. One of the CIA representatives was "David Morales," who seems to have been involved in almost every CIA assassination and coup plan directed against Castro in 1963.[53]

AMTRUNK was larger than the basically one-person Cubela operation, but far smaller than C-Day. AMTRUNK, however, was not able to recruit anyone high in the Cuban government, and the plan thus remained in its embryonic stages. A CIA report confirms that "in November 1963 the" AMTRUNK "program was still trying to develop leads into higher echelons of the military and civilian leadership."[54] However, AMTRUNK still served a purpose: Because it was less secret than C-Day, it could be talked about in general terms in Bobby's Cuban subcommittee meetings of the National Security Council. Also, AMTRUNK perhaps explains why the Kennedys were so eager to pursue the C-Day operation: It was the very thing the Kennedys had hoped for since February. C-Day fit perfectly into the Kennedys' existing plans, and it quickly surpassed AMTRUNK as their primary focus.

The CIA's case officers for AMTRUNK were the same as for the Cubela operation.[55] One told the Church Committee that it would be fair to say that "the AMTRUNK operation" was "comparable to the" Cubela "operation but simply involve[d] different characters."[56] In contrast, the case officers for C-Day were different—and weren't case officers in the traditional sense: They were assigned to assist Harry Williams and the other C-Day Cuban exile leaders, not to give them orders as was usually the case.

Since Tad Szulc worked on AMTRUNK and later wrote about events surrounding C-Day, we asked Harry Williams if Szulc worked on C-Day or knew about it in 1963, but Williams said no. Months after JFK's death and the end of C-Day, the CIA combined some elements of AMTRUNK with the Cubela operation and a few former C-Day Cuban exile leaders like Manuel Artime, which is probably when Szulc learned some information about C-Day.[57]

Szulc was active in AMTRUNK into the fall of 1963, as verified by a CIA memo about a meeting Richard Helms had at the White House about AMTRUNK.[58] Gus Russo found a note by Helms that states that the CIA was to "maintain periodic contact with Szulc on Cuban matters at Presidential request."[59] However, the AMTRUNK plan simply failed to produce any inroads into the high levels of the Cuban government needed to stage a coup against Castro.

In that way, AMTRUNK was similar to a plodding bureaucratic effort by a combined "DIA-CIA task force," which had worked for months to identify Cuban leaders who might be able to stage a coup. At the big November 12, 1963 subcommittee meeting about Cuba headed by JFK, the CIA's Desmond FitzGerald had updated the group about the DIA-CIA task force, saying they had "prepared a report covering some 150 Cuban . . . leaders" and that "out of this figure" there were "45 which look interesting." He then slipped in a reference to AMTRUNK, C-Day, and the Cubela operation, saying that the "CIA is in touch with three persons . . . in such circles."[60]

That covers all the major plans that the CIA had under way to get rid of

Castro in the fall of 1963, in addition to C-Day. There was also an ongoing program of minor sabotage and hit-and-run raids against Cuba, but those weren't seriously intended to topple Castro: Their main purpose was to keep Castro on edge and to provide a steady stream of covert activity so it wouldn't be obvious when the real action began as C-Day approached.

CHAPTER NINETEEN

US "Assets into Cuba"

ON NOVEMBER 22, 1963, several US assets were getting ready to go into Cuba in support of C-Day—and other Kennedy and CIA operations—in addition to Harry Williams. Harry told us that "I think there were many, many [US assets] going in that direction. Most of whom I didn't know . . . I was just one of them."[1] Before, during, and after the C-Day coup, it would be vitally important to have intelligence from US assets in Cuba. Declassified documents show why several young men in particular would try to get into Cuba starting in September 1963, with three attempting—and two succeeding—on November 22, 1963.

Shortly before the C-Day plan began in May 1963, a State Department "Memorandum for the President" said that "Aggressive, comprehensive, and continuing intelligence gathering in depth on Cuba should be identified as a primary objective of the national intelligence effort." Copies of the memo were also sent to the CIA, the Defense Department, the Justice Department, and the US Information Agency for their concurrence.[2] As we've noted, in May 1963 the Joint Chiefs of Staff were asking for "the introduction by CIA as soon as practicable of assets into Cuba for the development of intelligence" using "a suitable cover plan."[3] This confirmed earlier plans about the "liquidation of . . . Castro" noted earlier that included "increasing the volume and quality of [covert collection of] intelligence" using "assets trained and controlled by [the] CIA."[4]

As the plan for C-Day developed further, the need for certain types of assets increased. The Coup Plan by Secretary of the Army Cyrus Vance from September 1963 stressed that once the coup had started, "reliable reports from trained American observers in Cuba are essential to making a decision to intervene."[5] The Joint Chiefs pointed out that quickly getting such "observers" into Cuba after a coup had begun would be difficult, so that meant getting more assets into Cuba in advance of C-Day.[6] That's why Harry was going into Cuba prior to C-Day, as were others. Cuba is a large country, and the CIA would need to know how the average citizen was reacting to the coup not just in Havana, but in the major cities in other regions of Cuba.

However, the CIA was having problems with its usual methods of sneaking agents into Cuba by speedboats at night. As noted earlier, twenty-five of the CIA's operatives going into Cuba "had been either captured or killed," and even those who made it into Cuba weren't safe because outsiders were "viewed with suspicion."[7]

So the CIA had been trying other methods of getting intelligence assets into Cuba. If an asset could get into Cuba openly, as a friend of Cuba, he or she might not be "viewed with suspicion." By having a carefully constructed cover story, such a person could even be introduced to Cuban officials or proudly shown new facilities, instead of having to hide in the shadows.

A Kennedy administration official told us that since there wasn't a US Embassy in Cuba, "French and British" sources were used in Cuba for intelligence activity, "along with other NATO allies." However, because of the intense secrecy surrounding C-Day—which was not supposed to look like a deliberate, pre-planned invasion—this was not an option. Instead, US intelligence assets entered Cuba "usually through Mexico" with "some through Montreal."[8] Both Mexico City and Montreal had regular flights to Havana. The Kennedy administration official stated "there was a consistent effort" to get assets into Cuba during "the Spring . . . Summer and Fall of 1963." He said that "usually under the" CIA "they were always infiltrating and exfiltrating" people into and out of Cuba "for intelligence purposes."[9]

In addition to the need to get US assets into Cuba, Bobby Kennedy, the CIA, and the intelligence agencies that made up the DIA faced two other major problems. One was how to contain the Soviets in Cuba after Fidel and Raul were killed. The other problem was who would get the blame for killing Castro, since the Cuban populace could hardly be expected to follow someone who had killed the leader many of them still admired. The evidence indicates that getting a certain type of US asset into Cuba could effectively deal with both problems.

A solution appears to have arisen by September 1963, when Cyrus Vance submitted to the Joint Chiefs the thirteenth draft of the "Plan for a Coup in Cuba," cited earlier. The summary notes that "if the sympathy of the Cuban people was demonstrably on the side of the insurgents," then "the United

States would have a solid moral basis for action." It predicts that after the coup, "most of the population will probably remain passive but generally in sympathy with the insurgents." Yet the summary also notes that "Castro is the unchallenged leader of Cuba" and "an important minority of the Cuban people now apparently gives positive support to Castro," while "the majority passively accepts his regime."[10] But if most Cubans "support" or "accept" Castro's regime, then why would "most of the population" be "in sympathy with the insurgents," after those very insurgents had just killed Castro in a coup?

Harry Williams told us that while he knew that the C-Day coup leader would have Fidel and Raul killed, he made it clear that the coup leader didn't intend to take responsibility for their deaths. Regarding plans to set up someone to take the blame for Castro's death, Harry said "yeah, well, those were active." He said that after Castro's death, "if somebody goes on the ground and they pick him up . . . I guess they get the blame." But Harry said he didn't know any specifics about such plans, and implied that that was something Bobby and the CIA were handling, saying "I didn't know everything."[11] It made sense to leave Harry out of the loop on setting up a patsy. That way, if Harry were caught by hostile forces in Cuba, he could never be tortured into revealing something that he didn't know.

The CIA needed a patsy not only for C-Day, but also for the CIA's other fall 1963 plans to assassinate Castro. Whether you believe Cubela when he says the CIA was pressuring him to kill Castro, or the CIA's version in which Cubela wants to kill Castro, all the documents and testimony about Cubela show that he was very concerned about his own safety and didn't necessarily want to take the fall for killing Castro. However, despite Cubela's concerns, the CIA documents released so far say nothing about what the CIA was doing to address them. The AMTRUNK agents were probably equally concerned about their safety and not having to take the blame for killing Castro.

The Senate Church report confirms that in the fall of 1963, the CIA was paying the European QJWIN to recruit assassins for its "Executive Action" program to kill "foreign political leaders." But no experienced professional hit man would take on the task of killing a foreign official, especially on an island, unless he were also provided with someone to take the blame. Otherwise, the hit man himself would immediately become the focus of an intense manhunt. The same would apply to the CIA-Mafia plots, which still involved Johnny Rosselli in the fall of 1963. Rosselli knew the importance of having a patsy on hand, to be blamed and then quickly killed, to take the heat off the real killer. As we detail in Part II, the 1954 assassination of the

Alabama Attorney General–elect in Phenix City by Trafficante associates had been a fiasco that resulted in a massive crackdown and martial rule by the National Guard—all because there had been no patsy to take the blame. In contrast, the aftermath of the 1957 assassination of the president of Guatemala—linked to mob associates of Rosselli—had gone smoothly, since a seemingly lone patsy had been quickly blamed and killed. Once the Guatemalan patsy's room had been found to be full of Communist propaganda, that was all the motive the police, the press, and most people needed, and the investigation ended there.

If the person who took the fall for killing Castro was a US asset who was a Russian or Russian sympathizer, that would solve several problems for Bobby Kennedy, the CIA, and the US military: It would allow someone besides the coup leader to be blamed, and it would instantly neutralize the Soviet troops and influence in Cuba once the coup leader publicly blamed the Russians. One of Rosselli's CIA associates had considered setting up a Russian or Russian sympathizer to take the fall for the assassination of Castro, according to notes uncovered by the Church Committee. Desmond FitzGerald's predecessor in the anti-Castro operations was the hard-drinking, pistol-toting William Harvey. Until FitzGerald took over in early 1963, Harvey ran QJWIN and the CIA-Mafia plots to kill Castro under the CIA's "Executive Action" plan, part of which had the code name ZR/RIFLE.[12] William Harvey's handwritten notes for these plans say "Cover: planning should include provision for blaming Soviets." Harvey wanted to be sure that in case there were any problems with his assassination operations, the Soviets—or, if that wasn't possible, then their allies the Czechs—took the fall.[13] Harvey's notes even warned of the "Dangers of RIS (Russian Intelligence Service) counter-action . . . if they are blamed."[14]

Just a few months after Desmond FitzGerald took over CIA Cuban operations from William Harvey, C-Day planning began and the Joint Chiefs asked the "CIA" to find "a suitable cover" plan for their "assets" going into Cuba.[15] The CIA's existing "Cover: planning . . . for blaming Soviets" would have been ideal. When Harry was asked about a "blame the Russians" plan for C-Day, he replied "it makes sense to me."[16] As for having someone like that appear to be pro-Castro, so they could easily get into Cuba before C-Day, Harry said "that could very easily be . . . I am sure, it happened." Although, again, he cautioned us that he didn't know any specifics about that part of the C-Day plan, implying that they were handled by Bobby Kennedy and the CIA.[17]

Under the best of circumstances, it was difficult for the US to get intelligence assets into Cuba, even low-level informants. The US assets most likely to get into Cuba openly—those with ties to Russia and apparent Castro sympathies—would also meet William Harvey's "cover" criteria, to be able to blame the Soviets if there were any problems with an assassination attempt. At the same time, such an asset would have made an excellent patsy for C-Day or the CIA plots to kill Castro in the fall of 1963.

The low-level US "asset" would simply be an informant, someone to provide intelligence, with little idea of the main operation. But if the low-level informant was maneuvered to be in the right place at the right time by his handler, such an asset could have been very valuable as a patsy to the CIA for one of their plots to kill Castro.* The coup leader, an admired and popular figure to the Cuban people and respected in other parts of the world, would likely have been the one laying the blame on such a person. His pronouncements—and whatever evidence of guilt he could produce—would carry enough weight to convince most of the Cuban people. The evidence suggests several people of interest to US intelligence who could have been utilized like that for C-Day, including three young men in particular. They could have also been used—unknowingly, on their part—by the Mafia for their own purposes.

Each of the men was in his early twenties, and all three had Russian connections in their recent past. FBI and Warren Commission files show that all three young men tried to leave the US to get into Cuba from Mexico just after the JFK assassination, and two of them succeeded. For one of the three, it was his second attempt to get to Mexico and on to Cuba. A declassified Warren Commission memo says that one of the men was on a "mission," and another source says he was an asset for a US law enforcement or intelligence agency.[18] One of the men was a person of interest in the Chicago assassination attempt (Miguel Casas Saez); the second was a person of interest in the Tampa assassination attempt (Gilberto Lopez); and the third was the prime suspect in Dallas, Lee Harvey Oswald.[19]

We will detail much more about this in upcoming chapters. For example, when Oswald made his first attempt to get to Cuba by visiting the Cuban Embassy in Mexico City, CIA files show that two other young men (not the

---

* We do not want to suggest that the CIA would consider using a low-level intelligence "asset" or informant as an assassin. That would be left to a professional—in the case of C-Day, either the coup leader himself, an experienced revolutionary, or one of his trusted men. In the case of the CIA-Mafia plots, the CIA had turned to the Mafia and people like QJWIN because they were professionals.

Chicago and Tampa suspects) also linked to Artime and David Atlee Phillips visited the Embassy and tried the same thing. The odds of three young men linked to Artime and Phillips trying the same thing on the same day only two months prior to C-Day are remote at best, unless they were all part of the same program to get US intelligence assets into Cuba. This attempt by Oswald and the other two occurred just after Vance delivered his thirteenth draft of the Coup Plan to the Joint Chiefs.[20] We noted earlier a US official's comment that assets got into Cuba via either Mexico City or Montreal, and the only two foreign cities the Warren Commission received credible reports of Oswald visiting in 1963 were Mexico City and Montreal.[21]

Also, in the summer of 1963 Oswald had a very public confrontation in New Orleans with a Cuban exile who was formerly close to Rolando Cubela, making Oswald a suitable fall guy for that operation as well. As we document, the Cubela operation was penetrated by associates of Santo Trafficante, Rosselli's partner in the CIA-Mafia plots against Castro. Rosselli reportedly visited Oswald's employer in New Orleans in the summer of 1963. It's unfortunate if the CIA were using someone like Rosselli to set up a patsy for supposedly killing Castro, since the real target of Rosselli—and his allies Marcello and Trafficante—was JFK, not Castro. After Oswald was captured, his room was also found to be filled with recent American Communist propaganda, even though he had studiously avoided attending any Communist meetings since returning to America. That evokes the scene a few years earlier, following the assassination of the president of Guatemala by Rosselli associates, when the seemingly lone Communist patsy was found to have a similar stash of Red literature.[22]

While J. Edgar Hoover and Lyndon B. Johnson had little if any official knowledge of C-Day prior to JFK's death, both learned much (but not all) about the plan after LBJ became president. LBJ had a phone taping system in the Oval Office, which recorded the following exchange on November 28, 1963, six days after JFK's death: LBJ asked his trusted friend Hoover if Oswald "was connected to the Cuban operation with money," and Hoover replied "that's what we're trying to nail down now."[23] We believe the "Cuban operation" LBJ is referring to is probably C-Day. Keep in mind that for Hoover and LBJ, who learned about C-Day and some of the other plots only after the fact, C-Day, AMTRUNK, Cubela, and the CIA-Mafia plots might appear to be just parts of one big CIA operation against Castro.[24]

CHAPTER TWENTY

The Chicago and Tampa Assassination Attempts and C-Day

THE CUBA CONTINGENCY PLANS DISCUSSED in Chapter 12 were central to protecting C-Day, for dealing with the "assassination of American officials" if Castro found out about C-Day or the other plots and tried to retaliate in advance.[1] Efforts by key officials to keep C-Day and the other plots from being exposed helps to explain why the Chicago and Tampa attempts have remained secret for so long, and why "over one million" CIA documents related to JFK's death have still not been released.

The Cuba Contingency Plans were meant to buy time so the President could make a reasoned response that would not cause a needless rush to war. The thinking behind those plans appears to have been put into effect during and after the attempts to assassinate JFK in Chicago and Tampa, when news of the attempts was kept out of the press at the time. It's important to note that we say "the thinking behind those plans," because most of the mid-level officials actually making the plans didn't know about C-Day or those assassination attempts. However, higher officials seeing the planning—like Bobby Kennedy or Richard Helms—knew about C-Day and the attempts, and their actions would have been influenced by what they had read and the scenarios the Cuba contingency planners had developed.

The suppression of news about the assassination attempts by Bobby Kennedy and other officials, to allow time for a thorough investigation and prevent a hasty response while protecting C-Day, began in Chicago, continued in Tampa, and affected the release of information after Dallas. As detailed in Part III, the three attempts share several elements in common, such as reports in each of gunmen with high-powered rifles with scopes. In each city, one or more of the shooters would be in a building, and in each case the building overlooked or was near a sharp turn where JFK's motorcade would have to slow to a crawl. In Tampa and Dallas, the key buildings are strikingly similar, tall red-brick affairs with dozens of unguarded windows. Also, in each case at least one Cuban or seeming Cuban sympathizer was reported to be in the area and later became a focus of investigation. Each of the men seemed to be connected to C-Day, ensuring that the thinking behind the Cuba Contingency Plans would be put into effect, and much would have to be suppressed to protect C-Day. The fact that these men were reported in more than one of the three target cities, and other similarities in their movements preceding the assassination, demonstrates that they were being manipulated by the same people, for the same reason. As noted briefly in this and the following chapters—and documented extensively in Part II—each of the three attempts was also tied to the Mafia, specifically associates of Johnny Rosselli (part of the Chicago Mafia family), Santo Trafficante (godfather of Tampa), and Carlos Marcello (whose territory included Dallas). The mob bosses had one basic plan that was applied in each of the three cities, giving them a backup in case earlier attempts had to be called off.

In Chicago, CIA documents say that the Cuban reported in the area just prior to JFK's motorcade and the assassination attempt was named Miguel Casas Saez, aka Angel Dominguez Martinez, and he always seemed to be one tantalizing step ahead of the authorities.[2] He was conveniently reported to be in Chicago just before JFK canceled his November 2, 1963 motorcade there, in Florida shortly before JFK's Tampa motorcade, and in Dallas when JFK was shot. In other words, the Cuban was always reported to be in just the right place at the right time to trigger the cloak of secrecy of the Cuba Contingency Plans to protect C-Day. Whether the Cuban agent was a real person, or just an impression created by a series of coordinated informant reports, the point was that the CIA and other agencies like the FBI thought he was real. And his presence in places like Dallas caused consternation at the highest levels of the CIA, as was recently documented by veteran intelligence journalist Joseph Trento.[3] This also had the effect of hiding the three Mafia bosses' role in the assassination—not just in Dallas, but also in Chicago and Tampa.

The Chicago assassination attempt against JFK on November 2, 1963—three weeks before Dallas—is covered in detail later, but the following brief summary is from the files of former Senate investigator Bud Fensterwald. Five years after the attempt, he found several Chicago newsmen at the *Chicago Daily News* who knew about the four-man threat in Chicago, even though they did not write about it at the time. One of the newsmen said "at the time of JFK's scheduled visit to Chicago [on November 2, 1963] there were four men in town who planned an assassination attempt from one of the overpasses from O'Hare into town. They were seized but apparently not arrested." The assistant city editor also recalled "a disassembled rifle in the story." However, as Fensterwald's memo of the interview with the newsmen puts it, "for some reason" the story about the assassination attempt "did not get in the paper."[4] In the rush for news after JFK's death, many newspapers, even in Chicago, published all sorts of unverified rumors and speculation, but the four-man Chicago attempt was still not reported in the press at that time, even as a rumor.

The Kennedys and other officials were able to keep the Chicago assassination attempt out of the press in 1963 for a number of reasons. The Kennedys had an unusually good relationship with the news media, one of the factors that allowed them to stifle any mention of JFK's numerous extramarital affairs until almost a decade after his death. Also, when it came to matters of national security, the pre-Watergate, pre-Pentagon-Papers news media were especially accommodating. JFK himself talked about this in his prime-time TV news conference shortly after the Cuban Missile Crisis, when JFK told the television audience that "at least one newspaper learned about some of the details [of the Missile Crisis] on Sunday and did not print it for reasons of public interest." Regarding other news about the Missile Crisis, JFK told his audience that "there were obvious restraints on newspapermen."[5] One reason for the failure of the Bay of Pigs was that there were press reports before its launch, so the Kennedys realized the importance of keeping their covert Cuban operations out of the press. Miami was the center for most CIA covert Cuban activity, and two senior CIA officials later told Bill Moyers that "they had explicit arrangements with the press" in Miami "to keep their secret operations from being reported, except when it was mutually convenient."[6]

However, the Chicago story did circulate privately among journalists in the days following JFK's assassination. By December 9, the FBI had learned of the Chicago newsmen's story. The result was an "urgent" FBI teletype to the head of the Dallas FBI office from the head of the Chicago FBI office, concerning two of the same newsmen Fensterwald would locate five years later, in regard to an incident in which "four men [were] arrested [in] Chicago, Nov. Two," 1963, one of whom was linked to JFK's assassination. However, by that time Hoover had already announced that Oswald was the lone assassin, so the FBI's efforts were mainly directed at downplaying the Chicago story, not exploring the lead.

However, the FBI teletype does contain a very carefully worded response from Chicago Secret Service Chief Maurice Martineau, which changes the subject rather than explicitly deny the existence of the four-man threat.[7] Martineau was one of several Chicago Secret Service personnel who were reticent and evasive regarding the four-man threat, even when talking to Congressional investigators fifteen years after the incident. It was only in the 1990s that Martineau finally confirmed the existence of the threat. (The existence of the four-man threat was probably a key reason Martineau said that, based on "his own role in the investigation," he believed "there was more than one assassin" in Dallas.)[8]

Former Chicago Secret Service Agent Abraham Bolden had no problem confirming the four-man Chicago threat, and he told Congressional investigators and Fensterwald that it was handled differently from any other threat against the President. Bolden said that when Chicago Secret Service Chief Martineau first learned of the threat shortly before JFK's scheduled visit, he told Bolden and the other agents that "There were to be no written reports; any information was to be given to him orally." The chief would "report only by phone to" the head of the Secret Service, James "Rowley, personally."[9]

Instead of the usual file number, Bolden testified that any written information was put into a "COS" file, which stands for "Central Office" and "Secret." Bolden said COS "files were kept separate from all others and that" the Secret Service "could say they had nothing in their files on a subject when in fact a 'COS' file existed." After the last-minute cancellation of JFK's trip to Chicago due to the threat, Bolden says "the memos were then taken to O'Hare airport and given to a crew member of a commercial flight to Washington where he believes" a Secret Service "employee met the flight and delivered the material to [Secret Service] headquarters."[10]

But that wasn't the end of the secrecy about the four-man threat. Bolden said that "shortly after the [JFK] assassination," the Chicago Secret Service chief "called all agents into his office and showed them a memo from Washington to the effect that the Secret Service was to discuss no aspect of the assassination and investigation with anyone from any other federal agency now or any time in the future. Every agent . . . was made to initial this memo." Bolden thought this memo was directed at the "FBI" who "wanted to get the role of Presidential protection away from" the Secret Service.[11] Former Chicago "FBI Agent Thomas B. Coll," decades later, recalled that "Some people were picked up. And I'm telling you it wasn't ours. That was strictly a Secret Service affair . . . you'll get no more out of me."[12]

By the day of JFK's scheduled Chicago motorcade on November 2, 1963, only two of the four Chicago suspects had been detained, so there was still an active threat, with potential assassins on the loose. In addition, two of the suspects had Hispanic names—"Rodriguez" and "Gonzales"—indicating a possible Cuban connection. Combined with Immigration and Naturalization Service (INS) and CIA reports of a Cuban agent in the Chicago area, the situation looked like the worst-case scenario of the Cuba Contingency Plans: possible Castro retaliation for C-Day by "assassination of an "American official"—but on American soil, something the officials had considered "unlikely." The motorcade had to be cancelled at the last minute, even as Secret Service agents were at the airport to meet JFK, and people were already starting to line the motorcade route.

But a key reason for the cancellation—the assassination plot—could not be released to the press or most officials, because it could have led to C-Day. The initial reason given for JFK's sudden cancellation was a "cold," although that was quickly changed to the need for JFK to stay in Washington to deal with the aftermath of the assassination of Vietnamese President Diem. While Diem's death probably was a factor in JFK's decision, news services had already run a story saying that special equipment had been installed in Chicago so JFK could monitor the tragic events in Vietnam during his Chicago visit, and even Congressional investigators were unable to determine the real cause of JFK's last-minute Chicago cancellation.[13]

While some members of the press knew about the Chicago threat, the Kennedys couldn't allow it to be reported. If the threat were made public, and the four men turned out to be Cuban agents retaliating for C-Day, then C-Day could be exposed. That could have resulted in a dangerous confrontation with the Soviets, just a year after the Cuban Missile Crisis.

Remarkably, there is no evidence that those making the Cuba Contingency Plans were told about the Chicago threat. They were mid-level officials, and knowledge of the Chicago (and Tampa) threats appears to have been limited to higher officials, especially those in the Secret Service and FBI—two agencies not directly involved in the Cuban Contingency Planning. However, very high officials like Bobby Kennedy who were seeing the Contingency Plans did know about the Chicago threat, and it probably influenced their decisions to keep the lid on the Chicago and Tampa attempts.

Could the Mafia have been behind the reported presence of a Cuban agent in Chicago, a key main factor that triggered such extreme secrecy? Many recently declassified files confirm that the Mafia had penetrated many Cuban exile groups, even those involved in C-Day. Moreover, files and testimony clearly show that men working with Rosselli, Trafficante, and Marcello easily had the capability to bring someone from Cuba to the US or to manipulate informants to make it appear that way.

The Mafia had many ways to safely feed certain information—and disinformation—to federal and local agencies in Chicago, all linked to the Chicago mob's Johnny Rosselli. Rosselli was working for the CIA at the time, and was especially close to CIA official David Morales, the Chief of Operations at the huge Miami CIA Station, home base of the CIA's part of C-Day, code-named AMWORLD. Earlier, Rosselli had worked on the CIA-Mafia plots with Richard Cain, who in 1963 was the Chief Investigator for the Cook County (Chicago) Sheriff's Office.[14] CIA documents quoted later confirm that Cain not only knew about C-Day but was feeding information to the CIA about C-Day exile leader Tony Varona.[15]

Cain was also an FBI informant at the time, but his real loyalty was to Chicago godfather Sam Giancana, Rosselli's boss, since Cain was an actual "made" member of the Mafia (real name: Ricardo Scalzetti).[16] Other Rosselli associates in 1963 with the ability to spread disinformation were former Chicago FBI Chief Guy Banister and Chicago native Jack Ruby, both of whom knew about C-Day according to FBI reports. Banister had been the head of the Chicago FBI office in the 1950s, so he not only knew how to feed information to the FBI and how they would react, but he had also worked with other federal and local law-enforcement agencies in Chicago. Ruby had grown up in Chicago and cut his teeth on organized crime there—including a murder that Bobby Kennedy had written about a few years earlier—before being sent by the Chicago mob to Dallas.[17] Ruby still maintained ties to Chicago, and in the summer of 1963 Ruby was an informant for two Chicago police detectives.[18]

So Rosselli and his associates like Morales, Cain, Banister, and Ruby could easily make sure federal agencies knew that a possible Cuban agent was in the Chicago area—or at least make them think one was. It's no coincidence that government files and investigators link Rosselli, Morales, Cain, Banister, and Ruby not only to knowledge of C-Day but also to JFK's assassination. In fact, a declassified CIA document confirms that a key informant about the supposed Cuban agent at that time was one of David Morales's operatives, from the group code-named AMOT.[19] The Cuban agent's presence in places like Dallas caused consternation at the highest levels of the CIA, as recently documented by veteran intelligence journalist Joseph Trento.[20]

Later in the book, we'll document everything known about the seeming Cuban agent, who some CIA reports say was a very ordinary person, with little money ("a poor person, poorly dressed"), from a relatively small town in Cuba, certainly not the type of person Castro would send if he really wanted to commit sabotage or assassination.[21] Still, the reports of an alleged Cuban terrorist prior to JFK's visit to Chicago—as well as Tampa and Dallas—while C-Day was imminent were enough to trigger the thinking behind the Cuba Contingency Plans, which is what the Mafia needed to hide their own involvement in JFK's death. Because of all this talk about a supposed Castro agent, it should be noted that both Richard Helms and former CIA official David Atlee Phillips—both very active in the CIA's Cuban operations in 1963 and after—went "on the record" shortly before their deaths and wrote that they didn't think Castro had anything to do with JFK's assassination.[22] As Castro himself said after JFK's assassination, it would be foolish for him to do something that would justify a US invasion of his country.[23] Instead, in cases where CIA informants who tried to link Castro to JFK's death are named, almost all the "informants" turned out to have ties to associates of Marcello, Trafficante, or Rosselli.[24]

Secret Service Agent Abraham Bolden told us that he knew not only about the Chicago attempt to assassinate JFK, but also about the attempt in Tampa, during JFK's November 18 motorcade, just four days before Dallas.[25] This isn't surprising, since two of the Hispanic names that Bolden recalled from the Chicago investigation—Gonzales and Rodriguez—also came up in the Tampa investigation, according to a high Florida law-enforcement source.[26] While the Warren Commission may have read the brief FBI report of the Chicago JFK threat rumor, none of the Commission members or staff knew anything about the Tampa assassination attempt. That's because the very day Bolden was going to tell them about Tampa and Chicago, he was framed and arrested, in an incident detailed shortly.

In the weeks following the Chicago attempt, new reasons emerged for JFK and Bobby Kennedy to keep it secret and to suppress news reports of any threats that might emerge during JFK's upcoming November 18, 1963 trips to Tampa and Miami. Just five days after the Chicago attempt, American newspapers reported that Soviet leader Nikita Khrushchev had publicly warned the "US that attack on Cuba will lead to war."[27] That made it all the more crucial that no hint of C-Day, and any possible tie it might have to the threats in Chicago and Tampa (and, later, Dallas), could be make public.

Three days after Khrushchev's threat, the Kennedys were probably surprised by a front-page newspaper article that hinted at C-Day. Written by Al Burt, the journalist who later wrote the extensive article on Artime and C-Day quoted in Chapter 12, the article on the front page of the November 10, 1963 *Miami Herald* attracted little public attention at the time or in the years that followed. We only found it while poring over microfilm records of every edition of major Florida newspapers for November 1963. We were looking for unusual articles about Cuban operations, especially those that were dropped from later editions or never followed-up—which is how we discovered the Tampa assassination attempt against JFK.

In retrospect, it's obvious from reading Burt's November 10, 1963 *Miami Herald* article that his sources knew that something big was up. Burt wrote that "Recent events make it undeniable that a secret war is being waged against Fidel Castro." He said that "the full size and scope of the war has not been revealed," but the war was "like an iceberg—the part that shows only hints at the part that doesn't." Burt noted that "What is known reveals a well-organized and equipped military operation that . . . keeps opposition alive inside the island." He said that his "sources point out that the war stepped up its pace in the last three months, and that any new acceleration could change the possibilities [of overthrowing Castro]."[28]

Burt was right on the money, even though his article flew in the face of what most newspapers were reporting: stories about the recent US crackdown on Cuban exile raids. Burt's article also noted that "On Oct. 21 [1963], the Cuban Armed forces captured an armed band of infiltrators" who "admitted . . . their purpose was to . . . prepare the people for armed uprising."

Why would Burt's sources leak him information that even hinted at an operation as secret as C-Day, less than three weeks before the coup was to happen? The answer is in the next part that Burt wrote, when he said that "Fidel finds a US Central Intelligence agent behind every plot. If the US is involved to the extent Castro says, it is getting far less credit than deserved from those critics who say nothing is being done about Cuba." Apparently, Burt's sources were responding to an article from two days earlier in which "critics" had slammed JFK over Cuba. Two days before Burt's article, the *Miami Herald* had run a story from the *Los Angeles Times* wire headlined

"Kennedy Ducking Cuba Problem, GOP Says." The article said "The Republican Party warmed up the Cuban issue Thursday, with the charge that the
Kennedy administration had 'swept Cuban affairs under the rug' since the
Missile Crisis of October, 1962." Apparently, Artime or one of his lieutenants
had leaked information hinting at C-Day to Burt, to counter the Republican
criticism of JFK.

Burt's article apparently caught the attention of someone in Washington,
because there were no more such leaks prior to C-Day.

We do not think Burt would have written the article if it he'd known
about the actual C-Day plan—it would have been like a British journalist
writing a front-page article hinting at D-Day, shortly before the Normandy
invasion. Having a source like Artime (or someone close to him) and having
them hint to you that something very big is brewing is not the same as
knowing the date for C-Day, the identity of the coup leader, or facts about
the US military's invasion plans. Still, leaks like Burt's November 10, 1963
newspaper article added even more pressure for the Kennedys to launch C-
Day on schedule, and to keep a lid on anything that might expose it.

The Tampa Police Chief on November 18, 1963, J. P. Mullins, confirmed
the existence of the plot to assassinate JFK in Tampa that day. While all news
of the threat was suppressed at the time, two small articles appeared right
after JFK's death, but even then the story was quickly suppressed. Mullins
was quoted in those 42-year-old articles, and he didn't speak for publication
about the threat again until he spoke with us in 1996, firming not just the
articles but adding important new details.

The Tampa attempt is documented in full for the first time in any book
later; but, briefly, it involved at least two men, one of whom threatened to
"use a gun" and was described by the Secret Service as "white, male, 20,
slender build"[29] (a description far closer to Oswald than the initial description issued in Dallas after JFK's murder there). According to Congressional
investigators, "Secret Service memos" say "the threat on Nov. 18, 1963 was
posed by a mobile, unidentified rifleman shooting from a window in a tall
building with a high power rifle fitted with a scope."[30] That was the same
basic scenario as Chicago and Dallas.

Chief Mullins confirmed that the police were told about the threat by the
Secret Service prior to JFK's motorcade through Tampa, which triggered even
more security precautions. One motorcade participant still recalls com-

menting at the time that "at every overpass there were police officers with rifles on alert."[31]

In addition to Chief Mullins, we spoke with a high Florida law-enforcement source about the Tampa motorcade, a man who wishes to remain anonymous because of his efforts against the Mafia, though his veracity and position have been verified by the Tampa Chief of Police. The official said that he was certain there was going to be a hit on November 18 in Tampa and that JFK was informed of the threat. Perhaps that's why Kennedy appeared "handsome, tan, and smiling" when in front of the crowds, but backstage the official said he appeared "tired and ill."[32] Nevertheless, JFK went out of his way to present a fearless image in Tampa, in spite of the threat. After finishing one of his speeches, JFK "surged out into the crowd, which immediately engulfed him. The Secret Service men with him went crazy," according to a report in a local newspaper. The article also noted a motorcade participant's recollection of "how concerned everyone was when" JFK "stood up in the car as he rode through the streets of Tampa after his talk."[33] JFK had to project a confident façade to the media—and the coup leader in Cuba—in case news of the assassination threat leaked before JFK could give his important speech in Miami later that day, with passages written especially for the coup leader.

Tampa godfather Santo Trafficante had the means not only to know that the plan to kill JFK in Tampa had been uncovered by authorities, but also to know the suspects who were being sought, and that the plot was being kept out of the press (just as in Chicago). The high Florida law-enforcement official confirmed that Trafficante had a man in a key position in an important law-enforcement agency in the Tampa-St. Petersburg area, who had an important position helping with security for JFK's motorcade. The official felt that Trafficante's lawman had tipped off the godfather that the assassination plot had been uncovered.[34]

Chief Mullins and the Florida official confirm that local law-enforcement agencies were not told about the Chicago threat, just sixteen days earlier. However, when the heads of federal agencies got reports of suspected Cuban involvement in the Tampa attempt—including two of the same Hispanic names that surfaced in the Chicago attempt—their reaction was the same as in Chicago: A tight lid of secrecy was clamped down on all information about the threat.[35] As noted earlier, there was no mention of the Tampa assassination threat in the local or national press at the time—just two brief articles almost a week later, which received no follow-up. After JFK's death, the

Tampa threat still could not be made public, since there was still the chance that Oswald or other suspects might prove to have connections to Castro or C-Day. Even weeks or months after JFK's death, the public's faith in the Secret Service, already at a low ebb after Dallas, would have been shaken to the core if it had been revealed that they had covered up an assassination attempt in Tampa that had so many parallels with Dallas.

Top US officials who knew about C-Day or the Cuba Contingency Plans must have had several concerns about the assassination plots in Chicago and Tampa. First was whether or not the attempts were linked to Castro, and might be retaliation for C-Day or other US actions against Cuba. (Officials had been worried about that since September 1963, when work had begun on the Cuba Contingency Plans.) But to investigate any Cuban connections thoroughly, the assassination attempts had to be kept out of the news, to avoid pressure for quick action or a rush to judgment. Also, to ensure that C-Day remained a closely held secret and that there were no leaks to JFK's critics in Congress and potential rivals in next year's election, official paperwork about the threats and the investigation had to be minimized.

Secret Service agents in Tampa were probably subjected to the same pressure for secrecy as those in Chicago. That helps to explain why Chicago and Tampa Secret Service agents' testimony was so vague and unhelpful to Congressional investigators in the late 1970s.[36] It also explains why, in the mid-1990s, the Secret Service destroyed documents about JFK's motorcades in the weeks before Dallas, rather than turn them over the JFK Assassination Records Review Board as the law required.[37] As noted earlier, that destruction occurred just weeks after the authors had first informed the Review Board about the Tampa attempt.[38]

There is clear evidence that the Secret Service and other agencies handled the serious JFK assassination attempts in Chicago and Tampa far differently from earlier assassination attempts we've researched. Since just after JFK's election, most attempts to kill him would briefly make the newspapers at the time of the incident.[39] That was even true for minor, routine threats to JFK in Chicago and Tampa in the fall of 1963, attempts that were clearly unrelated to Cubans or C-Day.[40] However, these two threats were kept out of the newspapers at the time. No report of the Chicago attempt appeared in local newspapers for over ten years. The Tampa attempt was kept completely out of the news media at the time of JFK's visit, and for four days afterward. Only two small articles about the Tampa attempt finally appeared after JFK's death, one in Tampa on Saturday, November 23, and one in Miami on Sunday, and there were no follow-up articles in either paper.[41] The two articles went unnoticed by Congressional investigators and historians for decades, and this is the first book to ever quote them. The Tampa assassination attempt would not be mentioned in any newspaper article for the next four decades.

The thing that made the attempts to kill JFK in Chicago and Tampa (and later, Dallas) different from all previous threats was the involvement of Cuban suspects—and a possible Cuban agent—in each area. In addition, these multiperson attempts were clearly not the work of the usual lone, mentally ill person, but were clearly the result of coordinated planning. The Chicago and Tampa assassination attempts took place in the weeks prior to C-Day, when US officials were still making plans for dealing with the possible "assassination" of "American officials" in retaliation for US actions against Castro. Until it could be determined if that was the case in Chicago and Tampa, information had to be kept out of the news media and investigations conducted with the utmost secrecy.

Because of the cover-up of the Tampa attempt, both at the time and from each of the ensuing government commissions and Congressional committees, the many parallels between the Tampa and Dallas (and Chicago) attempts have never been listed, until this book. While they would have been apparent to high officials like Bobby Kennedy and J. Edgar Hoover, they have never been made public. There were almost a dozen parallels between Tampa and Dallas—detailed in later chapters—such as official concerns about the motorcade's hard left turn in front of a tall red-brick building with many unsecured windows. Just as the House Select Committee on Assassinations concluded that Dallas was most likely the result of a conspiracy involving Tampa godfather Santo Trafficante, Secret Service agent Sam Kinney revealed in 1996 that the threat in Tampa had "something to do with organized crime."[42] The high Florida law-enforcement official mentioned earlier was more direct, bluntly saying that Trafficante was behind the plot and explaining why he called it off at the last minute. Chief Mullins added that "he did not know if the other two" men who threatened JFK in Tampa "may have followed the Presidential caravan to Dallas."[43] We later document men linked to Jack Ruby and Trafficante who did travel from Tampa to Dallas between the two attempts.[44]

In both the Tampa and Dallas attempts, officials sought a young man in his early twenties, white with a slender build, who been in recent contact with a small pro-Castro group called the Fair Play for Cuba Committee (FPCC). In Dallas that was Lee Harvey Oswald, but the Tampa person of interest was Gilberto Policarpo Lopez, who—like Oswald—was a former defector to Russia.[45] We will document eighteen parallels between Dallas suspect Lee Harvey Oswald and Gilberto Policarpo Lopez, but here are a few:

Like Oswald, Lopez was also of interest to Naval Intelligence. Also similar to Oswald, Gilberto Lopez made a mysterious trip to Mexico City in the fall of 1963, attempting to get to Cuba. Lopez even used the same border crossing as Oswald, and government reports say both went one way by car, though neither man owned a car. Like Oswald, Lopez had recently separated from his wife and had gotten into a fist-fight in the summer of 1963 over supposedly pro-Castro sympathies.[46] Declassified Warren Commission and CIA documents confirm that Lopez, whose movements parallel Oswald in so many ways in 1963, was on a secret "mission" for the US involving Cuba, an "operation" so secret that the CIA felt that protecting it was considered more important than thoroughly investigating the JFK assassination.[47] Our high Florida law-enforcement source confirmed that Lopez was an asset for another agency, though he did not say whether Lopez was a "witting" or "unwitting" asset (agencies like the CIA use those two categories, since sometimes assets are the source of information or action without realizing the true nature of their associates).

Lopez's "mission" for a US agency involved trying to go to Cuba—via Texas and Mexico City—on the day the countdown to C-Day was to begin, November 22, 1963. This is yet another parallel to Oswald, since a long-overlooked memo written by Warren Commission Counsel David Belin says that on November 22, 1963, Oswald could have been trying to go from Texas to Mexico; regular flights to Cuba were available in Mexico City.[48] As with Oswald, the Mafia had found a way to link Lopez to the C-Day Cuban exile groups, by linking him to Oswald.[49] Oswald was linked to Lopez via informant reports of a visit by Oswald to Tampa and someone with its small Fair Play for Cuba Committee chapter, the same group Lopez visited on November 17, 1963, the day before JFK's Tampa trip.

We should note that our analysis of all the documented information about Tampa's Gilberto Lopez indicates that he had no knowing involvement with JFK's assassination. But he would have made a perfect patsy for the Mafia if

JFK had been assassinated in Tampa four days before Dallas. Government reports confirm that Lopez was in Texas the day after JFK's assassination, and indicate that he may have been there on the day of the assassination. Unconfirmed newspaper reports do place him in Dallas at the time JFK's death. If so, that means that if something had happened to Oswald before JFK's murder, there still would have been a similar patsy on hand to pin it on.[50]

If facts about the Tampa threat and its many similarities to Dallas had come out right after JFK's death, the public would never have bought the "Oswald-as-lone-assassin" theory. However, a truly wide-ranging investigation could have exposed C-Day, since the Mafia had been careful to tie Lopez to Oswald and therefore to the C-Day Cuban exile groups. That's why the Warren Commission was never told about the Tampa threat or C-Day.

Did Bobby Feel Responsible?

THE CHARACTERISTICS OSWALD AND LOPEZ shared would have also made both men ideal as US intelligence assets in Cuba for C-Day. It has long been known that both men attempted to go to Cuba prior to C-Day—unlike Oswald, Lopez actually succeeded—though they were just two of what Harry Williams called "many going in that direction."[1] If they were part of C-Day, that could explain reports that Bobby Kennedy felt responsible in some way for his brother's death.

Two declassified documents confirm that Gilberto Lopez was on a "mission" involving a highly secret US intelligence "operation" in November 1963. Most documents about Lopez were withheld even from the Warren Commission and later Congressional investigations, and most that have been released are often heavily censored.[2] However, one declassified memo confirms that when Lopez went from Florida to Texas to Mexico to Cuba in late November 1963, he was on a "mission" that the Warren Commission tried to learn more about.[3] They were not successful, which is why Lopez is not mentioned in their final Report.[4] A CIA document unavailable to the Warren Commission and finally declassified in 1994 confirms that Lopez was involved in an "operation" so secret that its name is still classified. The document in question was prepared by Richard Helms on December 4, 1963 for the CIA Station in Mexico City, where David Atlee Phillips was stationed. The memo is highly unusual in that Helms tells them "we assume you have not told" another agency about Lopez going to Cuba "on 27 November [1963] because you do not want to blow the [censored] operation. This problem is up to you."[5] Although Lopez was the subject of an urgent investigation by the CIA and the FBI to see if he had been involved in the JFK assassination, apparently the "[censored] operation" was considered by

Helms to be even more important.[6] Imagine the pressure to invade Cuba if a young Cuban like Lopez had been fingered for JFK's assassination instead of—or in addition to—Oswald.[7]

When the CIA's Richard Helms testified to the House Select Committee on Assassinations, he said that any intelligence interest in Oswald would have been handled by the "intelligence organs of the Defense Establishment."[8] In 1963, that would have meant General Joseph Carroll's recently created Defense Intelligence Agency (DIA), which oversaw the various military agencies like Naval Intelligence, its close affiliate Marine Intelligence, and Army Intelligence. Helms's comment makes sense for ex-Marine Lee Harvey Oswald, but it doesn't explain why secret Tampa FBI reports on Gilberto Lopez—a young male defector from Cuba who was never in the US military—were sent to several branches of the DIA, including Naval Intelligence, Army Intelligence, and the Air Force Office of Special Investigations.[9] If files on Lopez were being sent to several branches of the DIA after JFK's assassination, it raises a question as to whether one or more of the agencies had a file on Lopez prior to JFK's death.

Many of Oswald's military intelligence files were kept hidden from the Warren Commission and then destroyed. Investigative journalist Anthony Summers documented that "US Army Intelligence had a file on Oswald before the assassination. As a result, a Colonel in intelligence was feeding information to the FBI within an hour of Oswald's arrest."[10] However, he notes that "the Warren Commission was never supplied with the Army Intelligence file on Oswald."[11] Years later, when Congress tried to see the file, "Congressman Richard Preyer" told Summers that "those records had been destroyed." Congressman Preyer lamented that "the Army file on the Kennedy assassination has been destroyed, and we don't know why it was done."[12]

Why would the Army have a file on an ex-Marine, who would more logically fall under Naval Intelligence or Marine Intelligence? It makes sense when you consider that all of those agencies were part of the Defense Intelligence Agency under General Carroll. As the CIA C-Day document we quoted earlier showed, General Carroll was involved in C-Day. A confidential Naval Intelligence source—detailed later—explained to us that when Oswald was under "tight" surveillance prior to the assassination, they often had to keep tabs on him in areas where Naval Intelligence didn't have a lot of resources. In those cases, they used informants from other agencies, both military and CIA.[13]

We noted earlier that starting in May 1963, the Joint Chiefs asked the CIA to start getting "assets" into Cuba under a suitable "cover." A well-documented incident might be related to this. Journalist Jim Hougan writes that "in June 1963" the "Chief Security Officer of the State Department" named Otto "Otepka was ordered removed from office by Secretary of State Dean Rusk." This was because Rusk and the Kennedys suspected that Otepka had given classified information to the "ultra-conservative" head of the "Senate Subcommittee on Internal Security." But Rusk didn't just remove Otepka from his office: "Rusk also ordered his safe drilled open" and the contents removed. Apparently, there was something very sensitive that Rusk and the Kennedys didn't want leaked. However, "according to Otepka, the only 'non-routine' material in the safe at that time was a half-finished study on American defectors, including one Oswald, Lee Harvey. Coincidentally, Oswald had just received a new passport from the State Department on the day Otepka was ousted. According to Otepka, the study on defectors was initiated by him because neither the CIA nor military intelligence agencies would inform the State Department which defectors to the Soviet Union were double agents working for the United States. Asked whether Oswald was 'one of ours or one of theirs,' Otepka recently grouched, 'We had not made up our minds when my safe was drilled and we were thrown out of the office.'"[14]

Journalist Joe Trento, who has excellent CIA sources, once wrote about "a theory shared by some internal CIA investigators. They believe Oswald was working for US intelligence . . . and that this explains his life in Russia," referring to Oswald's highly unusual defection to Russia right after he left the Marines.[15] There are also indications that Oswald was still "working for US intelligence" in 1963. Earlier, we cited a CIA document about an operation directed at the Fair Play for Cuba Committee which involved both David Atlee Phillips and James McCord, alleged by *Vanity Fair* and FBI veteran William Turner to have been a CIA contact for Harry Williams during C-Day planning.[16] Both Oswald and Lopez had contact with the Fair Play for Cuba Committee in 1963. Former CIA officer Joseph Smith worked with David Atlee Phillips, and he told *Vanity Fair* that "I think Oswald may have been part of a penetration attempt" against the Fair Play for Cuba Committee.[17]

Former Senator Richard Schweiker says that in the summer of 1963, "Oswald was playing out an intelligence role . . . I personally believe that he had a special relationship with one of the intelligence agencies." Schweiker was in a good position to know, since he chaired—along with Gary Hart— the Church Committee's subcommittee which looked into the JFK assassination. This gave Schweiker access to much classified material, some of which has never been made public, such as Tad Szulc's secret AMTRUNK testimony. Schweiker said that "all the fingerprints I found during my eighteen months on the Senate Select Committee on Intelligence point to Oswald as being a product of, and interacting with, the intelligence community."[18]

A link between the Defense Intelligence Agency's General Joseph Carroll and Oswald comes from the files of former Senate investigator Bernard Fensterwald. After leaving the Senate, Fensterwald represented clients like James McCord, before becoming a leading Freedom of Information Act (FOIA) attorney and prying documents about the JFK assassination out of reluctant agencies. Fensterwald created a research center in Washington, D.C., to make those documents available to researchers. It was also a place where investigative journalists could share their files, and Fensterwald kept scrupulous notes of his conversations with journalists and investigators. Among these are the notes of a conversation he had with a source who told Fensterwald he had learned that "Lee Harvey Oswald had connections to an 'intelligence service.' . . . It was a 'new intelligence service that was formed in 1962 called the Defense Intelligence Agency . . . I got the name of the general who was the guy who supposedly made the arrangements and he won't talk. His name is General Joe Carroll, he was the founder of the DIA . . . obviously Army Intelligence was running what turned into the DIA. And that's probably why the Army was going nuts' over Oswald's part in the assassination."[19]

According to *Vanity Fair*, General Carroll and Army Intelligence weren't the only ones "going nuts" when Oswald's name quickly surfaced as a suspect after JFK's assassination. The magazine noted that when CIA veteran David Atlee Phillips died, he "left behind an unpublished manuscript for a novel." Phillips was the CIA agent who worked on C-Day and allegedly met Oswald in public two months before JFK's assassination. *Vanity Fair* states that Phillips's novel "features a character apparently modeled on himself, a CIA officer who served in Mexico City." Phillips's character says "I was one of the two case officers who handled Lee Harvey Oswald. We gave him the mission of killing Fidel Castro in Cuba . . . I don't know why he killed Kennedy. But I do know he used precisely the plan we had devised against Castro. Thus the CIA did not anticipate the President's assassination, but it was responsible for it. I share that guilt."[20]

Vanity Fair broke the story of Phillips's novelized confession in their December 1994 issue.[21] Former Senate investigator Gaeton Fonzi says that Phillips's meeting with Oswald and Menoyo's partner Antonio Veciana was

just a couple of months before the JFK assassination, around the time
Phillips was working on C-Day.[22] Veciana told us that Oswald and Phillips
were discussing what "we can do to kill Castro." Veciana made that revelation to us on June 2, 1993, a year and a half before *Vanity Fair* revealed that
Phillips wrote that he had given Oswald "the mission of killing Fidel Castro."
The fact that Veciana's story independently matched that of Phillips gives
credence to both accounts.

During his life, Phillips was adamant in his claims that he hadn't met
Oswald or Veciana in Dallas, even threatening and filing lawsuits over the
allegation, which dogged him the last fifteen years of his life.[23] So it was
quite surprising to most people to learn about Phillips's secret, novelized
confession, which was only discovered after his death. A confession like that
of David Atlee Phillips may be good for the soul, but keeping so much secret
while he was alive also kept him from uncovering the truth. Phillips may not
have known that Marcello, Trafficante, and Rosselli hadn't just penetrated
the CIA-Mafia plots and the QJWIN operation, but also C-Day. So, the mob
bosses had many ways to find out "precisely the plan we had devised against
Castro." Phillips was wasting his time trying to figure out "why he [Oswald]
killed Kennedy," when the historical record—detailed in Part II—clearly
shows that Marcello, Trafficante, and Rosselli "killed Kennedy" to stop
Bobby's relentless prosecution of them and their associates.

However, by penetrating C-Day and supporting operations like the US
assets into Cuba, the mob bosses made it appear as if somehow the C-Day
plan itself had backfired and resulted in JFK's murder. Harris Wofford was
one of Bobby's close associates, who later became a distinguished Senator
from Pennsylvania. In his book about JFK and Bobby, Wofford asked if Bobby
was, "to some significant extent, directly or indirectly, responsible for his
brother's death." Wofford wrote that "keeping from the public facts about the
CIA, the FBI, and the Mafia crucial to the investigation of his brother's"
murder "must have caused him [Bobby] special suffering." According to
Wofford, "There was nothing Robert Kennedy could see to do or say about
it. There was no way of getting to the bottom of the assassination without
uncovering the very stories he hoped would be hidden forever. . . . [Bobby]
took no steps to inform the [Warren] Commission of the Cuban and Mafia
connections that would have provided the main clues to any conspiracy."[24]

A more direct link between Bobby, C-Day, and Oswald comes from a man who Warren Commission and FBI documents confirm knew Oswald.[25] The man is Adrian Alba, who owned the parking garage next to Oswald's place of work in New Orleans in the summer of 1963. Oswald often talked to Alba and looked at his gun magazines. Also, "Alba had a contract to look after a number of unmarked cars belonging to the Secret Service and the FBI" in New Orleans.[26] Alba once saw Oswald take a large envelope from an FBI "agent from Washington." But more surprising was what Alba learned from a Secret Service agent after the assassination.

According to author Gus Russo, "Oswald's friend Adrian Alba . . . told *Frontline* investigator Scott Malone that RFK's network in New Orleans had considered recruiting Oswald for the Castro assassination plot." We should note that "RFK's network in New Orleans" included private detective Guy Banister, the former FBI chief in Chicago. Banister once shared an office with top Kennedy aide Carmine Bellino, and Banister had served in the FBI with DIA chief General Joseph Carroll. Banister was involved in anti-Castro operations tied to Bobby Kennedy, and two of Banister's close associates—including David Ferrie—knew about C-Day. Unfortunately for Bobby, Banister was also the private detective for godfather Carlos Marcello in 1963.

According to his interview with the PBS *Frontline* investigator, Adrian Alba said that "Oswald was one of ten dossiers given to RFK to assassinate Castro." Russo writes that "Alba's sources for this information" included "John Rice of the Secret Service (who parked his car in Alba's garage)." Alba's "sources also told him that after the assassination, RFK was seen in the Justice Department wailing, 'I've killed my own brother!'"[27]

Bobby's later comments to aides like Richard Goodwin and others show that he soon realized that Carlos Marcello was behind his brother's death. However, the Attorney General knew that proving that in a court of law was probably impossible, given the way top mob bosses insulated themselves from actual hits. Harris Wofford quotes Bobby as saying to a Senate Committee two months before JFK's death that for mob hits, top godfathers "have insulated themselves from the crime itself" so "to have somebody knocked off . . . the top man will speak to somebody who will speak to somebody else who will speak to somebody else and order it."[28] Plus, even trying to prosecute the mob bosses would have jeopardized Bobby's ongoing efforts to prosecute Marcello and Hoffa, and go after Trafficante and Rosselli, for crimes far less difficult to prove than a conspiracy to murder the Attorney General's own brother. Attempting a truly thorough investigation of the roles of Marcello and the others would have meant involving hundreds of investigators from many federal, state, and local agencies, which would have certainly exposed C-Day and probably cost still more lives.

We should note that neither Bobby nor David Atlee Phillips nor General Carroll would likely have ever considered having someone like Oswald actually try to shoot Castro. The record shows that Oswald was a terrible shot, even when he practiced frequently in the Marines, sometimes missing the entire target—and even the Warren Commission found no reliable record that he had practiced even once since returning from Russia. However, if someone like Oswald were in Cuba as a low-level intelligence asset, he could easily have been manipulated to be in the right place at the right time to help with a plot or to take the fall for Castro's death. With Oswald's recent stay in Russia, his Russian wife, and his recent visits and calls to the Soviet Embassy in Mexico City, it would have been easy for the C-Day coup leader to pin Castro's death on the Soviets, thus instantly neutralizing all the Soviets still in Cuba. Gilberto Lopez also had a connection to Russia—he had a brother undergoing military training in Russia—so he would have also made a good patsy for one of the plots to kill Castro.

Bobby's comment that "I've killed my own brother" and Phillips's comment that the person who shot JFK "used precisely the plan we had devised against Castro" are also echoed in an article by a familiar name: Pulitzer Prize–winning journalist Haynes Johnson. Johnson wrote the article in 1967, just four days after David Ferrie's sudden death soon after Jim Garrison's investigation had gone public. The article sums up Garrison's theory at that point, one that was soon lost as various parties started trying to sabotage and feed disinformation into his investigation (among them were Bobby Kennedy's top Hoffa aide Walter Sheridan, and Cuban exiles like Rolando Masferrer who were linked to the assassination). Haynes wrote that supposedly "Oswald was working with an anti-Castro right-wing organization and actually intended to kill Fidel; that Oswald's publicly pro-communist activities in New Orleans and his attempt to enter Mexico and secure a Cuban visa were a ruse to enable him to carry out that Castro assassination objective."[29]

Haynes Johnson's article also contains two more pieces of information that shed light on the case and how Oswald came to be involved. Johnson writes about David Ferrie—who worked for Carlos Marcello and Marcello's detective, Guy Banister—being a pedophile. He says that Ferrie was involved in a "morals case" with a "15-year old boy" who "said at the time that he had flown to Cuba with Ferrie on several occasions."[30] Ferrie was Oswald's Civil Air Patrol instructor when Oswald was about that age (a photo exists of them together), and Ferrie apparently encouraged Oswald to join the Marines.[31] Activities like the Civil Air Patrol and the Marines were hardly the activities one would expect from a budding Communist, but they make sense in light of Oswald's favorite TV show, *I Led Three Lives*, about a US agent who only pretended to be a Communist.[32] Oswald had lived that fantasy while he was a defector in Russia, being the center of attention in Minsk and living very comfortably. But when he returned from that assignment—and there was no attempt by the KGB to recruit him or his wife—Oswald seemed resigned to a drab and poor life in New Orleans. It was probably all too easy for his old associate Ferrie to interest him in a new assignment.

There are other indications that Oswald was doing intelligence work in the fall of 1963 and was under very close surveillance. In the 1960s, there was much cooperation between the police departments of large cities, military intelligence, and the CIA. One article from the summer of 1963 specifically noted such cooperation in Dallas, Texas.[33] When British Television asked Dallas Police Chief Jesse Curry if he believed reports that "Oswald was, or had been some kind of an agent," Chief Curry answered "I can believe it, yes."[34] Former FBI Director Clarence Kelley said that much was known about Oswald's activities in Mexico City, not just from "the wiretaps and cameras" that were eventually disclosed to the Warren Commission and Congressional investigations, but also from never-revealed "informants and other types of foreign intelligence techniques."[35]

Two *New York Times* articles document unusual US government surveillance of Oswald prior to JFK's death, related to Oswald's mysterious trip to Mexico City in late September 1963. On November 25, 1963—the day after Oswald's death—the *Times* reported that when Oswald crossed the border from Texas into Mexico, his "movements were watched at the request of a 'Federal agency at Washington,'" according to "William M. Kline, assistant United States Customs Agent-in-Charge of the Bureau's Investigative Service" at Laredo, Texas.[36] The following day, the *Times* reported from Mexico City that "there were reports here also that his [Oswald's] movements were followed in Mexico by an unidentified United States agency."[37] The CIA's official story has always been that they didn't even know, until after he had left, that Oswald had been in Mexico City. Much more evidence of Oswald's role in intelligence work is detailed later in this book.

Like Oswald, Gilberto Lopez was a troubled, unhappy young man. Just as Oswald was stymied in trying to get a good job because of his dishonorable discharge (something Oswald desperately wanted to change), Lopez was also stymied by the lack of a US government document. According to Lopez's wife, who talked with us in her first interview since a conversation she had had with the FBI in 1964, Lopez wanted to go back to Cuba very badly in 1963 because his mother still lived there. Lopez's wife said that he was worried about his mother and wanted to see her before she died.[38] But Lopez's US passport had expired several months after he made a mysterious trip from Florida to Cuba and back in 1962, around the time of one of the CIA-Mafia plots against Castro involving Johnny Rosselli and Tony Varona.[39] Due to the laws about Cuban exiles in effect in 1963, Lopez could not get a new passport. (Only Cuban exiles working for Artime or one of the other C-Day exile groups were able to easily travel outside the US, without regard to paperwork.). That left Lopez, like Oswald, subject to manipulation to get a government document he wanted. As we noted earlier, a high Florida law-enforcement official confirmed that Lopez was an "informant" for some agency. Declassified files confirm at least seventeen parallels between Oswald and Lopez and their actions in 1963, showing that they were being manipulated by the same people.

But Oswald and Lopez weren't the only unusual young men who attempted to get into Cuba via Mexico City in the fall of 1963. In addition to the Cuban cited earlier—Miguel Casas Saez, who seemed to shadow JFK in Chicago and Dallas—we know of two more, including one who appears in a Warren Commission document that wasn't published in their Report or twenty-six volumes of supporting material. This young man, Manuel Porras Rivera, just two years older than Oswald and Lopez, was from Costa Rica, where C-Day exile leader Manuel Artime had one of his bases. Investigative journalist Anthony Summers writes that Porras left Costa Rica and "traveled first to Miami," where, "by his own admission," he "had meetings with anti-Castro activists. Porras then proceeded to Mexico City with the intention of obtaining a Cuban entry visa." Summers notes that Porras just happened to visit "the Cuban Embassy on Saturday, September 26 [1963], a day when Oswald was also there." Porras left Mexico "on October 3, the same day as Oswald." Using the same border crossing as Oswald (who was being "watched" at the time "by a Federal agency"), Porras then "traveled to Dallas and then New Orleans." Summers says that "Costa Rican Intelligence" was "aware" that Porras "planned to infiltrate Cuba."[40] Two of the mysterious things about Oswald's trip to Cuba have always been the reports of his appearance (such as his height), which varied from the way he really looked, and documented calls in which a person claiming to be Oswald spoke

Spanish (Oswald couldn't speak Spanish).[41] Summers points out that Porras's height and physical description were "very much like the man remembered by witnesses in Mexico" as being Oswald.

There was yet another unusual young man whose actions also parallel those of Oswald, Gilberto Lopez, and Manuel Porras Rivera. Former *Time* magazine journalist Robert Sam Anson documented from Warren Commission records that "Gilberto Alvarado . . . said he was in Mexico City in September 1963" at the same time as Oswald. Alvarado said he went to the Cuban Embassy there "to get a visa for travel to Cuba, on 'a penetration mission for the Nicaraguan Intelligence Service.'"[42] Summers documented that "Alvarado was handled and debriefed by David Atlee Phillips," and CIA documents link Phillips to C-Day around this same time. In addition, Summers writes that the Nicaraguan government claimed that Alvarado was "a known Communist," even though "the Americans concluded Alvarado was [a] Nicaraguan intelligence agent—a fact he admitted."[43] The parallel to Oswald and Lopez, both of whom appeared to be Communists at times, but who also seemed to have intelligence connections, is striking. As a Nicaraguan agent, Alvarado would have been under the control of Nicaraguan strongman Luis Somoza, who was backing C-Day exile leader Manuel Artime at the time.

Summers points out that Alvarado used some of the exact same phrases used by the men who had tried, two months earlier, to link Oswald to C-Day leader Manolo Ray's JURE in Dallas. Further, one of the exiles in the JURE incident used phrases similar to a CIA report about Miguel Casas Saez containing information from one of David Morales's agents. The clear link to all three is Johnny Rosselli, who was working with Morales at the time of the Saez reports and who was close to Alvarado's handler, David Atlee Phillips. In addition, Rosselli had a close associate named John Martino who was linked to the JURE incident.

We only know about Alvarado, Oswald, Lopez, Porras, and Saez—all young men trying to get into Cuba via Mexico City around the same time— because they came to the attention of law-enforcement authorities after the JFK assassination. It's possible that others tried to get into Cuba, perhaps even succeeding like Lopez and Saez, but that their identities were never exposed. If some of these agents are still in Cuba, as Lopez and Saez may well be, it would be yet another reason for US intelligence to keep so much so secret for so long. (The names of Lopez and Saez have long been declassified and named in other books, so we are not endangering their lives by discussing them here.)

Earlier, we documented that the C-Day operations of Harry Williams, Artime, Menoyo, Ray, and Varona had been thoroughly penetrated by the Mafia, so it's likely that the plans to send US intelligence assets into Cuba prior to C-Day had been penetrated as well. The young men who were US assets would have only been focused on their intelligence mission, and would have known nothing about JFK's assassination or that some of those monitoring or directing their mission had other agendas. Oswald, Lopez, Porras, and Saez all spent time in the fall of 1963 in US cities controlled by Trafficante or Marcello, both of whom had ties to Alvarado's Nicaragua. Just as some of those working on C-Day were actually working for the Mafia, some of those working with US intelligence assets going into Cuba were also working for the Mafia. That certainly applies in the case of Oswald, who worked for Guy Banister and with David Ferrie in the summer of 1963, while both Banister and Ferrie were employed by Carlos Marcello.

Pieces of C-Day: Banister and Ferrie; Martino and Cain

US INTELLIGENCE OPERATIONS TO support C-Day in the summer and fall of 1963 could have also been used to support the other Kennedy plan to eliminte Castro—AMTRUNK—and the CIA's other Castro assassination operations. These supporting operations included getting US intelligence assets into Cuba prior to C-Day, and getting intelligence on various C-Day participants. In earlier chapters, we looked at the higher officials and aides involved in C-Day, like Bobby Kennedy, Harry Williams, Vance, Helms, FitzGerald, and Morales. As we've said before, only about a dozen US officials and aides were officially told anything close to the full scope of the C-Day plan. But there was also a lower level of operative, the men in the field who did what some might consider the "dirty work" on certain aspects of C-Day. Among those we have mentioned so far are John Martino, Richard Cain, David Ferrie, and Guy Banister. They may have had only small or supporting roles in C-Day, but documents and articles of the time confirm that they knew about it, and several of them had important roles in the Mafia penetration of C-Day.

Cain, Martino, Banister, and Ferrie are just some of the associates of mob bosses Marcello, Trafficante, and Rosselli who knew about or worked on aspects of C-Day. All of the dozen people knowingly involved in the Mafia plot to kill JFK were informants or assets of federal agencies.[1] They could not only feed disinformation to authorities before and after JFK's death, but their asset status often removed them from suspicion or let them divert suspicion to others.

At the same time the Kennedys were finalizing their plans for the C-Day coup against Castro, the Mafia bosses were culminating months of planning to penetrate C-Day. As detailed in Part II, their plan was to use parts of C-Day in the plot to kill JFK—first in Chicago, then Tampa, and finally

Dallas—forcing a cover-up by Bobby Kennedy and others in the government to protect national security and prevent a potential nuclear confrontation with the Soviets. The mob's men who had penetrated C-Day would be part of, and help spark, that cover-up. For example, a CIA memo says Cain was "deeply involved in the President Kennedy assassination case."[2] And Martino's hints about C-Day in the press and to the FBI were designed to force the government to back off from certain aspects of the investigation.

The mob ties of men like Martino, Cain, Banister, and Ferrie remained hidden from others working on C-Day in 1963 because of the highly sensitive, compartmentalized nature of C-Day and the management style of Bobby Kennedy, who often disdained traditional bureaucracy in favor of informal approaches. Richard Goodwin told us that "people who worked for Bobby were often in secretive cliques."[3] Bobby Kennedy's own Justice Department wasn't told about C-Day, according to two sources who worked with him.[4] This included both the Justice Department section targeting the Mafia, and the separate "Get Hoffa" squad. This was especially tragic, because those were the very experts who would have been able to detect the Mafia penetration of C-Day. On the other hand, Bobby hadn't been informed by the CIA about Varona's bribe from Rosselli's Chicago Mafia family, and the FBI hadn't told Bobby about the threats to JFK that their informants had picked up from associates of Trafficante and Marcello.

The closest the Justice Department came to C-Day was having some input into the Cuba Contingency Plan—although not knowing about C-Day would have certainly limited the effectiveness of their input. There's no record or testimony as to what high officials of the Secret Service were told about C-Day, or the Cuba Contingency Plans to protect it. Even J. Edgar Hoover apparently wasn't officially told about C-Day prior to the assassination. In hindsight, those omissions made it much easier for the Mafia to penetrate C-Day and use parts of it against JFK.

Former Chicago FBI Chief Guy Banister not only knew about C-Day, but, along with his close associate in 1963, Eastern Airlines pilot David Ferrie, he even worked on parts of C-Day. Declassified FBI files say that an associate of Ferrie "told the FBI" about Ferrie's activities with "Robert Kennedy" and their "dealings with the late Attorney General Robert Kennedy" and about "plans for a Cuban second invasion."[5] The FBI files make it clear that Guy Banister—a New Orleans private detective in 1963—was also involved in those activities, and we later document Banister's work on a project that year involving CIA officer David Atlee Phillips. One of Guy Banister's closest associates—who Banister later said talked too much about sensitive matters—wrote briefly about parts of C-Day in August 1963. It described "Kennedy Administration planning" for Cuba where Castro "would be the fall guy in a complete reorganization for the [Cuban] regime which will purportedly be free of Soviet influence. The plan calls for 'uprisings' and 'desertions' and 'guerrilla fronts.'" The article said that "a new government" for Cuba would be "set up with such men as . . . Manolo Ray."[6]

Banister's part-time employee in 1963, David Ferrie, was involved with the minor-league exile training camp outside New Orleans linked to Manuel Artime and Somoza that was mentioned in Chapter 12.[7] Two reporters for the *New Orleans States-Item* wrote that "one group, reportedly led by Ferrie, was instructed in guerilla warfare employing four to five man teams for infiltration purposes. The training was at a camp . . . a few miles outside of metropolitan New Orleans."[8] The training camp Ferrie visited had other possible connections to C-Day and the JFK assassination. The camp's owner said "he bought arms from Ferrie, who in turn got them from US Army personnel who had stolen them." That is similar to the stolen-military-arms ring we mentioned earlier, involving the Dallas gun dealer the *Washington Post* said sold the bullets found in Oswald's rifle and who gave remarkably accurate descriptions of C-Day to FBI informants a month before JFK's death.[9] The *Washington Post* writers also linked longtime gunrunner Jack Ruby to the same stolen-military-arms ring.

As for the "minor league" exile training camp linked to C-Day, author Anthony Summers writes that Guy Banister's secretary said "that Ferrie not only met Oswald but took him on at least one visit to an anti-Castro guerrilla training camp outside New Orleans."[10] The secretary told Summers that Ferrie was "one of the agents" of Banister and that Ferrie's "work was somehow connected" with the CIA. One of the men involved with the camp told an Assistant District Attorney for New Orleans that "General Somoza of Nicaragua had given them the green light" for the camp, so they assumed it had "at least tacit backing of the United States Central Intelligence Agency."[11] The "former Executive Assistant to the Deputy Director of the CIA" confirmed that "Ferrie had been a contract agent to the Agency [CIA] in the early sixties . . . in some of the Cuban activities" and that Richard "Helms stated that David Ferrie was a CIA agent" in the fall of 1963.[12]

By 1963, Banister and Ferrie had several years' experience in anti-Castro Cuban matters, having helped the New Orleans branch of the Kennedy-backed Cuban Revolutionary Council exile group when it included Tony Varona, Manuel Artime, and Manolo Ray.[13] As the former FBI chief of America's second largest city, Banister had numerous contacts in law enforcement and intelligence that reached all the way to the Kennedys, J. Edgar Hoover and the FBI, Naval Intelligence, and the Defense Intelligence Agency.[14] Banister's former business partner was close JFK aide Carmine Bellino, and Banister had worked at least two major FBI cases with General Carroll, who had become head of the Defense Intelligence Agency.[15]

In addition to David Ferrie, later chapters document that Guy Banister had another part-time employee in 1963 who also knew about C-Day, according to reports from the *New York Times*, the Secret Service, and former FBI Director Clarence Kelley. As documented in Part II, this part-time employee of Banister in the summer of 1963 was Lee Harvey Oswald. Kelley wrote in his memoirs that "Oswald . . . had information on a CIA plot to assassinate Fidel Castro."[16] A Secret Service report from December 1963 says that "citizens of the United States had entered into an agreement or plot to assassinate Premier Castro of Cuba and that Lee Harvey Oswald . . . learned of this plot."[17] An associate of David Ferrie was quoted in the *New York Times* as saying "Lee H. Oswald had boasted" about what he would do "if the United States attempted an invasion of Cuba."[18]

The tragic reality is that in the summer and fall of 1963, Guy Banister and David Ferrie were also working for New Orleans godfather Carlos Marcello, as documented by the House Select Committee on Assassinations (HSCA). As detailed in Parts II and III, Ferrie admitted doing extensive work for Marcello in the days right before the Chicago and Tampa attempts. Ferrie was with Marcello in court dealing with charges brought by Bobby Kennedy on the day JFK was shot, sparking Ferrie's unusual trip to Texas that night. The HSCA says that Ferrie admitted "he had also been critical of any President riding in an open car and had made the statement that anyone could hide in the bushes and shoot a President."[19] The *Washington Post* said that Ferrie "had been quoted as saying the President 'ought to be shot.'"[20]

We once asked Harry Williams about someone named "Feria"—not David Ferrie, but someone with a similar-sounding name—and Harry immediately asked if the man "was a pilot"—Feria wasn't, but Ferrie was. When we showed Harry a photo of David Ferrie, Harry said that "his face looks familiar," but said he was not part of C-Day—at least, not that Harry knew of.[21] However, Ferrie did have ties to both Manuel Artime and Tony Varona, as detailed in Part II.

Guy Banister provided the respectable front that allowed himself and Ferrie to penetrate C-Day. Although Banister did jobs for Marcello in 1963, the former FBI supervisor was never seen in public with the godfather.[22] That's because Banister was well known in law-enforcement and intelligence circles. According to former Senate investigator Bud Fensterwald, Banister did some work for Naval Intelligence, which by 1963 was part of the new Defense Intelligence Agency (DIA) run by General Carroll, Banister's former FBI colleague.[23] But Banister worked for other intelligence agencies as well. According to the *New Orleans States-Item*, "the veteran FBI agent [Banister] was a key liaison man for US government-sponsored anti-Communist activities in Latin America. 'Guy [Banister] participated in every important anti-Communist South and Central American revolution which came along,'" according to one Banister associate the newspaper interviewed.[24] This makes sense when you consider that New Orleans was the key shipping gateway between the US and Latin America; and, until the creation of the CIA, the FBI had responsibility for US intelligence in Latin America.[25] Banister was also very close to the New Orleans FBI office.

New Orleans even had a little-known role in the 1961 Bay of Pigs operation, and Banister was also involved.[26] E. Howard Hunt wrote that early in 1961, a Cuban exile leader "together with a hundred untrained followers, [were] sent to the CIA's amphibious base on Lake Pontchartrain, Louisiana," just outside New Orleans.[27] Gus Russo, a journalist with many CIA contacts, writes that in 1961 "Hunt served as the Agency's advisor to the Kennedy-backed Cuban Revolutionary Council [CRC], with its headquarters in Miami and New Orleans."[28] In 1961, the CRC Board of Directors included future C-Day leaders Manuel Artime, Tony Varona, and Manolo Ray. According to Russo, "FBI files indicate that Banister" helped the New Orleans office of the CRC, and a Congressional report confirms that Banister "ran background checks" for the CRC. It was a convenient arrangement, since "Banister's office was in the same building as the CRC office and it is known that" Banister "saw David Ferrie . . . with some regularity" since Ferrie was the assistant of the local CRC leader.[29]

By mid-1963, Ferrie was working directly for Banister and, according to Gus Russo, E. Howard Hunt was helping Harry Williams with C-Day.[30] A few years later, when questions arose within the CIA about the Bay of Pigs base outside New Orleans, the CIA chose David Atlee Phillips to prepare a detailed internal report about it.[31] Phillips's meeting with Banister is documented from court files in Part II.

Banister's personal and professional life had been on a slow but steady decline ever since his early retirement from the FBI in 1954, which may have been forced by J. Edgar Hoover due to Banister's heavy drinking and explosive temper. Both these problems only worsened as the fifties grew into the sixties. Banister's bread-and-butter business had been Commie-hunting and security checks for blacklists, both of which were long past their heyday by 1963. Banister tried to replace them with extreme racism, saying that integration was a Communist plot, but that didn't generate revenue the way company-wide security checks used to. Banister's intelligence work may have brought him contacts, influence, and prestige, but it was generating little direct revenue by 1963.

However, New Orleans godfather Carlos Marcello was more than willing to pick up the financial slack.[32] The work Banister did for Marcello apparently went far beyond routine detective work related to the legal case brought against Marcello by Bobby Kennedy's Justice Department. When Johnny Rosselli visited Banister's office, Rosselli was ostensibly working on anti-Castro plots for the government, while actually working on the plot to kill JFK.[33] All the evidence shows that Banister was doing the same thing—ostensibly helping the government while actually working to kill JFK.[34] One of Banister's business associates told an investigator for the New Orleans District Attorney that "he heard Banister remark on several occasions that someone should do away with Kennedy."[35]

The CIA admits that John Martino was one of its assets in 1963, yet Martino wrote the following remarkable description of C-Day for a small, right-wing journal. It was published on December 21, 1963; given the lead time of even small magazines, it must have been written within a couple of weeks of JFK's assassination. Martino wrote that "the Kennedy Administration planned to eliminate Fidel Castro . . . through a putsch . . . the plan involved a more or less token invasion from Central America to be synchronized with the coup. A left-wing coalition government was to be set up. . . ." Martino accurately said that "the plan involved US [military] occupation of Cuba," something that would not be declassified until over thirty years later. Martino mentioned that Lee Harvey Oswald had been linked to Manolo Ray's C-Day exile group JURE, when he wrote that "Oswald made . . . approaches to

JURE, another organization of Cuban freedom fighters, but was rejected." Called the "Odio incident" because of JURE member Silvia Odio, it would not become public knowledge until almost a year after Martino's article was published.[36] Martino knew about it because he was involved in the incident: Martino had met Silvia Odio's sister in Dallas around the time of the Oswald approach. Martino even used some of the same phrases with Silvia's sister as the "Oswald group" used with Silvia.[37] Martino learned about Silvia in the first place because a man described by the FBI as Martino's "close friend"— Rolando Masferrer—had a brother who lived in Silvia Odio's Dallas apartment complex.[38]

Martino gave other descriptions of C-Day in the days, weeks, and months after JFK's death, like this one he taunted FBI agents with on February 15, 1964: "President Kennedy was engaged in a plot to overthrow the Castro regime by preparing another invasion attempt against Cuba."[39] Clearly, Martino knew more about C-Day than all but a dozen top US officials had known prior to JFK's death. Martino used his knowledge of C-Day to keep the FBI and the Warren Commission from digging too hard into areas that could lead to his Mafia bosses like Trafficante and Rosselli. Martino did this by raising the specter of C-Day and the possibility that Castro had killed JFK in retaliation for it.

According to reporter Earl Golz, Martino later told his business partner that he "was a contract agent for the CIA."[40] Martino's wife told Congressional investigators that Martino's contact with the CIA and FBI was intense in 1962 and 1963 after Martino's release from a Cuban prison.[41] A *Village Voice* article by Dick Russell confirms that Martino was involved with Johnny Rosselli and Santo Trafficante in a CIA-Mafia plot against Castro in the late spring and early summer of 1963. The CIA first confirmed Martino's involvement with them when the Agency reviewed a manuscript by *Life* magazine writer Richard Billings, whose notes say that Martino was "a CIA go-between."[42] CIA documents declassified later confirm Martino's involvement in the spring CIA-Mafia plot code-named OPERATION TILT.[43] To the CIA, it looked like Martino was helping with Rosselli's CIA-Mafia plots to kill Castro, when in reality both men were actually targeting JFK.[44]

In 1963, John Martino was very close to Johnny Rosselli, who, along with Santo Trafficante, directed Martino's actions. Congressional investigators learned that he admitted his role in JFK's assassination shortly before his death. According to an article in *Vanity Fair*, Martino told his wife, prior to the assassination, that "They're going to kill him. They're going to kill him when he gets to Texas." Shortly before Martino's death, he told an award-winning *Newsday* reporter that "he'd been part of the assassination of Kennedy. He wasn't in Dallas pulling a trigger, but he was involved . . . delivering money, facilitating things." Martino told the reporter several details of the operation, such as the fact "that there had been two guns, two people involved" as well as "anti-Castro Cubans." *Vanity Fair* reports that Martino also revealed a few details about the assassination to his business partner, specifically that "Oswald wasn't the hit man" and that "he was to meet his contact at the Texas Theater." Martino's background and activities are detailed in Part II and Part III.

Richard Cain was another CIA asset who knew about, and worked on part of, C-Day: Congressional investigators wrote that Cain had "a reputation for experience in sabotage, polygraphs, and electronic surveillance" and was "fluent in Italian and Spanish and traveled extensively in Latin America."[45] Cain began working with the CIA in 1960, and the *Chicago Tribune* reports that Cain had bugged a Communist embassy in Mexico City for the CIA.[46] By the summer of 1963 and through the fall, Cain was a CIA informant about Tony Varona, one of Harry's five C-Day exile leaders.[47]

Cain's CIA reports include information relating to C-Day such as "On 23 August 1963 Richard Cain received information" about "a guerilla organization presently being formed in Central America . . . sponsored by the Pentagon."[48] Another version of the CIA memo provides more detail, saying that "Cain . . . had been approached by" a Cuban exile group which "attempted to recruit him to be trained in Central America." A representative for the exile group said they were being "sponsored 'by the Pentagon, which is in competition with [the] CIA., and therefore, all activities'" of the exile group "'must be kept secret.'"[49] It wasn't public knowledge at the time that "the Pentagon"—people like Secretary of the Army Cyrus Vance and the DIA's General Carroll—was involved with Cuban exiles at all, let alone with Artime's C-Day camps "in Central America."

Later Cain CIA memos about Varona's C-Day activities say that "Manuel Artime is considered to be a CIA employee" and that "Luis Somoza" is having difficulty getting arms "from the US Government." Cain's information matches what was really going on with C-Day at the time, and some of Cain's reports were routed to CIA C-Day coordinator Desmond FitzGerald's department.[50] Cain had been a key member of the Chicago Police Department and in 1963, while working for the CIA, Cain was Chief Investigator for the Cook County–Chicago Sheriff's Office, with a staff of forty. He was also an informant for the Chicago FBI.

The CIA admits that Cain first became a CIA informant in the "Fall of 1960" by "providing information on the activities of Cuban exile groups." The CIA admits that Cain was also active in "Mexico City."[51] The CIA says that Cain was a "current informant" in August 1963. A CIA memo says that on August 19, 1963, Cain met in Chicago with two CIA officials and that Cain "agreed to assist the [CIA] by providing information on undercover activities of the Cubans" and "providing names of any Cubans who might be used to [the] CIA."[52] The memo says that Cain told the CIA officials "he was also in contact with Cubans in the Chicago area who were involved in ventures which were not completely legal."[53]

As noted earlier, Richard Cain was not just a high Chicago lawman, CIA asset, and FBI informant in 1963; he was actually a "made" member of the Chicago Mafia named Ricardo Scalzetti, and the House Select Committee on Assassinations found that "Cain admitted that he had worked covertly for [Chicago Mafia boss] Giancana and been on his payroll while he was a member of the Chicago Police Department . . . and Chief Investigator for the Cook County Sheriff's Office from 1962–64."[54] Cain's Mafia family included Johnny Rosselli, and Cain had been part of the CIA-Mafia Castro assassination plots with Rosselli, Santo Trafficante, and Tony Varona. Richard Cain had also worked for Carlos Prio, the ex-Cuban president and Trafficante associate who had penetrated C-Day.[55]

Cain's ties to men like Rosselli and Trafficante are especially disturbing in light of CIA documents that show Cain's knowledge of C-Day in August and September of 1963. On the other hand, it makes perfect sense for Rosselli and Trafficante to involve Cain in penetrating C-Day and helping with the plot to kill JFK. Chicago godfather Sam Giancana was under "lockstep" surveillance by the FBI much of the time, due to pressure from Bobby Kennedy, so Giancana couldn't actively participate in the plot against JFK—but his trusted aide Cain could. Cain's previous work with Rosselli and Trafficante on the assassination plot against Castro surely made him acceptable to the Mafia bosses. Cain's status with the CIA would help him penetrate C-Day, while his law enforcement role with the Sheriff's Office in Chicago and informant status with the FBI would prove invaluable after JFK's death, when a CIA memo says Cain was "deeply involved in the President Kennedy assassination case."[56]

Cain's CIA file contains other disinformation he fed to them and to law enforcement about Oswald after the assassination. For example, a CIA "memorandum dated 29 November 1963 in the file of one Richard S. Cain" says that "Cain said that the Cook County Sheriff's Office . . . had strong sus-picions that Oswald was in Chicago in April [1963]" and tried to tie Oswald to the Fair Play for Cuba Committee there.[57] Part II details Cain's likely role in Oswald's unusual visits to the Cuban and Soviet embassies in Mexico City in the fall of 1963.

As an FBI informant, Cain gave up nothing of value, but he learned a great deal about what the FBI knew from the questions he was asked and the friendly banter he had with his FBI handler, Bill Roemer. Cain was also able to feed disinformation to the FBI that way. The FBI's Roemer never realized that Cain was fooling him and the FBI for all those years.[58] The FBI had prided itself on its bugging of Giancana in 1963, but it wasn't good enough to detect Giancana's contact with surveillance expert Cain. Author Peter Dale Scott writes that "In 1963," FBI agent Bill "Roemer was the FBI expert on Sam Gian-cana, in part because Roemer's chief mob informant (and close friend) was Richard Cain." Scott points out that Roemer's "young assistant" obtained the reports from local Mafiosi, saying things like "'Ruby was not outfit connected' that later found their way into the Warren Report," though such findings were eventually "demolished by the" House Select Committee on Assassinations.[59]

Cain had forty deputies working for him in Chicago in 1963, and with his connections to the FBI, the CIA, and the Mafia, he could keep tabs on any development that could implicate the Mafia in JFK's death. So it shouldn't be surprising that Richard Cain's CIA file includes references to "Abraham W. Bolden," the "former Secret Service agent serving time in Springfield" prison who "stated that he was prevented from testifying for the Warren Commission that the Secret Service knew of a plot to assassinate Kennedy in Chicago."[60]

We've mentioned Bolden before: the first black Presidential Secret Service Agent, who was arrested the very day he went to Washington to tell the Warren Commission about the Chicago and Tampa threats against JFK and about other problems he had observed. It took two trials, but Bolden was finally convicted on counterfeiting charges based only on the testimony of two criminals: one whom Bolden had previously arrested, and one who later admitted committing perjury against Bolden. Consequently, this agent with an excellent reputation and outstanding service record served six years in prison, sometimes in solitary confinement after he would try to draw atten-tion to his case.[61]

The criminal who later admitted he'd been pressured to commit perjury worked for a very close associate of Richard Cain named Sam DeStefano, one of Sam Giancana's most ruthless gangsters. Giancana had once tried to get DeSte-fano involved in the CIA-Mafia plots against Castro, with himself and Cain.

The Mafia knew that Bolden had to be—in the words of the CIA report—
"prevented from testifying for the Warren Commission" about the "plot to
assassinate Kennedy in Chicago." If the Warren Commission and the public
learned what Bolden knew about the attempts to assassinate JFK in Chicago
and in Tampa, no one would buy the "Oswald-as-lone-assassin" theory any
more. A truly thorough investigation, including the Tampa and Chicago
attempts, could eventually uncover the Mafia's role in JFK's death. With
Cain's connections in law enforcement, the CIA, and the FBI, he was in the
perfect position to find out what Bolden was about to do, and his criminal
connections would have enabled him to have his gangland associate, Sam
DeStefano, frame Bolden.

A Kennedy aide who worked on C-Day confirmed to us that Bobby
Kennedy was aware of Bolden's plight, but that Bobby felt he "couldn't" do
anything to help Bolden.[62] Any attempt by Bobby to intervene could have led
to the exposure of the Chicago and Tampa attempts and why they had to be
covered up, which would have exposed C-Day, which in turn could have
potentially created a nuclear confrontation with the Soviets. As Part III documents, the Mafia—specifically Cain, Martino, Rosselli, Masferrer, and
Artime—had planted so many "Castro killed JFK" stories (sometimes also
implicating the Soviets) that public or political pressure to invade Cuba or
retaliate against the Soviets might become overwhelming before the real Mafia
culprits could be identified. While Bobby told associates in private that Marcello was behind the assassination, proving it in court would be another thing.

Because of Richard Cain and the secrecy surrounding C-Day, Bolden had
to suffer in prison. In April 1973, the man Cain used to frame Bolden, Sam
DeStefano, was murdered in Chicago.[63] Though officially unsolved, Cain
was the prime suspect, but he'd constructed an alibi so strong that he
couldn't be prosecuted. However, someone close to Cain confirmed to us
that Cain was responsible for DeStefano's killing.[64] Later that same year,
Richard Cain "was slain in gangland fashion in a Chicago restaurant," in the
same fashion the Mafia had tried against Harry Williams.[65] Abraham Bolden,
long out of prison, still continues his decades-long quest for a pardon.

When looking at the actions of those involved with C-Day and in JFK's
assassination, it's important to keep in mind that they were working for Carlos
Marcello, Santo Trafficante, and Johnny Rosselli. Part II documents the three
mob bosses and their work together in new ways that explain not just how,
but also why, they penetrated C-Day and used parts of it against JFK.

PART TWO

SANTO TRAFFICANTE, CARLOS MARCELLO, AND Johnny Rosselli were willing to risk everything to kill JFK by 1963. By revealing the Mafia's ties with earlier CIA operations starting in the 1950s, Part II presents a clear, step-by-step picture of how the Mafia penetrated C-Day. It was those relationships that allowed the mob bosses to plan JFK's assassination in a way that would force Bobby Kennedy and key government leaders to suppress crucial evidence to protect C-Day and its participants.

Part II delineates the entire JFK assassination plot and how it was built one piece and one person at a time, using contacts and operations established earlier. The mob bosses used only people who had proved reliable time and again, ranging from high-level mob allies like Jimmy Hoffa to lower-level operatives such as Jack Ruby, John Martino, Richard Cain, Guy Banister, David Ferrie, and French Connection heroin mastermind Michel Victor Mertz. Each person the Mafia used in the JFK plot—less than a dozen in all—had been an asset or an informant for various intelligence or law-enforcement agencies.

We explain how the fortunes of the three mob bosses were intertwined with the rise of John and Bobby Kennedy, by depicting the Kennedys' onslaught against the Mafia. At the same time, we document how the Kennedys, or their close aides, met with a total of twenty-six associates of Ruby, Marcello, Trafficante, and Rosselli—yet another way the mob bosses were able to penetrate C-Day.* Part II finally explains several mysteries about Ruby and Oswald that have baffled government investigators for years, by showing how they were connected to the Mafia, C-Day, or previously secret CIA operations.

Marcello, Trafficante, and Rosselli

MARCELLO, TRAFFICANTE, AND ROSSELLI HAD several things in common, in addition to confessing their roles in JFK's assassination in later years. The three were close associates who met at least once or twice a year, sometimes at a secluded location free from FBI surveillance revealed in this book for the first time.[1] All three were under intense and unrelenting pressure from Attorney General Bobby Kennedy by 1963, pressure that had begun in 1957. All three were in business with Jimmy Hoffa, who was also under constant prosecution from Bobby Kennedy. But unlike Hoffa—a high-profile, very public figure—these three godfathers shunned the limelight and were unknown to the general public in 1963. All three had dealings with mobster Jack Ruby and had associates close to Lee Harvey Oswald. All three had links to the French Connection heroin ring. All three had worked for the CIA, in attempts to assassinate Castro.[2] And despite the Kennedys' best efforts, all three had operatives who had managed to penetrate the C-Day plan without the Kennedys' knowledge.[3]

Why these three Mafia bosses were willing to risk killing the President in 1963 can be explained only by looking at their operations before they came under assault by the Kennedys. That was the era they wanted to return to, a time when J. Edgar Hoover publicly denied that the Mafia even existed.

Carlos Marcello, Santo Trafficante, and Johnny Rosselli were each powerful in their own right by the 1950s. But the more they worked together, the more powerful they became. Their combined actions are rarely discussed outside of obscure government reports, old newspaper articles, and a few books, some long out of print. The House Select Committee on

Assassinations volumes had some good information on Marcello, less on Trafficante, and strangely little on Johnny Rosselli, so it never gave a clear sense of how the mob bosses worked together. The action they took together in 1963 to assassinate JFK was not the first time they had worked together or the first time they had assassinated public officials. Likewise, C-Day wasn't the first CIA operation the three mob bosses had infiltrated—that was something they had done several times in the years before they killed JFK.

CARLOS MARCELLO

The 1950s were a golden time for Carlos Marcello, the New Orleans godfather who headed America's oldest and—in many ways—most ruthless Mafia family. Marcello not only had his enemies killed, but sometimes even had their bodies dissolved in lye and dumped on his 6,500-acre private estate outside New Orleans. Marcello was a short bulldog of a man, with a prominent Roman nose befitting an emperor of crime.[4] His empire reached from Texas to Alabama, and the many ports (notably Houston and New Orleans) and Mexican border crossings in his territory made him an important part of the highly profitable French Connection heroin network.[5]

According to Marcello's biographer, noted historian John H. Davis, Marcello's "gambling wire" served "bookmakers in Louisiana, Texas, Oklahoma, Arkansas, Chicago, Alabama, Missouri, and Mississippi." In most of those locations, he also had a "call-girl ring," run by an associate of Jack Ruby.[6] Marcello's gambling and call-girl operations in Alabama were linked to the assassination of the Alabama attorney general-elect. The New Orleans godfather would eventually "extend [his] operations to California, Central America, the Caribbean, and beyond."[7]

Marcello's biographer says that "next to New Orleans, the most important city in the invisible empire of Carlos Marcello was Dallas." Since it "did not have a Mafia family of its own, . . . its underworld was a satellite of the Marcello organization and its leaders . . . took their orders from Carlos Marcello." Davis quotes "one law-enforcement official" as saying the "Marcello network in Texas was 'an independent, elaborately insulated operation'" where Marcello reaped the benefits while remaining behind the scenes. Carlos "Marcello's slot machines could be found almost everywhere in Texas" and, "according to a report by" the "Texas State Attorney General . . . the Marcello gambling syndicate in Texas" eventually "numbered 800 bookmakers handling gross revenues of $700 million."[8]

Long before Bobby Kennedy became US Attorney General, he knew about

"Marcello's representative in Dallas, Joe Civello," according to a recent history of the Federal Bureau of Narcotics (FBN). While chief counsel for the Senate "Rackets" Committee in the late 1950s, Bobby "suspected that Marcello, through Trafficante in Florida . . . played a dominant role in international drug trafficking. As Bobby was certainly aware, the FBN office in New Orleans believed that Marcello received narcotics from Trafficante in Florida on Teamsters trucks and that" Marcello had a front company that "smuggled drugs from Mexico 'without interference from customs.'"[9]

Frank Ragano, the lawyer for Jimmy Hoffa and Santo Trafficante, wrote that "Santo mentioned obliquely that Marcello's power extended to Texas, where he had placed an under-boss, Joe Civello, to run rackets out of Dallas. I recalled from newspaper stories that Civello, in fact, had represented Marcello at the Apalachin conference in 1957."[10]

Dallas newspaper reporter Earl Golz wrote that Marcello "knew Civello from rackets connections near Baton Rouge, La., before Civello moved to Dallas." These connections involved "a heroin and cocaine bust . . . that reached from Dallas to New Orleans to Chicago." It was "in 1950" that Marcello and Civello "quietly cemented a Dallas–New Orleans relationship" that lasted for decades. This relationship was confirmed when "Federal agents" found telephone "toll records which showed a number of calls between Civello and Marcello's" company in New Orleans. FBI agents were informed that Jack "Ruby was a frequent visitor and associate of Civello, after Ruby moved to Dallas." Ruby was linked by several witnesses to narcotics traffic, and "federal agents" found "telephone communications" between Civello and "a major trafficker in narcotics" from New York.

Golz also found that "Marcello invested heavily in Dallas area land and bankrolled bars, restaurants, and other businesses." The head of the New Orleans Crime Commission said that "there's been a long history of Marcello negotiations in connection with real estate in the Dallas area . . . he acquires land and properties, more often than not, in the names of straw men." In addition, "vending machine operators paid him a percentage of their take and so did gamblers, although Marcello doesn't gamble himself."[11] Shortly before JFK's assassination, a Marcello associate used a vending-machine executive to pay Jack Ruby several thousand dollars, according to JFK press secretary (and former Senate crime investigator) Pierre Salinger.

Marcello had what Golz considered "the Mafia's most expansive kingdom ruled by a single godfather."[12] Former Justice Department prosecutor Robert Goldfarb related a meeting with Robert Kennedy about Marcello, in which

Marcello was termed "a top syndicate member, if not *the* top Mafia boss" [emphasis in original].[13] Marcello's special position allowed him to undertake certain activities without the approval of the Mafia's national commission.

Marcello received special treatment not only from the national Mafia, but also from local, state, and even federal officials. According to a recent history of the FBN, "Marcello was protected at home; although FBI agents had arrested him in 1938 for possession of 23 pounds of pot, when he was known to be running one of the 'major narcotics rings in the New Orleans area,' Louisiana Governor O. K. Allen arbitrarily reduced his sentence and within nine short months Marcello was back on the streets."[14] Within a few years, Marcello was running one of the major narcotics rings not just in New Orleans, but in the whole country, along with his close ally Santo Trafficante.

The FBN history quotes Clarence Giarusso, a veteran New Orleans narcotic agent and later its chief of police, to explain Marcello's freedom from prosecution: "We don't care about Carlos Marcello or the Mafia. City cops have no interest in who brings the dope in. That's the job of federal agents."[15] However, even some federal agencies weren't interested in Marcello's heroin trafficking.[16] In 1959, FBN agent Tony Zirilli "was set up because he had gotten close to" making a case on "Carlos Marcello through Marcello's girlfriend."[17]

The history of the FBN goes on to say that Bobby "Kennedy wanted to nail Trafficante and Marcello, but the FBN had only four agents in its Miami and New Orleans offices, and the FBI—though it had the manpower—chose not to place wiretaps on them. These two were the only Mafiosi to receive such privileged treatment from J. Edgar Hoover." New Orleans FBI agent "Regis Kennedy even made the outrageous claim that Marcello was not involved in crime."[18] The FBI agent claimed that he considered Marcello merely a lowly "tomato salesman," long after Marcello's crime empire had been exposed by the Congressional hearings of John Kennedy and others.[19] The FBI's "hands-off" approach to Marcello might be explained by Johnny Rosselli's boasts to Jimmy "The Weasel" Fratianno that Hoover was once arrested for having gay sex in New Orleans.[20] Marcello wasn't even a US citizen, having been born in Tunisia, though for much of the 1950s that presented little problem for him thanks to his bribes and political influence.

Trafficante's lawyer Frank Ragano, who met Marcello on several occasions, wrote that "despite Marcello's prison record, despite being vilified by congressional committees and the press as an unsavory mobster, in Louisiana, he seemed invulnerable, operating his rackets with impunity." He pointed out that "Louisiana politicians and law-enforcement officials had a long history of being corrupted by the Mafia."[21]

Marcello's political savvy and largess extended to national politics, important to someone whose territory covered many states and who was subject to deportation by federal authorities. His influence in Washington sprang from several sources. Marcello employed a well-connected Washington, D.C. lobbyist whose clients included the Somoza family. Lyndon Johnson, then one of the most powerful members of the Senate, received support from Marcello during the 1950s, in the same way that powerful mobsters supplied money to powerful politicians in many parts of the country. Richard Nixon's connections to Marcello will be covered shortly.

John Davis writes that "Marcello's payoff man in Texas in the fifties . . . had been a principal financial backer of Lyndon Johnson's political campaigns in Texas from the late forties on, to the extent that it could be said that illegal profits from Marcello's slot machines in Dallas and Houston . . . were crucial to the success of Johnson's senatorial campaigns." Davis says that "Johnson, because of his dependence on" this money, "had helped kill in committee all antiracketeering legislative proposals that could have affected . . . Marcello's activities in Texas."[22]

Carlos Marcello himself told Mafia authority Michael Dorman that in 1960, Marcello had "promised his support at the convention to Lyndon Johnson" and indeed "the Louisiana delegation went for Johnson." Marcello said "Sure, I've got plenty of political connections; I don't deny that. I've been helping put people in office for years. I've spent a whole lot of money on campaign contributions and I've spread the word to people to support my candidates." Marcello even admitted "Well, naturally, I'm not goin' to support someone who's later goin' to go out of his way to try to hurt me. In the old days, when I was involved in gambling, I'd try to elect a governor or mayor or district attorney who took a lenient position on the gambling issue."[23]

It's important to put Marcello's support for LBJ in context. Like Nixon, LBJ was not part of the JFK assassination plot. But just as Marcello tried to support LBJ and Nixon over JFK in 1960, Marcello saw either man as preferable to JFK in 1963 and 1964. After JFK's death, Marcello's biographer, John Davis, writes that Marcello had "enough on Johnson so that the new President would not wish an investigation to turn up evidence of Carlos [Marcello's] complicity."[24]

When Marcello could not buy influence with government officials, he had no qualms about trying to kill them. According to one Mafia history, "in April 1955 . . . there was some reason to believe that [New Orleans Sheriff Frank] Clancy was talking to federal agents about Louisiana gambling." Earlier, "Clancy . . . had been a reluctant witness at the Kefauver [Crime] Hearings in 1950–51" where "he revealed that he had allowed the underworld to place 5,000 slot machines in his parish" and "New Orleans boss Carlos Marcello [had] opened three gambling casinos."

Now Clancy was talking to federal agents, so when Clancy was hospitalized for a medical condition, there was a "guard outside his door." However, a police report says "the guard was removed . . . by somebody representing themselves as the sheriff's wife." Someone then "walked into" a hospital "room and proceeded to smash" a patient's "skull with a cleaver." There was only one problem: The murdered man was a New Orleans bank teller who had the room next to Sheriff Clancy's room. But the sheriff got the message and "ceased giving information to federal agents." In fact, everyone got the message: "A nurses' aide who had seen the killer and provided police with a detailed description three days later suddenly recalled she had no idea what the man looked like."[25] The same type of witness intimidation would occur on several occasions after the JFK assassination.

Other Marcello hits were more successful. Aside from the usual small-time mob hits in Marcello's territory, the head of the New Orleans Crime Commission "was able to attribute at least three, possibly four, murders to Marcello, including the gangland-style killing of two of Marcello's former narcotics associates," and "for none of these crimes was Marcello ever charged."[26] One reason Marcello never faced prosecution for any of his murders might have been his philosophy, expressed in "a sign on the door leading out" of his office, that said THREE CAN KEEP A SECRET IF TWO ARE DEAD.[27]

Part of Marcello's gambling empire included "the most lavish illegal casino in the nation" called "the Beverly Club," which featured top entertainers and lavish furnishings. As the 1950s progressed, Marcello would expand his gambling interests into Las Vegas, with the help of Johnny Rosselli.[28]

Marcello was even closer to Santo Trafficante. Here are Trafficante's own words about Marcello, in sworn, immunized testimony to the House Select Committee on Assassinations in 1978: "Mr. Trafficante: I know Carlos Marcello about 30 years. I met him in New Orleans. My father had an operation there." Trafficante went on to say that "I see him once in a while when I go to New Orleans. He's come to Miami. . . ."[29] Trafficante admitted that he had discussions with Marcello "about Robert Kennedy . . . that Bobby Kennedy had him deported" and "put him on a plane with some marshals and dumped him in Guatemala." Trafficante agreed that Marcello "was pretty upset" about that and that Trafficante "felt that Robert Kennedy had mistreated" Marcello. Trafficante said that even seventeen years later, in 1978, "I still think he mistreated him."[30]

SANTO TRAFFICANTE

The violent barbershop murder scene in Francis Ford Coppola's first *Godfather* film was inspired by the real hit on New York mob boss Albert Anastasia in 1957. This daring killing made headlines across America, and Santo Trafficante's involvement in it first brought him to the attention of the Kennedy brothers. The Mafia godfather of Tampa and much of Florida, Trafficante's influence extended to New York City, Alabama, and even Cuba. Despite his deadly reputation, Santo Trafficante was highly intelligent and, according to his lawyer, "was an avid reader, who every day perused four or five newspapers from Florida, New York, and Chicago."

Trafficante was an average-looking man who preferred to stay out of the limelight. In the only photo of him in his Havana casino, Trafficante almost seems to blend into the background.[31] The Federal Bureau of Narcotics' (FBN) internal list of major heroin kingpins gives a very precise description of Trafficante (technically, "Santo Trafficante, Jr.," since he took over as godfather from his father of the same name): "Born in Tampa, Florida on November 15, 1914 . . . height 5' 10½"; weight 175 lbs . . . gun shot wound scar on upper left arm . . . visits major cities on the Eastern Seaboard of United States." The FBN document calls Trafficante "a powerful Mafia figure in Tampa, Florida" and notes that he "attended the underworld meeting at Apalachin, New York on November 14, 1957," which was called to deal with the aftermath of Anastasia's assassination.[32]

Santo Trafficante was a major casino owner in Havana before Castro took over, and Trafficante hid out in Cuba when Senator John Kennedy and his brother Bobby tried to subpoena him about the Anastasia hit for their Senate Organized Crime hearings in 1959. As described later, those hearings propelled JFK to the presidency—he even announced his candidacy in the same hearing room where Hoffa, Marcello, and others had been grilled by the committee.[33] While Trafficante was in Havana in 1959, government documents show that he met Jack Ruby, who had been running guns to Cuba, and

formed other alliances that would help him kill JFK a few years later. Among
Trafficante's "criminal associates" listed in the FBN report quoted above was
a man Jack Ruby told the Warren Commission he stayed with in Havana in
1959.[34] As detailed shortly, it is both ironic and tragic that one other mobster the Kennedys fruitlessly tried to find for their hearings in 1959 was a
low-level Mafia operative who smuggled arms to Cuba and was known to the
Kennedys only by his alias: "Jack La Rue."[35]

A large measure of Trafficante's power, wealth, and nationwide influence
came from his prominent role in the narcotics trade, which also included
Cuba. The Federal Bureau of Narcotics said that Trafficante worked with
"Cuban racketeers in Miami" and "knows most of the major sources of
supply of narcotics to Central and South America."[36] Among Trafficante's
"Criminal Associates," the FBN listed a gangster close to Jimmy Hoffa,
Frankie Dio. Frankie Dio would later be involved in a major heroin bust at
Fort Benning when it was a C-Day Army base, a bust that linked Trafficante,
Marcello, and French Connection kingpin Michel Victor Mertz.

One Mafia history notes that Trafficante's mob family is "one of the oldest
Mafia groups in the country" after New Orleans, and this allowed it to stake
out an early share of what would become known as the French Connection
heroin network. It says "the Tampa family, through the years, figured significantly in the narcotics trade and simply ignored requests or directives from
other crime families to curtail such activities." During the 1920s, "Tampa
became the American end of a drug pipeline extending from Marseilles,
France, through Cuba to Florida." By 1940, Santo Trafficante, Sr. was the
undisputed leader of the mob in Tampa, where he prospered "in the narcotics trade, especially with the French underworld."[37]

"Trafficante [Sr.] always wanted to make it big in Cuban casinos and dispatched his son, Santo Jr., to Havana in 1946 to operate mob casinos." Upon
Trafficante Sr.'s death in 1954, his son Santo "succeeded his father as boss of
Tampa."[38] Santo Trafficante also assumed his father's key role in the French
Connection heroin network. For example, just weeks after the heroin car
bust depicted in the famous *French Connection* film, Trafficante's key French
supplier got another heroin-filled car into New York with no problem.[39] As
we will show, those aspects of Trafficante's mob career—drugs, Cuba, and the
French Mafia—would all play key roles in the plot used to penetrate C-Day
and kill JFK.

Trafficante had a long history of murder and assassination. According to a recent history of the FBN, at the Kefauver (Crime) Committee Hearings in Florida in the early 1950s, "Santo Trafficante in Tampa was linked to fourteen murders over twenty years, including the June 1950 murder of" a Committee witness before he could testify. "Tampa's Police Chief told the Committee that the Mafia had a standard operating procedure for murder, which included the importation of hired killers from out of town, and setting up patsies to take the fall."[40] Also, an "FBI Agent . . . linked Marcello to Trafficante" and "identified drug trafficker Carlos Marcello as the main cog in Southern interstate crime."[41] Trafficante's proven techniques of working with Marcello, importing "hired killers from out of town," and "setting up patsies to take the fall" would be applied against JFK.

Possibly to compensate for his lack of higher education, Trafficante consumed biographies of powerful men—Churchill, Napoleon, Mussolini, and General George S. Patton—as well as histories of World War II.[42] His interest in Patton was also professional since—as we shall see—Patton once had tried to stamp out Trafficante and Marcello's rackets in notorious Phenix City, Alabama, across the river from Fort Benning. In that battle, even the great General Patton had been unable to defeat Santo Trafficante.

Trafficante also worked closely with mob boss Johnny Rosselli in the 1950s, even before they worked together on the second round of the CIA-Mafia plots to kill Castro beginning in 1960. But Rosselli was a very different kind Mafia don from either Trafficante or Marcello.

JOHNNY ROSSELLI

Johnny Rosselli's biographers noted that "Rosselli's combination of tact and muscle made him perfect for the job" of representing the Chicago Mafia in Las Vegas." He could be relied on to finesse delicate negotiations" yet "he could be crossed only at the risk of execution."[43] Noted historian Richard Mahoney points out why the Chicago Mafia needed a powerful mob boss in Nevada: "In Las Vegas, the Chicago outfit had controlling interest in no fewer than four casinos, which together threw off about $10 million in skim a year," in addition to their considerable reported profits.[44]

Rosselli's biography says that his "first deal in Las Vegas" was "the construction of the $50 million Tropicana," then the "most luxurious" casino "on the strip. The hidden ownerships represented the peaceable combination of the most powerful mob chieftains in the country, including . . . Carlos Marcello, the don of the New Orleans Mafia."[45] The Tropicana opened in

April 1957. According to Mahoney, "Rosselli unofficially managed the Trop-icana in Las Vegas in the late 1950s."[46]

One result of the Tropicana business partnership between Rosselli and Marcello would be the explosion of Las Vegas's golden "Rat Pack" era of the late fifties and sixties, thanks to another Rosselli associate, Frank Sinatra. In 1956, when construction on Rosselli and Marcello's Tropicana was started, Las Vegas needed glitzier casinos and more big-name entertainment to compete with the exotic tropical locale of Havana. Havana casinos at the time were also generally classier, while Havana itself offered more in terms of vice. In addition, Las Vegas can be cold in the winter and sweltering in the summer, in contrast to the year-round ocean breezes of coastal Havana. Las Vegas also needed a new super-hotel/casino like the Tropicana to com-pete with now-forgotten US gambling meccas like Hot Springs, Arkansas, whose quasi-legal casinos featured big-name entertainers like Nat "King" Cole.

Marcello was a logical partner for Rosselli's huge Tropicana venture, because since 1947 Marcello had been running "the most lavish illegal casino in the nation." Marcello's "Beverly Club in Jefferson Parish near New Orleans" had "huge crystal chandeliers, fine china for diners, and name entertainers like Sophie Tucker and Tony Martin."[47]

In the first major exposé of the mob's influence in Las Vegas—published the month JFK was assassinated—Mafia experts Ed Reid and Ovid Demaris give a description of Rosselli in 1963 that would have been just as valid in the 1950s: "Johnny Rosselli . . . lives the good life of a respected 'elder' in the Mafia."[48] Before *The Godfather* became a bestseller in the late 1960s, a more common term for a powerful mobster was Mafia "don." It's a sign of Rosselli's high rank when Reid and Demaris point out that "Don Giovanni, as he is known to the Mafiosi, is soft-spoken and polite. The rough edges of the old torpedo days have been polished to a fine patina of masculine gentility."[49]

Reid and Demaris paint a vivid picture of Rosselli's posh life in the years before the Kennedy assassination: "Rosselli spends his leisure hours . . . at the Desert Inn Country Club. He has breakfast there in the morning, seated at a table overlooking the eighteenth green. Between golf rounds, meals, steam baths, shaves, and trims, Twisting, romancing and drinking, there is time for private little conferences at his favorite table with people seeking his counsel for friendship. It may be a newsman, a local politician, a casino owner, a prostitute, a famous entertainer, a deputy sheriff, a US Senator, or the Governor of Nevada."[50] In Rosselli's case, his associates brought him surprisingly close not just to John and Bobby Kennedy, but also to Senator Barry Goldwater. Rosselli had two close friends of Senator Goldwater assassinated in the late 1950s.

Rosselli did not begin his life in such lavish surroundings, associating with friends of presidents and presidential candidates. Rosselli was born on the 4th of July, 1905—but in Italy, not the US; therefore, all his life Rosselli had to face the same deportation worries as his friend Carlos Marcello. Early in his criminal career, "Rosselli (born Francesco Sacco) had been arrested for peddling heroin in 1921," according to a history of the FBN.[51] Former Congressional investigator Gaeton Fonzi says that Rosselli "started as a street hood in Al Capone's Chicago mob. Over the years he transformed himself into a dapper, slick and consummately charming diplomat for Organized Crime, moving among the top family bosses as a broker of mutual interests," primarily "in Las Vegas and Hollywood."

Rosselli was a powerful behind-the-scenes influence in Hollywood. According to Gaeton Fonzi: "The story goes that Rosselli . . . 'suggested' to Harry Cohn, then head of Columbia Pictures, that Frank Sinatra get the Maggio role in *From Here to Eternity*, the part that subsequently saved the crooner's sinking career. Mario Puzo dramatized the incident in *The Godfather's* horse's-head-in-the-bed scene."[52]

In return, Johnny Rosselli would become a shadowy member of Frank Sinatra's "Rat Pack" during their glory days. Even before that, Rosselli brokered deals with the likes of Howard Hughes and other Hollywood studio heads. Court documents show that in 1947, Rosselli had been an uncredited producer on a minor "B" movie, *He Walks by Night*,[53] which depicted a murderous ex-serviceman who kept his rifle wrapped in a blanket. In one scene, he's stopped on a deserted street by a police car—but when the cop gets out to talk to him, the serviceman shoots him with a pistol and runs away. Sixteen years later, Rosselli would use all those same elements again, only this time in real life, to make it appear that an ex-serviceman in Dallas had shot Police Officer J. D. Tippit with a pistol and shot JFK with a rifle supposedly kept hidden in a blanket.

He Walked by Night was one of three films "produced in part by an actual gangster," according to Rosselli's biographers.[54] Producer "[Bryan] Foy once described him as an 'artistic consultant.'"[55] Rosselli's real role was probably in the influence he could bring to bear. For example, one film-noir history finds it "surprising" that the "notoriously low-budget studio, Eagle-Lion" was able to "provide" *T-Men* "with a massive publicity campaign," including a lavish "pictorial spread on the film" in "*Life* magazine, which usually lent its support only to the glossier efforts of the big-name studios," not minor "B" pictures.[56]

Rosselli's influence in Hollywood continued into the early 1960s, where he and his associates tried to prevent a film from being made of Bobby Kennedy's best-selling Mafia exposé *The Enemy Within*. But the roots of Rosselli's power in Hollywood—and the reason his name couldn't be listed in the credits of *He Walked by Night*—led directly to Rosselli's assassination of Arizona Senator Barry Goldwater's two good friends. These two assassinations from the 1950s are important in showing the extent of the power of Rosselli and his Chicago Mafia family, who could assassinate with impunity two friends of a US Senator, one of whom had recently been the mayor of Las Vegas. It also shows why Rosselli was not concerned about the possibility that the assassination of JFK might result in a Goldwater presidency after the 1964 elections: If Senator Goldwater was incapable of going after the man behind the assassination of his two good friends, the Mafia had little to fear from any investigation a President Goldwater might undertake into the JFK assassination.

In *The Green Felt Jungle*, Ed Reid and Ovid Demaris say that "along the strip in Las Vegas, [Senator] Barry Goldwater is known to the wags and older show girls as a real 'swinger,'" because of his frequent presence there in the 1950s. Then, "Barry Goldwater was a frequent visitor, occupying plush suites, first at the Flamingo and then later . . . at the Riviera.[57]

Las Vegas mayor Gus Greenbaum introduced Goldwater to "Willie Bioff, the convicted panderer, extortionist, and celebrated stoolie." By the late 1930s, Bioff and Rosselli had a highly profitable labor racket with the Hollywood studios, and Rosselli lived the glamorous lifestyle to the hilt. "But in 1941 . . . Bioff had been . . . convicted" on federal racketeering charges. After serving three years of a ten-year sentence, Bioff turned informer "and assisted the government in the prosecution of nine Chicago mobsters, including Johnny Rosselli," who was sent to prison.

By "1955 Bioff found an even more unlikely friend: the junior Senator from Arizona, Barry Goldwater. The two men were often seen together, and Goldwater . . . personally chauffeured Bioff in his private plane all over the Southwest to attend various parties. When questioned by reporters, Goldwater became indignant, protesting that he had no idea that his friend . . . was the notorious Willie Bioff. Later" Goldwater claimed Bioff "was . . . giving him a special insight into union racketeering."[58] Goldwater was able to make that claim because he served on the McClellan Crime Committee along with Senator John F. Kennedy and the committee's chief counsel, Bobby Kennedy.

According to Reid and Demaris, "in 1952 when Goldwater was seeking election for his first term in the [US] Senate," Willie "Bioff . . . contributed $5,000 to Goldwater's senatorial campaign."[59] However, Johnny Rosselli hadn't forgotten Bioff and the conviction that had sent Rosselli to prison and which kept him from having a real studio position. So, "on November 4, 1955, Willie Bioff" was killed at his home in Phoenix, when his truck exploded in his driveway, due to "a dynamite bomb wired to the starter."[60]

The case was never solved. Rosselli's biographers confirm that "the police never did question Johnny Rosselli about the murder of Willie Bioff." Johnny Rosselli had been so worried about the Bioff murder that he had immediately called "a Los Angeles reporter and stated for the record that he 'hadn't seen Bioff in years.'" And "Rosselli then called" a close friend "and asked if he might stay in" their "guest room until the excitement died down. 'They're going to be on my back instantly,' Rosselli explained. 'I'm going to need to lie low for a few days.'"[61] Like Marcello and Trafficante, Rosselli would soon learn the value of having a patsy on hand to take the fall for a major mob hit, to quickly take the heat off.

Unlike the mob murder of Bioff, the assassination of former Las Vegas Mayor Gus Greenbaum—also close to Goldwater—was meant to be attributed to the mob, so it didn't need a patsy. It was intended as a very public lesson, since Greenbaum was openly tied to the Mafia. Mayor Greenbaum had been a "close friend" of Barry Goldwater, and "some of the Senator's speeches were written in Las Vegas," with the aid of Greenbaum's "ghost-writer."[62] However, by 1958 Greenbaum was experiencing a variety of problems, including heroin addition, which the Mafia didn't permit for someone involved in casinos in Las Vegas.

According to Rosselli's biographers, "by the summer of 1958, when Rosselli had moved into the top position in Las Vegas, Greenbaum was ordered to sell out of the Riviera" casino, but "Greenbaum refused." So, "on December 3, 1958, Gus Greenbaum's body was discovered in his bedroom, nearly decapitated," and "his wife Bess" had had "her throat slashed with a butcher knife."[63] Reid and Demaris note that "the Greenbaum funeral was attended by three hundred mourners, including Senator Barry Goldwater."[64] As with the murder of Rosselli's nemesis Bioff, there was "no clue, no suspicion, no arrest," even though five years later, the authors of *Green Felt Jungle* were able to document the arrival of two hit men from Miami shortly before the murder, who left shortly after the hits in a private plane.[65]

Ruby, Hoffa, Heroin, and Gun-running

ROSSELLI, MARCELLO, AND TRAFFICANTE RULED their own kingdoms, but their work together in drug smuggling—and their common associates like Jack Ruby and Teamster boss Jimmy Hoffa—were crucial to their efforts to penetrate C-Day and kill JFK. While Trafficante's role as a major player in the French Connection heroin ring has long been known, few historians have focused on how much Ruby, Hoffa, Marcello, and associates of Rosselli were involved in that secure heroin network.

Jack Ruby grew up in a large, poor Jewish family in Chicago. A troubled youth in a troubled family, Ruby dropped out of school and tried a wide range of activities to make money, some of them criminal. According to Ruby biographer Seth Kantor, this included delivering "sealed envelopes at the rate of $1 per errand for Chicago's No. 1 racketeer, Al Capone."[1] Investigator Scott Malone says that "Ruby moved from Chicago to Los Angeles in 1933 and began selling handicappers' tip sheets at Santa Anita racetrack. Johnny Rosselli testified to the Kefauver Crime Committee in 1951 that he, too, had moved from Chicago to Los Angeles in 1933—to oversee gambling at Santa Anita for the Chicago mob." By 1939, Ruby was back in Chicago as a "secretary to the Waste Handlers Union" and was questioned "in connection with the murder of the secretary-treasurer of the local."[2] The union was "described by the FBI as 'largely a shakedown operation.'"[3] Malone points out "that murder enabled the mob, and eventually the Teamsters, to take over the union. (Bobby Kennedy, in his book *The Enemy Within*, called this episode a key step in the mob's rise to domination over the Teamsters.)" Luis Kutner, a Chicago lawyer who was the staff attorney for the Kefauver Committee, says Ruby "hobnobbed with Chicago mob boss Sam Giancana, and his crowd"—which would include Rosselli—"during this period."[4] A recent history of the Federal Bureau of Narcotics (FBN) by Michael Valentine says that Jack "Ruby and Rosselli had known each other since the 1930's and . . . they both knew George White," an FBN supervisor with CIA ties who later "often sent" his subordinate "to the airport to pick up Rosselli and bring him to the office."[5]

According to Valentine, "the Ruby family had a long history in the illicit drug trade." One of Jack Ruby's brothers "was convicted in 1939 of buying two ounces of heroin." The diary of the FBN's George White said that that brother of Jack Ruby "had been his informant since July 1946" and states that "in October 1947" Ruby's brother "betrayed [Paul Roland] Jones to FBN agents in Chicago."[6] Warren Commission and other files show that Jones had been involved in the Chicago Mafia's attempt to move into Dallas in 1947, a move that involved Jack Ruby, "according to former Dallas sheriff Steve Guthrie."[7] By 1950, the FBN's George White was also an investigator for the Kefauver Senate Crime Committee. That year, Jack Ruby "briefed the Kefauver Committee about organized crime in Chicago" according to Luis Kutner.[8] Kutner said his "staff learned that Ruby was 'a syndicate lieutenant who had been sent to Dallas to serve as a liaison for Chicago mobsters.'"[9] This is the first of many times Ruby would appear to cooperate with authorities, in return for protecting his criminal activities or finding out what the authorities knew.

Why isn't Ruby's role in narcotics and as an informant better known? "The FBN had a file on Ruby," according to FBN agent George Gaffney, "but there wasn't much in it . . . just that he was a source on numerous occasions, on unimportant suspects."[10] As he would do later with the Dallas Police, Ruby was just using the system to provide protection for his illegal activities. Even so, "right after Ruby shot Oswald," FBN agent "Mort Benjamin checked the files in the New York office and found one that indicated that Ruby had been an FBN informant since the 1940s. But the next time Benjamin looked for it, the New York file had gone missing, and Secret Service Chief Rowley," who had asked Gaffney to check the FBN headquarters file, "never returned the FBN headquarters file to Gaffney."[11]

Not surprisingly, the Dallas FBN office says they knew nothing about Ruby being an FBN informant and insists "the Mafia was not selling heroin" in Dallas, in spite of evidence to the contrary. After all, FBN agent "Jack Cusack had informed the McClellan Committee in January 1958 that Mafioso Joseph Civello ran the heroin business in Dallas" and "Cusack linked Civello with Marcello, Trafficante, and Jimmy Hoffa." The author of the FBN history notes that "Civello was Marcello's 'deputy in Dallas,'" and Bobby Kennedy himself would name Civello as an associate of Carlos Marcello, when Bobby grilled Marcello before the Senate McClellan Committee.[12]

According to Mafia expert David E. Scheim, soon after JFK's assassination "Civello stated to the FBI "that he had known Ruby casually 'for about ten years.'" An employee of Civello's told the FBI that "Ruby was 'a frequent visitor and associate of Civello.'" Investigative journalist "Ovid Demaris . . . reported that Civello told him, 'Yeah, I knew Jack—we were friends and I used to go to his club.'"[13]

The author of the FBN history poses the question: With all these connections between Ruby, his associates, and heroin, "how could the Dallas [FBN] office not know of" Civello's "narcotics activities or that Jack Ruby was part of his organization"? Perhaps the Dallas "police were able to keep the Dallas [FBN] agents in the dark. The Kefauver Committee concluded that big-city vice squads could limit the ability of federal agents to make cases. Civello was a [Dallas] police informant on narcotics cases," and "after Civello was convicted in 1931 on a federal narcotics charge," he "obtained early parole on the recommendation of Dallas Sheriff Bill Decker."[14]

Civello had other ties to law enforcement that would be useful for Ruby and Marcello after JFK's assassination. Investigative journalist Anthony Summers found that "not long after Civello's arrest at the famous Apalachin meeting of organized crime figures" in 1957, Joe "Civello had invited Sergeant Dean" of the Dallas Police Department "to dinner."[15] Dallas Police Sergeant Dean even boasted to historian Peter Dale Scott "of his longtime relationship with Civello. He justified being on good terms with Civello by the information Civello supplied him, in 'many, many dope cases I made.'"[16] Given Civello's top rank in the Dallas Mafia and well-documented ties to narcotics and Marcello, one imagines that Civello made sure the information he provided to Decker and Dean protected his major heroin traffic, while keeping low-level users and dealers in line. Along with Sheriff Decker, Sergeant "Dean of the Dallas Police Department was one of those responsible for security . . . when Ruby shot Oswald."[17]

Ruby "was well acquainted with virtually every officer of the Dallas Police force," according to the Warren Commission file on Ruby's best friend Lewis McWillie, who worked at casinos for Trafficante and Rosselli.[18] Dallas policemen never had to pay for a drink at Ruby's club, and sometimes they were even provided with women. A Warren Commission document bluntly calls Ruby "the pay-off man for the Dallas Police Department."[19] Another investigator noted that "Officer Tippit's attorney remarked: '[Dallas Police Captain Will] Fritz and Jack Ruby were very close friends. Jack Ruby, in spite of his reputation of being a 'hood,' was allowed complete run of the Homicide Bureau." According to FBI documents, Jack Ruby "took the Chief of Police" of Dallas to "Hot Springs, Arkansas" in 1956, when it was a gambling mecca.[20]

Investigative reporter Seth Kantor knew Jack Ruby and met him at Parkland Hospital shortly after JFK was shot. Kantor wrote a landmark biography of Ruby, and was told by "a retired Dallas police captain" that "the department 'was rotten from top to bottom . . . oh, there were some good cops. But man, it was a dangerous place to work in.'"[21] We should make it clear now that this book does not have evidence that any Dallas policeman was knowingly involved in JFK's assassination, though some might have been subject to unknowing manipulation by Ruby and his more powerful associates.

Congressional investigator Michael Ewing wrote that "Ruby had several dozen friends, employers, associates, and acquaintances who were significantly involved in organized crime."[22] He also noted "Ruby's close friendship" with the "chief" of "the special Dallas Police unit charged with investigating organized crime cases as well as narcotics and vice," whom "Warren Commission testimony shows regularly (sometimes nightly) visited" Ruby's "Carousel stripjoint."[23] Johnny Rosselli's biographers documented that "from 1947 to 1963, Jack Ruby . . . was arrested nine times in sixteen years, but developed connections to the Dallas police strong enough that he never faced a trial."[24]

According to a Warren Commission document, Ruby was active in the French Connection heroin network in Dallas. The document said that since 1956, "Jack Ruby of Dallas" gave "the okay to operate" for a "large narcotics set up operating between Mexico, Texas, and the East."[25] This was the tight-knit heroin network run by Trafficante, Marcello, and Michel Victor Mertz. FBN authority Michael Valentine says that while "the small FBN office in New Orleans . . . in 1963 had reasons to believe that" Marcello "was a major narcotics trafficker," the FBI "agents in New Orleans . . . never had the manpower or resources to make a conspiracy case on Marcello."[26]

The true extent of the French Connection heroin network involving Ruby, Marcello, Trafficante, and others was detailed by Valentine, with the help of retired FBI agents and internal FBN reports. Valentine says "the Mafia's courier from New York" to Texas, "Benjamin Indiviglio, was convicted of heroin trafficking in Houston in 1956." But after "the US Supreme

Court" reversed his conviction, Indiviglio "immediately went into business" with a close associate of Trafficante heroin supplier Michel Victor Mertz. "Indiviglio had shared a prison cell" with the Mertz associate—Joseph Orsini—who would later be involved with Mertz, Trafficante, and Marcello in the heroin bust at Fort Benning."[27] According to the DEA's official history of the French Connection, by "1959 . . . ninety kilograms of heroin a month" were going to "Indiviglio" and his associates, "who operated under the auspices of Santo Trafficante."[28] But the FBN didn't know at the time—and would only learn later—that part of this heroin network involved "deliveries from" French "SDECE agent Michel Victor Mertz, while Mertz was wearing his French Army uniform! This arrangement with . . . Mertz . . . lasted from 1960 until September 1964."[29] The SDECE was the French Secret Service; Mertz's role as a double agent for them, targeting rebellious French officers, would later play a role in the Mafia penetration of C-Day and JFK's assassination.

Two of Mertz's partners in this heroin network, Lucien Rivard and Paul Mondoloni, had ties to Trafficante and to associates of Jack Ruby. Rivard was imprisoned for a time in Cuba with Trafficante in 1959, while both Rivard "and Mondoloni were co-owners of the El Morocco club in Cuba with Norman Rothman," an American gangster and underboss who worked with Santo Trafficante and Jack Ruby. A November 24, "1958 memo to [FBN Chief Harry] Anslinger . . . said that Mondoloni's operation in Cuba, which had begun in 1955 with Norman Rothman and Trafficante, 'poses a most serious threat to the suppression of the illicit heroin traffic at the present time.' While Mondoloni's operation proceeded apace, Rothman and former Cuban President Carlos Prio were indicted for arms trafficking to Castro." Both Rothman and Prio were linked by Warren Commission documents to Cuban arms smuggling with Jack Ruby. However, "the CIA had the gangster set free. According to historian Peter Dale Scott, 'In 1978 Rothman told a CBS television interviewer that he had avoided conviction because of the CIA's interest in his gunrunning activities.'"[30] While Rothman was not involved in JFK's assassination, his use of a federal agency like the CIA to avoid prosecution would later be adopted by Trafficante, Mertz, Rosselli, and others for the JFK assassination.

Jimmy Hoffa's name has not often been linked in the public's mind to drug-running, but the evidence shows that he, too, was part of Trafficante's heroin network that included Marcello, Ruby, and Mertz. This well documented but rarely exposed part of Hoffa's background will also help to explain his supporting role in the plot that killed JFK.

Valentine's recent history of the FBN says that in Organized Crime hearings covered in the January 10, 1958 *New York Times*, a "district supervisor in Atlanta described the link . . . between the Civello family in Dallas and . . . Carlos Marcello in New Orleans, Santo Trafficante, in Tampa, and remarkably, with Jimmy Hoffa and gun-running in Cuba."[31] The FBN history goes to note that "as Chief Counsel on" the McClellan Crime Committee, "Bobby Kennedy learned how drug smuggling factored into the Mafia's relationship with the Teamsters." Bobby heard an FBN agent explain how a "Teamsters official . . . laundered drug profits through a union welfare fund," ways in which "Jimmy Hoffa had protected Detroit's major drug traffickers . . . by assigning them to" a certain local, "and that Trafficante had an office at a Teamsters local in Miami, which had been established by Mafia drug traffickers James Plumeri and Frank Dioguardia."[32] (Frank Dioguardia—aka Frankie Dio—would later be convicted for his role in the French Connection heroin smuggling ring at Fort Benning not long after C-Day, and Plumeri would be involved in the original 1959 CIA-Mafia plots to kill Castro, which were brokered by Hoffa.) Valentine writes that "Bobby came to realize that the FBN . . . had solid evidence that Hoffa was beholden to the mob, and that certain Teamster 'paper locals' (with no membership), like the one run by Johnny Dioguardia (Frank's brother) in New York, were providing logistical support to the Mafia's national drug distribution syndicate."[33]

Valentine notes that Hoffa had been involved with narcotics smuggling since the 1940s, when the head of the FBN "revealed [that] Detroit drug smugglers were receiving narcotics from Santo Trafficante in Tampa, via New Orleans. The connection was established in December 1945" by Carlos Marcello, Frank "Costello and [Meyer] Lansky," using gangster Frank Coppola, who grew close to Hoffa. "From Hoffa's headquarters in Detroit, the Teamsters facilitated the Mafia's national drug distribution system. After being received from overseas sources, Frank Coppola's narcotics were transported to Joe Civello in Dallas" by a trucking company.[34]

Former Teamster vice president Allen Friedman wrote that "Hoffa . . . worked with the mob," finding "ways to exchange favors, to gain mob influence" while "protecting organized crime members wherever he could." Friedman notes that some "French Connection . . . drug dealers were connected with Hoffa in legitimate business activities. Others were given union jobs." While not directly and personally involved in smuggling, Hoffa "understood the financial importance of narcotics to organized crime members who were friends of his. By helping the men . . . he was winning their gratitude. He gave them a certain amount of respectability and, in that way, protections from some of the investigators. He also knew that they would feel obligated to him, willing to help him win and maintain power, no matter what the cost."[35]

According to former Teamster Friedman, Hoffa's criminal ties also led to an odd alliance with Fidel Castro—which would eventually lead to Jack Ruby and the JFK assassination. Friedman says that "Jimmy Hoffa" was "aware of the Cuban revolution and the need for arms by both sides" and that "military surplus weapons were readily available through both legitimate and illegal sources." So Hoffa "decided to support both sides" in the revolution, "making the most money possible." Hoffa used Florida as a "shipping base" for the "guns and a few army surplus planes." Friedman says that "Hoffa wanted to continue gun-running after Castro took control of Cuba" and "wanted to utilize Teamster money . . . $300,000 . . . to aid friends involved with gun-running." This "was Hoffa's way of trying to help organized crime figures . . . it is believed that Hoffa's main interest was in helping Santo Trafficante," whose "Miami office was in Teamster Local 320."[36] Friedman also says that "Richard Nixon was becoming involved with Hoffa's people and the Cuban connection at this time. He regularly visited Cuba before the [1960] election, visiting Batista, and occasionally going to the casinos while he was a Senator."

Joe Franco, one of Hoffa's "most trusted lieutenants," would be with Hoffa the day he disappeared in 1975. He confirms that "when Fidel Castro was still a rebel fighting in the mountains of Cuba against Batista . . . one of the business agents" for a Teamster local in New York "was a strong supporter of the Castro movement and he left while Castro was still up in the mountains fighting guerrilla war, and he joined up."[37] Jimmy Hoffa "started handing over money to buy the arms" for Castro "and for a long time he continued to give money for arms for Castro and they got on a very solid basis and there was a few times when Jimmy asked that Castro send people over here to do little jobs for him."[38]

Several government documents link Jack Ruby to Cuban gun-running at this time, and we'll quote from many of them shortly. Jimmy Hoffa's son told Teamster expert Dan Moldea that "I think my dad knew Jack Ruby . . . so what?"[39] Moldea writes that in 1958, "Hoffa's friends in the underworld viewed Fidel Castro as a potential ally" so "the syndicate had shipped arms and ammunition to the revolutionary forces" of Castro "as well as to Batista, hoping that if Castro took over his cooperation could be bought in advance." According to a Hoffa associate who turned informer for Bobby Kennedy, Hoffa and several associates were "in the business of ferrying arms from south Florida to various points in Cuba. 'I was right there on several occasions when they were loading the guns and ammunition on the barges,'" the associate recalls, and "Hoffa was directing the whole thing.'"[40]

In the 1950s, Marcello, Trafficante, and Rosselli prospered in a vast criminal network that included associates ranging from powerful national figures like Jimmy Hoffa to lowly operatives like Jack Ruby. Cuba would play an increasing role in their operations, as would other Latin American countries like Guatemala. For a time, it seemed as if the Mafia bosses could operate with near impunity, and their horizon seemed limitless.

Nixon, Havana, and Assassinating an Attorney General

IN THE GOLDEN AGE OF Havana gambling in the mid-1950s, before Castro and the Revolution, several key relationships developed that would later allow the Mafia to infiltrate C-Day. The Mafia's National Commission worked hard to smooth operations in Cuba, so there were no bloody turf wars between Mafia families to scare away customers. The two major casino owners in Havana were Meyer Lansky and Santo Trafficante, though each took on partners from other Mafia families across America. According to Johnny Rosselli's biographers, "Santo Trafficante was assigned" the "direct control of the Sans Souci, and shares of the Capri, the Hilton, and the old Hotel Commodoro. Near the end of his life, Charles 'Lucky' Luciano said that Trafficante . . . 'was a guy who always managed to hug the background, but he is rough and reliable. In fact, he's one of the few guys in the whole country that Meyer Lansky would never tangle with.'"[1]

In Cuba, Trafficante was smart enough not to cast his lot completely with Cuban dictator Fulgencio Batista. Trafficante's lawyer confirms that in 1958, he was told by Trafficante that "he and his friends were secretly contributing to" Castro's "rebels, as well as to Batista. Santo figured that no matter who won the war, he would emerge safe and sound. All his bets were covered."[2] Trafficante's proclivity for playing more than one side would later surface in several aspects of the JFK assassination.

Rosselli's biographers write that "according to FBI and court records and interviews," Fidel "Castro received a steady supply of arms from Santo Trafficante and gambling boss Norman 'Roughhouse' Rothman, whose gunrunning network included a Dallas nightclub operator and onetime mob slugger named Jack Ruby."[3] Norman Rothman was an underboss for a Pennsylvania mob family, and his involvement with Trafficante in Cuba shows how Trafficante's leading role in Havana helped him form alliances with Mafia families throughout America. Rothman himself would play a role in the Mafia's activities with the CIA in Cuba in the late 1950s. However, he would not infiltrate C-Day because the Kennedys rebuffed his attempt to join their earlier Cuban operations in the spring of 1961.

Of more significance is "another weapons trafficker" cited by Rosselli's biographers, a "soldier of fortune" named "Frank Fiorini, who later gained fame as one of the Watergate burglars" and who "maintained intermittent contacts with both the CIA and Santo Trafficante." Fiorini—who later used the name Frank Sturgis—would be on the fringe of the Mafia's penetration of C-Day. However, Fiorini was not a significant part of JFK's assassination, probably because the Mafia knew he was a publicity-seeker who cultivated friendships and news stories from noted journalists like Jack Anderson. (Anderson, an associate of Johnny Rosselli, even paid Fiorini's bail after his Watergate arrest.) But Fiorini's "contacts with both the CIA and Santo Trafficante" would make him helpful in feeding information—and disinformation—to the CIA, and to the press after JFK's assassination.[4]

Johnny Rosselli performed "various functions" in "Havana's high-rise gambling district" according to his biographers, including "operating for a time in a management capacity at Trafficante's Sans Souci."[5] They note that "Rosselli's parallel in the intelligence community"—first in Havana and later in America—was "a man who played the same clandestine role for the American government that Rosselli did for the mob . . . David Sanchez Morales." Morales will play key roles in the various CIA plots to kill Castro starting in 1959, as well as C-Day.

New Orleans mob boss Carlos Marcello was not nearly as active in Cuba as Rosselli and Trafficante, perhaps because there was always the risk of being denied reentry into the US if he went to Cuba, since he was an illegal alien. (US authorities had not yet realized that Rosselli was an illegal alien.) Marcello's influence in Cuba was more indirect. New Orleans was a major port for trade with Cuba and the rest of Latin America, and Marcello controlled the docks, as well as related businesses and some union activity in New Orleans. Because of this, New Orleans developed a large Cuban exile community that would play a role in both C-Day and the Mafia's penetration of it.

In the 1950s, the Mafia flourished not only in Havana, but also in the US—due in large part to the lack of attention paid to prosecuting them by certain US officials. These officials included FBI head J. Edgar Hoover, who went so far as to deny the Mafia's existence, and Vice President Richard M. Nixon. Hoover's Mafia ties have become better known in recent years—in books such as Anthony Summers's *Official and Confidential*—so they won't be covered here. While the media pays much attention to real and alleged contacts between the Kennedy family and mob figures, little attention has been paid in recent decades to the far more extensive ties between Richard Nixon and the Mafia. Briefly publicized around the time of Watergate, Nixon's Mafia ties faded from public view after his pardon, but they are crucial to understanding the origins of C-Day, why it failed, and how that failure continued to affect US presidents after JFK, eventually costing Nixon his presidency.

Before the election of JFK in 1960 and Bobby's appointment as attorney general, the US had made little progress in prosecuting top Mafia godfathers. There were occasional hearings, arrests, or trials, but by and large the Mafia was allowed to flourish. Naturally, the mob bosses supported candidates of both parties, at all levels, usually using seemingly (or actually) legitimate businesses and businessmen as intermediaries. In some cases, the official would only find out he had received support from a mob figure when that person needed help or some favor. In that context, the relatively few mob ties of LBJ and Goldwater were not unusual for the times. On the other hand, Richard Nixon's having numerous Mafia ties, which spanned decades and involved well-known Mafia associates, is highly unusual in the annals of the US presidency. Nixon associates worked smoothly with Marcello, Trafficante, and Rosselli from the '50s to the '70s. These ties help explain Nixon's roles in the CIA-Mafia plots, in penetrating C-Day, and in the Watergate scandal, which eventually brought him down. They do not, however, implicate him in JFK's assassination. Nixon was probably as surprised as the rest of the country when that happened—otherwise it wouldn't have made sense for him to be on a highly publicized business trip in Dallas (which included nightclubbing with movie star Joan Crawford) just before JFK's death.

Los Angeles mobster Mickey Cohen, an early associate of Johnny Rosselli, confirmed the Mafia's support for Nixon from the beginning of his career. According to Nixon biographer Anthony Summers, "Cohen gave Nixon a check for five thousand dollars . . . about forty-four thousand dollars" in today's dollars, for his first run for Congress in 1946. During Nixon's 1950 Senate run, Cohen said he "was again asked by" Nixon aide "Murray Chotiner to raise funds" for Nixon. Cohen hosted a fund-raiser attended by several associates of Johnny Rosselli, which Cohen says raised "$75,000, a considerable sum in those days" for Nixon.[6] The Mafia's initial link to Nixon was through Chotiner, the notorious figure "who managed" Nixon's "1950 campaign" for the Senate and "who ran the 1952 campaign that took Nixon to the vice presidency." Murray Chotiner was well acquainted with the Mafia, since according to Summers, "Chotiner . . . had handled no fewer than 221 California bookmaking cases in one four-year period" in the early 1950s.[7]

Santo Trafficante also viewed Nixon favorably. "'Santo,' recalled his attorney Frank Ragano, 'viewed Nixon as a realistic, conservative politician who was not a zealot and would not be hard on him and his mob friends. The Mafia had little to fear from Nixon.'"[8] Trafficante may have known Nixon through Havana. A longtime associate of Carlos Marcello told Congressional investigators that "he heard stories that Nixon knew Norman Rothman and that Nixon had lost money gambling in the Caribbean."[9]

Summers notes that "Norman Rothman was a significant player in the organized crime apparatus that ran gambling in Havana. The casino he ran, the Sans Souci, was Cuba's classiest gaming palace, located in the heart of the Country Club district, home to the capital's elite families."[10] The actual owner of the Sans Souci would turn out to be Santo Trafficante. Rothman was later part of a gun-running operation to Cuba that involved Jack Ruby.

According to Anthony Summers, in 1954 "Sans Souci operator Rothman met with a Pennsylvania District Attorney . . . and stated 'categorically' that Nixon had indeed been in Havana . . . and had been gambling. Later still, in other interviews with law enforcement officers covering a range of matters, Rothman said that while" someone else had gotten the blame for writing a bounced "check, on a 1950 Nixon campaign account, it had been Nixon who actually lost money that night. Even more troubling was Rothman's assertion that he had covered up for Nixon, falsely telling a journalist in 1952 that Nixon had not been" involved and Rothman "claimed he had shielded Nixon by avoiding giving testimony in" a "lawsuit" about the matter.[11]

Historian Richard D. Mahoney documented that "Nixon's Mafia ties were wide-ranging: Bebe Rebozo . . . in south Florida, Carlos Marcello in New Orleans (a heavy Nixon contributor) . . . as well as Teamster mob chieftains like Anthony Provenzano."[12] He adds "Nixon's friend Bebe Rebozo was a well-known figure in various mob families."[13]

Summers confirms that latter assertion, saying that "in probing Nixon's possible links to gambling and to Cuba," Meyer "Lansky's name crops up again, as it has repeatedly in connection with Bebe Rebozo." According to one official, "'The really close friendship between Nixon and Rebozo,' said former IRS operative Norman Casper, 'began in Cuba.'" Casper told Summers that at Meyer Lansky's "Hotel Nationale in the early fifties . . . Nixon was gambling pretty heavily." He says "Nixon lost thousands of dollars," perhaps as much as fifty thousand dollars, "and Bebe picked up the marker on it. Bebe bailed Nixon out."[14] A former "OSS operative and a source of information on organized crime" told Summers that Bebe "Rebozo was involved in Lansky's gambling" and that when he "checked the name [Rebozo] with the Miami police, they said he was . . . very close to Meyer [Lansky]." He also saw documents confirming that "when Nixon stayed at the Hotel National [in Havana], which Lansky owned, they comped the whole deal—paid his bill. And it was the Presidential Suite." According to Summers, "an FBI document released in 2000 cites an informant who emphasized Rebozo's involvement with Nixon, and others in business ventures in Cuba during the Batista period."[15]

Summers also reveals that "as the 1952 presidential election approached," Chicago's "Sam Giancana, then a rising power in the national crime syndicate," was quoted as saying "I like Ike. But I like his running mate, Nixon, even better . . . I'm hedging my bets. We got campaign contributions to both sides: Our guys out in California are backing Nixon" while mob funds were also channeled to Adlai Stevenson.[16] At that time, "our guys out in California" meant Johnny Rosselli and his associates. Nixon's ties to Rosselli—and Marcello and Trafficante—laid the groundwork for the actions that would later cost Nixon his presidency.

Marcello, Trafficante, and Rosselli knew how to manage political figures —but what if a politician couldn't be bought? The Mafia's growing power in the mid-1950s led to one of their few setbacks in that era, when the decision was made to assassinate a state attorney general-elect who threatened the operations of Trafficante and Marcello. But even this setback was limited to just one small city, and the mob bosses learned from their mistake. The next time a high government official was assassinated—like the President of Guatemala in 1957—the mob bosses made sure to have a patsy on hand, to quickly take the blame and divert the media and investigators away from the real killers, avoiding the problems they had experienced in 1954 in Alabama.

In the fall of 1962, when Carlos Marcello told an FBI informant about his plan to end Attorney General Bobby Kennedy's prosecution of him, Marcello said it was important to kill JFK, not Bobby; otherwise, JFK might simply call out the Army in response. Marcello was speaking from experience, because that is exactly what happened in 1954, after the Attorney General-elect of Alabama was assassinated in Phenix City, Alabama. That assassination and its aftermath seriously impacted the operations of Marcello and Trafficante, and ultimately influenced their plans for the JFK hit.

Phenix City, Alabama lies on the boundary between the territories of Carlos Marcello and Santo Trafficante, though, according to one journalist, Trafficante had primary responsibility for it. Veteran Tampa reporter John Sugg wrote that "from his base in Tampa . . . Santo Trafficante for years ran rackets—prostitution, drugs, and notably, loan sharking—in Phenix City, Alabama, a town renowned for its lawlessness. The mob's primary 'clients' were the soldiers across the Chattahoochee River at Fort Benning, Georgia."[17] Fort Benning was part of Columbus, Georgia's second-largest city; and both the large, prosperous town and the huge military base provided a steady stream of clients to relatively small Phenix City (population 23,000).

Phenix City was a microcosm of the type of crime Trafficante and Marcello practiced in many other cities and towns. According to *National Guard* magazine, Phenix City "offered every conceivable vice: gambling, prostitution, bootleg whiskey, drugs" and even "backroom abortions and baby selling."[18] Many of the clubs were like more extreme versions of Jack Ruby's Carousel Club in Dallas, using "B-Girls" to hustle huge quantities of watered-down drinks, as well as sometimes to engage in prostitution.[19] According to a recent book, even "General George S. Patton, while training his troops at Fort Benning . . . was so enraged by the atrocities against his soldiers in Phenix City that he publicly threatened to take his tanks across the river and mash Phenix City flat." But General Patton was no match for the vice lords Trafficante and Marcello, and anyway Patton soon left for Europe. The crime in Phenix City continued; and, by 1954, "what was already bad had become incredibly worse."[20] It should be noted that while Phenix City was certainly the worst, many states in the 1950s and into the early 1960s had areas that were nearly its equal. That's why the crime crusade of the Kennedys—first in the Senate and later in the White House—received so much public attention and support.

Eventually, things got so bad that a local reform-minded lawyer named Albert Patterson ran for Attorney General of Alabama on a platform of cleaning up Phenix City. He felt he had no choice since, according to his son, state officials "looked the other way" and "the federal people did not get involved," even though Phenix City was notorious throughout the country.[21] The lack of federal action or interest in Phenix City is significant, given the interstate nature of the crimes and the fact that many of the victims were US soldiers—but neither J. Edgar Hoover, Vice President Richard Nixon, or anyone else in the Eisenhower administration did anything about it.

In a surprising upset, Albert Patterson won the Democratic nomination— which, in a one-party state like Alabama was at the time, meant that he was the Attorney General-elect. But on June 18, 1954, the new Attorney General-elect "was gunned down next to his car. He was struck three times: in the chest, in the arm and in the mouth, the death-mark for informers," according to *National Guard* magazine.[22] The assassination sent shock waves across not just the region, but the nation. And because no patsy was used it was immediately clear that the Mafia was responsible.

Corruption went so high in Alabama that the official response was slow, but public outrage grew by the day. According to one historian, two major vice lords fled to Florida—Trafficante's territory—while the "Phenix City night Police Chief," involved in a "protection racket" and a nightclub, fled to Marcello's territory in Texas.[23]

After being pressured by National Guard General Walter Hanna, the Alabama Governor finally went "to consult with President Dwight Eisenhower, FBI Chief J. Edgar Hoover, and constitutional lawyers" about shutting down the vice in Phenix City. The Governor returned with a drastic solution: martial rule of Phenix City by the National Guard, which required "the replacement of all elected law enforcement."[24] This US military occupation got plenty of publicity, and the assassination became the subject of a popular movie actually filmed in Phenix City (and featuring some of its citizens).

On June 23, 1954, the corrupt Alabama Attorney General Si Garrett (still in office; Patterson was not in office yet)—the target in a grand jury investigation into the assassination—told reporters he was going "to a psychiatric clinic in Galveston, Texas, for a rest."[25] Galveston, southwest of Houston, was in Marcello's territory and, according to the *Dallas Morning News*, was where "Jack Ruby was running guns and ammunition . . . to Fidel Castro's guerrillas in Cuba" in the mid-1950s.[26] Galveston was so safe for Marcello's people that David Ferrie went there in 1963, right after the JFK assassination.

Si Garrett was indicted for Albert Patterson's assassination; but, except for a brief stay at a hospital in Mississippi (also Marcello territory), he remained safely in Galveston—despite attempts to have him extradited—until 1963, and later his "case was dismissed."[27] Witness intimidation and murder, as well as official corruption, kept the investigation from reaching as high as Trafficante or Marcello. Among the four men indicted, only one was convicted of murder, and he served just seven years. Another was acquitted, still another "pleaded nolo contendere" to a minor charge, and corrupt former Attorney General Garrett was never even tried.[28]

Even though the *Columbus Ledger* was awarded "the 1955 Pulitzer Prize for their reporting of the Phenix City story and the political assassination of Albert Patterson" and a movie about the events was released, the story was soon forgotten by most Americans.[29] But not by Trafficante and Marcello, who would remember its lessons well in their planning for JFK's assassination. The lack of a logical patsy without an obvious connection to the real killers had been the biggest problem, one that would not be repeated in two later presidential assassinations.

Phenix City and its legacy would also impact C-Day. After the National Guard crackdown in 1954, the Mafia gradually revived some of its activities across the river in Georgia, even closer to Ft. Benning. However, the usual vice found near a huge Army base was kept much lower-key than it had been in Phenix City, to avoid publicity and notoriety. And as if to make up for lost profits, by 1963 the French Connection heroin ring involving Marcello, Trafficante, and Michel Victor Mertz was smuggling large quantities of heroin through Ft. Benning, hidden in cargo coming from Europe.[30] Unfortunately for JFK, that was at the same time the Kennedys had Cuban exiles training there for C-Day, giving the mob bosses yet another way to learn about and penetrate C-Day.[31]

Guatemala: The Mafia Assassinates a President, the CIA Stages a Coup

IN 1956, WHILE JOHNNY ROSSELLI and Carlos Marcello were finalizing their Las Vegas Tropicana partnership, Rosselli would take action linking him to the assassination of the President of Guatemala. At that time, Guatemala was ruled by a CIA-installed dictator named Carlos Castillo Armas, described by Rosselli's biographers as "a slight, malleable Army colonel." They note that Armas had replaced the democratically elected Jacobo Arbenz, "a liberal who initiated a sweeping land-reform program" and "was deposed in June 1954, in a coup orchestrated by the CIA, the State Department, and the United Fruit Company." They also point out that "the collapse of the Arbenz government opened the door to the Mafia, represented by John Rosselli."[1] According to their numerous sources, in Guatemala "Rosselli . . . cultivated relationships with the [Guatemalan] Army faction that was tempted by the potential financial rewards of casino gambling."[2]

Carlos Marcello needed help in 1956, help that only someone with enormous influence in Guatemala could provide. Marcello had been born in Tunisia; so, as both a convicted criminal and an illegal alien, he was theoretically subject to deportation at any time. The Mafia's close ties to Nixon had no doubt helped keep such concerns at bay, but in the event Ike and Nixon lost in 1956, that could change. Even if they won, as seemed likely, there was always the chance that unexpected publicity could force the US government to act.

Rosselli would have been sympathetic, since he, too, was both a convicted criminal and an illegal alien, having been born in the tiny Italian town of Esperia. What Marcello needed was a phony birth certificate from some foreign country, so that he could attain legal alien status. Even better, if deportation to that country was ever attempted, a "cooperative" (i.e., bribed) government could refuse to accept Marcello, preventing his deportation from the US. Several countries were considered, but Guatemala seemed ideal, for several reasons: Rosselli had tremendous influence in Guatemala, and his biographers have documented from two sources that "Rosselli's primary concern in Guatemala was to protect and advance the interests of" a company based in New Orleans with ties to Carlos Marcello.[3] Marcello had longstanding business ties to Guatemala. In addition, "Guatemala City was easily accessible to New Orleans by air, telephone, and telegraph"; so, according to Marcello's biographer, "in 1956," Carlos "Marcello . . . decided that Guatemala would be the most appropriate country" to obtain a phony birth certificate from. However, for the scheme to work, it would have to be done with the cooperation of those high in the government.

So a deal was struck with "the former law partner of Guatemala's prime minister" to have Marcello's name expertly forged into a church ledger in a small Guatemalan town. The lawyer then "produced an affidavit attesting to the accuracy of Marcello's birth" and "on the basis of that, the government of Guatemala issued citizenship papers for Marcello bearing the President's signature and seal." Marcello's representative later "testified that" he had paid "around $100,000" to the lawyer and the prime minister. However, there's no indication that Guatemalan President Armas was paid anything, or that he was part of—or even initially aware of—the scheme.[4]

CIA expert David Wise noted that "Castillo-Armas was generally regarded as an honest, proud and rather simple man who genuinely loved his country. But he had a covey of advisers, and some of them were less dedicated than their chief."[5] Accounts of Armas's involvement in corruption vary, but the evidence shows that he was far less corrupt than some of those around him—and it would cost him his life.

Wise goes on to say that "After the 1954 coup, American gambler types began drifting into Guatemala, and certain of the liberator's lieutenants were cut in. Castillo-Armas could not bring himself to realize that some of his followers were treacherous. A gambling casino was built in which various Army officers shared a heavy financial interest with the Americans."[6] A history of Guatemala says that "many leading officials of the new regime considered Castillo Armas' victory a license to steal money . . . a number became involved, some apparently in collaboration with American gangsters, in casino gambling, which was forbidden by the straitlaced" Armas.[7]

Rosselli's biographers confirm that "after the fall of the Arbenz government" and the installation of President Armas, "American gangsters reportedly enlisted Army officers in the operation of a plush new gambling hall which drew its clientele from the cream of the government and international community."[8] The "owner of the [Guatemala] casino was Ted Lewin, a globe-trotting gaming operator whose roots ran to Los Angeles," who "ran in the same circles as John Rosselli in the thirties and turned up in association with Rosselli again in Las Vegas in the middle 1960s."[9]

To Rosselli's biographers, an associate of Lewin confirmed that "Lewin knew John Rosselli, and that he and Lewin had seen Rosselli in Guatemala, 'around 1956.'"[10] Two other "informants contend that Rosselli was also active in labor and government affairs" in Guatemala "and possibly in helping Ted Lewin launch his casino. 'Johnny was a flywheel, and everything spun off from him,' said the underworld informant."[11] One of the informants worked for "the US International Cooperation Administration (ICA)." The ICA informant "confirmed that . . . Rosselli had been 'a major force' beneath the surface of events in Guatemala City and in other states in Central America." Rosselli "had access to everyone and everything that was going on there," including "the fruit companies, the Guatemalan Army, and the American delegation. 'He had an open door at the embassy in Guatemala, and in Costa Rica. He was in there plenty of times. I know because I saw him,'" according to the ICA source.[12]

An adviser to Armas told Rosselli's biographers that "'we thought it was a shame to see the gambling come in—after what had happened in Cuba. I was disgusted by it, and I know that Armas was very, very angry about it.' Castillo Armas was installed by the CIA in the coup against Arbenz, but he was, as one observer recalled, a 'man of great probity.'"[13]

A history of Guatemala notes that "Armas authorized several raids" against the casinos "but either through lethargy or indifference or possibly complicity, never completely stamped them out. In this area as in others," Armas "did not appear in full control of his administration."[14] But in his heyday, Johnny Rosselli was always in control. He had to do something about Armas—but what? If he couldn't be bribed—and apparently he couldn't, at least not by gangsters, since there's no evidence that he took any of Marcello's money for the phony birth records—then Armas would have to go.

But assassinating the president of a country would have to be done carefully, much more carefully than the assassination of the Alabama Attorney General-elect in 1954. To avoid those problems, Rosselli needed a patsy—and given the political instability in Guatemala, it would be better if the patsy died immediately, with no risk of a trial. The patsy had to be someone

with no connection to the Mafia, yet someone the public and press and especially the US government would be willing to immediately accept as a logical
assassin, so there would be no calls for a thorough investigation.

This was 1956—not too long after the McCarthy hearings, and in the
midst of the "Red Scare" decade and the Cold War. Armas had ostensibly
been installed to prevent a Communist takeover, so why not blame his death
on a Communist—or, at least, on someone who seemed like a Communist?
Trying to set up a real Communist was too risky, even assuming one could
still be found in repressive Guatemala. Assuming someone could be found to
be manipulated into being at the right place at the right time to take the fall,
how could he be made to look like a Communist?

The answer could be found the previous year, in Marcello's New Orleans,
a city that Rosselli was known to visit. Researcher Paul Hoch writes that "In
the Spring of 1956 . . . hearings were held" in New Orleans "by James Eastland's Senate Internal Security Subcommittee. They were preceded by a raid
on the home of" a black seaman. "The assistant police chief, who called his
take 'the finest collection of Communist literature in the South that I have
ever seen or heard of,' was Guy Banister. The New Orleans *Times-Picayune*
carried a photo of Banister posing with some of that literature."[15] (In 1963,
Dallas Police would photograph a similar cache in the rooming house of
former Banister employee Lee Harvey Oswald, after his death.) If the dead
Guatemala patsy could be found to have incriminating Communist material
on him or in his room after his death, President Armas's assassination could
easily be blamed on a seemingly lone Communist.

How much involvement Rosselli had in Armas's assassination is not—and
may never be—clear. Due to his extensive ties to local officials and the mob,
he was certainly at least aware of it, and—given its parallels to a later Rosselli
hit—probably more. Although Rosselli was visiting Guatemala around that
time, he wasn't spending his time managing Lewin's casino. One of Lewin's
associates told Rosselli's biographers that "Rosselli had nothing to do with
the casino. 'I'm not sure what he was doing down there,'" Lewin's associate
said.[16] What Rosselli was doing became clear in July 1957 when, according
to his biographers, Armas "moved to close the gambling casino" while
"jailing Ted Lewin. Four days later, Castillo Armas was murdered."[17]

A history of Guatemala says that "several shots rang out. Castillo Armas
collapsed and died almost immediately. Police found the assassin, an army
guard named Romeo Vasquez Sanchez, dead on the floor nearby, apparently a suicide."[18] A quickly issued government "communiqué . . . said he

immediately committed suicide with the same rifle he had used to kill the President."[19]

A historian confirms that "the police portrayed Vasquez Sanchez as a lone Communist fanatic" and "they even produced some leftist propaganda that had supposedly been found in his pockets and a suspicious 'diary,' but few if any Guatemalans believed the official explanation."[20] Rosselli's biographers agree, saying that "that scenario was quickly dismissed by observers on the scene as a fabrication." Instead, "a more plausible explanation, one that gained currency in Guatemala City at the time of the shooting, was that Castillo Armas had run afoul of an illicit alliance between corrupt factions of the Army and the Mafia."[21]

The parallels between the Armas patsy and Lee Harvey Oswald are striking. Oswald was a seemingly Communist ex-Marine who was able to get a job at a sensitive firm—a Dallas company that helped prepare maps based on U-2 spy plane photos—even after he returned from his "defection" to the Soviet Union. The government described the Guatemala patsy "as a 'Communist fanatic' who was expelled from the Guatemalan Army six months ago for 'Communist ideology,' but had" still been allowed to join "the Presidential Palace Guard."[22] Like Oswald, the Guatemala patsy was supposedly an ardent Communist, yet also like Oswald "no evidence ever turned up that" the Guatemalan patsy "was a member of the . . . Communist Party."[23]

So, both were ex-military men (under less than honorable circumstances), seemingly lone Communist nuts who killed a president with a rifle, conveniently left behind diaries and Communist propaganda, and were soon killed themselves. The 1957 assassination doesn't just provide a template for the use of a patsy in the 1963 JFK assassination; it probably also shows what was supposed to have happened in Dallas. In the case of the immediately killed Guatemala patsy, there was no trial or attempt at a thorough investigation—which is probably how things would have worked out if Oswald had been found dead in the sixth floor of the Texas Schoolbook Depository after apparently committing suicide—or if Oswald had been killed by a heroic Dallas policeman (like J. D. Tippit) after leaving his rooming house, which would have been quickly found to be filled with a wide array of Communist propaganda (unusual for someone who avoided real Communist party meetings and members).

The American press and officials quickly accepted the "lone Communist nut" theory in regard to Armas's assassination. Historian John Immerman says that President Eisenhower's son, John, concluded that the killer "had been acting under orders from Moscow." But Immerman is one of many who points out that "there is convincing evidence to suggest that the Communists were not responsible for Castillo Armas' murder."[24] That's because "John Eisenhower based his conclusion on a photostat of a letter alleged to have been found by the Guatemalan government on Vasquez Sanchez's body. Guatemalan authorities, while never producing the photostat, maintained that it was the bodyguard's correspondence to Moscow confirming his assignment to assassinate Castillo Armas. Major Eisenhower did not question the photostat's authenticity, despite the unlikelihood of the Kremlin copying such damaging evidence and returning it to Guatemala and Vasquez Sanchez carrying it with him on his dangerous mission."[25]

According to another journalist, "the evidence turned out to be a card from the Latin American service of Radio Moscow that read: 'It is our pleasure, dear listener, to engage in correspondence with you. We are very thankful for your regular listening to these programs.'" The journalist also notes that "when Oswald was arrested in New Orleans, he had the name of a Radio Moscow commentator on his person."[26]

Most scholars today don't buy the "lone Communist nut" theory of the Armas assassination. Even at the time, a history of Guatemala says that "there were whispers that mobsters from the United States, angered by" President Armas's "harassment of their incipient casino business, were responsible."[27]

There is no evidence that the CIA knew about the assassination in advance, but someone in the CIA must have been aware of the true nature of Armas's assassination after it happened. That's because David Atlee Phillips, one of the original CIA agents who first brought Armas to power, later planned to use the same patsy technique. This was in 1971, for an attempt to assassinate Castro in Chile using Antonio Veciana, a close associate of C-Day exile leader Eloy Menoyo. Veciana says that the plan "was similar to the Kennedy assassination. Because the person that" David Phillips had "assigned to kill Castro was going to get planted with papers to make it appear that he was a Moscow . . . agent and then he would himself be killed."[28]

Rosselli and Marcello were apparently happy with the results of the assassination. The new dictator not only went along with Marcello's false claim of Guatemalan citizenship, but he would initially welcome Marcello to Guatemala after the mobster was unceremoniously deported there by Bobby Kennedy in 1961.

The Kennedys Go on the Attack

THE DARING 1957 BARBERSHOP MURDER of New York mob boss Albert Anastasia demonstrates that when Santo Trafficante felt threatened, he wouldn't hesitate to help assassinate someone even more powerful than himself. Yet that very hit brought Trafficante to the attention of John and Bobby Kennedy, setting off a chain of events that would send JFK to the White House and focus Bobby on attacking Trafficante's empire.

By 1957, Cuba was a lucrative haven for Trafficante, Rosselli, and the Mafia. As a result of the close partnership between mob boss Meyer Lansky and Cuban dictator Fulgencio Batista, ever more lavish hotel-casinos were being built in Havana. Lansky's biographer noted that "the only casino operator in Havana for whom Meyer had any respect was Santo Trafficante," so Trafficante's role in the world of Havana casinos continued to grow.[1]

Fidel Castro was not yet seen as a serious threat, and neither were rumblings of new Senate crime hearings in Washington, so the only problem on the horizon for Trafficante and his Havana operations seemed to be New York City godfather Albert Anastasia. Among the New York Mafia families—the city was divided among several families, unlike New Orleans, Tampa, and Chicago—Anastasia was only rivaled by Vito Genovese. Anastasia had reached his peak of power by the mid-1950s, when he murdered with impunity four witnesses to prevent their testimony in a trial for "income tax evasion." Such actions also showed the public the need for the Kennedys' crime hearings. Even Lansky and Trafficante were taken aback when "Anastasia started working on plans to bring his own gambling setup into Cuba."[2] The *Washington Post* confirms that "Anastasia had been attempting to move in on Trafficante's Cuban Gambling operations."[3] According to one report, Anastasia even sent four hit men to Cuba to kill

Trafficante, but the Cuban police told the men they weren't allowed to do the hit in Cuba.[4]

Anastasia's moves threatened the high profits and tranquility of Trafficante and Lansky's criminal empire in Cuba, so Anastasia had to be eliminated. Since the hit would take place in New York City, Lansky and Trafficante had to get the approval of Vito Genovese, and the contract was passed to the "Gallo brothers" to either make the hit or get someone reliable to do it.[5] Trafficante went to New York City and met with Anastasia on October 24, 1957, in Anastasia's hotel suite. Trafficante was staying at the same hotel, under an alias. The following morning, Anastasia was murdered by two men while he was at the barbershop of the Park Sheraton Hotel. The barber was left unharmed, and Trafficante checked out of the hotel an hour later. The case was never officially solved, but suspicion for the widely publicized hit quickly fell on Trafficante, for having a role in setting up Anastasia for the hit. The *Washington Post* noted that Trafficante was "a leading suspect in the 1957 barbershop execution of Albert Anastasia."[6]

However, Trafficante was so confident—and the Mafia so powerful at that time—that he was back in New York state a couple of weeks later. The sudden removal of Anastasia from the scene left a power vacuum in New York, and there were still Cuban issues to deal with. A history of the FBN says that "Anastasia's assassination sent shockwaves through the underworld and prompted the Mafia Commission to schedule a . . . summit that November in Apalachin, New York, at the estate" of a Buffalo mob leader. "Insiders say" the summit meeting was "convened to anoint Vito Genovese as the Mafia's new boss of bosses" and also to discuss "how much support to give" increasingly popular rebel leader "Fidel Castro in Cuba."[7] Trafficante attended, while Carlos Marcello sent Dallas boss Joe Civello as his representative.

But state police noticed all the activity and raided the estate, forcing Mafiosi to flee into the surrounding countryside. Trafficante, Civello, and many others were arrested, fifty-eight in all. Coming at a time when J. Edgar Hoover still publicly denied the existence of the Mafia, the Apalachin raid generated tremendous national publicity, especially coming just two weeks after the Anastasia hit.

In the coming months, this new public and media focus on the Mafia would be a boon for Senator John F. Kennedy. He served on a Senate committee that had been investigating the Teamsters, but chief counsel Bobby Kennedy kept finding more and more connections between the Teamsters—

especially one of its vice presidents, Jimmy Hoffa—and the Mafia. Technically, the Senate Select Committee Hearings were an "Investigation of Improper Activities in the Labor or Management Field." But the names that kept coming up in the Kennedys' investigation of the Teamsters sounded like a who's-who of midwest Mafia figures, including many old associates of Jack Ruby.

One of the Teamster mob associates Bobby Kennedy grilled at the hearings was Paul Dorfman. In Bobby's own book about the hearings, *The Enemy Within*, he wrote that Paul "Dorfman took over as head of the Chicago Waste Handlers Union in 1939 after its founder and secretary-treasurer was murdered." Then Jimmy "Hoffa made a trade with Dorfman. In return for an introduction to the Chicago underworld, the Committee found, Hoffa turned over to Dorfman and his family" control of "the gigantic Central" States Teamster Pension Fund."[8] What Bobby left out of his book, published in 1960, was provided later by one of his investigators, Walter Sheridan, in his landmark work, *The Fall and Rise of Jimmy Hoffa*. Sheridan noted that at the time of the murder of the founder of the Chicago Waste Handlers Union, "the other official of the union at the time was a man named Jack Ruby, who achieved notoriety many years later."[9] As detailed later, in 1963 Bobby Kennedy and Walter Sheridan would hear reports that Ruby had accepted a large payoff from Dorfman's son in Chicago, shortly before JFK's assassination—a payoff finally explained in this book for the first time, using new information from Pierre Salinger.

While the hearings were officially chaired by Senator John L. McClellan, the Kennedys spearheaded much of the effort. In addition to Jack and Bobby, their team of investigators included JFK's future press secretary, Pierre Salinger; Bobby's future Hoffa prosecutor, Walter Sheridan; and even an accountant, Carmine Bellino, who had briefly been partners with Guy Banister after Banister had left the FBI. Senator Barry Goldwater, one of the McClellan Committee members, later said that "When the Committee was formed, we thought it was just a vehicle for Jack's campaign for President, but I can tell you it turned into a forced march and Bobby was like a Marine platoon leader."[10]

On August 20, 1957, two months before the Anastasia barbershop hit, John and Bobby Kennedy had their first public confrontation with Jimmy Hoffa at the hearings. Viewed now, that confrontation has a historical significance that was lacking at the time. At that point, Hoffa was not yet the

Teamster president—that was David Beck, and Dave Beck was a major target of the hearings. As investigator Walter Sheridan said, "Outside of the state of Michigan and the labor movement, few people had heard of James R. Hoffa in January, 1957." Hoffa was as ambitious as he was corrupt, and he even tried to get rid of Teamster president Beck "by arranging for one of Beck's own attorneys to feed information to [Bobby] Kennedy about Beck."[11]

The Anastasia hit and the huge Apalachin mob bust brought the Kennedys' hearings new visibility, especially after Jimmy Hoffa became president of the Teamsters in January 1958. Most of the godfathers detained at Apalachin got off with little or no punishment, since the meeting itself wasn't actually a crime, and this probably left the public hungry for some action against the mob bosses. Hoffa was combative in hearings, usually leaving it to his underlings to plead the Fifth Amendment, and counting on witness intimidation to keep a lid on damaging information. As the Kennedys—especially Bobby, who did most of the questioning at the hearings—found more links between Hoffa and the Mafia, a barrage of charges was leveled against Hoffa. This resulted in more bad blood between Hoffa and the Kennedys, which resulted in more charges and more publicity.[12] It also caused an ever-growing hatred on Hoffa's part toward the Kennedys, which would eventually lead to plans to assassinate Bobby in the summer of 1962 (before the target was changed to JFK, with the help of Hoffa's allies Santo Trafficante and Carlos Marcello).

Each hearing brought the Kennedys more revelations and headlines, which generated further hearings, all of which increased JFK's standing as a potential presidential nominee. Historian Richard D. Mahoney notes that "the McClellan Committee hearings made first-rate theater, with anywhere from 80 to 120 reporters in attendance. National radio and TV coverage was constant," along with "a succession of stories in the major news magazines of the day," where the focus "was usually about Bobby versus Hoffa, but the bounce was the photographs of the telegenic Kennedy brothers. *Look*" magazine alone "took eight thousand pictures of Jack and Bobby" to prepare the photo spreads for their magazine.[13]

While serving as a launching pad for JFK's political aspirations, the hearings were also targeting the very mob bosses who would later have JFK assassinated. Sam Giancana—Rosselli's boss—and even Carlos Marcello were dragged in front of the committee by the Kennedys. Such public exposure was one way to impact some of the godfathers' operations, even if federal authorities—like Vice President Nixon and FBI Director Hoover—did little or nothing about the Mafia's rampant and growing criminal activities.

Santo Trafficante did not have to appear at the hearings, instead hiding out safely in Havana. From there, it was easy for Trafficante to run his southeastern crime empire, since there were frequent flights to Florida and Trafficante often used couriers to transport money, information, and orders. In Cuba, Trafficante was safe from the Kennedys, and from authorities who wanted to question him about Anastasia's assassination. In the transcript of one of the hearings, Bobby Kennedy says that Trafficante "is the one that the authorities in New York have been trying to locate in connection with the slaying of Albert Anastasia."[14]

The Kennedys had other witnesses testify about Trafficante and his criminal empire. When the director of the Crime Commission of Greater Miami was questioned by Bobby Kennedy at the July 3, 1958 hearing, he confirmed that "Santo Trafficante" was "the key figure in the Mafia circles of Tampa." Regarding "gangland slayings in Tampa," he said that "until 1953 there were 21 gang killings in the 20-year period, none of which I believe were ever solved." The director added that "there have been several more since that time." Bobby Kennedy said "I understand from a telephone call I got last night there was another one yesterday." On one hand, it may seem stunning that Trafficante would okay a mob hit in Tampa while he knew hearings about him were going on. On the other hand, perhaps the hit was meant to intimidate witnesses who might be scheduled to testify, and to show other Mafia bosses that Trafficante wasn't going to be intimidated by the Kennedys.[15]

Bobby's witness went on to say that the mob hits in Tampa were "typical gangland type of killings" involving "moving automobiles, and from ambush."[16] The witness also noted that "the narcotics unit has found in the past that Tampa was intimately associated in the smuggling of narcotics."[17] As shown later, members of Trafficante's narcotics ring would eventually help to "ambush" JFK while he was in a "moving automobile."

Bobby Kennedy also made sure details about Trafficante's involvement in the Anastasia murder and the Apalachin raid came out in the hearings. Bobby also brought up mutual criminal associates of Trafficante, Marcello, and Hoffa, like "'Trigger Mike' Coppolo." Earlier that day, Bobby had grilled a less cooperative witness, mob boss James Plumeri (aka "Jimmy Doyle"), who pleaded the Fifth to almost every question. Still, Bobby's detailed questions gave the public the lurid details needed for news coverage by asking questions like "Isn't it a fact, Mr. Plumeri, that approximately five or six years ago you attempted to push a well-known singer out of a window in a New

York hotel because he would not marry a young lady that you wanted him to marry?" Bobby's questions also documented Plumeri's ties to Hoffa associates like mob boss "Russell Bufalino." The following year, Plumeri would be involved in the long-secret 1959 CIA-Mafia plots to kill Castro, along with Bufalino, in a deal brokered by Hoffa.

If Trafficante and Anastasia had been able to peacefully settle their dispute about Havana gambling, there might have been no headline-grabbing barbershop hit on Anastasia and no need for the Apalachin Mafia conference, whose bust made national headlines for weeks. Without the Anastasia hit or the Apalachin bust, it's possible that public interest in the Kennedy hearings would have waned and the hearings themselves would have simply died from lack of public interest. Instead, the hearings—and John and Bobby Kennedy—were in the right place at the right time to take advantage of the tremendous publicity and interest in the Mafia, and JFK eventually rode the hearings to the Democratic presidential nomination. And though Trafficante had found a temporary safe haven from the Kennedys in Cuba, by 1959 he would find himself in a Cuban prison, thanks to the island's new ruler, Fidel Castro.

Ruby, the Mafia, and the CIA Help Castro

THE ACTIONS OF THE MAFIA and the CIA in Cuba in the late 1950s are crucial for understanding the Mafia's penetration of C-Day and JFK's assassination in 1963, because so many of the same people were involved, doing similar things: Jack Ruby helping Trafficante, Hoffa, and Rosselli; the theft of arms from a National Guard armory by a ring that included Ruby; the involvement of numerous Trafficante associates who later penetrated C-Day, like John Martino, Frank Fiorini, Carlos Prio, and Rolando Masferrer; Mannlicher-Carcanos and the very Colt Cobra pistol that Ruby used to shoot Oswald. On the CIA side, both David Morales and David Atlee Phillips were involved in attempts to assassinate Castro in 1959 that were linked to various Mafia associates. Even future Kennedy aide Harry Williams and Che Guevara briefly ran across these crucial events.

The activities of Ruby, Trafficante, and their associates in Cuba have never been fully explained, because some of the most critical information was only declassified in the 1990s and much is still missing or withheld. This parallel with the secrecy surrounding the JFK assassination is no accident. Trafficante and Rosselli made sure to include, in their plot to kill JFK, people like Ruby and others who had been involved in CIA-sanctioned activities since the late 1950s. They knew this would force a cover-up about the JFK assassination to protect the CIA's own Castro assassination attempts with mobsters like Trafficante and Ruby. Whenever the remaining "over one million CIA" documents related to the JFK assassination are finally declassified, it will not be surprising to find that a good number of those files were first opened or very active in 1959.

Assembled here for the first time from a variety of documents and sources, this crucial information reveals how several of those involved in

C-Day originally began working together in Cuba, gaining the contacts and experience that would later allow the Mafia to penetrate C-Day and kill JFK.

Many of those in the CIA and the Mafia who would try to kill Castro in 1959 and later had actually been helping Castro just a year earlier, in 1958. Their help ultimately gave them the access needed to try to kill Castro, while their sense of betrayal—at having helped Fidel, only to have him seemingly turn against them—provided their shared motivation to kill him.

In the decade after Fulgencio Batista took power, weapons began to flow to Batista's opponents, ranging from the wealthy Carlos Prio to Fidel Castro's small but growing group of rebels. In response, Batista needed more weapons to fight the growing insurgency, causing the arms traffic to quickly expand. One historian noted that "with its decision to impose an arms embargo in March 1958" against sales of arms to places like Cuba, the US "State Department served notice that Batista's days were numbered."[1] However, a history of the arms trade notes that because "the US had slapped an [arms] embargo on Cuba" that "was not backed up by force, [it] had the effect of excluding only legitimate US arms dealers."[2] This made running guns and other arms to Cuba even more profitable for mobsters like Jack Ruby.

Becoming a gun-runner in the late 1950s was easy, since, according to an arms expert, "one had only to register with the . . . Department of State" to import guns and "pay a one-dollar fee to the Treasury Department" to sell them. Plus, "no applicant was required to be fingerprinted or checked for a criminal record."[3] So, obtaining guns legitimately was relatively easy, and it was then just a matter of smuggling them into Cuba, to sell to either rebel leader Castro or the dictator Batista. Several sold to both, providing the seller with a market and an ally, no matter who won.

A major investigative report in *Rolling Stone* found that "when Castro began his revolution in the Cuban hills, [Jack] Ruby initially supported him and sold him US-made weapons."[4] Jack Ruby wasn't high in the Mafia—he just happened to know several people who were close associates of Cuban mob kingpin Santo Trafficante. Organized crime expert David Scheim later documented that "In 1958, Ruby wrote a letter to the State Department's Office of Munitions Controls 'requesting permission to negotiate the purchase of firearms and ammunition from an Italian firm.' And the name 'Jack Rubenstein' [Ruby's birth name] was listed in a 1959 Army Intelligence report on U.S. arms dealers. Although located by clerks of these two federal agencies in 1963, both documents are today inexplicably missing."[5]

The disappearance of these documents has little to do with JFK's assassination, and everything to do with the fact that the gun-running of Ruby and his associates to Castro was often sanctioned by the CIA, who wanted to keep that fact—and any association with Ruby—away from the public. As anyone who has tried to get US documents declassified knows, if just one federal agency wants something kept secret, it can even keep other agencies from releasing that document (this is sometimes known as the "third agency" rule or exception).

Historian Anthony Summers documented in his recent biography of Richard Nixon that in 1958, "the CIA, hedging its bets, had acted benignly toward Castro in the months before the Revolution. It had facilitated the guerrilla's arms supplies and even sent an agent to join them in the mountains."[6] "Former CIA agent Ron Crozier, interviewed in 1996, says both Castro and Che Guevara knew he was with the" CIA.[7] Crozier later worked with David Atlee Phillips, and Crozier confirmed that Phillips used "Maurice Bishop" as one of his CIA aliases.[8]

One of the backers of Ruby's gun-running activities was Havana casino and slot-machine supervisor Norman Rothman, who reported to Trafficante. Rothman would soon complain to one of Bobby Kennedy's men about what he saw as unfair US prosecution for his CIA-sanctioned activities. In a CIA memo kept secret for over thirty years, mobster Rothman says "that [the] CIA used the same people in these gunrunning activities for which he (Mr. Rothman) was being prosecuted by the Federal Government . . . he said that CIA would truck the stuff to the point of ship pick-up, where he (Mr. Rothman) would supervise the loading of the ships."[9] Another CIA file calls mobster "Rothman a 'former witting collaboration'" with the CIA.[10] The long-secret files clearly show that the CIA was well aware of Rothman's criminal associates—indeed, it was their criminal reputation that made mobsters like Rothman and Ruby useful for the CIA. That way, the CIA could provide covert assistance to Castro while not openly antagonizing dictator Batista or publicly violating the US ban on weapons sales to Cuba.

Even with all this secrecy, information about Ruby's role with so many Trafficante associates began to surface in official circles after Ruby shot Oswald. The FBI had information in their files by October 1963 linking Dallas gun-running to reports of the top secret C-Day operation and the bullet found in Oswald's rifle. So, when FBI investigators like Atlanta FBI agent Daniel Doyle began picking up much information about Ruby's Cuban gun-running, J. Edgar Hoover had to cut off such investigations, since Hoover had already publicly said that Oswald had acted alone and there was no conspiracy. Ostensibly to protect C-Day, it would also prevent embarrassing information about the FBI from being exposed.

Uncovered less than a week after JFK's assassination, FBI Agent Doyle's information tied Ruby to a gun-smuggling ring that involved Carlos Prio (who, unknown to Doyle, had recently penetrated C-Day) and associates of mobster Norman Rothman. Journalist Anthony Summers wrote that "A former FBI agent" said "Daniel Doyle[,] found a number of significant links between Jack Ruby and the anti-Castro movement." According to the former FBI agent, "these leads were 'washed out' of the reports finally assembled for consumption in Washington. [FBI] Agent Doyle resigned soon afterward, reportedly disillusioned by his experiences in the service of the FBI."[11]

The FBI kept a lid on the explosive information about Ruby's gun-running with associates of Trafficante—as well as actual meetings between Trafficante and Ruby—in several ways. In a follow-up to FBI Agent Doyle's report about Ruby running guns with Carlos Prio, a former gun-runner in the ring, who used the alias "Don Eduardo," was interviewed by another FBI agent while "serving a three year sentence" in prison. But Warren Commission files show that the FBI agent warned "Don Eduardo" that "any statement he did make could be used in court, even against him at a later date," so naturally the man denied everything.[12] That technique was repeated in several FBI investigations: The FBI repeatedly asked subjects about illegal gun-running they had witnessed or were involved in with Ruby, putting their subjects in the position of having to back off their original statements if they didn't want to be charged with a crime. Moreover, the FBI used the threat of prosecuting them for perjury if they persisted in saying what Hoover didn't want to hear. Luckily, some of those questioned didn't back down, and other FBI records confirm that Ruby dealt with a Texas gun-runner who was indicted with Carlos Prio for arms trafficking.

As for the CIA, they kept a lid on things even decades later by withholding documents from government investigations, and more. One journalist notes that "the CIA's Office of Security files" on the gun-runner who used the alias "Don Eduardo" were "inadvertently destroyed in 1979 after the moratorium was lifted," after the House Select Committee's investigation.[13] Among the many reasons the "CIA's Office of Security" had for destroying the file of the gunrunner was the CIA's practice of sometimes having more than one agent or asset use the same alias. FBI veteran William Turner wrote that "Don Eduardo" was the alias used during C-Day planning by two CIA officers, one of whom allegedly worked for the CIA's Office of Security. The CIA wasn't trying to hide their knowing involvement in JFK's assassination by such actions; instead, like the FBI, they were ostensibly protecting C-Day while keeping potentially embarrassing information under wraps.

But enough documentation is still available to give a good indication of the size and scope of Ruby's involvement in Cuban gun-running, and his ties to associates of Trafficante and Rosselli. According to one journalist, government files and sources show that "Ruby told one of his business partners . . . he was a close friend of Mickey Cohen," the Los Angeles mobster. The FBI has documented numerous ties between Cohen's girlfriend and Ruby. Ruby was her manager, would try to get her an early parole, and would use her defense attorney in his own trial for shooting Oswald. "According to John Martino"—the Trafficante mobster who later wrote about C-Day right after JFK's death—"Mickey Cohen was involved in arms smuggling to Fidel Castro from 1957 to 1958," at the same time Jack "Ruby was involved in an identical venture."[14]

Another FBI document states that "a former Oklahoma law officer . . . says that an incident in 1958 definitely linked . . . Jack Ruby to gun-running. The guns and ammunition were being taken to Cuba." It said "an investigation by the Texas Department of Public Safety and the FBI revealed [the] involvement of" Jack Ruby, "owner of the Carousel Club in Dallas, in the gunrunning incident," which included "a car loaded with guns and ammunition."[15]

Ruby was also linked to gun-running in 1958 in the small Florida Key of Islamorada, then as now a noted sports fishing locale. It's known today as the longtime favorite tropical resort area for former President George H. W. Bush, who has frequented the key for decades. According to an FBI report, at the time Ruby was there, tiny Islamorada was also home to "Ted Williams, well-known professional baseball player" and a noted sports fisherman at the time. Ruby met the FBI's witness behind Ted Williams's cottage.[16] New research by the authors showed that in the late 1950s, mob boss Meyer Lansky owned a significant part of the small island. The man involved was definitely Jack Ruby, since the witnesses said Jack's "real name was Leon" (which was true of Ruby, who used that for his middle name), and that "Jack was originally from Chicago" and "ran a drinking place in Dallas." The witnesses also said that her brother—involved with Jack—"reportedly was a member of the Dallas, Texas, Police Department for a short time" and "had known Jack in Dallas."[17]

After the pressure exerted by Hoover on agents like Daniel Doyle, it should not come as a surprise that "the FBI did not interview" the brother who ran guns with Ruby, and "on January 23, 1964, an order went out from the" FBI Special Agent in Charge of "Dallas, to 'discontinue active investigation to locate'" the brother.[18] Likewise, it should be no surprise that years later, investigative journalist Scott Malone noted that the brother "has said he knew both . . . Ruby" and the gun-runner who used the alias "Don Eduardo."[19]

Malone also documented that "in 1958" Norman "Rothman . . . one of Santo Trafficante's closest associates, coordinated the smuggling of arms to Castro" while still "splitting his take from Cuba's slot machines with Batista's brother-in-law. The available evidence indicates that Ruby helped in Rothman's gun smuggling," as was borne out by the statements of several witnesses to the FBI.[20] Also in the FBI files on this operation is Frank Fiorini, the Trafficante bagman who would later be one of the Watergate burglars. Testimony indicates that some of the arms were provided by a "CIA proprietary."[21]

In addition to Trafficante associates Ruby and Fiorini, Rothman's gun-running ring was also linked to two associates of Trafficante's French Connection heroin partner, Michel Victor Mertz, who was deported from Dallas shortly after JFK's assassination. One of Mertz's associates was indicted along with Rothman over a huge theft ($13,500,000) of Canadian bonds, used to finance the arms smuggling. The other Mertz associate would soon be in prison in Cuba with Santo Trafficante. Rothman was also close to Rolando Masferrer, the Ruby associate who would penetrate C-Day, and help link Oswald to it. Also, Rothman's ring obtained some arms from a major theft at a US National Guard Armory—Rothman was convicted for that in February of 1960—the same type of operation the FBI uncovered in Texas in the fall of 1963 that was linked to C-Day and Jack Ruby.[22]

Another member of Rothman's arms ring, Frank Fiorini, testified under oath to Federal investigators that "Fidel told me in the mountains, here is what I have got . . . all different types of foreign-made rifles—for instance like the Italian carbine, you shoot that twice in rapid fire it would overheat and jam."[23] A journalist who later interviewed Fiorini noted that "many of the rifles" Fiorini "obtained" from a CIA-backed company for Fidel "were surplus 6.5 millimeter Mannlicher-Carcanos," of the type found in the Texas School Book Depository after JFK's assassination. When Fiorini "was asked about this coincidence," he replied "'I possibly could have purchased Mannlicher-Carcanos, if they had them, yes I could have. As a matter of fact, you are recalling something for me. . . .'"[24]

Mannlicher-Carcanos were just one of several types of cheap, unreliable guns that could be easily obtained in the late 1950s and early 1960s, either wholesale or retail, through dozens of ads in various gun magazines. An arms historian noted that in 1958, "The (Italian Mannlicher-) Carcano was also receiving notice in the United States" because "on May 13, 1958, Senator John F. Kennedy" had introduced a bill in Congress that would have prohibited the importation into the United States of "firearms manufactured for the Armed Services of any country." It was only in 1980 that researcher Paul Hoch discovered that "in just-released 1958 Senate Hearings, JFK specifically mentioned Italian Carcanos," which were being offered for sale in ads in *The American Rifleman* magazine at that time. Opposed by the NRA, the magazine's publisher, JFK's 1958 legislation failed.[25] The ads offering the cheap rifles would continue to run into 1963, when the cheap mail-order rifles would be the subject of Congressional hearings months before JFK's assassination. Those hearings got them into the news just before Lee Harvey Oswald would appear to have ordered one using an alias, even though Oswald had access to gun shops near his home with cheaper, much more reliable rifles, in an incident explained later.

How did a lowly Dallas nightclub operator like Jack Ruby become involved in such complex transactions? It was because of who he knew; plus, his role in these transactions was similar to the type of role Trafficante would use him for in the JFK assassination. The man that even Warren Commission reports call Jack Ruby's best friend—Lewis McWillie—worked for Norman Rothman and Trafficante at the time, in Havana. In addition, one of Ruby's other Dallas Mafia associates—R. D. Matthews—was also working in Havana. And Ruby was a trusted functionary on the Dallas part of the French Connection heroin network. A glad-handing hustler like Ruby could be counted on by the Mafia to work hard for relatively little, and to use his many connections to their benefit.

The Mafia could also count on Ruby to keep his mouth shut if he were ever interrogated by US or Cuban authorities. Ruby had taken his middle name, "Leon," from Leon Cook, his co-worker in the Waste Handlers Union, the official who was murdered in the takeover that Bobby Kennedy said first forged the alliance between Jimmy Hoffa and the Mafia. Ruby kept quiet when questioned by authorities about the murder. Ruby's ties to Hoffa—whose own Cuban gun-running was documented earlier—also no doubt helped Ruby's position, first in gun-running, then in the 1959 CIA-Mafia plots that Hoffa brokered, and finally in the JFK assassination.

Still more evidence proves that Ruby was heavily involved in the Mafia's CIA-sanctioned gun-running to Fidel Castro, despite a forty-year effort by some to ignore or minimize these activities. Ruby's gun-running contacts would pave the way for him to become involved in helping to get Trafficante out of a Cuban prison and meeting Trafficante personally, yet another contact that paved the way for Ruby's inclusion in Trafficante's plan to assassinate JFK.

Warren Commission counsel Leon Hubert wrote in an internal memo that "the probability that Ruby was involved in illegal activities in Cuba prior to 1959 . . . is supported by the statement of a Delta Airlines employee in New Orleans who recalled that" around 1957, Jack "Ruby flew from New Orleans to Havana. This airline employee stated that he overheard Ruby telephone his club in Dallas and state that his trip to Cuba was being paid for by someone else and that no one should be advised of his whereabouts."[26] Ruby's Cuban arms trading was glossed over in the Warren Commission's final report, since they didn't have the resources—or documents—to investigate it fully.

The *Dallas Morning News* reported in 1978 that "Jack Ruby was running guns and ammunition from Galveston Bay [southeast of Houston] to Fidel Castro's guerrillas in Cuba about 1957." They cited a Ruby associate who "told the FBI that he 'personally saw many boxes of new guns, including automatic rifles and handguns, stored in a 2-story house . . . and loaded on what looked like a 50-foot surplus military boat. He stated that each time that the host left with guns and ammunition, Jack Ruby was on the boat,' the FBI report said." The witness said that Ruby "was in command of" the ship and "went out every time it went. It was meeting a connection there in Cuba." The *Dallas Morning News* also noted that "by 1959, Castro had taken control of Cuba and Ruby was beginning to switch sides."[27]

Ruby wasn't the only one to switch sides not long after Castro took over Cuba. Trafficante, Hoffa, Rosselli, and other mobsters—as well as Havana CIA officers David Morales and David Atlee Phillips—would do the same.

1959: CIA-Mafia Plots and Coup Attempts

THREE RARELY NOTED DEVELOPMENTS IN 1959 had an enormous impact on C-Day and the Mafia's penetration of it: the 1959 CIA-Mafia plots to kill Castro, the CIA's first coup attempts against Castro, and how both affected the Kennedys' Senate crime hearings. All three have been mentioned in brief passages in just a handful of books and articles, so they have received attention from only a few historians. Because of the secrecy surrounding C-Day, even those historians didn't realize how many of the later participants in C-Day—and the Mafia's infiltration of it—began working together in 1959. In fact, many C-Day participants were chosen because of what they had done—or started doing—in 1959. By including people linked to the 1959 plots—like Jack Ruby—in their penetration of C-Day and JFK's murder, the mob had another way to ensure that a thorough investigation wouldn't be pursued.

The 1959 CIA-Mafia plots were uncovered by Senate investigators in the mid-1970s but were left out of their final report, which only covered the CIA's plots with the Mafia from mid-1960 to early 1963. The 1959 plots began due to pressure from Vice President Richard Nixon, and initially involved Trafficante associates like Rolando Masferrer and Frank Fiorini. When those failed, the CIA turned to Jimmy Hoffa—who was then involved in a complex arms deal using Jack Ruby—to recruit more powerful mobsters. Several were glad to help, since they wanted to be protected from the intense grilling the Kennedys were giving to mob bosses like Carlos Marcello.

In 1959, John and Bobby Kennedy, and even Harry Williams, came tantalizingly close to the people who would later penetrate C-Day and assassinate JFK—but intervention by the CIA (and probably the FBI) kept that from happening. Jack Ruby was one of those people, and his documented role as an FBI informant is explained in upcoming chapters for the first time, as are his meetings in Cuba with Santo Trafficante. Even the pistol Ruby used to shoot Oswald came out of Ruby's Cuban activities, and its use in 1963 was yet another way for the Mafia to close off certain aspects of the JFK assassination investigation.

While the CIA's David Morales handled aspects of the 1959 CIA-Mafia plots, he and David Atlee Phillips also supported early coup attempts against Castro that involved several men who would later have prominent roles in C-Day: Eloy Menoyo, Manuel Artime, Tony Varona, Manuel Ray, and Bernard Barker. Johnny Rosselli and John Martino also played small roles in the Mafia's 1959 activities in Cuba. The involvement of so many people later involved in C-Day is one reason most information about the 1959 CIA-Mafia plots and coup plans is still classified and was withheld from most government investigators.

The events in 1959 foreshadowed much that would happen in the fall of 1963, and they provide an important piece of the puzzle that has been missing from most previous accounts of the JFK assassination. It was in 1959 that associates of Trafficante and the other mob bosses learned that cooperating—or appearing to cooperate—with the FBI and the CIA could protect their activities, a crucial lesson that the Mafia chieftains would apply in 1963. The secrecy surrounding the 1959 plots resulted in crucial documents being withheld from the Warren Commission and Congressional committees that looked into JFK's assassination. Many of those documents have never been released, so the level of detail we have for the 1959 plots is far less than for the later CIA-Mafia plots, or even for C-Day.

The CIA's pursuit of plots with the Mafia, at the same time they were assisting coup attempts against Castro, is another parallel between 1959 and 1963, one that eventually had tragic consequences for JFK. The overlap of people and operations in 1963 had its roots in 1959. At times, the various 1959 CIA-Mafia Castro assassination plots and coup attempts appear to be separate operations—but at other times they blend together, using the same people at the same time. That is exactly what would happen in 1963, when the CIA was running its own Castro assassination plots while it was helping with C-Day, and the resulting crossover allowed the Mafia to penetrate C-Day. Also, in 1959 it was sometimes hard to tell which side certain participants were on—the same problem the CIA, Bobby Kennedy, and other agencies faced after JFK's assassination, when they tried to sort out who was really working to overthrow Castro and who was part of the plot that killed JFK.

It's also important to fully expose the 1959 CIA-Mafia plots because some former officials now give the impression that the CIA had no interest in trying to remove Castro, only taking actions because of the Kennedys. Some even give the impression that the CIA-Mafia plots began under the Kennedys.[1] While it's clear that the Kennedys pressed for action against Cuba, it's naïve to believe that the CIA was perfectly happy to have a Communist dictator like Castro only ninety miles from the US at the height of the Cold War. The historical record is clear regarding CIA actions to topple leaders seen as unsympathetic to US interests. And the record is equally clear that CIA actions to kill Castro not only predated JFK's taking office by more than a year, but that the CIA plots continued well after JFK's death.

The 1959 CIA-Mafia plots are different from the mid-1960 to early 1963 plots that the CIA officially acknowledges. In 1959, the CIA was not nearly as "hands-on" as it would become in the summer of 1960. Those later plots represented a "ratcheting up" of the plotting, with the CIA taking a guiding hand and trying to call the shots to the Mafia. By the summer of 1960, it was clear to the CIA that the Mafia needed more help if Castro were to be assassinated in time to help Richard Nixon's race for the presidency that fall.[2] The Mafia deliberately used veterans of its 1959 and 1960–63 plots with the CIA to help penetrate C-Day and in their plan to kill JFK, to force the CIA to withhold information from outside investigations.

Detailing the 1959 CIA-Mafia assassination and coup plots for the first time shows how many of those alliances and operations continued in a logical fashion to the fall of 1963. The threads documented so far—the assassination expertise of mobsters like Trafficante and the coup experience of CIA veterans like David Morales and David Atlee Phillips—come together for the first time in 1959. Following the actions of these people and their associates from 1959 to 1963 shows how some alliances shifted and others solidified. By 1963, Trafficante and his allies were leaving nothing to chance or to inexperienced amateurs—they had years of experience to know exactly how the key players would react.

NIXON'S PRESSURE SPARKS THE CIA-MAFIA PLOTS

In an odd confluence of events, it was Richard Nixon—along with Bobby Kennedy's subpoena to godfather Carlos Marcello—that brought the CIA and the Mafia together in 1959, to try to assassinate Fidel Castro. In the days following the triumph of Castro and the other revolutionaries on January 1, 1959, most of the people later involved with C-Day—either for the Kennedys or the Mafia—were all on the same side. Future C-Day exile leaders like Harry Williams, Varona, Artime, Menoyo, and Ray had all helped the Revolution. The same was true for those who later helped Trafficante penetrate C-Day: former Cuban President Carlos Prio, Trafficante bagman and Castro mercenary Frank Fiorini, and gun-runner Jack Ruby. Trafficante himself had played both sides, helping both fallen dictator Fulgencio Batista and Fidel Castro. The CIA, acting on behalf of the Eisenhower-Nixon administration, had also hedged their bets by helping Castro. Yet within just a few months, the situation would change radically, and many of Fidel's former allies would start to turn against him as he solidified his power. In the US, Richard Nixon took a leading role in pressing for CIA action to get rid of Castro.

When Vice President Nixon met Castro in April 1959, Nixon seemed suspicious yet ambivalent about Castro. Yet by June 1959, just two months later, a dramatic shift had taken place, and the US was backing moves to eliminate Castro. Before documenting that shift, it's important to note two important facts left out of many histories of Cuba-US relations. Castro was not the first president of the new revolutionary government after January 1, 1959—that was President Manuel Urrutia, viewed as a moderate. However, Castro was the Revolution's best-known symbol, and his political savvy was matched by his understanding of the importance of publicity—something that would help him successfully stage one coup in the coming months and survive two US-backed attempts against him. Second, while it is true that Castro ordered the mob-run casinos shut down soon after the Revolution, most accounts overlook that fact that they were soon reopened. A history of the Canadian arm of the French Connection notes that Castro allowed most "foreigners, especially the gangsters, to go about their business, re-opening casinos, gambling dens and night clubs. This was a kind of compensation for the financial and material aid (especially arms) which underworld leaders had supplied to the guerillas."[3] A CIA report says the Cuban "Cabinet on February 17, 1959 authorized reopening the casinos for the tourist trade" and that "*Time* magazine for March 2, 1959 announced that the casinos had been reopened the previous week."[4] Some casinos would stay open another two and a half years, allowing the Mafia to maintain an important foothold in Cuba.

When Fidel Castro visited the US in April 1959, his media savvy was at its peak. He spoke to a group of American newspaper editors, appeared on NBC's *Meet the Press*, met with the Senate Foreign Relations Committee, and gave talks "at Columbia, Harvard, and Princeton Universities."[5] According to one historian, "the CIA briefed him [Castro] for two hours on the Red menace."[6] President Eisenhower made sure he was out of town when Castro came to Washington, so the task of meeting with the controversial figure fell to Vice President Nixon. As Nixon noted in his memoirs, he had a "three-hour meeting with Castro" and then wrote a long memo for the president and other top officials, saying that Castro "is either incredibly naïve about Communism or under Communist discipline."[7]

Nixon had been a supporter of the dictator Batista, and probably viewed the new Cuban government with growing alarm. One historian said that as of May 1959, five months after the Revolution, "foreigners" still "own 75 percent of arable land" including "five US sugar companies" who "own or control more than two million acres in Cuba." Among the major land holders was the US fruit company that had pressed for the CIA's 1954 coup in Guatemala. On May 17, 1959, "Castro signs the first Agrarian Reform Law, putting a limit on land holdings and expropriating the remainder with compensation to the owners," with their land being "distributed among landless Cubans." "This new law limits privately owned sugar cane land to 3,300 acres per owner."[8]

Such actions added fuel to the fire for Nixon's hardening position against Castro. Another historian quotes Henry Kissinger as saying that Bebe Rebozo—Nixon's best friend—"hated Castro with a fierce Latin passion."[9] While most historians date the official US change of heart about Castro to March 1960—when an official National Security Council meeting authorized CIA planning against Castro—Nixon's own words confirm that secret US action against Castro began much earlier. In his book *Six Crises*, Nixon wrote that the secret anti-Castro "program had been in operation for six months before the 1960 campaign got underway." Since the 1960 Presidential campaign kicked off in January 1960, that means the secret US anti-Castro plots started in about June 1959. This is further confirmed by Nixon when he says that while he "was present at the" March 1960 "meeting in which Eisenhower authorized the CIA to organize and train Cuban exiles" to overthrow Castro, "it was a policy I had been advocating for nine months" prior to that, meaning since June 1959.[10] The historical record is full of US action against Castro around that time.

Many former CIA officials, especially Richard Helms, spent the last two decades talking about how much pressure they felt from the Kennedys—especially Bobby—to do something about Castro. While that pressure was certainly real, it obscures that fact that even the CIA admits that their Castro assassination plots began under Nixon, before the election. Nixon's "Press Secretary Herb Klein admitted" that Nixon "'was eager for the Republican Administration to get credit for toppling Castro before the election.'"[11] Historian Stephen Ambrose wrote that seven months before the election, "Nixon pushed as hard for action as he dared." This included sending "a memo to General Cushman (who was serving as his liaison man with the CIA people in charge of the Program). Nixon said the agents 'ought to get off their tails and do something'" about Castro.[12] As the evidence shows, Nixon was frustrated because the CIA had been trying to get rid of Castro—through assassination or coup or both—since at least June 1959.

But how to eliminate Castro? As we documented earlier, Nixon and his associates had ties to the Mafia, especially in Los Angeles and Florida. Nixon would soon be receiving a major cash contribution from Jimmy Hoffa and Carlos Marcello. And because of John and Bobby Kennedy's Senate crime hearings, Nixon's criminal supporters were strongly motivated to gain protection from the Kennedys by assisting US officials.

BOBBY KENNEDY GRILLS CARLOS MARCELLO

In the spring of 1959, the Kennedys' crime hearings were still generating headlines, and any godfather—or mob associate like Hoffa—would be interested helping US officials if doing so could keep their criminal activities from being exposed to the American public. Mob bosses didn't want to be subjected to the same kind of grilling Carlos Marcello faced from Bobby Kennedy on March 24, 1959.

Carlos Marcello had always tried to avoid publicity, preferring to wield his power over his vast criminal domain in relative secrecy. But he couldn't avoid the Kennedys' subpoena. While the Kennedys' hearings had originally been targeted at corrupt unions like the Teamsters, the public outrage from the Anastasia hit and the mob's Apalachin conference allowed the Kennedys to greatly expand the scope of their hearings. Marcello was just one of many godfathers they targeted, but it's clear from the questioning on March 24, 1959 that Marcello was a major focus of their investigation.

Several senators weren't present for Marcello's testimony, among them John Kennedy and Barry Goldwater. But Chief Counsel Bobby Kennedy was there and would do most of the questioning. "Assistant counsel" Pierre Salinger was there to provide information, since Marcello would plead the Fifth Amendment in response to most questions.[13]

Bobby Kennedy, Salinger, and the other investigators had clearly done their homework, and the questions themselves conveyed the points Bobby wanted to get on the record, like Marcello's control of Dallas and important parts of the heroin trade. Bobby asked Marcello: "You are an associate of Joe Civello of Dallas, Texas, who attended the meeting at Apalachin?" Marcello replied: "I decline to answer on the ground it may tend to incriminate me."[14] A later Senate report would make it clear that "Joe Civello . . . controls all rackets in Dallas and vicinity," and, as we noted earlier, Civello was over Dallas mobsters like Jack Ruby.[15]

Bobby Kennedy then asked if Marcello was an associate of "Sam Carolla, who was deported in 1947 as a narcotics trafficker." Marcello said only: "I decline to answer on the same ground."[16] But other witnesses and huge charts clearly showed the importance of Marcello and New Orleans to what would soon become known as the French Connection narcotics trade.

Since Marcello pleaded the Fifth Amendment repeatedly, most of the information about Marcello's huge criminal empire came from Pierre Salinger, who had gone to New Orleans to investigate Marcello, and from the head of the New Orleans Crime Commission. Even a brief summary of Marcello's extensive criminal and legitimate holdings and his criminal associates is far too long to list here, but they were summarized well in Marcello's biography, *Mafia Kingfish*, by John H. Davis.

Bobby Kennedy asked Aaron Kohn of the New Orleans Crime Commission: "Isn't it correct that Mr. Carlos Marcello has been under orders of deportation from the United States since about 1953?" Kohn replied that that indeed was the case, but that "ever since then he has been fighting the deportation" and "at the last count" Marcello "has been in court some 37 times in various appellate proceedings, and in various hearings."[17]

Senator Sam Ervin—whose Watergate Committee would secretly question Johnny Rosselli about the JFK assassination over a decade later—also questioned Marcello in 1959. After reminding Marcello of his two felony convictions, Ervin asked "how a man with that kind of record can stay in the United States for five years, nine months, twenty-four days after he is found to be an undesirable alien. . . . How have you managed to stay here?" Marcello eventually answered "I wouldn't know."[18] That question has never been satisfactorily answered.[19]

Marcello's lack of US citizenship meant that he could not frequent Cuba like Trafficante, because there was always the chance that he might not be allowed to reenter the US. But the Kennedys' hearings exposed how Marcello still managed to profit from Cuban gambling and drug smuggling. As jour-

nalist Robert Sam Anson notes, "Cuba was not an end in itself. The heroin
that came into its ports did not stay there. Neither did the cash that was generated by the casinos like the ones at Sans Souci and the Tropicana. The
island was merely an enormous funnel through which the cash and heroin
poured, bound for its next destination, the city of New Orleans." Anson says
the Kennedys' crime hearings "named New Orleans as the key distribution
point for heroin and syndicate cash." As one witness explained, "'There is
too much money here,' said a new Orleans chief assistant district attorney.
'We feel that it's flowing in from other Cosa Nostra organizations in other
parts of the country for investment by the local mob.'"[20] This helped to
solidify Marcello's close cooperation with other top mob bosses like Trafficante and Rosselli, which would culminate in their assassination of JFK.

Bobby Kennedy's grilling of Marcello set off a chain of events resulting in
Marcello's humiliating deportation to Guatemala, his return with the aid of
David Ferrie, and his prosecution by Bobby's men in the weeks leading up to
JFK's assassination. But in 1959, Marcello's forced appearance before Bobby
Kennedy—and the news media—no doubt made other mob bosses and asso-
ciates anxious to do whatever they could to avoid the same scrutiny. For
Trafficante, that would mean fleeing to Cuba. For others, it would mean
working with the CIA in plots to assassinate Fidel Castro, in return for the
CIA interceding with the Kennedys' Senate committee.

THE FIRST 1959 PLOTS AGAINST CASTRO FAIL

Before getting to the actual CIA-Mafia plots to kill Castro that were in full
swing by the summer of 1959, it's important to look at three earlier failed
attempts that laid the groundwork for them. These winter 1959 attempts
were more like CIA-monitored assassination attempts involving Trafficante
bagman Frank Fiorini and former Batista death-squad leader Rolando Masferrer. Their failure pointed out that later attempts would have to involve
more participation by the CIA, as well as by more powerful mob figures.

In the first months of 1959, official US policy toward Castro was still sympathetic, which is why even Fiorini admits that the US Embassy didn't give
him the go-ahead for one of the Castro assassination attempts. The former
hard-line US Ambassador, Earl E. T. Smith, had been replaced by Philip
Bonsal, who adopted a more conciliatory attitude toward Castro. A Cuban
exile historian confirms that Bonsal "clashed with" US diplomats who
"called for a strong stance against Castro," while Bonsal "urged continuance
of a hopeful and watchful wait-and-see policy."[21]

However, there were groups and individuals who wanted to see Castro assassinated even before Nixon's April 1959 meeting with Castro started having its effect on US policy. Rolando Masferrer, a former Cuban senator and Batista death-squad leader, had fled Cuba when Castro took power, and he wanted to see the old guard returned to power—perhaps with himself at the helm. Santo Trafficante and Jake Lansky, Meyer Lansky's brother, had briefly been detained, then released, in the winter of 1959, and Jake Lansky had immediately left Cuba. The Lanskys hadn't given Castro enough support during the Revolution—as had Trafficante—and were anxious to see Castro go.

Frank Fiorini was in a unique position in early 1959. A career criminal, he was one of several Americans who had helped Castro during the Revolution, and he was still trusted by Castro. Fiorini was especially close to a high official in the new Cuban Air Force, which was small and needed planes. He even gave advice to the woman Castro had put in charge of monitoring the reopened casinos, which gave Fiorini a legitimate reason to rub shoulders with many mobsters.

As a newspaper reported years later, one of Fiorini's associates said that Fiorini "was involved with the Pittsburgh Mafia," as well as "Trafficante and his boys" since "Trafficante was his backer."[22] To a journalist, Fiorini confirmed that in Cuba "I knew, I met, Santo Trafficante."[23] Fiorini also admitted under oath in secret testimony to the Rockefeller Commission in 1975 that in Cuba he knew "Santo Trafficante" as well as one of Trafficante's casino partners, "Norman Rothman," and gangsters like "Jake Lansky" and "Charles 'The Blade' Tourine."[24] Trafficante was at least aware of Fiorini's assassination plotting in 1959 and may have had a hand in it.

Fiorini also admitted under oath to the Rockefeller Commission that in 1959 he knew a man he believed "was [the CIA] Station Chief at the Agency" in Havana.[25] He told the Commission that he had set up one Castro assassination attempt, but never received the go-ahead from the CIA to proceed. A journalist who interviewed Fiorini extensively adds that "in early 1959," Fiorini "said that Charlie Tourine approached him and offered him one million dollars to assist the mob in killing Fidel Castro. Meyer Lansky had put out the contract on Castro," but Fiorini didn't get a "go-ahead from his contacts at the American Embassy, and discussed this with Trafficante" and "Charlie Tourine."[26]

Lansky's long-rumored million-dollar contract on Castro was finally confirmed by Nixon biographer Anthony Summers, who wrote that "according to"

Meyer Lansky's "close associate . . . Lansky was one of the first to propose the assassination of Castro and discussed it with CIA contacts as early as 1959. It was at this time . . . that Lansky reached out to" two Nixon associates "in the hopes of getting the administration to 'accept his assassination plan.'"[27]

A short time later in 1959, Fiorini said he "did arrange . . . another attempt at assassination of him [Castro] in the headquarters of the Air Force on the second floor."[28] Fiorini's second plot failed, but not because it didn't get CIA authorization, as we'll see shortly. As the situation in Cuba developed, Fiorini would be on the fringe of later CIA-Mafia plots and the fall 1959 coup attempt involving Manuel Artime. Even after Fiorini left Cuba, he would continue scheming against Castro while working for Trafficante and reporting regularly to CIA agent Bernard Barker. There's no reliable evidence that Fiorini was involved in the JFK assassination, probably because he was too much of a publicity-seeker who cultivated friendships with media figures like columnist Jack Anderson and, according to one report, Ben Bradlee. Fiorini would help spread disinformation favorable to Trafficante about JFK's death, though without the details about C-Day that characterized similar accounts by John Martino. Under a different name, "Frank Sturgis," Fiorini would be involved in Watergate, along with alleged C-Day veterans Bernard Barker, James McCord, E. Howard Hunt, and Manuel Artime. Fiorini told the Rockefeller Commission that "the Cubans knew me as Frank Fiorini, not as Sturgis," so Fiorini is the name we use for him in this book.[29]

Fiorini's second attempt to kill Castro in early 1959 involved another Trafficante associate, Rolando Masferrer, and—according to Cuban accounts—Havana CIA official David Morales. Fiorini told the Rockefeller Commission that "Rolando Masferrer . . . was a senator under Batista" and that Masferrer "was very much in touch with the crime syndicate, the American crime syndicate in Havana."[30] A journalist wrote that according to the *Washington Post* of March 27, 1959, "four of Rolando Masferrer's men were arrested in Havana for plotting to assassinate Fidel" Castro.[31]

The former head of Cuban State Security, Fabian Escalante, told a small conference of US historians and former US officials that "[David] Morales . . . from the United States Embassy in Havana" was part of "a conspiracy with Rolando Masferrer . . . to kill Fidel Castro to promote an armed uprising. This plot started in 1959." The Cubans learned about the plot when they "arrested one of the CIA agents that used to be a member of the Batista police" and "he identified David Morales" and said "Morales . . . had told him about a plot against Fidel Castro's life that he had headed in 1959. And that this plot was going on, to be carried out in the headquarters of the [Cuban] military Air Force." The Cubans think it's the same plot revealed by Fiorini.[32]

Apparently, this plot—involving CIA official David Morales and Trafficante associates Rolando Masferrer and Frank Fiorini—was stopped by the arrest of four of Masferrer's men, as reported in the *Washington Post*. But like Fiorini, Masferrer would go on to have roles in the 1959 CIA-Mafia assassination and coup plots. In the early 1960s, Masferrer would cause problems for the US government, especially the Kennedys, but he would seem to get protection from some US agency that allowed him to keep operating and avoid a long prison sentence or deportation. Eventually, Masferrer would be killed in a spectacular car bombing in Miami, at just the time the Church Committee's investigation into the CIA-Mafia plots and JFK's assassination was gearing up.

Masferrer's death may have been related to another associate he had in 1959: Jack Ruby. According to FBI veteran William Turner, "in 1959 [Jack] Ruby . . . made overtures to sell surplus jeeps to" Fidel Castro. Ruby wasn't a Castro supporter, but was instead an opportunist, and while in Cuba Ruby "boasted to at least two US citizens that he was 'in with both sides.' Most prominent of the anti-Castroites whose friendship he claimed was Rolando Masferrer, a Batista henchman."[33] Ruby's "friendship" with Masferrer developed at a time when both were involved in assassination and coup operations in 1959. The Ruby-Masferrer friendship would also be useful to Trafficante again in the fall of 1963, when both men penetrated C-Day—and Masferrer helped Trafficante operative John Martino link Lee Harvey Oswald to Manolo Ray's C-Day Cuban exile group in Dallas, two months before JFK's assassination.

The CIA Turns to Hoffa

SINCE THE CASTRO ASSASSINATION PLOTS of Rolando Masferrer and Frank Fiorini hadn't achieved the result the CIA's David Morales had hoped for, a more powerful criminal figure was brought into the plotting: Jimmy Hoffa. These 1959 CIA-Mafia plots helped set off a chain of events that not only led to Hoffa's involvement with Trafficante and the other mob bosses in the JFK assassination, but also led to Hoffa's own death in 1975, to keep the 1959 plots from being exposed.

The CIA needed Jimmy Hoffa in 1959 for several reasons. First, the CIA needed what's known as a "cutout" to deal with high-level mob bosses who could assassinate Castro. That way, if a plot backfired and the Mafia's role was exposed, it would be blamed on Hoffa and not the CIA. Also, Hoffa in 1959 was seen by many as a legitimate labor leader, and it was no doubt seen as far more palatable to deal with him than for the CIA to go to Mafia leaders directly. Plus, the CIA already had at least an indirect relationship with Hoffa, since he had been part of the CIA-sanctioned gun-running to Fidel Castro. The CIA was certainly aware that Hoffa had connections to top Mafia leaders who wanted to have Castro assassinated, as the Kennedys had shown in their Senate crime hearings.

Hoffa had another key advantage to the CIA: He was still actively trying to sell arms and planes to Fidel Castro in the spring and summer of 1959. This gave him both access to Castro, and a way to "cover" the assassination planning—an excuse for his men to be going in and out of Cuba. In all, there were at least four parts to the 1959 CIA-Mafia plot to kill Castro that Hoffa brokered, most of which were going on at the same time:

1. The assassination operation itself, organized with the help of several top Mafia bosses—like Russell Bufalino—who were Hoffa's associates, and using several lower-level criminals Hoffa knew. Jack Ruby played a small role in this part of the operation.

2. Coordinating the assassination plans with two different CIA-backed coup attempts, both involving future C-Day leaders such as Manuel Artime and Eloy Menoyo.

3. A deal to sell arms and planes to Fidel Castro, which provided cover for the assassination planning. Ruby played a larger role in this part of the operation, a role that was almost uncovered by the Kennedys.

4. Using stolen Canadian bonds to finance the sale of the planes to Castro, who was strapped for cash and credit at the time. This part included several of the people involved in the assassination and plane deals, as well as Norman Rothman and a French Connection heroin kingpin linked to both Trafficante and Michel Victor Mertz.

The goal for the mob was to plan the assassination using the arms-and-planes deal as a cover, thanks to money provided by Rothman's stolen bonds. Then the mob would assassinate Castro, coincident with a CIA-backed coup against Castro that would leave a Cuban leader like Menoyo, Varona, or Artime in charge of Cuba.

The complexity of this four-part arrangement has stymied investigators for decades. It was only through the efforts of Bobby Kennedy's investigators in 1959—and work by Dan Moldea, whose mentor was Bobby's top Hoffa investigator, Walter Sheridan—that the operation can be documented today, despite all the CIA files that remain classified.[1]

As the 1959 CIA-Mafia plots are detailed, it becomes clear that the one man who knew most of the participants was Santo Trafficante, who had the most extensive mob network in Cuba after Meyer Lansky fled. It's logical to ask why Trafficante wasn't actively involved in the 1959 CIA-Mafia plots, as he was the following year. The answer is that Trafficante could not be directly involved in 1959 because he had already been briefly jailed in Cuba shortly after the Revolution, and would soon be jailed for a much longer period of time. Cuba was under pressure to jail or deport Trafficante because the US Federal Bureau of Narcotics considered him a major drug kingpin. Yet Trafficante couldn't flee Cuba, because he was wanted by the Kennedys for the Senate crime hearings and by New York authorities for questioning in the

Anastasia hit. Since Trafficante had his own worries in 1959, Hoffa turned to other mob bosses he knew who had an incentive to see Castro assassinated.

Hoffa's role as the liaison between the CIA and the Mafia in 1959 was first reported to the public in a major investigative article that appeared in *Rolling Stone* in 1977, after the Church Committee had finished its investigation and just as the House Select Committee was gearing up for its own inquiry. The article said that "Jimmy Hoffa, who disappeared in July 1975 . . . served as a liaison between the CIA and the Syndicate in the Castro plot."[2] Yet because of the ongoing criminal investigation into Hoffa's disappearance at the time (as well as the unsolved murders around that time of Johnny Rosselli, Sam Giancana, Rolando Masferrer, and many others), as well as national security concerns relating to C-Day, Hoffa's role in the plots was left out of both the Church and House Select Committee reports and consequently overlooked by most historians and journalists since that time.

There had been one earlier article, in *Time* magazine on June 9, 1975, that had talked about the plots. The article didn't name Hoffa as the middleman between the CIA and the Mafia, and was vague about the year the plots started, but it did accurately name the mob bosses Hoffa had recruited: Russell Bufalino, James Plumeri, and Salvatore Granello, all from the Northeast. Senate records describe Russell Bufalino as "one of the most ruthless and powerful leaders of the Mafia in the United States," who was "engaged in narcotics trafficking and "labor racketeering" with Hoffa and mob bosses like Plumeri.[3] The *Time* article appeared at the height of the Church Committee investigation into CIA plots and the JFK assassination, and the article apparently came from sources close to the committee. The *Time* article caused consternation in two places: In the CIA, and in the ranks of top Mafia bosses.

A journalist recently found that "a document from the CIA's Office of the Inspector General" says that a "June 9, 1975 *Time* article [that] named mafiosi in connection with the CIA" caused a secret internal CIA "black book" on a Mafia case to be "brought to the attention of the [CIA] Inspector General." The Mafia case was somehow related to the fact that "in 1963 a CIA agent was used in support of an FBI investigation of Jimmy Hoffa . . . on Attorney General Robert Kennedy's authorization." The "mafiosi" named in the "*Time* article"—which caused such concern in the CIA—were "Russell Bufalino, James Plumeri, and Salvatore Granello."[4] Because so many documents are still withheld, it's difficult to explain more—and apparently the

CIA withheld their "black book" and information about CIA assistance with Bobby's 1963 Hoffa case from Congressional investigators. However, what was very clear to Bufalino from the June 1975 *Time* article was that his role in all those events was in danger of being exposed.

One Mafia expert writes that Russell Bufalino, "considered a major power behind the scenes in Teamsters Union affairs . . . has been considered by Federal authorities as the number one suspect in the disappearance of ex-union head Jimmy Hoffa," in July 1975.[5] That was just six weeks after the *Time* article linking Bufalino to the CIA-Mafia plots had appeared.

The mob didn't wait even that long for former Chicago godfather Sam Giancana, who was later brought into the CIA-Mafia plots and was also mentioned in the June 9, 1975 *Time* article—Giancana was murdered only ten days later, on June 19, 1975. What about Granello and Plumeri, the other mob bosses linked to Bufalino in the *Time* article about the CIA-Mafia plots? According to one crime writer, "in 1970"—after articles by Jack Anderson hinting at the CIA-Mafia plots had started to appear—Salvatore "Granello was found in a corn field in upstate New York" with "several bullets in his head. The following year James Plumeri was found in his car, strangled."[6]

The CIA-Mafia plots that Hoffa brokered in 1959 eventually led to alliances that resulted in JFK's assassination in 1963 by Trafficante, Marcello, and Rosselli. That is what Bufalino wanted to avoid having exposed, no doubt with the blessing of his allies at the time, Santo Trafficante and Carlos Marcello. Hoffa's role in the 1959 plots—overlooked by most historians—is based on multiple credible government informants who told—or tried to tell—their story to the Church Committee.

Dan Moldea wrote in 1979 that "Information had been leaked to the Church Committee that five underworld figures had been involved in the Castro plots" in 1959 and those five mob figures were "Russell Bufalino . . . and his associates from the Northeast . . . Hoffa was the original liaison between the CIA and the underworld in these plots" and "Hoffa was responsible for bringing Bufalino and his associates into the plots."[7] In 1993, Moldea reaffirmed that "strong evidence points to the fact that the original middleman between the CIA and the American underworld was Jimmy Hoffa." He said that Edward Partin, "a former Hoffa aide—later a government informant" for Bobby Kennedy—"believes his boss was the CIA's initial go-between with the Mob in the Castro murder plan."[8]

Moldea writes that "within a week after Giancana's death" on June 19, 1975—while Jimmy Hoffa was still alive—"Edward Partin," Bobby Kennedy's "key government witness against Hoffa in his 1964 jury-tampering trial, flew to Washington and met Senator McClellan," Bobby's old friend from the Senate crime hearings. Partin says he "'wanted to tell all I knew about Hoffa's involvement with the Mafia people who were trying to kill Castro. I thought that it was time the truth came out, and the Church Committee wanted to hear it.' But for unknown reasons Partin was never called to testify in either open or closed session."9

Another reliable government informant also tried to tell the Church Committee about Hoffa and the 1959 CIA-Mafia plots. Moldea names a former hit man for the Chicago mob, who said that "Hoffa had been the 'original liaison' between the CIA and the underworld. He strongly implied that it was Hoffa who had brought in Russell Bufalino and his associates." Moldea checked on the hit man's credibility with "a former Deputy Director of" the Bureau of Narcotics who "called the former syndicate figure 'absolutely reliable.'" In fact, the Bureau "used [the hit man's] information about the underworld's narcotics traffic in numerous successful prosecutions," when he had turned "informer for the Bureau of Narcotics."10

Moldea explains why Hoffa had originally recruited Bufalino and the others in 1959 to assassinate Castro for the CIA: "The CIA had learned of losses taken by . . . underworld figures and tried to capitalize on them." Bufalino, Granello, and Plumeri were partners in "a race track and a large gambling casino near Havana." As the *Time* article noted, when Bufalino, Plumeri, and Granello fled Cuba after the Revolution, they had to leave "behind $450,000" they had stashed.11 (Some accounts place the figure as high as $750,000.12) Moldea notes that Granello and Plumeri "had been helping" a Trafficante and Ruby associate named "(Dave) Yaras . . . get [Teamsters] Miami Local 320 started," where Trafficante would maintain an office. "Plumeri and Granello were also in business with Hoffa at the time, splitting kickbacks on loans from the Central States Pension Fund."13 Hoffa then "approached" the mob bosses and "suggested that in return for their cooperation [with the CIA] they might be able to recover their money" stashed in Cuba.14

Working with the CIA could provide protection to the mob bosses that even outweighed their share of the $450,000. So it's not surprising that Moldea found that "other underworld figures also tried to cash in on the CIA arrangements. Among them were two western Pennsylvania mob leaders, John LaRocca and Gabriel Mannarino, who had interests in Bufalino's Havana casino and the $450,000." These men were part of the same tight-knit group as Hoffa and the others, since "Mannarino had earlier sold his interest in Cuba's Sans Souci casino to Trafficante" and "LaRocca and Mannarino . . . had been involved in the same Cuban gunrunning operations in which Hoffa participated."[15] Mannarino and LaRocca were later rewarded by the CIA for their help in the 1959 CIA-Mafia plots—and for keeping them quiet. Noted journalist Robert Sam Anson writes that in 1971, Mannarino and LaRocca were acquitted on Teamster kickback charges when "one of the star witnesses" for their defense "turned out to be the local head of the CIA."[16]

Moldea makes it very clear that this 1959 CIA-Mafia plot brokered by Hoffa associates was separate from the Mafia plots that the CIA admits began in August 1960. He says the well-documented cutout who the CIA acknowledges using to contact the Mafia in August 1960—Robert Maheu—"denies having any role in or knowledge of the" 1959 CIA-Mafia plots, and that Maheu "concedes that 'things were happening before I became involved'" in the summer of 1960.[17]

Ruby's involvement in the 1959 CIA-Mafia plots also led to his being an informant for the FBI and having meetings with Trafficante that year—both of which probably proved crucial in Trafficante's decision in 1963 to use Ruby in the JFK assassination plot. Detailing Ruby's role in the complex 1959 plots also helps to show how the Mafia and their associates operated, with those at the top delegating to trusted associates down the food chain. That way, those at the top received the benefits while those at the bottom took most of the risk. Ruby wasn't a major player in the Mafia or the 1959 plots; he was simply a trusted low-level mob functionary who knew the right people and could be counted on not to talk.

How Jack Ruby became involved in the 1959 CIA-Mafia plots with Hoffa is easy to document, thanks to newly declassified documents and even long-overlooked Warren Commission files. Jimmy Hoffa not only knew Jack Ruby—according to Hoffa's son, now the head of the Teamsters—but Hoffa and Ruby had several associates in common, including Santo Trafficante. However, a mobster at the relatively low level of Jack Ruby would meet with people on the level of Hoffa and Trafficante only rarely. But Ruby had close associates who reported regularly to bosses like Trafficante, and to Trafficante's underbosses—and these contacts probably led to Ruby's inclusion in the 1959 plots.

The godfathers would want to insulate themselves from the actual dirty work, and therefore delegated the work to a trusted underboss who had easy access to Cuba. The underboss in turn would use managers he could trust, like those who were still running the Havana casinos after they reopened in 1959. Those managers would use people they could trust and could depend on to keep their mouths shut no matter what. These hierarchies were not necessarily the strict Sicilian Mafia patterns found in some cities; as Lansky and Ruby show, non-Sicilians were often used. Also, because the casinos often had multiple partners, one underboss might run a casino for several godfathers.

For the 1959 plots, those at the highest level were Hoffa, Bufalino, Plumeri, Granello, LaRocca, and Mannarino. At the next level we know of one under-boss, Norman Rothman, who was involved with both the 1959 CIA-Mafia plots and with Jack Ruby's gun-running. Working for Rothman was Lewis McWillie, a man Jack Ruby told Chief Justice Earl Warren he "idolized." R. D. Matthews, another mobster Ruby looked up to and befriended, was considered for the plots.[18] So, given Ruby's ties to Matthews, McWillie, Rothman, and Hoffa, it's not surprising that Ruby was able to hustle his way into the 1959 plots as one of the lower-level operatives. In addition, Ruby's gun-running to Castro gave him valuable contacts in Cuba.

There are two other things that most of the people involved had in common: Santo Trafficante and the city of Dallas. All of the participants knew, or were partners with, Trafficante, which again means that he was at least aware of what was going on, even if he was too busy with the Kennedys and Castro to be actively involved. And all of the mid- and lower-level people—Ruby, McWillie, Matthews, Rothman—had recently lived in Dallas. It shows that while Ruby wasn't a major player in the plots, he was from the right place at the right time and knew the right people. Even CIA agent David Atlee Phillips, who admitted running one of the Cuban coups for the CIA around this time, grew up in the Dallas area. Phillips's good friend (and later business partner) Gordon McLendon was a friend of Ruby, and often gave Ruby plugs on his Dallas radio station. Phillips's friend McLendon also had a mutual friend with Jack Ruby and McWillie, whose name surfaces around the time of Ruby's last trip to Cuba, when Ruby bought the pistol he would later use to shoot Oswald.[19]

Norman Rothman was first linked to the 1959 CIA-Mafia plots by the

New York *Daily News*, which first noted that Rothman was a partner with Trafficante in a Havana casino. It said at that time that "Rothman was in touch with several CIA agents" and "they had many meetings concerning assassination plots against Castro." Others named as being part of the plots included "Salvatore (Sally Burns) Granello."[20] It also indicated that Rothman may have been involved in one of Fiorini's early 1959 Castro assassination attempts.

A CIA file kept secret for thirty years after JFK's death confirms Rothman's association with several men tied to Trafficante and Ruby. It says that "Rothman has a long history of . . . illegal arms dealing" and "is known to CIA as a hoodlum with ties to pre-Castro Cuba." The CIA file confirms that "Rothman" knew "Frank Fiorini." It says that "Rothman first came to [the] CIA's attention in 1958 when he was residing in Dallas, Texas."[21] That was at the time when Ruby was part of Rothman's gun-running network. Still another CIA memo says that "Rothman has engaged in many exploits and deals with [Rolando] Masferrer," whom Ruby boasted was a friend of his.[22] The CIA document also says that "Rothman . . . claims to know [Carlos] Prio," the associate of Ruby and Trafficante whom CIA documents confirm would penetrate C-Day in the fall of 1963.[23]

Rothman was also tied to other aspects of the 1959 CIA-Mafia plots. He was later arrested (along with Sam Mannarino, brother of Gabriel) for the stolen Canadian bonds that were being used to finance Hoffa's sale of arms and planes to Castro.[24] That part of the plot also involved a French Connection heroin associate of Trafficante and Michel Victor Mertz. A Canadian historian says that "Rothman [was] an arms and drug trafficker" who was "closely linked to" the heroin network that included Trafficante, Mertz, and Jack Ruby.[25]

Rothman worked for the godfathers who Hoffa brought into the 1959 CIA-Mafia plots, which is probably how he came to be involved. But if, as seems likely, the 1959 CIA-Mafia plots were in response to pressure from Vice President Richard Nixon, that is yet another avenue to Rothman. In an incident mentioned earlier in Part II, Nixon biographer Anthony Summers notes that "Rothman had earlier played a central role in the gambling scandal involving Nixon and one of his friends and" Rothman "claimed he had covered up for Nixon. In his view, Nixon owed him a favor." Summers goes on to note that Rothman had "early contacts with the CIA" about assassinating Castro.[26]

Rothman, who was at the Tropicana in 1959, probably brought his employee Lewis McWillie—the "idol" of Jack Ruby—into the plots. When McWillie testified before the House Select Committee, he admitted that he met Rothman at the Tropicana, in Havana. An FBI document also notes that "McWillie solidified his syndicate connections through his association in Havana, Cuba, with Santo Trafficante." As the 1959 plots developed—and Trafficante faced troubles of his own—testimony shows that it was probably McWillie who arranged for Jack Ruby to soon meet with Trafficante in Cuba.

JACK RUBY, THE HOFFA PLANE DEAL, AND THE CIA-MAFIA PLOTS

When Jack Ruby's documented activities in 1959 are put into a timeline of the CIA-Mafia plots and coup actions, several long-standing mysteries about Ruby are explained. For example, Ruby's role in the 1959 CIA-Mafia plots— and Hoffa's plane deal that provided cover for it—involved several trips to Cuba that year. These trips have perplexed investigators for decades, because missing or withheld documents made determining the number or dates of the trips difficult. The House Select Committee found "documentary evidence that Ruby made at least two, if not three or more, trips to Havana in 1959," and "may in fact have been serving as a courier for underworld gambling interests in Havana."[27] Journalist Scott Malone noted that "FBI reports indicate that Ruby may have traveled to Havana six or more times. It wasn't hard to visit Cuba secretly in those days, leaving behind no records of the journey."[28]

Another lingering mystery is why Ruby—while in jail for shooting Oswald—seemed more worried about his gun-running to Cuba than facing trial for a first-degree murder committed live in front of a nationwide TV audience. This is especially odd since running guns to Castro had been seen as simply adventurous just a few years earlier. Castro had gradually changed from hero to villain to most Americans, so there was no particular stigma in what Ruby had done. Any legal issues relating to his gun-running were surely minor, compared to the death sentence Ruby was facing for murder. But even after Ruby's conviction and death sentence (which he probably hadn't expected), Ruby was still concerned about the gun-running. One of Bobby Kennedy's Mafia prosecutors wrote that Ruby told a friend "they're going to find out about Cuba. They're going to find out about the guns, find out about New Orleans, find out about everything."[29] The psychiatrist who examined Ruby at the Dallas County Jail wrote that "there is considerable guilt about the fact that he sent guns to Cuba."[30]

Ruby knew that his survival depended most immediately on no one finding out about the 1959 CIA-Mafia plots. That would link him—and his Mafia bosses Marcello and Trafficante—to JFK's assassination. Ruby knew that he would be killed if that happened, and long-overlooked Warren Commission testimony shows that he also feared for the life of his relatives. The quick deaths that Giancana and Hoffa suffered after the *Time* article about the 1959 CIA-Mafia plots shows that Ruby's fears were well-founded.

Another decades-long mystery about Ruby is why he briefly became an FBI informant in 1959. Almost certainly, one of the reasons Ruby became an FBI informant was to cover his role in Hoffa's planes-and-arms deal with Castro, which was itself a cover for the CIA-Mafia plots to assassinate Castro. Journalist Scott Malone wrote that "on March 11, 1959," Jack Ruby "was contacted by" FBI "Special Agent Charles V. Flynn of the Dallas" FBI office, about becoming "an informant for the Bureau," since "Ruby had long been an informer for the Dallas Police Department." (Either Ruby was lucky to have this opportunity drop in his lap or, more likely, one of Ruby's associates had put the word out that Ruby was interested in becoming an informant.) Malone used Warren Commission files to document that "the FBI dealt with Ruby on nine occasions between March 11 and October 2, 1959, during the height of his Cuban activities." While "the FBI maintains it received absolutely no useful information from Ruby . . . several present and former agents, including Representative Don Edwards (D-Calif.), say the Bureau never interviews an informant nine times if he is providing worthless information." According to a later Secret Service report, shortly after his first meeting with the FBI in 1959, "Ruby purchased over five hundred dollars worth of miniature tape-recording equipment," including "a wrist-watch which held a microphone . . . and also an instrument to bug a telephone."[31] Keeping in mind that this was three years before the first James Bond film ignited the spy craze of the 1960s, Ruby was clearly involved in a high level of intrigue for the owner of a small, sleazy Dallas nightclub.

Ruby's partner in the Hoffa plane deal was Dominick Bartone, according to Congressional testimony.[32] Bartone was a mob associate of a gun-runner who both Ruby and Rothman knew.[33] According to one journalist, "Dominick Bartone was a Cleveland gangster dating from the days of Al Capone who had worked with Ruby in smuggling arms to Fidel Castro between 1957 and 1959."[34] A CIA document links "Bartone . . . with Jimmy Hoffa of the Teamsters Union," and Bobby Kennedy uncovered much evidence showing that Bartone was working with Hoffa in 1959.[35] A memo from the Rockefeller Commission—the third US committee to investigate the JFK assassination—describes "Bartone" as a "Mafia member in Cleveland." The memo goes on to say that Bartone "was hired in 1959 . . . to help with assassination plotting against Fidel Castro." It also links Trafficante associate Frank Fiorini to the plan, though this was different from his earlier attempts to kill Castro.[36]

The 1959 CIA-Mafia plot to assassinate Castro was also supposed to be part of a CIA-backed coup attempt, involving future C-Day leader Eloy Menoyo and his associate William Morgan. A journalist found that in the summer of 1959, the CIA created an index card about Dominick Bartone "Regarding [his] Association with William Morgan." Bartone's CIA card also links his "association" with Menoyo's partner, William Morgan, to "Information Concerning a Plot to Assassinate Castro."[37]

The arms-and-planes deal involving Jimmy Hoffa, Jack Ruby, and Dominick Bartone was very complex, which is one reason the Kennedys' Senate Crime Committee was so important. Ordinary law enforcement was no match for the sophisticated financial maneuverings of Hoffa and his mob allies. Since J. Edgar Hoover was reluctant to let the FBI go after the Mafia or Hoffa in the 1950s, their complex criminal conspiracies could only be unraveled by Bobby Kennedy and his investigators, who included investigative accountants like Carmine Bellino.

Edward Partin, the Louisiana Teamster leader and Hoffa aide who became Bobby Kennedys' most important informant against Hoffa, explained Hoffa's plane deal to Dan Moldea: "Hoffa . . . and another person had bought a bunch of arms and were selling them to anyone who wanted them in Cuba. They bought some planes from the Army surplus, and they were ferrying these weapons and planes from Florida to Cuba."[38] Moldea notes that "after Castro overthrew the old regime, Hoffa tried . . . to obtain a $300,000 loan from the" Teamster "Pension Fund on behalf of a group of gunrunning friends. They formed a corporation" to sell "a fleet of C-74 airplanes to the new Cuban government. 'The whole . . . thing was purely and simply Hoffa's way of helping some of his mob buddies who were afraid of losing their businesses in Cuba,' says Partin. 'So they were trying to score points with Castro right after he moved in.'"[39] Bobby's top Hoffa prosecutor—Walter Sheridan—wrote that "on April 1 [1959] the Cuban government announced its intention to purchase from four to ten of the airplanes."[40]

Hoffa's dealings with Castro—which also involved Jack Ruby and his partner Bartone—gave Hoffa's mob allies the perfect cover for their plot to assassinate Castro in conjunction with a CIA-backed coup. At the time, Ruby and Bartone were dealing with two Cuban leaders who were going to lead the CIA-backed coup against Castro. As mentioned earlier, one of these was future C-Day exile leader Eloy Menoyo, whose rebel group the SNFE (Second National Front of Escambray) had played a major role in the Revolution. Menoyo's partner in the SNFE was the American soldier-of-fortune William Morgan. According to the FBI, "Morgan . . . claims he was once a bodyguard for Meyer Lansky," and Morgan had an extensive criminal record in America.[41] Tad Szulc wrote that Menoyo met Morgan in 1958 "in Escambray where . . . Morgan . . . seemed to be fighting there strictly for the money." In contrast to the mercenary Morgan, Eloy Menoyo was seen as being driven by his principles and not by money (his brother had been killed by Batista's troops during an unsuccessful attack on the Presidential Palace in March 1957). The former head of Cuban State Security noted that "Morgan had received his rank of Commander in the SNFE, and after January 1 [1959] he was assigned some military responsibilities" in the new Cuban government.[42]

CIA documents show how the Hoffa-Ruby-Bartone plane deal with Menoyo and Morgan was also part of the CIA-Mafia assassination and coup plans. One CIA memo says that on "March 26, 1959," a high-level informant told the "Acting Chief" of the CIA's "Western Hemisphere Division" that "he had been in Cuba about a week before." The informant told the CIA that William "Morgan claims 2,000 of his former troops are now in the Cuban Army and still loyal to him." The CIA informant said that "Morgan then came to Havana and met an American from Cleveland, Dominick Bartone, who is . . . trying to sell some [C-74] Globemasters to Fidel Castro. Dominick Bartone befriended Morgan and was paying for his room at the Capri." The CIA memo doesn't mention that Santo Trafficante was a major owner of the Capri.[43] A later CIA report talked about Morgan contacting the CIA and State Department in Havana. It also noted a trip Morgan made to Miami in late July 1959, where Morgan "reported to (censored) that he was the leader of a plot to assassinate Castro."[44]

Jack Ruby was in the middle of all this, meeting with William Morgan in Havana on behalf of Dominick Bartone. This statement is based on sworn testimony given to the House Select Committee in the late 1970s but kept secret until the 1990s, from an eyewitness account by another American soldier-of-fortune who CIA files confirm was in Cuba at the time. The earliest account of this meeting, by journalist Scott Malone, places Ruby at the Havana home of William Morgan in June 1959. Accompanying Ruby was Lewis McWillie, who worked for Norman Rothman and was also close to Trafficante.[45] Warren Commission files confirm that the previous month, Ruby had sent a message via a mutual female acquaintance to McWillie in Cuba, saying that he was coming to visit McWillie in Havana. The woman told the FBI that Ruby also handed her "five letters and numbers, which was a coded message" to give to McWillie. The woman worked at the airport in Dallas and "frequently saw Ruby and McWillie . . . coming and going on their frequent trips." When the woman gave the verbal message to McWillie in Cuba, he was at first cool to the idea of Ruby's visit.[46] But something soon changed McWillie's mind—either the coded message or the reaction of McWillie's criminal superiors like Norman Rothman—because within a short time McWillie was practically begging Ruby to come to Cuba, even arranging and paying for Ruby's plane tickets for at least one of his trips. As for why a verbal message and code would be needed for Ruby to communi-cate with McWillie in Cuba, McWillie later told the House Select Committee that "every [phone] call was monitored in Havana."[47] As for the trip's timing, there are several days between June 6, 1959 and June 17, 1959 when Ruby's whereabouts could not be established—and FBI files show that Jack Ruby met with his FBI handler on June 5 and June 18, 1959.

The Ruby-McWillie-Morgan meeting on behalf of Bartone was detailed in sworn testimony to the House Select Committee on Assassinations (HSCA) in the late 1970s, although the transcripts were kept secret until the late 1990s. However, even before their release, we were able to interview the HSCA witness—American soldier-of-fortune Jerry Hemming—about the meeting. He said the meeting took place at "Morgan's penthouse" in Havana. Prior to this, he said "Jack Ruby and McWillie and Bartone first sold postal-type jeeps to Batista. Then, they tried to sell them to Fidel." He pointed out "these were not combat jeeps; these were designed for use at airports and such." Then "Jack Ruby and Bartone tried to sell Globemaster planes" to Cuba. They thought Morgan had influence with Fidel and "would be the log-ical way to get to Castro, since no one was able to easily get an appointment to see Castro." He confirmed that "in the penthouse were Jack Ruby, McWillie, and William Morgan," in addition to himself and a Los Angeles newsman. He made it clear that "Ruby was acting on behalf of Bartone." In addition, "Bartone was also trying to sell Globemasters to [Rafael] Trujillo," the Dominican Republic's brutal dictator (as we show shortly, Ruby wasn't directly involved in the Trujillo deal, though another Hoffa associate was). The solder-of-fortune said that "Hoffa was involved for the financing kickbacks—he would have loaned Cuba the money to buy the planes." He also said that "Frank Fiorini had dealt with Jack Ruby about the planes, earlier." But "William Morgan didn't realize Jack Ruby and Bartone had already tried to cut a deal with Fiorini."[48]

There is much confirmation for this account. Corroboration for McWillie's involvement with Ruby in an earlier deal to sell jeeps to Castro comes from long-overlooked Warren Commission testimony by Jack Ruby's sister. When she was asked "What did Jack tell you about the jeeps?" Ruby's sister replied "This was the deal with McWillie at the time and we were on friendly terms" with Castro. Ruby's sister didn't know much about the deal, only that it involved a quantity of jeeps—"400 or 800 jeeps or 80 jeeps"— and it also involved "McWillie."[49] It's understandable that Ruby's sister didn't know the details, since Ruby's travel to Cuba was so secret that he didn't even tell her about it, even though she was also his business partner for their nightclubs.[50]

A related story about Ruby and jeeps is known to most historians, an approach Ruby made to Texas gun-runner Robert McKeown in early 1959 that involved selling jeeps to Castro in return for help in getting someone out of jail in Cuba. But often overlooked is that the gun-runner testified under oath and grant of immunity to the House Select Committee that Ruby told him he already had the jeeps and just needed help arranging the deal by getting a letter of introduction to Castro.[51] The Texas gun-runner said that Ruby dropped the matter with him in early 1959—and it's now clear that that was because Ruby decided to approach William Morgan instead.

More confirmation of Bartone's dealings with Morgan and Menoyo comes from a formerly "secret" CIA document from the file of C-Day leader Eloy Menoyo. It says "Bartone . . . previously connected with . . . Cuba-based effort which developed into a fiasco . . . involving William Morgan and Eloy Menoyo." This document was generated by the CIA four years after the Ruby-McWillie-Morgan meeting, when the CIA says that "notorious racketeer" Bartone was granted an interview with them because of the "request of [the] special assistant to the US Attorney General," Bobby Kennedy, on June 6, 1963.[52] This was shortly after Bartone's old partner, Jack Ruby, became part of the plot to kill JFK.

There is also evidence that gives credence to the claim that Ruby, McWillie, and Bartone first tried to cut a deal with Frank Fiorini. Fiorini admitted to a journalist that "I knew Dominick Bartone." Fiorini probably knew McWillie as well, since the journalist found that "an FBI document confirmed: 'In 1959 Frank Fiorini was a government inspector of gambling at the Tropicana night club, Havana, Cuba.'"[53] Mafia expert David Scheim documented that in 1959, Lewis "McWillie was manager of the mob-owned Tropicana Hotel in Havana."[54]

   That Ruby played a role in Hoffa's deal with Bartone, which included the Globemaster planes, is clear, as is the involvement of Ruby's friend Lewis McWillie. But why would McWillie—who managed the Tropicana, one of the finest casinos in Havana—want to work with a low-life like Ruby? On one hand, it's clear that Ruby would do anything McWillie wanted, since Ruby looked up to him. A few years later, when Chief Justice Earl Warren flew to Dallas to question Ruby (after the Warren Commission refused Ruby's request to be taken to Washington for questioning), Ruby was remarkably candid to Warren about his admiration for McWillie. Ruby said "I idolized McWillie. He is a pretty nice boy, and I happened to be idolizing him."[55] And Ruby's sister told the Warren Commission that McWillie was a very "high class . . . gambler." She said that "if you met" McWillie, "you would think he is a doctor or a lawyer." Before McWillie went to Havana, she said he "was the main guy at the high class club here" in Dallas "and the town sort of overlooks" his gambling "and they admire him."[56] Why would such a "high class" mobster be so anxious to have Ruby visit him in Cuba?
   It was because Ruby was involved in more than just the jeeps and Hoffa's plane deal. Those were covers for the CIA-Mafia plots Hoffa had brokered, and Ruby's contacts with the FBI during that time could help provide additional cover. Also, the CIA-Mafia assassination plots were coordinated with CIA-backed coup attempts, which also figure into the story. Plus, by the summer Santo Trafficante would need help getting out of detention in Cuba, and Ruby played a role there, too. On at least one of Ruby's trips to Cuba in the summer of 1959, Cuban records show he stayed at Trafficante's Capri Hotel, and Ruby admitted to Chief Justice Earl Warren that McWillie got Ruby his plane tickets "from the travel agent in the Capri Hotel."[57]
   Since Ruby was based in Dallas, he was technically beholden to Trafficante's close ally, mob boss Carlos Marcello, whose underboss Joe Civello presided over Dallas. The soldier-of-fortune who witnessed the Ruby-McWillie-Morgan meeting in Cuba said later that "Ruby was on the

periphery of deals Marcello was trying to cut with Castro."[58] That might explain where Ruby—always tight on cash—could get the financing for his involvement in the jeep deal, his earlier gun-running, and his small part of the Hoffa plane deal. Ruby also sometimes flew through Marcello's New Orleans on his way to Havana. Anthony Summers found Warren Commission documents confirming that "Ruby's airline acquaintance at the New Orleans airport overheard Ruby talking on the telephone before taking off on one of his flights" to Cuba. "He listened as Ruby instructed one of his employees not to disclose his whereabouts 'unless it were to the police or some other official agency.'" Summers points out that "the one 'other agency' known to have been in close touch with Ruby at that period was the FBI" and "the [FBI] agent dealing with Ruby has admitted that Ruby told him about one of his Cuban trips."[59]

Warren Commission files show that Jack Ruby met with his FBI handler on June 5, 1959, probably prior to Ruby's meeting with McWillie and Morgan about the Hoffa plane deal. Ruby also met with the FBI agent on June 18, the day before the FBI told the CIA about a major development in the CIA-Mafia assassination and coup plots.[60] More about that shortly.

Why wasn't Dominick Bartone at the Ruby-McWillie-Morgan meeting about the Hoffa plane deal, instead leaving Ruby to act on his behalf? According to former Hoffa prosecutor Walter Sheridan, "On May 22 [1959] Customs agents . . . arrested Bartone and his co-conspirators," seizing a "plane and its cargo just prior to its scheduled departure" for Trujillo's Dominican Republic. However, Sheridan made it clear that Bartone's partner—who used the alias "Jack La Rue"—was not one of those arrested with Bartone.[61] This makes sense, because Ruby wasn't involved in the Trujillo side of the plane deal, which was related to the CIA-backed coup designed to coincide with the CIA-Mafia assassination of Castro.

Even after Bartone's arrest, Bobby Kennedy's crime hearings make it clear that his dealmaking continued, and Bartone himself was soon back in the thick of the Hoffa plane deal and the CIA-Mafia Castro assassination plot. It's clear that Bartone was getting assistance from one (or more) government agencies to continue his activities, especially since his partner "Jack La Rue" was able to evade Bobby's usually thorough investigators. The reasons become clear when you look at the CIA-backed coup that was originally scheduled to coincide with the CIA-Mafia assassination of Castro.

Menoyo, Morales, and Phillips Plan a Coup

CIA FILES SHOW THAT IN Cuba, future C-Day exile leader Eloy Menoyo was starting to have doubts about Castro. A "March 3, 1959" CIA document using information from Havana says that Menoyo "is disturbed with Fidel Castro . . . because he is acting as though he thinks that he is another liberator like Simon Bolivar and because he is taking all of the honors of the revolution, rather than sharing them with any of the other revolutionary leaders." The same CIA document also notes the dissatisfaction of "Carlos Franqui," the journalist who Harry Williams would help to defect prior to C-Day in 1963.[1]

At the time, David Morales was running operations for the CIA from the US Embassy in Havana, while David Atlee Phillips operated as a CIA agent while seeming to be an ordinary businessman in Havana. The CIA's involvement in planning the assassination and coup planning in 1959 was far less "hands-on" than it would be in 1963, or even in 1960: In 1959, the CIA seemed content to monitor existing operations and provide "deniable" support when possible, in an attempt to get the results it wanted.

The former head of Cuban State Security says the CIA first starting plotting their coup in "February 1959." That's when a "CIA representative . . . met with [Dominican dictator] Trujillo and his chief of intelligence Colonel Johnny Abbes," regarding Castro's overthrow. Even the Cubans imply that the CIA was not yet operating with a heavy hand in planning the coup. They say the US "didn't have to give its public consent" to the coup. "It only had to look the other way and then, once the deed was done, pretend that it had just heard about it," meaning "once again the US could plausibly deny any involvement."[2] (We are cautious when using Cuban government accounts of CIA actions, for obvious reasons of potential bias. However, when you strip the Cuban accounts of their revolutionary rhetoric and focus primarily on actions that are backed up by other evidence, the most important points are often confirmed by both Cuban and US accounts.)

The CIA contact with Trujillo would soon evolve into the still-controversial coup attempt in the summer of 1959 by future C-Day leader Eloy Menoyo and William Morgan that included help from mobsters such as Bartone and Ruby. A young Fidel Castro had set his sights on toppling Trujillo years earlier, and that no doubt motivated Trujillo to be interested in helping to overthrow Castro. Bernard Spindel, Hoffa's top "wireman" who bugged Hoffa's enemies, handled the Dominican side of things for Hoffa—and sometimes the CIA—including the Dominican aspect of the Hoffa plane deal.[3] Spindel wrote in his autobiography that Trujillo had ruled the Dominican Republic with an iron fist since 1930, after engineering "the massacre of more than 45,000 people." To stay in power, Trujillo's ruthless security forces killed "four to six political prisoners every day . . . some by tortures so terrible they make the medieval torture chambers seem almost merciful by comparison." Spindel writes that "while Trujillo was bribing US public officials and newspaper people, the US was" sending him "$25,000,000 a year in foreign aid."[4]

In the early spring of 1959—well before the Ruby-McWillie-Morgan meeting—the US Embassy received an unusual visit from Menoyo and his partner in the SNFE, William Morgan. This account comes from Paul Bethel, a friend of CIA agent—and propaganda expert—David Atlee Phillips, and in it Phillips admits that he was involved in a 1959 coup attempt. Bethel's account was written years later, and in some ways it sounds like an attempt to put a benign face on documented US contacts with Menoyo and Morgan before their attempted coup. Unlike declassified internal CIA documents that were never intended for public consumption, Bethel's account appeared in a book he wrote for a right-wing publisher and provides candid details on several key points.

Bethel says he was the "Press Officer for the US Embassy in Havana" when he was visited by Menoyo and Morgan in the spring or late winter of 1959. He says that "Morgan" had "provided our embassy with details regarding the early Communist takeover of the Cuban government." Then one day Morgan, along with "Eloy Menoyo, came straight to the Embassy, causing a minor sensation by walking fully armed to the desk of the Marine guard in the foyer of the building and asking to see me." Bethel says future C-Day leader "Menoyo was dark and slender" while "Morgan was squat, blond, blue-eyed and tough." In talking with Bethel, Morgan mentioned that he was reluctant to go to Miami, "referring to the possibility that once he set foot on US soil he ran the risk of being picked up by Federal agents and trotted off to face a court martial for desertion from the Army of the United States." (Bethel doesn't mention that Morgan would soon feel free to travel to Miami.) Bethel says he left Menoyo with another US official, while he and Morgan "went to another room." Bethel admits that "this conversation (with Morgan) was to lead to a labyrinthian series of intrigues, plots and counter-plots, and finally to an 'invasion' of Cuba." Morgan was feeling out Bethel about US help for overthrowing Castro, saying that Menoyo's "SNFE was still intact, an entity apart from the Castro government" and that "the SNFE, where Menoyo had many followers and friends, was being quietly organized into a political party." After Morgan and Menoyo left the US Embassy, Bethel says he "carefully reported to the political section what had been told to me by Morgan." Bethel "was asked . . . to keep in contact with the SNFE" leaders and "follow the progress of the daring young men."[5]

Bethel tells us little in his book about what he did to "keep in contact with" Menoyo or Morgan and "follow the progress" they were making in their attempt to overthrow Castro. Bethel does say he talked to a press agent who had been hired by Menoyo and Morgan to raise Menoyo's profile prior to the coup. One wonders if "Press Officer" Bethel or propaganda expert David Atlee Phillips—also involved with Cuban coup planning—had advised Menoyo and Morgan to hire such a person. Bethel writes that after the press agent resigned, he told Bethel that "Morgan kept company with a very unwholesome American who lived at the Capri Hotel, whom he described as a 'gangster.'" The Capri was a Trafficante hotel where Ruby, Bartone, and other gangsters stayed. Bethel says that "contact was again renewed by Morgan a few months later when an attempt [was] made to implicate the American Embassy, through me, in a phony 'invasion' of Cuba from the Dominican Republic."[6] However, Bethel leaves out information contained in one of Menoyo's censored CIA files that has been released. It shows that by "June 18, 1959," some US official was trying to help Menoyo improve his public profile with a favorable article, saying that hyping Menoyo "is extremely important, politically" for the US.[7]

Why would the CIA be so concerned with improving Menoyo's public image? Because he was helping to lead the CIA-backed coup that would hopefully take over Cuba, after the CIA-Mafia plot had assassinated Castro.

According to noted historian and Kennedy confidant Tad Szulc, Dominican dictator Trujillo had expanded his coup plotting with the CIA to include "plotting with two Rebel Army comandantes . . . considered ready to betray Castro. One was an American mercenary named William Morgan and the other was a Spaniard named Eloy Menoyo."[8]

The CIA-Mafia assassination plot and the coup plan were part of the same overall operation. Cuban accounts say that "during the first days of March [1959], Morgan received a telephone call from a US mafioso" who "was Trujillo's messenger. A meeting then took place in a room in Havana's Hotel Capri." Morgan reportedly told the Mafioso that "for a million dollars he would turn the SNFE against the revolution and 'bounce Fidel Castro from power.'" Later, the "mafioso" confirmed a deal with Trujillo, whereby "Morgan would receive his million dollars. Half would be deposited in a bank account, and he would get the rest when he completed the operation." The Cuban accounts say that at an April 1959 meeting in Miami, Morgan met with several others involved in the coup, including a former "general in Batista's army."[9] Note that after talking with Bethel, Morgan was able to travel to Miami without fear of arrest by the US Army for desertion.

At the Miami meeting, Morgan and the others "expressed their belief that" Menoyo's "SNFE and the White Rose counterrevolutionary group could carry out this task. The White Rose was composed of various isolated cells throughout the island, mainly ex-soldiers of the Batista regime." The Cuban account says that "a week later Morgan returned to Miami" and "explained that Eloy Menoyo . . . had agreed to participate in the plot, but only on the condition that the US government supported it." (Menoyo had the same attitude in 1963, when Harry Williams was trying to get him to join C-Day.) The Dominican Consul in Miami "told them it was coordinated at the highest levels of [the US] government, and gave Menoyo the necessary assurances. The money for operating expenses would be distributed in $10,000 installments to two of Morgan's emissaries who traveled to Miami periodically."[10]

A journalist found an FBI report confirming that Morgan was getting money for "anti-Castro" activities at this time. He wrote that "on May 1, 1959, the FBI received a report of funds being funneled to William Morgan: 'Within the past few days $25,000 was delivered to William Morgan . . . William Morgan has reportedly agreed to establish a new revolutionary anti-Castro front in the Escambray area . . . Carlos Prio . . . and the Dominican

Republic are supplying the other arms and equipment.'"[11] Carlos Prio was the last elected president of Cuba (pre-Batista), who had originally supported Castro but had now turned against him. Frank Fiorini once said that "the closest friend" of "ex-President Carlos Prio" had been "involved so much with the U.S. underworld and drugs that the American Government at one time threatened . . . to stop the sale of all legal drugs into Cuba because of this man."[12]

Historian Hugh Thomas, who wrote his definitive book on Cuba prior to the release of many important US files, says "it is just possible that the CIA" was "involved" in Menoyo's coup plan.[13] But he also cites an account which says that a "CIA cover" company—which would later be "sued for the employ of US pilots in the Bay of Pigs invasion"—was involved in the plots going on in "June 1959." His book notes that the "CIA cover" company "had been incorporated on May 14, 1959."[14] The weight of the evidence now shows that the CIA was clearly involved. Also, in Cuba in 1959, were two important CIA agents involved in coup planning David Morales and—by his own admission—David Atlee Phillips.

THE CIA-MAFIA PLOTS AND THE COUP: DAVID ATLEE PHILLIPS AND DAVID MORALES

David Atlee Phillips and David Morales went from plotting coups and assassinations for the CIA in Guatemala in 1954 to attempting the same thing in Cuba in 1959. Their actions in 1959 are important because by 1963, both CIA operatives would be working on C-Day, with some of the same people from 1959. And by 1963, David Morales would be a prime link in the CIA-Mafia plots against Castro. The Mafia penetration of C-Day and the other 1963 CIA plots—which led to JFK's assassination—had its roots in the CIA-Mafia plots of 1959, with people like Morales involved at both times.

CIA agents Phillips and Morales played very different roles in the 1959 plots, based on their documented activities and future statements. Phillips appears to have worked more with the Cuban resistance—as he would continue to do—while Morales was described by a CIA official as being willing to deal with the Mafia. Rosselli's biographers confirm that "Morales distinguished himself . . . by cultivating relationships with the Mafia" and "it seems likely that" Morales "put those connections to work for him during his years in Havana."[15] Again, it's important to stress that the CIA wasn't trying to control every aspect of the plots, as would happen by 1963. In 1959, they appear to have had the more traditional CIA role in such plotting, trying to guide and shape things while remaining in the shadows, with the CIA's role being largely unseen and thus "deniable."

According to one account, David Atlee Phillips began working for the CIA in Havana in 1955, though he did have an important assignment in the Middle East from 1957 to 1958. One account says that "in 1957" David Atlee "Phillips . . . was posted to Beirut, Lebanon," arriving "at the same time as a CIA assassination squad whose target was the famed Soviet agent, Kim Philby." David "Phillips's cover in the area was provided by a close associate of John Connally, the rising Texas political power"—which is not surprising, since Phillips grew up in Fort Worth, Texas. The account says that Phillips was doing the same type of "psychological warfare" and propaganda that had been so effective for the CIA in Guatemala, and that Phillips would use again for the Bay of Pigs: "Phillips and his psychological warfare team" established "a network of illegal radio outlets" that called "itself the Voice of Justice" and "was soon locked into a bitter propaganda war with" Egyptian leader "Nasser's voice of the Arabs." But this time, Phillips's results were more like the Bay of Pigs disaster, because "in July 1958, Iraq 'fell' to anti-American nationalist forces, and Phillips narrowly escaped death. The CIA's clients, King Faisal and his uncle, as well as their puppet Iraqi premier, were all murdered" and "the next day, Eisenhower sent the Marines . . . to shore up" the US-backed President of Lebanon. This account says that "Phillips had to depart on the last commercial flight out of Beirut."[16]

David Atlee Phillips returned to Havana, where the CIA officer who had originally recruited Phillips in Chile was now CIA Chief of Station in Havana.[17] In Havana, Phillips used "the deep cover of David A. Phillips Associates, a public relations firm."[18] In other words, Phillips appeared to be an ordinary businessman, to cover his clandestine work for the CIA. By the spring of 1959, David Morales—Phillips's compatriot from the Guatemala coup and assassinations—had joined Phillips in Cuba; Morales was essentially running CIA operations from the US Embassy.

The CIA's switch from supporting Castro to trying to overthrow and assassinate him had only taken a few months. Originally, the CIA had seen supporting Castro as a way to hedge its bets and perhaps ride the tide of what seemed like a wave of Latin American dictators being overthrown. Journalist Tad Szulc points out that during the rise of Castro's revolution, Venezuela's dictator, Marcos Perez Jimenez, fell on "January 23, 1958," but that was only the latest in a series of similar events that included the 1957 toppling of Colombia's dictator, Gustavo Rojas Pinilla; the fall of Argentina's Juan Peron in 1955; and Peru's ruler, Manuel Odria, being deposed in 1956. We earlier noted how much support Szulc discovered the CIA had given to Fidel Castro and Che Guevara.[19]

But by the spring and early of summer of 1959, the CIA had a radically different attitude toward Castro, in tune with Vice President Nixon's hard-line stance toward Castro. Yet, on the surface, Phillips was simply a successful public relations man. Phillips wrote in his first autobiography that in Havana in 1959, "David A. Phillips Associates was the fastest growing public-relations business in the world." Unaware that Phillips was a CIA agent and the company his CIA cover, "foreign industrialists sought my advice on dealing with the new, alarmingly Socialist Castro government. The pendulum was swinging to the left, and I did well."[20]

In his autobiography, CIA agent David Atlee Phillips has some surprisingly nice things to say about revolutionary hero Che Guevara. This makes Phillips yet another C-Day veteran who has said highly complimentary things about Che, the others being Bobby Kennedy, Harry Williams, and Artime–CIA operative Felix Rodriguez. Phillips writes that "Che was quite a guy. He had the charisma and charm—he was simpatico—which are essential qualities for Latin Americans who aspire to greatness in any field of endeavor. I predicted to my friend that he would become the most successful revolutionary of our time." Phillips said this in 1959, when Che was already a high Cuban official and Phillips had a seemingly chance encounter with him. Phillips goes on to say "in any event, I admired him. That early morning encounter in the coffee house helped me understand the aspirations and convictions of men with whom I disagreed. . . ." Right after praising Che, Phillips starts talking about a coup in Cuba: "My [CIA] case officer asked me to undertake what he called a 'special' mission. A group of anti-Castro Cubans in Havana was planning the first coup attempt against the new regime," and Phillips was asked to assist the group.[21]

(Maurice Gatlin, an associate of Guy Banister, sent the following to the FBI on March 30, 1959, after a visit to Havana: "We also learned, through sources that I have found to be reliable, that [Che] Guevara . . . intend[s] to liquidate their communist front man, Fidel Castro, around June or July [1959], arranging his death so it will be attributed . . . to a 'gringo' for propaganda purposes."[22] It is not known if this was simply a rumor, or if Che might have had some role in one of the coup or assassination plans.)

David Atlee Phillips's work on this 1959 coup foreshadows his later work on C-Day. From his own very brief account, he worked primarily with the

Cuban resistance, as he would later do on C-Day in working with Cuban exiles. For Phillips's 1959 activity, his autobiographical account is all we have, since no documents about it have been released.

While David Atlee Phillips worked from the cover of his Havana PR firm, David Morales had a more traditional—and powerful—CIA role. Morales worked out of the US Embassy, under a State Department cover.[23] In 1959, "Morales was listed as a 'political attaché to the American consulate in Havana.'"[24] In reality, Morales handled the nitty-gritty of CIA operations, just as he would do later at Miami's huge CIA Station during C-Day.[25] According to one expert, "David Morales was probably the highest CIA operations person in Havana in 1959."[26] However, that information was kept hidden from the first five government committees that looked into the JFK assassination, just as the CIA didn't tell them that Morales was CIA Chief of Operations in Miami in the fall of 1963. (Of course, the CIA didn't tell any of those government committees about C-Day, either.) In 1959, Phillips was a much lower-level agent than the powerful Morales.

This means that CIA agent David Morales would have been at the center of the 1959 CIA-Mafia plots to assassinate Castro. This probably explains why he had a similar role by the summer and fall of 1963, while he was also working on C-Day. A recent CIA history quotes a high CIA official as saying that David Morales "would do anything, even work with the Mafia."[27] Morales would also have known Phillips's friend Paul Bethel—who met with Menoyo and Morgan—and Morales would have been part of the coup plotting. Unlike some US officials, Morales was against Castro from the start, since Morales had helped support the dictator Batista.[28]

Morales's CIA position was secret in 1959 and was later kept hidden from US investigating committees—but it was known at the time by a close associate of Santo Trafficante, Johnny Rosselli, and Rolando Masferrer. This mob associate who knew that David Morales was a key—perhaps *the* key—CIA figure in Havana was John Martino, the same mobster who would later penetrate and even write about C-Day in 1963. Martino's knowledge of Morales's CIA role in Havana in 1959 is easy to document, since Martino wrote about it in his book *I Was Castro's Prisoner*, published in 1963. Martino called "David Morales . . . an intelligent and patriotic public servant" who "sent voluminous reports to Washington" about "Fidel Castro."[29]

Morales expert Larry Hancock noted that "John Martino seems to have known far more about David Morales" in 1959 "than the CIA would reveal to House Select Committee investigators" two decades later.[30] How would a mobster like Martino know that Morales was a top CIA operative in Havana in 1959? Johnny Rosselli's biographers say it's likely that he was close to Morales in 1959, and Martino was also close to Rosselli. In addition, Hancock writes that John "Martino . . . was actually involved" in a casino that was partially owned by "Santo Trafficante," yet another associate of Rosselli. In addition, "two of John Martino's co-workers" there "were R. D. Matthews (an associate of both Santo Trafficante and the Campisi family in Dallas) and Lewis McWillie."[31] McWillie, Matthews, and even Trafficante were also all associates of Jack Ruby, and McWillie was partners with Ruby in Hoffa's plane deal that served as the cover for the 1959 CIA-Mafia plots to kill Castro.

John Martino was very likely engaged in some aspect of the 1959 CIA-Mafia plots, given his unusual activities that year and his ties to others involved in or aware of the plots, like McWillie, Matthews, Trafficante, Rolando Masferrer, and Frank Fiorini.[32] An FBI memo sent to J. Edgar Hoover in late July 1959 says that John "Martino has made twelve to fourteen visits to Cuba since January 1, 1959." It notes that "Martino was a close friend of . . . Rolando Masferrer (ex-Cuban Senator and political gangster) . . . and of many American gamblers such as Santo Trafficante, Top Hoodlum from Tampa, Florida." The FBI memo also says that "Martino was also engaged in a smuggling venture with Masferrer."[33] Why would Martino make so many trips to Cuba—according to the FBI, twelve to fourteen in just the first seven months of 1959? One expert on Martino says that "Martino was being a courier—for information and money—for Trafficante in 1959."[34]

Even the CIA later admitted that Martino was "a CIA go between" by the early 1960s, so it's likely that the mobster had some CIA contact in 1959, given his awareness of David Morales's CIA activities that year.[35] But Martino's 1959 activities for the Mafia—and possibly for Morales and the CIA—would come to an end just as the CIA had new reason to accelerate the Castro assassination and coup plots.

A Cuban account says that on July 17, 1959, Fidel "Castro criticizes [Cuban] President Urrutia in a speech" on television "and Urrutia resigns."[36] This soon made Castro the sole leader of Cuba, a position he would quickly move to consolidate, soon turning the country into a dictatorship. Historian Tad Szulc observes that "Castro had carried out a coup d'etat by television," something that no doubt made CIA propaganda expert David Atlee Phillips envious.[37] It probably confirmed the worst fears of Vice President Richard Nixon, and the CIA-Mafia plots and coup plans were likely stepped up after that.

Several days after Castro's "TV coup," mobster John Martino was back in Cuba on one of his frequent missions, this time taking his son along, possibly as "cover," according to one expert. But an FBI memo sent to J. Edgar Hoover says that "John Martino . . . was arrested July 23, 1959" in Cuba.[38] Martino's son was released, but "Martino was convicted and sentenced to 13 years" in jail, according to one account.[39] Martino would finally be released in 1962, though his horrible experiences in prison (including watching the slow execution of Menoyo's former partner, William Morgan) would leave him scarred and bitter toward the US government. This would lead to his involvement in the Mafia penetration of C-Day, and his acknowledgment, shortly before his death, of his role in JFK's assassination.

But even without the now-imprisoned Martino, the 1959 CIA-Mafia assassination plots and coup plans forged ahead. Martino was an expendable, lower-level mobster like Ruby. There were plenty of other Mafiosi for Morales to work with, and Phillips was still working on his coup plans. However, the public face of the US attitude remained less antagonistic. One historian noted with irony that "during the second half of 1959, President Eisenhower declared that the US was not accusing the Cuban government of being Communists" and even "General C. P. Cabell, Deputy Director of the CIA, affirmed that 'Fidel Castro is not a Communist.'"[40] Given the 1959 CIA-Mafia plots and coup attempts, it's possible that at least CIA Deputy Director Cabell's comments were meant to deflect suspicion that the US was trying to overthrow Castro.

HARRY WILLIAMS ENCOUNTERS THE 1959 CIA-MAFIA PLOT TO ASSASSINATE CASTRO

The public, both in America and Cuba, had no idea that the CIA and the Mafia had joined forces to assassinate Fidel Castro. But Harry Williams— later the key architect of C-Day for the Kennedys—knew better. Williams had a personal encounter with the highly secret 1959 CIA-Mafia plots. In 1959, Harry Williams was a successful mining engineer based in Havana, with a family. He had provided support earlier to Che and the Revolution, but now Harry viewed with alarm the increasing abuses—and power—of

Castro. But when he tried to take action to stop Castro, he came up against the CIA-Mafia plots.

It was in 1992 that Harry Williams told us about encountering the CIA-Mafia plots, feeling that after thirty-three years it was finally safe to discuss such things. The fact that Trafficante and Masferrer were dead—and Menoyo had been released from Cuban prison a few years earlier—were probably also factors in Harry's willingness to talk. He allowed the interview to be taped. Minor editing has been made in Harry's quotes for clarity, since Harry spoke in accented English and occasionally had trouble with English idioms.

Harry said he had grown so weary of all the disappearances and executions in Cuba, and of Castro's ever-growing power at the expense of more moderate leaders, that he felt he had to do something. Harry worried about his family and his country. He felt that Castro had to go, and soon. Harry was just a businessman and didn't know about how to go about such things. So he "went to the Mafia" to see about arranging things, a logical choice given the Mafia's still-prominent role in Cuba in "1959."[41]

First, Harry went to a friend of his who owned a small nightclub and said he wanted to see a mutual acquaintance, someone Harry had heard was "a little mixed up with the Mafia." Harry wanted "to get in touch with the people who take action, who do the Mafia type of thing. In other words, I want to see a hit man." Actually, Harry explained, he "wanted to see the guy who was the boss of a hit man," to see if it was possible to arrange a Mafia hit on Castro. Harry had no idea of what a mob hit on Castro would cost. He planned to find out first, then see if he could raise the money.[42]

Harry explained the rough plan he had in mind. He said that when he "had the idea of eliminating" Castro, Harry "lived next to the sea. And Castro had a lady—a Spanish lady—near there that Castro used to visit a lot. And Castro would visit with her and then they would always go to a [particular] restaurant," one that Harry also frequented. That was where Harry thought Castro could be "eliminated." But as for the actual killing, Harry's "idea was to leave that to the professionals. I mean if you . . . hire a professional killer, leave it to him." Also, by using a professional hit man, Harry hoped "to come out of things alive."

Harry evoked an old Spanish saying, "muerto el perro se ocabo la rabia." A Cuban source said it technically translates as "when the dog is dead, the rabies are over." Harry's English version was "a dead dog is not rowdy." In either case, the meaning is clear—to Harry, Fidel Castro was like a rabid dog who must be stopped. And Harry eventually "had a meeting with" the man who was "a little mixed up with the Mafia." Harry says the man "gave me a telephone number in Miami" to call.[43]

Harry called the number and, while he was waiting to hear back from his Mafia contact in Miami, got a call he wasn't expecting. Harry says that "I was called by a guy, a CIA man in Havana that I didn't [personally] know. But he called me and I had a meeting with him, a long meeting at night." Harry indicated that he knew of the CIA man by reputation—and his distinctive appearance—but had not met him before. Harry said "I used to call him . . . Blanco," which in English means "the White . . . he was dressed [all] in white. White suit, white shirt, necktie white, and shoes white. And he was a CIA man" who spoke "Spanish freely." Harry says he saw him during a later encounter with the CIA, after Harry had left Cuba, but by that time the CIA man "was dressed a little different," not so distinctively.[44] It is possible that Harry's CIA man dressed in all white was somehow related to the "White Rose" resistance group that Cuban accounts say was part of the Menoyo-Morgan coup plan backed by the CIA and the Mafia.[45]

It is clear that Harry's CIA man had some contact with the Mafia. That's because he told Harry not to bother with his recent attempt to hire a hit man, to leave it alone. He told Harry "to have patience." Harry found it odd at first that the CIA man was trying to talk him out of trying to eliminate Castro. But near the end of the conversation, the CIA man admitted that "we know everything. We even know you called this number" in Miami, trying to reach the Mafia.[46]

Harry was surprised, because he had called the Miami number from a pay phone, on the street. Usually, that would be impossible to trace to a particular person (which is why Trafficante always used pay phones for business). Then, it became clear to Harry that the CIA had been alerted to him by the Mafioso in Miami. And the CIA man was trying to let Harry know that he didn't need to proceed with his plan to hire a hit man, because the CIA was already taking care of that. The CIA was in contact with the same "boss of a hit man" that Harry had called in Miami.[47]

Since the CIA man was "telling" Harry to "drop the subject" of hiring a hit man, that's exactly what Harry did. Harry said he had never "even started raising the money" for the hit, since he hadn't yet found out what it would cost. Harry did remain friendly with the CIA man, however, and worked briefly with him on a later mission with the CIA.[48] Harry soon left Cuba and, by the fall of the following year, would be one of the oldest volunteers for the Bay of Pigs invasion of Cuba. There he would finally get a chance to kill

Castro, only to find his pistol empty of bullets. After that, Harry's final chance to eliminate Castro and bring democracy to Cuba would be his C-Day plan with the Kennedys in 1963.

In 1959, when Harry had his encounter with the CIA-Mafia plots, the Kennedys were hard at work on their Senate crime hearings—unaware that the CIA-Mafia plots would soon impact their efforts. The Kennedys had forced Trafficante to flee to Havana, to avoid having to testify about his role in the Anastasia hit and his extensive criminal empire in America and Cuba. For Trafficante, his sojourn in Cuba was about to take a dangerous turn.

Ruby, Trafficante, the Kennedys, and "Jack La Rue"

IN APRIL OF 1959, TRAFFICANTE had been briefly jailed in Cuba, along with Meyer Lansky's brother Jake. Both had been quickly released. Jake soon left Cuba, but Trafficante couldn't leave while the Kennedys' crime hearings were in progress and he was still wanted for questioning in the Anastasia assassination.[1] But a variety of circumstances would cause Trafficante to be rearrested in Cuba, and this time his detention would be longer and more serious. It would also lead to Trafficante's meetings with Jack Ruby, even as the Kennedys fruitlessly sought the Dallas nightclub owner for their crime hearings.

The new Cuban government had been under pressure from US officials in the early months of 1959 to deport Meyer Lansky and Trafficante because of their involvement in drug smuggling.[2] According to the House Select Committee on Assassinations, the Cuban government arrested Trafficante a second time in June 1959 due to a request from Harry Anslinger, the head of the Federal Bureau of Narcotics. However, it's also possible that the Cuban government detained Trafficante at that time because he knew all the Mafia participants in the CIA-Mafia plots and the CIA-backed coup attempts against Castro. The Cubans may have wanted to stop the plots by jailing Trafficante—his associates might think twice about trying to kill Castro while Trafficante was in custody—or to see if Trafficante, to win his release, would reveal what he knew about the plots. Though one account says "the Cuban Cabinet ordered the deportation of Trafficante due to his having been involved in heroin trafficking," for some reason the Cubans wanted to hold Trafficante and not deport him to the US at that particular time.[3]

At first Trafficante's detention seemed relatively benign. His American lawyer, Frank Ragano, wrote that "to a casual observer, Triscornia [Detention Center] could pass for a decent rooming house and the men chatting in rocking chairs on the porch looked like contented guests."[4] He said "there was a public pay phone inside that Santo used to telephone people in Havana and Florida."[5] Ragano observed that "no armed guards were present" and "Santo was dressed casually, as if he were relaxing in his apartment. He remarked that the Cuban food served at the center was good—quite a compliment from a man who prided himself on being a gourmet."[6]

Trafficante seemed to be given all sorts of special consideration at first. Ragano said that for Trafficante's "oldest daughter," the Tampa godfather was even allowed to make "arrangements for the [daughter's] wedding and reception at the Havana Hilton on Father's Day, June 21, 1959." And "Fidel Castro" himself "authorized a brief furlough for Santo to participate in the wedding."[7] Rosselli's biographers noted that "Trafficante testified later, 'We had it pretty good. It was like a big camp.'"[8]

Trafficante was allowed frequent visitors, and many of those who came to see him would later be involved in the events of 1963. Detained with Trafficante was Lucien Rivard, a major Canadian drug kingpin who was part of the French Connection network that included Trafficante, Michel Victor Mertz, and Jack Ruby.[9] According to journalist Dick Russell, another man detained with Trafficante was Loran Hall, who had been "working in Santo Trafficante's Hotel Capri casino" before he was sent to the "quonset-hut prison in which Trafficante was being held." Hall explained how Trafficante really got the gourmet food he wanted: "Santo has his meals catered. The food came out every night in a Cadillac." Russell writes that "according to Hall," one of the visitors to the prison "was Johnny Rosselli."[10]

Also detained with Trafficante was a British man named John Wilson Hudson, who did not have a criminal record like most of the others did. Hudson would cause a stir after the JFK assassination when he made another observation about Trafficante's meals. Hudson would tell authorities that he had met a man who "accompanied the person who brought Trafficante his meals," and that man was Jack Ruby.[11]

There is much more evidence that Ruby visited Trafficante's jail in Havana. But to understand why Ruby went there, what he was trying to accomplish, and why it would cause concern in the CIA into the 1970s (when even CIA Director George H. W. Bush was interested in it), it's important to see what preceded Ruby's visits.[12]

As discussed, Ruby's partner in the Hoffa plane deal, Dominick Bartone, was also involved in the CIA-Mafia plot to assassinate Castro and the CIA-backed coup plan by Eloy Menoyo and William Morgan. That coup plan was also backed by Dominican dictator Rafael Trujillo. But in a bizarre twist, Bartone was also involved in a tiny, mysterious attempt by Castro to invade Trujillo's Dominican Republic. A review of the basic facts shows that the tiny Cuban invasion of the Dominican Republic was probably just a provocation, to justify Trujillo's support of the much larger CIA-backed Menoyo-Morgan attempt to overthrow Castro.

Tad Szulc writes that in June 1959, "56 rebels," including ten Cubans, "landed in" the Dominican Republic. He says "the Dominican Army rapidly destroyed the invading force."[13] Official Cuban accounts admit that they sent a small revolutionary group to Trujillo's Dominican Republic. However, they claim that "the US Embassy—which was aware of the plans—supplied some resources for the enterprise through" Frank Fiorini.[14] Fiorini was friends with Dominick Bartone, and the implication is that the US backed the small Cuban force so that Trujillo would have a very public reason to back a coup against Castro. Trafficante bagman Frank Fiorini was more likely to be working for the Mafia than for the CIA, though David Morales doubtlessly would have liked the idea of embarrassing Castro while at the same time giving Trujillo a pretext to back the CIA's planned coup against him.

Whether Bartone tipped off Trujillo about the tiny invasion, or the CIA used Bartone to encourage an invasion sure to fail (or both), it's clear that Bartone was involved in the effort at the same time he was working to overthrow Castro. A CIA document says the FBI was told that "Dominick Bartone supplied a plane 'which was used by the Cubans and Dominicans for the invasion of the Dominican Republic which took place on June 19, 1959.'"[15] It's interesting to note that one day earlier, on June 18, 1959, Jack Ruby—Bartone's partner in the plane deal—had met with his FBI handler. The timing of the FBI report on Bartone, and of Ruby's meeting with the FBI, strongly suggests that Ruby was involved in passing the information along to the FBI. Why? Because passing along such information could keep Ruby from being dragged before the Kennedy crime hearings, as we will see.

Even though Bartone supplied the plane for Castro's tiny force, Bartone and the Mafia were still firmly supporting the CIA's coup and assassination plan against Castro. Bartone was meeting with William Morgan and arranging for a huge quantity of guns to be delivered to the Dominican Republic for Trujillo's men to use against Castro in Menoyo and Morgan's planned coup. This is confirmed by a Miami FBI document that says "On June 25, 1959 the Miami FBI was instructed to clarify 'the statement . . . that William Morgan was with Dominick Bartone, who was arrested May 22, 1959, by Customs, Miami. . . . Headquarters was advised that according to a source . . . William Morgan" had a meeting at the "Dupont Plaza Motel in Miami" in "a room registered to Dominick Bartone." The FBI was also told that "Morgan was awaiting arrival in the Dominican Republic of $200,000 worth of guns."[16] Even though Ruby's partner Bartone had been arrested, he was still able to continue his role in the Hoffa plane deal, because it was part of the CIA-Mafia plots and the CIA-backed coup attempt. Bartone would still have to appear before the Kennedys' crime committee, though he would be able to take the Fifth and not have to be asked about his mysterious partner, "Jack La Rue."

The Senate crime hearings of Jack and Bobby Kennedy continued to generate headlines by dragging top godfathers before the glare of public scrutiny. This surely provided further incentive for mobsters to cooperate with the CIA or the FBI, in order to be protected from having to appear before the committee. The Kennedys' grilling of mob bosses also motivated some of them to back JFK's assassination four years later. One of those was Chicago godfather Sam Giancana. Though Bobby Kennedy's tight "lockstep surveillance" would prevent Giancana from having an active role in JFK's assassination, his don Johnny Rosselli would be a key planner of JFK's murder.

On June 9, 1959, Bobby Kennedy verbally sparred with Sam Giancana, the first time most of the country had seen or heard of the mobster who would soon become the most well-known godfather in the country—until that publicity led to his downfall. Giancana pleaded the Fifth Amendment most of the time, but his sneering attitude caused Bobby Kennedy to ask things like "Is there something funny about it, Mr. Giancana?" and "Would you tell us anything about any of your operations, or will you just giggle every time I ask you a question? I thought only little girls giggled, Mr. Giancana." The latter was in response to Bobby Kennedy's query: "Would you tell us, if you have opposition from anybody, that you dispose of them by having them stuffed in a trunk? Is that what you do, Mr. Giancana?"[17] Sam Giancana was forced to plead the Fifth over three dozen times, but Bobby got information about his criminal activities on the record—and in the press—by questioning committee investigator Pierre Salinger.[18]

Noted journalist Sy Hersh, in a report for the *New York Times* that was confirmed by Bobby's aides, found that at least one mob boss had a way of avoiding being grilled.[19] Another journalist added to Hersh's account and wrote that "in 1959 when the three Mafia dons became CIA agents, Bobby [Kennedy] was counsel for the Senate Rackets Committee. Among the members of organized crime he was investigating were Bufalino, Plumeri and Granello. One . . . was brought in for questioning by Bobby." "The Mafia man said: 'You can't touch me. I've got immunity.' 'Who gave you immunity?' Bobby asked. 'The CIA. I'm working for them, but I can't talk about it. Top secret.' Bobby checked it out and sure enough, the CIA had made a deal with" the mobster.[20]

Since that article was written in the 1970s, other information has shown that the 1959 plots included other mob bosses besides Bufalino, Plumeri, and Granello, so it's not possible at this time to determine who the favored Mafia boss was. Still, it does show that one way to avoid the Kennedy hearings was to help in the CIA-Mafia plots that Hoffa brokered. And Jack Ruby found that it could work for small-time mobsters as well as for godfathers.

By late June 1959, Bobby Kennedy and his investigators had gathered a massive amount of information on Hoffa's plane deal with Jack Ruby and Bartone. But Bobby and his men didn't know about the 1959 CIA-Mafia plots that Hoffa had brokered, of which Hoffa's plane deal was an important part. As a result the Kennedys were unable to find Jack Ruby, just as they were blocked from talking to one of the mob bosses also involved in the plots. Perhaps when the remaining one million CIA documents related to JFK's assassination have been released, it will be possible to say if Ruby was being protected by the CIA for his role in the CIA-Mafia plots, by the FBI for being an informant at that time, or by both agencies.

After all, in 1959, John F. Kennedy was just a senator—not yet even a declared presidential candidate—and Bobby Kennedy only the chief counsel of a Senate committee. And at that time, and for years to come, even senators and congressmen recoiled from any confrontation with the powerful FBI Director, J. Edgar Hoover. And the CIA had not yet suffered a major public defeat like the Bay of Pigs, so they were also held in high regard and treated with deference by Congress. That left the Kennedys no recourse if mobsters were protected in the name of national security or law enforcement.

For the Senate crime hearings, only a few of the senators were usually present for most hearings. For example, JFK was present the day after Marcello testified, but not on the day of the mob boss's grilling by Bobby Kennedy. On the other hand, Bobby Kennedy was apparently present for every hearing, as the lead questioner. This doubtlessly helped the resulting headlines and news stories, since even on the days when JFK wasn't present, a Kennedy was always mentioned in relation to the hearings.

Transcripts show that on "Tuesday, June 30, 1959" for the "Jack La Rue" hearing, JFK wasn't there, but several other key senators were. Barry Goldwater was present, as was Senator Frank Church, who would later lead the Senate hearings into CIA assassination plots in the mid-1970s. Senator Sam Ervin—whose Southern drawl and folksy style would later gain national prominence in the Senate Watergate Hearings—was also in attendance. Also present at the 1959 "La Rue" hearing was "accounting consultant" Carmine S. Bellino, a Kennedy loyalist who would later be a top investigator for the Senate Watergate Committee. Also at the 1959 "La Rue" hearing was Pierre Salinger, then a committee investigator, but soon to be JFK's press secretary—and, decades later, the source of an account of Jack Ruby's Chicago Mafia payoff shortly prior to JFK's assassination.[21]

The purpose of the "Jack La Rue" hearing was to unravel Hoffa's very complicated plane deal, which—unknown to the Kennedys—also served as a cover for the 1959 CIA-Mafia plots. Bobby announced in his opening statement that he would first focus on one of Hoffa's men, "Mr. Louis Triscaro, who is second in charge of the Ohio Conference of Teamsters." Using information developed by his investigators, Bobby said the scheme involved giving Jack "'La Rue' and [Dominick] Bartone an option on *two* planes, which Bartone said he could sell in Cuba." Bobby said that "Dominick Bartone is a very important figure in the whole transaction," while Jack La Rue was Bartone's partner. The deal began on "January 21, 1959," at the time other accounts show that Ruby first began trying to get to Castro to cut a deal. According to Bobby, this operation was no small transaction, since "the price to the Cuban Government was to be some $400,000 apiece for the airplanes." But the transaction started to turn sour for several businessmen dealing with "the group known as La Rue & Bartone," since the businessmen were out "$1,050,000" for "*eleven*" planes and the deal with Cuba had stalled. So La Rue and Bartone offered them a "bailout deal" to "sell the whole thing to a group on the West coast." Bobby was unable to find out who the "West coast" backers of La Rue and Bartone were. Of course, Hoffa had mob allies on the West Coast—like Johnny Rosselli and Mickey Cohen—and the plane deal probably started to turn sour for the businessmen when Hoffa began using it more as cover for the CIA-Mafia plots than as a real business deal.[22]

Bobby Kennedy was clearly frustrated at his inability to not only locate "Jack La Rue," but to find out anything at all about him. Bartone's background could be well documented, as could that of other Hoffa men involved, like Triscaro and Bernard Spindel, who handled the Dominican side of the deal. But Bobby and his best investigators—who had compiled massive files on secretive figures like Marcello and Sam Giancana and numerous drug lords—could find absolutely nothing about "Jack La Rue." Here's an example, as Bobby Kennedy questions one of the businessmen:

Mr. Kennedy: "Did you know who Mr. La Rue was at the time?"

Businessman: "No, sir; I did not. . . ."

Mr. Kennedy: "Do you know where he came from? We have not been able to find him."

Businessman: "No, I don't."

Mr. Kennedy: "Do you know anything about him at all?"

Businessman: "No; I don't."

Mr. Kennedy: "Do you know if that's his real name? La Rue?"[23]

From Bobby Kennedy's questioning and the evidence presented, it soon becomes clear that Jimmy Hoffa was heavily involved, trying to use Teamster Pension Funds to help finance the deal. There are then several trips to Cuba, some involving Bartone. Bobby Kennedy asks one of the businessmen "Who was the contact from the Cuban government?" and the man replies "Mr. Bartone seemed to be the man who was the contact there . . . he seemed to have very close contacts with William Morgan, who was a leader of the rebels." Bobby and his men were unaware that at that very moment, Morgan and Eloy Menoyo were being backed by the CIA in a planned coup against Castro, a plot that also involved Bartone. However, the businessman did say that Morgan "had . . . formerly worked for Bartone in years past," which seems possible, given their similar criminal associates. Morgan, the most prominent American rebel leader in Cuba, had a criminal record for "robbery and escape" on three occasions in just one year. According to Bobby Kennedy, while Morgan "was in jail, he escaped and committed robbery again and escaped again and committed robbery" yet again.[24]

The Kennedy–La Rue hearings show that even as Jack Ruby, Lewis McWillie, and William Morgan were meeting in Cuba, the complex deal took yet another turn. This involved a "shipment of $1,250,000 worth of arms and ammunition" that would be taken to the Dominican Republic on one of the planes. According to one newspaper report they cited, the arms "were going to the Batista faction for the purpose of overthrowing Fidel Castro." This shows again how the Mafia and its allies like Hoffa would play both sides—on one hand trying to sell planes to Castro, while also trying to sell arms to those trying to kill him. This Dominican, anti-Castro aspect of the deal is only mentioned in conjunction with Bartone, not Jack La Rue—probably because wireman Bernard Spindel handled Dominican arrangements for Hoffa. And it was Bartone who was finally arrested in connection with that transaction.[25]

Bobby Kennedy actually managed to get the recently indicted Bartone into the Hearing Room—but before he could question him, Bartone's attorney pointed out that Bartone shouldn't have to testify, because anything he might say would affect his upcoming trial. So Bobby was reluctantly forced to excuse Bartone, without being able to question him about the mysterious "Jack La Rue." When Hoffa's man Louis Triscaro was called next, he refused to answer any questions (besides his name), instead repeatedly invoking the Fifth Amendment. So Bobby was unable to find out anything from him about the elusive "Jack La Rue." (Almost two decades later, Bobby's top Hoffa prosecutor would still consider the identity of "Jack La Rue" an unsolved mystery.) Instead, Bobby had his investigators' detailed chronology read into the record, which documented the trips of Bartone to Cuba and many calls from Jimmy Hoffa, culminating in Bartone's arrest in Miami on May 22, 1959. But Bartone had apparently been released on bond, and Teamster involvement in the deal continued. Just six days after Bartone's arrest, Hoffa's man "went to Miami and stayed in the same room at the Eden Roc Hotel with Bartone."[26]

According to Bobby's information, on "June 9," 1959, the Teamsters finally approved the huge loan for Bartone. But by that time, the Kennedy hearings on the matter were just three weeks away. Hoffa realized how bad it would look for the Teamsters' huge loan to a criminal like Bartone to be exposed at the Kennedy hearings, since one of the Kennedys' main goals was to expose the criminal ties and activities of Hoffa. So on "June 12," 1959, Hoffa made a call to the Pension Fund's attorney, and on "June 15" the loan was suddenly rejected, according to the detailed chronology compiled by the Kennedys' investigators. The Kennedys were able to track such complex transactions with the help of investigators like Pierre Salinger and Carmine S. Bellino, who also testified that day.[27] When the Kennedys later tried to get Hoffa's wireman Bernard Spindel to testify at his appearance before the committee on July 15, 1959, Spindel not only tried to take the Fifth, but also criticized Bellino and implied that Bobby Kennedy had tried to bribe him. According to Spindel's autobiography, Bellino came at Spindel after the hearing, and Spindel punched Bellino. It shows how high tensions were running at the time, and the growing animosity between Hoffa and his people, and Bobby Kennedy.[28]

JACK RUBY VISITS SANTO TRAFFICANTE

In July and August 1959, Jack Ruby's Cuban activities didn't only continue; they seemed to increase. This culminated in his meetings with Santo Trafficante and also coincided with a spectacular turn of events in the CIA-Mafia assassination and coup plot involving Eloy Menoyo and William Morgan.

On July 2, 1959, Warren Commission files show that Jack Ruby again met with his FBI handler. One day earlier, a journalist found that the *New York Times* had reported that the Kennedys' crime committee "had discovered that an aide of Hoffa's had shared a Miami hotel room with Dominick Bartone"— Ruby's partner in the Hoffa plane deal—"who had sought to sell airplanes to Cuba." Had the FBI wanted to ask Jack Ruby about the *New York Times* article that named Ruby's partner, Bartone? On July 21, Ruby met with his FBI handler yet again. A journalist notes that this time, the FBI agent says he "questioned Ruby about several bank robberies which Ruby said he had no knowledge of." Yet the FBI agent still "rated his informant as 'good,'" for some reason. But "in late July . . . the Dallas FBI Field Office Special Agent-in-Charge received information that something wasn't kosher about Ruby," and so he "sent Ruby's [finger] prints to FBI Headquarters so that he could get Ruby's rap sheet."[29]

Meanwhile, in Cuba, Trafficante's confinement in his Cuban jail continued. Though it was relatively comfortable—and Trafficante no doubt was glad he was avoiding the glare of the Kennedys' crime hearings—he was still confined. It was now clear that this wasn't going to be a very brief detention like his first one. With the continually changing situation in the Cuban government, as Castro consolidated his power and a CIA-aided resistance movement grew, Trafficante knew that he was in danger as long as he was confined. Plus, much of a godfather's power was based on his ruthless image, something that was diminished in the eyes of mob rivals and subordinates the longer Trafficante remained in prison.

The flurry of trips by mobster John Martino between Cuba and Miami was probably related to both maintaining Trafficante's control—by ferrying cash and information—as well as assisting efforts to get Trafficante released. Martino was also close to those involved in the CIA-Mafia plots. John Martino was someone Trafficante could trust. Noted historian Richard Mahoney, whose father worked as a troubleshooting diplomat for JFK, says that "John Martino" was "a Cuban-American" who "had installed security systems in Mafia casinos in Havana" and was an associate of godfather Trafficante and death-squad leader Masferrer, who were both involved in narcotics.[30] So when John Martino was arrested by Cuban authorities in late July 1959, Trafficante lost a valuable messenger. According to *Vanity Fair*, "although the Cubans charged" Martino "with trying to smuggle out a counterrevolutionary, Martino said that his principal mission had been to liberate gambling cash left behind by Trafficante."[31] Those funds were also essential for any attempt to buy Trafficante's release from his Cuban jail.

Trafficante's mob allies were trying to get him out of jail. According to Scott Malone, Congressional investigators found that those "who wanted Trafficante released included Johnny Rosselli and his boss, Sam Giancana—both of whom . . . visited Trafficante in jail in 1959."[32] Other accounts say that "Carlos Marcello attempted to free Trafficante. The" Mafia "wanted anyone who could influence Fidel Castro to intervene on Trafficante's behalf."[33] And it didn't matter if they were a Sicilian mobster or not, since the Tampa Police Chief would later testify that Trafficante's "operations . . . show, also, a characteristic Mafia method of utilizing non-Sicilian associates where it serves its criminal objectives."[34]

While Trafficante was in jail in Cuba, Jack Ruby made attempts at arms deals to help secure Trafficante's release, according to several accounts. Scott Malone found that "Congressional investigators" noted in a "briefing memorandum" that "in 1959 Jack Ruby traveled to Cuba and visited Santo Trafficante in jail." Other reports came from a "British journalist" who was "briefly jailed by Castro" and who "said that while in jail he 'knew a gambling-gangster type named Santo' who, he said, 'was visited frequently by another American gangster-type named Ruby.'"[35] A close friend of both Rosselli and Giancana who "testified before the Senate Intelligence Committee" in the 1970s "says Rosselli told him, 'Ruby was hooked up with Trafficante in the rackets in Havana.'"[36]

The "British journalist" briefly in jail with Trafficante was John Wilson Hudson, who said that Jack Ruby "accompanied the person who brought Trafficante his meals."[37] Hudson's report surfaced shortly after Ruby shot Oswald, and was briefly noted in one of the twenty-six Warren Commission volumes, though its importance was ignored by most journalists and the public at the time since CIA documents about the connections between Trafficante and the CIA-Mafia plots and the JFK assassination wouldn't surface for more than a decade.[38] Ruby had many associates in common with Trafficante, ranging from Rolando Masferrer to Dallas underboss Joseph Civello to R. D. Matthews. But the most likely person to have taken Ruby to see Trafficante was the "high class" gambling supervisor, Lewis McWillie, who was also involved with Ruby and Bartone in the Hoffa plane deal.

Many years later, when McWillie was interviewed by the House Select Committee on Assassinations, McWillie answered in a very nervously cautious manner. When asked if Ruby had accompanied him on his visits to Trafficante in prison, McWillie said: "It's possible he could have . . . I don't recall it, but he could have. I don't know for sure." When pressed, McWillie again said "I went out there with someone but I don't recall who it was. It may have been Ruby. I don't think so. He could have been. . . ."[39] Sometimes McWillie denied that Ruby had gone with him, but would quickly add that he didn't "know for sure." McWillie was testifying shortly after the murders of numerous Trafficante associates and government witnesses—Giancana, Rosselli, Hoffa, Masferrer, Nicoletti, and others. Since Trafficante was still alive and in power (and had ties to at least Rosselli's and Hoffa's murders), and McWillie was still working at casinos, his equivocation is as close to a "yes, Ruby went with me" as the committee could possibly expect.

However, as would later happen in the JFK assassination plot, Ruby had gone from a willing participant in the Cuban operations to being more reluctant. Whereas in May 1959 Ruby had been the one pressing to visit McWillie in Cuba, by early August 1959 McWillie was now the one who wanted Ruby to leave the safety of Dallas and come to Cuba. Perhaps Ruby was frightened by the arrest of Trafficante messenger John Martino. Or perhaps Ruby knew through his contacts with Bartone and Morgan that the coup and assassination plot against Castro was imminent. When that happened, there was no

way to predict what would happen in Cuba—or to Trafficante, or Trafficante's men, or to anyone who'd met with Morgan in Cuba, as Ruby had.

But Ruby couldn't ignore the pressure from McWillie and Trafficante.
Ruby's recent experience with the Menoyo-Morgan and Hoffa-plane-deal
aspects of the CIA-Mafia plots made him the ideal man to help Trafficante in
August 1959. So, as *Rolling Stone* noted in a major investigative article, "In
August 1959 Ruby visited Havana at the invitation of Lewis McWillie, the
Syndicate's manager at the Tropicana casino and a man Ruby said he 'idolized.' A friend of Ruby's recently told House investigators that the former
errand boy had been summoned to help arrange freedom for Santo Trafficante."[40] Ruby's testimony to Supreme Court Chief Justice Earl Warren in
Dallas makes it clear that in August 1959, it was McWillie who wanted Ruby
to come to Cuba. Also, keep in mind that Ruby was having to testify about
this in Dallas—in a building almost within sight of Dealey Plaza, the ultimate
reminder of what happens to those who cross the Mafia—since Warren
refused Ruby's request to be taken to Washington to testify.

Ruby testified that McWillie "wanted me to come down to Havana, Cuba;
invited me down there, and I didn't want to leave my business because I had
to watch over it." Ruby says that McWillie "was a key man over the Tropicana [casino] down there." Ruby originally told McWillie "I couldn't make
it. Finally he sent me tickets to come down, airplane tickets."[41] Ruby told
Earl Warren that McWillie "had a way of purchasing tickets from Havana
that I think he purchases them at a lesser price. He bought them from the
travel agent in the Capri Hotel."[42] Ruby didn't mention that the Capri was
mostly owned by Santo Trafficante (as noted by *Time* magazine in their May
2, 1959 issue). Ruby did tell Warren that "I made the trip down there via
New Orleans."[43] Ruby may have gone through New Orleans first, to get
instructions or funds from Marcello's people.

Ruby tried to say that he had made only this one McWillie-funded trip to
Cuba, while official US and Cuban records show a confusing array of several
trips, with unexplained gaps in the travel records. For example, Jack Ruby
told Earl Warren that he stayed at some apartments—which were later found
to be owned by front men for Trafficante—while Cuban records show that
he stayed at Trafficante's Capri Hotel and Casino. The truth is that Ruby
probably stayed at both places, but on different trips. Regarding McWillie,
Ruby testified "I was with him constantly" while Ruby was in Cuba "in
August of 1959." That no doubt included the times when McWillie went to
see Trafficante in prison.[44] Ruby's intrigues with McWillie and the CIA-Mafia

plots would continue for several more months, culminating in Ruby's purchase of the gun he would later use to shoot Oswald. But for now, it's useful to look at what was going on in Cuba in August 1959 to fully understand Ruby's mission to Trafficante for McWillie.

On August 6, 1959, Ruby met with his FBI handler again. Then, two days later, on August 8, Ruby flew to Cuba from New Orleans, listing the Capri Hotel and Casino as his destination on his Cuban tourist card.[45] In addition to being mostly owned by Trafficante, the Capri was where Ruby's partner—Dominick Bartone—had earlier stayed and had arranged for William Morgan's room.

Ruby's trips to Cuba, and the inconsistent travel records, have long perplexed historians and government investigators. For example, one researcher noted that "According to Cuban travel records, Jack Ruby entered Cuba from New Orleans on August 8, 1959; left Cuba September 11, 1959; re-entered Cuba from Miami on September 12, 1959; and returned from Cuba to New Orleans on September 13, 1959." However, "bank records, Dallas police records, and FBI records showed Ruby in Dallas August 10, 21, 31, and September 4, days which fall right in the middle of his supposedly continuous stay in Cuba. Somehow, Ruby was getting in and out of Cuba without the Cuban authorities detecting and recording it. Why was Ruby making multiple excursions to Cuba during this time? What were the nature of these visits and why did he choose to hide them?"[46] A review of other events in Cuba at that time—related to the CIA-Mafia plots and the related coup attempt by Menoyo and Morgan—provides the answer.

MENOYO'S COUP IS BETRAYED AND TRAFFICANTE IS RELEASED

The CIA's involvement in the summer of 1959 Menoyo-Morgan coup is verified by the earlier noted document from one of Menoyo's still-censored and grossly incomplete CIA files that has been released.[47] The letter in Menoyo's CIA file from "June 18, 1959" says that placing an article hyping Menoyo "is extremely important, politically" for the US. That is exactly the sort of thing someone like Havana PR expert and CIA agent David Atlee Phillips—or Phillips's friend, US Embassy Press Attaché Paul Bethel—would do. Bethel provides more confirmation of his dealings with Morgan about the coup in his heavily sanitized autobiography.

While assassination was part of the coup plans, those actions are linked to the mercenary and former mobster William Morgan, not to his partner in the coup, Eloy Menoyo. From all indications, Menoyo may have been unaware of the CIA-Mafia assassination side of the coup plan. But CIA documents confirm that Morgan was involved with the assassination component, including one memo in which "Morgan . . . said he was the leader of a plot to assassinate Castro."[48]

Paul Bethel writes that "in June [1959] William Morgan surfaced again." This was at the same time that Jack Ruby had been meeting with Morgan. Bethel says "Morgan turned to me and said: 'I have five thousand men, willing and able to fight against Communism.' He went on: 'Sure, Menoyo is the leader, but the boys follow me. Menoyo is also with us, though.'" Bethel told "Morgan that he most probably would be contacted by another person who would use my name in making that contact." Bethel says he "went immediately to the Embassy, wrote a long memorandum of the conversation and gave it to the deputy chief of the CIA."[49] That may have been David Morales or at least his close associate. Bethel says he and the CIA official "had a long conversation, during which he said he was not disposed to make contact with Morgan 'just yet.'"[50] At least, that is what Bethel says he was told; the record is clear that the CIA was already in contact with Morgan and Menoyo.

Planning continued for the coup and assassination attempt. Cuban records show that "on July 20," 1959, there was a meeting of Morgan and the other conspirators "in the Hotel Capri" about "smuggling arms into Cuba for use by" Menoyo's rebels. They note that "on July 28 [1959] Morgan again visited Miami" and "received a boatload of arms" for the upcoming coup.[51] It was between those two dates that Trafficante's courier, John Martino, was arrested by the Cubans.

Something unexpected happened around this time. According to Paul Bethel, "mysterious rumors began to circulate that something was afoot which involved the Dominican Republic." Bethel was referring to the Menoyo-Morgan coup plan, which was backed by Dominican dictator Trujillo. Bethel says "that Morgan learned that certain of his activities had come to the attention of Castro . . . we at the Embassy concluded that Morgan flipped completely over, and told Castro that he was acting as a double agent." In other words, to save his skin after someone had told Castro about the plot, "Morgan brought" Castro "in on the plot, saved his own hide and that of Menoyo, and decided to fight another day."[52]

Who had informed on the CIA's plot with Menoyo and Morgan? The dates involved strongly suggest that it was someone connected to Trafficante. After all, Trafficante mobsters from Lewis McWillie to John Martino to Jack Ruby were in a position to know about the plots. And Trafficante had every incentive to trade any kind of information as part of a deal to win his release from Cuban prison.

Ruby met with his FBI handler on August 6, 1959, then flew to Cuba on August 8, 1959—at McWillie's urging—to stay at Trafficante's Capri, site of a recent Menoyo-Morgan coup meeting. Cuban accounts say that after the coup, "the minister of government was to be . . . Rolando Masferrer," Ruby's associate.[53] A journalist documented that in August of 1959, the FBI "received information about an anti-Castro uprising sponsored by Rolando Masferrer." He notes that "most of this telex" is "still withheld" for some reason, even forty years later.[54]

Jack Ruby's partner Bartone was still in the thick of things after Ruby's arrival in Cuba. An August 10, 1959 CIA document quotes a "CIA source" reporting that "Morgan met with Bartone and several anti-Castro Cubans at Bartone's Miami home and Morgan was given $140,000 in cash." Also, the "CIA discovered Dominick Bartone sending Morgan money via [a] Panamanian bank." These transactions also raise the possibility that ex-mobster Morgan was bribed by his mobster associates—which included Jack Ruby and Bartone—to betray Menoyo and the CIA-backed coup. Trafficante would have had the cash and the incentive to do that, to get out of prison.[55]

Castro had Menoyo and Morgan continue their plans for the coup, while he monitored them. Historian Tad Szulc says "it is entirely possible that the two men were playing a double or triple game, depending on the most favorable outcome." (Again, it's important to note that Menoyo always seems to have been motivated by his beliefs, while former mobster Morgan was interested in money and fame.[56]) Neither man may have had any choice but to play along with Castro, once their plan had been exposed. A Cuban exile historian says that Morgan and Menoyo were "induced or forced by Castro to entrap the plotters."[57] They "urged the Dominican dictator [Trujillo] to dispatch arms and men to support the fake uprising. When Trujillo's plane landed, Castro and his aides, who were hiding near the airstrip, captured the invaders, [and] ordered the arrest of the plotters in Havana and other cities."

Castro played a masterful PR game, giving Trujillo and the CIA the impression that a revolt really was happening. It was exactly the type of propaganda operation that David Atlee Phillips had directed so well during the CIA's 1954 Guatemala coup and assassination operation, using phone press releases, news stories, and fake radio broadcasts—only now it was being used against Phillips's side. In retrospect, Phillips may have been happy enough that he wasn't arrested. He wrote in his autobiography that the CIA told him that "several" of his Cuban conspirators "have been arrested."[58] According to Cuban accounts, on "August 8 [1959], in Havana, Cuban State Security arrested two US Embassy officials," including one "detained while directing a meeting of" rebels "to carry out sabotage and other actions in support of" the coup. It's also interesting to note that the two US officials were arrested on the day Jack Ruby arrived in Cuba.[59] (As if there weren't enough figures from 1963 involved in these 1959 activities, yet another one shows up briefly in August 1959: David Ferrie.[60])

On August 12, 1959, the OAS (Organization of American States) convened a Foreign Ministers conference in Chile to "consider tensions in the Caribbean" and "the effective exercise of representative democracy," in response to widespread news reports of the ongoing coup in Cuba—phony reports that Castro himself was spreading. At the OAS meeting, the Cuban representative says the conference "is an obvious attempt . . . by the US to maneuver the OAS against the Cuban government."[61]

On August 14, 1959, Cuban accounts say that Castro finally pulled the plug on the whole CIA-backed Menoyo-Morgan coup operation, after luring Trujillo's plotters to Cuba and arresting many other plotters in Cuba. On that date, "Fidel Castro appeared before the national television cameras and revealed the entire saga" of Trujillo's conspiracy. The Cubans say it "had all the classic characteristics of a CIA operation: internal insurrection, destabilization and mercenary invasion linked to an OAS maneuver with the complicity of the traditional allies of the US in order to lend legitimacy to a military intervention with the 'altruistic purpose' of pacifying the island."[62] Stripped of its self-serving rhetoric, the Cuban account does a good job of summarizing many of the similarities between the August 1959 coup and other US coup operations, including C-Day. Some of the Cuban wording about the August 1959 coup is very similar to that found in the long-secret fall 1963 C-Day coup documents by the US Joint Chiefs of Staff, though the Cuban account was written two years before the first Joint Chiefs C-Day coup documents were released.

Four days after Castro's TV speech about the coup, Santo Trafficante was released from prison in Cuba. His lawyer, Frank Ragano, says that "on August 18, 1959, Santo called to say he had been officially released and that he was on his way back to Miami. Upon his return to Tampa," Trafficante told his lawyer that he had met with "Raul Castro (Fidel's brother). 'We worked out an arrangement,' he said cryptically." Ragano says that "most probably the meeting with Raul was decisive in getting him released" but that "nevertheless, there had to be a bribe at some point in the chain of events that led to his freedom."[63] Jack Ruby's exact role, and whether the "bribe" including selling out the Menoyo-Morgan coup plot, may never be known.

As for the participants in the coup, their fates varied. David Atlee Phillips's friend Paul Bethel wrote that the US "Ambassador [to Cuba] Bonsal was certain that Castro would attack the US, saying that the US, through its Press Attaché [Bethel], had been implicated in the plot." The CIA chief disagreed, and he "was right. Morgan and Menoyo apparently had said nothing about their contacts with the American Embassy for the simple reason that they had not stopped plotting against Castro."[64] Bethel was right. Cuban accounts say that "in November 1960, Morgan was arrested as he tried to organize— for the CIA—a band of" rebels in support of the upcoming Bay of Pigs invasion. Morgan's good friend, Trafficante courier John Martino—who was imprisoned with Morgan—wrote about Morgan's gruesome execution in his book *I Was Castro's Prisoner* (the same book that named Havana CIA official David Morales). But Morgan had almost been assassinated right after the failed August 1959 coup. An FBI report from that month talked about a meeting between Rolando Masferrer and Norman Rothman—both associates of Jack Ruby and Trafficante. The FBI report—from an unnamed informant—says that Masferrer met with "Norman Rothman, gangster, Miami Beach, concerning double cross of William Morgan, but Masferrer does not want anything to do with any plot to assassinate William Morgan. . . . Informant said that also they discussed having an American crime syndicate sign a contract to produce the assassination of Morgan."[65] But nothing was done about that, probably because the failure of Morgan's coup had resulted in the release from prison of a top member of the "American crime syndicate"—Santo Trafficante.

As for Menoyo, he finally left Cuba in January 1961. After allegedly having a falling-out with Trafficante over a failed arms deal, Menoyo was eventually wooed by Harry Williams to join the Kennedys' C-Day plan in the fall of 1963.

What about Jack Ruby? In spite of his dealings with William Morgan before the coup—or maybe because of them—Ruby suffered no repercussions after the failed coup. He continued to visit Cuba, stayed an FBI informant for a short time longer, and remained a low-level part of the CIA-

Mafia plots for a few more months. Now that Trafficante was safely out of
Cuba, the Mafia could once again set its sights on helping the CIA assassinate Fidel Castro, this time with a new cast of future C-Day leaders.

September 1959:
Artime, Varona, and Ruby
Target Castro

IN THE FALL OF 1959, the CIA geared up for yet another coup attempt against Castro, this time involving Manuel Artime, Tony Varona, and Bernard Barker. The CIA's David Morales and David Atlee Phillips remained in Cuba, presumably working on the new CIA coup plan in some capacity. Jack Ruby continued his FBI informant status and Cuban activities, which would eventually result in his purchase of the pistol he later used to shoot Oswald.

Before heading back to Cuba, Ruby met with his FBI handler on August 31, 1959. A journalist notes that "by this time," Ruby's FBI handler "had received word from his superior to dump Ruby." But the FBI handler responded that "While Ruby has not furnished any positive information to date, there is no indication of emotional instability or unreliability. It is recommended Potential Criminal Informant be continued."[1] As we said above and as several writers have commented, it is highly unusual to keep meeting with an informant who produces no "positive information."

Ruby was in Cuba at various times in September; and, again, the existing records simply don't match up. Some Warren Commission files show that Ruby was in Havana for Labor Day weekend, where he met and talked with three businessmen from Chicago. INS records show Ruby not traveling to Cuba except for a quick trip from Miami to Cuba on September 12, with a return on September 13 to New Orleans from Havana. Ruby told Warren Commissioner Gerald Ford that he spent "eight days in Havana." (Ruby also told Ford that he stayed with friends of McWillie who were later linked by the HSCA to narcotics traffic.) The bottom line is that Ruby made several trips to Cuba in the fall of 1959, and not all his travels are reflected in official records. And as with Ruby's earlier trips, there were still coup and assassination plots brewing in Cuba.

William Attwood, who would later become an aide to JFK, wrote in *Look* magazine in September 1959 that Castro was "the world's likeliest target for an assassin's bullet." Attwood would later carry out JFK's secret peace negotiations with Castro in the fall of 1963, and, ten years after that, Attwood would spearhead the Pulitzer Prize–winning investigation that first brought attention to the heroin network of Michel Victor Mertz and Trafficante. But in 1959, Attwood was a Havana correspondent for *Look* magazine, who perceptively wrote that Fidel Castro's "former associates are calling him a Red or plotting his assassination . . . you can smell a police state in the making."[2]

Cuba had still not yet been taken over by Communism, and Che's men still used the term to insult their rivals. In fact, a Cuban exile historian notes that "violent quarrels erupted at the Tenth Labor Congress [in Cuba] between the Communist militants shouting 'Unity!' and the 26th of July activists" from Che's party "chanting 'Melons!' The latter suggested that the Communists were like watermelons—on the outside olive green, the color of Castro's Rebel Army uniform, but red inside."[3]

While the US was still trying to put on a good public face about tolerating Castro, some in the government—ranging from Vice President Richard Nixon to David Morales—were still determined to see Castro go, by any means necessary. So another CIA-backed coup was ramped up, even as the CIA-Mafia assassination plots continued. The coup participants this time would include several people who would later work with Nixon during Watergate, and with David Morales during C-Day—and in some cases they worked on both C-Day and Watergate. At least three of them were also later involved with Trafficante.

Cuban accounts and CIA documents indicate that the following were involved: Future C-Day leader Manuel Artime, who was also involved in Watergate for Nixon. Artime would also be linked to Trafficante, and a Congressional investigator was told that Artime had "guilty knowledge" of JFK's assassination. Another future C-Day leader involved in the fall 1959 coup was Tony Varona, who the CIA admits was working on the CIA-Mafia plots with Trafficante by the following year. Also involved in 1959 was Varona's mentor, ex-Cuban President Carlos Prio, who was also linked to Trafficante and drugs. Assisting Artime and his eventual escape from Cuba in the fall of 1959 was Bernard Barker, the future Watergate burglar for Nixon. As a CIA agent, Barker allegedly assisted E. Howard Hunt during C-Day, and Barker's

CIA file from 1963 is full of reports about his regular informant, Frank Fiorini. In the fall of 1959, Fiorini—who had fled Cuba a few months earlier, and would later work on Watergate with Barker, Artime, and Hunt— would be linked to air support for Artime's coup.

Cuban accounts say that the fall 1959 coup plan included as its leaders "Manuel Artime" and "Huber Matos . . . the head of" Castro's "Rebel Army" in one of the provinces. Artime had joined Castro's Revolution before it triumphed, and by mid-1959 Artime was one of the "directors of agricultural development" in eastern Cuba. According to the Cubans, "Artime elaborated a plan, with the support of [former Cuban President Carlos] Prio" and future C-Day exile leader Tony "Varona . . . to organize subversion in the eastern part of the country." As part of the coup, "they planned an uprising . . . under Artime's command . . . which they expected to quickly spread to the rest of the country."[4]

CIA files confirm that Artime and Varona were working for the CIA at the time. The archivist for Miami-Dade County uncovered a CIA file which confirms that Manuel Artime was a CIA "operational asset utilized" beginning in "1959."[5] Information on Varona comes from his censored CIA Security Office "summary"—the same summary which later confirms Varona's payoff from Rosselli's Chicago Mafia during C-Day. This CIA summary says that on "August 28, 1959 Varona is granted Operational Approval-amended" by the CIA. This represents a change in his status from the previous year, when Varona had gotten "operational approval for . . . use as an informant in Cuba by" the CIA's Western Hemisphere Division.[6] The documents detailing the new role that Varona assumed for the CIA on August 28, 1959 are still classified "secret" by the CIA and have not been released. However, Varona's summary does confirm that he was close to gangster "Dino Cellini." FBI files confirm that Cellini was an associate of Jack Ruby's "idol" Lewis McWillie.[7] Cellini had also been detained for a while at the same prison camp as Trafficante.[8]

Overseeing Artime's role as an "operational asset" in the coup—and Varona's new role—would have been David Morales, who still ran operations for the CIA from the US Embassy. It is not clear if David Atlee Phillips, still running his CIA activities using the cover of his Havana public relations firm, was involved in this coup operation, since Phillips's file from that time is still classified.

As we noted earlier, Jack Ruby was in Havana in early September, and Cuban accounts date the start of the coup planning from that time. They say that "in the first days of . . . September [1959], a social gathering was held" in Havana. Among the guests were "the First Secretary of the US Embassy" and conspirators including "Manuel Artime." Artime, Huber Matos, and a third Cuban "retired to a back room," where they plotted the coup. According to the Cubans, "the US Embassy pulled the strings of the con-spiracy . . . the link with Artime was Bernard Barker, an old police official of the Batista dictatorship and future Watergate" burglar. "Through this con-duit, Artime kept the [US] Embassy informed about developments." But even the Cubans admit that Artime wanted to be in charge, not just acting on the orders of the US. That way, Artime told his fellow conspirators, "we will be the ones selected to form the new government, organize the next elec-tions, and then. . . ."9 It echoes Artime's stance during C-Day, when he and Harry didn't take orders from the CIA. Also like C-Day, it shows that the goal of the coup was free elections, not just replacing one dictatorship led by Castro with another dictatorship led by Artime or the others.

One of Bernard Barker's CIA files—several have been released, each dif-ferent and all heavily censored—confirms that Barker began working for the CIA "in mid-1959," having been recruited by the CIA's Chief of Station in Havana. One CIA-Barker file shows that on April 2, 1959, the Havana CIA station where Morales worked sent a memo to the CIA Director saying "clearance urgently requested" on Barker, since he was "in position [to] gather info [about] commie penetration [of the Cuban] government and military."10

This was at a time when Frank Fiorini—Barker's future key source during 1963 and his partner in Watergate—was very active against Castro. Barker's clearance was granted on April 17, 1959, while Castro was visiting the US. There is a large gap in Barker's released file from late April 1959 until November 1959, during the time of the Menoyo and Artime coup attempts.11 However, E. Howard Hunt's memoir confirms that Barker worked with Artime in 1959.12 Within a few months, a few CIA documents show that Bernard Barker was using the CIA code name of AMCLATTER-1. This was the code name Barker was using in 1963, at the time of C-Day. However, docu-ments with that code name are often missing or censored from the first Bernard Barker personnel file that the CIA released.13 In an interesting twist, a few months after Artime's fall 1959 coup attempt, David Atlee Phillips's name appears on one of Barker's CIA documents—and CIA files confirm that

David Atlee Phillips was using the CIA code name of "Lawrence F. Barker" in the early 1960s and at the time of C-Day.[14] (That was only one of at least three code names that Phillips was using at the time, probably for his roles in different operations.)

Further indication of CIA involvement in Artime's coup comes from noted historian Hugh Thomas. He writes that "on October 11 [1959] one aircraft dropped three bombs on a sugar mill in" Cuba, "the first of many such occasions." He asks if "the CIA were now prepared to help the exiles with arms, as Vice-president Nixon had proposed?" He notes that "among twenty men captured by the [Cuban] government in" the province near the bombing, "two were US pilots; the whole group had been supplied from Florida, no doubt unofficially, as the US government said, but how unofficial was the CIA in Miami?"[15]

For Artime's fall of 1959 coup, some historians have suspected that the second most popular revolutionary in Cuba, Commander Camilo "Cienfuegos, head of the Rebel Army," was part of the attempt. In 1959, Cienfuegos was even more popular among the Cuban people than Che Guevara.[16] In that way, it was similar to the Kennedys' 1963 C-Day plan involving a very high Cuban official, a known hero of the Revolution. It was therefore different from other CIA plots to topple Castro.

While Artime's coup was being planned with Tony Varona and others, Jack Ruby was still making trips to Cuba. While in Cuba, Ruby later testified that he spent most of his time with Lewis McWillie, whose associate Dino Cellini was close to Tony Varona. On October 2, 1959, Jack Ruby was back in Dallas and had his last meeting with his FBI handler.[17] According to one account, FBI records show that even though Ruby's FBI handler wanted to continue working with Ruby, the FBI agent was "told by his superior to drop" Ruby as an informant.[18]

Artime and Varona's coup got under way on October 19, 1959, on the same day an assassination attempt was made on Castro. The coup was not a well-coordinated effort, and its poor results would doubtless influence the future coup efforts of Artime and others. On October 19, Cuban accounts say that Artime's ally "Huber Matos, head of the Rebel Army regiment in Camaguey Province . . . publicly resigned" due to "communists" in "the government."[19] Historian Hugh Thomas adds that "fourteen officers resigned with him."[20] This was the signal for the coup to begin.

Artime and his allies had picked a good time to start their coup, because "at that time a convention on international tourism was being held in" Havana "which had attracted hundreds of delegates and journalists from all over the world," according to Cuban accounts. Hugh Thomas adds that "Castro himself was in Havana at this time, addressing the Travel Agents Conference. He went immediately to the television station to denounce the US for at least passive complicity" in the coup. At that time, a man Thomas identifies as "Roberto Salas Hernandez tried unsuccessfully to kill" Fidel Castro "with a knife."[21]

Paul Bethel, the US official who admits meeting with Menoyo and Morgan before their coup attempts, writes that "there were three bombs hurled that night, one at the offices of Revolucion" and "two more bombs . . . in the Havana suburb of Marianno."[22]

Two days later, "on October 21," Cuban accounts say that Trafficante bagman Frank Fiorini and a pilot "scattered thousands of leaflets over the city of Havana, exhorting the population to rise up against the revolution."[23] There were rumors of planes strafing and bombing Havana, in the same way that Cuban sugar mills and factories had recently been bombed. Hugh Thomas says the Cuban government quickly issued a pamphlet about the raid called *Havana's Pearl Harbor*, while the Cuban press "came out with headlines as large as those which might have proclaimed a world war: THE AIRPLANES CAME FROM THE US." Those reactions only increased the public's concern and hysteria about the revolt.

Historian Tad Szulc says that Artime's coup attempt "held immense dangers for Castro in assuring the unity and loyalty of the Rebel Army, and potentially it was his worst political crisis since he assumed power."[24] For help, Castro turned to Commander Camilo Cienfuegos, head of the Rebel Army and the second most popular figure in the Revolution after Fidel.

Even piecing together the various accounts of historians and Cuban officials, the story of Artime's coup gets murky at this point, as if something has been left out of the official version. For example, two days before the October 19, 1959 start of the coup, Fidel Castro had appointed "his brother Raul Castro" to become "Minister of the Armed Forces."[25] There is no indication why Fidel took that action—if Fidel had grown suspicious of the popular Commander Cienfuegos for some reason—or how Rebel Army head Cienfuegos reacted to what was essentially a demotion. But when Fidel ordered Commander "Cienfuegos . . . to go to Camaguey to make the" rebels "surrender," Cienfuegos didn't feel the need to take his army to confront Huber Matos and the rebels.[26]

Historian Tad Szulc says that Commander Cienfuegos "led a revolutionary crowd in a march on the provincial military headquarters to preempt whatever rebellion may have been brewing."[27] Commander Cienfuegos was then seemingly able to simply talk Matos out of his rebellion. That wasn't enough for Castro, who felt the need to go to Camaguey himself to meet with both Commander Cienfuegos and Matos. Was Castro suspicious that Commander Cienfuegos had been part of the coup? Or that Matos was talking him into joining it? We may never know—but soon after Fidel returned to Havana with Matos as his prisoner, the popular Commander Cienfuegos died under mysterious circumstances.

The last gasp of the coup occurred on October 23, 1959, when "Manuel Artime circulated an open letter to Fidel in which he resigned . . . and accused Fidel of having surrendered to 'international communism,'" according to Cuban accounts.[28] But by then it was too late. Artime's ally Matos was under arrest, and the hysteria of the "leaflet bombing" of Havana had subsided. So, according to Cuban accounts, Artime asked the CIA Chief at the US Embassy for help, and he ordered "Bernard Barker to activate his contacts to spirit" Artime off the island.[29] Confirmation of Barker's role in helping future C-Day exile leader Artime escape comes from CIA officer E. Howard Hunt, who later wrote that "Artime" was "exfiltrated to the US" from Cuba "by [the] CIA through Bernard L. Barker."[30]

Official Cuban accounts say that "on October 28 [1959] after defeating the revolt, Commander "Cienfuegos . . . died in a tragic accident" while "returning to Havana in an Armed Forces plane."[31] A Cuban exile historian says that "Cienfuegos, the commander-in-chief of the Rebel Army, the most popular man in Cuba after Castro, was reportedly lost over the sea in a flight to Havana. A major search was carried out, but not a single trace of the alleged accident was found. Suspicions of a government purge rapidly spread and created further unrest."[32]

Hugh Thomas is even more suspicious, saying "Cienfuegos was never found. Foul play was immediately suspected. Was not Cienfuegos anti-Communist? Had he been killed by Raul Castro," who "brought the news to a cabinet meeting?" Thomas wrote that "one observer who accompanied Castro on a search for Cienfuegos by air later recalled that Castro seemed in fact in no way upset by the course of events." In addition, he notes that "Cienfuegos' aide, Major Naranjo, was shortly afterwards killed and his assassin, Major Beaton, also killed in 1960." Plus, the "Captain of the base from which Cienfuegos was supposed to have taken off, suggested that the flight was a put-up job, that no one saw Cienfuegos in the airplane, and that several others either killed themselves or were overpowered."[33]

US official Paul Bethel adds more intrigue to the disappearance of Cienfuegos after Artime's coup: "Sent to arrest Huber Matos only a few days earlier, Cienfuegos had refused to accept an order from Raul Castro to do so. Fidel finally had to give the order." Bethel admits that the CIA "actually managed to plant a tape recorder in Matos' office," though "the quality of the taped conversation between Matos and Cienfuegos was" too bad to understand.[34]

With Artime being spirited out of Cuba by the CIA—and the role of Varona in the coup apparently undetected at that time—what about Artime's other partner in the coup, Huber Matos? His life was saved by yet another future C-Day leader, Manolo Ray. Hugh Thomas writes that "In the [Cuban] Cabinet, Matos' execution was also proposed. The leading moderates still in the cabinet"—including Manolo Ray—"opposed this," and Matos was sent to prison instead of being shot. But in the cabinet meeting, "Castro insisted to the Cabinet that he was an anti-Communist . . . Castro put his arm around Ray's shoulders and said 'Have confidence in me.'"[35]

The friendly relationship between Castro and Manolo Ray didn't last. A year and a half later, Ray would join Artime and Varona in trying to unseat Castro with the Bay of Pigs invasion. Two years after that disaster, Ray, Artime, and Varona would join forces again—this time with Menoyo and Harry Williams—in the Kennedys' C-Day coup attempt.

The CIA's fall 1959 coup with future C-Day leaders Manuel Artime and Tony Varona had failed, as had their earlier effort with Menoyo. CIA-backed coup attempts obviously needed to be bigger and better organized—and more closely integrated with the CIA's Castro assassination plots. That's exactly what the CIA would do the following year, when planning for the Bay of Pigs invasion began and the CIA ramped up more extensive CIA-Mafia plots in the summer of 1960 that included Tony Varona as a very active participant. But in late 1959 and early 1960, the CIA still had the original Hoffa-brokered CIA-Mafia plots and there is some evidence that Hoffa associate Jack Ruby had one more role left to play.

Starting in late October 1959, both mob boss Meyer Lansky and the CIA faced new pressure to get rid of Fidel Castro, resulting in the first written

CIA memo (that has been released so far, anyway) about the CIA and Castro's assassination. Shortly after that, Lansky associate Lewis McWillie, the suave Havana casino manager, got in touch once again with lowly Dallas mobster Jack Ruby, asking his fawning admirer for a favor. This favor involved Cuba, the CIA-Mafia plots, and the Colt Cobra revolver that Ruby would later use to assassinate Lee Harvey Oswald.

Some of what happened next is well documented, and some is the source of many conflicting accounts by the participants. But a careful analysis of all the available evidence shows that in January of 1960, Lewis McWillie wanted Ruby to buy four Colt Cobra revolvers—legally—at a particular hardware store in Dallas, and bring them to Havana. This way, the pistols could not be connected to any of the earlier CIA-sanctioned gun-running in Cuba, as might be the case with any pistol a gangster like McWillie could easily obtain in Havana. Ruby discussed his upcoming Havana trip with at least two associates who originally planned to go with him.

Then, for some reason, Ruby again became reluctant to go to Cuba on his mission for McWillie in January 1960. Perhaps Ruby got cold feet, since Trafficante courier John Martino was still languishing in a brutal Cuban prison. McWillie then asked Ruby to have the Dallas hardware store's owner ship the four pistols directly to McWillie in Cuba, and Ruby testified that he did so (though the store owner later denied this). It's not clear if the store owner shipped those four pistols to McWillie at that time, though on at least one occasion he did ship a pistol to McWillie—at Jack Ruby's request—at a much later date.[36] Several months later in 1960, a similar revolver was used in an attempt by a "gangster" to assassinate Fidel Castro, according to a detailed Cuban account.[37] What is well established is that during these unusual activities with McWillie, on January 19, 1960, Jack Ruby bought at least one Colt Cobra revolver at the Dallas hardware store: The Warren Commission found that this was the gun Ruby used to shoot Lee Harvey Oswald. Coupled with Ruby's earlier ties to the 1959 CIA-Mafia plots and coup attempts (through his involvement as "Jack La Rue" with Bartone and William Morgan), it was just one more reason why the Mafia used Jack Ruby—and that particular pistol—in their JFK assassination plot. It would be a signal that digging too deeply into Ruby and his Mafia ties could expose all sorts of deadly secrets that the CIA and other US agencies did not want exposed.

The catalyst for this round of CIA-Mafia plots were the mutual interests of the CIA and Havana godfather Meyer Lansky. Lansky had the bad timing to have sunk much of his personal fortune into the Havana Riviera, which his biographer, Robert Lacy, described as a "spectacular hotel-casino," Havana's finest. Lacy adds that "Meyer Lansky invested much more than his money in the Havana Riviera. He invested himself. He gambled everything— and, as he later put it, 'I crapped out.'" According to an account in a *New York Times* story on November 23, 1959, "Fidel Castro . . . kicked out the mobsters from the casino and put in his own men."[38] While the idea of Cuban revolutionaries running Havana's finest casino may seem almost comical, for Lansky it was deadly serious—and the following year the Cuban government officially "announced the confiscation and nationalization of the Havana Riviera hotel."[39]

Meyer Lansky continued with his "million-dollar contract" on Castro's life. As noted earlier, Anthony Summers documented that it was in "1959 . . . that Lansky reached out to" two Nixon associates "in the hopes of getting the Administration to 'accept his assassination plan'" for Castro. Summers also found evidence of the many ties between Nixon's best friend, Cuban exile Bebe Rebozo, and Meyer Lansky's men.[40]

In this case, the interests of Meyer Lansky were similar to those of Nixon and the CIA. On the same day that the Cuban government had confiscated Lansky's Havana Riviera, they had also nationalized and confiscated "165 other American enterprises, including the Cuban subsidiaries and franchises of Kodak, Woolworth, Canada Dry, Westinghouse, and Goodyear," according to Lansky's biographer—who noted that "Meyer Lansky was in distinguished company."[41] Vice President Nixon was regarded as very close to big American corporations, and something had to be done.

One result was the first CIA memo—at least, the first to have survived and been declassified—about the CIA assassinating Castro. Hoffa biographer Dan Moldea writes that "on December 11, 1959, the Western Hemisphere Division head of the Central Intelligence Agency"—J. C. King—"wrote a memorandum to Allen Dulles, the CIA chief, advocating the 'elimination' of Castro." Moldea says that "Dulles approved of the plan in a handwritten note" and that "both President Eisenhower and Vice President Nixon were informed of these discussions during meetings of the National Security Council, of which Dulles was a member. Perhaps because he 'knew' Cuba, Nixon was delegated to be the White House's liaison to the CIA on the matter."[42]

The December 11, 1959 CIA memo about Castro's assassination may have been the first time it had been put in writing at such a high level, but it was not the start of CIA assassination plans for Castro. Plenty of testimony from CIA and other officials shows that they avoided putting talk of assassination in writing whenever possible, to preserve "plausible deniability," for the officials involved and especially for the president. The few times assassination memos were written, they had usually been preceded by months of discussion and, often, action. This December 1959 memo represents not the first step, but the *next* step in a process that had begun by June of 1959, as Nixon himself had written on two occasions. The previous, very loosely controlled CIA-Mafia plots had failed, so things needed to be kicked upstairs; hence the memo to the CIA Director.

In Havana, CIA operations director David Morales was still at the US Embassy and David Atlee Phillips was still undercover in Havana, although, after the arrest of his coup participants, his autobiography says he was making plans to leave Cuba with his family. After Castro's recent denunciation of the US following the failed Menoyo and Artime coups, the CIA could not afford to have any evidence tying them to another Castro assassination attempt. But there was someone connected to the earlier CIA-Mafia plots, someone from the Dallas-Fort Worth area where David Atlee Phillips grew up, who might be able to help.

An FBI document confirms that in addition to being close to "Santo Trafficante," Lewis McWillie had "solidified his" Mafia "connections" to "Meyer and Jake Lansky."[43] Like any Lansky associate, McWillie would certainly have been interested in a share of the million-dollar bounty on Castro. Earlier, we noted McWillie's role with Ruby in the Hoffa plane deal, which was part of the 1959 CIA-Mafia plots. Scott Malone quotes a US mercenary as saying that the Mafia "was using McWillie just prior to the Bay of Pigs on the hit job [against Castro] and some other intelligence stuff."[44] So there's no reason to believe that, between June 1959 and early 1961, McWillie suddenly lost his nerve, especially when a million dollars was at stake. But in late 1959, communicating by phone with someone in the States who could help him with such a project would be risky. However, a mobster friend of Ruby—and McWillie—named R. D. Matthews was leaving Havana in late 1959 to return to Dallas, so it would be safe to send a message to Ruby through Matthews.

Like McWillie and Jack Ruby, R. D. Matthews was also a Trafficante associate who has been linked to the early Castro assassination plots.[45] Matthews was on McWillie's level, and was someone else Ruby looked up to. Matthews was involved in the Dallas narcotics trade, as was Ruby, and Matthews even duplicated Ruby's close relationships with law enforcement, though on a much higher level. According to one account, R. D. Matthews was close to Dallas "Sheriff Bill Decker. In 1959 the FBI questioned Sheriff Decker about his alleged mob ties. Sheriff Decker admitted that he had known R. D. Matthews all of his adult life."[46]

By late 1959 and early 1960, the ever-hustling Ruby would have been receptive to some new action, especially since his earlier Cuban gun-running had dwindled. His role in the Hoffa airplane deal with Bartone was over, and he hadn't been in Cuba since September 1959. Ruby was no longer an FBI informant, and he had been officially dropped from the "FBI (Potential) Criminal Informant rolls" on November 6, a month after his last meeting with the FBI.[47]

The timing of Ruby's purchase of one of the Colt Cobra pistols McWillie requested makes it easy to establish the time frame of the operation. FBI Reports in Warren Commission Exhibits 2993 and 2994 clearly show that "Jack Ruby purchased a Colt Cobra revolver . . . on January 19, 1960." The serial number of the revolver is the same as the one taken from Ruby after he shot Oswald. The gun-store owner and his wife said that "Ruby was accompanied by a Dallas policeman at that time," and "a prizefighter was with them." One prizefighter Ruby definitely knew was Barney Baker, described as "a close associate of Jimmy Hoffa" who "worked . . . under Hoffa's direct orders" at that time, according to Mafia expert David Scheim. Bobby Kennedy called Baker "one of Hoffa's 'roving emissaries of violence.' The FBI identified him as a 'reported muscle and bagman'" for Hoffa, and he "maintained close and frequent contacts with notorious mobsters throughout the country."[48] Baker's presence might be an indication that Hoffa still had a role in the CIA-Mafia plots he had first brokered the previous year.[49] Barney Baker, Hoffa's enforcer, would also have documented contact with Ruby less than two weeks before Ruby shot Oswald, using the Colt Cobra purchased on January 19, 1960.

Regarding a later pistol that Ruby would ask the same hardware store owner to send McWillie in the spring of 1963—around the time of a well-documented CIA-Mafia plot with Johnny Rosselli to kill Castro with pistols—two journalists asked: "Was Ruby supplying the pistols to the Las Vegas gambler McWillie so they could be passed on to Rosselli, another Las Vegas" mobster, to be "used in a plot against Castro? If the Rosselli assassination squad was apprehended, it would be very difficult to trace the pistols back to the CIA since Ruby had purchased them in an out-of-the-way gun store in Texas."[50] The same reasoning would apply to the earlier CIA-Mafia plots and the four revolvers McWillie had asked Ruby to send to Havana. As for using a Colt Cobra pistol in an assassination, Ruby himself proved on national TV that it is an easily concealed, effective weapon.

While he was in the Dallas jail for shooting Oswald, Ruby talked about the four Colt Cobras McWillie had wanted in January of 1960 with several noted investigators, including Chief Supreme Court Justice Earl Warren and (now Senator) Arlen Specter. It was usually Ruby who brought the subject up, and he made it clear that he really wanted to be questioned about them. For example, Ruby testified that "I wanted that question put to me in reference to" the gun dealer and "my trip to Cuba and my association with the Underworld." Ruby insisted on making a very big deal over what seemed like a tiny incident to the investigators.[51] Then again, they didn't know at the time about the CIA-Mafia plots that had begun in 1959.

Regarding McWillie's request to have Ruby get the hardware store owner to send four Colt Cobras to Cuba, Ruby testified: "Now, this is incriminating for me because all I did—like a tool—got myself involved by relating a message that somebody else wanted . . . this is incriminating me very bad." Ruby's statements often raise more questions than they answer. "Involved" in what? Why is Ruby worried about a call regarding the sale of four pistols being "incriminating," when he is in jail for first-degree murder? As for Ruby's use of the phrase "like a tool" instead of "like a fool," it isn't possible from the Warren volumes to see if that is a transcription error or a Freudian slip.[52]

Ruby makes a big point of the fact that the hardware store owner denies that Ruby ever asked him to ship four Colt Cobras to McWillie in Cuba (though the owner did admit sending one much later to McWillie in Las Vegas). Ruby told Chief Justice Warren that McWillie "wanted some four little Cobra guns—big shipment." Ruby says the hardware store owner "denies I ever called . . . maybe he feels it would be illegal to send guns out of the country. I don't know if you gentlemen know the law. I don't know the law." To which Chief Justice Earl Warren replies "I don't know [the law]"— not one of his finest legal moments. But Ruby goes on about the hardware store owner's denial, saying "This definitely would do me more harm, because . . . that makes it look like I am hiding something."[53]

Ruby was certainly hiding something, and while sometimes it sounds like he really wants Warren and the investigators to look more closely at "Cuba and my association with the Underworld," at other times he tries make excuses for why McWillie wanted the Cobras. Ruby tries to say McWillie wanted them right after Castro took over, just for "protection." But Castro had been in power for over a year when Ruby bought his Colt Cobra, and Cuba was still awash in guns at that time, many originally provided with US help to Castro or Batista. Ruby seems truly conflicted about the Colt Cobras, for some reason never made clear to investigators at the time. A psychiatrist who talked to Ruby in jail noted that "there is considerable guilt about the fact that he sent guns to Cuba."[54] Now, using information not available to the psychiatrist or the Warren Commission, it's clear that—to Ruby—sending guns to Cuba led to his being in jail. That's because he knew that the same mobsters he'd dealt with in those days—like Trafficante—were behind the JFK murder conspiracy, the reason Ruby had to shoot Oswald.

There are several reasons why the hardware store owner would deny being asked by Ruby to send four Colt Cobras to McWillie in Havana in 1960. It was illegal to send guns to Cuba at that time, but that's no reason for the hardware store owner to deny even being asked. He could easily have said "maybe Ruby asked, but I didn't send them, it was against the law." Instead, the owner was adamant in his insistence that it never even came up. Yet Ruby remembered the conversation vividly, saying that, when told about McWillie's request, the hardware store owner said "Oh, I know Mr. McWillie very well . . . I've done business with him constantly."[55] Yet no records of McWillie buying guns from the hardware store were found (the one pistol Ruby had the store send to McWillie two years later was returned, unclaimed).

This raises the possibility that the hardware store owner did send the four Colt Cobras to the gangster McWillie in Cuba in 1960 like Ruby asked—only it was off the books, like McWillie's earlier purchases must have been. In that case, it would make sense for the hardware store owner to deny not just sending the guns, but that the conversation Ruby remembers so well ever took place. It is also possible that the store owner was telling the truth, but it is clear that the store owner wanted to distance himself as much as possible from anything that might indicate that Ruby was involved in any type of conspiracy. When a journalist asked the hardware store owner about the incident in 1977, the owner said "Jack Ruby is as far from Fidel Castro and the Mafia as Billy Carter is to Lady Bird Johnson." When Lewis McWillie was asked about the incident by the House Select Committee, they mistakenly used the date 1959 instead of 1960. McWillie was careful to include their wrong year in his reply, when he said "No reason I would have wanted guns in 1959."[56]

In addition to buying one Colt Cobra and asking that four of the revolvers be shipped to McWillie in Cuba, Ruby was also making plans to visit Cuba at that time, in late January or early February 1960. The time can be pinned down independent of Ruby's gun purchase. Journalist A. J. Weberman cites House Select Committee testimony when he writes that one of Ruby's planned companions for the Cuba trip had to cancel, saying that "he never made the trip because a big show, starring Frank Sinatra, Dean Martin and Sammy Davis Jr. was scheduled for the same time." Weberman says "the date of the Sinatra-Martin-Davis show . . . took place from January 20, 1960 to February 16, 1960." This means that Ruby originally planned to visit Cuba during that time frame, which began the day after Ruby bought his Colt Cobra. Another of Ruby's original companions for his planned January 1960 Cuba trip was a mutual acquaintance of Ruby's good friend Gordon McLendon. McLendon was also friends—and later business partners—with CIA agent David Atlee Phillips, then based in Havana.[57]

According to a Cuban government report provided to Senator George McGovern, several months after Havana mobster McWillie asked Jack Ruby about the Colt Cobra revolvers, a "gangster" (not McWillie) was involved in "a plot against" Fidel Castro along with "the CIA." The "gangster" and his associate were captured by Cuban authorities, along with their "material and equipment." A photo of their "equipment" shows that it included a revolver similar to the one Ruby bought—and the four he discussed with McWillie— just a few months earlier.[58] Whether it was exactly the same type of pistol is not possible to tell from the photo in the report, but it is interesting that a "gangster" would have been using a light, easily concealed weapon in a "plot" with "the CIA" several months after Ruby had been involved with similar pistols regarding Cuba.

1960 and 1961:
New CIA-Mafia Plots,
the Bay of Pigs, and
RFK's War Against Marcello

WE'VE DOCUMENTED THAT MANY OF the people linked to C-Day, the Mafia's penetration of it, or JFK's assassination were involved to some degree in events in Cuba in 1959 and early 1960. This includes Trafficante, Rosselli, Marcello, their close ally Hoffa, and their henchmen like Ruby, Martino, Fiorini, Prio, and Masferrer. On the CIA side were David Atlee Phillips, David Morales, and Bernard Barker, as well as C-Day leaders Varona, Artime, Ray, and Harry Williams. About the only ones missing were patsies Lee Harvey Oswald and Gilberto Lopez; CIA officials Howard Hunt, James McCord, and Richard Helms; and mobsters Charles Nicoletti and Michel Victor Mertz—all of whom would soon be added to the mix. Even the Kennedys were involved in 1959, in terms of having their hearings harmed by the CIA-Mafia plots.

As we move forward into 1960 and beyond, more of the basic historical framework is well established for events central to the Mafia penetration of C-Day such as the later CIA-Mafia plots and the Bay of Pigs, so we will be able to cover things far more quickly. Yet even in those years, well-documented events critical to the Mafia penetration of C-Day are missing from most historical accounts, so covering those will be a primary focus. The reason that that information is missing from most accounts is because much of it has only been declassified in the last ten years—mostly due to the JFK Assassination Records Review Board—long after most accounts of the era were written. These new documents also call into question previously accepted accounts of CIA and Mafia operations in the early 1960s.

Recently declassified documents call into question even internal CIA accounts of the CIA-Mafia plots which "began" in the summer of 1960, plots that the CIA admits involved Santo Trafficante, Johnny Rosselli, and Tony

Varona in leading roles. Those plots were first detailed in a long-secret 1967 CIA Inspector General's Report (hereafter called the IG Report) that President Lyndon Johnson had asked CIA Director Richard Helms to have prepared after the first news stories appeared hinting at the CIA-Mafia plots (leaked to Jack Anderson by Rosselli to avoid prosecution).

LBJ was given only an oral summary of the IG Report by Helms, and the full report later became a bitter point of contention between CIA Director Helms and Richard Nixon before and during Watergate. Much of the report was kept classified until the 1970s, parts weren't released until the 1990s, and some of it is still classified today. While for years historians thought it was being kept secret for what it revealed, the more complete versions show that it was being kept secret because of what it left out—various CIA operations ranging from the 1959 CIA-Mafia plots to 1963's C-Day (AMWORLD) and AMTRUNK, which are clearly established by many other declassified CIA documents.

The IG Report has been the source of much misinformation over the years, and it is just as important for what it leaves out as for what it includes. The IG Report was prepared in 1967, when there was a chance that Bobby Kennedy or Richard Nixon could have been elected president while Helms was still CIA Director. Also at that time, New Orleans District Attorney Jim Garrison's investigation had become public—but his prime suspect David Ferrie had died, meaning other individuals connected to the CIA might face prosecution for JFK's assassination. Consequently, the report appears to be not only an attempt to explain the CIA-Mafia plots, but also to whitewash what had happened for the "benefit" of LBJ or future presidents, protecting Helms and others in the CIA from charges that their operations had somehow been compromised and used in JFK's assassination.

In fact, some noted authorities, including Peter Dale Scott, have pointed out that Helms's IG Report ignores the very issue that LBJ had asked Helms to investigate, which was whether plots by Bobby Kennedy and the CIA against Castro had somehow backfired against JFK. Helms was able to ignore the issue because, while LBJ had been generally informed about C-Day and some of the CIA-Mafia plots after JFK's death, there were many details about both operations that he apparently hadn't been told. Helms simply left out information about the 1959 CIA-Mafia plots and Jack Ruby, as well as the CIA-Mafia plots going on in the fall of 1963. The IG report relegated mention of C-Day (AMWORLD) and AMTRUNK to just one brief sentence, which did not even use their CIA code names.

The IG Report itself admits "this reconstruction of Agency involvement in plans to assassinate Fidel Castro is at best an imperfect history" since "as a matter of principle no official records were kept of planning, of approvals, or of implementation. The few written records that do exist are either largely tangential to the main events or were put on paper from memory years afterward." The CIA report often uses phrases like "skeletal notes," "cryptic references," and "fragmentary." It admits that "we have had to rely on information given to us orally by people whose memories are fogged by time" and "hazy." (Yet this is April 1967, only three and a half years after JFK's death and eight years after the first of the CIA-Mafia plots.) There is no indication that Helms, who had worked on many of the operations in question, was ever asked to provide his own records or recollections about the events. It's as if Helms wanted to see what his subordinates (or perhaps his replacement) could find and what interpretation they would put on it. In this way, Helms did not have to get the authors of the report to lie for him; he simply had to make sure that they had limited access to certain people and materials.[1]

In a glaring omission, the IG Report's authors admit that they didn't talk to "Mr. Dulles," the CIA Director during the 1959 CIA-Mafia plots, or "General Cabell," the Deputy Director at that time—the very people who would have approved the 1959 CIA-Mafia plots. Nor are there any indications, in the parts of the report that have been released so far, that CIA officers David Morales or David Atlee Phillips were interviewed about either the 1959 CIA-Mafia plots or coup attempts, Morales's extensive contacts with Johnny Rosselli in 1963 (documented by Congressional investigator Gaeton Fonzi), or Phillips's operations against the Fair Play for Cuba Committee and contact with Lee Harvey Oswald.

The IG Report's authors say things like "We cannot overemphasize the extent to which responsible Agency officers felt themselves subject to the Kennedy administration's severe pressures to do something about Castro and his regime"—but the existing draft shows that the word "Kennedy" was added at a later point. The sentence just quoted is grossly incomplete, since the CIA IG report admits that the planning began under the Eisenhower-Nixon administration, before JFK was even elected—and other evidence, apparently not available to the IG Report's authors, shows that the plotting had been going on for well over a year at that point. While the Kennedys' pressure was undoubtedly "severe," the pressure from Nixon by 1960 must have been extreme for the CIA to have dealt directly with mob bosses like Rosselli, Trafficante, and Giancana.

The CIA IG report admits that "those who have some knowledge of the episodes guessed at dates ranging from 1959 through 1961. The March-to-August [1960] time span we have fixed may be too narrow, but it best fits the limited evidence we have." The report likes to focus on anti-Castro plots involving "poison cigars" and a plan "to destroy Castro's image as 'The Beard' by causing the beard to fall out," in lieu of the plots involving Jack Ruby, Jimmy Hoffa, pistols, or the extensive plots going on in the fall of 1963. The CIA often floats these stories to the media whenever more serious information about CIA-Mafia plots starts to surface, as during the Church Committee hearings in the 1970s or when many CIA documents were getting declassified in the 1990s.

While the remainder of Part II will utilize the CIA's IG Report for some information and brief summaries, it will more often focus on the documented CIA, FBI, and other information that the CIA left out of that report. As might be expected, those are the portions that clearly show the Mafia's penetration of several CIA operations, including the CIA's side of C-Day (AMWORLD).

NIXON'S OCTOBER SURPRISE: ASSASSINATING CASTRO
Traditional history says that following a March 1960 meeting of Eisenhower's National Security Council, the CIA began preparing for what eventually became the Bay of Pigs invasion. In addition, in the summer of 1960, high CIA officials began meeting personally with top mob bosses like Johnny Rosselli and Santo Trafficante about assassinating Castro. The CIA likes to focus on silly things like the "exploding cigar" plan, but does admit preparing poison pills for the Mafia to give Castro. Although these CIA-Mafia plots and the Bay of Pigs planning were going on at the same time by the same CIA officials, the CIA tries to pretend that there was really no connection between the two—or between them and the assassinations of two other foreign leaders around the same time. After Nixon's defeat in November 1960—and the Bay of Pigs disaster in the early months of JFK's administration—the CIA admits that their Castro assassination plots with the Mafia continued until early 1963, when they claim that they ended. Which was lucky timing for the CIA, because that way there could be no connection between the CIA-Mafia plots involving Rosselli and Trafficante, and JFK's assassination in November 1963. End of story. Except that dozens of key CIA documents declassified in recent years—many withheld from Congressional investigating committees—and much testimony show that that account is at best grossly incomplete.

The newly documented history is quite different: According to many sources—including President Eisenhower—the March 1960 meeting authorized neither a huge Bay of Pigs invasion force not the CIA-Mafia plots. Instead, its general resolution involving support for anti-Castro operations was used by Nixon to press for more action on the CIA-Mafia plots, which had yet to show results. In response, the CIA's "Colonel Sheffield Edwards, Director of the Office of Security," and "the Chief of the Operational Support Division of the Office of Security," James O'Connell, started meeting with Rosselli and Trafficante, according to the Senate Church Committee Report.[2] But this time, instead of Jimmy Hoffa, they used a different "cutout"—Robert Maheu, a Las Vegas Howard Hughes operative who had helped the CIA before.

However, sworn testimony shows that one of the high CIA officials already knew Rosselli prior to the meeting with Maheu. The CIA claims that Rosselli and Trafficante were needed to get to Tony Varona, to involve him in the plots. Yet the CIA's own records show that the CIA had already been using Varona since at least 1958, with an upgrade to his status in 1959. The reality was that the CIA was assuming a leading role in the assassination and coup plots that had been going since 1959. And instead of dealing indirectly with a half dozen mobsters like Norman Rothman and Bufalino though Hoffa, the CIA was now dealing directly with Rosselli, Trafficante, and Rosselli's boss Sam Giancana. Other mob associates used by the mob bosses in the plots include Frank Fiorini, wireman-lawman-mobster Richard Cain, and Chicago mob hit man Charles Nicoletti, all of whom would play a role for the mob during or after JFK's assassination.

With the November 1960 election fast approaching, Nixon needed the boost that toppling Castro would provide. While the CIA plotted Castro's assassination with Rosselli and Trafficante, Carlos Marcello and Jimmy Hoffa were also trying to help Nixon. Around the time of the first JFK-Nixon debate, Bobby Kennedy's most trusted Hoffa informant witnessed a meeting in New Orleans between Marcello and Hoffa. The purpose of the meeting was a suitcase filled with $500,000 in cash destined for Nixon—only half of a promised $1,000,000 contribution organized by the two.[3] Rosselli, on the other hand, played both sides so he would have an advantage no matter who won the presidency—he introduced Senator John F. Kennedy to a lovely young woman named Judith Campbell, who was also close to Rosselli's boss Sam Giancana and Frank Sinatra.

Prior to the 1960 election, only a few Cuban exiles were being trained by the CIA: not nearly enough for even a small invasion force, but enough to go into Cuba right after Castro's assassination, to help install someone like Tony Varona as the new leader of Cuba. Journalist Haynes Johnson reportedly told an interviewer that Vice President Richard "Nixon was very influential at [the] top of the B[ay] of P[igs] planning."[4]

However, the CIA-Mafia plots failed to assassinate Castro prior to the election, which JFK narrowly won. In the election's aftermath, the CIA greatly expanded the exile operations that Eisenhower had authorized in March 1960, into what would become the 2,000-man Bay of Pigs invasion force. But the CIA was running two other operations in the fall of 1960 that would facilitate the Mafia's penetration of C-Day and JFK's assassination. One was the CIA's use of an assassin recruiter named code-named QJWIN, a European criminal tied to narcotics smuggling. (QJWIN's name is still withheld by the CIA, but his identity is discussed in a later chapter.) This CIA assassination program was named ZRRIFLE, and CIA agent QJWIN appears to have been involved in events leading up to the assassination of Congo leader Patrice Lumumba. Overlooked until recently was the fact that in late 1960, the CIA had looked at using a close mob associate of Johnny Rosselli in the ZRRIFLE program, meaning that the CIA-Mafia plots and the ZRRIFLE assassination operation with QJWIN were really just two aspects of one CIA operation.

The other CIA operation of interest in late 1960 that would have big repercussions the following year—and for JFK's assassination—was possibly a joint effort with Naval Intelligence. It involved staging a fake attack on the US Navy base at Guantanamo, Cuba, using US-supported exiles pretending to be Fidel's troops. This provocation would provide an excuse for a US invasion of Cuba in December 1960, before Vice President Nixon had to leave office, at least letting him go out on a high note. However, on "December 3, 1960, Cuban State Security arrested more than 40" participants and "at their trial . . . the alleged CIA agent and Anti-Communist League of the Caribbean Head of Action and Sabotage . . . testified and publicly unmasked the CIA's participation." While that event is not noted by most US historians, its consequences are, since "just a few days later, the Eisenhower administration decided to break relations with Cuba" and "on January 3, 1961, the US Embassy closed its doors."[5] Those actions tremendously limited JFK's options when he took office shortly after that, since CIA operations in any country were usually run out of the local US Embassy.

JFK would be harmed even more by someone linked to the December 1960 Guantanamo provocation: Guy Banister. The Cubans asserted that the

CIA had used the "Anti-Communist League of the Caribbean" in the operation, and FBI veteran William Turner discovered that Guy "Banister was also instrumental in the Anti-Communist League of the Caribbean, a pet project of Nicaragua's General Somoza."[6] The *New Orleans States-Item* reported that Banister "was a key liaison man for US government-sponsored anti-Communist activities in Latin America," quoting "a close friend and advisor of Banister's" as saying that "Guy participated in every important anti-Communist South and Central American revolution which came along."[7]

Confirmation of this can be found in one of the only Naval Intelligence documents ever released about Guy Banister. Quoted here for the first time, it confirms that Banister was working for the "General Counsel" of the "Anti-Communist League of the Americas." On "August 31, 1960"—a few months before the planned date of the first Guantanamo provocation—Banister wrote to a Naval Intelligence contact in New Orleans for the League, saying that "to have a successful revolution to overthrow the Castro government . . . a unit of the Armed Forces must lead the revolution."[8] By 1963, Banister would be working for Carlos Marcello, but in 1960 he was still a former FBI supervisor high in New Orleans intelligence and far-right circles. The Cubans say the "the Anti-Communist League of the Caribbean . . . was run by the CIA and was in contact with the US Embassy" in Havana, "on the 5th floor of the Embassy."[9] That would indicate that Havana CIA operations director David Morales was also involved in this first Guantanamo provocation.

The next attempt by US intelligence to stage a phony attack on Guantanamo would help cause the Bay of Pigs disaster in 1961.

ROSSELLI, TRAFFICANTE, MARCELLO, AND THE BAY OF PIGS

Starting in 1961, the Kennedys tried to fight what they saw as two separate wars, one against Castro and the other against the Mafia and Hoffa. But that year, as in the fall of 1963, it would turn out that the two wars weren't separate after all, and the results would be disastrous. After taking office, President Kennedy let the CIA handle the growing US covert war against Castro, while Attorney General Bobby Kennedy fought Marcello, Trafficante, and the Mafia. But the Mafia's involvement in the CIA's anti-Castro efforts was one reason the US-backed Cuban exile invasion known as the Bay of Pigs was such a colossal failure, and it laid the groundwork for the Mafia penetration of C-Day two years later.

Historians, former officials, and Cuban exiles still argue about the reasons for the failure of the Bay of Pigs, but the CIA-Mafia plots and yet another

Guantanamo provocation were key factors that are often overlooked. The blame is sometimes laid to JFK's failure to back up the Cuban exiles with the US military, even though, in the weeks before the invasion, he had publicly promised America and the world not to do that. Some blame the press, for reporting widely on the supposedly secret invasion prior to the event; but if that was a reason for the failure, why didn't the CIA simply delay the invasion a few months, so they could catch Castro by surprise? Was there a reason that the CIA's invasion had to take place at that particular time? Others say that the invasion failed because the Cuban populace didn't rise up against Castro as expected—yet CIA Director Allen Dulles and other CIA officials have said that that was never part of the plan. If Dulles is correct and no uprising was expected, then how could the CIA have thought that a 2,000-man invasion force could conquer all of Cuba? And why is some information about the Bay of Pigs still classified SECRET today? One key reason is that many of those involved later had roles in C-Day—or in the Mafia's penetration of it.

The entire Bay of Pigs operation actually had six components, only two of which are widely known, though most of the others are well documented. Known to all historians is the 2,000-man Cuban exile invasion force, most of which was based in Guatemala and commanded by Pepe San Roman, with assistance from Manuel Artime and Harry Williams. Also widely known was the Cuban Provisional Government-in-exile, the Cuban Revolutionary Council, which included future C-Day exile leaders like Tony Varona and Manolo Ray and their CIA handlers. CIA coordinator E. Howard Hunt, whose assistant was Bernard Barker, thought Manolo Ray was too liberal to be included, so he quit the project. David Atlee Phillips handled propaganda for the project, and CIA operations specialist David Morales—in America by that time, along with Phillips—also worked on the Bay of Pigs.

But four other parts of the Bay of Pigs aren't widely known, and would help to lay the groundwork for the penetration of C-Day. First was the CIA-Mafia plots, which were clearly coordinated with the invasion. The "secret" invasion couldn't be postponed, even after it became an open secret, because it had to coincide with Castro's assassination. However, the CIA-Mafia plots were so tightly held within the CIA—known to only a handful of officials— that miscommunication resulted in the plots' failure. The new leaders-in-exile like Tony Varona were put in protective custody by the CIA just prior to the invasion, so that one of them couldn't try to get into Cuba and take control first, before the others could get there. But Varona's man in Cuba had the CIA's poison pills, and was only awaiting Varona's signal to use them against Castro—a signal that never came, because of Varona's detention. Several mob bosses who had cooperated in the earlier 1959 CIA-Mafia plots were waiting off the coast of Cuba at this time, ready with money to go in and reopen the casinos—apparently the CIA's way of repaying them for their earlier help.[10]

It is possible that, if Castro had been assassinated, JFK might have reevaluated his stance against using the US military, since he could have rationalized that he was sending in US forces to a now-unstable Cuba to prevent civil war. But the CIA had yet another way to prod JFK into committing massive US forces to the invasion: another Guantanamo provocation. While most of the US-backed Cuban exiles had trained in Central America, one group had trained at a special CIA camp near New Orleans. Linked to that camp were CIA agent David Atlee Phillips and the New Orleans office of the CIA-created anti-Castro group, the Cuban Revolutionary Council (CRC). Active in the New Orleans CRC branch were New Orleans detective Guy Banister and David Ferrie.[11]

Supposedly, the CIA-trained Cuban exiles would leave New Orleans on a ship named the *Santa Ana* and head for an area near the US base at Guantanamo, to stage a "diversionary landing" while the real invasion took place far away. In reality, once the ship got near Guantanamo, the Cuban exiles were told that they were to put on the Cuban uniforms of Castro's troops and stage a fake attack on Guantanamo. This provocation would let the CIA and US Navy press JFK, who did not know about the operation, to respond against Castro with massive US military force. However, the Cuban exiles refused to undertake the bizarre, possibly suicidal, landing and attack. They were there to risk their lives fighting Castro's troops, not the US military.

Even if both the fake attack against Guantanamo and the CIA-Mafia plot to assassinate Castro had been successful, the CIA would still have been faced with a new governing coalition that could have been troublesome, since it had to include more moderate and liberal elements, at the Kennedys' insistence. A White House memo shows that Kennedy officials only learned months after the Bay of Pigs that the CIA had formed a small group called Operation 40—which, according to some accounts, included Trafficante bagman Frank Fiorini—supposedly to assassinate more progressive elements of a new Cuban government. JFK aide Arthur Schlesinger, Jr., wrote a memo to Richard Goodwin about it, saying that "liberal Cuban exiles believe that the real purpose of Operation 40" after the Bay of Pigs was to first "'kill

Communists'—and, after eliminating hard-core Fidelistas, to go on to eliminate first the followers of Ray, then the followers of Varona and finally to set
up a right-wing dictatorship, presumably under Artime."[12] Newly released
documents show that David Morales was involved with Operation 40.[13]

Finally, one element of the Bay of Pigs, reported here for the first time, is
that there were several mid-level Cuban officials willing to openly support
and join the new US-backed Cuban government, either after Castro's death
or once it became clear that the US military was taking part in the invasion.
On that list is Rolando Cubela, the mid-level official and former leader of a
rebel group called the DR.[14] Cubela's star would continue to fall in the
coming months, and he would be contacted again by the CIA for assassination plots shortly before the Cuban Missile Crisis and yet again in the
summer of 1963, just after C-Day first developed.

It's interesting to note that on the list of disgruntled Cuban officials for the
Bay of Pigs, the C-Day coup leader is missing. At that time, that hero of the
Revolution still sided with Castro, as he would tell a future C-Day exile
leader captured in the invasion. Yet it would be Castro's growing prestige and
power after the failed US invasion that would start the future C-Day coup
leader on the path that would bring him into partnership with the Kennedys
by late 1963.

It was after the Bay of Pigs that Harry Williams, lying severely injured in
a crude Cuban field hospital, almost accomplished what the Mafia could not
do—shoot Fidel Castro, had not the bullets been removed earlier from his
pistol by his friends. One of the leaders of the Bay of Pigs told us that one
reason JFK did not send in the military to help with the invasion—or rescue
Williams and the other prisoners right after the invasion—was Russian
leader Nikita Khrushchev's threat to attack the US portion of Berlin if JFK
intervened. JFK did tell Castro that if the prisoners were executed—as it was
rumored would happen—he would attack Cuba, which probably saved their
lives. A few months after the Bay of Pigs, Kennedy aide Richard Goodwin
met with Che Guevara at a conference in South America. Their talks almost
began a dialogue between the countries, until Goodwin's meetings were
denounced by conservatives in Congress. But in some ways, seeds had been
laid for secret talks that would resume in a different way in 1963.

The CIA had not been successful in assassinating Castro, but they were
able to help assassinate Dominican dictator Trujillo the following month, in
May 1961. According to Trujillo's chief of security, this CIA plot included
Johnny Rosselli and a future CIA C-Day coordinator. Trujillo was killed in

his car, in a hit very similar to one Rosselli's Chicago Mafia was famous for, the assassination of New York mob boss Frankie Yale. Perhaps because of Rosselli's success, the CIA continued to use Rosselli and Santo Trafficante in plots to assassinate Castro—but without telling the Kennedys. Other mob associates tried to get in on the action and get close to the Kennedys, but the Kennedys weren't biting. Trafficante associates Frank Fiorini and ex-Cuban president Carlos Prio met JFK briefly in 1961. Ruby's old gun-running associate Norman Rothman talked to Kennedy friends and officials about helping to assassinate Castro, but those talks went nowhere.[15] Based on comments JFK made to Tad Szulc and others, the Kennedys seemed ambivalent about assassinating Castro, though they wanted to find some way to overthrow his government.

By the end of 1961, the Kennedys were backing a new, massive anti-Castro program called OPERATION MONGOOSE. The top CIA officials responsible for the Bay of Pigs disaster—Director Allen Dulles, Deputy Director General Charles Cabell, and Deputy Director for Plans Richard Bissell—had resigned. Bobby Kennedy was now in charge of coordinating the plan among several agencies, and the US military would now have the lead role in covert invasions, not the CIA. However, it is still not clear how much the Kennedys ever learned about the CIA's phony Guantanamo provocation or the CIA-Mafia plots. Those operations, coupled with the CIA's Operation 40 that involved mobsters like Fiorini, gave the Mafia leverage over the CIA—and, as one high CIA official put it, the potential to blackmail the CIA.

Other 1961 CIA activities would impact events in 1963 and beyond. According to sworn court testimony, in 1961 a CIA man named "Phillips" met with Guy Banister and the New Orleans branch of the Cuban Revolutionary Council, to discuss a TV show promoting the group.[16] That type of media propaganda had been the specialty of David Atlee Phillips since the time he handled propaganda for the CIA's 1954 Guatemalan coup. Phillips and the CIA also targeted left-wing groups and publications that supported Castro. In 1961, CIA documents confirm that David Atlee Phillips was involved in penetrating the Fair Play for Cuba Committee (FPCC), a small pro-Castro group, and mounting an operation against it.[17] Phillips's FPCC operation lasted from February to July 1961. On June 29, 1961, the CIA ordered forty-five copies of a new pro-Castro pamphlet titled *The Crime Against Cuba*, apparently for use in some future propaganda operation.[18] The CIA received copies of the first edition of the pamphlet, which quickly sold out and was into its fourth printing by the end of the year. As detailed in later chapters, the first-edition pamphlets and David Atlee Phillips would come together in August 1963 in another operation targeting the Fair Play for Cuba Committee, this time involving Lee Harvey Oswald.

Working with Phillips on the 1961 FPCC operation was CIA Security Office official James McCord, the future Watergate burglar and alleged C-Day official.[19] CIA documents confirm that McCord had one other Cuban assignment in 1961 and into 1962: trying to help get three CIA men out of prison in Cuba, where they had been detained after what columnist Jack Anderson called a "Watergate-style break-in" at the Chinese Embassy in Havana.[20]

In early 1961, Bobby Kennedy focused on his battles with the Mafia and Hoffa, firing the opening salvos in what was to become the largest war on organized crime in US history. While Trafficante and Rosselli's boss Sam Giancana were the focus of major efforts, Bobby Kennedy targeted New Orleans mob boss Carlos Marcello for special attention, since Marcello had defied US Immigration authorities for years, despite a deportation order. Bobby beefed up the Justice Department's special prosecutors and organized them into Organized Crime and "Get Hoffa" sections. Bobby's men even went to Central America to investigate Marcello's phony Guatemalan birth certificate, where they were sometimes shadowed by Marcello's pilot, David Ferrie.

Shortly before the Bay of Pigs—even as the CIA was secretly working with Trafficante and Rosselli—Bobby Kennedy had Marcello suddenly arrested, thrown on a plane, and deported to Guatemala (ironically, the country where the CIA was training the Bay of Pigs exile invaders). Marcello's biographer, John H. Davis, writes that on "April 4, 1961, Carlos Marcello" and his lawyer "paid his required tri-monthly visit, as an alien, to the offices of the Immigration and Naturalization Service . . . in New Orleans." Marcello was told he was being deported to Guatemala, then he was handcuffed, taken "to a waiting car" along with his lawyer, and rushed to the airport in a "three-car convoy." He was refused permission to make any calls to his family or his special deportation lawyer in Washington, or to get any clothes or money for the trip. "Once at the airport the immigration convoy was immediately surrounded by police, and Marcello was escorted by a small army of police and immigration officials to the plane, engines already running"—and it took off as soon as Marcello boarded.[21] "Attorney General Kennedy publicly announced that Marcello had been deported to Guatemala and he was taking full responsibility for the expulsion of the New Orleans crime boss. Kennedy stated that . . . he was 'very happy Carlos Marcello was no longer with us.'"[22] Adding insult to injury, several days later "on April 10 back in New Orleans, the Internal Revenue Service had filed tax liens in excess of $835,000 against Carlos" Marcello and his wife, "instigated by Attorney General Kennedy."[23]

Marcello's exile in Central America started well, but he was soon tossed out of Guatemala and forced to trek through the jungle—all the while cursing Bobby Kennedy and swearing vengeance. Marcello's biographer wrote that "Carlos Marcello spent two harrowing months of exile in Central America— in Guatemala, El Salvador and Honduras."[24] Marcello was forced to leave Guatemala when that country's president responded to pressure from a major local newspaper. Marcello and his attorney were simply left at "an army camp in the Salvadorian jungle near the Guatemala-Salvador border, where they were left at the mercy of Salvadorian soldiers." Marcello and his attorney were then taken by bus "20 miles into Honduras" and "unceremoniously dumped off the bus like baggage thrown in the dust, left to fend for themselves on a forested hilltop with no signs of civilization in sight."

Marcello barely managed the 17-mile trek to a tiny village, and another trek through the jungle to finally reach a small airport. "Still wearing their city clothes and their city shoes stuffed with cash," Marcello and his associate "had little to drink or eat . . . Marcello found breathing difficult along the mountain-top road. He collapsed three times in the dust, complaining that he could not go on any farther, that he was finished, and that it was that rich kid Bobby Kennedy who had done this to them. 'If I don't make it . . . ,' Carlos told [his associate] at one point as he lay exhausted in a roadside gutter, 'tell my brother when you get back, about what dat kid Bobby done to us. Tell 'em to do what dey have to do.'" Before arriving at the small airport, the exhausted Marcello plunged "down a pathless slope. They ended up in a burrow, bleeding from thorns, bruised by rocks, with Marcello complaining of a severe pain in his side" from "three broken ribs."[25] All the while, Marcello swore vengeance on the man who had done this to him, Bobby Kennedy. After a couple of months, Marcello was able to secretly reenter the US—according to one US agency, with the help of David Ferrie— although he would remain in an ever-escalating legal war with Bobby Kennedy until November 22, 1963.

The War Against the Godfathers and Targeting RFK

AS 1962 PROGRESSED, THE KENNEDYS tried to continue their two-front war against Castro and the Mafia, but the two kept crossing over, sometimes with their knowledge and sometimes without. The pressure on the Mafia nationwide had increased many times over what it had been in the 1950s, but the attention that Justice Department prosecutors—and, at Bobby's urging, the FBI—paid to Marcello, Trafficante, Rosselli, Sam Giancana, and Jimmy Hoffa was especially intense.

In addition to the $850,000 tax assessment, Marcello faced "the indictment for illegal reentry, the McClellan committee hearings, the indictment . . . for conspiracy and perjury, and now the deportation order upheld after an unsuccessful appeal," says Davis, adding, "People close to the Marcellos at this time have remarked that . . . the family's hatred of Robert Kennedy knew no bounds." He points out that Marcello "did make at least one attempt to resolve his problems with Bobby Kennedy through diplomacy," according to an FBI transcript of a conversation between two gangsters who—unlike Marcello— were bugged. On July 17, 1962, Pennsylvania godfather Angelo Bruno told Russell Bufalino that Marcello had "asked Mafia bosses Santo Trafficante and Sam Giancana to persuade their friend Frank Sinatra to intervene in his behalf." But, "according to Bruno, Sinatra's intervention made matters worse" and "only made Bobby more determined than ever to go after Marcello." John Davis notes that "the failure of this diplomatic effort meant that Marcello now had only one recourse in his struggle with Bobby Kennedy: war."[1]

Even while Trafficante and Rosselli were working on the CIA-Mafia plots, they weren't immune from the Kennedys' unrelenting pressure. Trafficante's gambling operations were busted in Orlando by the IRS, and two of his family members were even arrested.[2] According to historian Richard

Mahoney, "the IRS had launched an audit of Rosselli's tax records in February 1962" and an "FBI detail . . . secretly scrutinized all his banking and stock transactions."[3] He notes that "Rosselli . . . grew openly bitter. 'Jesus,' he told [Norman] Rothman in July 1962, 'I'm being run right into the ground—it's terrible.'" Rosselli "voiced his frustration to an associate" and "specifically referenced the 'screwing' he was getting from Bobby Kennedy. 'Here I am helping the government, helping the country, and that little son of a bitch is breaking my balls.'"[4] Rosselli's boss, Chicago godfather Sam Giancana, was also facing pressure from the FBI at Bobby's urging.

The Mafia did get two lucky breaks in 1962 that would help them penetrate C-Day the following year, using the CIA's other anti-Castro plots. When the head of the Federal Bureau of Narcotics (FBN), Harry Anslinger, reached the mandatory retirement age in 1962, a recent history of the FBN notes that "in view of Bobby Kennedy's ethnically charged war on the Mafia, a political decision was made that an Italian American would get the job. The choice was between Charlie Siragusa and Henry Giordano, and the key decision maker was Bobby Kennedy's consigliere, Carmine Bellino."[5]

Charles Siragusa had been the FBN's top man in dealing with the Mafia and the CIA. In fact, the CIA had originally talked to Siragusa about joining the ZRRIFLE operation and becoming the CIA's assassin recruiter code-named QJWIN, but he turned them down. Likewise, the CIA had asked Siragusa at one point to hire the Mafia for them, to break out the three CIA agents captured in Cuba who were later the responsibility of CIA agent James McCord. While the CIA saw Siragusa as having close ties with the Mafia, Siragusa was good at penetrating the Mafia and their operations for the FBN.

The bottom line is that if Charles Siragusa had become head of the FBN, with his Mafia knowledge and experience with the CIA, it's likely that the mob would have had a much more difficult job in compromising the CIA-Mafia plots, QJWIN, and ZRRIFLE, and using their key heroin operatives like Michel Victor Mertz in the JFK assassination. But Bobby's man, Carmine Bellino—the former partner of Guy Banister—chose the other candidate (Henry Giordano) instead, and Mafia-CIA expert Siragusa was denied the top slot.

The Mafia's other lucky break in 1962 that would impact JFK's assassination occurred in Chicago. One of the people linked to both the JFK assassination and the CIA-Mafia plots in the fall of 1963 was Chicago hit man Charles Nicoletti. After being caught by police "on May 2, 1962" in a car specially modified for hits and assassinations, Nicoletti was released—which later allowed him to be involved in the fall 1963 assassination plots. US Senate hearings about what came to be known as Nicoletti's "hit car" show the lengths the Mafia would go to for even routine hits. According to the Senate hearings, Nicoletti and another mobster—both linked to narcotics by earlier cases—were caught hiding in "a 1962 Ford sedan"; "under the dashboard of this automobile were concealed three switches. Two of these switches enabled the operators of the car to disconnect the taillights. Without taillights, the police would have difficulty in following the car at night. The third switch . . . opened a hidden compartment in the back rest of the front seat . . . fitted with brackets to hold shotguns and rifles." It was also large enough "that a machine gun could be secreted in the compartment."[6] If Nicoletti and Rosselli's Chicago mob would go to that much trouble for routine hits, one can only imagine the lengths they would go to in preparing for JFK's assassination.

Meanwhile, the CIA's assassination plots with the Mafia continued, although a hitch developed that finally brought more details of the operation to the Kennedys, just as the Kennedys' own Mafia connection was boiling to the surface. An FBI memo confirms that in the spring of 1962, Bobby's Justice Department had to suppress the prosecution of an associate of Richard Cain, who had been wiretapping "Dan Rowan, member of Rowan and Martin comedy team" who was reportedly "engaged to Phyllis McGuire, girl friend of top hoodlum Sam Giancana and member of McGuire Sisters singing trio." While Rowan was a few years away from the superstardom of *Rowan and Martin's Laugh-In* TV show, the McGuire Sisters were then one of America's top singing groups. The prosecution of Cain's associate had to be suppressed to avoid exposing the CIA-Mafia plots to kill Castro.[7]

On May 7, 1962, CIA General Counsel Lawrence "Houston and the CIA's Director of Security, Colonel Sheffield Edwards, briefed the Attorney General about the details of the CIA-Mafia plot to kill Castro, including Rosselli's recent operational prominence."[8] There are indications that a year earlier, Bobby had learned in general terms about the CIA's use of Giancana during the Bay of Pigs, but it's unclear whether he knew that Giancana was involved in assassinations, or thought he was just helping to provide intelligence. In any event, the CIA admits that Bobby hadn't known that the plots had continued—or that the CIA would continue the plots after telling Bobby that they had stopped.

One of the CIA officials who met with Bobby, Director of Security Sheffield Edwards (James McCord's superior), testified later that "I talked with Johnny [Rosselli] on several occasions" about the CIA-Mafia plots to kill Castro. Edwards confirmed that "the plan was [originally] approved by Allen W. Dulles and General Cabell, his deputy." Edwards added that "I briefed Robert Kennedy, who cautioned . . . that he was to know about these things—words to that effect."[9] An FBI memo says that "on 5/9/62 [Bobby] Kennedy discussed with the Director [Hoover]" an "admission by CIA that" a Rosselli associate "had been hired by that Agency to approach Sam Giancana to have Castro assassinated at a cost of $150,000. Kennedy stated he had issued orders that CIA should never undertake such steps again without first checking with Department of Justice."[10]

Bobby Kennedy was no doubt angry that the unauthorized CIA operation had interfered with his war against the Mafia—although he would have been even more angry if he or JFK had found out that the CIA-Mafia plots were continuing without their knowledge. Bobby knew that mobsters could be the source of good intelligence, as he would demonstrate later in 1962 with Hoffa informant Grady Edward Partin, and in 1963 with the celebrated Joe Valachi hearings. Bobby himself would have a CIA agent meet with Mafia types regarding intelligence about Cuba in 1962. But Bobby didn't need the CIA to use the Mafia to assassinate Castro—Bobby had his own, much more extensive plan for dealing with the Cuban dictator, OPERATION MONGOOSE.

At the same time that Bobby was dealing with the CIA's revelations about the CIA-Mafia plots, a Mafia connection of the Kennedys was also boiling to the surface. J. Edgar Hoover was anxious not to meet the same fate as the FBN chief upon reaching mandatory retirement age. Historian Richard Mahoney notes that "on January 6, 1962 . . . columnist Drew Pearson predicted that the Attorney General would get rid of the FBI Director." So, on February 27, 1962, Hoover sent "a top-secret memorandum to" Bobby "that summarized Judith Campbell's telephone contact with the President as well as her association with Sam Giancana. A copy of the memo was also sent to a top JFK aide, saying 'I thought you would be interested in learning of the following information which was developed in connection with the investigation of John Rosselli.'" This led to "Hoover's lunch with the President on March 22," 1962, which a JFK aide described as "bitter" and "which went on for no less than four hours."

According to Mahoney, "the concession the [FBI] Director sought was confirmation in his post as head of the FBI."[11]

After the meeting, Hoover leaked a story about Campbell to "Walter Winchell's nationally syndicated column" that "finally surfaced on May 9, 1962: 'Judy Campbell of Palm Springs and Bevhills is Top No. 1 in Romantic Political Circles.'" Although the story didn't mention JFK, the message to the President and Bobby was clear, and "Hoover was confirmed in his position" as FBI Director.[12] Some have suggested that Hoover arranged JFK's assassination to keep the Kennedys from removing him; but with Hoover having such information, it would have been impossible for the Kennedys to ever fire him.

While Hoover got what he wanted, historian Richard D. Mahoney points out that "Hoover may have been manipulated . . . by" Johnny "Rosselli. First, Rosselli arranged the introduction of his former paramour and friend Judy Campbell to President Kennedy. Second, Rosselli knew about the FBI wiretap of his phone in his LA apartment, and therefore that his conversations would be transcribed and analyzed by federal authorities. He also knew of the war going on between the Attorney General and the FBI Director. Finally, Rosselli allowed Campbell to stay at his apartment when he was away from Los Angeles, which was often."[13] So Rosselli not only enabled the Mafia-compromised Hoover to stay on as FBI Director, but he also ensured that JFK and Bobby knew that he and Giancana had potential blackmail material on JFK. (It should be noted that Judy Campbell continuously embellished one aspect of her story over the years—about secret missions and messages between JFK, Giancana, and Rosselli—and has no evidence to support it, according to Johnny Rosselli's biographers.[14])

The other person in the Rosselli-Giancana-Campbell story was Frank Sinatra, the good friend of all three. According to Mahoney, "the day the [FBI] Director lunched with the President . . . Bobby called Jack and told him that he had to cease all contact with Frank Sinatra—that under no circumstances could he stay, as planned, at Sinatra's home in Palm Springs." "Sinatra . . . had installed twenty-five phone lines, built cottages for the Secret Service near his home, and even put a gold plaque in the bedroom where the President was to stay." After the President's brother-in-law Peter "Lawford informed Sinatra of the decision, the singer went berserk." He "picked up a sledgehammer and began smashing the concrete pad that had been specially built for the President's helicopter."[15] However, even without Sinatra—or an ongoing relationship between Campbell and JFK—to use as leverage against JFK, Rosselli still had one card left to play. JFK, and perhaps even Bobby, had another occasional lover who also knew Sam Giancana and Sinatra. This woman was far more famous than Judy Campbell, so getting the President or his brother into a compromising position or scandal with her would be even better for the Mafia. In May 1962 she sang "Happy Birthday, Mr. President" at a huge gala for JFK—but just over two months later, Marilyn Monroe would be dead.

If Jimmy Hoffa had had his way, Bobby Kennedy would have died around the same time as Marilyn Monroe. The House Select Committee on Assassinations (HSCA) found that "Hoffa and at least one of this Teamster lieutenants . . . did, in fact, discuss the planning of an assassination conspiracy against President Kennedy's brother Attorney General Robert F. Kennedy, in July or August of 1962. Hoffa's discussion about such an assassination plan first became known to the Federal Government in September 1962." Hoffa's lieutenant-turned-informant, Louisiana Teamster official Grady Edward Partin, passed an FBI lie detector test about the matter, and "the Justice Department developed further evidence . . . that Hoffa had spoken about the possibility of assassinating the President's brother on more than one occasion." Partin told the HSCA that "Hoffa had believed that having the Attorney General murdered would be the most effective way of ending the Federal Government's intense investigation of the Teamsters and organized crime."

The informant also said that "he suspected Hoffa may have approached him about the assassination proposal because Hoffa believed him to be close to various figures in Carlos Marcello's syndicate organization." The HSCA "noted the similarities between the plan discussed by Hoffa in 1962 and the actual events of November 22, 1963" such as "the possible use of a lone gunman equipped with a rifle with a telescopic sight, the advisability of having the assassination committed somewhere in the South, as well as the potential desirability of having Robert Kennedy shot while riding in a convertible." The HSCA notes that "references to Hoffa's discussion about having Kennedy assassinated while riding in a convertible were contained in several Justice Department memoranda received by the Attorney General and FBI Director Hoover in the Fall of 1962." Apparently, "Hoffa believed that by having Kennedy shot as he rode in a convertible, the origin of the fatal shot or shots would be obscured."[16] At that time, Hoffa was referring to shooting Bobby Kennedy, not JFK. But the basics would still be the same for JFK's assassination.

More details about Hoffa's plan to assassinate Bobby Kennedy came from Bobby's top Hoffa prosecutor, Walter Sheridan, who talked with Partin on many occasions. Sheridan also saw the parallels between what Hoffa had planned for Bobby and what happened to JFK. Sheridan told Dan Moldea it's "the kind of thing that makes you wonder. . . ." Kennedy would be shot to death from some distance away; a single gunman would be enlisted to carry it out—someone without any traceable connection to Hoffa and the Teamsters; a high-powered rifle with a telescopic sight would be the assassination weapon. According to Partin, "Hoffa had a .270 rifle leaning in the corner of his office and Hoffa said, 'I've got something right here which will shoot flat and long. . . .' The 'ideal setup,' Hoffa went on, would be 'to catch [Bobby] Kennedy somewhere in the South,'" and have someone to "throw investigators off the track by being blamed for the crime."[17]

Though Hoffa had been talking about killing Bobby Kennedy, the parallels with JFK's assassination are uncanny.

Is there any indication that Hoffa or his allies actually tried to put their plan to kill Bobby into effect in the summer of 1962? There is one documented instance of a threat against Bobby, but it's not in "the South," as we usually think of it, but rather southern California. Investigative journalist Anthony Summers—who first broke the now widely accepted story of JFK's affair with Marilyn Monroe—writes that "on July 26," 1962, "Robert Kennedy came to Los Angeles" to make "a speech to the National Insurance Association. At midday, as he was on his way to the engagement, the Los Angeles office of the FBI received an anonymous call, warning of a plan to kill him. The caller said 'gangland characters' were plotting the murder."[18] The person who made the call to the FBI has never been identified.

There was a person who had recently been with "gangland characters" who were associates of Hoffa, people who wanted to get rid of Bobby Kennedy, and this person might have wanted to warn Bobby. Writer Nick Tosches raised the possibility that the caller might have been Marilyn Monroe, who had been at Giancana's Cal-Neva lodge at Lake Tahoe just weeks earlier, and on July 26— the date of the anonymous call—Monroe was preparing to make another visit.[19] The official Nevada State Web site says that "Marilyn Monroe is known to have made her last visit to Lake Tahoe . . . during the weekend of July 27–29, 1962, just prior to her apparent suicide."[20]

Whether Monroe or someone she knew made the call about Bobby

Kennedy, it's evident that Monroe was subject to blackmail after that weekend, because of Sam Giancana. If Giancana, Rosselli, and other allies of Hoffa were the ones who had planned to kill Bobby Kennedy on July 26, they might have wanted to force Marilyn Monroe into some type of compromising situation, to force Bobby to back off.

Former Chicago FBI agent Bill Roemer writes that Sam "Giancana had been at Cal-Neva, the Lake Tahoe resort, with Frank Sinatra and Marilyn the week before she died. There, from what I had been able to put together, she engaged in an orgy. From the conversation I overheard, it appeared she may have had sex with both Sinatra and Giancana on the same trip." Unlike Marcello and Trafficante, one of Giancana's offices was bugged (one reason he couldn't have an active role in the JFK plot), and Roemer related a conversation in which Rosselli said to Giancana, 'You sure get your rocks off fucking the same broad as the brothers, don't you?'" Marilyn Monroe had been friends with Johnny Rosselli since the late 1950s, which put her in very dangerous company in the summer of 1962. Roemer goes on to say that Sam Giancana's younger brother later said that "unbeknown to" Marilyn, Sam Giancana "had orchestrated the invitation" to the Cal-Neva Lodge that weekend. The younger Giancana also confirmed that Sam boasted of having sex with Marilyn that weekend.[21] Marilyn had also been at Giancana's lodge four weeks earlier.

Marilyn's presence at Giancana's Cal-Neva Lodge on the weekend before her death has been confirmed by numerous witnesses found by Anthony Summers, ranging from the "Bell Captain" at the Cal-Neva to the co-pilot of Sinatra's private luxury plane, who flew Marilyn and Peter Lawford there. Summers found another witness who confirmed that Marilyn complained shortly before she died about "Peter Lawford because he was having orgies." In addition, "a film processor . . . says he developed pictures of Marilyn, taken by Frank Sinatra, that last weekend" that "showed Marilyn in utter disarray." Summers said that "Marilyn talked about the Cal-Neva visit to her masseur, Ralph Roberts. 'She told me it was a nightmare, a dreadful weekend,' Roberts recalls. 'She didn't want to go particularly.'"[22] She apparently called Joe DiMaggio for help, and DiMaggio "came to Lake Tahoe" but could "not actually enter the Cal-Neva 'because there was a feud between him and Sinatra at the time.'" A friend of DiMaggio's confirms that "She went up there, they gave her pills, they had sex parties."[23]

Even more ominously, Summers writes that "Paul (Skinny) D'Amato," who "represented Giancana's interests at the Cal-Neva Lodge, confirmed . . .

that Marilyn had been there just before she died." D'Amato also said "There was more to what happened than anyone has told. It would've been the big fall for Bobby Kennedy, wouldn't it?"[24] In the countless books written about Marilyn Monroe's death, one scenario that has received little attention is the possibility that Marilyn Monroe committed suicide because—in addition to her many emotional and professional problems—she was being pressured or blackmailed into compromising Bobby Kennedy. The photos taken of her that last weekend at Giancana's Cal-Neva Lodge would have made her subject to pressure from the Mafia, who might have wanted her to arrange one last meeting with Bobby Kennedy. In those days, a photo of Bobby Kennedy leaving Marilyn Monroe's house late at night would have been so explosive as to have forced the attorney general to resign, or it could have been used as blackmail to force him to back off his Mafia prosecutions. Summers writes that shortly before her death, Monroe had been "talking about her career to *Life* magazine" and "Marilyn had said, 'It might be kind of a relief to be finished. It's sort of like I don't know what kind of a yard dash you're running, but then you're at the finish line and you sort of sigh—you've made it! But you never have, you have to start all over again.'"[25]

Summers found that after Monroe returned from Giancana's Cal-Neva Lodge, "on July 30, 1962, Marilyn made her final call to the Justice Department, as logged in the surviving telephone records. The call lasted eight minutes, and she made it on the Monday of her last week alive."[26] Six days later, Monroe was dead. Summers notes that "by midmorning on the day after Monroe's death," the records of Marilyn's recent phone calls "were removed from the headquarters of General Telephone . . . by the FBI." This was confirmed to Anthony Summers by "the company's division Manager" and "a former senior FBI official." "If mobsters had hoped to use the Monroe connection to destroy Bobby Kennedy, they were thwarted by the successful cover-up" which "worked largely thanks to [J.] Edgar [Hoover]. By grabbing the telephone records on their behalf, he made the Kennedys more beholden to him than ever."[27] When the authors looked at Bobby Kennedy's phone logs in the National Archives—the same ones that list so many calls between Bobby and Harry Williams—the pages for the days just before and after Marilyn Monroe's death were missing, and had probably never been turned over to the Archives.

Perhaps in one more attempt to compromise the Kennedys—or simply to remind the Kennedys of what the Mafia knew—Summers notes that Rosselli's and Giancana's friend "Judith Campbell called the White House twice the next day—once in the afternoon and again in the evening," but "a note in the log indicates that [President] Kennedy was in conference with the scrawled addition 'No.'"[28] Information flowed to the Kennedys—in one case, from Trafficante's home base of Tampa—to make sure they didn't dig into Marilyn's death too deeply, or it could expose other things. Nick Tosches writes that "on August 16 [1962], J. Edgar Hoover sent a personal memorandum to" Bobby "Kennedy. It conveyed information Hoover had received from the FBI field office in Tampa: 'Before the last presidential election, Joseph P. Kennedy [the father of President John Kennedy] had been visited by many gangsters with gambling interests and a deal was made which resulted in Peter Lawford, Frank Sinatra, Dean Martin and others obtaining a lucrative gambling establishment, the Cal-Neva Hotel, at Lake Tahoe. These gangsters reportedly met with Joseph Kennedy at the Cal-Neva.'"[29]

There may have been one more attempt by Johnny Rosselli and Carlos Marcello to compromise the Kennedys, which is detailed here for the first time. A former anti-Castro activist, whose CIA and FBI files are extensive, claims that Bobby Kennedy actually met Johnny Rosselli on one occasion in Miami. The meeting occurred in "1962," sometime "before the Cuban Missile Crisis" of October 1962. The setting for this historic meeting was the distinctive houseboat used as the setting for the briefly popular TV series *Surfside Six*. The houseboat would later become infamous as the place where Gianni Versace's murderer Andrew Cunanan was captured.[30]

The man who is said to have introduced Bobby Kennedy to Johnny Rosselli was Sam Benton, a private investigator who worked for Carlos Marcello and also sometimes for Santo Trafficante. However, Bobby knew Benton as someone closely associated with a major gambling figure named Mike McLaney (also close to Trafficante and Ruby's friend Lewis McWillie). In 1962 and into 1963, McLaney was involved in a well-documented feud and legal dispute with the Kennedys' close friend Carroll Rosenbloom, a gambler who was the owner of the Baltimore Colts NFL football team.[31] A Bobby-Rosselli-Benton meeting could have been related to the problem between Rosenbloom and McLaney, since Bobby did meet with McLaney, and the NFL soon afterward hired someone Bobby had recommended to deal with gambling problems. It's also possible that a meeting between Bobby and Rosselli could have been related to the release of the Bay of Pigs prisoners, since Rosselli was a contributor to a failed 1962 attempt to ransom them.

The Mafia bosses would have had their own reason to engineer the meeting between Rosselli and Bobby Kennedy. It occurred around the time when the CIA had admitted to Bobby that they had continued the CIA-Mafia plots with Rosselli (though the CIA lied to Bobby when they said they had ever stopped), and when the Kennedys had broken off contact with Rosselli associates Frank Sinatra, Judy Campbell, and Marilyn Monroe. The meeting linked Bobby Kennedy directly to someone involved in the CIA-Mafia plots, and to the dark swirl of events intended to compromise or destroy the Kennedys. It also put Bobby in a face-to-face meeting with one of the mob bosses he was trying to destroy. This meeting might also explain why Bobby's Mafia prosecutors would fail to closely question Rosselli's boss, Sam Giancana, in court the following year when they had the opportunity. If pressed, Giancana could have opened up a Pandora's box about the CIA-Mafia plots and this meeting. Even though the CIA-Mafia plots had begun under Nixon, exposing the 1962 meeting between Bobby and Rosselli could have proven a major embarrassment for Attorney General Kennedy.

Shifting the Target to JFK

BY THE FALL OF 1962, evidence shows that the Mafia had taken a big step in its war against the Kennedys: Marcello and Trafficante were now talking to trusted associates about assassinating President Kennedy, not Bobby. Gone was the chance of stopping the Kennedys' onslaught against the mob bosses with anything short of assassination: Sinatra, Judy Campbell, and Marilyn Monroe were no longer possible sources of leverage against the Kennedys.

The JFK assassination plans that Trafficante and Marcello discussed with FBI informants were not reported to the Warren Commission, but were thoroughly investigated by the House Select Committee on Assassinations in the late 1970s, which found them credible. In addition, "the Committee's extensive investigation led it to conclude that the most likely family bosses of organized crime to have participated in" the JFK "assassination plan were Carlos Marcello and Santo Trafficante."[1] Information withheld by the CIA from the committee—like the existence of C-Day and its penetration by many associates of Marcello, Trafficante, and Rosselli—only buttresses the committee's findings.

Carlos Marcello made two documented statements about his plans to assassinate JFK, one that the committee knew about and one that came out only years after the House Select Committee had finished its work. Still, "the Committee found that Marcello had the motive, means, and opportunity to have President John F. Kennedy assassinated," although, without knowing about C-Day, "it was unable to establish direct evidence of Marcello's complicity."[2] As to how Marcello could plan even a small conspiracy without being detected, the committee found that "Marcello was never the subject of electronic surveillance coverage by the FBI." In addition, "the FBI determined in the 1960s that because of Marcello's position as head of the New Orleans Mafia family (the oldest in the United States, having first entered the country in the 1880s), the Louisiana organized crime leader had been endowed with special powers and privileges not accorded to any other Las Cosa Nostra members. As the leader of 'the first family' of the Mafia in America, according to FBI information, Marcello has been the recipient of the extraordinary privilege of conducting syndicate operations without having to seek the approval of the national commission."[3]

The best account of Marcello's fall 1962 statement about assassinating JFK comes from the biography of Johnny Rosselli. It says that "Ed Becker, a private investigator and free-lance businessman, was meeting with Marcello and his longtime associates Carlo Roppolo and Jack Liberto when their boss (Marcello) pulled out a bottle and poured a generous round of scotch. The conversation wandered until Becker made an off-hand remark about Bobby Kennedy and Marcello's deportation. The reference struck a nerve, and Carlos jumped to his feet, exclaiming the Sicilian oath, 'Livarsi na pietra di la scarpa!' (Take the stone out of my shoe!)." Marcello didn't speak Sicilian, but was repeating an old saying he had heard many times from those who did. "Reverting to English, Marcello shouted, 'Don't worry about that Bobby son-of-a-bitch. He's going to be taken care of.'"

Becker responded that killing Bobby would get Marcello "'into a hell of a lot of trouble.' In answer, "Marcello invoked an old Italian proverb: 'If you want to kill a dog, you don't cut off the tail, you cut off the head.'" Becker says the implication was that "Bobby was the tail" and "if the President were killed then Bobby would lose his bite. Marcello added that he had a plan, to use 'a nut' to take the fall for the murder . . . then Marcello abruptly changed the subject, and the Kennedys were not mentioned again."[4]

According to all accounts of the incident, "Becker related his encounter with Marcello to the FBI soon after the meeting, and well before the Kennedy assassination, but no action was taken by the Bureau." In addition, a "former FBI agent," named in Rosselli's biography, "who was familiar with Becker at the time, corroborates Becker's account."[5]

Marcello also made a later threat against JFK, which was only uncovered in 1988. His biographer says that "in the Spring of 1963," Marcello was "at his lodge" with "close friends from the old Sicilian families of New Orleans" one weekend. "While having a scotch with one of them in the kitchen," the friend "made a casual reference to an article he had read . . . about the Supreme Court upholding" Marcello's deportation order. "At the mention of

Bobby Kennedy's name, Carlos suddenly seemed to choke, spitting out his scotch on the floor. Recovering quickly, he formed the southern Italian symbol of . . . 'the horn,' with this left hand." "Holding the ancient symbol of hatred and revenge above his head, he shouted: 'Don't worry, man, 'bout dat Bobby. We goin' to take care a dat sonofabitch.'"

The friend asked if Marcello was going to "give it to Bobby," but Marcello replied "What good dat do? You hit dat man and his brother calls out the National Guard. No, you gotta hit de top man and what happen with de next top man? He don't like de brother." Marcello declared to his friend that "Sure as I stand here somethin' awful is gonna happen to dat man."[6]

Marcello knew that if he killed the Attorney General, JFK would order the National Guard or the Army into Marcello's compound, similar to what happened in Phenix City, Alabama, after Trafficante's associates killed the Alabama Attorney General-elect in 1954. This would render meaningless the political figures in Louisiana and elsewhere whom Marcello had corrupted and could usually rely on for protection. So, to Marcello and his associates, the answer was to kill JFK, not Bobby. The animosity between Bobby and LBJ—who would be the new president—was well known, and LBJ had never made prosecuting the Mafia any sort of priority.

History would prove Marcello's reasoning to be correct. According to historian Richard Mahoney, "As Bill Hundley, head of the [Justice Department's] Organized Crime Section, put it, 'The minute that bullet hit Jack Kennedy's head, it was all over. Right then. The organized crime program just stopped, and Hoover took control back.' Marcello had been right: Cut the dog's head off and the rest of it would die."[7] More confirmation for Marcello's approach comes from the FBI's "own electronic surveillance transcripts" of a "conversation between Sam Giancana and a lieutenant" two weeks after JFK's death, in which the lieutenant told Giancana: 'I will tell you something, in another 2 months from now, the FBI will be like it was 5 years ago."[8] The Mafia wanted a return to the "good old days" of the 1950s, before the Kennedys and when J. Edgar Hoover and Richard Nixon could be counted on not to press them. Killing JFK was the only way to achieve that.

In the fall of 1962, around the time of Marcello's first mention of a plan to assassinate JFK, Trafficante made a similar comment to an associate named Jose Aleman, who was on the fringe of the 1959 CIA-Mafia plots. Trafficante confirmed to Congressional investigators that he knew Aleman, and acknowledged having met with him about business approximately three times, although some accounts put the number much higher.[9]

Aleman's family had long-standing Mafia ties; William Turner notes that Jose Aleman's grandfather "had been Lucky Luciano's lawyer in Havana." Aleman's family had recently helped Jimmy Hoffa gain control of a Miami bank that Hoffa could use to launder money from his criminal activities. Also, Aleman also knew Rolando Cubela, the disgruntled mid-level Cuban official and CIA asset.[10] In later testimony to the House Select Committee on Assassinations (HSCA), Aleman said: "Mr. Cubela . . . I talked to him many times to do something against the regime of Castro."[11] Aleman was referring to talks he had with Cubela in 1959, the year Trafficante also met with Cubela while Trafficante was in jail in Cuba.

According to the *Washington Post*, Jose "Aleman had been a rich young revolutionary in Havana" whose "considerable wealth" included "Miami real estate, including the Miami Stadium." But after losing "his land holdings in Cuba to the revolution" and the death of his father, Aleman "was forced to sell the Miami Stadium" and other Miami real estate, except for "the three story . . . motel" where Aleman would meet with Trafficante in 1962. By the fall of that year, Aleman "was in debt," though his contacts and reputation could still be of use to someone like Trafficante, who was always looking for seemingly legitimate fronts for money-laundering and other scams.[12] The *Post* notes that "Aleman . . . became involved with Trafficante in 1962 through his cousin, (Rafael) Garcia Bango," who was a "resourceful lawyer" for Trafficante.[13] (In 1965, the CIA learned that Trafficante's attorney, Bango, knew about Cubela's plot with the CIA to assassinate Castro.)

Aleman testified under oath to the HSCA that in 1962, an associate of Trafficante "came to me and he said Santo wants to meet you." Aleman said he was initially reluctant, since he "had to testify against Santo's people in 1960," in a complex case involving Trafficante associates like "Norman Rothman." Rothman, the gun-running associate of Jack Ruby mentioned earlier, had been involved in the 1959 CIA-Mafia plots. Aleman had been a reluctant witness against Rothman, and his testimony had not been especially damaging. Aleman said that "in spite of" his initial "reluctance," he did "ultimately go to . . . meetings with Trafficante."[14]

"Aleman said that Trafficante" made the threat against JFK as "part of a long conversation that lasted from sometime during the day until late at night."[15] Aleman said "the conversation" with Trafficante "came about because" Bango (a distant cousin of Aleman) had helped to get "someone out

of a Cuban jail" and Trafficante "wanted to help Aleman get out of his financial difficulties in return."[16] To the Congressional investigators, "Aleman
attempted to explain why" Trafficante "would have contact with him, much
less offer him assistance, in view of the fact that Aleman had testified for the
State in the Rothman trial. Aleman said he explicitly told" Trafficante about
"his adverse testimony" against Rothman, but Trafficante "laughed out loud
and said not to worry about it, that it didn't matter at all."[17] According to the
Washington Post, Aleman had been subpoenaed by the FBI to testify against
Rothman, and Aleman "tried to avoid testifying, but the FBI reminded him
that, if he did not cooperate, he might be subject to prosecution for illegal
gunrunning."[18]

According to the *Washington Post*, "Aleman . . . had at least three meetings
with Trafficante."[19] Trafficante and Aleman "had been in contact with each
other for some time, and Trafficante had offered to arrange a million-dollar loan
for Aleman . . . from the Teamsters Union" which "had 'already been cleared by
Jimmy Hoffa himself.' It was natural that the conversation turned to Hoffa when
Trafficante met Aleman at the Cott-Bryant Hotel in Miami in September 1962."
Aleman told HSCA investigators that Trafficante complained about JFK, saying
"have you seen how his brother is hitting Hoffa . . . mark my word, this man
Kennedy is in trouble and he will get what is coming to him.' When Aleman disagreed with Trafficante and said he thought . . . Kennedy would be re-elected,"
Trafficante said "You don't understand me. Kennedy's not going to make it to the
election. He is going to be hit." Aleman told the government investigators "that
Trafficante 'made it clear . . . he was not guessing about the killing, rather he was
giving the impression that he knew Kennedy was going to be killed.' Aleman
said he was 'given the distinct impression that Hoffa was to be principally
involved in the elimination of Kennedy.'"[20]

According to historian Richard Mahoney, "Aleman later maintained that
he reported this comment to two Miami FBI agents."[21] Another historian
confirmed that, saying that, "Disturbed by what had transpired at that
meeting, Aleman immediately began informing on Trafficante to" two FBI
agents at "the FBI's Miami Field Office. Trafficante had offered to get him a
loan from Jimmy Hoffa's Teamsters Union, Aleman told the FBI and . . . Trafficante had mentioned, in passing, that because of the Kennedy administration's harassment of certain individuals, JFK was finished. According to
Aleman, Trafficante had said simply, 'He is going to be hit.' Such words
would seem ominous enough in hindsight, but Trafficante's hints were
apparently judged mere gangland braggadocio."

The historian goes on to write that "although, thirty years later, Aleman's accusations would resist positive confirmation, with Bureau records of his debriefings remaining classified," one of the Miami FBI agents, "when advised of Aleman's allegations, would affirm: 'He's a reliable individual.'"[22] The *Washington Post* notes that "Aleman's relationship with the FBI had initially been hostile," but "after his testimony in the Rothman trial, Aleman's relationship with the Bureau grew very close. The FBI men came to rely on him." A retired FBI agent said that Aleman "is a real nice fellow . . . he's a reliable individual."[23]

Part of Trafficante's plan to kill JFK included C-Day and Cuba, which would raise the possibility to high US officials that Castro had killed JFK in response to C-Day or the CIA's Castro assassination attempts. As we document in later chapters, this would prevent a thorough investigation of JFK's assassination, to protect C-Day. Trafficante associates John Martino and Rolando Masferrer would be involved in spreading such stories, and there would even be reports linked to David Morales of a shadowy Cuban agent following JFK as he went to Chicago, Tampa, and Dallas.

Perhaps having learned of Aleman's contacts with the FBI by the summer of 1963, Trafficante used Aleman to lay the groundwork for those stories. In a part of Aleman's story long overlooked by most investigators, the *Washington Post* reported that by the summer of 1963, Aleman said "he got little interest from the FBI when" he started telling them that "three Cubans he had known in Havana appeared in Miami, and then left for Texas. Aleman suspected them of being Cuban agents and, he later said, told this to the Bureau. 'I advised the FBI in long conversations that I thought something was going to happen,' Aleman said. 'I was telling them to be careful.'"[24]

The House Select Committee found Aleman and Trafficante's threats credible. "The Committee found that Santo Trafficante's stature in the national syndicate of organized crime, notably the violent narcotics trade, and his role as the mob's chief liaison to criminal figures within the Cuban exile community, provided him with the capability of formulating an assassination conspiracy against President Kennedy."[25] In addition, the HSCA's "examination of the FBI's electronic surveillance program of the early 1960s disclosed that Santo Trafficante was the subject of minimal, in fact almost nonexistent, surveillance coverage. During one conversation in 1963, overheard in a Miami restaurant, Trafficante had bitterly attacked the Kennedy administration's efforts against organized crime, making obscene comments about 'Kennedy's right-hand man'" who had recently coordinated various raids on

Trafficante gambling establishments. In the conversation, Trafficante stated that he was under immense pressure from Federal investigators, commenting "I know when I'm beat, you understand."[26] Like Marcello and Rosselli, Trafficante felt like he had been backed into a corner by the Kennedys, and so had nothing to lose by trying to assassinate JFK.

Nothing else had worked, not even trying to intimidate Bobby's Justice Department prosecutors. Ronald Goldfarb—one of those Mafia prosecutors—writes that he "had been looking into a potential case in Tampa, Florida involving a local underworld character . . . it produced the only moment when I experienced personal threat. In the middle of the night, upon returning from an investigation in Tampa, I was awakened by a caller, purporting to be from Tampa. He said, gruffly: 'Tell your wife to come outside, Mr. Goldfarb.'" Goldfarb reported the call to his superior at Justice, "who contacted the FBI; fortunately, nothing more happened."

It's unfortunate that the CIA had withheld information on C-Day from the HSCA, or the whole JFK assassination plot might have been unraveled at that time. Also, the HSCA did not look as closely at Johnny Rosselli as it did at Trafficante and Marcello, which meant that they were missing yet another crucial piece of the puzzle.

It should also be noted that the fact that the Marcello and Aleman threats were reported to the FBI doesn't mean that J. Edgar Hoover was part of the JFK assassination plot. At that time, the FBI was having to deal with thousands of pieces of information about the Mafia—dealing with it seriously for the first time, because of Bobby Kennedy—and it's only in hindsight that the threats take on crucial significance. (Hoover was concerned when he learned that Marcello's threat was going to appear in a book in the late 1960s.) Also, J. Edgar Hoover was actually planning to try to take over presidential protection from the Secret Service in late 1963, so it would have been in his interest to use the threats to help accomplish that. Instead, Hoover and his FBI were left embarrassed by their actions concerning Oswald, and any thoughts Hoover had of trying to move presidential protection to the FBI were abandoned.

While it may seem unusual for people like Marcello and Trafficante to think about assassinating a US president, they and their associates like Rosselli hadn't hesitated to kill heads of state (the president of Guatemala and Trujillo, dictator of the Dominican Republic) or other officials who got in their way. Also, assassination attempts against heads of state were in the headlines quite often in the early 1960s. In addition to occasional reports of assassination attempts against Castro, which Trafficante and Rosselli some-times assisted in their work for the CIA, there were many others that an avid newspaper-reader like Trafficante would have known about in the fall of 1962. In the previous two and a half years, there had been over a dozen attempted assassinations of heads of state, and three successful ones.[27]

Of special interest to Trafficante and Marcello would have been several widely reported attempts to assassinate French President Charles de Gaulle, including those on May 25, 1962 and August 22, 1962. The latter attempt helped inspire the novel *Day of the Jackal* and involved a former associate of Michel Victor Mertz, Trafficante's French Connection heroin kingpin. There had been an earlier attempt to assassinate de Gaulle on September 8, 1961, which was stopped by Mertz himself, while Mertz was working undercover for the French Secret Service (SDECE). Saving de Gaulle gave Mertz even more clout with French intelligence, and apparently kept Mertz's name out of US Congressional hearings in the early 1960s, even though all of his close associates were exposed.[28]

An earlier assassination that attracted much attention was that of the Congo's Patrice Lumumba on January 17, 1961. Lumumba had originally been targeted by the European assassin recruiter code-named QJWIN as part of the CIA's ZRRIFLE "Executive Action" program.[29] CIA asset QJWIN had numerous parallels to Michel Victor Mertz, which are documented in a later chapter. By 1962 and 1963, ZRRIFLE and QJWIN were being used by the CIA for their Castro assassination plots with the Mafia, a fact that Trafficante could exploit in his plot to kill JFK.[30]

The CIA-Mafia Plots, Operation Mongoose, Plans to Invade, and the Cuban Missile Crisis

IMPORTANT NEW INFORMATION ABOUT THE Cuban Missile Crisis continues to emerge, even after more than forty years. For example, historians now know that the tactical nuclear weapons in Cuba were under local control, meaning that a quick military strike by the US—as advocated by the Joint Chiefs and many others at the time—would certainly have triggered a nuclear war. Still overlooked until recently by many historians are the roles that the CIA-Mafia plots and US invasion plans may have played in triggering the crisis. In addition, US actions against Cuba in the summer and fall of 1962, which included the Kennedys' OPERATION MONGOOSE as well as the CIA's Castro assassination plots with the Mafia, are important because they laid the groundwork for C-Day and the Mafia penetration of it. The way C-Day was structured and run by Bobby Kennedy was designed to minimize many of the problems the Kennedys had encountered in 1962.

In the summer of 1962, as in 1963, the Kennedys were running their own program to eliminate Castro, using the military and the CIA, while some in the CIA were running their own Castro assassination operations without telling the Kennedys. In each case, problems resulted when the CIA assassination operation disrupted the Kennedys' plans. The Kennedys' OPERATION MONGOOSE was a loose collection of actions directed at Cuba, which included support for exile groups, sabotage, and plans for military action. It was coordinated by the CIA's General Edwin Lansdale, but was backed by the Kennedys, the US military, and the National Security Council. Lansdale was considered a maverick within the CIA, and had been the real-life basis for both Graham Greene's *The Quiet American* and William J. Lederer and Eugene Burdick's *The Ugly American*.[1] As an outsider, Lansdale was not part of Richard Helms's ongoing CIA-Mafia plots, and neither was CIA Director John McCone.

MONGOOSE had started at the end of 1961, but by June of 1962 it was producing no real results. Perhaps that's why Helms and William Harvey used Johnny Rosselli and Tony Varona to send an assassination team into Cuba on June 21, 1962.[2] That was just six weeks after the CIA had officially told Bobby Kennedy about the CIA-Mafia plots and had assured him that they had been stopped, as was noted in Chapter 35. Varona reported that the assassination team had made it into Cuba, but, according to the CIA, they were never heard from again.

In addition to the CIA-Mafia plots, the CIA was juggling a variety of other anti-Castro plots in the summer of 1962, like ZRRIFLE with European assassin recruiter QJWIN. There were also plots with the many CIA-backed Cuban exile groups. Historian Richard Mahoney notes with concern that the many CIA assassination operations had "brought together Cuban mob henchmen like Eladio del Valle and Rolando Masferrer—both Trafficante couriers" with Trafficante bagman Frank Fiorini and "CIA case officers like . . . David Morales."[3] Del Valle was also close to David Ferrie, who would be involved with Masferrer the following year in penetrating C-Day for Trafficante and the JFK assassination plot.[4]

Some historians believe that despite CIA documents and testimony to the contrary, the Kennedys must have known about—or have been directing— the CIA's assassination plotting, and that it must have been part of OPERATION MONGOOSE. However, a MONGOOSE planning meeting in August 1962 seems to make it clear that most US officials involved didn't realize that the CIA was involved in ongoing efforts to assassinate Castro. Historian Richard Mahoney writes that at a "meeting in [Secretary of State] Rusk's office on August 10," 1962, "Secretary of Defense Robert McNamara . . . got up to leave and voiced an opinion that 'the only way to take care of Castro is to kill him. I really mean it.'"[5]

Bobby Kennedy was absent from that particular meeting, but CIA Director John McCone was angered by the suggestion that Castro be assassinated. Mahoney writes that "later, [General] Lansdale referred to 'the liquidation of leaders' in a memorandum to the group." CIA officer "[William] Harvey described" putting such things in writing "as 'stupidity.' [Richard] Helms agreed with Harvey."[6] *Newsweek* editor Evan Thomas notes the irony that for Lansdale to mention "liquidation" in a memo, he must not have known about the ongoing CIA-Mafia plots. On the other hand, the two men who objected to having it in writing—Helms and Harvey—were running the plots, without authorization from Lansdale, McCone, or the Kennedys.[7]

There were other unauthorized CIA actions just before and during the Missile Crisis. Congressional investigator Gaeton Fonzi found that in early September 1962, "when only Washington's intelligence insiders were aware of a brewing Cuban missile crisis, Maurice Bishop directs Alpha 66 leader Antonio Veciana to launch a commando attack on . . . two Cuban cargo vessels." Fonzi says the Bishop alias was used by David Atlee Phillips, and on "October 8, 1962, under the strategic direction of Maurice Bishop, Antonio Veciana orders commandos of Alpha 66 to attack Soviet merchant ships in Havana harbor."[8]

In the days before the Cuban Missile Crisis became public, these were extraordinarily provocative acts, seemingly designed to provoke a response from the Soviets or Cubans that would justify an all-out US attack on Cuba. It fits a pattern that Phillips would continue to use with Alpha 66 throughout 1963—when it was allied with Menoyo's C-Day exile group, the SNFE—and even in the days following JFK's assassination. Phillips would try to take advantage of situations, by manipulating events or information, to prompt a US invasion of Cuba at times when only a few officials were aware that such invasion plans were already under discussion.

In the summer of 1962, most of the Bay of Pigs prisoners were still in Cuban jails, including Manuel Artime. Harry Williams and some other injured prisoners had been released in an attempt to jump-start talks with the US to get the rest ransomed, but those efforts stalled during the summer, as the Kennedys focused on toppling Fidel with OPERATION MONGOOSE. As part of that effort, a huge variety of Cuban exile groups was getting a massive amount of support from the CIA at this time. They included the Cuban Revolutionary Council of Tony Varona, Manolo Ray's JURE, and Eloy Menoyo's SNFE (and its close affiliate, Alpha 66), but they also included hundreds of others. *Washington Post* editor Jefferson Morley writes that "In Miami the DRE-in-Exile quickly attracted the support of CIA covert operations officers such as David Phillips and Howard Hunt."[9] Morley says that the DRE "won headlines around the world for sensational actions such as attempting to assassinate Castro outside a Havana hotel in August 1962." The DRE had grown out of the DR, a revolutionary group originally founded by Cuban official Rolando Cubela—and the CIA resumed its contact with Cubela in the summer of 1962.

OPERATION MONGOOSE was in many ways a very unfocused, uncoordinated plan, which Sy Hersh said "cost American taxpayers at least $100 million." He said that "its ambitions, outlined by [General] Lansdale in a series of top-secret documents in early 1962," indicated that "there were to be six phases to the elimination of Castro and his regime, moving from guerrilla operations by midsummer to open revolt in the first two weeks of October [1962]. In one paper Lansdale set a target date of October 20, 1962, for the installation of a new Cuban government."[10]

According to Sy Hersh, "Pentagon . . . planners had been instructed to prepare for a pitched battle in Cuba in the fall of 1962, in the event" MONGOOSE "paid off and Cuba was in revolt . . . hundreds of thousands of American soldiers and sailors took part in military exercises in the Caribbean, under the watchful eye of Cuban intelligence. In August more than 65,000 men participated in OPERATION SWIFT STRIKE II, obviously meant to simulate an attack on an island like Cuba. Later, 7,500 US Marines conducted a mock invasion of an island near Puerto Rico named 'Ortsac'—Castro spelled backwards. In the fall of 1962, the Pentagon was ordered to begin prepositioning troops and materiel for a massive invasion of Cuba. If the President so ordered, an estimated 100,000 troops in military bases along the East Coast could hit the beaches of Cuba in eight days."[11] This plan gives an idea of what was in store for C-Day, the following year.

Hersh quotes a Naval Institute Oral History by "Admiral Robert Dennison, commander in chief of the Atlantic Fleet," who said he had "five army divisions and the Second Marine Division, reinforced by elements of the First Marine Division" for a Cuban invasion in the fall of 1962 that would "require Naval and Air Force support." He said the "plans were approved by the Joint Chiefs of Staff and . . . were known to the President." However, unlike C-Day the following year, effective plans for a viable post-invasion government in 1962 were lacking; the Admiral said that "having captured Cuba and occupied it, the United States would have had a terrible problem in rehabilitation, establishing a government."[12]

This was before the Cuban Missile Crisis, so it is not in reaction to the crisis, and in fact may have helped precipitate it. Hersh quotes Yale historian John Lewis Gaddis, who said in 1997 that "given the unprecedented level of American military activity in the Caribbean in the months and particularly the weeks before the [Cuban Missile] crisis broke, it seems foolish to claim that the next step [invading Cuba] would never have been taken—especially if one of the CIA's many assassination plots against Castro had actually succeeded."[13]

As with C-Day, Bobby Kennedy took a leading role in all this planning, but personality clashes constantly hampered his efforts. Historian David

Corn writes that "Harvey and Lansdale could not stand one another. More serious was the enmity between Harvey and the Cuban show's true overseer, Bobby Kennedy." In private, "Harvey routinely referred to Kennedy as 'that fucker.' He criticized the Kennedy brothers as 'fags' who did not have the guts to take on Castro" and "in one White House meeting . . . offered the observation that those in attendance wouldn't be in this goddamn pickle if the Kennedy brothers had displayed balls in earlier days."[14]

Foreshadowing CIA concerns about Bobby and the C-Day exile leaders, David Corn writes that at the huge Miami CIA Station in 1962, "there was real fear that Bobby Kennedy was too close to the exiles. [Station Chief] Ted Shackley sent into Cuba an agent who had met Bobby Kennedy in Washington" so the agent could "evaluate resistance groups on the island." The agent was captured, and the CIA "received reports the agent was undergoing torture. [CIA] Station officers feared he might tell the Cubans of his encounter with the President's brother," and "any public statement along such lines would embarrass the White House."

"The agent was tried and executed, and when the Miami station received a report on the trial, its officers let out a collective sigh" because "their man had not talked."[15] In light of that concern, one can only image how serious things were the following year, when—on November 22, 1963—several high CIA officials met with Harry Williams, on the day he was leaving for a secret meeting inside Cuba with the C-Day coup leader.

According to some current historians, the Cubans reacted to the steady buildup of US action against Cuba in the summer of 1962 by requesting protection from the Soviets. In response, the Soviets sent missiles to Cuba, thus sparking the Cuban Missile Crisis at the very time the original OPERATION MONGOOSE timetable had designated for toppling Castro, October 1962. But an unauthorized assassination mission by CIA officer William Harvey could have triggered World War III—and the resulting personnel shuffle after the Missile Crisis would have an enormous impact on the Mafia penetration of C-Day and on JFK's assassination.

Richard Helms's biographer, Thomas Powers, writes:

> at the height of the Missile Crisis Bobby Kennedy told [CIA Director] McCone that he wanted an immediate halt to all operations against Cuba, and McCone passed on the order to [William] Harvey. But . . . on October

21 [1962], the day before President Kennedy announced a blockade of Cuba in a television speech, a CIA team headed by Eugenio Martinez [a future Watergate burglar] landed two agents on the northern coast of Cuba. At least one other team made a similar landing the same night. Later, at a meeting of the NSC executive committee . . . Harvey was asked if all operations had been halted. "Well," he said, "all but one." He told them several agents had already landed, there was no way to communicate with them, and thus no way to recall them.[16]

Another account of one of William Harvey's teams was uncovered by the New York *Daily News*, which quoted "intelligence sources" as saying:

The CIA sent an execution squad into Oriente Province in [early] November 1962 to ambush Castro near Santiago de Cuba as he drove to a memorial service for his fallen guerrillas. Snipers hid among trees and bushes lining the road to the cemetery where the service was to be held. On the morning of the scheduled ceremony, a motorcade of five jeeps approached the graveyard . . . machine guns and rifles sprayed the second jeep with bullets, killing the driver and his passenger, who turned out to be Castro's lookalike bodyguard, Capt. Alfredo Gamonal. The assassins escaped.[17]

Bobby Kennedy was livid that William Harvey had sent two teams into Cuba, at the most tense moments of the Cuban Missile Crisis, without authorization. Action by either team after a deal had been reached with the Soviets could have been disastrous. Thomas Powers says that CIA Director "McCone wanted to fire" William Harvey in late 1962, but "Helms talked him out of it, and the following year [1963] had Harvey assigned as Chief of Station in Rome."[18] William Harvey was the CIA's main link with Johnny Rosselli and QJWIN, and Harvey's replacement in the CIA assassination plots was David Morales, who was even closer to Johnny Rosselli.

Morales was chosen because of his experience, which included CIA assassination plotting in 1954 in Guatemala and running operations at the Havana CIA station when the 1959 CIA-Mafia plots were first developed. After leaving Cuba in 1960, Morales had been involved in training special teams for the Bay of Pigs, and by early 1963 he was the Operations Chief for the CIA's huge Miami CIA Station, code-named JMWAVE.

William Harvey retained some contact with Rosselli and QJWIN in the spring and early summer of 1963, but responsibility for at least Rosselli gradually shifted to Morales as the year progressed. This would mean that even as Rosselli was finalizing the JFK assassination plot with Marcello and Trafficante in the summer and fall of 1963, Rosselli was often in the company of the CIA's David Morales.

After the Missile Crisis, Bobby Kennedy focused on working with Harry Williams to get the Bay of Pigs prisoners released. Even that effort had been penetrated by the Mafia, specifically Johnny Rosselli. According to historian Richard Mahoney, "former Eisenhower Ambassador (and Flying Tiger co-founder) William D. Pawley, who had become a sort of godfather of Cuban exiles in south Florida, approached Kennedy through aide Richard Goodwin. Pawley wanted to raise money to pay the ransom of the imprisoned Bay of Pigs fighters through the sale of Cuban government bonds. It was a venture long on creative quality and short on financial sense, but Kennedy looked at it. One of the major subscribers was Johnny Rosselli," but "it is not known whether Bobby Kennedy knew Rosselli was a subscriber."[19] If he did, that might be one reason that particular plan wasn't pursued.

Before leaving the Missile Crisis and its aftermath, it's important to look at the actions of Lee Harvey Oswald in the fall of 1962. Oswald, seemingly an ex-Marine defector, had left the Soviet Union with his Russian wife Marina and returned to Texas in June 1962. Congressional investigator Gaeton Fonzi notes that on "October 11, 1962," Lee Harvey "Oswald is hired by . . . a Dallas photographic firm that has a contract with the US Army Map Service which involves information obtained from U-2 spy flights."[20] Less than two weeks later, similar maps will become well known throughout the world, as President Kennedy and UN Ambassador Adlai Stevenson use them to show the world the existence of Soviet missiles in Cuba. Defense Intelligence Agency (DIA) head General Carroll is credited with the analysis of the U-2 photos that uncovered the missiles. Working at a firm that prepared the wording for U-2 maps would be perfect for Oswald's role as an intelligence "dangle" for the DIA's Office of Naval Intelligence. As described by Edward Epstein, the firm did "highly classified work" involving "lists of names of cities and areas in the Soviet Union, China and Cuba which were" going to appear on maps based on the U-2 photos. "Oswald had complete access to the worktables on which the secret lists of place-names for the Army Map Service were kept," including when "Cuban names" appeared "on the list" during the Cuban Missile Crisis.[21]

It was no doubt hoped that Oswald's employment at such a firm—especially at such a sensitive time—would make him an irresistible target for

KGB agents to try to recruit. As we document shortly, Oswald was under "tight" surveillance by Naval Intelligence (with the assistance of other US agencies), and any such approach would be carefully monitored and would allow the US to find out how the KGB recruited American assets.

Such an intelligence role for Oswald also explains why the employment of a recent Soviet defector at a firm that set type for U-2 spy-plane maps aroused no concern on the part of US intelligence agencies or the FBI, even at the height of the Missile Crisis. Only four days before Oswald got his job at the U-2 map firm, Congressional investigator Gaeton Fonzi found that Oswald had first met a US intelligence asset who would become Oswald's best friend in Dallas for several months. Oswald's mother said this man— George De Mohrenschildt—had "already arranged a job for her son in Dallas."[22] The intelligence connections of De Mohrenschildt—and the unusual "friendship" of this cultured and aristocratic White Russian with Lee Oswald—are documented in an upcoming chapter.

The actions of US intelligence and Oswald regarding his job at the firm that helped with U-2 maps, and Oswald's strange friendship with De Mohrenschildt, have been seen as conspiratorial by some—but they make perfect sense when viewed in the light of Cold War tensions and the US intelligence connections of those involved. It was the responsibility of US intelligence to uncover the KGB network that recruited Americans, and they would have been remiss in their responsibilities if they had not tried to use valuable assets like Oswald. Such activities were clearly authorized by US officials, and were in the national interest. However, the KGB didn't try to approach either Oswald or his wife Marina; and by the end of the year, Oswald's use as a "dangle" at the map firm had produced no tangible results for US intelligence. Perhaps Oswald's background could make him more useful in a different assignment.

1962 ended on a high note for the Kennedys: The remaining Bay of Pigs prisoners were released, and JFK had redeemed himself from the Bay of Pigs fiasco by his strong performance during the Missile Crisis. To America and the world, JFK had forced the Soviets to back down, bringing the world back from the brink of nuclear war. Cuba was finally off the front pages, and it's easy to see why JFK and his officials didn't want to remind the world—and especially the Soviets and the Cubans—that the lack of UN inspections for nuclear weapons of mass destruction prevented a true end to the crisis. OPER-

ATION MONGOOSE was over, but the Kennedys weren't finished with Cuba. Something would have to be done with the newly released Cuban exile prisoners, including their leaders like Manuel Artime. As noted earlier, JFK's remark at the Orange Bowl ceremony about returning the Cuban brigade's flag in a free Havana had not been planned, but JFK intended to try to make it a reality. Bobby Kennedy would play an even bigger role in Cuban operations in the coming year, juggling that responsibility with his role as attorney general.

Unfortunately, the CIA continued to deal with mobsters like Rosselli without telling the Kennedys, setting the stage for disaster in 1963.

1963: Targeting Castro and the Mob Targeting JFK

AS 1963 DAWNED, THE KENNEDYS were ready to deliver their final assault on the Mafia and were developing a new strategy against Castro after the quiet failure of OPERATION MONGOOSE. They thought their two wars—against Castro and the Mafia—were separate and tried to keep them that way, but the Mafia had been working on the CIA's Castro assassination plots far too long for that to be possible. From the perspective of Marcello, Trafficante, and Rosselli, the time period of January 1963 to late October 1963 can be divided into two parts: For the first five months, they made plans to assassinate JFK—and prevent a thorough investigation—by using their ties to the CIA-Mafia anti-Castro plots and other US intelligence operations and assets. Starting in mid-May 1963, their plans would change as C-Day started to develop and the Mafia bosses could infiltrate a plan actually controlled by the Kennedys. However, the historical record shows that the mob chieftains had been making extensive plans to kill JFK well before C-Day gave them an even better opportunity.

In 1963, the Kennedys increased their already intense pressure on Marcello, Trafficante, and Rosselli, as well as Rosselli's boss Sam Giancana and Jimmy Hoffa. Marcello's biographer notes that on May 27, 1963, the US "Supreme Court . . . declined to review the Marcello deportation action," which was "prominently reported in the New Orleans papers" and "meant that all Carlos's appeals were exhausted." With that defeat, "the pressure" on Marcello to take action against the Kennedys in order to preserve his freedom and his empire "increased many times over."[1] The other mob bosses faced similar pressure due to the Kennedys in 1963.

Santo Trafficante faced ever-increasing scrutiny from the Kennedys, who busted his operations and made increasing use of IRS tax liens against him. Bobby had also made the very private and reclusive Trafficante the focus of major Congressional hearings.[2] Finally, the Kennedys had broken what Trafficante considered an unwritten law by subpoenaing Trafficante's wife. Trafficante did plenty of philandering, but godfathers' wives had been considered "off limits" during the previous decade.

Johnny Rosselli was still dogged by the FBI—except when he was working for the CIA—and his boss, Sam Giancana, was put under "lockstep" surveillance by the FBI at the urging of Bobby Kennedy, crippling Giancana's ability to function (and preventing him from having an active role in JFK's assassination).[3] Rosselli's power in Las Vegas and Hollywood flowed from his high position with the Chicago mob, so unless Rosselli could eliminate Bobby's pressure on Giancana, Rosselli's own future looked dim. Rosselli continued his close relationship with Frank Sinatra and "in 1963" Rosselli "was sponsored for membership in" the exclusive "Friar's Cub in Beverly Hills . . . by Frank Sinatra and Dean Martin," according to crime writer Ed Reid.[4] But Sinatra could no longer help Rosselli with the Kennedys, since the Kennedys had broken with Sinatra the previous year.

Even Rosselli's work for the CIA on the CIA-Mafia plots to kill Castro didn't give Rosselli any leverage with Bobby, since the plots had begun before JFK was elected and the CIA had assured Bobby and CIA Director McCone that the plots had ended; however, CIA officials at the level of Richard Helms, William Harvey, and David Morales were continuing the plots to kill Castro with Rosselli in the spring, summer, and fall of 1963. Rosselli's ongoing work with the CIA gave Rosselli access to contacts and information that would be useful in the JFK assassination.[5]

In 1963, Rosselli's associates continued to successfully assassinate government officials. According to investigative journalist Dan Moldea, a "close friend of [Jack] Ruby" was "credited by law enforcement officials with the murder of" Chicago alderman "Benjamin F. Lewis." The Chicago official was found dead on "February 28, 1963 . . . face down in a four-foot-wide pool of blood" after "the back of his head had been shot off by three bullets." His assassination was "the 977th unsolved underworld hit in Chicago since the early 1900s."[6]

It was clear that Rosselli and his associates wouldn't hesitate to kill JFK. But if Rosselli, Marcello, and Trafficante could find a trusted ally, to spread the risk and the expense, so much the better. One person who fit the bill was Jimmy Hoffa.

Hoffa also faced a barrage of charges and prosecutions in 1963. Hoffa's lawyer, Frank Ragano—who also worked for Trafficante—explained how Hoffa came to back the JFK assassination plot of Trafficante and Marcello. Ragano wrote that "in the first months of 1963, Jimmy [Hoffa] was consumed by the prospect of looming indictments and his animosity to the Kennedys. A day rarely went by without him unleashing his customary obscenities at 'Booby,' his unflattering sobriquet for the Attorney General."[7] Ragano says that "one evening in March" 1963, he was "in Jimmy's $1,000-a-day suite at the Edgewater Beach Hotel." Hoffa asked Ragano and another "long-time lawyer . . . who had Mafia relatives . . . 'What do you think would happen if something happened to Bobby?'" Hoffa's other lawyer replied that "John Kennedy would be so pissed off, he would probably replace him with someone who would be more of a son-of-a-bitch than Bobby." Hoffa posed another question: "Suppose something happened to the President, instead of Booby." Hoffa's other attorney replied: "'Lyndon Johnson [the vice president] would get rid of Bobby.' 'Damn right he would,' Jimmy said. 'He hates him as much as I do. Don't forget, I've given a hell of a lot of money to Lyndon in the past.'"[8]

So "in March 1963, Jimmy [Hoffa]" ordered Ragano to go to New Orleans, to meet with Carlos Marcello and Santo Trafficante. Ragano writes that "Santo and Marcello were bosom friends . . . Santo had spoken frequently in my presence about Marcello, referring to him as a 'good friend,' which meant in his covert language that he was a trusted Mafia ally." In New Orleans, "the two [Mafia] dons greeted each other with affectionate hugs and handshakes. 'How ya doing, man,' Marcello repeated as they embraced and kissed each other's cheeks." But Trafficante wasn't doing well, for the same reason Marcello kept facing more and more legal problems. "'Except for that son-of-a-bitch Bobby Kennedy, everything would be all right,' Carlos said. Turning to Santo, he asked, 'I guess they're still on your back, too.'" To which Marcello replied: "'Yeah, you better believe it . . . [and] Jimmy's in the same boat we're in, except a lot worse.'"[9]

Apparently, Trafficante and Marcello were testing Ragano, to see how he would react to hints of the plan they had been talking about with trusted associates since the previous fall. "'You know,' Carlos said, 'it's a goddam shame what those Kennedys are putting Jimmy through.'" "'Yeah,' Santo agreed. 'If Kennedy hadn't been elected, Jimmy never would have been indicted.'" "'You, Jimmy, and me are in for hard times as long as Bobby Kennedy is in office,' Carlos said to Santo, his face turning ruddy. 'Someone ought to kill that son-of-a-bitch. That fucking Bobby Kennedy is making life miserable for me and my friends. Someone ought to kill all those goddam Kennedys.'"10

Later that evening, Trafficante told Ragano: "Bobby Kennedy is stepping on too many toes. You wait and see, somebody is going to kill those sons of bitches. It's just a matter of time."11

Ragano says "in the early spring of 1963, Santo and I returned to New Orleans" to meet with Carlos Marcello.12 On "May 9, 1963, [Hoffa] was indicted for jury tampering along with six co-defendants," including "Allen Dorfman, the insurance broker for the [Teamster] pension fund."13 (Dorfman would later be tied to two mobsters who penetrated C-Day, Jack Ruby and Richard Cain.) Ragano notes the barrage of charges against Hoffa that just kept coming: "Another indictment followed in June [1963]." Bobby Kennedy's "Get Hoffa Squad cobbled two years of exhaustive investigations into a massive indictment accusing Jimmy . . . of booking $25 million in fraudulent loans from the pension fund . . . the breadth and the complexity of the double indict-ment against the head of the nation's largest union was staggering."14

Hoffa responded to the pressure by trying to kill Bobby Kennedy one more time, before signing on to the plan Trafficante and Marcello had been working on for months to kill JFK. Ragano writes that in order to look at the evidence Bobby had against Hoffa, Ragano and Hoffa went to the Justice Department to meet with Bobby Kennedy at the Justice Department in July 1963. Ragano says that "Forty-five minutes after we arrived, Bobby Kennedy strolled in with a large dog on a leash. 'Where the hell do you get off keeping me waiting while you're walking your fucking dog,' Jimmy said. 'I've got a lot of important people to see.' Bobby made no reply. He smirked at Jimmy, a condescending expression that said, 'I'm in charge, not you.' 'You son-of-a-bitch,' Jimmy snarled, lunging at Bobby, knocking him against the wall. He started choking Bobby with two hands and hollering, 'I'll break your fucking neck! I'll kill you!' He had a killer's look in his eyes."15

Ragano says that "Bobby tried futilely to pry Jimmy's powerful hands from his throat as" Ragano and the others "struggled to pull Jimmy away" and the "combined efforts of Bobby" and the others "finally broke his chokehold. I am positive Robert Kennedy would have died before our eyes if we had not intervened." However, "Bobby must have realized that arresting Jimmy for assaulting him would have been more embarrassing to himself than to Jimmy. It would have diminished Bobby's image as a two-fisted, hard-nosed scrapper and demeaned the office he held." But Ragano says that "after his encounter with Kennedy, Jimmy was increasingly distraught . . . the pressure of the two indictments was corrosive. He knew that the odds of winning in the courtroom eventually would turn against him, and there were rumors more indictments were coming."[16]

Ragano says that "on Tuesday, July 23," he "was preparing to leave Washington . . . for a meeting in New Orleans with Santo and Carlos," but first Ragano met with Hoffa. "'Something has to be done,' [Hoffa] muttered bitterly. 'The time has come for your friend [Trafficante] and Carlos to get rid of him, kill that son-of-a-bitch John Kennedy.'"[17] Hoffa's switch to talking about killing JFK instead of Bobby makes it clear that Hoffa had heard from one of the other mutual associates he had with Marcello and Trafficante, about the godfather's plan to focus on killing JFK. Hoffa couldn't mastermind the plot to kill JFK himself, because aside from the risk, Hoffa was worried that he was being bugged by Bobby's men.[18]

Regarding JFK's assassination, Hoffa says "'This has got to be done. Be sure to tell them what I said. No more fucking around. We're running out of time— something has to be done.'" The next day, in New Orleans, Ragano told Trafficante and Marcello that Jimmy "'wants you to do a little favor for him . . . you won't believe this, but he wants you to kill John Kennedy.'" Ragano says their reaction was "Silence. Santo and Carlos exchanged glances." So Ragano continued: "'He wants you to get rid of the President right away.' Their facial expressions were icy. Their reticence was a signal that this was an uncomfortable subject, one they were unwilling to discuss" even with a trusted non-Mafia associate like Ragano. Ragano says he "interpreted their mutual silence as embarrassment that I had blindly intruded into a minefield that I had no right to enter: that without my knowledge the thought of killing the President had already seriously crossed their minds." Ragano didn't realize that the mob bosses had been carefully, cautiously making plans to assassinate JFK since the fall of 1962. Hoffa's final agreement to go along with their plan would put the Teamster boss in their debt and give them access to millions more in lucrative Teamster Pension Fund loans.[19]

Ragano says that "none of us spoke again of Jimmy's incredible request" to Marcello and Trafficante.[20] However, there would be two documented celebrations on the day JFK was assassinated, and one of them involved Frank Ragano. The first celebration was in New Orleans, where Marcello's associates were ostensibly celebrating Marcello's acquittal of charges brought by Bobby (thanks to juror bribery). The other celebration was in Tampa, where Trafficante openly toasted JFK's death with Ragano, at the very hotel where

JFK had delivered a speech just four days earlier. Ragano's fiancée was so horrified at the joyful actions of Trafficante and Ragano that tragic day that she fled in tears from the restaurant.[21]

In the early months of 1963, Trafficante, Marcello, and Rosselli had the motive to kill JFK, and the CIA's anti-Castro operations would be the means. Some of those CIA plots involved the Mafia, so the mob bosses could use their activity with the CIA to hide their own plotting against JFK. By using people linked to those operations, the Mafia could send messages and people and equipment for seemingly legitimate CIA operations—only they would later turn out to have been used in the JFK assassination, forcing a CIA cover-up. In 1963, the US government couldn't afford to let the world know that they were trying to kill a foreign leader like Castro, especially just months after the Cuban Missile Crisis. Plus, officials like Helms, Harvey, and FitzGerald hadn't even told their own CIA Director about some of the plots; this fact would force those officials into even more cover-ups to protect their positions. Prior to C-Day, the CIA seems to have responded to the anti-Castro pressure from the Kennedys by trying a wide variety of Castro assassination plots, and the Mafia had ways of learning about—and often participating in—all of them.

A key to the Mafia's penetration of the CIA's Castro assassination plots was the close relationship between Johnny Rosselli and David Morales, the "Chief of Operations" at the huge Miami CIA station, "the largest, best financed and most active CIA station ever run outside of [the CIA's] Langley headquarters." Former Congressional investigator Gaeton Fonzi writes that "Johnny Rosselli" was "using an action group [of Cuban exiles] that, obviously, came under the supervision of the station's Chief of Operations, David Morales." Fonzi notes that Morales also worked closely with CIA officer David Atlee Phillips, then based in Mexico City, and "Morales was away from the [Miami CIA] Station a lot" in 1963, "usually . . . on trips to Mexico City."[22] While this no doubt meant that Phillips knew (from Morales) what Rosselli was doing in regard to Castro assassination plots, it also meant that Rosselli could learn from his close friend Morales what Phillips was working on as well.

Bradley Ayers was an Army officer assigned to the CIA in 1963 to help train Cuban exiles in support of actions planned against Cuba in the fall of 1963. He saw Johnny Rosselli—called "Col. Rosselli"—at the CIA headquarters in

Miami, with David Morales. He later said "I further state with certainty, that 'Dave' [Morales] controlled John Rosselli." Ayers says that "I was unwitting at the time that John Rosselli was, in fact, a Mafia functionary, but I did know that he was involved in the planning and execution of the [attempted] assassination of Fidel Castro." Ayers notes that "Morales held sway with Ted Shackley," the Miami CIA Station Chief, "and dominated the entire operational agenda at the [CIA] Station." However, Morales chafed at orders from Washington. "Morales was often demonstrably irritated with changes to planned [CIA] covert/paramilitary operations that were handed down by CIA headquarters at Langley or by orders from [Bobby Kennedy's] Special Group that seemed to be micro-managing the secret war against Castro."[23]

With his high position and key role heading CIA Operations in Miami, Morales had a hand in all the CIA actions against Castro in 1963, both before C-Day developed in May 1963 and after. For example, CIA files confirmed that "Dave Morales—CIA" was at an early AMTRUNK meeting at a "safe house in Washington, D.C.," along with "Tad Szulc, *New York Times* Reporter," someone from the State Department, and two other CIA agents.[24] Morales had taken over the CIA-Mafia plots with John Rosselli after William Harvey had been reassigned. Harvey kept the European assassin recruiter on the CIA payroll during all of 1963—possibly meeting with him in Miami that year— so it's likely that Morales became involved with QJWIN as well.

The CIA's IG Report ignores the contacts between Rosselli and Morales and tries to present the contacts between Harvey and the CIA and Rosselli as gradually declining during 1963. However, according to presidential historian Richard Mahoney, CIA files show that "on February 18, 1963, Harvey and Rosselli had drinks together in Los Angeles. According to Harvey's later testimony, they agreed to put the assassination plotting on hold but leave the bounty on Castro of $150,000 where it was . . . but there is evidence that Harvey's collaboration with Rosselli continued. In April [1963], Harvey submitted an expense sheet to CIA administrators covering the period April 13 to 21. A hotel receipt indicated that Harvey had paid the bill of a 'Mr. John A. Wallston' at a Miami hotel. Rosselli's CIA alias was variously 'John A Ralston' or 'John Ralston.' The entry also gave the client's address as '56510 Wilshire Boulevard, Los Angeles.' Further, Harvey chartered a boat at Islamorada, Florida (Key Largo), which he also charged to the Agency after the fact. With a veritable navy of CIA craft in the vicinity, renting a boat seems a curious choice."[25]

According to Mahoney, the CIA admits that "on June 20 [1963], Rosselli

flew into Dulles airport in Washington and was picked up there by Bill
Harvey . . . after dinner, Rosselli accompanied the Harveys to their home,
where he spent the night. Harvey was later to characterize the meeting as
social, but one old Rosselli retainer, DC police inspector Joe Shimon,
thought the overnight stay at Harvey's home 'unlike Johnny unless, of
course, they were doing business.'"[26] Richard Mahoney, a respected historian
given special access to Kennedy papers, is forced to conclude that "under the
CIA penumbra, Rosselli could move guns and assassins in relative secrecy.
All experienced murderers seek cover. By putting the Agency's fingerprints
on [Mafia] operations, the mob could anticipate that the CIA would cooperate in the cover-up" of JFK's assassination."[27]

Mahoney goes on to note that in early 1963, Rosselli "set up shop at an
upscale motel in Key Biscayne" and "hooked up with John V. Martino, a
former mob electronics technician in the Havana casinos who had just been
released from prison in Cuba. . . . Martino would eventually end up on the
periphery of the plot to kill President Kennedy and provide critical testimony
of what really happened." The FBI continued monitoring Rosselli, but "when
Rosselli left Florida, the FBI had difficulty tracking his movements, as FBI
telexes of the time attest."[28] (Miami FBI surveillance records of Rosselli in
the critical months before 11/22/63 would disappear from official files in the
mid-1970s.) Mahoney says that "the tap" the FBI "had put on Rosselli's
apartment phone in LA revealed little of value" since "Rosselli likely knew of
its existence." In addition, "Rosselli was also hard to track because he either
rented cars or used those of friends" and "he had no retinue of bodyguards"
and "when he traveled by air, which was often, Rosselli never made reservations. He would show up at the airport ten minutes before a flight and pay
for his ticket in cash. Accordingly, Rosselli rarely showed up on the flight
manifest . . . he was visible only when he chose to be, otherwise disappearing."[29]

Rosselli's work on the CIA-Mafia plots continued, and journalist Scott
Malone writes that "in early March 1963 . . . one of Rosselli's hit squads,
equipped with high-powered rifles and walkie-talkies, was picked up on a
Havana rooftop."[30] FBI veteran William Turner notes that later, "Rosselli told
columnist Jack Anderson that he obtained scoped rifles from Mafia sources."
However, "the CIA insisted on substituting 'sanitized' Belgian FAL assault
rifles, of the type used by the Cuban Army, and communist ammunition so
that if the assassination team were nabbed, it could not be proved it had
come from the United States."[31] It's unclear what kind of "scoped rifles"

Rosselli obtained "from Mafia sources" and if any of them surfaced in later Rosselli or CIA operations.

The CIA continued their Castro assassination plots with Rosselli in the spring of 1963 even though the Kennedys' own official emissary—James Donovan—was in Cuba at that time, negotiating for the release of twenty-seven prisoners, including three CIA agents.[32] That the CIA would try to assassinate Castro and endanger their own men—as well as the Kennedys' own representative—shows the lengths to which some people in the CIA would go to eliminate Castro. CIA Director John McCone didn't know about the CIA-Mafia plots at that point, so it's likely that the highest approval rested with CIA Deputy Director for Plans Richard Helms. Helms was at the heart of the anti-Castro plotting in 1963, having approved the continued employment of CIA assassin recruiter QJWIN. However, assassinations were not the CIA's only dangerously provocative actions.

In March of 1963, CIA propaganda and PR expert David Atlee Phillips ordered the Alpha 66 Cuban exile group to attack a Russian ship in a Cuban port. Former Congressional investigator Gaeton Fonzi writes that on March 19, 1963, "at a press conference in Washington arranged by" Phillips, using his "Maurice Bishop" code name, "Alpha 66 leader Antonio Veciana announces that his anti-Castro forces have raided a 'Soviet fortress' and ship in a Cuban port east of Havana, causing a dozen Soviet casualties and serious damage. Veciana says his purpose is 'to wage psychological warfare.'"[33] (The use of the media, and even of terms like "psychological warfare," are hallmarks of Phillips's operations going back to the CIA's 1954 Guatemala coup.) Fonzi notes that "The *New York Times* says the Kennedy administration is 'embarrassed by the incident.'"[34] Livid was more like it, and Alpha 66 was denounced by the administration. This would soon lead to an odd situation for C-Day. Alpha 66 was not part of C-Day, because of that incident. Yet its leader, Antonio Veciana, was so closely allied with C-Day exile leader Eloy Menoyo (and his SNFE group) that one US agency considered Menoyo's SNFE and Alpha 66 to be one and the same.

The Phillips-engineered press conference about the Alpha 66 attack was held on March 19, 1963, just six days after a March 13, 1963 CIA-Mafia Castro assassination attempt engineered by Rosselli and Morales. According to the *Miami Herald*, that plot had included "a plan to assassinate Castro from a house near the University of Havana by firing a mortar . . . bazookas, mortars, and machine guns were taken." Cuban State Security photographed all the captured men and equipment, although the attempt received little publicity in the US at the time. Then, on "April 7, 1963," the Cubans stopped a plot "involving 16 men armed with pistols and fragmentation grenades, who were to attack Castro at the Latin American Stadium."[35] (Kennedy emissary James Donovan was still in negotiations with Castro at that time, since the prisoners would not be released until April 23, 1963.)

Confirmation of CIA involvement in that assassination attempt also comes from Harry Williams. Harry was working closely with Bobby Kennedy at that time, although the C-Day plan was still a month away from developing. When asked about the April 7, 1963 assassination attempt with pistols, Harry said "I know about that. But I was not involved at all." However, he added that "a lot of those people used to work for the CIA."

The use of pistols in that attempt in the spring of 1963—and possibly a later one—brings Jack Ruby back into the picture. Warren Commission Exhibit 2993 says "that on May 10, 1963, a .38 Smith and Wesson Centennial revolver . . . had been shipped to L. C. McWillie" in "Las Vegas." Jack Ruby had asked a Dallas gun shop to ship the pistol to his friend and "idol" Lewis McWillie in Las Vegas, where Johnny Rosselli held sway. McWillie had been linked to the CIA-Mafia plots prior to the Bay of Pigs, and to Ruby's planned visit to Havana that coincided with an earlier shipment of four Colt Cobras to McWillie (one of which Ruby purchased and kept himself). As noted earlier, an investigative journalist had asked, regarding the May 1963 pistol shipment, "Was Ruby supplying the pistols to the Las Vegas gambler McWillie so they could be passed on to Rosselli, another Las Vegas" mobster, to be "used in a plot against Castro? If the Rosselli assassination squad was apprehended, it would be very difficult to trace the pistols back to the CIA since Ruby had purchased them in an out of way gun store in Texas."[36]

Perhaps the pistol Ruby had sent was planned for use in the next CIA-Mafia assassination attempt, on "July 26, 1963," when the *Miami Herald* says was there was a plot to "assassinate the Minister of the Armed Forces, Raul Castro," Fidel's brother. But this particular pistol was not used, because the Warren Commission document notes that the pistol was "later returned" to Dallas in May 1963 because "McWillie did not pay for the gun." This pistol shipment to McWillie in May 1963 may have been a test in manipulating Ruby as he was starting to be drawn into the JFK assassination plot.

Ruby owed a small fortune to the IRS by May 1963 and was desperate for money. But starting in late April 1963, Ruby had clearly become of great interest to powerful Mafia figures. The former director of the House Select Committee on Assassinations (HSCA) wrote that "though the [Warren]

Commission apparently believed that press speculation about the President's trip [to Dallas] did not begin until September 13, 1963 . . . a story in the *Dallas Times Herald* on April 24, 1963 . . . quoted Vice President Johnson as saying that President Kennedy might 'visit Dallas and other major Texas cities [that] . . . summer.'" Starting the following month, the HSCA "discovered a pattern of telephone calls to individuals with criminal affiliations, calls that could only be described as suspicious."[37]

Like many mob figures, Ruby probably made many calls from pay phones—but even his documented long-distance calls provide a clear record that he was becoming involved in something quite unusual for him by May 1963. From making fewer than ten long-distance calls in April 1963, Ruby suddenly more than doubled that total to twenty-five in May and more than thirty in June. He continued on that approximate pace through September, then his total skyrocketed to over eighty long-distance calls in October 1963 and over 110 in just the first three weeks of November.[38] Long-distance calls were far more expensive, and less routine, in those days, when only AT&T provided phone service and there was no competition.

As in 1959, Ruby was not a major player, but he knew the right people. Ruby worked in a city controlled by Carlos Marcello and had met and tried to help Trafficante. Ruby had begun in Rosselli's Chicago Mafia (and probably had first met Rosselli in the 1930s), and Jimmy Hoffa's own son admits that his father knew Jack Ruby. The mob bosses and Hoffa had more than a dozen associates in common with Ruby, making it easy to communicate with Ruby through intermediaries. Ruby had the connections with the Dallas Police to arrange for any patsy used in Dallas to be quickly killed. If that didn't happen, Ruby would have to do the job himself.

In preparation for Ruby's help with the JFK plot, he may have been given a small role in the CIA-Mafia Castro assassination plots. By the fall of 1963, Jack Ruby would be having face-to-face meetings with Johnny Rosselli in Miami, while the CIA-Mafia plots to kill Castro were continuing.

In the spring of 1963, before C-Day developed, Marcello, Trafficante, and Rosselli needed something more than the CIA-Mafia plots and QJWIN to use as "cover" for their JFK assassination plan. That those plots were active was unknown outside the CIA; even the Kennedys didn't know that they were still going at that point. To provoke a wide official cover-up after JFK's assassination, the mob bosses needed an operation known outside the CIA, one known even to Robert Kennedy. So the Mafia decided to create its own operation and then get the US government to back it.

Trafficante and Rosselli used John Martino—recently released from Cuban prison—to help put together a plan the CIA would eventually name OPERATION TILT. Using some of the same people working on the CIA-Mafia plots in the spring of 1963, TILT involved sending a Cuban exile team into Cuba to retrieve Soviet technicians supposedly ready to defect and reveal the existence of Soviet missiles still on the island. The chance to find proof of Soviet missiles was supposed to be irresistible to the CIA and the Kennedys, and there was initially interest from Kennedy associates, some in the CIA, and even *Life* magazine.

In actuality, there were no Soviet technicians. The team sent into Cuba with CIA and Kennedy backing and equipment would never return.[39] If evidence were planted during JFK's assassination linking some of those people and that equipment to JFK's death, it would appear that the exiles had been captured by Castro, "turned around" by the Cubans, and used against Kennedy. This would prompt a widespread cover-up to protect not just that operation, but years of CIA-Mafia plots and Castro assassination attempts. Johnny Rosselli actually floated that story about the assassination on several occasions. Historian Richard Mahoney confirms that OPERATION TILT "fit nicely with Rosselli's later claim that President Kennedy was assassinated by an anti-Castro sniper team sent in to murder Castro, captured by the Cubans, tortured, and redeployed to Dallas." However, "the handiwork of Rosselli's assistant, John Martino, the CIA, *Life* magazine, [William] Pawley, and Senator Eastland were all variously implicated" in OPERATION TILT.[40] However, OPERATION TILT was largely abandoned by the Mafia, after C-Day presented a real Kennedy operation that the Mafia could penetrate, an operation that involved even more government agencies and the military.

Someone to Take the Fall: Lee Harvey Oswald

EVEN BEFORE C-DAY DEVELOPED IN May 1963, the Mafia had begun to develop at least two patsies. One is a name familiar to everyone—Lee Harvey Oswald—while the other would only have become infamous if JFK had been assassinated in Tampa: Gilberto Policarpo Lopez. Regardless of where JFK was killed, having a patsy to quickly take the blame was the only way to make sure that all escape routes out of town—airlines, small aircraft, trains, even roads—were not blocked after the assassination in a huge manhunt. Having a patsy to divert blame from the Mafia would also prevent the massive military retaliation that Trafficante's operations in Phenix City had suffered when a patsy wasn't used there. The Mafia's use of a Cuban-linked patsy, to blame JFK's assassination on Castro, is really just another variation of the thinking behind the Guantanamo provocations in 1960 and in 1961, both linked to Guy Banister. Those phony attacks were designed to provoke a US retaliatory attack on Cuba, and a JFK patsy who appeared to have Cuban ties was intended to accomplish the same thing, further taking the heat off the Mafia and preventing a thorough investigation of the assassination.

Marcello had mentioned using someone who the public would regard as a "nut," someone the public and press would believe capable of killing JFK. If such a person could be found who also had or could develop connections to Cuba—and to US intelligence—that would be ideal. The public would have a logical culprit, while officials would have to withhold crucial information from police and other investigators to protect US intelligence operations and assets. Both Guy Banister and David Ferrie had done work for US intelligence on Cuban matters; and in 1963 both were working for Carlos Marcello. And all three had previous ties to a young man who would make an excellent patsy: Lee Harvey Oswald.

The "official story" of Oswald is that he became a Communist as a teenager, joined the Civil Air Patrol, then joined the Marines, was discharged, defected to Russia, got married and came back, then was of no interest at all to Marine or Naval Intelligence or to the CIA—in spite of the fact that he got a job at a Dallas photo company that prepared material for secret Army maps made from U-2 spy plane photos.[1] That official version has long been discredited by many critics, who have pointed out its glaring inconsistencies in many books and articles over the past four decades.[2]

New evidence about Oswald and Naval Intelligence, coupled with our discoveries about C-Day, allow us to present a comprehensive, alternative version of Oswald's life for the first time. Instead of simply picking apart many facets of the official version, the following scenario uses documented evidence to explain all of Oswald's actions, even those that have baffled investigators for decades. Because we have few official sources to fill in the gaps in the "over one million CIA records" related to JFK's assassination that have not yet been released, the following is not on the same level of completeness as our chapters proving the existence of C-Day, the Mafia penetration of it, and the assassination plots in Chicago, Tampa, and Dallas. But the existing evidence presents a very different version from the official one that paints Oswald as a teenage Communist sympathizer. That's because Oswald's three biggest idols when he was growing up weren't Communists, but were his brothers—both in the military—and Commie-hunter Herbert Philbrick, the inspiration for Oswald's favorite TV show, I Led Three Lives.

Oswald grew up in difficult circumstances, without a strong father figure. His own father died two months before Oswald was born. Oswald and his brothers lived in crime-filled areas of New Orleans before they moved to Texas, where the family continued to struggle. Robert Benton wrote that Oswald had an IQ of 118, well above average, but observes that "Oswald was probably dyslexic" and "his writing shows difficulties out of sync with his intelligence. This learning disability would explain Oswald's trouble in school," since little help was available for such disabilities in those days. Oswald also reportedly had some hearing loss. School must have been very frustrating for him, unable to make good grades even though he was highly intelligent. His older brother, Robert, and his half-brother, John Pic, both joined the service. While Pic was in the Coast Guard stationed in New York, Oswald and his mother moved there, but Oswald developed truancy problems and was briefly placed in a youth house.[3]

However, after Oswald's mother took him back to New Orleans, he suddenly turned his life around. Oswald developed an interest in astronomy, joined the Civil Air Patrol, and began trying to join the military. The formerly troubled truant seemed to have found a purpose in life and wanted to follow in his half-brother's footsteps. Pic wasn't just in the Coast Guard in New York—he was in the Coast Guard Port Security Unit (PSU), described by researcher Greg Parker as working "hand in glove with the FBI and the Office of Naval Intelligence searching out subversives in the maritime industry." Oswald "idolized Pic," and Pic planned to eventually join the Air Force, which probably spurred Oswald's interest in the Civil Air Patrol and astronomy. However, US Air Force guidelines say that "waivers for hearing loss are not granted by USAF, although hearing loss may be waived by other services on very rare occasion." So Oswald eventually dropped the Civil Air Patrol in favor of the Marines, where he could still be in the service like his older brothers—and also pursue intelligence work like Pic.[4]

We know that Oswald was interested in undercover intelligence work because his brother said Lee's favorite TV show around this time was *I Led Three Lives*, about a seemingly average man—Herbert Philbrick—who had a secret life as a Communist.[5] But the man also had a third life, his true calling: helping US intelligence.[6] Any interest Oswald showed in Communism as a teenager was probably in preparation for filling such a role himself, especially since then—as later—he carefully avoided attending regular meetings of real American Communists. In the Cold War 1950s, the Red-scare McCarthy era and its aftermath, it's doubtful that a real teenage Communist would have been found in the Civil Air Patrol, let alone trying to join the US Marines before he was even old enough.

When Oswald was making these crucial decisions that would shape his life, *I Led Three Lives* was typical of the Red-menace hysteria then sweeping the country. As one journalist described the series: "Those sweet little old ladies who lived in the house on the corner were, it turned out, evil-doing reds; the elevator operator was a Commie, too; so were the butcher, the baker, and the candlestick maker. If the percentage of Communists to the total population had actually been as high as portrayed on that series, the Communists could have elected the president and held a majority in Congress." Yet 600 stations ran its 117 episodes from 1953 to 1956.[7] Philbrick, the real-life inspiration for the series, received high praise from J. Edgar Hoover and maintained a lucrative lecture career into the 1960s.

The show Oswald watched religiously was just part of a wave of similar Red-menace entertainment at that time. The TV show *I Led Three Lives* was inspired by its producer's earlier success with the radio drama series *I Was a Communist for the FBI*, also based on a true story. The radio drama, which no doubt would have appealed to Oswald, was based on a successful movie, also called *I Was a Communist for the FBI*. According to one author, it featured scenes of "red goons" using "lead-pipes wrapped in Yiddish newspapers to beat and silence union leaders" and "Reds boasted they would infiltrate churches, force American women to work in brothels to service Red occupiers of the country, and all Americans would live in harsh labor camps while being brainwashed." However, "while most critics blasted the movie, reviewers tended to get in laudatory words about" the real-life subject of the movie (Matt Cvetic), "making him something of a noble folk-hero." Like Philbrick, Cvetic went on to a lucrative speaking career, talking about his long years undercover before finally revealing his true loyalties and reaping the accolades of friends, family, and US officials.[8]

One can imagine Oswald dreaming of doing years of undercover work pretending to be a Communist, only to finally be embraced by his family and society—and reaping considerable rewards, like men like Philbrick. (In 1963, Oswald would talk of writing a book about his Russian exploits, just as Philbrick and Cvetic had written books. Oswald's radio and TV appearances in the summer of 1963—one of which involved a group that would include Philbrick on its board of directors—showed that Oswald had the potential to be a decent public speaker.[9]) But Oswald was not alone in being captivated by the exploits of agents and assets like Philbrick and Cvetic. *I was a Communist for the FBI*, the highly fictionalized movie about Cvetic, was a typical full-length Hollywood B-movie of the period, a low-budget affair with no memorable actors or actresses. Yet such was the Red-menace hysteria of the times that it was nominated for an Academy Award in 1951—as Best Documentary! It was the only Oscar nomination that its producer—Johnny Rosselli's business partner and close friend at the time, Bryan Foy—ever received.

There is clear evidence that David Ferrie had known Lee Oswald since the 1950s. By the early 1960s, Ferrie would be linked to the anti-Castro activities of the CIA and Robert Kennedy, in addition to being a pilot for Carlos Marcello. However, in the 1950s, David Ferrie had been a pilot for Eastern Airlines when it was one of the largest US airlines and when pilots were one of the most respected US professions. In his crisp pilot's uniform, the tall Ferrie was said by Congressional investigators and others to have had a commanding presence that particularly impressed teenage boys.

According to investigative journalist Anthony Summers, a David Ferrie associate "said Ferrie once told him about a youth who had witnessed a sex act in which Ferrie had taken part, and then [the youth] joined the Marines and left New Orleans."[10] In fact, according to Oswald's mother, Oswald "joined the Marines and left New Orleans" after originally getting encouragement from a uniformed man who "influenced [him] while he was with the Civil Air Cadets. She said the man came to the Oswald apartment, with sixteen-year-old Lee in tow, to persuade her to let the boy join up while still underage," a plan that included having her sign a fake birth certificate stating that Lee was a year older than he really was. Summers points out that "it seems unlikely that a genuine recruiting officer would have tried to persuade a cadet's mother to connive at breaking the law," but the House Select Committee on Assassinations noted "that David Ferrie 'urged several boys to join the armed forces.'" In addition, Summers says that Ferrie "had a personal penchant for the fakery of personal documents." Finally, photos of Ferrie in uniform while in the Civil Air Patrol reveal a man who looks very much like a military officer. As noted earlier, at least one photo of Oswald and Ferrie together in the Civil Air Patrol does exist and was shown on PBS. Summers writes that "a phony Oswald birth certificate was created," but "the Marines spotted the forgery."[11] But Oswald was persistent and, just days after he turned seventeen, he managed to join the Marines.

David Ferrie was the type of pedophile who preyed on teenage boys, something he was later prosecuted for, though it's not known if Ferrie victimized Oswald in that way.[12] Numerous allegations about Oswald being gay or bisexual were known to the Warren Commission, though they were only mentioned once in the final Warren Report. However, the supporting volumes contain almost two dozen statements of witnesses who were questioned about Oswald's possible homosexuality and his close association with gays.[13] Summers found that

> in the Marines, some wondered about Oswald's sexuality. He reportedly took friends to the Flamingo, a bar for homosexuals on the Mexican

border that he appeared to have visited before. In Japan, he seemed comfortable in a "queer bar." One fellow Marine, David Murray, kept his distance from Oswald because of a rumor that he was a homosexual. "He had
the profile of other homosexuals I'd known or come in contact with,"
former Marine sergeant Dan Powers recalled in 1994.[14]

The information about Oswald is not conclusive, as it is in the case of Jack
Ruby, whose homosexuality is clearly established in almost forty instances in
the Warren volumes and confirmed by extensive evidence. What matters for
the JFK conspiracy is not whether Oswald was gay or bisexual or—because
he was victimized by Ferrie in adolescence—a sexually confused young man.
But it is clear that Oswald interacted with those in gay circles, which could
indicate that Oswald was simply ahead of his time and comfortable around
gays. In the repressive era of the '50s and early '60s, gays were expected to
stay in the closet, even marry and have children. Gay life had to be secretive;
public exposure could not only end one's career or marriage—or military
service—but could send one to prison. Thus, people in those secretive circles were constantly subject to blackmail. This made someone like Oswald
ideal for manipulation, either by US intelligence or, later, by the Mafia. For
the mobsters manipulating Oswald, doing so via the secretive gay realms of
Dallas and New Orleans was simply one more way to keep things hidden
before and after the assassination. For example, anyone witnessing a meeting
between Oswald and someone else in one of the five gay bars in Dallas in
1963 would be risking their career, home life, and freedom if they revealed
what they saw to authorities.

None of this should be taken as any reflection on gays at the time or in
general; it's merely one more way that the Mafia was able to use what was
then a secretive, shadowy world for their own purposes. The Marcello and
Trafficante associates involved in the JFK assassination in this way were not
typical gays—they were middle-aged men who preyed on young teenage
boys. In addition to David Ferrie, others involved in the conspiracy said to
share this criminal tendency (older men preying on teenage boys) included
Jack Ruby and Ferrie's friend Eladio del Valle (Masferrer's business partner
who was later murdered the same day Ferrie died).

Numerous books have pointed out the flaws and inconsistencies in the
Warren Commission version of Oswald's military files, so we won't try to

cover them all here. Many of the most important records have never been released, or were destroyed. Anthony Summers writes that Congressional investigators were astonished to learn in 1978 that Oswald's Army Intelligence file "had been destroyed" five years earlier.[15] This file had never been shown to the Warren Commission, even though it figured prominently in the early investigation of Oswald's possible role in the JFK assassination. At that time, Army Intelligence was part of the Defense Intelligence Agency, as was Naval Intelligence. As detailed later, a Naval Intelligence source told us that they began destroying their files on Oswald immediately after Oswald's arrest for JFK's assassination—files that included a CIA contact number.

After Oswald joined the Marines, records and testimony show that he became involved with US intelligence. This was highlighted by Senator Richard Schweiker, one of two Church Committee members—along with Gary Hart—who formed a special subcommittee that looked closely into Oswald and JFK's assassination. According to Anthony Summers, Senator Schweiker "had access to many classified US intelligence files" and told Summers that "I personally believe that [Oswald] had a special relationship with one of the intelligence agencies." Schweiker went on to say that all the indications he saw during his "eighteen months" on the Church Committee "point to Oswald . . . being a product of, and interacting with, the intelligence community." Regarding Oswald's defection to Russia after leaving the Marines, Senator Schweiker told Summers that he seriously considered the possibility that "we trained and sent [Oswald] to Russia."[16]

Summers himself points out the obvious: that notes of Oswald's very overt apparent interest in Communism throughout his Marine career "do not crop up in any Naval file" on Oswald, "at least none the public has been permitted to see."[17] It's all the more incredible that the Marines would give a seeming Communist like Oswald a security clearance and assign him to the secret U-2 spy plane base in Atsugi, Japan. This was prior to the famous incident when Gary Powers's U-2 was shot down over Russia, when the public, and most of the world, had no idea that the top-secret U-2 spy plane even existed. This was also an era when people in all walks of life with even moderately progressive views were often blacklisted, even renowned actors like Charlie Chaplin, Zero Mostel, and John Garfield. It is impossible to believe that Oswald would have been sent to a U-2 base—or even allowed to stay in the Marines—if his superiors thought his seeming Communist sympathies were genuine.

Edward J. Epstein, a noted journalist for publications like the *Wall Street*

Journal, uncovered compelling information about Oswald's time in Japan through Oswald's fellow Marines and Epstein's own intelligence sources. Epstein found that "there were times" in Japan "when Oswald would disappear to Tokyo on a two-day leave" where he was apparently spending time with "a hostess at the Queen Bee [nightclub] in Tokyo." Epstein says this "was extraordinary" because "the Queen Bee, known for its more than 100 strikingly beautiful hostesses, was then one of the three most expensive nightclubs in Tokyo" and "catered to an elite clientele . . . including U-2 pilots . . . not to impoverished Marine privates." That's because "an evening at the Queen Bee . . . could cost anywhere from $60 to $100," about what Oswald took home in an entire month. Yet "Oswald went out with this woman from the Queen Bee with surprising regularity, even bringing her back to the base area several times." They were seen by "other Marines" who "were astonished that someone of her 'class' would go out with Oswald at all." Epstein says that "Naval Intelligence was also interested in the possibility that hostesses from the Queen Bee were being used at the time to gather intelligence" from US military personnel.[18]

The answer to Oswald's odd exploits at the Queen Bee comes from a Marine who served with Oswald in California, after Oswald left Japan. According to journalist Dick Russell, in 1959 Oswald and several other Marines there were told "to report to the military's Criminal Investigation Division," where they met a civilian intelligence operative. Oswald "indicated later" to his fellow Marine "that the civilian had also been his intelligence contact at the Atsugi (U-2) base."[19] This former Marine who served with Oswald told historian Henry Hurt that "he and his fellow mercenaries were never sure of the identity of the real organization" the civilian represented, "although he said they believed it to be the CIA."[20]

As recounted by researcher Michael Benson, Oswald told his fellow Marine that when he was "stationed in Atsugi that he had been alone in a bar when he was approached by a woman who was curious about the details of his 'top secret' work. Oswald reported the incident to his superior officer, who arranged for Oswald to meet a civilian. The civilian told Oswald that the woman was a known KGB agent. The man gave Oswald money and told him he could do his country a great service by feeding the woman false information regarding the U-2 spy plane flown out of Atsugi."[21]

Oswald had finally gotten the chance to be an agent for US intelligence at the Atsugi U-2 spy plane base. Like his *I Led Three Lives* idol, Oswald was first a Marine, then someone who seemed interested in betraying his country; but he was really working for US intelligence—either the CIA or military intelligence, or both working together. There are many cases of military men being assigned to the CIA, while retaining their rank or after they appear to have left military service. Henry Hurt noted that in sworn testimony in 1978, former CIA Director Richard Helms "considered that Oswald somehow retained an official connection with the Marine Corps. In the same testimony, Helms referred several times to the Navy's hypothetical responsibility for Oswald."[22] Hurt also found "there is at least one example of US intelligence recruiting a Marine out of the service in order to work in Cuba—a Marine who served with Oswald in Japan."[23] However, Oswald wasn't destined for an assignment in Cuba—at least, not yet. Instead of going to Cuba for US intelligence in 1959, Dick Russell reports that Oswald told his fellow Marine "that he was to be discharged from the Marines and go to the Soviet Union—on behalf of American intelligence."[24]

Once Oswald was stationed back in the US, his overt Communist comments became so frequent that his fellow Marines called him "Oswaldovitch." He tried to teach himself Russian, and the Marine Corps gave him a Russian proficiency test (a clear sign that high officials were well aware of Oswald's seeming Communist activities), which he failed. However, he was soon able to speak Russian very well, perhaps because—as the Warren Commission's chief counsel said in a closed session classified "top secret" for ten years—Oswald had "studied at the Monterey School of the Army" some type of language. As Summers notes, that school, "now the Defense Language Institute . . . provided highly sophisticated crash courses in languages . . . in 1959, while Oswald was based in California."[25]

Oswald was given an early discharge, ostensibly to return home to help his mother, but he went to Russia instead. As with Oswald's military service, numerous books have devoted many chapters to covering the discrepancies in the official record of Oswald's travels and finances in getting to Russia, so we won't cover those here. We believe the evidence shows that Oswald was on another mission like the one he had performed in Japan, only on a much larger scale. The "former" Marine would appear to defect to Russia, then return at a specified point with a Russian wife. The true goal of the operation would be to see how the KGB would try to contact Oswald—or his wife—in America. Allowing a returning Russian defector like Oswald—with an "undesirable" discharge from the Marines and a Russian wife—to get a job at a Dallas company that provided copy for secret maps based on U-2 spy plane photos makes perfect sense when viewed in this context. Such a job was no doubt intended by Naval Intelligence and/or the CIA to make Oswald and his wife more appealing targets for recruitment by KGB spies in America.

Henry Hurt found more evidence of the US intelligence role Oswald had played while he was in Russia. Hurt wrote that "while interviewing Naval Intelligence personnel" for another book, he

> encountered a startling assertion from a high Naval officer serving in an intelligence capacity. The officer, who served as an intelligence man in Moscow during the latter days of Oswald's defection, stated: "I felt that there was a CIA man under cover in the Naval attaché's office that I believe was sort of like a handler for Oswald . . . there was more CIA connection to Oswald than has ever met the eye." This Naval officer . . . stated that he never worked for the CIA—only for Naval Intelligence.[26]

In addition, Hurt found that in 1963

> the State Department was engaged in a study of US defectors to the Soviet Union . . . one of its aims, according to Otto Otepka, the official in charge of the study, was to determine which "defectors" were genuine and which were US intelligence operatives on espionage missions. In June 1963, Otepka was ousted from his position at the State Department. He was barred from entering his safe or from access to the contents, which included the incomplete study of US "defectors," one of whom was Lee Harvey Oswald.[27]

US intelligence couldn't afford to have Oswald exposed at that point, because he was one of the low-level intelligence assets being used in operations related to C-Day.

Oswald wasn't unique when he went to Russia in 1959, but rather was part of a small, tightly held US intelligence operation. Journalist Dick Russell observed that Oswald was one of "five American defectors over a four-month period." Furthermore, "there would be two more in 1960" and "six of these seven eventually . . . returned home" to America.[28] Russell says that a US "consular official present at the time" of Oswald's visit to the American Embassy in Moscow told "the Warren Commission that he believed Oswald 'was following a pattern of behavior in which he had been tutored by a person or persons unknown.'"[29]

According to *Vanity Fair*,

> the official story has it that when Oswald defected he went to the American
> Embassy in Moscow only once, visiting only the consular office on the
> ground floor. Yet the widow of the assistant naval attaché, Joan Hallett,
> who worked as a receptionist at the embassy, said Consul Richard Snyder
> and the security officer "took him upstairs to the working floors, a secure
> area where the Ambassador and . . . military officers were. A visitor would
> never get up there unless he was on official business. I was never up there."
> According to Hallett, Oswald came to the embassy "several times" in 1959.

Vanity Fair also points out that the CIA "had previously employed Consul
Snyder," and the HSCA "was 'extremely troubled'" by the fact that the CIA
couldn't explain a reference in Snyder's CIA "file to 'cover.'" The implication
is that Snyder was under CIA cover at the time—perfectly reasonable in
those Cold War days—and that Oswald was on a mission for US intelligence.

Once Oswald made it through the rigors of Soviet questioning and
probing, his life in the Soviet Union was far better than he could have
expected in America. He was a local celebrity, often the center of attention in
Minsk. Dick Russell points out that when Oswald first arrived there, "the
mayor personally greeted him" and gave "him a rent-free apartment . . . with
a private balcony offering a panoramic view of the city" and "the salary he
received as an apprentice" at a TV factory "coupled with a stipend he
received from the Soviet government" meant "Oswald earned as much
money as the factory's director."[30]

Still, being far from home, along with the pressure of knowing that he was
being monitored by the KGB, would start to wear on him. (According to one
account, "KGB files indicate that all of his dates were government agents or
informants."[31]) Oswald was probably relieved when he was able to return
home to the US after marrying a Soviet wife, Marina, and they had a child.
Similarly, an ex-Navy man who defected "just two weeks prior to Oswald"
also returned to the US with a new wife and child "just two weeks before
Oswald came home." It's as if the former servicemen were following the same
schedule, a schedule prepared by Naval Intelligence and the CIA. Oswald
even asked the US Embassy about the similar defector, and the Russians were
no doubt suspicious as well.

Marina Oswald reportedly had an uncle in the Soviet MVD (more similar to the FBI than the KGB), and he or someone else may have tried to influence events without Marina's knowledge.[32] Dick Russell writes that a "US intelligence check into Marina Oswald's background found an address matching that of" the other defector's "Leningrad apartment building in her address book. And Marina herself, some years later in America, told an acquaintance that her husband had defected after working at an American exhibition in Moscow. The trouble was, that defector was not Oswald, but" the other defector whose actions were so similar to Oswald's.[33]

"TIGHT SURVEILLANCE" ON OSWALD AFTER HE RETURNS TO THE US

The authors obtained the first confirmation from a former military source that Oswald was under "tight surveillance" from the time he returned to the US from the Soviet Union: Until the assassination, Oswald was under surveillance by the Office of Naval Intelligence and its close affiliate, Marine Intelligence, both part of the recently created Defense Intelligence Agency (DIA).[34] In coordination with the CIA, these agencies compiled extensive information on Oswald using mail intercepts, phone intercepts, and physical surveillance. This close monitoring of Oswald helps to explain why so many documents about Oswald were destroyed or kept secret for years, and why many are still secret.

Time magazine recently described the military's practice of using seemingly former soldiers for special assignments. An article about the US Special Forces commandos sent into Iraq, months before the actual invasion, said: "If a soldier is assigned highly clandestine work, his records are changed to make it appear as if he resigned from the military or was given civilian status; the process is called sheep dipping, after the practice of bathing sheep before they are sheared."[35] Oswald's background fits that description much better than that of being a lone assassin. It explains why a seemingly Communist teenager like Oswald joined the US Marines, why the Marines gave a supposedly Communist soldier a security clearance and assigned him to its U-2 spy-plane base in Japan, and why Oswald wasn't arrested once he returned to the US.[36] The surveillance also accounts for Oswald easily obtaining a job at the Dallas firm involved with maps from U-2 photos during the Cuban Missile Crisis, and why Oswald was never put on the FBI's watch list of security risks, or any government watch list of potential subversives.[37]

Since Naval Intelligence had limited resources in comparison to agencies like the CIA and FBI—especially in landlocked cities like Dallas—they often relied on assets of those agencies to monitor Oswald. This explains the large number of US intelligence assets that swirled around Oswald after he returned to the US. A few of these people would be known to Oswald as intelligence assets, while others would not. The physical surveillance of Oswald—and the type of assets used to conduct it—could not be too obvious, or it might scare away the KGB agents that Naval Intelligence and the CIA were hoping Oswald and his wife would attract. In this way, the "tight surveillance" of Oswald was the opposite of the "lockstep surveillance" that Bobby Kennedy had the FBI using against Chicago mob boss Sam Giancana. For Giancana, the FBI agents hovering close to Giancana at restaurants and even on the golf course were meant to be seen by Giancana and others, to impair his ability to conduct business. For Oswald, the goal of US intelligence was to avoid having any obvious surveillance that the KGB might spot. In many cases, even Oswald would be unaware that some of his associates, and those of Marina, were reporting to US intelligence assets or were assets themselves.

Among the US assets who befriended Oswald was George De Mohrenschildt, the distinguished White Russian whom Oswald met in the fall of 1962, just four days before getting his job at the U-2 map firm in Dallas. De Mohrenschildt numbered among his associates Texas oil executive George H. W. Bush and Jackie Kennedy, whose mother and aunt he had known.[38] The close relationship that quickly developed between someone as highly refined and cultured as De Mohrenschildt and Oswald has long puzzled historians— but De Mohrenschildt was part of the "tight surveillance."

De Mohrenschildt's contact with the CIA predated his contact with Oswald. According to Congressional investigator Gaeton Fonzi, records show that "in 1961" De Mohrenschildt had "showed up at a Guatemalan camp being used by the CIA to train Cuban exiles for the Bay of Pigs" and on another occasion "a CIA memo written . . . by Deputy Director Richard Helms credits De Mohrenschildt with providing valuable foreign intelligence."[39]

The *Wall Street Journal* reported that just before De Mohrenschildt committed suicide in the 1970s, he admitted to the *Journal*'s reporter "that he had been asked to keep tabs on Oswald" by a CIA official in Dallas. De Mohrenschildt agreed to help the CIA, in the hope that the CIA "might help him in future ventures."[40] The *Journal*'s reporter for this story, Edward Jay Epstein, has a long history of access to US intelligence sources. Anthony Summers documented that "De Mohrenschildt had told Epstein that he had had extensive contact with CIA agent J. Walton Moore, of the CIA's Domestic Contacts

Division. Moore had told" De Mohrenschildt "that the CIA had an 'interest' in Oswald even before he left the Soviet Union." After Oswald returned "to Dallas, De Mohrenschildt said he had embarked on his improbable relationship with the lowly ex-Marine only at the urging of Moore and one of his CIA associates."[41]

According to Summers, even "a branch chief in the CIA's Soviet Russia Division in the early sixties"—who admits "a long relationship with De Mohrenschildt dating back to before World War II"—says he "'believed' he met with De Mohrenschildt in the spring of" 1963. This was "shortly after De Mohrenschildt had seen Oswald for the last time," and the CIA official reluctantly told Summers that De Mohrenschildt "'may' have spoken with him about Oswald."

According to former FBI agent William Turner, there were other links between De Mohrenschildt and the CIA in 1963, such as "a declassified CIA Office of Security file dated April 29, 1963" which said "[Deleted] Case officer had requested an expedite check of George De Mohrenschildt for reasons unknown to Security." April 29, 1963 was just after De Mohrenschildt had finished his Oswald assignment and was leaving Dallas. According to Turner, shortly after that date "former CIA contract agent Herbert Atkin" says De Mohrenschildt's "real mission" at that time "was to oversee a CIA approved plot to overthrow the [Haitian] dictator 'Papa Doc' Duvalier.'"[42] The CIA wasn't De Mohrenschildt's only intelligence contact, since Turner notes that his CIA file says that in May 1963 "De Mohrenschildt arranged a meeting between" a business associate and "the Assistant Director of the Army Office of Intelligence, the US Army's liaison with the CIA" that was part of the Defense Intelligence Agency.[43]

On March 29, 1977, an elderly De Mohrenschildt finally revealed his monitoring of Oswald for the CIA to journalist Edward J. Epstein, while both were in a Palm Beach hotel room. At the same time, Congressional investigator Gaeton Fonzi was meeting with De Mohrenschildt's daughter at their south Florida home, to arrange an official interview with her father. This was after numerous people linked to JFK's assassination—Trafficante associates like Rosselli, Giancana, Hoffa, and Masferrer—had recently been murdered.

After his interview with reporter Epstein, De Mohrenschildt apparently committed suicide, dying of a gunshot wound in the mouth. It's interesting to note that De Mohrenschildt was one of several witnesses who died just before they could be officially interviewed by Congressional investigator Gaeton Fonzi—who was clearly on the right track. It's even more interesting to note that on the same day De Mohrenschildt died, Rosselli hit man Charles Nicoletti—part of the CIA-Mafia anti-Castro plots and also wanted for questioning by Congressional assassination investigators—was murdered with three shots to the head. Gaeton Fonzi later turned up information linking De Mohrenschildt's former business partner to Trafficante bagman Frank Fiorini.[44]

In 1963, De Mohrenschildt's reports on Oswald would have gone to the CIA, while the CIA would send them to Naval Intelligence, part of the newly created Defense Intelligence Agency (DIA) run by General Joseph Carroll, a former FBI colleague of Guy Banister. The notes of an interview with Congressional investigator James P. Kelly discuss a source "in DIA who spilled much of their techniques . . . said they watched De Mohrenschildt as a possible asset."[45]

From the fall of 1962 to the spring of 1963—when De Mohrenschildt left Dallas shortly before Oswald moved to New Orleans—George De Mohrenschildt appears to have been one of the primary US intelligence assets monitoring Oswald. However, even before the two men left Dallas, there are indications that Oswald was in contact with the two US intelligence assets who would monitor—and manipulate—Oswald from late spring 1963, through the summer, and into the fall of 1963: former FBI Chicago chief Guy Banister and his associate, pilot David Ferrie.

As noted in Chapter 22, both Banister and Ferrie had the experience and credentials to make them logical candidates for US intelligence to use in the "tight surveillance" of Oswald. Banister was a decorated FBI veteran who had served on two major cases with the man who would later head the DIA, General Carroll. In 1954, Banister had been the Special Agent In Charge of America's second-largest city, Chicago. After that, Banister had briefly been partners with Carmine Bellino, who was now a top Kennedy adviser. Banister was also a former New Orleans police official, and he maintained contacts with the FBI, the ONI, and the CIA. Banister had played a role in supporting the New Orleans aspect of the Bay of Pigs, the secret training ground linked by a CIA memo to David Atlee Phillips.[46] (At that time, one of Banister's anti-Castro groups had even used Oswald's name for a truck purchase, when Oswald was still in Russia and not in a position to object to the use of his name.[47])

Banister and Ferrie had long assisted—and sometimes shared a small

office building with—the New Orleans chapter of Tony Varona's Cuban Revolutionary Council, which was financed by the CIA with the approval of
Robert Kennedy. So, from the perspective of US intelligence, Guy Banister
was a logical choice to help monitor Oswald.

David Ferrie's intelligence resume was far less extensive than Banister's,
but he had helped with various anti-Castro operations, including Varona's
Cuban Revolutionary Council. In addition, Ferrie had known Oswald in the
Civil Air Patrol and was probably still an authority figure Oswald would
trust. By early 1963, Ferrie was working for Banister part-time, in return for
Banister's assistance with Ferrie's case against Eastern Airlines, who had dismissed Ferrie because of his pedophiliac activities with teenage boys. While
activities like this might seem to make Ferrie less acceptable to US intelligence, such charges actually gave intelligence agencies potential leverage
over Ferrie.

While Oswald was in New Orleans in early 1963, someone would need to
pick up the "tight surveillance" of him, so Guy Banister and David Ferrie
would be logical choices, from the perspective of US intelligence. While
most historians date the start of Oswald's 1963 activities in New Orleans
from late April 1963—when he moved to New Orleans to live with his uncle,
a bookie for Carlos Marcello—the Senate Church Committee investigation of
US intelligence found evidence of Oswald in New Orleans earlier in 1963.
This often-overlooked New Orleans activity by Oswald in early 1963 appears
tied to intelligence activity related to Cuba.

The Immigration and Naturalization Service (INS) inspector who told
Senate investigators about his interview with Oswald in early 1963 could not
have been confusing it with Oswald's well-publicized activities in New
Orleans in the summer of 1963, or his actions after Oswald moved to New
Orleans in late April. The inspector was transferred from New Orleans on
April 1, 1963, and he recalls meeting Oswald "shortly before" his transfer,
which would place his Oswald interview in March 1963, or perhaps as early as
February or late January 1963. The INS inspector interviewed Oswald while
Oswald was an inmate in the New Orleans jail, where "he is certain that
Oswald 'was claiming to be a Cuban alien' and that he talked to Oswald 'to
prove or disprove this status.'" Oswald spoke no Spanish, outside perhaps of a
few phrases he had learned informally, so the inspector "quickly ascertained
that Oswald was not a Cuban alien . . . and left Oswald in his jail cell."[48]

New Orleans police had no record of Oswald's being in jail at that time—
though, since Oswald was claiming to be a Cuban alien, he was likely using

an alias. Former New Orleans police official Guy Banister could easily have dealt with any records of Oswald's detention, since it resulted in no court action. At this time, Oswald was being groomed for use in some operation related to Cuba, and his Cuban activities would escalate throughout the spring, summer, and fall of 1963, culminating in his mysterious alleged visits to the Cuban Embassy in the early fall of 1963.

At the same time that Banister and Ferrie renewed their interest in Oswald in early 1963, both men were also working for Carlos Marcello, who had been looking for "a nut" who could take the fall for JFK's assassination. Even before C-Day developed a few months later, someone with Oswald's intelligence background seemed ideal to take the blame for JFK's murder, since Oswald's covert activities would prevent a thorough investigation. A close probe of Oswald's true background wouldn't just risk exposing Oswald as a US government asset, but could expose the Americans who went into Russia around the same time as part of the same operation—some of whom were still in Russia.

Former FBI supervisor Guy Banister and David Ferrie were in the perfect position to assist Marcello. Their legitimate monitoring of Oswald for US intelligence could cover their manipulation of him to take the fall for JFK's assassination. Since the KGB hadn't taken the bait while Oswald worked at the firm involved with U-2 maps, US intelligence needed to raise Oswald's profile and prepare him for use in another operation. Banister and Ferrie could help with that, knowing that, at the same time, Oswald's higher-profile activities would make him look even more guilty after JFK's assassination. Likewise, if Banister wanted Oswald to do something or be somewhere without US officials knowing about it at the time—to make him a better patsy—it was easy for Banister to submit false information about Oswald's whereabouts and activities. Plus, Banister had enough experience, contacts, and reputation left to be able to deal with local—and even some national—officials without having to give detailed explanations.

It's important to be clear about the type of surveillance Banister and Ferrie would have been providing. We don't want to give the impression that they were filing voluminous written reports in triplicate on a weekly basis. Banister was good friends with Guy Johnson, formerly with Naval Intelligence and still said to be an asset.[49] It would be a simple matter to pass information on Oswald to Johnson—or any of Banister's other trusted intelligence and FBI contacts in New Orleans—on an informal basis. Those men would carefully pass that information on to their contacts or superiors.

Since Oswald's tight surveillance was highly classified, it wouldn't be overtly shared with most local officials or agencies. Even within US agencies, evidence cited later shows that most officials wouldn't know about the "tight surveillance" of assets like Oswald, to protect against leaks and moles.

Was the INS incident in which Oswald was detained and pretended to be Cuban part of a US intelligence operation, or part of setting Oswald up as a patsy? The fact that it remained secret until the mid-1970s—when most evidence even remotely implicating Oswald as a lone Communist assassin came out quickly in the hours, days, and weeks after the assassination—argues for it being an early step in a US intelligence operation regarding Cuba. The same is true for the fact that no record of the INS inspector's meeting with Oswald—or Oswald's detention—is in police files. Cooperation between US intelligence and local police was so common in that era that a 1963 magazine article detailed the close ties between police officials and US intelligence, especially as it pertained to dealing with operations targeting "subversives"—i.e., Communists.

Still, because Oswald's New Orleans contact (and sometime employer) Guy Banister could act on behalf on US intelligence and Marcello, it's possible that Oswald's Cuban act served both purposes, if Oswald did it at Banister's behest. If Banister was only helping to monitor Oswald at that point, Oswald's actions in that operation might have been what first brought Oswald to Banister's attention as a suitable patsy for the JFK assassination that Marcello was planning. The INS incident is only one of many ways that Oswald could have come to the attention of Banister—and Marcello—as a potential patsy. Earlier, we noted Ferrie's prior contacts with Oswald, and Banister's use of Oswald's name two years earlier, while Oswald was still in Russia. Oswald would live for part of 1963 with his uncle, a longtime bookie for Carlos Marcello. Marcello would later claim that Oswald worked for his organization briefly, as a "runner." And Guy Banister's friendship with Naval Intelligence asset Guy Johnson was yet another way Banister could have become aware of Oswald's status in early 1963.

Banister had several ways to become aware of Marcello's need for a patsy in the JFK hit. Banister sometimes worked for Marcello in 1963, and he knew Marcello's attorney, G. Wray Gill, and Marcello's pilot, David Ferrie. As noted later in Part II, testimony also links Johnny Rosselli to Banister's office.

Rosselli would have seen many advantages to using Oswald as a fall guy for the JFK hit, in the same way that the assassination of the president of Guatemala in 1957 was quickly blamed on a lone, seemingly Communist patsy. Rosselli would have been familiar with the concept of someone like Oswald—a US asset posing as a Communist—since his movie-producer partner's only Academy Award nomination had come for *I Was a Communist for the FBI*.[50] Even the CIA admits that in early 1963, Rosselli was still working with it on CIA plots to kill Castro, and had been doing so for at least two and a half years (originally with Trafficante), giving Rosselli a seemingly legitimate reason for his interest in a US asset. Rosselli was also close to Miami CIA Operations Chief David Morales, allowing Rosselli insight into additional CIA operations. There are ample ways that Oswald could have come to the attention of Rosselli and Marcello as a patsy who could be manipulated by Guy Banister. But why would a former high FBI official like Banister join a plot to assassinate the President of the United States?

America in 1963 was very different from the Commie-hunting, blacklist days of Banister's heyday in the FBI and his first years in private business. In the early 1950s, targeting Communists—and others who weren't Communists but were liberal or progressive about things like civil rights—was a high priority for J. Edgar Hoover's FBI. Even after Banister left the FBI, he maintained a lucrative business checking the backgrounds of people employed for large companies with government contracts. But by 1963, the Red-menace hysteria of the 1950s had started to fade. Communists had never been more than a tiny part of the American political scene; and, by 1960, it was said that one fourth of all Communist party members were reporting to the FBI. That market was saturated, and Banister no longer had big corporations willing to pay highly to see if their current or prospective employees had ever been linked to progressive organizations. While Banister continued his Commie-hunting on college campuses—apparently for his own satisfaction—Banister's paying clients had dwindled to Marcello associates and others involved in far-right, racist causes.

Congressional investigators found plenty of evidence that Banister was an ardent segregationist and white supremacist, involved with several of the most extreme groups. To Guy Banister, JFK was the enemy, someone to be despised for his efforts on civil rights. Such sentiments were not uncommon in the Deep South at that time (and even much later, as David Duke showed decades after this), which is probably one reason Banister's intelligence contacts were seemingly unconcerned about his racism. However, Banister was extreme even among segregationists at the time. For Banister, America was moving in the wrong direction, at the same time Banister's fortunes were in steep decline with little prospect of improvement. From that perspective, it

makes perfect sense that Banister would quite willing to become part of Marcello's plot to kill JFK, for political, personal, and financial reasons.

Why would Oswald be willing to take a quick trip to New Orleans in early
1963, get himself arrested or detained by police, then attempt to fool an INS
inspector with an obviously phony claim that he was Cuban? This was a step
in Oswald taking on a new intelligence assignment. Clearly, the KGB hadn't
tried to contact him since his return to the US, even when he was working
at the company involved with U-2 maps at the height of the Cuban Missile
Crisis. So something new had to be tried. Oswald had been undercover for
over three years at that point, not as long as the nine years of his childhood
idol Philbrick, but Oswald's time had not been spent in the comfortable
middle-class life Philbrick had maintained.

Oswald and the world had changed greatly since Oswald had first been
taken with the idea of living as an undercover asset until his "big reveal," to
use today's terminology. After his time in the Marines—much of it overseas—and in Russia, America in 1963 must have seemed a very different
place than it had been when he left civilian life in 1957. Gone was the Red
menace lurking around every corner, and in its place was a much more complex Cold War world. Oswald himself had also matured, after experiences in
the military and in Russia that few other people had undergone.

From Oswald's writing, it's clear that he viewed the world and his place in it
in a much more complex way. In his notes found later by the FBI, and left out
of the Warren Commission's Report (but included in their rarely seen twenty-
six volumes of supporting material), Oswald writes that the US and Russia
"have too much to offer to each other to be tearing at each other's throats in an
endless cold war. Both countries have major shortcomings and advantages, but
only in ours is the voice of dissent allowed opportunity of expression." Oswald
makes it clear in these notes that he still hates Communism, writing "there are
possibly few other Americans born in the US who [have] as many personal reasons to know—and therefore hate and mistrust—Communism." According to
the Warren Commission, Oswald made these "Notes for a speech by Lee
Harvey Oswald," but the speech was never given.[51] It was the kind of speech
Oswald could only have given after he was no longer undercover and had been
revealed as a US asset, perhaps by testifying in court (like Philbrick) or before
Congress (like the hero of I Was a Communist for the FBI).

In order to ever be able to give such a speech—and reap the respect,
money, and comfortable life it would bring—Oswald would either have to
get the KGB to recruit him, or to undertake another intelligence assignment

that would fit with his current cover. Oswald had been interested in Cuba in 1959, when one of his Marine buddies was recruited by US intelligence for a Cuban operation, so it makes sense that Oswald would be receptive to helping with anti-Castro operations. While Castro had been a sort of glamorous figure in 1959, by 1963 he was clearly the type of Communist that Oswald said he hated, a brutal dictator.

In fact, Oswald had no other good options besides whatever Banister and US intelligence offered him. To the residents of conservative Dallas and New Orleans, he was a former defector who still seemed to be a Communist—an appearance Oswald had to maintain, to keep from blowing his cover and wasting all the years he had spent working undercover. His discharge had been changed to "undesirable"—no doubt to help preserve his cover—so getting a really good job on his own would be difficult. (Oswald tried to get his "undesirable" discharge changed before his death, without success.) Though he had an above-average IQ and was well read considering his background, his writing skills were compromised by his learning disability, further limiting his options. (The notes we quoted above were corrected for grammar and punctuation; Oswald's handwritten notes are clearly the work of someone with learning difficulties. On the other hand, some of his manuscripts published in the Warren Volumes are very polished and extremely articulate, a discrepancy that has been explored by many other authors. They could have been extensively corrected and rewritten by those who typed them. Or perhaps some were extensively revised by a polished and articulate writer Oswald is reported to have met in 1963, David Atlee Phillips.)

Three Oswald Riddles

THREE DEVELOPMENTS IN EARLY 1963 linked to Oswald have long been the source of controversy: guns ordered through the mail with an alias Oswald used; a shooting involving far-right icon General Edwin Walker; and Oswald's sudden interest in the Fair Play for Cuba Committee. These controversies become much clearer when looked at in the context of Oswald's contacts with those involved with US intelligence and with mob bosses Marcello, Trafficante, and Rosselli.

It seems odd that Oswald would order guns through the mail when cheaper and more reliable weapons were easily available in Dallas. Likewise, it seems strange for Oswald to suddenly develop a great interest in Cuba and begin a phony one-man chapter of a small organization called the Fair Play for Cuba Committee, when there were legitimate leftist and socialist organizations in Dallas and New Orleans that he could have joined. Dr. George Michael Evica noted that in early 1963—as the JFK conspiracy was coming together—two related Congressional committees were looking into the Fair Play for Cuba Committee and into mail-order gun sales by the very firms Oswald ordered from. Not only were both hearings in the newspapers of the time—making it easy to see where Banister or the mob bosses got the idea to take advantage of them—but members of both Congressional committees had ties to Trafficante operatives Frank Fiorini and John Martino, who was also close to Johnny Rosselli.

Oswald was probably encouraged to join the Fair Play for Cuba Committee (FPCC) to further legitimate US intelligence objectives: to make him more attractive for KGB recruitment; to lay the groundwork involving Oswald in anti-Castro operations; as part of David Atlee Phillips's efforts to penetrate the FPCC—or for all those reasons. Ordering the guns was probably at the behest of someone working for the Mafia—though Oswald's associates like Banister were working with both the Mafia and US intelligence, making it all too easy for the Mafia to manipulate Oswald under the guise of furthering some US intelligence activity. Banister was part of the same racist circles as General Walker—associates of the two had been at a racist conference in New Orleans just four days before someone shot into Walker's home—so any role Oswald had in that incident was probably at Banister's behest, to plant evidence that would make Oswald look murderously violent after he was arrested for JFK's assassination.

The three Oswald riddles begin when someone using the name "Alek Hidell" ordered a pistol and rifle through the mail in early 1963. The rifle was alleged to be the one used in JFK's assassination, and the pistol to murder Officer J. D. Tippit. When authorities encountered numerous problems in making both of those connections, the rifle was then said to link Oswald to a single shot fired into the home of racist General Edwin Walker in Dallas. However, numerous problems with those assertions have been documented at length in many books over the past forty years, and it would take an entire book to cover them all now.[1] We believe that related events in early 1963 linked to Oswald, Banister, and their associates show how the gun orders, the Walker shooting, and Oswald's sudden interest in the Fair Play for Cuba Committee fit into a pre-C-Day plan to tie Oswald to the murder of JFK, in a way that would prevent a thorough investigation of the assassination.

The guns tied Oswald's actions to a Senate committee investigating mail-order weapons, some of whose members were also investigating the Fair Play for Cuba Committee at the same time. In a book praised by the *Washington Post* and other major newspapers, journalist Henry Hurt wrote that the theory "that Oswald chose to acquire his guns by mail order has never made much sense. Its only value is to the official version of events," by creating a "chain of documentary evidence to link Oswald to the weapons supposedly responsible for the murders of President Kennedy and Officer Tippit," even though "the same make of rifle and revolver could have been purchased by Oswald at stores only a few blocks from where he worked in Dallas." Hurt points out that under the laws at the time, "there would have been no record of his purchase and ownership" at a store, as there would be for mail-order guns.[2] This meant that by using the mails, Oswald appears to have deliberately left much more of a trail than if he'd made the same purchase by spending a few minutes at a busy gun shop's counter.

The largely unregulated sale of guns through the mail was much in the news at the time, since the US Senate had begun hearings on the matter in January 1963 under Senator Thomas J. Dodd (father of current Senator Christopher Dodd*). Someone using an alias linked to Oswald ordered a pistol from Seaport Traders in California on January 25, 1963 and ordered the infamous Mannlicher-Carcano rifle from Klein's in Chicago on March 13, 1963. Hurt points out that "the major gun houses under investigation by the Dodd Committee" at that time in "1963 included Seaport Traders of California" and "Klein's of Chicago," while "one of the weapons whose unregulated traffic" caught the attention of the Senate "was the Mannlicher-Carcano."[3]

Hurt, Evica, and other authors have noted unusual activity by lower-level staffers and informants for the Dodd Committee. For example, "one young Dodd Committee investigator—after getting into trouble with the police on the Mexican border . . . was subsequently discovered by authorities trying to check two Thompson submachine guns, a pistol, and 5,000 rounds of ammunition through to Hyannis Port, Massachusetts, while President Kennedy was visiting there." Hurt writes that "part of the effort of the Dodd Committee was to show that absolutely anyone with a few dollars could successfully order weapons through the mails" at that time. He suggests that if Oswald "thought he was working for" someone connected to the Dodd Committee, "this represents a convenient way to get him to order the weapons and leave a perfect paper trail linking himself to the guns" later seemingly involved in JFK's assassination.[5]

Senator Thomas Dodd himself was above reproach, but his areas of concern brought his staff into contact with those who were not. In early 1963, Dodd was not only investigating mail-order guns, but also narcotics traffic; and he also served on Senator James O. Eastland's committee investigating the Fair Play for Cuba Committee (FPCC). Several historians have noted that Dodd's investigations into mail-order guns, the FPCC, and narcotics traffic brought Dodd and his staff into contact with numerous informants, Cuban exiles, and various intelligence assets.[6] This included associates of

---

*As a Congressman, Christopher Dodd later sat on the House Select Committee on Assassinations (HSCA), which pointed toward a conspiracy involving Carlos Marcello and Santo Trafficante. However, Congressman Christopher Dodd felt compelled to add additional remarks to the HSCA's final report, stating that "I remain convinced that the preponderance of the evidence supports the finding of the committee that a gunman fired from the grassy knoll."[4] Christopher Dodd followed in his father's footsteps and became a US Senator himself, and he played a key role in creating the JFK Assassinations Review Board in the 1990s.)

Trafficante, men such as John Martino and Frank Fiorini. Dr. Evica notes that in the hearings, "Dodd had taken testimony from several important Castro defectors, including" a close friend of Trafficante bagman Frank Fiorini—and Fiorini himself "later admitted to having intelligence connections to" Dodd's committee."[7]

Early in his career, Dodd had been an FBI agent for a year on a major case that included Guy Banister. Guy Banister had earlier assisted Dodd's colleague Senator Eastland, who led the FPCC investigation, so the committee's staff would have been receptive to information provided by a former FBI supervisor. In passing information to Dodd's staff, men working for Marcello and Trafficante would also be in a position to learn what Dodd was targeting—and to manipulate someone into thinking that they were acting on behalf of Dodd's staff by joining a group like the FPCC and ordering certain weapons from certain companies. Paul Hoch, whose work has assisted several government assassination investigations, wrote that "Oswald [might have] thought he was placing the gun orders as part of [the Dodd] . . . effort, on the instructions of whoever he was working for."[8] Dr. Peter Dale Scott notes that the "purchase of a pistol from Seaport Traders on January 27, 1963"—using an alias linked to Oswald—"without even minimum proof of identification, was only two days before the Dodd subcommittee hearings on the matter opened on January 29. Sometime later, a corresponding purchase in Texas from Seaport Traders"—Oswald's order—"was duly noted in the committee's sample statistics."[9]

Between Oswald's conveniently timed mail-order gun purchases and his contact with the Fair Play for Cuba Committee, Dr. George Michael Evica notes that "Oswald could not have set up a more consistent pattern had he been working (whether directly or indirectly) for Dodd's" committees.[10] Which may be exactly what Oswald thought he was doing. Oswald may well have imagined himself some day testifying before Congress like his boyhood hero Philbrick, by going along with what Banister or others told him to do. Oswald would think he was assisting the Committee—in showing that a former Russian defector and Fair Play for Cuba Committee member could easily order a rifle and pistol through the mail—when in actuality he was being set up as a patsy.

This also helps to explain why someone using an Oswald alias ordered an Italian Mannlicher-Carcano, a notoriously unreliable weapon. An FBI expert later testified to the Warren Commission that it was a "cheap old weapon," which seemed to surprise Warren Commissioner Hale Boggs, who was well aware—as were the other commissioners—that a rifle would have to be very accurate and reliable to come even close to doing what they claimed it had done. Author Sylvia Meagher cites an FBI report showing that the shipment Oswald's rifle was part of was so poorly constructed and maintained that one of the gun companies involved went to court claiming that the rifles "were defective." Another Warren Commission exhibit cites a Secret Service report saying that a former classmate of Oswald had "an Italian rifle of the same type" and "he shot the rifle several times, but it is so poorly constructed he decided that it was best not to shoot it any more for the reason it would explode."

When a TV documentary recently tried to recreate JFK's shooting using a gun like Oswald's, they found that it jammed 25 percent of the time, and that was after they had it overhauled by an expert gunsmith. One Dallas gun dealer told the FBI "the rifle was 'real cheap . . . real flimsy . . . very easily knocked out of adjustment,'" and another said it was so "cheap" that "it could have been purchased for $3 each in lots of 25."[11] However, the rifle had to be cheap because Oswald was always short of money, and it could blow his carefully maintained cover—or make authorities suspicious after the JFK assassination—if he were seen or photographed with an expensive rifle.

There are three reasons why those who killed JFK would want to involve that particular rifle. First, because it was the subject of Senate hearings at the time it was ordered, so it could be linked to the Senate Committee. (This was before the emergence of C-Day, so the Mafia needed as many ways as possible to link Oswald to a government body, to help prevent a thorough investigation.) Second, an FBI report states that "in the 1930's Mussolini ordered all arms factories to manufacture the Mannlicher-Carcano rifle. Since many concerns were manufacturing the same weapon, the same serial number appears on weapons manufactured by more than one" factory. As author Sylvia Meagher notes, "the FBI communication . . . suggests that there may be as many Mannlicher-Carcano rifles bearing the serial number C2766 in circulation as there were arms factories in Italy in the 1930's."[12] That would make it easy to pin JFK's assassination on the rifle ordered under the Oswald alias, when in fact other rifles—either Mannlichers completely rebuilt and overhauled to be accurate and reliable, or a rifle using the same caliber of ammunition—were actually used to shoot JFK. Having another rifle (or two) with the same serial number could be vitally important for setting Oswald up as a JFK patsy without his knowledge. Third, the firm the Mannlicher was ordered from was in Chicago, where the second-ranking man in the Cook

County Sheriff's department was Richard Cain, a made member of the Mafia who had worked on CIA Castro plots with Johnny Rosselli and Santo Traffi-cante. If needed, Cain could assist in obtaining—and widely publicizing—the records of the gun order, after JFK's assassination.

The rifle later linked to JFK's murder was now linked to an alias used by Oswald in early 1963 (and to Oswald's post office box, though there is no evi-dence that he picked up the guns there). Next, it was time to make the usually nonviolent Oswald seem capable of violent murder. Banister also needed to see if Oswald could be manipulated effectively, to put him in proximity to a violent act. To set up Oswald in this manner, Banister could use his associates in racist and reactionary circles. Banister had several mutual associates with former General Edwin Walker, and just four days after they were at a confer-ence in New Orleans, at least two men were involved in firing a shot into Walker's home in Dallas. A week after JFK's death, as public doubts mounted about the assassination being the work of a lone gunman, Oswald's name con-veniently surfaced in connection with the Walker shooting.

Major General Edwin A. Walker had been relieved of his command in Europe just two years earlier, for trying to force Army personnel to read racist and reactionary literature. After leaving the Army, Walker had been "arrested by federal authorities"—and held for mental tests on the orders of the Kennedys—during the fall 1962 riots by white protesters at the Univer-sity of Mississippi when black student James Meredith tried to enroll.[13] Walker had also tried unsuccessfully to parlay his notoriety into political prominence. But by the winter of 1963, Walker was long out of the main-stream news, with nothing on the horizon to get him any more national—or even regional—publicity. As Guy Banister was finding as well, the ultra-con-servative, white supremacist movement was fading from the mainstream of American life, its adherents pushed farther and farther to the fringes of society for its financing and support. For Banister, this included taking on Marcello as a client. For both Banister and Walker, it also meant becoming involved with some of the more reactionary anti-Castro Cubans.

The rifle from Klein's arrived at Oswald's post office box on March 25, 1963. On March 31, Oswald conveniently had his wife, Marina, take the famous photos of him holding the rifle, photos that would be found after

JFK's death. (Oswald's trip to New Orleans, where he had been interviewed by the INS inspector, had to have occurred before this incident.) On April 4–6, 1963, several mutual associates of Banister and Walker were at a major conference for racists and reactionaries in New Orleans. (Also attending was white supremacist Joseph Milteer, who would reveal details about the JFK assassination to a government informant prior to JFK's death.) On April 10, 1963, someone took a shot at General Walker's house.[14]

The Warren Commission and others have tried to pin the Walker shooting exclusively on Oswald, to show a propensity for murderous violence that is otherwise missing in Oswald's background. But numerous journalists and authors have pointed out many problems with that theory. Oswald couldn't drive and didn't have a car, raising the ludicrous spectacle of Oswald walking along the sidewalk or suspiciously skulking through alleys with his rifle, or taking his rifle on the bus to Walker's home. Even if the rifle had been disassembled, it would still have been so long as to have provoked the suspicions of those he would have encountered, at least the following day when they learned about the shooting and recalled seeing someone in the area with an unusually long package.

Also, witnesses saw at least two people at the shooting, and at least two cars were involved in suspicious activity around Walker's house. None of the witnesses said any of the men looked like Oswald, and Walker's night watchman said the driver of a suspicious 1957 Chevrolet he spotted casing the house a few days earlier looked "Cuban." Right after JFK's assassination, the Dallas police put out a lookout for a 1957 Chevrolet. Among Oswald's effects after the assassination was found a photo of the rear of General Walker's home where a 1957 Chevrolet was parked—but when the photo was published by the Warren Commission, the license tag on the Chevrolet was blacked out. Several historians and journalists have pointed out that when the same photo was published in the memoir of Dallas Police Chief Jesse Curry, the tag was not blacked out, though the photo was too small to read the license plate. Some have suggested that that is an indication that the car, someone linked to it, or Oswald was involved in some type of undercover work.[15]

Others were involved, though Oswald's statements to Marina and his CIA monitor George De Mohrenschildt make it clear that Oswald was as well. But research by Dick Russell and Anthony Summers indicates that it was not an assassination attempt. Instead, it was a way to get publicity for General Walker's fading career as a reactionary extremist. Walker's breathless story to reporters that he was almost killed—and would have been shot in the head if he hadn't bent down at just the right moment—generated tremendous regional and national publicity. However, we had only Walker's word that he was even in the room when the shot was fired. Otherwise, an incident involving a shot fired into an empty room would be little more than a case of serious vandalism. Walker's long-standing pattern of lies and exaggerations in regard to civil rights and minorities calls into question his overly dramatic story.

Guy Banister got what he wanted: publicity for a white supremacist ally, a test in manipulating Oswald with firearms, and several actions on Oswald's part that would incriminate him after JFK's death. All these things fit into the plan of Carlos Marcello. As for General Walker, the shooting's publicity at the time—and briefly again after JFK's assassination—was his last taste of national or even regional fame. He didn't make national news again until 1976, when the *Washington Post* reported that Walker had been arrested for "making a homosexual advance to a plainclothes policeman in a men's room."[16] It turns out that Walker—intolerant and hateful toward minorities—had been leading a double life all along. (And raising yet another possible reason why Walker's name and home phone number would be in Oswald's address book.)

The Walker shooting incident was known to the CIA at the time, so it was likely also part of their new plan for Oswald. Someone like Guy Banister—working for godfather Carlos Marcello while also in contact with US intelligence—would be in a perfect position to suggest something like the Walker incident that would advance the interests of US intelligence, while at the same time leaving a trail of evidence that would make Oswald look guilty after JFK's death. Since Oswald had begun the Cuban phase of his covert activity just ten days before the Walker incident—with a letter to the national chairman of the small Fair Play for Cuba Committee—Oswald's actions in relation to Walker were probably designed to test his abilities for his new assignment. Unlike Oswald's previous "defect and return" assignment, anti-Castro operations demanded a new set of skills, from surreptitiously arranging and attending planning meetings (and keeping them secret from his wife) to dealing with firearms in a covert way. The Walker incident was a chance to see if Oswald—who had never served in combat—could handle a different type of assignment. Given Oswald's dramatic increase in

Cuban activity in the months after the Walker incident, he obviously passed the test.

Guy Banister clearly took on more than a surveillance role with Oswald in 1963, increasingly manipulating Oswald's actions as the year progressed. This made him different than the other US intelligence assets who only monitored Oswald as part of his "tight surveillance," like the distinguished George De Mohrenschildt, Oswald's seeming best friend in Dallas. Many years later, when Edward J. Epstein asked De Mohrenschildt if he had "reported the Walker incident—and the telltale photograph (of Oswald holding the rifle)—to" his CIA handler in Dallas, De Mohrenschildt "said, after a long, almost painful hesitation, 'I spoke to the CIA both before and afterward. . . .'"[17] Nine days after the Walker incident, De Mohrenschildt left Dallas. The following month, De Mohrenschildt had the meeting mentioned earlier in Washington, D.C., with a CIA official and a high-ranking member of Army Intelligence (part of the DIA).

The Walker shooting incident leads directly into explaining the next major riddle of Oswald's activities in early 1963: Oswald's sudden interest in Cuba. General Walker had many documented contacts with anti-Castro Cuban exiles in 1963. This is yet another thing he had in common with fellow racist activist Guy Banister, and another reason the presence of a "Cuban" in one of the suspicious cars connected to the shooting indicates that the incident was a set-up. Investigative journalist Anthony Summers notes that "apart from the race issue, Cuba was the General's favorite rabble-rousing topic in 1963. In his speeches and actions throughout the year Walker was, in his own words, 'raising holy hell with the government over Castro and the communists.'"[18]

Another major racist in 1963 was also focusing on Cuba, in particular the Fair Play for Cuba Committee that was to play an increasingly prominent role in Oswald's activities for US intelligence in 1963. Mississippi "Senator [James] Eastland was at the time the most powerful racist in the Senate and perhaps indeed in the country," according to Dr. Peter Dale Scott.[19] So it should come as no surprise that just a few years earlier, ardent racist Guy Banister had met and worked with Senator Eastland in an anti-Communist operation. This was the Louisiana operation that yielded what Banister told one newspaper at the time was "the finest collection of Communist literature in the South that I have ever seen" and probably gave Banister the idea for the incredible collection of Communist literature found and photographed in Lee Oswald's rooming house after JFK's assassination—an amazing assemblage, considering that Oswald avoided real American Communists and Communist party meetings like the plague.[20] In the winter and spring of 1963, the investigation of Senator Eastland and his colleagues into the Fair Play for Cuba Committee and other matters would cause them to become supporters of a CIA-backed operation being run by Santo Trafficante and Johnny Rosselli—an operation that Rosselli would later link to JFK's assassination.

Most Americans first heard of the Fair Play for Cuba Committee right after the JFK assassination, when hundreds (if not thousands) of news stories said that Oswald was a member of the organization. However, it had briefly been in the news in the winter and spring of 1963, when Senator Eastland targeted the tiny organization in Senate hearings. The hearings were called "Castro's Network in the United States (Fair Play for Cuba Committee)" and were part of "Hearings before the Subcommittee to Investigate the Administration of the Internal Security Act and other Internal Security Laws," which was part of the Senate Judiciary Committee. Other senators involved included John McClellan (the Kennedys' mentor in the Mafia hearings), gravelly-voiced Senator Everett Dirksen, and Sam Ervin, later chairman of the Senate Watergate Hearings. Eastland's vice-chair was Senator Thomas Dodd, who was holding his own hearings on mail-order guns around the same time, meaning that there was some overlap in staff between the two Senate committees.[21]

The counsel for Senator Eastland's Fair Play for Cuba Committee (FPCC) hearings was Julian Sourwine, who directed much of the questioning and staff work (as Bobby Kennedy had done a few years earlier for JFK and McClellan's Senate organized crime committee). On February 14, 1963, Sourwine grilled FPCC head Vincent Lee, an enigmatic Army veteran. Sourwine commented on the FPCC head's criticism of Rolando Masferrer, since Vincent Lee had pointed out in a much earlier newspaper article that Masferrer, a "onetime Batista executioner, was roaming around free on the streets here, all deportation proceeding against him mysteriously left pending or dropped."[22] FPCC head Vincent Lee's testimony would not be published until May, but it obviously caught the attention of those manipulating Oswald, which was not difficult since Sourwine was linked to Trafficante associates Frank Fiorini and John Martino (who was also Johnny Rosselli's roommate at the time).

Dr. John Newman, the historian and retired Army major with twenty years' experience working with military intelligence, discovered that the Chicago FBI office launched a major "investigation of the FPCC . . . on March 8 [1963], four days before Oswald" seems to have "ordered the rifle from Chicago." Of course, Banister was a former FBI chief in Chicago. Dr. Newman also notes that word of the FBI investigation of the FPCC "was transmitted to the CIA" for some reason.[23] (As we will soon see, the reverse was not always true: The CIA did not always inform the FBI of its own FPCC operations.) There were more FPCC hearings on March 13, 1963—the same day Oswald appears to have ordered his rifle—and little more than two weeks after that, Lee Harvey Oswald wrote his first letter to FPCC head Vincent Lee. That was the day Oswald had his wife Marina take the famous photos of him holding his recently arrived mail-order rifle. (In the photo, Oswald was also holding two different Communist newspapers, from factions strongly opposed to each other.)[24] More Senate FPCC hearings were held on April 3, 1963, and little more than two weeks later, Oswald wrote another letter to FPCC head Vincent Lee.

At the time of the hearings, Oswald was writing to other Communist organizations, all of whom were under close surveillance by the FBI. Journalist Dick Russell notes that "despite Oswald's history in the USSR and his flurry of correspondence with the Communist Party, USA, the Socialist Workers Party, and the Fair Play for Cuba Committee—much of which was known to the FBI at the time—his name was never included on either part of the [FBI's] Security Index, not even after he went on to set up his highly visible"—one-man—"Fair Play for Cuba chapter." Russell asks "had the FBI received word from someone to keep a relative distance from Oswald . . . because he was considered part of another intelligence operation?"[25]

It's not as if FBI headquarters was unaware of Oswald at this time, since his case was eventually assigned to an agent in their Dallas office. In addition, Dr. Newman found that the FBI was targeting the FPCC, including "collecting dirt on FPCC leaders" and "using the incendiary tactic of planting disinformation" about the organization and its members. Dr. Newman writes that "these tactics dramatize the lengths to which the FBI was willing to go to discredit the FPCC, whose chapters in Chicago, Newark and Miami were infiltrated early on by the" FBI, and "during Oswald's tenure with the FPCC, FBI break-ins to their offices were a regular occurrence."[26] Such activity could have been known to former Chicago FBI Chief Guy Banister, the staunch anti-Communist who maintained close contact with FBI personnel in 1963.

As Senator Eastland and Sourwine continued their FPCC hearings during the spring of 1963, both men became involved in a plot hatched by Santo Trafficante and Johnny Rosselli. Earlier in Part II, we briefly discussed OPERATION TILT, the CIA's name for an operation put together by John Martino, who was fronting for his boss Santo Trafficante and his roommate Johnny Rosselli. Martino, who had met with a representative of the Kennedys about OPERATION TILT, and Frank Fiorini had also been providing information to Senator Eastland and Sourwine, and may have persuaded them to support their operation. The House Select Committee on Assassinations confirmed that "Julian Sourwine, counsel to the Senate [FPCC] subcommittee, 'was involved in financing the operation which has come to be known as'" OPERATION TILT "and that it 'saw evidence that the CIA knew of Sourwine's involvement.'"[27]

Even as the Mafia was beginning to use OPERATION TILT as cover for their plans to assassinate JFK, C-Day would present the mob bosses with a better opportunity. For OPERATION TILT, the plan would have been to blame JFK's assassination on a quickly killed Oswald (and his mail-order rifle), while leaving signs that those sent into Cuba for OPERATION TILT had been captured, tortured, and sent back by Castro to kill JFK. While JFK's assassination would have been done by professional hit men, the mob bosses would have hoped that because of the intelligence links of Oswald (ONI-DIA and CIA) and OPERATION TILT (CIA, Senator Eastland, and a Kennedy associate), the government would not have been able to allow a thorough investigation of the assassination and the case would be closed with just Oswald. However, although that plan would have compromised the CIA, it would not have compromised the FBI or Robert Kennedy very much (since he didn't know that the CIA-Mafia anti-Castro plots with Rosselli were continuing, and neither he nor JFK had wound up supporting OPERATION TILT). However, the three mob bosses were desperate for anything that would provide cover for their planned JFK hit. It's easy to see why the Mafia chiefs abandoned OPERATION TILT soon after C-Day presented a much better opportunity, one that involved Robert Kennedy—and other government agencies—much more extensively, in a much more sensitive operation.

The efforts of Banister and others working for the Mafia would not be wasted. Much of what they had Oswald do in the winter and spring of 1963 would make him look very guilty right after JFK's assassination. In addition, the CIA and Naval Intelligence were continuing their use of Oswald in operations against the Fair Play for Cuba Committee and against Cuba. David Atlee Phillips had been a key player in the CIA efforts against the FPCC since 1961, and he would play an increasingly important role in those activities as 1963 progressed.

David Atlee Phillips and Fair Play for Cuba, Marcello and Oswald, Oswald and Gilberto Lopez

ACCORDING TO *VANITY FAIR*, "A former CIA Clandestine Services officer, Joseph Smith, who worked with [David Atlee] Phillips," said the CIA's "attitude toward the Fair Play for Cuba Committee" (FPCC) "was 'one of great hostility . . . we did everything we could to . . . smear it and I think to penetrate it. I think Oswald may have been part of a penetration attempt."[1] Smith's autobiography describes Phillips as "a good writer" and "a great snake oil salesman," and Smith confirms that JFK was "encouraging the CIA to work for the overthrow of Castro at the time he was killed."[2] It's ironic that just as the Mafia would penetrate C-Day, much evidence shows that Phillips was doing something similar by using Oswald to penetrate the FPCC. By having Oswald use the FPCC to build a very public (and well-documented) pro-Castro cover—for use in CIA anti-Castro operations—Phillips played right into the hands of Banister and others planning JFK's assassination.

In the early 1960s, Banister and Phillips both worked to help the Cuban Revolutionary Council (CRC), the Cuban exile group that Tony Varona would head by mid-1963. The CRC received official support from the CIA and the Kennedys, and Banister assisted the New Orleans branch of the CRC (sometimes using adjacent office space), while Phillips handled propaganda for the group.[3] According to a sworn deposition in a court case involving a *Playboy* magazine interview, a "Mr. Phillips" attended a meeting in New Orleans with Guy Banister at Banister's office. "Mr. Phillips" was "from Washington," implied that he was with an intelligence agency, and "seemed to be running the show." Also present was the local head of the CRC. As researcher Lisa Pease wrote, "the project that Banister," the local CRC head, and "Mr. Phillips were working on, according to the witness, was to be a televised anti-Castro propaganda program, something that would have been in the direct purview of David Phillips as chief of propaganda for Cuban operations at that time."[4] Phillips and Banister worked with the CRC through November of 1963, giving Banister plenty of time to manipulate the situation for Marcello's benefit.

While Phillips was working to help the CRC, he had been working against the small Fair Play for Cuba Committee (FPCC) since 1961. At that time, he was working with another CIA official alleged to have been a case officer for C-Day in 1963: future Watergate burglar James McCord. Dr. John Newman quotes declassified CIA documents showing that in early 1961, "James McCord and David (Atlee) Phillips . . . launched a domestic operation against the FPCC." According to the declassified documents quoted (and shown) by Dr. Newman in his book *Oswald and the CIA*, the operation involved surveillance on a young American male who had "returned from Cuba under the sponsorship of the FPCC." Newman quotes a "February 1, 1961" CIA memo saying "Subject's case was coordinated with Mr. McCord of SRS" (the CIA's Security Research Service) and "Mr. McCord expressed the opinion that it was not necessary to advise the FBI of the operation at this time . . . the file of the Subject, along with that of the W(estern) H(emisphere Division) man who is supervising the operation (David Atlee Phillips number 40695) will be pended for the attention of Mr. McCord on 1 March 1961" [parentheses in original].[5]

According to Newman, the operation "was conceived and authorized" by James McCord, while it was actually run by David Atlee Phillips. Phillips essentially had a CIA employee get close to, and spy on, a former school friend who greatly admired Castro. Dr. Newman writes that "it is fitting that one of the (CIA's) legendary disinformation artists, David Atlee Phillips, should have been in charge of the CIA's C(ounter) I(ntelligence) and propaganda effort against the FPCC. Phillips would reappear in Mexico City at the time Oswald visited there," in an operation documented later in Part II. Dr. Newman quotes other declassified cables about this operation, quoting one informant as saying "I have been advised by Mr. Phillips . . . to continue my relationship with" the subject. This is the same type of surveillance the CIA was helping Naval Intelligence conduct on Oswald, from the time of his return from the Soviet Union in June 1962 until his death on November 24, 1963. In the case of the 1961 Fair Play for Cuba subject, the FBI eventually uncovered the CIA's informant, and after July 1961 Dr. Newman says "the CIA pulled its employee out of David Phillips C(ounter) I(ntelligence) operation against the FPCC" [parentheses in original].[6] This same type of bureaucratic lack of cooperation between agencies—not sharing information about operations or informants—would continue in 1963 regarding Oswald, with deadly consequences.

The CIA's David Atlee Phillips would continue his operations against the Fair Play for Cuba Committee in 1963, using Lee Harvey Oswald and several items the CIA actually had ordered in the summer of 1961. As detailed in an upcoming chapter, Oswald would receive extensive local media exposure— TV, radio, newspaper—in the summer of 1963 for passing out pro-Castro literature on the streets of New Orleans and getting into a fist-fight over it—which led to still more media coverage, including a radio debate between Oswald and his alleged attacker. For decades, it's been known that some of the pro-Castro literature Oswald passed out was hand-stamped with the office address of the staunchly anti-Castro Guy Banister. However, it wasn't until 1992 that author James DiEugenio discovered that some of the literature Oswald had been given to pass out had been ordered by the CIA on June 28, 1961, while Oswald was still in Russia.[7]

The CIA ordered these particular pro-Castro pamphlets at the same time David Atlee Phillips was still running his anti-Fair Play for Cuba Committee operation in June 1961. It's lucky they did, because the pro-Castro pamphlet—*The Crime Against Cuba*, by peace activist Corliss Lamont—was popular, and the CIA got some of the last copies of the first printing. By December 1961, it was already in its fourth and final printing. Oswald was still in Russia at that time, but copies of the fourth printing were still available after he returned to the US from Russia in June 1962. The fourth printing was also still available for order in the summer of 1963, when Oswald was passing out copies of the pamphlets on the streets of New Orleans. However, Warren Commission documents show that Oswald was passing out copies of the *first* printing, which had sold out over two years earlier, a year before he returned to the US. Where could Oswald have obtained that many copies of the long-sold-out first printing?[8]

The pamphlet's author was ninety years old when DiEugenio found him, but he had saved a copy of the "28 June 1961" purchase order he received for "45" copies from the "Central Intelligence Agency, Mailroom Library, Washington 25, D.C." for "$3.00."[9] As documented in an upcoming chapter, the operation Oswald used the pamphlets for in the summer of 1963 involved both Guy Banister (which is why Oswald hand-stamped Banister's address on them) and CIA propaganda expert David Atlee Phillips (which is why Oswald received so much press coverage for his actions involving the pamphlets). We also explain Oswald's meeting with David Atlee Phillips in Dallas shortly after the pamphlet operation, and how both incidents relate to C-Day.

Oswald was being used by the CIA (and probably Naval Intelligence) regarding the Fair Play for Cuba Committee before C-Day developed, at the same time Oswald was also being manipulated by men, like Guy Banister, who were working for Carlos Marcello. That explains why Oswald started writing to the Fair Play for Cuba Committee while the Senate hearings on them were in progress. It also explains why Oswald didn't associate with other Cuba sympathizers or Communists—instead, he formed phony chapters of the FPCC in Dallas and New Orleans with only one member: himself. As *Vanity Fair* confirmed from "CIA releases," the "CIA . . . penetration of the Fair Play for Cuba Committee . . . was directed by . . . 'Dave Phillips.'"[10] His role with Oswald in that regard may be among the "over one million CIA documents" relating to JFK's assassination that have not yet been released.

Or, as former CIA Chief Allen Dulles explained to his fellow Warren Commission member Louisiana Congressman Hale Boggs, there may be no written record. For contact between a CIA agent and an asset, Dulles explained, "the record might not be on paper." And if it was on paper, it might "have hieroglyphics that only two people knew what they meant, and nobody outside of the CIA would know" what they stood for. When Chief Justice Earl Warren asked Allen Dulles if the CIA supervisor who recruited the agent would "tell" about agents "under oath," former CIA Chief Dulles replied "I wouldn't think he would tell it under oath, no . . . he ought not tell it under oath. Maybe not tell it to his own government." Another Warren Commissioner asked Dulles if the CIA supervisor would at least "tell . . . his own chief" about the agent he recruited, but Dulles replied "he might or might not."[11] The Warren Commission didn't grill any CIA officials about their agents, and the Warren Commission meeting transcript was kept secret for several years after their report was issued.

Many years later, David Atlee Phillips came to realize that he and Oswald had been manipulated by those responsible for JFK's assassination. During his life, David Atlee Phillips was a staunch defender of the CIA in his public statements.[12] But shortly before he died, Phillips told a former staff member of the House Select Committee on Assassinations "that JFK was done in by a conspiracy, likely including rogue American intelligence people."[13] In addition to Guy Banister, one of those he may have had in mind was Miami CIA Chief of Operations David Morales, Johnny Rosselli's good friend in

1963. The very things that made Oswald a good asset for US intelligence also made him a good patsy for those planning JFK's assassination for Marcello, Trafficante, and Rosselli. And, as we'll document shortly, the Fair Play for Cuba Committee was also used to provide cover for another US asset for a "mission" to Cuba—this time in Trafficante's territory, and this asset was also suspected by the CIA in JFK's assassination—and Phillips would have been aware of that as well.

CARLOS MARCELLO AND LEE HARVEY OSWALD

Carlos Marcello had numerous links to New Orleans native Lee Harvey Oswald by 1963, and evidence shows that Oswald was being manipulated with regards to the JFK assassination plot by April of that year. On April 25, 1963, "Oswald moved in to the New Orleans apartment of his Uncle Dutz" Murret, a Marcello bookmaker.[14] Also in "April 1963," FBI reports say that a "young ex-Marine" named Eugene De Laparra was working at a New Orleans bar allegedly backed by one of Marcello's brothers, "who traveled regularly to Dallas where De Laparra believed Marcello owned a nightclub." De Laparra "took care of one of" Marcello's brother's "racehorses, and doubled as an informant for the FBI," providing "them with 'reliable information' on illegal gambling." De Laparra told authorities about hearing a brother of Marcello say "the word is out to get the Kennedy family." In one of De Laparra's reports, he mentions someone called "The Professor" at the bar at the time, who was one of several people "looking at an advertisement in a detective magazine for a foreign-made rifle which sold for $12.95." One of the men said "this would be a nice rifle to buy to get the President . . . somebody will kill Kennedy when he comes down south."[15] David Ferrie, Marcello's pilot, was sometimes called "Doctor" or "Professor"—an FBI report on Ferrie cites a source who calls him "Dr. Ferrie," and there was Ferrie's bogus claim to hold a "Doctor's Degree in Philosophy."[16]

Marcello's biographer John H. Davis notes that "at about the time Eugene De Laparra heard . . . there was a plot in the works to assassinate President Kennedy, a visitor to New Orleans from Darien, Georgia, was having dinner one evening at the Town & Country restaurant" in the same complex where Carlos Marcello had his headquarters. The Georgia businessman later told authorities that he witnessed Lee Harvey Oswald get "a wad of money . . . passed under the table" to him by a man later identified as a "high-ranking member of the Marcello criminal organization."[17] Davis also documents that FBI informant Joe "Hauser claims he received from Carlos" Marcello "a casual admission that both Lee Harvey Oswald and his uncle Dutz Murret had worked in his downtown bookmaking network and that during the summer of 1963 Oswald worked as a 'runner' for" one of his "bookmaking establishments . . . in the French Quarter."[18] Oswald had grown up around the French Quarter, and Oswald's only documented New Orleans job in 1963—at the Reily Coffee Company—only lasted from May 9 to July 19. So, Oswald had no documented job in part of April—when the Georgia businessman witnessed him getting money from a Marcello associate—and during much of the summer, when he supposedly worked as a "runner" in Marcello's operation. As noted shortly, Oswald is also reported to have worked part-time for Guy Banister in the summer of 1963, at the same time Banister was working for Marcello.

Oswald was not the only patsy used by the Mafia in the JFK assassination plot. In some ways, many of those being used by the mob bosses in the plot would have made logical patsies in a pinch, or if the plot had ever started to unravel. The following assassination participants all had the combination of a logical motive to kill JFK and prior intelligence connections to make them acceptable patsies if needed: Jack Ruby (IRS problems), John Martino (his long Cuban imprisonment), David Ferrie (anger over the failure of the Bay of Pigs), Guy Banister (anger over JFK's civil rights policies), Michel Victor Mertz (busts in his heroin network), and Rolando Masferrer (prosecuted by JFK and Bobby). However, if things worked properly, those people would never be investigated for the assassination. Still, at least one more patsy like Oswald was desirable, in case anything should happen to Oswald.

PARALLELS BETWEEN LEE HARVEY OSWALD AND TAMPA'S GILBERTO LOPEZ
While Marcello knew Oswald had the right connections to be an excellent patsy, there was also someone in Trafficante's territory who would make a good fall guy for JFK's assassination: Gilberto Policarpo Lopez, a young Cuban exile. Trafficante's home was in Tampa, but he spent much of his time in Miami, where he had much influence and shared an office with the Teamsters. In early 1963, Lopez lived south of Miami in the Florida Keys, but by the fall of 1963 he had moved to Tampa. Trafficante surely knew what would happen if a Cuban exile were paraded in front of TV cameras as the supposed assassin of JFK (or had been found dead, a "suicide" after killing JFK). The pressure to invade Cuba in retaliation would have been overwhelming—and

Trafficante would know that the US was poised, ready, and had plans to do just that, because so many of his associates had penetrated C-Day. Later we will have more information about Lopez, but consider the following parallels between Oswald and Lopez, especially their activities in 1963, all from government documents and sources:

- Both were white males, twenty-three years old during most of 1963.
- Both had returned to America in the summer of 1962 from a Communist country.
- Both spent part of 1963 in a Southern city that was headquarters for one of the two mob bosses that the House Select Committee on Assassinations says were most likely behind the Kennedy assassination.
- During 1963, each was frustrated by the lack of a government document, which could hamper his employment and the prospects for his future. This need to get a favorable determination on his status could make him amenable to taking risks for a US agency or make him subject to manipulation by someone saying they could help with his document problem.
- Both are said by various sources to have been assets or informants for some US agency, and both were of interest to Naval Intelligence, who kept files on them.
- In mid-1963, both men and their wives moved to another city and then became involved with the Fair Play for Cuba Committee.
- In the summer of 1963, some of their associates saw them as being pro-Castro, while others saw them as being anti-Castro. Both were living in a city where there was much anti-Castro activity.
- In the summer of 1963, both were involved in fist-fights over "pro-Castro" statements they made.
- Though both appeared at times to be "pro-Castro," neither joined the Communist Party and neither regularly associated with local Communist party members.
- In the summer of 1963, their backgrounds would have made both of them a good, deniable, low-level intelligence asset inside Cuba. In addition to sometimes appearing to be a Castro supporter, each had a Russian connection in their background, meaning that the CIA could blame any problem on the Russians if they were caught. These same attributes would also make both good Mafia patsies for the JFK assassination.

- By September 1963, both men were living apart from their wives as the result of marital difficulties.
- In the fall of 1963, both crossed the border at Nuevo Laredo and made a mysterious trip to Mexico City, where they were under photographic surveillance by the CIA. Both were trying to get to Cuba.
- Both went by car on one leg of their Mexico City trip. Neither was a very good driver and neither man owned a car.
- In the fall of 1963, each had a job in the vicinity of JFK's route for one of his November motorcades.
- A trusted FBI informant and a Tampa police informant placed both men in Tampa in the fall of 1963, in conjunction with the Fair Play for Cuba Committee.
- The week of 11/22/63, both men were in a Texas city where assassination was in the works for JFK.
- Following the events in Dallas, both men were investigated for involvement in JFK's assassination.
- Declassified documents indicate that both men were the subject of unusual US intelligence activity.
- For years after the assassination, government agencies tried to keep much of the material about both men classified, even from Congressional committees like the HSCA. Much still remains classified today, because both were involved in highly sensitive covert US operations in 1963.

Eighteen parallels like that in the months before JFK's murder demonstrate that both Oswald and Lopez were being manipulated by the same people, for the same purposes. Neither man realized that he was being manipulated by the Mafia, in addition to whatever intelligence function he was also fulfilling. Because much of the investigation of Lopez by the CIA and FBI was kept secret from Congressional investigators, far less is known about him than Oswald. Yet, by having Oswald visit Tampa shortly before the assassination—or at least planting information that he had—the Mafia also managed to link the two patsies. This meant that much of the activity that seemed to incriminate one of the men could also be used to incriminate the other.

The Warren Commission got only fragments of information about Tampa's Gilberto Lopez, though they did learn enough to know that Lopez was on a "mission" at the time of JFK's assassination. However, the Warren Commission was never told about the attempt to assassinate JFK in Tampa, or that local authorities considered Lopez a person of interest in the matter because Secret Service agent Abraham Bolden was framed and arrested the day he was going to Washington to testify about the Tampa and Chicago attempts.

With all their parallels, there is a key difference between Oswald and Gilberto Lopez, based on all the evidence about Lopez that has been released in recent years. In 1963, Oswald was emulating his childhood hero, living "three lives" as a seemingly average man pretending to be a Communist, who was really helping US intelligence. The evidence shows that Oswald—like Lopez—was on a "mission" for US intelligence when they undertook their actions in November 1963, and that instead of intending to kill JFK on November 22, 1963, Oswald planned to go to Cuba as part of a US intelligence operation.[19] In fact, after the Tampa assassination attempt, Lopez went to Texas, then actually made it into Cuba shortly after JFK's death, according to surveillance by the CIA.[20]

However, while all the evidence shows that Oswald was knowingly involved with US intelligence, the same is not necessarily true for Gilberto Lopez. Even Lopez's alleged role as an informant for a US agency may have been on an unwitting basis: Lopez may not have known that a friend or associate of his was reporting his information to a US agency. In the same way, Lopez's actions could have been manipulated by a friend or associate who played on Lopez's hopes of getting a valid passport, or for other reasons. Just as Oswald's prospects were limited (in case he ever decided to quit his covert activities before completing his mission) by his "undesirable" discharge, Lopez needed a valid US passport to freely travel between the US and Cuba (where his family still lived, except for a brother who was in Russia).

Gilberto Lopez came to the US "soon after Castro took over." He was issued a US passport in July 1960 that was valid until January 1963. So, by the spring of 1963 (and into the summer and fall), Lopez was unable to travel freely between the US and Cuba to see his family. Until the numerous parallels with Oswald begin to occur in 1963, there is nothing in Lopez's background to suggest an interest or involvement in espionage—with one possible exception: In July 1962, Lopez made a mysterious trip back to Cuba for several weeks, claiming to Cuban authorities that "he was homesick." He quickly returned, and then suddenly married an American woman. His marriage to her was as troubled as Oswald's was to Marina, and they eventually separated and lived apart, at the same time as Oswald and Marina.[21]

The authors were the first investigators to talk to Lopez's wife since the

FBI had spoken with her in 1964—which seems strange, since Lopez was investigated by both the Senate Church Committee and the House Select Committee on Assassinations in the 1970s. She said that Lopez had never told her about his brief trip back to Cuba in July 1962, just before he married her. This seems unusual, but there may be an innocent explanation. On the other hand, US intelligence expert Joseph Trento has written that the Miami CIA station was by 1963 "the largest CIA station in the world, with six hundred case officers. These mostly inexperienced case officers interrogated the" flood of "Cuban refugees coming into Florida every day. It was from among this group that relatives were recruited back home in Cuba to spy on the hated Castro regime." Since Lopez had a brother in Russia, it's possible that the CIA attempted to recruit Lopez before he made his brief trip back to Cuba in July 1962 or upon his return to the US. Lopez was briefly back in Cuba just days after a CIA report says Johnny Rosselli had sent an assassination team into Cuba, as part of the CIA-Mafia plots with Tony Varona. July 1962 coincides with the buildup of activity for OPERATION MONGOOSE and the renewal of CIA contact with mid-level Cuban official Rolando Cubela, but there is no evidence linking Lopez to any of those activities.[22]

Lopez's many parallels with Oswald in 1963—especially actions that would have incriminated him if JFK had been killed in Tampa instead of Dallas—show that Lopez was also being manipulated by someone working for Marcello, Trafficante, and Rosselli. According to newspaper reports, Gilberto Lopez "worked in the construction industry in Tampa—which has had a long-established organized crime connection with Key West—before traveling to Texas at the time of the assassination. His movements and activities suggest that he was a possible participant in Trafficante's activities."[23] From all the evidence we have seen—which includes every file on Lopez that has been released, material regarding attempts to get more of his files released, and an exclusive interview with his wife—we do not think that Lopez had any knowing involvement in JFK's assassination or Trafficante's criminal activities. Lopez's unusual actions that seemed to link him to JFK's assassination were likely the result of unknowing manipulation by someone working for Trafficante. A likely candidate would be David Ferrie's close associate in Florida, Eladio del Valle. Del Valle was a businessman and Cuban exile who was involved in running narcotics for Santo Trafficante and was partners with Rolando Masferrer.

Targeting Harry Williams

BEFORE C-DAY DEVELOPED IN May 1963, the Mafia had begun trying to set up their own Chicago-based exile group, eventually called the "Junta of the Government of Cuba in Exile," often shortened to "the Junta" or JGCE. It began forming in April 1963, but newspaper reports quickly tagged the group as being backed by mobsters linked to Havana casinos. Historian Richard Mahoney writes that on May 19, 1963, "the *Miami News* reported in an article titled 'Gamblers Pop Out of the Exile Grab Bag' that Chicago-based gangsters were behind the" Junta, including "a Trafficante asset."[1] The Junta made attempts to join C-Day, but they were cordially rebuffed by Harry Williams, who referred them to the State Department, which was not part of C-Day. The Junta organization had folded by November 1963. The Mafia also provided funds to other exile groups like the DRE; but, as those groups were passed by for C-Day, they became of little use to the Mafia.[2]

Once C-Day began to develop in late May 1963, it presented the Mafia with a golden opportunity to get "cover" for their planned assassination of JFK. To briefly recap, in the buildup to the C-Day coup, US intelligence assets would get into Cuba either covertly or openly (if they had suitable cover or nationality). Castro would be killed by the high Cuban official and Revolutionary hero who was the coup leader, but Castro's death would be blamed on someone else, preferably with a connection to Russia, to turn the Cuban people against the thousands of Russians who remained in Cuba. Harry Williams would be in Cuba when Castro was killed, and after his death the "five fingers" would converge on Cuba from their various bases: Manuel Artime, Tony Varona, Manolo Ray, Eloy Menoyo, and the leaders of the Army's Cuban exile group at Fort Benning would join Harry Williams and the coup leader in a new Provisional Government. The Cuban exile troops from Fort Benning would be the first US military forces into Cuba, but the Provisional Government would ask for more US military assistance if needed.

That's the way the plan was supposed to work, with Bobby Kennedy calling the shots and the US military (Cyrus Vance, Chairman of the Joint Chiefs General Maxwell Taylor, and DIA Chief General Joseph Carroll) having the leading official role, with the CIA (Helms, FitzGerald, Morales, Phillips, and allegedly McCord and Hunt) having key supporting roles—like getting US intelligence assets into Cuba. Contingency plans were also made to protect C-Day in case Castro found out and tried to retaliate, though this planning was complicated because some of those involved didn't know about the real C-Day plan; they only knew about lower-level disgruntled Cuban officials like Cubela/AMLASH or those involved in AMTRUNK—and none of those working on the Cuba contingency plans knew about the threat to JFK from the Mafia.

In reality, every segment of the C-Day plan would be penetrated by associates of Marcello, Trafficante, and Rosselli. Each of the five fingers was compromised in some way, and Harry Williams himself was targeted by Trafficante and his men. The Mafia compromised the CIA on many levels, including the intelligence assets they were trying to get into Cuba openly via Mexico City, like Oswald and Gilberto Lopez. The Mafia had also compromised the CIA's other plots to kill Castro, including the Cubela/AMLASH operation, the European assassin recruiter QJWIN and other plots with French nationals, and of course the ongoing CIA-Mafia plots to kill Castro. The Mafia even had ways to feed disinformation to the US military planners, including Vance and the DIA, through men like Guy Banister and John Martino.

Rosselli, Marcello, and Trafficante each had gambling empires, so all three could see that the odds were in their favor. At least fourteen associates of Marcello, Trafficante, and Rosselli learned about C-Day—and six of those men actually worked on C-Day. In addition, more than two dozen associates of the mob bosses or Jack Ruby had met with JFK, Bobby Kennedy, or their close aides.

Associates of Rosselli, Marcello, and Trafficante who knew about C-Day included Miami CIA Chief of Operations David Morales, John Martino, Frank Fiorini, Tony Varona, David Ferrie, Eloy Menoyo, Guy Banister, Carlos Prio, Jack Ruby, Lee Harvey Oswald, Rolando Masferrer, Richard Cain, Manuel Artime, and a CIA operative. Six of those who actually worked on C-Day in an official capacity, according to government documents, include

Morales, Varona, Menoyo, Artime, David Ferrie, and a CIA operative. However, just because a person had dealt with Trafficante in the past does not
mean that the person was a knowing participant in the JFK assassination
plot. For example, according to government documents and his partner
Antonio Veciana, Eloy Menoyo had engaged in arms deals with Trafficante—
but all the evidence shows that Menoyo had no knowing involvement in the
death of JFK. Menoyo's focus was strictly on overthrowing Castro.

The large number of associates of Jack Ruby or his Mafia bosses who had
met with the Kennedys (or their close aides) also created ways in which the
Mafia could learn about or compromise C-Day. This list includes Guy Ban-
ister, David Morales, Dominick Bartone, Sam Benton, Judy Campbell, a CIA
operative, David Ferrie, Sam Giancana, William Harvey, Jimmy Hoffa, David
Morales, Peter Lawford, Mike McLaney, Dean Martin, John Martino,
Menoyo, Marilyn Monroe, Edward Partin, Carlos Prio, Frank Ragano,
Johnny Rosselli, Norman Rothman, Frank Fiorini, Frank Sinatra, and Tony
Varona.

Some parts of C-Day were easy for the Mafia to compromise, while others
took repeated effort. Cuban exile leader Tony Varona was relatively easy,
since he had been working with Trafficante and Rosselli on the CIA-Mafia
plots since 1960. Varona's group—the Cuban Revolutionary Council—had
been active in New Orleans and had shared office buildings and other activities with Guy Banister and David Ferrie. Harry Williams and the Kennedys
viewed Varona as important for the new Provisional Government, but not
Varona's problematic organization, so the funding for the organization had
been cut in May 1963. This cut made Varona amenable to a bribe from
Rosselli's Chicago Mafia family, to bring the banned Rolando Masferrer
secretly into Varona and Artime's part of C-Day. In addition, Varona had long
been the protégé of corrupt former Cuban president Carlos Prio, a relationship he maintained through the fall of 1963.

As for the other "five fingers," the Mafia's attempts to link them to JFK's
assassination are detailed in the following pages. The Mafia first targeted
Artime through his minor-league training camp outside New Orleans, a
camp that Ferrie and Oswald visited. After Menoyo's earlier dealings with
Trafficante, he was apparently wary, so the Mafia arranged to have Menoyo's
partner—Antonio Veciana—meet Lee Harvey Oswald. Manolo Ray proved
incorruptible, so Trafficante had John Martino and Rolando Masferrer

arrange to have Oswald (or someone posing as Oswald) meet with one of Ray's supporters in Dallas. Fort Benning was home to the largely incorruptible and well-trained Cuban-exile Army troops. However, Fort Benning—across the river from the formerly notorious Phenix City—was also a stop on the French Connection heroin network of Trafficante, Marcello, and Michel Victor Mertz. A major bust would be made there shortly after C-Day was cancelled, and a few Cuban-exile soldiers were later linked to drug smuggling.

Harry Williams himself was the target of three attempts by the Mafia to penetrate C-Day, one of which almost cost him his life. While staying at Bobby Kennedy's Manhattan apartment, Harry had to face down Rolando Masferrer, Trafficante's associate and the former leader of Cuba's most feared death squad. Masferrer and his two "gangsters" wanted in on the Kennedys' plan, but Harry rebuffed their attempt. Harry Williams also survived a personal meeting with Mafia godfather Santo Trafficante, well known for eliminating those who crossed him. Trafficante tried to make Harry an attractive offer that he couldn't refuse at the meeting, which Harry says he was taken to by a CIA official later involved in Watergate. Finally, Harry barely survived an assassination attempt by two hit men in a restaurant.

MASFERRER CONFRONTS HARRY AT BOBBY KENNEDY'S NEW YORK APARTMENT
While laying the groundwork for C-Day, Harry had grown close to Bobby Kennedy. They had learned to trust one another during the tense negotiations for the release of the Bay of Pigs prisoners, and they built on that relationship in the spring of 1963 to put together a plan to topple Castro, a plan that would become C-Day. In addition to Washington, D.C. and Bobby's Virginia estate at Hickory Hill, one of the places Harry met with Bobby Kennedy was New York City. Bobby—later a New York senator—stayed at his father's large Manhattan apartment, and he sometimes asked Harry to stay there as well; "so, I stayed with him, same apartment," Harry told us.

Harry says Bobby would walk "with me in the streets of New York," and sometimes as late as "10 or 11 at night, he would invite me to a place . . . he knew close to the St. Patrick's Cathedral, that he liked." And while walking back to the Kennedy apartment, Harry remembers being amazed that if Bobby's shoe became untied, Bobby would just "sit down on the sidewalk and start tying his shoe." The sight of the Attorney General of the United States, the second most powerful man in the world, sitting on a New York sidewalk in the middle of the night—as traffic and people went by—apparently unnerved the cautious Williams. Harry warned Bobby that "you got thousands" of people who don't like you, "all these Mafia people" and "if some son of a bitch comes out here and starts shooting. . . ." Harry says he told Bobby, "they're going to try to kill you," but Bobby didn't seem concerned or cautious about his own safety. At that time, Harry didn't know that Bobby had already gotten wind of Hoffa's earlier plans to assassinate him.

In the spring of 1963, Harry Williams was at the Kennedy apartment in New York one day without Bobby. The secret groundwork for C-Day was being laid, but word was already circulating in Cuban exile circles that Harry had the backing of the Kennedys. This was at a time when CIA support for most exile groups was being cut back, so the word was out that Harry was the man to see if you wanted the Kennedys' backing. Rolando Masferrer had tried to see JFK at the White House a couple of years earlier, and now Masferrer somehow found out that Harry was at the Kennedys' New York apartment and went to see him there.

Harry was surprised to see Masferrer, accompanied by two "gangsters." Harry described the two men with Masferrer in New York as looking like classic Mafia torpedoes, thugs to back up Masferrer. The former death-squad leader demanded to become part of Harry's operation. Harry was familiar with Masferrer, and told us later that he "had a very strong organization," but that Masferrer was a "Mafia type, there is no question about it." Harry explained he had "been told that" Masferrer and his men sometimes "scared some of the Cubans, for money"—raising money through intimidation, like a classic Mafia protection racket. Harry said that "is why I dropped him" from any consideration for C-Day.[3]

Harry said that Masferrer was "enraged" at being turned down, but Harry refused to be intimidated. Finally, Masferrer and his two thugs left. Bobby Kennedy was no doubt glad when Harry related the incident, since Bobby had been trying to prosecute Masferrer since 1961 and had his activities monitored by the FBI.

HARRY MEETS WITH THE CIA, BUT IS SURPRISED TO FIND TRAFFICANTE THERE
As C-Day developed during the summer of 1963 and Harry's plan got even more backing from the Kennedys—as well as the CIA and the military—Trafficante decided to try a more direct approach to Harry Williams. Neither the Kennedys or Harry Williams realized that the CIA-Mafia plots against Castro were continuing, nor that Trafficante's close associate Johnny Rosselli con-

tinued to meet regularly with Miami CIA Operations Director David Morales. It's likely that both Rosselli and Morales had a hand in setting up the meeting between Harry Williams and Santo Trafficante.

On one hand, Morales could make a case that the CIA's Security Office needed to see if Harry was "on the take" from Trafficante, and Morales could easily find out when Harry would be in Miami to meet with one of the CIA officials assigned to assist him. On the other hand, Johnny Rosselli would be very interested in setting up a meeting between Harry and Trafficante. At best, Trafficante would be able to bribe Harry. At the very least, having the CIA set up a meeting between Harry and Trafficante would be one more link between the Mafia and C-Day, something else the CIA would have to cover up after the JFK assassination.

Harry went to meet the CIA official at a Miami restaurant. The CIA official left for a few minutes, and then Harry was surprised to see Santo Trafficante in the bar. Trafficante got Harry's attention, and said he wanted to talk. Harry said he "knew Trafficante's reputation" as a "Mafia guy." Yet when Harry "met him in Miami," he was surprised that "he looked like kind of an old man." Harry said Trafficante actually "looked to me very gentle, like a gentleman." Harry explained that "you know, sometimes you meet a guy you know that is involved in some [very unsavory] things" but he looks very "different" from his reputation.

The meeting lasted only minutes, and Trafficante quickly came to the point. Harry says Trafficante wanted "to see me to give me money." No specific numbers were mentioned, but Trafficante implied "it would be big." Trafficante said "look, I am a businessman . . . I want to go back to Cuba and I want to recover what I got" there. If "you win, I want my casinos back." That was Trafficante's proposition.

Harry politely declined the godfather's offer and excused himself. Minutes later, the CIA official returned, and didn't mention Trafficante. It's difficult to say if the CIA official took Harry to the restaurant intentionally to meet Trafficante, or if Morales had learned of the meeting and passed the word to Rosselli, who told Trafficante. Harry says he was contacted "by the FBI . . . two weeks" later. They must have had Trafficante under surveillance, because they told Harry "you had a conversation in a bar in such and such a place. What are you doing with that guy?" Harry told the FBI agent "none of your business," and he says the agent just "laughed." After all, the FBI wasn't after Harry, they were after Trafficante. FBI records were surely generated about the meeting between the FBI agents and Harry, and probably about

Harry's meeting with Trafficante, yet none have yet been released. It's just one more example of what the CIA and FBI would have to cover up after JFK's assassination, ostensibly to protect C-Day—but it also covered up a Mafia attempt to penetrate it.

Having failed to bribe or intimidate Harry, to Trafficante there was only one thing left: kill him. If Harry were dead, then Manuel Artime—later tied to Trafficante—would become the de facto exile head of C-Day, and Trafficante's man Tony Varona would have an even greater role. In addition, Harry was the only exile leader who really wanted to include the more liberal Manolo Ray and Eloy Menoyo (though both had the support of the Kennedys). Without Harry, they might go as well, and that could create openings for Trafficante associates Carlos Prio and Rolando Masferrer.

AN ATTEMPT TO ASSASSINATE HARRY LEADS TO A RESTAURANT SHOOTOUT

Harry occasionally went to Guatemala in 1963, where Artime had one of his C-Day bases. Shortly before one such trip, Harry had been warned by an FBI man close to Bobby Kennedy that his life was in danger. Harry at first thought the FBI agent meant that Castro wanted to kill him, but the FBI agent explained that he meant someone on the same side as Harry. The FBI man "advised" Harry to "take a gun" and to "have a gun with you" at all times. So Harry took his pistol with him to Guatemala. Harry had been to Guatemala before, during his Bay of Pigs training, and was well aware of the 1954 CIA-backed coup there and the 1957 assassination of the president of Guatemala. Harry was not aware of the ties of Johnny Rosselli and Carlos Marcello (and David Ferrie) to Guatemala.

When Harry got to the restaurant in Guatemala City for his meeting, he was careful to get a corner table so that he could see anyone entering the restaurant. Harry and his companion were having their meeting in the restaurant's back corner, near the kitchen. Harry said "it was open enough you could see the people that were coming in, you know, about ten steps, so I was watching all the time." Before they finished their meal, Harry noticed two nervous young men enter the dining area. Their leather jackets were in stark contrast to the evening attire of the diners and staff. "These two men came in, you could see that they were . . . not professionals," not real hit men, but "naive" young thugs. Harry told his companion to "get out, get out through the kitchen . . . get out the back door and if you hear anything" like shots "get out" and if you "don't hear anything, come back."

One of the punks pulled a gun, "but before he [could] shoot, I shot him,"

Harry said. He said that that thug "dropped and then the other guy started running and I got out of the restaurant myself." Harry went straight to his "hotel" and was surprised that "nobody said anything. It was not in the papers, there was nothing. Just like it didn't happen . . . no police, nothing."

Harry says "I called Bobby from Guatemala. I said 'look here, Bobby, they just took a shot at me.' Bobby asked 'What happened, did they catch you?' I say 'nothing happened to [one] guy, [but] I killed the other guy. There were two of them. The other guy just ran like hell." Harry immediately went to the airport and left the country. Harry said he feels that whoever was behind the hit "was somebody that had pull, because you don't kill a guy in a restaurant and you don't shoot it out in a restaurant without at least coming in the paper." As noted in Chapter 26, Johnny Rosselli reportedly had that kind of "pull." One CIA document says that Manuel Artime was involved in the CIA-Mafia plots to kill Castro, at the same time the CIA was supporting Artime, which raises the question of Artime's possible role in, or knowledge of, the attack on Harry.

No mention of the shootout or the death of the hit man ever made the papers. However, indirect confirmation of it surfaced years later, via a very similar attack. In 1972, the *New York Times* reported on another assassination attempt in a restaurant in Guatemala City, only this one was successful. A Guatemalan official was shot in a restaurant by two men with pistols, who fled the scene and were never captured.[4] The victim had recently begun working with an old friend of Harry's—Manuel Artime.[5] According to the *Miami Herald* and *San Francisco Chronicle*, at the time Artime was working on an offshoot of the Watergate "plumbers" operation and the official's assassination occurred shortly after the Watergate break-in.[6]

A couple of years before the attack on Harry, while David Ferrie was working for Marcello, Ferrie had stalked one of Bobby Kennedy's Mafia prosecutors in Guatemala. This raises the possibility that Ferrie might have had some involvement in the attack on Harry in Guatemala. The attack occurred in the late summer or fall of 1963. The HSCA found that David "Ferrie said he went to Guatemala on business for Marcello from October 11 to October 18 [1963] and from October 30 to November 1."[7] When shown a picture of David Ferrie, Harry said it "looked familiar," though he couldn't place where he had seen Ferrie before.

The French Connection Heroin Network and the Plan to Kill JFK

A CIA MEMO NAMES MICHEL Victor Mertz, notorious assassin and mastermind of the French Connection heroin network involving Trafficante and Marcello, as being in Dallas when JFK was murdered.[1] Mertz's French Connection heroin network was a key link between the operations of Marcello, Trafficante, and Rosselli, and was vital to their plan to assassinate JFK. Mertz's network included key participants in JFK's assassination, from those behind the scenes like Jimmy Hoffa to active participants like Jack Ruby. In Mertz, the mob bosses had an experienced killer to coordinate JFK's assassination on the ground. While Mertz had perfected the classic technique of hiding heroin in cars shipped from France to America on ocean liners as depicted in the *French Connection* film, he had learned how to manipulate French authorities to gain immunity and special treatment—something that would be useful before, during, and after the JFK assassination.

For decades, Mertz had skillfully played both sides in various conflicts so that he always came out on top. In World War II, Mertz initially sided with the Nazis—until the tide of war turned, at which time he joined the French Resistance. According to Pulitzer Prize–winning reporter Robert Greene, Mertz did so in spectacular fashion, gaining his Resistance reputation by taking a "machine gun into" a French café, leaving "15 Germans slaughtered."[2] This and other feats earned Mertz France's highest medal, the French Legion of Honor, which he used to cover a variety of criminal activities. When the authorities could no longer ignore his crimes, he joined French Intelligence—an organization called the SDECE (similar to the US Secret Service and the CIA)—to gain additional protection. For the French SDECE, Mertz infiltrated Jean Souetre's OAS officers who were opposed to independence for the French colony of Algeria. Souetre confirmed that "he and Mertz had served together in two units in Algeria in 1958–59, but had not seen each other after that time."[3]

In 1959, the French rebel officers of the OAS tried to assassinate French President Charles de Gaulle, but were stopped by the timely intervention of Israeli leader Shimon Peres.[4] That was only the first of more than a dozen attempts to assassinate de Gaulle, and the SDECE used a variety of criminals in its battle against the rebel officers.

After helping the SDECE, Mertz returned to his main criminal activity, smuggling heroin to the US hidden in cars on ocean liners.[5] Later, when the rebel officers were once more planning to assassinate de Gaulle, Mertz went undercover again. According to *The Marseilles Mafia*, Mertz's job was to infiltrate the OAS. Back in mainland France "in June (1961), he was arrested for distributing OAS propaganda leaflets in the Paris streets, and" was jailed. *The Marseilles Mafia* notes that "the flimsiness of the pretext seems to indicate it was a maneuver on the part of the" SDECE.[6] Once Mertz was imprisoned with the OAS rebels, he revealed their plot to the French authorities in the nick of time, saving de Gaulle's life and earning even more protection for Mertz.

According to Fensterwald, and confirmed by a Pulitzer Prize–winning series in William Attwood's *Newsday*, Mertz's heroin network was "closely connected with the Trafficante organization in Florida." But "several times during the 1960s, the US asked France to take action against Mertz, but the French refused because of his SDECE and Gaullist connections. He was literally known as one of the 'untouchables.'"[7] While Mertz's connections protected him from arrest, his heroin network had suffered a major setback in late 1962 when one of its shipments going into Houston had been busted. A history of the Federal Bureau of Narcotics (FBN) describes the "November 7, 1962 bust . . . in Houston" of "twenty-two pounds of heroin from" a close associate of Mertz. The heroin was destined for a New York mobster who was "a former co-owner of the Sans Souci casino in Havana with . . . Santo Trafficante."[8] One of Bobby Kennedy's Mafia prosecutors, Ronald Goldfarb, confirmed that the "big narcotics case in Houston" was "associated with Trafficante."[9]

For heroin going through Houston, the case would have also involved Carlos Marcello. The loss of twenty-two pounds of heroin was significant, as was another bust of Mertz's network the following year, also in Texas, when thirty-four kilos of heroin were seized from a Mertz courier by US Customs officials. That bust also involved an anti-Castro Cuban named Fulgencio Cruz Bonet.[10] However, Trafficante and Marcello had a way that Mertz could utilize his unique skills, connections, and background to make up for these tremendous losses.

By July 1963, Mertz was taking steps that linked him to C-Day and to the JFK assassination. Johnny Rosselli or QJWIN could have covered their dealings with Mertz by telling the CIA that they were considering using Mertz in a Castro-assassination plot. Mertz's involvement in the JFK plot was probably due to his huge heroin losses, but there were other factors as well. Though it's often overlooked by historians, the Kennedys were making headlines in early 1963 with their "Presidential Advisory Commission on Narcotics and Drug Abuse" that recommended "rehabilitation for addicts rather than imprisonment," along with a "massive attack on [heroin] importers and distributors."[11] In addition, Mertz was watching his heroin network partners Trafficante and Marcello, and Rosselli's Chicago Mafia, suffer increasingly at the hands of the Kennedys. For Trafficante and Marcello, Mertz's network included all the right places for their plans to kill JFK: Texas; Florida; the upper Midwest and Montreal; and even Fort Benning, where some of the C-Day Cuban exiles were training.

The reason that Mertz was in Dallas on November 22, 1963 can be traced to three critical issues regarding assassins that the CIA's Richard Helms was dealing with in June of 1963. The three assassins were Johnny Rosselli, QJWIN, the CIA's European assassin recruiter, and Jean Souetre, member of a rebel French Army group. Rosselli, QJWIN and Souetre all had links to Mertz, whom a CIA memo says was "expelled from the US at . . . Dallas 48 hours after the assassination of President Kennedy."[12] Helms's concerns with Rosselli, QJWIN, and Souetre in June 1963 help to explain how Mertz was able to penetrate C-Day and influence the actions of Lee Harvey Oswald three months before JFK's murder.

While Rosselli's connection to JFK's assassination has been discussed in several books, the roles of Mertz, QJWIN, and Souetre have baffled investigators since the first CIA reports about them surfaced in the 1970s. By compiling all the known information about them and putting it in the context of C-Day and Mertz's other documented activities, the roles of all three in the events surrounding JFK's death become much clearer. Our revelations build on the work of former Senate investigator Bud Fensterwald; a Pulitzer Prize–winning series published by JFK's special ambassador, William Attwood; and new information from Jean Souetre himself via French journalist Stephane Risset.

As C-Day developed in 1963, we noted in Part I that CIA Deputy Director for Plans Richard Helms reactivated or renewed three other CIA assassination operations—QJWIN (of the ZRRIFLE "Executive Action" program), Rolando Cubela (AMLASH), and Johnny Rosselli—in the CIA-Mafia plots. These were assets that only the CIA controlled, unlike C-Day in which the CIA played only a supporting role. While it took until the mid-1970s for Cubela's identity to be revealed, the CIA has never officially revealed QJWIN's true name—probably because all those operations were penetrated by the Mafia and linked to JFK's assassination.

QJWIN had originally been used by the CIA in attempts to assassinate Congo leader Patrice Lumumba, an effort that began prior to JFK's election in 1960. William Harvey later began using QJWIN in his ZRRIFLE assassination program, the one famous for its use of the term "Executive Action" to describe its goal of assassinating foreign leaders. Harvey and Richard Helms continued to use QJWIN in 1962 and 1963. But after angering Bobby Kennedy by sending a hit team into Cuba during the Missile Crisis, Harvey was being phased out of his role in Cuban operations in 1963, in favor of Desmond FitzGerald.

In June 1963, Harvey had one final meeting with Johnny Rosselli, whose handling was apparently turned over to Miami CIA operations chief David Morales. Harvey also wrote a memo about QJWIN on June 27, 1963, which appears to involve some sort of transition: Harvey said that QJWIN was "capable of operating in certain circles in Europe where we have very few assets," but Harvey explained that the CIA's continued use of QJWIN depends on whether "he can be used by any other" CIA "informant as a long term unofficial cover agent." (In the original memo, the word "informant" is overwritten by hand with a word that looks like "operation" or "operative.")[13]

The day after Harvey's QJWIN memo, the CIA issued its first memo establishing the AMWORLD operation, the CIA's code name for their portion of C-Day. The AMWORLD memo says that memos about it are to be coded with the terms RYBAT SECRET TYPIC YOBITE AMWORLD. Those terms appear on many of the CIA C-Day documents that have been released. The RYBAT term had previously been used by the CIA on some—but not all—of the QJWIN documents. Most of QJWIN's monthly payment records did not have the "RYBAT" term (like those for his May 1963 salary, paid in June, or his June salary, paid in July). But by the time of his October 1963 salary—paid on November 22, 1963—QJWIN's payment memos bear the RYBAT code word.[14] RYBAT appears on the few QJWIN documents the CIA has released after that date. Just as Johnny Rosselli was picked up by another CIA handler in June of 1963, this raises the possibility that assassin recruiter QJWIN was also picked up by David Morales or another CIA officer, for use in one of the CIA's Castro assassination operations.

William Harvey seems to imply something of that nature when he says in his June 27, 1963 memo that QJWIN was "on ice as far as any operational assignments are concerned" and "as far as the ZRRIFLE aspects of this operation which have been covered under the QJWIN authorization . . . except for one precautionary 'life line,' aspects of this case have been terminated."[15] What—or who—this "life line" was has never been revealed. But we do know that Desmond FitzGerald was aware of QJWIN. That's because a CIA accounting memo—about a financial discrepancy from the time the CIA dispatched QJWIN to the Congo to try to assassinate Congolese leader Lumumba—was copied to Desmond FitzGerald's Special Affairs Staff (SAS). The primary goal of FitzGerald's SAS in the summer and fall of 1963 was the elimination of Castro.

The CIA's assassination operations were a closely guarded secret, kept even from JFK's CIA Director, John McCone. FitzGerald, and his superior in these matters Richard Helms, may have been the highest CIA officials who knew about the assassination aspects of QJWIN, which was also true for the assassination aspects of the Cubela operation. Just as McCone and some other government officials were aware of Cubela only as an intelligence asset—not as an assassin—evidence indicates that the same was true for QJWIN. QJWIN was run out of the CIA's Luxembourg station, and was paid from the CIA's Paris station, and there are indications that they—and McCone—were not fully informed about QJWIN's assassin-recruitment activities. So, in addition to the CIA-Mafia plots with Rosselli, and the Cubela assassination plot, QJWIN was yet another CIA assassination operation being kept from JFK's CIA Director.

There are documented ties between the CIA-Mafia plots with Johnny Rosselli and the QJWIN operation: According to William Harvey's handwritten notes, the expenses for his meetings with Rosselli in Miami were reimbursed under the QJWIN program. As for QJWIN himself, he was being paid only $7,200 a year, plus operational expenses, to recruit potential CIA assassins from the elite of Europe's criminals, from jewel thieves to heroin smugglers. Some underworld figures were paying CIA assets far more to compromise CIA operations, as verified by the CIA memo that says that in July 1963, four members of Rosselli's Chicago mob paid C-Day exile leader Tony Varona "$200,000."[16] QJWIN's European CIA handler wondered whether QJWIN "really intended to commit himself to [his CIA] assignment," since he has a "habit of hedging his bets."[17]

Just as French Intelligence would keep an eye on Cubela in the fall of 1963, French Intelligence may have also been keeping tabs on QJWIN, if not actively assisting him. In an interview with former Senate investigator James P. Kelly, who had worked for Bobby Kennedy in the late 1950s, Kelly mentioned "contacts in French Intelligence who approached US with capacity to hit Castro."[18] Kelly was referring to the early 1960s, using information he uncovered while working for Congressional committees in the 1970s.

Another report says that in May 1978, a Congressional investigator interviewed Phillipe de Vojoli, who headed French intelligence in the US in 1963, who "talked generally about plots against Castro and an offer by French Intelligence to the CIA to carry out the Castro assassination for them."[19] French Intelligence may have been at least monitoring QJWIN, and—given the many potential assassination candidates QJWIN and William Harvey reviewed who were French—may have overtly or covertly assisted him. At least three well-known French criminals had well-documented ties to Cuba, either through marriage or because of their heroin-smuggling or nightclub interests there, ties that would have been helpful in a Castro assassination attempt. All three French criminals with ties to Cuba—Paul Mondoloni, Jean Baptiste Croce, and Ansan Bistoni—were key members of the French Connection heroin network of Santo Trafficante and Michel Victor Mertz.

QJWIN had one assassination in his background, but seemed better suited to recruiting others. In QJWIN's case, his CIA file says he was "arrested" in "1919 in Geneva for complicity in an assassination."[20] That would make QJWIN at least in his early sixties by 1963, though some documents in his CIA file give the impression of a younger man. In fact, the age of QJWIN is not easy to pin down, based on the CIA documents that have been released, which are sometimes at odds with the testimony of CIA officials. For example, Richard Helms testified about QJWIN that "if you needed somebody to carry out murder, I guess you had a man who might be prepared to carry it out." That seems odd to say about someone whose last documented murder was over forty years before he was recruited by the CIA.[21] One would hope that with all the resources of the CIA, they could find a more recently experienced assassin, and one not in his sixties, but perhaps Helms was confusing QJWIN with one of the killers QJWIN had recruited.

Problems with CIA testimony and files about QJWIN are due in part to the intense level of secrecy surrounding CIA assassination operations. The QJWIN and ZRRIFLE operations began in the summer of 1960, at the very time the CIA was ramping up its assassination efforts with Castro by reaching out to Johnny Rosselli and Santo Trafficante. This was an era when Congressional oversight was lax and journalists rarely exposed top-secret government operations. Yet even then, William Harvey and his superiors knew that what they were doing had to be kept secret, even from most others in the CIA. They never dreamed of a time when the Freedom of Information Act would allow their internal memos to be widely published. Still, Harvey's notes about QJWIN/ZRRIFLE show that he wanted the files on the project to be "forged and backdated."[22] That would serve to protect the operations, even within the CIA—and provide cover for those involved, if they should ever be the subject of an internal CIA investigation. (Which is what happened after the JFK assassination, although the CIA's own JFK investigators weren't told about ZRRIFLE, QJWIN, or the CIA-Mafia plots.)

In addition to QJWIN's real name, much information about him and his activities has never been declassified, and other information may have been "forged and backdated" after the fact. One released document briefly refers to an important meeting QJWIN had with his European case officer in August 1963, but the actual reports of that meeting have never been released, even though numerous similar reports—dating from the much earlier era of the Lumumba assassination—have been declassified.[23] Unlike QJWIN's termination notice ("termination" as in "let go," not killed) in early 1964 after the JFK assassination, none of the 1963 reports of QJWIN's European case officer have been declassified. The QJWIN files that have been released so far are often censored, some so heavily that entire pages are blank. For example, a cable sent by the CIA Director to the Luxembourg CIA Station nine weeks after JFK's assassination is totally blank except for a handwritten "eyes-only" notation. There may also be evidence of tampering in some of the files that have been released: One QJWIN file has a typed date of 1962, but a date stamp of being processed in 1965.[24] QJWIN was paid monthly, the same amount each month, but there are two payment dispatches for QJWIN's April 1963 monthly salary in his file, one dated May 10, 1963 and the other dated May 17—both identical, except for the date.[25]

Records and testimony are also unclear as to whether and when QJWIN and ZRRIFLE were applied to Castro's assassination. One cautiously worded CIA report from the 1970s says that—based on existing records and testimony— it wasn't. But an internal CIA Inspector General's report says that "after Harvey took over the Castro [assassination] operation, he ran it as one aspect of ZRRIFLE."[26] There are declassified expense notes for QJWIN written by William Harvey in early 1963 for an operation based in Miami, some of which clearly relate to his activities with Johnny Rosselli.[27] In addition, William Harvey admitted in his Senate testimony that some of his "notes" about ZRRIFLE were "missing" and "had been destroyed."[28]

One should be cautious about reading too much into the evidence that has been released so far, especially as it relates to Cuba. Take, for example, Harvey's June 27, 1963 memo about looking for a new operation for QJWIN, followed by the big June 28 CIA memo about C-Day/AMWORLD, followed by QJWIN's August 1963 meeting with his European case officer in which QJWIN is prodded to take action. It might be tempting to assume that QJWIN—based in Paris and trying to recruit assassins—had some connection to the CIA's September 28, 1963 assassination plot against Castro in which a Frenchman was captured. William Harvey had been sent a report about the Frenchman a year earlier.[29] But in that particular instance, there may not be a connection, since the Frenchman was a longtime Cuban resident and a member of a well-established Cuban exile group, meaning there was no reason to go through QJWIN to get to him. C-Day exile coordinator Harry Williams told us that he had heard about the Frenchman's capture, but indicated that it had nothing to do with C-Day.

QJWIN and ZRRIFLE first became publicly known during the Church Committee hearings about CIA abuses in the 1970s, and more information has been gradually released about them in the decades since, though some is still secret. Even in the mid-1970s, testimony between Harvey and other CIA officials about them varied, and sometimes an official's "testimony varied" over "the course of several appearances before the Committee."[30] Adding to the problem is the often-overlooked footnote in the Church Report that says ZRRIFLE had two parts, "the Executive Action assassination capability" and a "second program . . . meant to provide a cover for any Executive Action operation." However, the Committee felt that the "second program" was "not part of the subject matter of this Report," and it was not closely investigated.[31] How a "cover" program for CIA assassinations could not be within the scope of a report entitled "Alleged Assassination Plots Involving Foreign Leaders" is hard to fathom. Then again, as noted earlier in Part II, Bobby Kennedy's former top Hoffa informant was ready to tell the Committee about the 1959 CIA-Mafia plots, but that was not included in the Church Report either. So much was withheld from the Church Committee—from C-Day to the fall 1963 CIA-Mafia plots—that they never had the chance to see if

ZRRIFLE's "second program" cover operation had any ties to those operations, or to the JFK assassination.

ZRRIFLE's "second program" probably came in handy for keeping others in the CIA from learning about the assassination aspect of QJWIN. QJWIN was officially run (probably the "second program") through the Luxembourg CIA Station, and paid through the Paris CIA Station; and, at least by the fall of 1964, CIA Director John McCone knew about QJWIN. But there are indications that he didn't know about the assassination aspect of QJWIN. For example, sometime after September 30, 1963, the office of CIA Director McCone asked the Luxembourg CIA Chief for an "accounting for funds advanced to QJWIN" that was "long overdue. Request immediate action. . . ." McCone (or his office) didn't seem to realize that QJWIN had been run—at least through June 1963—by William Harvey, or that Desmond FitzGerald's SAS still maintained an interest in QJWIN. McCone hadn't been told about the ZRRIFLE assassination project, just as he hadn't been told about the CIA-Mafia plots until August 1963, when a story about them and Giancana surfaced in the press—and even then, McCone was not told that the plots were continuing.

Six months after QJWIN's termination in early 1964, Director McCone suddenly cabled someone (apparently the Luxembourg CIA Chief, though the memo is hard to read) for a "brief roundup of QJWIN Project and activities up to time of termination last February and any knowledge you have of him since that time." Apparently, someone at CIA headquarters warned McCone that he might learn more than he wanted to know, because the next day McCone sent a new cable saying "please destroy" the previous cable requesting the QJWIN "roundup."[32] (As detailed in a later chapter, just weeks after the "please destroy" cable—on the one-year anniversary of JFK's murder—an especially appropriate type of retribution would be exacted in Europe against someone with numerous links to QJWIN: French Connection heroin kingpin Michel Victor Mertz.)

The CIA's Richard Helms and William Harvey kept QJWIN on the payroll throughout all of 1963, when he was apparently not producing any results in establishing his "cover" or making progress of any kind. From some of the CIA's testimony and documents, it appears that QJWIN didn't do anything at all of substance. But this is belied by the many pages of censored notes and files about European assassins and smugglers that QJWIN and William Harvey considered at some length for various CIA operations.[33]

The CIA and Church Committee documents released so far do not address the question of who was handling or supervising the assassination aspect of

QJWIN in October and November 1963. By that time, William Harvey had been eased out of his previous roles in the Castro assassination plots with Johnny Rosselli, and out of Cuban operations in general. Those duties had been taken over by SAS head Desmond FitzGerald. Yet FitzGerald was a patrician blue-blood more at home in a Georgetown club than in the field, unlike the more rough-and-tumble Harvey. Just as David Morales took over Johnny Rosselli from William Harvey after June 1963, perhaps Morales also assumed responsibility for the assassination aspect of QJWIN. It's also possible that the assassination side of QJWIN was not closely supervised at that time. Either option presented opportunities for Rosselli, Trafficante, and Marcello.

We know from an incident in August 1962 that William Harvey—and the CIA in general—were loath to put anything about assassinations in writing, so it's possible that written records of the assassination side of QJWIN from the fall of 1963 don't exist or were among those destroyed. Much of QJWIN's assassination operation was handled on an EYES ONLY basis, one of the most secret CIA classifications. Some important documents do exist, like one dated February 19, 1962, when Richard Helms sent Harvey a memo saying that "for the purpose of ZRRIFLE activities, you are hereby authorized to retain the service of principal agent QJWIN and such other principal agents and subagents as may be required . . . through 31 December 1963 subject to renewal at that time." QJWIN's salary was given as $7,200, plus Helms authorized an additional $13,800 for expenses. Apparently the additional amount is so large because it had to cover expenses for the "other principal agents and sub-agents"—who, in one instance, included Johnny Rosselli. Immediately after that memo, however, Helms quickly sent an almost identical memo that adds a crucial item: "It is requested that this activity be handled strictly on an EYES ONLY basis" [capitalization in original].[34]

Even forty-five years after QJWIN was first hired by the CIA, his true identity is still secret; it was withheld even from members of the Church Committee like Senator Gary Hart. Today, based on the 1919 arrest report in one CIA file, QJWIN himself would have to be over a hundred years old if he were still alive. Because of the EYES ONLY basis and the "forged and backdated" documents, it has not been possible for historians and researchers to piece his identity together from released documents, as has sometimes been the case with other CIA operations.

Tampa investigative reporter H. P. Albarelli, Jr., writes that "QJ/WIN is sometimes erroneously identified by the aliases: Mozes/Moses Maschkivitzan; Jean Voignier; Michael Mancuso; and Jose/Michael Mankel. Complicating WIN's identity is the fact that there was more than one CIA contract-agent who operated under this moniker that was originally intended to include 'principal agents and sub-agents.'"[35] Based on the documents that have been released, European smuggler Michael Mankel (full name also given as Joe Marie Andre Mankel) seems the most likely choice, but in William Harvey's own handwritten notes, even his name is accompanied by a question mark. Historian Richard D. Mahoney's father worked for JFK as a diplomat in Africa shortly after QJWIN worked there, and he names Moses Moschkivitzan as QJWIN, and he is one of several men who appear in Harvey's QJWIN notes.[36] Since the late 1970s, others have pointed to the many parallels between QJWIN and Michel Victor Mertz.

Several people were considered for the role of QJWIN, including Charles Siragusa, a high official with the Bureau of Narcotics, and many more for the "principal agents and sub-agents," so it can sometimes be hard to tell who was the recruiter and who was the recruited. In the case of Rolando Cubela, whose code name was AMLASH, he was actually AMLASH 1, and there were also exiles assisting him named AMLASH 2 and AMLASH 3. The same could be true for QJWIN.

So much official CIA secrecy after forty-five years makes no sense for a man who—from most CIA accounts—accomplished nothing. In some ways, the secrecy surrounding the CIA's 1967 Inspector General's Report about the CIA-Mafia assassination plots provides an important clue. As noted earlier, that report was so secret that the CIA did not give (or show) it to the presidents who asked for it—LBJ and Nixon. It has only gradually been released starting in the mid-1970s, with the full report having only been released in the late 1990s (and even then with a few passages still censored).

When historians were finally able to see the report (almost) in full, the big surprise wasn't what it said—it was what it *didn't* say. It left out almost completely the 1959 and fall 1963 CIA-Mafia plots, and mentioned C-Day only obliquely, in one sentence—incredible omissions, since the report was supposed to look at the ties the Castro assassination plots might have had to the JFK assassination. That was the real reason for the secrecy—the fact that the report was so grossly incomplete. (The report was prepared at the direction of Richard Helms, who knew far more than was included in the report, but didn't bother telling his own investigators.) Something similar may well be true for QJWIN's true identity. The real secret might not be who QJWIN really was, after all; instead, the reason for so much secrecy might be something else—like the identity of one or more of the many European criminals he recruited for the CIA. Or that QJWIN's own identity—or cover identity—might have been used without the CIA's knowledge in a way that the CIA would be loath to ever admit.

Unless every QJWIN document the CIA has declassified is a "forgery" that has been "backdated," several things are clear. QJWIN spent time in Paris and was involved in smuggling, including drug smuggling. He targeted French criminals for recruitment on several occasions. For example, in November 1960, a CIA document says "QJWIN recommended two French contacts who agree [to] undertake unspecified job." Later, "during April 1961, QJWIN spotted some candidates in France."[37] Most of the CIA files naming potential assassins considered by Harvey and QJWIN are heavily censored. Some files were "destroyed," and others—ranging from one to twenty-three pages—are still withheld by the FBI and Drug Enforcement Administration (formerly the Federal Bureau of Narcotics). These include the alphabetical files where potential assassins with names starting with "M" would have been.[38] That makes it hard to see if Mankel, Moschkivitzan, Mancuso, or Michel Mertz were considered for recruitment by QJWIN—or *were* QJWIN.

There are two dozen parallels between Michel Mertz and QJWIN—both QJWIN the individual and QJWIN the program, as described in CIA documents. Both Mertz and QJWIN worked for French Intelligence, were involved in drug smuggling, and were seen as Nazi collaborators in France early in World War II before joining the Resistance. Their activities in the early 1960s parallel each other and intersect in many different areas, including Africa, Paris, Brussels, Frankfurt, and Switzerland. Even their backgrounds are similar—QJWIN was born and grew up in the tiny country of Luxembourg, while Mertz was born and grew up on the border between France and Luxembourg. Mertz also matches many of the criteria for the QJWIN program, such as his ties to Corsican mobsters, the Middle East, Paris, and the specific type of potential assassins Harvey and QJWIN were looking for. Mertz was born in 1920, and Harvey's notes show that he used or considered using one criminal named "(censored) born around 1921" in "France" who was still a "French national" and who was "in French underground with QJWIN 1943–45," the same time Mertz was in the underground.[39] The parallels between Mertz and QJWIN are too numerous to detail here, but all are contained in the following endnote.[40]

Some researchers, like former Senate investigator Bud Fensterwald, who led the legal fight to get many of the documents about QJWIN and Mertz declassified, thought that QJWIN probably was Michel Mertz. However, new

CIA documents released since Fensterwald's death make it appear more likely that Mertz—or one of his close associates—was one of the criminals QJWIN recruited for the ZRRIFLE operation. Mertz was exactly the type of criminal who QJWIN was supposed to recruit for CIA assassinations and other operations. William Harvey was looking at so many European—and especially French—criminals like Mertz and his associates that it would be unusual if they hadn't been considered. Also, Mertz had well-documented aliases that he sometimes used, like Maurice Valentin, so he could have also been used or considered under another name. The numerous parallels between Mertz and QJWIN raise another possibility as well—it would have been relatively easy for Mertz to have learned about QJWIN and assumed his identity for a limited period of time.

We noted earlier that Mertz was getting protection from some US agency, which kept his name not only out of the 1963 Congressional hearings on organized crime and narcotics—when all his close associates were named—but also out of the files of the Bureau of Narcotics until 1965. That was while Mertz was one of America's major heroin suppliers. As detailed in an upcoming chapter, there is considerable evidence that Mertz was one of possibly two men who were deported from Dallas shortly after the JFK assassination. Mertz almost always made his frequent flights between the US and Europe alone; for example, there was one in October 1963. But after that, and only for a short time in the weeks following JFK's assassination, government files show that Mertz started being accompanied by "an unnamed colleague of Mertz, whose travels parallel Mertz."[41] Perhaps that person was QJWIN or someone who worked for QJWIN or was using his identity, since shortly after Mertz's name surfaced in the JFK assassination investigation in Europe in February 1964, QJWIN was terminated from the CIA.

As mentioned earlier, Michel Victor Mertz utilized another CIA-connected name in his activities leading up to—and during—JFK's assassination in Dallas. That was Jean Souetre, a former French officer who was part of the 1962 assassination attempt against French President Charles de Gaulle that inspired the book and film *The Day of the Jackal*. By the summer and fall of 1963, the real Souetre was a fugitive, spending much of his time in Spain. Travel to a country like the US or Canada was out of the question for Souetre. Even though he had a fake US passport, he would have been arrested as a major fugitive if he had ever been caught in North America, not just deported but extradited to a French prison. Mertz, on the other hand, could—and did—travel freely to America at any time, frequently visiting New York City, Montreal, and Mexico City, all major stops in the heroin network that supplied Marcello and Trafficante as well as Rosselli's Chicago mob family.

Souetre—later pardoned by the French government in an amnesty for the officers who took part in the many assassination attempts against de Gaulle—says that Mertz had used his (Souetre's) name as an alias before, and was using it again in 1963, including when Mertz was in Dallas on November 22, 1963. Another stop on Mertz's heroin network was New Orleans, the port of entry for the heroin that went through Georgia's Fort Benning, home of the Cuban exile officers completing their training for C-Day. According to a memo to the Justice Department by former Senate investigator Bud Fensterwald, in the late spring of 1963 a Frenchman using the name Jean Souetre "went to New Orleans and met with" a Cuban exile who admits meeting Oswald and "to Lake Pontchartrain and helped train anti-Castro Cubans."[42]

Fensterwald's memo also links Alpha 66 to the camp, which at that time was closely allied with Menoyo's C-Day exile group. That also appears to be the same camp that Manuel Artime used as a kind of minor-league training camp there for a few months and the camp Ferrie and Oswald reportedly visited. More than ten years after Fensterwald's memo, in the 1990s, Army Intelligence declassified files stated that "Artime" said "he had obtained aid and instructors from Europe" for his Cuban exile operation.[43]

A Frenchman calling himself Souetre may well have been at the exile camp outside New Orleans—but the real Jean Souetre was in Europe at that time. Souetre did not visit America at all in the 1960s, while he was a wanted fugitive. However, INS and BNDD (Bureau of Narcotics and Dangerous Drugs, the successor to the FBN) records show that Michel Victor Mertz was in America in the summer of 1963. After being in the US for almost a month, Mertz left New York City for Cologne on June 19, 1963. Mertz could fly a small plane, so it was easy for him to get around the US—especially to a place like New Orleans, where Carlos Marcello's Churchill Farms had its own airstrip. If Mertz visited New Orleans and the exile training camp, he could have used "Souetre" as an alias. It would have been easy for Guy Banister to feed information to the FBI or some other federal agency long after Mertz had left, claiming that the real Souetre had been in the area. A close associate of Souetre confirmed to Fensterwald that Souetre had once met Banister, giving Banister a way to know about the real Souetre.[44] The FBI would always be seemingly one step behind Souetre in their search for him in America.

For the three mob bosses, Souetre was a critical name to link to C-Day and JFK's assassination, for several reasons. First, Souetre's conviction for the "Day of the Jackal" attack on de Gaulle's car would make authorities—and the public, if it came to that—view him as a logical assassin of JFK, because JFK supported de Gaulle's stance on Algeria. Second, the FBI had been looking for Souetre since at least April 1963, because of a Christmas card sent to Souetre by a Houston dentist. The card wound up in the US Post Office in New York, and since Souetre's name was on an international fugitive watch list, it generated a flurry of FBI memos. Given Banister's proximity to Houston, the New Orleans area's relatively large French population, and Banister's ties to right-wing French extremists, it's possible that the former FBI supervisor—who still maintained close ties to the FBI—might have been asked to check with his many informants for any sign of Souetre.

Most important for the Mafia, Souetre had been in recent contact with the CIA. His May 1963 CIA contact in Europe is well documented in CIA files, and one unconfirmed report says that Souetre even met with a CIA officer who was allegedly working on C-Day by the fall of 1963. Souetre's contact with the CIA was part of a long series of contacts between his OAS anti–de Gaulle group and the CIA. In a CIA exposé published in 1962, *Inside the CIA*, Andrew Tully had written about "a top-secret luncheon in Washington on December 7, 1960" between Richard Helms's predecessor, Richard Bissell, and an OAS leader who would later lead a coup against de Gaulle.[45] The coup attempt occurred in April 1961, and a former CIA case officer alleges that his predecessor "met with OAS leader General Raoul Salon in Paris just before the OAS mutiny . . . in Algeria in April 1961."[46] Tully writes that "when Pierre Salinger arrived in Paris on May 2," 1961, he had to contend with numerous press reports that the CIA had been behind the recent coup attempt against de Gaulle.[47] Fensterwald writes that "on December 12, 1961 . . . the 'high command of the OAS' met with" the "CIA Station Chief in Paris" about CIA help for an OAS coup against de Gaulle. The OAS "asked for equipment for an army of 50,000; in return" the CIA "asked for trade preference in the 'New Algeria' and US bases in the Sahara. A tentative deal was stuck and a draft agreement was rushed back to Washington . . . President Kennedy, who had been a strong advocate of Algerian independence since the mid-1950s, took a very dim view of the proposal, and he killed it."[48]

The CIA interest in the OAS predated JFK's presidency, and it continued after his death. The *Chicago Tribune* reported in June 1975 that "Congressional leaders involved in the Central Intelligence Agency investigation have been told of CIA involvement in a plot with French dissidents to assassinate the late Gen. Charles de Gaulle" that "dated to the mid-1960s" when "dissidents in the de Gaulle government contacted the CIA to seek help in a murder plot" during "the Johnson administration."[49]

So, Jean Souetre's approach to the CIA in Europe in May 1963 was just one in a long list of contacts between OAS representatives and the CIA. Souetre's approach eventually reached the desk of Richard Helms, who didn't pursue Souetre's proposal. At the time, Helms had his hands full dealing with assassins like QJWIN, the CIA-Mafia plots, and Cubela, as well as Helms's work known to the Kennedys on AMWORLD and AMTRUNK. Helms wrote a memo on July 10, 1963 about Souetre's CIA meeting in Europe, which was copied to the FBI.[50] That probably prompted another small flurry of activity on the part of the FBI, though those files—and the FBI's copy of Helms's July 10, 1963 memo—have not been released. That may be because the FBI followed the trail of someone they thought was Souetre to the Dallas area, only to lose track of him just before JFK's assassination.[51]

Mertz was able to cover his tracks while participating in JFK's assassination by using names that would cause alarms to go off at the FBI and CIA when they surfaced in conjunction with JFK's assassination. Probably with the help of his heroin partner—Marcello's private detective, Guy Banister—Mertz was able to use names like Souetre and links to QJWIN to force agencies to conduct secret—rather than public—investigations, and go into cover-up mode. As noted earlier, Mertz was just one of several participants in JFK's assassination linked to heroin trafficking. That's because the heroin trade was the Mafia's most secure, tight-knit, ruthless, and profitable business.

Other drug traffickers involved in the JFK plot included Rolando Masferrer and his associate Eladio del Valle. An investigator for the Senate Internal Security Subcommittee told a journalist in 1975 that del Valle "was a gun for hire . . . anything that had to do with smuggling, gun-running, del Valle was with it. Both a bagman and a hitman." He also indicated a possible connection to a CIA operative who was involved with C-Day and Trafficante.[52] Journalist Anthony Summers points out that "del Valle . . . was a close friend and associate of David Ferrie" and "also had contact with Trafficante." Summers also mentions that del Valle "headed the Free Cuba Committee in Florida," an anti-Castro group.

As noted earlier, a Warren Commission document—not cited in their final report—said that Ruby was part of the French Connection heroin network in Dallas, something later confirmed by a recent history of the Federal Bureau of Narcotics. The Warren Commission document said that since 1956, "Jack Ruby of Dallas" gave "the okay to operate" for a "large narcotics set up operating between Mexico, Texas, and the East."[53]

Also, a recent history of the FBN says that "the Church Committee notes that in 1962, QJ/WIN 'was about to go on trial in Europe on smuggling charges,' but the CIA wished to 'quash charges or arrange somehow to salvage QJ/WIN for our purposes.'"[54] While the CIA kept QJWIN out of jail, if he lost a quantity of drugs as had Mertz, that could have made QJWIN subject to manipulation by Mertz and Trafficante.

Mertz had several easy ways to get out of the US after JFK's death, in addition to using QJWIN's identity. If Mertz had ever been detained in the US— either before or after JFK's assassination—it would have been easy for him to get out of custody and the US by revealing his true identity. As a Legion of Honor winner with protection from French Intelligence, a hero who had recently saved de Gaulle's life, Mertz could use diplomatic means to leave the US if need be. Or, to avoid involving French Intelligence while he was still in the US, Mertz could pretend to be someone who was required to be immediately deported if they were ever detained or discovered in the US. Mertz had two close associates who had not joined the Resistance in World War II and who were wanted war criminals in France.[55] If Mertz posed as one of them and he were ever arrested, he would immediately be expelled from the US and deported (and once in France, Mertz could use his own clout to quickly get released). According to reports from two United States INS officials detailed later, that's exactly what happened in Dallas right after JFK's assassination, which explains the CIA report saying Mertz had been "expelled from the US at . . . Dallas 48 hours after the assassination of President Kennedy."[56] Imagine how Marcello—still smarting over his own deportation ordeal at the hands of Bobby Kennedy—must have felt after JFK's assassination, when one of his own hit men was deported to safety by the US government.

We noted earlier that Mertz had been part of an intelligence operation in France that involved his pretending to be pro-OAS, passing out pro-OAS leaflets, then being jailed. The same thing happened to Oswald in August 1963—only involving pro-Castro leaflets—in a well-documented incident detailed in the following chapters. However, it's not widely known that Oswald was also reportedly seen passing out pro-Castro leaflets in Montreal, where Mertz had a base and was a frequent visitor.

Either Oswald was in Montreal or someone impersonating him was, according to a report sent to the US Secret Service a week after JFK's assassination from the "Senior Customs Representative, US Treasury Department Bureau of Customs, Montreal, Canada." The report says that "several persons have contacted this office recently and advised that Lee Oswald, suspected of assassinating the late President Kennedy, was seen distributing pamphlets entitled 'Fair Play for Cuba,' on St. Jacques and McGill Streets, Montreal, during the summer of 1963. Mr. Jean Paul Tremblay, Investigator, Customs and Excise, Montreal stated on November 27, 1963 that he received one of the above-mentioned pamphlets from a man on St. Jacques Street, Montreal, believed to be in August 1963, and he is positive that his person was Oswald. Mr. Tremblay also stated that . . . he believes he could identify the three persons that accompanied Oswald and that the reason for paying special attention to these persons was because he was working on cases involving Cuba at the time."[57]

Perhaps the obscure Montreal incident was a "dry run" for Oswald's well-publicized activities of a similar nature in New Orleans—which, upcoming chapters document, involving Guy Banister. Jean Souetre says that Mertz was using his name in 1963, which accounts for reports of Souetre's meeting with "General Edwin A. Walker at Dallas" and with an exile "group led by Rolando Masferrer," and at the training camp linked to Artime "on the bank of Lake Pontchartrain in 1963" that Oswald reportedly visited with David Ferrie.[58] A French investigator told Fensterwald that the arms used by the Cuban exiles at the camp "were furnished by the intermediary at the Guantanamo Naval Base" and "training took place at the New Orleans region" and the headquarters for the activity "was 544 Camp Street." Journalist Dick Russell notes "544 Camp Street . . . was Guy Banister's office, and the address stamped on Oswald's (pro-Castro) Fair Play for Cuba literature."[59] In each of those cases, the man using Souetre's identity was Michel Victor Mertz, who was also involved in heroin smuggling through New Orleans with Marcello's organization.

Oswald
and the Summer of 1963

MARCELLO'S ATTEMPT TO SOLIDLY LINK Oswald to C-Day ended with the closure of Artime's minor-league camps outside of New Orleans. When another camp nearby was raided by the FBI and a large cache of weapons and explosives was discovered Artime's camp was closed. Marcello's men Guy Banister and David Ferrie then found a new way to link Oswald to C-Day, using the same technique that had helped Michel Victor Mertz infiltrate the OAS. This would fit well with CIA Officer David Atlee Phillips's plan to build Oswald's public pro-Castro persona, in preparation for getting him into Cuba as a US asset to support C-Day and the CIA's other anti-Castro plots. It would also damage the reputation of the Fair Play for Cuba Committee, something Phillips had been working on since 1961. However, Phillips wouldn't be aware that he was being used by Marcello's men, in much the same way that Phillips was using Oswald. Phillips's efforts to get Oswald into Cuba as a US asset were infiltrated by associates of Marcello, Trafficante, and Rosselli, in order to make Oswald look more guilty after JFK's death. They were successful and Oswald's actions generated four mysterious incidents that have stymied historians and government investigators for decades.

All four incidents make sense when put in the context of C-Day and the actions of CIA agent David Atlee Phillips. Three were legitimate US intelligence operations, penetrated by the Mafia, while the other was an attempt by associates of Trafficante and Rosselli to link Oswald to a C-Day exile group. The four incidents all occurred in seven-week period from early August to late September 1963, just two months before JFK's assassination. In order, the incidents were:

- Oswald's well-publicized "fight" with an anti-Castro activist, and

Oswald's subsequent media appearances on New Orleans TV and
radio.

- A Dallas meeting between Oswald, David Atlee Phillips, and Antonio
  Veciana, the partner of C-Day exile leader Eloy Menoyo.

- The "Odio Incident" in Dallas, when Oswald was used to try to compromise the JURE C-Day group of Manolo Ray, during an approach to
  JURE member Silvia Odio.

- Oswald's trip to Mexico City and dealings with the Cuban and
  Russian embassies, where some of the contacts involved someone pretending to be Oswald.

All four incidents have been the source of immense problems for government investigators, starting with the Warren Commission, because of
missing evidence—like the CIA photos and tapes of Oswald in Mexico
City—and constantly shifting official explanations. But newly released files,
when added to the work of researchers like Dr. John Newman, an Army
major with twenty years' experience with military intelligence, and *Washington Post* editor Jefferson Morley, allow the full story to be told here for the
first time. Like so many other puzzles from the JFK assassination, the keys
to unlocking the mysteries are the secrecy surrounding C-Day and the CIA's
other Castro assassination plots, the Mafia's penetration of those efforts, and
CIA propaganda expert David Atlee Phillips.

CIA documents confirm that David Atlee Phillips had at least three different roles for the CIA, and all help explain the four mysteries from the
summer of 1963. First, Phillips played a major role in the CIA's anti-Castro
operations, ranging from C-Day (AMWORLD) and other CIA plots to handling
non-C-Day Cuban exile groups like the DRE and Alpha 66. Second, Phillips
handled anti-Castro propaganda and worked against the US-based Fair Play
for Cuba Committee. Third, Phillips was the number-three man at the CIA
station in Mexico City, where he handled anti-Castro operations.

To carry out these three roles in 1963, declassified documents and testi-
mony show that Phillips used at least three code names and cover identities
in 1963: Maurice Bishop, Lawrence F. Barker, and M. C. Choaden.[1] Some of
Phillips's CIA roles and operations were separate, while others overlapped.
Some of Phillips's most sensitive anti-Castro operations for CIA official
Desmond FitzGerald in Washington were kept secret from most others in the
CIA, including the CIA Chief of Station in Mexico City, Win Scott.

As noted in Part I, by the summer of 1963, the CIA—at the request of the

Joint Chiefs—was trying to get more intelligence assets into Cuba in preparation for the upcoming C-Day coup. Since the US no longer had an embassy in Cuba to use for recruiting or handling spies, this meant that the CIA had to either sneak CIA assets into Cuba at night by boat or find some legitimate way to get them into Cuba. In 1963, some Fair Play for Cuba Committee members were able to get into Cuba openly by going through Mexico City, which had regular flights to Havana. For the C-Day coup, having US assets that could walk the streets freely and even meet with Cuban officials and student leaders would be important in gauging public acceptance of the coup and the new post-coup Cuban government. Out of this pool of US assets could also come someone whom the CIA could logically blame for Castro's death. If Castro's death were publicly blamed on the C-Day coup leader, Harry Williams, or any anti-Castro Cuban exile who had sneaked into Cuba by boat, much of the Cuban populace and officialdom would oppose them. However, if Castro's death were blamed on a seeming Soviet sympathizer who had entered the country openly—and if the C-Day coup leader and noted exiles like Williams were seen as helping to restore order and prevent a Soviet takeover—the Cuban populace would rally around them.

In addition to C-Day, the CIA had its own plots going in the summer of 1963. They were getting ready to resume contact with Rolando Cubela, the disgruntled mid-level Cuban official who the CIA had been working with, on and off, since early 1961. While the CIA told other US officials that Cubela was just to support C-Day objectives and provide intelligence on it, the CIA would actually be pressing Cubela to assassinate Castro. However, Cubela would be reluctant to act alone or take the blame for Castro's death—so the CIA would need to provide someone to address Cubela's concerns. During the Revolution, Cubela had co-founded the group (the DR) that later grew into the DRE exile group, and Cubela had stormed the Presidential Palace with Carlos Bringueir, who now headed the one-man DRE chapter in New Orleans.[2] Out of those connections and concerns would come Oswald's unusual activities and media appearances in New Orleans.

To deal with all those issues, David Atlee Phillips took actions that resulted in the four Oswald mysteries from the summer of 1963. The secrecy surrounding C-Day helped obscure what had really happened for over forty years, but now it provides a logical explanation—not just for each mystery, but it also shows how all were connected and why they all occurred so close together.

- Oswald's well-publicized "fight" and media appearances on New

Orleans TV and radio were designed by CIA propaganda expert Phillips to build Oswald's credibility as a pro-Castro activist who should be allowed into Cuba openly. Unfortunately, the people Phillips used in New Orleans to help with this operation—Guy Banister and David Ferrie—were also working for Carlos Marcello.

- The Dallas meeting between Oswald and David Atlee Phillips was to debrief Oswald after his New Orleans media appearances, and to prepare him for his next assignment: going to Mexico City to obtain Cuban permission to go to Havana. Phillips allowed Antonio Veciana—the partner of C-Day exile leader Eloy Menoyo—to see Oswald at the meeting, so that when Oswald or his photo surfaced in conjunction with actions in Cuba, the Cuban exile would know that Oswald was actually working for Phillips. However, news of Phillips's planned meeting with Oswald could have quickly reached the Mafia, via Phillips's close associate David Morales, who was also working closely with Johnny Rosselli on the CIA-Mafia plots to assassinate Castro.

- An incident in Dallas where Oswald apparently tried to join the C-Day group of Manolo Ray was *not* one of Phillips's operations: It was an attempt by Rosselli and Trafficante associates John Martino and Rolando Masferrer—both of whom knew about C-Day—to link Oswald to Ray's group. That way, after Oswald was blamed for JFK's assassination, it would tarnish Ray and his group by directing suspicion at them. The removal of Ray and his group from the C-Day coalition government would also create an opening for Masferrer and the Mafia, and increase the clout of the remaining C-Day exile leaders like Trafficante associate Tony Varona.

- Oswald's trip to Mexico City and contacts with the Cuban and Russian embassies were part of the CIA's and Phillips's effort to get Oswald into Cuba legitimately, as a low-level asset for C-Day and the other CIA assassination operations. However, the Mafia had penetrated CIA surveillance of Communist embassies. Trafficante and Rosselli associate Richard Cain had actually worked for the CIA on such surveillance the previous year in Mexico City. So the contacts with the Cuban and Soviet embassies involving someone pretending to be Oswald were intended to incriminate Oswald, after he had been blamed for JFK's assassination. It worked as expected, triggering CIA cover-ups from government investigators from 1963 until today.

Before detailing how exactly the Mafia had penetrated each of these operations—and all the evidence linking the real Oswald's actions to Phillips and
his CIA operations—it's important to note the following: While Phillips had
some knowing assistance in his operations from a few US intelligence assets
like former FBI supervisor Guy Banister, most of the others involved in
Phillips's operations would have no reason to know the true nature of what
they were involved in. They would simply react the way Phillips knew they
would react in certain situations. For example, the Cuban exiles Oswald
sought out in New Orleans were sure to be angry after Oswald first pretended he wanted to join their anti-Castro group, only to soon find him
passing out pro-Castro leaflets in a pro-Castro demonstration. New Orleans
TV and radio and newspapers could be counted on to cover a "fight" connected with Oswald's seemingly pro-Castro demonstrations, since such
demonstrations were very rare in the conservative South. A New Orleans
anti-Communist propaganda group could be counted on to publicize Oswald
on radio for their avowed purpose, without needing direct orders from
Phillips (though several of the group's leaders had ties to the CIA that could
have been used if needed).

What happened to Oswald—and to Phillips—was an example of how a
small, tightly held secret US intelligence operation can have a big impact,
even though it is carried out with only a handful of knowing participants.
Oswald was told only the bare minimum he needed to know at a particular
time—and probably nothing at all about the overall operation. This meant
that Oswald didn't have to act surprised when he was suddenly ambushed
with information about his defection during his New Orleans radio appearance. Oswald's surprised reaction was exactly what Phillips would have
expected, and helped to discredit the Fair Play for Cuba Committee while
building Oswald's reputation as a Communist—something that took work,
since Oswald never joined the Communist party and avoided meetings of
real American Communists and socialists where he might be exposed. When
Phillips met with Oswald in Dallas a few days later, he probably explained to
Oswald that Oswald had passed with flying colors and was ready for his next
step, going to Mexico.

In addition to his roles in Mexico City and working with exile groups like
the DRE, Phillips also worked on C-Day for Desmond FitzGerald.
FitzGerald's small group in the CIA was known as the Special Affairs Staff
(SAS), and it was under Deputy Director for Plans Richard Helms, who also
worked on C-Day. *Washington Post* editor Jefferson Morley has written that

"the SAS was created in January 1963," after William Harvey was reassigned, and FitzGerald's SAS was a new bureaucratic entity tasked by the Kennedy White House with hastening the overthrow of the government of Cuba without too much "noise," meaning political consequences . . . the Kennedy brothers didn't care what SAS did as long as the White House had plausible deniability. The SAS operatives tried everything from assassination conspiracies to propaganda to political action to psychological warfare, the contemporary term of art for espionage that deceived and disoriented and divided the communists. Along the way, some of the SAS men became interested in the very obscure character named Lee Harvey Oswald.[3]

Morley says that Phillips's jobs for the SAS were his familiar roles of "propaganda . . . political action" and "psychological warfare." Phillips's actions with Oswald in the summer of 1963 would involve all three, as would Phillips's role in C-Day.[4]

Morley conducted an interview about these matters with a former CIA operative, with the help of Dr. John Newman. After interviewing the CIA operative and reviewing all the relevant documents with Newman, Morley—who did not know about C-Day—concluded that "if you insist there was a plot by a faction in the Special Affairs Staff (SAS) to provoke an invasion of Cuba in late 1963, I would say you might well be right." Morley also noted that "whatever" Phillips and his subordinates "did in 1963 it certainly had the approval of the late Dick Helms," who had overall control of FitzGerald's "SAS faction that was holding information about Oswald tightly under their control" and away from most others in the CIA. Part of that operation involved "running a psychological warfare operation designed to link Lee Harvey Oswald to the Castro government without disclosing the CIA's hand."[5]

OSWALD'S RADIO AND TV APPEARANCES IN NEW ORLEANS

For Phillips and his CIA superiors like Helms and FitzGerald, Oswald's well-publicized arrest for pro-Castro leafleting in New Orleans in August 1963—and his subsequent TV and radio interviews—were designed to help him get into Cuba as a CIA asset for C-Day and other CIA operations. Yet Guy Banister assisted the operation, and possibly even suggested it, because he knew that when all that publicity quickly surfaced after JFK's death and was replayed repeatedly across the country, it would also make Oswald look guilty of the assassination. (As detailed later, Harry Williams was contacted by a New Orleans Cuban exile just hours after JFK's assassination, in an attempt to ensure that NBC ran the Oswald footage.) Thousands of pages have been written about Oswald's well-publicized August activities, but by focusing on long-overlooked aspects and their connections to C-Day participants, it's easy to see that this was one more way the Mafia used activities related to C-Day for its own ends.

The incident that sparked so much local press coverage was a carefully planned altercation between the only member of a phony New Orleans "chapter" of the Fair Play for Cuba Committee (FPCC) and the only New Orleans member of a Cuban exile group called the DRE.[6] What is documented now—but was unknown to the Warren Commission—was that the FPCC had been targeted and used by the CIA's David Atlee Phillips and that the DRE was "run" for the CIA by the same David Atlee Phillips. The incident and its aftermath have all the hallmarks of a well-crafted, deniable covert propaganda operation, the type Phillips had been running for years.

As in any effective covert operation, Phillips would only tell a few of those involved anything about it, and even those few would be told only what they needed to know, usually through others ("cutouts") or by indirect messages. Most of those involved would be manipulated unknowingly, since Phillips could easily predict how Cuban exiles or right-wing radio personalities would react to certain events or people based on past experience. That would preserve the intelligence goals of compartmentalization and deniability, and ensure that the whole operation might actually seem real to the public in both America and Cuba.

As we highlight the cluster of key dates in Oswald's well-publicized activities, it's important to remember the numerous witnesses and evidence cited in earlier chapters, which showed that Oswald was working for Guy Banister at this time—and that Banister was working for New Orleans godfather Carlos Marcello.

August 3, 1963: Oswald wrote a letter to the New York office of the Fair Play for Cuba Committee (FPCC), which Warren Commission files confirm was postmarked the following day. In the letter, Oswald says his "street demonstration was attacked" by "some Cuban-exile(s)" and he was "officially cautioned by police." However, that incident would not actually occur until August 9, six days after Oswald wrote and mailed his letter.[7]

August 4: Jack Ruby called key Marcello lieutenant Nofio Pecora in New Orleans, for reasons that will become clear.

August 5: Oswald sought out DRE Cuban exile leader Carlos Bringueir and "offer[ed] to train anti-Castro guerrilla fighters." Bringueir was a friend of David Ferrie, and Oswald made a show of being anti-Castro to Bringueir.[8]

August 9: Oswald passed out pro-Castro leaflets on a New Orleans street, and "has a street altercation with Bringueir and is arrested."[9] Oswald's arrest and subsequent trial were "prominently reported in the New Orleans papers" and on TV.[10] A New Orleans attorney later testified to the Warren Commission that "Oswald had told him he was being paid to hand out pro-Castro leaflets on the streets of New Orleans."[11] As documented in Chapter 41, some of these leaflets apparently came from a batch ordered by the CIA when David Atlee Phillips had targeted the Fair Play for Cuba Committee.[12] They were later hand-stamped by Oswald with the address of Banister's office building. A New Orleans police lieutenant who talked to Oswald after his arrest later testified to the Warren Commission that Oswald "seemed to have set them [the exiles] up, so to speak, to create an incident."[13] The police lieutenant also said that Oswald "liked the President," a sentiment shared by most people who ever heard Oswald mention JFK.[14] A police sergeant observed that Oswald "knows very little about" the FPCC "that he belongs to and its ultimate purpose or goal."[15]

August 10: According to the Director of the House Select Committee on Assassinations, Oswald's release from jail was arranged by an associate of Marcello lieutenant Nofio Pecora; Pecora had been called by Jack Ruby just six days earlier.[16]

August 12: At his trial, Oswald pleaded guilty to disturbing the peace, even though the DRE leader "was by all accounts the antagonist in the incident." Oswald was fined, while the DRE leader walked "off scot free."[17] The trial was covered by WDSU-TV and, according to Dr. John Newman, the event "was well attended by local television and newspaper reporters." In fact, Oswald got so much attention from the press that "after the hearing, when the news media surrounded Oswald for a statement," one Cuban exile "said he 'got into an argument with the media and Oswald because the Cubans were not being given an opportunity to present their views.'"[18]

August 16: Evidently unworried about being attacked or arrested again, Oswald again passed out pro-Castro leaflets on a New Orleans street. Though unemployed, Oswald "reportedly hired two helpers, paying them $2 apiece to help pass out his pro-Castro leaflets." One of the men, who appeared Hispanic, has never been identified. Oswald passed out leaflets "for only a few minutes, yet the demonstration was filmed by WDSU-TV."[19]

August 17: Oswald was contacted by a WDSU radio host and invited to be interviewed on his weekly radio show. The radio personality "admits he had been briefed by the FBI on Oswald's background."[20] Oswald did well in the interview.

August 21: The WDSU radio host moderated a radio debate between Oswald, Carlos Bringueir, and Ed Butler, who worked with an anti-Communist propaganda group called INCA. Oswald did well in the debate—until he was confronted on the air about his defection to Russia, which he had not mentioned. According to journalist Dick Russell, "after the taping, Oswald popped into the WDSU-TV studio for a quick interview" and said "on film that he was a Marxist."[21]

Late August or early September 1963: Oswald went to Dallas for a meeting with David Atlee Phillips. A few weeks later, Oswald traveled to Mexico City, where he was one of several young men—all linked to C-Day leader Artime—who were trying to get into Cuba.

For Phillips, Oswald's publicity efforts were an important part of making Oswald look enough like a pro-Castro activist that he would be allowed into Cuba, to help with C-Day and the CIA's other anti-Castro operations. The ambush of Oswald during the radio debate also helped to discredit the Fair Play for Cuba Committee, another goal of Phillips and the CIA. While much evidence indicates that Oswald's actions were part of a CIA-backed propaganda operation, that was probably unknown to most of the people Oswald came into contact with during the incidents.

Ed Butler, one of the participants in Oswald's radio debate, represented the anti-Communist propaganda group known as INCA (Information Council of the Americas), founded in 1961 when Phillips was coordinating anti-Castro propaganda for the CIA. Journalist Anthony Summers found that "recently released CIA records show that the CIA had repeated contacts with Butler in the sixties," including one saying that Butler was "very cooperative" and "seems to welcome any opportunity to assist the CIA." In addition, "INCA's manager, in the summer of 1963, was a member of the Cuban Revolutionary Council (CRC)," the organization headed by C-Day exile leader Tony Varona.[22, 23]

Carlos Bringueir may have been the sole New Orleans member of the

DRE in the summer of 1963, but he told the Warren Commission that he was the "Secretary of Publicity and Propaganda" for the CRC "in New Orleans" until "July 1962," when he resigned from the CRC and joined the DRE.[24] As noted previously, CIA officer E. Howard Hunt told Congressional investigators that David Atlee Phillips ran the DRE for the CIA.[25] Phillips had been doing "propaganda and media relations for the Cuban Revolutionary Council (CRC) starting in 1961, while also running the DRE exile group."[26] According to Anthony Summers, a "former DRE leader . . . told the [House] Assassinations Committee . . . he 'recalled Bringuier's contact with Oswald and the fact that the DRE relayed that information to the CIA at the time.'"[27] Bringueir wrote a press release mentioning "Mr. Lee H. Oswald," calling him a "Castro agent" and asking people to "write to your Congressman . . . for a full investigation of" Oswald. The DRE then issued an "Open Letter to the People of New Orleans" that denounced "Lee H. Oswald."[28] Perhaps that was too much attention on Oswald, because *Washington Post* editor Jefferson Morley found "declassified CIA cables" showing that an associate of Phillips "demanded that the group [DRE] clear their public statements with him."[29]

Phillips and the CIA might have had a reason for having Oswald approach Carlos Bringueir, in particular, one that Bringueir would not have known. As noted earlier, by August 1963 the CIA was resuming contact with Bringuier's old colleague from the original DR student group and the Cuban revolution, Rolando Cubela (AMLASH). Since storming the Cuban Presidential Palace together, Bringueir and Cubela had followed different paths, with Bringueir becoming an anti-Castro exile with the DRE while Cubela remained in Cuba, an increasingly irrelevant mid-level official who was able to travel freely throughout the world. However, since 1961—when Cubela had contacted the CIA about helping them against Castro—both Cubela and Bringueir had essentially been on the same side.

CIA supervisor Desmond FitzGerald ran the Cubela operation, at the same time he was helping coordinate the CIA's portion of C-Day, AMWORLD. By bringing Oswald into contact with Cubela's old colleague Bringueir, the CIA was helping set up Oswald for a role in the Cubela operation as well as C-Day. To someone like FitzGerald, AMWORLD and AMLASH were simply two parts of an overall CIA effort to eliminate Castro. The testimony of Cubela's CIA case officers shows that Cubela was willing to take part in a plan to kill Castro, but he didn't want to take the blame or face certain death even if he succeeded. Because of Oswald's contact with the DRE, Oswald would have been a good candidate to take the fall if Cubela had been able to assassinate Castro. This also helps explain the continued CIA secrecy about their use of the DRE in 1963, which we detail shortly, since Bobby Kennedy had not been told about the assassination side of the Cubela operation. The bottom line is that if all the publicity generated for Oswald in August 1963 helped him get into Cuba, he would be useful in several of the CIA's operations there, from C-Day to Cubela, and even the CIA-Mafia plots (since the Mafia wouldn't be anxious to take the blame for killing Castro either, if they hoped to reopen their casinos with the support of the Cuban people).

Several Mafia connections are evident upon close inspection of Oswald's August 1963 activities. John Martino's son told a former Congressional investigator that in August 1963, Martino "saw Lee Harvey Oswald passing out pro-Castro leaflets in New Orleans."[30] In a few weeks, Martino would be part of an attempt to link Oswald to Manolo Ray's C-Day exile group, an attempt Martino would later write about in his article that threatened to reveal C-Day. This attempt to link Oswald to C-Day, known to historians as "the Odio incident" because it involved a Dallas Cuban exile named Silvia Odio, will be detailed shortly. Silvia Odio's uncle—a friend of C-Day exile leader and Mafia associate Tony Varona—was in the courtroom when Oswald pleaded guilty for his "fight" and was fined.

We've documented in earlier chapters that in 1963, Banister was doing work for Carlos Marcello, as was David Ferrie—and both were clearly part of the plot to assassinate JFK.[31] An investigator for the New Orleans district attorney interviewed a man who "had business dealings with Banister" beginning in 1963, who told the DA's investigator that "he had heard Banister mention on several occasions his feelings and bitterness toward the Kennedy administration." He "further stated that he had heard Banister remark on several occasions that someone should do away with Kennedy." It should be noted that these remarks were made before Banister had been publicly linked to JFK's assassination in the press.[32]

Historian Richard Mahoney, whose father was close to JFK and part of his administration, found that "Six witnesses confirm seeing Ferrie and Oswald together in Louisiana in the summer of 1963."[33] This is in addition to the witnesses we cited earlier who saw Banister and Oswald together, including some who said Banister told them Oswald was working for him. One of Oswald's former Civil Air Patrol buddies—at a time when David Ferrie was one of its advisers—said that "Banister had a great deal of personal loyalty to David Ferrie."[34]

As documented earlier, Banister and Ferrie also knew about C-Day and worked on it. One Banister associate even wrote an article hinting about C-Day in August 1963—though one of Banister's investigators said that Banister considered that associate a "loose mouth." This investigator said that Banister told him the person passing out Fair Play for Cuba Committee leaflets "was one of mine."[35] Why would Phillips and the CIA use someone like Banister for an aspect of C-Day? The same investigator told the New Orleans DA's office that he still had "letters from Banister to him concerning Banister's providing him with false credentials and a cover for infiltrating Communist groups," including a "code name." Banister's experience in dealing with undercover assets posing as Communists was clearly a plus to someone like Phillips.

Banister had so many ways to have learned about C-Day that it would have been easy for him to seek out an assignment related to it. There were his ties to C-Day leader Tony Varona's CRC (Varona's name was in the index to Banister's file, with two file numbers).[36] The CRC had been created by the CIA, in particular by David Atlee Phillips and E. Howard Hunt. The New Orleans branch had received special attention from Bobby Kennedy while it shared an office building with Banister. As previously noted, Banister had served in the FBI with General Joseph Carroll, now head of the Defense Intelligence Agency. Banister also had ties to Somoza, who ran Nicaragua, home to Manuel Artime's C-Day bases. Despite Banister's fiery temper and a growing drinking problem, as a former FBI supervisor he still maintained his contacts with the FBI and was probably trusted by some in the US intelligence community.[37]

To preserve secrecy, someone like Phillips would have told Banister as little as possible, perhaps not even the true reason for wanting to get Oswald into Cuba. But Banister had other ways to learn about C-Day. Banister worked for Marcello, so he could have first learned about C-Day that way. Rosselli was close to David Morales, the Miami CIA operations chief who was working on C-Day with Phillips, and we noted earlier that Rosselli had reportedly visited Banister in the summer of 1963. Banister's chief investigator said that Rosselli's name sounded familiar to him and he remembered having "some contact with" Trafficante bagman Frank Fiorini "around New Orleans."[38] As noted earlier, Fiorini admitted that he stayed at Marcello's headquarters—the Town and Country Motel—when he visited New Orleans.

Historians and investigators have long tried to figure out Oswald's widely publicized actions in August 1963; but, without knowing about C-Day, they couldn't put all the pieces together. For example, Anthony Summers wrote that Oswald's "FPCC 'chapter' in New Orleans was entirely fiction. Lee Oswald was the sole member of a group which existed only on paper, but it was a role he exploited to the full," leaving a very public (and paper) trail of his alleged pro-Castro sympathies. He went on to say that "Oswald's effort brought the publicity he was courting" but, after that, "Lee Oswald would never again venture out in public support of the Castro regime. He did not need to, for now he was indelibly stamped as a [pro-]Castro militant" in the public record. "Clearly Oswald had successfully carried out part of a plan. What plan?" Summers asks. He says information, most of it unavailable to the Warren Commission, "suggests Oswald may have been part of a covert intelligence scheme involving Cuba."[39] But that's as far as Summers or other historians could go, without knowing about C-Day.

Dr. John Newman, a twenty-year veteran of military intelligence, could only ask "Why did Oswald come into contact with so many people with CIA connections in August and September 1963?"[40] He named five individuals, but there are actually more, counting people like John Martino (whom the CIA admits was a CIA asset) and David Atlee Phillips himself, whom Oswald met in late August 1963. One of those Newman named was William Gaudet, the CIA asset who worked for INCA's Dr. Ochsner. It's now clear that Gaudet was part of the "tight surveillance" on Oswald mentioned earlier. A former Senate investigator wrote that "before his death in 1981, Gaudet admitted witnessing Oswald's distribution of pro-Castro leaflets in" New Orleans.[41] Historian Richard Mahoney says that when "Oswald applied for and received a Mexican tourist card (FM 824085) in New Orleans on September 17 (1963), the individual who received the tourist card with the previous number (FM 824084) was William George Gaudet . . . who had close ties to the local office of the CIA. Gaudet later admitted under oath that he had seen Oswald one day 'in deep conversation with [Banister] on Camp Street . . . they were leaning over and talking and it was an earnest conversation.' Gaudet said his impression was that Banister was asking Oswald to do something for him."[42]

As we've documented, C-Day/AMWORLD was the most closely guarded CIA operation, both in 1963 and in the decades that followed. So it should be no surprise that the CIA lied to the House Select Committee on Assassinations about their role with the DRE Cuban exile group at the time of its contact with Oswald and that, even in 2005, the CIA still refuses to release its files about it. Dr. Newman and Jefferson Morley, an editor at the *Washington Post*, have taken a leading role in documenting the CIA's deception in this matter. What they have uncovered sheds more light on why the CIA is still reluctant to release these forty-two-year-old documents.

Morley wrote that in the early 1960s "in Miami the DRE quickly attracted the support of CIA covert operations officers such as David Phillips and Howard Hunt" and that "both men took care in their memoirs to praise the leaders of the DRE."[43] E. Howard Hunt stated under oath that Phillips ran the DRE, but Phillips increasingly had other responsibilities in 1963; so while he maintained overall control, the day-to-day operations were given to Miami CIA officer George Joannides. According to Jefferson Morley, by the end of July 1963, Joannides started to focus exclusively on his work with the DRE, and he met with national DRE leaders on August 8, 1963 in Miami, the day before Oswald's arrest in New Orleans.[44]

Jefferson Morley goes on to write that "whatever" Joannidies "did in 1963 it certainly had the approval of the late Richard Helms" since "George Joannides was part of the SAS faction" of Desmond FitzGerald "that was holding information about Oswald tightly under their control." Unknown to Morley, both Richard Helms and Desmond FitzGerald also worked on C-Day/AMWORLD with Bobby Kennedy. Morley writes that "in his job evaluation from the summer of 1963, Joannides was credited with having established control over the" DRE. Morley points out "it was Joannides's job to make sure that his actions could not be traced to the U.S. government. He was, judging from his job evaluations in 1963, very good at his job."[45]

Joannides continued to cover his tracks in the 1970s, when he became the second CIA liaison with the House Select Committee on Assassinations (HSCA), after the first liaison had been caught tampering with evidence. As CIA liaison, Joannides would tell the HSCA that the CIA had had no contact with the DRE in 1963. In reality, Morley writes that "according to a CIA memo found at the JFK Library, Joannides was giving $25,000 a month (about $150,000 in today's dollars) to the DRE at the time when the group's New Orleans delegation decided to collect intelligence on and publish propaganda about Oswald." It's important to stress that Joannides was not acting on his own—"the CIA's Miami station chief Ted Shackley specifically cited Joannides' handling of the propaganda efforts of the DRE in awarding him the highest possible grades. Shackley concluded that Joannides had proven he could 'translate policy directives into meaningful action programs.'"[46]

What Morley and others have been unable to figure out is what "action programs" were involved, and why are they still so secret. It was not revealed by the CIA until 2005—and then only after a lawsuit by Morley—that Joannides had been awarded a promotion and a pay raise in December 1963 for his good work with the DRE in the summer and fall of 1963. Further, Morley says he was told that "the CIA admits that it has records about George Joannides's operational actions in late 1963 when the Cuban students under his guidance were gathering and publicizing information about Oswald. The CIA will not say how many such records it has. Even more remarkably, the CIA asserts that it will not publicly release any of these JFK assassination-related files in any form."[47] This is in spite of the JFK Assassinations Records Act that created the Review Board (since disbanded), which says such records must be released.

Morley did not realize that the DRE records were part of the "more than one million CIA records" related to JFK's assassination that have not yet been not released. Many of those records are probably about C-Day/AMWORLD. Even though the DRE was not one of the five official C-Day groups, that is one reason they were still valuable to the CIA. It would be too risky for the CIA to build Oswald's pro-Castro public image by bringing him into contact with one of the "five fingers" of C-Day. By bringing Oswald into contact with the DRE, the CIA was able to both mount a propaganda effort against the Fair Play for Cuba Committee, and to build Oswald's pro-Castro image so that he could enter Cuba openly through Mexico City—the same route discussed in Senator Eastland's FPCC hearings earlier in the year.

However, the CIA records on Joannides, Phillips, and the DRE would also reveal things embarrassing to the CIA. For example, Joannides was based in Miami, where David Morales was in charge of operations. Morales would have known everything Joannides and Phillips were doing with the DRE— but Morales was also working closely with Johnny Rosselli at the time on the CIA-Mafia plots to kill Castro. The CIA's records could raise troubling questions about how the CIA's operations were infiltrated and used by Rosselli in the JFK assassination. Again, it's important to stress that outside of Morales, Banister, Ferrie, and the Mafia members, the authors don't feel that others named in the preceding section—including Carlos Bringueir—had any role in JFK's assassination.

By late August 1963, Oswald had gotten what he and his handlers wanted: A huge amount of publicity, the kind any real Communist could only dream of, that made him look pro-Castro. Even with all the publicity, Oswald had avoided getting any members for his phony Fair Play for Cuba chapter, which was in keeping with his practice of avoiding meetings of real American Communists and socialists. Instead, Oswald was preparing for the next step in his mission by checking out James Bond novels from the library, including *From Russia with Love* and *Goldfinger*. He also read a book by America's most famous James Bond fan, a man Oswald's associates heard him talk about only in admiring terms: John F. Kennedy. The book was *Profiles in Courage*, and Oswald would need a lot of that for his mission of getting into Cuba.[48] But first, Oswald would meet David Atlee Phillips.

Oswald and David Atlee Phillips: His Next Assignment

FROM THE POINT OF VIEW of Marcello, Trafficante, and Rosselli, the meeting between Lee Harvey Oswald and the CIA's David Atlee Phillips in Dallas near the end of August 1963 had two benefits. First, it tied a CIA officer to the one of the men the Mafia bosses planned to use as the patsy for JFK's assassination. Second, it tied Oswald indirectly to C-Day exile leader Eloy Menoyo, whom the Mafia had been unable to bribe as they had Tony Varona. Perhaps this was because Menoyo was a man of high principles, or maybe because Menoyo was cautious about dealing with Trafficante after a bad gun deal the previous year (detailed in CIA documents and confirmed by a close associate of Menoyo). In any case, the Mafia had to find another way to compromise Menoyo or his organization, and they got their wish when Menoyo's closest associate—Antonio Veciana—met in public with Oswald and Phillips.

Following Oswald's spate of publicity, his actions in the time period from August 22, 1963 to September 17, 1963 have been the source of great controversy. In spite of all the investigations after the assassination and in the ensuing decades, Congressional investigator Gaeton Fonzi wrote that the "House (Select) Committee on Assassinations (HSCA) says there is no corroborated whereabouts for Oswald during this period" (with the exception of Oswald being seen yet again with David Ferrie).[1] However, the HSCA did uncover evidence that Oswald had a meeting in Dallas with David Atlee Phillips in late August (or early September) 1963, showing that Oswald was engaged in work for US intelligence during this time.

While working with the HSCA and after, Gaeton Fonzi developed conclusive evidence that Oswald met Phillips in a Dallas office building, while Phillips was also meeting with Cuban exile Antonio Veciana. Veciana was the head of Alpha 66, the violent exile group disliked by the Kennedys that was closely aligned with C-Day exile leader Eloy Menoyo's SNFE group. Veciana says the longtime CIA contact he met with in Dallas used the cover identity of "Maurice Bishop," though every description he gave of "Bishop" and his career fits perfectly with that of David Atlee Phillips.

In a book-length study, Fonzi has conclusively proved from numerous intelligence sources that he uncovered while working with the HSCA that David Atlee Phillips used the alias "Maurice Bishop" in his CIA work. This was years before newly released documents showed that Phillips used at least two other cover identities for his Cuban operations in the early 1960s, "Michael Choaden" and "Lawrence Barker." However, Veciana was reluctant to confirm Phillips's use of the Maurice Bishop alias, for several reasons. After Veciana had a falling-out with the CIA in the early 1970s—following a Castro assassination attempt in South America that historians have linked to David Atlee Phillips—Veciana was sent to prison, after he says he was set up on a drug charge. After Veciana was released from prison, numerous Congressional witnesses were killed, or died suddenly, either just before or just after their testimony. The list includes names familiar to the readers of this book: Masferrer, Artime, Prio, Rosselli, Hoffa, Giancana, Nicoletti, and those who were murdered earlier like Richard Cain and Eladio del Valle. When we interviewed Veciana, he said had known Eladio del Valle, and mentioned that del Valle had been murdered near Veciana's house.

So we want to make it clear that Veciana did not confirm to us that his CIA contact who used the name Maurice Bishop was indeed David Atlee Phillips. Indeed, given Veciana's cautious Congressional testimony in the 1970s, to do so now could open up Veciana to charges of perjury. However, Veciana pointed us to the name he came up with for his group, Alpha 66, saying "I used the name Alpha because it's the first letter of the alphabet, and I used the 66 because I was driving down the street and saw a Phillips 66 station and took that name." (The first letter of the alphabet is also the middle initial for David A. Phillips.) We believe that the evidence compiled by the HSCA and Gaeton Fonzi, and detailed in Fonzi's book *The Last Investigation*, is conclusive, so we will use "Phillips/Bishop" in this chapter when discussing Veciana's CIA controller.

One reason so much information was withheld from Congress about Phillips and Alpha 66 was that Alpha 66 was yet another 1963 CIA anti-Castro operation that had not been authorized by the Kennedys. Phillips had directed Alpha 66 in several attacks against Cuba in the spring of 1963, including one that damaged a Soviet ship, "causing a dozen Soviet casualties." Veciana had trumpeted the attacks in a carefully coordinated PR campaign that included a press conference in Washington—a hallmark of propaganda expert Phillips—much to the consternation of the Kennedys. In those Cold War times, and in the months just after the tense standoff with the Soviets during the Cuban Missile Crisis, such attacks could have triggered a nuclear confrontation, so the Kennedys didn't want any CIA support going to Alpha 66. However, Phillips/Bishop had been working with the group and Veciana for several years, and the CIA continued to support and direct Alpha 66, just as it continued backing Rosselli and the CIA-Mafia plots long after Bobby Kennedy had been told that the plots had been stopped.

Veciana told us bluntly that his goal in working with Phillips/Bishop in 1963 was "the killing of Castro." Veciana said that that was his full-time job in 1963, and the meeting in Dallas—where Oswald showed up—was about "plans to kill Castro." This plot with Alpha 66 can be added to the long list of CIA operations to kill Castro in the fall of 1963, only two of which—C-Day/AMWORLD and AMTRUNK—were fully authorized by the Kennedys. The unauthorized CIA operations include the CIA-Mafia plots, plots with French nationals, Cubela/AMLASH, and the ZRRIFLE operation with assassin recruiter QJWIN. At times, the CIA overlapped personnel among these operations. In fact, when QJWIN was mentioned to Veciana in our interview, he briefly related an incident that involved a meeting in New York, a dollar bill torn in half to later be matched for identification, and the CIA official who originally recruited David Atlee Phillips into the CIA (who worked with Phillips in Havana at the same time Veciana began his work for Phillips/Bishop).[2]

The CIA's contact with unauthorized groups like Alpha 66, the DRE, and those in the CIA-Mafia plots had to be carefully hidden, even within the labyrinth of the CIA and its massive filing systems. Much money and personnel was involved and had to be tracked, but the files needed to be concealed even more than usual so they couldn't easily be found in case there was ever a shakeup at the CIA that involved more than just the top job. The fact that Richard Helms stayed in the CIA for another ten years (rising to director), Phillips remained longer than that, and others who worked on C-Day and related operations stayed in the CIA into the 1980s, is one reason the real CIA files on groups like the DRE and Joannides didn't start to trickle out until the late 1990s, and most remain secret even today. Since Phillips ran the DRE and Alpha 66 for the CIA at the same time, the Alpha 66 files are likely also being similarly withheld.

Before detailing the Phillips-Oswald meeting, it's important to put Veciana in context, since he was also at the meeting. Veciana's public image in 1963 was defined by an angry, defiant photo from the time of the spring 1963 attacks that Phillips/Bishop had ordered. The Kennedys did not want to support Veciana or his group, Alpha 66. However, Veciana was closely allied with Eloy Menoyo, the progressive exile leader of the SNFE. While technically separate groups, FBI and other files show that they were so closely allied that they almost operated as one. Veciana had a very close relationship with Menoyo then, one that continues to this day—Veciana had seen Menoyo just two hours before our interview with him. Many Cuban exiles saw Menoyo as too progressive, almost socialist, but Veciana stuck by him. Even Phillips/Bishop told Veciana that "he had very little faith in Menoyo," and Veciana says "the CIA didn't want to give Menoyo anything."

However, in the summer and fall of 1963, the Kennedys wanted to give Menoyo a great deal, in order to get him to be part of C-Day. CIA documents confirm that Harry Williams tried to woo Menoyo throughout that time, to join the C-Day plan. Harry Williams—and the Kennedys—saw Menoyo as the kind of progressive leader needed for the new Provisional Government after C-Day, if it was to gain broad support from the Cuban people. However, in spite of being given support by the Kennedys and wooed by Harry Williams, Menoyo was reluctant to fully commit to C-Day, probably for two reasons. One, mentioned in Part I, was that Harry was apparently reluctant to reveal the identity of the C-Day coup leader, the revolutionary hero high in the Cuban government, to Menoyo until he had fully committed.

The second reason Menoyo was probably reluctant to join C-Day was because his close ally, Antonio Veciana of Alpha 66, could not be part of C-Day. Menoyo was likely reluctant to leave behind his longtime ally who had stood by him when most others wouldn't. Harry made it clear to us that Veciana was not one someone he wanted in C-Day. Veciana confirmed to us that Menoyo had not told him about his negotiations with Harry Williams, and such confidentiality was probably a condition of Harry's negotiations with Menoyo. Veciana had only heard rumors that Manuel "Artime was the 'pretty boy' of the CIA . . . who would take over Cuba if Castro fell," and Artime would then be "the puppet" of the CIA.

It would have been clear in the close-knit community of Cuban exile leaders that in the summer and fall of 1963, the Kennedys were starting to funnel support to Menoyo for some reason. The Mafiosi who had penetrated C-Day would know that the support was an attempt to woo Menoyo for C-

Day, making Menoyo's close ally Antonio Veciana a tempting target. If Menoyo's partner Veciana could be linked to Lee Harvey Oswald, it would force Bobby Kennedy and the CIA into a huge cover-up after the JFK assassination was blamed on Oswald. It would also probably result in the removal of Menoyo from C-Day, meaning more power for the already-bribed Tony Varona and creating openings for the mob-backed Carlos Prio and Rolando Masferrer.

As with so many aspects of Oswald and Phillips's actions in 1963, it's helpful to look at their meeting from the perspective of both US intelligence and the Mafiosi who were planning to kill JFK and pin the blame on Oswald. From Phillips's perspective, meeting with Oswald—and Veciana—in Dallas made sense. Phillips himself was from adjacent Fort Worth, so he was quite familiar with the Dallas area.[3] Oswald had just finished his role in the highly publicized operation to raise his public profile as being pro-Castro, and was ready for his trip to Mexico City, where he would attempt to get a visa to get into Cuba. As for Veciana, the CIA was accelerating all its unauthorized Castro assassination plots by September 1963, either in support of—or possibly to preempt—C-Day. So meeting with Veciana at this time about Alpha 66 plots to kill Castro also made sense for Phillips/Bishop.

But why have Oswald encounter Veciana at the meeting? Or, from the other perspective, why have Veciana come into contact with Oswald? Intelligence operations are usually kept tightly compartmentalized from each other, to avoid exposure or contaminating one operation if another is blown. Veciana confirmed to us that he usually met with Phillips/Bishop "alone," except for this one time when Veciana briefly encountered Oswald. So, the Veciana-Oswald encounter was apparently arranged on purpose.

Veciana's meeting in Dallas seemed odd to him in other ways. Veciana says he "couldn't understand why [Phillips/Bishop] only wanted to meet with him for only five or ten minutes." Veciana had been in Miami, and flew to Dallas just for the meeting, then flew back to Miami the same day. Veciana confirms that the meeting was the idea of Phillips/Bishop: "He . . . called me here in Miami and asked me to fly to Dallas. He wanted me to come to discuss plans . . . to kill Castro."

Veciana says "I had the meeting with him in downtown . . . it was in the newest building in Dallas at that time. In the lobby of an office building. In a public place." Veciana says "there was a young guy who was with him" and "according to the pictures I saw in the paper later, the man with him was Lee

Oswald." Veciana says "I'm sure that the individual was Lee Harvey Oswald" and that "he was a shy and timid man and very nervous . . . he wanted to get out and leave." Veciana says that Oswald "was talking about something that we can do to kill Castro." However, Phillips/Bishop "thinks besides killing Castro that we can set up a marine guerrilla against Castro to try to convince the US that they must finish Castro." It's not clear what Veciana meant when he said Phillips/Bishop used the term "marine guerrilla." Journalist, Kennedy confidant, and AMTRUNK originator Tad Szulc called the Artime side of C-Day (AMWORLD) "Second Naval Guerrilla" in several articles. Or "marine guerrilla" could refer to former Marine Oswald. In any event, Phillips/Bishop meant doing something "to try to convince the US that they must finish Castro."

Phillips likely saw Oswald and Veciana as part of the same general CIA plan to "kill Castro." Phillips wanted Veciana to see Oswald, and vice-versa, since they were on the same general operation. Perhaps they would need to recognize each other, once both men were in Cuba. Or Veciana might need to recognize newspaper or TV photos of Oswald, if Oswald were arrested for Castro's assassination. If Oswald were being groomed by Phillips as a possible patsy for one of the CIA's Castro assassination operations—a long list that included Veciana's Alpha 66—it's possible that Phillips had Veciana see Oswald because Phillips intended to have Oswald take the fall if Alpha 66 killed Castro.

Beyond just being one of the US "assets into Cuba," Oswald's role could have included being a patsy for any of the CIA operations to kill Castro, including C-Day. His Soviet past would make him ideal to take the blame, because the US could claim that the Soviets were really controlling his actions. Oswald's recent spate of pro-Communist activity and TV/radio appearances and his upcoming trip to the Soviet Embassy in Mexico City would only buttress that. For C-Day, the patsy couldn't have any obvious links to Harry Williams, and thus to the Kennedys. So it makes sense that Harry said he doesn't recall ever meeting Phillips, among all the CIA people he encountered. Phillips's role seems to have involved overseeing CIA-backed exile groups that were not officially part of C-Day (like Alpha 66 and the DRE), but which had some connection to exile groups that were—the DRE was connected to Artime's minor-league training camp outside New Orleans, while Alpha 66 was allied with Menoyo's C-Day group.

From the Mafia's perspective, Veciana would have made a viable patsy for JFK's assassination, due to his public antagonism with the Kennedys. He also had links to both C-Day (through Menoyo) and the CIA, which would ensure government cover-ups. David Morales could have manipulated Phillips into having Oswald and Veciana at the same brief meeting. Morales was senior to Phillips in 1963, and Morales could have been acting on behalf of his partner in the CIA-Mafia plots, Johnny Rosselli. It would have been easy for the Mafia to have someone like Guy Banister get word to Phillips that Oswald wanted a face-to-face meeting with a US intelligence official before proceeding with the next, more dangerous part of his mission (going to Mexico City and then to Cuba). As for Veciana, it would have been easy for the Mafia to be aware of him as well. Veciana told us that he knew least three Trafficante associates: Eladio del Valle, Frank Fiorini, and Jose Aleman.

Still, for the mob bosses, the biggest benefit of the meeting was that it linked Oswald—one of their primary patsies for the JFK assassination—with both C-Day (Veciana through Menoyo) and a CIA official. The Mafia immediately took advantage of this by linking Oswald to another C-Day group and to JFK's assassination, with the help of Trafficante associates John Martino and Rolando Masferrer. The mob bosses knew how the CIA would react after JFK's assassination when they realized that one of their own CIA officers had met with Oswald in Dallas less than three months before JFK's murder. The cover-ups at CIA—and DIA's Naval Intelligence, which was running surveillance on Oswald—would be enormous, to protect their agencies.

The Dallas meeting between Oswald and David Atlee Phillips probably eliminates Phillips from knowingly being involved in JFK's assassination. It would make no sense for Phillips to meet with someone like Oswald in public just three months before JFK's murder, if Phillips were knowingly involved in the plot. Phillips did cover up after the JFK assassination, and for decades, but it was probably to protect his own reputation, that of the CIA (who were undertaking so many unsanctioned operations), and that of authorized operations like C-Day. Phillips's post-assassination attempts to blame JFK's murder on the Cubans—and thus prompt a US invasion of Cuba—could be seen as simply trying to make the best of a bad situation. JFK was dead, and even Bobby Kennedy felt—as he told Harry Williams and President Johnson—that a free Cuba was the best memorial his slain brother could have. Phillips quickly backed off his post-assassination attempts to blame JFK's death on Castro, as soon as it became clear that President Johnson was not going to continue C-Day.

Perhaps because of his meeting with Oswald, there is evidence that David Atlee Phillips later came to feel that he might have been manipulated by others, and that some US intelligence people were involved in JFK's assassination. As one might expect for someone who had written so much effective propaganda for the CIA, David Atlee Phillips was an accomplished writer, with several books to his credit. In his unpublished, autobiographical novel found after his death, Phillips's character said: "I was one of the two case officers who handled Lee Harvey Oswald . . . we gave him the mission of killing Fidel Castro in Cuba." But instead, JFK was killed with "precisely the plan we had devised against Castro. Thus the CIA did not anticipate the President's assassination, but it was responsible for it. I share that guilt." However, at the time he penned his autobiographical novel, Phillips seemed to feel that Oswald had shot JFK and he wrote "I don't know why he killed Kennedy."[4]

Phillips did not have access to the results of Naval Intelligence's secret assassination investigation we discuss in an upcoming chapter, which showed that Oswald could not have done the actual shooting. Perhaps Phillips learned more, because, before he died, *Vanity Fair* confirmed that Phillips told a former HSCA staff member that "JFK was done in by conspiracy, likely including rogue American intelligence people." Phillips's close associate in 1963, David Morales, was in the perfect position to pass along Phillips's Castro assassination plans to Morales's good friend Johnny Rosselli. As noted by historian Richard Mahoney, Rosselli later confessed his role in the JFK assassination plot, as did both Trafficante and Marcello.[5]

As for Phillips' statement that the CIA "gave" Oswald "the mission of killing Fidel Castro," there is other evidence, beyond Veciana's account of his meeting with Oswald, that supports Oswald being involved in the CIA's plots against Castro. *Vanity Fair* author Anthony Summers wrote that "a senior CIA officer, Frank Hand, told a colleague that the CIA had placed a 'control agent'—not [George] de Mohrenschildt—close to Oswald and his wife to monitor their activities. Hand, the file shows, was involved in a high-level discussion of the plots to kill Castro." Since Oswald lived apart from his wife Marina after they left New Orleans in September 1963, the "control agent" must refer to someone in New Orleans, like Guy Banister or David Ferrie.

We want to make it clear that Oswald's involvement in any Castro assassination plot probably did not involve him being a shooter, since Oswald was such a bad shot in the Marines (where he at least had the chance to practice) that he frequently missed the target altogether.[6] Some authors and documentaries make much of the fact that Oswald's impressive-sounding score of 191 on his Marine shooting test qualified him as a "marksman."[7] But they fail to say that "marksman" is the lowest of the three Marine shooting titles, and that the lowest possible score on the test is 190, with the highest being

250.[8] In other words, anyone would get a score of at least 190 and be a "marksman" on that test—and before Oswald left the Marines he only scored one point above that. No US intelligence agency would logically give someone like that a role as a shooter, any more than the Mafia would. But that still left other roles for Oswald, from helping with intelligence to staging a diversion to taking the fall.

It may sound cold to talk about the CIA looking at using someone like Oswald as a patsy in a Castro assassination plot. However, many nonfiction intelligence accounts show that—by necessity—covert intelligence operations are a cynical, ruthless business. And Oswald didn't have many viable choices by September 1963, given his background and desire for undercover work that he had craved since his teenage years. If Oswald quit taking assignments, all his long years of undercover work would be for nothing, and there would be no big payday at the end of the rainbow as there had been for Herbert Philbrick. Oswald was in a troubled marriage, had an "undesirable" discharge, and his Communist-defector reputation was even bigger now thanks to his recent spate of publicity. Oswald couldn't just quit and try to "come out" on his own. The same carefully constructed cover designed by Naval Intelligence and the CIA to fool the KGB left Oswald with no obvious way to prove that he had been acting for US intelligence all along. And the CIA had been careful to give Oswald only small amounts of money, so that he was never able to save a meaningful amount and was always near poverty. Oswald was above average in intelligence and was becoming well read, but his learning disabilities and lack of formal education would always keep him from getting work that was really challenging for him.

So, if Oswald were told that the next part of his assignment involved a dangerous mission to Cuba, but was one that could bring democracy to Cuba instead of the Communism that Oswald said he "hated"—as well as fame, money, and recognition for Oswald—he would not have a difficult time making a decision, even if he were told there was a chance he could be killed. Oswald's background and experience showed when he had agreed to a dangerous life-or-death mission in the past—going into the Soviet Union alone as a spy in 1959, at the height of the Cold War. Now, Oswald was probably ready for more of the international intrigue that he had previously experienced in Japan and Russia. In addition, Oswald's notes for a speech indicate that he was starting to chafe under the far-right reactionary Banister.

As for the Mafia, they were now ready to link Oswald to talk of assassinating JFK and to another C-Day group, Manuel Ray's JURE. They were going to link Oswald to a Dallas JURE member, Silvia Odio. It's interesting to note that Alpha 66's Antonio Veciana may have known Silvia Odio, even though she was part of another exile group (as we showed with Carlos Bringueir, crossover between the exile groups was common). In our interview with Veciana, when we first asked if he knew Silvia Odio, he said "she called me." Then Veciana got an alarmed look and quickly said "I don't remember speaking with her." Then he grudgingly added that "maybe she went to a meeting."

According to Gaeton Fonzi, Silvia Odio told him that she had seen Veciana in Dallas. Veciana's reaction does not indicate any conspiratorial activity on his part—and, for the record, we do not think he had anything to do with JFK's assassination. But because both Veciana and Odio met Oswald in Dallas the space of a few weeks—under unusual circumstances—it strongly suggests that someone who knew both of them had a hand in the Odio incident. Silvia Odio lived in the same Dallas apartment complex as the brother of Rolando Masferrer, whose partner was Eladio del Valle. Veciana said he knew del Valle, who was also close to Santo Trafficante and David Ferrie.

THE ODIO INCIDENT: THE MAFIA LINKS OSWALD TO C-DAY

The Mafia was unable to bribe C-Day exile leader Manolo Ray or penetrate his group, JURE, so they did the next best thing: They linked Oswald to JURE, just seven weeks before JFK's assassination, while also planting evidence tying Oswald to JFK's assassination. That way, the Mafia hoped to achieve three goals: First, they incriminated Oswald; second, by tying Oswald to JURE, they stymied a thorough investigation; third, after JFK's assassination—when JURE and Manolo Ray were tarnished because of the link to Oswald—the Mafia hoped that the suspicion would eliminate Ray from the post-C-Day Provisional Government. This would increase the stature of the previously Mafia-bribed Tony Varona, while creating openings in the Provisional Government for Trafficante associates Masferrer and Prio.

The Mafia operation that linked Oswald to Manolo Ray and JURE is called "The Odio Incident" by historians, and it has been investigated by the Warren Commission, the Senate Church Committee, the House Select Committee on Assassinations (HSCA), and the JFK Assassination Records Review Board. Gaeton Fonzi investigated it for the Church Committee and the HSCA, and he wrote that someone "wanted it to appear that Oswald was associated with JURE, in order to implicate JURE, a politically left-of-center group, in the Kennedy assassination."

For the Mafia, the timing was important. Linking Oswald to Manolo Ray's C-Day group JURE had to occur after Oswald had met in person with a CIA officer like David Atlee Phillips, to ensure a cover-up by the CIA and Phillips. On the other hand, linking Oswald to Ray's C-Day group needed to occur before Oswald went to Mexico City to try to get into Cuba, since there was always the chance that Oswald would be allowed into Cuba (although the Mafia had a way to try to prevent that). Timing was also important in that the CIA was not supposed to know about Oswald's contact with a member of Ray's JURE C-Day group until after Oswald was a suspect in JFK's assassination.

The Dallas member of Ray's JURE C-Day group that Oswald met was Silvia Odio, the Cuban exile daughter of a prominent resistance leader then in prison in Cuba. Silvia told Congressional investigator Gaeton Fonzi that "her father was well known. He was a millionaire who helped Fidel in the mountains. He transported all the arms" for the Revolution. Silvia said that her father "was described in *Time* magazine as the 'transport tycoon' of Latin America. . . . We were very strong supporters of Castro until we felt betrayed by him." Her father joined the resistance against Castro—Manolo Ray's group JURE—and stayed in Cuba, on his large estate. After a failed assassination attempt against Castro by Antonio Veciana—on the orders of David Atlee Phillips—Veciana's accomplice sought refuge on her family's farm, where he and her parents were captured. Her father was imprisoned as well, where he remained in September 1963.

Silvia and her two sisters wound up in Dallas, dependent on the local exile community and others for assistance. In their apartment complex lived one of Rolando Masferrer's brothers.[9] FBI documents had linked Rolando Masferrer to Trafficante and John Martino since 1959. Martino was the Trafficante operative who was imprisoned in Cuba during the 1959 CIA-Mafia plots. By 1963, Martino was roommates at times with Johnny Rosselli and had helped to arrange the CIA's OPERATION TILT for Rosselli and Trafficante. After that operation was no longer needed—because C-Day developed—Martino went on a speaking tour to promote his upcoming book about his imprisonment, a convenient way to travel extensively without arousing suspicion.

Martino was a CIA asset and also had ties to military intelligence (the DIA), giving him two ways to feed disinformation to US authorities. But his allegiance was to the Mafia, which is how Martino learned about C-Day (which he would write about shortly after JFK's assassination, and mention the Odio incident in the same article). Shortly before his death, Martino confessed his role in the JFK assassination. John Martino met Silvia's sister,

Sarita, at one of his talks shortly before the staged meeting between Silvia Odio and Oswald took place. As noted earlier, Martino had seen Oswald several weeks earlier, while Oswald was passing out leaflets in New Orleans in an incident staged by the CIA, with the assistance of Banister and Ferrie. This time, however, the Mafia would be staging the incident without the knowledge of the CIA.

Between Rolando Masferrer and John Martino, the Mafia had two ways to have become aware of Silvia Odio. There were also others: Silvia's uncle in New Orleans—Dr. Augustin Guitart—was close to both C-Day leader Tony Varona and the DRE's Carlos Bringueir, who was friends with David Ferrie. In fact, Silvia's uncle had been in court the day Oswald was sentenced for the street altercation. So, the Mafia had many ways to have learned about Silvia, who they no doubt saw as a weak link in the otherwise tight JURE structure. It was well known in Dallas exile circles that Silvia was having emotional difficulties adjusting to her newly reduced circumstances and to her parents being in prison.

Silvia Odio told the FBI that in late September 1963 she was "contacted . . . by two Cuban males who stated they were members of . . . JURE, an anti-Castro Cuban organization headed by Manuel [sic] Ray . . . these two Cubans were accompanied by an individual that they introduced as Leon Oswald, who Miss Odio states is identical with Lee Harvey Oswald. These Cubans contacted Odio and requested her help in soliciting funds from Dallas businessmen, which she refused because both her parents are presently in jail in Cuba, and she feared for their safety. A few days later one of these individuals" called Silvia Odio and "stated that they were going to have nothing further to do with Oswald since he was 'loco.' Oswald told them he was an ex-Marine and wished to help them in their Cuban underground." The caller also claimed "Oswald told them 'I am sure you Cubans would want to shoot President Kennedy for what he did to you at the Bay of Pigs.'"[10]

The Warren Report contained additional details, saying that when the three men met Silvia, "the men did not state their full names, but identified themselves by 'war names,'" which were Leopoldo and Angelo; and other reports say the men knew her father's "war name," something not widely known. The report also says that "Mrs. Odio said the men told her they had just come from New Orleans." It also adds that Silvia said the man who called after the meeting said that Oswald "had been in the Marine Corps and was an excellent shot, and that the American said the Cubans 'don't have any guts because President Kennedy should have been assassinated after the Bay of Pigs, and some Cubans should have done that.'"

The Report also says that while Silvia Odio didn't think the men were really "members of JURE, she was certain that the American who was introduced to her as Leon Oswald was Lee Harvey Oswald" as did "her sister, who was in the apartment at the time of the visit by the three men, and who stated she saw them."[11]

Gaeton Fonzi's interview with Silvia Odio for the Senate Church Committee clarified some additional details. Silvia said the leader of the three, the one who called her later and made the incriminating statements about Oswald, wanted her to write fund-raising letters for them, "in the name of JURE," and he wanted her "to write them in English, very nice letters," that the men could use to raise "some funds." Silvia said she "remembers specifically that Oswald's name was said twice, once by the man introduced him and once by Oswald himself. The man who introduced Oswald was the one who later made the call that incriminated Oswald, so it's clear he wanted to make sure Silvia remembered Oswald's name. Silvia also remembered "that Oswald had a slight beard and more of an indication of a moustache, as if he hadn't shaved in a day or so or (as they said) had just come from a trip."[12] (Oswald lived in New Orleans at the time.)

Silvia said "the thing she remembers most about one of the" other men, not Oswald, "is that he had a 'funny kind of forehead. It just sort of went back, with no hair on the side. It was peculiar and it's hard to explain.'" She said he "had pockmarks on his face and a very bad complexion. He also had a 'funny kind of head,' a lot of hair but 'big entrance on the side.'"

It's also interesting that "she says that when the three men came to the door they first asked for Sarita," her sister. That was the one who John Martino had met not long before. Silvia said that when she told them Sarita wasn't there, "they seemed confused, but when she told them she was Silvia and that she was the oldest they said it was she they wanted to talk with." Silvia also said that when one of the men called her back and "told her about Oswald talking about killing Kennedy," it was two days later.[13]

Before JFK's assassination, Silvia Odio told at least three other people about Oswald's visit. Researcher Paul Hoch checked Odio's raw deposition at the National Archives against her published testimony, and found that Odio had originally said that she had told three other people about the incident, when it was still "fresh."[14] One of those three was her uncle, Dr. Augustin Guitart, described by one exile leader as Tony Varona's "right-hand man" in New Orleans.

When Silvia saw Oswald's picture on TV on November 22, 1963 as the assassin of JFK, she fainted and had to be hospitalized. Her account eventually reached the FBI and the Warren Commission. The FBI eventually came up with an explanation for the incident—involving an associate of John Martino and Santo Trafficante—which was put into the Warren Report at the last minute, but it was later shown to be false. In the following decades, the "Odio Incident" continued to perplex investigators, but it finally becomes clear when put in the context of C-Day:

1. Earlier in 1963, Harry Williams turned down Masferrer's demand to join C-Day, during their confrontation at Bobby Kennedy's New York apartment.

2. In July 1963, Tony Varona became part of C-Day, and a CIA document confirms that Rosselli's Chicago Mafia paid Tony Varona a bribe of $200,000 (in 1963 dollars, over a million in today's dollars).

3. In August 1963, a CIA memo says Tony Varona met with Rolando Masferrer, an associate of John Martino. Varona said he would get Masferrer into C-Day, after certain "obstacles" had been removed. Varona, Masferrer, and Martino were all associates of Santo Trafficante, who was already plotting JFK's assassination.

In late September 1963, the Odio Incident laid the groundwork for getting rid of the "obstacles" of both JFK (who was opposed to Masferrer) and Manolo Ray. It would be a ticking time bomb, ready to go off after JFK was assassinated—whether in Chicago, Tampa, or Dallas—and Silvia Odio saw Oswald again. With her fragile reputation, the Mafia was sure she would have a traumatic reaction (which she did) and that word of the incident would reach authorities (which it did), making Oswald look even more guilty. But the indication of Oswald being in contact with a C-Day group like JURE would cause consternation and cover-ups at high levels (which it did). Imagine if Silvia had written letters for the men on behalf of JURE, and those letters had been found after JFK's assassination in Oswald's rooming house or even on him, after his arrest. Just to make sure that the authorities got the message, John Martino mentioned the Odio Incident in his article that also mentioned C-Day. Martino's article came out just weeks after JFK's assassination, long before the Odio Incident was made public, showing that Martino had inside knowledge of the incident.

Oswald in Mexico City: A CIA Operation Compromised

WHILE THE THREE PREVIOUSLY EXPLAINED Oswald mysteries have been the subject of much controversy over the decades, none can match Oswald's Mexico City trip—seven weeks before JFK's assassination—for the amount of CIA stonewalling, obfuscation, and withholding evidence from Congressional investigators. The reasons are twofold: First, Oswald was in Mexico City as part of a CIA anti-Castro operation, which accounts for much of the secrecy at that time and even today. Most of those in the CIA were not aware of this operation, which is why some information about Oswald was withheld by one part of the CIA from another part. Second, it started to become clear to Congressional investigators in the 1970s—and was amply proven by document releases in the 1990s—that an impersonator made several of the phone calls attributed to Oswald that CIA wiretaps picked up in Mexico City. The CIA (and FBI) were surprised when they discovered this right after JFK's assassination, but the Mafia's ties to Mexico City—and their penetration of C-Day—explain the reason for this deception.

According to most official accounts, Oswald's time in Mexico City lasted from about September 27, 1963 until approximately October 1, 1963.[1] For many years, historians assumed that the reason the CIA withheld so much information about Oswald's trip to the Cuban and Soviet embassies in Mexico City—and released so much evidence that was contradictory—was to protect the CIA's photo and phone surveillance of the embassies. However, that CIA surveillance became widely known in the mid-1970s, and in fact was never much of a secret to the Soviets and Cubans. But the CIA's withholding of information persisted even after that; and whenever new information was pried out of the CIA, it only raised new questions and pointed out new contradictions. There was so much secrecy, so much information that was withheld or destroyed, and so many signs of an Oswald impostor in phone calls and photos that some felt that Oswald had not gone to Mexico City at all.

While the official Warren Commission story of Oswald's trip quickly started to crumble after the publication of its report, the CIA doggedly clung to the story they had maintained right after JFK's assassination: that, until after JFK's death, they had had no idea that Oswald had gone to the Cuban Embassy. Over the years, more and more evidence showed that not only had the CIA known about Oswald's visits to the Cuban Embassy, but that they had arranged them as part of a CIA operation. That's what they've been protecting all these years. And the target of the CIA mission with Oswald was Cuba, not Russia, which is why so much remains withheld about Oswald's Mexico City trip even after the fall of the Soviet Union.

The solution of the mystery of Oswald's visit to Mexico City becomes clear when put in the perspective of C-Day, and the Mafia's penetration of it as part of their plan to kill JFK. At the heart of Oswald's CIA mission in Mexico City—and most of the secrecy surrounding it—is David Atlee Phillips. CIA documentation for C-Day, code-named AMWORLD, confirms that Phillips was involved with C-Day regarding Mexico City at this time. However, Phillips was also working with Miami CIA operations chief David Morales, whose close ties to Johnny Rosselli made it easy for the Mafia to use its long-standing contacts in Mexico City to take advantage of the situation.

No ordinary American wanting to go to Cuba or Russia in 1963, even a former defector, would still be the source of so much CIA secrecy more than forty years later. In Oswald's case, however, his C-Day mission cut across several layers of CIA secrecy, including different departments within the CIA itself. CIA officials like Phillips, Desmond FitzGerald, and Richard Helms weren't just withholding information from the FBI or the Warren Commission; they were withholding some sensitive information about Oswald from others in the CIA, both in Washington and in Mexico City. Before explaining why, it's important to recall that Phillips had at least three CIA roles at the time, and—as part of those three different roles—was bouncing between CIA stations in Mexico City (where he was based), Washington, D.C. (where Desmond FitzGerald and Helms were based), and Miami (where David Morales was based).

When Oswald went to Mexico City—and we believe, after reviewing all the available evidence, that he did go—he was picked up by the CIA's regular surveillance of the Cuban and Soviet embassies, both phone taps and photo surveillance. However, at the time, Oswald was still under the additional "tight surveillance" by Naval Intelligence, with assistance from other federal agencies. This was confirmed by our Naval Intelligence source, who saw a photo of the real Oswald in Mexico City, something the CIA has never admitted existed, as well as by other evidence which briefly surfaced right after Oswald's death.

According to the *New York Times*, "there were reports" that Oswald's "movements were followed in Mexico by an unidentified United States agency."[2] According to author Sylvia Meagher, after Oswald's death "the *New York Post* reported that William Kline, chief of US Customs at Laredo, had said . . . that Oswald's movements had been watched at the request of 'a federal agency at Washington.'" She also noted that "the *New York Herald-Tribune* reported" that another "US Customs official, Oran Pugh, had said that . . . 'US Immigration has a folder on Oswald's trip'" and that the way "Oswald had been checked by US Immigration officials on entering and leaving Mexico . . . was not the usual procedure."[3] Secret Warren Commission transcripts show Senator Richard Russell saying Oswald "came back in a car" from Mexico, when Oswald didn't drive or even own a car, even though the official story in the Warren Report said he returned by bus.[4]

Finally, in recent years, Dallas FBI Agent James Hosty—assigned to watch Oswald prior to JFK's death—"repeated a conversation he had with a friend of his who had been working in Mexico City at the time, agent Michael DeQuire. DeQuire had informed Hosty, after the assassination, that Oswald was under surveillance in Mexico City outside of his visits to the embassies, and that he had been separately photographed near a fountain at one time during the surveillance."[5] This new information meshes perfectly with what our Naval Intelligence informant had told us years earlier. The ultimate goal was to catch the KGB trying to recruit Oswald or Marina, which explains why Oswald (and the US intelligence agents controlling his actions) had to be careful with his trips and expenses. There always had to be a seemingly logical (and documentable) sequence to his actions, in case Oswald was being watched by the KGB prior to their contacting him.

In addition to Oswald's "tight surveillance" and the CIA's usual embassy surveillance of photos and wiretapped phones, Oswald came into contact with a much more sensitive type of CIA embassy monitoring: CIA assets inside at least the Cuban Embassy. This accounts for some of the continuing secrecy, but cannot account for the CIA's withholding or destroying its photos and phone tapes that had nothing to do with these CIA assets.

At the heart of the remaining secrecy is Oswald's real mission at the time, which was getting into Cuba in support of C-Day and the CIA's other Castro assassination plots. As new documents reveal, that operation was very tightly held in the CIA, known only to a few, not even to the CIA's chief of station in Mexico City. Others in the CIA were apparently aware that Oswald was involved in some type of operation against the Fair Play for Cuba Committee, as a way of accounting for some of the special attention Oswald was getting, but that was mainly a cover. It was better if a Soviet or Cuban mole (or electronic eavesdropping) in our embassy picked up word of an operation against the Fair Play for Cuba Committee, than if they learned that Oswald was being manipulated as part of a plot to topple Castro. That's probably why the Mexico City CIA chief wasn't told about Oswald's role in C-Day, and why meetings about it involving David Phillips were held far from Mexico City, in Washington, D.C. and Miami. Unfortunately, while the CIA was worried about the Russians and the Cubans, each of the CIA operations described above had also been penetrated by the Mafia and its allies in Mexico City.

Oswald's goal for the CIA in going to Mexico City was to get into Cuba. To avoid appearing too obvious, he claimed at the embassies that he really wanted to go to Russia, but their rules required him to get a Cuban visa first. The Cubans weren't about to let someone like Oswald, who wasn't part of an organized group and had no one to vouch for him, into Cuba. But they would let him into Cuba if he had a Russian visa and was just using Cuba as a transit point. However, even the Warren Report admits that "the evidence makes it more likely [Oswald] intended to remain in Cuba" rather than go on to Russia.[6] But when the Russians said it would take at least four months before he got the Russian visa that would enable him to go to Cuba, "Oswald, upset at this response, shouted, 'This won't do for me! This is not my case! For me, it's all going to end in tragedy."[7] Oswald knew that his mission depended on his getting into Cuba, and much sooner than four months from then. Though Oswald would not have known the exact date of C-Day, he had certainly been given a deadline by Phillips, since C-Day was only two months away at that point.

Oswald's trip from Texas to Mexico City via Nuevo Laredo, in an attempt to get into Cuba, presaged what Gilberto Lopez would do several weeks later—only Lopez managed to actually get into Cuba. A secret Warren Commission memo said that Lopez was on a "mission" at the time, and the same was true for Oswald. Lopez made his trip from Texas to Mexico City after

JFK's death, and Oswald was apparently planning another trip to Mexico City at the same time. Another secret Warren Commission memo even documented how Oswald could have been planning to go to Mexico City on the day of the assassination, noting such things as the bus schedules and the amount of money Oswald had.

Another reason for so much secrecy and confusion about Oswald's visits to the Cuban Embassy in Mexico City is that Oswald was just one of three young men linked to C-Day leader Manuel Artime who were all trying to get into Cuba at the same time, even on the same day. The other two young men were discussed in Part I, and one of them fits the description by two Cuban Embassy officials of "Oswald" being "blond" better than the actual dark-haired Oswald does.

The CIA was generally trying to "get assets into Cuba" at that time, and if Oswald had succeeded, it would have been positive for the CIA and those working on C-Day David Atlee Phillips. If Oswald didn't succeed, even his attempt would hopefully increase his interest to the KGB, who might then try to recruit the former Marine at a later time. (That is why Oswald remained under "tight surveillance" until JFK's death.) Oswald could always try to get to Cuba again at a later date, using an alias and fake identity like "Hidell," the ID and name he originally used when arrested in Dallas.

In some ways, the Mafia wouldn't have minded if Oswald had gone to Cuba for a brief period, as long as he returned. A recent sojourn to Cuba would make him look all the more guilty in the eyes of the American press and public. But the planned attempt to kill JFK in Chicago was only a month away at that point. If Oswald managed to stay in Cuba, the Mafia could lose its best patsy for the JFK hit. Because the Mafia did not want Oswald to go to Cuba, it arranged the phony "Oswald" calls made to the Soviet Embassy. These calls were made by someone who spoke Spanish, unlike Oswald, and who spoke Russian very poorly, unlike Oswald, helping to ensure that Oswald didn't get the Russian transit visa that would have allowed him into Cuba.

While Oswald's defection already made it possible to blame Castro's death on the Soviets if Oswald were fingered for the murder, Oswald strengthened that Russian connection in Mexico City. He spoke to a KGB officer at the Soviet Embassy, which could easily be used by the C-Day coup leader as evidence that the KGB had been behind Oswald's actions in killing Castro. For years, some people, both in the CIA and not, made sinister implications about Oswald's contact with the KGB official (including that Oswald was acting on KGB orders when he killed JFK). However, after the fall of the Soviet Union, that official and the others Oswald dealt with were extensively interviewed, and more Soviet documents about Oswald were released. One of the Soviet officials even wrote a book and attended a conference about JFK's assassination, where he was questioned by researchers and journalists. It turns out that the Soviets were very suspicious of Oswald being a US intelligence agent. Other US documents dispel any notion that Oswald was being manipulated by the Soviets, or the Cubans.

David Atlee Phillips's multiplicity of roles in 1963—which included working on C-Day, running CIA Cuban operations out of Mexico City, and being the number three man at the Mexico City station (in charge of monitoring the Soviet and Cuban Embassies)—is the reason he figures into many of the lingering controversies about Oswald in Mexico City. Congressional investigator Gaeton Fonzi notes that when David Atlee Phillips was testifying to Congress in the 1970s, or giving interviews to newspapers, Phillips was a mass of contradictions regarding the tapes of Oswald's phone calls and the reasons why no surveillance photographs existed of Oswald at the Cuban consulate—even though there were numerous photos of others at the same time (including a heavyset man the CIA claimed at one point it thought was Oswald). Such disinformation by Phillips would make sense if Oswald had been part of a US intelligence operation in the fall of 1963, one that neither the Warren Commission nor the Congressional committees of the 1970s were privy to. The one relevant operation that fits such a description—and which Phillips was working on at the time—was C-Day, AMWORLD (since the CIA-Mafia plots, AMTRUNK, QJWIN, and Cubela/AMLASH had all been at least partially revealed at that point). Of course to Phillips, and certainly to David Morales, C-Day was just one of several CIA plots at the time to get rid of Castro. So, Oswald's actions in Mexico City could have also helped the other CIA assassination operations, all of which had been penetrated by the Mafia.

CIA documents show that both Phillips and the Miami CIA station, where operations were headed by David Morales, were working on C-Day in the fall of 1963. David Morales made frequent trips to Mexico City, where Phillips was stationed. Phillips also went to Morales's Miami CIA station, right after Oswald left Mexico City. While Oswald was in Mexico City, Phillips was in

Washington, where Richard Helms and Desmond FitzGerald were based.[8] It's clear from all this activity that plans for C-Day were moving swiftly, and Phillips was a key player. But Morales probably ranked higher than Phillips at the time, meaning that Morales was in a position not only to know what Phillips knew about C-Day (and relay it to Johnny Rosselli), but also to influence (directly or indirectly) Phillips to take certain actions. Morales was working with Johnny Rosselli at the time on the same goal, overthrowing Castro, so Morales may not have even realized that he was being indiscreet or being used by Rosselli.

While most C-Day files remain among the "over one million CIA documents" related to JFK's assassination that have not yet been released, some have slipped through. One of them links Phillips's actions in Mexico City in October 1963 to C-Day. This declassified document has the official CIA code name for their part of the operation, AMWORLD, and C-Day leader Manuel Artime is code-named AMBIDDY-1, a code name not revealed until recently and unknown to previous Congressional investigating committees. David Atlee Phillips is code-named "Michael C. Choaden," which the Assassinations Records Review Board has confirmed was actually Phillips. Translating the code names to make it clearer, the cable says that "in regard to providing C-Day operation with safehouse facilities in your area [Mexico City]. The safehouse would serve as a meeting place between members of the Headquarters staff component in charge of C-Day and Manuel Artime. As discussed with David Atlee Phillips, Artime will be conveyed to the safehouse by. . . ."

The memo refers to an earlier CIA memo about AMWORLD from September 12, 1963—just two weeks before Oswald's visit to Mexico—that has not yet been released. Given that three men linked to Artime were trying to get into Cuba around this time, a meeting involving Artime and Phillips makes perfect sense. The cable was sent to J. C. King, the chief of the CIA's Western Hemisphere Division, who had worked with Phillips (and Morales) since their days together on the 1954 CIA Guatemala coup/assassination operation.[9]

Another CIA cable doesn't have the AMWORLD code name (usually censored from most documents), but does refer to Phillips by the "Michael C. Choaden" code name used in the AMWORLD cable. It says that on October 1, 1963—the date of one of the phony Oswald calls to the Russian Embassy— the CIA's Mexico City station said that a diplomatic pouch sent the same day should be held until it could be picked up by Phillips. The cable notes that Phillips is on temporary duty at that time to CIA headquarters. Phillips's trips at that time were authorized by Desmond FitzGerald.[10] On October 1, the

Mexico City CIA station also sent a cable directing that a diplomatic pouch, sent on October 1 to Washington, should be held in the registry until picked up by "Michael C. Choaden [i.e., Phillips] presently TDY [temporary duty] HQS."[11]

When writing about his time at the CIA station in Mexico City from 1962 to 1964, David Atlee Phillips is quite revealing in his first autobiography, written—and approved by the CIA—before his name became so prominent in two Congressional JFK assassination investigations: He says he "reported for work at the Mexico City station to take over the covert action desk" and "much of my time was spent on anti-Castro propaganda operations. This called for many hours of coordination with the station officer whose . . . job was to maintain 'total coverage' of the Cuban embassy." Phillips adds that "the CIA is not authorized to watch American citizens abroad unless they are clearly engaged in the espionage game." Since the CIA routinely photographed everyone who went in and out of the Cuban and Soviet embassies—and recorded all the calls made to them—Phillips's statement seems ridiculous. But given the Cold War mentality of the times, perhaps their justification would be that any American going to the Cuban or Soviet embassies was potentially engaged in espionage.

Phillips writes that the CIA's overall coordinator for Cuban Operations (and C-Day) "Desmond FitzGerald visited Mexico City . . . to review the station's Cuban efforts." The CIA station chief in Mexico City, Win Scott, was not fully informed about C-Day—he only knew about the Artime side of AMWORLD in a general sense. However, he is the source for key information cited later that is at odds with the official version of Oswald's visit, so it's helpful to know that according to Phillips, "Win [Scott] had a near-photographic memory." Phillips writes that when he was first recruited into the CIA, "'We intend to dangle you,' my Case Officer said... A dangle operation is when something or someone of interest is intentionally put into the path of another intelligence service with the hope it will bite.'"[12] That is what Phillips hoped the Cuban Embassy would do, with a tasty morsel like Oswald.

Phillips's autobiography also shows one of the places he got the idea to manipulate Oswald and the other Artime-linked men. He writes about an American from Texas who attempted to contact the Cuban Embassy in Mexico City in July 1963. In this case, the American seems (one never knows, hence we won't use his name) to have been interested in helping the Cubans. But Phillips found out about it using his surveillance, then manipulated the man while keeping him under surveillance. What is unusual is that a cable about this American was put into Oswald's file well before JFK's assassination—even though the CIA officially maintains to this day that they were unaware that Oswald had any contact with the Cuban Embassy until after the assassination.[13] Why would a cable about an American being manipulated by Phillips be put into Oswald's file prior to JFK's death? The CIA has no explanation, but it's clearly because Phillips was also manipulating Oswald and the other Artime-linked young men.

Phillips's dual role—helping to direct the surveillance of the Cuban Embassy, while at the same time running operations designed to take advantage of it—led to many of the controversies of Oswald's Mexico City visit. Far more people in the CIA were aware of the embassy surveillance than knew about various operations, especially extremely sensitive ones like C-Day/AMWORLD. This is nowhere more evident than in the disappearing tapes, transcripts, and photos of Oswald's visits. The official CIA version is that no tapes of Oswald's calls (real or alleged) exist, that only a few transcripts survive (and at least one of those is missing). They claim that the tapes were routinely destroyed before JFK's assassination. However, there is ample evidence that the tapes weren't destroyed prior to the assassination, and survived for months if not years (and may still exist).

For example, FBI chief J. Edgar Hoover told President Lyndon Johnson in a recorded call that "we have up here the tape and the photograph of the man who was at the Soviet Embassy, using Oswald's name. That picture and the tape do not correspond to this man's voice."[14] In addition, "former Warren Commission lawyers William Coleman and David Slawson told" journalist Anthony Summers "they listened to the tapes—courtesy of the CIA—several months after the assassination." In addition, "the senior CIA officer who had played them the tapes . . . confirmed that the tapes indeed existed as late as the spring of 1964."[15]

The CIA had several reasons to suppress or destroy the tapes. First, as Dr. John Newman points out, they record someone who could speak good Spanish but only broken Russian. That meant that Oswald was impersonated by phone at least five times (too many to be a simple mistake or error) by perhaps two different people.[16] Second, as Dr. Newman says, "there is substantial . . . evidence that other Oswald-related telephone calls were intercepted and transcribed by the CIA in Mexico City."[17] This evidence includes an account written by the chief of the Mexico City station at the time of Oswald's visit, who describes a call with Oswald spelling his name slowly, something that is not in any of the existing transcripts.

The impersonated Oswald calls appear to have only have two possible explanations. While they could be part of Phillips's C-Day operation with Oswald, their sloppy manner (not having the caller speak English or good Russian) seems at odds with the care such operations usually had. On the other hand, if the calls were made to help ensure that Oswald didn't get his Russian visa—and thus couldn't get into Cuba—that would fit perfectly with the needs of the Mafia. Did the Mafia know about the CIA's phone surveillance of Communist embassies in Mexico City? The answer is that the Mafia not only knew about it, but one of them helped to set some of it up—and the mob's allies ran it—as we document shortly.

The photos of Oswald in Mexico City are just as problematic, but for a different reason. Here, the culprit isn't the Mafia impersonations, but what the photos would show. The official CIA story is that no photos of Oswald in Mexico City exist, because the cameras weren't working, and other explanations which have changed over the years. However, the *Washington Post* says that Mexico City CIA station chief Win "Scott, for example, stated unequivocally that his subordinates in the Mexico City station had photographed Oswald during his visit. The CIA denies that any picture of Oswald was ever taken in Mexico City. Yet Stanley Watson . . . Scott's deputy in Mexico City, said in secret sworn testimony to congressional investigators in 1978 that the Mexico City station's Oswald file contained two surveillance photos of Oswald."[18]

Congressional investigator Gaeton Fonzi found that the deputy CIA chief for Mexico City at the time of Oswald's visit recalled being "shown a photograph of Lee Harvey Oswald" by CIA station chief Win Scott, but "two or three other people were in the photo." The CIA man said "discussion centered on who Oswald was and who the other people were" in the photo with Oswald.[19]

So photos did exist—but at least one showed Oswald with other people in the photo. This was a problem for Phillips because Oswald went to Mexico City alone and had no friends there. If the people in the photo were innocent, casual acquaintances, there would be no reason to hide the photos. So the people in the photo with Oswald must have been problematic for Phillips.

Our Naval Intelligence source saw one photo of Oswald in Mexico City in their files, before the assassination, which presents another dilemma for the

CIA, one which may explain the missing photos. Under what is known as the "third agency rule," if an agency like the CIA is helping another arm of the federal government—like Naval Intelligence—in an operation, then the CIA cannot release or declassify any information about that operation without permission from the first agency, in this case Naval Intelligence. Since the CIA was assisting the "tight surveillance" of Oswald for Naval Intelligence—and gave at least one photo of Oswald in Mexico City to them—the CIA is legally not obliged to declassify that photo or any of the others without permission from Naval Intelligence.

C-Day, the "tight surveillance," and the Oswald impersonation phone calls probably account for all the secrecy and missing evidence relating to Oswald. And some of the evidence may still exist (along with other evidence Congress was never told about). For example, the House Select Committee on Assassinations report about Oswald in Mexico City is 500 pages long, and was written by staff members after they reviewed what must have been thousands of pages of documents and transcripts of interviews. However, it says that "this Committee has not seen all of the photographs produced by the [CIA] photo surveillance operations in Mexico City. Hence, it cannot conclude that a photograph of Oswald does not exist among those photographs it has not seen." The still partially censored report goes on to say that "the production from (censored) the second base that covered the Soviet Embassy entrance, and the pulse camera that covered the Cuban Consulate entrance, has not been made available for review."[20] So, among the "well over a million CIA records" may yet be photos of Oswald—with others—in Mexico City.

Because of his many roles, David Atlee Phillips even deceived and withheld information from some people in the CIA, including his own superior in Mexico City, Win Scott. Peter Dale Scott writes that "As Chief of Covert Action in the Mexico City CIA station, and later as Chief of Cuban Operations, David Phillips oversaw" the phone "intercept operations. Simultaneously he held a second operational responsibility in the Special Affairs Staff, which in 1963 was coordinating all covert operations (including assassinations) against Castro." In the fall of 1963, the latter job took precedence over the former, meaning that details about C-Day and CIA assassination operations (like Morales's CIA-Mafia plots with Rosselli) were kept from the CIA Mexico City chief. Even without the C-Day documents, Scott used declassified documents to state that "there was a pre-assassination CIA operation involving Oswald and Cuba. Such an operation, at least in its Mexico City aspects, would almost certainly have been directed by David Phillips."[21]

Much work on Oswald in Mexico City has been done by Dr. John Newman and *Washington Post* editor Jefferson Morley. They analyzed thousands of documents and got an "on the record" interview with a CIA operative who worked with some of the Mexico City cables. The CIA officer told them "there had to be a reason" for Desmond FitzGerald's Special Affairs Staff "to withhold information about Oswald" from other parts of the CIA. As noted earlier, FitzGerald's Special Affairs Staff handled C-Day and CIA Castro assassination plots, and had David Phillips working for it at this time. Jefferson Morley writes that the "simplest and most plausible explanation is that" the CIA "sought to protect . . . a covert operation involving Lee Harvey Oswald in the fall of 1963."[22]

Morley didn't know about C-Day or Oswald's role in it, but he came tantalizingly close to documenting it. Morley's article pointed out that the CIA officer "said that newly declassified CIA records suggested that members of the CIA's Special Affairs Staff (SAS) seemed to be carefully guarding information about Oswald in the weeks before Kennedy was killed." The CIA officer "was not only acknowledging that somebody in SAS was interested in Oswald six weeks before Kennedy was shot. She was stating that whoever that somebody was made an affirmative decision to withhold information about him from other CIA officers before November 22, 1963." Who? The CIA officer said that "responsibility for the cable on Oswald . . . belonged to . . . Dick Helms's right hand man."

Dr. Newman asked the CIA officer if that was "indicative of some sort of operational interest in Oswald's file?" The CIA officer replied "Yes . . . to me it's indicative of a keen interest in Oswald held very closely on the need to know basis." The CIA officer added "Well, the obvious position . . . would be that they thought that somehow . . . they could make some use of Oswald . . . I would think that there was definitely some operational reason."[23] There *was* an operational reason, one that Morley and Newman came close to uncovering, and that the CIA officer probably was not aware of (otherwise, she wouldn't even have given them an interview in the first place): The operation was C-Day/AMWORLD.

As we've noted earlier, one of those working on that operation was Miami CIA operations chief David Morales. Morley says that because "CIA officers in anti-Castro operations hid the nature of their interest in Lee Harvey Oswald before and after President Kennedy was killed . . . their actions may have had the inadvertent effect of insulating Oswald from scrutiny on his way to Dealey Plaza."[24]

Actually, Oswald was subject to too much scrutiny, of the wrong kind. He was under tight surveillance to see if the KGB was ever going to take the bait and contact him. As we noted earlier, some of the very people helping with that surveillance were also working for Marcello, Trafficante, and Rosselli, who were planning to kill JFK.

The Mafia penetration of C-Day includes Mafia ties to the CIA's surveillance operations in Mexico City during Oswald's visit. Johnny Rosselli probably learned of Oswald's planned trip to Mexico City from his good friend David Morales, or from Guy Banister, whom Rosselli visited around this time. As for the CIA surveillance, Rosselli didn't even have to go outside the "family" to learn about that, and to learn how to use it to compromise Oswald. Richard Cain was a "made" member of Rosselli's Chicago Mafia (real name: Ricardo Scalzetti). Richard Cain talked about knowing Johnny Rosselli, and they seemed very close, according to Mike Cain, Richard's half-brother. He said that Richard Cain was extremely close to Sam Giancana, and also knew Charles Nicoletti.[25] CIA files confirm that Cain was part of the CIA-Mafia plots along with Trafficante, Rosselli, Giancana, and future C-Day exile leader Tony Varona (Cain also did occasional work for Varona's mentor, Carlos Prio).[26] Cain admitted being part of the CIA-Mafia plots, once getting as far as one of Castro's rooms, and he talked about making a number of trips to Cuba. However, Cain wore glasses and had terrible eyesight, so shooting Castro—or JFK—with a rifle was not something he would have tried.[27]

Cain was also the number-two man in the Cook County (Chicago) Sheriff's office. He was also a bugging and wiretap expert. In 1962, one year before Oswald's trip to Mexico City, Congressional investigators found that Cain had helped install electronic eavesdropping equipment in a Communist embassy in Mexico City. CIA documents confirm that Cain was still in contact with the CIA during August and September 1963, and that he knew about C-Day. Cain was also in touch with the Chicago branch of the DRE exile group in August 1963, the same month that Oswald came into contact with the New Orleans branch.[28] Cain was said by CIA documents to "be deeply involved in the President Kennedy assassination case" in 1963.[29]

Just as the work of Dr. John Newman and Jefferson Morley showed that information about Oswald's trip to Mexico City flowed along two paths within the CIA, the same is true for Richard Cain. For Oswald, Newman and Morley documented that much sensitive information was kept from most of the CIA, even the Mexico City CIA station chief. False information was sometimes put in Oswald's file instead, with the most sensitive information about Oswald only being known to a few CIA officials like Richard Helms, Desmond FitzGerald, and David Atlee Phillips—all of whom were working on C-Day.

Cain's CIA file—as released so far—shows that his information flowed along two paths as well, include the same super-secret path as Oswald's. Thus, most CIA personnel who looked at Cain's file simply saw him as a high-level informant on Cuban exiles. In August 1963, as the Chicago assassination approached and C-Day was developing, Cain made a new and successful play to become a regular CIA informant. The CIA confirms that on August 19, 1963, "Cain met" two CIA officials and told them "he also was in contact with Cubans in the Chicago area who were involved in ventures which were not completely legal. Cain . . . agreed to assist the Agency by providing information on undercover activities of the Cubans."[30] Some of Cain's information involved exiles wanting to buy weapons. And FBI memo says that the C-Day groups "JURE" and "Alpha 66" had small chapters operating "in Chicago during 1963."

The DRE exile group, run by David Atlee Phillips, was also operating in Chicago in 1963. That was one of the groups Cain was reporting on to the CIA in the summer and fall of 1963. The DRE told Cain that the "group was sponsored by 'the Pentagon, which is in competition with [the] CIA.'"[31] However, the CIA had a different view of the DRE. A September 1963 CIA memo in Cain's file quotes a CIA official in Washington—whose name is censored—as saying: "Apparently the DRE is a MOB-controlled organization which, at times, seems to act independently of its monitor." Beside that comment, a CIA official has written by hand "AMEN!" That is capitalized in the original, as is the word "MOB." It's unclear if "its monitor" refers to the mob, or to the man who was really running the DRE, David Atlee Phillips.[32]

The CIA's "Domestic Contact Services office in Chicago used" Cain "as an informant and dealt with him on a variety of matters from 1960 to September 1964." When the Chicago CIA office "requested the [CIA] Office of Security to grant a contract approval in September 1963," the Security Office "furnished the" Chicago office "available derogatory information on" Cain. Yet even with that "derogatory information," the Chicago CIA admits that they kept using Cain until September 1964.[33] This allowed Cain to continue to keep track of what the CIA was interested in, and to feed them disinformation.

Cain's CIA files exist on two levels, those that most CIA personnel could see and those that only certain CIA personnel were allowed to see. For example, most CIA files say that the informant who told the CIA about C-Day exile leader Tony Varona getting a $200,000 payoff from the Chicago Mafia was "probably not Cain." However, a cover sheet for one of Cain's CIA files shows that it indeed was Cain who told the CIA about Varona's huge bribe: It clearly says that "Richard Cain, Chief Investigator, Sheriff's Office . . . Chicago" was the source for information in mid-August 1963 about "Cuban exiles' interest in purchasing arms/financial contribution from Chicago underworld." Notations on this Cain file show that it was sent to Desmond FitzGerald's deputy and to the CIA staffer who handled key Mexico City cables about Oswald—putting Cain's information on the same super-secret path as Oswald's.

C-Day was at the root of the extreme secrecy within the CIA about both Oswald and Cain. Just three days before Oswald arrived in Mexico City for his mission, Cain was talking to C-Day exile leader Tony Varona about C-Day. In Cain's CIA report—which omits Cain's name—Cain says that on September 23, 1963, Varona, "while visiting Chicago, told me that the President of Honduras had offered him the use of an island off Honduras as a base for anti-Castro activities. He also said that Manuel Artime is considered to be a CIA employee and makes no move whatsoever unless CIA approves."[34]

Cain had another connection to Oswald's Mexico City trip: Cain knew about the CIA's surveillance of Communist embassies in Mexico City. The corrupt Mexican DFS (Dirección Federal de Seguridad) manned the monitoring stations for the CIA, and Cain had helped them bug a Communist embassy in Mexico City the previous year. The DFS was also tied to narcotics trafficking, as was the Chicago Mafia (Giancana himself would eventually move to Mexico and expand the traffic). This allowed Cain to ensure that Oswald didn't get into Cuba—which would have cost the Mafia its best patsy—by having fake Oswald calls made to the Soviet Embassy (whose permission was necessary for Oswald to get into Cuba).

Peter Dale Scott documented that "the DFS was involved in the" CIA's phone monitoring of Communist embassies "and probably manned the listening posts. The DFS may have been assisted in this . . . project by Richard Cain." Scott notes that "Richard Cain" may have "trained and possibly helped recruit the Mexican" CIA call-intercept "monitors."[35]

To the CIA, Richard Cain was a trusted intelligence and electronics expert. To the Mafia, he was the perfect way to find out about—and manipulate—the CIA's surveillance of Oswald in Mexico City. To the CIA, the DFS was a trusted Mexican agency who helped them man their listening posts for calls made to Communist embassies in Mexico City. Scott writes that "DFS officials worked closely with the Mexico City station of the" CIA and "the DFS passed along photographs and wiretapped conversations of suspected intelligence officers and provocateurs stationed in the large Soviet and Cuban missions in Mexico City." But to the Mafia, high officials of the DFS were allies who were "deeply involved in the international drug traffic," according to extensive documentation compiled by Scott. He writes that while "the DFS had links to the Mexico-Chicago drug traffic, dating back to the 1940s," after 1963 "the DFS and the Mexican drug traffic became increasingly intertwined," so much so that "the last two DFS Chiefs were indicted, for smuggling and for murder; and the DFS itself was nominally closed down in the midst of Mexico's 1985 drug scandals."[36] Between Cain and the DFS, it would have been easy to rig the phony Oswald phone calls to the Russian Embassy, to make sure that Oswald didn't get his transit visa that would allow him to go to Cuba before JFK's death.

After Oswald's visit to Mexico City, on October 4, 1963, two CIA documents that are still partially censored say that "David Phillips will arrive" at the JMWAVE CIA station in Miami "for consultation." Both memos were sent from the CIA Director to the Miami station. One of the CIA documents makes it clear that Phillips went to the Miami CIA station in his capacity as the Chief of Cuban Operations for Mexico City, so the operation Phillips was coming to Miami to discuss was clearly an anti-Cuban operation involving Mexico City.[37] The head of operations at Miami was David Morales, and a portion of C-Day (AMWORLD) was being run out of Miami at a high, very secretive level. So Phillips was coming to Miami to talk to Morales about C-Day (and related operations), possibly to brief him about the actions of Oswald and the other young men who had just tried to get into Cuba.

TIGHT SURVEILLANCE ON OSWALD CONTINUES

From their years of various forms of vice, corruption, and intimidation, Marcello, Trafficante, and Rosselli knew that human nature was predictable in a practical way that could benefit them. If a seemingly pro-Castro person appeared to have killed JFK—or even a far-right extremist—it would make sense to the average person or reporter. Most officials and Congressmen would also accept that scenario, and most of the additional information they might get through law-enforcement and intelligence contacts would seem to support that. Some agencies would have to cover up or sanitize legitimate contacts they might have had with those seemingly involved, to protect reputations and other operations. Congressmen with especially good sources might, at most, be told quietly that further investigation might endanger US intelligence operations.

A few key officials who knew about C-Day and other secret US operations—like Bobby Kennedy, Richard Helms, and others—would also believe that Oswald had done it (at least initially), but not for the reasons most others did. They would think that a US asset like Oswald had "turned," for some reason. Yet that reason couldn't be publicly revealed—or even fully investigated—without exposing C-Day, as well as many other agents and operations (this would include the fake defector program and others who were under the same special surveillance as Oswald).

This last point is important, because it explains much of the secrecy surrounding the JFK assassination that doesn't directly relate to C-Day. As confirmed by the summer 1963 Dallas newspaper article cited earlier, when "penetrating so-called subversive or radical groups," police in major cities throughout America—including Tampa and Chicago—worked with a wide variety of federal agencies. The general public remained largely unaware of these domestic surveillance operations until the late 1960s. But the mob bosses—through their associates like former FBI supervisor Guy Banister and Chicago law-enforcement official Richard Cain—knew that such networks existed and would have to be protected, even if one of their targets (or assets) appeared to be involved in the JFK assassination.

The tight Naval Intelligence surveillance of Oswald—which included assets from other agencies like the CIA—would have to be protected, for example, and their reports withheld from any public investigation or court trial. In addition, information about the particular programs Oswald was in before C-Day would have to be protected—the false defector program and whatever overall operation the CIA and military intelligence were running against groups like the Fair Play for Cuba Committee. Also, information would have to be covered up or destroyed regarding the roles Oswald and others like him were playing in C-Day. In sum, the many cover-ups during the JFK assassination investigation were generated to avoid exposing many operations and dozens of assets, and perhaps even to avoid endangering other operatives who were still in Communist countries.

There were several developments in Oswald's surveillance by Naval Intelligence in October 1963, but one development in particular would allow us to uncover the surveillance decades later. Now, when we talk about "Naval Intelligence," we are referring to both the Office of Naval Intelligence and its close affiliate, Marine Intelligence, referred to on some Oswald documents as "G2-USMC."[38] They worked closely together, and while both were nominally under the command of the newly created Defense Intelligence Agency (DIA), there are instances in which Naval Intelligence apparently kept—or considered keeping—some information about Oswald secret even from DIA chief General Joseph Carroll.

A confidential source who worked with Naval Intelligence in the fall of 1963 saw Oswald's surveillance file in October 1963, a month or so prior to the JFK assassination. The source cannot be named because after helping with the secret Naval Intelligence investigation of Oswald, he signed a special confidentiality agreement. Many people think such agreements have been waived in the past, at least for Congressional investigations, but that is not the case. The only time a waiver has been given covering even a few people was for those at JFK's autopsy to testify before the House Select Committee on Assassinations in the late 1970s. Such confidentiality agreements are one reason that so much about JFK's assassination still remains secret, and they explain how C-Day remained secret for so long. To avoid violating National Security law, we used a nonmilitary intermediary in communicating with this source.[39]

The Naval Intelligence source was based in Washington, D.C., in 1963. The source said he first looked at Oswald's file in October 1963 because he saw Oswald's picture and thought he was someone from his home town. After studying the photo, he decided he was mistaken. However, the source said he did see, in the file, photos of Oswald in Mexico City. These photos have never been released; in fact, no photos of Oswald in Mexico City have ever been released. The CIA has only released photos of a heavyset stranger it claimed it once thought was Oswald. However, photos of the real Oswald, similar to what our source saw, have been described by several officials, including Mexico City CIA station chief Win Scott.[40]

Our source said Naval Intelligence had a "thick" file on Oswald. The file documented the "tight" surveillance on Oswald after his return to the US from the Soviet Union. The source was familiar with such "tight surveillance," and said it consisted of visual sightings, phone taps, and mail intercepts. (Agencies like the FBI have admitted intercepting mail sent to groups like the Fair Play for Cuba Committee, but have not admitted targeting

Oswald specifically.) The source said one name he recalled participating in the visual surveillance of Oswald was William Gaudet, mentioned in an earlier chapter as being in line right behind Oswald when Oswald got his Mexican tourist card in New Orleans.[41]

Gaudet had many ties to Guy Banister, providing a way for Carlos Marcelloto take advantage of the Naval Intelligence surveillance of Oswald. Gaudet told journalist Anthony Summers that he saw "Oswald discussing various things with [Guy] Banister" and that David "Ferrie . . . was also with Oswald" in the summer of 1963. Gaudet's status as a CIA asset has been detailed by Dr. John Newman, historian Richard D. Mahoney, and former Senate investigator Bud Fensterwald. Gaudet admitted observing Oswald passing out leaflets in New Orleans on several occasions, when Gaudet was doing a newsletter for the founder of INCA, the group that helped give Oswald's leafleting activities so much publicity prior to JFK's death. People who worked at Banister's office building confirmed to Summers that "Banister did know Gaudet and that Gaudet had on occasion visited" Banister's "office in the summer [of] 1963." Gaudet's activities in relation to Oswald were clearly being coordinated, if not directed, by Guy Banister, who had ties to Naval Intelligence through his closest friend, Guy Johnson.

As for Gaudet, after talking "at length of Oswald's physical appearance and personality, assessing him from personal observation as a 'very nervous, frail, weak man,'" Gaudet said he "did not believe Oswald killed the President," saying "I think he was a patsy. I think he was set up on purpose." Gaudet's conclusion about Oswald is similar to that reached by Naval Intelligence after their secret investigation (an investigation confirmed by both an additional, independent source and a Congressional investigation), which concluded that "Oswald was not the shooter" and that "Oswald was incapable of masterminding the assassination."[42]

Gaudet admitted to the House Select Committee on Assassinations that he was a CIA asset in the summer of 1963, and said "they told me frankly when I did things for them that if something went awry, they would never recognize me or admit who I was."[43] One can't help being reminded of Oswald in police custody the night after JFK's assassination, asking on TV for someone to please "come forward" to help him, still hopeful that Banister or some official would make a call that would extricate him from his predicament without Oswald's having to prematurely blow the cover he had worked so hard to maintain for so many years.

Our Naval Intelligence source confirmed that "Gaudet" was part of the 'tight' surveillance for" Oswald's "Mexico trip," providing additional evidence that Oswald's activities in Mexico City were not only monitored by US intelligence, but were undertaken at its direction. The source said that "a note on the top of the file jacket" for Oswald "said to contact the CIA if Oswald was arrested or got into any trouble. There was a name and some sort of code given for someone at the CIA."[44] Given Oswald's meeting with CIA official David Atlee Phillips, it's likely that the name was either Phillips—or one of his several code names like Maurice Bishop, Michael Choaden, or Lawrence Barker—or one of his close associates. Paul Hoch has spent decades studying the many anomalies in the CIA and military files on Oswald, while helping to get many documents declassified. In analyzing missing items in the existing Oswald Naval Intelligence files—items referred to but not now present in the files—Hoch found indications that certain CIA cables about Oswald had apparently been "forwarded to some unit within Naval Intelligence which had a special Oswald file."[45]

The reason that our Naval Intelligence source had access to Oswald's file before JFK's assassination was because the source was in a group doing "domestic surveillance." He said he "usually tracked a lot of liberal types," the same type of domestic surveillance that the obscure 1963 Dallas newspaper article talked about regarding police cooperation with military intelligence.[46] Further confirmation for how common this was in the early 1960s comes from a high Florida law-enforcement source who was involved with security for JFK's Tampa motorcade, four days before Dallas. The law-enforcement official said that "military intelligence had a large domestic spying role on groups in the 1960s which has never been written about." He even named a particular group—the "902 unit"—and named the retired general who commanded it.[47] Preventing the discovery of such domestic spying by the US military helps to explain why the Army destroyed its Oswald file in 1973, and why Army intelligence files under Oswald's name—and his alias "Alek Hidell"—were withheld from the Warren Commission, even though Army personnel testified as to their existence.

Since Oswald began his career in the US Marines, Naval Intelligence would have had the most files on him of all the service branches. Paul Hoch found indications in declassified government memos and reports that implied that there were more Naval Intelligence files on Oswald than were provided to the Warren Commission. He found references to three files, as well as a "supplemental file" on Oswald, that was never explained or provided to any government committee.[48] Our Naval Intelligence source did not get to see Oswald's "supplemental file," and thus did not know what operations Oswald was involved in.[49] The source's job was strictly surveillance, a good example of the compartmentalization that typifies so many of the intelligence operations we've discussed, of which C-Day is only one example.

Fall 1963: Rosselli, Robert Kennedy, and Ruby

WHILE C-DAY PROGRESSED IN OCTOBER 1963—with Bobby Kennedy and Harry Williams trying to get the "five fingers" to function together, while dealing with the C-Day coup leader in Cuba—the CIA's other activities provided fertile ground for Rosselli and the mob bosses. Most of the five Kennedy-sanctioned groups were supposed to be operating outside the continental US, except for the US Army's exiles in training at Fort Benning, Georgia. But the CIA was authorized to have a few small camps in Florida, where exiles were trained. These camps were tightly controlled by the CIA and used to stage small raids against Cuba. The raids were not expected to have any great impact, but they helped to cover the infiltration and exfiltration of US covert agents into Cuba. They ensured that exile commandos would be experienced and ready to help support C-Day, which was only weeks away at that point. Although these small camps were sanctioned by JFK and Bobby Kennedy—and even visited by Bobby—they were also used by Johnny Rosselli, with the approval of his close friend David Morales.

An insight into how tightly Rosselli had insinuated himself into yet another sensitive US intelligence operation is provided in a first-hand account by Bradley Ayers, a US Army captain assigned to work with the CIA to train exiles. Though officers on the level of Capt. Ayers were not told about C-Day, it's clear in hindsight that his work was part of the support structure for the upcoming C-Day coup. Captain Ayers's account was first published in 1976, long before hundreds of pages of documents supporting it and C-Day were released.

Cooperation between the military and the CIA was much closer than the often-difficult relationship between the CIA and the FBI. Military personnel—like Capt. Ayers, an experienced Ranger instructor—were sometimes assigned to the CIA. Earlier in 1963, Ayers describes going to the Pentagon's "Special Operation Section, Special Warfare, Office of the Deputy Chief of Staff for Army Operations." There, Capt. Ayers and other officers met with Lt. General Victor Krulak of the US Marines, "a personal friend of the President and a long-time military friend of General Maxwell Taylor, the chairman of the Joint Chiefs of Staff."[1] General Krulak served on one of Bobby Kennedy's secretive Cuban committees of the National Security Council along with Secretary of the Army Cyrus Vance and the CIA's Richard Helms.[2] Krulak also received copies of the "Plan for a Coup in Cuba" in the fall of 1963.[3]

General Krulak asked Capt. Ayers and other officers to volunteer to train Cuban exiles in Florida, explaining that "his country has been carrying on covert paramilitary and espionage activities against the regime of Fidel Castro . . . some of these raids and paramilitary operations are being conducted independently by ill-equipped, poorly organized exile groups, but most of the operations are being planned and conducted under the supervision of the CIA, using carefully selected Cuban exile volunteers, from bases in southern Florida and elsewhere in the Caribbean. The CIA has not been achieving the success hoped for. The Army has been ordered to provide the CIA direct support in two critical areas—the training of small commando units for raids and infiltration, and the planning and use of demolitions and explosives." General Krulak made it clear that "this matter has top priority and is receiving attention at the highest levels of government . . . you will have to sever all ties with the Army, forget that you ever were in the military . . . if you accept this mission, you will become undercover agents for the Central Intelligence Agency.'"[4]

By October 1963, Capt. Ayers—now ostensibly a civilian CIA operative—had been training Cuban exiles in Florida for about five months, though Ayers says that "because of this compartmentalization" and secrecy, "no one person could fully describe the Cuban program." Ayers explains that "our cover stories . . . must conceal our true status even from certain other CIA personnel." To maintain their "cover stories, the CIA had a "cover branch" that "was able to create new people, to change identities, appearances, credentials, passports, or whatever might be necessary for a specific mission. Some agents had as many as three or four identities, each used for different tasks."

Ayers's account of these activities parallels the development of C-Day, starting when he says that "during late May and early June 1963, there was a pronounced increase in exile raids and bombings."[5] In June 1963, Ayers even briefly met Bobby Kennedy at a "CIA social function" at "an expensive stucco house overlooking Biscayne Bay." Ayers noted that Bobby "Kennedy had great influence in the Administration, and I'd heard he chaired the Special Group. His presence tonight reinforced my belief that the Cuban situation and Castro were prime concerns to the White House."[6]

Bobby made a more unusual visit in the fall of 1963, when Ayers says "the Administration was ready to begin making an even more concerted effort to unseat Castro" because "the election year of 1964 was rapidly approaching, and President Kennedy's Cuban-policy critics were putting on the heat."[7] He notes that "by early October [1963], all programs for which I had been given responsibility were actively engaged or ready to begin."[8] A co-worker told Ayers that "there's something pretty big going on around here. I went to a couple of meetings while you were away last week; and it looks like things are really moving into high gear."[9] Ayers was taken to a meeting in south Florida that involved "thirty minutes of travel across open swampland and deep canals" by airboat, to a place where there were only "two small Quonset" huts and "two helicopters parked in the shadows." He says "four men emerged" from "the Quonsets," including "the deputy chief" of the Miami CIA Station—and "Attorney General Robert Kennedy," who "shook hands with each of us, wishing us good luck and God's speed on our mission."[10]

Capt. Ayers was soon told by his CIA superior that "during the next six weeks we want you to eat, sleep, and live this mission with the Cubans twenty-four hours a day . . . no one but you is to know the location of the training site. Once the commandos are there, they will not be permitted to leave until the mission is run." The exact mission was still left vague, but Ayers was told by his CIA superior that it could involve "two-man submarines" and that "an airborne commando raid [into Cuba] may not be far off."[11] Captain Ayers was told that "we had to be ready to go any time after the first of December," 1963.[12] It's clear from that date that Capt. Ayers was training exile commandos who would go into Cuba in support of C-Day, either just before or just after the C-Day coup.

Unfortunately, Johnny Rosselli was also using the CIA camps. A year and a half earlier, Bobby Kennedy had ordered the CIA not to use mobsters like Rosselli without informing him. In October 1963, Bobby's men were pressuring and prosecuting both Rosselli and his boss, Sam Giancana. Yet Ayers writes that "from time to time a man called 'Colonel' John Rosselli, who worked out of CIA headquarters in Washington, used" an exile "team for raids and other clandestine operations. Rosselli . . . was one of the few Americans authorized [by the CIA] to actually go on commando missions into Cuba."

The team that Rosselli sometimes used included a "sharpshooter" who did "daily marksmanship practice . . . rehearsing for the day when he could center the cross hairs of his telescopic sight on Fidel Castro." This was no poor shot like former Marine Lee Harvey Oswald, but someone capable of killing "three cormorants at a range of nearly five hundred yards." Though that team—separate from Ayers—had an official supervisor, the supervisor "admitted" a "lack of supervision at the safesite." According to Capt. Ayers, the official supervisor "wasn't aware, or pretended not to be, that" his "team was doing target practice with live ammunition."[13] In hindsight, this was clearly a dangerous situation rife with opportunities for exploitation by Johnny Rosselli.

Mob boss Johnny Rosselli was able to gain access to the CIA camps thanks to his close friend and associate David Morales. Captain Ayers says that "Dave [Morales], the big New Mexican Indian who ran" the CIA's Miami Operations branch, "was the only branch chief who treated us less than respectfully. He ran all the station's activities with a heavy hand and was famous for his temper . . . to cross him in any way was to invite trouble."[14] While the military's relationship with the CIA was far better than that between the CIA and the FBI, Ayers writes that "the CIA "people treated us with detachment and suspicion, regarding us as intruders in their secret, bureaucratic domain. There seemed to be an atmosphere of forced accept-ance and it reaffirmed our belief that we'd been 'jammed down the throat' of the CIA by" Bobby Kennedy's "Special Group."[15] Captain Ayers was unaware of another reason some in the CIA resented military personnel like himself: because C-Day was being run primarily by the military, with the CIA in only a supporting role.

Rosselli, a smooth operator always quick to take advantage of any situa-tion, also ingratiated himself with the military. Ayers writes that a fellow Army officer told him that "he and John Rosselli, the dapper American agent in charge of the continuing attempts to assassinate Fidel Castro, had been on a weekend binge together. They'd become close friends as they worked together . . . their drinking friendship was a natural extension of their duty relationship."[16] Ayers had even unofficially "heard that a new effort to assas-sinate Castro was being organized."[17] To Ayers at the time, Rosselli was just one of several CIA operatives with a team of Cuban exiles; Ayers didn't seem to be aware of Rosselli's extensive—but low-profile—criminal background.[18]

Training exiles in remote locales left little time to follow the news that fall, which featured stories about Bobby Kennedy's increasing prosecutions of Rosselli's mob allies.

THE CIA-MAFIA PLOTS CONTINUE AND ROSSELLI MEETS WITH JACK RUBY

In the fall of 1963, the CIA-Mafia plots with Johnny Rosselli continued, giving the mob bosses even more ways to cover their planning for JFK's assassination. What appeared to be CIA-Mafia plotting to kill Castro went on in Miami, but the Mafia was actually finalizing their plans to kill JFK. The *Miami Herald* places Chicago hit man Charles Nicoletti in the CIA-Mafia plots at this time.[19] Given reports of Nicoletti's presence in Dallas during the JFK assassination, it's clear that Nicoletti's real target was JFK, not Castro.

Also at a fall 1963 Miami meeting about the CIA-Mafia plots was Marcello operative Sam Benton, the man who reportedly once introduced Bobby Kennedy to Johnny Rosselli.[20] Benton had also been involved with an exile training camp, outside New Orleans, that had been raided by the FBI in the summer of 1963. Benton's involvement in the CIA-Mafia plots helps explain why, years later, Marcello claimed to have been involved in the CIA-Mafia plots: Marcello's biographer John Davis writes that "during an FBI sting operation against Marcello" in the late 1970s that eventually sent him to prison, "Marcello told [a] government undercover agent . . . that he" participated "in the CIA-Mafia plots to assassinate Castro." Davis says that "Marcello at the time was quite close to Santo Trafficante . . . the two met frequently and both were financial backers of Cuban exile groups."[21] The main exile group Marcello supported was the New Orleans branch of Tony Varona's Cuban Revolutionary Council, which involved David Ferrie.[22]

Jack Ruby apparently became involved in the fall 1963 CIA-Mafia anti-Castro plots with Johnny Rosselli, though it was really just a cover for Ruby's part in the JFK assassination. Investigative journalist Scott Malone confirmed that Jack "Ruby met secretly with Johnny Rosselli in Miami" and that "two meetings between" them "occurred during the two months preceding the Kennedy assassination on November 22, 1963."[23] That would put the meetings in late September or early October of 1963.[24] Malone says that "Rosselli was under FBI surveillance" during some of that time, and "an FBI agent familiar with the case says that Rosselli was indeed in Miami when the meetings with Ruby are supposed to have occurred" and "investigators were able to identify the exact motel rooms" where "the meetings occurred."[25] Congressional investigator Michael Ewing wrote a meticulously detailed nine-page analysis of Scott Malone's six-page article after it was released—noting anything even slightly in error—without pointing out any problems with the article's description of the fall 1963 Ruby-Rosselli meetings in Miami.[26]

Peter Dale Scott notes that David Atlee Phillips was at the CIA's "Miami JMWAVE station from October 7–9. There are reports that Rosselli, who had good standing in the JMWAVE station, met on two occasions in Miami . . . with Jack Ruby" around that time. Scott goes on to point out that "David Phillips even had one friend, Gordon McLendon, in common with Jack Ruby. McLendon, a sometime intelligence officer and Dallas owner of radio stations, had known Phillips since both men were in their teens. (The two men would in the 1970s join in forming the Association of Retired Intelligence Officers.)" Scott says that "what has not yet been explained is why McLendon, whom Ruby described as one of his six closest friends, embarked on a sudden and surprising trip with his family to Mexico City in the fall of 1963."[27]

Again, it's important to look at someone like Jack Ruby from the perspective of US intelligence at that time. Ruby had had a small role in the 1959 CIA-Mafia plots, and had been an informant for the FBI and narcotics officers. With Ruby's background in Cuban gun-running, if Rosselli had told David Morales that Ruby would be helpful in the fall 1963 CIA-Mafia plots, Morales would have had no reason to doubt him. Even Phillips could have been receptive, since he had a good friend in common with Ruby.

Malone notes that "columnist Jack Anderson says that Rosselli admitted knowing Ruby. 'One of our boys' is how Rosselli described him to Anderson. And a Rosselli friend says that in the course of various conversations over the years, Rosselli often referred to Ruby as 'that crazy Jew.'"[28] Ruby's long-distance phone calls were also starting to skyrocket, from just under 30 in September 1963 to around 80 in October, and 110 in the first three weeks of November 1963.[29] While Ruby and the Mafia had prepared a cover story—problems with the union that represented his strippers—to explain his sudden increase in phone calls and travel, the HSCA noted that Ruby's "labor problems do not necessarily explain all significant aspects of his actions and associations during that period," since "the explanations provided by several of the organized crime-connected figures Ruby was in touch with have not been corroborated and seem to have lacked credibility."[30] It's important to stress that this doesn't imply any massive conspiracy. In most cases, Mafia associates were simply passing a brief coded message to or from Ruby, with the Mafia associates having no knowledge of the JFK assassination plot.

Ruby's calls dramatically increased as newspapers started to report more about JFK's upcoming trips to Chicago, Tampa, and Dallas. Historian Richard Mahoney points out that "on September 13, 1963, the *Dallas Morning News* confirmed that President Kennedy would be visiting Dallas on November 21 or 22. Several days later, Jack Ruby began telephoning Mafia and Teamsters Union operatives and hit men all over the country, and made trips to New Orleans, Miami, and Las Vegas"—three cities where Marcello, Trafficante, and Rosselli wielded tremendous influence.[31]

Phone records also show how David Ferrie could communicate with an associate of Jack Ruby—in this case Lawrence Meyers, whom Ruby would be with the night before JFK's assassination. Meyers was from Chicago, and his companion when he met with Ruby that night was a woman named Jean Aase. An investigator notes that "Jean Aase [in Chicago] . . . received a phone call" from "David Ferrie on Sept. 24, 1963, the same day Oswald left New Orleans." Years later, "Miss Aase, whom the HSCA was unable to locate, indicated in 1993 that the Sept. 24 [1963] call from Ferrie (fifteen minutes in length) was probably for Meyers, and [she] was relieved to know . . . that [Meyers] is now dead."[32] It's possible that the call was related either to Oswald (perhaps his reported trip to Chicago) or a trip Ruby would soon make to Chicago, to receive a large sum of money shortly before the attempt to assassinate JFK there.

More Kennedy Pressure on the Godfathers

THE KENNEDYS' UNRELENTING PRESSURE ON Rosselli, Marcello, and Trafficante increased during the fall of 1963. Any hesitancy the mob bosses might have felt at attempting to murder JFK was no doubt overcome by the real prospect they all faced of having their operations exposed, being sent to prison, or—in the case of Rosselli and Marcello—being deported.

Ever since the days of Chicago's Al Capone, mobsters in general—and Chicago gangsters in particular—had feared the use of the IRS against them, and Rosselli was no exception. In coordination with Bobby Kennedy's Justice Department, the IRS had launched two thousand tax investigations against mobsters in 1963. One of their targets was Johnny Rosselli (and another was an associate of his, ex-Chicago mobster Jack Ruby). On various charges, the Justice Department had indicted 318 mob figures in 1963.[1] Due to pressure from Bobby Kennedy, the FBI kept Johnny Rosselli under close surveillance, watching for any offense that might allow an indictment. Earlier in 1963, a memo to J. Edgar Hoover from the Special Agent in Charge (SAC) of Los Angeles said that "Rosselli told Las Vegas SAC Dean W. Elson that he had told his new apartment manager that he should get a discount" on his rent because of "the FBI detail that would move into the neighborhood and bring down the number of burglaries and street crime."[2] The only time Rosselli seemed to be able to shake his FBI surveillance was when he was working on the CIA-Mafia plots against Castro.

Rosselli's power in Las Vegas and Hollywood flowed from his position in the Chicago Mafia, and the head of that family—Sam Giancana—faced even tougher surveillance than Rosselli. According to Chicago FBI agent Bill Roemer, "we literally lockstepped" Giancana. "We used nine men on each twelve-hour shift, twenty-four hours a day. If he went to dinner, we went with him. If . . . he got up from the table to go to the men's room, I'd get up and be at the next urinal."[3]

Historian Richard D. Mahoney pointed out that Giancana's lockstep surveillance "completely disrupted the Chicago Outfit's effort to establish casinos in the Dominican Republic by making it impossible for Giancana to meet with his top gambling experts." Such expansion was important, both because the Mafia no longer had casinos in Havana and because Bobby Kennedy was preparing a major assault against mob-controlled casinos in Las Vegas. Mahoney notes that "against the advice of his lieutenants, Giancana filed suit against the United States Government in federal court" in the summer of 1963, "claiming that he had been 'harassed . . . humiliated . . . [and] embarrassed' and asking for an injunction to protect his civil rights." As a result, "the court . . . ordered that the FBI maintain specified distances between its agents and Giancana. The Circuit Court of Appeals reversed the lower court's injunction two weeks later." Mahoney also notes that "the outcome coincided with a leak . . . to *Chicago Sun-Times* reporter Sandy Smith that Sam Giancana had done work for the CIA."[4] But even that leak failed to end Bobby Kennedy's assault on Giancana (though some speculate that it caused Bobby to move more cautiously against Giancana). If Giancana went down, it could seriously affect Rosselli.

FBI Agent Roemer often said that Sam Giancana—and by implication, any of his key people in the Chicago mob like Rosselli—could not have been involved in the JFK assassination. That's because in addition to the FBI's lockstep surveillance, they also had some electronic monitoring on Giancana. Roemer later used Richard Cain as an informant until the early 1970s. However, the FBI and Roemer had no idea that Cain was working for Giancana in 1963— according to the CIA, the FBI didn't even learn that Cain was a mobster until 1967. This shows that even with the FBI surveillance, Cain— and others like Rosselli and Nicoletti—had secure ways of communicating with Giancana in 1963 that were beyond the reach of the FBI.

Rosselli was also facing the imminent publication of *The Green Felt Jungle*, the Las Vegas exposé mentioned earlier that would focus an unwelcome spotlight on the publicity-shy Rosselli. Mahoney wrote that it would blow "Johnny Rosselli's cover" and would depict him as a "sophisticated and glamorous don."[5] Slated for release in mid-November 1963, its publication would greatly complicate Rosselli's covert work for the CIA. If Rosselli was going to take advantage of his CIA activities to provide cover for his work on the JFK assassination plot, he would have to do so soon.

The Green Felt Jungle also detailed Bobby Kennedy's new initiative against Las Vegas mobsters. It said that "the Justice Department has assigned eighty-six investigators to Las Vegas since Robert F. Kennedy took over as Attorney General. The new attack is called 'Operation Big Squeeze.'"[6] It quoted Bobby Kennedy as saying "Top racketeers always deal in cash, and there are innumerable ways to conceal cash from the very best investigators . . . one is the 'skimming' operation conducted behind barred doors, in which a large percentage of the proceeds of so-called legal gambling is skimmed off and then hidden."[7] The claims of *Green Felt Jungle* were more accurate than the authors knew, since such funds and Las Vegas would play a role in Rosselli, Trafficante, and Marcello's murder of JFK. Jack Ruby would make a trip to Las Vegas just before the Tampa attempt to kill JFK, and an alleged casino courier would be detained by police in Dallas shortly after JFK's assassination there. Ironically, the leak of an FBI report on Las Vegas several months earlier may have prevented electronic surveillance from picking up some hint of the Mafia's plot against JFK. Historian Mahoney notes that earlier in 1963, J. Edgar Hoover gave "the Justice Department a single copy of a two-volume document titled 'The Skimming Report,' which detailed the inner mechanics of the Mafia's massive and untaxed diversion of gambling profits in Las Vegas . . . based on two years of electronic surveillance of the homes and hotel officers of some twenty-five mafiosi in the Las Vegas Area. Three days after the report was handed to Justice, however, someone gave a copy to the Mafia" and "FBI bugs began picking up commentary among gangsters that revealed that the government had been compromised." Mahoney writes that while "the FBI promptly pointed" to one of Bobby's Justice Department prosecutors "as the one responsible for the leak," it was "Hoover, who was strongly opposed to revealing FBI sources and was himself compromised by the mob," who "had the motive as well as the means to leak the highly charged materials." After the leak, Bobby Kennedy "ordered that the bugging of Mafia offices and homes in Las Vegas be stopped," with the result that "the leak of the Skimming Report . . . may well have kept the FBI from detecting evidence of a plot to murder the President."[8]

Bobby Kennedy's attacks against Rosselli, Giancana, and Las Vegas gave the Mafia plenty to worry about in the fall of 1963. The nation was riveted by the Valachi Hearings in Congress, which began in late September 1963 and continued until the end of October. This first-ever exposé of the inner workings of the Mafia generated massive newspaper and TV coverage, allowing Americans to hear from an actual "made" member of the Mafia about an organization that, just a few years earlier, J. Edgar Hoover had reportedly said did not exist.

The Valachi Hearings had such a tremendous impact because up until that time, no "made" member of the Mafia had publicly broken the oath of secrecy. Initially, Valachi hadn't broken the secrecy oath even after two narcotics convictions that would keep the fifty-seven-year-old mobster in jail for thirty-five years. It was only after Valachi killed a fellow inmate he thought was going to attack him—and was facing the death penalty—that he finally cracked and started revealing the secret structure of the Mafia.[9]

JFK and Bobby Kennedy had learned by experience in the late 1950s how important Congressional hearings could be in getting publicity and galvanizing the public against the Mafia. So, in the fall of 1963, the country was treated to the Valachi Hearings—in front of the Kennedys' old friend, John McClellan.[10] The focus of the hearings was "Organized Crime and Illicit Traffic in Narcotics," which struck at the heart of Trafficante and Marcello's lucrative French Connection.

Using testimony and incredibly detailed charts of criminal hierarchies—provided with the help of Bobby's Justice Department—the hearings clearly laid out their huge drug network and its many affiliates. Michel Victor Mertz's close associates in Canada and Mexico City were also identified, although Mertz himself was not named at all in the hearings, for reasons that are still unclear. Mertz associates who were named included Paul Mondoloni, Ansan Bistoni, and Jean Baptiste Croce, all of whom also operated in Havana. According to the hearings, Bistoni was "believed to have interests in the Eve, Cupidon, and Pigalle nightclubs" in "Havana, Cuba," while "Croce . . . owns two nightclubs in Havana, Cuba."

The hearings also named Canadian Lucien Rivard—who had been incarcerated in Cuba with Trafficante at the time he was visited by Jack Ruby—and those who worked with Mertz on the French Connection case dramatized later in the book and movie, Jean Jehan and Marius Louis Martin. The Valachi hearings even covered Mertz's French associates like Joseph Orsini, who had "been convicted in France for . . . collaboration with the Germans during World War II" and "Antoine D'Agostino," who "had been sentenced to death in absentia" for his "wartime collaboration with the Germans."[11] Mertz would use their World War II backgrounds as a cover story to get himself deported from Dallas shortly after JFK's assassination.

Glaring by his absence is Mertz himself, since all of his close associates in America, Montreal, Mexico City, and France were listed in the hearings. Perhaps diplomatic pressure kept his name out of the hearings. It's also possible that his many parallels with the life of CIA assassin recruiter QJWIN played a role. In any event, his heroin network was detailed, including "operations in Mexico City whereby large amounts of heroin were sent to the United States." The hearings also noted heroin routes that included New York, Florida, Texas, and Chicago.

When talking about Chicago mob boss Sam Giancana—"Gilormo Giangono, alias Momo Salvatore Giangono, alias Sam Mooney Giancana"—the hearings mentioned two of his longtime associates who figure into the story of JFK's assassination and its aftermath: Sam DeStefano and Charles Nicoletti, whose special "hit car" mentioned earlier was also cited in the hearings. Huge charts even showed photos, aliases, and FBI ID numbers for Giancana, Nicoletti, and DeStefano. Nicoletti looks like a handsome, snappy dresser, while DeStefano looks like a stereotypical thug. DeStefano would later be linked to the framing of Chicago Secret Service Agent Abraham Bolden and the death of Rosselli mob associate—and CIA asset—Richard Cain. Charts in the Valachi Hearings also included pals of Jack Ruby, like Lenny Patrick and Dave Yaras.[12] And singled out by the hearings for special attention was Ruby's associate from 1959, Santo Trafficante.

On October 15, 1963—just two weeks before the planned assassination of JFK in Chicago—Trafficante's activities were exposed in the national spotlight of the Congressional crime hearings. Among those present were Senator John McClellan, Bobby Kennedy's former mentor, and Senator Edmund Muskie.[13] Testimony about Trafficante came from Tampa Police Chief Neil G. Brown. In an ominous foreshadowing of JFK's assassination and its aftermath, Chief Brown said that it was quite "difficult . . . to obtain evidence sufficient for successful prosecution of Mafia members, because the witnesses who might offer such evidence have always been reluctant to do so." This was due to "fear of Mafia reprisals, since it is common knowledge in Tampa that the Mafia does not hesitate to murder for such reprisals." He pointed out "the relative infrequency with which such professional murders are successfully prosecuted." The chief noted statistics showing that only one of twenty-three Mafia homicides in Tampa had been solved—and the single exception was not typical—compared to a 97percent success ratio in solving non-Mafia murders in Tampa.

The Mafia's relative impunity when it came to murder helps explain both Trafficante's belief that he could get away with killing JFK, and how the Mafia was able to keep their attempt to assassinate JFK in Tampa secret for so many decades. Chief Brown noted the difficulty in prosecuting Mafia murders in Tampa "because of witnesses who are reluctant to give" police "any information whatsoever." Senator McClellan—who had been hearing such testimony for the past six years—said bluntly that such witnesses "know that the penalty for them talking would be death," and Chief Brown agreed. Brown even pointed out three Mafia reprisal murders in Tampa due to "the Mafia's knowledge . . . that the victims had given to legal authorities evidence incriminating Mafia members."[14]

In yet another chilling foretaste of JFK's assassination, one of these murders involved a victim whose "head was blown off" while the victim "was seated in his automobile," and then the chief "suspect in this killing . . . was himself murdered."[15] After such public testimony just weeks before JFK's murder, one cannot help but imagine the reaction of law enforcement and the public if Trafficante's name had surfaced as a suspect soon after JFK's assassination or in conjunction with the Tampa attempt.

Tampa Chief Brown directed the Committee to a large chart of the Tampa mob, with the "Top Man" being "Santo Trafficante." Chief Brown said "Santo Trafficante is the boss of this criminal group," then gave a detailed biography of Trafficante, exposing Trafficante's private life to public scrutiny for the first time. Chief Brown testified that "Santo Trafficante, Jr., was born in Tampa on November 14, 1914" and lives "today in Tampa and in Miami." He noted Trafficante's "gambling casinos" in Cuba, and Trafficante's ties to the "Mannarino brothers . . . Meyer Lansky . . . Sam Giancana" and "Joe Stassi," the mobster tied to the French Connection heroin bust in Houston the previous fall. Brown said Trafficante's Tampa Mafia has "interstate and international ties to other Mafia groups" and "we have witnessed and documented many visits of out-of-town racketeers with Santo Trafficante"—including at least one from Chicago—and "these visitors give further indications that Trafficante is associated with Mafia members in other cities."[16]

Chief Brown noted that Trafficante had "been picked up by the police for questioning about the gangland slayings of three men," and that "Trafficante was a suspect in the Albert Anastasia murder" after Anastasia attempted "to move in on Trafficante's gambling operations in Cuba." Unlike Carlos Marcello—who controlled numerous legitimate concerns—Brown knew "of no legitimate businesses that are owned or controlled by Santo Trafficante." He said that Trafficante "owns no real estate, nor any other property" since "his house, automobile, and all his other possessions are held in the names of others." However, Trafficante's family wasn't safe from prosecution by the Kennedys, and Chief Brown pointed out that "both brothers" of Trafficante had been "indicted by the Federal government for tax law violations." The chief noted the earlier arrest of "two cousins of Santo Trafficante" thanks to an IRS gambling raid, and a "July 1963 raid on a" Trafficante "gambling house . . . by the IRS agents" in coordination with local police, which was linked to yet another Trafficante cousin.

In response to "the difficulty of protecting witnesses against the Mafia," Chief Brown noted "Attorney General Kennedy's request for additional funds for that purpose, which . . . I strongly endorse."[17] The chief also endorsed "strongly the Attorney General's strong recommendation before this sub-committee that the Congress authorize the use of wiretapping in fighting organized crime," because "it is almost impossible for the Police Department of the City of Tampa, or any other municipality, to cope effectively with the activities of a national or international crime syndicate."[18]

Chief Brown was right, as events in the coming weeks in Chicago, Tampa, and Dallas would show. Brown would resign as police chief just weeks after his testimony and prior to JFK's November 18, 1963 motorcade in Tampa. His replacement—J. P. Mullins—would find himself dealing not only with an attempt to assassinate JFK, but also with having to keep it secret. Until we talked to Mullins in 1996, he had not discussed the Tampa assassination attempt with any journalist in thirty-three years, since a brief discussion with one reporter the day after JFK's death.

As noted above, several of Trafficante's relatives had been caught in prosecutions resulting from the increasing pressure by Bobby Kennedy. A recent history of the Federal Bureau of Narcotics (FBN) notes that in 1963, "Miami agents conducted narcotics investigations" on "Tampa resident Santo Trafficante." It says that "as part of the on-again, off-again surveillance," an FBN agent even "monitored Trafficante's daughter's wedding." This surely angered Trafficante, since usually noncriminal family members were considered off-limits by law enforcement. However, "that was as close as any FBN agent ever got to" Trafficante, according to one agent. He explained that "the CIA made weekly visits to our office, but they never helped us make cases. It was a one-way street" where "we helped them."[19] But the CIA didn't help the FBN against targets like Trafficante, who had worked on the CIA plots to kill Castro.

Carlos Marcello faced the most immediate threat of all: By mid-October 1963, his trial in New Orleans on federal charges was just two weeks away, and he faced another deportation. Marcello was clearly guilty of the charges Bobby Kennedy had brought against him; so, according to his biographer, "Marcello's principal strategy was to terrorize and possibly eliminate" the key witness against him and to "bribe as many jurors as" possible.[20] But Marcello knew that even if he were successful in using that strategy for this trial, Bobby would keep bringing new charges against him as long as JFK remained president.

Marcello's only hope was to eliminate JFK, and, as soon shown, Marcello used his meetings with David Ferrie—supposedly about the trial—to cover for planning the final details of the JFK assassination. Bobby Kennedy's top Marcello prosecutor, John Diuguid, told us in a recent interview that Marcello was not bugged or wiretapped at this time, which meant that such planning went undetected. The following year, one Bureau of Narcotics informant would wear a wire into Marcello's lair on just one occasion, but that was the extent of electronic surveillance of Marcello for many years, because local FBI officials in New Orleans later told Congressional investigators that they considered Marcello a simple tomato salesman at this time, with no connection to organized crime.

Given the extensive material about Marcello's criminal empire exposed by John and Bobby Kennedy—with the help of Pierre Salinger—in their 1959 Senate hearings, the FBI's stance strains credulity. The FBI had also warned Bobby's federal prosecutors to stay away from New Orleans District Attorney Jim Garrison. As Bobby's Marcello prosecutor John Diuguid explained to us, "we didn't take Jim Garrison seriously when we first went down there, because of the FBI's attitude toward Garrison. But in retrospect, Garrison had some interesting stuff [about Marcello] and perhaps we should have taken him more seriously."[21] If Bobby's prosecutors had been in close contact with Garrison around the time of JFK's assassination, their combined efforts might have turned the tide when David Ferrie first came under suspicion in the days immediately following JFK's death.

The Godfathers' Plan to Kill the President

FOR JOHNNY ROSSELLI, CARLOS MARCELLO, and Santo Trafficante, the only way to end the relentless pressure from Bobby Kennedy was to murder his brother, the source of Bobby's power. As Marcello had said a year earlier when referring to JFK's murder, if you cut off the head of a dog, the tail stops wagging. Rarely prone to impulsive action, the three mob bosses had had plenty of time to consider all their options and the possible outcomes, and to plan accordingly. With Marcello set to go on trial, and the others facing increasing pressure, they could wait no longer to put their plan into motion.

Marcello, Trafficante, and Rosselli planned the assassination using a combination of secret meetings and several low-tech, but secure, ways of passing messages. Though Marcello was free from bugging in 1963—and Trafficante was bugged only four times that year, in a restaurant—there was always the possibility that their conversations might be wiretapped. Their ally, Jimmy Hoffa, employed his own "wiremen" to check for bugs and was constantly worried that Bobby Kennedy was monitoring him, even if the tapes might not be admissible in court. So the mob bosses would have taken every precaution in planning the assassination of JFK.

Those at the top would insulate themselves from the dirty work by delegating tasks to trusted associates and using intermediaries when possible. The number of associates knowingly involved would be kept to an absolute minimum—about a dozen. Only trusted, experienced people would have significant roles, and they would always have a cover story to account for their actions. Some people with small roles would know nothing about the real plan—they would just do what they always did, or behave as the mob bosses knew they would behave, based on past experience. Certain aspects of the operation would be kept compartmentalized from other aspects, so a leak in one part wouldn't jeopardize the other parts. There would always be a backup plan, and preferably even the backup plan would have a backup.

Santo Trafficante's lawyer, Frank Ragano, wrote that Trafficante was extremely cautious and "there was no certainty where he would appear on any given day in Tampa. He had no office, no hotel suite, no habitual bar or clubhouse. Afraid that his home phone was vulnerable to tapping, he never used it for business purposes. He relied mainly on public telephones to transact his deals and to conduct business. His pockets were filled with packs of quarters and he often stopped at payphones to hold lengthy long-distance conversations.

For arranging meetings and relaying messages, a low-level mobster like Jack Ruby could be very useful. Ruby had the right background, since he lived in Marcello's territory of Dallas, frequently visited New Orleans, was from Chicago, and sometimes visited Tampa (where he had been stationed during World War II). A Ruby visit to New Orleans wouldn't arouse suspicion, and Marcello's biographer notes that "after the Kennedy assassination, several Bourbon Street denizens remembered Ruby prowling the area in mid-October" 1963.[1] Other messengers were involved as well, such as Trafficante's attorney, Frank Ragano, who delivered Hoffa's request about killing JFK to Trafficante and Marcello.

There were at least two places where the mob bosses could safely meet away from prying eyes and any type of government surveillance—one revealed here for the first time. One meeting place long known to historians was Carlos Marcello's Churchill Farms, outside of New Orleans. This 6,500-acre tract of swampy land with one house—and, according to some accounts, an airstrip—was the place where Marcello mentioned his plan to kill JFK to an FBI informant in the fall of 1962.

During the visits of Trafficante and Rosselli to New Orleans in 1963, Churchill Farms would have been the perfect place to discuss the JFK assassination. David Ferrie would later admit plotting strategy with Marcello there the weekend after the Chicago assassination attempt and the weekend just before the Tampa assassination attempt.[2] Of course, Ferrie claimed that they were only plotting legal strategy for Marcello's ongoing trial. More likely they were discussing the JFK plot, as borne out by something New Orleans district attorney investigators later found. They discovered "notations in the margins of one of" David Ferrie's "books, a reference manual on high-powered rifles," showing "that Ferrie had measured exactly how many feet an empty cartridge flew when ejected from that rifle and at what angle."[3] An odd thing to measure, unless you wanted to know how someone should place spent cartridge shells to make a convincing "sniper's nest." In addition to meeting at Churchill Farms, Marcello's biographer notes that "during October" 1963, "Ferrie met with Marcello several times at the Mafia boss's office in the Town & Country Motel."[4]

A Florida law-enforcement source told us of the resort where "Rosselli would often visit Trafficante," which, still in operation today, catered primarily to a Jewish clientele.[5] In the early '60s, racism in the Deep South extended not just to blacks but also to Jews, and rarely was either group represented in most law-enforcement agencies at the time. That left local law enforcement with no way to easily place undercover officers in a large, secluded resort with primarily Jewish guests and a staff that was Jewish and black. Local law enforcement was aware of Rosselli or Marcello visiting Trafficante at the resort, but their clandestine surveillance stopped at the gates.

For planning at lower levels, there were several ways that Marcello's men like Guy Banister and David Ferrie could carry out their operations. First, they weren't subject to intense law-enforcement surveillance like some of the Mafia godfathers. It was just the opposite for Banister, who—with his long ties to local and national law enforcement and intelligence—assisted those agencies in conducting various types of surveillance. In addition, Banister operated in the secretive circles of the far-right, racist movements of the era, who had their own code of secrecy and channels of communication—which helped to prevent many of the most notorious racially motivated crimes of the era from being solved for decades.

For planning other aspects of JFK's assassination, pilot David Ferrie could easily leave the country—and there is evidence that he did so. According to FBI files, David Ferrie left New Orleans on October 11, 1963 for Guatemala, and he didn't return until October 18, 1963. He flew a commercial airliner on those flights—but once in Guatemala, he could have flown anywhere during that week. The same is true for the period of October 30, 1963 to November 1, 1963, when he again flew to Guatemala. November 1, 1963 is the date the Chicago assassination attempt was uncovered by Secret Service agents there. This means that Ferrie was safe from prying eyes on October 31, when the final arrangements were being made. And even on November 1, Ferrie might have flown to Chicago instead of back to New Orleans, if the Chicago assassination plan had not been uncovered and the attempt canceled.[6]

John H. Davis notes that Carlos Marcello had a well-documented method of operating; he "always dealt through intermediaries." Davis writes that

"Marcello would have employed the same modus operandi" in the JFK assassination: "The individuals who actually performed the assassination would have come from out of state or from outside the country and would have had no direct contact with Marcello . . . they would have accomplished their mission and quickly left the country." Davis says "Ferrie's principal role would have been that of adviser to Marcello and framer of Lee Harvey Oswald."[7]

The plan to kill JFK involved targeting him first in Chicago, with Tampa as a backup and then Dallas as their last opportunity before C-Day. This three-city approach had several advantages. First, it spread the risk among the three Mafia families. Second, JFK had long motorcades scheduled in all three cities, and the three visits fell in a time period just three weeks long, so the mob bosses could come up with one basic plan that could be applied to all three. Because the opportunities were so close together, the same personnel could mostly be used for each attempt. Finally, having three cities meant that even the backup plan (Tampa) had a backup (Dallas).

Each of the three target cities had a key Mafia operative close to law enforcement, to monitor any leaks about—or investigations into—the JFK hit. In Chicago, it was Richard Cain, the mobster who was the chief investigator for the Cook County sheriff. The CIA continued to deal with Cain in the fall of 1963, giving him a pipeline into not only law enforcement but intelligence as well.[8] In Tampa, Trafficante's man was actually a prominent member of one of the area's law-enforcement agencies whose identity was verified by a high Florida law-enforcement source.[9]

In Dallas, Jack Ruby would serve a similar function. Though Ruby wasn't a member of law enforcement, as we noted earlier, his friendly contacts with Dallas police were long and deep. According to government files, Ruby knew at least seven hundred of the twelve hundred Dallas policemen, with several officers and Ruby associates saying that Ruby actually knew *every* policeman. Ruby was particularly close to several corrupt cops, and a Warren Commission document calls Ruby "the pay-off man for the Dallas Police Department."[10] Ruby's Chicago roots would also let him assist there if needed, and by the fall of 1963 Ruby was also cultivating his informant status with Chicago law enforcement.

One key part of the assassination plan that was the same for Chicago, Tampa, and Dallas was that JFK be killed in public, while in a moving car.

Any attempt away from the public eye that was not immediately fatal could have resulted in the Mafia's worst nightmare: Bobby Kennedy essentially running the country—and tracking down his brother's attackers—while hiding the true extent of his brother's injuries. With all the resources of the US government at Bobby's command—and with his knowledge of C-Day and other CIA operations—Bobby would likely have been able to unravel the mystery, even using secret investigations to avoid exposing C-Day. The Mafia bosses also hoped that killing JFK in public—and blaming his death on a patsy linked to Cuba—would also cause a public outcry for a quick invasion of Cuba in retaliation. Unlike the American public, the mob chieftains knew that the US was poised and almost ready to invade Cuba in support of C-Day. They hoped that all the US officials would need was a spark to prompt an invasion.

While a moving car might seem harder to hit than a stationary target, in this case it gave the Mafia several advantages. The mob bosses would know from earlier motorcades—like JFK's spring 1963 trip to Chicago—that Secret Service agents rode with the motorcade and were not on the ground, except at the beginning and end of the route. This meant that if JFK were shot en route, there would be no Secret Service agents on the ground at the site of the shooting. Even better for them, shooting JFK in a car—as opposed to blowing it up—would take the Secret Service agents away from the crime scene, since they would have to stay with the motorcade to protect the President's car on the way to the hospital.

Johnny Rosselli and his Chicago mob had plenty of experience assassinating notable individuals while they were in cars, starting with their killing of New York mob boss Frankie Yale. And just two years before Dallas, Johnny Rosselli had been linked to the assassination of Dominican dictator Rafael Trujillo while he was in a moving car. In those cases, the shooters were also in moving cars, a much more difficult operation. But in Dallas, the shooters would be stationary while firing at a slowly moving target.

For the JFK hit, experienced marksmen would be used, and there would be at least two of them firing from two different locations. That way, the final shooter would not just be a backup in case something happened to the first shooter, but also insurance, in case JFK were only injured by the first shots. This explains why no shots were fired at JFK until he was close to the grassy knoll, where JFK aides Dave Powers and Kenneth O'Donnell saw the shots. The best shot from the Texas School Book Depository would have been while the car was approaching the Depository, or while it was directly below making its slow turn, or just after the turn. From the Depository—looking down—that would have been like shooting fish in a barrel. However, the first shot was not fired until JFK was clearly visible from the grassy knoll, when JFK's limo was getting farther away from the Depository.

There are several indications that the Mafia's plan to kill JFK was constructed in a way very similar to the CIA's plan to kill Castro for C-Day. This would be to ensure that the CIA, Bobby Kennedy, and other high officials realized immediately that there was a link between JFK's death and C-Day at the first reports of the tragedy. That would guarantee immediate steps on the part of those officials to preserve the secrecy of the impending C-Day coup and invasion, helping to obscure the role of the Mafia in JFK's death. The shooters the CIA had been training, and the CIA's assassination plans for Castro, could have been intended for Rosselli's CIA-Mafia plots, for QJWIN and ZRRIFLE, to assist AMLASH, or as backup for C-Day. While Bobby Kennedy hadn't been told about the first three, it's possible that Richard Helms or Desmond FitzGerald might have told Bobby that they were making backup plans in case the C-Day coup leader got cold feet at the last minute or had trouble arranging Castro's assassination.

Earlier, we noted the observation of Army Capt. Ayers who—while assigned to the CIA in the summer and fall of 1963—observed that Johnny Rosselli sometimes utilized a team of CIA-trained Cuban exiles whose "sharpshooter" was "rehearsing for the day when he could center the cross hairs of his telescopic sight on Fidel Castro." Another indication of similarity between the Mafia's murder of JFK and plans the CIA had made to kill Castro is CIA officer David Atlee Phillips's statement that "we gave him the mission of killing Fidel Castro in Cuba . . . I don't know why he killed Kennedy. But I do know he used precisely the plan we had devised against Castro."[11] Phillips was saying that about Oswald in the context of an autobiographical novel, but it could indicate that the CIA's "plan we had devised against Castro" was similar to the way JFK was killed.

Bobby Kennedy provides further indications of similarity between the JFK and Castro assassination plans. As mentioned previously, something made Bobby tell a Pulitzer Prize–winning journalist, Haynes Johnson, "one of your guys did it" (i.e., killed JFK) just hours after JFK's death. Johnson was working on a book at the time with C-Day exile leaders Manuel Artime and

Harry Williams. Bobby's comment referred to Artime, not Harry. Bobby said that "at the time" of JFK's death, he "asked [CIA Director John] McCone . . . if they had killed my brother, and I asked him in a way that he couldn't lie to me, and they hadn't." This statement is important, because Bobby said he asked McCone "at the time" JFK died, meaning something about JFK's murder made him quickly suspect that the CIA might have been involved.

Second, how could Bobby ask McCone "in a way that he couldn't lie to me" unless there was some particular operation both men knew about? Clearly, Bobby was asking CIA Director McCone if a plan meant for Castro had been used on his brother instead. That plan had to be C-Day, since Bobby and McCone both knew about C-Day, but neither knew about the CIA-Mafia plots with Rosselli at the time or the assassination aspects of the Cubela plot. Richard Helms was apparently the highest-ranking CIA official who knew about all those operations. Because CIA Director McCone hadn't been told about the ongoing CIA-Mafia plots with Rosselli, McCone quickly assured Bobby that the CIA "hadn't" killed JFK. Bobby Kennedy also said that "McCone thought there were two people involved in the shooting."[12]

More indications of similarity between the JFK hit and plans to kill Castro come from one of the later AMWORLD documents dealing with Manuel Artime. In it, a Castro assassination plan is discussed that involves killing Castro "when he goes to Varadero," where Castro had a beach house. Artime was given "the details and the exact locations where Fidel spends every Saturday and Sunday and specifically every Sunday at Varadero."[13] One would assume that Castro's beach house would be very secure and well guarded; but if Castro regularly drove or was driven there every Sunday, having two or three shooters ambush him in his vehicle before he got there would be a viable option. While this particular document was written after the JFK assassination, since it involved Artime and AMWORLD it may well reflect the thinking involved in the plans for killing Castro for C-Day.

Varadero Beach would be perhaps the only reliable opportunity to assassinate him.[14] After the fall of Batista, Castro went to Havana in an open jeep, a 600-mile trip, and since that time Castro has eschewed limousines in favor of jeeps. To maintain his Revolutionary image, Castro often uses jeeps, even for long distances (Varadero is about 75 miles from Havana).

The sad irony is that the Mafia may have taken the very plan that the CIA had intended to use against Castro in an open jeep, and used it instead to kill JFK in an open limousine. That could account for the comments of Bobby and David Atlee Phillips after JFK's death, and for much of the CIA's cover-up (along with C-Day). The indications are that Rosselli not only knew about the CIA's Castro assassination plans, but was actually working on them in the fall of 1963, with his friend David Morales.

The CIA's considerations in assassinating Castro were similar to those the Mafia had to consider in killing JFK. For the C-Day coup plan to work properly, it would be much better to kill Castro in public, as opposed to in private. Otherwise, Raul Castro or Soviets in Cuba might simply hide the fact of Castro's death for days or even weeks, until they were ready to take control. For the CIA and the C-Day coup leader in Cuba, having Castro killed in public would also allow a logical patsy to be quickly blamed. Only an obvious murder—preferably in public—would allow the chain of events necessary for an effective coup. The CIA's attempt to kill Castro at a stadium in the spring of 1963 had not worked, since the limited entrances and exits at such a facility made getting weapons inside—or escaping afterward—too difficult. So, killing Castro in a car on his way to a speech or event—or on his regular Sunday trip to Varadero Beach—might have been part of the C-Day plan. Until all the C-Day documents are declassified, it's hard to be more definitive.

Harry Williams was kept separate from the assassination details for the same reason he was kept separate from the arrangements for the patsy— because he had been linked to Robert Kennedy in the press in May 1963. Harry would have learned those details once he got into Cuba on November 23, 1963 and met with the C-Day coup leader. If Harry were captured inside Cuba before he was able to rendezvous with the C-Day coup leader, he couldn't reveal what he didn't know. While Harry was the primary person in communication with the C-Day coup leader, the CIA had begun to have some communication with him as well, to complete the arrangements for his $50,000 payment and the CIA "protection" of one of his relatives in another country (to ensure his cooperation). Through those same channels, it's possible that the CIA and the C-Day coup leader had communicated about the Castro assassination plan and potential patsies to take the blame. Or the CIA may have simply been making backup plans for the assassination and patsies, in case the coup leader needed help with either.

The steps taken by the Mafia ensured that after the JFK assassination, information about it would unfold on two levels. First would be what the police would find and the press would publicize (obvious things like Oswald's ordering a rifle, writing to the Fair Play for Cuba Committee, being on TV and radio in New Orleans, etc.). Second would be what key authorities in Washington would find or suspect but couldn't publicize—that JFK's assassination seemed to have some connection to US efforts to kill Castro and that there were hints from informants that Castro himself might be involved. That would stymie a thorough investigation of JFK's assassination for national security reasons and possibly even prompt a US invasion of Cuba, further distracting US authorities.

Marcello, Trafficante, and Rosselli took advantage of the lack of cooperation between federal intelligence and law-enforcement agencies. These interagency rivalries allowed them to penetrate C-Day and other anti-Castro plots while feeding disinformation to agencies that implicated Lee Harvey Oswald, Gilberto Policarpo Lopez, and Miguel Casas Saez in JFK's assassination. The goal was to make it look like Fidel Castro was behind JFK's death, which would at least divert suspicion away from the Mafia—while causing a large amount of official secrecy to protect C-Day—and at best prompt a US invasion of Cuba.

Investigative journalist Howard Kohn found that even the Warren Commission staff considered such a scenario, though they didn't include it in their report or even in their 26 supporting volumes of evidence. Kohn uncovered a "theory advanced by two of the [Warren] Commission's lawyers" regarding "anti-Castroites" using Oswald in their plot to kill JFK. Kohn pointed out that this theory could apply to Marcello, Trafficante, and Rosselli, since they worked with various anti-Castro types supported by US intelligence. (Neither Kohn nor the Warren Commission lawyers knew that Marcello had employed Oswald, and that the three mob bosses knew about C-Day, which makes the lawyers' theory even more compelling.) In a memo kept classified for ten years, the Warren Commission lawyers wrote that "the motive of" the "anti-Castroites" using Oswald "would, of course, be the expectation that after the President was killed," that "Oswald would be caught or at least his identity ascertained. Law-enforcement authorities and the public would then blame the assassination on the Castro government, and the call for its forcible overthrow would be irresistible."[15]

The Warren Commission lawyers didn't pursue this theory very far, perhaps because—unlike the Mafia bosses—they didn't know about C-Day and that a US invasion of Cuba was already planned and ready to go at the time of JFK's death. Kohn also notes that Jack Ruby "allegedly told a jailhouse visitor that he had expected Kennedy's assassination to incite a second Bay of Pigs invasion."[16]

To the public, Oswald appeared to be ardently pro-Castro. In actuality, he appears to have been an undercover agent being used by the CIA and Naval Intelligence, in an operation designed to help Oswald get into Cuba in support of C-Day and the CIA's other anti-Castro operations. Marcello, Trafficante, and Roselli knew that Oswald's public pro-Castro stance would make him an ideal patsy for JFK's assassination. At the same time, Oswald's connections with intelligence agencies would prevent a truly thorough or public investigation of the assassination.

By mid-October 1963, the key players in the Mafia plot to kill JFK were set. Of the dozen or so knowingly involved, several have either confessed— or documents confirm—that they knew about C-Day. At the top were Marcello, Trafficante, and Rosselli. Next came key planners like former FBI supervisor Guy Banister and French Connection mastermind Michel Victor Mertz. Chicago hit man Charlie Nicoletti—a veteran of the 1960 CIA-Mafia plots, who had rejoined them in October 1963—was also probably involved.[17] Unconfirmed reports place Nicoletti in Dallas during the assassination, and Nicoletti was murdered during the same time period when several other key participants also died.

On the next level would come key operatives like Jack Ruby, Chicago law-enforcement official (and Mafioso) Richard Cain, David Ferrie, and Eladio del Valle. Other Trafficante associates involved include John Martino and his associate Rolando Masferrer. Another person involved on some level was Jimmy Hoffa's enforcer in Puerto Rico, Frank Chavez (an associate of Jack Ruby who would later attempt to kill Bobby Kennedy). Former government investigators such as Gaeton Fonzi are highly suspicious of the CIA's David Morales, because of his close relationship to Rosselli, and also because of statements he made about JFK, including a brief apparent confession to being part of the assassination. Morales probably engaged in business with Trafficante associate John Martino in the years after JFK's death. On the other hand, Morales may have simply provided inadvertent help and information to Rosselli during his nighttime drinking binges. As for David Atlee Phillips, his knowing involvement seems very unlikely. Thanks to the research of Larry Hancock, we now know that in 1963 David Morales ranked higher in the CIA than David Atlee Phillips, which means that Morales was in a position to manipulate Phillips by feeding him disinformation or certain operations.

As for other CIA officials, there is no evidence of their involvement.

Cover-ups by Richard Helms and others can be explained by other reasons, such as protecting their reputations, the CIA, or sensitive operations like C-Day. In addition, Washington CIA officials on the level of Helms and Desmond FitzGerald would know that killing JFK would cause an immediate halt to C-Day. There is no evidence indicating that Vice President Lyndon Johnson had been told about C-Day before JFK's death, and he certainly had no role in it. Johnson's antipathy toward Robert Kennedy was well known in government circles, and that would certainly extend to Bobby's pet projects like C-Day. So any CIA official involved in JFK's assassination had to want to see JFK dead far more than they wanted to see Castro overthrown. Or they would have had to be so politically unsophisticated as to think that LBJ could be prodded to continue C-Day or invade Cuba. Based on his statements, David Morales is the only CIA official who fits those criteria.

Former FBI agent William Turner and Dr. John Newman, an Army major with twenty years' experience in military intelligence, also concluded that the CIA as an institution—and its highest officials—were not knowingly involved in the JFK assassination. After his presentation at a conference at MIT in 1995, Newman said "Why in the hell would [the CIA] plan to kill Kennedy and use one of their own people and write cables to the FBI, Navy, and the State Department and sign their names on the bottom of them? That would draw attention to themselves . . . the extent to which Oswald is being used and involved in all of these low-level CIA operations is in a sense exculpatory in terms of the 'institutional plot' theory. However, the type of information that I have shown you tonight I think is entirely consistent with the theory—and I say just that, a theory—that a renegade faction, or a bad apple or two or three, set up Oswald. He was the perfect patsy by virtue of all of the sensitive offices that held files on him and the type of operations that he was becoming involved in."[18]

C-Day exile leader Tony Varona had some involvement, though how much is not known. Varona had worked with Trafficante, Rosselli, and Cain and accepted a huge bribe from the Chicago Mafia. Both the CIA and Bobby Kennedy must have had some suspicions about Varona, because he was the only C-Day exile leader who was quickly cut off after JFK's assassination. The other four continued to receive official US support.

The possible involvement of C-Day exile leader Manuel Artime in JFK's assassination is even less clear. Senate investigators were told that Artime had "guilty knowledge" of JFK's assassination. Also, Bobby Kennedy seemed to be implicating Artime when Bobby told Artime's co-author Johnson "one of your guys did it." But Artime's "guilty knowledge" could simply be the "guilt" that David Atlee Phillips wrote about, if he realized after the fact that some of his men or equipment had been diverted and used in the JFK assassination, or that some of his associates were involved. On the other hand, Artime continued to have dealings with Trafficante associates, and Artime's protégé later became one of Florida's biggest drug kingpins.

Looking at those involved in the JFK assassination, most were informants or operatives for various US intelligence or law-enforcement agencies. Rosselli, Trafficante, Marcello, Nicoletti, Ruby, Cain, and Varona had all worked on the CIA-Mafia plots. Banister, Ferrie, del Valle, Martino, Fiorini, Masferrer, and the CIA agent had all been involved in CIA-backed anti-Castro operations. Such connections not only let all those people feed disinformation to the CIA and other agencies; it also gave them potential blackmail leverage to use against those agencies if they were ever suspected of involvement in JFK's assassination. In fact, one former Kennedy administration official told us that he considered Artime "unreliable and very slick" because he "exploited the guilt the Kennedys felt over the Bay of Pigs" and also "blackmailed (in a general way) the CIA, because once Artime" had done things for the CIA, he "could then use that information to make sure the CIA had to keep supporting" him.[19]

CIA memos raise the issue of Artime's ties to the Mafia around the time of JFK's assassination, which could have at least made Artime subject to manipulation by Johnny Rosselli. As briefly mentioned in Chapter 12, a CIA memo not revealed in any previous book implies a connection between Johnny Rosselli and Artime at the time of AMWORLD. The CIA memo was written in 1976 when the Miami police were seeking information from the CIA to help them investigate the brutal murder of Johnny Rosselli. The memo was written by the CIA's Inspector General's office to the Deputy Director of the CIA (the Director at the time was George Bush). It says that when Manuel "Artime and his group were supported by the CIA," Artime "was used by the Mafia in the Castro operation." This link between Artime and Rosselli is not detailed in any of the existing CIA documents about the CIA-Mafia plots. This information linking Artime to the CIA-Mafia plots with Rosselli had been withheld from the Senate Church Committee, which concluded its hearings shortly before the memo was written. Not surprisingly, the CIA memo about Artime and Rosselli's CIA-Mafia plots says "This information should not be released."[20]

The CIA document admitting that Artime "was used by the Mafia in the Castro operation"—written thirteen years after JFK's assassination—raises an important question. Does it mean "used," as in "'utilized' by the Mafia?" Or does it mean "used" as in "'taken advantage of' by the Mafia?" By 1976, some in the CIA would have certainly been aware of what the House Select Committee on Assassinations (HSCA) would conclude just three years later, that some of the very people the CIA used in the CIA-Mafia plots had killed JFK. If the "taken advantage of" definition was intended by the CIA, it could indicate an awareness or suspicion that some of the CIA's own assets could have been "used" in killing JFK. This could help explain the massive amount of stonewalling and deception that the CIA would undertake against the HSCA, and the earlier withholding of information from the Church Committee. In any event, Artime's previously unknown role in the CIA-Mafia plots gave Rosselli yet another way to monitor developments with C-Day, since Artime was in frequent contact with Bobby Kennedy.

One AMWORLD memo suggests a way the CIA can take advantage of Artime's Mafia ties. The memo says that one way "to cover CIA support" for Artime was to attribute it to the "Mafia." It says this could work because "rumors of Mafia support" for Artime "had long pervaded" Artime's "organization" and "Artime claimed to have been contacted in the past by the Mafia for the sale of arms." So, the CIA memo says, "certain air deliveries could be made attributable to . . . the Mafia."[21] Still, Artime's "guilty knowledge" that Senate investigators were told about could have come after JFK's death. In fact, a CIA AMWORLD memo from the first week of November 1963 (after the Chicago assassination attempt, but before the Tampa attempt) makes it clear that Artime wanted JFK to stay in power. This CIA memo says that one of Artime's men had said "that while President Kennedy is in power it will be impossible to defeat Castro." But Artime "does not share this opinion" and is ready to carry "the war into Cuba."[22]

C-DAY'S ROLE IN THE MAFIA PLAN TO ASSASSINATE JFK

By mid-October 1963, Marcello, Trafficante, and Rosselli had penetrated or compromised every aspect of C-Day in some way. From Harry Williams to the "five fingers" to the bullets that would be found in the patsy's rifle to the tight surveillance of the patsy, all those C-Day connections would play a role in the unfolding drama of JFK's assassination. At the very least, so many connections to C-Day would prevent high officials from pursuing a thorough investigation of the assassination. At best, the pending C-Day invasion would go forward thanks to a seemingly pro-Castro patsy, and the Mafia might someday be able to reopen their casinos. But that would be icing on the cake. Their main goal was to kill JFK to stop Bobby's prosecution of them, and it couldn't happen soon enough for the three mob bosses.

As noted earlier, the C-Day exile troops were training at Fort Benning, across the river from Phenix City, with others being trained at Fort Jackson, South Carolina. Unknown to authorities at the time, a French Connection drug route linked to Michel Victor Mertz and Santo Trafficante was operating through Fort Benning (and would be busted over a year later).[23] While the Cuban exile military leadership there was above reproach, as were most of the troops, such a ring did create an opportunity for the Mafia to learn about that part of the C-Day operation. In fact, one of the Fort Jackson Cuban exile soldiers, Alberto Sicilia-Falcon, later established what a Drug Enforcement Administration (DEA) director described as a gigantic heroin ring—which included a top associate of Johnny Rosselli and Santo Trafficante.[24]

Various CIA files have been released for CIA agent Bernard Barker that show how Trafficante's men were getting close to C-Day. One of Barker's CIA reports from August 14, 1963 says that Barker "is known to most of his contacts as a channel to US intelligence." Barker CIA files show that he was being fed a steady stream of information by Trafficante bagman Frank Fiorini. (Fiorini would continue providing information to Barker, which Barker would pass along to his CIA superiors, until at least February 1965.[25] In 1972, Fiorini and Barker would be two of the Watergate burglars, along with former CIA officer James McCord, in an operation directed by former CIA officer E. Howard Hunt.)

According to former Senate investigator Bud Fensterwald, "both Barker and" Fiorini "have admitted being close to" Carlos Prio, and Prio "himself has admitted coordinating Cuban exile demonstrators at the 1972 political conventions—under the initial guidance of his friends, Barker and" Fiorini.[26] Fensterwald also notes that "Prio was once arrested for Cuban gun-running with an associate of Jack Ruby."[27]

On March 18, 1963, CIA files show that Barker "reported the formation" of a new exile group "with financial backing from ex-President Prio" and "an infiltration and caching operation" in Cuba "by Frank Fiorini."[28] Since at least July 1962, Barker had been reporting on the "activities of Frank Fiorini." For example, in May 1963, Barker reported on "Frank Fiorini's agreement to participate in [an] Air Strike against Cuba" and a "request by [a] Venezuelan national that Frank Fiorini purchase arms for him." In June

1963, Barker passed along to his CIA superiors two items "from Frank Fiorini," including "current activities of Frank Fiorini."[29] Barker also produced a report "from Frank Fiorini," according to Barker's "Operational Progress Report" for November 1, 1963 to December 31, 1963 that was sent from the Miami CIA station to Desmond FitzGerald in Washington.

One item reported to the CIA by Barker on May 27, 1963 was "Possible cooperation between Tony Varona and Manuel Artime"—a report that coincides perfectly with the start of C-Day.[30] Neither Barker nor E. Howard Hunt have ever confirmed working on C-Day. But Gus Russo, an author with many CIA sources, wrote that Harry "Williams' CIA case officers were E. Howard Hunt and Bernard 'Macho' Barker."[32] Also, only a handful of CIA documents have been released under Barker's CIA code-name "AMCLATTER-1, and the name itself wasn't declassified until 1998."[32] Barker documents from the relevant time period show him reporting on things like "Unification of activities by Manolo Ray" and "Plans of [Manolo] Ray . . . to infiltrate Cuba for JURE" after November 1, 1963.[33] In November 1963, the CIA says that Barker "was also instructed to be especially alert for rumors of impending raids on Cuba" and "several of his reports included such leads." An August 1963 CIA Barker report mentions "Plan Omega," a name some exiles used for C-Day.[34]

That Barker dealt with Trafficante associates like Fiorini and Prio should not be a reflection on Barker—it was part of his job as a CIA agent to get information from, and about, unsavory sources. For example, several Barker reports in the summer of 1963 discuss the Chicago-based exile group known as the "Junta," which was allegedly backed by Mafia money.[35] But all the various CIA reports about Varona, Barker, Prio, Fiorini, Artime, Ray, Harry Williams, General Joseph Carroll, and others from the fall of 1963 show how associates of Trafficante had been able to get close to those involved in C-Day in the days, weeks, and months prior to JFK's assassination.

As documented in Part I, even the bullet found in Oswald's rifle was linked by FBI memos to C-Day in October 1963. These memos link Eloy Menoyo's C-Day group to the Dallas gun dealer who apparently sold the bullets used in Oswald's rifle—while the same gun dealer was describing C-Day to a government informant. At the same time, the informant—US Army Capt. George Nonte—was involved in a gun-running operation involving an associate of Jack Ruby. The investigation in October 1963 involved Army Intelligence (part of the Defense Intelligence Agency), the FBI, and the Treasury Department. After JFK's assassination, a Warren Commission document says that a former employee of Jack Ruby placed Ruby himself in an operation that sounds identical to Nonte's ring.[36]

The arms were being stolen from Fort Hood by Capt. Nonte, who was never prosecuted for the thefts. Since Nonte had a "top-secret clearance," perhaps this lack of prosecution was because some authority in Washington approved or encouraged the "thefts" as a way to covertly supply Kennedy-backed Cuban exile groups with weapons. FBI documents from late October 1963 quote "Army Intelligence" as saying that "on 10/24/63" the Dallas gun dealer "had asked Captain George Charles Nonte, Fort Hood, Texas . . . if he knew anyone who might be interested in buying information concerning large-scale military operations in [the] Caribbean." The information "was obtained from [a] weapons buyer . . . who had recently been through Dallas seeking arms" and who "had previously been involved in . . . Alpha 66," which was so closely aligned with Menoyo's SNFE C-Day group that the FBI considered them the same. The Dallas gun dealer didn't know the date, but said the military operation "would be directed against Cuba by large rebel forces . . . at unknown Caribbean bases." The gun dealer was "implying" to Nonte that "considerable money could be made on [the] stock market by [a] person having such data."[37]

The FBI and Treasury focused on the Dallas gun dealer far more than on Capt. Nonte, and tried to figure out what big upcoming military operation against Cuba the gun dealer had been referring to. An FBI memo says that regarding the "large-scale attack being planned" against Cuba, "consideration was given to possibility this might be Central Intelligence Agency (CIA) operation; however, CIA on 9/28/63 in discussing anti-Castro activities in Nicaragua, advised that it was not organizing any Cuban invasion forces."[38]

The CIA was clearly keeping information about C-Day away from the FBI, since the FBI had no official role in C-Day. But as we soon document, the FBI was also withholding crucial information from the CIA. Such lack of cooperation, just days before the first attempt to assassinate JFK in Chicago, would eventually prove fatal to JFK in Dallas. In addition, it would spawn numerous cover-ups after the assassination, preventing a thorough investigation of JFK's death. Once J. Edgar Hoover's good friend President Johnson had told him about C-Day, one can only imagine Hoover's reaction to finding that the Dallas gun dealer talking about C-Day had also been the one to sell the bullet found in Oswald's rifle. Also imagine Hoover's reaction when he realized that—as *Vanity Fair* noted—"Jack Ruby's auto mechanic, Donnell

Whitter, was arrested in possession of stolen weapons" linked to Capt. Nonte's ring "just four days before the assassination."[39]

David Ferrie would also be linked to the stolen weapons, according to an investigator for the New Orleans district attorney. The investigator interviewed an anti-Castro activist who knew both Ferrie and Oswald, who said "he bought arms from [David] Ferrie who in turn got them from US Army personnel who had stolen them."[40] That statement was made decades before the FBI documents about the thefts quoted earlier were declassified. If the CIA and DIA wanted to get US arms to C-Day groups without supplying them directly, then having the arms "stolen" from an Army base and sold to David Ferrie or associates of Jack Ruby would fit well with the CIA memo about AMWORLD, the memo that suggested using "the Mafia" as a cover for supplying a C-Day exile group. However, after Ruby shot Oswald—and Ferrie quickly became a suspect in JFK's assassination—it's not hard to imagine the consternation and cover-ups that would have ensued.

PART THREE

Laying the Groundwork for Chicago

IN THE WEEKS BEFORE THE scheduled November 2, 1963 presidential motorcade, the Mafia started laying the groundwork for the Chicago attempt to kill JFK. The plan for Chicago would be refined for Tampa and Dallas, but its basic elements would stay the same: experienced gunmen brought in for the hit; a local patsy in place to take the fall; links to someone seemingly pro-Castro to trigger secrecy concerns about C-Day and divert suspicion; and Jack Ruby in charge of arranging for the patsy to be killed or doing the job himself. Richard Cain would be able to monitor any law-enforcement knowledge about the plot. The Chicago attempt would occur in conjunction with crucial activity related to a CIA Castro assassination plot, to also help force a cover-up. Each of those events would have mob ties that can be traced to associates of Marcello, Trafficante, and Rosselli.

Oswald's trip to Chicago in the weeks after his well-publicized New Orleans incident, prior to the Chicago attempt, isn't known by most historians. Several factors distinguish it from the welter of alleged Oswald sightings that emerged in the months after JFK's death, including supporting evidence for the trip from a variety of independent sources. Oswald's trip seemed designed to ensure that a few people would remember him; and while its purpose may have seemed to Oswald to be simply part of his activities to build his pro-Castro credentials, it would also link him to the Chicago attempt and make it appear as if he had been stalking JFK.

Oswald's trip to Chicago included a brief stop in Atlanta. In the late summer of 1963, JFK had originally planned to visit Atlanta and give a major speech, but local Democrats had urged him to cancel or scale back the appearance because of concerns about JFK's stance on civil rights.[1] Apparently, plans had already been made for Oswald to visit Atlanta en route to

Chicago, and his trip continued. The author of an investigation into the Ku Klux Klan writes that "one of her sources told her that Oswald, in the summer of 1963, had called on [Klan] Imperial Wizard James Venable in his office in Atlanta seeking the names of right-wing associates. Venable confirmed . . . that he was fairly sure that Oswald had been there for that purpose."[2] Oswald indicated to Venable that he was on his way to Chicago. Klan leader Venable made his statement to the journalist in the 1980s, at a time when the Klan was still the subject of surveillance and prosecution by the FBI. It's difficult to see why Venable would make up an Oswald encounter, especially since it tended to link Oswald with Venable's "right-wing associates," thus potentially giving the FBI reason to interview or investigate them.

According to FBI files, they received reports of Oswald's brief stay in Atlanta from several individuals, including Hal Suit, the highly respected news director of Atlanta's largest TV station and later a candidate for governor. Some of the reports to the FBI mentioned Oswald's leaving behind a pistol at a Holiday Inn motel after he checked out.[3] Oswald soon retrieved the pistol, but such an incident would tend to incriminate Oswald after JFK's assassination, whether it had happened in Chicago or Dallas. The Oswald pistol incident occurred in the suburb of Marietta, northwest of Atlanta, not far from the home of notorious racist J. B. Stoner, an associate of Venable. Both Stoner and Venable were close to a man we document shortly, Joseph Milteer, who, prior to the Tampa and Dallas attempts, talked to a police informant (on tape) about plans to assassinate JFK. Stoner, Venable, and Milteer were part of the same extreme racist inner circles as Guy Banister, who reportedly employed Oswald in the summer of 1963.

David Ferrie's long-distance phone records show a phone call placed from the Atlanta suburb of Marietta to Ferrie in New Orleans on August 16, 1963. For the call to show up on Ferrie's phone records, it had to be a collect call placed from Marietta to Ferrie's number in New Orleans. There's a longer collect phone call placed from Atlanta to Ferrie on August 18, 1963, and that's followed by a brief collect phone call from Atlanta to Ferrie's number on August 20, 1963.[4]

Oswald's best friend in Dallas, CIA asset George De Mohrenschildt, once made an unusual comment about Oswald's activities in Atlanta, saying they were as important as those in New Orleans and Mexico City—yet Oswald had no official contact with the city, except for flying through its airport after his return from Russia. However, Jack Ruby had several associates in Atlanta in 1963 who owned local nightclubs, and Atlanta had a significant Cuban exile community at the time.[5] When De Mohrenschildt made his comment, there had been no publicity yet about the Oswald-in-Atlanta FBI reports, or Venable's claim; as noted earlier, as noted earlier, even today most researchers aren't aware of them.

Oswald apparently continued on to Chicago, but first stopped at the University of Illinois at Urbana. An FBI memo says Oswald reportedly inquired at the office of the assistant dean of students about Cuban student organizations, and asked the secretary "if . . . she had ever seen him on TV in New Orleans."[6] The FBI memo says Oswald "expressed interest in any campus organization advocating humanist views" to the secretary.[7] From the report in the FBI memo, Oswald seems to have made sure that he would be remembered as being very interested in leftist causes. Oswald's actions at the University of Illinois echo those observed at what is now the University of New Orleans. Desegregated in 1958, it was targeted for special attention by racist Guy Banister. Historian Dr. Michael L. Kurtz, while a student in 1963, witnessed Guy Banister with Oswald there, both at various times debating students about integration.[8] There are other indications that Oswald was aware of, and possibly monitoring for Banister, leftist and progressive professors in New Orleans.

Since Oswald was under tight surveillance by Naval Intelligence in the days, weeks, and months leading up to the Chicago attempt on JFK's life, questions arise: Was it the real Oswald who was near Chicago after his TV appearance in New Orleans? And if it was Oswald, did Naval Intelligence know about or direct all or part of Oswald's trip? Whether the man who stopped by the University of Illinois and Atlanta was Oswald or not, someone wanted to leave a trail connecting Oswald to Chicago, prior to the attempt to assassinate JFK there. If someone like Guy Banister was providing surveillance for those helping Naval Intelligence, it was also possible for Oswald to take a trip without its appearing in Naval Intelligence files. On one trip, Oswald was linked to left-wing pro-Castro and right-wing groups, just as in New Orleans he'd first tried to join the right-wing anti-Castro organization before his pro-Castro demonstration.

Jack Ruby's Chicago Payoff

Jack Ruby's trip to Chicago in the fall of 1963, where he received a large payoff from an associate of Jimmy Hoffa, is revealed here for the first time thanks to JFK's press secretary, Pierre Salinger.[9] A longtime trusted associate of Salinger, James Allison, was an eyewitness to the incident. As noted in Part II, Salinger first began working for the Kennedys as an investigator for the

Senate crime hearings in the 1950s, where he focused on Hoffa and Carlos Marcello. Neither Salinger nor eyewitness Jim Allison knew that stories of Ruby's Chicago payoff from a Hoffa associate had surfaced in secret FBI memos within hours of Oswald's murder. The sources in the FBI memos were completely independent of Allison. Though one of the initial FBI sources was Bobby Kennedy's top Hoffa prosecutor, Walter Sheridan, the investigation into the Ruby-Chicago-payoff story was quickly squelched by the Justice Department to avoid harming their ongoing prosecution of Hoffa.[10]

Jack Ruby—who had ties to all three cities in the JFK plot, Chicago, Tampa, and Dallas—probably had the same role in Chicago that he had in Dallas: making sure the patsy was quickly rubbed out in what seemed like a logical way, unconnected to the mob. Having Richard Cain make such arrangements would have been too risky, since Cain was much too close to Rosselli and Giancana to simply order one of his deputies to be in a position to kill the patsy. Risking exposure of Cain's ties to the Mafia, which wouldn't become known to the FBI for another four years, was not an option. Ruby had all the right connections—to Marcello, to Trafficante, to Hoffa, and recently to Rosselli—but they were much less obvious. (Ruby's connections to the Mafia didn't start becoming publicly known until the late 1970s.) Ruby had grown up in Chicago, had moved back for a time as recently as the early 1950s, and had close relatives and many friends in the city. For example, just two months before the Chicago attempt, journalist Seth Kantor says Ruby had "met in Dallas with two Chicago detectives to provide them information."[11] Beginning an informant relationship like this before an assassination echoes what Ruby did when he became an FBI informant before—and during—his involvement in the 1959 CIA-Mafia Castro assassination plots. Ruby had other contacts with people connected to Chicago in the weeks and months prior to the Chicago assassination attempt. For example, on October 7, 1963—just three weeks before the Chicago assassination attempt—Ruby had met in Dallas with the Chicago businessman David Ferrie had called on September 24, 1963. The same Chicago businessman would be in Dallas meeting with Ruby the night before JFK's assassination, and staying at a Hoffa-financed hotel.

Salinger put us in touch with Jim Allison, a respected businessman who in 1963 was involved in the public relations field, which brought him into contact with "lots of colorful characters, including mob types." One of those was a man who called himself "A. G. Hardy" ("A. Gordon Hardy"), who Allison met at a fine hotel in London when Hardy was talking to two men from France. As a result of that meeting, Allison helped Hardy get more business in Europe.[12]

Later, Hardy introduced Allison to Jimmy Hoffa in Chicago. Allison had been staying at Chicago's Bismarck Hotel, while trying to get some business from a local merchant. Hardy took Allison to Hoffa's large suite in the same hotel, introduced them, and Hoffa made a call to the local merchant—who soon began doing business with Allison. Later, Allison learned that the company Hardy worked for was actually controlled by the Teamsters and its boss, Hoffa—so when Allison had helped Hardy get more business in Europe, he was actually helping Hoffa. Allison also learned that Hoffa controlled a business that operated a large fleet of trucks in Florida.[13] Later, Hardy took Allison "to a restaurant in Chicago that was a Mafia–Teamster hangout." Around this time, Allison came to realize that the company Hardy worked for also had ties to the Mafia. It's clear that Hardy came to view Allison as someone he felt he could trust and who knew how to be discreet, even though Allison was a completely legitimate businessman.[14]

Allison was a football fan, and he was lucky to have a friend like Hardy in Chicago in 1963: That was the year the Chicago Bears football team won the NFL championship in a game that left New York Giant quarterback Y. A. Tittle bloodied and on his knees, in one of the most famous sports photographs of the 1960s. Allison was in Chicago on business the weekend of October 27, 1963, and wanted to see the Bears play the Philadelphia Eagles. But the Bears were on a roll, and good seats were hard to come by on such short notice.[15]

Hardy told Allison getting tickets would be "no problem," and told Allison to meet him on Sunday morning at the coffee shop at the Bismarck Hotel. Apparently, Hardy had already made plans to meet someone else there on Sunday morning. Allison was having a late breakfast at the coffee shop when Hardy showed up with the football tickets. While Allison was talking with Hardy, "a little guy came in" to the coffee shop and caught Hardy's eye. Hardy asked Allison to excuse him, saying that he had to give the guy money to pay for his breakfast. Hardy smiled as he pulled out a #10 business envelope and—feeling Allison was a friend he could trust—gave Allison a look at the inch-thick stack of $100 bills inside. Hardy then went over to the "little guy" and gave him the envelope. Allison soon left the coffee shop, went to the football game, and didn't think anything more about the payoff in the coffee shop until just over three weeks later.[16]

On November 24, 1963, Allison was watching the transfer of Oswald from the police station to the county jail on NBC, along with much of the rest of the country. When he saw Ruby shoot Oswald live on TV, and the ensuing coverage, Allison realized "it was the man at the coffee shop" he had seen receiving the envelope stuffed with money from the Hoffa associate. However, Allison was reluctant to tell the authorities. After all, he'd just seen someone murdered on live TV in a police station—by someone his friend Hardy apparently knew—and admits he was nervous. In addition, "by that time [Allison] realized Hardy's company had Mafia connections," so he says he was simply afraid to go to the authorities.[17] Allison also had a former client who had been murdered, and when he had been routinely "interviewed by the FBI, it wasn't a pleasant experience." Allison said he "didn't want to face FBI grilling again." "Two or three months after JFK's assassination"Allison says he "went to see" Hardy in Chicago. This was to be their first meeting since the coffee-shop incident. However, Allison was shocked when Hardy's secretary told him that Hardy had died of a sudden heart attack. Allison thought that "was suspicious," since Hardy had appeared to be only in his late thirties and in good health. By then, Allison had started to hear the occasional news reports of other suspicious deaths related to the JFK assassination, so Hardy's death was yet another reason not to go to the authorities. It was also possible, with Hardy dead, that Allison's information might lead investigators to Jimmy Hoffa himself—not an appealing prospect, given Hoffa's ruthless reputation and well-known explosive temper.[18]

It is unlikely that Hardy had any idea what the money he had given Ruby was for, or that Ruby would soon become so notorious; otherwise, he wouldn't have met Ruby in front of witnesses. Hardy had probably simply been asked by Hoffa or one of Hoffa's men to give this man Ruby from Dallas an envelope stuffed with money. In terms of the compartmentalization and "need to know" that characterized mob operations, that's all Hardy needed to know.

Allison didn't tell anyone about the Chicago payoff, even his good friend Pierre Salinger, until 1991. During the rising tide of JFK assassination publicity between the twenty-fifth anniversary in 1988 and the release of the Oliver Stone *JFK* film in 1992, when there was talk of new information coming out, Allison decided to talk to Salinger. Allison still didn't want to talk to authorities—the press was full of even more suspicious deaths by then—but indicated that he would be willing to talk in confidence to a trusted writer or journalist.[19] Salinger eventually told *Vanity Fair* author Anthony Summers about Allison and the Ruby payoff in Chicago. Summers thought the information credible, but was on such a tight deadline that he didn't have time to interview the witnesses. Years later, we were able to follow up with Salinger, and we talked to Allison in detail in 1998. We found Allison to be honest and credible, and we were able to find corroboration for what he witnessed. Allison passed away three years later.[20]

Neither the Warren Commission nor the House Select Committee on Assassinations (HSCA) could find any record of Ruby's being in Dallas on October 27, 1963, one of the few days in the months before JFK's assassination they could not account for.[21] Ruby had called a number in Chicago the previous day, after he had called Los Angeles—Johnny Rosselli's home base. Ruby kept late hours, and it would have been easy for him to take a commercial flight—under an assumed name, which was easy in those days—to Chicago early in the morning after his club had closed. Or he could have been flown by a private pilot like David Ferrie, who had recently returned from a trip to Guatemala.

The FBI and Justice Department reports about a rumored payoff to Jack Ruby prior to JFK's death named Teamster businessman Allen Dorfman—a close Hoffa associate—as supplying the money. Allen Dorfman was a seemingly legitimate businessman who was nonetheless heavily involved in criminal activity, often involving high finance. Ruby knew Allen Dorfman's father, Paul Dorfman. One of the FBI reports notes that Ruby "in the 1940s was an organizer for Paul Dorfman's Waste Handler's Union in Chicago" which "is now reportedly affiliated with James Hoffa's Teamsters Union."[22] What the FBI report doesn't mention is that Ruby kept his mouth shut—when questioned by police—about a murder that allowed Dorfman, the Mafia, and eventually Hoffa to take over the Waste Handlers. The murder Ruby kept quiet about was so important in forging an alliance between the Mafia and the Teamsters that Bobby Kennedy himself highlighted it in his book about the Mafia, *The Enemy Within*.[23]

Allen Dorfman was exactly the type of financial expert Jimmy Hoffa would have turned to for a cash payoff in untraceable money that could have gone to Hardy for Ruby. (Years later, *Time* magazine reported that Allen Dorfman had provided $500,000 in Teamster-connected funds to Richard Nixon, to include a parole condition preventing Hoffa from taking back the Teamsters after his release from prison.[24]) The call Ruby made to Chicago on October 26, the day before he received the payoff was to an associate of Allen

Dorfman. When the Allen Dorfman associate was questioned by the FBI about the call soon after JFK's assassination, he initially "refused to provide any information about this call" and "subsequently furnished a series of contradictory explanations."[25] Many years later, when Allen Dorfman was murdered in 1983, someone close to Chicago mobster and law-enforcement official Richard Cain was a suspect in the still-unsolved crime.[26]

Jim Allison knew Allen and Paul Dorfman, but not through Hardy or Jimmy Hoffa. Allison said he had met the Dorfmans "through a New York gangster named 'Big Al' who always went around New York City with a sack full of quarters, which he used in pay phones" to ensure that the law wasn't listening to his calls. Again, we want to reaffirm that Allison wasn't a mobster, but a legitimate and respected PR man whose business occasionally brought him into contact with such characters.

On the afternoon of November 22, a Dallas bank official saw Ruby with a significant amount of cash that was almost certainly the money he had received in Chicago. Before finding that information, we had estimated the amount of money Ruby had gotten in Chicago, by duplicating what Allison saw: a #10 business envelope with an inch-thick stack of $100 bills. We found that seventy random bills from a bank in such an envelope measured out to one inch in thickness, equaling $7,000. Later, we were surprised to find that according to journalist Seth Kantor, "the loan officer at" Ruby's bank "vividly remembers Ruby standing in line" at his Dallas bank "on the afternoon of November 22, after President Kennedy was slain." According to the loan officer, "Jack was standing there crying and he had about $7,000 in cash on him the day of the assassination . . . I warned him that he'd be knocked in the head one day, carrying all that cash on him."[27] Ruby didn't put the money in the bank, however—bank records show that Ruby's only bank transaction that day was a withdrawal for $31.87. Ruby needed the money to help him murder Oswald. Ruby was crying when the banker saw him because he knew that since Oswald had not been killed by J. D. Tippit or any other officer, he was finally going to have to do what he didn't have to do in Chicago or Tampa: risk his life by going into a police station to kill the patsy. Gaining assistance from one or more corrupt cops must have cost Ruby less than $5,000, since he had over $2,000 on him when he was arrested.[28] As for what Ruby did with the $7,000 from the time he got it in Chicago until November 22, 1963, FBI reports show that Ruby's employees say he bought a safe sometime between October and November 8, 1963.[29]

Ruby wasn't the only one of Marcello's men to visit a bank with $7,000 in

November 1963. After David Ferrie returned from his trip to Guatemala on November 1, 1963, he deposited $7,000 in his bank account.[30] (Apparently, $7,000 was the down payment for helping on the JFK hit at the level of Ferrie and Ruby.) Ferrie's $7,000 was supposedly for his work on Marcello's trial—which began on November 1, 1963—so Ferrie had a plausible reason for suddenly having so much money, while Ruby had to keep his in a safe or safety deposit box. Ruby was in dire financial straits in October and November of 1963, and it would have looked very suspicious for him to have suddenly deposited $7,000 for even a short time.

In 1963, Jack Ruby owed the IRS $39,000 (close to $250,000 in today's dollars), which was no doubt his prime motivation for participating in the JFK assassination plot. Ruby's life had been a string of business failures and business problems, and now he was facing his worst problem yet. The IRS had already filed tax liens against him for the full amount he owed. The days of earning easy extra money running guns to Cuba were long over, and his club was struggling. Nonetheless, as the dates for JFK's assassination drew near, Ruby started acting like someone expecting to get a lot of money, soon. Five days before getting the money in Chicago, Ruby was shown a new location for his club by a realtor, according to a Congressional report. In early October, the report says the cash-strapped Ruby had told a former "*Dallas News* nightclub reporter who is now in the travel business that he is interested in a Caribbean cruise." One of Ruby's Dallas friends, who also knew Lewis McWillie, told a Congressional investigator that "on the morning of the assassination," Ruby visited him and "told him he was moving into a new apartment starting Monday, that cost $190 a month (up from the $100 that Ruby had been paying). The new address was 21 Turtle Creek . . . Ruby said 'I've scrimped all my life and now I want to live a little.'" In 1963, the Turtle Creek area was one of the nicest in Dallas, not the kind of place Ruby could have ever dreamed of affording before.[31]

Ruby's $7,000 was apparently just a down payment for his role in the JFK plot, since Ruby owed the IRS over five times that amount. Three days after getting the $7,000 in Chicago and returning to Dallas, Ruby called a Marcello lieutenant named Nofio Pecora, in New Orleans. Talking to a Congressional investigator about Ruby and Hoffa years later, Walter Sheridan "stressed [the] potential importance of Nofio Pecora" in the JFK assassination. Sheridan said he viewed "a combination Marcello/Hoffa conspiracy . . . as credible," and investigators have long felt that Pecora was acting as an intermediary between Marcello and Ruby.[32] For October 31, 1963—one day after

Ruby's call to Pecora—neither the Warren Commission nor Congressional investigators could find any documented evidence that Ruby was in Dallas. Perhaps Ruby was en route, or getting ready to go, to Chicago, since JFK was due to be assassinated there on November 2. But the Chicago plot was uncovered, so Ruby stayed in—or returned to—Dallas. However, Ruby did call Chicago on November 1, 1963.[33]

Like most of those the mob bosses were using in their plan to kill JFK, Ruby had informant status and ties to past and current CIA operations, and to Chicago itself.[34] In case Ruby's role in the JFK plot ever became known, his role in the 1959 CIA-Mafia plots would also keep authorities from digging too deeply into his past. Ruby's old partner in the 1959 plots with Hoffa, Dominick Bartone, was mentioned in an October 29, 1963 *New York Times* article, which reported that Bartone had won a US Supreme Court decision on a case related to his gun-running.[35] That article's timing was a coincidence, but Bartone's approach to Bobby Kennedy's aide four months earlier was probably not. Bartone had contacted an aide to Bobby Kennedy, offering to help with anti-Castro operations, when C-Day was getting under way and the exile guidelines for C-Day were being drafted. The same CIA summary that linked Bartone to Eloy Menoyo in 1959 said that on June 6, 1963, the CIA interviewed Dominick Bartone at the request of the special assistant to the attorney general. Bartone's approach was clearly an attempt to penetrate C-Day, with Bartone saying he had "'connections' in acquiring aircraft, weapons, etc."—the very things the C-Day exile groups would need to acquire without being traceable to the US government.[36] Bartone's approach occurred after Jack Ruby's phone records show that Ruby had become involved in the JFK assassination plot. Bartone's June 1963 offer apparently wasn't accepted by the CIA or Bobby Kennedy, but its record in the files would serve as a reminder of what might be exposed if Ruby's name surfaced in JFK's assassination and investigators delved too deeply.

Yet another Jack Ruby connection is significant to events in Chicago at the time of the JFK assassination threat. Earlier, we mentioned FBI reports that Ruby knew Hoffa enforcer Frank Chavez in the early 1960s. Ruby had even met with Chavez—and another unidentified Teamster official—at least once in Puerto Rico, where Chavez held sway.[37] Teamster expert Dan Moldea later uncovered a "Justice Department memorandum" dated two days after Ruby shot Oswald that "refers to 'a connection between Ruby and Frank Chavez and Tony Provenzano.'" But, Moldea notes, "the specific information alluded to was not included in the memorandum."

Provenzano was a high Teamster official and Mafia captain, and was later convicted of murder. Tony Provenzano would be a prime suspect in Hoffa's 1975 disappearance, and was mentioned in one of Carlos Marcello's confessions to JFK's assassination. It's possible that Provenzano was the unidentified Teamster official who met with Ruby and Chavez in Puerto Rico. (Chavez would be linked to JFK's murder within hours of his death in Dallas, and would later try to assassinate Bobby Kennedy.)[38] Based on Marcello's comment and Provenzano's role in Hoffa's murder, Provenzano could have had a role in JFK's assassination, perhaps in regard to either Jack Ruby or Chavez's activities in Puerto Rico, or both. As a Mafia captain—in a New York crime family—and a Teamster vice president, Provenzano would have been in a perfect position to help Chavez manipulate the movements of someone like Miguel Casas Saez, the putative Castro agent who traveled all over the US, always one step ahead of the US authorities.[39] After Saez traveled from Cuba to Puerto Rico—where Chavez reigned—one CIA report says Saez was "headed for New York"—where Provenzano was based. Saez was then reported in Chicago at the time of the threat to JFK's motorcade, before heading to Dallas, where Saez was alleged to be at the time of JFK's assassination.[40]

The Cuba Contingency Plan and the Phony Cuban Agent

THE REPORTED PRESENCE OF THE shadowy Saez in Chicago on November 1, 1963—right before the JFK assassination attempt planned there for November 2, 1963—was no doubt designed by the Mafia to trigger a cover-up in relation to the Cuba Contingency Plans and its protection of C-Day.[1] Those plans were being developed in case Castro tried to retaliate against the US by assassinating American officials. The reported presence of Saez in the area during a threat to assassinate JFK would play right into those plans and point suspicion for the assassination toward Castro.

It has recently been confirmed that the CIA's Chief of Counterintelligence—James Angleton—actually believed that Miguel Saez was involved in JFK's assassination.[2] However, a close analysis of the CIA documents about the agent that have been released shows that the CIA reports about Saez appear highly suspect. CIA documents also confirm that some of the original information about Saez originated with an operative working for Miami CIA operations chief David Morales.

The suspicious reports about Cuban Miguel Casas Saez apparently shadowing JFK are just one of several streams of information that tried to implicate Castro. Like the other streams, it falls apart upon close inspection. But because Saez investigations by the CIA, FBI, and other agencies were kept secret at the time, such a close analysis was not possible by Congressional investigators until more than a decade later, and it took historians and journalists more years to pry even heavily censored documents out of federal agencies. Like other "Castro did it" streams that eventually proved false, the Saez incident has direct ties to associates of Johnny Rosselli, Santo Traffi-cante, and Carlos Marcello.

In this case, the connection to Rosselli is a CIA program called "AMOT," which provided key early information on Saez prior to JFK's assassination. A formerly secret CIA document declassified in 1998 says that "AMOT's were Cubans in Miami . . . controlled by JMWAVE (CIA Miami) Station who gathered information on Cubans, primarily from debriefing of Cuban refugees."[3] New research confirms that David Morales was in charge of this operation.[4] The AMOT program involved more than two dozen people and lasted for several years, so it would have been a viable way for Morales's friend Johnny Rosselli to feed information to US authorities. It's likely that Morales himself had learned about the Cuba Contingency Plans to protect C-Day, information that he possibly could have shared with Rosselli in the fall of 1963. In any event, the information that AMOT-28 and other CIA sources conveyed about Miguel Saez matched perfectly what the closely held Cuba Contingency Plans were looking for.

The information that the CIA received about Saez prior to JFK's death also would have made him a viable patsy for JFK's assassination. The report from CIA agent AMOT-28, still heavily censored, says that Saez came "to the United States" on an infiltration mission for "sabotage"—and sabotage was a major concern of the Cuba Contingency Plan to protect C-Day, along with assassination. The CIA report describes Saez as belonging "to the Communist shock troops" and "the G-2 and DTI" Cuban intelligence agencies. AMOT-28 even noted that Saez "took a course on the Russian Language in the University of Santa Clara," and another CIA report says that Saez "speaks Russian quite well." Just like Oswald and Gilberto Lopez, Saez had a Russian link.

The sources of other information the CIA received about Saez are still classified, but they say that Saez "left Cuba by small boat" and "ended up in Puerto Rico. Entered Miami from Puerto Rico." Once in Miami, Saez "tried to buy a boat for unknown purposes" and adopted the alias of "Angel Dominguez Martinez."[5] Under that name, Saez would be investigated by the US Immigration and Naturalization Service the day before JFK's scheduled Chicago motorcade. Saez had supposedly gone to Chicago from Miami the previous day.[6] The CIA's "recheck with INS revealed" that Saez, using an alias, was "possible [sic] located in Chicago. INS office requested his file 1 Nov 63." But the CIA was unable to locate Saez.[7]

There weren't just one or two reports about Saez, but a steady stream: before the Chicago attempt, three days after the Chicago attempt, two days before the Tampa attempt, and several after JFK's assassination in Dallas. However, US authorities always seemed to be one step behind him. Saez's wide travels were probably supposed to make him look like he was part of some vast Cuban plot, since Saez was reportedly able to travel so extensively, from Puerto Rico to Miami to Chicago to New York City to Dallas to Mexico City and then back to Cuba. However, there is a much more logical explanation for his travels, and for the suspicious information the CIA kept receiving about Saez.

As we document more extensively in a later chapter, after JFK's death the CIA received extremely provocative information from suspiciously vague sources implicating Saez in JFK's assassination. Saez "had firing practice in militias and [was] capable of doing anything," said one report, using wording very similar to that regarding Oswald's alleged visit to Dallas Cuban exile Silvia Odio. To drive the point home even more directly, the CIA would receive reports saying that Saez "was in Dallas on the day of the assassination of Kennedy," and that when Saez left Cuba he was "a poor person, poorly dressed," but after returning from Dallas "now he dresses well, has a lot of money, owns large amounts of t-shirts, jackets and shoes, all American made." The CIA reports claimed that Saez had left Dallas with two others after JFK's death, had crossed the border at Nuevo Laredo after it reopened, and was then flown from Mexico City to Cuba.[8] Some reported additional suspicious activity related to that flight. The information was meant to put Saez in the middle of a Cuban plot that killed JFK. If the information had become public right after JFK's death, the pressure to invade Cuba would have been enormous.

The CIA and INS reports of a possible Cuban agent being near Chicago at the time of the JFK assassination attempt there no doubt helped to fuel the official secrecy surrounding that attempt. That is exactly what the Cuba Contingency Plans had been designed for, though apparently the non-CIA personnel on the committee making those plans were not told about Saez. The information about Saez being in Dallas at the time of JFK's assassination, and then fleeing back to Cuba, now with lots of money, should have sent up all sorts of red flags at the CIA and FBI. And it did—for a while. But the CIA and FBI soon noted problems with the story. Much of the information was second- or even third-hand. In one Saez document, for example, the "Source" (censored) got the information from a "Sub-source" (also censored) "who received the information in a letter from (censored)." Apparently, the sources weren't considered sufficiently reliable by the CIA.

The FBI, for its part, didn't find any evidence of the suspicious flight activity that took Saez back to Cuba. A handwritten note on a CIA memo says that "in view of the vagueness of the original report" and its "unknown sources," the writer recommends "I'd let this die its natural death, as the Bureau [FBI] is doing."[9] While CIA counterintelligence chief James Angleton was suspicious that Saez and Tampa's Gilberto Lopez were Cuban agents, CIA officials much closer to C-Day and the other Cuban operations in 1963 saw through the ruse: Both Richard Helms and David Atlee Phillips said, shortly before their deaths, that Castro was not behind JFK's assassination.[10]

However, Saez's reported actions cover all the right bases for Rosselli, Trafficante, Marcello, and their ally Jimmy Hoffa: Cuba, Puerto Rico, Miami, Chicago, New York City, Dallas, and Mexico City. One CIA report lists Saez as a "follower of Raul Castro," and Trafficante himself admitted meeting Raul Castro. Some experts think Raul and Trafficante struck a smuggling deal as part of the arrangement that got Trafficante released from Cuban prison; if true, that might have provided a way for Trafficante and Hoffa to manipulate Saez's reported travels. Hoffa lieutenant Joe Franco said that after Castro came to power, "for a long time" Jimmy Hoffa "continued to give money for arms for [Fidel] Castro and they got on a very solid basis and there was a few times when Jimmy asked that Castro send people over here to do little jobs for him."[11] Those jobs were probably a routine smuggling operations for Hoffa and Trafficante, to get around the US embargo against Cuba. That would account for the "large amounts of t-shirts, jackets and shoes, all American made" the CIA was told Saez took back to Cuba. One CIA document says that Saez gave his occupation as a "buyer," the perfect cover for routine smuggling. Smuggling on behalf of Teamster boss Hoffa and Trafficante would also explain how Saez—with no car and no apparent source of funds—was apparently able to travel so extensively all over the country.

One particular type of smuggling linked to Trafficante and Cuba was the transshipment of drugs through Cuba (supposedly allowed by Castro's government as long as the drugs were kept away from the Cuban people). Saez's reported travels near JFK assassination attempts echo the reports the FBI received about Frenchman Jean Souetre, at a time when heroin kingpin Michel Victor Mertz was using Souetre's name as an alias. Hoffa was also linked to Mertz's French Connection ring, and both Mertz and Rolando Masferrer (also linked to drugs) had bases in New York City, where Saez reportedly traveled. Having Saez use the same border crossing (Laredo/Nuevo Laredo) that Oswald had used just weeks earlier—and on the same day as Tampa patsy Gilberto Lopez, who was heading to Cuba at the same time as Saez—ensured that Saez would be viewed with suspicion by authorities after he was back in Cuba.[12]

The odd journey of Miguel Casas Saez was just one of several attempts to divert suspicion for JFK's assassination onto Fidel Castro. In the days, weeks, and months after JFK's assassination, several associates of Rosselli and Trafficante would make additional efforts. This would include radio, newspaper, and magazine stories—some of which hinted at C-Day—by John Martino, the longtime associate of Trafficante, Rosselli, and Masferrer. In the course of promoting his book, Martino occasionally hinted to the media and officials about C-Day, thus ensuring that even the FBI had to treat him cautiously. Martino had even described his associate David Morales as a CIA officer in his book, *I Was Castro's Prisoner*, giving the CIA an additional reason to avoid bringing attention onto Martino or closely investigating him. Martino would later confess to having a small role in JFK's assassination, as Congressional investigators confirmed shortly after Martino's death. "Rolando Masferrer" said in October or early November 1963 "that JFK is going to be assassinated," according to journalist Dick Russell. Masferrer would later spread phony stories to the FBI implicating Castro in JFK's death.[13] Frank Fiorini did the same—though, unlike Martino, Fiorini and Masferrer's stories never hinted at C-Day.

Saez's movements would be worrisome to CIA officials like Richard Helms and Desmond FitzGerald not only because of C-Day, but also because of the other Castro assassination plots the CIA was running in October and November 1963. Just as the CIA had juggled several plots during the Bay of Pigs, hoping one would come through, Helms was doing the same in the fall of 1963. He had at least three Castro assassination plots active by late October 1963, in addition to the Kennedy-authorized C-Day/AMWORLD and AMTRUNK operations. These included the CIA-Mafia plots (still with Rosselli), the ZR/RIFLE operation with European assassin recruiter QJWIN, and the Cubela/AMLASH operation.

Cubela (AMLASH) says the CIA was pressing him to assassinate Castro in October, an indication that the CIA saw Cubela as an alternative to C-Day, one they alone could control. According to one declassified memo, the "CIA hoped to avoid a bloody coup."[14] In 1963, a CIA memo confirms that "Cubela has no official position in the government," putting him in a poor position to stage a coup himself. However, his friendships with people like Raul Castro and Cuba's former "Ambassador to the USSR" could make it possible to help arrange Castro's assassination—or to be a logical fall guy for one of the CIA's other plots.[15] The CIA says they also wanted Cubela "to get into contact with his old friends from the DR"—which had become the DRE exile group and was run for the CIA by David Atlee Phillips.[16] This was around the time that Lee Harvey Oswald made his highly publicized contact with the DRE in New Orleans, which included Cubela's old associate Carlos Bringueir.

Miami CIA operations chief David Morales was not only working on C-Day and the CIA-Mafia plots with Johnny Rosselli, but also on the CIA's assassination plot with Rolando Cubela. Cuban officials say that "Morales was identified by Rolando Cubela as 'one of the officials' who spoke with him in Paris . . . about assassinating Castro."[17] Morales was in charge of providing the foreign-made rifles with scopes to Cubela. This may be significant when one looks at the unusual timing of later Cubela meetings in Paris with CIA officials, as documented by the Senate Church Committee.

CIA officer Desmond FitzGerald himself would meet with Cubela on October 29, 1963, just four days before the Mafia's scheduled attempt to assassinate JFK in Chicago with rifles. FitzGerald would claim to be a US Senator and the personal representative of Robert Kennedy, and would discuss providing Cubela with "rifles with telescopic sights" to use in assassinating Castro. Later, just two days after the failure of the Tampa attempt to kill JFK, the CIA would contact Cubela and tell "him there will be a meeting on November 22," 1963, which is also the date of JFK's motorcade in Dallas. On that date, a CIA officer would meet with Cubela and tell him that "rifles with telescopic sights will be provided," to use in assassinating Castro. "As the meeting breaks up, they are told President Kennedy has been assassinated," according to the Senate Church Report.[18]

The timing of such a meeting—at the very time JFK was being assassinated with "rifles with telescopic sights"—seems beyond coincidence, seems designed to force the CIA into a cover-up. The same would have been true if JFK had been assassinated in Chicago, four days after FitzGerald had met with Cubela in Paris. Not only was the Cubela operation withheld from the Warren Commission (along with C-Day/AMWORLD, AMTRUNK, the CIA-Mafia plots, and QJWIN), but the CIA admits that its own internal JFK assassination investigation was not told about the Cubela operation.[19] FitzGerald and the CIA officer meeting with Cubela were not involved in JFK's assassination and would have no reason to compromise their own operation. However, since David Morales was involved with Cubela and was also working with Johnny Rosselli, Morales may have been in a position to influence the timing of the meetings.

Morales wasn't the only person linked to Rosselli, Trafficante, or Marcello to be in a position to either influence Cubela or monitor Cubela's actions. Trafficante himself knew who Cubela was, since he admitted under oath to having met Cubela in 1959. Jose Aleman, the exile businessman in Miami who heard Trafficante's threat against JFK and reported it to the FBI, also knew Cubela, and he testified that prior to 1963 "I talked to him many times" about doing "something against the regime of Castro."[20] Trafficante's Cuban lawyer, Rafael Bango, was Aleman's cousin, and the CIA admits that by 1965 Bango was talking about Cubela's being involved in a CIA assassination plot.

The CIA admits, in an October 3, 1963 report entry, that "at the time of" the meetings between Cubela and the CIA in Paris, "it was discovered that the French were unilaterally keeping Cubela under surveillance." To keep French Intelligence (the SDECE) from becoming suspicious, the "CIA informed the French that our contacts with Cubela were for the purpose of defecting him."[21] Also working for French Intelligence at that time was Michel Victor Mertz. Three days after Cubela met in Paris with his CIA handler—and requested a meeting with Bobby Kennedy—INS records show that Mertz flew from Europe to New York City and stayed in America for ten days.[22] Mertz traveled under his real name for that trip, but he would soon return to the US using the alias of "Jean Souetre" for the JFK assassination.

In addition, a "lifelong friend of Cubela" was also linked to the French drug trade. According to an analysis of recently declassified documents and testimony by researcher Larry Hancock, Cubela's lifelong friend "was living in Miami in 1963 and operating in association with old Havana gambling network members such as" Marcello's man "Sam Benton." In fact, Cubela's friend had been taken into custody along with Benton after the FBI's July 31, 1963 raid on a Cuban exile training camp just outside New Orleans. By the early fall of 1963, Benton was acting as Marcello's representative in Miami for Rosselli's CIA-Mafia plots. As for Cubela's friend, his associate would later tell Congressional investigators that sometime after 1963, Cubela's friend had "ended up in a French prison doing an extended sentence for drug smuggling/dealing."[23]

All those connections made Cubela subject to monitoring and manipulation by the Mafia from two directions, through the CIA (via Morales, on behalf of Rosselli) and by Cubela's associates linked to Trafficante and Marcello. Congressional investigators and most historians have concluded that

Cubela was not a double agent for Castro. In addition to Cubela's denial, they cite Cubela's thirteen-year prison sentence after his trial in 1966 and the fact that Cubela didn't reveal the CIA's involvement with him at his trial (Castro double agents usually widely publicize their CIA contacts). Castro apparently only became aware of Cubela's CIA contacts in 1964, after the CIA put Cubela in touch with Manuel Artime. The remarkable timing and content of Cubela's CIA meetings that parallel JFK assassination attempts was either incredible coincidence or the result of Mafia influence. Even a long-secret CIA report seemed incredulous that "at the very moment President Kennedy was shot a CIA officer was meeting with a Cuban agent (Cubela) in Paris and giving him an assassination device for use against Castro."[24] That doesn't even address the additional "coincidence" that JFK was shot with a foreign-made, scoped rifle, similar to the type of weapon the CIA was arranging to provide Cubela the day JFK was shot.

In addition to the unusual timing of the November 22, 1963 Cubela–CIA meeting (and the one just before the Chicago assassination attempt), it seems unusual that, according to the CIA, Cubela had asked in October 1963 to meet personally with Bobby Kennedy. Historians didn't start to grasp Bobby Kennedy's leading role in Cuban affairs until the mid-1970s and the Church Committee investigation, and it wasn't widely known for years after that. In 1963, people knew Robert Kennedy as the US Attorney General and the brother of the President, not as someone heading highly secret Cuban subcommittees.

We may never know the full story behind the timing of the Cubela meetings and his request for scoped rifles, because there are so many inconsistencies within the surviving reports and the later testimony by the participants. Another complicating factor is that FitzGerald "requested written reports on" the Cubela "operation be kept to a minimum," an order the CIA says FitzGerald issued on November 19, 1963—the day after the Tampa assassination attempt and three days before Dallas—when FitzGerald "approved telling Cubela he would be given . . . high power rifles w/scopes."[25]

Neither Desmond FitzGerald or his supervisor, Richard Helms, bothered to ask Bobby Kennedy before FitzGerald's trip to Paris to meet with Cubela, where Cubela claimed to be Bobby's personal representative. The Church Report says that FitzGerald went to "Helms, who agreed that FitzGerald should hold himself out as a personal representative of Attorney General Kennedy." As to why Helms didn't ask Bobby Kennedy, Helms said "because

this was so central to the whole theme of what we had been trying to do"—
which the Church Committee said was trying to "find someone inside Cuba
who might head a government and have a group to replace Castro." Helms
said that "This is obviously what we had been pushing, what everybody had
been pushing for us to try to do, and it is in that context that I would have
made some remark like this."[26]

However, Bobby Kennedy didn't need Cubela to assassinate Castro,
because Bobby already had a much bigger, more advanced plan—C-Day—to
eliminate Castro. Putting someone else into the mix could risk complicating
things. Bobby Kennedy and the non-CIA members of his secret subcommittees only knew about Cubela as a potential source of intelligence, not as part
of an assassination operation. That explains the discovery by Evan Thomas
that on the same day that Cubela made his request to meet with Bobby
Kennedy, Bobby's "phone records show a call from Desmond FitzGerald."[27]
FitzGerald was keeping Bobby generally informed about Cubela as an intelligence asset—just not about the assassination part or Cubela's request to
meet with Bobby.

There are two other uses the CIA may have had for Cubela, one of which
might have involved Bobby Kennedy. FitzGerald and Helms may have seen
Cubela as a sort of backup plan for C-Day; if so, this would not be the first
time Cubela had been used like that by the CIA. A newly released CIA document indicates that Cubela was used as a backup for the 1960–61 CIA-
Mafia plots, which involved Rosselli, Trafficante, and Varona, and passing a
poison capsule to an associate of Varona's—Juan Orta, who was close to
Castro—prior to the Bay of Pigs. However, apparently at the same time, the
CIA was using Cubela in a similar plot, since a December 19, 1960 CIA document says that "assurances received of ability to deliver capsule to Rolando
Cubela." This document was only released in 1999, and it contradicts much
that the CIA has previously said about Cubela, even in the CIA's own internal
secret reports.[28] It shows that there may be other facets to the CIA's use of
Cubela that remain to be uncovered.

The time frame of the CIA's accelerating contacts with Cubela in the
summer and fall of 1963 parallels the development of C-Day, raising yet
another possible role for Cubela. It's clear from former officials, numerous
documents, and testimony that the Cubela operation (AMLASH) was separate
from the main coup plan, C-Day/AMWORLD. Cubela could provide intelligence about C-Day participants, without being told about it, as a way to see
if word of C-Day was leaking. (There is considerable evidence that Cubela

was not told about C-Day.) Cubela might also serve as a backup for C-Day, though it was not realistic to think that he could lead any kind of coup. A declassified CIA memo admits that in 1963 "Cubela has no official position in the [Cuban] government."[29] Cubela had a military rank, but it was ceremonial and he commanded no troops or government agency.

Cubela was not even close to Fidel. The CIA was working with Johnny Rosselli on the CIA-Mafia plots in the fall of 1963, and his men had their own highly skilled sharpshooters. So why did the CIA court Cubela so aggressively in the fall of 1963? The answer may be found in the CIA's Castro assassination plan's earlier guideline of "blaming the Soviets." A September 27, 1963 CIA memo about Cubela indicates that his influence in Cuba comes from his friendships with other officials, including Cuba's former "Ambassador to the USSR."[30] Cubela's friendship with Cuba's ex-Russian ambassador—coupled with Cubela's travel to Communist countries controlled by Russia—would have made him an excellent patsy to take the fall for Castro's death. A patsy was needed by the CIA, both for C-Day and for the CIA-Mafia plots. The Mafia intended to reopen their casinos if they helped assassinate Castro, but they could hardly do so with the support of the Cuban people if the Mafia were blamed for Castro's death. Likewise, even if a CIA exile sharpshooter—like those Rosselli sometimes used—succeeded in killing Castro, the blame would need to go someplace else if there was to be a viable Provisional Government supported by most of the people remaining in Cuba. The same would also be true for the CIA's AMTRUNK operation. Cubela's one assassination in 1956 had been unusual for him, but it gave him what little public notoriety he had in Cuba, and that notoriety would make it easy for the Cuban people to accept that he had assassinated their beloved Fidel, on the orders of the Soviets. When coupled with Cubela's travels, which gave him plenty of opportunity to meet Soviets (he even had a trip scheduled to Soviet-controlled Prague soon after JFK's death), it made Cubela a viable patsy for Castro's assassination. It's interesting to note that the CIA accelerated their contacts with Cubela even more after Oswald was unable to get into Cuba in late September 1963.

Harry Williams said that while he was sure there were arrangements being made for someone to take the fall, he wasn't involved with that, and he implied that Bobby Kennedy and the CIA would handle it. That might also explain FitzGerald's call to Bobby on the day of the CIA's October 11, 1963 meeting with Cubela in Paris. To FitzGerald and Richard Helms, another viable Castro assassination patsy like Cubela would be helpful not only for

C-Day, but also for the plots they were keeping secret from Bobby and CIA Director McCone.

The CIA was also keeping their contacts with Cubela secret from J. Edgar Hoover and the FBI. That led to a crucial intelligence failure on October 10, 1963, the day before Cubela met with his CIA case officer in Paris and reportedly asked for a meeting with Bobby Kennedy. An October 10 FBI report from a Miami informant said that Cubela was talking with the CIA. According to a Senate report, "The FBI informant [even] knew the date and location of one of the meetings."[31] The Miami informant's information about Cubela and the CIA was sent to FBI headquarters in Washington. J. Edgar Hoover usually delighted in letting the CIA know that one of their operations was insecure, as when the FBI uncovered the Phillips–McCord operation against the Fair Play for Cuba Committee in 1961. However, Hoover did not tell the CIA that word of their meeting with Cubela in Paris had reached a Miami FBI informant, though it's unclear why he didn't.

The October 10, 1963 leak to the FBI informant didn't include the fact that Cubela was plotting Castro's assassination with the CIA—but it did when the FBI informant made another report in July 1964. The FBI didn't tell the CIA about that leak either, even though the FBI felt that the Cubela–CIA talks might involve a "U.S. hoodlum element and Cuban exile plan to assassinate Castro"—in other words, the CIA-Mafia plots. It's not known whether the FBI suspected that the October 10, 1963 Cubela–CIA leak might also involve the CIA-Mafia plots; but it did involve the same informant, and the FBI was aware in the fall of 1963 that Johnny Rosselli was visiting Miami.[32] Also, the source of the informant's Cubela information in 1964 was Cubela's close friend who was tied to Marcello's operative and to French drug smuggling, meaning it's possible that he tipped off the same informant in October 1963.

The Church Committee uncovered still another intelligence failure related to the CIA's contact with Cubela, finding that "FitzGerald's Special Affairs Staff, which was responsible for Cuban operations, was . . . both plotting with" Cubela "and at the very same time" working on the Cuba Contingency Plans for dealing with "possible Cuban retaliation." Deciding that "Cuban attack against US officials within the US" was an unlikely response, FitzGerald and Helms "made the decision to escalate the level of CIA covert activity against Cuba," including more meetings with Cubela.[33]

The Mafia's bottom line for Cubela and the JFK assassination was compromising the CIA and Bobby Kennedy, probably using subtle influence from either the CIA–Morales side, or the Cubela-associate side, or both. Imagine if JFK had been assassinated in Chicago on November 2, 1963, using scoped rifles—while, just four days earlier, a high CIA official claiming to represent Bobby Kennedy had been talking with a Cuban official about assassinating Castro with scoped rifles. And this was the same CIA official— Desmond FitzGerald—who was playing a key role in Bobby Kennedy's C-Day plan. The cover-ups to protect C-Day and national security and reputations would have been enormous. Almost as big as they would be on November 22, 1963, when one of FitzGerald's men was meeting with Cubela about assassinating Castro with scoped rifles "at the very moment President Kennedy was shot."[34]

By late October, things were in high gear for Bobby Kennedy, Harry Williams, and the other "five fingers" of the C-Day plan. Artime, Varona, and the Fort Benning exile officers were almost ready, and while Manolo Ray and Eloy Menoyo weren't fully on board yet, they were getting support from the Kennedys and ramping up their operations. The military side of C-Day was also progressing rapidly, as the various drafts of coup plans cited earlier demonstrate. The Navy had been reluctant to have the CIA run covert operations through Guantanamo by 1963, but Bobby Kennedy was determined to have his way. "A Naval Intelligence officer stationed in Guantanamo in the fall of 1963" told author Gus Russo that "in 1963, the Kennedys sent down Joseph Califano—the head of Bobby Kennedy's Cuban Coordinating Committee—and he fired everybody."[35] In only a few weeks, Harry Williams planned to go to Guantanamo, were he would slip into Cuba to meet with the C-Day Coup Leader, ten days before C-Day. That's when Castro would be killed, and the "five fingers" (including the exile troops) would rush into Cuba, joining Harry and the coup leader in forming the new Provisional Government.

Most of the key Cuban exile officers were completing their training at Fort Benning, but some were at other bases—and they were getting anxious by the end of October 1963, according to an Army Intelligence report. It says "a group of officers with the Cuban Officers Training Program at Lackland Air Force Base" are contemplating "submitting their resignations if the United States has not done anything for the freedom of Cuba by December 1963." To preserve secrecy, the exile officers hadn't been told that C-Day was scheduled for December 1, 1963. The report goes on to say that "many officers have indicated their desire to resign in order to join Manuel Artime who is supposedly organizing a training camp in Nicaragua. Artime has some contacts that have been undermining the present training program by spreading dissention among their fellow officers."[36] While it was known in the exile community that Artime was getting increasing support from the US government, because of secrecy, the exile officers didn't realize that they and Artime were part of the overall plan.

Three Weeks Before Dallas: The Chicago Assassination Attempt

TWO VERY DIFFERENT MEN FIGURE prominently in the story of the attempt to assassinate JFK in Chicago on November 2, 1963: Richard Cain and Abraham Bolden. Both seemingly on the side of law enforcement during the Chicago attempt, they were in fact at opposite ends of the spectrum, Cain being a career criminal while Bolden was an outstanding law-enforcement agent. Yet within months, because of the Chicago attempt, Bolden would be the one in prison.

Richard Cain's unique roles in law enforcement, the CIA, and the Mafia gave the Mafia a level of insight and influence into how government agencies would react before and after JFK's assassination. In 1963, CIA documents confirm that Cain was the "Chief Investigator" for the Cook County Sheriff's Office, Chicago."[1] Cain had forty to fifty deputies working for him, and was the chief of the Special Investigations Unit, which the Cook County Sheriff had created just for him. The sheriff—like the FBI at the time—had no idea that Cain was a full member of Giancana's Chicago mob family[2] For the JFK assassination plot, Cain was in the perfect position to feed disinformation to—and learn real information from—all the local, state, and federal law-enforcement and intelligence agencies that the sheriff's office in America's second-largest city usually dealt with.

For instance, Cain would have been in a position to know about the cover-up of a threat against JFK's spring 1963 motorcade in Chicago. A Secret Service memo confirms that a written warning was received "threatening the life of the President during the motorcade from O'Hare Field to the Conrad Hilton Hotel" scheduled for "March 23, 1963." The memo says that all Chicago Secret Service agents "and senior supervisory officers for the Chicago Police Department were apprised of this development." More motorcycles were added to JFK's motorcade as a result, and in the end there was no assassination attempt. However, "the Chicago Police Department was requested to keep the information concerning the threat confidential."[3] We know from analyzing other threat reactions in Tampa and Dallas that the Chicago sheriff's office would have also been told about the threat—and the need to keep it quiet. Cain's knowledge of the spring 1963 cover-up would influence the Mafia's approach in the fall of 1963, allowing them to develop one plan to kill JFK that could be applied in three cities, confident that even if an attempt had to be aborted, it would probably not be made public.

Richard Cain's role in the Chicago attempt can be judged based on his actions in relation to Dallas, where CIA files confirm that "in 1963" Cain "became deeply involved in the President Kennedy assassination case."[4] Only a handful of those documents have been released, but they show Richard Cain spreading disinformation about Oswald. This includes Cain planting reports to the CIA and Chicago media that "the Cook County Sheriff's Office . . . had strong suspicions that Oswald was in Chicago in April" and that "the assassination of President Kennedy" had been discussed "at a secret meeting of the Fair Play for Cuba Committee held in Chicago in February 1963." The memo said that "Cain" even "inferred he might be able to get the information to the FBI 'off the record'" about those matters.[5] If the FBI had been slow to get the mail-order records of Oswald's rifle from the Chicago firm that sold it, Cain was in a position to make sure that that carefully laid paper trail wasn't overlooked. Cain was in position to do everything he did after Dallas for the earlier Chicago assassination attempt, and more. As the story of the Chicago attempt unfolds, it's important to keep in mind Cain's role and his true loyalty to the Mafia.

Much information about Cain is missing or still classified by the CIA and FBI. But one CIA document that has been released also talks about Chicago Secret Service agent Abraham Bolden. Much of what is known about the Chicago assassination attempt is due to the efforts of Bolden, who "was prevented from testifying for the Warren Commission that the Secret Service knew of a plot to assassinate Kennedy in Chicago by members of a dissident Cuban group." This 1967 CIA memo then says that "an unsavory character known as Richard S. Cain . . . who was in touch with the CIA's contact office in Chicago in 1963 passed information of a similar import to the CIA's Chicago office."[6] The CIA memo briefly mentions that Bolden is in prison, but doesn't mention that Bolden was framed by a Chicago mobster on the eve of his attempt to tell the Warren Commission about the Chicago and Tampa assassination attempts. As detailed in later chapters, the mobster who framed Bolden was a close associate of Richard Cain.

A former Senate investigator wrote that Abraham Bolden "worked his way through college, graduating cum laude from Lincoln University." He worked for Pinkerton for one year, then spent "four years as an Illinois State Trooper" where "his record was so outstanding that he became an Eisenhower appointee to the US Secret Service in" 1959. Bolden worked counterfeiting cases in Chicago, eventually winning "two commendations for cracking counterfeiting rings." In the summer of 1961, John F. Kennedy appointed Bolden the first black agent to work presidential protection as part "of the Secret Service White House detail."[7]

According to Congressional investigators, "Bolden spent only 3 months in" the White House "detail and was evidently shocked at what he saw." Bolden "resented the slurs against blacks" he occasionally heard from some of the white agents, as well as "the separate housing facilities for black agents on southern trips." Bolden "complained to his supervisor . . . and to James Rowley, then head of Secret Service, about the general laxity and the heavy drinking among the agents who were assigned to protect the President." But Bolden's warnings went unheeded, and the straitlaced agent "was transferred back to Chicago."[8] In Chicago, Agent Bolden resumed his focus on counterfeiting cases. But two of the cases would come back to haunt him several months after JFK's death, and would result in the fact that both the Chicago and Tampa assassination attempts remained secret for years.

Few historians know about the November 1963 Chicago assassination attempt, and the account that follows is one of the longest ever compiled. It relies heavily on the work of Congressional investigators, FBI agents, former Senate investigator Bud Fensterwald, and investigative journalist Edwin Black, as well as Vince Palamara and other researchers in America and England. All of the available declassified documents have been consulted. Most of all, this account is possible because of the efforts of ex-Secret Service agent Abraham Bolden, who has tried to focus attention on these important events for over forty years. The Chicago attempt has been confirmed by multiple sources and documents, including the head of the Chicago Secret Service at the time, Maurice Martineau; Bolden; FBI agent Thomas Coll; and several Chicago newsmen.

The pattern set by Rosselli, Trafficante, and Marcello in Chicago would be refined in Tampa and perfected by Dallas. The Chicago plot would involve killing JFK with high-powered rifles with scopes, as happened in Dallas and as the Secret Service admits was planned for the day of JFK's Tampa visit. The Chicago hit men planned to kill Kennedy while he was on a long motorcade, again just as in Tampa and Dallas.

JFK's scheduled visit to Chicago on November 2, 1963 was important politically, and would help lay the groundwork for launching his re-election campaign in just over two months. Mayor Richard Daley was one of JFK's crucial supporters, and the November 2, 1963 motorcade and football game attendance were supposed to make up for the previous October, when JFK had been forced to suddenly cut short his trip to Chicago.

After arriving in Chicago in October 1962—just before the Cuban Missile Crisis—JFK attended "a $100-a-plate dinner of the Cook County Democratic Committee" and had "gone to a late-night pep talk to mayor Richard Daley's precinct captains," according to historian Richard Reeves, when Bobby Kennedy called to say that the situation with Cuba had worsened and JFK needed to cancel the rest of his trip. JFK had not yet announced the Missile Crisis—and JFK didn't want to offend the politically powerful Mayor Daley—so the cancellation had to be done carefully. JFK felt fine, but he called in press secretary Pierre Salinger and told him to "tell the press that I'm returning to Washington on the advice of Admiral Burkley," JFK's personal physician. Before Salinger left the room, JFK called him back and said "we better be sure we're all saying the same thing." JFK wrote on a pad "slight upper respiratory . . . 1 degree temperature . . . weather raw and rainy . . . recommended return to Washington . . . cancelled schedule." After their stories were perfectly coordinated, Salinger made the announcement.[9] In many ways, this foreshadows what would happen in November 1963.

JFK's motorcade on Saturday, November 2, 1963 was to proceed from Chicago's O'Hare Airport to Soldier Field, where JFK would watch the Army–Air Force game with Mayor Daley and other dignitaries. The motorcade route was eleven miles long, and aroused several concerns.[10] As Edwin Black found, JFK was supposed "to arrive at O'Hare around 11 A.M., motorcade down what was then known as the Northwest Expressway to the Loop. At Jackson [Street]," JFK's motorcade "would lumber up the Jackson exit, make that slow, difficult left-hand turn onto the street and shuttle over to the stadium." The Jackson turn was problematic, because "as in Dallas, JFK's limousine would be forced to make a difficult 90-degree turn that would slow him to practically a standstill." In addition, "JFK's limousine would pass through a warehouse district—which Secret Service advance men consider ten times more deadly than any office building corridor" since warehouses often have entire floors empty, with no one to notice unusual activity.[11] Dallas's Texas School Book Depository was essentially a high-rise warehouse, with offices at that time only on the lower floors. Tampa's motorcade route would be even longer than Chicago's, going past all sorts of buildings— including one high-rise that was impossible to secure, a warehouse that overlooked a ninety-degree turn for JFK.

According to Abraham Bolden's interview with Congressional investigators, there were only "13 agents in the Chicago Secret Service office at the time," not many for America's second-largest city.[12] While agents in the White House detail would travel with the President, the local office would need to handle any local threat to the President. "Around October 30, 1963," the House Select Committee on Assassinations Report cites Bolden as saying "the FBI sent a teletype message to the Chicago Secret Service office stating that an attempt to assassinate the President would be made on November 2, by a four-man team using high-powered rifles."[13] The FBI's source remains a mystery.

Bolden told Congressional investigators that "he recalled" it was "a long teletype message" and that "it was unusual, he told us, for the FBI to cooperate on any cases with the Secret Service." J. Edgar Hoover had made no secret of the fact that he wanted to add presidential protection to the FBI's responsibilities. But for some reason, Hoover's FBI was eager to pass this threat along to the Secret Service, instead of handling it themselves and perhaps reaping enough publicity to take over presidential protection. Bolden says the telex from the FBI was taken to acting Chicago Secret Service chief Martineau. Also, "prior to the telex," Bolden remembers, "there was a phone call from the FBI."[14]

As Bolden explained to former Senate investigator Fensterwald, there was also a call to Chicago chief Martineau from the head of the Secret Service, James J. Rowley. "Martineau called in all" of the Chicago agents "and told them of Rowley's call. He also informed them . . . 1. There were to be no written reports; any information was to be given to Martineau orally; 2. Nothing was to be sent by" telex, that Martineau "was to report only by phone to Rowley, personally; 3. No file number was to be given to this case." In addition, all of the agents in Chicago were "shown four photos of the men allegedly involved in the plot." There may have been names to go with all four at the time, but Bolden only remembered two of the names: "Gonzales and Rodriguez."[15]

The Secret Service's special conditions for investigating the four-man assassination team make sense in the light of the thinking that was going into the Cuba Contingency Plans to protect C-day. The Cuban agent or the four men—at least two of which were Hispanic—could be the retaliation for C-Day that Bobby and the other officials had worried about. Or, the men could be disaffected Cuban exiles, bitter about JFK and the Bay of Pigs or angered by JFK's recent crackdown on all but the handful of C-Day exile groups. Bolden knew what usual investigative conditions were like in the Secret Service, and had seen how the spring 1963 threat against JFK had been handled, but these conditions were like nothing he had ever experienced. However, officials in Washington who knew about C-Day—like Bobby Kennedy—would insist on secrecy in this investigation.

Bolden and the other Secret Service agents were not told that at the time, the CIA and the Immigration and Naturalization Service (INS) were looking for suspected Cuban agent Miguel Casas Saez, aka Angel Dominguez Martinez, in Chicago. However, it is hard to believe that the INS would not have told Chicago's Martineau, or at least Rowley in Washington, about a possible Cuban terrorist being in the city JFK was about to visit. The confluence of possibly threatening Cuban or Hispanic individuals with a visit by JFK would seem sure to trigger the thinking behind the Cuba Contingency Plans, in order to protect C-Day. They were designed to deal with Cuban agents trying to "assassinate" a US official. However, those plans were still in progress, and neither the Secret Service, nor the FBI, nor the INS were part of that official process. Still, if the threats were well enough known to be shared between agencies (FBI to Secret Service for the four men, and CIA to INS for the Cuban agent), it's likely that one or both threats did become known to high officials who were at least aware of the Cuba Contingency Planning. If Hoover would have the FBI tell the Chicago Secret Service office about the four-man threat, he would certainly also tell the Attorney General.

In fact, Hoover was dealing closely with both JFK and Bobby at this time, as he was burying the story of one of JFK's mistresses in return for being "confirmed in his position as [FBI] Director" and getting Bobby's "approval for four new wiretaps on Martin Luther King Jr." As noted by historian Richard D. Mahoney, JFK had one of his rare lunches with Hoover on October 31, 1963, so Hoover may well have told JFK personally about the four-man Chicago threat that his FBI had uncovered.[16] Likewise, while the CIA kept certain secret operations away from Bobby Kennedy (like the ongoing CIA-Mafia plots), once the CIA was dealing with the INS about the suspected Cuban agent being near Chicago, it's likely that they would have told Bobby Kennedy about it. Bobby tried to run all things Cuban for the CIA—plus once the INS was involved, that would create a paper trail in another agency and the prospect that the INS would tell Bobby if the CIA didn't.

The significance of the names "Gonzales and Rodriguez" would become clear only three weeks later, around the time of the Tampa attempt. "Gonzales and Rodriguez" were the names of two men close to Gilberto Lopez and the Tampa Fair Play for Cuba Committee (FPCC). Unlike Oswald's phony one-man FPCC chapter, the Tampa chapter of the FPCC was a real chapter with real members, as was the one in Chicago. By the fall of 1963, Lopez was an informant for a government agency, according to a high Florida law-enforcement source. Lopez was also getting ready for his "mission"—as a secret Warren Commission memo called it—to Cuba. If JFK had been killed in Chicago, the names "Gonzales and Rodriguez"—even if they were aliases—could have linked JFK's death to Lopez, whether or not Lopez had gone to Chicago.[17]

Based on other actions of Marcello and the mob bosses, at least two of the men were probably from out of town. Out-of-town hit men were frequently used by the Mafia, because they made investigations much more difficult, since the hit man would have no local ties, couldn't be recognized by anyone, and could easily get away with using an alias if he were detained for any reason. The Secret Service found the four men staying at a rooming house in Chicago, another indication that at least some of the men weren't local.

According to one unconfirmed source close to Cuban exiles at the time, "some narcotic cops" were involved somehow in messing up the surveillance of the four suspects. The source also says that "the organizer of the Chicago attempt was out of Montreal" and that the organizer "had some type of operation to 'cover' the Chicago assassination attempt."[18] Michel Victor Mertz was a major narcotics trafficker who had a base in Montreal at the time and several cover operations to hide his heroin smuggling. This raises the possibility that Canadian authorities or someone connected to Mertz could have been the source of the FBI's tip. Just four months after the Chicago attempt, the FBI would be given information by French authorities linking Mertz to JFK's assassination. Another possibility, based on a later incident in Dallas involving a former FBI informant, is that a supporting participant in the assassination plot—not one of the four suspects—who had already received some of his money might have tipped off the FBI.[19]

It's possible that one or two of the hit men were local. Charles Nicoletti might seem like a logical candidate, but Nicoletti was well known to Chicago law enforcement—having been found in the specially modified "hit car" earlier—so it's more likely that he would have kept his distance or used an intermediary. The same would not be true for Tampa and Dallas, where Nicoletti wasn't known and could easily use an alias or assumed identity. It's doubtful that Jack Ruby was one of the hit men, since that wasn't his usual role. As in Dallas, Ruby was probably meant to just ensure that the patsy was quickly killed after the assassination, by a local officer or—if that failed, as it did in Dallas—by himself. We noted earlier that Ruby could have been in Chicago on October 31, not the thirtieth when the warning was received.

Michel Victor Mertz or his associates, or those considered for recruitment by QJWIN, would also be possible candidates for the four men. Mertz could not only speak Spanish (and pass for Hispanic), he could also speak unaccented English and pass for an American. Bolden was never shown photos of Mertz or his associates by Congressional investigators. According to Edwin Black, "the suspects were rightwing paramilitary fanatics, armed with rifles and telescopic sights."[20] David Ferrie might qualify, but Bolden didn't recognize photos of Ferrie when shown them by Congressional investigators. Nor did he recognize photos of Eladio Del Valle, Trafficante, and Masferrer. However, Trafficante had several Hispanic hit men, some linked to right-wing paramilitary exile groups, who could have been involved and have been linked to JFK's assassination by other exiles and Cuban authorities. Bolden was never shown their photos.

According to Abraham Bolden's testimony, "Surveillance was undertaken by the" Chicago Secret Service "agents on two of the four subjects identified with the threat. Bolden" and another black agent in the Chicago office "were excluded from the 'north side' Chicago surveillance because it was a predominantly white neighborhood." Bolden was still able to keep track of the around-the-clock surveillance on the rooming house where the two men were staying, "partly from his monitoring the Secret Service radio channels in his car" and "partly from office" talk by the other agents.[21]

With JFK's trip only three days away, Chicago chief Martineau told Congressional investigators "We got a telephone threat. The caller was not identified, that Kennedy was going to be killed when he got to Jackson Street." Recall that Jackson was the exit with the difficult ninety-degree turn for JFK's motorcade.[22] It's not clear if the anonymous tipster was referring to the four-man team, or to the main Chicago patsy who was about to emerge.

ANOTHER EX-MARINE PATSY FOR CHICAGO

The report of the HSCA confirms that "on October 30, 1963, the Secret Service learned that an individual named Thomas Arthur Vallee, a Chicago resident who was outspokenly opposed to President Kennedy's foreign policy, was in possession of several weapons."[23] That same day, according to an FBI report, two Secret Service agents conducted a "pretext interview of Vallee . . . and noted that he had two M-1 rifles in his possession, along with [a] .22 caliber revolver and an estimated 1,000 rounds" of "ammunition."[24] Unlike the other ex-Marine patsy, Oswald, Vallee was serious about guns. The Secret Service agents returned to the office and reported their concerns to Martineau.[25]

Of great concern, writes Edwin Black, Vallee's place of employment looked "out over the Jackson Street exit ramp where Kennedy's limousine would have been" traveling during the motorcade.[26] Vallee worked for a printing company, and British researcher Paul Byrne was able to confirm that that street "would be the logical choice for a dignitary to disembark from the Expressway leading from O'Hare and heading to Soldier's Field." He found that "the print shop was high up, overlooking this street" and "was on the correct side of the building." A Chicago alderman talked to "the owner of the print shop where Vallee worked and confirmed for himself that the windows did overlook the unused motorcade route."[27]

Like Oswald, Vallee was an unusual ex-Marine. Of French-American extraction, Edwin Black writes that Vallee was "born and raised in Chicago."[28] A small *Chicago Daily News* article reported that Vallee spent "seven years in the Marines, where he was awarded the Purple Heart and oak leaf cluster for wounds suffered in the Korean War." It notes that "Vallee said he returned to his native Chicago from New York City last August."[29] That was the same time that Oswald began his highly publicized New Orleans activities and met David Atlee Phillips, who was talking about assassinating Fidel Castro with exile Antonio Veciana. That was just weeks before Oswald moved from New Orleans to Dallas, where Oswald lived briefly at a YMCA in October 1963 before moving to a rooming house. At the end of October, ex-Marine Vallee moved from a local YMCA to a rooming house, according to a Secret Service report.[30]

Vallee told Edwin Black that earlier in 1963, prior to his return to Chicago, he had been "recruited . . . to train members of a fiercely anti-Castro guerrilla group" for "the assassination of Fidel Castro." The "training locale" was "in and around . . . Long Island."[31] The area around New York City may seem an unlikely place for Cuban exiles, but there were several large groups of exiles in the area. FBI files confirm that Rolando Masferrer was often based in the New York City area, and less than a year after the Chicago attempt, C-Day exile leader Tony Varona would be there as well. Two discoveries by researcher Bill Adams lend credence to Vallee's claims. He confirmed that Vallee did live for a time in Hicksville, Long Island, and that Vallee had a former housemate there who had been arrested for gun dealing.[32] Cracking down on gun dealing to Cuban exiles was a major focus of the Treasury Department and the Secret Service at the time. In addition to the Dallas incident mentioned earlier— linked to the bullets in Oswald's rifle and C-Day—the Chicago Secret Service had an active case in November 1963 about gun dealing to Cuban exiles that would later appear tied to JFK's assassination.

Like his fellow ex-Marine Oswald, Vallee was intelligent but troubled. According to the FBI, Vallee had completed "two years of college." Vallee was older than Oswald and had been in the Marines from 1949 to 1952, when he was honorably discharged. Vallee re-enlisted in the "Marine Corps Reserve" on February 9, 1955 and entered active duty on November 28, 1955. He was honorably discharged the following September, with some disability, though he had seen no combat during that time. Vallee was diagnosed by the Marines as "schizophrenic reaction, paranoid type . . . manifested by preoc- cupations with homosexuality and femininity." Homosexuals were rarely given honorable discharges by the Marines, but Vallee's psychiatric evalua- tion found indications of possible "organic difficulty" perhaps related to two episodes of possible concussions, once from an exploding mortar shell in Korea and the other in "an auto accident that required hospitalization for two months," an accident in which his father died. It also noted "homicidal threats . . . and chronic brain syndrome associated with brain trauma."[33]

Vallee's status with the Marines raises several questions. First, why was he allowed to reenlist, only to be discharged a year and a half later? If his mental problems were so severe as to be considered for disability at his discharge, why weren't they noticed when he reenlisted? The unenlightened attitudes toward gays at the time don't make things any clearer. In the 1950s, most doctors—and especially the US military—considered homosexuality to be a mental illness. Was Vallee really schizophrenic, or were the doctors just trying to find a "reason" for his homosexuality, so he could be given an hon- orable discharge and considered for disability? Were the US Marines just being nice to a combat veteran who had been injured years earlier? Or had Vallee engaged in—or agreed to engage in—some special activity for the Marines, or for Naval Intelligence, to rate his special treatment?

Sometimes in the 1950s, US military personnel who had recovered from injuries were given domestic surveillance assignments by military intelligence, almost exclusively targeted at Communist and left-wing groups. However, by the early 1960s, military domestic surveillance began to focus sometimes on far-right groups that were seen as extremist.[34] This was especially true after April 1961, when "Major General Edwin Walker, commander of the 24th Infantry Division in Europe . . . was accused of indoctrinating his troops with right-wing literature from the John Birch Society. With the agreement of President John F. Kennedy, Defense Secretary Robert McNamara relieved Walker of his command and announced an investigation."[35] This was the same General Walker involved in the phony "assassination" incident linked to Oswald, just over six months before the Chicago attempt.

In its brief article, the *Chicago Daily News* said that Vallee's "apartment contained John Birch Society literature" and that Vallee himself claimed "he is a 'disaffiliated' member of the John Birch Society."[36] It's unclear what "disaffiliated" means in relation to Vallee, but maybe it means he didn't really associate with Birchers and only pretended to be one, while having their literature in his apartment. That would be similar to Oswald, who only pretended to be a pro-Castro Communist—while avoiding real American Communists and Castro sympathizers—even though Oswald's apartment was filled with pro-Castro, Communist literature. While the HSCA report says the Secret Service learned that Vallee "was a member of the John Birch Society," there is no evidence of that in the released documents, or in interviews with any fellow members who knew him.[37]

The John Birch Society is not well known today, but it had a much higher public profile in the early 1960s as perhaps the leading conservative movement of its era. The society had been founded in 1958 by candy magnate Robert Welch as an ultra-conservative organization that used anti-Communism as cover for a pro-corporate, anti-union agenda that was seen by many as racist. Welch's views were extreme, and he "circulated a letter calling President Dwight D. Eisenhower a 'conscious, dedicated agent of the Communist Conspiracy.' It may sound silly today, but in the early 1960s it was taken quite seriously and was considered "mainstream" in many parts of the country. 1964 Republican presidential candidate Barry Goldwater publicly courted John Birch Society members and leaders, though others viewed it as an extremist group that needed to be monitored. Agencies ranging from the FBI to military intelligence kept an eye on it, using informants and infiltrators.

A member of the John Birch Society would have made a logical patsy for

JFK's death, based on their newsletter that appeared just one month before the Secret Service put Vallee under surveillance. Amid articles about the move "to impeach Earl Warren" because he has a "ninety-two percent Communist voting record" and a cartoon of JFK with vampire fangs is an article about Cuba. As part of their "Free Cuba in '63" campaign, the article asserts that nothing can be done to free Cuba from Castro until the "communist influences" in Washington are eliminated, because "what keeps the Cubans enslaved under Castro is the same power in Washington [underline for emphasis in original] that propels this Administration into surrendering our military forces, and our security, into Communist hands." If JFK's death had been blamed on Vallee, the American public could have easily believed that a troubled ex-Marine could have been influenced by such propaganda to take drastic action.[38]

According to researcher Vince Palamara, "Mr. Vallee claimed he was framed by someone with special knowledge about him, such as his 'CIA assignment to train exiles to assassinate Castro.'"[39] They may have also known about his Bircher activities, whether they were real or part of some domestic surveillance operation. It is unusual that right after Vallee moved back to Chicago, Oswald supposedly visited a Klan leader in Atlanta, asking for the names of far-right associates in Chicago. And just after Vallee finished training Cuban exiles with regards to killing Castro for the CIA, Oswald met with David Atlee Phillips, who was talking with Antonio Veciana about killing Castro. It appears that whoever was aware of—and manipulating—Oswald's movements was doing the same with Vallee.

In Oswald's case, one of the people who reportedly directed his actions was Guy Banister, who had extensive ties to far-right causes, ranging from the Klan to the John Birch Society. Banister had Oswald pretend to be a right-wing, paramilitary type interested in guns when he first approached the DRE leader in New Orleans, only to have Oswald publicly reveal himself as a pro-Castro Communist a few days later. Witnessing Oswald's public display in New Orleans was John Martino, who was then on a nationwide speaking tour to promote his book about his imprisonment in Cuba. It is notable that Martino, a close associate of Rosselli and Trafficante, is featured with a photo, in the John Birch Society newsletter for September 1963, as part of their Speakers Bureau.[40] With such credentials, it would have been easy for someone like Martino to monitor or influence Vallee. John Martino also knew David Morales, who had a hand in all the CIA-backed Castro assassination plots at the time, and would have also been in a position to know about, monitor, or influence someone like Vallee. In short, the same small group who manipulated Oswald could have done the same for Vallee.[41]

As Abraham Bolden stated to investigators on many occasions, and as Chicago Secret Service chief Martineau finally confirmed in 1993, the Chicago Secret Service considered the Vallee threat completely separate from the four-man assassin team the FBI had warned them about.[42] With the pressure of both serious threats, and JFK's upcoming motorcade to plan for, the possibility that Vallee was the fall guy for the four-man team of assassins didn't occur to anyone at the time. Whether it occurred to any Secret Service agents or officials later isn't known, but if it did, it might help account for the reluctant testimony, withheld files, and destroyed documents relating to the Chicago attempt.

On or about Thursday, October 31, 1963—one day after the Chicago agents' pretext interview of Vallee—"Vallee's landlady called the [Secret] Service office and said that Vallee was not going to work on Saturday," according to the testimony of Agent Edward Tucker to Congressional investigators. The agent testified that because Saturday was "the day of JFK's visit to Chicago," this information "resulted in the [Secret] Service having the Chicago Police Department surveil Vallee."[43] A later FBI report says that as a result of the Secret Service request to the Chicago police, "a 24-hour [a day] surveillance was placed on Vallee and his activities by the Chicago Police Department."[44]

It seems incredible that the Secret Service wouldn't have requested the surveillance if Vallee's landlady had not called, that it was comfortable with the idea that a heavily armed man who had said threatening things about JFK would be at his job with a clear shot at JFK's motorcade. Yet that is what some of the files indicate. Another report says that Secret Service agents were concerned about Vallee's weapons and his comments about JFK when they returned to the office after the pretext interview.

Except for Bolden and Chicago chief Martineau, the other Chicago agents have been reluctant to admit the existence of the four-man threat to government investigators over the years. But unless the agents were busy with the four-man threat, it seems unlikely that the Secret Service would delegate the surveillance of a heavily armed suspect like Vallee to the local police.

Protecting the president was the Secret Service's number one job, one that the FBI was trying to take away. It's hard to believe that the Chicago Secret Service would trust the surveillance of a suspect like Vallee—and their own reputations and that of the Secret Service itself—to a few Chicago cops. Unless the Chicago Secret Service office had a far greater threat to worry about, and other more important suspects to keep under their own 24-hour surveillance.

On Friday, November 1, 1963, David Ferrie and Carlos Marcello were no doubt ready to see JFK killed the following day, cutting off the major source of Bobby Kennedy's power. Marcello's biographer writes that "on the morning of November 1, 1963, in a federal courtroom in New Orleans, the final showdown began in Carlos Marcello's ten-year battle to avoid deportation." Bobby had sent his own Justice Department lawyers to prosecute Marcello, who was charged with "'conspiracy to defraud the United States government by obtaining a false Guatemalan birth certificate' and 'conspiracy to obstruct the United States government in the exercise of its right to deport Carlos Marcello.'"

At some point in the day, David Ferrie joined Marcello in the courtroom, since Ferrie had just "returned from his last mission to Guatemala on November 1."[45] Marcello had been plotting JFK's death for just over a year at that point, and now his goal was just a day away. For John F. Kennedy to die the day after Marcello's trial started would no doubt be sweet revenge for Marcello, revenge for all the prosecutions—which he viewed as persecutions—and the harrowing ordeal of his humiliating deportation. After court adjourned, Ferrie would be available Friday night and Saturday morning to take care of any last-minute problems or to fly to Chicago if needed.[46]

While the Chicago Secret Service left the surveillance of Vallee to the local police, Secret Service agents kept watch on two of the four-man assassin team. But, as Agent Bolden later told Congressional investigators, "through a series of blunders, the surveillance" of the two assassins "was 'blown.'"[47] According to investigative journalist Edwin Black, the agents had only been able to pick up the trail of two of the four men, and had been watching the rooming house where they were staying. When the two men left, one Secret Service agent followed them in an unmarked car. However, when the car with the two men suddenly reversed direction on a narrow street and began doubling back, the two men wound up going past the Secret Service agent's car. They overheard the agent's radio, and realized that they were under surveillance.[48] With their surreptitious surveillance blown, the Secret Service felt it had no choice but to go ahead and detain the men, so "the two subjects were apprehended and brought to the Chicago Secret Service office," Bolden told investigators.[49] Black writes that "the two men were taken into custody (but not actually arrested or booked) in the very early Friday hours and brought to the Secret Service headquarters. There are no records that any weapons were found in their possession or back at the rooming house."[50]

The lack of any weapons—and the premature ending of the surveillance before the two men had committed any sort of crime—presented a problem for the Chicago agents. Threatening the president was not a federal crime at the time. The only information about the two men being a threat came from the FBI, which was loath to share informants or information with other federal agencies. Without knowing the source or circumstances of the original information about the four-man threat, the Chicago Secret Service faced two problems: how to find out where the other two men were, and how long they could justify detaining the two men they did have in custody.

Once the two men were detained by the Secret Service, no doubt various checks on them—or at least on the aliases they were using—were run in an attempt to find an outstanding warrant or other reason to hold them. Chief investigator for the Sheriff's Department Richard Cain would realize at that point that the assassination plot had been blown, and the plan was no doubt called off. The remaining two men were probably quickly gotten out of town. Jack Ruby called Chicago on November 1.[51] Somehow, word was gotten to Ruby that his services would not be needed in Chicago after all.

The mob was a professional organization, and they hadn't gotten away with—by one estimate—over a thousand unsolved mob hits in Chicago without being able to deal with problems when they arose. The fact that the two men detained by the Secret Service had nothing illegal on them—or in their rooming house—like illegal weapons, traceable stolen cash or property, drugs, etc.—shows that they were experienced professionals. Any names they gave would have had no outstanding warrants. Otherwise, the agents would have found some small thing to charge them with. No doubt frustrated—and with the start of JFK's motorcade rapidly approaching—they didn't want to face a similar situation with Vallee, so the agents probably told the Chicago police watching Vallee to be alert for any tiny infraction of the law and to arrest him at the first opportunity.

    With JFK set to arrive in Chicago around 11 A.M. on November 2, 1963, the Chicago Secret Service, Bolden, the Chicago police, Vallee, and some members of JFK's administration were all facing a critical moment. Congressional investigators wrote that "on Saturday morning, November 2, Bolden was in the [Secret Service] office early." Bolden "recalls that the interrogation rooms were littered with cigarette butts and coffee cups, evidence of a night-long interrogation. He saw only one of the two men" the Secret Service "had apprehended" of the four-man assassin team. Bolden described the man as "swarthy, stocky, 'a truck driver type' . . . 5′ 9″ or 5′ 10″, wearing a jacket and shirt with open collar. His hair was dark and he had a crew cut which is described as 'Detroit style.'"[52]

    Years later, Congressional investigators showed Bolden photos of Vallee from that same time period, and Bolden said it wasn't the man he saw at the Chicago Secret Service office that morning. Which is accurate, because Vallee was never detained there. Also, Vallee was only 5′ 6″, three or four inches shorter than the suspect Bolden saw, was not "stocky," and Vallee's features would be described as Nordic instead of "swarthy." The only photo Bolden was shown by Congressional investigators that looked something like the Chicago suspect was one whose "facial structure" looked "similar to that of the" Chicago suspect Bolden saw in the office. That particular photo—of a man wearing a hat, coat, and sunglasses—was taken in Dealey Plaza in Dallas just after JFK's death; his identity has never been firmly established.[53]

    Bolden's recollection of the names "Gonzales and Rodriguez" suggests that those were the names of the two men who were detained at the Chicago Secret Service office. Bolden said that "Secret Service agents took their pictures with a Polaroid camera. The men remained in custody, while the Secret Service knew their two compatriots were still at large. The agents' interrogations had apparently gotten them no information of value in finding them. It was now almost 9:00 A.M., and JFK's arrival was just two hours away.

    In another part of town, Thomas Vallee was heading into the city, but he wasn't going to work. According to Congressional investigators, he had put one of his M-1 rifles and his pistol in the trunk of his car, where he also had

3,000 rounds of ammunition. Vallee wore a shirt with an open collar, and a jacket—similar to what at least one of the four-man assassin team was wearing. Vallee also had a crew cut and dark hair. Vallee was several inches shorter than the assassin suspect; but if seen at a distance or glimpsed quickly, Vallee could fit the same general description as the assassin suspect (at least as well as Oswald fit the first description issued by the police in Dallas).

Our analysis of all the available government reports and of Vallee's statements indicates that he was not on his way to murder JFK, or anyone else, that morning. Instead, he was likely going ahead with a meeting whose time and place had probably been set before the landlady's call, and therefore before the two assassin suspects were detained. It would have been easy for a supposed weapons buyer to have arranged to meet Vallee that morning, saying he wanted to buy Vallee's M-1 rifle and the 3,000 rounds of ammunition. Vallee's recent housemate had been arrested for gun dealing, and Vallee had trained Cuban exiles. Chicago exile groups—some with links to the Mafia—were looking for weapons in Chicago at that very time, including one case involving Chicago Secret Service agents. (One group in particular was partially funded by Johnny Rosselli.[54]) Vallee's meeting might have been set for a secluded spot or warehouse near Vallee's place of work on Jackson, along JFK's motorcade route. Everyone's attention would be focused on the imminent arrival of JFK's motorcade, not on Vallee as he waited for his contact to show up. However, the contact would never appear, because it was all a setup to get Vallee in the right place at the right time with the right weapons and appearance.

If the warnings about Vallee and the four-man team had not been received, JFK could have been shot by two of the four-man team positioned near Jackson, using M-1's and the same type of ammunition as in Vallee's trunk. If anyone happened to catch a glimpse of one of the shooters, it would have matched Vallee in terms of his crew cut and style of dress. And Vallee would be found quickly in the area, with an M-1 and the same type of ammunition. The scenario would be that a troubled ex-Marine and Bircher killed JFK, either at the behest of the pro-Castro Oswald, who had been seeking someone like Vallee several weeks earlier, and/or of the shadowy Cuban Saez, reportedly in Chicago. Government cover-ups would have ensued because of Oswald's Naval Intelligence surveillance, C-Day, and Vallee's recent training of Cuban exiles in a Castro assassination plot.

Because of the tips about the four-man team and Vallee, JFK was able to live another three weeks. A later newspaper account says that Vallee was "arrested on a concealed weapons charge less than an hour before the late President Kennedy was to arrive here Nov. 2."[55] According to Edwin Black, Vallee was arrested around 9:00 A.M., about two hours before JFK's scheduled touch-down at O'Hare. The two police officers following Vallee pulled him over for "left turn without a proper signal," and also found a "hunting knife in [his] front seat."[56] That was all the pretext the Chicago police needed to search his car. According to the Report of the House Select Committee on Assassinations, the police found "an M-1 rifle, a handgun and 3,000 rounds of ammunition in his automobile." An FBI file says a subsequent "search of Vallee's home" by Chicago police "discovered an M-1 rifle, a carbine rifle and about 2,500 rounds of ammunition."[57] A different FBI file says that Chicago police "charged him with an 'assault with a deadly weapon' charge."[58]

JFK's Chicago Motorcade: Cancelled at the Last Minute

VALLEE WAS OFF THE STREET, but two suspects from the four-man threat remained at large. JFK would have to leave Washington for Chicago within the hour, and people were already starting to line his motorcade route in anticipation of seeing the President. Mayor Daley and other local dignitaries were also ready and waiting. It's unclear how much the Secret Service had been told about the report of Miguel Casas Saez being in Chicago. The CIA and INS knew about Saez and probably would have told one or more key Washington officials in the Kennedy administration, to protect themselves in case something happened. It's hard to imagine that Bobby Kennedy or one of his aides would not have been told at some point. However, as reported in the *Chicago Daily News* at the time, "At 9:15 A.M. Chicago time, White House Press Secretary Pierre Salinger called newsmen in Washington. 'The President is not going to the football game,' Salinger said."[1] The motorcade, and JFK's entire trip to Chicago, was suddenly cancelled.

JFK's presidency is one of the most studied and well-documented in history. Yet even the House Select Committee on Assassinations (HSCA)—with access to classified material not available to historians for years later, and with subpoena power—"was unable to determine specifically why the President's trip to Chicago, scheduled for November 2, was cancelled." The HSCA said "the possibilities range from the condition of his health to concern for the situation in South Vietnam following the assassination of President Diem to the threat received on October 30" about Vallee.[2] But Vallee was either in custody, or under surveillance and about to be arrested, before the trip cancellation, suggesting that the real reason was the four-man threat, since two of those suspects were still at large. It's unclear how much the HSCA knew about the report of alleged Cuban agent Saez being in Chicago, but that could also have been a factor, especially since he could have been one of the two at-large suspects.

Salinger's initial explanation of JFK's having a cold was quickly jettisoned, probably because it was the same excuse JFK had used the previous year. The new explanation was the assassination of the dictator of South Vietnam, Ngo Dinh Diem. Most historians agree that JFK had approved the coup to replace the corrupt leader, so the coup itself wasn't an unexpected event—but the murder of Diem and his brother was. JFK seemed genuinely shocked to learn that the dictator and his family hadn't simply been allowed to go into exile, and a famous photograph captured JFK's anguish at hearing the news.

On November 2, around 8:30 A.M. Chicago time—after Diem's murder was hitting the news—Pierre Salinger had "announced . . . that a special communications facility would be rush constructed under the Soldiers Field bleachers to keep the President informed on up-to-the-minute developments in coup-torn South Vietnam. He reiterated Kennedy would not cancel the trip."[3] Yet just forty-five minutes later, Salinger announced the trip's cancellation.

When interviewed by a researcher years later, a Secret Service agent in the White House detail at the time said "I don't know if he [JFK] would cancel a motorcade. . . ." The researcher took that to mean that the Secret Service—not JFK—would be the ones to cancel a trip because of a security threat that was too great. But even the Secret Service seems to have been caught by surprise in this case. Chicago Secret Service chief "Martineau confirmed that the motorcade was cancelled 'at the last minute—I was already out at the airport' to meet JFK's plane when this occurred."[4] Another Chicago agent was already at Soldier Field, and one of the White House agents set to drive in the motorcade had already arrived in Chicago and was awaiting the President's arrival." Almost in unison, Secret Service agents at the time described JFK's trip as being canceled "at the last minute" or "at the last moment." What they can't agree on—or wouldn't reveal to Congressional investigators—is the reason for the cancellation. The only reason several agents gave for JFK's sudden cancellation was "the Cuban Missile Crisis," which had happened over a year earlier.[5]

If JFK didn't cancel the motorcade—as one agent implied—and the Secret Service didn't cancel it, since they seemed as surprised as anyone, then who did? We may never know for sure, unless copies of the Chicago files the Secret Service destroyed in 1995 are among the "one million" CIA documents related JFK's assassination that have not yet been released. However, a quick look at all the key players suggests that Bobby Kennedy may have played a role. While JFK was still alive, J. Edgar Hoover was still reporting important information to Bobby, who was technically Hoover's boss, so Bobby may have been aware of the four-man threat. Bobby also had his hands in all aspects of the administration and was his brother's fiercest protector. JFK's two top White House aides, Kenneth O'Donnell and Dave Powers, were also close to Bobby. So Bobby was one of the few people in position to have known about the four-man threat, Vallee, and the suspected Cuban agent. Plus, his own Justice Department prosecutors had their own sources, informants, and ongoing investigations that could have turned up related information.

When HSCA investigators questioned Secret Service agents about the cancellation fifteen years later, they seemed stunned by the often evasive, incomplete, and sometimes deliberately incorrect (in the case of Chief Martineau) responses many of the agents and staff gave. The investigators were amazed at the collective amnesia about this cancellation, even when one subject was confronted with memos from the time contradicting what they had said. It was similar to the evasive answers some agents gave regarding the threat on November 18, 1963, the day of the Tampa threat. However, in the late 1970s during the time of the HSCA, committee director G. Robert Blakey stated that he did not believe a federal agency would deliberately withhold information from his committee—a position that he has since changed. He and his staff did not realize the extraordinary lengths the Secret Service would go to, in order to keep information about Chicago and Tampa secret. By 1995, those lengths would include destroying records about the trips, even though the law mandated that the records be turned over to the JFK Assassination Records Review Board.

One possibility that has never been considered is that the agents might have been told that if they ever talked about the four-man team of assassins with the Hispanic names or the suspected Cuban agent or Vallee's Cuban exile training, it could trigger another nuclear standoff like the Cuban Missile Crisis. The agents couldn't be told about C-Day, but telling them that certain matters could trigger national security secrets that could cause World War III would have had the desired effect both then and in the following decades.

The real issue isn't whether the motorcade was canceled only because of one reason, when Diem's death, the four-man threat, the report of the Cuban agent, and Vallee's Cuban exile assassination training all probably played a role. Whatever the case, JFK's cancellation foiled any chance the Mafia had to kill him in Chicago. But all the official secrecy—which also extended to the news media—meant that the Mafia was free to try again. Especially after what happened next.

By Saturday night, November 2, 1963, all the suspects who were in custody—Vallee and the two who were part of the four-man team—had been released. As Abraham Bolden told Congressional investigators, "The two suspects in Chicago were turned over to the Chicago police who took them away in a patrol wagon."[6] According to Edwin Black, who had several Chicago police sources, since no evidence had been found to justify holding the men, they were released.[7] As for the heavily armed Vallee, the HSCA report says that he was "released from [Chicago police] custody on the evening of November 2."[8] Vallee was apparently never even brought to the Secret Service office for an interview, then or in the coming weeks. This seems odd, since a far-right threat against JFK surfaced the following week in Florida involving a high-powered rifle, like those Vallee owned. The Secret Service didn't even talk to ex-Marine Vallee in the weeks after the Dallas assassination was blamed on fellow ex-Marine Oswald, even though Secret Service records—dozens of which are still classified and known only by title—show that they maintained an interest in Vallee for at least the next seven years.

Abraham Bolden revealed to Congressional investigators the secrecy procedures used for the four-man threat, and there are indications that some of those procedures may have been used for some of Vallee's files as well. Bolden said that Secret Service head "Rowley called from Washington and suggested that [Chicago chief] Martineau use a COS file number." Bolden explained that "a CO (for Central Office) number was issued only in or from Washington headquarters and an 'S' for secret or sensitive was given when they wanted to sequester information contained in the file." The reason was that "these files were kept separate from all others and" so the Secret Service "could say they had nothing in their files on a subject when in fact a 'COS' file existed."[9]

(One might think that having information like that would have helped the JFK Assassination Records Review Board look for those files in the 1990s. Unfortunately, Bolden's HSCA interview revealing the COS designation for the files on the four-man threat was declassified one year after the Secret Service destroyed files relating to the Chicago and Tampa threats.)

Bolden says the Chicago "agents' notes" about the four-man threat "were typed up and the memos were then taken to O'Hare Airport," where they were flown to Washington.[10] With the notes gone and the suspects released, the four-man threat disappeared into a black hole—until after JFK's assassination, when Chicago chief Martineau and a Secret Service inspector from Washington would personally visit the rooming house where the four-man team had stayed. By then, however, it was too late to piece together the whole story.[11] So all the Chicago agents were then ordered by Washington, in writing, to "discuss no aspect of the assassination and investigation with anyone from any other federal agency now or any time in the future," and each agent "was made to initial this memo."[12] This helps to explain why, over thirty years later, the Secret Service destroyed files about Chicago and Tampa rather than turn them over to the JFK Assassination Records Review Board as required by law.

There are several reasons why the Secret Service would have turned over to the Chicago police the two men they'd apprehended from the four man-team, and they are some of the same reasons the Chicago police would have subsequently released the two men. First, it's important to note that the Vallee incident shows how authorities were able to find an excuse to arrest someone if they really wanted to. In Vallee's case, authorities used a minor traffic violation and the mere presence of a hunting knife on Vallee's front seat to haul him in. The fact that the Chicago Secret Service turned the two men over to the Chicago police indicates that they had some reason for not wanting to hold them. If they had wanted to hold them, the Secret Service could have—for example—found some minor discrepancy in their testimony and charged them with lying to a federal official. The point wouldn't have been to convict the two men, but simply to hold them while a more complete investigation was done and the search for their two compatriots continued. Instead, they were handed over to the Chicago police. It's also significant that even though the original warning to the Secret Service came from the FBI, the two were not handed over to the local FBI.

One possible reason for the sudden release of the two was that they were assets or informants of some other law-enforcement or intelligence agency that came forward and vouched for the men. Otherwise, it's difficult to imagine the Secret Service letting them go so quickly, since, in the aftermath of JFK's cancellation, they would have more time and manpower to investigate the two men in custody and look for the other two. Instead, it's as if some authority told them "they're okay, they work for us, don't worry." With such assurance, the Secret Service would not have thought the two would resume stalking JFK. It's even possible that the two detainees claimed that they were working undercover in dealing with the other two, perhaps investigating narcotics or illegal arms sales. The two could have claimed that the Secret Service interference blew weeks or months of work.

The Chicago police records from late October and early November had been thoroughly scrutinized for any sign of the two men, but to no avail. The only men named "Rodriguez" who were arrested in that time frame were taken into custody on October 29, 30, and 31, not November 2.[13] Either the paperwork has been removed, or the two weren't formally booked, or they were quickly turned over to another agency.

Historian Philip H. Melanson wrote that several decades ago, "the CIA provided a wide range of services to metropolitan police departments: seminars, briefings, workshops in bugging, clandestine action, disguise techniques and lock picking." He found that an "important payoff of its police ties was that the CIA could deal directly with its police friends in matters involving CIA employees." Melanson cites a CIA "memo entitled 'Relationships with Police,'" which "makes it clear that 'if CIA staff, contract or service employees' have interactions with police—whether as the victim or alleged perpetrator of the crime—the CIA would contact friendly police to get their help in 'resolving certain personal problems of employees.'" Melanson goes on to say that "CIA contacts with police were exercised through the police intelligence squad or unit."[14] So, the Chicago Police Intelligence Unit could have released the men after being contacted by the CIA or some other federal agency. It is interesting to note that in August 1963, when the CIA had an interest in Lee Harvey Oswald (as did Naval Intelligence), the "Commander of the Intelligence Division" of the New Orleans Police interviewed Oswald. The police commander later testified after the assassination that, based on his conversations, "as far as dreaming or thinking that Oswald would do what it is alleged he had done, I would bet my head on a chopping block that he wouldn't do it."[15] Recall also that the Senate Church Committee found evidence that Oswald had been seen in New Orleans police custody in the winter of 1963 by a local INS official, even though no police records of Oswald's arrest at that time—or paperwork about the INS visit—were ever found.

It's also possible that the Chicago police quickly turned the two men over to the INS for deportation, as happened right after JFK's death in Dallas, or to another agency, like the Chicago sheriff's office. Richard Cain's Special Investigations Unit at the sheriff's office was similar to a police intelligence unit. The INS was already trying to locate Cuban Miguel Casas Saez in Chicago at the time. But we only know about the INS investigation of Saez from CIA records—no INS records detailing their investigation have been released.

The Chicago sheriff's office—in the person of CIA asset and mobster Richard Cain—could have easily gotten the two men released by the Chicago police. Acting for his Mafia bosses, Cain could have claimed that the two were informants or assets, or pretended that he was acting at the "request" of someone like Miami CIA operations chief David Morales.

A 1967 CIA memo cited earlier, which talks about Richard Cain, may provide a clue to the two suspects' identities. The memo said that Abraham Bolden "was prevented from testifying for the Warren Commission that the Secret Service knew of a plot to assassinate Kennedy in Chicago by members of a dissident Cuban group."[16] A review of almost all the known articles and interviews with Bolden—including our own—doesn't show him using the phrase "dissident Cuban group." From what we have been able to find, Bolden said only that two of the suspects were named "Gonzales" and "Rodriguez," not that they were Cuban or part of any sort of exile group. The CIA memo was dated December 12, 1967 and was probably prompted by an Associated Press article about Bolden, headlined in the December 6, 1967 *New York Times* as "Plot on Kennedy in Chicago Told."[17] That was the first revelation to the public about the Chicago attempt, but it doesn't mention a "dissident Cuban group." While it's possible that the term came from some other story about Bolden, it's also possible that the CIA was relaying its own information accurately in ascribing the Chicago attempt to dissident Cuban exiles.

As noted previously, many Cuban exiles were angry at JFK because of the crackdown on most exile groups. The Cubans in the C-Day exile groups could hardly be called "dissident," due to all the support they were receiving from the Kennedys, but other groups were not so fortunate. However, even some of the groups excluded from C-Day, like DRE and Alpha 66, were still receiving support and direction from the CIA, specifically David Atlee Phillips and his associates. Other Cubans involved with the CIA included exile hit men linked to David Morales, some drug-linked exile operatives of Phillips in Mexico City, and those being trained at the camps frequented by Rosselli in south Florida. The latter might include exiles used in Rosselli's CIA-Mafia plots and the ZRRIFLE operation, and it's possible that exiles were recruited by the CIA's QJWIN. Those categories are not necessarily mutually exclusive, and it should be noted that Santo Trafficante had several Cuban exiles who worked for him and who have been linked to JFK's assassination.

Assuming that the CIA memo is correct about Cuban exiles and the

Chicago threat, there would still be a level above the four shooters and spotters on the ground. The mob bosses would want one or more highly experienced people to coordinate an assassination; three possibilities cited by some experts are Chicago hit man Charles Nicoletti, French assassin Michel Mertz, and Johnny Rosselli. All three were reportedly in Dallas when JFK was shot. In fact, it's possible to speculate that the Chicago plot failed—as did Tampa—because men like those had delegated too much to others, whereas in Dallas they were on the ground to make sure things worked properly.

As with Dallas and Tampa, there were probably fewer than a dozen people knowingly involved in the Chicago assassination attempt, with perhaps a few more on the periphery. In the background would have been Sam Giancana and Jimmy Hoffa, who were under such intense prosecution that they couldn't be actively involved. Hoffa frequently visited Chicago, and two of his prosecutions were based in Chicago and Tampa, but he would have to use intermediaries—like A. G. Hardy—to ensure that his actions didn't catch the attention of Bobby's prosecutors. Sam Giancana's lockstep surveillance by the FBI would ironically give him an ironclad alibi for JFK's assassination, if suspicion should be directed his way by those who remembered the verbal sparring between him and Bobby Kennedy at the 1959 Senate crime hearings. Giancana's close associates Johnny Rosselli, Charles Nicoletti, and Richard Cain were probably his representatives in the plot. Since all three were currently CIA operatives or informants, this gave them a large degree of protection, since they could always claim that their association with a suspicious person or weapons was because of their anti-Castro work for the CIA.

Because of Johnny Rosselli's ongoing role in the CIA-Mafia plots to kill Castro, he could play a larger role in the plotting to kill JFK. (Trafficante and Marcello had also been involved in those plots, giving them blackmail leverage over the CIA if suspicion in the JFK assassination was ever directed their way.) Rosselli knew he was under FBI surveillance, but he was able to elude that surveillance in Florida and Las Vegas when necessary. Also, Rosselli's close friendship with David Morales gave him ways to take advantage of the CIA's many Castro plots in October and November 1963, since Morales had official roles in C-Day, AMTRUNK, Cubela/AMLASH, the CIA-Mafia plots, and probably the ZRRIFLE and QJWIN operations.

There are plenty of signs that indicate that there was some type of official secrecy about the Chicago attempt at the time, secrecy that continued in the decades that followed. While the Secret Service doesn't like to publicize any assassination attempts or any incidents that make the Service look bad, the nature and duration of the secrecy indicate that this was something more, probably related to national security. It's also difficult to imagine that the CIA and INS would be tracking suspected Cuban agent Miguel Casas Saez in Chicago on November 1, 1963, the day before JFK's scheduled visit, and not tell the Secret Service—but no Secret Service files about Saez have yet been found or declassified. We think it's likely that at least Secret Service chief Rowley in Washington was told about Saez: Imagine how the INS and CIA would have looked if JFK had been killed and it became known that those two agencies had not bothered to inform the Secret Service about a possible Cuban agent in the area.

There are also indications that an unusual concern for secrecy impacted the Vallee arrest. For example, a November 6, 1963 Secret Service report about Vallee—finally declassified more than thirty years later—is more notable for what it leaves out than for what it says. It does not mention Vallee's arrest by Chicago police. Although it is supposed to be a report summarizing the Vallee incident, it doesn't mention information contained in other Secret Service and FBI reports, like the fact that Vallee had said he wasn't going to go to work on the day of JFK's motorcade. It says "no Form 1609 has been executed, Form 1641 is not applicable as no arrest was made, no Form 1599 was obtained," and "no fingerprints were obtained." The last point is especially odd, since the Secret Service's job is to maintain files on the large number of people who have threatened the president or have been suspected of doing so. The report appears to indicate that because Vallee didn't threaten JFK to Secret Service agents when they first talked to him on a pretext interview—something any potential assassin would be unlikely to do with two strangers he had just met—Vallee wasn't deemed important. This report even says that "it is not believed that this subject is to be considered dangerous."[18]

Contrast that benign conclusion with the findings of the House Select Committee on Assassinations, which found that "the Secret Service continued "a record of extensive, continued investigation of Vallee's activities until 1968."[19] The oddly incomplete November 6, 1963 report on Vallee was originally considered too secret to release when it was first considered for declassification on July 24, 1993. However, after the Secret Service destroyed documents about the Chicago threat in January 1995, it was then deemed safe to release the November 6, 1963 Secret Service report in full.[20]

The incomplete Secret Service report of November 6, 1963 makes sense if Vallee were an asset of some intelligence or law enforcement agency, or because of national security concerns, or both. It would also explain the following odd omission. Congressional investigators wrote that the Secret Service learned that Vallee "was a Marine Corps veteran with a history of mental illness . . . a member of the John Birch Society and an extremist in his criticism of the Kennedy administration, and he claimed to be an expert marksman." And yet that information on "Vallee was not forwarded to the agents responsible for the president's trip to Texas," though Dallas was known as a hotbed of far-right activity and the Secret Service had received other reports in mid-November of a far-right plot in which a marksman would shoot JFK. The investigators noted that while the Vallee information wasn't shared with the agents responsible for the Dallas trip, it "was transmitted to the Protective Research Section" of the Secret Service in Washington.[21] Apparently, information about the Chicago threats couldn't be shared between field offices, but only at the Washington headquarters level.

Despite Vallee's arrest in Chicago on the morning of JFK's planned motorcade with "an M-1 rifle, a handgun and 3,000 rounds of ammunition in his car," and despite his threats against JFK, he was not interviewed by the Secret Service or FBI in the days, weeks, or even months after the Tampa attempt or JFK's murder in Dallas.[22] Not one interview, to see if he might know anything about Tampa or Dallas, or about anyone who might be involved. This is an especially glaring omission in the hours and days right after JFK's death, before authorities had settled on the "lone assassin" theory. That's when even casual acquaintances of Tampa's Gilberto Lopez were having their phones bugged (based on the many pages of transcripts in the FBI files). Although the Warren Commission was aware of both Vallee and the rumors of the four-man threat, they never bothered to interview Vallee, and neither did the HSCA or any other government committee investigating the JFK assassination. Yet the Secret Service deemed Vallee important enough to monitor his activities for the rest of the 1960s. Even today, dozens of Secret Service files on Vallee have not been released—more than a decade after his death—and they are deemed so sensitive that they can't even be released in heavily censored versions, like many documents are. One explanation for all these anomalies about Vallee is that he was doing work for the CIA as he claimed, related to a still-secret Cuban operation designed to kill Castro. The other alternative is that he was working for Naval Intelligence in some capacity— or, like Oswald, he was involved with both Naval Intelligence and the CIA.

It's unclear if Oswald's trip to Chicago allowed some connection to be made between him and Vallee, or—if JFK had been killed in Chicago and Vallee arrested—if something connecting the two ex-Marines would have been found in Vallee's small apartment. Based on the files that have been released, it was only five days after JFK's assassination, "on November 27, 1963," that the Secret Service made a "notation . . . of the similarity between" Vallee's "background and that of Lee Harvey Oswald."[23] Yet they didn't bother to interview Vallee until 1966, and then only about rifle serial numbers.

When journalist Edwin Black interviewed Vallee in the mid-1970s, using the pretext of being a soldier of fortune, Vallee was remarkably forthright, and his answers gave clues about one of the reasons for so much secrecy about the Chicago attempt. When asked about the events of November 2, 1963, Vallee said "Soldiers Field. The plot against John F. Kennedy. I was arrested." While admitting everything about his guns and his arrest, "he patently denied he actually threatened the President or even considered doing him any harm. Vallee claimed he was framed . . . because with his openly anti-Kennedy sentiments, he could easily be believed to have threatened the President."

In addition, Vallee "also gave specifics about his CIA assignment to train exiles to assassinate Castro."[24] That's why even Vallee's case came to be cloaked in the same type of official secrecy as the four-man threat. Just as ex-Marine Oswald was a Naval Intelligence asset who was brought into contact with C-Day on several occasions—at Artime's minor-league camp, in the meeting with Phillips and Menoyo's partner Veciana, and with the female member of Manolo Ray's JURE group—ex-Marine Vallee was probably in a similar situation. At the very least, his Cuban exile training could have involved one of the CIA's Castro assassination plots. Just as Oswald's legitimate intelligence activities in the months before C-Day were manipulated by associates of Marcello, Trafficante, and Rosselli like Banister, Ferrie, Martino, and possibly Morales, the same is also probably true for Vallee.

Vallee confirmed to author Edwin Black that "he was never called to testify before the Warren Commission"; even Vallee "thought that was remiss."[25] The FBI didn't bother to talk to Vallee at all. Such a "hands-off" approach—while, as the HSCA said, the Secret Service maintained a close eye on Vallee for five years after JFK's death—would be consistent with Vallee's being an asset for another US agency.

Contrast the benign approach of the Warren Commission, Secret Service, and FBI to Vallee with that of Chicago Police Sergeant Lawrence Coffey, who told Edwin Black in 1975 that "Naturally, I remember every detail" of the Vallee case. "How often is anyone involved in a threat against the President's life? One involving a lot of heavy weapons like this Vallee character." And an FBI memo confirms the serious nature of the case, saying that at "the interrogation of Vallee by Chicago Police Officers, Vallee revealed he was very much against the" JFK "administration." Yet even with all Vallee's weapons, and the reported threats against JFK, Vallee was only convicted a month and a half after JFK's death of "'Unlawful use of a weapon' and in addition was imposed a $5 suspended fine on a traffic violation."[26]

The four-man team and Vallee were clearly hot potatoes for the Secret Service, and for other federal agencies as well. When FBI Agent Thomas B. Coll was asked by Edwin Black about the four-man team in mid-1970s, he reportedly responded: "I remember that case. Some people were picked up. And I'm telling you it wasn't ours. That was strictly a Secret Service affair. That whole Soldier Field matter was a Secret Service affair . . . you'll get no more out of me. I've said as much as I'm going to on that subject. Get the rest from the Secret Service." Apparently, the FBI found the four-man threat problematic, which is probably why Hoover and the FBI referred it to the Secret Service instead of pursuing it themselves.

Researcher Vince Palamara wrote that "Abraham Bolden was adamant that [Chicago Secret Service Chief] Martineau knew about" the four-man "plot to kill JFK on November 2, 1963. In 1993, Martineau himself confirmed the existence of the plot to Palamara, and said "he assumed everyone knew about it." Martineau also added that he believed JFK was killed as a result of a conspiracy and that there was "'more than one assassin' on November 22, 1963."[27] That is not a surprising conclusion, given the similarities between the attempts to kill JFK in Chicago and Dallas (and Tampa), similarities Martineau would have known about.

It's important to note that Martineau's statements were made in 1993, at an important point in time. In the wake of the furor over Oliver Stone's *JFK* film, thousands of CIA documents had been released, and President Clinton and the Congress had created the JFK Assassination Records Review Board to release thousands more. Martineau's own testimony to investigators for the House Select Committee on Assassinations in the late 1970s was still classified secret. The Secret Service had not yet destroyed the documents about Chicago and Tampa, as they would in January 1995. So Martineau was simply being honest to a young researcher, Palamara, about things he figured were already known or would soon come out.

Contrast that with Martineau's attitude a decade and a half earlier, to investigators from the House Select Committee on Assassinations, in testimony not declassified until 1996. They wrote that Martineau "visibly stiffened" when "the HSCA asked about threats to JFK in the Chicago area in November 1963." He claimed to "recall no threat that was significant enough to cause me to recollect it at this time," and "his answers became vague and less responsive." He said he did not recall "any all-night interrogation of any suspects in the Chicago office" or "surveillance involving Cuban or Latin types."[28] His last two answers seem oddly precise, and exclude, for example, long interrogations that lasted only most of the night and surveillance of Americans who might have used Hispanic aliases. Unfortunately, Martineau was never asked by investigators about contacts between the Chicago Secret Service's office and Richard Cain or Cain's unit at the Chicago sheriff's office.

Martineau's unresponsive responses to the House Select Committee on Assassinations (HSCA) investigators were typical, and indicate that all those from the Chicago Secret Service office were operating under the same constraints for secrecy and national security. The investigators were able to find one Chicago agent in addition to Bolden who said that there had been a threat in Chicago during that period," but that agent "was unable to recall details."[29] Otherwise, the HSCA investigators hit a brick wall, not only on the four-man threat, but even on the well-documented Vallee threat. Some agents claimed to remember nothing about JFK's last-minute cancellation, or even that he was scheduled to come to Chicago that day. One staff member's amnesia to HSCA investigators led her to say that she "had no recall about any threats during her twenty years in the Chicago office."[30] When Edwin Black had first contacted some of the agents about the Chicago threat a few years prior to the HSCA, some hinted that there was something there, but refused to confirm anything or provide any details.

We feel that the Chicago and White House Secret Service agents and staff were following orders based on national security concerns, causing all but ex-agent Bolden to stonewall even Congressional investigators. Many of the agents interviewed were still working for the Secret Service when they were interviewed, and would have been aware of the years Abraham Bolden spent in prison after he attempted to tell the Warren Commission about the Chicago and Tampa threats.

News reports about the four-man assassin team were suppressed at the time of the attempt and after JFK's death, though the FBI confirmed that it was discussed among Chicago newsmen. Even Vallee's arrest received scant media attention at the time, not surfacing in any detail until over a month after the arrest, in a small *Chicago Daily News* article of December 3, 1963, more than a week after JFK's murder. In that article, Vallee made it clear that he "had no intention of trying to assassinate the President."[31] The spring 1964 newspaper articles about Bolden's arrest didn't mention the Chicago attempt, and it was not until a December 6, 1967 *New York Times* article about Bolden that the public first learned about the Chicago attempt. That revelation about Chicago attracted little attention at the time, when the public and media were focused on the investigation of New Orleans DA Jim Garrison. There was a little more publicity about the Chicago attempt in the mid-1970s at the time of Edwin Black's article. While the article sparked investigations at several Secret Service offices across the country—and attempts by the HSCA a few years later to find out more—the general public and most historians remained unaware of the Chicago attempt.

However, newsmen were aware of the story at the time of the Chicago attempt. The files of Senate investigator Bud Fensterwald contain notes from 1969 interviews with four reporters and editors with the *Chicago Daily News* who all recalled that "at the time of JFK's scheduled visit to Chicago" in 1963, "there were four men in town who planned an assassination attempt from one of the overpasses from O'Hare into town. They were seized but apparently not arrested." One of the newsmen recalled "a disassembled rifle in the story," and made it clear that this was different from the Vallee arrest. However, the newsman said that "for some reason" the story of the four-man assassin team "did not get in the [news]paper."[32] Just after JFK's death, two of the newsmen appear in FBI reports about stories of the four-man Chicago assassin team circulating among reporters. The editor at the heart of the story "received information from a police source indicating that four men had been arrested in various parts of the city on 11-2."[33] It's interesting that the editor gave a "police source" as the basis for the story, since it would be more than a decade before it was publicly reported that Bolden said that two of the four-man team had been turned over to Chicago police.

What happened with the news suppression in Chicago was simply the start of what happened again after the Tampa attempt, and after Dallas. The news suppression wasn't designed to protect JFK's assassins, but to protect sensitive anti-Castro Cuban operations, like C-Day and the other CIA plots.

The Cuba Contingency Plans to protect C-Day were still being developed, so they weren't ready to be put into effect on a strict basis. But the thinking behind them was known to officials like Bobby Kennedy, Richard Helms, and Desmond FitzGerald. They would have worried that any threat against JFK that could involve Cubans—whether suspected agents like Miguel Casas Saez or the two suspects with Hispanic names—could be the advance retaliation, or "preemptive strike," by Castro for the C-Day operation they had been planning for. As detailed later, it's ironic that the lower-level officials actually writing the Cuba Contingency Plans apparently weren't told about the Chicago threat, and they certainly couldn't read about it in the newspapers. If they had, their planning might have gone quite differently. Then again, some of those working on the Contingency Plans hadn't even been told about C-Day, and only knew generally about the nonassassination aspects of the AMTRUNK and Cubela operations.

The cover-up of the Chicago attempt—by JFK, Bobby, the Secret Service, the FBI, and probably other agencies like the CIA—went far beyond the usual cover-up of presidential assassination attempts.[34] The Secret Service routinely tried to keep attempts out of the press as much as possible, to avoid copycats and prolonged negative publicity, but the secrecy surrounding the Chicago attempt went much farther than any cover-up that had been attempted before. The cover-up in Chicago was successful, with just a handful of leaks, most after JFK's death. Even historians remained largely unaware of the Chicago attempt until the late 1970s, and it is still not widely known by the public or most journalists. The same cover-up techniques would be refined and applied again by the Kennedys and federal authorities in Tampa, with even greater success. After Tampa and Chicago, the ability of the Secret Service, FBI, CIA, Bobby Kennedy, and others to cover up key events relating to JFK's death in Dallas was finely honed, and is yet another reason so much has remained secret until this book.

Laying the Groundwork for Tampa

DURING THE FIRST TWO AND a half weeks of November 1963, Marcello, Trafficante, and Rosselli were finalizing their plan to kill JFK in Tampa, while the Kennedys were putting the finishing touches on C-Day. Planning for both intensified as the month progressed, but the mob bosses had the advantage of not building to one C-Day, but rather of having two more chances to kill JFK. When the Chicago attempt remained secret in the days and weeks that followed, the mob was able to refine their plan for the attempt in Tampa. After the Tampa attempt, which resulted in no arrests and was again kept from the public, the mob bosses were ultimately able to use the same basic plan and personnel again in Dallas just four days later.

The Mafia learned from its mistakes in Chicago, but the attempt had shown the mob bosses that their basic plan was capable of provoking a cover-up, and even of getting two of their men out of custody when they were detained. For the Tampa attempt—as in Chicago and Dallas—fewer than a dozen people would need to be knowingly involved in the plot. Most would have ties to law-enforcement or intelligence agencies, to help if they were arrested on even a minor charge and to force cover-ups by the agencies if they were ever suspected in JFK's murder. The mob bosses would again bring in several experienced gunmen. A local patsy—Gilberto Lopez—would be in place to take the fall, having been linked to Oswald and thus to C-Day. Someone like Ruby would no doubt make sure the patsy was quickly killed, even if it meant doing the job himself. An official in the Tampa–St. Petersburg area in a position similar to Richard Cain's would help to monitor law-enforcement knowledge of the plot and its aftermath. If JFK were killed in Tampa, the presence of Cubans such as Gilberto Lopez (who lived in Tampa) and Miguel Casas Saez (recently reported in Florida) allegedly linked to the assassination would ensure that US authorities had to cover up much information after JFK's death, to protect C-Day and other anti-Castro operations.

The Tampa attempt had even more parallels to Dallas than Chicago: a long presidential motorcade in an open limo, a hard left turn to slow JFK's limo in front of a tall red-brick building with many unsecured windows, a gunman with a high-powered rifle planning to shoot from a building, and reports to officials of organized crime involvement. A key suspect in Tampa, Gilberto Lopez, was a young white male of slender build, a government asset, linked to the Fair Play for Cuba Committee, and a former defector who had a Russian connection in his background. Like Oswald, Lopez was seen as apolitical or anti-Castro by some, yet had gotten into a fight over seemingly pro-Castro statements. Lopez was also linked to Oswald prior to the Tampa attempt, tying Lopez to C-Day.

Security was the Mafia's highest priority, and several of the knowing participants had ties to the Mafia's highly secure—and brutally ruthless—heroin network. The usual steps the Mafia took to evade Bobby's prosecutions and any possible electronic surveillance—intermediaries, messengers, coded phone messages, and pay phones—were increased. Jack Ruby's suspicious long-distance phone calls for November are too numerous to detail, though we will note the most important. Most of the calls were brief, simply passing or initiating messages to trusted Mafia or Hoffa associates. There were several layers of intermediaries, most not involved knowingly in the plot and simply passing coded phrases that were meaningless to them.

Although the press secrecy surrounding the four-man Chicago threat appeared to be holding, the three mob bosses couldn't be sure at that time that it would remain secret. A single story in the press about the Chicago attempt would increase security arrangements for Tampa and Dallas, or even cause their cancellation (as in Chicago) or postponement. Just in case the Chicago threat blew wide open, Johnny Rosselli tried yet another way to get some type of leverage over JFK, either to make Bobby back off his Mafia prosecutions or to lure JFK into a trap: Rosselli had Judith Campbell contact JFK, even though most accounts say that JFK had not seen Campbell in well over a year. Richard D. Mahoney wrote that "on November 4," 1963, "a memo to Hoover . . . informed him that Judith Campbell was back in 'telephonic contact' with" JFK's "secretary, Evelyn Lincoln . . . the information was apparently derived from an FBI bug." The FBI also found that Campbell had resumed talking to Johnny Rosselli and Sam Giancana at the same time, and they were clearly behind her renewed attempt to see JFK.[1] But JFK didn't take the bait this time, so planning continued for the Tampa attempt.

Because of Bobby Kennedy, Marcello was on trial in New Orleans, but he had men like Guy Banister and David Ferrie to continue the assassination plan. According to John H. Davis, "on the second day of" Marcello's "trial, November 5," David Ferrie "bought, by his own admission, a .38 revolver, and several days later the normally impecunious Ferrie deposited in his account in the Whitney National Bank the $7,093" he had been paid for his work on the Marcello case.[2] On November 7 and 8, 1963, Jack Ruby—who had gotten what looked like approximately $7,000 from Hoffa's man the previous week—"has long phone calls with two associates of Jimmy Hoffa."[3] Ruby could also be useful in Tampa, since he had been stationed there during World War II and in recent years had made trips to Tampa to recruit strippers there for his club. Ruby had been in Tampa the previous year on such a visit, so he knew the city and could go there on a similar pretext for the assassination attempt.

On November 9, Ruby's recent visitor from Chicago—Lawrence Meyers—was in New Orleans and called Chicago.[4] David Ferrie, called by Meyers just over a month earlier, and Carlos Marcello spent the weekend of November 9–10 working on strategy at Marcello's huge, secluded Churchill Farms outside of New Orleans. It wasn't legal strategy they were planning, as Ferrie later claimed to the FBI, since Marcello had top local and national attorneys handling that. They were meeting in the same farmhouse where FBI informant Ed Becker had heard Marcello swear to kill JFK the previous year. Marcello had boasted that he'd use a "nut" in the assassination, to quickly take the blame. In Lee Harvey Oswald, Marcello had a near-perfect patsy, since the seemingly pro-Castro Oswald was involved with both Naval Intelligence and the CIA. Since early October, Oswald had been living alone in Dallas, away from his family. He was probably told to do that because it would make it easier for him to make preparations for another attempt at getting into Cuba. In reality, having him live away from his family made it easier to manipulate him in the days before the attempts to assassinate JFK in Chicago, Tampa, and Dallas. Now Oswald was also being linked to Tampa and Gilberto Lopez.

A Secret Service report says that Dallas Secret Service agent "William Patterson" was told by Dallas FBI agent James Hosty that "Oswald had contacted two known subversives about two weeks before the assassination."[5]

This report has never been clearly explained, and was part of a little-known Secret Service attempt to reopen the Warren Commission investigation. But prior to the Tampa attempt, there are reports that Oswald was in Tampa, meeting with members of the Fair Play for Cuba Committee, whom the FBI would certainly call "subversives."[6] The supposed Oswald trip to Tampa can't be dated precisely, but most reports place it somewhere in the few weeks leading up to the day before the November 18 Tampa attempt. Whether Oswald was really in Tampa or not isn't important to the Mafia plot. What is important is that one or more informants reported that Oswald was in Tampa meeting with people from the Fair Play for Cuba Committee, which was linked to Gilberto Lopez, the Tampa patsy. By linking Oswald to Lopez, Oswald's connections to C-Day would force a government cover-up if Lopez were blamed for JFK's death.

Hosty was the Dallas FBI agent assigned to Oswald, and he had earlier talked twice with Oswald's wife Marina, who no longer lived with Oswald and only saw him on most weekends. If Dallas FBI agent Hosty said that Oswald was contacting "two known subversives about two weeks before" JFK's death, that would be around November 8. Four days later, on November 12, 1963, Oswald himself went to Hosty's Dallas FBI office and left a note for him. This incident was covered up at the time and from the Warren Commission, and was later the subject of a Senate investigation. Author Larry Hancock has researched all the available documentation and interviewed Agent Hosty. Hancock writes that after JFK's death, "Agent Hosty was ordered to destroy" Oswald's note. "Hosty did so and made no mention of the note in any of his official reports or statements. In addition . . . the FBI actually had (a partial copy of) Lee Oswald's personal notebook retyped . . . to remove a note regarding a contact between Hosty and Oswald." "Agent Hosty also" told Dallas police "Officer Jack Revill on November 22 . . . that Oswald . . . had been under observation. When Revill protested that the information had not been shared with the Dallas police intelligence unit, he was reminded of the FBI policy forbidding sharing of information pertaining to espionage."[7]

The last comment sheds additional light on Oswald's relationship with the FBI, since Oswald was under tight surveillance by Naval Intelligence, which sometimes used assets of the CIA, FBI, and other agencies to help with that surveillance. However, Oswald was not an FBI informant per se, and poor Dallas FBI agent Hosty seems to have been left out of the loop as to what Oswald was really up to. (Which was actually positive for Naval Intelligence and the CIA, since any unusual treatment of Oswald or Marina by Hosty could have tipped off KGB agents who might have been considering contacting the two.) Even some New Orleans FBI agents may have known more than Hosty, since they at least had ex-FBI supervisor Guy Banister who could fill them in on an informal basis.

Even the Senate investigation couldn't pin down the contents of the note Oswald left for Hosty, since it was ordered destroyed right after JFK's assassination. Hosty said it was along the lines of "stop bothering my wife, talk to me if you need to," while the secretary said it was more ominous, like a threat to "blow up" the FBI office. We believe the note may have been an attempt by Oswald to keep Hosty from "blowing" Oswald's carefully crafted image and his role in the upcoming Cuban operation. Oswald's willingness to go into the FBI office shows that he had been perfectly willing to talk to Hosty directly, if Hosty had been in the office—hardly the act of a lone assassin who had kept the FBI from finding out where he lived. But it is consistent with a frustrated Naval Intelligence and CIA asset who knows that his upcoming "mission" to Cuba might be jeopardized by Hosty's actions. Because the FBI had no official role in C-Day, or any of the other CIA anti-Castro plots, Agent Hosty had no way of knowing that he might be interfering.

Oswald was anxious because all his years of undercover work were about to pay off. Hancock cites FBI reports with evidence that on November 9, 1963, "Oswald test drove a new car from the Downtown Lincoln-Mercury dealership, gave his name and stated he would soon have enough money to buy the car."[8] While this incident has been known to historians for years, British researcher Ian Griggs compiled surprising evidence from other FBI reports supporting the idea that Oswald thought he would be getting a significant amount of money soon and buying his first car. In an FBI interview with Marina Oswald only released in October 1995, Marina states that "she had insisted on several occasions that Oswald buy a car but he objected that he did not have sufficient money to buy it. . . ." Obviously, she's responding to concerns that the FBI had raised about Oswald buying a car, showing that the FBI took Oswald's actions seriously. The woman Marina and the children were living with, Ruth Hyde Paine, said that "on "Saturday, November 9, 1963," she "took Marina and Lee Oswald in my station wagon to the Texas Automobile Drivers Bureau in the Oak Cliff section of Dallas, Texas, to enable Lee Oswald to make application for an automobile driver's learner permit," but it was closed. Griggs also cites a report that Lee "returned to the Automobile License Bureau the following Saturday [16th] but although 'he had arrived before closing time [it was] still too late to get in because there was a long line ahead of him.'" There was other testimony about Oswald learning how to drive, talking to a co-worker about taking a driver's test, and visiting an insurance office to see about buying "automobile liability insurance."9

Oswald's well-documented interest in buying a car is completely at odds with the idea that he was a lone Communist nut getting ready to sacrifice his life to kill JFK. But it is consistent with someone who believes he will soon be coming into a good deal of money. It fits with Oswald's long-overlooked speech from Warren Commission files that we cited in Part II, seemingly written to be given as part of his speaking tour after his "big reveal." Oswald no doubt envisioned the same lucrative speaking tour his idol Herbert Philbrick and other undercover Communists for the FBI had been rewarded with after their years of undercover work. For Oswald to be making plans to get a car in Dallas also shows that Oswald thought his big payday was coming soon, and that he was not facing yet another long, deep cover assignment. He must have been told he would be going to Cuba soon, via Mexico City, but that his assignment would be over relatively quickly. That's consistent with Oswald being an asset for C-Day, which was planned to happen in a month or less. Oswald would not have been told much about C-Day, only that he was going into Cuba in support of some very important, US-backed action against Castro. In reality, once Oswald was in Cuba, he could have been used for any of the CIA plans against Castro.

The CIA's plots against Castro in November 1963 included not only C-Day (AMWORLD), but also AMTRUNK, Cubela (AMLASH), the CIA-Mafia plots, and QJWIN. A CIA memo based on information from early November 1963 shows that a US asset with a Russian connection like Oswald (or Gilberto Lopez, or even Miguel Casas Saez) would be useful to take the fall for any of those plots. The CIA memo shows the friction between Castro and Russia at the time, and Castro's worries that something is afoot that might result in a revolt. With so many CIA plots in action—especially AMTRUNK, which involved several Cuban officials looking for higher Cuban officials willing to stage a coup—it's not surprising that Castro's effective intelligence service had an inkling that something was brewing.

The information in the CIA memo is dated November 6, 1963, but it was sent later—and wasn't disseminated within the CIA until much later. The memo's subject is "Fears by Fidel Castro relative to an internal . . . revolt." The source of the information is a "Cuban who was closely associated with the 26 of July Movement," the movement that included Che Guevara. The memo says that in "the early part of November 1963, Fidel Castro, during the course of a private conversation . . . expressed his fear of the possibility of 'commando insurrections' which might take place in large scale in Cuba, as the Cuban economy was such that he could not maintain a state of military alert for a long time." The CIA memo states that "to negate this possibility, Castro was undertaking an intensive propaganda campaign to give confidence to his troops and to limit the occurrence of any internal uprising."[10]

In addition to a possible revolt, Castro was also concerned about handling the public-relations fallout from all the news reports about his problems with the Soviet Union. The CIA memo says that "Fidel Castro admitted to 'some difference' between Cuba and the Soviet Union, but explained that the two countries had . . . an agreement for a controlled release of news relative to such difference and thereby win some time." Like a consummate politician or corporate PR expert, Castro was trying to control the flow of news about his difficulties with Russia.[11] Such efforts were needed because in just a couple of weeks, the *New York Times* would have a front-page story headlined "Political strains develop" between Cuba and Russia, saying that that "conclusion [was] reached in high Government quarters here on the basis of the available intelligence estimates." Those "intelligence estimates" may well have included the CIA information we just cited. The *Times* went on to say that "Castro irritated Moscow with his expressions of friendship toward Communist China."[12] Castro's calculated ploy to play Russia against China had resulted in many similar stories the world over, giving the CIA an opportunity to divert the blame for Castro's death away from the US. If the person blamed for Castro's death were seen as a Russian sympathizer, it would be believable in the eyes of the world, given the recent strains between Castro and Russia.

A patsy for Castro's death who could be painted as a Russian sympathizer would also deal with another critical problem. The CIA memo mentioned above cited their source in Cuba as saying that "according to Fidel Castro . . . in early November [1963], the bulk of the Soviet equipment was still under Soviet control and would be used (by the Soviets?) [question mark in original] if necessary."[13] Blaming Castro's death on a Russian sympathizer was the only way to instantly neutralize the thousands of Russians—and all their equipment—that remained in Cuba. The coup leader may have had a real Russian patsy in mind, but it's likely that the CIA was leaving nothing to chance, preparing its own. Oswald would fit the bill for the CIA, as would

Tampa's Gilberto Lopez (whose brother was studying in Russia), or even Miguel Casas Saez (who had learned Russian in Cuba from Russian instructors). The irony is those very things also helped to make them effect patsies for the Mafia, to take the blame for JFK's death.

Almost like clockwork, the CIA received a report about the enigmatic "Cuban agent" Miguel Casas Saez on November 5, 1963, just three days after the Chicago attempt. The CIA would receive another report about Saez three days before the Tampa attempt, from a CIA asset working for David Morales.[14] Like the earlier CIA reports about Saez, these were always one step behind the elusive Cuban—but their real purpose seems to have been to ensure that the thinking behind the Cuban Contingency Plans was put into effect after JFK's death, to invoke a veil of secrecy to protect C-Day (and possibly also prompt an invasion of Cuba).

A week after the Chicago attempt, plans for the next attempt to kill JFK, in Tampa on November 18, were in full swing. On November 9, 1963, someone who knew of the plot—and traveled in the same circles as Guy Banister—was talking to a government informant about it and was able to describe the plot with remarkable accuracy.

THE PLAN FOR TAMPA—AND DALLAS AND CHICAGO—IS DESCRIBED TO AN INFORMANT

Just nine days before the Tampa assassination attempt, a "rightwing extremist" named Joseph Milteer told a Miami police informant about a plan "to assassinate the President with a high-powered rifle from a tall building."[15] The House Select Committee on Assassinations confirms that the description was taped at the time, though the tape was never provided to the Warren Commission.[16] While known to historians since the 1970s, the full significance of the plan was not clear to Congressional investigators, since they were never told about the Tampa attempt. The plan describes what was supposed to happen in Tampa, and also matches the Chicago attempt seven days earlier and what would happen in Dallas in less than two weeks. In other words, it is a description of the basic plan the Mafia bosses had developed to use in all three cities. Milteer had ties to associates of Guy Banister, and even got two secretive payments totaling $7,000 just weeks before Jack Ruby and David Ferrie got the same amount.[17]

The following description of the plan by ardent racist Joseph Milteer is compiled from the actual November 9, 1963 tape that was provided to the Secret Service and FBI three days later: Milteer said on the tape that once JFK was assassinated "with a high-powered rifle from a tall building," authorities "wouldn't leave any stone unturned." So, to divert attention from the real assassins, the plotters will make sure authorities "will pick up somebody within hours afterwards . . . just to throw the public off." As for how the assassins would have gotten their weapons into the high building they planned to shoot from, Milteer says you can "disassemble a gun, you don't have to take a gun up there [in one piece], you can take it up in pieces, all those guns . . . you can take them apart." While in one place the sniper's nest is referred to as being planned for an "office building" (like the Texas School Book Depository in Dallas), at another point Milteer says "somebody could be in a hotel room across the way there, and pick him off just like" that. In Tampa, authorities worried that JFK would be shot from a hotel room, since his motorcade had a hard left turn in front of the tallest building in Tampa at the time, the Floridian Hotel.[18]

After JFK was killed, but before Oswald was shot by Ruby, Milteer told Miami police informant William Somersett that "Oswald hasn't said anything and he will not say anything." When the informant asked "Why do you think that?," Milteer said "He will just not say anything, and nobody has any worry." Milteer soon added that he and his far-right associates "had no worry as to being exposed, because this group that this Oswald belonged to which was pro-Castro had been promptly infiltrated, and of course, money had been put into [the] right hands, furnished to the right people to do the job without throwing anything on" Milteer and far-right extremists (a group that could include Guy Banister). Later, Milteer warned the informant that "We are not under no [sic] circumstances to give the impression to our people that we had infiltrated this Oswald pro-Castro organization and had the job done."[19] Milteer's ties to associates of Guy Banister explain how he seemed to have a fairly good idea of how the Fair Play for Cuba Committee (FPCC) had been used to frame Oswald. However, as we soon document, the plotters also used the Tampa chapter of the FPCC to help set up the patsy there, Gilberto Lopez.

Somersett, the Miami police informant, told authorities that Milteer "knows the people in Miami or New Orleans" involved with Oswald's FPCC chapter, and "that is where the infiltration was made into" Oswald's "group, it was either Miami or New Orleans." It was New Orleans, where Guy Banister was helping to orchestrate Oswald's highly publicized, one-man FPCC chapter. Milteer said it "had been infiltrated by" right-wing extremists who "arranged from there to have the execution carried out, and drop the responsibility right into the laps of the Communists, their association, or Castro." That's an accurate description of how right-wing extremists Guy Banister and David Ferrie, both working for Carlos Marcello, tried to pin JFK's assassination on Oswald and Lopez, who appeared to be pro-Castro affiliates of the FPCC. Milteer made it clear that despite what he might say in public, he knew that JFK's murder was not a Communist plot and "that Oswald was not connected with Moscow, or any big communist leaders." Based on what Milteer told him, the Miami police informant said that "the agreement was reached" about the JFK assassination plot "probably in New Orleans or in Miami, maybe New York, maybe Chicago." Of course, Marcello was based in New Orleans, Trafficante had a base in Miami, and Rosselli's mob family controlled Chicago. As for New York, that was a base for Michel Victor Mertz, Rolando Masferrer, and mob boss Tony Provenzano. As to the main place the JFK conspiracy was based, the informant Somersett said "from the impression that I got from" Milteer, "this conspiracy originated in New Orleans, and probably some in Miami. . . ."[20]

Milteer knew other things about JFK's assassination, such as "that this has been in progress for some time." By November 1963, it had been more than a year since Carlos Marcello first revealed to an FBI informant that JFK would be assassinated, to end the threat from Bobby Kennedy. Milteer seemed to know the significance of that as well, telling Somersett that after the assassination, "Bobby Kennedy . . . had no more power in Washington." Milteer added "I think you will see that Bobby Kennedy will resign, and that Johnson will put another Attorney General in"—which is exactly what happened.[21]

Milteer added, "Of course there was a lot of money" involved in the assassination, "and it came not only from the" far-right extremists, "but from men who could afford to contribute." When Somersett asked more specifically where the big money came from, Milteer wouldn't say, and only "mentioned the name Leander H. Perez (Sr.) . . . a judge down there . . . right outside of New Orleans . . . this Milteer seems to be a friend to him, or to know him very well, and several other people in the state of Louisiana and Texas."[22] Leander Perez, the political boss of two parishes (counties) outside New Orleans, had several close ties to Guy Banister. Some, easily documented from New Orleans newspapers, put the two men together at a far-right political rally in May 1963, which later resulted in Banister being appointed to run as a racist elector in a district controlled by Leander. In addition, Banister's mistress/secretary in November 1963 was close to Leander.[23] Banister was low on funds by 1963, so the big money Milteer referred to probably came from Banister's employer, Carlos Marcello, laundered through the far-right political machine of Perez.

Milteer himself may have gotten some of that money. According to an investigation by *Miami* magazine, Milteer opened a savings account under an assumed name in Utah "on July 31, 1963." There is no evidence that Milteer, who was wealthy, ever used an assumed name for any other accounts. "There were only two other deposits" to the secret Utah account, "one of $5,000 and another of $2,000 on August 20 and September 24 [1963] respectively."[24] That totals $7,000—just four weeks before Jack Ruby got his $7,000 in Chicago from a Hoffa associate and five weeks before David Ferrie deposited $7,093 from a Marcello associate.

Banister likely would have used Milteer in a supporting role for the JFK plot, not as a shooter or major planner. As with most of those in the JFK plot, Milteer himself would have made a logical person to take some of the blame if needed, given his far-right credentials and public anti-Kennedy stance. Milteer seemed to have good insight into how Banister had framed Oswald using the Fair Play for Cuba Committee, so perhaps Milteer had had a hand in manipulating Oswald or one of the other parties. Milteer was from the small south-Georgia town of Quitman and often made trips to Atlanta. Milteer knew the Klan leader Oswald (or someone posing as Oswald) visited in Atlanta on his way to Chicago in the late summer of 1963. Also on that trip, Oswald left a pistol at a Marietta Holiday Inn, which was just a few miles from the home of another associate of Milteer, notorious racist J. B. Stoner. Since Oswald was on his way to Chicago, and Milteer traveled widely for far-right extremist causes, Milteer would have also been ideal to manipulate the Chicago patsy, Thomas Vallee, a far-right extremist himself. Somersett had cited Chicago as one of the places Milteer implied that the JFK plot was discussed.

In his talks with Somersett, Milteer had all the basics of the JFK plot correct. He had some details and speculation wrong, and Milteer seems to have gotten his information from a far-right extremist—such as Banister—so Milteer seemed to view it as a far-right plot. *Miami* magazine described Milteer as "a wealthy rabble-rousing racist" who "devoted his life to right-wing causes, belonging to at least four ultra-conservative organizations" including "The National State's Rights Party" and "The Dixie Klan." Milteer's literature "blasted Kennedy, Jews, Communists, the UN"—all targets of the John Birch

Society.[25] Congressional investigators noted that Milteer had traveled extensively throughout the United States and had associates who were suspected of having committed violent acts, including the bombing of a Birmingham, Alabama, church in which four young girls had been killed."[26]

Miami magazine noted that "the FBI in its documents about the incident called [William] Somersett 'a source who has furnished reliable information in the past.'"[27] Somersett had "extensive right-wing political ties" and "was a Klansman," but he didn't like violence and offered his services as an informant to Miami police after a series of Miami bombings. Though the Miami police didn't know it, Somersett "had worked for the FBI, off and on, for about a decade."[28] Somersett first met Milteer "in April 1963" in "New Orleans" where both men had gone "for a meeting of the Congress of Freedom party . . . a confederation of right-wing political groups."[29] Milteer seemed confident that he could trust Somersett, since they traveled in the same far-right circles. Somersett told authorities that Milteer "doesn't seem to be suspicious, because he told me that he has never been arrested, he has never been brought in by anyone or questioned about any activities." That's probably because the FBI had a very inconsistent record in dealing with far-right radicals in the early and mid-1960s, sometimes reflecting the racist attitudes of its director, J. Edgar Hoover.

After having Somersett's November 9, 1963 tape of his conversation with Milteer about plans for JFK's assassination transcribed, the Miami police gave copies to the FBI. The Miami police knew that JFK's visit to their city was less than nine days away at that point, so on November 12, 1963, Miami police intelligence officers met with Secret Service agents and gave them a copy of the transcript.[30] Unfortunately, the Miami police were apparently not told about the recent Chicago attempt against JFK, so they didn't realize that Milteer's comments were also related to that. On the tape, after Milteer says JFK will be shot "from an office building with a high-powered rifle," informant Somersett seems incredulous, asking "They are really going to try to kill him?" Milteer makes it clear that he is not guessing or speculating, saying "Oh, yeah, it is in the works." Somersett then says "I don't know how them Secret Service agents cover all them office buildings everywhere he is going. Do you know whether they do that or not?" Milteer replies, "Well, if they have any suspicion, they do that, of course. But without suspicion, chances are that they wouldn't."[31] Milteer had no idea, as he spoke those words, that he was giving authorities all the suspicion they needed.

After hearing Milteer talk about the plan to assassinate JFK, the Secret

Service and FBI both swung into action, although—for some reason—neither agency put Milteer under surveillance or tapped his phones. (Coupled with the lack of action against Milteer after JFK's assassination—when the FBI accepted Milteer's statement that he hadn't threatened JFK, even though the FBI had tapes and interviews proving otherwise—and the fact that Milteer had never been arrested or even questioned about his activities, this raises the question of whether Milteer had some type of protection as an informer or asset, perhaps through Banister or some agency.) An Atlanta FBI agent in 1963, Don Adams, said that "Two weeks prior to the assassination, I got a call to investigate a plot against the President." According to a newspaper article, Adams "was assigned to develop a background on a Joseph A. Milteer, a right-wing radical involved in the plot. Adams turned the report over to the Atlanta office and the Secret Service."[32]

The FBI and Secret Service also got wind of the plot Milteer was talking about through a different informant, shortly after they got Somersett's information from the Miami police. Milteer was part of the far-right National States Rights Party, and the FBI learned that "a militant group of the National States Rights Party plans to assassinate the President." This informant had apparently gotten his information second- or third-hand, probably from Milteer or one of Milteer's associates, during his "travels throughout the country" as "a member of the Ku Klux Klan." As such, the informant told the FBI he didn't think JFK's assassination was "planned for the near future." The FBI thought this informant was just trying "to make some sort of deal with them" to reduce his criminal car theft charges, so the FBI told the Secret Service "no information developed that would indicate any danger to the President in the near future or during his trip to Texas."[33]

Before Dallas, JFK would be in great danger in Tampa, as well as in Miami. However, there was no big public motorcade scheduled for Miami, as there was for Tampa. Over the years, perhaps because of the Milteer tapes, a rumor developed that a JFK Miami motorcade was cancelled, but the House Select Committee on Assassinations (HSCA) could find no evidence of that.[34] However, the HSCA was never told about the Tampa threat on the same day as Miami, so they never investigated any links between the Milteer threat and Tampa. Since the Milteer-Somersett conversation was being taped in Miami, it was assumed that that was the city Milteer was talking about, when his remarks really apply to Tampa.

The HSCA stated that the "Secret Service failed to follow up fully" on the Milteer threat.[35] But it's possible that the Milteer threat was pursued more fully than the released documents indicate. For example, the background material on Milteer that FBI Agent Don Adams turned over to the Secret Service has never surfaced. Researcher Vince Palamara has found evidence that a Secret Service agent may have been tasked with "monitoring mortal threats to JFK's life made in the month of November, and" this "was covered up after" JFK's death.[36] Perhaps the increased scrutiny after the Milteer threat surfaced helped authorities uncover the threat in Tampa linked to "organized crime" and the Fair Play for Cuba Committee. Of course, they were really all the same plot. That's why more material about the Milteer threat may have wound up in the suppressed files about the Tampa attempt, files that were withheld from the HSCA and which the Secret Service "destroyed" instead of turning them over to the JFK Assassination Records Review Board. The public only learned about the Milteer threat several years after it happened because it had originally been uncovered by Miami Police Department, which had no role in protecting C-Day or the CIA's other anti-Castro plots.

Mid-November 1963: The President Prepares a Message for the Coup Leader

WHILE MILTEER WAS DESCRIBING THE JFK assassination plot that was attempted in Chicago and slated to be used again in Tampa, CIA officials were unaware that the same plotters were using several CIA operations in their plot. Key CIA officials like Richard Helms, Desmond FitzGerald, and David Atlee Phillips were probably too busy with C-Day and their other operations to realize what the Mafia was really up to. David Morales's close personal and working relationship with Johnny Rosselli makes it difficult to tell if he was equally distracted, or if he was actively or passively assisting Rosselli in the JFK plot.

In the aftermath of Chicago, the key CIA officials were probably concerned with why they always seemed to be one step behind shadowy Cuban Miguel Casas Saez, and what connections the CIA may have had to the "dissident Cuban group" involved in the Chicago attempt. They may have been trying to make sure Thomas Vallee's arrest didn't blow any of their Cuban exile operations. Meanwhile, Johnny Rosselli continued his work on the CIA-Mafia plots to kill Castro, meaning that the CIA would have assumed that Rosselli's meetings with people like Jack Ruby and Charles Nicoletti were part of that operation. Expenses for CIA work with Rosselli had been reimbursed under the QJWIN assassin-recruiter program, which also seems to have been co-opted by the Mafia for the JFK plot.

David Morales had a key role that has never received attention in the CIA's operation with Rolando Cubela (AMLASH). While the CIA's contact with Cubela was known generally to at least one of Bobby Kennedy's Cuban sub-committees, the assassination aspect of the Cubela plan was known only to Helms, FitzGerald, and a few others in the CIA—not even to CIA Director McCone. Depending on who you believe, either the CIA was pressing Cubela to kill Castro using high-powered rifles that the CIA would provide, or Cubela was begging the CIA to give him the scoped rifles to kill Castro. (Even Congressional and internal CIA reports say that "FitzGerald's recollection . . . conflicts with the case officer's sworn testimony" about Cubela.[1]) Regardless, it's now clear that as Miami CIA operations chief, Morales would have handled the operation designed to provide the "rifles and telescopic sights" to Cubela, as part of a weapons drop in Cuba.

In later Senate testimony, Miami CIA station chief Ted Shackley—Morales's immediate superior in Miami—admitted that "this operation often was tasked to get weapons into Cuba," but "he could not recall being tasked to get rifles and telescopic sights into Cuba." However, the Senate Church Committee found that "the documentary record reveals, however, that the" CIA's Miami "station was tasked to supply the explosives, rifles, and telescopic sights to" Cubela.[2] Perhaps Morales's boss was evasive in his testimony about the rifles for Cubela because he really didn't remember the rifles—because Morales didn't tell him about them. Or, by the time Shackley testified in 1976, he may have suspected that there had been some problem with Morales's actions. Regardless, the fact is that Morales was in charge of getting high-powered rifles to Cubela, at the same time Morales's friend Johnny Rosselli was part of a plot that involved shooting JFK with high-powered rifles. While the rifles eventually provided to Cubela after JFK's assassination were Belgian FAL rifles, there is no way of knowing if they were originally going to be M-1's, rebuilt Mannlicher-Carcanos, or whatever rifle was going to be used against JFK in Tampa.

In mid-November 1963, "FitzGerald had told the case officer" for Cubela "that he was authorized to tell" Cubela "that the rifles, telescopic sights, and explosives would be provided." But the CIA admits those weren't the only assassination weapons the CIA was going to provide Cubela." The Senate Church Committee also found that in mid-November, Cubela's "case officer also waited at [CIA] Headquarters while a ballpoint pen was fashioned with a needle on it which could be used to inject a lethal dose of poison." However, "the pen proved difficult to fashion and it was not ready until a few days before the November 22 meeting" between Cubela and his case officer in Paris.[3] As we will document, the timing of that fateful November 22, 1963 meeting wasn't dictated by Cubela, but by someone in the CIA who would have dealt with David Morales.

The CIA was also prodding the AMTRUNK agents to produce results and find Cuban military leaders willing to stage a coup, no doubt in case something happened to the C-Day coup leader. AMTRUNK had been in operation since its first meeting in February 1963, which included *New York Times* journalist Tad Szulc (who came up with the idea) and David Morales.[4] Though Szulc was given the internal CIA code name of AMCAPE-1, he had very little to do with the plan after that, the plan being run by CIA officers like Morales.[5] CIA files say that on November 9, 1963, the CIA sent a radio message to "the AMTRUNK's in Cuba" and "asked if they had developed any leads into the higher echelons of the Rebel Army, and who at higher levels appeared to be good prospects for recruitment." The CIA also hinted at C-Day/AMWORLD to the AMTRUNK agents in Cuba, by telling them about rumors that persons in top positions of the Cuban government "were dissatisfied to the point that they may have been thinking of plotting against Fidel."[6]

The Kennedys and the CIA had worked hard to keep any hints of C-Day out of the press, so they must have been worried when the following article appeared in the *Miami Herald* on November 10, 1963. Detailed earlier in Part I, the large front-page article was headlined "War in Cuba: Fidel Battling an 'Iceberg,'" and said "A secret war is being waged against Fidel Castro" but "the full size and scope of the war has not been revealed." So "the war then is viewed like an iceberg—the part that shows only hints at the part that doesn't." The author, Al Burt, got information from Manuel Artime which allowed him to say that "the war stepped up its pace in the last three months" and "the US . . . is getting far less credit than deserved from those critics who say nothing is being done about Cuba." The article was in response to two recent events, one being an article two days earlier in the *Miami Herald*, headlined "Kennedy Ducking Cuba Problem, GOP Says." The other event behind Burt's article was probably JFK's upcoming trip to Miami, slated for November 18, 1963.

While JFK's Miami visit wouldn't have a long, public motorcade like Tampa (JFK would be taken to the hotel by helicopter), there would be an airport arrival and the probability of crowds around the hotel where JFK would be speaking. Because of the Bay of Pigs and JFK's clampdown in recent months on most non–C-Day exile groups, security for JFK's Miami trip was a big worry. It's possible that Burt's article was meant to convey to exiles in Miami that JFK really was taking action against Castro. But it was a delicate balancing act to get JFK credit for action against Castro while not blowing C-Day—and someone in the administration may have felt that the information

Artime or his men leaked to Al Burt went too far. There would be no more articles hinting at C-Day while JFK was President.

As JFK got ready for his Miami trip, his big Tampa motorcade, and trips to Houston, Fort Worth, and Dallas after that, he had his hands full with C-Day, the Cold War, and dealing with the aftermath of the coup in Vietnam. It's easy to see why C-Day had been delegated to Bobby, but there were still aspects of C-Day that JFK would have to discuss with Bobby and others, such as Joint Chiefs Chairman General Maxwell Taylor and DIA head General Joseph Carroll. JFK had an Oval Office taping system like Richard Nixon and Lyndon Johnson. But meetings about C-Day—as well as dealing with the fallout from the cancellation of his Chicago trip, the threat there, and discussions about the threat in Tampa—may explain why a Senate Church Committee counsel found that there were no tapes from the last two weeks of JFK's administration.[7]

JFK and Bobby had their hands full with recent developments that would impact C-Day, such as the November 7, 1963 *New York Times* story saying "Khrushchev warns US that attack on Cuba will lead to war. . . ."[8] The stakes were high for C-Day, and a wrong move could spark an international confrontation. It's easy to see why being able to blame Castro's death on someone besides US-backed exiles or the US military was so important. Harry Williams said he wasn't directly involved with them, but plans to find someone to take the blame for Castro's death "were active . . . I am sure it happened."[9] Since Harry wasn't involved, Bobby would have needed the help of the CIA or Naval Intelligence, or both. Oswald was involved with both agencies, and FBI reports on Tampa's Gilberto Lopez were routinely forwarded to Naval Intelligence.[10] To maintain the concept of "plausible deniability" to protect the President, it's doubtful that Bobby would have told JFK any details about that part of C-Day, though JFK certainly would have wanted assurance from Bobby that Castro's death would not obviously be the work of the US.

JFK had still not given up on finding a peaceful solution with Castro, before C-Day. On November 6, 1963, a meeting of one of Bobby's Cuban subcommittees—the "Special Group"—was told that "it has come to the attention of the White House that Castro would like to have a talk designed to bring about some arrangement with the US." This was an update on the attempts by Special UN Envoy William Attwood, sparked by journalist Lisa Howard, that were detailed in Part I. The Special Group decided to put off making a decision, to study the matter further—but some of the members didn't realize the urgency of the situation because they didn't know about C-Day, which was just over three weeks away.[11] So JFK and Bobby had Attwood pursue his efforts, though little progress was being made. As noted in Part I, in Cuba the French journalist Jean Daniel had been waiting since late October to see Fidel Castro. Daniel carried yet another message to Castro from JFK, trying to spark one last attempt at a peaceful solution to the Cuban problem.

But C-Day was almost ready. The first payment of $50,000 had been delivered to the coup leader, and one of his relatives was under CIA observation and "protection" in a foreign country. With C-Day less than three weeks away, and so much compartmentalization among the various agencies and subcommittees—where some knew about C-Day and some didn't—a meeting of key Washington officials was needed to keep things on track. This led to the unusual meeting on November 12, 1963, presided over by JFK, that was detailed in Part I. Some of the fourteen participants knew about C-Day, while others only knew generally about AMTRUNK and the nonassassination aspects of Cubela; but even for those in the latter group, the presence of JFK would signal the high stakes involved.

Of the fourteen officials at the November 12 meeting, the CIA was represented by four: Director McCone, Helms, FitzGerald, and one person usually not at such meetings—Miami CIA station chief Ted Shackley, Morales's boss.[12] Shackley's presence gave Morales a way to know what was happening at the highest reaches of government—something that the heavy-drinking, sometimes loose-lipped Morales could have shared with his drinking buddy, Johnny Rosselli. Morales already knew much of what the CIA men might say, but the comments of people like Joint Chiefs Chairman General Maxwell Taylor would provide a perspective on military operations that Morales—and Rosselli—could find useful. At the big meeting, FitzGerald cautiously shared information about C-Day exile leaders Manuel Artime and Manolo Ray, though a CIA "official involved in" the Cubela operation confirmed to Evan Thomas that "FitzGerald consciously played down the [Cubela] operation" in the meeting.[13]

A MISSED OPPORTUNITY TO PREVENT THE ASSASSINATION OF JFK?

While the caution displayed by FitzGerald and others at the big November 12 meeting helped preserve the secrecy of C-Day, a smaller meeting at the same time shows how the US government was too compartmentalized when it came to protecting JFK from assassination. Also on November 12, 1963, one of Bobby's secretive groups—the "Subcommittee on Cuban Subversion" of the "Interdepartmental Coordinating Committee on Cuban Affairs"—had a crucial meeting about assassinations. The meeting was a "Status Report on assigned Contingency Papers," what we call the Cuba Contingency Plans to protect the secrecy of C-Day and other anti-Castro operations in case Castro found out about them and retaliated. As described in Part I, the meeting discussed Contingency Plans to deal with "attempts at . . . assassination of American officials." But just like their plans to deal with retaliatory sabotage by Castro, those present decided only to focus on the possibility of Castro assassinating a US official in "Latin America."[14] Earlier, they had decided that an assassination attempt against a US official inside the US was "unlikely."

The memo is heavily censored, so it's difficult to determine the exact list of all those who attended, but we have spoken to one former Kennedy administration official who was part of the planning process—who told us that they weren't told crucial information. He confirms that they had not been told about the Chicago attempt at all. They had also not been told about the reported presence of possible Cuban agent Miguel Casas Saez in Chicago on the day before JFK's visit there. Likewise, they had not been told anything about the recent reports, from the Milteer informant, of a plot to assassinate JFK. While individual members of the subcommittee might have known about one or more of those events through their own agencies, it was not brought up at the meeting and shared with the others. If the whole subcommittee had known about any or all of those things, it could have had a tremendous impact on the Cuba Contingency Planning and the security for JFK in his upcoming Tampa and Dallas motorcades. Then again, the former Kennedy administration official who was our source had not been told about C-Day— he only knew in general about the nonassassination aspects of the CIA's Cubela operation. With so many crucial pieces of information being withheld from him, he didn't see any particular urgency in their planning or that they should be looking at possible assassination attempts within the US.[15]

JOHN AND ROBERT KENNEDY SEND A MESSAGE TO THE C-DAY LEADER IN CUBA
When JFK was targeted for assassination in Tampa on November 18, 1963, JFK was also set to deliver a crucial message to the C-Day coup leader in Cuba. That high Cuban official and hero of the Revolution would hear words of support from JFK himself, thanks to the Kennedys' savvy use of the news media. John and Bobby Kennedy made remarkable use of the media in

planning C-Day. We've already noted how stories were planted and squelched, to cut off unwanted publicity and get out information they felt was important. Even before JFK's personal message would be delivered in his own words to the coup leader, the Kennedys were preparing for the successful aftermath of C-Day.

The Kennedy's PR offensive after C-Day would include a book and a prime-time network TV special. The book was *The Bay of Pigs* by Haynes Johnson, written in conjunction with Harry Williams, Manuel Artime, and two other leaders of that failed invasion. According to author Gus Russo, Haynes "Johnson had been hand-picked by Bobby Kennedy to chronicle the Bay of Pigs story."[16] An unconfirmed account says that some of the book was written—or at least conceptualized—on weekends at Bobby Kennedy's Hickory Hill estate in Virginia. In Bobby Kennedy's Oral History at the John F. Kennedy Presidential Library, Bobby says that "some of my people in the Department of Justice . . . are working on" the book. Bobby also confirms that he read the original manuscript of the book before publication, and considered it accurate.[17] In the Introduction to the book, Haynes Johnson says that "the manuscript was completed before the assassination of President Kennedy."

But why would politically savvy Bobby want a book about JFK's biggest disaster to come out at the start of the 1964 campaign? The answer is that, to Bobby, the *Bay of Pigs* book wouldn't bring unwanted attention to a political embarrassment—it would end with JFK's greatest triumph. The book was apparently held for publication until July 1964, but had JFK not died, the already completed book would surely have been published much sooner.[18] If C-Day had been a success, it probably would have included an afterward highlighting the fact that the book's co-authors like Harry Williams and Manuel Artime were now part of the new Provisional Government in a free Cuba.

At the same time the book was being completed in November 1963, the Kennedys and Harry Williams were helping with a prime-time TV special called "Cuba: Bay of Pigs." It was slated to run on NBC on December 3, 1963. Now, the third anniversary of the Bay of Pigs wouldn't be until April 1964, and the first anniversary of the release of the Bay of Pigs prisoners wouldn't be until Christmas—so why run the special in early December? We think it was because C-Day was scheduled for December 1, 1963. If C-Day was a success, the TV show wouldn't be about a disaster, but would be a potent public relations tool about the US military operation then going on in Cuba, supporting the new Provisional Government (which would include prominent Bay of Pigs veterans). Even if C-Day failed, at least the Bay of Pigs would have been covered well before the 1964 campaign really got under way.

The members of the NBC news team that was part of the special were Chet Huntley and David Brinkley, then America's leading TV journalists. In 1963, there were only three networks, so even if the NBC *Bay of Pigs* special was third in the ratings, it would still draw viewership that would dwarf today's most popular TV series. Bobby made sure that the TV show got his personal attention and cooperation, to ensure that it would present his brother in a good light.

Harry Williams met Chet Huntley and David Brinkley in Bobby Kennedy's Virginia home. Harry and Chet Huntley immediately hit it off and became friends.[19] This would lead to Harry's call to Huntley on the afternoon of JFK's death, in which Harry passed along information that he had just received from a New Orleans Cuban exile named Alberto Fowler. As we document shortly, Fowler would shadow JFK the day before the Tampa attempt, and would later spread publicity designed to immediately convict Oswald in the eyes of the world.

As the date for C-Day drew near, the coup leader in Cuba wanted a signal, from JFK himself, that the President would back the coup after Castro had been eliminated. This led directly to key passages in the speech JFK would give in Miami on November 18, 1963, just after his Tampa motorcade. Senate investigators found a "CIA paper" citing "Kennedy's speech of November 18, 1963" which said "the CIA intended President Kennedy's speech to serve as a signal to dissident elements in Cuba that the US would support a coup . . . the paper states that Cuban dissidents 'must have solemn assurances from high level US spokesmen, especially the President, that the United States will exert its decisive influence during and immediately after the coup.'"[20] It's clear that JFK's speech was intended for the C-Day coup leader, since documents show that Rolando Cubela (AMLASH) and the Cubans in AMTRUNK weren't told about the speech until after it had been given (four days later, in the case of Cubela).[21]

The crucial paragraphs in JFK's speech have been the source of disagreement between the CIA and some in the Kennedy administration, particularly Arthur Schlesinger, Jr. In 1978—three years after the first public revelations about the CIA and Cubela, and almost fifteen years before the existence of

AMTRUNK was revealed—Schlesinger wrote that "the CIA told Cubela that Desmond FitzGerald had helped write the speech and that" one particular "passage . . . was meant as a green light for an anti-Castro coup." Schlesinger says that "Richard Goodwin, the chief author of the speech, intended to convey" support for the Attwood negotiations, not to help FitzGerald or Cubela. Schlesinger says that "a search of the JFK papers shows that Goodwin, Ralph Dungan, Bundy, Gordon Chase of Bundy's staff, and I were involved in discussions about the speech. No evidence was uncovered of any contribution from FitzGerald and the CIA."[22]

On the other hand, a Church Committee attorney told journalist Sy Hersh that "Seymour Bolton, a senior CIA officer . . . had 'carried a paragraph [to the White House] to be inserted into Kennedy's November 18 speech.'" Bolton told the attorney (around 1975) that the paragraph was "the President's signal of support for Cubela."[23] However, even the CIA's own internal report on Cubela indicates that neither Helms nor FitzGerald—nor anyone else in the CIA—had told JFK or Bobby about their discussions with Cubela regarding the assassination of Castro. Bolton, who died in 1985, had been a key assistant to Desmond FitzGerald in 1963. Recently released CIA documents show that Bolton was aware of AMWORLD (the CIA's part of C-Day)—unlike the Church Committee, which wasn't told about C-Day, which is probably why Bolton only told the committee about Cubela.

JFK aide Richard Goodwin confirmed to us that he had not been told about C-Day, and that he also didn't know about Cubela. We feel that the CIA may well have crafted the paragraph Sy Hersh described, as a signal of support for C-Day and the coup leader in Cuba. If the CIA paragraph was taken to the White House, it may well have been JFK's contribution to the speech, which wasn't finalized until the weekend (November 16–17) prior to its delivery. JFK often took a hand in his speeches, and if he gave the passage to Goodwin, Schlesinger (who didn't know about C-Day either), and the others, they may not have realized its true significance or CIA origins. As we noted earlier, Goodwin's contribution to JFK's speech was unusually well publicized in newspapers at the time.

On November 18, 1963, JFK's speech was planned to cap a well-publicized spate of activity designed to reassure the coup leader that the US Commander in Chief would stand behind him. On Saturday, November 16, JFK was scheduled to watch the submarine launch of a new Polaris missile, which would be front-page news in most Florida newspapers the following day. JFK would also have a "secret session" at MacDill Air Force Base, with the Commander of the US Strike Force Command and other military leaders. For a "secret session," it was also well publicized. In all, the missile launching, the Strike Force meeting, and the Miami speech would indicate JFK's willingness to back the C-Day coup with the full force of the US military.

The Tampa part of the trip, with four speeches and a long motorcade, was also important for JFK politically. According to one writer, JFK "needed desperately to carry Florida, a state he had lost to Richard Nixon in 1960 by only 46,776 votes out of 1,544,180 total ballots." JFK's "position in the South concerned party officials, which explains why his November schedule included trips to both Texas and Florida." Mindful of the recent Chicago threat, "the Secret Service sent an advance party one week ahead of the President," where security preparations were intense and "the motorcade route through Tampa was reviewed by the Secret Service at 3 A.M. one morning."[24]

As JFK made plans for his Florida trip, the Mafia was busy with its plan to assassinate him in Tampa. This apparently included a trip by Jack Ruby to Las Vegas, on the weekend prior to JFK's Monday Tampa motorcade. Journalist Seth Kantor notes that Ruby's trip was left out of the Warren Commission chronology for Ruby, "even though the FBI spoke to witnesses who confirmed Ruby's presence in Las Vegas."[25] Researcher Larry Hancock cites three FBI documents saying that "Jack Ruby was reported in Las Vegas on November 16" and possibly the seventeenth by two informants, one reporting to the FBI and another to the Las Vegas sheriff. "Both sources placed Ruby at the Tropicana, a hotel in which John Rosselli had originally been very much involved," along with Carlos Marcello.[26] Rosselli's biographers cite one account that "alleges that Ruby met with Rosselli during a trip he made to Las Vegas November seventeenth."[27] While FBI accounts don't show Rosselli being in Las Vegas until November 19—when the FBI lost his trail for the next seven days—Hancock cites unusual travel by Rosselli from Los Angeles to Phoenix that weekend which might have afforded Rosselli a chance to slip away to Las Vegas.[28] Investigators for the House Select Committee on Assassinations (HSCA) could find no documentation that Ruby was in Dallas on November 17.[29]

Carlos Marcello and David Ferrie were also busy plotting strategy that weekend, and John H. Davis notes that "Ferrie, by his own admission, spent the weekends of November 9, 10 and 16, 17 with Marcello at Churchill Farms."[30] Marcello was still on trial, thanks to Bobby's Justice Department prosecutors, but he had found a way to bribe a key juror to get an acquittal.

Still, that was only a short-term solution—he would soon be prosecuted for the bribe as well—so killing JFK was the only permanent solution to the ever-increasing pressure that he, Rosselli, Trafficante, and their allies faced.

The mob bosses continued to take advantage of CIA operations and personnel for their JFK plot. On November 15 (Friday), one of David Morales's AMOT informants reported still more information about the mysterious Cuban, Miguel Casas Saez, saying he was in the US on a "sabotage" mission. While there is no direct report of Saez in Tampa, he had been reported in Florida just over two weeks earlier, and his whereabouts between the Chicago and Dallas attempts is unclear.[31] Still, the report of Morales's informant seems suspect, since he got it from a sub-source who got the information from still someone else. Because it was third-hand, it appears not have attracted too much attention at most levels in the CIA—but to those who knew about C-Day and the Cuban Contingency Plans (like Desmond FitzGerald or Richard Helms), it was exactly the type of thing they'd been planning for.

It's not clear exactly what operations the CIA or David Atlee Phillips were running against the Fair Play for Cuba Committee (FPCC) in 1963, though Anthony Summers writes that "the CIA had penetrated the FPCC with its own agents," who "were supplying the" CIA "with photographs of documents and correspondence purloined secretly from FPCC files."[32] Still, the Mafia would have been well aware that in recent weeks, new Congressional hearings into the FPCC had started to get press attention. This made Oswald even more valuable to them as a patsy, and arrangements were made for Gilberto Lopez to be at a real FPCC meeting in Tampa the day before JFK's motorcade there on November 18. Even better, new FPCC hearings were scheduled for Monday the eighteenth, meaning that if the patsy in JFK's death was linked to the FPCC, journalists and the public would literally have information about the tiny, obscure group at their fingertips.

Anthony Summers points out that the witness scheduled for Monday, a young ex-serviceman named John Glenn, had many parallels to Lee Oswald. Glenn had "joined the US Air Force, where he became an intelligence operative" and "received a 'crypto' clearance and studied Russian. His career as a left-wing activist began soon after he left Air Force intelligence." Glenn "traveled to the Soviet Union" and, after his trip to Cuba, Glenn had recently returned from Europe with his fare paid by the US State Department, "just as Oswald's fare home from Russia had once been paid by the State Department." After joining the FPCC, Glenn "had tried to visit Cuba, at first by traveling through Mexico, eventually succeeding by "summer 1963." Also, "like Oswald, Glenn used a post-office box as [a] mailing address and subscribed to the *Militant* newspaper," one of the two opposing Communist newspapers Oswald is holding in the infamous backyard photos along with his mail-order rifle. Summers writes that "the result of [Glenn's] foray to Cuba" would be a well-publicized "appearance before the [House] Un-American Activities Committee, one which effectively smeared [the] Fair Play for Cuba Committee as a Communist-front organization."[33] It's not hard to imagine Oswald seeing the reports of those hearings, and imagining himself the subject of similar press attention after his next mission and his final "big reveal."

Gilberto Lopez probably had other concerns, chiefly finding a way to get back to Cuba. But Lopez also had many things in common with Oswald—such as a background that reportedly made him useful to some agency as an informant, but which would also make him a viable patsy for JFK's assassination. Lopez and his wife had both moved to Tampa from Key West in June 1963. But in August 1963, Lopez's wife moved back to Key West because of marital problems, just a few weeks before Oswald sent Marina to live in Dallas because of their marital problems.[34]

Like Oswald, many of Lopez's family and associates saw him as pro-Castro, while others saw him as anti-Castro. Like Oswald, Lopez had gotten into a fist-fight over his seemingly pro-Castro sympathies. Oswald had already been linked to Lopez, who was part of the Tampa Fair Play for Cuba Committee (FPCC) chapter. Unlike Oswald's phony one-man New Orleans chapter, Tampa had a real chapter with several members and regular meetings. According to former FBI undercover asset Joe Burton, Oswald had recently visited Tampa and met with a key member of that chapter. (A pilot like David Ferrie could have easily flown Oswald to Tampa and back on a weekend day.) *Vanity Fair* magazine confirmed from the FBI that Burton was "'a valuable and reliable source' and was paid for his services" as an informant.[35] In addition, a high Florida law enforcement source independently told us about a reported meeting in Tampa between Oswald, Lopez, and a key member of the Tampa FPCC chapter shortly before JFK's assassination.[36] The two Hispanic last names that surfaced in the Secret Service investigation of the Chicago assassination attempt match those of two close associates of Lopez.[37] One matches the name of someone linked to the Tampa FPCC, while the other is the same as a man who crossed the border at the same place and day as Oswald, when Oswald returned to Texas after his mission to Mexico City. While some of the name links might be coincidence, the bottom line is that the Mafia had a back-up fall guy, seemingly pro-Castro, linked to Oswald.

A 2003 newspaper report pointed out how Lopez might have come to the attention of the Mafia, saying that "Gilberto Policarpo Lopez, former Key West resident, worked in the construction industry in Tampa—which has had a long-established organized crime connection with Key West—before traveling to Texas at the time of the assassination. His movements and activities suggest that he was a possible participant in Trafficante's activities." We would add that based on our analysis of all the declassified Lopez documents and other research, if Lopez was manipulated by the Mafia, it was as an unwitting participant.[38]

When we interviewed Lopez's wife (they were never divorced, though she hasn't seen him since he went to Cuba in late November 1963), she said we were the first people to talk with her about the case "in a long time," since "some FBI agents" talked to her back in 1964. She called Lopez "Gilbert" and said he "was a loner," apparently very private—he never even told his wife about the brief trip he made back to Cuba in the summer of 1962, shortly before they were married. Lopez was "a painter by trade," and when she "left him in Tampa, he was working painting a big building . . . across from where they lived in Ybor City." (The small Ybor City enclave in Tampa was frequented by Santo Trafficante, since it was home to his favorite restaurant.) She echoed others interviewed by the FBI when she told us that she didn't know whether Lopez was pro- or anti-Castro, and seemed to indicate that he didn't feel strongly one way or the other. She said that Lopez had wanted to go back to Cuba very badly because of his mother, that he was worried about her and wanted to see her before she died.[39]

Lopez had no passport and little money, didn't drive, and had no car, so his desire to return to Cuba could have given someone a way to manipulate him if it would help him get to Cuba. On Sunday, November 17, Lopez's fortunes would suddenly change while he was at a Tampa FPCC meeting. According to an FBI report, Lopez, who "spoke very little English . . . was expecting [a] telephone call from Cuba that day, in order to get word on his departure for Cuba."[40] The Church Committee adds that Lopez "was at a get-together at the home of a member of the Tampa Chapter of the Fair Play for Cuba Committee . . . for some time waiting for a telephone call from Cuba which was very important. It was understood that it all depended on his getting the 'go ahead order' for him to leave the United States. He indicated he had been refused travel back to his native Cuba."[41] The part about Lopez having "been refused travel back to his native Cuba" doesn't appear in any Lopez files declassified so far (though some are heavily censored, and others withheld). Lopez's US passport had expired, but there are no indications that he had actually been "refused" at any point, which echoes Oswald's experience seven weeks earlier, when he was denied permission to travel to Cuba.

On another occasion, Lopez made it sound as if his problem in getting to Cuba was financial. Congressional investigators wrote that "in a later letter, Lopez told his wife he had received financial assistance for his trip to Cuba from an organization in Tampa. His wife explained that he would not have been able to pay for the trip without help."[42] And though his letter said he'd gotten money from "an organization in Tampa"—a seeming reference to the FPCC or a member of it—it's not clear why that would have required Lopez to "wait . . . for a telephone call from Cuba."

Lopez apparently gave a variety of reasons for wanting to return to Cuba, according to the Church Committee. On one hand, Lopez "told FBI sources that he had originally left Cuba to evade Cuban military service. Nevertheless, some sources told the FBI that [Lopez] had returned to Cuba in 1963 because he feared being drafted in the US." It seems odd that Lopez would return to Cuba because of the US draft, because it was being reported in US newspapers that Cuba had announced that it was instituting a draft, which would start in December 1963. While some sources said Lopez wanted to return because he was worried "about his parents," others gave Lopez's concern "about his own health" as the reason he wanted to return (Lopez reportedly had epilepsy).[43]

Lopez's trip was also unusual because he didn't own a car or drive, yet he would embark on a long journey to get to Cuba by going by car to Texas, then into Mexico, then catching a flight from Mexico City to Havana.[44] The "FBI concluded he crossed in a privately owned automobile owned by another person."[45] Yet the car's owner or driver has never been identified. Other information about Lopez missing from the released files include his employer's name and location for the last week he was in Tampa, and even whether or not Lopez was at work on November 18.

One possible explanation for the many unusual aspects of Lopez's trip may come from a report from a high Florida law-enforcement official that Lopez was an informant for some agency. Also, a Warren Commission memo refers to Lopez's trip to Mexico and then Cuba as a "mission," not simply a trip. Lopez would cross into Mexico on November 23, but the border had been closed after JFK's death, so Lopez may have originally planned to get into Mexico and on to Cuba on November 22. We've noted earlier that Lopez had a brother "studying in the Soviet Union" at the time, which could have made Lopez useful to US intelligence. Lopez's many parallels to Oswald and the odd nature and timing of his trip could indicate that he was being used as "an asset into Cuba" for US intelligence. That might explain Lopez's having to wait on a call from Cuba about his return (even though he was getting his funds for the trip in the US), since at that time David Morales had at least one agent in Cuba.[46]

According to the *Tampa Tribune*, "on Nov. 17, 1963—one day before Kennedy visited Tampa . . . Lopez attended a meeting in the home of a member of the Tampa chapter of the Fair Play for Cuba Committee. Another person thought to have been at that meeting was Lee Harvey Oswald." They go on to say that "recently declassified FBI files quote 'operatives' as saying Oswald met with a member of the Fair Play for Cuba Committee in Tampa on that date. That information was never confirmed. Lopez's attendance at the meeting, however, was confirmed."[47]

A high Florida law-enforcement source stated that an "informant said that he'd met Oswald at an FPCC meeting in Tampa with several other people present, just before JFK's motorcade. The informant remembered Oswald's appearance, but not" his name, so if it was Oswald, he may have been using an alias. This informant was different than the one cited by the *Tampa Tribune*, Joe Burton, who was known to our source as someone who helped "the FBI."[48]

According to John H. Davis, "over the weekend of November 16, 17 [1963], the real Oswald disappeared entirely from view and his whereabouts on those two days still remain unknown."[49] For the Tampa assassination attempt, the point is not whether the real Oswald was in Tampa or not on November 17, 1963; what is important is that someone wanted authorities to *think* he was, or might have been. And if it wasn't Oswald in Tampa, they knew enough about Oswald's movements to know that information could be planted indicating that he was in Tampa and it couldn't be refuted.

There is one report of Oswald in Texas on November 17, which ties Oswald to a close associate of C-Day exile leader Tony Varona. According to the *Dallas Morning News*, "in Abilene, Texas . . . a local exile activist and friend of Tony Varona in Miami received a note. The note was . . . seen by a good friend and exile supporter," and it said "'Call me immediately—Urgent' with two Dallas telephone numbers and the name Lee Oswald."[50] Larry Hancock notes that two Caucasian males "also attended a meeting with" Varona's associate "a couple of months before the assassination—a young man resembling Oswald and 'a little dried up Anglo from New Orleans, about 5′ 8″ appearing to be in his 50's and with a weathered complexion.' This description could easily be applied to John Martino."[51]

Leaving a note with Oswald's name the day before the Tampa attempt—and just five days before Dallas—seems almost to be a setup, as if to intentionally tie one of Varona's men to Oswald. That fits with the pattern of trying to tie Oswald to C-Day. Perhaps it was also a way of ensuring that Varona wouldn't talk, after JFK's death was blamed on Oswald. Varona had been in New Orleans on November 14 and 15, staying with the "uncle of Silvia Odio," Silvia Odio being the member of Manolo Ray's C-Day group who said she had been visited by Oswald in September 1963.[52]

Varona's associates in C-Day, Harry Williams and Manuel Artime, were meeting with Bobby Kennedy in Washington on November 17, 1963. According to a DIA memo declassified in 1997, Bobby, Harry, and Artime were scheduled to meet again on November 21 or November 22. But that would depend on the reaction of the C-Day coup leader to JFK's speech on the eighteenth.[53] First, though, Bobby asked for Harry's help with security for the upcoming Florida trip. Bobby was especially worried about security for JFK's Miami visit: He worried that some non–C-Day exiles might create a disturbance—or worse—before JFK's important speech to the Inter-American Press Association, the speech that contained lines written for the C-Day coup leader.

Harry told us that "the FBI and the Secret Service told me that they were afraid of JFK being killed in Miami. They took me aside and told me how JFK was going to come into and out of Miami. I was amazed that they'd tell me that. And I told them about these two or three guys and they were killers." Harry said there were "3 or 4" Bay of Pigs veterans who "had threatened to kill JFK." Harry called them "hotheads" who "would do anything. They would kill Kennedy if they thought they could." Harry made it clear that these weren't men working with him on C-Day, but were fellow exiles he'd known at the Bay of Pigs.[54]

Harry offered to help the authorities in Miami "try to get the" exiles "out of the way, and so they asked me to take them to the [Florida] Keys and babysit them." Harry "took them to . . . Marathon Key" until JFK's Florida trip was over. He "bought them drinks, women, everything . . . for two days." Secret Service files for the Miami trip show that that's where the Secret Service's main concern was, due to all the disgruntled exiles, and other exile leaders like Harry were used in an attempt to keep things quiet during JFK's trip.

Unknown to Harry, while he was busy getting those exiles out of the way during JFK's visit, another friend of his had been stalking JFK. On Sunday, November 17, JFK had been at the Kennedy Palm Beach estate with Goodwin and his other aides, putting the finishing touches on his big speech for the following day, with its passage for the C-Day coup leader. JFK was no doubt pleased with the front-page stories in the Sunday newspapers, with photos of him watching a Polaris missile being fired "from a submarine," which was described as "spectacular." In the articles, JFK "voiced his warm appreciation for the demonstration of [US] naval power." JFK was quoted as talking about the US having "control of the seas" and "the most modern weapons system in the world." It was exactly the image of strength he wanted to convey to the C-Day coup leader, ninety miles away in Cuba.[55] Coupled with coverage of his visit to the US Strike Command and his speech in Miami, JFK no doubt hoped it would provide enough reassurance for the coup leader to proceed.

However, in the house next door, JFK was being monitored by Alberto Fowler, a Bay of Pigs veteran. Fowler was from a well-to-do Cuban family, described by another exile as "high society." He'd fought at the Bay of Pigs and wound up a prisoner, until Harry helped Bobby secure the release of all the men. However, Fowler was left very bitter by his experience. Fowler later admitted to the New Orleans *Times-Picayune* that "I had been resentful of Kennedy, in fact I had even written a long article for *US News and World Report*, showing my resentment for the lack of air cover that had been promised for that invasion." Fowler's article had appeared less than two weeks after his release from prison in Cuba.[56] Fowler got a job at New Orleans's International Trade Mart, where he worked with Clay Shaw.

However, Fowler was described as rather rigid and somewhat intolerant toward some minorities, including gays. Someone else who had an office at the Trade Mart was William Gaudet, the CIA asset who helped monitor Oswald. Alberto Fowler may have also been a CIA asset, since a CIA memo from 1967 censors almost three lines of description about Fowler's ties and activities. Fowler later joined Herbert Philbrick on the International Advisory Committee for INCA, the group that helped sponsor (and publicize) Oswald's radio debate.

Fowler's exile associates were connected to Artime's minor-league training camp outside New Orleans, the one that was reportedly visited by David

Ferrie, Lee Harvey Oswald, and possible Michel Mertz (using the alias Jean Souetre).[57] Fowler was not part of C-Day, but he was friendly with Harry like many Bay of Pigs veterans. Fowler told the New Orleans *Times-Picayune* that on the weekend of November 17, he and some other exiles "had taken the house next to" JFK's estate. Fowler says "we spent the whole weekend—he was there preparing a speech he was to make." Fowler told the newspaper that he was just trying to annoy JFK by playing Cuban music loud—but if JFK's Secret Service detail had known that a bitter Bay of Pigs veteran was next door, it's not hard to guess what their reaction would have been, given all the security concerns about Cuban exiles for the Miami trip.[58] Fowler also had at least one friend in common with Trafficante's man Frank Fiorini. That may explain the provocative call about Oswald that Fowler would make to Harry on the afternoon JFK was shot, and why Fowler was in position to point Jim Garrison away from the Mafia, when Fowler began working for the New Orleans District Attorney on the JFK case in 1967.

November 18, 1963:
The Attempt to Assassinate
JFK in Tampa

BY LATE SUNDAY, NOVEMBER 17, or early Monday, November 18, 1963, the Secret Service was extremely concerned that an attempt would be made to assassinate JFK during his motorcade in Tampa, Florida. This threat, detailed here for the first time, has not appeared in any previous book. Information about the threat was confirmed by Tampa's police chief at the time, J. P. Mullins; by a high Florida law-enforcement official involved in security for JFK's motorcade; and by Secret Service agents such as Abraham Bolden. Secret Service documents about the Tampa attempt were destroyed "in an apparent violation of the JFK Act" in 1995, according to the JFK Assassinations Records Review Board.[1] We had first informed the Board of the Tampa attempt just a few weeks earlier, after finding what appear to be the only two articles about it which briefly surfaced in two Florida newspapers in the days after JFK's death (no articles about the threat appeared while JFK was still alive). One small article appeared in the *Tampa Tribune* on November 23, and part of that article was excerpted in a small article in the *Miami Herald* on November 24. However, by that time "the FBI, Secret Service, and local officers declined to discuss the matter," and no further articles appeared in either paper.[2]

This plot to kill JFK was different from the minor threats reported against JFK in Tampa in May 1963 and October 1963 (the latter involving a businessman named John Warrington, who had nothing to do with the serious threat).[3] The Tampa threat was not revealed to the Warren Commission or any of the later government committees that investigated aspects of JFK's assassination, until we brought it to the attention of the Review Board in 1995. The House Select Committee on Assassinations had a few documents which in retrospect did concern the serious Tampa threat, but since the

HSCA had not been officially informed of that threat, they apparently assumed that those documents only applied to the Joseph Milteer threat.

One of the two surviving small articles mentions "a memo from the White House Secret Service dated Nov. 8 [that] reported: 'Subject made statement of a plan to assassinate the President in October 1963. Subject stated he will use a gun . . . Subject is described as white, male, 20, slender build, etc.'" That memo—cited in a November 23, 1963 article in the *Tampa Tribune*—may no longer exist in Secret Service files. The suspect's description in the memo matches either Gilberto Lopez (described by the FBI "23, 5' 7", 125 lbs. . . . fair complexion") or Lee Harvey Oswald far better than the initial description that would be issued in Dallas four days later, after JFK was shot, which put out a lookout for a thirty-five-year-old man. The article also quoted Mullins as saying that there were two people involved in the threat, and "he did not know if the other two may have followed" JFK "to Dallas."[4] Just as in Chicago, there were two suspects on the loose prior to a JFK motorcade—only this time, on this day, there could be no cancellation if JFK were going to convey a convincing image of strength to the C-Day coup leader in Cuba.

More information about the threat comes from Secret Service files that still existed in the late 1970s. Some of those found by a Congressional investigator "made it clear that the threat on Nov. 18, 1963 was posed by a mobile, unidentified rifleman shooting from a window in a tall building with a high power rifle fitted with a scope." There are two highly unusual things about the information in that Secret Service memo. First is how closely the timing and wording in that memo matches a long-secret internal CIA memo from November 19, 1963, in which Desmond FitzGerald "approved telling [Rolando] Cubela he would be given . . . high powered rifles w/scopes" in a weapons cache. As noted earlier, providing those weapons would have been the job of David Morales, who was also in position to know about the plot of Rosselli and the other mob bosses to kill JFK. One can only imagine the reaction of FitzGerald and Helms if JFK had been killed in Tampa by the type of weapon they were going to provide to Cubela—or how they felt when they heard how JFK had been shot in Dallas with a "high powered rifle" with a scope, at the very moment their agent was meeting with Cubela in Paris.

Second, even when one of the Secret Service agents who wrote the memos was shown a copy, Congressional investigators say he "experienced difficulty in recalling detailed information of any kind" and had "virtually complete loss of memory," saying he "had 'no recall' of these facts even when his own recollection was refreshed by his own memoranda."[5] Just like the Chicago attempt, information about Tampa would be covered by an intense veil of official secrecy. Secret Service agent deFreese was willing to admit to Congressional investigators that "a threat did surface in connection with" JFK's Florida trip and "there was an active threat against the President of which the Secret Service was aware in November 1963 in the period immediately prior to JFK's trip to Miami made by 'a group of people.'" However, he focused only on the Miami part of JFK's trip, not on Tampa.[6] In the 1990s, the Secret Service agent who drove the car immediately behind JFK in Tampa (and Dallas), Sam Kinney, told researcher Vince Palamara that the threat that day had "something to do with organized crime" and "one of the unions."[7] Santo Trafficante controlled organized crime in Tampa and most of south Florida, and, as we know now, Teamster head Jimmy Hoffa was backing Trafficante's plot to kill JFK.

In his first interview about the subject since 1963, former Tampa Police Chief J. P. Mullins confirmed the existence of the plot to us in 1996. He indicated that it wasn't a far-right threat that was based on the Milteer information, which he didn't recall having been shared with the Tampa police. Chief Mullins also said that they had not been told about the recent Chicago plot to kill JFK. However, when given the full names of the two men linked to Gilberto Lopez whose last names were Rodriguez and Gonzales, Mullins thought they sounded familiar, but he couldn't say for sure. He recalled that no suspects were arrested that day, but said that if a suspect wasn't taken "into custody on some legal pretext, they'd keep them under surveillance," echoing what happened to Vallee and the other suspects in Chicago. He said that since "they were worried about the guy who fit the description in the newspaper" article, it was more likely that suspects "were kept under surveillance." He said that "the Secret Service gave us names to watch for, and our own Intelligence Unit had names to watch for," but Oswald's name "wasn't on any [watch] list."[8]

Mullins described Trafficante as "their main mobster," and he said that in general they "tried to keep the heat and surveillance on him," which eventually caused Trafficante to spend more time in Miami, away from Tampa. Mullins was familiar with Trafficante's attorney, Frank Ragano. Mullins had become police chief again just weeks before JFK's motorcade, after having been replaced for a time by Chief Neil Brown, whose Senate testimony from September 1963 we cited earlier. Mullins had a good reputation for being honest and against the Mafia. He had been acting chief in 1958 and full chief in 1960, before being dropped back to number two under a new mayor.

When the mayor changed again, Mullins became chief again. However, local politics would cause back-and-forth changes in the Tampa Police Department's leadership that would eventually lead to the files about the Tampa threat being destroyed. Under Mullins, the Tampa PD had "huge files on Trafficante" (with a code like "CI-60," because they began in 1960), and files on the Tampa JFK attempt. But eventually, another official told us that a new Tampa mayor and his new police chief had those files "destroyed . . . so they couldn't be subpoenaed" by any of the JFK investigating committees.[9]

Regarding the Tampa motorcade, Mullins said a "Secret Service agent told him it was the President's longest exposure in the US—the only one longer was in Berlin." JFK's motorcade was scheduled to go from MacDill Air Force Base to Al Lopez Field, then to downtown Tampa and the National Guard Armory, then to the International Inn, and finally back to MacDill. According to an article about the motorcade, "the Tampa police alone supplied 200 of the department's approximately 270 uniformed force." In addition, "four hundred men from federal law enforcement agencies such as the US Air Force also saw duty," including "law enforcement officers from the state, six counties, and the cities of St. Petersburg and Clearwater."[10] With a total of six hundred trained professionals guarding JFK, it's clear how serious the security concerns were.

One of those other officials also spoke to us about the Tampa threat. Chief Mullins was eighty-two when we spoke to him, but he was still alert, and he recalled the key points of that historic day. But he felt that this other individual might remember more, since he was several years younger than Mullins, and he suggested that we talk to him. Mullins vouched for this official's honesty and integrity, which we were able to confirm, along with the official's position in 1963. The official was active in the fight against the Mafia in Florida, so he would prefer to remain anonymous. This high Florida law-enforcement official was "convinced there was going to be a hit in Tampa" against JFK on November 18, 1963.

Like Mullins, the Florida official said that he and his agency hadn't been told about the Chicago attempt. The official recalled that one of the three places that especially concerned the Secret Service was a bridge, though he didn't understand why at the time. Once we informed him that Chicago newsmen had told a former a Senate investigator that the Chicago plot involved a "planned assassination attempt from one of the overpasses," the official said he finally understood the Secret Service's concern about the bridge.[11] The other two places the Secret Service was concerned about were "a place where gangsters hung out" and the Floridian Hotel (sometimes referred to as the Grand Floridian).

Chief Mullins had told us that the Floridian Hotel was a special problem, because "it was the tallest building in town at the time"—and yet JFK's motorcade had to make a hard left turn right in front of it. That would slow the motorcade to a crawl in front of a tall, red-brick building with dozens of unguarded windows, in the days when hotel windows weren't sealed shut. Mullins said for the other tall buildings—he recalled a couple of "bank buildings" in particular—"his men went through looking for anything unusual" and would sometimes "leave an officer posted [there]." However, as the tallest hotel in town—with a great view overlooking JFK's motorcade route—the hotel was going to be packed with visitors on Monday, November 18, making security extremely difficult. Aside from all the windows, there was all the luggage that could contain weapons, and in those days using an alias or fake ID to register was incredibly easy. So Mullins said he depended on hotel staff to keep him abreast of any suspicious or strange people.[12] The Florida official confirmed Mullins's account, but still thought the hotel would have been an ideal place from which assassins could shoot at JFK.

The Florida official recalled being briefed about the minor threat regarding the jailed businessman, but said it was different from the main threat, which he implied was connected at the time somehow to Cubans or the local chapter of the Fair Play for Cuba Committee (FPCC). He said anti-Castro groups were not that big in Tampa, because Castro was relatively popular and had many supporters who weren't Communists. He said the Tampa police received no security help from Cuban exiles, in the way Harry Williams and some other exiles had assisted in Miami. Mullins said that a group of anti-Castro Cubans had "asked for a permit to demonstrate during JFK's motorcade, but" Mullins "turned them down." Instead, the exiles were content to run an ad in Monday's newspaper condemning JFK.

The high Florida law-enforcement official identified the full name of a man linked to Gilberto Lopez and the Fair Play for Cuba Committee, who "was watched closely in conjunction with JFK's visit." The man's last name was "Rodriguez." The official was aware of Gilberto Lopez—whom he called "Gilbert"—and "thought he was an informant" for some agency. However, he didn't connect Lopez at the time to the JFK threat; that would come later, after JFK's death, when the FBI and others began investigating Lopez.

It's unclear when Bobby Kennedy learned about the Tampa threat; but on Monday morning, November 18, it is clear that he certainly had a lot on his plate. After dealing with Harry and Artime the previous day, he would be anxious about how the C-Day coup leader would receive the special message for him in the speech JFK was giving in Miami that night. In addition, Bobby's war against the Mafia was reaching a crucial stage. Richard Mahoney wrote that "on Monday, November 18, the last week of the trial to deport Carlos Marcello for good began" and "Bobby was monitoring it closely." There would be meetings later in the week with many of his Justice Department prosecutors, to map out strategy against Trafficante and other mob bosses. Also, Monday had seen the first of a major five-part series in the *New York Times* about the ties between the Mafia, Hoffa's Teamsters, and Las Vegas. The *Times's* investigation had been supported by Bobby, who had provided crucial information and quotes. Bobby was no doubt aware that in a separate story, the previous day's *Times* had spotlighted the Mafia ties of one of JFK's potential rivals, when it reported that "Sen. Goldwater admits association with Willie Bioff, labor racketeer slain in 1955 and Gus Greenbaum, gambler slain in 1958," ties that are "divulged in forthcoming book *The Green Felt Jungle* by Ed Reid and Ovid Demaris." Bobby would have known that both the Bioff and Greenbaum murders had ties to Johnny Rosselli. Somewhere amidst all those items on Bobby's agenda would have been the news of the Tampa threat. Bobby of course knew about the Chicago threat and cancellation, as well as the Cuban Contingency Planning. He also knew how important that Monday's events were to JFK and to C-Day, but it's not known what—if any—advice he gave to JFK about the Tampa threat. All that is known is what JFK did in response to the threat.

The Florida official confirmed that "JFK had been briefed he was in danger."[13] However, JFK knew that he couldn't afford to cancel another motorcade so soon after Chicago without raising suspicion. Plus, he couldn't afford to appear weak on the day that he needed to project an image of strength and confidence, along with the message written for the C-Day coup leader in Cuba. Canceling the motorcade simply wasn't an option. JFK was set to use the same limousine he was scheduled to use in Dallas, the SS-100-X, but he knew that the "bubble-top" occasionally used during inclement weather wasn't bulletproof; also, using it wouldn't send the message he wanted (any photos of his motorcade would be sent to the coup leader). So JFK decided to proceed with the motorcade as planned, in an open car.

JFK must have been under enormous stress, and it showed. The Secret

Service had told the Florida official that JFK was not well, and he told us that that was quite evident. At least the first stop was MacDill Air Force Base, which was very secure, with newspapers saying that "more than half of the 150 Air Police were detailed to the President's visit."[14] While there, JFK had his "secret session" with the Strike Force Commander, as well as with commanders of the Tactical Air and Continental Army units brought in from Virginia for the session.[15]

While JFK was at the secure military base, the Secret Service and other agencies tried to ensure JFK's safety on his upcoming motorcade through downtown Tampa. The Miami Secret Service office had police informant William Somersett call Joseph Milteer at his Georgia home, just to make sure that he was there and not in Tampa. As Mullins would later tell the *Tampa Tribune* for their small article following JFK's death, "Tampa police and Secret Service agents scanned crowds for a man who had vowed to assassinate the President here."[16] One of the few surviving Secret Service documents about the Tampa motorcade—since it was provided to Congressional investigators—says that "underpasses [were] controlled by police and military units, [while the] Sheriff's office secured the roofs of major buildings in the downtown and suburban areas."[17] According to the *St. Petersburg Times*, a local dignitary in the motorcade "recalls that 'it was weird being in the motorcade and we commented at every overpass [that] there were police officers with rifles on alert.'"[18]

The main motorcade would last about forty minutes, and would make the left turn in front of the Floridian Hotel at approximately 2:30 P.M. before going over a bridge to the Armory, where JFK would give another speech. JFK didn't have Jackie accompanying him, as she would in Dallas, and it must have been very tense being alone and aware that assailants were at large among the teeming crowds. Tampa was considered the Deep South at that time; but, as in Dallas, the crowds were large and enthusiastic for JFK. To aid with security and scan the throngs, two Secret Service agents, Don Lawton and Charles Zboril, rode on the back of JFK's limousine much of the time.

Photos of the Tampa motorcade show that for much of it, JFK stood up in the limousine. It certainly made for great photos, but it also made him an easy target. It's unclear whether he was doing that to send a message, whether it was because of his back problems, or whether he didn't want the Secret Service agents towering over him much of the time. Regardless, it was a courageous thing to do under those tense circumstances. A man later recalled for the *St. Petersburg Times* that he remembered "how concerned everyone was when [Kennedy] stood up in the car as he rode through the streets of Tampa."[19]

One can only imagine what JFK must have thought when "someone from the crowd threw a" small, cylindrical red item "at the motorcade" that "landed with a 'thud' on the hood of the Secret Service follow-up car. Thinking it could be a lethal stick of dynamite, Agent Emory Roberts pushed the object forcefully off the hood" of the follow-up limo. As noted by researcher Vince Palamara, when they realized that the object was a "'Powerhouse' candy bar . . . Roberts and the other agents shared a laugh."[20]

In contrast to the concern about the threat, accounts of the day say "it was the kind of day the Chamber of Commerce prays for: blue skies, balmy breezes, lots of sunshine," which sounds very much like the way it would be in Dallas four days later. JFK made it past the Floridian without incident and gave his speeches at the Armory and, later, the International Inn for the United Steelworkers Union. After one speech, newspaper reports say that "as soon as the President finished his talk, he surged out into the crowd, which immediately engulfed him. The Secret Service men with him went crazy."[21]

In spite of the pressure he must have been under, from both the threat and his packed schedule, JFK remained gracious, with the charm that had captured much of the nation. According to one account, when JFK walked into the International Inn he "was immediately spotted by a bellboy who yelled, 'This way, Mr. President.' Kennedy immediately went over and shook hands with several bellboys and clerks at the desk."[22] As his time in Tampa drew to a close, back at MacDill, a member of the Tampa police motorcycle detail told the *St. Petersburg Times* that "Chief of Police J. P. Mullins introduced each of us to the President,'" who was no doubt grateful that he had survived the motorcade unharmed.[23]

JFK didn't realize that just as in Chicago, someone in law enforcement in the Tampa–St. Petersburg area was feeding information to the mob bosses involved in the assassination plot. This mob lawman actually had a position very similar to that of Richard Cain. According to the high Florida law-enforcement source, the mob's lawman was not a "made" member of the Mafia like Cain, but openly boasted of his ties to the Mafia and was feeding information to Trafficante at the time. The Florida official thought it likely that the mob lawman could have tipped Trafficante off that the threat had been uncovered. Later, the Florida official heard rumors that the hit for Tampa had been cancelled because some of the older dons in the local Mafia had worried that killing JFK there would bring down too much heat on their operations.[24] Of course, Trafficante would have also known that there was still one more chance to kill JFK, in Marcello's territory of Dallas.

After JFK's death, the Florida official tried to run down reports of Jack Ruby being in Tampa, but couldn't confirm anything. He later came to believe that Frank Fiorini had had some type of involvement in the JFK assassination. His agency eventually had an "inches-thick file" on the motorcade security preparations and the JFK assassination investigation, though it was later destroyed, as was the information that the Tampa police had compiled under Chief Mullins.[25]

Mullins said they provided much information to the FBI at the time of the Tampa threat. Those documents have never surfaced in declassified FBI files. After Gilberto Lopez became a suspect in JFK's assassination, the FBI documents released about him to date don't even answer such basic investigative questions as whether Lopez was at work on the day JFK was in Tampa. In contrast, files from the Tampa FBI office reviewed at the National Archives contain many pages of transcripts of bugged telephone calls involving casual Tampa acquaintances of Lopez. These imply a much more intense FBI interest and investigation than the declassified Lopez documents indicate.[26]

Chicago Secret Service agent Abraham Bolden told us that he had been told about the Tampa threat.[27] It makes sense that the Chicago office would be told, in light of the very similar threat there just sixteen days earlier. It would be logical to check the Tampa details and suspects against those in Chicago, but no Secret Service documents about that have been uncovered. In fact, no Secret Service documents about the main Tampa threat have ever been released, aside from a few references in reports by HSCA investigators in the late 1970s. Even those were always assumed by the investigators to refer only to Joseph Milteer, since the HSCA was never told about the main Tampa threat.

In fact, Milteer himself commented on the aborted hit to Miami police informant William Somersett, after JFK's death. Somersett told investigators that Milteer "said that Kennedy could have been killed" on his trip to Florida, "but somebody called the FBI and gave the thing away, and of course, he was well guarded and everything went 'pluey,' and everybody kept quiet and waited for Texas."[28]

Once in Miami, JFK was ready to give his important speech to the Inter-

American Press Association, with its special message to the C-Day coup leader. JFK said:

> The genuine Cuban revolution, because it was against the tyranny and corruption of the past, had the support of many whose aims and concepts were democratic. But that hope for freedom was destroyed.
>
> The goals proclaimed in the Sierra Maestra were betrayed in Havana.[29]
>
> It is important to restate what now divides Cuba from my country and from the other countries of this hemisphere. It is the fact that a small band of conspirators has stripped the Cuban people of their freedom and handed over the independence and sovereignty of the Cuban nation to forces beyond the hemisphere. They have made Cuba a victim of foreign imperialism, an instrument of the policy of others, a weapon in an effort dictated by external powers to subvert the other American republics.
>
> This, and this alone, divides us.
>
> As long as this is true, nothing is possible. Without it, everything is possible. Once this barrier is removed, we will be ready and anxious to work with the Cuban people in pursuit of those progressive goals which a few short years ago stirred their hopes and the sympathy of many people throughout the hemisphere.
>
> No Cuban need feel trapped between dependence on the broken promises of foreign Coummunism and the hostility of the rest of the hemisphere. For, once Cuban sovereignty has been restored, we will extend the hand of friendship and assistance to a Cuba whose political and economic institutions have been shaped by the will of the Cuban people.[30]

The audience received JFK politely; but, as we noted earlier, Richard Goodwin told us that it really wasn't JFK's type of audience. But unknown to Goodwin, the audience that JFK really wanted to reach was ninety miles away, in Cuba. Now, JFK, Bobby, and Harry would have to see if the message had been what the C-Day coup leader wanted to hear.

The following day's headlines are notable both for what they say and what they don't say. First, several newspapers seem to pick up very well on what JFK had been trying to get across—in some cases, almost too well. For example, the November 19, 1963 *Dallas Times-Herald* headlined their UPI story with "Kennedy Virtually Invites Cuban Coup." The story said that in his Miami speech the previous day, "President Kennedy all but invited the Cuban people today to overthrow Fidel Castro's Communist regime and promised prompt US aid if they do. Kennedy's encouragement of a Cuban coup was contained in a major foreign policy speech. . . . The President said it would be a happy day if the Castro government is ousted."

Some other newspapers also had provocative headlines based on the same UPI story, saying "Kennedy Encourages Cuba Coup" and "Says US will Aid in Ouster."[31] While headlines like those ensured that the coup leader in Cuba would get the intended message, they made JFK's carefully crafted words almost too clear. However, most newspapers were more restrained in their headlines and stories. The *New York Times*, for example, headlined theirs a more restrained "Kennedy says US will aid Cuba once Cuban sovereignty is restored under a non-Communist government."[32]

The headlines on November 19, 1963 were also notable for what they lacked: any mention of the main Tampa threat. Even in the local Tampa-area newspapers, there was no mention of it. We confirmed this by scanning microfilm of every edition on that day and those that followed (in the early 1960s, newspapers sometimes went through three or more editions each day). No story about the main Tampa threat appeared while JFK was alive.

Concerns about the Tampa threat had been broad enough that surely it must have caught the attention of some reporters. Even if only a few dozen of the six hundred officials and officers helping with security knew anything of substance about the threat, it's difficult to imagine that one wouldn't have told a journalist or reporter. Especially since the motorcade had gone so well, it would be logical for some official to boast about the good job dealing with the threat, or even more logical for officials to widely publicize the description of the two suspects who were at large. But neither happened, probably for the same reason that there was no publicity about the four-man Chicago threat, even though several Chicago newsmen knew about it at the time.

For Bobby Kennedy and the other officials working on C-Day, there were too many other considerations to allow the threat to be publicized. The possible Cuban connection that our high Florida law-enforcement source was told about shows how any public investigation could bring unwanted attention to any connections that pro-Castro or anti-Castro suspects might have. If pro-Castro suspects were publicly announced or uncovered, would the C-Day coup leader worry that Castro had uncovered his role and was retaliating? What if an investigation accidentally uncovered exiles working for

Artime or one of the other C-Day exile groups? That could also lead to embarrassing questions from the media at a critical time. As was probably a consideration in the Cuba Contingency Planning, any further investigations of the Tampa threat were probably done very quietly and in secret, and any news and publicity about it was avoided.

In hindsight, the tragedy in such an approach is apparent. If the Dallas police had known about Tampa, they no doubt would have prepared their security very differently. Even if they'd only been informed after the assassination, at least they would have investigated the case far differently. If the public had known what almost happened in Tampa, they would have been even more skeptical of the official version of events in Dallas. Most of all, if the Tampa threat had been exposed in the press, it's hard to imagine that the mob bosses would have proceeded with basically the same plan just four days later.

There were only faint echoes of the events of November 18, 1963 in the days to come. On November 19, the CIA took advantage of JFK's message for the C-Day coup leader by using it to encourage their AMTRUNK agents in Cuba. They sent one of them a secret message "asking that he tune into Radio Americas a Voz del Jercito Rebelde all nights except Sundays" because it "would carry two major guarantees from U.S. govt. Program was designed to inspire rebel army to unite and rise in coup against Fidel."[33] Apparently, the broadcast was going to include JFK's speech or a report about it. As mentioned earlier, on November 22 in Paris, a CIA agent would tell Rolando Cubela (AMLASH) that the crucial part of the speech had been meant for him.

The following day, the first of two small newspaper articles finally slipped through in the *Tampa Tribune*. Quoted earlier, it apparently caught the attention of other reporters. The following day in the *Miami Herald*, an article quoted a small part of the *Tribune* article and tried to advance the story. But "when asked to comment on published reports that the Secret Service had alerted local authorities that an assassination attempt might be made on Mr. Kennedy when he visited here last Monday," they only "drew a 'no comment'" from officials.[34] No further stories about the threat appeared in either paper, even though both papers were filled with many other stories about JFK and the assassination for weeks to come.

We noted earlier the stonewalling that Congressional investigators faced from the Secret Service about the threat in the late 1970s, and the document destruction that occurred after we first told the JFK Assassination Records Review Board about Tampa. In addition, the Review Board's Final Report stated that "the Secret Service 'was a very difficult agency to work with,' said a Board member . . . 'they seemed to believe that terrible things would happen if they released documents.'" Another staff member told the Board, "Some agencies were more cooperative than others. Secret Service was the most difficult. They were a brick wall. They destroyed records after the law was passed."[35] We feel that this shows how sensitive C-Day, and the security precautions to protect it and its participants, were—not just in 1963, but for decades to come. Unfortunately, the secrecy at the time—which was not just the responsibility or decision of the Secret Service, but which must have had the approval of JFK and Bobby—allowed the mob bosses to regroup and try once more, in Dallas.

November 19–21:
Regrouping for Dallas

WITH THE FAILURE OF THE Tampa attempt to kill JFK, Trafficante, Marcello, and Rosselli still had one more clear chance to eliminate JFK. Dallas would be one of the last opportunities of any kind to kill JFK before C-Day and the Thanksgiving holidays, and the only chance to use the same basic plan that had been developed for Chicago and Tampa. Since both the Secret Service and Florida law enforcement had picked up indications of Mafia involvement in the Tampa attempt, Trafficante would not be able to play a larger role in the plot. Even though Dallas was Carlos Marcello's territory, he couldn't be more actively involved either, since he was in court in New Orleans each day facing Bobby Kennedy's Justice Department prosecutors. Bobby's top prosecutor there, John Diuguid, told us recently that he had not been told at the time—or ever—about the Tampa assassination threat. However, at the mention of Tampa, he immediately said "that must be Trafficante." He added that as far as Marcello and Trafficante being behind JFK's assassination, it was both "possible" and "feasible." Diuguid also said that he learned later from the FBI that while he was working on the Marcello case in Guatemala, David Ferrie and another had been shadowing him there.[1]

With Marcello and Trafficante under too much heat, that left Johnny Rosselli to take on a larger role in the plot. His biographers confirm that "the FBI surveillance of Rosselli loses his trail on the West Coast between November 19 and November 27." Rosselli had Judy Campbell move "into a suite of rooms at the Beverly Crest Hotel in Los Angeles two days before the assassination." That was possibly to ensure that she didn't become a loose cannon after JFK's death, or perhaps for her blackmail potential in case the Dallas attempt didn't accomplish its goal. Rosselli's biographers say that "Jimmy Starr, the Hollywood gossip columnist and a friend of Rosselli's," told them: "What I heard about the Kennedy assassination was that Johnny was the guy who got the team together to do the hit."[2] Rosselli apparently began taking a more hands-on role in the plot by heading to Tampa.

Florida was one place where the FBI had difficulty monitoring Rosselli, apparently because of his work for the CIA there. An analysis of FBI and CIA records by researcher Larry Hancock shows that in April 1963, "Rosselli had managed to elude his [FBI] surveillance during the exact window in which" Rosselli met with CIA officer William Harvey about the CIA-Mafia plots in Miami. Hancock notes that many of the FBI surveillance reports on Rosselli for August to November 1963 are missing—the only missing reports out of a several-year period—and that "there are absolutely no reports from the Miami [FBI] office, this despite well-documented travel by Rosselli to Miami as part of his CIA work."[3] As we noted earlier, our Florida law-enforcement source said that "Rosselli would often visit Trafficante"; they would usually meet at the previously mentioned coastal resort in Trafficante's territory that catered to a Jewish clientele. Free from surveillance by the FBI or local police officials, Rosselli would have been able to meet with Trafficante to finalize details for Dallas. As far as the CIA would know, "Col. Rosselli" was simply working on the CIA-Mafia plots to kill Castro, with his former partner in those efforts with the CIA, Trafficante.

There is an unconfirmed report of Rosselli being in Tampa on November 20, before flying to New Orleans the next day. The report comes from a pilot named W. Robert Plumlee, described by Congressional investigators as "an associate of John Martino."[4] Plumlee told William Turner that earlier in 1963, he had flown Rosselli to meetings with Carlos Prio, as what appears to be part of the CIA-Mafia Castro assassination plots.[5] Plumlee says that Rosselli stayed in Tampa the night of November 20, before being flown in a private plane to New Orleans on November 21. He says the group then went to Houston, before going on to Dallas on the morning of November 22. Plumlee says the flight was authorized by "military intelligence" with "the CIA" in a supporting role.[6] If Plumlee's account is accurate, it buttresses the possibility that Rosselli was using his work on the CIA-Mafia anti-Castro plots to cover for his work on the JFK plot.

On November 19, the *Dallas Morning News* reported that on the previous day, "a 60-mile-an-hour police chase ended in the capture of two ex-convicts hauling a load of stolen machine guns. Nabbed were" Lawrence R. Miller and

Donnell D. Whitter. The police found "two air-cooled .30-caliber machine guns, a .45 caliber 'grease gun' sub-machine gun and two Browning automatic rifles. The weapons were identified as part of the loot from the Wednesday burglary of the Texas National Guard armorer's shop at Terrell."[7] According to an article many years later in the *Washington Post*, Whitter was "Jack Ruby's [auto] mechanic," and Whitter and Miller "were suspected of supplying guns to anti-Castro groups that were planning to mount an invasion of Cuba in the last week of November 1963." This was the same arms network we've detailed earlier, when FBI reports from October 1963 cited a Dallas gun dealer talking about what sounds very much like C-Day. The *Washington Post* said that the gun dealer "gave a sworn deposition to the House Select Committee on Assassinations acknowledging that the ammunition" used in Oswald's rifle (including the bullet found in Oswald's rifle after JFK's death) probably came from his gun shop."[8]

The arms ring was actually being investigated from two directions, by the FBI and by the Dallas Police, as well as by what is now known as the Bureau of Alcohol, Tobacco, and Firearms (ATF) and its lead agent on the case, James Ellsworth. Agent Ellsworth, acting undercover, had arranged to buy weapons from the Dallas gun dealer on the evening of November 18, but the police-FBI bust of Whitter and Miller put an end to that. Ellsworth arrested the Dallas gun dealer the following day, though the man behind arms thefts at US bases in Texas, US Army Capt. George Nonte, was never arrested. Instead, Nonte—whom the *Post* notes "had a top secret clearance"—went on to become "one of the world's leading experts on firearms, eventually authoring many books on guns."[9]

The benign treatment of Nonte leaves the impression that perhaps his role in the affair was sanctioned, a way for some US agency to provide arms to certain exile groups without being overt about it. The bottom line for all this unusual activity was that a ring with links to Oswald and Ruby was providing arms to Alpha 66, the group that was essentially the same as Eloy Menoyo's SNFE C-Day exile group. The authors of the *Washington Post* article tie the ring to the DRE exile group; and, as we've noted earlier, David Atlee Phillips was reportedly involved with both groups. The plan was that if Ruby and Oswald were investigated for involvement in JFK's assassination, such connections could quickly squelch certain avenues of investigation, to protect C-Day (AMWORLD) and other CIA anti-Castro operations. Indeed, many documents about the ring were kept secret until the 1990s. One wonders what steps the CIA might have taken after their arrest was publicized, to make sure that no CIA anti-Castro operations were compromised, since the two men were part of a ring apparently dealing with Alpha 66 and the DRE.

Wednesday, November 20 was Bobby Kennedy's thirty-eighth birthday. According to John H. Davis, Bobby celebrated "at a raucous party in his office at the Justice Department" and "later in the day he was briefed by an aide on the progress of the Marcello trial and was assured all was going well. A favorable verdict was expected in a couple of days. For Friday [November] 22, [Bobby] Kennedy had scheduled a top-level meeting on organized crime to be attended by his personal staff and US attorneys from all over the nation. He was looking forward to giving them the good news from New Orleans as soon as it came in. On Thursday, November 21, the defense rested" in the Marcello case.[10]

As documented extensively in Davis's biography of Marcello, *Mafia Kingfish*, Marcello had bribed key jurors and knew he would be acquitted on Friday. Marcello knew that with a little luck, the verdict would be rendered at the same time JFK was being assassinated. Being in court that day would not only give Marcello an ironclad alibi for JFK's murder; it also allowed him to plan a celebration for the afternoon, ostensibly to celebrate his acquittal.

Marcello, Trafficante, and Rosselli's plan to kill JFK in Dallas was essentially the same as for Chicago and Tampa, though they continued to learn from their mistakes. Once again, they would try to kill JFK in public, in a moving car. High-powered rifles with scopes would be used, the same type of weapon the CIA would be discussing with Cubela in Paris at the time of the JFK hit, and possibly the same type of weapon and attack that was being considered for C-Day. Once more, they would try to link JFK's death to a patsy linked to Cuba—Lee Harvey Oswald—both to divert blame and to possibly prompt a public and Congressional outcry that would demand the invasion of Cuba that the mob bosses knew was being planned anyway.

The mob bosses knew that their basic plan was capable of provoking a government cover-up, and those involved in the plot would have ties to law-enforcement or intelligence agencies. Fewer than a dozen people would have to be knowingly involved, including experienced gunmen brought in from outside Dallas. There would be reports of firing from at least two locations, including the Texas School Book Depository, whose many windows presented a similar opportunity to the Floridian Hotel in Tampa. Jack Ruby would make sure that the patsy was quickly killed, even if he had to do the job himself. Oswald's connections to C-Day, and the reported presence of not just a Castro sympathizer but actual Cubans like Gilberto Policarpo Lopez and Miguel Casas Saez, was sure to evoke the thinking behind the Cuban contingency planning, to close off many avenues of any public investigation.

The Mafia continued to learn from its successes and mistakes. Because of the problem with Vallee in Chicago, the Mafia knew to avoid suspicion by making sure that the patsy went to work on the day of the assassination attempt. Also, the patsy didn't even have to take a rifle to work with him—which could be a problem if the person he was riding with happened to be stopped for a traffic violation or were involved in even a minor car accident. All the patsy needed was a package that *looked* like it could hold a disassembled rifle, and the actual rifle incriminating him could already be in place.

Just as Gilberto Lopez had been waiting for a phone call about going to Cuba on November 17, we feel that the evidence shows that Oswald thought he was going to Cuba via Mexico on November 22 as part of a mission for US intelligence. Oswald had tried to do that in late September 1963, when he crossed the border at Nuevo Laredo and went to Mexico City—the same route Lopez would take just after JFK's death. One of Oswald's co-workers at the Book Depository told police that "during the lunch breaks, Oswald usually made several phone calls, which were usually short in length."[11] Oswald's only close friend in Dallas, George De Mohrenschildt, had left the country almost seven months earlier, so, outside of Marina, it is not known who Oswald could have been calling. It would have been easy for someone who Oswald trusted (like David Ferrie) to tell Oswald to wait until no one was around during lunch on November 22, then call a certain number from the pay phone—and someone would soon call him back with the final instructions on where to go regarding his impending trip to Mexico and then on to Cuba. As we document shortly, that would account for many of the known Oswald sightings around the Book Depository lunch room near the time of JFK's death. In addition, Joseph Milteer had told William Somersett that "he thought [Oswald] was downstairs in the Book Depository rather than on the upper floor" when the shots were fired at JFK.[12]

There is one unconfirmed report from a mob associate that some type of demonstration or incident relating to Cuba was planned for Dealey Plaza that day.[13] Oswald may have been told that some sign would be unfurled from a window, or otherwise displayed, that would embarrass JFK with a pro-Castro message, and that this would create news stories like he'd had in New Orleans—supposedly causing the Cubans to welcome him this time when he tried to get into Cuba.

CIA and FBI files confirm that the man who ended up getting into Cuba—Gilberto Lopez, who had so many parallels to Oswald—went to Texas after the Tampa attempt.[14] A CIA memo says that Lopez had gotten a 15-day tourist card in Tampa on November 20, 1963.[15] That's what Oswald had done, just before his trip to Mexico City in an attempt to get to Cuba. In Oswald's case, right behind him in line was CIA asset William Gaudet, an associate of Guy Banister. The possibility exists that a similar CIA asset was watching Lopez when he got his Mexican tourist card.

As for the Mafia, several of the participants would again be part of their secure and ruthless heroin network. This would include reports of French Connection mastermind Michel Victor Mertz himself being in Dallas. Jean Souetre told our associate, French journalist Stephane Risset, that Mertz was in Dallas and using Souetre's name as an alias, which is why CIA and FBI files indicate that a man using those names was in Dallas on November 22, before being deported early the next day.

Former Senate investigator Bud Fensterwald, in a sworn statement to the Justice Department as part of a Freedom of Information lawsuit, said that "the FBI had traced Souetre to Dallas a day before the assassination and then lost him." We've earlier documented that the FBI had begun looking into Souetre in the spring and early summer of 1963, regarding a Christmas card sent to Souetre by a Houston dentist who had known him many years earlier. That was also the time when Souetre was talking with the CIA, culminating in Richard Helms's summer 1963 memos about Souetre.

While Souetre was a wanted fugitive because of his role in a 1962 attempt to assassinate Charles de Gaulle, there are no indications that the FBI was looking for Souetre very hard in the summer and early fall. Why they suddenly began looking for him in November, prior to JFK's death, is unclear. However, given the recent attempts to assassinate JFK in Chicago and Tampa that the FBI would have known about, both of which resulted in two suspects still at large, the FBI may have worried a French assassin could have been involved. Or, the FBI may have thought Souetre might be a threat to JFK in Texas, particularly Houston, which JFK would visit before Dallas. They also may have picked up reports of someone using Souetre's name around New Orleans, in the camps linked to former FBI supervisor Guy Banister.

According to Fensterwald, the FBI later told the Houston dentist that "the FBI felt Souetre had either killed JFK or knew who had done it," and "they wanted to know who in Washington had had him flown out of Dallas."[16] The man the FBI thought was Souetre was actually Mertz, who was using "Souetre" as an alias while the real Souetre was in Europe. Because of his past, both as a winner of the French Legion of Honor and as having saved de Gaulle's life in 1961, Mertz had enormous influence with French Intelligence. As Fensterwald wrote in his statement to the Justice Department, "Several times during the 1960s, the US asked France to take action against Mertz but the French refused because of his SDECE and Gaullist connections. He was literally known as one of the 'untouchables.'"[17] Some US agency even managed to keep Mertz's name out of the fall 1963 Congressional hearings on organized crime and narcotics. As we noted earlier, Mertz also had many parallels to the CIA's European assassin recruiter, QJWIN. In an unfortunate bit of timing, declassified CIA files show that the date of QJWIN's November pay voucher was November 22, 1963.

Mertz was using Souetre's identity as an alias, and may have been using QJWIN or his identity as well, but he was also using yet another alias, one much more innocent. The CIA file about Mertz's deportation gives another alias for Mertz, Michel Roux, a young Frenchman who arrived in Texas on November 20, 1963. Roux happened to be taking a brief vacation in the Dallas area just before and after November 22, 1963. "Michel Roux" is yet another alias listed in the CIA document about Mertz's deportation. However, the real Roux was not deported; he left Texas quite openly on December 6, 1963 and eventually returned to Paris.[18] The use of so many aliases and identities is not unusual in the context of Mertz's overall criminal exploits, but it has made it difficult for investigators and historians to accurately piece together this story.

The presence of Mertz in Dallas might explain FBI reports that never made it to the Warren Commission. John H. Davis wrote that on the morning of Wednesday, November 20, 1963,

> two police officers on routine patrol entered Dealey Plaza . . . and noticed several men standing behind a wooden fence on the grassy knoll overlooking the plaza. The men were engaged in what appeared to be mock target practice, aiming rifles over the fence in the direction of the plaza.

The two police officers immediately made for the fence, but by the time they got there the riflemen had disappeared, having departed in a car that had been parked nearby. The two patrol officers did not give much thought to the incident at the time, but after the assassination . . . they reported the incident to the FBI, which issued a report of it on November 26. For reasons that have never been satisfactorily explained, the substance of the report was never mentioned in the FBI's investigation of the assassination, and the report itself disappeared until 1978, when it finally resurfaced as a result of a Freedom of Information Act request.[19]

Historian Richard D. Mahoney confirms that "the FBI report was never part of the Warren Commission's investigation."[20] Neither was the CIA document about Mertz's deportation (and his use of the aliases Souetre and Roux), though reports of FBI investigations into the travels of people named "Roux" and "Mertz" and similar names do appear without explanation among the thousands of pages of Warren Commission documents.[21]

As noted many times previously, Jack Ruby was involved with narcotics, particularly the arm of the French Connection ring that went through Texas, and had been the subject of busts in Houston, in November 1962, and in Laredo, earlier in the fall of 1963.[22] That was yet another thing that made Ruby attractive to the mob bosses for the JFK plot, in addition to his need for money to pay his huge IRS bill and his past work as an FBI informant, Cuban gun-runner, and his involvement in the 1959 CIA-Mafia plots. We also noted that on October 30, Ruby had called Marcello lieutenant Nofio Pecora in New Orleans. The head of the New Orleans Crime Commission once described Pecora's "extensive past history in the heroin trade" and said he "directed a call-girl ring" operating in Louisiana and the surrounding area. That leads us to a woman on the lowest rung of the heroin network that involved Ruby and Mertz, a heroin courier and prostitute traveling from Florida to Dallas after the Tampa attempt, who tried to warn of JFK's impending assassination.[23] Her story has been the subject of much misinformation over the years, but we relied only on the accounts of Congressional investigators, law-enforcement officials, and media personnel. Their accounts show that at least one member of the tight-knit heroin network, which stretched from Marcello's Dallas and New Orleans to Trafficante's Florida, had learned of the mob's plan to kill JFK in Dallas, and told others about it before JFK's death.

The evidence confirms that a woman using the name of Rose Cheramie had worked for Ruby and was a low-level part of the heroin network that included Marcello, Trafficante, and Michel Mertz—and that on Thursday, November 21, 1963, she told law-enforcement and medical personnel that JFK was going to be assassinated in Dallas on Friday, November 22, 1963. It's possible that two men, further described below, who were with her were involved in the plot to assassinate JFK in some fashion as she claimed, although that can't be confirmed at this late date.

"Rose Cheramie" was one of many (at least thirty!) aliases used by Melba Christine Marcades, a woman with a long history of prostitution and other arrests since she had turned eighteen. Approximately thirty-four years old in 1963, she had worked as a B-girl for Jack Ruby and had been mainlining heroin for nine years.[24] She also had a small child, a boy. According to a Louisiana Police report, in mid-November 1963 "she worked as a dope runner for Jack Ruby" and had "worked in the night club for Ruby and that she was forced to go to Florida with another man whom she did not name to pick up a shipment of dope to take back to Dallas, and that she didn't want to do this thing but she had a young child and that they would hurt her child if she didn't."[25] Another man would accompany Cheramie and her original companion from Florida back to Dallas.

More details come from the Congressional testimony of Francis Fruge, a lieutenant with the Louisiana State Police in 1963. Fruge asked Cheramie what she was going to do in Dallas: "She said she was going to, number one, pick up some money, pick up her baby, and to kill Kennedy." This was late on the night of November 20, 1963, when Fruge and a secretary from his office were accompanying Cheramie on a trip to the East Louisiana State Hospital for treatment of heroin withdrawal. He testified that Cheramie "related to me that she was coming from Florida to Dallas with men who were Italians or resembled Italians. They had stopped at this lounge . . . and they'd had a few drinks and had gotten into an argument or something. The manager of the lounge threw her out and she got on the road and hitchhiked to catch a ride, and this is when she got hit by a vehicle." She had been initially treated for those injuries at a private hospital and released. While in jail "to sober up," she began exhibiting acute symptoms of heroin withdrawal. So Fruge and a secretary accompanied Cheramie on the "1 to 2 hour" ride to the state hospital, where she could be treated. During the trip, Fruge "asked Cheramie some 'routine' questions" and said "during these intervals that Cheramie related the story [about JFK] she appeared to be quite lucid."[26]

Fruge paid little attention to Cheramie's story about Kennedy, as did the doctors and nurses at the hospital when Cheramie was admitted early on the morning of November 21. As Dr. Victor Weiss, head of the Psychiatry Department at East Louisiana State Hospital, told Congressional investigators and also in a filmed interview for journalist Jack Anderson, "Rose Cheramie was absolutely sure Kennedy was going to be assassinated in Dallas on Friday and kept insisting on it over and over again to the doctors and nurses who were attending her Thursday morning [November 21]." Dr. Weiss said that Cheramie had told them "word was out in the New Orleans underworld that the contract on Kennedy had been let."[27] However, according to the Louisiana Police Report, "Dr. Weiss said that he didn't really pay much attention to a woman of this type until after the assassination occurred."[28]

Lt. Fruge also started paying attention, but it was Monday (November 25) before Cheramie was well enough to be interviewed again. That's when Cheramie told him that

> the two men traveling with her from Miami were going to Dallas to kill the President. For her part, Cheramie was to obtain $8,000 from an unidentified source in Dallas and proceed to Houston with the two men to complete a drug deal. Cheramie was also supposed to pick up her little boy from friends who had been looking after him. Cheramie further supplied detailed accounts of the arrangement for the drug transaction in Houston. She said reservations had been made at the Rice Hotel in Houston. The trio was to meet a seaman who was bringing in 8 kilos of heroin to Galveston by boat. Cheramie had the name of the seaman and the boat he was arriving on. Once the deal was completed, the trio would proceed to Mexico.

In addition, "Cheramie told him she had worked for Ruby" and indicated that Ruby and Oswald had known each other.[29]

Fruge was able to confirm that Cheramie had worked for Ruby as a B-girl, that she had a child and who was holding it, and to confirm many of the details of the drug-smuggling deal in Houston. Narcotics was not Fruge's specialty, so he didn't realize that the Houston–Dallas leg of the drug deal was part of a larger network that included Mexico City, New Orleans, and parts of Florida. He also didn't know that it was run by men like Marcello, Trafficante, and Michel Victor Mertz, and that it also included Jack Ruby. This same ring—with chemically identical heroin, according to Bobby Kennedy's

Justice Department—had been busted in Houston in 1962 and in Laredo in the fall of 1963, a prosecution Bobby had personally taken an interest in.[30]

However, on November 21, 1963, no one was paying attention to Rose Cheramie's warnings. It's unclear whether the two men who were with her were actually going to have a role in JFK's assassination. While it would be tempting to link them to the two at-large suspects in the Chicago attempt and the two at-large suspects in the Tampa attempt, the evidence is not adequate to make that leap at this late date. But it is clear that Rose's role in the heroin network and association with Ruby had allowed her to know about the impending plan to assassinate JFK on November 22.

In Washington, Bobby Kennedy and the CIA were busy with C-Day and their other Cuban operations. On November 19, historian Michael Bechloss writes that Richard Helms had shown Bobby Kennedy a Cuban rifle from a "three-ton Cuban arms cache left by terrorists on a Venezuelan beach, as well as blueprints for a coup [by Castro] against" the president of Venezuela. Bobby sent them over to see JFK at the White House, who viewed the rifle with interest. Helms said that "we had been for a long time looking for hard evidence that the Cubans were exporting revolution to Latin America," and now apparently the CIA had found it. Helms admitted "he presumed that any efforts the President was making for an accommodation with Castro were at best 'a feint,'" just part of a "try-everything approach," but that JFK's "'real energy' on Cuba was going into covert action." We feel that, given the timing, Helms's presentation was meant to convey a message, either to forget about negotiating with Castro and forge ahead with C-Day, or to help cover and justify Helms's unauthorized Castro assassination programs. According to Bechloss, JFK "reminded Helms that he was leaving soon for Texas: 'Great work. Be sure to have complete information for me when I get back from my trip. I think maybe we've got him now.'"[31]

Either that day or the next, JFK, Bobby, and Helms received the response they'd been waiting for from the C-Day coup leader in Cuba: his reaction to JFK's message to him in his November 18 Miami speech. JFK's assurances had been enough. The C-Day coup was a "go." In response, Bobby arranged for Harry Williams to meet on Friday, November 22, with a group of CIA officials for a final C-Day planning meeting. After a session that would stretch from morning to afternoon, Harry Williams would leave for the US base at Guantanamo on November 23, and from there go into Cuba, to meet personally with the coup leader and await the coup on December 1. The ten days from November 22 to December 1 would essentially be the countdown for C-Day, and once Harry Williams was inside Cuba, there would be no turning back for JFK and Bobby.

Gus Russo wrote that on November 20, Bobby "wrote a memo to National Security Council advisor McGeorge Bundy concerning Cuba, the contents of which remain secret. Only Bundy's response is known: 'The Cuban problem is ready for discussion now . . . so we will call a meeting as soon as we can find a day when the right people are in town.'" JFK was getting ready to leave for Texas the next day, and several cabinet members like Dean Rusk would be flying to the Far East on the same day. Early the following week would be the soonest all the administration's top officials could be gathered. That may well have been the meeting at which officials like Rusk would finally be told about C-Day, since at that point the coup would have been less than a week away.[32]

C-Day could not come too soon if its secrecy were to be maintained. One of David Morales's AMOT informants reported hearing from a woman whose "sister's husband . . . is [a] member [of the] SNFE, that" its leader "Eloy Menoyo commented" on November 21, 1963 "that something very big would happen soon that would advance [the] Cuban cause." While the declassified version of the CIA cable doesn't have the AMWORLD code name, it does have the code-word series RYBAT TYPIC YOBITE that the first AMWORLD document said was to be on all AMWORLD documents.[33]

Richard Helms had still not given up on his own unauthorized Castro assassination operations, including AMLASH (Rolando Cubela). According to the Church Report, "on November 19, AMLASH told a CIA officer that he planned to return to Cuba immediately."[34] But a November 19 CIA memo says "FitzGerald approved telling Cubela he would be given a [weapons] cache inside Cuba. Cache could, 'if he requested it, include . . . high power rifles w/scopes."[35] So, on November 20, 1963, a CIA officer telephoned AMLASH and asked him to postpone his return to Cuba in order to attend a meeting on November 22" in Paris.[36]

The actions of FitzGerald and his supervisor for this project, Helms, are significant on several counts. It's clear that the CIA set the tragic timing of the November 22 meeting, not Cubela. We're not pointing the finger at the CIA officer who relayed the message (who probably knew nothing about C-Day or the recent attempts against JFK), but we are suggesting that the man in charge of delivering the weapons cache to Cubela—David Morales—may have had a hand in choosing that particular date and time.

Meanwhile, in Cuba, French journalist Jean Daniel finally had the meeting with Castro that he'd been waiting for since late October. According to Arthur Schlesinger, after "spending three fruitless weeks in Havana," Jean Daniel was surprised by a visit from Fidel Castro at 10 P.M., the night before Daniel was scheduled to leave Cuba. Daniel and Castro talked until 4 A.M., and Daniel conveyed Kennedy's wishes from late October about his desire for dialogue. Daniel and Castro arranged to have lunch again, to continue their discussion—on November 22, 1963. Not only is the date ironic, but the location of their lunch was to be Castro's "villa at the beach," at Varadero—the very place one later AMWORLD document says would be a good place to assassinate Castro.[37] If JFK had not been assassinated, November 22 might well have been remembered by history as a crucial date in American–Cuban relations, either because of a last-minute breakthrough by JFK's emissary Jean Daniel, or because the countdown for C-Day began on that day, or because of AMLASH.

Meanwhile, the Secret Service, the FBI, and the CIA all had security concerns related to JFK's visit to Texas. Unfortunately, many of those concerns weren't being shared among the three agencies. It doesn't look as if the Secret Service had been told that the FBI had lost the trail of someone using the name "Jean Souetre" in Dallas on November 21, 1963. The FBI didn't realize that it wasn't Souetre in Dallas at all, but Michel Victor Mertz using Souetre's identity. Also, the CIA wasn't telling the Secret Service or the FBI that it was still using criminals like Johnny Rosselli or European assassin recruiter QJWIN in their Castro assassination plots. The CIA hadn't informed either agency about Rosselli's Chicago Mafia's payoff to Tony Varona, and that Manuel Artime would also be used in the CIA-Mafia plots.

The Secret Service had its hands full trying to make sure JFK's visit to Texas, especially conservative Dallas, went off well. There were still at-large assailants from Chicago and Tampa to be concerned about. Perhaps that's why Secret Service agent Forrest Sorrells would later testify to the Warren Commission that "while making a security survey of the route" in Dallas "with some Dallas Police Department officers, he remarked to those present that shooting JFK with a high-powered rifle with a scope would not be difficult."[38] Even JFK would reportedly make a similar comment the morning of November 22. It wasn't idle speculation on either man's part, simply the realization that what could have happened in Chicago or Tampa was still a possibility.

At least no definite threat had surfaced in Dallas, as it had in Chicago and Tampa. The extraordinary security in Tampa, which involved police searching key buildings along the motorcade route, is borne out by the Secret Service's own regulations. They state that "In general, the Secret Service does not inspect buildings along a moving [motorcade] route except under three circumstances: 1. Presidential inaugurations, 2. Visits by a king or president of a foreign country, or 3. When the motorcade route has been known for years."[39]

On Thursday, November 21, 1963, in Dallas at the Texas School Book Depository, Lee Harvey Oswald asked his co-worker Wesley Frazier for a ride home after work. Oswald was living in a rooming house in the Oak Cliff section of Dallas, while his wife, Marina, and their children lived with a woman named Ruth Hyde Paine. Oswald usually only went home to Marina on weekends (though he hadn't on the previous weekend), but he told Frazier that he wanted to get some curtain rods. Oswald planned to spend the night at Ruth Paine's, then ride to work with Frazier on Friday, with the curtain rods.

Based on all the evidence, we feel that Oswald was planning to leave work the following day, in order—he thought—to go meet his contact at the Texas Theater (as John Martino said) in order to get to Mexico City, and then on to Cuba, as part of a mission for a US intelligence agency (either the CIA or Naval Intelligence, or perhaps both). Oswald would bring something with him the following morning, wrapped in brown paper, but it probably wasn't curtain rods. It also wasn't the Mannlicher-Carcano rifle that Oswald kept wrapped in a blanket, just like the murderous ex-serviceman in Johnny Rosselli's old B-movie film noir *He Walked by Night*. Frazier's sworn testimony would preclude that, since the Mannlicher was too long, even when disassembled, to be held the way Frazier saw Oswald holding the package (with the base cupped in his hand, with the package vertical under his arm).[40]

Warren Commission counsel David Belin outlined in a memo (not in the Warren Report) how Oswald could have gotten to Mexico on November 22, using bus connections and the amount of money he had.[41] While that makes sense from the perspective of Oswald's maintaining his lowly, far-left cover for a mission, it doesn't make sense to try to escape on public transportation after having shot the president of the United States. In fact, any scenario for Oswald shooting the president as a lone assassin doesn't make sense. If Oswald had truly been a Communist, doing it for some ideological reason (even laying aside the fact that Oswald wrote that he hated Communism, and the fact that he never joined the party or associated with real American Communists), he avoided claiming credit or making his ideological points when he had the chance at his Friday-night press conference. If Oswald hoped to get away, killing Kennedy and then trying to escape by bus and cab—to get to a rooming house where he had no car or driver's license—that also makes no sense. Oswald would have known that once he left work, he would quickly be fingered for the crime, and he had no way to get out of Dallas without taking public transportation.

If Oswald were a lone Communist assassin, it makes no sense for the Mafia to risk having Jack Ruby kill him in a police station, on live TV. As one of Bobby Kennedy's former Justice Department prosecutors, G. Robert Blakey, told Congress, the American public might have believed "one lone assassin in November in Dallas, but two surely asks for more than many have been willing to accept." It's also hard to believe that the mob would have gone against decades of experience and hired someone like Oswald to kill JFK. If Oswald had gotten more experience driving and had acquired a car prior to JFK's death, perhaps one could attempt to make a case that he was hired to do the hit; but the thought of the Mafia having a hit man flee a major assassination using public transportation seems ludicrous.

Even if Oswald was a low-level US intelligence asset who "turned," it still doesn't make sense for him to have assassinated JFK. Oswald wouldn't have been told much about his assignment in Cuba, but even if—as some reports indicate—he realized that he was part of some effort to overthrow Castro and he turned against the US, Oswald blew his chance to expose the US to the world by keeping quiet about it at his Friday-night press conference. Our view is just the reverse and fits the facts: that Oswald knew that he was a low-level part of some US effort against Castro, and that he had been told that his cover must be maintained at all costs to avoid blowing an important operation, one that could cost lives if it were discovered.

For someone who had withstood KGB pressure and scrutiny in Russia for years, dealing with the Dallas police for a couple of days—until someone came forward to help him—would present few problems. In fact, Dallas Police Chief Jesse Curry later said that "One would think that Oswald had been trained in interrogation techniques and resisting interrogation techniques." The Dallas district attorney at the time said that he "was amazed that a person so young would have had the self-control he had. It was almost as if he had been rehearsed or programmed to meet the situation he found himself in."[42] Actually, we feel that Oswald had been trained (or retrained) to deal with Cuban intelligence, probably prior to his Mexico City trip seven weeks earlier. Unfortunately, some of the US intelligence assets directing Oswald were also associates of mobsters like Marcello and Rosselli, so he found himself in a far different situation than he had expected. The mob bosses knew that Oswald had to be silenced before he broke his intelligence cover and said too much to local investigators, an attorney, or the press.

Four different unconfirmed reports from mob associates place Johnny Rosselli in Dallas on November 22, 1963. Most of the accounts also include hit man Charles Nicoletti, the man with the specially modified "hit car" in Chicago. One of the accounts also places Rosselli in Houston the night before JFK's death. None of the accounts meets the standards for reliability or corroboration that we generally apply. To us, the number of independent accounts only suggests the possibility that Rosselli and Nicoletti might have been in Dallas. It is worth noting, however, that no alibi for either Rosselli or Nicoletti has emerged for November 22, despite the fact that these allegations have been public for many years.[43]

There were credible reports made to the FBI that Jack Ruby was in Houston on the afternoon of November 21, a couple of hours before JFK was scheduled to arrive there. Ruby was sighted one block from the President's entrance route to and from the Rice Hotel, where the President would be staying. Several people saw Ruby on the 400 block of Miami Street, around 3:00, and Ruby also called a Houston booking agent.[44] According to one account, Ruby didn't leave Houston until after JFK's arrival.[45] If Ruby was in Houston, he may have been there to observe security preparations for JFK, or to meet someone, or both. Just two days earlier, Ruby had seen his tax attorney and "said he had a connection who would supply him money to settle his long-standing government tax problems," which totaled over $40,000. On that same day, Seth Kantor notes that "Ruby's Carousel checking account" had $246.65 in it, about the usual amount.

At this point, with the assassination scheduled for Dallas, and with Ruby's extensive ties to numerous policemen, Ruby was firmly enmeshed in plans for the JFK hit. Over the next two and a half days, Jack Ruby would be a very busy man, and it's not surprising that he said at one point that he'd taken a considerable amount of Dexedrine that weekend. His job appears to have been making sure that Oswald was quickly killed after JFK was shot. That could have involved having Oswald killed before he left the Book Depository, or soon after, as well as having to do the job himself if he couldn't arrange for a policeman to do it.

Back in Dallas on Thursday evening, November 21, Ruby had dinner with one of his friends and business associates, Ralph Paul.[46] Paul was "associated with Austin's Bar-B-Cue," where one of the part-time security guards was Dallas policeman J. D. Tippit.[47] Congressional investigators determined that the married Tippit had been carrying on a long-term affair with a waitress at Austin's.[48] Author Henry Hurt talked to the woman, who confirmed that, at the time, she thought she was pregnant by Tippit.[49] This would have made Tippit subject to pressure or blackmail by one of Ralph Paul's associates—like Ruby. It could have simply been a matter of Tippit being told that he needed to be in the right place at the right time on November 22 to make a big arrest, with no advance indication to Tippit of what was going to happen to JFK.

November 22: JFK is Murdered

SO MUCH HAS BEEN WRITTEN about the events of November 22 and its aftermath that it could fill—and has filled—hundreds of books. Our focus in the coming chapters is to provide the most relevant facts based on what we were told by several Kennedy associates and by our best evaluation of all the available evidence. This will help to explain what drove the actions of Bobby Kennedy and other officials in the hours, days, and weeks after JFK's assassination. The Warren Report's limited view of events has existed for decades—though, within just a few years of its publication, researchers like Sylvia Meagher and dozens of others used information in the Warren Commission's twenty-six volumes of supporting material to challenge many of the Report's official conclusions. Other researchers found important witnesses who had not been interviewed by the commission, or who had additional information they had not been able to provide. The release of tens of thousands of pages of Warren Commission documents in the following years provided more ammunition for critics. For example, David Ferrie isn't mentioned at all in the Warren Report, and his name appears only a couple of times in the twenty-six volumes—yet the Warren Commission documents contain many pages of FBI reports dealing with him. Later government investigating committees had access to much more information denied to the Warren Commission, such as the CIA-Mafia plots, though, as we've noted, much remains secret even today.

To cover as much as possible, we will give brief passages in approximate chronological order. Where times are given, they should be considered approximate, as are dates when events happened very late at night or very early in the morning. Since most of the key events occurred in Texas, Central time is used unless otherwise indicated, so JFK's assassination occurred at 12:30 P.M., CST. Some meetings or incidents that we've covered extensively in earlier chapters are mentioned only briefly here, to show them in the context of other important events.

NOVEMBER 21, NIGHT, DALLAS

1:10 P.M.: Jack Ruby dines on a steak at the Egyptian Restaurant and Lounge in Dallas with one of his "three best friends," the restaurant's owner, Joseph Campisi. Campisi is extremely close to Carlos Marcello and also runs gambling tours from Dallas to the Flamingo Hotel in Las Vegas. The meal lasts about 45 minutes.[1]

Midnight: Ruby stops at the Bon Vivant Room restaurant in the Teamster-financed Cabana Hotel. With Ruby is Chicago businessman Lawrence Meyers, who has checked into the Cabana earlier that day. Meyers is linked to mobsters in Chicago and Las Vegas. Though married, Meyers has traveled to Dallas from Chicago with a woman named Jean Aase, who also goes by the name of Jean West. Meyers said that he'd picked her up at the 20 East Delaware Lounge in Chicago. According to some researchers, David Ferrie had called West's number to speak to Meyers, for a fifteen-minute call on September 24, 1963.[2] Earlier that evening, Meyers had been at Ruby's Carousel strip club.[3] It appears that Meyers is a mob messenger or courier.

NOVEMBER 22, VERY EARLY MORNING HOURS, DALLAS–FT. WORTH

2 A.M.: After the Fort Worth Press Club has closed, at least six off-duty Secret Service agents show up at Fort Worth's Cellar club, which Warren Commission files describe as a "night spot that poses as a beatnik place," a coffee shop where customers bring their own liquor.[4] After the recent stress of the Chicago and Tampa threats, it's not surprising that the agents would be ready for some relaxation, especially since no threat had emerged for the next day's Dallas visit. The owner of the Cellar club knew both Jack Ruby and Lewis McWillie.[5]

2:30 A.M.: Jack Ruby calls the Carousel club from the Cabana Hotel.[6]

2:45 A.M.: Most of the Secret Service agents are still at the Cellar Door in Ft. Worth.[7] The owner of the Cellar club, Pat Kirkwood, said in a filmed interview for Jack Anderson in 1988 that several strippers who worked for Jack Ruby had come to the club late that night, and he indicated that Jack Ruby may have sent them over on purpose.[8] Kirkwood also claimed that some of the agents "were drinking pure Everclear [alcohol]."[9] Warren Commission documents confirmed that some of Ruby's strippers knew Kirkwood.[10] Whether or not the women were sent by Ruby on purpose—or whether the Cellar was one of the few late-night places open in the Dallas–Ft. Worth area when they got off work—the fact that Secret Service agents were out so late the night before Kennedy's visit was important information for someone like Ruby. Their presence indicated that the Mafia's plan for Dallas hadn't leaked, as it had in Chicago and Tampa. None of the Secret Service limo drivers were involved. This is the type of behavior that Chicago Secret Service agent Abraham Bolden had tried to warn his superiors about, which resulted in his transfer away from the White House detail.

5:00 A.M.: The last Secret Service agent leaves the Cellar Door club in Ft. Worth.[11] The agents have to report for duty at 8:00 A.M., just three hours away.

6:45 A.M.: Oswald wakes up and dresses for work without waking his wife Marina or Ruth Paine. Oswald leaves his wedding ring in a cup on the dresser and $170 in a wallet in a dresser drawer. He walks over to Wesley Frazier's house, about a hundred yards away. Marina wakes up later to find her husband gone, and the items he left.[12]

7:25 A.M.: Wesley Frazier's sister sees Oswald walking across the lawn toward Wesley's car, carrying something in a long paper bag. He rides in to work with Wesley, saying that curtain rods are in the brown paper bag.[13]

7:30 A.M.: JFK wakes up in the Hotel Texas in Fort Worth. Later that morning, he reportedly makes a comment to Kenneth O'Donnell about how easy it would be to assassinate him with a high-powered rifle. According to historian Michael Bechloss, JFK also tells Jackie how easy it would have been to assassinate him the night before, by someone using a pistol.[14]

8:00 A.M. (approx.): Oswald arrives at his place of work, the Texas School Book Depository, with Wesley Frazier. Wesley sees Oswald cup the bag in his palm and under his arm, giving the package a maximum length of around 23 inches. That is too short for even a disassembled Mannlicher-Carcano, which would be too long to hold in such a fashion. Oswald hurries ahead (unusually, according to Frazier) and walks on in, ahead of Frazier, who remains behind and doesn't actually see Oswald enter the building. No one in the building sees Oswald with the package. No one sees Oswald enter the building except for Jack Dougherty, who thinks he remembers Oswald but not the package. This raises the possibility that Oswald's package was passed off to someone waiting near the Book Depository or the parking lot.[15]

November 22, Morning, Washington, D.C.

Harry Williams has his most important meeting about C-Day with several CIA officials, who reportedly include the CIA officers assigned to assist him, as well as Lyman Kirkpatrick. Kirkpatrick had been the CIA's Inspector General who had looked into the Bay of Pigs disaster, so it's logical that he would be there to grill Harry and the others about their plan.[16] It's possible that Helms and FitzGerald were there at some point as well, though no names are given to Harry for the high CIA officials, since he will be inside Cuba within two days. However, both Haynes Johnson and a Kennedy aide said to others that the top official at the meeting was Kirkpatrick, the CIA's Executive Director. Kirkpatrick is just below the CIA's Director and Deputy Director, and above Helms and Angleton and FitzGerald. As noon (Eastern time) approaches, the men break for lunch. Harry leaves to have lunch separately from the CIA men, and they will resume their meeting after lunch.

Aside from C-Day, Helms and FitzGerald are also concerned with their other plans. They know that in Paris, Rolando Cubela (AMLASH) is meeting with his CIA case officer to get a poison pen and to discuss the weapons caches, including foreign-made, high-powered rifles with scopes.[17] It's also likely that Helms and the CIA are continuing to try to get "assets into Cuba" in preparation for C-Day and their other plots. Three young men who might have roles in such an operation—Lee Harvey Oswald, Gilberto Policarpo Lopez, and Miguel Casas Saez—are all in Texas at this point, reportedly in Dallas. In addition, there might be fallout to deal with from the arrest of the men linked to the arms ring in Texas, the one that had ties to C-Day, Alpha 66, and the DRE exile groups. Dallas-area native David Atlee Phillips would be a logical person to deal with both of these matters, and there is one unconfirmed report that Phillips told his brother he was in Dallas that day.[18]

At the Justice Department, Bobby Kennedy is in a meeting on organized crime with forty of his attorneys from the Racketeering division. According to John H. Davis, "major items on the agenda were the investigations of"

Rosselli's boss "Sam Giancana, Santo Trafficante, Jimmy Hoffa, and Carlos Marcello."[19] Bobby is told that the verdict in the Marcello case in New Orleans could come as early as today. The last subject before they break for lunch is Sam Giancana and corruption in Chicago.[20] Bobby goes home for lunch, to his Hickory Hill estate in Virginia.

NOVEMBER 22, LATE MORNING, DALLAS

11:38 A.M.: Air Force One lands at Love Field with JFK and Jackie aboard. On the presidential wavelength of the Secret Service radio net, JFK and Jackie are referred to by their code-names of Lancer and Lace. An open limo driven by Secret Service Agent Bill Greer—age 54, with 35 years of experience—is waiting to take them through Dallas.[21]

11:40–11:45 A.M.: Oswald asks another employee why a crowd is gathering outside, and when told the President is visiting, Oswald replies, "Oh, I see."[22] When his co-workers go to lunch, Oswald remains on the upper floor, where he is working.[23]

Jack Ruby is at the *Dallas Morning News* building.[24]

11:50 A.M.: Oswald is seen on the first floor, near a telephone.[25]

11:50 A.M.: JFK's motorcade leaves Love Field.[26]

12:00 noon: Four witnesses say that Oswald is downstairs, around the lunch room, at this time.[27] Book Depository employee Bonnie Ray Williams returns to the sixth floor to eat his lunch.[28]

At this point, it's important to describe the area around the Book Depository and Dealey Plaza. The Book Depository is at the corner of Elm and Houston streets (Houston runs approximately north–south, and Elm approximately east–west). However, the building actually fronts what is called the Elm Street extension, which is the street that runs west from Houston at a ninety-degree angle; Elm street proper, the portion that runs eastward from Houston, is at a ninety -degree angle to Houston in that direction. To the west of Houston, Elm Street proper heads off to the southwest (a 120-degree left turn if you're heading north on Houston), away from the Book Depository.

Dealey Plaza is an approximately triangular (or, more descriptively, funnel-shaped) area south of Elm Street, bounded on its south side by Commerce Street doing the same thing that Elm Street does—in mirror image— from two blocks south on Houston Street, and bounded on its east end by Houston. The triangle formed by the small parklike area *north* of Elm Street, between Elm Street and the Elm Street extension, is the area known as the "grassy knoll," which is to the west-southwest of the Book Depository. It has a small concrete monument, and beyond that a wooden picket fence. Behind the monument and the fence is a parking lot, and, beyond that, several railroad tracks and a small railroad tower. Main Street, parallel to Elm and Commerce east of Houston and halfway between them, continues straight when it crosses Houston and bisects Dealey Plaza. All three streets—Elm, Main, and Commerce—converge and go under the Stemmons Expressway a couple of blocks to the west.

11:55–12:25 A.M.: At 11:55, Lee Bowers, in the tower in the railroad yard behind the grassy knoll, sees a dirty 1959 Oldsmobile station wagon enter the parking lot behind the picket fence. The driver, a middle-aged white male with partially gray hair, drives around slowly, then leaves. The car has out-of-state plates and a "Goldwater for '64" sticker in the rear window. According to his statement to police, completed on November 22 and in Warren Commission Volume 24, "at about 12:15 another came into the area with a white man about 25 to 35 years old driving. This car was a 1957 Ford, black, 2-door with Texas license. This man appeared to have a mike or telephone in the car. Just a few minutes after this car left at 12:20 P.M., another car pulled in. This car was a 1961 Chevrolet Impala . . . color white, and dirty up to the windows. This car also had a 'Goldwater for '64' sticker. This car was driven by a white male about 25 to 35 years old with long blond hair . . . he left the area about 12:25 P.M."[29]

12:15 P.M.: A witness sees a man—dark-haired, maybe Caucasian or a Latin with a fair complexion—with a rifle and scope on the westernmost end of the sixth floor of the Depository (toward the grassy knoll). There is a dark-skinned man visible at the easternmost end (near the apparent "sniper's nest" found after the shooting). One of the men is described as wearing a very light-colored shirt, white or a light blue, open at the collar, unbuttoned about halfway, with a regular T-shirt beneath it. (Oswald said he was wearing a red or reddish shirt at work that day; a neighbor described his shirt that day as "tan.") At 12:23, another witness sees "two men standing back from a window on one of the upper floors of the Book Depository," and she notices that "one of the men had dark hair . . . a darker complexion than the other." At the time, she felt the man "might have been a Mexican," and "she had the impression the men were looking out, as if 'in anticipation of the motorcade.'"[30]

12:15 P.M.: Mrs. R. E. Arnold, a Book Depository secretary, sees Oswald standing in the hallway between the front doors leading to the warehouse, on the first floor. She puts the time at 12:15 or a little later. Oswald claims he ate his lunch in the first-floor lunch room, alone, except for a black man named Junior who walked through with a short black man. Both of the men are later identified, and were in the lunch room at times between noon and 12:25. The short man, Harold Norman, later said "there was someone else in there," but he couldn't remember who. Oswald says that when he finished his lunch, he went up to the second floor, to get a Coke.[31]

12:15–12:20 P.M.: Book Depository employee Bonnie Ray Williams finishes his lunch on the sixth floor and leaves that floor. He leaves behind the scraps of his lunch, which will be initially assumed by the police to have been Oswald's. The FBI later reported that it takes six minutes to assemble a Mannlicher-Carcano, using a dime (since no tools were found)—so that leaves 4 to 9 minutes for Oswald alone to supposedly move all the 50-pound boxes into position in the "sniper's nest."[32]

12:15–12:20 P.M.: Jack Ruby had been seen sitting on the second floor of the *Dallas Morning News* building, in the only chair from which he can see the site where Kennedy will be killed. However, both shortly before and after the shooting, Ruby is not seen in the offices, meaning that he could have slipped away for a time. An FBI report says that "Hugh Aynesworth, reporter, *Dallas Morning News* . . . said he has known Jack Leon Ruby for a long time and Ruby had been observed by him around the *Dallas Morning News* building about noon, November 22, 1963. Also, Ruby was seen there by other employees of the newspaper but was missed for a period of about 20 to 25 minutes and Aynesworth had no information as to where Ruby had gone during this interval of time, nor did other employees."[33]

12:20 P.M.: Two men who work for the city and county see a man in the sixth-floor window, only he's staring "transfixed" at the area of the grassy knoll, and not at the motorcade. One of the men remarks to the other that the man in the window looks "uncomfortable," like he "must be hiding or something." The man in the window is wearing an "open neck . . . sport shirt or a T-shirt . . . light in color, probably white" and they mention a "sport shirt . . . yellow." One of them later says "he did not think the man in the window was Oswald, insisting that the man in the window had 'light-colored hair.'"[34]

12:20 P.M.: JFK's motorcade is greeted by huge, enthusiastic crowds. John Connally later said "the crowds were extremely thick . . . there were at least a quarter of a million people on the parade route that day." He recalled that even with the throngs, "there was this little girl—I guess she was about eight years old—who had a placard that said, 'President Kennedy . . . will you shake hands with me?' . . . Well, he immediately stopped the car and shook hands with this little girl, and of course, the car was mobbed." Later, "there was a nun, a sister, with a bunch of schoolchildren . . . right by the car. And he stopped and spoke to them," too.[35]

12:24 P.M.: Prisoners in the Dallas County Jail—which overlooks Dealey Plaza—see two men, at least one of whom had a dark complexion, on the sixth floor of the Book Depository, adjusting the scope on a rifle.[36]

12:27 P.M.: Twenty-two-year-old soldier Gordon Arnold is walking behind the picket fence on the grassy knoll, in the parking lot, when he's confronted by someone who "showed me a badge and said he was with the Secret Service and that he didn't want anybody up there." Arnold then goes on the other side of the fence, on the grassy side of the knoll. Warren Commission files confirm that there were no Secret Service agents on the knoll, or in Dealey Plaza at all. They were all either with the motorcade, or miles away at the site of JFK's upcoming speech at the Dallas Trade Mart.[37]

12:28 P.M.: Lee Bowers, in the railroad tower overlooking the parking lot behind the grassy knoll's fence, told attorney Mark Lane that he noticed two men behind the stockade fence, looking up toward Main and Houston. One of the men is "middle-aged" and "fairly heavy-set," wearing a white shirt and dark trousers. The other, about ten to fifteen feet away from the first man, is "mid-twenties in either a plaid shirt or plaid coat."[38]

12:29 P.M.: JFK's limo has turned onto Houston Street, and is heading toward the Book Depository. JFK's driver, Secret Service agent William Greer, testified that "when they got to Houston from Main Street, he felt relieved. He felt they were in the clear, the crowds were thinning and . . . he did begin to feel relieved. . . ."[39]

However, the limo is getting closer and closer to the Book Depository and the alleged "sniper's nest" at the easternmost window on the sixth floor of the building, closest to Houston. For almost a minute, anyone in that perch would have a totally unobstructed shot at a slow-moving car, with a target that is getting larger with each passing second. The limo has to slow even more as it makes the 120-degree turn onto Elm, passing directly underneath the "sniper's nest," still with no trees or obstructions of any kind. As JFK's limo continues down Elm, away from the Depository, the view from the "sniper's nest"—or any of the sixth-floor windows, for that matter—starts to be obscured by the branches of a large tree that is part of the small park that includes the grassy knoll.

12:30 P.M.: Mrs. Nellie Connally, riding in the limo with JFK, Jackie, and Nellie's husband John Connally, tells JFK, "Mr. Kennedy, you can't say Dallas doesn't love you." JFK, impressed by the huge, enthusiastic throngs which are only now starting to thin out, replies "That is very obvious."[40]

12:30:12 P.M.: One shot is fired at the President's limousine. JFK raises his hands to his neck. One of the emergency physicians, Dr. Carrico, will later describe the small wound in JFK's throat as an entrance wound. In the limo directly behind JFK's, Secret Service agent Sam Kinney would later say that "the first shot 'hit the President in the throat.'"[41] Kennedy aide David Powers, in the limo directly behind JFK's, is sure that the shot came from the right front—the grassy knoll—as is another Kennedy aide, Kenneth O'Donnell, who is in the limo with Powers. Soldier Gordon Arnold, on the grassy knoll, said "the shot came from behind me, only inches over my left shoulder. I had just gotten out of basic training . . . and I hit the dirt."

According to Texas Senator Ralph Yarborough, who was two cars behind JFK, "immediately on the firing of the first shot I saw the man . . . throw himself on the ground . . . he was down within a second, and I thought to myself, 'There's a combat veteran who knows how to act when weapons start firing.'" (Yarborough was a World War II combat veteran himself.) Secret Service agent Lem Johns, in the limo behind Yarborough, later testified that "the first two [shots] sounded like they were on the side of me towards the grassy knoll. . . ."[42] JFK's limo, which has gotten back up to a speed of around 11 miles an hour after making the turn onto Elm, slows down. Powers told us that he felt they were riding into an ambush, which explains why JFK's limo initially slowed down so much. John Connally turns to the right, because he thinks the sound came from over his right shoulder. Not seeing JFK out of the corner of his eye, Connally starts to turn back toward his left.[43]

1.65 seconds later: One or more shots are fired from above and behind JFK's limo. JFK's limo continues to slow, as the driver looks back toward the back seat. David Powers is adamant that "the same bullet that hit JFK did *not* hit John Connally," meaning one of these shots probably hit Connally.[44]

Secret Service agent Glenn Bennett, in the limo with Powers and O'Donnell, "saw what appeared to be a nick in the back of President Kennedy's coat below the shoulder. He thought the President had been hit in the back."[45]

At some point, a shot is fired that misses JFK's limo entirely and strikes a curb on Main Street near the bridge that forms the triple underpass with Elm, Main, and Commerce. The shot knocks up a chip of concrete that strikes an onlooker, James Teague.[46]

5.91 seconds later: Lee Bowers, in the railroad tower behind the grassy-knoll parking lot, notices a flash of "light or smoke" from the two men behind the fence overlooking the grassy knoll. Bowers says that he thought one of the men might have been standing on the bumper of a car backed up to the fence. This shot blows away a large portion of the President's skull, rendering him brain-dead, though his heart continues to beat. Officer Hargis, riding on a motorcycle behind and slightly to the left of Kennedy, is splattered with blood and brain matter. Powers and O'Donnell are certain that this shot came from the front, from the fence on the grassy knoll. It's possible that a shot is fired from above and behind at almost exactly the same time, hitting Kennedy in the back. Secret Service Agent Paul Landis, in the limo with Powers and O'Donnell, says he believes the final head shot came from the grassy knoll, but that an earlier shot came from above and behind him (in the direction of the Book Depository). After a moment, JFK's limo finally speeds toward Parkland Hospital, four miles away.[47]

12:31 P.M.: A railroad yardman sees someone behind the fence on the grassy knoll "throw something in a bush." From the roof of the Terminal Annex Building near the Depository, J. C. Price sees a man (about twenty-five, with long dark hair) running full-speed away from the fence and toward the railroad yard. The man is carrying something in his right hand that "could have been a gun." He is wearing a white dress shirt, no tie, and khaki-colored trousers.[48] Dallas Sheriff Bill Decker, riding in the front car of the motorcade, radios for all available men to head for the railroad yard behind the fence on the grassy knoll.[49] Some witnesses say they saw a rifle barrel in one of the high windows of the Depository. As is clearly shown in photos, most of the crowd surges toward the grassy-knoll area, including many deputies. In fact, one researcher found that of the twenty deputies who gave statements, "sixteen thought the assassin had fired from the area of the grassy knoll" while three had "no opinion" and one "decided the shots came from" the Book Depository.[50]

12:31:30 P.M.: Less than ninety seconds after the last shot, Oswald is seen on the second floor of the Depository, in the lunch room drinking a Coke, by a policeman and Oswald's supervisor. Oswald is not winded. After the supervisor vouches for him, Oswald "saunters out of the building," looking calm as he passes a clerical supervisor.[51]

12:32 P.M.: Dallas Police Officer Joe Smith, accompanied by a deputy, runs behind the fence on the grassy knoll and smells gunpowder (as did many of the witnesses on or near the knoll). He pulls out his gun and confronts a well-dressed man. According to Officer Smith's statement to the FBI, the man pulls out ID "and showed me he was a Secret Service agent" and is allowed to go. However, Smith says the "Secret Service" agent is dressed in a sports shirt and sports pants, not in a suit. Also, even though he was well dressed, he "looked like a mechanic" and his hands were dirty. (Possibly from assembling or quickly disassembling a weapon.) Later, Secret Service Chief James Rowley confirms that all Secret Service agents in the area were riding in the motorcade and went to the hospital with the President—none were stationed on the ground. Yet Sheriff's Deputy Seymour Weitzman also told the Warren Commission he saw "Secret Service, as well" behind the fence. Weitzman later said the man who he thought was Secret Service showed him ID and said that he had everything under control. Although Weitzman is one of the first people behind the fence, he finds "numerous kinds of footprints that did not make sense because they were going in different directions." Officer Smith searches the interior of a 4-door, off-white 1960 or 1961 Chevrolet sedan parked by the fence, but not the trunk.[52]

Smith and Weitzman are soon joined by three (of seven) railroad employees who had watched the motorcade from an overpass approximately fifty feet in front of the Presidential limousine, and heard shots coming from the grassy knoll and saw a cloud of smoke hanging from the trees there. The railroad men also see all the footprints on the ground and two muddy footprints on the bumper of a station wagon parked there. One of the railroad men says that near the "station wagon there were two sets of footprints that left . . . they could've gotten in the trunk compartment of this car and pulled the lid down, which would have been very easy." None of the trunks of the cars parked behind the knoll are searched.[53]

According to Anthony Summers, "within minutes of the shooting" off-duty policeman John Tilson was driving near the knoll and "saw a man 'slipping and sliding' down the railway embankment behind the knoll." He later "described the man as '38–40 years, 5' 8" . . . dark hair, dark clothing.' Tilson comments that he looked like Jack Ruby, whom he knew, but does not claim it was Ruby." Officer Tilson said the man "had a car parked there, a black car. He threw something in the back seat and went around the front hurriedly and got in the car and took off." Tilson tried to follow the car but lost it. Around this time, a car is reported speeding through downtown Dallas, bearing a stolen Georgia license plate.[54]

Journalist Robert McNeil wrote that "a crowd, including reporters, converged on the grassy knoll believing it to be the direction from which the shots that struck the President were fired." He "saw several people running up the grassy hill beside the road. I thought they were chasing whoever had done the shooting and I ran after them."[55]

12:32 P.M.: At the Book Depository, James Worrell told police and the Warren Commission that he saw a man in his early thirties, 5' 8" to 5' 10", dark hair and average weight, in a dark sports jacket open in front with lighter colored pants, no hat or anything in his hands, emerge from the back entrance of the Book Depository and run off down Houston Street, toward the south. About three minutes earlier—one or two minutes before the shots—another witness, Richard Carr, had seen a man he described as heavy-set, with horn-rimmed glasses and a tan sports jacket, in a window on the top floor of the Book Depository. Shortly after the shots, Carr sees the same man "walking very fast" south on Houston Street to Commerce, then east on Commerce one block to Record Street. Then the man gets into a 1961 or 1962 gray Rambler station wagon, which is parked just north of Commerce on Record Street. The station wagon, which has a Texas license plate, is driven away by a young black man, in a northerly direction, away from Dealey Plaza.[56]

Two witnesses, one of them a sheriff's deputy, see "a light colored Nash (Rambler) station wagon" pulled up in front of the Book Depository "and a white male came down the grass-covered incline between the building and the street and entered the station wagon after which it drove away in the direction of the Oak Cliff section of Dallas." Deputy Roger Craig also saw the incident and said "I heard a shrill whistle and I turned around and saw a white male running down the hill from the direction of the" Depository, while "a light colored Rambler station wagon" pulled over and the man "who had been running got into this car. The man driving this station wagon was a dark complected white male." Deputy Craig "reported this incident at once to a Secret Service officer, whose name I do not know"—though again, no real Secret Service agents were in the area. Craig saw Oswald at police headquarters later, and felt that he had been the running man.[57]

Behind the Depository, Police Sergeant D. V. Harkness encounters "several 'well-armed' men dressed in suits. They tell Sergeant Harkness they are with the Secret Service." But, again, no real Secret Service agents are in or around Dealey Plaza or the Book Depository at that time.[58]

Several witnesses and officers have directed attention to the Book Depository. But one witness on the street who later claims to have identified Oswald as standing in the window on the sixth floor initially describes the man as much older and heavier than Oswald, and fails to pick Oswald out of a lineup later. The Depository has not attracted as much attention as the area behind the grassy knoll, and is not sealed off until twenty-eight minutes after the shooting.[59] Within minutes of the shooting, Oswald walks out of the building without being noticed—and if Oswald can leave the building without being noticed, anyone else can, too.

According to most accounts, Oswald walks north one block, then turns right and goes east on Pacific. He swings back to Elm Street. He pauses in front of the Blue Front Inn, seven blocks east of the assassination site. He possibly boards the Marsalis Street bus, on Griffin Street. When the bus becomes stalled in traffic, Oswald asks for a transfer and gets off the bus at the same time as another passenger. Oswald heads south on Lamar Street. He pauses in front of the Greyhound bus terminal, three blocks from where he left the bus. He takes a cab, which goes southeast down Zangs Boulevard and turns south on to Beckley.[60]

12:35–1:00 P.M.: In separate incidents, police arrest or detain two men at the Dal-Tex building, across Houston Street from the Book Depository. Some researchers feel that one or more shots may have been fired from a Dal-Tex window near the corner of Elm and Houston, where the line of sight to JFK's limo would not have been obstructed by tree limbs as it was from the Depository. Some witnesses stated that "when the shots were fired [at JFK], they sounded as if they came from the direction of the Dal-Tex building." One of the men arrested at the Dal-Tex is a young man wearing a black leather jacket and black gloves. He is later released, and no records were kept of his arrest. The other man arrested is from Los Angeles. According to Anthony Summers, the man "was detained for 'acting suspiciously.'" Many years earlier, the Los Angeles man "had been observed in the company of James Dolan"; Dolan "knew Jack Ruby well" and Dolan was described by Congressional investigators as "an acquaintance of both Carlos Marcello and Santo Trafficante." The man from Los Angeles sometimes did business from the seventeenth floor of the Pierre Marquette Building in New Orleans, where he received mail. Summers writes that "in his work for Marcello, [David] Ferrie worked out of" a different office on the same floor. The man from Los Angeles is released within hours. Police search the Dal-Tex building.[61]

In all, at least twelve men—possibly more—are detained by police, then released. In some cases, no records are kept about their detainment. In addition, some men from the Book Depository, besides Oswald, were questioned closely by police.[62]

12:35 P.M. (approx.): "Officer J. D. Tippit, who had been parked at" a Texaco service "station watching traffic . . . suddenly sped off towards Oak Cliff," according to "three attendants" at the station interviewed by William Turner. The station was located "on the Oak Cliff end of the Houston Street Viaduct that the fleeing Oswald traveled in a taxi . . . just a few blocks west of the triple underpass in Dealey Plaza."[63]

12:37 P.M.: At Parkland Hospital, JFK is rushed into the trauma room, where faint signs of life are detected. The first doctor to see Kennedy (and the only one to see him before his clothes were removed), Dr. Charles J. Carrico, sees a small, round bullet-entry wound (3–5 mm wide) on his throat, above his shirt and tie. Carrico is soon joined by other doctors, who note the huge head wound, which they estimate to be about 35 square centimeters (by the time the autopsy on Kennedy is performed that night, this wound will be described as four times bigger). They characterize this wound, at the right rear of the head, as an exit wound (indicating that the shot came from the front). At the small, round bullet-entry wound in his throat, a tracheotomy incision is performed. Also, external cardiac massage is performed. Emergency room doctors don't have any reason to turn Kennedy's body over, so they don't notice the wound in his back. Connally lies wounded in a second trauma room a few yards away.[64]

JFK's limo is left unattended in the parking lot and is soon surrounded by people. Eventually someone, probably a Secret Service agent, starts scrubbing the blood off the President's limo, unintentionally removing what would have been crucial evidence.[65]

12:40 P.M. (approx.): Jack Ruby is seen again at the *Dallas Morning News* building. "Hugh Aynesworth, reporter, *Dallas Morning News*" told the FBI that "shortly after" Jack Ruby had been "missed, people began to come to the office of the newspaper announcing the assassination of President John F. Kennedy and Ruby appeared shortly thereafter and feigned surprise at this announcement and gave some show of emotion over the news that had been received."[66]

12:44 P.M.: The Dallas police broadcast a description of the President's attacker, which is too old and heavy to be a good description of Oswald: white, 5' 10", 160 pounds, 30 years old, armed with a .30-cal. rifle.[67]

12:45 P.M.: Officer Tippit is ordered into the Oak Cliff area of Dallas, though the veracity of this transmission is considered problematic by some researchers, since it was missing from some early accounts. Jack Ruby and Lee Harvey Oswald live in different parts of the small Oak Cliff neighborhood.[68]

12:45 P.M. (1:45 Eastern): J. Edgar Hoover calls Bobby Kennedy, who is having lunch at his home in Virginia, to tell him that "the President has been shot. I think it's serious. I am endeavoring to get details. I'll call you back when I find out more." Bobby calls CIA Director John McCone at Langley CIA Headquarters and asks him to come right over (it's only about a mile away).[69]

12:50 P.M.: Secret Service agent Forrest Sorrells arrives at the Book Depository after leaving Parkland Hospital. He is able to enter the rear of the building without presenting any identification.[70]

12:54 P.M.: Officer Tippit radios that he is in the area, and he is instructed to "be at large for any emergency."[71]

12:58 P.M.: Police Capt. Will Fritz arrives at the Book Depository after leaving Parkland Hospital. Twenty-eight minutes after the shooting, Fritz orders that the building be sealed off.[72]

12:59 P.M. (approx.): Two men working at a record shop in Oak Cliff say Tippit hurried into the shop, made a call, apparently got no answer, and hung up after about a minute and rushed from the store. Dallas reporter Earl Golz interviewed the two men, whose shop was one block from the Texas Theater (where Oswald would be apprehended) and seven blocks from where Tippit would be killed. The men knew Tippit because he sometimes stopped in the store to use their phone.[73]

1:00 P.M.: **John F. Kennedy receives the last rites of the Catholic Church and is pronounced dead at Parkland Hospital.**

RFK's Suspicions and
C-Day is Put on Hold

THOUGH JFK WAS PRONOUNCED DEAD at 1:00 P.M. in Dallas, the public would not know that for another half hour. Events continued to unfold at a dizzying pace in Dallas, but Oswald's actions can be explained by looking at them from two points of view: Oswald's perspective, and that of the Mafia chiefs behind the assassination.

By 1:00, Oswald must have realized that things had gone terribly, horribly wrong for some reason. Yet he probably felt that he still had a mission to complete for US intelligence. It most likely involved leaving work after lunch and going to a prearranged meeting at the Texas Theater, as part of getting to Mexico and on to Cuba. The reality of Oswald's mission, and how much was made up or exaggerated by men like Ferrie and Banister, may never be known; but, as someone who had accepted the risks involved in defection to Russia at the height of the Cold War, Oswald would have known the value of following orders.

CIA asset John Martino, whose associates ranged from Rosselli to David Morales, said that Oswald was supposed to meet his "contact" at the Texas Theater, then be eliminated.[1] As for the use of movie theaters as clandestine meeting places, consider the autobiography of someone who had reportedly met Oswald in Dallas just three months earlier, David Atlee Phillips. In his autobiography published in 1977, just before Phillips became part of the JFK controversy, Phillips wrote that when he was a young man starting in the intelligence business, he "told a case officer on the telephone I would meet him at the Roxy Theater at eleven . . . I learned recognition procedures: 'You go into the men's room at the movie with a copy of *Newsweek* in your left hand. You say to the agent, 'Haven't we met in Cairo?'"[2] At the Texas Theater, Oswald would have something unusual with him, half of a box-top, as if he was supposed to meet someone with the other half. Oswald would sit next to at least two people in the theater, then move, as if he was waiting for them to say a code phrase or produce the other half of the box-top.[3] As noted earlier, the "torn half" matching technique was used in 1963 by both the CIA officer who had originally recruited Phillips (with Antonio Veciana) and by members of Michel Mertz's heroin ring—most recently, in the Texas–Mexico City heroin run that was busted at Laredo at the time of Oswald's return from Mexico.

Rosselli and his associates needed to quickly have JFK's death blamed on Oswald, to avoid a massive manhunt in Dallas. They also needed him to be killed quickly, before he could talk about Ferrie, Banister, or other connections that could lead authorities to Marcello and the other mob bosses. Based on Oswald's past experience, he could be counted on to maintain cover for a time if he were apprehended; but for Rosselli and the others, the sooner he was dead, the better. As noted earlier, it's possible that Oswald was supposed to have died at or near the Book Depository just after the shooting. The delays in JFK's motorcade may have caused problems with that part of the plan. Because of Rosselli's ties to men like Banister and Morales, he could have known what Oswald was supposed to do when he was scheduled to leave work after lunch to begin his mission to Mexico and Cuba. This gave the mobster more opportunities to have Oswald killed in a seemingly logical fashion. As noted earlier, Jack Ruby was apparently a key part of this plan, either to arrange for a Dallas policeman to be in the right place to shoot Oswald or to do the job himself, if there was no other way.[4]

If a Dallas policeman was in the right place to confront Oswald, Rosselli would win, no matter what the outcome. Rosselli knew that the police—having discovered that Oswald was missing from the Depository—would soon find the "empty blanket" that formerly held the Mannlicher-Carcano, at the house where Oswald had stayed the previous night. If the police killed Oswald, the slain man would be blamed for the President's death. If Oswald, or whoever might be with him, killed the policeman and then fled, that was also good for Rosselli. The police would quickly catch up to the cop-killer, who would be fleeing on foot and dependent on public transportation, and the angry Dallas cops might well shoot to kill. Rosselli knew that the basic elements, a murderous ex-serviceman hiding his rifle in a blanket and using his pistol to shoot a patrolman on the street beside his squad car, had been accepted by the audiences for the then-obscure B-movie he'd helped produce in 1948 (*He Walked by Night*), and there was no reason to believe the public wouldn't buy it now.[5]

THE SLAYING OF OFFICER J. D. TIPPIT

At 1:00 P.M. in the Oak Cliff neighborhood of Dallas, Earlene Roberts, the housekeeper at Oswald's rooming house, saw Oswald run into the rooming house.[6] Also at 1:00, Dallas police headquarters radioed the patrol car of Officer J. D. Tippit, but he did not answer.[7] At 1:02, Earlene Roberts saw a Dallas police car pull slowly up to the rooming house. The police car parked directly in front of the house and sounded its horn twice, and then slowly pulled away. She says she saw two policemen in the car. However, William Turner points out that Tippit's uniform jacket was "was on a hanger in the car's window," and she may have mistaken that for a second officer. The housekeeper, who had poor eyesight, said she thought the car's number was "107"—Tippit's number was "10."[8]

At 1:05 P.M., Roberts saw Oswald running out of the rooming house. Oswald had probably changed shirts, to a long-sleeved rust-brown shirt with a white T-shirt beneath it. He was also probably packing his revolver by this time. The housekeeper last saw him waiting at a bus stop, for a bus which would take him back downtown.[9] At 1:08, Tippit radioed headquarters, but headquarters didn't reply.[10]

Two people at the Texas Theater, Butch Burroughs and Jack Davis, say they observed Oswald inside the Texas Theater as early as 1:15, according to researcher Larry Harris. He writes that "Burroughs, who was working the concession counter, remembered waiting on Oswald."[11] However, sometime between 1:10 and 1:15—most likely around 1:12—Dallas Police Officer J. D. Tippit was shot at the 400 block of East Tenth Street, between Denver and Patton streets, by a man who was "kind of short" and "kind of heavy," and wearing "khaki and a white shirt" according to eyewitness Acquilla Clemons. This man then motioned another man with him to "go on." Another witness saw a man with a long coat, which ended just about at his hands, looking at Tippit—fallen, on the ground—then running to his car (a 1950–51 gray, maybe a Plymouth) and driving off. Also, most witnesses say that the man who was talking with Tippit had been walking west—toward Oswald's rooming house, not away from it. Also, there were many evidence problems noted with some of the bullets in Tippit and shells found at the scene not matching, initial descriptions of the weapon, and a discarded jacket.[12]

Thousands of pages, even entire books, have been written just about the Tippit slaying, so we cannot cover here all of the evidence and the problems with the theory of Oswald as a "lone assassin" of Tippit. Oswald may have killed Tippit, someone with Oswald may have killed Tippit, or Oswald may have been in the theater totally unaware of Tippit's death. We will look briefly at some events that call into question the Warren Commission version of events, which appears to have been based on incomplete evidence. For example, two days after the Tippit slaying, a policeman told witness Acquilla Clemons that she might get hurt if she told anyone else what she saw, and she never spoke to the Warren Commission about it. As noted by Anthony Summers, witness "Warren Reynolds was shot in the head two days after telling the FBI he could not identify Oswald," and after his recovery Reynolds "agreed he thought the fleeing gunman had been Oswald after all." The chief suspect in the Reynolds shooting was a heroin addict named Darrell Wayne Garner. Though Garner drunkenly boasted of the shooting and confessed to being at the scene, he was released when provided with an alibi by Nancy Mooney, a former employee of Jack Ruby. Eight days later, Mooney was arrested; she "was later found hanged in her cell" by her pants, "presumably a suicide." Another Tippit slaying witness, Domingo Benavides, "was anonymously threatened after the Tippit killing," and "his brother Edward was murdered by an unknown assailant" soon afterward.[13] We feel that Jack Ruby's mob associates in Dallas—especially those who also knew Rosselli, Trafficante, and Marcello—were capable of having key witnesses intimidated or attacked.

Two key witnesses in addition to Clemons were not heard by the Warren Commission. According to researcher Larry Harris, "Frank Wright, who lived on the next block . . . heard gunshots, went out to see what was happening and saw a man standing near a police car. He insisted the man ran and jumped in a gray car parked beyond" Tippit's car "and sped away west on Tenth Street. Jack Tatum told House Assassination Committee investigators that he . . . had just passed a police car when the shooting broke out; Tatum paused and watched the gunman walk behind the squad car and take careful, deliberate aim before firing one more shot into Tippit." The HSCA Report said "This action, which is commonly described as a coup de grace, is more indicative of an execution."[14] That is something that one might expect of an experienced hit man. We have included other problems with key Warren Commission witnesses who identified Oswald as Tippit's lone slayer in this endnote.[15] Even the Dallas Assistant District Attorney at the time, William Alexander, later told Anthony Summers regarding the Tippit slaying that "Oswald's movements did not add up then and they do not add up now. No way. Certainly he may have had accomplices." And when Oswald went to the Texas Theater, "was he supposed to meet someone?" and "did he miss a connection?"[16]

At 1:22, officers on the scene of the Tippit shooting broadcast a description of the assailant, describing him as a white male about 30 years old, 5' 8", "black wavy hair," slender build, wearing a white jacket, white shirt, and dark slacks.[17] William Turner cites Dallas police radio logs as saying that "shortly after 1:41 P.M., Sergeant Hill came on the air: 'A witness reports that he [the Tippit suspect] was last seen in the Abundant Life Temple about the 400 block. We are fixing to go in and shake it down.' On an alternate channel, Car 95 ordered 'Send me another squad [car] over here to Tenth and Crawford to check out this church basement.'" However, another call came in, erroneously reporting that the suspect was at a library, where police converged. Then police were called to the Texas Theater, and the Abundant Life Temple was never searched.[18]

According to the Warren Commission version, Johnny Calvin Brewer, the owner of a shoe store six blocks away from the slaying site, heard a report on the radio about a policeman being shot in the neighborhood. He looked up to see a man hide from a passing police car by stepping into his doorway. He followed the man, Oswald, who ducked into the nearby Texas Theater. Brewer alerted the cashier, who called the police. However, some researchers think that Oswald had been inside the theater since shortly after 1 P.M., either having bought a ticket or using a ticket someone had bought earlier and given to him. As noted earlier, witness Jack Davis says that once in the theater, Oswald sat next to him for a few minutes; then Oswald moved to sit next to another person for a few minutes; then Oswald got up and went to the lobby, as if he was looking for someone. The alternate theory says that Oswald got worried when he couldn't find his contact, the person who would have the other half of the torn box-top, so Oswald walked out to the lobby, and then onto the sidewalk, looking for his contact. He saw a police car go by and ducked into the doorway of the shoe store, then went back into the theater to await his contact's arrival.[19] In any event, police broadcast an alarm at 1:45 to converge on the Texas Theater.

At approximately 1:48, police arrived at the Theater, and the shoe store owner pointed out Oswald to the officers. However, Oswald was not the first patron approached. First, an officer frisked two men sitting in the center of the theater before going on to Oswald. Did one or more of the policemen hope Oswald would make a run for it, allowing them to shoot the possible cop-killer? Assistant DA William Alexander had gone to the Theater, and says the assumption at the time was that the person who killed Tippit had also killed JFK. Oswald was arrested between 1:51 and 1:55, after a scuffle.

As noted by author Henry Hurt, "there is conflicting testimony among arresting officers about just what happened during the arrest," and "most of the dozen or so patrons scattered about the theater . . . were never canvassed and questioned in any inclusive fashion by the FBI or the Warren Commission."[20] There is also some evidence calling into question what ID Oswald had on him at the time, and whether an additional wallet was found at the Tippit slaying scene.

At 2:00, Oswald arrived at the Dallas police station. He was found to have $13.87 on him. He also may have had David Ferrie's library card.[21] At 2:30, a police call went out to look for a 1957 Chevy sedan, last seen in the vicinity of the Tippit slaying. The alert said that the car's occupants should be checked for illegal weapons.[22] Later, police searched Oswald's small apartment at the rooming house. In a sea bag, they found a tiny Minox spy camera, three other cameras, a 15-power telescope, two pairs of field glasses, a compass, and a pedometer. There were also several rolls of exposed Minox film.[23] At approximately 3:00, police arrived at the home of Ruth Hyde Paine, where Oswald's wife Marina lived and Oswald had spent the previous night. Two weeks earlier, Marina had noticed what appeared to be Oswald's rifle wrapped in a blanket in the garage. Now, police found the blanket empty.[24] The case against the ex-serviceman who kept his rifle wrapped in a blanket and shot a patrolman on the street seemed cinched, except for one more important piece of evidence.

The "magic bullet," the cornerstone of the Single Bullet Theory required for one lone presidential assassin, was found at Parkland Hospital around the time Oswald was being arrested at the Texas Theater. This is the almost-pristine bullet that supposedly caused JFK's back and throat wounds and all of Connally's injuries. According to Henry Hurt, citing medical reports, it "'literally shattered' his fifth rib, leaving five inches of it 'pulverized,'" and then "struck Connally's right wrist" and "shattered the radius bone at the largest point"—all while, according to the Single Bullet Theory, Connally continued to grip "his white Stetson hat" with that hand. The bullet then buried itself in Connally's thigh, from which it supposedly fell out, later, emerging in almost perfect condition. Thousands of pages have been written that point out the many problems with the Single Bullet Theory and its magic bullet, by critics such as Dr. Cyril Wecht. These problems include fragments from the pristine bullet left in Connally's body, and other sizable fragments that were removed from his wrist, some visible on X-rays and others seen by doctors, a nurse, and a Texas State Trooper that never made it into evidence.[25]

Around 1:30, about fifteen minutes before the magic bullet would be discovered, Jack Ruby was seen at Parkland Hospital by two reliable witnesses, including noted journalist Seth Kantor. Kantor later remembered the brief encounter and even speaking with Ruby. However, Ruby later lied to authorities about the encounter, saying that he hadn't gone to Parkland that day. This raises the question of why he would deny his presence there— unless he was engaged in some illegal activity, such as planting evidence. Ruby may have planted the magic bullet, or may have given it to someone else to plant.[26]

At about 1:45, Parkland Hospital Senior Engineer Darrell Tomlinson found the nearly pristine bullet. It was on one of two stretchers close together in a hallway, one of which had probably been used to transport Connally, while the other hadn't been used for either Kennedy or Connally. Both stretchers had probably been unattended for thirty minutes, in a hall with various people milling about. According to one account, the stretcher had probably held a bleeding child within the hour, so its fresh blood stains might have been enough to cause a person to think it had been Kennedy's or Connally's stretcher.[27] Regardless of who placed the pristine bullet on the stretcher, it was used to link Oswald's rifle to the shooting of JFK and Connally.

OTHERS HEAR THE NEWS OF JFK'S ASSASSINATION

In New Orleans, the trial of Carlos Marcello was in its final stages. At 1:30 P.M. CST, Judge Herbert Christenberry "had just delivered his fifteen minute charge to the jury," according to John H. Davis, when "a bailiff suddenly strode into the courtroom and . . . handed the judge a note." After reading it, the shocked judge announced that JFK had been shot and might be dead. The judge "handed the case to the jury and called for an hour's recess."[28] Court resumed session at 3:00. However, Bobby's lead Justice Department prosecutor on the case, John Diuguid, told us that while David Ferrie had been in the courtroom with Marcello's team before the break, he thought that Ferrie wasn't in court when everyone returned.[29]

With remarkable speed, at 3:15 the jury delivered its verdict. The juror Marcello had bribed reportedly boasted later "that not only had he voted not guilty . . . but he had also convinced several of his fellow jurors to vote not guilty." Marcello had also threatened the key witness against him during the trial. Consequently, Marcello was pronounced "not guilty" on both counts of perjury and conspiracy.[30]

There was a celebration at the Marcello home, but Davis writes that Marcello left the party and "went to his office at the Town and Country" motel, according to one source "looking as if he had something urgent on his mind."[31] There were loose ends that still needed to be taken care of if Marcello didn't want to face far more serious charges than those he had just escaped.

In Paris, a CIA case officer was meeting with Rolando Cubela (AMLASH). They had discussed Cubela being provided with several items, including "two high-powered rifles with telescopic sights."[32] According to the Church Committee, the case officer "tells AMLASH the explosives and rifles with telescopic sights will be provided. The case officer also offers AMLASH the poison pen device but AMLASH is dissatisfied with it. As the meeting breaks up, they are told President Kennedy has been assassinated."[33]

In Washington, D.C., Harry Williams had returned from lunch to resume his meeting with the CIA officials. According to CIA Director John McCone's desk calendar, now at the National Archives, McCone had lunch that day, starting at 1 P.M. (Eastern), with Richard Helms, Lyman Kirkpatrick, and two other officials. By the time Harry's meeting resumed, everyone had heard that JFK had been shot. Harry told us that the highest official at his meeting, apparently Lyman Kirkpatrick, began eyeing him with suspicion. Harry said he was trying to play it cool, but he felt that perhaps the CIA official took it the wrong way. The meeting broke up within minutes, with all plans put on hold, and Harry returned to his room at the Ebbitt Hotel.[34]

Someone in the Presidential party in Dallas called Bobby at his Hickory Hill estate in Virginia, to give him the tragic news that JFK was dead. That was followed by a flood of calls over the four phones in Bobby's large house, from LBJ, Hoover, and others. While taking a break from the flurry of calls, according to Richard Mahoney, Bobby confided to Ed Guthman, his press secretary and friend, that "I thought they'd get one of us, but . . . I thought it would be me."[35]

After John McCone arrived at Bobby's estate, probably between 2:45 and 3:00 (Eastern), Mahoney writes that Bobby "went out of the lawn with him. 'I asked McCone,' Kennedy was to tell his trusted aide Walter Sheridan, 'if they had killed my brother, and I asked him in a way that he couldn't lie to me.'" Mahoney points out that "McCone was one of Bobby's closest friends in the Administration, and this extraordinary question revealed a deep and terrible suspicion about the CIA, something born of some knowledge, or at least intuition, and not simply the incontinence of grief."[36] Neither McCone or Bobby knew about the ongoing CIA-Mafia plots, or the assassination side of the Cubela (AMLASH) and QJWIN operations, so we feel that Bobby's question is likely in reference to some aspect of C-Day/AMWORLD. Bobby's suspicion could have been triggered by the way in which JFK was killed, by the link of Oswald (or Oswald's alias) to the crime, by some activity related to C-Day being staged in Dallas, or by all of those things.

As we noted earlier, McCone told Bobby that the CIA hadn't killed his brother. Yet "autonomous" exiles like Manuel Artime weren't actually part of the CIA, and within an hour, Bobby would apparently focus his suspicion more directly in that direction.[37] Not long after the assassination, Arthur Schlesinger, Jr. notes, CIA Director McCone told Bobby that "he thought there were two people involved in the shooting."[38] By 5:00 (Eastern), McCone was back at CIA Headquarters, meeting with Richard Helms, Lyman Kirkpatrick, and two other officials.[39]

JFK's assassination was reverberating throughout the US government, as information, misinformation, and possible disinformation about Oswald started to be uncovered. Peter Dale Scott says that "FBI Agent James Hosty, who handled the Oswald file in Dallas, has written that he learned later from two independent sources that at the time of Oswald's arrest, fully armed warplanes were sent screaming toward Cuba. Just before they entered Cuban airspace, they were hastily called back. With the launching of airplanes, the entire U.S. military went on alert." Scott notes that "these planes would have been launched from the U.S. Strike Command at MacDill Air Force Base in Florida," but Scott was unaware that that was the very base that JFK had visited just four days earlier, for a secret session with the Strike Force Commander and other leaders. Scott points out a declassified "cable from U.S. Army Intelligence in Texas, dated November 22, 1963, telling the Strike Command (falsely) that Oswald had defected to Cuba in 1959 and was "a card-carrying member of the Communist Party." Later, even Hoover would erroneously tell "Bobby Kennedy that Oswald 'went to Cuba on several occasions, but would not tell us what he went to Cuba for.'"[40]

According to FBI agent Hosty, after JFK's murder in Dallas "the Pentagon ordered us to Defense Condition 3, more commonly known as Def Con 3— the equivalent of loading and locking your weapon, and then placing your finger on the trigger. The power cells within Washington were in a panic."[41] However, the alert status soon diminished. *U.S. News & World Report* notes that "the Air Force and the CIA sent a 'Flash' worldwide alert for all" US surveillance flights "to return to their bases lest the Soviet Union be provoked."[42]

In Havana, French journalist Jean Daniel was having lunch with Fidel Castro, discussing JFK's proposal for talks between the two countries. When Castro was informed of Kennedy's death, Castro said three times, "This is very bad." (Other accounts have Castro saying "This is very bad news.")[43]

In Tampa, Police Chief J. P. Mullins was reading a letter from the Secret Service thanking him for protecting JFK when his wife called and said JFK had been shot.[44] In Chicago, Secret Service chief Martineau later told an FBI agent that "his office had verified" that on 11-22-63, "[Thomas] Vallee was employed at his place of business during the entire day" at a printing company at "625 West Jackson, Chicago."[45] Vallee had been arrested on the day of JFK's canceled Chicago motorcade, and soon released. It's not known if Vallee had been put under any type of surveillance after the very similar Tampa threat surfaced. It seems unusual that Vallee was apparently not interviewed after JFK's death, to see if he knew or had ever met his fellow ex-Marine, Lee Harvey Oswald.

In Miami, Jimmy Hoffa called Frank Ragano, the attorney he shared with Trafficante, and gloated over the assassination of JFK. However, Hoffa's mood would change later after he got a call from a Teamster official in Washington. Hoffa was furious that two Teamster leaders at the union's Washington headquarters had closed the office, lowered its flag to half-mast, and sent condolences to the President's widow. Hoffa yelled at his secretary for crying, hung up on the people in Washington, and left the building.[46] In San Juan, Puerto Rico, FBI reports say, a Teamster organizer told the Secretary-Treasurer of the local Teamsters Hotel and Restaurant Workers Union that "We killed Kennedy and the next will be Ramos Ducos," an honest union official. The Teamster organizer was an associate of Frank Chavez, linked to Jack Ruby by FBI reports. Chavez would later attempt to kill Bobby Kennedy, and several reporters would come to suspect that Chavez had been involved in JFK's assassination.[47]

HARRY WILLIAMS TRIES TO GET FOOTAGE OF OSWALD ON TELEVISION

As described in earlier chapters, by around 4 P.M. (Eastern) in Washington, D.C., reporter Haynes Johnson had joined Harry Williams in his room at the Ebbitt Hotel. Harry had been helping Johnson with his upcoming *Bay of Pigs* book, and Johnson had also worked closely with Manuel Artime. Harry was on the phone with Bobby Kennedy, who told him that C-Day was on hold, so Harry wouldn't be leaving for Guantanamo the next day. Bobby then asked to speak to Johnson, also a friend of Bobby's. As Haynes wrote, Bobby "was utterly in control of his emotions when he came on the line and sounded almost studiedly brisk as he said: 'One of your guys did it.'"[48] Haynes didn't mention Bobby's comment to Harry, and Bobby never said anything about it—or said anything similar—to Harry.

Though historian Richard Mahoney didn't know about C-Day, he was perceptive when he wrote that Bobby's comment to Haynes Johnson "clearly was referring to embittered Cubans deployed by elements in the CIA" who might have been "acting at a deniable distance."[49] As we noted earlier, we feel that Bobby's comment related somehow to Manuel Artime's operations, which had several ties to associates of Marcello, Trafficante, and Rosselli.

Haynes Johnson soon left Harry at the Ebbitt Hotel. Harry then received a call that appears to have been an attempt to make sure that the footage of Oswald on TV in New Orleans—appearing to be an ardent Castro supporter—was quickly given a national audience. As described previously, NBC was preparing a Bay of Pigs special to run in early December, and Bobby had introduced Harry Williams to Chet Huntley and David Brinkley, who anchored America's most widely watched evening newscast. Chet and Harry "hit it off" and became friends. Huntley told Harry to call him whenever he wanted to pass along some news, to feel free to call him at any time.[50] In working on the TV special, Huntley may have sensed that something big was brewing about Cuba, and, as Bobby's closest Cuban-exile confidant, Harry would be one of the first to know of any new developments.

Apparently, Harry's friendship with Chet Huntley became known to some of the other exiles. So, after Haynes Johnson left, Harry was called by Cuban exile Alberto Fowler, from New Orleans. As we noted earlier, Fowler had shadowed JFK in Palm Beach on November 17, 1963, the day before the Tampa assassination attempt. Fowler, who lived in New Orleans, says he "had taken the house next to" JFK's estate for "the whole weekend."[51] Fowler was a Bay of Pigs veteran who had been left bitter at JFK because of his long imprisonment in Cuba. Fowler worked with Clay Shaw at the International Trade Mart in New Orleans, where CIA asset William Gaudet had an office; Fowler may have been a CIA asset as well, since a CIA memo from 1967 had three lines about Fowler's ties and activities censored. Fowler would soon join the International Advisory Committee for INCA, the group that helped to promote Oswald's radio debate.

Fowler was a member of Tony Varona's Cuban Revolutionary Council, and Varona may have told Fowler how to contact Harry. Harry knew Fowler as he knew many Bay of Pigs veterans, but it was a casual acquaintance and Fowler was not part of C-Day. Fowler's associates were linked to Artime's camp outside New Orleans that had reportedly been visited by Oswald, Ferrie, and Michel Mertz (using the alias Jean Souetre).[52] Fowler also had a friend in common with mob associate Frank Fiorini.

It is not known who, if anyone, put Fowler up to calling Harry in Washington, but the timing is suspicious. Fowler told Harry that Oswald had been passing out pro-Castro leaflets in New Orleans and making statements on TV and radio, and that he should let Bobby Kennedy or his friends in the news media know, immediately. Harry tried Bobby, but he had already left his home for the Pentagon. Harry then called NBC, trying to reach Chet Huntley, who had been on the air almost constantly covering the assassination. Harry was able to leave a message with someone else in the newsroom.[53]

It's not known if Harry's call had any effect, but by 7:00 P.M. (Eastern), Chet Huntley was introducing the audio portion of Oswald's August 21, 1963 interview with WDSU-TV in New Orleans. By 7:43, NBC was running the video portion of the interview as well, allowing millions of viewers to see and hear Oswald say "I would definitely say that I am a Marxist" and then outlining the aims of the Fair Play for Cuba Committee.[54]

Fowler's actions could have been innocent, or he could have been manipulated by those wanting to get a message across to Bobby Kennedy and the American public. Fowler had first asked Harry to let Bobby know, and, as we saw from Bobby's comment to Haynes Johnson, Bobby's initial reaction was to link JFK's assassination to anti-Castro exiles. The TV footage of Oswald would help frame JFK's assassin as just the reverse, pro-Castro. If Fowler's actions were being manipulated by those who knew about C-Day (mob associates like Varona or Artime), then they might have felt that getting quick, wide exposure for such footage could have the effect of prompting a US invasion of Cuba. Alberto Fowler doesn't resurface in the JFK story until 1967. After the sudden death of David Ferrie, the prime suspect at the time of New Orleans District Attorney Jim Garrison's investigation, Fowler began assisting Garrison. Shortly after that, Garrison's new prime suspect became Clay Shaw, Fowler's co-worker at the Trade Mart, who was later acquitted. Fowler may also have steered Garrison away from exiles like Varona and Artime.

TRAFFICANTE CELEBRATES IN TAMPA, BUT PROBLEMS EMERGE IN NEW ORLEANS
According to David Ferrie's statement to the FBI, Carlos Marcello's celebration—ostensibly of his acquittal—lasted until at least 9 P.M. at the Royal Orleans hotel. But, as we noted, Marcello wasn't there to enjoy it. However, Santo Trafficante was able to enjoy his own more intimate celebration in Tampa. Trafficante had earlier arranged to meet his lawyer, Frank Ragano, and Ragano's girlfriend—Nancy Young (later Ragano)—for dinner. The place would be Tampa's International Inn, where JFK had delivered a speech just four days earlier, and certainly the irony was not lost on Trafficante. It wasn't lost on Ragano either, who realized that in "the same hotel lobby I was crossing to meet Santo, Kennedy had shaken hands and waved at admirers" earlier in the week.

Ragano found that the normally crowded restaurant was almost empty that Friday night. He says that "A smiling Santo greeted me at our table. 'Isn't that something, they killed the son-of-a-bitch,' he said, hugging and kissing me on the cheeks. 'The son-of-a-bitch is dead.'" Ragano noted that Trafficante's "generally bland face was wreathed in joy." As Trafficante drank Chivas Regal, he proclaimed "This is like lifting a load of stones off my shoulders . . . now they'll get off my back, off Carlos's back, and off [Hoffa's] back. We'll make big money out of this and maybe go back into Cuba. I'm glad for [Hoffa's] sake because [Lyndon] Johnson is sure as hell going to remove Bobby. I don't see how he'll keep him in office." Ragano said that Trafficante "talked more excitedly than usual and it was unclear to me what he meant about returning to Cuba." Ragano didn't realize that Trafficante and several of his men knew about C-Day, and hoped that, by spreading stories in the coming days to the effect that Oswald had somehow been acting for Castro, the US would go ahead and invade Cuba in retaliation.

After a Trafficante toast, Ragano's girlfriend arrived. Ragano says that "when her drink came, Santo and I raised our glasses again and Santo said merrily, 'For a hundred years of health and to John Kennedy's death.'" Then, Trafficante "started laughing" and began another toast. Horrified by the public spectacle, Ragano's girlfriend "banged her glass on the table and rushed out of the restaurant." Ragano stayed with the "jubilant" Trafficante, who "continued toasting in Sicilian to the bountiful times he was certain were coming."[55]

Trafficante could tell from the news that Oswald was being blamed as a lone assassin. In the FBI, that conclusion had already been reached. Around 5:15 P.M. (Eastern), J. Edgar Hoover had issued an internal memo stating that police "very probably" had Kennedy's killer in custody. He called Oswald a nut and a pro-Castro extremist, an "extreme radical of the left." Hoover would also start to exert pressure on senior FBI officials to complete their investigation and issue a factual report supporting the conclusion that Oswald was the lone assassin. While it wasn't a federal offense for one person acting alone to kill a president, it was a federal offense for two or more people to conspire to "injure any officer of the US engaged in discharging the duties of his office." Thus, proclaiming Oswald the "lone" assassin kept it a local and not a federal prosecution—thus keeping it out of the hands of Bobby Kennedy's Justice Department.[56]

Hoover would have had plenty to worry about if Bobby Kennedy had ever been able to take control of Oswald's prosecution and the investigation. Not that Hoover was involved in JFK's assassination, but there had been many missed warnings along the way, like Ed Becker's warning to an FBI agent about Marcello's threat, and Jose Aleman's similar warning to an FBI agent about Trafficante. In fact, several hours after the assassination, Jose Aleman was visited by two FBI agents. Apparently, they came in reaction to Aleman's earlier warnings about Trafficante's threats against JFK. The agents kept pressuring Aleman until he told them that Trafficante didn't say *he* was going have JFK killed, just that JFK was going to be hit. The FBI agents reportedly told Aleman to keep his account of the Trafficante threat confidential, which Aleman did until the late 1970s.[57]

Hoover's early decision to pronounce Oswald a lone assassin—even before JFK's autopsy had been performed—had several effects. It no doubt signaled to many agents in the field what they should be looking for, and it's clear that there was a gradual shift from agents pursuing every lead vigorously, to a focus on trying to prove Oswald's guilt and that he had acted alone. It addition, because of the quick decision of no conspiracy, there was no large manhunt in Dallas for other conspirators. Roads and airports weren't closed, making escaping the city far less difficult for those involved in the assassination. There are unconfirmed reports of various private planes taking off from small airports around Dallas, particularly Redbird, but nothing close to conclusive. Because authorities already assumed they had their man, and there was only one assassin, even seemingly routine arrests or detentions made by Friday night or Saturday would not attract any special attention from authorities.

However, in New Orleans, things were starting to unravel just a bit. The mood at Guy Banister's office had been joyous earlier in the day. Though his temporary secretary said Banister wasn't there "at all that day," she said that Banister's mistress, Delphine Roberts, was in the office. Roberts "received a call to inform her that the President was assassinated and to turn on the TV. When Delphine Roberts turned on the TV, she jumped with joy and said 'I am glad.'"58

In the evening, after the secretary had left, Banister finally made it in to the office after visiting a neighborhood bar. He was preceded by Jack Martin, a private-detective associate and drinking buddy of Banister's. According to Delphine Roberts, Martin arrived first and went to a filing cabinet. Banister entered and accused Martin of stealing files. They argued, and Martin yelled, "What are you going to do—kill me, like you all did Kennedy?" Banister then pulled out a pistol and struck Martin on the head several times, causing him to bleed. Martin would later call an assistant District Attorney to say that Ferrie was a longtime colleague and tutor of Lee Oswald. Since Martin had fallen out with Ferrie over a fraudulent ecclesiastical order (the Holy Apostolic Catholic Church of North America) and was an alcoholic, there was some doubt at the time about his reliability. But Martin's actions would set off a chain of events that would lead to Ferrie's arrest by Monday, November 25.59

However, on Friday evening, Ferrie had more to worry about than just the accusations Martin would make: a report that Ferrie's name was on a library card found on Oswald at the time of his arrest. According to an FBI report, Marcello's lawyer, G. Wray Gill, is reported to have "stated that he had gotten word that Lee Oswald, when he was picked up, had been carrying a library card with David Ferrie's name on it." On Sunday, November 24, Gill would stop by Ferrie's residence and leave word that "Ferrie should contact, him, Gill, and he would represent him as his attorney. In addition, Gill said that Jack Martin . . . had gone to the police and the FBI and said that Ferrie had stated in his presence that the President should be killed."[60]

That was on Sunday, but according to the House Select Committee on Assassinations "Oswald's former landlady in New Orleans, Mrs. Jesse Garner, told the committee she recalled that Ferrie visited her home on the night of the assassination and asked about Oswald's library card." In addition, "a neighbor of Oswald's" in New Orleans also said "that Ferrie had come by her house after the assassination, inquiring if" her husband "had any information regarding Oswald's library card."[61] Later, the Secret Service would ask Ferrie whether he had ever loaned Oswald his library card.[62] But on Friday, November 22, Ferrie didn't want the authorities to connect him to Oswald in any way, so he set off on an odd journey that would last two days.

There has been much speculation that David Ferrie's sudden trip to Texas was part of a getaway scheme for the assassins of JFK. However, the fact that Ferrie took two young men with him would argue against that. While Ferrie's travels and actions on the trip were considered bizarre and unusual by investigators, we feel that it's possible that Ferrie's trip was to retrieve the library card. Guy Banister might have been able to use his law-enforcement or intelligence contacts to get someone on the Dallas police force to pull the card, by mentioning Ferrie's work with Varona's anti-Castro Cuban group, the CIA-backed Cuban Revolutionary Council. Banister could have told a contact that Ferrie had simply been helping with the tight surveillance of Oswald, and had innocently loaned Oswald his library card. Or Marcello's associates might have been able to use their contacts to get a policeman to do them a favor. Mobster Joe Civello ran Dallas for Marcello, and Dallas Police Sergeant Patrick Dean boasted to Peter Dale Scott about his "longtime relationship" with Civello. Patrick Dean was also good friends with Jack Ruby. In fact, according to Scott, "Dean would be in charge of security in the Dallas [Police Department] basement when Oswald was murdered" and later fail "a lie detector test about Ruby's access to" it.[63] Someone who ranked even higher than Dean, Homicide Captain Will Fritz, was also "very close friends" with Jack Ruby, according to J. D. Tippit's attorney.[64] Fritz was also in charge of the Oswald investigation. So there were several ways Ferrie's library card could have been surreptitiously retrieved from evidence.

It would have been important for Ferrie to get his library card back, so that he could produce it if he were ever asked by investigators in New Orleans. Shortly before his death, Ferrie would tell Garrison's staff that "he had some business for [G. Wray] Gill to take care of" when he suddenly went to Texas.[65] Ferrie told the FBI that "he had been in New Orleans until at least 9 P.M. on November 22, celebrating Marcello's trial victory at the Royal Orleans" hotel. Ferrie suddenly decided to drive to Houston through a heavy rainstorm, with two young men. Ferrie went to a Houston ice-skating rink, where he "spent a great deal of time at a pay telephone, making and receiving calls," according to Anthony Summers. In the early morning hours of November 23, Ferrie checked in to the Alamotel in Houston, which was owned by Carlos Marcello. Congressional investigators confirmed that Ferrie made "a collect call . . . to the Town and Country Hotel, Marcello's New Orleans headquarters." He also made calls to Marcello attorney G. Wray Gill that weekend. But while still registered at the Houston Alamotel, Ferrie drove to Galveston and checked into another motel there. Congressional investigators couldn't understand why hotels in Houston and Galveston both listed Ferrie as staying there during the same twelve-hour period.[66]

We feel the explanation is that someone in Galveston or Houston may have been bringing David Ferrie his library card. For example, there were men in each city who had just come from Dallas, shortly before Ferrie's arrival. One was an associate of Jack Ruby, and the other had been arrested in Dealey Plaza just after JFK's assassination. Ruby had made several calls to Galveston around the time of Ferrie's arrival there. While we're not saying that either of those two men was delivering Ferrie's card, this demonstrates how it could have been done.

JACK RUBY'S FIRST ATTEMPT TO PLUG A LEAK

Richard D. Mahoney writes that "Subsequent to the Kennedy assassination, Ruby, a man described by Rosselli himself as 'one of our boys,' stalked, murdered, and thereby silenced Oswald. This act shines out like a neon sign through the fog of controversy surrounding the President's death."[67] Ruby would constantly stalk Oswald at the police station, while continuing to try to find a policeman willing to silence Oswald for him. Ruby's association with hundreds of policemen made him well suited to the task. Tippit's attorney, mentioned earlier, said that not only was Ruby "very close friends" with Homicide Captain Will Fritz, who was running the Oswald investigation, but that "Ruby, in spite of his reputation of being a 'hood,' was allowed complete run of the Homicide Bureau."

Ruby didn't waste any time, and he admitted later that he was packing a pistol when he went to police headquarters that night. At 6:00 P.M., Ruby was seen on the third floor of police headquarters by John Rutledge, a reporter for the *Dallas Morning News*. At 7:00 P.M., Ruby spoke to Detective August Eberhardt at Dallas police headquarters, on the third-floor hallway. Finally, at some time after that and before 8:00 P.M., Ruby tried to open the door to Capt. Fritz's office, where Oswald was being interrogated. However, two officers stopped him and one told him, "You can't go in there, Jack." It seems obvious that if Ruby had managed to get into Fritz's office while Oswald was there, Ruby would have done what he would finally do on Sunday—shoot Oswald.[68]

Frustrated at his first attempt, Ruby regrouped for a bit. Ruby called the home of his friend Gordon McLendon, owner of KLIF radio, who was close to David Atlee Phillips and had a connection to Marcello. Ruby then called a radio DJ, offering to help him set up a telephone interview with District Attorney Henry Wade. Such an effort would give Ruby an excuse to ingratiate himself with Wade, and would also give him still more access at the police station. Around 9:50 P.M., Ruby even dropped by Temple Searith Israel, where Ruby seemed depressed when he talked with Rabbi Hillel Silverman. Ruby didn't mention JFK's assassination—because that's not what he was depressed about: He was probably worried about what might happen to him if he tried to shoot Oswald in a room full of cops with guns.[69]

During Oswald's interrogation, around 10:30 P.M., one of the officers got a phone call from Ruby, offering to bring them some sandwiches. The officer declined. By 11:30, Ruby was back at the police station, where he was seen by a policeman among the throngs of reporters.[70] Finally, after midnight, Ruby would get a chance to see Oswald—but he would be too far away to have a clear shot. Ruby was packing his pistol, and carrying some sandwiches, when he attended a third-floor briefing at Dallas police headquarters. There, Chief Curry and District Attorney Henry Wade announced that Oswald would be shown to newsmen at a press conference in the basement. Ruby attended the chaotic press conference in a basement assembly room, where Oswald was shown to reporters to counter stories that he had been beaten. When Wade said that Oswald belonged to the "Free Cuba Committee" (an anti-Castro group headed by Eladio del Valle), Ruby—standing on a table in the back of the room—corrected him, saying that it was really the "Fair Play for Cuba

Committee" (a communist, pro-Castro group).[71] As we've noted before, Eladio del Valle was close to David Ferrie and knew Trafficante.

That's as close as Ruby would get to Oswald that night. Ruby went to the radio station with the sandwiches. While there, Ruby called Oswald a good-looking guy who resembled Paul Newman; Ruby expressed no bitterness toward Oswald.[72] Around 2:00 A.M., Ruby left the radio station and met a Dallas police officer and his girlfriend, a dancer for Ruby, at Simpson's garage. There are numerous discrepancies about the duration of the meeting and the participants, but the police officer said the meeting with Ruby lasted two to three hours. Some researchers have speculated that Ruby was trying to either get the officer to shoot Oswald, or to help Ruby find an officer who would.[73]

NATIONAL SECURITY CONCERNS ABOUT OSWALD'S FILE AND JFK'S AUTOPSY
Two Naval facilities in Washington would be the focus of unusual activity related to national security on Friday, November 22, and into the early morning hours of November 23. First was the Office of Naval Intelligence. The confidential Naval Intelligence source we've mentioned in earlier chapters was called back to his office in Washington after Oswald's name surfaced in the assassination. Along with his co-workers, he says, he helped to destroy and sanitize much of the Oswald "tight" surveillance file that their group had maintained since Oswald's return from Russia. At that point, it appeared that Oswald's file might become the subject of at least an internal military investigation, and, at worst, aspects of the surveillance might even be brought up or exposed at Oswald's trial. While national security was no doubt the overriding concern in the document destruction ordered by our source's superiors, it would also help to avoid embarrassment to those higher in the chain of command who had been aware of Oswald's special status.

The FBI apparently encountered the results of the Naval Intelligence destruction of Oswald documents. According to researcher Paul Hoch, an FBI memo dated April 2, 1964 by T. N. Goble stated that three of Oswald's fellow Marines "said they had been interviewed about Oswald." However, "Goble noted that no such statements or interview reports had been located" in Oswald's Marine or Office of Naval Intelligence files that had been provided to the FBI. "In a postscript for the" FBI headquarters file, "Goble did not suggest any doubt that such interviews had taken place. Their absence from USMC and ONI files 'indicates that perhaps they have been destroyed,'" Goble wrote.[74]

There were more national security concerns at Bethesda Naval Hospital, the site of John F. Kennedy's autopsy. There had already been problems in Dallas, when JFK's body was removed from Parkland Hospital only after a confrontation between Kennedy's people and the local authorities.[75] Then there were discussions while Air Force One was in the air about whether to have the autopsy at Bethesda or at Walter Reed Army Hospital. Once Bethesda was settled on, elaborate precautions were set up to get JFK's body from Air Force One to the hospital, including the use of a decoy ambulance and military guards for the real one.

The controversies surrounding JFK's autopsy are far too numerous to list here, but they can be accounted for by national security concerns related to C-Day. The major controversies include JFK's back wound, the entrance wound in his throat, the direction and extent of his head injuries, and missing X-rays and photographs—as well as JFK's missing brain. The magic-bullet theory attempted to tie together the wounds and the missed shot in a way that pointed to only one shooter, from the rear. This involved describing the back wound (six inches below the base of JFK's neck) as a back-of-the-neck wound instead. It also meant calling the front throat wound an exit, not an entrance, wound. Many witnesses have taken issue with that theory, most recently FBI Agent James W. Sibert, who was at the autopsy. He says now that the single-bullet theory is false, since the back wound wasn't a back-of-the-neck wound and thus "there's no way that bullet could go that low then come up, raise up and come out the front of the neck, zig zag and hit Connally and then end up in a pristine condition over there in Dallas. . . . There's no way I'll swallow that."[76]

There is considerable evidence that there was a preliminary, rushed examination at Bethesda, prior to the start of the official autopsy. Researcher David Lifton interviewed many of those involved in transporting and guarding the body, finding much documentation that the ambulance with JFK's body was away from its military guard for a period of up to thirty minutes. There is also much confusion—and unaccounted-for time—in all the official accounts and records of the arrival of the body and the start of the autopsy. There is also photographic evidence and testimony showing exploratory wound alteration prior to the official autopsy. For example, the small, neat tracheotomy incision made by Dallas doctors over JFK's small throat wound was much larger and very ragged by the start of JFK's official autopsy.[77] Many authors, including leading forensic pathologists like Dr. Cyril Wecht, have detailed these issues in books and articles over the years.

For years, some researchers have dubbed this first, rushed examination prior to the official autopsy a "national security autopsy." We concur, since by that time there were concerns about JFK's assassination in terms of a conspiracy. David Powers and Kenneth O'Donnell—who both saw shots from the front—were at Bethesda with Bobby. On Friday night, November 22, it looked as if an official autopsy would have to be used at Oswald's trial. Any examination to determine if there were national security concerns (e.g., shots from two directions, indicating a conspiracy that could involve Cubans or Cuban exiles and potentially expose C-Day) would have to be done prior to the official autopsy. This reflects the thinking behind the Cuba Contingency Planning we've detailed earlier. While those plans weren't completed, and hadn't focused on the assassination of a US official on US soil (only in a foreign country), Bobby and others at the autopsy were familiar with the planning. We interviewed two people who were at Bethesda with Bobby Kennedy that night, and we feel that such security considerations played a role in events at the autopsy and any preliminary examination that occurred.[78]

National security is also why Bobby Kennedy wanted JFK's autopsy held at a military facility in Washington, instead of in Dallas—where Kennedy's aides and the Secret Service had to practically hijack JFK's body and force their way out of Parkland Hospital.[79] Keep in mind that those writing the Cuba Contingency Plans were expecting any assassination—if it did occur—to happen outside of the US, in a Latin American country. In such a case, if the US Ambassador to a Latin American country were assassinated, it would be important to hold the autopsy at a US military facility, for national security reasons. This would be important so the release of information could be carefully controlled, giving the President time to decide if and when to retaliate against Cuba. Think of the disaster if a president ordered military strikes against Cuba, only to find out later that the Ambassador had really died from an accident or a simple robbery. While the Cuba Contingency Plans weren't yet completed—and they hadn't counted on the President being killed—the basic thinking remained the same.[80] In fact, Admiral Burkley wrote a report for the Warren Commission saying that, at the time, he told Jackie that JFK's autopsy site "should be a military hospital for security measures."[81]

One fact that's often overlooked is that Bobby Kennedy was at Bethesda, comforting Jackie Kennedy in a seventeenth-floor suite in the same building as the autopsy room—and the evidence shows that it was Bobby who actually controlled the autopsy. JFK's personal physician, Admiral George Burkley, was in the autopsy room. In his official Oral History at the JFK Presidential Library, Dr. Burkley says that "during the autopsy I supervised everything that was done . . . and kept in constant contact with Mrs. [Jackie] Kennedy and the members of her party who were on the seventeenth floor in the suite at that level."[82] That's confirmed by Dr. J. Thornton Boswell, one of the autopsy physicians, who said that "Dr. Burkley was basically supervising everything that went on in the autopsy room and that the commanding officer was also responding to Burkley's wishes."[83]

The man giving orders to Dr. Burkley was Bobby Kennedy. According to Gus Russo, JFK aide General Godfrey McHugh testified later "that Bobby Kennedy frequently phoned the autopsy suite, inquiring 'about the results. . . .'" Dr. Robert Karnei, who assisted at the autopsy, said "Robert [Kennedy] was really limiting the autopsy." The Commander of the Bethesda Naval Medical School, Capt. John Stover, said that "Bobby went so far as to periodically visit the autopsy room during the procedure."[84] In addition, Bobby had someone to assist him in dealing with Dr. Burkley and the autopsy.

An extremely sensitive confidential source, a Kennedy aide who knew about C-Day, confirmed to the authors that he helped to act as an intermediary between Bobby Kennedy and Dr. Burkley, relaying Bobby's wishes to Burkley.[85] This Kennedy aide's presence at Bethesda during the autopsy has been confirmed by an official account, and his credibility, integrity, and position with the Kennedys have been confirmed by numerous other sources, including Dean Rusk, Harry Williams, FBI Agent Courtney Evans (the liaison between Bobby and Hoover), and others.[86] We feel it's significant that someone who knew about C-Day would be in such a key position during the autopsy. It's important to note that this Kennedy aide was also of the opinion that JFK was killed by a conspiracy involving Marcello, Rosselli, and Trafficante.[87] In addition in 1982, Dr. Burkley—the only doctor at both Parkland Hospital and the autopsy—said that he thought Kennedy was murdered as the result of a conspiracy, and he implied that he didn't even agree with the Warren Commission's conclusion as to the number of bullets that entered the President's body.[88]

At 3:56 A.M. (Eastern), or possibly later, the ambulance with JFK's body left Bethesda Naval Hospital, headed for the White House. JFK's body and funeral arrangement were given over to others who had been working on aspects of the top-secret C-Day plan. As noted in Part I, for several months, Col. Alexander Haig had been helping Cyrus Vance and Joseph Califano with parts of the C-Day plan, including the Cuba Contingency Plans.[89] Long-secret notes from the first meeting about the Contingency Plans, where possible Cuban "attacks against US officials" were discussed, were signed on "September 12, 1963" by "A. M. Haig, Lt. Col.," and they say that "Mr. Califano" also attended that meeting.[90]

In his autobiography, Haig wrote that "I was assigned the duty of helping with the preparations for the President's funeral. November 22, 1963, the day Kennedy died, was a Friday, and I spent Saturday . . . handling details concerning the burial site . . . I worked far into the night and came in again early on Sunday morning."[91] And Califano writes that after the assassination, he went straight to the Pentagon, where Secretary of the Army Vance put him in charge of arranging JFK's burial at Arlington, including meeting Bobby there the next day.[92] Haig and Califano were the right people for Vance and Bobby to use, in case any problems had developed relative to C-Day. While Califano and Haig have said they didn't know as much about Bobby's plans as Vance, they knew enough that it would have only taken moments for Vance to explain the full scope of C-Day, if any problems had arisen. Haig and Califano already knew most of the key participants in C-Day, like Harry Williams, and had been part of many of Bobby's secretive Cuban subcommittees.

CHAPTER SIXTY

Another Mob Hit in Dallas Devastates Bobby

CHICAGO AND TAMPA BEGAN TO figure in the assassination investigation as early as Saturday. The rifle found in the Book Depository after JFK's murder might have a paper trail that could be traced, if authorities could determine where and how it had been purchased. According to historian Richard D. Mahoney, "CIA files . . . reveal that the first lead as to the location of the rifle came from the chief investigator of the Cook County Sheriff's Office, Richard Cain, a Rosselli-Giancana confederate." The staff at Klein's, a major purveyor of mail-order rifles, began searching their records and "on November 23 at 4:00 A.M., CST, executives at Klein's Sporting Goods in Chicago discovered the American Rifleman coupon with which Oswald had allegedly ordered the Mannlicher-Carcano."[1] As we noted earlier, a CIA memo said that Cain was deeply involved in the JFK assassination investigation, but he probably had other concerns in Chicago as well. For Johnny Rosselli, Cain could also see if the recent four-man Chicago threat surfaced in the news media, in addition he could plant false information that Oswald had received support from the small Fair Play for Cuba Committee chapter in Chicago.

Chicago Secret Service agent Abraham Bolden "received a call at home from a Dallas [Secret Service] agent who wanted 'instant' information on Klein's Sporting Goods store and Oswald's rifle and the possibility that Oswald received money from Chicago, as alleged by the *Chicago American*." However, "neither Bolden, nor any other Secret Service agent, could get any information on either lead and they were preempted by the FBI, who had gotten to Klein's and the newspaper first, and who had warned all concerned to talk to no one, including the Secret Service."[2] This was just part of an ever-increasing lack of cooperation between the FBI and the Secret Service that would hinder the assassination investigation.

On Saturday, November 23, the *Tampa Tribune* printed the small article we quoted earlier, the one that said that prior to JFK's visit, the Secret Service and police had learned that the suspected assassin in Tampa was "a young man" who "stated he will use a gun" and was "described as white, male, 20, slender build."[3] Ironically, that description fits Oswald much better than the initial lookouts issued in Dallas for the slayers of JFK and Officer Tippit.

However, when the *Miami Herald* tried to find out more about the small article in the Tampa paper, the *Herald* reported the next day that "The FBI, Secret Service, and local officers declined to discuss the matter." The newspaper got no further with the Secret Service in 1963 than Congress or the Kennedy Assassination Review Board would in the decades to come. The *Herald* reported that "The Secret Service . . . when asked to comment on published reports that the Secret Service had alerted local authorities that an assassination attempt might be made on Mr. Kennedy when he visited here last Monday [11-18-63], drew a 'no comment.'"[4] A wall of secrecy seemed to descend over the story, and neither paper featured any type of follow-up. This was in stark contrast to the huge number of other assassination stories that filled newspapers in the days and weeks that followed, which reported any detail or rumor. The sheer mass of stories, along with the "no comment" in the *Herald* story, probably helped the two articles to escape the notice of other journalists at the time, and of historians in the decades to come. Since Oswald appeared to be a lone assassin, the Secret Service and the FBI probably saw no value in revealing either the Tampa or Chicago attempts at this point. If either agency revealed that it had kept those two attempts out of the press, the public might wonder about what Dallas stories the agencies might be suppressing.

At 9 A.M. (Eastern) on November 23, 1963, CIA Director John McCone talked to Bobby Kennedy. McCone was set to meet with Lyndon Johnson at 12:30, so it's not hard to imagine that McCone and Bobby must have discussed what McCone was going to tell LBJ about C-Day. At that point, LBJ had had no involvement in C-Day and probably didn't even know that such a plan existed. Now, as president and commander-in-chief, he would have to be brought up to speed, and quickly. McCone knew about C-Day, but there were probably many details the CIA Director couldn't be expected to know, since they were handled by his subordinates like Helms and FitzGerald, or by men like Harry Williams and Cyrus Vance who reported to Bobby

Kennedy. We think it's doubtful that Bobby provided any additional information about C-Day to McCone to pass along to LBJ.

McCone was about to find out a bit more about the AMLASH operation with Rolando Cubela. According to Evan Thomas, on November 23 Desmond FitzGerald finally told "Walt Elder, the executive assistant to McCone, that he had met with Cubela in October and that one of his agents had been meeting with the Cuban turncoat the very moment Kennedy had been shot. But he did not tell Elder that AMLASH had been offered a poison pen or promised a rifle." Without knowing about the scoped rifles, "Elder was struck by FitzGerald's clear discomfort. 'Des was normally imperturbable, but he was very disturbed about his involvement.' The normally smooth operator was 'shaking his head and wringing his hands. It was very uncharacteristic. That's why I remember it so clearly.'"[5] Just two days later, FitzGerald would tell Cubela's case officer to delete a reference to the poison pen in a memo, so McCone will continue to be in the dark about the assassination side of the AMLASH operation.

FitzGerald and Helms would have been concerned, as information linking the assassination to C-Day continued to trickle in to authorities. Given the CIA's extensive liaison with local law enforcement, they probably learned of information like that received by the Dallas police from an informant on November 23, who said that Oswald had attended meetings of an anti-Castro group at a Cuban's house in Dallas, but that the Cuban had left the house in the last few days. The house was the local headquarters of Alpha 66, the close affiliate of Eloy Menoyo's SNFE C-Day exile group. Researchers and historians over the years have noted that many such leads were never fully explored or resolved, but we feel it's likely that in at least some cases authorities were asked to curtail investigations that could have run across covert CIA operations and impacted national security.[6] It's unclear how much information linking C-Day to the assassination managed to work its way past Helms and others to reach Director McCone. At any rate, McCone seemed to focus on information that seemed to link Oswald to Castro, just as numerous associates of Rosselli and Trafficante had planned.

John McCone met with Lyndon Johnson at either 12:30 P.M. (Eastern), according to McCone's desk calendar in the National Archives, or at 9:19 A.M. (which would have been just after McCone met with Bobby). It's very important to look at what McCone could have told LBJ in those early hours, since it would shape LBJ's opinions—and US policy—in the coming days, months, and years. McCone probably told LBJ at least the broad outlines of C-Day.

McCone also would have told LBJ about AMTRUNK, the so-far-ineffective plan to try to find Cuban military leaders to revolt against Castro. McCone might have known what his aide had just learned about FitzGerald and Cubela (AMLASH); but, if not, McCone probably told LBJ the following day. However, McCone didn't know about the assassination side of the Cubela operation, so he couldn't have told LBJ about that. As for the CIA-Mafia plots, McCone had only learned about those in August, and had been told they were long over—which is probably what he repeated to LBJ. So neither LBJ or McCone would have known that the CIA-Mafia plots were continuing, with Rosselli working David Morales and, apparently, Manuel Artime. Likewise, McCone doesn't seem to have been aware of QJWIN (at least the assassination side of it), so he couldn't have told LBJ about that.

This information would shape much of LBJ's outlook about the assassination, along with another bit of news that McCone reportedly conveyed to LBJ on either November 23 or at their meeting on November 24. According to historian Michael Bechloss, McCone told LBJ that "the CIA had information on foreign connections to the alleged assassin, Lee Harvey Oswald, which suggested to LBJ that Kennedy may have been murdered by an international conspiracy."[7] Peter Dale Scott adds that "a CIA memo written that day reported that Oswald had visited Mexico City in September and talked to a Soviet vice consul whom the CIA knew as a KGB expert in assassination and sabotage. The memo warned that if Oswald had indeed been part of a foreign conspiracy, he might be killed before he could reveal it to U.S. authorities." Scott says that "Johnson appears to have had this information in mind when, a few minutes after the McCone interview, he asked FBI Director J. Edgar Hoover if the FBI "knew any more about the visit to the Soviet embassy."[8]

According to a second- or third-hand account noted by Gus Russo, the concern McCone conveyed was directed at the Cubans. Russo cites LBJ's former speechwriter, Leo Janos, as saying he heard the following from the spouse of an aide to Johnson: "'When Lyndon got back from Dallas, McCone briefed him' on the cause of the assassination, allegedly saying: 'It was the Castro connection.' The information was contained in a file McCone brought with him to LBJ's vice-presidential residence." "According to Janos, Johnson immediately called Senator Richard Russell, relayed to him McCone's conclusion, and asked, 'What do we do?' Russell replied, 'Don't let it out. If you do, it's World War III.' Johnson swore Russell to secrecy, and proceeded to destroy McCone's file."[9]

The CIA and FBI would soon start getting a stream of accounts linking

Oswald, and even Ruby, to Castro, though most would eventually be shown to have originated with associates of Johnny Rosselli, Santo Trafficante, or David Morales. One CIA cable that weekend tried to urge caution in dealing with such reports, but it went unheeded, at least initially. This cable doesn't have the AMWORLD code name for the CIA's side of C-Day, but it does have the RYBAT TYPIC YOBITE code words that were to be used on all AMWORLD cables. It says that "rumors are now circulating among exile Cubans" about "possible [Castro] involvement in Kennedy's death." It says the "authors [of] these rumors [are] not identified, but it is clear this [is] being done primarily in [an] attempt [to] provoke strong US action against Cuba."[10] Soon, the "authors" of the rumors would have names, and they would include John Martino, Rolando Masferrer, and Frank Fiorini. But for the first several weeks after JFK's death, the rumors—coupled with the fact that Oswald had visited the Cuban and Soviet embassies in Mexico City—seemed to find traction with McCone, LBJ, and other officials.

It's possible, perhaps likely, that McCone (and thus LBJ) wasn't told that Oswald was in Mexico City visiting the Cuban and Soviet embassies as part of a closely held operation run by Desmond FitzGerald's SAS unit. As we noted in Part II, Dr. John Newman has demonstrated from declassified CIA cables that there were two streams of information about Oswald flowing to Washington from Mexico City. The most secret of those streams was known only to officials like Helms and FitzGerald, not even to the CIA's Mexico City station chief, Win Scott. (Information about Richard Cain was also part of that secret stream of information.) If Helms and FitzGerald were keeping so much else from McCone—like the ongoing CIA-Mafia plots and the assassination aspects of the Cubela/AMLASH operation—it's possible that their use of Oswald was kept from McCone as well, especially after Oswald was blamed for assassinating the President. Both FitzGerald and Helms would get promotions in the coming years, something that would not have been the case if it had looked like their use of Oswald had failed horribly. (One reason Helms and FitzGerald had the high positions they did in 1963 was because both men had avoided the taint of the Bay of Pigs fiasco.) In addition, Oswald was involved with Naval Intelligence, and, as Helms himself once implied in testimony, that meant that Oswald was the responsibility of the Defense Department, not the CIA.

For the rest of his life, LBJ seemed to focus primarily on Castro as a probable culprit, though by at least 1967 LBJ also started to voice suspicions about the Mafia and even the CIA. Amidst learning his new job as president

Johnson was quickly being brought up to speed and learning about C-Day, AMTRUNK, the nonassassination side of Cubela/AMLASH, and in general about the CIA-Mafia plots. To LBJ they probably all seemed like just different facets of one big CIA or Bobby Kennedy operation. Johnson would tread cautiously in such murky waters, though he would keep some of the anti-Castro operations alive much longer than many of his former officials like to admit.

Yet McCone himself wasn't fully informed about some of the very operations—the ongoing CIA-Mafia plots and QJWIN—that would have most affected LBJ's understanding of JFK's assassination. So, even when McCone briefed LBJ about Cuban operations again on Sunday, November 24, there were limits to how much LBJ could find out.[11] The same was true when McCone apparently briefed Secretary of State Dean Rusk at noon on the same day. This may be when Rusk first learned about C-Day, since he told us that he learned about it soon after JFK's death.

The relationship between LBJ and Bobby was never good, and the strains that were apparent on Saturday, November 23 began to get worse. Just after Bobby's own talk with McCone, Bobby had been angered that LBJ seemed to be moving into the White House too quickly. Later that afternoon, Evan Thomas wrote that Bobby "at first refused to attend" LBJ's "first cabinet meeting . . . RFK arrived late, interrupting Johnson's opening remarks. Some cabinet members stood up when RFK came through the door, but LBJ remained seated. Kennedy stared at him with undisguised loathing. Johnson showed no expression, but he felt humiliated and believed that Kennedy had intentionally upstaged him."[12] Their growing animosity would not only affect the possibility of continuing C-Day, but would also prevent each man—and the public—from learning the full story behind JFK's assassination.

The CIA's European assassin recruiter, QJWIN, was still drawing his monthly salary, but McCone wouldn't develop an interest in him for almost another year. Meanwhile, the French Connection kingpin and notorious assassin with so many parallels to QJWIN, Michel Victor Mertz, was reportedly in Dallas. Mertz was using the aliases of fugitive Jean Souetre (in Europe at the time) as well as a young Frenchman named Michel Roux (who really was in Fort Worth at the time), and probably others. Mertz would escape Dallas in a novel way: by deportation. In an earlier chapter, we cited the CIA document saying that Mertz was deported from Dallas within 48 hours of JFK's assassination. Two Dallas officials of the Immigration and

Naturalization Service (INS) remembered incidents that appear to be related to Mertz's deportation.

In 1980, noted researcher Gary Shaw talked to Virgil Bailey, who was an investigator for the INS in Dallas in 1963. "Bailey immediately remembered picking up a Frenchman in Dallas shortly after the assassination of President Kennedy." Bailey and another investigator "picked up the Frenchman . . . and brought him to [the] INS offices. Bailey was unable to remember why the pickup was ordered, who ordered it, or what was done with the Frenchman after he was brought in." Bailey was able to give a description of the man, saying he was "6' 1" or 6' 2" ft. tall," appeared to be "in his 50s, 210 to 215 pounds, well built [but] not fat," with "greying hair." That is a fairly accurate description of Michel Victor Mertz, who was 6' 1" tall, weighed around 200 pounds, and was well built but not fat, and appears to have had graying hair (the only two known printed photos of Mertz are of poor quality, and the originals reportedly disappeared from the files of *Newsday* after their Pulitzer Prize–winning exposé of his heroin network).[13]

Mertz would have been forty-three, but he looked older and French authorities say he often used a cover identity (Maurice Valentin) that was age forty-eight at the time. The man Bailey remembered was certainly not Jean Souetre, who was only thirty at the time. Bailey remembered another important fact that distinguished the man from the ordinary: "The Frenchman . . . had been tried in absentia in France and was under a death sentence for collaboration with the Nazis during World War II." Mertz had two associates with that background, Joseph Orsini and Antoine D'Agostino, who both had earned "a death sentence in absentia" for collaborating with the Nazis. (Orsini's nephew would be arrested in conjunction with the French Connection heroin bust at Fort Benning that would eventually send Mertz to jail.)[14] Of course, there is no record of a real collaborator being deported to France at this time, and the CIA memo says the deportation was to Canada or Mexico, which makes it appear that the war crimes angle was simply a cover story.

But the cover story is even more complicated, since Bailey also thinks he recalls that the man was "a chef or maitre d' in an unknown Dallas restaurant." Michel Roux, the other man whose name Mertz was using as an alias, would later become a well-known chef in New York. Yet the man Bailey remembers couldn't be the real Roux, because Roux was just in his early twenties and travel records show that he was never detained or deported, but left the Dallas–Fort Worth area legally several days after JFK was killed. It appears that Mertz simply used elements from several people to construct a suitable cover identity that would obscure his trail.

Virgil Bailey's supervisor at the time, Hal Norwood, recalls what might be another aspect of the story. While he didn't remember the same details as Bailey, Norwood told Gary Shaw about "the arrest of another individual who might have been French which occurred shortly after the killing of the President. The Dallas police called INS and requested that they come to city jail to investigate a foreigner that they had in custody. The reason for his being in jail was unknown to Norwood. INS men . . . went to the jail and picked up the man. He thought Virgil was one of the men he sent. The man in question was a wanted criminal and shortly after INS took him into custody the head of Washington INS investigations called requesting a pickup on the man. They were surprised that he was already a prisoner." Norwood said "the Washington INS office was VERY interested in the man and called twice regarding him."[15] From Norwood's account, it appears that the man deported could have been one of those detained after JFK's assassination for some reason. And the INS interest at the Washington level could be an indication of the kind of clout Mertz had with the French government, and apparently with some US agency (that kept his name out of the fall 1963 Congressional hearings on organized crime and narcotics, though each of his associates was named extensively). The bottom line is that apparently Mertz was in Dallas during JFK's assassination, and was deported soon after.[16]

Other members of Mertz's heroin network—from Carlos Marcello to Jack Ruby—were also busy on November 23, 1963. In New Orleans, Marcello no doubt monitored the progress of David Ferrie, who was still apparently trying to get back the library card he had loaned Oswald. In addition, Jack Martin, angry over the beating from Guy Banister, was talking to an assistant New Orleans district attorney, and word of Martin's allegations was reaching other authorities and the media. Marcello probably didn't realize that Rose Cheramie, his lowly heroin courier, was in a Louisiana mental hospital undergoing heroin withdrawal. It's interesting in retrospect just how close Marcello's plan came to being uncovered.

Also, two lawyers who were asked to represent Oswald had ties to Marcello. One was Clem Sehrt, an associate of Carlos Marcello who had known Oswald's mother since the 1950s. The other is Dean Andrews, who knew David Ferrie.[17] Neither man contacted Oswald before his death. Meanwhile,

Oswald was still maintaining cover, and when he was visited by the president of the Dallas Bar Association, who offered to get a lawyer for him, Oswald declined. Wanting to maintain his cover as being far-left, Oswald said he wanted noted civil-rights lawyer John Abt or someone from the ACLU.[18]

Jack Ruby was very busy again on November 23, as he once again stalked Oswald. We noted earlier Ruby's friendship with Dallas Police Sergeant Patrick Dean and Homicide Captain Will Fritz. But also among the hundreds of men on the force who Ruby knew was Police Chief Jesse Curry. According to one account, Ruby was friends with Curry, and had taken him to Hot Springs, Arkansas (then a noted center for gambling) in 1956.[19] At noon, Chief Curry called Captain Fritz to see if Oswald could be transferred to the county jail—and the jurisdiction of the sheriff—at 4:00 P.M.[20] Also at noon, Ruby was again at the police station. At 1:30, Ruby placed a call from the Nichols Garage, next door to his Carousel Club, and told someone the whereabouts of Chief Curry, which must mean that Ruby was talking to or keeping tabs on Curry. At 3:00 P.M., Police Sergeant D. V. Harkness, expecting Oswald to be moved at 4:00 P.M., started clearing a crowd that was blocking a driveway entrance to the county jail. Harkness saw Ruby in the crowd. Sometime after 3:00, Ruby placed another call from the Nichols Garage, about the transfer of Oswald, and Ruby said "You know I'll be there." An announcer for KLIF said Ruby called him to offer to cover the transfer of Oswald for the station. Finally, at 4:00, Ruby was at the police station, expecting Oswald to be moved—but for some reason the transfer was called off and rescheduled.[21]

However, at 7:30 P.M., Chief Curry inadvertently told two reporters wanting dinner—but not wanting to miss Oswald's transfer—that if they were back by 10:00 Sunday morning, "they won't miss anything."[22] About an hour later, Ruby called his friend and business associate Ralph Paul, and someone overheard Paul saying "Are you crazy? A gun?" Finally, at 10:20 P.M., Chief Curry announced at a press conference that Oswald would be moved the next morning, in an armored truck.[23] That meant Ruby would have to wait until the next day to complete his assignment.

But Ruby would have a dry run, of sorts, that evening. His cover story for Sunday, November 24, would be that he needed to go downtown to wire $25 to one of his dancers, Karen Carlin, and while downtown, on the spur of the moment, he happened to walk over to the basement of the police station and just happened to be able to get close enough to Oswald to shoot him. To set up the background for this story, on Saturday night Ruby and Karen Carlin and several others staged an odd incident at the Nichols Garage. One day earlier, after JFK had been shot, Carlin had been called by an associate of Ruby and Lewis McWillie, who ordered her to meet him "in about 20 minutes" and "if you're not down here, you won't be around too long." After that, Carlin was apparently willing to do what she was told. So, on Saturday night, she and several others went to the garage, where Ruby called the attendant and told him to give Carlin a loan of $5, but to time-stamp a receipt for the amount, and he'd pay him back shortly. (Apparently, this was supposed to provide evidence that Ruby was a good guy who'd loan his dancers money.)

Ruby showed up perhaps thirty minutes later. The cover story was that Carlin needed another $25, since her rent was supposedly due; and since Ruby had temporarily closed his club after JFK's death, he could only give her $5 now and wire her the rest tomorrow. However, everyone present later told authorities a different version of what happened that night. Plus, Ruby had plenty of money—if not on him, then next door, in the Carousel's safe— so he could have easily loaned Carlin the $25 that night. But that wasn't the point—the money wire the next day was just a cover, an excuse for Ruby to be downtown, one block from the police station, at the right time.[24]

Meanwhile, far from Dallas—in Mexico—Gilberto Policarpo Lopez and Miguel Casas Saez had crossed the border when it had reopened on November 23 (it had temporarily been closed right after JFK's death). Both men were en route to Cuba, via Mexico City. Both men were later reported to have been in Dallas during JFK's assassination. Lopez had left Tampa sometime after November 20, and the FBI concluded he crossed "the border at Nuevo Laredo—the same border crossing used by Oswald—" in a privately owned automobile owned by another person." However, he wouldn't check into his Mexico City hotel until Monday, November 25, and his whereabouts on the twenty-third and twenty-fourth are unknown. It's almost as if someone had been keeping him on ice, just in case some type of evidence emerged (perhaps photographic) proving that more than one gunman was involved, or in case Oswald needed an accomplice to make the scenario of his guilt believable. Lopez may well have been an unwitting asset for some US agency, focused only on getting back to his native Cuba. But just as Oswald was manipulated by those with intelligence connections who were also working for the Mafia, the same could have been true for Lopez.[25]

The actions of Miguel Casas Saez also appear to have been manipulated by someone wanting him to look suspicious. Some reports say that Saez flew out of Dallas on a private plane and made a mysterious airport rendezvous in Mexico City, where he transferred directly to a Cubana Airlines plane without going through Customs or Immigration. The plane had supposedly been waiting on him for five hours, and he then rode in the cockpit, thus avoiding identification by the passengers. The reports made Saez sound like a Cuban assassin, being given special treatment after fleeing Dallas. However, the House Select Committee looked into that account, and found that it wasn't true. Other reports say that Saez left Dallas with two friends after JFK was shot, and crossed the border Nuevo Laredo. Since some of the reports about Saez originated with David Morales's AMOT informants, we find the whole scenario suspect, as did—eventually—the CIA and FBI.[26]

Still, either or both men would have made excellent patsies for JFK's death if anything had happened to Oswald or if someone else was needed to shoulder some of the blame. At the same time, each may also have been serving (or thought they were serving) some legitimate role for US intelligence.

NOVEMBER 24, 1963

Jack Ruby may not have gotten much sleep the night before he shot Oswald, and not just because he'd claim to have taken thirty Dexedrine tablets in the hours and days before shooting Oswald.[27] On one hand, the jail time he faced—or might face—could be minimal. "Dallas Policeman Elmo Cunningham" told Gus Russo that "in those days in Texas, a murderer could have expected two to ten years, with time off for good behavior."[28] In Texas, when murders involved "sudden passion, the sentence could not only be as low as two years, but the jury can also recommend probation," according to CNN.[29]

On the other hand, the police station had been a crowded madhouse ever since JFK's murder, and the idea of shooting a man in a room full of cops with guns was probably starting to wear on Ruby. It would only take one policeman, reaching for his gun and firing to stop Ruby, to cost him his life. $7,000—or even almost $50,000 (enough to pay all of his back taxes with a little left over)—would be small consolation if Ruby were killed or left seriously injured or crippled.

As John H. Davis writes, "Sometime during the early morning of Sunday, November 24, the Dallas County Sheriff's Office and the local field office of the FBI received nearly identical warnings from an anonymous caller that Lee Harvey Oswald would be killed in the Dallas Police Headquarters basement during his transfer from headquarters to the county jail. The caller further stated that he hoped the police would hold their fire so innocent people would not get killed. The sheriff's office and the FBI duly reported the warnings to the Dallas Police."[30] One Dallas law-enforcement official says he recognized Ruby's voice as the caller.

In South Carolina, Miami police informant William Somersett was with Joseph Milteer, the white supremacist who on November 9 had described the basic plan for killing JFK. On November 23, Somersett had observed that Milteer "was very happy over" JFK's death "and shook hands with me. He said: 'Well, I told you so. It happened like I told you, didn't it? It happened from a window with a high-powered rifle.'" Milteer told Somersett he had recently been to several cities, including "Houston, Ft. Worth, and Dallas, Texas, as well as New Orleans."[31] On the morning of November 24, Somersett said "Milteer advised that they did not have to worry about Lee Harvey Oswald getting caught because he 'doesn't know anything.'"[32] However, apparently just to make sure, Milteer went away briefly to make a phone call.

Jack Ruby knew he'd soon be facing the biggest audience he'd ever seen, and he wanted to dress the part. Though recently in financial straits, Ruby put on a silk necktie with a gold-plated tie clasp, an imported leather belt, a ring with three diamonds, and a 14-carat gold Le Coultre diamond-studded watch. At 8 A.M. (Central), a television crew saw Ruby in front of the police station. Some time after that, Ruby's housekeeper called the Ruby home to see about coming over to clean. She had a strange conversation with a man who said he was Jack, but who didn't seem to recognize her voice. In addition, since the woman worked for Ruby regularly, she probably would have recognized the voice of George Senator, Ruby's roommate.[33]

Also that morning, Ruby's good friend Patrick Dean had been assigned security in the basement for the transfer of Oswald (Dean would later refuse to testify to the House Select Committee on Assassinations, threatening to get Melvin Belli to represent him if he was subpoenaed). At 9:30, Oswald was checked out of his cell and taken to Captain Fritz's office for one final round of questioning. Also at 9:30, a minister named Ray Rushing had a brief conversation with Ruby during a ride on an elevator in the police station. He said later that Ruby was going to the floor where Oswald was being held. Oswald's originally scheduled 10:00 A.M. transfer time passed while his questioning continued. Some reporters in the basement were already aware that the transfer had been rescheduled.[34]

At 10:19 A.M., dancer Karen Carlin in Fort Worth called Ruby's residence and supposedly asked Ruby to send her money for rent and groceries. There is a phone record of the call, but some authors doubt that Ruby was even there. In an interview Carlin had later that day with Secret Service Agent Roger C. Warner, Carlin said that Oswald, Ruby, and other individuals unknown to her were involved in a plot to assassinate Kennedy, and that she would be killed if she gave any information to authorities.[35] At approximately 10:45, a television crew saw Ruby in front of the police station. Ruby came to the window of their truck and asked, "Has he been brought down yet?"[36] Fifteen minutes later, Sergeant Patrick Dean may have removed guards from an interior door into the basement.[37]

Around 11:15, Oswald's interrogators were told that their time for questioning was up, and Oswald was ready to be moved. Some authorities still felt that their case against Oswald was weak. Chief Curry said later, "We don't have any proof that Oswald fired the rifle." Curry also said that "no one has been able to put him in that building with a gun in his hand." Perhaps that is why Curry, who had ridden in the car directly in front of JFK, told Vanity Fair that he "believed two gunmen were involved" in the assassination.[38]

The transfer party left Fritz's office with Oswald in handcuffs. Police escorts guided Oswald down through the basement, to the ramp of the garage. However, the transfer car wasn't in position, so they had to slow down to wait on it. Also present in the basement were seventy to seventy-five police officers and forty to fifty newsmen. Someone had to have sent word to them that Oswald's questioning was finished.[39]

At 11:17 A.M., Ruby wired Carlin the money from the Western Union office. He then left for the Dallas police station, one block away. One minute later, Tom Howard, Ruby's attorney, entered the police station through the Harwood Street entrance and walked up to the jail office window. Howard saw Oswald being brought off the jail elevator, then turned away from the window and walked back toward the Harwood Street door. As Howard passed Detective H. L. McGee, he waved and said "That's all I wanted to see."[40]

By about 11:19, Ruby had entered the basement from an alley that separates the Western Union office from the police headquarters, and which runs from Main Street to Commerce Street. At the midpoint of the alley is a door to the first floor of the police HQ, and Ruby got to the basement by a fire stairway. The door to the fire stairway could be opened only from the inside and was supposedly secured by Sgt. Dean, but John Servance and two other maintenance workers say that it wasn't secured. According to the Warren Commission, Ruby entered the basement by way of the Main Street ramp. However, Patrolman Roy E. Vaughn swore repeatedly—and passed a lie-detector test—that Ruby never came down the Main Street ramp. Seven other police officers and witnesses agreed with Vaughn.[41]

At around 11:20, Captain Fritz came to the jail office door and asked if everything was ready. Then someone shouted "Here he comes!," and Oswald came through the door, his right wrist handcuffed to Detective J. R. Leavelle's left and with Detective L. C. Groves walking to his left. As Oswald became visible to the spectators in the police basement, a car horn let out a blast.[42]

At 11:21 A.M., when Oswald was about ten feet from the jail office door, Ruby emerged from between a newsman and a policeman. Ruby extended his right hand, which was holding a .38 caliber revolver, and fired one bullet at Oswald's abdomen. Ruby was immediately grabbed by shocked officers. Oswald, on the floor, was asked if he wanted to make a statement, but shook his head no. Before he was put in an ambulance, someone applied artificial respiration, the worst thing to do since it would aggravate internal bleeding.[43]

In South Carolina, Joseph Milteer had rejoined William Somersett after making a long-distance phone call from a pay phone. Right after they heard on the radio that Oswald had been shot, "Milteer said, 'That makes it work perfect. . . . Now, we have no worry.'"[44]

When Ruby's roommate, George Senator, heard that Oswald had been shot, he called one of Ruby's lawyers even before Ruby had been identified as the killer. Five different attorneys were called by Senator and others, and the attorneys all converged on the police station, prepared to have Ruby released on bail. John H. Davis writes that "former Dallas police officer Don Ray Archer . . . had taken custody of Jack Ruby immediately after he shot Oswald." While "Oswald was being rushed to Parkland Hospital, Ruby had appeared to Archer as being extremely agitated and nervous, continually inquiring whether Oswald was dead or alive."[45]

At 1:07, Oswald was declared dead at Parkland Hospital, and the TV net-works were soon broadcasting reports of his death.[46] According to Davis, "It was not until another officer . . . told Ruby that Oswald was dead, that Ruby calmed down." Even when the other officer told Ruby "'it looks like it's going to be the electric chair for you' . . . Ruby immediately relaxed and even managed a wan smile. To Archer, it seemed at the time that Ruby felt his own life depended on the success of his mission, that if Oswald had not died, he, Jack Ruby, would have been killed."[47]

When the charge of "assault with intent to kill" was changed to "murder," all five of the attorneys left, except for Tom Howard. Given his criminal background and presence at the police station that morning, perhaps Howard didn't leave because he wasn't surprised when the charge became "murder." Ruby was taken upstairs and questioned by Sergeant Dean and three other police officers. FBI Agent Ray Hall and Secret Service Agent Forrest Sorrels were present during only parts of the interrogation. Ruby at times seemed unsure of how he should answer certain questions. Then Ruby was allowed to speak with Tom Howard.

At 3:15 P.M., Ruby was taken before Captain Will Fritz. After talking to attorney Tom Howard, Ruby no longer answered with uncertainty to some questions—he just said "No comment."[48] But Howard was just a local attorney, and Ruby was now a national figure. According to Peter Dale Scott, "after Oswald was murdered, Ruby's brother approached one of Hoffa's attorneys to represent Ruby."[49]

Among Ruby's possessions were found: the business card of the chief of the Narcotics Division in Austin, passes to his club for Dallas Assistant District Attorney William Alexander and two city hall officials, and a list with the names of Sheriff Decker's secretary, Deputy Sheriff Buddy Walthers, Deputy Sheriff Clint Lewis, and County Clerk Deputy Travis Hall. Ruby was also carrying $2,000 in cash.[50]

In Washington, D.C., Evan Thomas says that "President Lyndon Johnson broke the news to" Bobby Kennedy and then demanded that, as Attorney General, "you've got to do something, we've got to do something. We've got to get involved. It's giving the United States a bad name in the rest of the world."[51]

Within hours of Ruby's shooting Oswald live on national TV, a November 24, 1963 FBI report says that Bobby's top Mafia prosecutor—Walter Sheridan—had information that "Ruby had recently been in Chicago where" he picked "up a 'bundle of money' from . . . a close associate of Jimmy

Hoffa."[52] Sheridan reported the information to Bobby's personal liaison with J. Edgar Hoover, FBI agent Courtney Evans, the FBI agent Bobby trusted most. Bobby would have certainly found out about rumors of Ruby's Chicago payoff from either Sheridan or Evans, and later reports of the rumor added names Bobby would recognize immediately, like Hoffa and Mafia associate Paul Dorfman. Bobby must have realized or suspected that not only had his Cuban operations backfired somehow, but that Hoffa and the mob had taken their vengeance on his brother. The two crusades that had been Bobby's biggest passions—battling the Mafia and Hoffa, and trying to topple Castro—had somehow become intertwined in some terrible way that had led to his brother's death. And with the death of Oswald, perhaps any chance of finding out for sure who was behind JFK's death had died with him. Bobby was all too aware that mob hit men rarely talked, and that the godfathers they worked for were too well insulated by intermediaries to successfully prosecute.

As Evan Thomas put it, "Without question, [Bobby] worried that his own aggressive pursuit of evil men had brought evil upon his own house." Bobby had been running on adrenaline since Friday afternoon, and his energy was slowly fading, but the Oswald shooting forced him anew to face the horrible reality that the wars he had been waging against the Mafia, Hoffa, and Castro had been turned somehow against him. Thomas points out that unlike the rest of his family and even Jackie, Bobby Kennedy "seemed devoured by grief," a grief that was "overwhelming" and "all-consuming."[53]

A firsthand account not published before comes from Marcello biographer John H. Davis. In addition to being an acclaimed historian, Davis was also Jackie Kennedy's cousin, so he was at the White House on Monday night, November 25, 1963, after JFK's funeral. There, he saw his cousin Jackie being "strong" while "greeting 104 heads of state" from all over the world, like Charles de Gaulle. "Ted Kennedy was often beside her solid and strong. Upstairs, Rose Kennedy was stoic, while also cordial and outgoing." Davis says that Bobby had always been outgoing as well, always extroverted. But now he looked like "a destroyed man" who had been "crushed by the death of his brother." He sometimes just walked in circles, or went alone down a hallway. Bobby was normally articulate, but Davis now couldn't understand what he was saying, because he only mumbled. Davis felt at the time that Bobby's reaction was so extreme, so different from the rest of the family because he "seemed to be suffering under an intense feeling of guilt"— though Davis points out that in 1963, no one had any idea why.[54]

As Evan Thomas and other Kennedy biographers have noted, all the air seemed to go out of Bobby's fight against the Mafia after his brother's death. As for C-Day, Harry Williams told us that he saw Bobby a few days after JFK's death, at Bobby's Virginia estate. It was a somber meeting. There was no real talk about JFK's assassination, still an incredibly painful subject for Bobby, who told Harry that with Johnson as president, "things were going to change" regarding C-Day. It was on hold; but as far as Bobby was concerned, it had not yet been canceled. C-Day wasn't dead, but it was on life support. As would become evident over the coming days and weeks, Bobby hadn't given up the thought of trying to bring democracy to Cuba. Given all that his brother had been through with the Bay of Pigs and the Cuban Missile Crisis, Bobby told Harry that the best memorial to JFK would be a free and democratic Cuba.

The Legacy of Secrecy

CARLOS MARCELLO'S ROLE IN THE JFK plot was never closer to being uncovered than on November 25, 1963. David Ferrie was under arrest in New Orleans, along with two of his associates, and Jack Martin's allegations were being investigated by the FBI and the Secret Service. The news media had started to get wind of not just Ferrie, but even Marcello, as possibly being involved in JFK's death. But Martin was an unstable individual and quickly backed away from his charges, and within forty-eight hours the entire incident had blown over. This was in spite of the fact that Ferrie admitted to the FBI he had "severely criticized" JFK and possibly said "he ought to be shot," and that he had "been critical of any president riding in an open car" and said that "anyone could hide in the bushes and shoot a President." Ferrie was also able to produce his library card when the agents asked, so he was released and the investigation dropped. Former FBI supervisor Guy Banister was not investigated, and may have played a role in stopping the investigation. Statements by the local FBI to the press seemed to place responsibility for the whole incident on District Attorney Jim Garrison, something that would trigger a new investigation of Ferrie three years later, in response to a secret *New York Times* investigation of the roles of Ferrie and Marcello in the JFK assassination.[1]

Marcello probably didn't know about Rose Cheramie's statements about a plot to kill JFK and new statements she made about Jack Ruby on Monday, November 25 to State Police Lieutenant Fruge. Fruge investigated and confirmed her claims about the heroin ring operating in Texas, and that she had worked for Ruby as a B-girl. But authorities in Houston lost track of the heroin courier Cheramie had identified, and closed the case. Congressional investigators found that in 1965, Cheramie tried to tell the FBI "about a heroin deal operating from a New Orleans ship," and even though "the Coast Guard verified an ongoing narcotics investigation of the ship," the FBI decided not to pursue the case. One month after she contacted the FBI, Cheramie was found mortally wounded under unusual circumstances on a desolate road in Texas, and she died on September 4, 1965.[2]

Marcello wouldn't have to worry about a longtime mob associate like Jack Ruby revealing anything to authorities, especially after Ruby was visited in jail by men like Dallas restauranteur Joe Campisi, who was close to Marcello. Ruby was in the county jail, under the control of Sheriff Bill Decker, who had a long history of mob ties that included Campisi and Russell Mathews, a Trafficante associate. Ruby was sometimes in a cell that reportedly over- looked Dealey Plaza, a telling reminder of what happened to those who crossed Marcello. When a polygraph examiner first asked Ruby "Do you think members of your family are now in danger because of what you did?" Ruby said yes; when asked the question later, Ruby refused to answer. Ruby's sister testified that he talked to her about visualizing nightmarish scenes of "his brother, Earl, being dismembered" and "Earl's children" being "dis- membered" with their "arms and legs . . . cut off." Ruby may well have developed some mental problems the longer he stayed in jail, but such delu- sions could have been based on actual threats, since they were similar to cases of retribution carried out by associates of Marcello and Rosselli (including sadistic, psychopathic killer Sam DeStefano, whom Richard Cain would use to frame Abraham Bolden).[3]

Melvin Belli would soon take over Ruby's defense; his law partner had been called on November 24 by someone from Las Vegas connected with mobsters who'd had casinos in Havana. The Las Vegas caller wanted Belli to defend Ruby, who was described as "one of our guys." Belli was close to Los Angeles gangster Mickey Cohen, and a CIA memo says that Belli "was reportedly involved in illicit drug traffic." Belli took Ruby's case, and instead of using the "sudden passion" defense available in Texas—which can result in a sentence as short as two years served, or even just probation—Belli use a bizarre "psycho-motor" defense that had never been attempted before, and lost.

Marcello, Rosselli, and Trafficante didn't want more situations like the Ferrie investigation, so their men supplied a steady stream of stories implying that Castro had ordered JFK's death. This kept national security concerns alive in Washington, and the "Castro did it" stories of John Mar- tino even contained hints of C-Day. Other mob associates linked to such sto- ries include Rolando Masferrer, Frank Fiorini, and Manuel Artime. The eager audience for these stories included officials such as CIA Director John McCone, J. Edgar Hoover, and Lyndon Johnson. Alexander Haig wrote that Cyrus Vance took one such report seriously and ordered him to destroy it. Even within the CIA, there were suspicious (eventually discredited) "Castro did it" reports involving Miguel Casas Saez and Gilberto Lopez. David Morales and especially David Atlee Phillips were sources for such stories. The stories originating with Phillips never hinted at C-Day, unlike those of John Martino. Phillips could have been acting on behalf—or at the suggestion—of David Morales (who knew Martino). Or Phillips might have seen his actions as a way to prod the new president to go ahead with C-Day. Since even Bobby Kennedy wanted C-Day to continue at that point, in a way Phillips shared the same goal.[4]

National security concerns—that Castro might have been behind JFK's death in response to US actions against him—played a key role in the actions of LBJ, Hoover, and others. Hoover had almost certainly been told at least in general terms about C-Day, by his good friend LBJ. As former FBI agent Harry Whidbee told *Vanity Fair*, "We were effectively told, 'They're only going to prove [Oswald] was the guy who did it. There were no co-conspirators, and there was no international conspiracy.'" An FBI supervisor at the time told *Vanity Fair* that "Within days, we could say the [JFK] investigation was over. . . . The idea that Oswald had a confederate or was part of a group or a conspiracy was definitely enough to place a man's career in jeopardy."[5] LBJ pulled out all the stops in telling men like Senator Richard Russell why they should join the Warren Commission, declaring "We've got to take this out of the arena where they're testifying that Khrushchev and Castro did this and did that and kicking us into a war that can kill forty million Americans in an hour."[6] The creation of the Warren Commission was announced on November 29, but Hoover had already told the American people that Oswald was the lone assassin—and the Commission would have to depend on Hoover's FBI for most of their investigative work.

The reticence to dig deeply that was held by the FBI, some of the people on the Warren Commission, and other agencies had the unfortunate side effect of allowing the Mafia bosses and their associates to largely escape close scrutiny. It also allowed various officials and agencies to cover up their own intelligence failures. In addition, agencies were forced into an ongoing cover-up of their earlier cover-ups, like those of the Tampa and Chicago assassination attempts and the Naval Intelligence surveillance of Oswald. It probably seemed to some officials that there would never be a time when those could suddenly be revealed to the American public without triggering a firestorm of anger and suspicion at what else had been covered up.

Since so much couldn't be investigated publicly, or even revealed to the Warren Commission, there were many secret investigations. The CIA, Naval Intelligence, LBJ (he asked Richard Helms to conduct one for him), and the FBI all had their own internal, secret investigations of the JFK assassination. However, their results weren't shared between, or often even within, agencies. Our Naval Intelligence source told us that after Oswald died, they quit shredding and sanitizing his surveillance files, and began a lengthy investigation into the assassination. Naval Intelligence concluded that "Oswald was incapable of masterminding the assassination or of doing the actual shooting." The existence of this investigation and its conclusions were independently confirmed to us by the son of an admiral who saw a copy of the report while serving on a Navy base the early 1970s. The House Select Committee on Assassinations learned of a similar investigation by Marine Intelligence, which reached similar conclusions.[7]

At various times, Bobby Kennedy asked trusted associates to look into JFK's assassination for him. In most cases, the results pointed toward Carlos Marcello, and possibly Cuban exiles and intelligence types. In the first few weeks after JFK's death, the tide of conflicting evidence probably kept Bobby confused about who exactly had done it. But he seems to have become confident that C-Day was still secure enough to continue. A formerly "top secret, eyes only" memo "from Gordon Chase of the National Security Council Staff" implies that McGeorge Bundy, the "President's Special Assistant for National Security Affairs," was able to provide some type of "assurances re Oswald" on December 3, 1963 that indicated that Oswald was not a Castro agent.[8] Another Kennedy administration official told us that "nothing ever surfaced" to make him think Castro was involved in JFK's murder, though he did say it "was looked at over the course of the days and weeks" after JFK's death.[9]

By the end of the first week of December, Bobby Kennedy was determined to get C-Day back on track. Time was still critical. LBJ would be dubious about continuing any risky Kennedy initiative, but he would be even less likely to pursue it in an election year. Although the coup leader in Cuba was still in place and willing, the new draft there would have an increasingly disruptive influence on his followers. Harry Williams had not spoken with LBJ at this point, and since he was key to the whole operation, Bobby apparently suggested that Harry try to arrange a meeting with the new president. Harry said that he called Joe Califano, whom he had worked with before. LBJ's response was not encouraging. Harry recalled that Califano said that President Johnson replied "the Bay of Pigs is the responsibility of Kennedy. And I don't want to see any god damn Cuban, especially that son of a bitch Williams."[10]

Bobby knew Desmond FitzGerald socially, and may have pressed through him for a continuation of C-Day. On December 9, 1963, a memo was sent to CIA Director McCone about plans "for a coup in Cuba," that pushed for LBJ to get behind the plan. The memo evoked JFK's November 18, 1963 speech with the passage for the coup leader, and suggested that LBJ could do something similar.[11]

But the following day, McCone received news that would greatly impact any plans he might have been considering. As noted in a previous chapter, a December 10, 1963 cable from the Miami station said that "a Western diplomat . . . had learned from" someone in the Cuban government "that Che Guevara was alleged to be under house arrest for plotting to overthrow Castro."[12]

When LBJ held his first big National Security Council meeting on Cuba on December 19, 1963, Bobby was not present. At the meeting, detailed in Part I, LBJ made it clear to Desmond FitzGerald and others that he would tread cautiously when it came to Cuba. The prospects for any type of major Cuban operation looked dim. However, the support to Artime and a few other exile leaders continued for the time being.[13]

As mentioned in Part I, Che Guevara appeared on TV in Cuba on December 26, 1963, as if nothing were wrong.[14] Cuban journalist Carlos Franqui, whom Harry Williams had helped defect to Paris with a large payment from the Kennedys, had returned to Cuba by December. Castro didn't even realize Franqui's long vacation had been a defection. Franqui saw Che at a reception on January 2, 1964, for the first time since their Paris meeting the previous summer.[15]

In the second week of January 1964, Bobby and Harry talked again about trying to persuade LBJ to go ahead with C-Day. Bobby still felt a free Cuba would be a fitting memorial for his brother. For there to be any chance of persuading LBJ, Bobby would have to approach Lyndon directly. Things were still tense between them, but LBJ had tried at times to reach out to Bobby, so perhaps this could be a first step toward finding common ground. LBJ still refused to see Harry Williams, but Bobby went to speak to LBJ about C-Day personally.

We can only speculate about what was said. There is still a good chance that neither Bobby nor Helms had told LBJ everything about C-Day at this point. Bobby would have had little incentive to tell LBJ everything, until it was clear that LBJ was going to continue C-Day—or at least give it serious consideration. In having to assume control of the country so quickly, and with little time to devote to Cuba, LBJ would still probably view what he knew about C-Day, AMTRUNK, Cubela, and the CIA-Mafia plots as one overall Kennedy–CIA program that had probably triggered in some way his predecessor's death. Anyway, whatever Bobby told LBJ at their meeting wasn't enough: LBJ told him C-Day was finished.

LBJ said that ending C-Day would also involve shutting down the special military training programs for Cuban exiles at Fort Benning and other bases. LBJ agreed to meet the following day with one Cuban exile leader—not Harry, but one of the top Cuban officers who'd been trained at Fort Benning—to explain his reasoning. After leaving the White House, Bobby gave Harry the news. Harry was philosophical about it, telling Bobby that they had given it all they could, and perhaps it was time to move on. We asked Harry how he could just walk away at that point, given all that he had struggled to achieve since 1959, during the Bay of Pigs, his imprisonment, his efforts to free the remaining prisoners, and in trying to meld a coalition for C-Day. He explained that anything he did, he did one hundred percent. It was dangerous business trying to stage a coup, and if you didn't have every resource possible, the odds of success were very low while the chance of catastrophic failure was very high. He said he knew that he and the other exiles would never again have the resources and backing of the US government that they'd had when JFK was alive. Plus, Bobby had given it everything he could and made a last-ditch appeal to LBJ. What more could Harry ask of him? Harry said that when he thought of his own family, and the price Bobby had paid, he felt that he had given it his best, and it was time for him to leave dealing with Castro to others.

For Bobby as well, leaving behind the idea of C-Day and staging a coup was a turning point. He would never again so aggressively pursue such a Cold War endeavor, and, instead, was beginning his journey toward the persona he is remembered for today, one that would eventually lead him to oppose the war in Vietnam.

Bobby took the Cuban exile officer to meet with LBJ, who explained that the time just wasn't right for major action against Cuba. The officer tried to make his case, but LBJ had already made his final decision the night before. After leaving the brief meeting with LBJ, Bobby and the officer went to the Pentagon, where they met with a group that included Cyrus Vance, Alexander Haig, and Joseph Califano. In his recent autobiography, Califano writes that he "was told to deliver [LBJ's] message to Cuban Brigade officers still in the US military. In late February 1964, I traveled around the country to" offer them the choice of either continuing in the regular armed forces or receiving help in returning to civilian life.[16]

LBJ's refusal to continue with C-Day probably made a bad relationship between Bobby and Johnson even worse, and it would indirectly have a big impact on America for the next eleven years. LBJ's special assistant, attorney Harry McPherson, echoed that, saying "LBJ realized another Bay of Pigs debacle would be trouble, especially with the Vietnam problem."[17] For LBJ, the decision to terminate C-Day and the exile military program allowed him to focus his attention on Vietnam. Under JFK, the Vietnam War had cost fewer than one hundred American lives.[18] Since LBJ didn't want to act against Cuba, he would make a tough stand against Communism in Vietnam, at the eventual cost of 57,000 American lives.

Some accounts say that LBJ shut down all anti-Castro operations when he took over, but the record shows that substantial US support for some—like Artime—continued. According to Castro, assassination attempts against him actually increased under LBJ. But now, things were controlled completely by the CIA, with Bobby and Harry having no role. Without Harry, the coup leader in Cuba was no longer involved. So, the CIA combined parts of C-Day/AMWORLD—Artime, Menoyo, and Ray—with what was left of AMTRUNK and, eventually, Rolando Cubela (AMLASH).[19]

Tony Varona was not involved any more, and his quick fall from grace raises suspicions that someone in the CIA such as Helms, or perhaps Bobby, suspected that Varona was involved somehow in JFK's death. Helms had access to the Varona–Chicago Mafia payoff–Masferrer memos, and would have known about Varona's ties to Rosselli and Trafficante through the CIA-Mafia plots. Peter Dale Scott notes that an "agreement was in force from the mid-1950s to the mid-1970s, exempting the CIA from a statutory requirement to report (to the Justice Department) any criminal activity by any of its employees or assets." If Helms knew or suspected that Varona—or other CIA assets—had any involvement in JFK's death, he might simply have dealt with it himself.[20] Congressional investigators found that "Varona . . . had to leave Miami in early 1964 and move to New York to seek employment, giving up his full-time activities," and a CIA memo from August 1964 noted a *New York Times* article about Varona headlined "Cuban Anti-Castro Chief by Day Selling Cars in Jersey by Night."[21]

Artime, Menoyo, and Ray initially worked together in the early months of

1964—their operation was sometimes called Plan Omega—but strains soon developed, since Artime received the lion's share of the CIA's support. The CIA continued to call Artime's operation AMWORLD, and by February 1964, Artime was working closely with David Morales (ZAMKA), and was "singing [the] highest praises of" training he got from Morales.[22]

Strains soon developed between Artime, Ray, and Menoyo. A CIA document from March 1964 notes that Manolo Ray's group "JURE [had] animosity toward Manuel Artime" and quotes an exile as saying that "he has found it impossible to work in an atmosphere in which everyone wants to devour one another."[23] Ray's involvement soon faded, though Menoyo continued to be involved.[24] The CIA began working to bring Artime and Cubela together, and they finally met in Madrid. However, AMWORLD documents from 1964 show that Artime felt that Cubela was too weak to effectively lead a coup, and someone else was needed. The AMTRUNK operation was also looking for someone powerful enough to stage a coup. At this point, AMTRUNK, Artime, Cubela (AMLASH), and Menoyo were all part of one combined operation that the CIA still called AMWORLD, but they lacked someone to lead a coup in Cuba.

The combined operation reached a critical juncture in December 1964. AMTRUNK's Tad Szulc met in New York City with Che Guevara for "several hours" on December 13, 1964.[25] On Che's eight-day trip to the UN in December, he also had secret meetings with Senator Eugene McCarthy and former ABC reporter Lisa Howard, who had told the White House "Che has something to say to us." At that time, historian Jorge Castaneda says Che's relationship with Castro was at a low ebb and "his situation [with Castro] was untenable."[26]

On December 23, 1964—five days after Che left New York—one of Eloy Menoyo's CIA files talks about the "imminent infiltration [into Cuba] of Cuban exiles allegedly involved in [Castro] assassination plot." Shortly after that, Menoyo slipped into Cuba on a secret mission. On December 30 Artime was meeting in Madrid with Rolando Cubela about the assasination plot. According to a CIA report Menoyo was "captured by Cuban authorities January 4, 1965." Menoyo was "forced to go on Cuban television to publicly confess" after beatings that resulted in having "all his ribs broken" and Menoyo losing "all his hearing from one ear." Menoyo was "accused by the regime of having conspired to kill Castro" and began serving a life sentence.[27]

After leaving New York, Che didn't return to Cuba for three months. When he finally returned, Tad Szulc wrote that "In Havana on March 15 [1965] . . . the thread [between Castro and Che] was broken and Che was never seen [in public] again—except dead, two and a half years later in Bolivia. It is an absolute mystery what happened."[28] On the same day Che returned to face Castro, a Congressional report says that Trafficante's "lawyer contacted the CIA to inform the agency" that he was in contact with a "group of Cuban . . . leaders who were planning to eliminate Castro and take over the government."[29] Artime lieutenant Felix Rodriguez wrote that by April 1965, "rumors circulated . . . that [Che] had been executed by Fidel for political reasons."[30]

Che wasn't dead, but he was sent on a seemingly doomed mission to the Congo, a mission that seemed to be a death sentence.[31] Before leaving, he wrote a document in which he gave up everything, "resigning from all his posts and titles and his Cuban citizenship; in which he renounced all power . . . after giving up all his worldly possessions," according to Castaneda.[32] Without telling Che, several months later Castro read Che's declaration to the nation in a radio address in which he didn't say whether Che was dead or alive, and with Che's wife dressed in black on the platform with Fidel. Three weeks later, it was reported that "even Che's father believed he was dead."[33]

The Congo mission completely collapsed, and when Che returned to Cuba, he made no public appearances and avoided most friends. When Rolando Cubela was arrested and put on trial in early 1966, Che was conspicuously absent. Che was then sent by Castro on another doomed mission, to Bolivia, where even the Bolivian Communists and local peasants didn't support the revolt. Castro refused Che's repeated requests for supplies and help.[34] When Che was captured and executed, those present in the area included Felix Rodriguez, a "CIA colleague" called "Eduardo" and David Morales."[35] Fidel Castro was "frankly euphoric" over Che's death, according to Carlos Franqui.[36]

Harry Williams had one more encounter with his former colleague Manuel Artime, when Artime's CIA-funded operations were being shut down after financial irregularities surfaced and the Cubela part of the operation had been blown. In Miami, Harry happened to drop by a friend's house—and was surprised to find Artime and two CIA men there, including a Trafficante associate. Harry says "they were planning the selling of the equipment" and I "advised them don't do that." Instead, apparently Artime sold the equipment and kept the money.[37] In 1964, the mob bosses did whatever it took to keep their ties to JFK's assassination from being exposed. In some cases, it

involved witness intimidation, threats, or murdering people when necessary.[38] Marcello probably considered himself lucky when Guy Banister died in
June 1964, while the Warren Commission was still in session, eliminating any
possibility that he could ever be called to testify. In the case of Abraham
Bolden, the Chicago mob had to take a more active role to keep information
from the Warren Commission.

Bolden sacrificed his career and his freedom trying to tell the Warren
Commission about the Chicago and Tampa assassination attempts. As
Bolden revealed to us for the first time, a criminal he once arrested "did odd
jobs for Sam DeStefano."[39] DeStefano was one of the Chicago Mafia's most
ruthless killers, close to Sam Giancana, Charles Nicoletti, and Richard Cain
as well as part of the French Connection heroin network. DeStefano, either
acting on Cain's behalf or getting his orders directly from Johnny Rosselli,
apparently planned to frame Abraham Bolden before he could tell the
Warren Commission about the Chicago and Tampa attempts.[40]

On the very day Bolden went to Washington hoping to talk to Warren Commission staff, he was arrested on a bogus counterfeiting charge. Bolden had a
sterling reputation, and the only evidence against him was the word of two Mafia
henchmen, one of whom was the DeStefano thug whom Bolden had arrested
before. One of his accusers later admitted that he had lied when he implicated
Bolden. But Bolden was convicted by a Chicago judge and sent to prison for six
years, where he did hard time, sometimes in solitary. Sam DeStefano was murdered in 1973, probably by Richard Cain, and Cain himself was murdered soon
after. Bolden has spent the last forty years seeking to clear his name.[41]

A series of events that began in February 1964 almost exposed the actions
of Michel Mertz in Dallas. A February 18, 1964 article in an obscure French
newspaper caused a brief flurry of investigative activity in Europe and
America, directed at Jean Souetre, Michel Roux, and Michel Mertz. This may
have been a factor in the CIA's termination of QJWIN around that time. This is
also when the CIA memo was issued about Mertz (using the Souetre/Roux
aliases) being deported from Dallas after JFK's death. However, either the
case proved too complex or Mertz's intelligence pull was too strong, and the
investigation soon ended.

In the fall of 1964, CIA Director John McCone briefly tried to look into
QJWIN's activities, before quickly sending a follow-up cable saying to "please
destroy" his original request for information. The author of a recent history

of the Federal Bureau of Narcotics, Douglas Valentine, points out that Bobby Kennedy maintained an interest in the Mexico City–Texas arm of the French Connection heroin ring. He says that "based on [an] anonymous letter [about the ring], and reports written by Hank Manfredi and other CIA agents, Bobby may have believed that the plan to assassinate JFK was effected in Mexico through" a "protected drug route."

Still, just over a year after JFK's murder in Dallas, Mertz was the victim of an unusual crime in France. In November 1964, one of his cars laden with a million dollars worth of heroin was stolen off the street in a fashionable part of Paris. The heroin—chemically traceable—never turned up, and seems to have simply vanished. Just over a month later, Mertz's heroin ring was busted at Fort Benning, Georgia. The ring had been operating for years (while Cuban exile troops were training there), and it also involved New Orleans and Trafficante. It would take years, but Mertz would eventually go to prison briefly for his role in the ring in 1971. Sentenced to five years, he only served two months. After that Mertz lived well, occupying, according to one report, "a gigantic estate in Loiret region near Orleans, measuring about five miles on one side by about six or seven miles on the other.[42] While Jean Souetre eventually talked to journalists and allowed himself to be photographed, Mertz remained reclusive and threatening to investigators until his death on January 15, 1995. Even his death was kept relatively secret, hindering efforts to get US government files about him released.

In 1964, while Bobby Kennedy was still attorney general he had his hands full trying to prosecute Hoffa and Marcello for various crimes, while trying to keep any possible role they had had in JFK's death from tainting those prosecutions. Bobby also had to keep C-Day from being exposed, which was difficult when Hoffa and his lawyers sought to bring sensitive Cuban issues into the case. Bobby's prosecutors had some success with Hoffa, but none with Marcello. Marcello was acquitted on every charge Bobby attempted.

Starting in late 1966, the roles of Marcello and others in JFK's assassination were almost uncovered by investigations on several occasions. However, each time national security concerns related to C-Day kept crucial facts from emerging. In addition, the timely deaths (often by suicide or murder) of key witnesses prevented government investigators from getting closer to the truth.

In November 1966, the *New York Times* and other New York newspapers were investigating the JFK assassination anew. The *Times* wrote to the New Orleans Chief of Police, listing 32 questions about the assassination, primarily focused on David Ferrie, including Carlos Marcello. The police chief gave a copy of the letter to New Orleans District Attorney Jim Garrison, who had Ferrie brought in for questioning in December 1966.[43] Garrison lost the chance to learn anything from another Marcello associate on January 3, 1967, when Jack Ruby died. Ruby had been diagnosed with cancer three days after winning a December 7, 1966 appeal for a new trial, to be held in Wichita Falls.[44]

Garrison tried to conduct his investigation in secret at first, but it was leaked to the media, resulting in a firestorm of publicity that centered around Ferrie. At the height of the controversy on February 22, 1967, David Ferrie died of an apparent suicide. That same night, Ferrie's friend Eladio del Valle—an associate of Trafficante and Masferrer—was murdered in Florida. In the weeks and months that followed, Garrison's investigation was targeted by a variety of people offering to help, some of whom should have been investigated themselves, such as Masferrer and Alberto Fowler.

After Ferrie's death, Garrison had begun focusing on Clay Shaw, a coworker of Albert Fowler. Bobby had his close associate Walter Sheridan go to New Orleans to look into Garrison's charges. Eventually Sheridan began to undermine Garrison's investigation. Johnny Rosselli appears to have made attempts to find a way to influence Garrison. The Garrison investigation wound up becoming a media circus, and it was further undermined by some of his own investigators.

Johnny Rosselli was also being prosecuted at the time, so he began leaking hints of the CIA-Mafia plots and plots involving Robert Kennedy to columnist Jack Anderson, in an attempt to get the government to back off. LBJ asked Richard Helms—by then, CIA Director—for a report on the plots and any links they might have had to JFK's assassination. Helms met with Bobby Kennedy around this time and the resulting Inspector General's report delivered by Helms (detailed in Part 2) contained no information about C-Day, Rosselli's actions in the summer and fall of 1963, or the 1959 CIA-Mafia plots involving Hoffa and Ruby. In July 1967, Desmond FitzGerald died of natural causes.

Bobby Kennedy was assassinated on June 4, 1968, and many of the details of C-Day died with him. His convicted assailant, Sirhan Bishara Sirhan, was first represented by Johnny Rosselli's attorney. Sirhan had recently worked for a Cuban exile associate of Los Angeles mob boss Mickey Cohen. A frequent gambler who often lost, Sirhan "had written in his diary about receiving money from" a low-level mobster, prior to shooting Bobby.[45]

Watergate and its exposure involved a dozen people linked to various aspects of C-Day. Their roles, and the reasons for their actions, are too complex to detail in the space we have remaining, but they include: members of the Watergate operation such as Manuel Artime, Carlos Prio, Frank Fiorini (Sturgis), Eugenio Martinez, Bernard Barker, E. Howard Hunt, James McCord (whose letter to Judge Sirica revealed the cover-up), Richard Helms, and Richard Nixon (named in a C-Day document about Prio). As Fiorini later said, the real goal of the break-ins at the Watergate were a report (in both English and Spanish) prepared by Castro, about attempts against his life by the CIA, plots that had originated under Vice President Richard Nixon. Three others linked to C-Day actually helped bring the Watergate scandal to light and to a resolution: Nixon advisor Al Haig, Joe Califano (counsel for the Democratic Party and the *Washington Post* at the time), and Alexander Butterfield (who revealed Nixon's taping system). In 1973, both Haynes Johnson and Harry Williams gave interviews linking several Watergate figures to C-Day. However, Johnson's interview was only published in an obscure computer magazine, while Harry's interview would not be published until 1981, so they were never brought to the attention of the Senate Watergate Committee.[46]

After being tipped off by Jimmy Hoffa the Senate Watergate Committee in a secret session interviewed Johnny Rosselli about the CIA-Mafia plots against Castro. The Watergate Committee wasn't told about C-Day, though staff member Fred Thompson (later a senator) and a young Hillary Clinton (part of a small group looking into JFK's actions) may have came close to uncovering it. Revelations and leaks about assassinations coming out of the Watergate Committee spurred President Gerald Ford to create the Rockefeller Commission. Controversies arising out of the Rockefeller Commission investigation led Congress to create its own panels, the Pike Committee and the far better known Church Committee, to investigate CIA operations, domestic surveillance, and assassination plots.

On June 13, 1975, Richard Helms testified to the Church Committee in closed session about CIA assassination plots, including those with the Mafia. Former Chicago mob boss Sam Giancana was slated to testify, but on June 19, Giancana was murdered at his home in Chicago. The gun used in the slaying was later traced to Florida, and this begins a series of slayings related to the JFK assassination, most of which are either linked to Trafficante or occur in his home state of Florida. On July 30, 1975, Jimmy Hoffa disappeared before he could be called to testify. Trafficante made it clear to his attorney Frank Ragano that he knew what had happened.

In the summer of 1975, John Martino died, apparently of natural causes, two months after confessing his role in the assassination to a friend. On October 31, 1975, Rolando Masferrer's car was blown up. In June 1976, former CIA official William Harvey died of apparently natural causes.[47] In July of 1976 Johnny Rosselli disappeared in Florida, a short time after he had met with Traficante. His body was discovered, dismembered, and floating in an oil drum, several days later. In response to the resulting publicity, and other events, the House Select Committee on Assassinations (HSCA) was established. Church Committee investigator Gaeton Fonzi went to work for the HSCA, and he planned to interview Oswald's friend and CIA asset, George De Mohrenschildt, while other investigators tried to contact Chicago hit man Charles Nicoletti. On March 29, 1977, Fonzi was in south Florida to interview De Mohrenschildt—but on that day De Mohrenschildt committed suicide by shooting himself before Fonzi could see him. The same day, in Chicago, Charles Nicoletti was shot three times in the back of the head. By November 1977, Fonzi had spoken briefly with Manuel Artime, who agreed to a formal interview. But Artime became ill and died that month. In early May 1978, David Morales was told he would have to speak with Congressional investigators. He died of apparently natural causes on May 8, 1978.[48]

Even with the sudden deaths of people Harry Williams had known—Artime, Prio, and Masferrer—he volunteered to speak with the HSCA. The executive director of the HSCA was Robert Blakey, a former Justice Department prosecutor for Bobby Kennedy, but Harry's offer was never pursued. At that time, Jimmy Carter was president, and his secretary of state was Cyrus Vance; also in Carter's cabinet was Joseph Califano. On March 29, 1979, the HSCA issued its final report, which singled out Carlos Marcello and Santo Trafficante as likely being behind JFK's assassination. Both were also the targets of prosecution efforts by the federal government at that time.

In 1979, the government had targeted Marcello with a wired informant, finally resulting a successful prosecution. Marcello spent most of the 1980s in prison, and, while incarcerated, his comments to others about the JFK assassination were eventually reported to the FBI. An FBI report says that "on December 15, 1985 . . . Carlos Marcello discussed his intense dislike of former President John Kennedy as he often did. Unlike other such tirades against Kennedy, however, on this occasion Carlos Marcello said, referring to President Kennedy, 'Yeah, I had the son of a bitch killed. I'm glad I did it. I sorry I couldn't have done it myself."[49] Marcello became plagued by ill health in prison, and while being treated, drifting in and out of consciousness, Marcello ranted that he was "going to get Kennedy when he came to Dallas," and also said: "That Kennedy, that smiling motherfucker, we'll fix him in Dallas."[50] When later interviewed about these statements, Marcello denied them.[51] One additional confession by Marcello was obtained by the FBI in 1988—in which Marcello mentions Ruby, Ferrie, and Oswald—but the declassified version is so heavily censored that it is impossible to determine the informant's credibility or when Marcello made the comments.[52]

In the mid-1980s, there were unconfirmed reports that Trafficante had put a contract on Marcello's life. Trafficante was in ill health by March 1983, when he reconciled with Ragano (they'd had a falling out in 1976) and spoke to him for the last time. Without long to live, Trafficante looked back at his life and told Ragano that he felt he and Marcello should have killed Bobby Kennedy instead of JFK. Trafficante died four days later, on March 17, 1987. Ragano waited until January 1992 to reveal Trafficante's comments and his own role in carrying messages related to the assassination from Hoffa to Marcello and Trafficante.[53] Trafficante's family took issue with Ragano's statements, but an investigation by the *St. Petersburg Times* found corroborating evidence supporting Ragano.[54] In addition, Jack Newfield, who had worked with Bobby Kennedy, published an article that for the first time spotlighted Bobby's own comments to an associate that the godfather from New Orleans, Marcello, was responsible for his brother's death.[55] Marcello was released from prison in 1989 and died in March 1993 after a series of strokes.

Eloy Menoyo was finally released from a Cuban prison in 1986, after twenty-one years. Tony Varona passed away in 1992. As a consequence, when we approached Harry Williams in 1992, he finally felt free to talk about C-Day. In addition Harry thought that with all the publicity surrounding Oliver Stone's *JFK* film and the release of declassified documents, it was all going to come out soon anyway.

A few years after our first interviews with Harry, we shared with him some of the first AMWORLD documents that had been released, including one in which an informant had detailed Harry's November 1963 meeting with Menoyo. Harry was amazed at the accuracy of the report, but wondered how many of his other hundreds of meetings and phone calls about C-Day had been similarly documented by the CIA.

One man who would have known the answer to Harry's question was David Atlee Phillips, but he had passed away in 1988. Another who would have known was Richard Helms, who passed away on October 23, 2002 after completing his memoirs. Helms was the last person with first-hand knowledge of almost all aspects of C-Day. He mentioned the plans for a 1963 coup in Cuba in just one paragraph of his memoirs.

Two Cuban exiles sum up the unfinished business of US-Cuba relations: Eloy Menoyo and Luis Posada, both involved with various aspects of the Kennedys' C-Day plans in 1963. In 2003, Eloy Menoyo returned to Cuba, to work for nonviolent, peaceful change. On the other hand, Luis Posada has been accused of continuing the violent struggle to overthrow Castro that in some ways began for him at Fort Benning in 1963. Castro himself remains one of the world's longest-reigning rulers—yet another reason C-Day had to remain secret for so long. There was never a time when CIA or US military officials could consider all of the old files and personnel "old news." Instead, we're sure that invasion plans and US intelligence asset files have continued to be maintained. Into the 1980s some of Artime's men worked for US intelligence including contra operations in Central America and may still have roles and so their files must be massive at this point.

We realize that not all files related to C-Day can or should be released as they might legitimately jeopardize people's lives or US operations. But many of them can be released, and either a new (or reconstituted) Review Board and staff should be given the time and resources to make that determination.[56] Noted experts such as Dr. John Newman should be used to help identify the most important records that can be released. Our research shows that most of those who knowingly participated in JFK's assassination are either dead or have served time for crimes at least indirectly related to the assassination. Instead of further prosecution, which would be difficult after so many years, we recommend the establishment of a Truth Commission, capable of granting amnesty and waiving secrecy agreements, to take testimony before it's too late for several elderly participants. What is also needed is justice for Abraham Bolden, who has suffered far too long for trying to tell the truth.

When Harry Williams passed away in Miami on March 10, 1996 it attracted little notice, aside from surviving veterans of the Bay of Pigs. That's exactly how Harry would have wanted it, since he had avoided publicity for the last forty years. With the publication of this book, we hope to finally gain Harry the recognition he deserves, as well as bring attention to the efforts of other exiles who risked their lives for a cause they believed in.

PHOTO APPENDIX

Detail (right) from a photograph (above) of U.S. Attorney General Robert F. Kennedy and Harry Williams greeting a group of Bay of Pigs veterans, many of whom had just been released from Cuban prison due to the efforts of RFK and Williams. *Courtesy AP/Wide World Photos.*

Harry Williams with author, Lamar Waldron, Colorado, February 24, 1992. *Courtesy Thom Hartmann.*

President John F. Kennedy confers with Attorney General Robert F. Kennedy, outside of the Oval Office, March 1963. *Courtesy of Robert Knudsen, White House/John Fitzgerald Kennedy Library, Boston.*

Cyrus Vance, Secretary of the Army. *Courtesy of The John F. Kennedy Presidential Library, Boston.*

ABOVE: President John F. Kennedy, Director of the CIA Allen Dulles, and Director-designate of the CIA John McCone, September 1961. *Courtesy of Robert Knudsen/John F. Kennedy Presidential Library, Boston.* BELOW: Richard Helms, CIA Deputy Director for Plans in 1963. *Courtesy of AP/Wide World Photos.*

General Maxwell D. Taylor, Chairman of the Joint Chiefs of Staff, at his swearing-in ceremony in the Rose Garden, October 1, 1962, with President John F. Kennedy and Attorney General Robert F. Kennedy. *Courtesy of Abbie Rowe/John F. Kennedy Presidential Library, Boston.*

Secretary of State Dean Rusk was not fully informed about the "Plan for a Coup in Cuba" until after JFK's death. *Copyright © Carl Mydans/Time Life Pictures/Getty Images.*

ABOVE: Godfathers Carlos Marcello and Santo Trafficante (second and third from left) with Frank Pagano (fourth from left), attorney for Trafficante. *Copyright © Paul DeMaria/New York Daily News.* BELOW: Johnny Rosselli, the Chicago Mafia's man in Las Vegas and Hollywood. *Courtesy of the National Archives—JFK Assassination Records Collection.*

Lee Harvey Oswald with Dallas Police Officers. *Courtesy of the National Archives— JFK Assassination Records Collection.*

David Atlee Phillips, one of the CIA officers who worked on AMWORLD. *Courtesy of AP/Wide World Photos.*

ABOVE LEFT: Guy Bannister. *Courtesy of the National Archives—JFK Assassination Records Collection.* ABOVE RIGHT: David Ferrie. *Courtesy of the National Archives—JFK Assassination Records Collection.* LEFT: Chicago hit man Charles Nicoletti. *Courtesy of AP/Wide World Photos.*BELOW: Jack Ruby, in his office in the Carousel Club. *Courtesy of the National Archives—JFK Assassination Records Collection.*

DOCUMENT APPENDIX

On the following pages are just a sampling of the thousands of pages of government documents cited in *Ultimate Sacrifice*. Many more can be viewed at www.ultimate sacrificethebook.com. All government documents are from the National Archives and Records Administration, near Washington, DC, and have been declassified.

This June 1963 document signaled the start of AMWORLD, the long-secret codename for the CIA's supporting role in the Kennedys' coup plan.

TOP SECRET SENSITIVE   30 September 1963

A STATE - DEFENSE CONTINGENCY
PLAN FOR A COUP IN CUBA

1. **Problem.** To determine whether a coup in Cuba meets the criteria for
U. S. support and to provide for sufficient US assistance to an anti-
communist coup in Cuba to assure the replacement of the Communist government with one acceptable to the United States.

2. **Assumptions.**

a. The leaders of the coup may or may not be aware, from previous
contact with CIA, that if they agree to and appear capable of meeting
certain specified conditions (see paragraph 2.d. below), their revolt
will be supported by the US if a US "special team" (see paragraph 3.b.(1)
below) confirms that the criteria for support have been met. Thus, the
coup could be triggered in one of two ways: the leaders, in secure radio
contact with CIA, implement their plan with US concurrence and establish
a Provisional Government in full expectation of forthcoming US support
barring a complete and immediate crushing of the uprising; or, less ac-
ceptably, the leaders, in the belief that they can meet probable criteria
for US support, initiate the coup without consulting with or obtaining
the concurrence of the US but establish a Provisional Government, hoping
that the US will intervene.

b. If the US had prior knowledge of the coup, up to forty-eight hours
would be required after initiation of the action to introduce into Cuba
and receive reports from a "special team" which would obtain the information on which to base a decision to support the insurgents; if the US
did not have prior knowledge, a longer time would be required.

c. US intervention would be based on:

(1) A pre-arranged call for help from a Provisional Government
set up by the insurrectionists (preferably to the OAS, although US action
would not await formal OAS approval), or

(2) A call for help from the insurrectionists after a coup had
started without prior US concurrence, if the US determined that the
insurgents met generally the criteria for support, or

TOP SECRET SENSITIVE

The US military had a leading role in the coup plan, as shown by this draft of the
"Plan for a Coup in Cuba" document.

TOP SECRET SENSITIVE

contingency plan has concluded that the only way to be certain that
these criteria have been met without undue loss of time is to have
CINCLANT introduce a special CIA/DOD/State team within twenty-
four hours of the first report of the coup. It is proposed that this
special team would operate as indicated in the attached plan.

JCS comments are requested by October 21, 1963.

Cyrus R. Vance
Secretary of the Army

Attachment
As Stated

The "Plan for a Coup in Cuba" document (previous page) was sent to Maxwell
Taylor, Chairman of the Joint Chiefs, by Secretary of the Army Cyrus Vance.

APPROVED FOR RELEASE 1993
CIA HISTORICAL REVIEW PROGRAM

84804

RYBAT TYPIC YOBITE AMWORLD

1. NASIN ELIAS HAS ASKED NAVY IN GUANTANAMO BASE TO PASS FOLL MSG TO ▮▮▮▮

2. GENERAL UPRISING SCHEDULED FOR 1 DEC. PARTICIPATING GROUPS FND. MRR AND MID.

3. ON 14 NOV NASIN'S SOURCE MET WITH (UNIDENTIFIED) COORDINATOR-GENERAL OF FND WHO INDICATED FND, MRR, MID AND SUB-ORGANIZATIONS PLAN GENERAL UPRISING BEFORE 1 DEC. UPRISING PLANNED AS RESULT OF MIL SERVICE ACT WHICH IN OPINION OF GROUP LEADERS WOULD TREMENDOUSLY REDUCE CLANDESTINE MOVEMENT IN CUBA. SINCE MANY ANTI-REGIME PERSONNEL HAVE REMAINED INACTIVE WAITING FOR CHANCE TAKE EFFECTIVE ACTION, AND SINCE DRAFT WILL SOON PREVENT SUCH ACTION, SOURCE FELT PROBABLY THEY WILL JOIN FIGHT, EVEN WITHOUT WEAPONS. IT DECIDED GROUPS WOULD MAINTAIN PASSIVE STATUS UNTIL 23 NOV IN ORDER ENABLE OVERALL COORDINATOR ARTIME BUERA TO PROVIDE INSTRUCTIONS AND SUPPLIES. IF UPRISING WERE SUPPORTED, IMMEDIATE SUPPLY OF EQUIPMENT WOULD BE

REPRODUCTION BY OTHER THAN THE ISSUING OFFICE IS PROHIBITED.

The date for the Kennedys' coup in Cuba was eventually set for December 1, 1963, according to this CIA AMWORLD cable. *Courtesy Dr. John Newman.*

APPROVED FOR RELEASE 1993
CIA HISTORICAL REVIEW PROGRAM

DIR CITE WAVE 8058

HYBAT TYPIC YOBITE AMWORLD

1. ON 18 NOV 63 [   ] SAID DR. LUIS (DUANY), EXILED DENTIST WHO WORKED FOR (U S GOV ., INSISTING LAST TWO MONTHS THAT LEADERS MRP - ALPHA 66 - SFNE ALLIANCE MEET WITH ENRIQUE (RUIZ) WILLIAMS. DUANY ALLEGEDLY HAS NO DOUBT RUIZ "TRUE PERSONALITY IN CUBAN SITUATION AND ALL US PLANS BEING COORDINATED THROUGH HIM.

2. ON 13 NOV [   ] ELOY (GUTIERREZ) MENOYO, DUANY, AND ESTEBAN (ZORRILLA) JR. MET AT RUIZ'S HOME. DURING MEETING RUIZ SAID CUBANS MUST UNITE TO PRODUCE ACTION INSIDE CUBA, WHICH WILL BE INCREASING, AND THIS WILL WEAKEN REGIME WITH EACH PASSING DAY. HE (RUIZ) CERTAIN "US WILL LEND NECESSARY AID FOR FINAL FALL".

3. RUIZ SAID HAD NO DOUBT JFK WOULD RESOLVE PROBLEM BEFORE ELECTIONS. [   ] SAID THOUGHT REFLECTION WOULD BE SUCCESSFUL WHETHER OR NOT PROBLEM RESOLVED. RUIZ MADE NO COMMENT.

4. RUIZ SAID HE COORDINATOR BETWEEN "OFFICES OF THIS COUNTRY AND CUBAN GROUPS." HAD DEDICATED HIMSELF SMOOTHING THINGS OVER AFTER RFK AND [   ] HAD STRONG DISCUSSIONS FOLLOWING

11/74

In this CIA AMWORLD document, a noted exile says he "has no doubt Ruiz (Harry Williams)" is the "true personality in (the) Cuban situation and all US plans being coordinated through him." *Courtesy Dr. John Newman.*

e. __WAVE 8563 (IN 74654) 6 Dec 1963:__

   Information from AMPALM-4 from Francisco CHAO Hermida
who attended 10 Nov 63 meeting with Miguel A. "Cuco" LEON – involved
PLAN JUDAS. Leon told Chao that while in Washington, D.C. he met
with Enrique RUIZ Williams. RUIZ informed him that he (RUIZ) was
to lead new Cuban republic and had been so named by Robert Kennedy
who had gone to New York to interview him. Kennedy allegedly said
that RUIZ could work with any or every sector he wished but inportant
point was that RUIZ was to be the boss.

This detail from a CIA summary document again shows that Harry Williams (Enrique Ruiz-Williams) was the leading Cuban exile figure in the Kennedys' coup plan in the fall of 1963. Harry worked with a handful of other exile leaders, like Tony Varona. *Courtesy Stuart Wexler and Larry Hancock.*

E. Report of a "confidential informant" of the Field Office, Chicago—(probably not Cain) . On Aug 7, 1963 Informant stated he had learned that while Varona was in Chicago recently (July 1963), four underworld figures made a contribution # of $200,000 to him. Two of the figures are unknown. The other two are Moe Ginacana and Murray (The Canal) Humphreys. He also said Miro Cardozo (Cardona???) wanted to buy guns. Cardozo is employed by American National Insurance Co., Chicago Ph.# 522-7437 (7337)

This CIA memo documents that members of Johnny Rosselli's Chicago mafia family bought their way into the coup plan, with a $200,000 bribe to exile leader Tony Varona. Beginning in 1960 under then Vice-President Richard Nixon, Varona had worked with Rosselli and Santo Trafficante on the CIA-Mafia Castro assassination plots.

MARTINO was a close friend of many former members of the Batista government, such as ESTEBAN VENTURA, ROLANDO MASFERRER (ex-Cuban Senator and political gangster), FRENALDO GARCIA BAEZ (ex-head of Cuban Army Intelligence), and of many American gamblers such as SANTOS TRAFFICANTE, Top Hoodlum from Tampa, Florida.

This detail from an FBI memo to J. Edgar Hoover shows that Trafficante worked with two other Cuban exiles, John Martino, and Rolando Masferrer.

16

Commission No. *657*

UNITED STATES DEPARTMENT OF JUSTICE

FEDERAL BUREAU OF INVESTIGATION

*In Reply, Please Refer to
File No.*

Miami, Florida

RE: LEE HARVEY OSWALD;
INTERNAL SECURITY - RUSSIA - CUBA.

On February 15, 1964, John V. Martino, born
August 3, 1911, at Atlantic City, New Jersey, and resident,
with his family, at 2326 Alton Road, Miami Beach, Florida,
stated he was aware of the article which had appeared in
the Memphis, Tennessee, "Press-Scimitar," on January 30,
1964. Mr. Martino said he had been interviewed by Kay
Pittman of the "Press-Scimitar" on the day before he gave
a lecture in Memphis on the situation in Cuba. With regard to the content of the newspaper article, Mr. Martino
said it had been completely twisted by the reporter, and
he had reprimanded her for it while in Memphis. He said,
specifically, that he had never stated that Oswald had been
paid to assassinate President Kennedy. He said he does not
work with the Cuban underground, as quoted in the article,
although he has sources of information concerning activities in Cuba. He said he was quoted correctly in the statement that his sources informed him that President Kennedy
was engaged in a plot to overthrow the Castro regime by
preparing another invasion attempt against Cuba.

Martino refused to divulge the sources of his information or how they might know what plans President Kennedy
might have had. He said it was the opinion of his sources,

In this FBI document, part of the Warren Commission documents (#657), Rosselli
and Trafficante associate John Martino taunts the FBI with his knowledge of the
Kennedy coup plan (in the last three lines of the first paragraph).

NLK · 71 · 473

MEMORANDUM TO: The Chairman,
                Interdepartmental Coordinating Committee
                on Cuban Affairs

        FROM: Subcommittee on Cuban Subversion

     SUBJECT: Status Report on Assigned Contingency Papers

        The Subcommittee was assigned the preparation of contin-
gency plans to counter the following possible actions by
Castro:

        a) Sabotage of U.S. commercial or industrial installations
in Latin America, including ships and aircraft.

        b) Isolated or coordinated demonstrations or attacks on
U.S. Government property.

        c) Attempts at kidnapping or assassination of American
officials and/or citizens.

        d) Intensified subversion against Latin American govern-
ments.

        After carefully considering this problem, the Subcommittee
has concluded that these particular lines of attack by Castro do
not readily lend themselves to the usual contingency planning
providing for a direct United States response to Cuban actions.
Because the basic protection against attacks occurring within
the jurisdiction of another country must be provided by the
police and security forces of that country, the United States
has little choice but to depend upon these safeguards. Under
these circumstances the most practical counter-action open to
the United States is: (1) the continued strengthening of the
internal security capabilities of the Latin American countries
to deal with these situations, and (2) the alerting of our diplomatic missions and American communities in Latin America in
order that they may up-date, in conjunction with local security
agencies, plans for defending themselves against sabotage and
terrorism.

                              SECRET

                                          SANITIZED

                                    Acting Archivist (NLK-78-473)
                                    BY ____ NARS, DATE 5/6/80
                                          SECRET

ARA/CCA:JJMullon:dr 11/12/63

This two-page document shows that as the date for the Kennedys' coup drew near,
US officials made plans for dealing with "assassination of American officials" (item
"c"). As the 11-12-63 date on the second page (bottom) shows, this was just ten days
before Dallas.

★ ★ ★

Threats On Kennedy Made Here

Tampa police and Secret Service agents scanned crowds for a man who had vowed to assassinate the President here last Monday, Chief of Police J. P. Mullins said yesterday.

In issuing notice to all participating security police prior to the President's motorcade tour in Tampa, Mullins had said: "I would like to advise all officers that threats against the President have been made from this area in the last few days."

A memo from the White House Secret Service dated Nov. 8 reported:

"Subject made statement of a plan to assassinate the President in October 1963. Subject stated he will use a gun, and if he couldn't get closer he would find another way. Subject is described as: White, male, 20, slender build," etc.

Mullins said Secret Service had been advised of three persons in the area who reportedly had made threats on the President's life. One of the three was—and still is—in jail here under heavy bond.

Mullins said he did not know if the other two may have followed the Presidential caravan to Dallas.

Sarasota County Sheriff Ross E. Boyer also said yesterday that officers who protected Kennedy in Tampa Monday were warned about "a young man" who had threatened to kill the President during that trip.

Four days before Dallas, the Mafia planned to assassinate JFK in Tampa, Florida. JFK knew about the threat, but proceeded with his motorcade anyway. The attempt was stopped and then covered up by officials at the time, and this small article about the attempt appeared only once in the *Tampa Tribune*, four days later. (*Tampa Tribune*, 11-23-63)

NOTES

About sources, quotes, and interviews:

All government documents cited in these endnotes have been declassified and are available at the National Archives facility in College Park, Md., near Washington, D.C. Information about many of them, and full copies of a few, are available at the National Archives and Records Administration Web site.

Regarding interviews conducted by the authors for this book, for brevity we have used "we" to refer to interviews conducted by the authors, even if only one of us was present for a particular interview.

Within quotes in the book, we have sometimes standardized names (such as "Harry Williams") for clarity.

Introduction

1. Army copy of Department of State document, 1963, Record Number 198-10004-10072, Califano Papers, Declassified 7-24-97. CIA memo, AMWORLD 11-22-63, #84804, declassified 1993.

2. The last government committee, The Assassinations Records Review Board, was finally unofficially informed of the Coup Plan by one of the authors, via written testimony sent on 11-9-94 for the Review Board's 11-18-94 public hearing in Dallas, as noted in the Board's FY 1995 Report. The earlier committees were the Warren Commission, the Watergate Committee, the Rockefeller Commission, the Pike Committee (and its predecessor, the Nedzi Committee), the Church Committee, and the House Select Committee on Assassinations.

3. "A Presumption of Disclosure: Lessons from the John F. Kennedy Assassination Records Review Board," by OMB Watch, available at ombwatch.com.

4. *NBC Nightly News* with Tom Brokaw 9-29-98.

5. John F. Kennedy address at Rice University, 9-12-62, from *Public Papers of the Presidents of the United States*, v. 1, 1962, pp. 669–670.

6. Army document, Summary of plan dated 9-26-63, Califano Papers, Record Number 198-10004 10001, declassified 10-7-97.

7. Army copy of Department of State document, 1963, Record Number 198-10004-10072, Califano Papers, Declassified 7-24-97.

8. Army document, Summary of plan dated 9-26-63, Califano Papers, Record Number 198-10004-10001, declassified 10-7-97.

9. Interview with Harry Williams 7-24-93; interview with confidential C-Day Defense Dept. source 7-6-92; classified message to Director from JMWAVE, CIA/DCD Document ID withheld to protect US intelligence asset but declassified 3-94.

10. The following is just one of many: Joint Chiefs of Staff document, dated 12-4-63 with 11-30-63 report from Cyrus Vance, Record Number 202-10002-101116, declassified 10-7-97.

11. CIA cable to Director, 12-10-63, CIA 104-10076-10252, declassified 8-95; David Corn, *Blond Ghost: Ted Shackley and the CIA's Crusades* (New York: Simon & Schuster, 1994), p. 110.

12. House Select Committee on Assassinations vol. X, p. 77.

13. Interview with Harry Williams 2-24-92; interview with confidential Kennedy C-Day aide source 3-17-92; interview with confidential C-Day Defense Dept. source 7-6-92.

14. Interview with Dean Rusk 1-8-90.

15. *Foreign Relations of the United States*, Volume XI, Department of State, #370, 10-8-63; 12-6-63 CIA Document, from JMWAVE to Director, released during the 1993 CIA Historical Review Program.

16. From the John F. Kennedy Presidential Library, NLK 78-473, declassified 5-6-80.

17. John H. Davis, *Mafia Kingfish: Carlos Marcello and the Assassination of John F. Kennedy* (New York: McGraw-Hill, 1989), pp. 49, 64, many others.

18. *Ibid.*

19. FBI DL 183A-1f035-Sub L 3.6.86 and FBI Dallas 175-109 3.3.89, cited by A. J. Weberman; CR 137A-5467-69, 6-9-88, cited by Brad O'Leary and L. E. Seymour, *Triangle of Death* (Nashville: WND Books, 2003).

20. David Talbot, "The man who solved the Kennedy assassination," Salon.com, 11-22-03.

21. Jack Newfield, "I want Kennedy killed," *Penthouse* 5-92; Frank Ragano and Selwyn Raab, *Mob Lawyer* (New York: Scribners, 1994), pp. 346-54, 361; "Truth or Fiction?" *St. Petersburg Times*, 4-18-94. Charles Rappleye and Ed Becker, *All American Mafioso: The Johnny Rosselli Story* (New York: Barricade, 1995).

22. William Scott Malone, "The Secret Life of Jack Ruby," *New Times* 1-23-78; Bradley Ayers, *The War that Never Was: An Insider's Account of CIA Covert Operations Against Cuba* (Canoga Park, Calif.: Major Books, 1979), pp. 59, 129; The CIA's Inspector General's Report on the CIA-Mafia plots.

23. Malone, *op. cit.*; HSCA Final Report and volumes, many passages.

24. Phone interviews with Pierre Salinger 4-3-98, 4-10-98; interview with confidential source 4-14-98.

25. Warren Commission Exhibit #2818. (In mid-December 1963, after JFK's death and LBJ put C-Day on hold, Ruby placed the date for the invasion in May 1964.)

26. *Atlanta Journal-Constitution* 5-19-02, pp. C-1, C-6; John Sugg, "Time to Pull the Sharks' Teeth," *Creative Loafing* weekly newspaper, Atlanta edition, 12-11-03, p. 27.

27. G. Robert Blakey and Richard N. Billings, *The Plot to Kill the President* (New York: Times Books, 1981), p. 288.

28. Charles Rappleye and Ed Becker, *All American Mafioso* (New York: Barricade, 1995), p. 315.

29. Church Committee Report, Vol. V, officially *The Investigation of the Assassination of President John F. Kennedy: Performance of the Intelligence Agencies*, pp. 19-21; 8-30-77 CIA document, "Breckinridge Task Force" report, commenting on Church Committee Report, Vol. V, document ID 1993.07.27.18:36:29:430590, declassified 1993; Thomas G. Paterson, *Contesting Castro: The United States and the Triumph of the Cuban Revolution* (New York: Oxford University Press, 1994), p. 261, citing Bundy memo, "Meeting with the President," Dec. 19, 1963; Arthur Schlesinger, Jr., *Robert Kennedy and His Times* (New York: Ballantine, 1979), p. 598; Gus Russo, *Live by the Sword: The Secret War against Castro and the Death of JFK* (Baltimore: Bancroft Press, 1978), p. 278.

30. Haynes Johnson, "One Day's Events Shattered America's Hopes and Certainties," *Washington Post* 11-20-83.

31. ABCNEWS.com, 11-20-03, "A Brother's Pain," interview with Evan Thomas.

32. Phone interviews with Pierre Salinger 4-3-98, 4-10-98; interview with confidential source 4-14-98.

33. Re: Arthur M. Schlesinger, Jr., *Parade* magazine 6-7-98 citing Jack Newfield; re McCone: Schlesinger, *op. cit.*, p. 664; Blakey, *op. cit.*, many passages; re Sheridan: John H. Davis, *The Kennedy Contract* (New York: HarperPaperbacks, 1993), p. 154, and Evan Thomas, *Robert Kennedy*, p. 338; re O'Donnell: William Novak, *Man of the House: The Life and Political Memoirs of Speaker Tip O'Neil* (New York: Random House, 1987), p. 178; Jack Newfield, "I want Kennedy killed," *Penthouse* 5-92; re Burkley, Gus Russo, *Live by the Sword* (Baltimore: Bancroft Press, 1978), p. 49; Ronald Goldfarb, *Perfect Villains, Imperfect Heroes: Robert F. Kennedy's War against Organized Crime* (New York: Random House), pp. 258–299.

34. ABCNEWS.com, *op. cit.*

35. *Ibid.*

36. Joseph A. Califano, Jr., *Inside: A Public and Private Life* (New York: PublicAffairs, 2004), p. 125.

37. In addition, the predecessor of the Pike Committee—the Nedzi Committee—got close to aspects of JFK's assassination and C-Day when it investigated CIA activities during Watergate.

38. The following document was "systematically reviewed by JCS on 19 Oct 1989 Classification continued"—Joint Chiefs of Staff document, dated 12-4-63 with 11-30-63 report from Cyrus Vance, 80 total pages, Record Number 202-10002-101116, declassified 10-7-97.

39. "A Presumption of Disclosure: Lessons from the John F. Kennedy Assassination Records Review Board," by OMB Watch, available at ombwatch.com.

40. Interview with ex-Secret Service Agent Abraham Bolden 4-15-98; House Select Committee on Assassinations Report 231, 232, 636, *New York Times* 12-6-67; Abraham Bolden file at the Assassination Archives and Research Center.

41. Michael R. Beschloss, *The Crisis Years: Kennedy and Khrushchev, 1960–1963* (New York: Edward Burlingame Books, 1991) pp. 670, 671.

42. John Mitchell—the commander of JFK's PT boat unit—would become attorney general under Nixon, before his conviction due to a scandal related to C-Day.

43. Myra MacPherson, "The Last Casualty of the Bay of Pigs," *Washington Post* 10-17-89.

44. From the John F. Kennedy Presidential Library, NLK 78-473, declassified 5-6-80; article by Tad Szulc in the *Boston Globe* 5-28-76 and a slightly different version of the same article in *The New Republic* 6-5-76

45. Interview with Dave Powers 6-5-91 at the John F. Kennedy Presidential Library.

46. Novak, *op. cit.*, p. 178.

Part I

Chapter One: The Cuban Missile Crisis and C-Day

1. Interview with Dean Rusk 1-5-90.

2. Harold W. Chase and Allen H. Lerman, eds. and annotators, *Kennedy and the Press: The News Conferences*, with an introduction by Pierre Salinger (New York: Crowell, 1965), pp. 333-339.

3. Chase and Lerman, *Kennedy and the Press*, pp. 333-339; John F. Kennedy address at Rice University 9-12-62, from *Public Papers of the Presidents of the United States*, v. 1, 1962, pp. 669-670.

4. Michael R. Beschloss, *The Crisis Years: Kennedy and Khrushchev, 1960-1963* (New York: Edward Burlingame, 1991), pp. 555, 556.

5. Their Web site has a vast array of important documents and information on the US and Cuba, and covert CIA operations (www2.gwu.edu or www.gwu.edu).

6. Laurence Chang and Peter Kornbluh, eds., *The Cuban Missile Crisis 1962* (New York: The New Press), 1992.

7. *Ibid.*, pp. 235, 236.

8. *Ibid.*, p. 236.

9. *Ibid.*, Document 72

10. Chase and Lerman, *op. cit*, pp. 333-339.

11. *Ibid.*

12. Carlos Franqui, *Family Portrait with Fidel: A Memoir* (New York: Random House, 1984), p. 200.

13. Chang and Kornbluh, *op. cit.*, Document 78 and p. 237.

14. *Ibid.*, pp. 234-237, 394, others. Their book documents that it was President Richard Nixon who later formalized such a pledge.

15. Joint Chiefs of Staff document, dated 12-4-63 with 11-30-63 report from Cyrus Vance, Record Number 202-10002-101116, declassified 10-7-97.

16. *New York Times* 5-10-63, Section 1, p. 1, Section 2, p. 2.

17. *New York Times* 6-1-63, Section 3, p. 5.

18. Foreign Relations of the United States, Volume XI, Department of State, #347, 6-14-63

19. *Ibid.*, #352, 6-25-63

20. *Ibid.*, #322, 4-23-63.

21. *Ibid.*, #322, 4-23-63.

22. *Ibid.*, #323, 4-25-63.

23. Rockefeller Commission Document prepared for David Belin 5-1-75, Record Number 157-10005-10201, declassified 3-24-94

24. Gus Russo, *Live by the Sword* (Baltimore: Bancroft Press, 1978), p. 178.

25. Army copy of Department of State document, 1963, Record Number 198-10004-10072, Califano Papers, declassified 7-24-97.

26. *Ibid.*

27. Schlesinger, *Robert Kennedy and His Times*, pp. 510-511; cf 514.

28. Interview with Harry Williams 2-24-92.

Chapter Two: Harry Williams

1. Haynes Johnson, "The CIA's Secret War on Cuba," *Washington Post* 6-10-77, B1.

2. Interview with confidential Kennedy aide source 3-17-92. This former aide requested confidentiality, due to his position. But his knowledge of C-Day and impeccable reputation for honesty have been confirmed by numerous documents and non-confidential sources, including Harry Williams, Dean Rusk, and Courtney Evans (the highly respected FBI Agent who had the unenviable job of being the liaison between Bobby Kennedy and J. Edgar Hoover).

3. Evan Thomas, *Robert Kennedy: His Life* (New York: Simon & Schuster, 2000), pp. 177, 178, 238, 239.

4. Myra MacPherson, "The Last Casualty of the Bay of Pigs," *Washington Post* 10-17-89, pp. C-1, C-4

5. RFK Oral History at the JFK Library; Edwin O. Guthman and Jeffrey Shulman, eds., *Robert Kennedy: In His Own Words: The Unpublished Recollections of the Kennedy Years* (Toronto, New York: Bantam, 1988), pp. 376, 377.

6. 8-63 State Department memo, declassified 10-31-80. This exile wasn't one of the five C-Day exile leaders, so Harry and Bobby were passing the exile doctor off to State, which didn't know about C-Day at that time.

7. Evan Thomas, *Robert Kennedy*, pp. 238-9.

8. Warren Hinckle and William Turner, *The Fish Is Red: The Story of the Secret War Against Castro* (New York: Harper & Row, 1981), p. 151.

9. Willam Turner, "Men who Killed Kennedy," History Channel; Interview with confidential C-Day Defense Dept. source 7-6-92; Interview with confidential Kennedy C Day aide source 3-17-92.

10. Evan Thomas, *Robert Kennedy,* pp. 177-8.

11. Hinckle and Turner, *The Fish Is Red,* p. 190.

12. Evan Thomas, *Robert Kennedy,* pp. 238-9.

13. Haynes Johnson, "One Day's Events Shattered America's Hopes and Certainties," *Washington Post* 11-20-83.

14. William Turner interview with Harry Williams 11-28-73.

15. RFK Oral History at the JFK Library, and Guthman and Shulman, *op. cit.,* pp. 376-7.

16. "Enrique Ruiz-Williams," *Mines* July/August 1996, provided by the Colorado School of Mines Alumni Association.

17. William Turner interview with Harry Williams 11-28-73.

18. *Ibid.*

19. Interview with Harry Williams 2-24-92.

20. Interview with Harry Williams 7-24-93.

21. Haynes Johnson with Manuel Artime and others, *The Bay of Pigs: The Leaders' Story of Brigade 2506* (New York: Norton, 1964), many passages.

22. Nestor T. Carbonell, *And the Russians Stayed: The Sovietization of Cuba: A Personal Portrait* (New York: Morrow, 1989), p. 189.

23. Johnson and Artime, *op. cit.,* p. 177.

24. Interview with Harry Williams 2-24-92.

25. *Ibid.*

26. Johnson and Artime, *op. cit.,* p. 177.

27. *Ibid.,* many passages.

28. Interview with Harry Williams 2-24-92.

29. Carbonell, *op. cit.*

30. Richard D. Mahoney, *Sons & Brothers: The Days of Jack and Bobby Kennedy* (New York: Arcade, 1999), p. 218.

31. Carbonell, *op. cit.*

32. *Ibid.*

33. Interview with Harry Williams 2-24-92.

34. Johnson and Artime, *op. cit.,* many passages.

35. Carbonell, *op. cit.,* p. 191.

36. *New York Times* 5-23-63 (2:4; Kennedy transcript 18:4,5).

37. Evan Thomas, *Robert Kennedy,* pp. 238-9.

38. *Ibid.,* pp. 177-8.

39. 12-6-63 CIA Document, from JMWAVE to Director, released during the 1993 CIA Historical Review Program, with another copy released in 1994; best copy is courtesy of Dr. John Newman.

40. Evan Thomas, *Robert Kennedy,* pp. 177-8.

41. Interview with Harry Williams 2-24-92.

42. "A Presumption of Disclosure: Lessons from the John F. Kennedy Assassination Records Review Board," by OMB Watch, available at ombwatch.com.

43. Interview with Harry Williams 2-24-92.

44. Interview with confidential Kennedy aide source 3-17-92. Note to readers—multiple interviews were conducted on that date, so it's pointless to try to figure out the identity of any one source based on the interview date.

45. 5-10-63 Associated Press article quoted in Paris Flammonde, *The Kennedy Conspiracy: An Uncommissioned Report on the Jim Garrison Investigation* (New York: Meredith Press, 1969).

46. Phone interview with Harry Williams 11-13-92.

47. *Ibid.*

48. Interview with Harry Williams 4-92; names and dates of Defense Department interviews withheld to protect sources.

49. Interviews with Harry Williams 2-24-92, 7-24-93.

50. Daniel James, *Che Guevara: A Biography* (New York: Stein and Day, 1969), p. 285.

51. Interviews with Harry Williams 2-24-92, 7-24-93.

52. Harry Williams interview 7-24-93.

53. Confidential Kennedy Foreign Policy Advisor source 4-18-96; Jorge G. Castaneda, *Compañero: The Life and Death of Che Guevara* (New York: Vintage, 1998), pp. 242-255 and many others; interviews with Harry Williams 4-92, 7-24-93.

54. Laura Bergquist, "Cuba: A revisit with 'Che' Guevara," *Look*, 4-9-63.

55. Laura Bergquist, "A 2:30 A.M. interview with 'Che' Guevara," *Look*, 11-8-60.

56. JMWAVE cable to headquarters, December 2, 1963, cited in David Corn, *Blond Ghost: Ted Shackley and the CIA's Crusades* (New York: Simon & Schuster, 1994), p. 110 and note 433.

57. Interviews with confidential Kennedy administration official source 3-6-95, 3-8-96, and 4-18-96.

58. Foreign Relations of the United States, Volume XI, Department of State, #337, 5-10-63.

59. National Intelligence Estimate, Washington, June 14, 1963 in Foreign Relations of the United States, Volume XI, #347.

60. Foreign Relations of the United States, Volume XI, Department of State, #338, 5-13-63.

61. Interviews with Harry Williams 2-24-92, 7-24-93.

62. Foreign Relations of the United States, Volume XI, Department of State, #337, 5-10-63. It should be noted that it's unclear what, if anything, the authors or recipient of the memo knew about C-Day. It could be just a case of the coup leader's contact fitting perfectly with plans that the Kennedy Administration was already discussing.

63. *Ibid.*

64. Interviews with Harry Williams 2-24-92, 7-24-93.

65. Hugh Thomas, *Cuba: Or, Pursuit of Freedom* (London: Eyre & Spottiswoode, 1971), p. 1319.

66. Laura Bergquist, "Cuba: A revisit with 'Che' Guevara," *Look*, 4-9-63.

67. Foreign Relations of the United States, Volume XI, Department of State, #374 11-8-63 and #379 11-25-63 and others; Interview with Harry Williams 2-24-92.

68. Interviews with Harry Williams 2-24-92, 7-24-93.

69. *New York Times* Index 5-11-63 (2:1), "New drive to unify exiles into single orgn to overthrow Castro reptd; Castro lauds US ban on raids as step toward peace, TV int with L Howard."

Chapter Three: The C-Day "Plan for a Coup in Cuba"

1. Arthur Schlesinger, Jr., "An Open Letter to Bill Moyers," *Washington Star* 7-10-77; "JFK, Castro--and Controversy," *Newsweek* 7-18-77.

2. Edwin O. Guthman and Jeffrey Shulman, eds., *Robert Kennedy: In His Own Words* (Toronto, New York: Bantam, 1988).

3. Seymour M. Hersh, "Aides say Robert Kennedy told of CIA Castsro plot," New York Times 3-10-75.

4. Evan Thomas, *The Man to See* (New York: Touchstone, 1992), pp. 339-344.

5. Testimony of Richard Helms, HSCA Vol. 4, pp. 158, 159, 173, 174.

6. Richard Reeves, *President Kennedy: Profile of Power* (New York: Simon & Schuster, 1993), p. 714.

7. Gus Russo, *Live by the Sword* (Baltimore: Bancroft Press, 1978), p. 460.

8. Michael R. Beschloss, *The Crisis Years* (New York: Edward Burlingame, 1991), pp. 138-9.

9. Russo, *op. cit.,* p. 96, citing Helms testimony before the Church Committee.

10. Russo, *op. cit.,* p. 431, citing "The CIA: America's Secret Warriors," The Discovery Channel, 1997.

11. Evan Thomas, *The Very Best Men: Four Who Dared: The Early Years of the CIA* (New York: Simon & Schuster, 1995), p. 300.

12. Beschloss, *The Crisis Years*, pp. 138-9.

13. Reeves, *op. cit.,* p. 713.

14. Army document, Summary of plan dated 9-26-63, Califano Papers, Record Number 198-10004-10001, declassified 10-7-97.

15. Joint Chiefs of Staff document 5-1-63 (revised 5-13-63) "Courses of Action Related to Cuba", Record Number 202-10002-10018, declassified 7-23-97.

16. Reeves, *op. cit.,* p. 306.

17. ABC News Web site, *Friendly Fire: US Military Drafted Plans to Terrorize US Cities to Provoke War with Cuba*, May 1 and also dated 11-7-2001.

18. Warren Hinckle and William Turner, *Deadly Secrets* (New York: Thunder's Mouth, 1992), pp. 84, 85, 89, 93-4.

19. *Ibid.*

20. *Reeves, op. cit.,* p. 373. Taylor took command on 10-1-62.

21. Joint Chiefs of Staff document 5-1-63 (revised 5-13-63) "Courses of Action Related to Cuba", Record Number 202-10002-10018, declassified 7-23-97.

22. *Ibid.*

23. *Ibid.*

24. *Ibid.*

25. Joint Chiefs of Staff document, 5-1-63 (revised 5-13-63) "Courses of Action Related to Cuba", Record Number 202-10002-10018, declassified 7-23-97.

26. Joint Chiefs of Staff document, dated 12-4-63 with 11-30-63 report from Cyrus Vance, 80 total pages, Record Number 202-10002-101116, declassified 10-7-97.

27. *Ibid.*

28. Haynes Johnson, "Rendezvous with Ruin at The Bay of Pigs," *Washington Post* 4-17-81.

29. Hinckle and Turner, *Deadly Secrets,* pp. 170, 171.

30. Interview with Harry Williams 2-24-92.

31. Interview with Harry Williams 2-24-92; Interview with confidential C-Day Defense Dept. source 7-6-92; Interview with confidential Kennedy C Day aide source 3-17-92.

32. HSCA Vol. X, March 1979, page 77.

33. *Ibid.*

34. Foreign Relations of the United States, Volume XI, Department of State, #346, 6-8-63.

35. *Ibid.*

36. *Ibid.*

37. *Ibid.*

38. Church Committee Report, Vol. V, many passages; U.S. Senate, Select Committee to Study Governmental Operations with Respect to Intelligence Activities, *Alleged Assassination Plots Involving Foreign Leaders* (New York: Norton, 1976), many passages; CIA document, record number 104-10400-10133, Chronology of Significant documents in AMTRUNK file, prepared 4-77.

39. Hal Hendrix, "Backstage with Bobby," *Miami Herald* 7-14-63.

40. Foreign Relations of the United States, Volume XI, Department of State, #346, 6-8-63.

41. *Ibid.*

42. Interview with Harry Williams 2-24-92.

43. Church Committee Report, Vol. V, p. 13.

44. Russo, *op. cit.,* pp. 173-4.

45. Robert Kennedy phone logs at the National Archives. In addition to the 25 calls during 1963, they also document 13 phone calls from Harry Williams to Robert Kennedy from 7-31-62 to 10-22-62.

46. Richard D. Mahoney, *Sons & Brothers* (New York: Arcade, 1999), p. 170.

47. Interview with Harry Williams 2-24-92.

48. Evan Thomas, *The Very Best Men* (New York: Simon & Schuster, 1995); Dick Russell, *The Man Who Knew Too Much: Hired to Kill Oswald and Prevent the Assassination of JFK: Richard Case Nagell* (New York: Carroll & Graf/R. Gallen, 1992), p. 148.

49. Interview with Harry Williams 7-24-93.

50. HSCA Vol. X, March 1979, p. 11.

51. Russo, *op. cit.,* pp. 174, 175

Chapter Four: AMWORLD: *The CIA's Portion of C-Day*

1. CIA 104-10315-10004, 6-28-63 AMWORLD memo, declassified 1-27-99.

2. The 2004 AMWORLD document trove was discovered in the National Archives by researcher Stuart Wexler, who provided them to author Larry Hancock, who recognized their significance and provided them to the authors. We gratefully acknowledge their work in making these documents public.

3. CIA 104-10315-10004, 6-28-63 AMWORLD memo, declassified 1-27-99.

4. *Ibid.*

5. CIA #104-10098-10093, 10-31-63 AMWORLD Dispatch, declassified 6-20-96.

6. 6. Jefferson Morley, "The Good Spy," Washington Monthly 12-03.

7. Gaeton Fonzi, *The Last Investigation* (New York: Thunder's Mouth, 1994), p. 371.

8. David Corn, *Blond Ghost* (New York: Simon & Schuster, 1994), p. 85.

9. Phone interview with Larry Hancock 2-18-05.

10. David Atlee Phillips, *The Night Watch* (New York: Atheneum, 1977), p. 49.

11. Kate Doyle and Peter Kornbluh, *CIA and Assassinations: The Guatemala 1954 Documents,* National Security Archives Web site.

12. CIA #104-10098-10093, 10-31-63 AMWORLD Dispatch, declassified 6-20-96.

13. Warren Hinckle and William Turner, *The Fish Is Red* (New York: Harper & Row, 1981), p. 153. As might be expected for a long-time CIA veteran whose writings indicate that he still holds the CIA in high esteem, McCord declined to comment when contacted by us regarding his work with Harry Williams.

14. Quote is from James McCord, *A Piece of Tape: The Watergate Story: Fact and Fiction* (Rockville, Md.: Washington Media Services, 1974), back cover bio and from McCord's Web site http://www.mccordfamilyassn.com/endpage.htm#Endpage:

%20The%20purpose%20of%20this%20book, both say that McCord worked on European matters; John Newman, *Oswald and the CIA* (New York: Carroll & Graf, 1995), p. 240.

15. William Turner interview with Harry Williams 11-28-73, transcript courtesy of Mr. Turner.

16. Newman, *op. cit.*, pp. 95, 236, 240, 243, 396, 474.

17. Gus Russo, *Live by the Sword* (Baltimore: Bancroft Press, 1978), p. 165.

18. *CBS Reports: The CIA's Secret Army*, broadcast 6-10-77, from transcript at the Assassination Archives and Research Center.

19. Bernard Fensterwald, Jr., and Michael Ewing, *Coincidence or Conspiracy* (New York: Zebra Books, 1977), p. 517.

20. Hinckle and Turner, *The Fish Is Red*, p. 153.

21. Tad Szulc, "Cuba on our Mind," *Esquire*, February 1973.

22. Tad Szulc, *Compulsive Spy: The Strange Career of E. Howard Hunt* (New York: Viking, 1974), pp. 96, 97; it should be noted that Szulc places the operation more in 1964 and 1965, when some of the remnants of C-Day had been combined with Szulc's AMTRUNK and the CIA's Cubela operation.

23. Tad Szulc, "Cuba on our Mind," *Esquire*, February 1973. It should be noted that Szulc calls the second Cuban invasion "Second Naval Guerilla," a name which none of our sources or government documents has ever used. It's possible that Szulc coined the name as a descriptive reference, the same way we did for "C-Day," to avoid using the real CIA code name. That may explain why, when James McCord wrote the CIA asking for any information they had on "Second Naval Guerilla," he was told that they couldn't find any (his letter and the CIA response were on file at the Assassination Archives and Research Center, which was founded by one of McCord's lawyers, Bud Fensterwald). McCord's letter indicated that he hadn't participated in any such operation. On the other hand, when William Turner's 1981 book linked James McCord to Harry Williams, there was apparently no response from McCord.

24. Szulc, *Compulsive Spy*, pp. 96, 97.

25. Hinckle and Turner, *The Fish Is Red*, p. 153; William Turner interview with Harry Williams 11-28-73, transcript courtesy of Mr. Turner.

26. *CBS Reports: The CIA's Secret Army*, broadcast 6-10-77, from transcript at the Assassination Archives and Research Center.

27. James Hougan, *Secret Agenda: Watergate, Deep Throat, and the CIA* (New York: Random House, 1984), p. 18.

28. Richard D. Mahoney, *Sons & Brothers* (New York: Arcade, 1999), p. 265.

29. Summary Record of the 20th Meeting of the Standing Group of the National Security Council, in Foreign Relations of the United States, Volume XI, Department of State, #356, 7-16-63, declassified 1997.

30. Seth Kantor, *The Ruby Cover-Up* (New York: Zebra Books, 1992), pp. 376-382.

31. Russo, *op. cit.*, p. 173.

32. *Ibid.*, p. 547, note 31.

33. *Ibid.*, p. 174, citing *Orlando Sentinel Star* 6-12-77.

34. CIA Blind Memo dated 8-21-63, cited in Russo, *op. cit.*, p. 174.

35. *New York Times* 7-17-63 (2:1, 6, 7).

36. *New York Times* 7-22-63 (3:6).

37. Hal Hendrix, "Backstage with Bobby," *Miami Herald* 7-14-63.

38. August 1963 *Washington Post* article cited in Harold Weisberg, *Oswald in New Orleans: Case of Conspiracy with the C.I.A.* (New York: Canyon Books, 1967), p. 147.

39. Myra MacPherson, "The Last Casualty of the Bay of Pigs," *Washington Post* 10-17-89.

Chapter Five: The Kennedy Men: Vance, Haig, and Califano

1. Foreign Relations of the United States, Volume XI, Department of State, #342, 5-22-63.

2. Church Committee Report, Vol. V, pp. 15, 16, and others.

3. Standing Group Record of Actions 4-16-63, Cuba papers, NSA, cited in Richard Reeves, *President Kennedy: Profile of Power* (New York: Simon & Schuster, 1993), pp. 473, 727.

4. National Archives and Records Administration, Califano Papers Web page.

5. Alexander M. Haig, Jr., *Inner Circles: How America Changed the World: A Memoir* (New York: Warner Books, 1992), p. 109.

6. National Archives and Records Administration, Califano Papers Web page.

7. Joseph A. Califano, Jr., *Inside* (New York: PublicAffairs, 2004) p. 116.

8. Gus Russo, *Live by the Sword* (Baltimore: Bancroft Press, 1978), pp. 163, 164

9. Califano, *Inside*, p. 504.

10. Roger Morris, *Haig: The General's Progress* (New York: Playboy Press, 1982), p. 61.

11. Authors' interview with Harry Williams 2-24-92.

12. William Turner interview of Harry Williams 11-28-73, transcript courtesy of Mr. Turner. It's interesting to note that the

interview occurred just days after the 10th anniversary of JFK's assassination and while the Watergate investigation (which involved many C-Day veterans) was in high gear.

13. SSCIA index card summaries, prepared June-July 1975, record number 157-10011-10002, declassified 3-1-94.

14. Califano, *Inside*, p. 121.

15. ABC News Web site, *Friendly Fire: US Military Drafted Plans to Terrorize US Cities to Provoke War with Cuba*, May 1 and also dated 11-7-2001.

16. Army document, 7-19063, Memo from Alexander Haig to Captain Zumwalt, Califano Papers, Record Number 198-10004-10005, declassified 10-7-97.

17. Califano, *Inside*, pp. 118, 122.

18. Haig, *op. cit.*, p. 106.

19. *Ibid.*

20. *Ibid.*, p. 108.

21. *Ibid.*, p. 111.

22. *Ibid.*

23. ABC's *Nightline*, 12-29-97, cited in Russo, *op. cit.*, p. 163.

24. Interview with confidential Kennedy aide source 3-17-92.

25. CIA document, from Director to (censored) and JMWAVE, 30 Nov 63, #86031, released in 1994 by the CIA Historical Review Program; from "Carlos Prio Socarras [soft file]."

26. Interview with Harry Williams 2-24-92.

27. Interview with confidential C-Day Defense Department source 7-92.

28. Phone interview with confidential Kennedy Foreign Policy Adviser source 4-18-96.

29. Califano, *Inside*, p. 122.

30. *Ibid.*, p. 119.

31. *Ibid.*, pp. 122, 124.

32. *Ibid.*, p. 124.

33. *Ibid.*

34. *Ibid.*, p. 125.

35. *Ibid.*

36. *Ibid.*, p. 121.

37. Haig, *op. cit.*, p. 112.

38. Russo, *op. cit.*, p. 241.

39. Califano, *Inside*, p. 125.

40. Califano, *Inside*, pp. 383-389; Adrian Havill, *Deep Truth* (New York: Birch Lane, 1993), pp. 182, 183.

41. *The Surveillant*, May-June 1992, p. 176.

42. Joseph J. Trento article in the 1-10-81 *Wilmington News-Journal*, cited in Warren Hinckle and William Turner, *Deadly Secrets* (New York: Thunder's Mouth, 1992), pp. 412, 413. The authors wish to emphasize that we are only reporting Trento's article, not endorsing it. Likewise, we do not feel that Haig or Califano had any role in JFK's assassination or in criminal activity related to Watergate. Just the opposite—we feel that both men played important roles during Watergate that benefited the country.

43. Evan Thomas, *Robert Kennedy: His Life* (New York: Simon & Schuster, 2000), p. 272.

44. *Ibid.*, p. 449.

45. Haig, *op. cit.*, p. 119.

46. Russo, *op. cit.*, pp. 249, 250.

47. Church Committee Report, Vol. V, pp. 15, 16.

48. Department of the Army documents dated 9-14-63 and 9-27-63, provided by the State Department, in SSCIA record number 157-10005-10372 dated 3-27-76, declassified 2-18-94. Department of the Army documents dated 9-14-63 and 9-27-63, provided by the State Department, in SSCIA record number 157-10005-10372 dated 3-27-76, declassified 2-18-94.

49. Evan Thomas, *Robert Kennedy*, p. 449.

Chapter Six: Harry Williams, RFK, and the Coup Leader

1. *New York Times* 8-30-63 (7:1).

2. Tad Szulc, "Castro Reported Quarreling Again with Red Backers," special to the *New York Times*, 9-2-63.

3. *Ibid.*

4. CIA Document 12-6-63, from JMWAVE to Director, released during the 1993 CIA Historical Review Program, with another copy released in 1994; best copy is courtesy Dr. John Newman.

5. Classified Message to Director from JMWAVE, CIA/DCD file, declassified 3-8-94.

6. Jon Lee Anderson, *Che Guevara: A Revolutionary Life* (New York: Grove Press, 1997), p. 213; Carlos Franqui, *Family Portrait with Fidel: A Memoir* (New York: Random House, 1984), pp. 156, 157.

7. Franqui, *op. cit.*, p. 13.

8. C. Cabrera Infante, "Portrait of a Tyrant as an Aging Tyro," in Franqui, *op. cit.*, p. viii.

9. Army document, Summary of plan dated 9-26-63, Califano Papers, Record Number 198-10004-10001, declassified 10-7-97.

10. Gaeton Fonzi, *The Last Investigation* (New York: Thunder's Mouth, 1994), pp. 371-379; Charles Nicoletti obituary, UPI dispatch 3-30-77; Bradley Ayers, *The War that Never Was* (Canoga Park, Calif.: Major Books, 1979), pp. 36-38; The CIA's Inspector General's Report on the CIA–Mafia Plots (often called the IG Report).

11. Confidential interview with C-Day Cuban exile leader source 7-92.

12. CIA Office of Security Varona File Summary, Record Number 180-10144-10405, declassified 8-23-95; CIA Confidential Information Report 8-30-63, Document ID number 1993.07.29.17:58:19:340059; declassified 7-29-93.

13. Warren Commission Document #1553D pp. 1, 3—Kiki Masferrer, who lived in Silvia Odio's apartment complex, was Rolando Masferrer's brother; FBI 7-31-59 memo from Havana for J. Edgar Hoover says Rolando was a "close friend" of John Martino; Silvia Odio's sister met John Martino at a small meeting shortly before the Mafia tried to link Oswald to JURE using Ms. Odio.

14. *New York Times* 6-18-72 p. 11, 6-27-72 p. 43, 7-13-72 p. 9, first cited in A. J. Weberman Web book (http://www.ajweberman.com/coupt5.htm) chapter 21; Henrik Krüger, *The Great Heroin Coup: Drugs, Intelligence & International Fascism* (Boston: South End Press, 1980), p. 161; Warren Hinckle and William Turner, *Deadly Secrets* (New York: Thunder's Mouth, 1992), pp. 355, 356, 363, 389, 399, also citing: *Miami Herald* 8-17-73; *San Francisco Chronicle* 6-6-74, 11-26-75.

Chapter Seven: The "Plan for a Coup in Cuba": December 1, 1963

1. [a] Army document, Summary of plan dated 9-26-63, Califano Papers, Record Number 198-10004-10000, declassified 10-7-97; [b] Army document, Summary of plan dated 9-26-63, Califano Papers, Record Number 198-10004-10001, declassified 10-7-97.

2. *Ibid.* [a]; *Ibid.* [b].

3. *Ibid.* [a].

4. *Ibid.* [a].

5. Harry Williams told us that the C-Day plan eventually provided for the death of Raul, as well as Fidel. Also, while several other top Cuban government leaders are mentioned, including Che Guevara, the document makes it clear that killing them isn't an essential part of the plan.

6. Interview with Harry Williams 2-24-92.

7. Army document, Summary of plan dated 9-26-63, Califano Papers, Record Number 198-10004-10001, declassified 10-7-97.

8. Army document, Summary of plan dated 9-26-63, Califano Papers, Record Number 198-10004-10000, declassified 10-7-97.

9. Army document, Summary of plan dated 9-26-63, Califano Papers, Record Number 198-10004-10001, declassified 10-7-97; Joint Chiefs of Staff document, dated 12-4-63 with 11-30-63 report from Cyrus Vance, 80 total pages, Record Number 202-10002-101116, declassified 10-7-97.

10. Army document, Summary of plan dated 9-26-63, Califano Papers, Record Number 198-10004-10001, declassified 10-7-97.

11. *Ibid.*

12. Army document, Summary of plan dated 9-26-63, Califano Papers, Record Number 198-10004-10000, declassified 10-7-97.

13. *Ibid.*

14. Tad Szulc, "Castro Reported Quarreling Again with Red Backers," *New York Times* 9-2-63.

15. Interview with Harry Williams 2-24-92.

16. Interview with confidential Kennedy C-Day official source 3-17-92.

17. Army document, Summary of plan dated 9-26-63, Califano Papers, Record Number 198-10004-10001, declassified 10-7-97.

18. Foreign Relations of the United States, Volume XI, Department of State, #347, 6-14-63.

19. Army document, Summary of plan dated 9-26-63, Califano Papers, Record Number 198-10004-10001, declassified 10-7-97.

20. *Ibid.*

21. *Ibid.*

22. Interview with Harry Williams 2-24-92; Interview with confidential Kennedy aide source 3-17-92; Interview with confidential C-Day Defense Department source 7-6-92.

23. Army document, Summary of plan dated 9-26-63, Califano Papers, Record Number 198-10004-10001, declassified 10-7-97.

24. *Ibid.*

25. Haynes Johnson, "One Day's Events Shattered America's Hopes and Certainties," *Washington Post* 11-20-83; Interview with confidential Kennedy C-Day official source 3-17-92; Interview with Harry Williams 2-24-92.

26. Army document, Summary of plan dated 9-26-63, Califano Papers, Record Number 198-10004-10001, declassified 10-7-97.

27. *Ibid.*

28. *Ibid.*

29. *Ibid.*

30. *Ibid.*

31. *Ibid.*

32. *Ibid.*

33. *Ibid.*

34. *Ibid.*

35. *Ibid.*

36. *Ibid.*

37. *Ibid.*

38. *Ibid.*

39. *Ibid.*

40. *Ibid.*

41. Interview with Harry Williams 2-24-92. In 1963 dollars, the total payoff for the C-Day coup leader approved by the Kennedys was going to be $500,000, and a first installment of $50,000 (in 1963 dollars; $289,000 in 2003 dollars) was actually paid.

42. Army document, Summary of plan dated 9-26-63, Califano Papers, Record Number 198-10004-10001, declassified 10-7-97.

43. CIA Document 12-6-63, from Director, released during the 1993 CIA Historical Review Program, courtesy Dr. John Newman.

44. Gus Russo, *Live by the Sword* (Baltimore: Bancroft Press, 1978), p. 285.

45. *New York Times* 11-13-63 (10:4).

46. Interview with Harry Williams 2-24-92.

47. CIA Document 12-6-63, from Director, released during the 1993 CIA Historical Review Program, courtesy Dr. John Newman.

48. Joseph B. Smith, *Portrait of a Cold Warrior* (New York: Ballantine, 1981), pp. 377, 378.

49. Interview with confidential Kennedy C-Day official source 3-17-92.

50. Anthony Summers, *Not In Your Lifetime* (New York: Marlowe & Co., 1998), p. 247.

51. Interview with Dean Rusk 1-5-90; interview with confidential Naval Intelligence Investigator source 10-27-91; this subject is covered in detail in later chapters.

52. Tony Sciacca, *Kennedy and His Women* (Manor, 1976), pp. 83-90. The only reason given for JFK's transfer from Washington shortly after Pearl Harbor is usually given as JFK's affair at the time with Ingrid Arvid. However, JFK's affair with her continued even after he was transferred to Charleston, and, as Rusk told us, others involved with the Pearl Harbor intelligence failure were also transferred out of Washington

53. Army document, Summary of plan dated 9-26-63, Califano Papers, Record Number 198-10004-10001, declassified 10-7-97; Joint Chiefs of Staff document, dated 12-4-63 with 11-30-63 report from Cyrus Vance, 80 total pages, Record Number 202-10002-101116, declassified 10-7-97.

54. Army document, 7-19063, Memo from Alexander Haig to Captain Zumwalt, Califano Papers, Record Number 198-10004-10005, declassified 10-7-97.

55. Richard Reeves, *President Kennedy: Profile of Power* (New York: Simon & Schuster, 1993), p. 47.

56. Interview with confidential Kennedy C-Day official source 3-17-92.

57. Military historian W. J. Davis writes that "At the time of the 1960 elections, there were only a few more than 300 Cubans undergoing military training in Guatemala, and the count was going down, not up." W. J. Davis, Ph. D., *S. L. A. Marshall, Marine* (Author, 1987), p. 123.

58. Michael R. Beschloss, *The Crisis Years* (New York: Edward Burlingame, 1991), p. 427.

59. Russo, *op. cit.,* p. 170.

60. [a] Foreign Relations of The United States, Volume XI, Department of State, #367, 9-18-63; [b] Johnson Library, National Security File, Country File, Cuba, contact with Cuban Leaders, 5/63-4/65.

61. *Ibid.* [a]; *Ibid.* [b]

62. *New York Times* 9-24-63 (1:8).

63. For example, see the *New York Times* for 5-20-63 (1:8), 5-23-63 (2:4), 6-7-63 (1:5), 7-18-63 (1:2), 7-23-63 (44:1), 9-6-63 (1:2), 9-12-63 (21:2, 20:6), 9-21-63 (12:6), 9-28-63 (7:5), and many others.

64. HSCA Vol. X, p. 13.

65. Nestor T. Carbonell, *And the Russians Stayed* (New York: Morrow, 1989); Haynes Johnson with Manuel Artime and others, *The Bay of Pigs* (New York: Norton, 1964).

66. Carbonell, *op. cit., p. 191.*

67. On 4-16-76, Dave Powers returned the 70 by 49-inch flag to an attorney for the Brigade, who had requested its return: Peter Wyden, *Bay of Pigs* (New York: Touchstone, 1980), p. 303.

68. *New York Times* 12-3-63 (87:4); Interview with Harry Williams 2-24-92.

Chapter Eight: The Contingency Plans

1. Church Committee Report, Vol. V, p. 16; Former Senator Gary Hart—a member of the Church Committee—confirmed to the authors that the Church Committee did not uncover the C-Day plan, though they did uncover some of the other CIA plots to topple Castro.

2. Interviews with confidential Kennedy administration official source 3-6-95, 3-8-96, 4-18-96.

3. Interview with confidential Kennedy C-Day official source 3-17-92.

4. From the John F. Kennedy Presidential Library, NLK 78-473, declassified 5-6-80.

5. National Security Archive new release 10-12-02, 40th Anniversary Conference on the Cuban Missile Crisis.

6. Army document, Summary of plan dated 9-26-63, Califano Papers, Record Number 198-10004-10001, declassified 10-7-97.

7. Interviews with confidential Kennedy administration official source 3-6-95, 3-8-96, 4-18-96; Interview with confidential Kennedy C-Day official source 3-17-92.

8. Department of the Army documents dated 9-14-63 and 9-27-63, provided by the State Department, in SSCIA record number 157-10005-10372 dated 3-27-76, declassified 2-18-94.

9. Church Committee Report, Vol. V, pp. 15, 16.

10. *Ibid.*, Vol. V, p. 16, footnote 29; Department of the Army documents dated 9-14-63 and 9-27-63, provided by the State Department, in SSCIA record number 157-10005-10372 dated 3-27-76, declassified 2-18-94.

11. Department of the Army document 9-14-63, provided by the State Department, in SSCIA record number 157-10005-10372 dated 3-27-76, declassified 2-18-94. It might appear that "rash of covert activity" refers to the hit-and-run raids the US had been engaged in for years against Castro. But this makes little sense, because the level of that activity was no greater then than it had been for months—in fact, by most measures, the level of hit-and-run activity was declining at that time, since the non-C-Day Cuban exile groups were being reined in at the meeting. However, since not everyone at the meeting knew about C-Day, some excuse had to be given for the meeting for those who hadn't been told about C-Day.

12. Department of the Army document 9-14-63, provided by the State Department, in SSCIA record number 157-10005-10372 dated 3-27-76, declassified 2-18-94.

13. *Ibid.*

14. Department of the Army document 9-27-63, provided by the State Department, in SSCIA record number 157-10005-10372 dated 3-27-76, declassified 2-18-94.

15. Department of the Army documents dated 9-14-63 and 9-27-63, provided by the State Department, in SSCIA record number 157-10005-10372 dated 3-27-76, declassified 2-18-94.

16. Department of the Army document 9-27-63, provided by the State Department, in SSCIA record number 157-10005-10372 dated 3-27-76, declassified 2-18-94.

17. *Ibid.*

18. *Ibid.*

19. Interview with Dave Powers 6-5-91 at the John F. Kennedy Presidential Library.

20. From the John F. Kennedy Presidential Library, NLK 78-473, declassified 5-6-80.

21. *Ibid.*

22. Gus Russo, *Live by the Sword* (Baltimore: Bancroft Press, 1978), pp. 163, 164.

23. From the John F. Kennedy Presidential Library, NLK 78-473, declassified 5-6-80.

24. *Ibid.*

25. Eric Lichtblau, "FAA alerted on Qaeda in '98, 9/11 Panel said," *New York Times* 9-14-05; US officials thought an attack within the US was "unlikely," and decided that attacks were "more likely" outside the US, in wording that echoes the Cuba Contingency Plans.

26. Interviews with confidential Kennedy administration official source 3-6-95, 3-8-96, 4-18-96; Church Committee Report, Vol. V, several passages.

27. Interviews with confidential Kennedy administration official source 3-6-95, 3-8-96, 4-18-96.

28. Interview with confidential Kennedy C-Day official source 3-17-92.

29. *Ibid.*

30. *Ibid.*

31. Reference withheld to protect source; however the information cited is publicly available and will be revealed—along with the name of the source—after the source's death.

32. Numerous JFK biographies, and testimony of the participants, have detailed the struggle over JFK's body at Parkland Hospital in Dallas.

33. David S. Lifton, *Best Evidence: Disguise and Deception in the Assassination of John F. Kennedy* (New York: Carroll & Graf, 1988), pp. 403-405.

34. Testimony to JFK Assassination Review Board and earlier testimony to the HSCA released by the Board; David Lifton, *op. cit.*, many passages and photographs.

35. Dr. George Burkley's Oral History at the JFK Presidential Library.

36. David Lifton, *op. cit.*, many passages.

37. Alexander M. Haig, Jr., *Inner Circles* (New York: Warner Books, 1992), pp. 113, 114.

38. *Ibid;* if a concern had arisen regarding National Security in terms of JFK's body or burial, because of the recent work of Haig and Califano on the coup plan and the Cuba Contingency Plans, they would have been able to quickly grasp the gravity of the situation and how the Cuba plans needed to be protected.

39. Peter Dale Scott, *Crime and Cover-Up: The CIA, the Mafia, and the Dallas-Watergate Connection* (Santa Barbara, Calif.: Open Archive Press, 1993), pp. 9-12; Peter Dale Scott, *Deep Politics II* (Skokie, Ill.: Green Archive Publ., 1995), many passages.

40. Russo, *op. cit.*, p. 250.

41. Tad Szulc articles in the *Boston Globe* 5-28-76 and the *New Republic* 6-5-76.

42. *Ibid.*

43. FBI document, record number 124-10271-10082, declassified 7-11-94. However, the FBI did mention something called "SENSTUDY 75 Project material" that may be related to the Cuba Contingency Plan—though this material has never been made public.

44. Tad Szulc, "Cuba on our Mind," *Esquire*, February 1973; Tad Szulc, *Compulsive Spy* (New York: Viking, 1974)

45. Tad Szulc articles in the *Boston Globe* 5-28-76 and the *New Republic* 6-5-76.

Chapter Nine: "Playing with Fire"

1. For example, it was discussed at the Cuba subcommittee meeting on 11-5-63, which included Bobby, CIA Director McCone, Cyrus Vance, Richard Helms, and others—see Foreign Relations of the United States, Volume XI, Department of State, #373, 11-5-63.

2. Foreign Relations of the United States, Volume XI, Department of State, "Memorandum from William Attwood to Gordon Chase of the National Security Council Staff."

3. Interview with Dean Rusk 1-8-90.

4. Anthony and Robbyn Summers, "The Ghosts of November," *Vanity Fair*, December 1994.

5. RFK Oral History at the JFK Library; Edwin O. Guthman and Jeffrey Shulman, eds., *Robert Kennedy: In His Own Words* (Toronto, New York: Bantam, 1988), p. 376.

6. Richard Reeves, *President Kennedy: Profile of Power* (New York: Simon & Schuster, 1993), p. 473.

7. Foreign Relations of the United States, Volume XI, Department of State, #373, 11-5-63.

8. Foreign Relations of the United States, Volume XI, Department of State, #379, 11-25-63.

9. Foreign Relations of the United States, Volume XI, Department of State, #384, 12-3-63.

10. Jorge G. Castañeda, *Compañero: The Life and Death of Che Guevara* (New York: Knopf, 1997), pp. 271-273.

11. Miriam Ottenberg, *The Federal Investigators* (Englewood Cliffs: Prentice-Hall, 1962), p. 93.

12. Laurence Chang and Peter Kornbluh, eds., *The Cuban Missile Crisis 1962* (New York: The New Press, 1992), p. 357; several documents in the FRUS document series from the US State Department; Mark Riebling, *The Soldier Spies: The Secret History of the Defense Intelligence Agency*, upcoming, advance draft available at markriebling.com.

13. 12-6-63 CIA Document, from JMWAVE to Director, released during the 1993 CIA Historical Review Program, courtesy of John Newman; another copy was released in 1994.

14. James Carroll, *An American Requiem: God, My Father, and the War That Came Between Us* (New York: Houghton Mifflin, 1996).

15. Anthony Summers, *Not In Your Lifetime* (New York: Marlowe & Co., 1998), pp. 222-233, 238-241, 255, 294; Bernard Fensterwald files and FOIA filings on Guy Banister from the Assassination Archives and Research Center.

16. Phone interview with confidential Naval Intelligence investigator source 10-27-91; HSCA vol. XI pp. 542-51.

17. 12-6-63 CIA Document, from JMWAVE to Director, released during the 1993 CIA Historical Review Program, courtesy of John Newman; another copy was released in 1994; Foreign Relations of the United States, Volume XI, Department of State, #370, 10-8-63; "Central Intelligence Agency Official Routing Slip," undated but between documents dated 9-17-63 and 9-20-63, released in 1994 by the CIA Historical Review Program.

18. CIA Document 12-6-63, from JMWAVE to Director, released during the 1993 CIA Historical Review Program, courtesy John Newman; another copy was released in 1994.

19. CIA104-10408-10029; 8-25-76 CIA memo.

20. "Central Intelligence Agency Official Routing Slip," undated but between documents dated 9-17-63 and 9-20-63, released in 1994 by the CIA Historical Review Program.

21. Foreign Relations of the United States, Volume XI, Department of State, #370, 10-8-63.

22. Army document, Summary of plan dated 9-26-63, Califano Papers, Record Number 198-10004-10001, declassified 10-7-97.

23. Army document 10-21-63, Califano Papers, Record Number 198-10004-10004, declassified 10-7-97.

24. Page 2 of Army document 10-21-63, Califano Papers, Record Number 198-10004-10004, declassified 10-7-97, notes that it was handled by "A. M. Haig."

25. Army document 10-21-63, Califano Papers, Record Number 198-10004-10004, declassified 10-7-97.

26. Ibid.

27. Interview with confidential C-Day Defense Department source 7-6-92.; Interview with Harry Williams 2-24-92.

28. Army document 10-21-63, Califano Papers, Record Number 198-10004-10004, declassified 10-7-97.

29. Joint Chiefs of Staff document 5-1-63 (revised 5-13-63) "Courses of Action Related to Cuba", Record Number 202-10002-10018, declassified 7-23-97.

30. Army document 10-21-63, Califano Papers, Record Number 198-10004-10004, declassified 10-7-97.

31. September 27, 1963 "Contingency Paper Assignments re Possible Retaliatory Actions by Castro Government" memo to The Interdepartmental Coordinating Committee of Cuban Affairs.

32. Interview with confidential C-Day Defense Department source 7-6-92.

33. Army document, Summary of plan dated 9-26-63, Califano Papers, Record Number 198-10004-10000, declassified 10-7-97.

34. Joint Chiefs of Staff document, dated 12-4-63 with 11-30-63 report from Cyrus Vance, 80 total pages, Record Number 202-10002-101116, declassified 10-7-97.

35. Ibid.

36. Ibid.

37. Ibid.

38. Ibid.

39. Warren Hinckle and William Turner, The Fish Is Red (New York: Harper & Row, 1981), p. 195.

40. Evan Thomas, Robert Kennedy: His Life (New York: Simon & Schuster, 2000), p. 273. The Senior CIA official was involved in the Cubela operation, and his overhearing a call like this might have contributed to the controversy over whether or not the CIA had ever informed JFK or Bobby about the Cubela assassination operation. If the Senior CIA official wasn't in the loop about C-Day, he might have assumed that FitzGerald was talking to JFK about the Cubela operation, even though Cubela was much too minor an official to lead a coup against Castro. Plus, the CIA was still in the talking stages with Cubela in November of 1963, unlike C-Day, which was ready to go and set to happen in a matter of weeks.

41. New York Times, 11-7-63, section 2, page 4.

42. New York Times, 11-8-63, section 2, page 4.

43. Foreign Relations of the United States, Volume XI, Department of State, #387 12-13-63.

44. For example, the official record of the 10-3-63 "Minutes of the Special [Cuba] Group" meeting of October 3, 1963 say that "It should be noted that page 1 of these minutes has the underscored item 'see special minutes for additional items'. There is no indication of what these additional items refer to." Whatever these "additional items" were, it must have been highly sensitive, since the rest of the notes "discussed infiltration operations and sabotage." Similar wording about "special minutes" appears in the minutes for a Special Group meeting on 11-6-63 attended by Bobby Kennedy and the CIA's Richard Helms, as well as for the meeting on 11-15-63. There's no indication that those "special minutes" still exist, but from all the available evidence, we feel it's likely that the "special minutes" were discussions relating to the highly sensitive C-Day operation.

45. SSCIA index card summaries, prepared June-July 1975, record number 157-10011-10002, declassified 3-1-94.

46. Evan Thomas, Robert Kennedy, p. 449.

47. Foreign Relations of the United States, Volume XI, Department of State, #375, 11-12-63.

48. Jefferson Morley, "What Jane Roman Said," 12-02, available at: http://mcadams.posc.mu.edu/morley1.htm.

49. Foreign Relations of the United States, Volume XI, Department of State, #375, 11-12-63.

50. Ibid.

51. Ibid.

52. Ibid.

53. For an explanation of the "black" term in intelligence operations, see L. Fletcher Prouty, The Secret Team: The CIA and its Allies in Control of the United States and the World (Englewood Cliffs: Prentice-Hall, 1973), p. 23.

54. Foreign Relations of the United States, Volume XI, Department of State, #376, 11-12-63.

55. *Ibid.*

56. *Ibid.*

57. *Ibid.*

Chapter Ten: The Countdown for C-Day Begins: November 22, 1963

1. Foreign Relations of the United States, Volume XI, Department of State, #368, 10-1-63.

2. *Ibid.*

3. Tampa Tribune 11-17-63.

4. Church Committee Report, Vol. V, pp. 20, 21, 31, citing CIA Memorandum for the DCI, "Considerations for US Policy Toward Cuba and Latin America," 12-9-63.

5. Foreign Relations of the United States, Volume XI, Department of State, #388, 12-19-63.

6. Gus Russo, *Live by the Sword* (Baltimore: Bancroft Press, 1978), p. 276.

7. Arthur Schlesinger, Jr., *Robert Kennedy and His Times* (New York: Ballantine, 1979), pp. 598.

8. Richard Goodwin, *Remembering America: A Voice from the Sixties* (Boston: Little, Brown, 1988), pp. 190-208.

9. St. Petersburg Times 11-18-63.

10. Authors' interview with Richard Goodwin 4-15-98.

11. CIA document, record number 104-10400-10133, Chronology of Significant documents in AMTRUNK file, prepared 4-77.

12. Church Committee Report, Vol. V, pp. 19, 20, citing case officer testimony 2-11-76.

13. Army document, from Director of Foreign Intelligence to Office, Secretary of the Army attn: Mr. Joseph Califano, General Counsel; 12-11-63, Califano Papers, Record Number 198-10004-10011, declassified 10-7-97.

14. *Ibid.*

15. HSCA 180-10074-10394, cited in JFK Assassination Records Review Board Update presentation by Joseph Backes at the JFK Lancer Conference, 11-96.

16. HSCA Secret Service interviews declassified by the Assassinations Records Review Board, cited by Vince Palamara in *Deep Politics* magazine 4-97.

17. Phone interview with confidential high Florida law-enforcement source 12-10-96.

18. Church Committee Report, Vol. V, pp. 19-21; CIA document 8-30-77, "Breckinridge Task Force" report, commenting on Church Committee Report Vol. V, document ID 1993.07.27.18:36:29:430590, declassified 1993; Thomas G. Paterson, *Contesting Castro: The United States and the Triumph of the Cuban Revolution* (New York: Oxford University Press, 1994), 261, citing Bundy memo, "Meeting with the President," Dec. 19, 1963; Schlesinger, *Robert Kennedy and his Times*, p. 598; Russo, *op. cit.*, p. 278.

19. *St. Petersburg Times* 11-18-63; *Tampa Tribune* 11-18-63.

20. *Marietta Daily Journal* 11-19-63.

21. JFK speech, *New York Times* 11-19-63.

22. CIA document 8-30-77, "Breckenridge Task Force" report, commenting on Church Committee Report Vol. V, document ID 1993.07.27.18:36:29:430590, declassified 1993.

23. *Dallas Times Herald* 11-19-63, p. 1A; Warren Commission Exhibit #2695.

24. *Miami Herald* 11-20-63, cited in Peter Dale Scott, *Deep Politics II* (Skokie, Ill.: Green Archive Publ., 1995), p. 57.

25. Army document, from Director of Foreign Intelligence to Office, Secretary of the Army attn: Mr. Joseph Califano, General Counsel; 12-11-63, Califano Papers, Record Number 198-10004-10011, declassified 10-7-97.

26. CIA Document 12-6-63, from Director, released during the 1993 CIA Historical Review Program, courtesy Dr. John Newman.

27. Haynes Johnson, "One Day's Events Shattered America's Hopes and Certainties," *Washington Post* 11-20-83; Haynes also referred to the meeting in an earlier *Washington Post* article on 4-17-81.

28. Handwritten notes of Richard E. Sprague's interview with Haynes Johnson at the Madison Hotel in Washington, D.C., dated 1-12-73—the notes are on file at the Assassination Archives and Research Center in Washington. Keep in mind that the quotes are Sprague's notes of what Haynes was saying, so the wording might not be exact. Some of the interview was published a short time later. When contacted by the authors, Haynes Johnson preferred not to make any additional comments; Haynes Johnson with Manuel Artime and others, *The Bay of Pigs* (New York: Norton, 1964).

29. Handwritten notes of Richard E. Sprague's interview with Haynes Johnson at the Madison Hotel in Washington, D.C., dated 1-12-73.

30. *Ibid.*

31. *Ibid.*

32. Interview with Harry Williams 7-24-93.

33. Interviews with Harry Williams 7-24-93, 2-24-92.

34. Interview with confidential C-Day Defense Department source 7-6-92; Interview with Harry Williams 2-24-92.

35. Haynes Johnson, "One Day's Events Shattered America's Hopes and Certainties," *Washington Post* 11-20-83; Interview with Harry Williams 2-24-92.

36. Haynes Johnson, "One Day's Events Shattered America's Hopes and Certainties," *Washington Post* 11-20-83.

37. *Ibid.*; Anthony and Robbyn Summers, "The Ghosts of November," *Vanity Fair,* December 1994.

38. Harry Williams interview 4-92.

Chapter Eleven: Harry Williams and the Cubans

1. RFK Oral History at the JFK Library; Edwin O. Guthman and Jeffrey Shulman, eds., *Robert Kennedy: In His Own Words* (Toronto, New York: Bantam, 1988), p. 377.

2. Phone interview with Harry Williams 11-13-92.

3. Foreign Relations of the United States, Volume XI, Department of State, #355, 7-13-63.

4. Interview with Harry Williams 2-24-92.

5. State Department memo, declassified 10-31-80.

6. Interview with Harry Williams 2-24-92.

7. HSCA Vol. X, March 1979, pg. 78, citing FBI file No. 97-4546, sec. 1—correlation summary, 5-30-63.

8. Interview with Harry Williams 7-24-93.

9. E. Howard Hunt deposition, November 3, 1978, document #180-10131-10342, declassified 2-9-96, cited by *Fair Play* magazine.

10. See Chapter 44 for details and complete references.

11. *New York Times Index* 6-13 (1:4), 6-21-63 (8:3), 6-28-63 (9:6), 7-9-63 (10:5), 10-22-63 (16:4).

12. Interviews with Harry Williams 2-24-92, 4-92, 7-1-92, 11-13-92, 7-24-93, 2-21-95.

13. Foreign Relations of the United States, Volume XI, Department of State, #345, 5-28-63.

14. *Ibid.*

15. *Ibid.*

16. Jane Franklin, *The Cuban Revolution and the United States: A Chronological History* (Melbourne, Australia: Ocean, 1992), pp. 62, 63.

17. Foreign Relations of the United States, Volume XI, Department of State, #345, 5-28-63.

12. Interviews with Harry Williams 2-24-92, 4-92, 7-1-92, 11-13-92, 7-24-93, 2-21-95.

19. Foreign Relations of the United States, Volume XI, Department of State, #345, 5-28-63.

20. E. Howard Hunt, *Give Us This Day* (New Rochelle: Arlington House, 1973), pp. 11, 12.

21. Foreign Relations of the United States, Volume XI, Department of State, #345, 5-28-63.

12. Interviews with Harry Williams 2-24-92, 4-92, 7-1-92, 11-13-92, 7-24-93, 2-21-95.

23. Foreign Relations of the United States, Volume XI, Department of State, #347, 6-14-63.

24. Interview with Harry Williams 2-24-92.

25. Warren Hinckle and William Turner, *Deadly Secrets* (New York: Thunder's Mouth, 1992), p. 101.

26. CIA Classified Message, to Director from JMWAVE, 9-14-63, released in 1994 by the CIA Historical Review Program, from "Carlos Prio Socarras [soft file]."

27. Evan Thomas, *Robert Kennedy: His Life* (New York: Simon & Schuster, 2000), pp. 449-450.

28. Hinckle and Turner, *Deadly Secrets*, p. 167.

29. CIA document from JMWAVE to Director, 11-23-63. Document assistance provided by Dr. John Newman.

30. CIA Document 12-6-63, from JMWAVE to Director, released during the 1993 CIA Historical Review Program, with another copy released in 1994; best copy is courtesy of Dr. John Newman.

31. Interview with Harry Williams 2-24-92; Confidential interview with C-Day Cuban exile leader source 7-92.

32. TV program on WPLG (ABC affiliate), Miami, 5-22-76. Interviewers were Carolyn Wright and Glenn Rinker, transcript from the files of the Assassination Archives and Research Center in Washington, D.C.

33. A dozen people allegedly linked to C-Day in some way later show up in the Watergate affair: Eugenio Martinez, Bernard Barker, E. Howard Hunt, James McCord, Richard Helms, Manuel Artime, Al Haig, Joe Califano (counsel for the Democrats and the *Washington Post* during Watergate), Alexander Butterfield (went to work for Haig and Califano after JFK's death, when C-Day was winding down), Carlos Prio, Trafficante bagman Frank Fiorini (calling himself Frank Sturgis), and Richard Nixon, whom many of the preceding figures worked for and who is named in a C-Day document about Prio.

34. Handwritten notes of Richard E. Sprague's interview with Haynes Johnson at the Madison Hotel in Washington, D.C., dated 1-12-73.

35. *Ibid.*

Chapter Twelve: Manuel Artime

1. E. Howard Hunt, *Give Us This Day* (New Rochelle: Arlington House, 1973), pp. 11, 12.

2. Gus Russo, *Live by the Sword* (Baltimore: Bancroft Press, 1978), p. 171.

3. *Ibid.*, p. 548, quoting "CIA Internal Memo, 'CIA Involvement with Cubans and Cuban Groups,' 8 May 1967."

4. *New York Times* 9-1-63 (19:1).

5. *New York Times* 9-7-63 (6:3).

6. Foreign Relations of the United States, Volume XI, Department of State, #357, 8-9-63.

7. *Ibid.*

8. *Ibid.*

9. 7-29-75 testimony, U.S. Senate Select Committee to Study Governmental Operations with Respect to Intelligence Activities (Church Committee), record number 157-10011-10125, declassified 7-12-94.

10. HSCA Vol. X, March 1979, pp. 67, 68.

11. Al Burt, "Cuban Exiles: The Mirage of Havana," *The Nation*, 1-25-65.

12. *Ibid.*

13. Decades later, David Corn was writing a biography of Ted Shackley, the CIA's Miami station chief in 1963, when he found CIA memos suggesting that Burt was a witting CIA asset at the time. But Corn talked to Burt, who denied the charge. Corn wrote that "in no way did Burt consider himself" an "asset" of the CIA's Miami Station Chief, and he points to Burt's revealing articles—subjects that the CIA's Miami station chief surely "wanted under wraps." We agree with Corn's assessment. If Burt had been working for the CIA, there is no way he would have ever written his *Nation* article about Artime. (See David Corn, *Blond Ghost* [New York: Simon & Schuster, 1994], p. 114.)

14. Burt, *op. cit.*

15. *Ibid.*

16. *Ibid.*

17. *Ibid.*

18. *Ibid.*

19. *Ibid.*

20. Felix I. Rodriguez and John Weisman, *Shadow Warrior* (New York: Simon and Schuster, 1989), p. 116.

21. *Ibid.*, pp. 116-119.

22. *Ibid.*, p. 119.

23. *Ibid.*

24. *Ibid.*

25. *Ibid.*, pp. 120, 121.

26. *Ibid.*, p. 123.

27. *Miami News* 7-2-77.

28. Tad Szulc, "Cuba on Our Mind," *Esquire*, February 1973; Michael Benson, *Who's Who in the JFK Assassination: An A-to-Z Encyclopedia* (New York: Citadel, 1993), pp. 287, 368.

29. *Miami News* 7-2-77.

30. *Ibid.*

31. *Ibid.*

32. *Ibid.*

33. Evan Thomas, *Robert Kennedy: His Life* (New York: Simon & Schuster, 2000), p. 238.

34. *Ibid.*

35. Warren Hinckle and William Turner, *The Fish Is Red* (New York: Harper & Row, 1981), p. 238.

36. *Ibid.*, pp. 239, 240.

37. Interviews with confidential Kennedy administration official source 3-6-95, 3-8-96, 4-18-96.

38. Interview with Harry Williams 4-92.

39. Phone interview with Harry Williams 2-21-95.

40. Interview with Harry Williams 2-24-92.

41. Tad Szulc, "Cuba on Our Mind," *Esquire*, February 1973. Szulc's article places the date for the attack in 1965, but by the time he was writing his article, he knew the original C-Day plan had been postponed after JFK's death, then somewhat revived by the CIA in 1964 and 1965.

42. *Ibid.*

43. *Ibid.*

44. Tad Szulc, *Compulsive Spy* (New York: Viking, 1974), pp. 96, 97.

45. *Ibid.*

46. Hunt, *op. cit.*, p. 11.

47. *Ibid.*, p. 221.

48. *Miami News* 7-2-77.

49. Interview with confidential C-Day Cuban exile leader source 7-92.

50. Tad Szulc, "Cuba on Our Mind," *Esquire*, February 1973.

51. Gaeton Fonzi, *The Last Investigation* (New York: Thunder's Mouth, 1994), pp. 40, 41.

52. Haynes Johnson, "One Day's Events Shattered America's Hopes and Certainties," *Washington Post* 11-20-83.

53. Haynes Johnson with Manuel Artime and others, *The Bay of Pigs* (New York: Norton, 1964).

54. Warren Hinckle and William Turner, *Deadly Secrets* (New York: Thunder's Mouth, 1992), p. 89.

55. John H. Davis, *Mafia Kingfish* (New York: McGraw-Hill, 1989), p. 312.

56. Peter Dale Scott, *Crime and Cover-Up: The CIA, the Mafia, and the Dallas-Watergate Connection* (Santa Barbara, Calif.: Open Archive Press, 1993), pp. 16-18; Peter Dale Scott, *Deep Politics and the Death of JFK* (Berkeley: University of California Press, 1993), p. 120.

57. Burt, *Cuban Exiles.*

58. CIA "Information Report," "31 October 1963," released in 1994 by the CIA Historical Review Program; CIA document, "to Director from JMWAVE," "7 Nov 63," released in 1994 by the CIA Historical Review Program.

59. Scott, *Crime and Cover-Up*, pp. 9-13, citing numerous Warren Commission documents.

60. Warren Commission Document #1000-D, cited in Scott, *Crime and Cover-Up*, p. 10.

61. Warren Commission Vol. XV (index).

62. Henrik Krüger, *The Great Heroin Coup* (Boston: South End Press, 1980), p. 161; A. J. Weberman Web book (http://www.ajweberman.com/coupt5.htm) chapter 21; Hinckle and Turner, *Deadly Secrets*, pp. 355, 356, 363, 389, 399.

63. Hinckle and Turner, *Deadly Secrets*, p. 355.

64. CIA 104-10408-10029 8-25-76 CIA memo.

65. CIA Office of Security Varona File Summary, Record Number 180-10144-10405, declassified 8-23-95; CIA Confidential Information Report, 30 August 1963; Document ID number 1993.07.29.17:58:19:340059, declassified 7-29-93.

66. HSCA Vol. X, p. 68.

67. We do not want to leave the impression that Artime's exile associates were involved in criminal activities. For example, two such exiles worked for Artime were never linked to criminal behavior, Pepe San Roman and his brother Roberto. Pepe was the official leader of the Bay of Pigs, and the *Washington Post* noted that he was left emotionally shattered by the experience and eventually committed suicide. Pepe's brother Roberto San Roman was probably the closest exile to Bobby Kennedy on a personal basis, after Harry. Like Harry, during the Cuban Missile Crisis Roberto had also agreed to go with US troops on a suicide raid to rescue the Bay of Pigs prisoners if needed.

Chapter Thirteen: Manolo Ray

1. HSCA Vol. X, p. 137, citing CIA cable to Director 11-17-60.

2. Interviews with confidential Kennedy administration official source 3-6-95, 3-8-96, 4-18-96; Interviews with Harry Williams 2-24-92 and 7-1-92; Interview with confidential C-Day Defense Dept. source 7-6-92.

3. HSCA Vol. X, March 1979, pg. 78.

4. E. Howard Hunt, *Give Us This Day* (New Rochelle: Arlington House, 1973), pp. 11, 12.

5. Tad Szulc, *Compulsive Spy* (New York: Viking, 1974), p. 93.

6. HSCA vol. X, p. 77; Foreign Relations of the United States, Volume XI, Department of State, #388, 12-19-63.

7. HSCA vol. X, pp. 139, 140, citing CIA cable to CIA Director John McCone 6-19-63.

8. CIA 1993.07.27.18:36:29:430590, sometimes called the Breckenridge Report or the Task Force Report.

9. Foreign Relations of the United States, Volume XI, Department of State, #350, 6-22-63.

10. HSCA Vol. X, p. 140, citing CIA memo 8-23-63.

11. HSCA Vol. X, p. 140.

12. HSCA Vol. X, p. 78.

13. Interview with James P. Hosty by A. J. Weberman in August 1993, in Weberman Web book (http://www.ajweberman.com/coupt5.htm) chapter 21.

14. HSCA Vol. X, March 1979, p. 78.

15. Warren Commission Document #1085, Declassified 11-3-70.

16. Interviews with confidential Kennedy administration official source 3-6-95, 3-8-96, 4-18-96.

17. HSCA Vol. X, p. 78, citing CIA dispatch 7-22-63.

18. HSCA Vol. X, p. 29.

19. Interview with Harry Williams 7-24-93.

20. HSCA Vol. X, p. 138.

21. Interview with Harry Williams 7-24-93.

22. CIA Document dated 3-19-64, Document ID #1993.07.31.12:25:16:530059, declassified 7-31-93.

23. American Heritage Dictionary.

24. HSCA Vol. X, p. 77, citing CIA cable 9-11-63, also pp. 19-35.

25. HSCA Vol. X, p. 19-35; Gaeton Fonzi, *The Last Investigation* (New York: Thunder's Mouth, 1994), many passages.

26. Some researchers have speculated that if Odio had given the letters of support from JURE, one would have been found among Oswald's effects after he had been blamed for JFK's assassination, causing JURE to be excluded from C-Day and creating an opening for a mob-backed exile like Masferrer.

27. HSCA Vol. X, p. 19-35; Fonzi, *op. cit.,* many passages.

Chapter Fourteen: Eloy Menoyo

1. RFK Oral History at the JFK Library; Edwin O. Guthman and Jeffrey Shulman, eds., *Robert Kennedy: In His Own Words* (Toronto, New York: Bantam, 1988), pp. 376, 377.

2. *New York Times* 9-7-63 (19:1).

3. E. Howard Hunt, *Give Us This Day* (New Rochelle: Arlington House, 1973), pp. 11, 12.

4. Warren Hinckle and William Turner, *Deadly Secrets* (New York: Thunder's Mouth, 1992), p. 172.

5. Harry Williams interview by William Turner 11-28-73, transcript courtesy of Mr. Turner.

6. Telephone interview with Harry Williams 2-21-95.

7. HSCA Vol. X, pp. 39, 99, 100; Menoyo's group's initials are sometimes given as the Spanish version "SFNE" in documents, but we've standardized it to "SNFE," since that's what Congressional investigators used.

8. Interview with Harry Williams 7-24-93; RFK Oral History at the JFK Library; Guthman and Shulman, *op. cit.,* pp. 376, 377.

9. Standing Group Record of Actions 4-16-63, Cuba papers, NSA, cited in President Kennedy: Profile of Power by Richard Reeves, pp. 473, 727.

10. Miami FBI Report dated 6-3-64, Warren Commission number 1085c8.

11. Jane Franklin, *The Cuban Revolution and the United States: A Chronological History* (Melbourne, Australia: Ocean, 1992), pp. 62, 63.

12. Interviews with confidential Kennedy administration official source 3-6-95, 3-8-96, 4-18-96.

13. CIA document to Director (John McCone) from JMWAVE (Miami CIA Station) 11-23-63. Document assistance provided by Dr. John Newman.

14. CIA document to Director (John McCone) from JMWAVE (Miami CIA Station). The authors are withholding the exact date and other identifying information until the CIA code name for C-Day—which is on the document—is officially declassified. Document assistance provided by Dr. John Newman.

15. *Ibid.*

16. Interview with Antonio Veciana, 6-2-93.

17. Phone interview with Harry Williams 2-21-95.

18. CIA document, HSCA, Record Number 180-10143-10209, CIA Segregated Collection, Agency File Number 28-43-01, Declassified 8-16-95.

19. *Ibid.*

20. Warren Commission Document #1085, Declassified 11-3-70, released 1-8-71.

21. *Ibid.*

22. CIA Document, undated but apparently from 1978, Record Number 180-10143-10178, CIA Segregated Collection from the HSCA, Agency File Number 28-30-0, Box 28, Folder 30, released 8-14-95.

23. FBI Document, 12-3-63, Record Number 124-10009-10097, Agency File Number 62-109060-900, declassified 6-24-93.

24. FBI document 12-6-63, Record Number 124-10019-10445, Agency File Number 62-109060-1830, declassified 1-28-94.

25. As was also the case with investigations into Silvia Odio (linked to Ray's exile group), John Martino (linked to Artime's exile group), and others.

26. CIA "Information Report" 10-31-63, released in 1994 by the CIA Historical Review Program.

27. NARA CIA 1993.07.22.08:55:23:460530 - CIA DBA 28528, cited in A. J. Weberman web book (http://www.ajweberman.com/coupt5.htm) chapter 12.

28. Interview with Harry Williams 7-24-93.

29. Interview with Antonio Veciana 6-2-93.

30. CIA document 11-30-63 provided by Dr. John Newman, declassified in 1993 as part of the CIA Historical Review Program.

31. Phone interview with Harry Williams 11-13-92.

32. Dick Russell, *The Man Who Knew Too Much* (New York: Carroll & Graf/R. Gallen, 1992), pp. 511, 514.

33. HSCA Vol. X, p. 39.

34. HSCA Vol. X, p. 39.

35. Gaeton Fonzi, *The Last Investigation* (New York: Thunder's Mouth, 1994).

36. *Ibid.*, p. 307.

37. HSCA Vol. X, p. 47.

38. HSCA Vol. X, p. 39.

39. HSCA Vol. X, p. 37.

40. HSCA Vol. X, p. 40.

41. HSCA Vol. X, p. 41.

42. HSCA Vol. X, p. 41.

43. Interview with Antonio Veciana 6-2-93.

44. See Chapter 44; E. Howard Hunt deposition, 11-3-78, document #180-10131-10342, declassified 2-9-96, cited by *Fair Play* magazine.

45. Fonzi, *op. cit.,* p. 141.

46. Warren Commission Document #1085, Declassified 11-3-70, released 1-8-71.

47. Undated CIA Document, apparently from 1978, Record Number 180-10143-10178, CIA Segregated Collection from the HSCA, Agency File Number 28-30-0, Box 28, Folder 30, released 8-14-95.

48. Burt Griffin memo to Warren Commission Counsel David Slawson 4-16-64, cited in Ray and Mary La Fontaine, *Oswald Talked: The New Evidence in the JFK Assassination* (Gretna: Pelican, 1996), p. 282.

49. Ray and Mary La Fontaine, "The Fourth Tramp," *Washington Post* 8-7-94.

50. Phone interview with Harry Williams 11-13-92.

51. FBI airtel to "Director, FBI" from "SAC, San Antonio", 11-8-63, HSCA #1801007810062, declassified 11-29-93; FBI airtel to "Director, FBI" from "SAC, San Antonio", 11-1-63; HSCA #1801007810064, declassified 11-29-93; these and other documents in this series provided by Bill Adams.

52. HSCA #1801007810066, FBI document to "Director, FBI" from "SAC, San Antonio."

53. La Fontaine, *Oswald Talked,* p. 286.

54. *Ibid.,* p. 207.

55. Investigation of Improper Activities in the Labor or Management Field, Senate Select Committee Hearings, June 30, 1959; CIA document, HSCA, Record Number 180-10143-10209, CIA Segregated Collection, Agency File Number 28-43-01, declassified 8-16-95.

56. FBI airtel to Director, FBI from SAC, Dallas, 11-29-63, HSCA #1801007810057.

57. La Fontaine, *Oswald Talked,* p. 286.

58. Evan Thomas, *Robert Kennedy: His Life* (New York: Simon & Schuster, 2000), p. 238.

59. CIA 104-10308-10080 AMWORLD, citing 6/64 meeting.

60. CIA document, HSCA, Record Number 180-10143-10209, CIA Segregated Collection, Agency File Number 28-43-01, declassified 8-16-95.

61. Jorge G. Castañeda, *Compañero: The Life and Death of Che Guevara* (New York: Knopf, 1997), many passages.

62. Enrique G. Encinosa, *Cuba: The Unfinished Revolution* (Austin: Eakin, 1988), p. 196.

63. "Exile leader stays in Cuba," CNN.com 8-7-03.

Chapter Fifteen: Tony Varona

1. E. Howard Hunt, *Give Us This Day* (New Rochelle: Arlington House, 1973), pp. 11, 12.

2. Warren Hinckle and William Turner, *Deadly Secrets* (New York: Thunder's Mouth, 1992), pp. 77-81.

3. Charles Rappleye and Ed Becker, *All American Mafioso* (New York: Barricade, 1995), p. 192

4. 1967 CIA Inspector General's Report.

5. Hinckle and Turner, *Deadly Secrets,* pp. 77-82.

6. U.S. Senate, Select Committee to Study Governmental Operations with Respect to Intelligence Activities, *Alleged Assassination Plots Involving Foreign Leaders* (New York: Norton, 1976), p. 125.

7. HSCA Vol. X, pp. 57-63, 105-136.

8. Foreign Relations of the United States, Volume XI, Department of State, #325, 4-25-63.

9. *Ibid.*

10. *New York Times* 6-25-63 (8:4).

11. Classified Message 5-29-23 to Director from JMWAVE, declassified 1994.

12. Army document, from Director of Foreign Intelligence to Office, Secretary of the Army attn: Mr. Joseph Califano, General Counsel; 12-11-63, Califano Papers, Record Number 198-10004-10011, declassified 10-7-97.

13. Phone interview with Harry Williams 2-21-95.

14. Interviews with confidential Kennedy administration official source 3-6-95, 3-8-96, 4-18-96.

15. Charles Rappleye and Ed Becker, *All American Mafioso* (New York: Barricade, 1995), p. 192.

16. Charles Rappleye and Ed Becker, *All American Mafioso* (New York: Barricade, 1995), p. 219.

17. CIA Office of Security Varona File Summary, Record Number 180-10144-10405, declassified 8-23-95.

18. CIA Confidential Information Report, 30 August 1963; Document ID number 1993.07.29.17:58:19:340059; declassified 7-29-93.

19. *Ibid.*

20. Warren Commission document #1553D pp. 1, 3.

21. Anthony Summers, *Not In Your Lifetime* (New York: Marlowe & Co., 1998), p. 446.

22. *Ibid.*, p. 292.

23. Phone interview with Harry Williams 2-21-95.

24. Charles Rappleye and Ed Becker, *All American Mafioso* (New York: Barricade, 1995), p. 192.

25. Gaeton Fonzi, *The Last Investigation* (New York: Thunder's Mouth, 1994), p. 36.

26. *Ibid.*, p. 305; Warren Commission Exhibit #3063, also related #3064-3066.

27. CIA "Confidential" report on Prio, dated "December 1957" and "Not releasable to Foreign Nationals" released in 1994 by the CIA Historical Review Program.

28. Foreign Relations of the United States, Volume XI, Department of State, #345, 5-28-63.

29. CIA document, to Director from (censored), 8-8-63, released in 1994 by the CIA Historical Review Program.

30. Phone interview with Harry Williams 2-21-95.

31. CIA dispatch from Chief, Special Affairs Staff to Chief of Station, JMWAVE, 23 August 1963, released in 1994 by the CIA Historical Review Program.

32. *Excelsior* 10-17-63, clipping from the CIA's Carlos Prio file released in 1994 by the CIA Historical Review Program.

33. CIA document, "Telegram Information Report," 9-10-63 date of info (info acquired 9-19-63; distributed 9-27-63); released in 1994 by the CIA Historical Review Program.

34. CIA document, JMWAVE to Director, 12-5-63, released in 1994 by the CIA Historical Review Program.

35. *Ibid.*

36. *Ibid.*

37. Hinckle and Turner, *Deadly Secrets*.

38. The authors wish to thank Dr. John Newman for providing one of the copies of this memo.

39. CIA document, "Telegram Information Report," 10-7-63, info from 9-30-63, released in 1994 by the CIA Historical Review Program.

40. CIA document, "Information Report," 12-20-63, released in 1994 by the CIA Historical Review Program.

41. CIA document, to Director from JMWAVE, 11-7-63, released in 1994 by the CIA Historical Review Program.

42. CIA Office of Security Varona File Summary, Record Number 180-10142-104306, declassified 8-8-95. Note that several different versions of Varona's CIA file have been released, some revealing more information than others.

Chapter Sixteen: Cuban-American Troops on US Military Bases

1. Gaeton Fonzi, *The Last Investigation* (New York: Thunder's Mouth, 1994), p. 370.

2. Warren Hinckle and William Turner, *The Fish Is Red* (New York: Harper & Row, 1981), p. 153.

3. Fonzi, *op. cit.,* p. 370.

4. HSCA Vol. X, March 1979, p. 77.

5. Haynes Johnson, "Rendezvous with Ruin at The Bay of Pigs," *Washington Post* 4-17-81.

6. Transcript of JFK's 4-3-63 press conference cited in Harold W. Chase and Allen H. Lerman, eds. and annotators, *Kennedy and the Press: The News Conferences,* with an introduction by Pierre Salinger (New York: Crowell, 1965).

7. Chase and Lerman, *op. cit.*

8. Nestor T. Carbonell, *And the Russians Stayed* (New York: Morrow, 1989), p. 191.

9. Names and dates withheld to protect identity of confidential source; will be released upon the source's death.

10. Interview with confidential C-Day Defense Department source 7-92.

11. *Ibid.*

12. Felix I. Rodriguez and John Weisman, *Shadow Warrior* (New York: Simon and Schuster, 1989), p.115-119; declassified Artime files 105-117233-19 and 105127182-4, from the collection of J. Gary Shaw.

13. Interview with confidential C-Day Defense Department source 7-92.

14. Harold Feeny, "No Regrets—We'd Do It Again," *The Nation* 4-19-86.

15. Joint Chiefs of Staff document 5-1-63 (revised 5-13-63) "Courses of Action Related to Cuba", Record Number 202-10002-10018, declassified 7-23-97.

16. Army document, Summary of plan dated 9-26-63, Califano Papers, Record Number 198-10004-10001, declassified 10-7-97.

17. Joint Chiefs of Staff document, dated 12-4-63 with 11-30-63 report from Cyrus Vance, 80 total pages, Record Number 202-10002-101116, declassified 10-7-97.

Chapter Seventeen: Che Guevara: A Reassessment

1. Jorge G. Castañeda, *Compañero: The Life and Death of Che Guevara* (New York: Knopf, 1997).

2. David Corn, *Blond Ghost* (New York: Simon & Schuster, 1994), pp. 110, 433; CIA Record #104-10076-10252 dated 12-10-63.

3. Andrew Sinclair, *Che Guevara* (New York: Viking Press, 1970), p. 102.

4. Daniel James, *Che Guevara: A Biography* (New York: Stein and Day, 1969), pp. 284, 285.

5. Under oath, Fiorini said he only gave advice to the woman Castro had put in charge of monitoring the reopened casinos: Rockefeller Commission interview with Frank Fiorini (Frank Sturgis), 3-3-75, NARA SSCIA 157-10005-1012, reproduced by A. J. Weberman at ajweberman.com/nodules/nodule6.htm.

6. *New York Times* 9-30-61, cited on page 20 of the CIA's Inspector General's Report.

7. Senate Committee on Government Operations, Permanent Subcommittee on Investigations: Organized Crime and Illicit Traffice in Narcotics, Sept./Oct. 1963, originally cited by Peter Dale Scott.

8. Jorge G. Castañeda, *Compañero: The Life and Death of Che Guevara* (New York: Knopf, 1997), pp. 249, 250, 1997.

9. *Ibid.*

10. Carlos Franqui, *Family Portrait with Fidel: A Memoir* (New York: Random House, 1984), p. 213.

11. C. Cabrera Infante, "Portrait of a Tyrant as an Aging Tyro," in Franqui, *op. cit.*, p. xiv.

12. Franqui, *op. cit.*, pp. 212, 213.

13. Arthur Schlesinger, Jr., *Robert Kennedy and His Times* (New York: Ballantine, 1979), p. 861.

14. Evan Thomas, *Robert Kennedy: His Life* (New York: Simon & Schuster, 2000), p. 310, Simon & Schuster, New York.

15. Richard Goodwin, *Remembering America: A Voice from the Sixties* (Boston: Little, Brown, 1988), p. 530.

16. *Ibid.*, pp. 190-208.

17. *Ibid.*, p. 205.

18. *Ibid.*, pp. 204, 205.

19. Interview with Harry Williams 2-24-92.

20. William Turner interview of Harry Williams 11-28-73, transcript courtesy of Mr. Turner.

21. Interview with confidential C-Day Cuban Exile Leader Source, 7-92.

22. Interview with Harry Williams 2-24-92.

23. Franqui, *op. cit.*, p. 4.

24. House Select Committee handwritten summary of Manolo Ray CIA File, record #180-10143-10454, declassified 8-17-95.

25. Franqui, *op. cit.*, p. 4.

26. 8/11/75 document of the Senate Select Committee to Study Governmental Operations with Respect to Intelligence Activities, pp. 3, 4, Record Number 157-10005-10259, declassified 4/25/94.

27. Castaneda, *op. cit.*, p. 251.

28. *Ibid.*, p. 252.

29. Hugh Thomas, *Cuba: Or, Pursuit of Freedom* (London: Eyre & Spottiswoode, 1971), p. 1376.

30. Franqui, *op. cit.*, p. 209.

31. *Ibid.*, p. 200.

32. *Ibid.*, p. 209.

33. *Ibid.*, p. 50.

34. Hugh Thomas, *op. cit.*, p. 1376.

35. Tad Szulc, *Fidel: A Critical Portrait* (New York: Morrow, 1986), p. 603.

36. Castaneda, *op. cit.*, p. 253.

37. *New York Times* 6-20-63 (3:3).

38. Franqui, op. cit., pp. 210, 213.

39. Ibid., p. 56.

40. Nestor T. Carbonell, And the Russians Stayed (New York: Morrow, 1989), p. 47; Jon Lee Anderson, Che Guevara: A Revolu-
    tionary Life (New York: Grove Press, 1997), p. 213.

41. Martin Ebon, Che: Making of a Legend (New York: New American Library, 1969), p. 52.

42. Franqui, op. cit., pp. 210, 223.

43. Ibid., p. 210.

44. Memorandum to National Security Council Staff, 11-63.

45. Memorandum from William Attwood to Gordon Chase, in Foreign Relations of the United States #379.

46. Franqui, op. cit., p. 159.

47. Hugh Thomas, op. cit., p. 880.

48. Castaneda, op. cit., pp. 250-254.

49. Ibid., pp. 248-250.

50. Ibid.

51. Ibid.

52. Ibid., pp. 387, 404.

Chapter Eighteen: The Other Plots Against Castro

1. Interview with Harry Williams 4-92.

2. 12-6-63 CIA Document, from JMWAVE to Director, released during the 1993 CIA Historical Review Program.

3. The CIA's Inspector General's Report on Plots to Assassinate Castro admits on page 9 that Castro assassination plots could have
   begun in "1959" and claims that "seriously-pursued" plots with the Mafia began in August of 1960, but Congressional investigators and other documents clearly show that the CIA–Mafia plots began in 1959 and were initially brokered by Jimmy Hoffa
   (for example, see several passages in Dan Moldea and Sy Hersh, "The Hoffa Wars," New York Times 3-10-1975).

4. Interview with confidential Kennedy C-Day official source 3-17-92.

5. Senate Church Committee Report, officially called Alleged Assassination Plots Involving Foreign Leaders, pp. 85, 86; Evan
   Thomas, The Very Best Men (New York: Simon & Schuster, 1995), p. 402.

6. Bilingual report detailing CIA Plots Against Castro; also New Times, January 1982, p. 28.

7. Charles Rappleye and Ed Becker, All American Mafioso (New York: Barricade, 1995), p. 307; Warren Hinckle and William
   Turner, Deadly Secrets (New York: Thunder's Mouth, 1992), pp. 194-197; 1988 Jack Anderson TV special.

8. Interview with confidential Kennedy C-Day official source 3-17-92.

9. CIA 6-18-64 memo sent on 3-7-75 by the Assistant to the CIA Director to David Belin, Executive Director of the Rockefeller
   Commission (Commission on CIA activities within the United States); CIA's Inspector General's Report on Plots to Assassinate Castro.

10. Bradley Ayers, The War that Never Was (Canoga Park, Calif.: Major Books, 1979), pp. 58, 59.

11. Gaeton Fonzi, The Last Investigation (New York: Thunder's Mouth, 1994), p. 373.

12. Ibid., p. 376.

13. Ibid., pp. 309, 387.

14. CIA104-10408-10029 CIA memo from Deputy Inspector General to Deputy Director of the CIA, 8-25-76.

15. Rappleye and Becker, op. cit., pp. 146, 147.

16. Phone interview with Larry Hancock 2-18-05.

17. Charles Nicoletti obituary UPI dispatch 3-30-77.

18. Hinckle and Turner, Deadly Secrets, pp. 242-243.

19. Rappleye and Becker, op. cit., p. 245.

20. Malone revealed the Ruby–Rosselli meetings on 1-23-78 in an article for New Times magazine (this was a different New Times
    than the one referred to earlier), while Nicoletti had been murdered on 3-29-77 while being sought by Congressional
    investigators and Rosselli had been killed the previous year.

21. Sy Hersh, New York Times, 3-10-1975; Senate Church Committee Report, Alleged Assassination Plots Involving Foreign
    Leaders, many pages.

22. When McCone finally found about earlier CIA–Mafia plots in August of 1963, he was told they had long since been stopped.

23. Senate Church Committee Report, Alleged Assassination Plots Involving Foreign Leaders (New York: Norton, 1976), many
    passages.

24. Ibid., many passages; Church Committee Report, Vol. V, many passages; 1967 CIA Inspector General's Report, many passages.

25. Church Committee Report, Vol. V, p. 13.

26. Anthony Summers, *Not In Your Lifetime* (New York: Marlowe & Co., 1998); Hugh Thomas, *Cuba: Or, Pursuit of Freedom* (London: Eyre & Spottiswoode, 1971).

27. 7-29-75 testimony of case officer #1, US Senate Select Committee to Study Governmental Operations with Respect to Intelligence Activities (Church Committee), record number 157-10011-10125, declassified 7-12-94.

28. Detailed in chapters 18 and 43.

29. Cuban Officials and JFK Historians Conference, 12-7-95.

30. Anthony Summers, *Conspiracy* (New York: McGraw-Hill, 1980), pp. 350-352. Though Cubela was in a Cuban prison when Summers interviewed him, Summers was allowed to talk to him at length and film portions of the interview. Summers was allowed to ask any questions, and to sometimes talk to Cubela "out of earshot of officials."

31. 1967 CIA Inspector General's Report.

32. Evan Thomas, *The Very Best Men* (New York: Simon & Schuster, 1995), p. 300.

33. *Ibid.*, p. 303.

34. Interviews with confidential Kennedy administration official source 3-6-95, 3-8-96, 4-18-96.

35. For example, see several passages in Gus Russo, *Live by the Sword* (Baltimore: Bancroft Press, 1978).

36. Interview with confidential Kennedy aide source 3-17-92.

37. Evan Thomas, *The Very Best Men*, p. 300.

38. CIA Document 12-6-6, from JMWAVE to Director, released during the 1993 CIA Historical Review Program; Church Committee Report, Vol. V, pp. 67-75.

39. Evan Thomas, *The Very Best Men*, p. 307.

40. Church Committee Report, Vol. V, p. 31.

41. April 1966 CIA report on Cubela.

42. 8-1-75 testimony, US Senate Select Committee to Study Governmental Operations with Respect to Intelligence Activities (Church Committee), record number 157-10005-10258, declassified 4-25-94, pp. 8, 9.

43. *Ibid.*, pp. 35, 36.

44. 7-29-75 testimony, US Senate Select Committee to Study Governmental Operations with Respect to Intelligence Activities (Church Committee), record number 157-10011-10125, declassified 7-12-94, pp. 12-14, 42-44.

45. *Ibid.*, pp. 12-14.

46. *Ibid.*, pp. 16, 60-62.

47. *Ibid.*, p. 87.

48. *Ibid.*, pp. 23, 24.

49. CIA's Inspector General's Report on Plots to Assassinate Castro p. 99; 7-29-75 testimony, US Senate Select Committee to Study Governmental Operations with Respect to Intelligence Activities (Church Committee), record number 157-10011-10125, declassified 7-12-94, p. 137.

50. Church Committee Report, Vol. V, p. 74.

51. 5-23-67 CIA's Inspector General's Report on Plots to Assassinate Castro, declassified 1992.

52. CIA document 4-25-77, Record Number 104-10400-10123, Russ Holmes Work File, Subject: AMTRUNK Operation, declassified 10-26-98.

53. CIA document, Russ Holmes work file, 4-77.

54. CIA document 8-30-77, "Breckinridge Task Force" report, commenting on Church Committee Report Vol. V, document ID 1993.07.27.18:36:29:430590, declassified 1993.

55. Senate Church Committee Report, *Alleged Assassination Plots Involving Foreign Leaders* (New York: Norton, 1976), p. 86.

56. 7-29-75 testimony, US Senate Select Committee to Study Governmental Operations with Respect to Intelligence Activities (Church Committee), record number 157-10011-10125, declassified 7-12-94, pp. 123, 124.

57. CIA document; 4-77, Record Number 104-10400-10133, Russ Holmes Work File, Chronology of Significant documents in AMTRUNK file, declassified 10-26-98.

58. *Ibid.*

59. Russo, *op. cit.*, p. 180.

60. Foreign Relations of the United States, Volume XI, Department of State, #376, 11-12-63.

Chapter Nineteen: US "Assets into Cuba"

1. Interview with Harry Williams 7-24-93.

2. Army copy of Department of State document, 1963, Record Number 198-10004-10072, Califano Papers, declassified 7-24-97.

3. Joint Chiefs of Staff document, 5-1-63 (revised 5-13-63) "Courses of Action Related to Cuba," Record Number 202-10002-10018, declassified 7-23-97.

4. Foreign Relations of the United States, Volume XI, Department of State, #346, 6-8-63.

5. Army document, Summary of plan dated 9-26-63, Califano Papers, Record Number 198-10004-10001, declassified 10-7-97.

6. Army document 10-21-63, Califano Papers, Record Number 198-10004-10004, declassified 10-7-97.

7. Foreign Relations of the United States, Volume XI, Department of State, #376, 11-12-63.

8. Interviews with confidential Kennedy administration official source 3-6-95, 3-8-96, and 4-18-96.

9. *Ibid.*

10. Army document, Summary of plan dated 9-26-63, Califano Papers, Record Number 198-10004-10001, declassified 10-7-97.

11. Harry Williams interviews 4-92, 7-24-93.

12. Senate Church Committee Report, *Alleged Assassination Plots Involving Foreign Leaders* (New York: Norton, 1976), p. 182.

13. Declassified ZR/RIFLE notes of William Harvey, also cited in Senate Church Committee Report, *Alleged Assassination Plots Involving Foreign Leaders* (New York: Norton, 1976).

14. Senate Church Committee Report, *Alleged Assassination Plots Involving Foreign Leaders* (New York: Norton, 1976), p. 183.

15. Joint Chiefs of Staff document, 5-1-63 (revised 5-13-63) "Courses of Action Related to Cuba", Record Number 202-10002-10018, declassified 7-23-97.

16. Harry Williams interview 7-24-93.

17. Harry Williams interview 4-92.

18. Warren Commission internal memo 4-30-64 (document #674-279); Phone interview with confidential high Florida law-enforcement source 12-10-96.

19. Lopez and Saez are covered extensively in later chapters.

20. John Newman, *Oswald and the CIA* (New York: Carroll & Graf, 1995), p. 356 and many others.

21. See chapters 43 (Montreal) and 46 (Mexico City).

22. See Chapter 26.

23. 11/29/63 tape from the Lyndon Johnson Presidential Library, cited in Michael Beschloss, *Taking Charge: The Johnson White House Tapes, 1963-64* (New York: Simon & Schuster Audio, 1997).

24. Some have taken the comments as a reference to a bribe that bogus reports said Oswald received from the Cuban Embassy. If so, it's odd that LBJ didn't say "Cuban Embassy" or "Cuban government" or "Cuban official."

Chapter Twenty: The Chicago and Tampa Assassination Attempts and C-Day

1. From the John F. Kennedy Presidential Library, NLK 78-473, declassified 5-6-80.

2. Miguel Casas Saez document1-27-64, F82-0272/1, declassified 8-16-83; CIA F82-0272/1, 82-1625 (4).

3. Joseph J. Trento, *The Secret History of the CIA* (Roseville, Calif.: Prima, 2001), pp. 226, 227.

4. *Chicago Daily News* interviews 5-28 and 5-29-68, from the files of Bud Fensterwald at the Assassination Archives and Research Center in Washington, D.C.

5. Harold W. Chase and Allen H. Lerman, eds. and annotators, *Kennedy and the Press: The News Conferences*, with an introduction by Pierre Salinger (New York: Crowell, 1965).

6. *CBS Reports: The CIA's Secret Army,* broadcast 6-10-77.

7. FBI Teletype "urgent" 12-9-63, to SAC Dallas from SAC Chicago, 62-6115-69, from the Chicago FBI files at the National Archives.

8. Vincent Michael Palamara, *The Third Alternative* (Pennsylvania: 1993), Chapter 10.

9. Bernard Fensterwald interview of Abraham Bolden 3-29-68.

10. HSCA Document #180-10070-10273, interview of Secret Service Agent Abraham Bolden by HSCA staffers Jim Kelly and Harold Rese.

11. Bernard Fensterwald interview of Abraham Bolden 3-29-68.

12. Vincent Michael Palamara, *op. cit.,* Chapter 10.

13. *Chicago Daily News* 11-2-63; HSCA Report p. 231. It should be noted that Pierre Salinger, JFK's press secretary, had not been told about C-Day or the highly sensitive four-man Chicago threat. So even he could not be informed of the real reason for the Chicago cancellation.

14. HSCA Vol. X, pp. 161, 172-175, 193; additional information provided by Mike Cain.

15. The ties between Cain, the CIA, and Varona are detailed in Chapter 46.

16. HSCA Vol. X, pp. 161, 172-175, 193; additional information provided by Mike Cain.

17. Robert F. Kennedy, *The Enemy Within* (New York: Popular Library, 1960), p. 87; Seth Kantor, *The Ruby Cover-Up* (New York: Zebra Books, 1992), many passages.

18. Kantor, *The Ruby Cover-Up* (New York: Zebra Books, 1992), p. 275.

19. CIA memo about Saez released 8-16-93, still partially censored.

20. Trento, *The Secret History of the CIA*, pp. 226, 227.

21. Miguel Casas Saez document1-27-64, F82-0272/1, declassified 8-16-83.

22. David Atlee Phillips, *Secret Wars Diary* (Bethesda, Md.: Stone Trail Press, 1989), p. 166; Richard Helms with William Hood, *A Look Over My Shoulder: A Life in the Central Intelligence Agency* (New York: Random House, 2003).

23. HSCA Vol. III, pp. 197-281.

24. Peter Dale Scott, *Crime and Cover-Up: The CIA, the Mafia, and the Dallas-Watergate Connection* (Santa Barbara, Calif.: Open Archive Press, 1993). Informants who tried to blame Castro include John Martino, Rolando Masferrer, Frank Fiorini, and several associates of Manuel Artime.

25. Interview with ex-Secret Service Agent Abraham Bolden 4-15-98.

26. Phone interview with confidential high Florida law-enforcement source 12-10-96.

27. *New York Times* 11-7-63, section 2, page 4.

28. *Miami Herald* Sunday 11-10-63; "by Al Burt, *Herald* Latin America Editor," pgs. 1A and 16A.

29. "Threats on Kennedy Made Here," *Tampa Tribune* 11-23-63.

30. HSCA 180-10074-10394, cited in JFK Assassination Records Review Board Update presentation by Joseph Backes at the JFK Lancer Conference, November 1996.

31. Mary Everett, "Charm takes over in Tampa," *St. Petersburg Times* 11-11-99.

32. Phone interview with confidential high Florida law-enforcement source 12-10-96.

33. Mary Everett, "Charm takes over in Tampa," *St. Petersburg Times* 11-11-99.

34. Phone interview with confidential high Florida law-enforcement source 12-10-96.

35. Phone interview with J. P. Mullins 12-10-96; Phone interview with confidential high Florida law-enforcement source 12-10-96.

36. See Chapter 53.

37. Kennedy Assassination Records Review Board Final Report, 1998; "A Presumption of Disclosure: Lessons from the John F. Kennedy Assassination Records Review Board," by OMB Watch, available at ombwatch.com.

38. Authors' written testimony sent on 11-9-94 for the Review Board's 11-18-94 public hearing in Dallas, as noted in the Board's FY 1995 Report.

39. For example, the young man arrested in Mobile the day Oswald arrived in Mobile, to give a talk at a local seminary on 7-27-63. (A noted priest at the seminary was friends with Johnny Rosselli, according to historian Richard D. Mahoney.) The young man arrested had been in "New Orleans to attend a meeting which would lead to the assassination of John F. Kennedy," according to a memo by Andrew J. Scaimbra, Assistant D.A. of New Orleans, 5-8-67. The young man's arrest made the local newspapers for several days.

40. For example, when a lone man—Thomas Vallee—was arrested in Chicago prior to JFK's motorcade for having a trunk full of weapons and allegedly threatened JFK, that was duly reported in the Chicago newspapers at the time. And when a mentally ill businessman in Tampa sent JFK threatening letters prior to JFK's trip, that man's arrest was also noted in several newspaper articles.

41. "Threats on Kennedy Made Here," *Tampa Tribune* 11-23-63. "Man Held in Threats to JFK," *Miami Herald* 11-24-63.

42. Phone interview with Vince Palamara 12-10-96.

43. "Threats on Kennedy Made Here," *Tampa Tribune* 11-23-63.

44. "Threats on Kennedy Made Here," *Tampa Tribune* 11-23-63.

45. Senate Church Committee Report, *Alleged Assassination Plots Involving Foreign Leaders* (New York: Norton, 1976), many passages; HSCA Report pp. 118-121.; Trento, *op. cit.*

46. See Chapter 41.

47. Warren Commission internal memo 4-30-64 (document #674-279); CIA 1994.04.06.10:28:12:530005.

48. Warren Commission draft by David Belin, 7-11-64, cited in Seth Kantor, *The Ruby Cover-Up* (New York: Zebra Books, 1978), pp. 386-389.

49. Skip Johnson and Tony Durr, "Ex-Tampan in JFK Plot?," *Tampa Tribune* 9-5-76; phone interview with confidential high Florida law-enforcement source 12-10-96; Rory O'Connor, "Oswald Visited Tampa," *Tampa Tribune* 6-24-76.

50. Trento, *The Secret History of the CIA*, pp. 226, 227; Tim Gratz and Mark Howell, "The Strange Flight of Gilbert Lopez," *Key West Citizen* 11-20-03.

Chapter Twenty-One: Did Bobby Feel Responsible?

1. Interview with Harry Williams 7-24-93.

2. For example, the CIA simply waited out the document requests from the House Select Committee on Assassinations, until their authorization expired.

3. Heavily censored April 30, 1964 Warren Commission memo, document # 674-279, FOIA Review 8-76.

4. Gilberto Lopez does not appear in the Warren Report or the twenty-six volumes.

5. CIA document, 12-3-63, document ID 1994.04.06.10:28:12:530005, declassified 4-6-94.

6. HSCA Report, pp. 118-121; Joseph J. Trento, *The Secret History of the CIA* (Roseville, Calif.: Prima, 2001), pp. 226, 227. At the time the CIA memo was declassified, the CIA's surveillance operations on persons leaving for Cuba from Mexico City were already known, making it unlikely that that operation is what Helms was referring to.

7. HSCA Report, pp. 118-121.

8. HSCA Vol. 4, p. 184.

9. For example, 10-26-64 Tampa FBI memo document ID 105-126109-13 and Mexico City FBI memo 1-31-64 document ID 105-126109-8.

10. Anthony Summers, *Not In Your Lifetime* (New York: Marlowe & Co., 1998), p. 84.

11. *Ibid.*, p. 118.

12. *Ibid.*, p. 84.

13. Phone interview with confidential Naval Intelligence investigator source 10-27-91; interview with confidential ex-Navy source.

14. Jim Hougan, *Spooks: The Haunting of America—The Private Use of Secret Agents* (New York: Morrow, 1978), pp. 118, 371.

15. Article by Joe Trento and Jacquie Powers in the *Wilmington [Delaware] Sunday News Journal* 8-20-78.

16. John Newman, *Oswald and the CIA* (New York: Carroll & Graf, 1995), pp. 95, 236, 240-244; Anthony and Robbyn Summers, "The Ghosts of November," *Vanity Fair,* December 1994, p. 100; Warren Hinckle and William Turner, *The Fish Is Red* (New York: Harper & Row, 1981), p. 153.

17. Anthony and Robbyn Summers, "The Ghosts of November," *Vanity Fair*, December 1994, p. 132.

18. Anthony Summers, *Conspiracy* (New York: McGraw-Hill, 1980), p. 296.

19. Memo of August 21 conversation with investigative journalist, on file at the Assassinations Archives and Records Center in Washington, DC.

20. Anthony and Robbyn Summers, *op. cit.,* p. 139.

21. *Ibid.*

22. Gaeton Fonzi, *The Last Investigation* (New York: Thunder's Mouth, 1994), many pages.

23. David Atlee Phillips, *Secret Wars Diary* (Bethesda, Md.: Stone Trail Press, 1989), several passages.

24. Harris Wofford, *Of Kennedys and Kings: Making Sense of the Sixties* (Pittsburgh: University of Pittsburgh Press, 1992), pp. 6, 415.

25. Warren Commission Exhibits 1933, 1934, 3119 (p. 769).

26. Anthony Summers, *Not In Your Lifetime* (New York: Marlowe & Co., 1998), p. 219.

27. Gus Russo, *Live by the Sword* (Baltimore: Bancroft Press, 1978), p. 551; Adrian Alba interview with W. Scott Malone, 2-27-93.

28. Wofford, *op. cit.,* pp. 412, 413.

29. Haynes Johnson, "The New Orleans Plot," *Washington Sunday Star*, 2-26-67.

30. *Ibid.*

31. Summers, *Not in Your Lifetime*, p. 235.

32. Robert L. Oswald, "He was my brother," *Look* 10-17-67.

33. Philip H. Melanson, "Dallas Mosaic: The Cops, the Cubans and the Company," *The Third Decade*, Vol. 1 #3, March 1985.

34. Interview transcript with Jesse Curry from British television show *Panorama*, on file at the Assassination Archives and Research Center.

35. John Newman, *Oswald and the CIA* (New York: Carroll & Graf, 1995), pp. 376, 377.

36. "Oswald made visit in September to Mexico," *New York Times* 11-25-63, page 8. When called before the Warren Commission months later, Kline and another official gave cautiously and carefully worded denials that didn't address the issue. For example, one denied to talking to a reporter who didn't even write the article in question—and didn't mention the reporter who did write the article; see Sylvia Meagher, *Accessories After the Fact: The Warren Commission, the Authorities, and the Report* (New York: Vintage, 1992), pp. 311, 312.

37. Paul P. Kennedy, "Oswald visited Mexico seeking Visas," *New York Times* 11-26-63.

38. Interview with the former Mrs. Lopez, 3-2-96.

39. HSCA Report, pp. 118-121; 1967 CIA Inspector General's Report.

40. Warren Commission Document #936.17/19, cited in Summers, *Not in Your Lifetime*, pp. 442, 443.

41. Newman, *op. cit.,* p. 356 and many others.

42. Robert Sam Anson, *"They've Killed the President!": The Search for the Murderers of John F. Kennedy* (New York: Bantam, 1975), p. 256; Warren Commission Document 1084.

43. Anthony Summers, *Conspiracy* (New York: Paragon House, 1989), p. 518. Alvarado also made a false claim indicating that

Oswald was paid by the Cubans to kill JFK, which was debunked by FBI investigators—see *Conspiracy* (Paragon House, 1989), pp. 415-419.

Chapter Twenty-Two: Pieces of C-Day: Banister and Ferrie; Martino and Cain

1. For example, as even the Warren Commission admitted, Jack Ruby had been an informant for the FBI in 1959, and continued to be a narcotics informant in 1963; 1967 CIA Inspector General's Report.

2. Memo for Director of Security, December 19, 1969, Subject: Cain, Richard Scully, #272 141 pp. 1, 2, cited in Peter Dale Scott, *Deep Politics II* (Skokie, Ill.: Green Archive Publ., 1995) p. 132.

3. Authors' interview with Richard Goodwin 4-15-98.

4. Authors' interview with former Justice Department prosecutors Marvin Loewy and Thomas Kennelly, 11-4-93.

5. FBI 62-109060-251; FBI 62-109060-7077 2.26.73; FBI 62-109060-5815 10.13.67; also A. J. Weberman Web book (http://www.ajweberman.com/coupt5.htm) chapter 24.

6. *Independent American* 8-12-63.

7. Rosemary James and Jack Wardlaw, *Plot or Politics? The Garrison Case and Its Cast* (New Orleans: Pelican, 1967), p. 132; Interview with Lauren Batista and Alberto Fowler by Jim Alcock, Assistant District Attorney, 2-5-67.

8. James and Wardlaw, *op. cit.,* p. 132.

9. Ray and Mary La Fontaine, "The Fourth Tramp," *Washington Post* 8-7-94; FBI airtel to "Director, FBI" from "SAC, San Antonio" 11-8-63; HSCA #1801007810062, declassified 11-29-93; HSCA #1801007810066, FBI document to "Director, FBI" from "SAC, San Antonio"; to Director, SAC, Dallas, and Miami; from SAC San Antonio; 10-25-63 HSCA #180-10078-10069-1, declassified 11-29-93; all provided by Bill Adams.

10. Anthony Summers, *Not In Your Lifetime* (New York: Marlowe & Co., 1998), p. 236.

11. Interview with Lauren Batista and Alberto Fowler by Jim Alcock, Assistant District Attorney, 2-5-67.

12. Summers, *Not in Your Lifetime,* p. 233; *People and The Pursuit of Truth,* Vol. 1 No. 1, May 1975.

13. Gus Russo, *Live by the Sword* (Baltimore: Bancroft Press, 1978), p. 141.

14. John H. Davis, *Mafia Kingfish* (New York: McGraw-Hill, 1989), many passages.

15. Banister files at the Assassination Archives and Research Center, Washington, D.C.; Miriam Ottenberg, *The Federal Investigators* (Englewood Cliffs: Prentice-Hall, 1962), p. 93.

16. Clarence M. Kelley and James Kirkpatrick Davis, *Kelley: The Story of an FBI Director* (Kansas City: Andrews, McMeel & Parker, 1987), pp. 268-9, cited in Peter Dale Scott, *Deep Politics II* (Skokie, Ill.: Green Archive Publ., 1995), p. 95.

17. Secret Service Report in Warren Commission document #320.

18. *New York Times* 11-27-63, cited in Paris Flammonde, *The Kennedy Conspiracy* (New York: Meredith Press, 1969), p. 123.

19. HSCA vol. X, pp. 107, 117.

20. *Washington Post* article by George Lardner, Jr., 2-25-67, cited in Harold Weisberg, *Oswald in New Orleans: Case of Conspiracy with the C.I.A.* (New York: Canyon, 1967), p. 65.

21. Interview with Harry Williams 4-92.

22. Davis, *Mafia Kingfish* (McGraw-Hill, 1989), many passages.

23. Letters from Bud Fensterwald to the Naval Investigative Service 5-27-82, 6-18-82.

24. Ross Yockey and Hoke May, "Oswald Agent for CIA," *New Orleans States-Item* 5-5-67.

25. Mark Riebling, *Wedge,* markriebling.com.

26. Warren Hinckle and William Turner, *Deadly Secrets* (New York: Thunder's Mouth, 1992); Davis, *Mafia Kingfish* (McGraw-Hill, 1989).

27. E. Howard Hunt, *Give Us This Day* (New Rochelle: Arlington House, 1973), pg. 156.

28. Russo, *op. cit.,* p. 165.

29. *Ibid.,* p. 141.

30. *Ibid.,* p. 165.

31. David Phillips memo to Chief, CI/R & A: CIA OGC 67-2061, CIA MFR 2.14.68 Sarah K. Hall, cited in A. J. Weberman Web book (http://www.ajweberman.com/coupt5.htm) chapter 7.

32. HSCA Vol. X, pp. 110-112, 118, 120-122, 124-136; Davis, *Mafia Kingfish* (McGraw-Hill, 1989); Summers, *Not in Your Lifetime.*

33. Anthony Summers, *Conspiracy* (New York: McGraw-Hill, 1980), p. 579.

34. Davis, *Mafia Kingfish* (McGraw-Hill, 1989); Summers, *Not in Your Lifetime.*

35. Memo to Jim Garrison by Douglas Ward, Investigator, 12-30-66.

36. *Human Events* article by John Martino, 12-21-63; Charles Rappleye and Ed Becker, *All American Mafioso* (New York: Barricade, 1995); FBI report on John Martino 7-31-59.

37. Harold Weisberg interview with Colonel Castorr, on file at the Assassinations Archives and Records Center.

38. FBI memo to J. Edgar Hoover, July 31, 1959; Warren Commission Document #1553D, pp. 1, 3.

39. Warren Commission Document #657, 2-15-64 FBI interview with John Martino.

40. Earl Golz notes of Fred Classen interview, late summer 1978, on file at the Assassination Archives and Research Center.

41. HSCA memo Fenton from Fonzi and Gonzales 10-7-77.

42. Richard Billings notes from the CIA review of his manuscript with G. Robert Blakey of *The Plot to Kill The President*, on file with other papers of Richard Billings at the Assassination Archives and Research Center.

43. Larry Hancock, *Someone Would Have Talked* (Southlake, Tex.: JFK Lancer, 2003), pp. 1-22; David Corn, *Blond Ghost* (New York: Simon & Schuster, 1994).

44. Anthony and Robbyn Summers, "The Ghosts of November," *Vanity Fair*, December 1994, pp. 112.

45. HSCA Vol. X, p. 193.

46. *Chicago Tribune* 12-28-73, p. 16; Peter Dale Scott, *Deep Politics II* (Skokie, Ill.: Green Archive Publ., 1995), p. 132.

47. CIA Office of Security Varona File Summary, Record Number 180-10144-10405, declassified 8-23-95.

48. CIA memo, 3, 272, 992, released 1993.

49. CIA Office of Security Varona File Summary, Record Number 180-10144-10405, declassified 8-23-95.

50. For example, CIA "Process Sheet for OO/C Collections" from Cain's file, reports number 28925 and 28499, both released in 1993.

51. CIA Memo for Chief, Western Hemisphere Division, Subject: Salvadore Giancana and Richard Cain, 1-10-74, released 1994.

52. *Ibid.*

53. *Ibid.*

54. HSCA Vol. X, p. 172.

55. Charles Rappleye and Ed Becker, *All American Mafioso* (New York: Barricade, 1995), p. 178

56. Memo for Director of Security, December 19, 1969, Subject: Cain, Richard Scully, #272 141 pp. 1, 2, cited in Peter Dale Scott, *Deep Politics II* (Skokie, Ill.: Green Archive Publ., 1995), p. 132.

57. CIA memo to Chief, LEOB/SRS, 12-11-67, released 1992.

58. Confidential interview with close relative of Richard Cain.

59. Scott, *Deep Politics II*, pp. 136, 137; William F. Roemer, Jr., *War of the Godfathers: The Bloody Confrontation between the Chicago and New York Families for the Control of Las Vegas* (New York: Donald I. Fine, 1990), pp. 141, 220.

60. CIA memo for Director of Security, 12-12-67, 272141, released 1992.

61. Bernard Fensterwald file on Abraham Bolden, Assassination Archives and Research Center.

62. Interview with confidential Kennedy aide source 3-17-92.

63. John Kidner, Crimaldi, *Contract Killer: A True Story* (Washington: Acropolis, 1976), pp. 203-297.

64. Confidential interview with close relative of Richard Cain.

65. HSCA Vol. X, p. 193.

Part II

Chapter Twenty-Three: Marcello, Trafficante, and Rosselli

1. Phone interview with confidential high Florida law-enforcement source 12-10-96.

2. Many passages from the following: Ronald Goldfarb, *Perfect Villains, Imperfect Heroes: Robert F. Kennedy's War against Organized Crime* (New York: Random House, 1995); Charles Rappleye and Ed Becker, *All American Mafioso* (New York: Barricade, 1995); John H. Davis, *Mafia Kingfish* (New York: McGraw-Hill, 1989); Frank Ragano and Selwyn Raab, *Mob Lawyer* (New York: Scribners, 1994); The Staff and Editors of *Newsday*, *The Heroin Trail* (New York: Holt, Rinehart and Winston, 1975); Henrik Krüger, *The Great Heroin Coup* (Boston: South End Press, 1980).

3. One example of C-Day penetration by the godfathers is CIA Office of Security Varona File Summary, Record Number 180-10144-10405, declassified 8-23-95 and CIA Confidential Information Report, 30 August 1963; Document ID number 1993.07.29.17:58:19:340059; declassified 7-29-93.

4. G. Robert Blakey and Richard N. Billings, *The Plot to Kill the President* (New York: Times Books, 1981), p. 242; many passages in Davis, *Mafia Kingfish* (McGraw-Hill, 1989).

5. *Dallas Morning News* article by John De Mers 1-24-82; GPTV 1999 showing of documentary on Marcello in the *Lords of the Mafia* series, narrated & produced by Robert Stack.

6. Davis, *Mafia Kingfish* (McGraw-Hill, 1989), p. 64; Michael Benson, *Who's Who in the JFK Assassination: An A-to-Z Encyclopedia* (New York: Citadel, 1993), p. 359.

7. Davis, *Mafia Kingfish* (McGraw-Hill, 1989), p. 49.

8. *Ibid.*, p. 138; gambling statistics cited by Davis are for 1972, since he points out that no figures were available for 1963.

9. Douglas Valentine, *The Strength of the Wolf: The Secret History of America's War on Drugs* (London, New York: Verso, 2004), p. 254.

10. Ragano and Raab, *op. cit.*, p. 135.

11. Earl Golz, "Mafia boss Carlos Marcello in Dallas," *The Iconoclast* 11-12-76.

12. *Ibid.*

13. Goldfarb, *op. cit.*, p. 73.

14. Valentine, *op. cit.*, p. 75.

15. *Ibid.*, p. 63.

16. Valentine, *op. cit.*, p. 254; Davis, *Mafia Kingfish* (McGraw-Hill, 1989).

17. Valentine, *op. cit.*, p. 189.

18. *Ibid.*, p. 254.

19. Many chapters in Davis, *Mafia Kingfish* (McGraw-Hill, 1989).

20. Anthony Summers, *Official and Confidential: The Secret Life of J. Edgar Hoover* (New York: G. P. Putnam's Sons, 1993), pp. 241, 242.

21. Ragano and Raab, *op. cit.*, p. 134.

22. Davis, *Mafia Kingfish* (McGraw-Hill, 1989), pp. 273, 518.

23. Michael Dorman, *Payoff: The Role of Organized Crime in American Politics* (New York: Berkley Medallion, 1973), pp. 108, 109.

24. Davis, *Mafia Kingfish* (McGraw-Hill, 1989), pp. 273, 518.

25. Carl Sifakis, *The Mafia Encyclopedia* (New York: Facts On File, 1987), pp. 46, 47.

26. Davis, *Mafia Kingfish* (McGraw-Hill, 1989), p. 71.

27. *Ibid.*, p. 65.

28. Rappleye and Becker, *op. cit.*, p. 163.

29. HSCA Vol. V, p. 372.

30. *Ibid.*, p. 373.

31. Ernest Havemann, "Mobsters Move In on Troubled Havana and Split Rich Gambling Profits with Batista" *Life* magazine, 1958.

32. FBN International List Book, #234, reproduced in Valentine, *op. cit.*, p. 471.

33. Evan Thomas, *Robert Kennedy: His Life* (New York: Simon & Schuster, 2000), p. 360.

34. Warren Commisssion Vol. V, pp. 205, 206, 208; FBN International List Book, #234, reproduced in Valentine, *op. cit.*, p. 471.

35. U.S. Senate, McClellan Committee Hearings (officially Investigation of Improper Activities in the Labor or Management Field, Senate Select Committee Hearings), 6-30-59.

36. FBN International List Book, #234, reproduced in Valentine, *op. cit.*, p. 471.

37. Sifakis, *op. cit.*, pp. 325, 326.

38. *Ibid.*

39. The Staff and Editors of *Newsday, op. cit.*, p. 112; *Newsday* won the 1974 Pulitzer Prize for their original series of articles, compiled in this book, which named Trafficante as a major heroin figure and linked him to Cuban Exiles who had worked for the CIA.

40. Valentine, *op. cit.*, p. 87.

41. *Ibid.*

42. Ragano and Raab, *op. cit.*, p. 77.

43. Rappleye and Becker, *op. cit.*, p. 163.

44. Richard D. Mahoney, *Sons & Brothers* (New York: Arcade, 1999), p. 49.

45. Rappleye and Becker, *op. cit.*, p. 163.

46. Mahoney, *op. cit.*, p. 384.

47. Rappleye and Becker, *op. cit.*, p. 163.

48. Ed Reid and Ovid Demaris, *The Green Felt Jungle* (New York: Pocket Books, 1964), p. 191.

49. *Ibid.*

50. *Ibid.*

51. Valentine, *op. cit.*, p. 224.

52. Gaeton Fonzi, *The Last Investigation* (New York: Thunder's Mouth, 1994), p. 373.

53. Rappleye and Becker, *op. cit.*, pp. 120, 121. *He Walks by Night* was only released on video in the late 1990s, which may be why the parallels between its scenes and the Tippit shooting and other aspects of the framing of Oswald went unnoticed for so long.

54. *Ibid.* Rosselli's biographers note that though Rosselli "was never listed in the screen credits, he later testified under oath that he was an associates producer of the three films, and court documents reflected a 10 percent interest in the pictures." For his work "at Eagle Lion" Studios, Rosselli "reported a total of $16,171" in salary "to the IRS." Reid and DeMaris also confirm that "In his 1950 appearance before the Kefauver Committee," Rosselli said "Since 1947 I have been in the picture business . . . at Eagle Lion Studios. I later was assistant producer to Brian Foy [the head of the studio at the time] and associate producer with Robert T. Cain productions."

55. *Ibid.* The films do have various bits that ring true for the Mafia and Rosselli. For example, Rosselli liked steam baths, and a victim in one of the films—*T-Men*— is also fond of steam baths and dies in a dramatic scene renowned in film noir circles. That particular character was called "The Schemer," and the movie makes it clear that to squeal on the mob means certain death. The fact that the character and his actions bear a great resemblance to Jack Ruby is probably just a coincidence, though Rosselli had probably met Ruby years earlier.

56. Nicholas Christopher, *Somewhere in the Night: Film Noir and the American City* (New York: Free Press, 1997), p. 171.

57. Reid and DeMaris, *op. cit.,* p. 40.

58. *Ibid.,* pp. 42, 43.

59. *Ibid.,* p. 206.

60. *Ibid.*

61. Rappleye and Becker, *op. cit.,* pp. 140, 141.

62. Reid and DeMaris, *op. cit.,* p. 40.

63. Rappleye and Becker, *op. cit.,* p. 167.

64. Reid and DeMaris, *op. cit.,* p. 48.

65. *Ibid.*

Chapter Twenty-Four: Ruby, Hoffa, Heroin, and Gun-running

1. Seth Kantor, *The Ruby Cover-Up* (New York: Zebra Books, 1992), p. 195.

2. William Scott Malone, "The Secret Life of Jack Ruby," *New Times* 1-23-78.

3. Howard Kohn, "Execution for the Witnesses," *Rolling Stone* 6-2-77.

4. Malone, *op. cit.*

5. Douglas Valentine, *The Strength of the Wolf: The Secret History of America's War on Drugs* (London, New York: Verso, 2004), p. 311.

6. *Ibid.,* p. 309.

7. Michael Benson, *Who's Who in the JFK Assassination: An A-to-Z Encyclopedia* (New York: Citadel, 1993), pp. 224, 225.

8. Valentine, *op. cit.,* p. 309.

9. Dan E. Moldea, *The Hoffa Wars: Teamsters, Rebels, Politicians, and the Mob* (New York: Charter, 1978), p. 167.

10. Valentine, *op. cit.,* p. 309.

11. *Ibid.,* pp. 309, 310.

12. John H. Davis, *Mafia Kingfish* (New York: McGraw-Hill, 1989), p. 74; Valentine, *op. cit.,* p. 310.

13. David E. Scheim, *The Mafia Killed President Kennedy* (New York: SPI Books, 1992), pp. 125, 126.

14. Valentine, *op. cit.,* p. 311.

15. Anthony Summers, *Conspiracy* (New York: Paragon House, 1989), pp. 467, 468.

16. Peter Dale Scott, *Deep Politics and the Death of JFK* (Berkeley: University of California Press, 1993), p. 131.

17. Benson, *op. cit.,* p. 79.

18. Warren Commission Exhibit #1697, cited in Scheim, *Contract on America: The Mafia Murder of President John F. Kennedy* (New York: Zebra, 1989).

19. Scheim, *Contract on America,* pp. 141-142; Warren Commission Hearings Vol. 23, p. 335; Warren Commission Documents Vol. 4, p. 529.

20. FBI 44-24016-275; C.Ray Hall Warren Commission Exhibit 3; FBI DL 44-1639; LL R: BC D-cover page, cited by A. J. Weberman.

21. Seth Kantor, *The Ruby Cover-Up* (New York: Zebra Books, 1992), p. 31.

22. "The Marcello-Hoffa Areas," detailed memo by Michael Ewing on file at the Assassinations Archives and Records Center.

23. *Ibid.*

24. Charles Rappleye and Ed Becker, *All American Mafioso* (New York: Barricade, 1995), p. 241.

25. Warren Commission Exhibit #1761.

26. Valentine, *op. cit.,* p. 310.

27. *Ibid.,* p. 311.

28. *Ibid.*, pp. 4, 331.

29. *Ibid.*, p. 366.

30. *Ibid.*, p. 187.

31. *Ibid.*, p. 178; since the FBI agent read from a 100+ page report, the *New York Times* of 1-10-58 could cover only the briefest highlights of his testimony.

32. *Ibid.*, pp. 253, 254.

33. *Ibid.*, p. 177.

34. *Ibid.*, pp. 74, 75; see also Scott, *Deep Politics.*

35. Allen Friedman and Ted Schwarz, *Power and Greed: Inside the Teamsters Empire of Corruption* (New York: F. Watts, 1989), p. 132.

36. *Ibid.*, p. 154.

37. Joseph Franco with Richard Hammer, *Hoffa's Man: The Rise and Fall of Jimmy Hoffa as Witnessed by His Strongest Arm* (New York: Prentice Hall, 1987), pp. 197, 198.

38. *Ibid.*, p. 198.

39. Moldea, *The Hoffa Wars* (Charter, 1978), p. 448.

40. *Ibid.*, p. 122.

Chapter Twenty-Five: Nixon, Havana, and Assassinating an Attorney General

1. Charles Rappleye and Ed Becker, *All American Mafioso* (New York: Barricade, 1995), p. 145.

2. Frank Ragano and Selwyn Raab, *Mob Lawyer* (New York: Scribners, 1994), p. 48.

3. Rappleye and Becker, *op. cit.*

4. *Ibid.*

5. *Ibid.*, p. 145.

6. Anthony Summers with Robbyn Swan, *The Arrogance of Power: The Secret World of Richard Nixon* (New York: Viking, 2000), p. 55.

7. *Ibid.*, pp. 51, 52.

8. *Ibid.*, p. 213.

9. HSCA "Outside Contact Report" 11-2-78. In the original, "Rolando" is transposed as "Orlando."

10. Summers and Swan, *op. cit.*, p. 127.

11. *Ibid.*, p. 126.

12. Richard D. Mahoney, *Sons & Brothers* (New York: Arcade, 1999), p. 383.

13. *Ibid.*, p. 385.

14. Summers and Swan, *op. cit.*, p. 127.

15. *Ibid.*, p. 128.

16. *Ibid.*, p. 129.

17. John Sugg, "Time to Pull the Sharks' Teeth," *Creative Loafing* weekly newspaper, Atlanta edition, 12-11-03.

18. John Goheen, "Phenix Raised," *National Guard* magazine Web site, August 2004.

19. Margaret Anne Barnes, *The Tragedy and the Triumph of Phenix City, Alabama* (Macon, Ga.: Mercer University Press, 1998), pp. 250, 251.

20. *Ibid.*, prologue.

21. Goheen, *op. cit.*

22. *Ibid.*

23. Barnes, *op. cit.*, pp. 286, 287, 315, 319.

24. *Ibid.*, pp. 223, 224.

25. *Ibid.*, p. 209.

26. Earl Golz, "Jack Ruby's gunrunning to Castro claimed," *Dallas Morning News* 8-18-78.

27. Barnes, *op. cit.*, pp. 213, 286, 314.

28. *Ibid.*, pp. 307, 308.

29. *Ibid.*, p. 307.

30. The Staff and Editors of *Newsday, The Heroin Trail* (New York: Holt, Rinehart and Winston, 1975), pp. 114-119; Douglas Valentine, *The Strength of the Wolf: The Secret History of America's War on Drugs* (London, New York: Verso, 2004), pp. 364-371

31. Declassified Artime files 105-117233-19 and 105127182-4, from the collection of J. Gary Shaw; Warren Hinckle and William Turner, *The Fish Is Red* (New York: Harper & Row, 1981), p. 153. While most of the exiles at Ft. Benning were

exemplary, a few still-living exiles who trained there have been linked to drug trafficking. We can't list their names for legal reasons, but they aren't hard to find using Internet search engines.

Chapter Twenty-Six: Guatemala: The Mafia Assassinates a President, the CIA Stages a Coup

1. Charles Rappleye and Ed Becker, *All American Mafioso* (New York: Barricade, 1995), p. 148.

2. *Ibid.,* p. 154.

3. *Ibid.,* pp. 150, 151.

4. John H. Davis, *Mafia Kingfish* (New York: McGraw-Hill, 1989), pp. 160, 161.

5. David Wise and Thomas B. Ross, *The Invisible Government* (New York: Bantam, 1964) p. 195.

6. *Ibid.,* p. 195.

7. Stephen Schlesinger and Stephen Kinzer, *Bitter Fruit: The Story of the American Coup in Guatemala* (Garden City: Doubleday, 1982), pp. 234.

8. Rappleye and Becker, *op. cit.,* p. 148.

9. *Ibid.,* p. 149.

10. *Ibid.*

11. *Ibid.,* p. 151.

12. *Ibid.,* p. 150.

13. *Ibid.,* p. 149.

14. Schlesinger and Kinzer, *op. cit.,* p. 234.

15. Paul Hoch in "Echoes of a Conspiracy" 8-28-91, citing *New Orleans Times-Picayune* 3-31-56 and the work of J. P. Shinley.

16. Rappleye and Becker, *op. cit.,* p. 149.

17. *Ibid.*

18. *Ibid.,* p. 148.

19. Research by A. J. Weberman, cited at www.ajweberman.com/nodules/nodule6.htm.

20. *Bitter Fruit* by Stephen Schlesinger and Stephen Kinzer, p. 235.

21. Rappleye and Becker, *op. cit.,* p. 148.

22. Weberman, *op. cit.*

23. *Ibid.*

24. Richard H. Immerman, *The CIA in Guatemala: The Foreign Policy of Intervention* (Austin: University of Texas Press, 1982), p. 200.

25. *Ibid.,* p. 258.

26. Weberman, *op. cit.*

27. Schlesinger and Kinzer, *op. cit.,* pp. 235, 236.

28. Donald Freed with Fred Simon Landis, *Death in Washington: The Murder of Orlando Letelier* (Westport, Conn.: Lawrence Hill, 1980), p. 48. It should be noted that Antonio Veciana denied to government investigators that Phillips was his handler, Maurice Bishop, though the key government investigator, Gaeton Fonzi, and many others believe the evidence clearly shows that Phillips was Bishop.

Chapter Twenty-Seven: The Kennedys Go on the Attack

1. Robert Lacey, *Little Man: Meyer Lansky and the Gangster Life* (Boston: Little, Brown 1992), p. 286, many others.

2. Carl Sifakis, *The Mafia Encyclopedia* (New York: Facts On File, 1987), pp. 11-13.

3. George Crile III, "The Mafia, the CIA, and Castro," *Washington Post* 5-16-76.

4. Ed Reid, *The Anatomy of Organized Crime in America: The Grim Reapers* (Chicago: Regnery, 1969), pp. 93-95.

5. Carl Sifikas, *op. cit.,* pp. 11-13; Douglas Valentine, *The Strength of the Wolf: The Secret History of America's War on Drugs* (London, New York: Verso, 2004), p. 176.

6. "The Mafia, the CIA, and Castro" by George Crile III, the *Washington Post* 5-16-76.

7. Douglas Valentine, *The Strength of the Wolf: The Secret History of America's War on Drugs* (London, New York: Verso, 2004), p. 176.

8. Robert F. Kennedy, *The Enemy Within* (New York: Popular Library, 1960), p. 32.

9. Walter Sheridan, *The Fall and Rise of Jimmy Hoffa* (New York: Saturday Review Press, 1972), p. 32.

10. Richard D. Mahoney, *Sons & Brothers* (New York: Arcade, 1999), p. 26.

11. Sheridan, *op. cit.,* p. 32.

12. *Ibid.,* p. 32 and many others.

13. Mahoney, *op. cit.,* p. 32.

14. Investigation of Improper Activities in the Labor or Management Field, Senate Select Committee Hearings, June 1959.

15. *Ibid.*, July 1958.

16. *Ibid.*

17. *Ibid.*

Chapter Twenty-Eight: Ruby, the Mafia, and the CIA Help Castro

1. George Black, *The Good Neighbor: How the United States Wrote the History of Central America and the Caribbean* (New York: Pantheon, 1988), p. 104.

2. George Thayer, *The War Business: The International Trade in Armaments* (London: Paladin, 1970), p. 129.

3. Henry S. Bloomgarden, *The Gun: A "Biography" of the Gun that Killed John F. Kennedy* (New York: Bantam Books, 1976), pp. 49, 50.

4. Howard Kohn, "Execution for the Witnesses," *Rolling Stone* 6-2-77.

5. David E. Scheim, *The Mafia Killed President Kennedy* (New York: SPI Books, 1992), p. 221. It's possible that the Italian arms Ruby was referring to were American Thompson submachine guns that Ruby's later business partner—mobster Dominick Bartone—was planning to import from Italy.

6. Anthony Summers with Robbyn Swan, *The Arrogance of Power: The Secret World of Richard Nixon* (New York: Viking, 2000), p. 180.

7. *Ibid.*, p. 501.

8. Gaeton Fonzi, *The Last Investigation* (New York: Thunder's Mouth, 1994), p. 307.

9. CIA file summary by the HSCA, document #180-10143-10179, released 8/8/95.

10. CIA file summary by the HSCA, document #180-10142-10322, released 8/8/95.

11. Anthony Summers, *Conspiracy* (New York: McGraw-Hill, 1980), p. 492.

12. Warren Commission Exhibit #3063.

13. A. J. Weberman database 27.

14. *Newsweek* 8-9-79; Mickey Cohen, *Mickey Cohen, In My Own Words: The Underworld Autobiography of Michael Mickey Cohen, as Told to John Peer Nugent* (Englewood Cliffs, N.J.: Prentice-Hall, 1975); FBI Los Angeles- 44-895 GAP: mel cover page G; Warren Commission Exhibit #1228; Hank Messick, *Lansky* (New York: Putnam, 1971); Warren Commission Exhibit #1306; FBI 44-24016-56; HSCA Vol. 9 paragraph 1054; John Martino with Nathaniel Weyl, *I Was Castro's Prisoner: An American Tells His Story* (New York: Devin-Adair, 1963); Warren Commission Exhibit #2284; all cited (and compiled) by A. J. Weberman.

15. FBI memo 4-14-64, part of HSCA #180-10095-1001.

16. FBI memo 12-3-63, part of Warren Commission Exhibit #3065.

17. FBI memo 44-24016-308, cited by A. J. Weberman.

18. FBI memo 44-24016-1019, cited by A. J. Weberman.

19. Scott Malone memo 9-24-77 on file at the Assassinations Archive and Records Center, found by Mike Sylwester.

20. In addition to Malone's considerable evidence, A. J. Weberman cites information in the 3-13-58 *Miami Herald*, which links Rothman to Morolla, who is linked to FBI informant Mack Blaney Johnson who is linked to Ruby and the gunrunner using the alias "Don Eduardo."

21. William Scott Malone, "The Secret Life of Jack Ruby," *New Times* 1-23-78.

22. Jean-Pierre Charbonneau, *The Canadian Connection* (Ottawa: Optimum, 1976), pp. 143, 148, 256; FBI HO 165-689 and other information cited by A. J. Weberman; also research by Mike Sylwester.

23. Rockefeller Commission interview with Frank Fiorini (Frank Sturgis), March 3, 1975, NARA SSCIA 157-10005-1012, reproduced by A. J. Weberman at ajweberman.com/nodules/nodule6.htm.

24. Interview with Frank Fiorini by A. J. Weberman, database 6.

25. Bloomgarden, *op. cit.*, pp. 65, 66; Paul Hoch, "Echoes of a Conspiracy," 12-23-80.

26. Warren Commission memo Leon Hubert and Griffen 3-20-64, cited by A. J. Weberman.

27. Earl Golz, "Jack Ruby's gunrunning to Castro claimed," *Dallas Morning News* 8-18-78.

Chapter Twenty-Nine: 1959: CIA-Mafia Plots and Coup Attempts

1. See many passages in Seymour M. Hersh, *The Dark Side of Camelot* (Boston: Little, Brown, 1997) and Gus Russo, *Live by the Sword* (Baltimore: Bancroft Press, 1978). Russo is Hersh's former researcher.

2. Michael Beschloss writes in *The Crisis Years* (New York: Edward Burlingame, 1991) (p. 30) that "Nixon . . . was privately prodding the CIA to get the job done before Election Day." Dr. John Newman wrote in *Oswald and the CIA* (New York: Carroll & Graf, 1995) (p. 202) that "Nixon, having secured the Republican nomination for President, had sent his chief lieutenant, General Robert E. Cushman, into the working levels of the CIA that were concerned with Cuban operations. It is thus likely that Nixon knew some of the details about the CIA's cooperation with the Mafia."; Anthony Summers

with Robbyn Swan, *The Arrogance of Power: The Secret World of Richard Nixon* (New York: Viking, 2000), pp. 190-194; CIA Inspector General's Report on the CIA–Mafia Plots.

3. Jean-Pierre Charbonneau, *The Canadian Connection* (Ottawa: Optimum, 1976), pp. 153, 154.

4. CIA Inspector General's Report on the CIA–Mafia Plots.

5. Jane Franklin, *The Cuban Revolution and the United States: A Chronological History* (Melbourne, Australia: Ocean, 1992), p. 26.

6. George Black, *The Good Neighbor* (New York: Pantheon, 1988), p. 104.

7. Richard M. Nixon, *Six Crises* (London, 1962), pp. 351-352.

8. Franklin, *op. cit.*, p. 26.

9. Fawn M. Brodie, *Richard Nixon: The Shaping of His Character* (New York: Norton, 1981), p. 396.

10. *Ibid.*, p. 399.

11. *Ibid.*, p. 396.

12. Stephen E. Ambrose, *Nixon* (New York: Simon and Schuster, 1987), p. 550.

13. Investigation of Improper Activities in the Labor or Management Field, Senate Select Committee Hearings, March 1959.

14. John H. Davis, *Mafia Kingfish* (New York: McGraw-Hill, 1989), p. 74.

15. Senate Committee on Government Operations, Permanent Subcommittee on Investigations: Organized Crime and Illicit Traffice in Narcotics, Sept./Oct. 1963.

16. Davis, *Mafia Kingfish* (McGraw-Hill, 1989), p. 74.

17. Investigation of Improper Activities in the Labor or Management Field, Senate Select Committee Hearings, March 1959.

18. Davis, *Mafia Kingfish* (McGraw-Hill, 1989), p. 78.

19. The extensive mob associations of Vice President Richard Nixon—which would include getting a $500,000 contribution from Marcello the following year—may provide a clue.

20. Robert Sam Anson, *"They've Killed the President!": The Search for the Murderers of John F. Kennedy* (New York: Bantam, 1975), pp. 309, 310.

21. Nestor T. Carbonell, *And the Russians Stayed* (New York: Morrow, 1989), p. 62.

22. *Westmoreland Tribune Review* 10-25-77 article by Doris O'Donnell and Robert K. Brown interview with Richard Whatley 9-16-72, cited by A. J. Weberman.

23. Interview with Frank Fiorini by A. J. Weberman, database 7.

24. Rockefeller Commission interview with Frank Fiorini (Frank Sturgis), March 3, 1975, NARA SSCIA 157-10005-1012, reproduced by A. J. Weberman at ajweberman.com/nodules/nodule6.htm.

25. *Ibid.*

23. Interview with Frank Fiorini by A. J. Weberman, database 7.

27. Summers and Swan, *op. cit.*, p. 498.

28. Rockefeller Commission interview with Frank Fiorini (Frank Sturgis), March 3, 1975, NARA SSCIA 157-10005-1012, reproduced by A. J. Weberman at ajweberman.com/nodules/nodule6.htm.

29. *Ibid.*

30. *Ibid.*

31. *Washington Post* 3-27-59, cited by A. J. Weberman.

32. Cuban Officials and JFK Historians Conference, 12-7-95.

33. William Turner, "The Inquest," *Ramparts* magazine, June 1967.

Chapter Thirty: The CIA Turns to Hoffa

1. Sheridan's protégé was Dan Moldea, whose work is cited extensively in this chapter. Also, declassified documents obtained by A. J. Weberman were also important in confirming Jack Ruby's role.

2. Howard Kohn, "Execution for the Witnesses," *Rolling Stone* 6-2-77.

3. Ed Reid, *The Anatomy of Organized Crime in America: The Grim Reapers* (New York: Bantam, 1970), pp. 288, 289.

4. NARA document 1993.08.12.15:54:36:560007, cited by A. J. Weberman.

5. Carl Sifakis, *The Mafia Encyclopedia* (New York: Facts On File, 1987), p. 54.

6. Tony Scaduto, "The CIA–Mafia Connection," *Genesis*, January 1976.

7. *Clandestine American*, Vol. 3 #2, July-Aug/Sept.-Oct. 1979, p. 9, article by Dan Moldea.

8. Dan E. Moldea, *The Hoffa Wars: Teamsters, Rebels, Politicians, and the Mob* (New York: Charter, 1978), pp. 5, 12.

9. *Ibid.*, p. 387.

10. *Ibid.*

11. "Mafia Spies in Cuba," *Time* 6-9-75.

12. Tony Scaduto, "The CIA–Mafia Connection," *Genesis* January 1976.

13. Moldea, *The Hoffa Wars* (Charter, 1978), pp. 129, 130.

14. *Ibid.*, p. 130.

15. *Ibid.*

16. Robert Sam Anson, *"They've Killed the President!": The Search for the Murderers of John F. Kennedy* (New York: Bantam, 1975), p. 296, cited in Peter Dale Scott, *Deep Politics and the Death of JFK* (Berkeley: University of California Press, 1993), pp. 174, 352. Scott adds that "the witness, Mario Brod, was a New York lawyer and salaried CIA contract officer" who "worked for CIA Counterintelligence Chief James Angleton." Angleton's biographer confirms that "in this capacity" Brod "had contacts with the Mafia." (Tom Mangold, *Cold Warrior: James Jesus Angleton: The CIA's Master Spy Hunter* [New York: Simon & Schuster, 1991], pp. 104-105.)

17. Moldea, *The Hoffa Wars* (Charter, 1978), pp. 130, 131.

18. Mathews and Ruby: Peter Dale Scott, in *Deep Politics*, p. 118, says "R. D. Matthews" was "a former co-worker of [John] Martino's at the Hotel Deauville casino," and by 1963 "Matthews now resided in Dallas and knew Ruby." A. J. Weberman says "A 1959 FBI report stated R.D. Matthews move to Cuba was made on behalf of Trafficante. . . . A 1962 FBI report confirmed this: A FBI informant overheard a conversation between R. D. Matthews and . . . 'during which both men admitted having worked for Trafficante.'"

19. HSCA Vol. V pp. 28-87, 134, 172 and Vol. IX p. 167, cited by A. J. Weberman.

20. Paul Meskil, "How US Made Unholy Alliance with the Mafia," *New York Daily News* 4-23-75.

21. CIA document #1993.06.30.11:37:09:370410, approved for release 1993 by the CIA Historical Review Program.

22. CIA File Summary from the CIA Segregated Collection, document #180-10144-10409, released 8/23/95.

23. *Ibid.*

24. Anson, *op. cit.*, p. 309.

25. Jean-Pierre Charbonneau, *The Canadian Connection* (Ottawa: Optimum, 1976), p. 143.

26. Anthony Summers with Robbyn Swan, *The Arrogance of Power: The Secret World of Richard Nixon* (New York: Viking, 2000), p. 194.

27. HSCA Final Report, 1979, p. 173.

28. William Scott Malone, "The Secret Life of Jack Ruby," *New Times* 1-23-78.

29. G. Robert Blakey and Richard N. Billings, *The Plot to Kill the President* (New York: Times Books, 1981), p. 302.

30. "Psychiatric Examination of Jack Ruby by Werner Tutear, MD.

31. Malone, *op. cit.*

32. Investigation of Improper Activities in the Labor or Management Field, Senate Select Committee Hearings, 6-30-59; HSCA deposition of Gerry Hemming 3-21-78.

33. FBI memo Miami MM 87-8756 4.4.62 - Lenihan, cited by A. J. Weberman about Bartone's connection to alleged Ruby and Rothman gunrunning associate.

34. A. J. Weberman Web site (http://www.ajweberman.com/coupt5.htm).

35. CIA document # 1993.07.30.18:29:27:340046, 1-22-64, declassified 7-30-93.

36. CIA document RCD 5.6.75 that was mistakenly labeled by the National Archives as HSCA 180-10107-10419, cited by A. J. Weberman.

37. Cited by A. J. Weberman, and possibly related to CIA document RCD 5.6.75 that was mistakenly labeled by the National Archives as HSCA 180-10107-10419.

38. Moldea, *The Hoffa Wars* (Charter, 1978), p. 107.

39. *Ibid.*, pp. 122, 123.

40. Walter Sheridan, *The Fall and Rise of Jimmy Hoffa* (New York: Saturday Review Press, 1972), p. 110.

41. 1959 FBI report regarding William Morgan, quoted by A. J. Weberman, database 1.

42. Fabían Escalante *The Secret War: CIA Covert Operations Against Cuba, 1959–62* (Melbourne: Ocean, 1995), p. 19.

43. CIA report regarding 3-26-59 information to acting Director, Western Hemisphere Division about William Morgan, quoted by A. J. Weberman, database 1.

44. CIA report 8-13-59 regarding information provided by William Morgan, quoted by A. J. Weberman, database 1.

45. William Scott Malone, "The Secret Life of Jack Ruby," *New Times* 1-23-78.

46. Warren Commission Documents 84.215 and 84.216, cited in Anthony Summers, *Conspiracy* (New York: McGraw-Hill, 1980), pp. 462, 463, 497.

47. Summers, *Conspiracy* (McGraw-Hill, 1980), p. 462.

48. Phone interview with Gerry Hemming, 12-14-97. Ruby says at that meeting, Ruby was using the alias of "Bob Brown," while Bartone and McWillie used the aliases of "Bob Smith" and "Bob Jones." Hemming said he'd heard of Spindel's involvement, but not of anyone using the alias of LaRue. Hemming now says he thinks the meeting would have been in Sept. or Dec. 1959, instead of the June 1959 date he apparently recalled twenty years earlier to journalist Scott Malone. If the later

dates are correct, it would still fit Ruby's known schedule, since he was definitely in Cuba in September 1959, and talked with friends about making a trip around December 1959. When Hemming testified to the House Select Committee in the late 1970s, he placed the date in September of October 1959.

49. Warren Commission Vol. XIV, pp. 460, 461.

50. Warren Commission Vol. XIV, p. 461.

51. HSCA Vol. IX, pp. 587-801.

52. CIA document #1110910, "Eloy Gutierrez Menoyo" file.

53. FBI document quoted by A. J. Weberman, database 7.

54. David E. Scheim, *The Mafia Killed President Kennedy* (New York: SPI Books, 1992), p. 130.

55. Warren Commission Vol. V, p. 201.

56. Warren Commission Vol. XIV, p. 445.

57. Warren Commission Vol. V, p. 202.

58. Warren Commission Documents #732 and 302.159; HSCA Report p. 151; HSCA Vol. V p. 281; Scott Malone, "Rubygate," *New Times* 1-23-78; all cited in Summers, *Conspiracy* (McGraw-Hill, 1980), p. 466.

59. Warren Commission Vol. V, p. 202.

60. CIA document OS 8.24.62, Sheffield Edwards, cited by A. J. Weberman.

61. Walter Sheridan, *The Fall and Rise of Jimmy Hoffa* (New York: Saturday Review Press, 1972).

Chapter Thirty-One: Menoyo, Morales, and Phillips Plan a Coup

1. CIA Document #1994.04.28.14:42:11:720005, declassifed 4/28/94 by CIA Historical Review Program.

2. Fabián Escalante, *The Secret War: CIA Covert Operations Against Cuba, 1959–62* (Melbourne: Ocean, 1995), p. 19.

3. According to one account, Spindel may have also used the alias of "Jack LaRue" for his part of the Hoffa plane deal.

4. Bernard B. Spindel, *The Ominous Ear* (New York: Award House, 1968), pp. 74, 79.

5. Paul D. Bethel, *The Losers: The Definitive Report, by an Eyewitness, of the Communist Conquest of Cuba and the Soviet Penetration in Latin America* (New Rochelle: Arlington House, 1969), pp. 137-139.

6. *Ibid.*, p. 140.

7. CIA 1994.04.26.09:51:24:690005, declassified 4-26-94.

8. Tad Szulc, *Fidel: A Critical Portrait* (New York: Morrow, 1986), p. 499.

9. Escalante, *op. cit.*, p. 20.

10. *Ibid.*, pp. 20, 21.

11. FBI 105-70973 - Morgan, cited by A. J. Weberman.

12. Rockefeller Commission interview with Frank Fiorini (Frank Sturgis), March 3, 1975, NARA SSCIA 157-10005-1012, reproduced by A. J. Weberman at ajweberman.com/nodules/nodule6.htm.

13. Hugh Thomas, *Cuba: Or, Pursuit of Freedom* (London: Eyre & Spottiswoode, 1971), p. 1238.

14. *Ibid.*, p. 1243.

15. Charles Rappleye and Ed Becker, *All American Mafioso* (New York: Barricade, 1995), pp. 146, 147.

16. Donald Freed with Fred Simon Landis, *Death in Washington: The Murder of Orlando Letelier* (Westport, Conn.: Lawrence Hill, 1980), p. 44.

17. Joseph B. Smith, *Portrait of a Cold Warrior* (New York: Ballantine, 1981), p. 329.

18. Freed with Landis, *op. cit.*, pp. 44, 45.

19. Tad Szulc, *Fidel*, pp. 427-429.

20. David Atlee Phillips, *The Night Watch* (New York: Atheneum, 1977), p. 77.

21. *Ibid.*, pp. 80-81.

22. FBI 64-29230-95, cited by A. J. Weberman.

23. Larry Hancock, *Someone Would Have Talked* (Southlake, Tex.: JFK Lancer, 2003), p. 307.

24. Rappleye and Becker, *op. cit.*, pp. 146, 147.

25. Gaeton Fonzi, *The Last Investigation* (New York: Thunder's Mouth, 1994), p. 383.

26. Phone interview with Larry Hancock 2-18-05.

27. David Corn, *Blond Ghost* (New York: Simon & Schuster, 1994), p. 85.

28. John Simkin, David Morales biography at the British educational website www.spartacus.schoolnet.co.uk.

29. John Martino with Nathaniel Weyl, *I Was Castro's Prisoner: An American Tells His Story* (New York: Devin-Adair, 1963), p. 47.

30. Hancock, *op. cit.*, p. 92.

31. *Ibid.*, p. 12.

32. For Martino-Fiorini: A. J. Weberman, database 10.

33. FBI memo from Director to Legal Attache, Havana, subject John Martino, 7-31-59.

34. Phone interview with Larry Hancock 2-18-05.

35. Notes and letters between the CIA and G. Robert Blakey regarding the book by Blakey and Richard Billings, part of the papers of Richard Billings on file at the Assassination Archives and Research Center.

36. Jane Franklin, *The Cuban Revolution and the United States: A Chronological History* (Melbourne, Australia: Ocean, 1992), p. 27.

37. Szulc, *Fidel*, p. 505.

38. FBI memo from Director to Legal Attache, Havana, subject John Martino, 7-31-59.

39. A. J. Weberman, database 10.

40. Nestor T. Carbonell, *And the Russians Stayed* (New York: Morrow, 1989), p. 82.

41. Interview with Harry Williams 2-24-92.

42. *Ibid.*

43. *Ibid.*

44. *Ibid.*

45. Escalante, *op. cit.,* pp. 20, 21.

46. Interview with Harry Williams 2-24-92.

47. *Ibid.*

48. *Ibid.*

Chapter Thirty-Two: Ruby, Trafficante, the Kennedys, and "Jack La Rue"

1. Charles Rappleye and Ed Becker, *All American Mafioso* (New York: Barricade, 1995), p. 177.

2. *New York Post* 2-17-59, *New York Times* 2-21-58, *Time* 1-12-59, all cited by A. J. Weberman.

3. HSCA Vol. V, p. 294 and other information by A. J. Weberman.

4. Frank Ragano and Selwyn Raab, *Mob Lawyer* (New York: Scribners, 1994), p. 57.

5. *Ibid.,* p. 58.

6. *Ibid.*

7. *Ibid.,* p. 55.

8. Rappleye and Becker, *op. cit.,* p. 177.

9. Jean-Pierre Charbonneau, *The Canadian Connection* (Ottawa: Optimum, 1976), pp. 103, 153, 154.

10. Dick Russell, "Loran Hall and the Politics of Assassination," *Village Voice* 10-3-77.

11. A. J. Weberman, database 27.

12. Memo from "George Bush" to "DDCI" on "September 15, 1976" saying "he would like to see" a "CIA Cable" about "Jack Ruby visiting Trafficante in jail." Page 16 of a FOIA release on file at the Assassination Archives and Research Center.

13. Tad Szulc, *Fidel: A Critical Portrait* (New York: Morrow, 1986), p. 499.

14. Fabián Escalante, *The Secret War: CIA Covert Operations Against Cuba, 1959–62* (Melbourne: Ocean, 1995), p. 18.

15. CIA document OS 8.24.62, Sheffield Edwards, cited by A. J. Weberman; Tad Szulc gives the date of the invasion as June 14, 1959; Szulc, *Fidel*, p. 499.

16. FBI document 100-344127-NR 7.2.59, cited by A. J. Weberman.

17. Investigation of Improper Activities in the Labor or Management Field, Senate Select Committee Hearings, June 1959.

18. Richard D. Mahoney, *Sons & Brothers* (New York: Arcade, 1999), pp. 33, 34.

19. Seymour M. Hersh, "Aides say Robert Kennedy told of CIA Castro plot," *New York Times* 3-10-75.

20. Tony Scaduto, "The CIA-Mafia Connection," *Genesis* January 1976.

21. Investigation of Improper Activities in the Labor or Management Field, Senate Select Committee Hearings, June 30, 1959.

22. *Ibid.*

23. *Ibid.*

24. *Ibid.*

25. *Ibid.*

26. *Ibid.*

27. *Ibid.,* June 1959.

28. *Ibid.,* July 15, 1959; Bernard B. Spindel, *The Ominous Ear* (New York: Award House, 1968), pp. 207-210. In his autobiography, Spindel left out much information about Hoffa's criminal activities and the 1959 CIA-Mafia plots. Spindel has also been the source of many of the rumors over the years about secret audio tapes that supposedly recorded the Kennedys' meetings with Marilyn Monroe. According to one account, Spindel sometimes used the alias "Jack LaRue." That could be true, since covert operations often used one alias for two or more people, as in C-Day and Watergate. And someone had to handle the Dominican side of Hoffa's plane deal, since no evidence links Ruby to trips to the Dominican Republic.

But it's clear from all the evidence that Spindel was not the "Jack LaRue" being sought by Bobby Kennedy. Bobby's men already knew about Spindel's activities with Hoffa in June 1959. And even after Spindel's autobiography came out—which discussed Spindel's Dominican activities in 1959—Bobby's top Hoffa prosecutor Walter Sheridan still considered the identity of the "Jack LaRue" Bobby sought to be a mystery.

29. Michael Canfield and Alan J. Weberman, *Coup d'État in America: The CIA and the Assassination of John F. Kennedy* (New York: Third Press, 1975), p. 155, and other documents and information by A. J. Weberman.

30. Mahoney, *op. cit.*, pp. 271-273.

31. Anthony and Robbyn Summers, "The Ghosts of November," *Vanity Fair* December 1994.

32. William Scott Malone, "The Secret Life of Jack Ruby," *New Times* 1-23-78.

33. A. J. Weberman, database 27.

34. Senate Committee on Government Operations, Permanent Subcommittee on Investigations: Organized Crime and Illicit Traffice in Narcotics, Sept./Oct. 1963.

35. Malone, *op. cit.*

36. *Ibid.*

37. A. J. Weberman, database 27.

38. They only started to emerge when the Senate Church Committee investigation began in 1975.

39. HSCA Vol. V, pp. 2-240.

40. Howard Kohn, "Execution for the Witnesses," *Rolling Stone* 6-2-77.

41. Warren Commission volume V, p. 201.

42. *Ibid.*, p. 202.

43. *Ibid.*, p. 201.

44. *Ibid.*

45. G. Robert Blakey and Richard N. Billings, *The Plot to Kill the President* (New York: Times Books, 1981), pp. 292-302.

46. HSCA Vol. V, pp. 197-198, 204, 205, 221, cited in Lisa Pease, "Gunrunner Ruby and the CIA," *Probe* magazine.

47. For example, one document from Menoyo's file from March 1959 has censored the name of the "Project" associated with Menoyo, though the document itself was routed to many high levels in the CIA and was associated with the Deputy Director for Plans, which handled operations.

48. CIA report 8-13-59 regarding information provided by William Morgan, quoted by A. J. Weberman, database 1.

49. Paul D. Bethel, *The Losers: The Definitive Report, by an Eyewitness, of the Communist Conquest of Cuba and the Soviet Penetration in Latin America* (New Rochelle: Arlington House, 1969), pp. 187-189.

50. *Ibid.*

51. Fabian Escalante *The Secret War: CIA Covert Operations Against Cuba, 1959–62* (Melbourne: Ocean, 1995), p. 24.

52. Bethel, *op. cit.*, pp. 189-192.

53. Escalante, *op. cit.*, pp. 22-24.

54. FBI document 100-344127NR 5.13.59, 26; FBI 109-584-305, both cited by A. J. Weberman.

55. A. J. Weberman, database 27.

56. Szulc, *Fidel*, p. 499.

57. Nestor T. Carbonell, *And the Russians Stayed* (New York: Morrow, 1989), p. 70.

58. David Atlee Phillips, *The Night Watch* (New York: Atheneum, 1977), p. 82.

59. For the CIA's version of the coup, see *ibid.*; for the official Cuban version, see Escalante, *op. cit.*

60. HSCA Vol. X, p. 109. According to the House Select Committee on Assassinations: "In August 1959, while in Miami, Ferrie was put under 24-hour surveillance by customs agents who believed he was involved in gun smuggling. Following a brief investigation, including a tapping of his telephone conversations, it was determined that Ferrie was not involved in any illegal activity, but merely planning an outing for his 'scouts.' The investigation was dropped."

61. Jane Franklin, *The Cuban Revolution and the United States: A Chronological History* (Melbourne, Australia: Ocean, 1992), p. 27.

62. Escalante, *op. cit.*, p. 29.

63. Ragano and Raab, *op. cit.*, pp. 60, 61.

64. Bethel, *op. cit.*, pp. 189-192.

65. FBI document 100-344127-26, cited by A. J. Weberman.

Chapter Thirty-Three: September 1959: Artime, Varona, and Ruby Target Castro

1. A. J. Weberman, database 27.

2. Fawn M. Brodie, *Richard Nixon: The Shaping of His Character* (New York: Norton, 1981), p. 398.

3. Nestor T. Carbonell, *And the Russians Stayed* (New York: Morrow, 1989), p. 75.

4. Fabián Escalante, *The Secret War: CIA Covert Operations Against Cuba, 1959–62* (Melbourne: Ocean, 1995), pp. 32-37.

5. CIA file from the National Archives with no RIF number, 10-8-76 memo to Director of Security by Curtis R. Rivers, "handwritten note at bottom of RIF sheet: 'To NARA—Please replace previously released version of this document with the attached.'" From Miami-Dade Archivist Gordon Winslow at http://cuban-exile.com.

6. CIA document #180-10145-10211, declassified 8-29-95.

7. William Scott Malone,"The Secret Life of Jack Ruby," *New Times* 1-23-78.

8. G. Robert Blakey and Richard N. Billings, *The Plot to Kill the President* (New York: Times Books, 1981), p. 301.

9. Escalante, *op. cit.,* pp. 34-36.

10. CIA file 1994.03.08.08:15:51:120007, "CIA files on Bernard Barker as reviewed by Pat Orr," declassified 3-8-94.

11. *Ibid.*

12. E. Howard Hunt, *Give Us This Day* (New Rochelle: Arlington House, 1973), p. 11.

13. CIA Document #104-10110-10498, 1-15-1960 cable from CIA Director to Havana, released 3-4-98.

14. CIA file 1994.03.08.08:15:51:120007, "CIA files on Bernard Barker as reviewed by Pat Orr," memo from Havana to CIA Director written 4-19-60 and date-stamped 4-20-60, declassified 3-8-94; CIA document #104-10015-10341, declassified 12-10-93.

15. Hugh Thomas, *Cuba: Or, Pursuit of Freedom* (London: Eyre & Spottiswoode, 1971), p. 1243.

16. Escalante, *op. cit.,* p. 37.

17. Earl Golz, "Jack Ruby's gunrunning to Castro claimed," *Dallas Morning News* 8-18-78.

18. A. J. Weberman, database 27.

19. Escalante, *op. cit.,* p. 37.

20. Hugh Thomas, *op. cit.,* p. 1244.

21. *Ibid.,* p. 1246.

22. Paul D. Bethel, *The Losers: The Definitive Report, by an Eyewitness, of the Communist Conquest of Cuba and the Soviet Penetration in Latin America* (New Rochelle: Arlington House, 1969), p. 200.

23. Escalante, *op. cit.,* p. 37.

24. Tad Szulc, *Fidel: A Critical Portrait* (New York: Morrow, 1986), p. 505.

25. Jane Franklin, *The Cuban Revolution and the United States: A Chronological History* (Melbourne, Australia: Ocean, 1992), p. 28.

26. Escalante, *op. cit.,* pp. 37, 38

27. Szulc, *Fidel,* p. 505.

28. Escalante, *op. cit.,* p. 37.

29. *Ibid.,* p. 38.

30. Hunt, *op. cit.,* p. 11.

31. Escalante, *op. cit.,* p. 38.

32. Nestor T. Carbonell, *And the Russians Stayed* (New York: Morrow, 1989), p. 76.

33. Hugh Thomas, *op. cit.,* pp. 1247, 1248.

34. Bethel, *op. cit.,* pp. 198, 199.

35. Hugh Thomas, *op. cit.,* p. 1247.

36. Warren Commission Vol. XIV, pp. 543, 544; Warren Commission Exhibits 2993 and 2994.

37. Cuban Report, 7-30-75 office of Senator George McGovern.

38. *New York Times* 11-23-59, cited by A. J. Weberman.

39. Robert Lacey, *Little Man: Meyer Lansky and the Gangster Life* (Boston: Little, Brown 1992), p. 324.

40. Anthony Summers with Robbyn Swan, *The Arrogance of Power: The Secret World of Richard Nixon* (New York: Viking, 2000), p. 498.

41. Lacy, *op. cit.,* p. 324.

42. Dan E. Moldea, *The Hoffa Wars: Teamsters, Rebels, Politicians, and the Mob* (New York: Charter, 1978), pp. 126, 127; Senate Church Committee Report, *Alleged Assassination Plots Involving Foreign Leaders* (New York: Norton, 1976), p. 92.

43. FBI Memo 4-14-64, part of HSCA #180-10095-1001.

44. Malone, *op. cit.*

45. HSCA Vol. IX, pp. 524-586; George O'Toole, *The Assassination Tapes: An Electronic Probe into the Murder of John F. Kennedy and the Dallas Coverup* (New York: Zebra, 1977), pp. 290-295.

46. HSCA Vol. IX, p. 527; A. J. Weberman.

47. Blakey and Billings, *op. cit.,* pp. 292-302; A. J. Weberman, database 27.

48. David E. Scheim, *The Mafia Killed President Kennedy* (New York: SPI Books, 1992), pp. 118, 119.

49. A minor boxing figure Ruby knew in 1960 was a mobster from Chicago who had worked for Trafficante and Marcello,

named James Henry Dolan. He also had contact with Ruby two months before JFK's assassination. See Scheim, *Contract on America*, pp. 293, 298, 413, 414; also information from Dolan's son, James Dolan. Dolan had only boxed briefly in the 1940s, whereas Barney Baker like to tout his boxing prowess, which was good for his reputation as Hoffa's "muscle."

50. Michael Canfield and Alan J. Weberman, *Coup d'État in America: The CIA and the Assassination of John F. Kennedy* (New York: Third Press, 1975), p. 171.

51. It should be noted that Warren, Specter, even Ruby often use a variety of different dates for the Colt story, but the 1-19-60 purchase date was confirmed by the FBI and the hardware store records. The timing of Ruby's planned trip to Cuba can also be dated from the January 20 to February 16 performances by Frank Sinatra that caused one of Ruby's companions to drop out of the trip.

52. Warren Commission Vol. XIV, pp. 543, 544.

53. Warren Commission Vol. V, pp. 201, 202.

54. "Psychiatric Examination of Jack Ruby by Werner Tutear, M.D.

55. Warren Commission Vol. XIV, pp. 543, 544.

56. A. J. Weberman, database 27, citing FBK, Warren Commission, and HSCA documents.

57. House Select Committee Vol. V pp. 28-87, 134, 172, vol. IX p. 167, and other information cited by A. J. Weberman.

58. Cuban Report, 7-30-75 office of Senator George McGovern.

Chapter Thirty-Four: 1960 and 1961: New CIA-Mafia Plots, the Bay of Pigs, and RFK's War Against Marcello

1. 1967 CIA Inspector General's Report.

2. Senate Church Committee Report, *Alleged Assassination Plots Involving Foreign Leaders* (New York: Norton, 1976), pp. 74-77.

3. Dan E. Moldea, *The Hoffa Wars: Teamsters, Rebels, Politicians, and the Mob* (New York: Charter, 1978), p. 108.

4. Handwritten notes of Richard E. Sprague's interview with Haynes Johnson at the Madison Hotel in Washington, D.C., dated 1-12-73.

5. Cuban National Preparatory Committee of the XI World Festival of Youth and Students, *CIA: Cuba Accuses* (1979), p. 23.

6. Warren Hinckle and William Turner, *The Fish Is Red* (New York: Harper & Row, 1981), p. 205.

7. *New Orleans States-Item* article by Ross Yockey and Hoke May, 5-5-67.

8. 7-29-82 Department of the Navy release to Bernard Fensterwald, #110-6-212-58.

9. Cuban National Preparatory Committee, *op. cit.,* p. 23.

10. Warren Hinckle and William Turner, *Deadly Secrets* (New York: Thunder's Mouth, 1992).

11. FBI 62-109060-4759 and CIA MFR 2.14.68 cited by A. J. Weberman; Gus Russo, *Live by the Sword* (Baltimore: Bancroft Press, 1978), many passages.

12. SSCIA 157-10002-10057, 6-9-61.

13. New CIA documents cited by Larry Hancock in *Someone Would Have Talked* (Southlake, Tex.: JFK Lancer, 2005, advance draft).

14. CIA 104-10315-10003, memo to CIA Director from JMWAVE regarding "Ability to Deliver Capsule to Cubela," cited by by Larry Hancock in *Someone Would have Talked* (Southlake, Tex.: JFK Lancer, 2005, advance draft).

15. L. Gonzales-Mata, *Cygne* (Grasset, 1976); 1967 CIA Inspector General's Report; Rothman CIA files 1993.06 .30.11:37:09:370410, 180-10143-10179, 180-10142-10322, 180-10142-10319, and 180-10144-10409; Interview of Frank Fiorini by A. J. Weberman.

16. Deposition in a libel case against *Playboy* magazine—several years prior to David Phillips's name being connected to the JFK assassination—cited by Lisa Pease in *Probe*, Vol. 3 No. 3, March-April 1996.

17. John Newman, *Oswald and the CIA* (New York: Carroll & Graf, 1995), pp. 95, 236-243, 396.

18. James DiEugenio, *Destiny Betrayed: JFK, Cuba, and the Garrison Case* (New York: Sheridan Square Press, 1992), pp. 218-220.

19. *Ibid.*

20. Documents at the National Archives, including CIA 1993.08.11.18:17:58:620028 - Breckinridge, CIA Memo 6-21-72 Osborne to Parman, CIA, CIA FPIA #2795-1, 1993.08.11.18:16:27:590028, CIA Memo SDB to MFF 7.3.74, Shackley memo C/EAD 7/6/74, all quoted by A. J. Weberman at Database 10. McCord's role would have been at the "headquarters planning" level, and another of those CIA memos says files about this operation would be under the highly restricted "Black Tape wrapping, Job #67-86/78." That's the same high level of "black tape" security that a CIA handbook from 11-15-74 says would apply to files coded "RYBAT," one of the code words appearing on CIA AMWORLD documents.

21. John H. Davis, *Mafia Kingfish* (New York: McGraw-Hill, 1989), pp. 90, 91.

22. *Ibid.,* p. 92.

23. *Ibid.,* p. 94.

24. *Ibid.*

25. *Ibid.,* pp. 94-100.

Chapter Thirty-Five: The War Against the Godfathers and Targeting RFK

1. John H. Davis, *Mafia Kingfish* (New York: McGraw-Hill, 1989), pp. 104, 105.

2. Senate Committee on Government Operations, Permanent Subcommittee on Investigations: Organized Crime and Illicit Traffice in Narcotics, Sept./Oct. 1963.

3. Richard D. Mahoney, *Sons & Brothers* (New York: Arcade, 1999), p. 195.

4. *Ibid.*, p. 196.

5. Douglas Valentine, *The Strength of the Wolf: The Secret History of America's War on Drugs* (London, New York: Verso, 2004), p. 280.

6. Senate Committee on Government Operations, Permanent Subcommittee on Investigations: Organized Crime and Illicit Traffice in Narcotics, Sept./Oct. 1963; Carl Sifakis, *The Mafia Encyclopedia* (New York: Facts On File, 1987), pp. 154, 155.

7. FBI memo March 6, 1967, Sullivan to Wannall.

8. Mahoney, *op. cit.*, p. 159.

9. Interview of Colonel Sheffield Edwards by David Belin for the Rockefeller Commission, April 9, 1975.

10. FBI memo March 6, 1967, Sullivan to Wannall.

11. Mahoney, *op. cit.*, p. 156.

12. *Ibid.*, pp. 157, 158.

13. *Ibid.*, p. 157.

14. Rosselli's biographers noted many huge inconsistencies in Campbell's stories over the years. While she certainly had a relationship with JFK, the tales of being a courier between Sam Giancana and JFK simply aren't supported by the evidence. See Charles Rappleye and Ed Becker, *All American Mafioso* (New York: Barricade, 1995), pp. 208, 209.

15. Mahoney, *op. cit.*, p. 158.

16. House Select Committee on Assassinations Report, pp. 176, 177.

17. Dan E. Moldea, *The Hoffa Wars: Teamsters, Rebels, Politicians, and the Mob* (New York: Charter, 1978), p. 148.

18. Anthony Summers, *Goddess: The Secret Lives of Marilyn Monroe* (New York: New American Library, 1986), p. 339.

19. Nick Tosches, *Dino: Living High in the Dirty Business of Dreams* (New York: Dell, 1993), p. 356.

20. "Marilyn Monroe: Mystery and Myth" by Guy Rocha, Nevada State Archivist, from the official website of the Nevada State Library and Archives, Department of Cultural Affairs.

21. William F. Roemer, Jr., *Roemer: Man Against the Mob* (New York: Ballantine, 1991), p. 175.

22. Summers, *Goddess*, pp. 334-336.

23. *Ibid.*, p. 337.

24. *Ibid.*, p. 338.

25. *Ibid.*, pp. 339, 501.

26. *Ibid.*, p. 339.

27. Anthony Summers, *Official and Confidential: The Secret Life of J. Edgar Hoover* (New York: G. P. Putnam's Sons, 1993), p. 301.

28. *Ibid.*, p. 301.

29. Tosches, *op. cit.*, p. 357.

30. Phone interview with Gerry Patrick Hemming, 4-10-96.

31. Dan E. Moldea, *Interference: How Organized Crime Influences Professional Football* (New York: Morrow, 1989), many passages.

Chapter Thirty-Six: Shifting the Target to JFK

1. House Select Committee on Assassinations Report (New York: Bantam, 1979), p. 169.

2. *Ibid.*

3. *Ibid.*, p. 172.

4. Charles Rappleye and Ed Becker, *All American Mafioso* (New York: Barricade, 1995), pp. 237, 238.

5. *Ibid.*, p. 360.

6. John H. Davis, *Mafia Kingfish* (New York: McGraw-Hill, 1989), p. 114.

7. Richard D. Mahoney, *Sons & Brothers* (New York: Arcade, 1999), p. 304.

8. House Select Committee on Assassinations, *op. cit.*, p. 169.

9. HSCA Vol. V, pp. 373, 374.

10. Warren Hinckle and William Turner, *The Fish Is Red* (New York: Harper & Row, 1981), p. 297.

11. HSCA Vol. V, p. 315.

12. George Crile III, "The Mafia, the CIA, and Castro," *Washington Post* 5-16-76.

13. *Ibid.*

14. HSCA Vol. V, p. 303; some accounts place the dates of Trafficante's threats as June or July 1963, but most date them to around September 1962.

15. HSCA Vol. V, p. 314.

16. *Ibid.,* p. 319.

17. *Ibid.,* p. 320.

18. Crile, *op. cit.*

19. *Washington Post* 5-17-76 cited in Anthony Summers, *Conspiracy* (New York: Paragon House, 1989), p. 585.

20. Summers, *Conspiracy* (Paragon House, 1989), p. 434.

21. Mahoney, *op. cit.,* pp. 196, 197.

22. Mark Riebling, *Wedge,* Chapter 8, online edition at markriebling.com.

23. Crile, *op. cit.*

24. *Ibid.*

25. House Select Committee on Assassinations, *op. cit.,* p. 173.

26. *Ibid.,* p. 175.

27. 5-13-62 attempt against President Sukarno of Indonesia; 1-21-62 attempt against President Olympio of Togo; attempts on 8-1-62 and 9-9-62 against the President of Ghana; attempt against King Mahendra of Nepal on 1-22-62; attempt against President Diem of South Vietnam on 2-27-62 (he would be assassinated three weeks before JFK the following year). There was an attempt on 9-26-62 against a leader of Yemen and the successful assassination of the Premier of Burundi on 10-13-61. There was also the assassination of the Prime Minister of Jordan on 8-29-60, and attempts against the Premier of Japan on 7-14-60, the President of Argentina on 3-28-60, the President of Venezuela on 6-24-60, and the Premier of South Africa on 4-9-60; all listed in Murray Clark Havens, Carl Leiden, and Karl M. Schmitt, *The Politics of Assassination* (Englewood Cliffs, N.J.: Prentice-Hall, 1970), p. 166.

28. Memorandum by Bernard Fensterwald, submitted to the US Justice Department 7-13-82 as part of a Freedom of Information request; The Staff and Editors of *Newsday, The Heroin Trail* (New York: Signet, 1974), pp. 109-118; Henrik Krüger, *The Great Heroin Coup* (Boston: South End Press, 1980), pp. 95, 96.

29. U.S. Senate, Select Committee to Study Governmental Operations with Respect to Intelligence Activities, *Alleged Assassination Plots Involving Foreign Leaders* (New York: Norton, 1976), several passages.

30. CIA 104-10431-10050, declassified 12-16-98, has handwritten expense notes from William Harvey from the spring of 1963 charged to "QJWin / ZRRifle" regarding an operation based in south Florida, particularly the Florida Keys and Miami, that also includes calls to Los Angeles (where Johnny Rosselli was based). 1967 CIA Inspector General's Report; Richard D. Mahoney, *Sons & Brothers* (New York: Arcade, 1999), pp. 91-93, 108, 135, 166, 175, 215, 268, 269.

Chapter Thirty-Seven: The CIA-Mafia Plots, Operation Mongoose, Plans to Invade, and the Cuban Missile Crisis

1. Evan Thomas, *Robert Kennedy: His Life* (New York: Simon & Schuster, 2000), pp. 148-152.

2. 1967 CIA Inspector General's Report, p. 104.

3. Richard D. Mahoney, *Sons & Brothers* (New York: Arcade, 1999), p. 175.

4. Warren Hinckle and William Turner, *The Fish Is Red* (New York: Harper & Row, 1981), p. 206.

5. David Arron Memorandum to Bill Miller, Fritz Schwarz, Curt Smothers, Bill Bader, Subject: Assassiantions—Castro, May 27, 1975, HSCA, cited in Mahoney, *op. cit.,* p. 175.

6. Mahoney, *op. cit.,* p. 175.

7. Evan Thomas, *Robert Kennedy,* p. 159

8. Gaeton Fonzi, *The Last Investigation* (New York: Thunder's Mouth, 1994), pp. 418.

9. Jefferson Morley, "Directorio Revolucionario Estudiantil (DRE) Cuban Student Directorate," *Washington Post,* January 2000, Cuban Information Archives.

10. Seymour M. Hersh, *The Dark Side of Camelot* (Boston: Little, Brown, 1997), p. 285.

11. *Ibid.,* p. 292.

12. *Ibid.,* pp. 292, 293.

13. *Ibid.,* p. 293.

14. David Corn, *Blond Ghost* (New York: Simon & Schuster, 1994), pp. 82, 83.

15. *Ibid.*

16. Thomas Powers, *The Man Who Kept the Secrets: Richard Helms & the CIA* (New York: Knopf, 1979), p. 162.

17. Paul Meskil, "How US Made Unholy Alliance with the Mafia," *New York Daily News* 4-23-75.

18. Powers, *op. cit.,* p. 162.

19. Mahoney, *op. cit.,* pp. 170, 171, 400.

20. Gaeton Fonzi, *The Last Investigation* (New York: Thunder's Mouth, 1994), pp. 418.

21. Edward Jay Epstein, *Legend: The Secret World of Lee Harvey Oswald* (New York: Reader's Digest Press, 1978), pp. 192, 193.

22. Fonzi, *op. cit.*, pp. 418.

Chapter Thirty-Eight: 1963: Targeting Castro and the Mob Targeting JFK

1. John H. Davis, *Mafia Kingfish* (New York: McGraw-Hill, 1989), pp. 123.

2. Many passages in G. Robert Blakey and Richard N. Billings, *The Plot to Kill the President* (New York: Times Books, 1981) and Frank Ragano and Selwyn Raab, *Mob Lawyer* (New York: Scribners, 1994).

3. Charles Rappleye and Ed Becker, *All American Mafioso* (New York: Barricade, 1995), several passages.

4. Ed Reid, *The Anatomy of Organized Crime in America: The Grim Reapers* (New York: Bantam, 1970), p. 187.

5. 6-18-64 CIA memo sent on 3-7-75 by the Assistant to the CIA Director to David Belin, Executive Director of the Rockefeller Commission (on CIA activities within the United States); Charles Nicoletti obituary UPI dispatch 3-30-77; Bradley Ayers, *The War that Never Was* (Canoga Park, Calif.: Major Books, 1979), pp. 36-38.

6. Dan E. Moldea, *The Hoffa Wars: Teamsters, Rebels, Politicians, and the Mob* (New York, SPI, 1993), pp. 153, 154. This wasn't the first time that that particular Ruby associate had been linked to the assassination of a government official. Moldea writes on p. 153 that "In 1947 . . . the [Chicago] police captain who instigated [an] indictment" of this Ruby associate for another murder "was found dead in his garage, his jaw torn off by a .45 caliber bullet." The original murder indictment "was dropped" after "two witnesses against" the Ruby associate "were murdered" and "two others refused to testify."

7. Ragano and Raab, *op. cit.*, p. 140.

8. *Ibid.*, pp. 140, 141.

9. *Ibid.*, pp. 132-133.

10. *Ibid.*, pp. 134, 135.

11. *Ibid.*, p. 135.

12. *Ibid.*, p. 136.

13. *Ibid.*, p. 141.

14. *Ibid.*

15. *Ibid.*, pp. 142, 143.

16. *Ibid.*

17. *Ibid.*, pp. 144, 145.

18. *Ibid.*, several passages,

19. Blakey and Billings, *op. cit.*

20. Ragano and Raab, *op. cit.*, pp. 144, 145.

21. *Ibid.*, pp. 147-149.

22. Gaeton Fonzi, *The Last Investigation* (New York: Thunder's Mouth, 1994), pp. 369-376.

23. Sworn affidavit by Bradley Ayers, 11-3-89, on file at the Assassinations Archives and Records Center.

24. "Chronology of Significant Documents in AMTRUNK File," 3-77, Russ Holmes Work File.

25. Richard D. Mahoney, *Sons & Brothers* (New York: Arcade, 1999), p. 268.

26. *Ibid.*

27. *Ibid.*, pp. 268, 269.

28. *Ibid.*, p. 124.

29. *Ibid.*, pp. 124, 125.

30. William Scott Malone, "The Secret Life of Jack Ruby," *New Times* 1-23-78.

31. Warren Hinckle and William Turner, *Deadly Secrets* (New York: Thunder's Mouth, 1992), p. 195.

32. David Wise and Thomas B. Ross, *The Invisible Government* (New York: Bantam, 1964), pp. 275, 276.

33. Fonzi, *op. cit.*, p. 419.

34. *Ibid.*

35. *Miami Herald*, 7-31-75, citing report provided by Senator George McGovern.

36. Michael Canfield and Alan J. Weberman, *Coup d'État in America: The CIA and the Assassination of John F. Kennedy* (New York: Third Press, 1975), p. 171.

37. Blakey and Billings, *op. cit.*, p. 303.

38. HSCA Vol. IX, p. 191.

39. Warren Hinckle and William Turner, *The Fish Is Red* (New York: Harper & Row, 1981), p. 169.

40. Mahoney, *op. cit.*, pp. 271-273.

Chapter Thirty-Nine: Someone to Take the Fall: Lee Harvey Oswald

1. Examples of this version of Oswald's life include the Warren Commission Report (1964) and Gerald L. Posner, *Case Closed: Lee Harvey Oswald and the Assassination of JFK* (New York: Random House, 1993).

2. John Newman, *Oswald and the CIA* (New York: Carroll & Graf, 1995); Sylvia Meagher, *Accessories After the Fact* (New York: Vintage, 1992); Anthony Summers, *Conspiracy* (New York: McGraw-Hill, 1980); and dozens of others.

3. Michael Benson, *Who's Who in the JFK Assassination: An A-to-Z Encyclopedia* (New York: Citadel, 1993), pp. 329, 330.

4. Robert Oswald testimony Warren Commisssion Vol. I, pp. 264-469; John Edward Pic testimony Warren Commission Vol. VIII, pp. 196-202; Greg Parker article 10-21-04.

5. Robert L. Oswald, "He was my brother," *Look* 10-17-67.

6. Herbert Philbrick, *I Led Three Lives* (New York: Grosset & Dunlap, 1952).

7. Roger M. Grace, "Channel 11 Loads Its Schedule with Syndicated Shows," *Metropolitan News-Enterprise* 1-22-2003.

8. Wesley Britton, "They were Communists for the FBI," August 2004; Britton also cites Daniel J. Leab, *I Was a Communist for the F.B.I.: The Unhappy Life and Times of Matt Cvetic* (University Park: Pennsylvania State University Press, 2000).

9. INCA promotional literature on file at the Assassination Archives and Research Center.

10. Anthony Summers, *Not In Your Lifetime* (New York: Marlowe & Co., 1998), p. 234.

11. *Ibid.*, p. 235.

12. Technically, one who preys on adolescents is an ephebophile; Ferrie also fits the definition of a pederast. However, we will use the term "pedophile" when referring to Ferrie, since that is the term most commonly used in the criminal justice system.

13. Sylvia Meagher, in collaboration with Gary Owens, *Master Index to the J. F. K. Assassination Investigations: The Reports and Supporting Volumes of the House Select Committee on Assassinations and the Warren Commission* (Metuchen, N.J.: Scarecrow Press, 1980), p. 363.

14. Summers, *Not in your Lifetime*, p. 234.

15. Anthony Summers, *Conspiracy* (New York: Paragon House, 1989), p. 61.

16. Summers, *Conspiracy* (McGraw-Hill, 1980), pp. 142, 296.

17. Summers, *Conspiracy* (Paragon House, 1989), pp. 122, 123.

18. Edward Jay Epstein, *Legend: The Secret World of Lee Harvey Oswald* (New York: Reader's Digest Press, 1978), pp. 71, 72.

19. Dick Russell, *The Man Who Knew Too Much* (New York: Carroll & Graf/R. Gallen, 1992), pp. 178, 179.

20. Henry Hurt, *Reasonable Doubt* (New York: Henry Holt, 1987), p. 243.

21. Michael Benson, *Who's Who in the JFK Assassination: An A-to-Z Encyclopedia* (New York: Citadel, 1993), p. 63.

22. Hurt, *op. cit.*, p. 243.

23. *Ibid.*

24. Russell, *op. cit.*, pp. 178, 179.

25. Summers, *Conspiracy* (Paragon House, 1989), p. 125.

26. Hurt, *op. cit.*, pp. 243, 244.

27. *Ibid.*, p. 245.

28. Russell, *op. cit.*, pp. 210, 716.

29. *Ibid.*, p. 200.

30. *Ibid.*, p. 202.

31. Benson, *op. cit.*, p. 335.

32. *Ibid.*

33. Russell, *op. cit.*, p. 212. Marina's proximity to the other defector should not be taken as an indication of any knowing intelligence activity on her part. In a police state like the Soviet Union at the time, subtle manipulation from friends or relatives is far more likely.

34. Phone interview with confidential Naval Intelligence investigator source 10-27-91; interview with confidential ex-Navy source; House Select Committee on Assassinations Vol. XI, pp. 539-551.

35. Douglas Waller, "The CIA's Secret Army," *Time* 2-3-03.

36. Epstein, *op. cit.*

37. *Ibid.*, pp. 192-195; Anthony Summers, *Not In Your Lifetime* (New York: Marlowe & Co., 1998), many passages.

38. House Select Committee on Assassinations Vol. XII, many passages.

39. Gaeton Fonzi, *The Last Investigation* (New York: Thunder's Mouth, 1994), p. 191.

40. Edward Jay Epstein, "Who Was Lee Harvey Oswald," *Wall Street Journal* 11-22-83, cited in Paul Hoch, "Echoes of a Conspiracy," 3-12-84.

41. Summers, *Not in Your Lifetime*, p. 167.

42. Warren Hinckle and William Turner, *Deadly Secrets* (New York: Thunder's Mouth, 1992), p. 193.

43. *Ibid.,* p. 194.

44. Russell, *op. cit.,* p. 381; Fonzi, *op. cit.,* pp. 186-194, 313. The authors want to make it clear that they in no way mean to imply that Edward Jay Epstein—or Gaeton Fonzi—had anything to do with the death of De Mohrenschildt.

45. Interview of James P. Kelly by Kevin Walsh, 12-11-79, on file at the Assassination Archives and Research Center.

46. HSCA outside contact report on Joseph Oster, 1-27-78, JFK document 005207; FBI 62-109060-4759 and CIA MFR 2.14.68 cited by A. J. Weberman.

47. Summers, *Conspiracy* (New York: Paragon House, 1989), pp. 382-384.

48. Church Committee Report, Vol. V, p. 91.

49. *New Orleans Times-Picayune* 3-17-55, p. 5, cited by Jerry Shinley, says that Johnson recently worked with Naval Intelligence. For Guy Johnson's continuing role with Naval Intelligence, see numerous Guy Banister files at the Assassination Archives and Research Center, many compiled by investigators for the New Orleans district attorney.

50. Rosselli's business parter who had produced *I Was a Communist for the FBI*—Byron Foy—would have been very much on Rosselli's mind at the time, even though they had had a falling-out years earlier. They hadn't spoken to each other since Rosselli had punched Foy because of an indiscretion. In 1963 Foy was producing a movie that was sure to have Rosselli's attention: *PT-109,* the story of John F. Kennedy's exploits during World War II.

51. Warren Commission Vol. 16, Exhibit 102, pp. 441-442. In these notes for a speech, Oswald also makes it clear that he doesn't want to be just a "pseudo-professional communist like Herbert Philbrick or [former Senator] Joe McCarthy." It's important to draw a distinction between what Philbrick did—befriend numerous people for years, only to turn on them in court—and what Oswald did. That may be yet another reason why Oswald avoided Communist party meetings in the US, because he saw befriending and developing close, personal relationships with people—only to betray those individuals, even for a good cause—as different from the type of undercover work he was doing. On a more practical level, in giving speeches like the one these notes were for, Oswald would have been competing with Philbrick for speaking engagements, so distinguishing himself from his competion would also make sense.

Chapter Forty: Three Oswald Riddles

1. Sylvia Meagher, *Accessories After the Fact* (New York: Vintage, 1992); Anthony Summers, *Conspiracy* (New York: McGraw-Hill, 1980); Henry Hurt, *Reasonable Doubt* (New York: Henry Holt, 1987); George Michael Evica, *And We Are All Mortal: New Evidence and Analysis in the John F. Kennedy Assassination* (West Hartford, Conn.: Evica, 1978), Peter Dale Scott, *Deep Politics and the Death of JFK* (Berkeley: University of California Press, 1993).

2. Hurt, *op. cit.,* pp. 300-302.

3. Evica, *op. cit.,* p. 253.

4. *The Final Assassinations Report* by the House Select Committee on Assassinations (New York: Bantam, 1979), p. 643.

5. Hurt, *op. cit.,* pp. 300-302.

6. *Ibid.;* Dr. George Michael Evica, "And We Are All Still Mortal," *Assassination Chronicles,* March 1996.

7. Dr. George Michael Evica, "And We Are All Still Mortal," *Assassination Chronicles,* March 1996.

8. Paul Hoch, "Echoes of a Conspiracy," 11-30-77.

9. Scott, *Deep Politics,* pp. 248, 249.

10. Dr. George Michael Evica, "And We Are All Still Mortal," *Assassination Chronicles,* March 1996.

11. Meagher, *op. cit.,* p. 101; A&E JFK documentary 11-03.

12. Meagher, *op. cit.,* p. 105. Some might have the same serial number with a different letter prefix.

13. Dick Russell, *The Man Who Knew Too Much* (New York: Carroll & Graf/R. Gallen, 1992), p. 718.

14. *Ibid.,* pp. 718, 719.

15. Summers, *Conspiracy* (Paragon House, 1989), pp. 205-217.

16. *Washington Post* 7-9-76, cited in Bernard Fensterwald, Jr. and Michael Ewing, *Coincidence or Conspiracy?* (New York: Kensington, 1977), pp. 571, 581.

17. Anthony Summers, *Not In Your Lifetime* (New York: Marlowe & Co., 1998), p. 167.

18. Anthony Summers, *Conspiracy* (New York: Paragon House, 1989), pp. 216, 217.

19. Scott, *Deep Politics,* p. 114.

20. *New Orleans Times-Picayune* 3-23-56 and 3-31-56, cited by J. P. Shinley.

21. *Castro's Network in the United States (Fair Play for Cuba Committee)* Hearings, Judiciary Committee, Part 1, 2-14-63.

22. *Ibid.*

23. John Newman, *Oswald and the CIA* (New York: Carroll & Graf, 1995), pp. 274-276.

24. Russell, *op. cit.,* p. 719.

25. *Ibid.,* p. 274.

26. Newman, *op. cit.*, pp. 243, 244.

27. HSCA Vol. XI, p. 65, cited in Scott, *Deep Politics*, p. 116.

Chapter Forty-One: David Atlee Phillips and Fair Play for Cuba, Marcello and Oswald, Oswald and Gilberto Lopez

1. Anthony and Robbyn Summers, "The Ghosts of November," *Vanity Fair*, December 1994, p. 139.

2. Joseph B. Smith, *Portrait of a Cold Warrior* (New York: Ballantine, 1981), pp. 229, 230.

3. *Ibid.*, p. 339.

4. Article by Lisa Pease in *Probe*, Vol. 3 No. 3, March-April 1996.

5. John Newman, *Oswald and the CIA* (New York: Carroll & Graf, 1995), pp. 95, 236, 240-244.

6. *Ibid.*

7. James DiEugenio, *Destiny Betrayed: JFK, Cuba, and the Garrison Case* (New York: Sheridan Square Press, 1992), pp. 218-220.

8. *Ibid.* Researcher Paul Hoch notes that Oswald had apparently ordered copies of the pamphlet in his own handwriting. That is what one would expect of an asset like Oswald, trying to maintain his cover. However, we feel that Oswald had apparently distributed or used all of the fourth-printing pamphlets he would have received from his order (there are reports of earlier pamphlet/flyer distribution efforts that did not result in any arrest). Then, Oswald was given additional pamphlets by someone who did not notice the fine print showing they were from the first printing that had sold out long before Oswald returned to the US. The CIA had ordered and received copies of the first printing at a time when David Phillips was running operations against the FPCC, and testimony links Phillips to Banister after that, so we feel it's likely that that's how Oswald obtained the first-printing pamphlets he was distributing in August 1963 while he was working for Banister, just prior to Oswald's meeting with Phillips.

9. DiEugenio, *op. cit.*, pp. 218-220.

10. Anthony and Robbyn Summers, "The Ghosts of November," *Vanity Fair*, December 1994, p. 132.

11. Officially transcribed Warren Commission meeting notes, 1-27-64, in Harold Weisberg, with legal analysis by Jim Lesar, *Whitewash IV: Top Secret JFK Assassination Transcript* (Frederick, Md.: Weisberg, 1974).

12. Several chapters in David Atlee Phillips, *Secret Wars Diary* (Bethesda, Md.: Stone Trail Press, 1989).

13. Anthony and Robbyn Summers, "The Ghosts of November," *Vanity Fair*, December 1994.

14. John H. Davis, *Mafia Kingfish* (New York: McGraw-Hill, 1989), p. 123.

15. *Ibid.*, pp. 119, 120.

16. FBI Airtel 10-30-61, declassified 2-14-86.

17. Davis, *Mafia Kingfish* (McGraw-Hill, 1989), pp. 120, 121.

18. *Ibid.*, p. 434.

19. 12-4-63 "secret" "classified message" from the office of CIA Director John McCone (though signed by Richard Helms) about the Tampa suspect and not wanting "to blow the [censored] operation," declassified 4-6-94, Document ID 1994.04.06.10:28:12:530005; censored 4-30-64 Warren Commission memo Document Number 674-279 (much of the information about the Tampa suspect—from the CIA, FBI, and the many other agencies with an interest in him, like Naval Intelligence—is heavily censored and was even withheld from the House Select Committee on Assassinations).

20. Phone interview with Blanche Andrea Leon 3/2/96. Warren Commission Document 205; Church Committee Report Vol. V, pp. 30, 61-63; House Select Committee on Assassinations Report, pp. 118-121.

21. Phone interview with Blanche Andrea Leon 3/2/96; Warren Commission Report and volumes, many passages.

22. 1967 CIA Inspector General's Report, p. 104; Phone interview with Blanche Andrea Leon 3/2/96; Joseph J. Trento, *Prelude to Terror: The Rogue CIA, and the Legacy of America's Private Intelligence Network* (New York: Carroll & Graf, 2005), p. 29.

23. Tim Gratz and Mark Howell, "The Strange Flight of Gilbert Lopez," *Key West Citizen* 11-20-03.

Chapter Forty-Two: Targeting Harry Williams

1. Richard D. Mahoney, *Sons & Brothers* (New York: Arcade, 1999), p. 270.

2. The authors want to make it clear that doesn't necessarily mean the leaders of the Junta or the DRE knew that their group was receiving money from the Mafia, since it would usually be funneled through seemingly legitimate channels (like an employer).

3. Interview with Harry Williams 4-92.

4. *New York Times* 6-18-72 p. 11, 6-27-72 p. 43, 7-13-72 p. 9, first cited in A. J. Weberman Web book (http://www.ajweberman.com/coupt5.htm) chapter 21.

5. Henrik Krüger, *The Great Heroin Coup* (Boston: South End Press, 1980), p. 161; A. J. Weberman web book (http://www.ajweberman.com/coupt5.htm) chapter 21.

6. Warren Hinckle and William Turner, *Deadly Secrets* (New York: Thunder's Mouth, 1992), pp. 355, 356, 363, 389, 399; *Miami Herald* 8-17-73; *San Francisco Chronicle* 6-6-74, 11-26-75.

7. HSCA Vol. X, pp. 105-132.

Chapter Forty-Three: The French Connection Heroin Network and the Plan to Kill JFK

1. CIA 1993.08.05.12:35:37:460006, declassified 8-5-93 (more heavily censored versions were being released as late as 1998). It's often overlooked that this one page was item #8 from a longer document that appears to still be classified. Also, while some FBI follow-up documents from the resulting Jean Souetre investigation have been released, almost no follow-up documents on the FBI and CIA investigations of Mertz have been released (aside from a few FBI documents regarding airline passengers named Mertz).

2. Phone interview by Gary Shaw with *Newsday* reporter Robert Greene 4-17-79.

3. Memorandum by Bernard Fensterwald, submitted to the US Justice Department 7-13-82 as part of a FOIA request.

4. Recent accounts indicate that one possible outcome of the warning Peres gave de Gaulle in 1959 was help from the grateful de Gaulle in developing the Israeli nuclear program.

5. The Staff and Editors of *Newsday, The Heroin Trail* (New York: Signet, 1974), pp. 109-118; Memorandum by Bernard Fensterwald, submitted to the US Justice Department 7-13-82.

6. Pierre Galante and Louis Sapin, *The Marseilles Mafia: The Truth Behind the World of Drug Trafficking* (London: W. H. Allen, 1979), p. 53

7. Memorandum by Bernard Fensterwald, submitted to the US Justice Department 7-13-82.

8. Douglas Valentine, *The Strength of the Wolf: The Secret History of America's War on Drugs* (London, New York: Verso, 2004), p. 327.

9. Ronald Goldfarb, *Perfect Villains, Imperfect Heroes: Robert F. Kennedy's War Against Organized Crime* (New York: Random House, 1995), p. 139.

10. Valentine, *op. cit.,* p. 327.

11. *New York Times* 4-5-63, 4-12-63

12. CIA 104-10434-10381, declassified 11-19-98.

13. CIA 1994.03.11.16:03:49:940005, declassified 3-11-94.

14. CIA 1994.04.06.10:53:49:400005, declassified 4-6-94.

15. CIA 1994.03.11.16:03:49:940005, declassified 3-11-94.

16. CIA Office of Security Varona File Summary, Record Number 180-10144-10405, declassified 8-23-95.

17. CIA 104-10431-10050.

18. Interview of James P. Kelly by Kevin Walsh, 12-11-79.

19. Notes regarding James P. Kelly, on file at the Assassination Archives and Research Center.

20. CIA 1994.04.06.10:47:29:710005.

21. H. P. Albarelli, Jr., *The Mysterious Death of CIA Scientist Frank Olson* (http://crimemagazine.com/olson2.htm), 12-14-02.

22. CIA 1994.03.11.16:03:49:940005, declassified 3-11-94.

23. CIA 104-10431-10050.

24. CIA 1994.04.06.10:53:49:400005, declassified 4-6-94.

25. CIA 1994.04.06.10:53:49:400005, declassified 4-6-94.

26. 1967 CIA Inspector General's Report; U.S. Senate, Select Committee to Study Governmental Operations with Respect to Intelligence Activities, *Alleged Assassination Plots Involving Foreign Leaders* (New York: Norton, 1976), p. 182.

27. CIA 1994.04.06.10:53:49:400005, declassified 4-6-94.

28. Senate Church Committee Report, *Alleged Assassination Plots Involving Foreign Leaders* (New York: Norton, 1976), p. 184.

29. CIA 1993.07.15.15:07:34:780340.

30. Senate Church Committee Report, *Alleged Assassination Plots Involving Foreign Leaders* (New York: Norton, 1976), p. 184.

31. *Ibid.,* p. 182.

32. CIA 1994.03.11.16:07:16:500005.

33. CIA 104-10431-10050.

34. CIA 1994.03.11.16:03:49:940005, declassified 3-11-94.

35. H. P. Albarelli, Jr., *The Mysterious Death of CIA Scientist Frank Olson* (http://crimemagazine.com/olson2.htm), 12-14-02.

36. Richard D. Mahoney, *Sons & Brothers* (New York: Arcade, 1999), pp. 92, 93.

37. CIA 1994.03.11.16:07:16:500005.

38. CIA 1994.03.11.16:05:55:410005.

39. CIA 1994.03.11.16:05:55:410005.

40. Twenty-four parallels between QJWIN and Michel Mertz (lettered A-X):

A. According to Helms, QJWIN was capable of murder, while other testimony described him as a man of few scruples, capable of anything including assassination. Mertz began his reputation as a cold-blooded killer during World War II, killing Germans (he once machine-gunned 15 as they sat in a cafe). His reputation as a cold-blooded killer continued during his service for French Intelligence and the Corsican mob in the 1950s. Even into the 1980s, researchers were warned that just trying to talk to Mertz could prove fatal.

B. QJWIN suspected of Nazi collaboration in France during World War II. Mertz was a Nazi collaborator in France during World War II, until the tide of war started to turn against the Nazis.

C. William Harvey's notes recommend using former French Resistance personnel, and QJWIN was in the Resistance from 1943 to 1945. Mertz was a decorated member of the French Resistance in World War II.

D. In 1960, QJWIN was recruited in Frankfurt, Germany. QJWIN was originally approached "in connection with an illegal narcotics operation into the US." Michel Mertz frequently visited Frankfurt (he made 5 documented visits to Frankfurt in 1962 and 1963). Also, Mertz is one of the primary "French Connection" heroin smugglers into the US.

E. In November 1960, QJWIN was in the Congo, working for the CIA. In addition, QJWIN was supposed to go to another African nation for an unspecified mission. Some of Lumumba's UN guards were from Morocco, and Mertz had previously worked extensively in Morocco for French Intelligence—so that may explain why CIA officials in the Congo thought QJWIN might be able to get to Lumumba (in fact, a Moroccan guard reported Lumumba's escape that eventually led his to death).

F. In late December 1960, QJWIN finished his mission for the CIA in the Congo and returned to Europe. Mertz resumed working on his heroin smuggling operation (January 1961) only after QJWIN had finished his mission in the Congo.

G. In February 1961, according to a CIA document, QJWIN visited Switzerland and Italy. Mertz frequently visited Switzerland, since his illegal profits were deposited in the bank accounts of himself and his wife there. Since he was preparing to run a carload (220 pounds) of heroin into the US in early March 1961, it's logical that he would make preparations to handle the money in Switzerland prior to that.

H. On March 31, 1961, QJWIN was in Frankfurt, Germany. On March 27, 1961, Mertz returned to Paris from the US, where he'd smuggled a carload of heroin into New York City. Thus, Mertz was just a few hours away from Frankfurt, a city he often visited.

I. On March 31, 1961, the CIA gave QJWIN a lie detector test to see if he was "presently working for" another coutry's intelligence service—and he wasn't. However, the same document establishes that QJWIN had worked in the past for French Intelligence (and Luxembourg, Belgium, and West Germany). Prior to that time, Mertz had done work for French Intelligence, the SDECE. And Mertz was just getting ready to do more work for the SDECE (his assignment was to start in April). However, at the time in question, Mertz was not actually working for the SDECE.

J. QJWIN, on March 31, 1961, said he was known to French and Belgian police departments in connection with his illegal business transactions, and engaged in some activities concerning Belgium. Mertz, though based in France, frequently traveled through Belgium for his illegal activities. Mertz often traveled to the US via Brussels, and even received a US Visa in Belgium on October 7, 1964.

K. March 1961 CIA document that says QJWIN is a citizen of Luxembourg. The town where Mertz was born and raised, Waldvisse, France, is on the border with Luxembourg. Mertz used a variety of aliases and passports from different countries (he even had a US passport), and the fact that he spoke perfect German in addition to French (the two major languages of Luxembourg), coupled with his growing up next to Luxembourg, would have made it easy for him to pass as a Luxembourg citizen. And using this nationality in documents would be a good way of "backstopping" the QJWIN documents, as Harvey had outlined, to help obscure QJWIN's identity. Though QJWIN is supposed to be a Luxembourg citizen, QJWIN's monthly salary (at least for 1963, for which there are many monthly records) is paid through Paris—where Mertz lives—not Luxembourg.

L. QJWIN had a wife during the early 1960s. Also, the wife must have been someone of significiance, since CIA documents make references to her, which is very unusual (offhand, the authors can't recall seeing another agent's wife referred to in the many thousands of pages of declassified documents we've seen). She is also referred to as "extremely discreet." She is aware of QJWIN's unsavory activities. She even has her own bank account, which is used for one large payment to QJWIN. This would make sense for Mertz, since his wife was the daughter of one of the most powerful Canadian and French mob bosses and brothel owners, Charles Martel. Later law enforcement investigations showed that she maintained her own bank accounts, which were used to launder large drug payments.

M. In December 1961/January 1962, QJWIN began working on establishing cover for the CIA operations. Mertz had finished with his assignment for the French SDECE a couple of months earlier and would have been free to begin this assginment for the CIA.

N. In 1962, QJWIN was supposed to go on trial in Europe on smuggling charges. But the CIA somehow intervenes and a trial is never held. Considering that CIA documents indicate that QJWIN had worked for the French, Luxembourg, Belgian, and West German intelligence services, it's not clear why QJWIN would need the assistance of the American CIA instead of using his own influence with one of the European intelligence agencies he'd worked for. One of Mertz's French

Connection heroin shipments was busted in New York City in January 1962. An arrest was made in the US of a French citizen and the shipment was traced back to France (and to Mertz's group), but no trials were ever held in France in connection with the bust. Since the original bust had occurred in the US, it's logical to assume that the French government would have to have the concurrence of some US agency in order to let the investigation drop. In this case, it could have been the CIA protecting Mertz.

O. QJWIN's contract was terminated in April 1964. In March 1964, Mertz's name surfaced in a US document as allegedly being in Dallas on the day of the assassination. Also, an article had appeared in France in late February 1964 about the Mertz/Soutre/Roux incident, which had prompted an investigation of Mertz/Soutre/Roux by French officials (who urged US officials to do the same). Thus, the CIA could have had every interest in terminating QJWIN (if he was Mertz) to avoid an embarrassing connection to the assassination.

P. At the time of his termination in April 1964, QJWIN had received clearances to go ahead with a business venture involving a "shop" of some sort in Cologne, Germany. Mertz had a history of opening a wide variety of "cover" businesses, such as a New York company that arranged rebuilding of engines for the French military; a company in Columbus, Ohio; and an automotive company in New Jersey. Mertz had some tie to Cologne, as he arrived there, from New York, on June 19, 1963.

Q. William Harvey's notes recommend using Corsicans, since "Sicilians could lead to the Mafia." Mertz was part of the French Corsican Mafia, though not Corsican himself (the same way the Jewish Jack Ruby worked for the Mafia).

R. William Harvey notes recommend use of "Silverthorne" and his "stable in Paris." Silverthorne (whom some researchers believe to be the CIA's Arnold Silver) is later part of QJWIN's recruitment. Mertz's main base of activity at the time was Paris.

S. QJWIN suggested to Harvey that leaders of a gambling syndicate in the Middle East had a "pool of assassins." Mertz worked for French Intelligence in Turkey and Morocco, and was part of the Corsican mob, so this would be a logical thing for him to say.

T. Someone dealing with QJWIN was supposedly 44 years old as of March 31, 1961, according to one CIA document. Mertz (DOB April 20, 1920) was almost 41 at that time, and one of his main "cover identities"—Maurice Valentin—would have been 46 at that time (the fake DOB for Valentin was February 3, 1915). Thus, the age given for QJWIN is within the range of ages that Mertz could pass for.

U. February 19, 1962: Richard Helms authorized Harvey to use QJWIN through the end of the year. Mertz was in the US from January 11, 1962 until February 25, 1962, so it would have been possible for him to meet with William Harvey during this time, which could have resulted in Helms's authorization.

V. QJWIN was applied to the ZR/RIFLE assassination program in 1962 and 1963, under William Harvey; the primary focus of Harvey during that time was assassinating Castro. This would make sense for Mertz, since he had close French associates who maintained ties to Cuba after Castro took over and the American gangsters were expelled. Peter Dale Scott's *Crime and Cover-up* and Congressional hearings name these as Ansan Albert Bistoni, Jean Baptiste Croce, and Paul Damien Mondoloni. All had nightclub interests in Havana circa 1963, and it's unclear when, if ever, Castro forced them to leave.

W. On March 6, 1963, Richard Helms authorized QJWIN's activities through the end of 1963. Just one week earlier, on February 27, 1963, Mertz was able to get a passport renewal in New York City, despite his long criminal record. It's unclear whether this was a US passport or a French passport.

X. QJWIN's identity is still being kept classified, 40 years after his CIA activity, and his activity was obscured from even the Church Committee and the HSCA. This is despite the fact that several former employees of the CIA that were still alive could have easily identified WIN for either committee—and that senators like Gary Hart were very suspicious about the possible connections between QJWIN and the JFK assassination. Two reasons for the CIA to keep WIN's identity secret would be that WIN is either still alive (though according to one file, he would have to be over 100 years old), or that revealing his identity would prove an embarrassment to the CIA. Mertz was alive until 1995, though news of his death was kept quiet for several years. Also, Mertz's later drug conviction for the bust at Fort Benning—and his alleged presence in Dallas on the day of the assassination—could prove extremely problematic for the CIA.

41. Background report on the travels of Mertz, with dates and places of entry and exit from the US, Bud Fensterwald Mertz files at the Assassination Archives and Research Center.

42. Memorandum by Bernard Fensterwald, submitted to the US Justice Department 7-13-82.

43. Army Intelligence memos on the Cuban Officer Training Program prepared by 112th Intelligence Corps Group, San Antonio, Tex., 11-1-63, cited in Larry Hancock, *Someone Would Have Talked* (Southlake, Tex.: JFK Lancer, 2003).

44. French informant letters to Bud Fensterwald 10-9-81 and 1-11-82, on file at the Assassination Archives and Research Center.

45. Richard Deacon, *The French Secret Service* (London: Grafton, 1990), pp. 194-198.

46. Valentine, *op. cit.*, p. 270.

47. Andrew Tully, *CIA: The Inside Story* (New York: William Morrow, 1962), pp. 45-53.

48. Memorandum by Bernard Fensterwald, submitted to the US Justice Department 7-13-82.

49. "De Gaulle Plot Reported," UPI in *Dallas Morning News* 6-15-75.

50. CIA 104-10419-10342.

51. Memorandum by Bernard Fensterwald, submitted to the US Justice Department 7-13-82.

52. Dick Russell, *The Man Who Knew Too Much* (New York: Carroll & Graf/R. Gallen, 1992), p. 292.

53. Warren Commission Exhibits 1761, 1762, 3058-3062.

54. Valentine, *op. cit.*, p. 230.

55. The Staff and Editors of *Newsday, The Heroin Trail* (New York: Signet, 1974), p. 152; Jean-Pierre Charbonneau, *The Canadian Connection* (Ottawa: Optimum, 1976), pp. 47, 262; Norman Garett, "Across the Border," *Hush-Up* magazine 9-55.

56. Gary Shaw phone interviews with former INS officials Virgil Bailey (4-26-80, 4-28-80) and Hal Norwood (4-28-80).

57. US Treasury Dept. letter to US Secret Service by Senior Customs Representative Aurelien Chasse, 11-29-63.

58. Anthony Summers, *Conspiracy* (New York: Paragon House, 1989), p. 304; French informant letters to Bud Fensterwald 10-9-81 and 1-11-82, on file at the Assassination Archives and Research Center.

59. Russell, *op. cit.*, p. 562.

Chapter Forty-Four: Oswald and the Summer of 1963

1. (Bishop) Gaeton Fonzi, *The Last Investigation* (New York: Thunder's Mouth, 1994), pp. 306-309. (Choaden) According to Peter Dale Scott in *Deep Politics III*, "'M.C. Choaden' has been identified by ARRB (Assassination Records Review Board) staff as David Phillips." (Scott goes on to say that "the identity of [Lawrence F.] 'Barker' with Phillips is revealed by comparing the role of 'Barker' in the CIA cable reporting the Eldon Hensen story [MEXI 5448 of 20 July 1963; NARA #104-10015-10044; PS #66-14] with Phillips's first-person narration of it [*The Night Watch*, 126-28].")

2. According to a 6-3-64 FBI report at the National Archives, a "source . . . in the New Orleans area advised on May 28, 1963, that the DRE has to his knowledge no members in New Orleans but . . . a single delegate, namely Carlos Bringuier." Another FBI "source reported in 1963 that the only activity of the DRE at New Orleans was carried on by Carlos Bringuier." Both "added that the activities of the" DRE "in New Orleans in 1963 were limited to propaganda-type efforts of Carlos Bringuier . . . in any available channel of the news media." (From the Odio files of Paul Hoch.) While other members may have joined the New Orleans DRE from time to time, it was in any event a very small organization in 1963.

3. Jefferson Morley, "What Jane Roman Said," *Washington Post* (http://mcadams.posc.mu.edu/morley1.htm), 2003.

4. Morley, *op. cit.*

5. *Ibid.*

6. 6-3-64 FBI report at the National Archives.

7. Warren Commission Vol. XX, pp. 524, 525, cited in Dick Russell, *The Man Who Knew Too Much* (New York: Carroll & Graf/R. Gallen, 1992), pp. 391, 392.

8. Paris Flammonde, *The Kennedy Conspiracy* (New York: Meredith Press, 1969), p. 22; Russell, *op. cit.*, p. 721.

9. Russell, *op. cit.*, p. 721.

10. John H. Davis, *Mafia Kingfish* (New York: McGraw-Hill, 1989), p. 128.

11. *Ibid.*, p. 129, citing testimony of Dean Andrews.

12. The CIA would have originally ordered the pamphlets openly for two reasons: 1. To avoid an accusation of domestic spying. 2. To avoid having to rely on or tell the FBI about the CIA's current operations using the FPCC; Phillips had initially avoided telling the FBI about his FPCC operation in the winter of 1961. Usually, when the CIA wanted to obtain something like the pamplets surreptitiously, it would have ask the FBI to stage a "black bag" job and steal them, according to other CIA and FBI documents from 1963.

13. WDSU news footage, 8-23-63 cited in Oliver Stone and Zachary Sklar, *JFK: The Book of the Film* (New York: Applause Books, 1992), p. 35.

14. *Ibid.*

15. Russell, *op. cit.*, p. 391.

16. G. Robert Blakey and Richard N. Billings, *The Plot to Kill the President* (New York: Times Books, 1981), p. 342; Anthony Summers, *Conspiracy* (New York: McGraw-Hill, 1980), p. 341, which says that according "to an FBI report," the Pecora associate "contacted 'someone else' who arranged Oswald's release."

17. WDSU news footage, 8-23-63 cited in Stone and Sklar, *op. cit.*, p. 35.

18. John Newman, *Oswald and the CIA* (New York: Carroll & Graf, 1995), p. 337.

19. Russell, *op. cit.*, p. 400.

20. Russell, *op. cit.*, p. 401.

21. WDSU news footage, 8-23-63 cited in Stone and Sklar, *op. cit.*, p. 36.

22. Anthony Summers, *Not In Your Lifetime* (New York: Marlowe & Co., 1998), p. 216, 217.

23. INCA was a far-right group that produced anti-Communist propaganda primarily for distribution throughout Latin America, and it had numerous ties to US intelligence. The chairman of INCA was Alton Ochsner, a very prominent New Orleans

doctor who numbered among his friends the personal physician of Luis Somoza, the strongman of Nicaragua (where Artime had some of his C-Day bases). Both Somoza and his physician were part of the Anti-Communist League of the Caribbean, the group Guy Banister worked for (INCA file, from the Assassination Archives and Research Center; James DiEugenio, *Destiny Betrayed: JFK, Cuba, and the Garrison Case* [New York: Sheridan Square Press, 1992], p. 216.) One researcher found "an undercover agent and investigator employed by Guy Banister" who "confirmed that Banister and Ochsner did know each other well" (Edward T. Haslam, *Mary, Ferrie & the Monkey Virus* [Albuquerque: Wordsworth, 1995], p. 162). According to Dr. Ochsner's son, the doctor also knew David Ferrie (Interview with Alton Ochsner, Jr. by A. J. Weberman, April 1993, cited at www.ajweberman.com.)

Four other people notable in Oswald's life would also be involved with INCA. One writer found that "William Reily of Reily Coffee Company, where Oswald worked that summer, also donated funds" to INCA (DiEugenio, *op. cit.*, p. 217). Soon to be a member of the "INCA International Advisory Committee" was none other than Herbert Philbrick, of *I Led Three Lives*. Another member of the committee would be Alberto Fowler, a Bay of Pigs veteran who contacted Harry Williams right after JFK's assassination, in an attempt to get the August 1963 TV footage of Oswald on NBC (INCA file, from the Assassination Archives and Research Center). Dr. Ochsner sponsored a small newspaper about Latin America, and its editor—William G. Gaudet, an admitted CIA asset—would soon be monitoring Oswald as part of the "tight surveillance" of Oswald (Peter Dale Scott, *Crime and Cover-Up: The CIA, the Mafia, and the Dallas-Watergate Connection* [Santa Barbara, Calif.: Open Archive Press, 1993], p. 15.)

In addition, Peter Dale Scott notes that "at least three of INCA's backers and Cuban employees had previously been associated with the CIA-backed Cuban Revolutionary Council at 544 Camp Street" (Scott, *Crime and Cover-Up*, p. 15). Again, most of those involved with INCA or Oswald's radio debate simply saw it as another chance to expose a Communist.

24. Warren Commission Vol. X, p. 34.

25. E. Howard Hunt deposition, November 3, 1978, document #180-10131-10342, declassified 2-9-96, cited by *Fair Play* magazine.

26. Larry Hancock, *Someone Would Have Talked* (Southlake, Tex.: JFK Lancer, 2003), p. 6.

27. Summers, *Not In Your Lifetime*, p. 216.

28. Warren Commission Vol XIX, pp. 175, 176.

29. Morley, *op. cit.*

30. Gaeton Fonzi, *The Last Investigation* (New York: Thunder's Mouth, 1994), p. 325.

31. Dan E. Moldea, *The Hoffa Wars: Teamsters, Rebels, Politicians, and the Mob* (New York, SPI, 1993), p. 161.

32. Memorandum by Douglas Ward, December 30, 1966, on file at the Assassination Archives and Research Center.

33. Richard D. Mahoney, *Sons & Brothers* (New York: Arcade, 1999), p. 229.

34. "David Ferrie and Friends," File 111NPH, from the Assassination Archives and Research Center.

35. Summary of interviews with former Banister investigator on 4-12-68, 4-16-68, 4-17-68 by Barbara Reid, on file at the Assassination Archives and Research Center.

36. Guy Banister file index notes, on file at the Assassination Archives and Research Center.

37. Henry Hurt, *Reasonable Doubt* (New York: Henry Holt, 1987), p. 290.

38. "Guy Banister—Notes from New Orleans Investigation," 8-16-78 interview with Chief Investigator, on file at the Assassination Archives and Research Center.

39. Summers, *Not In Your Lifetime*, pp. 210-212.

40. Newman, *op. cit.*, p. 347.

41. Memo by Bud Fensterwald on file at the Assassinations Archives & Records Center.

42. Mahoney, *op. cit.*, p. 229.

43. Morley, *op. cit.*

44. Presentation by Jefferson Morley, JFK Lancer Conference.

45. Morley, "What Jane Roman Said."

46. Jefferson Morley, "Celebrated Authors Demand that the CIA Come Clean on JFK Assassination," Salon.com, 12-17-03.

47. E-mail from Jefferson Morley, 1-30-05.

48. Warren Commission Exhibit #2650.

Chapter Forty-Five: Oswald and David Atlee Phillips: His Next Assignment

1. Gaeton Fonzi, *The Last Investigation* (New York: Thunder's Mouth, 1994), p. 421.

2. Joseph B. Smith, *Portrait of a Cold Warrior* (New York: Ballantine, 1981), p. 329.

3. Donald Freed with Fred Simon Landis, *Death in Washington: The Murder of Orlando Letelier* (Westport, Conn.: Lawrence Hill, 1980), p. 40.

4. Anthony and Robbyn Summers, "The Ghosts of November," *Vanity Fair*, December 1994, p. 139.

5. Richard D. Mahoney, *Sons & Brothers* (New York: Arcade, 1999), p. 229.

6. Warren Commission Vol. VIII, pp. 228-265.

7. For example, Gerald L. Posner, *Case Closed* (New York: Random House, 1993), p. 20.

8. Sylvia Meagher, *Accessories After the Fact* (New York: Vintage, 1992), p. 107.

9. Warren Commission Document #1546, p. 213.

10. NARA 124-10158-10186; Warren Commission Document #1546.

11. Warren Commission Vol. XI, pp. 367-389.

12. Gaeton Fonzi, *The Last Investigation* (New York: Thunder's Mouth, 1994), pp. 111-115; Gaeton Fonzi interview with Silvia Odio 1-16-76, for the Senate Church Committee.

13. Gaeton Fonzi interview with Silvia Odio 1-16-76, for the Senate Church Committee.

14. E-mail from Paul Hoch 1-14-98: The edited version of Odio's testimony is at Warren Commission Vol. II, p. 378l; In later questioning in that session, Odio said February (1964), but Hoch thinks that Odio's first reponse was the most accurate.

Chapter Forty-Six: Oswald in Mexico City: A CIA Operation Compromised

1. John Newman, *Oswald and the CIA* (New York: Carroll & Graf, 1995), p. 356.

2. *New York Times* 11-26-63.

3. Sylvia Meagher, *Accessories After the Fact* (New York: Vintage, 1992), pp. 313, 314; citing *New York Post* 11-25-63 and *New York Herald-Tribune* 11-26-63. Meagher points out that the Warren Commission affidavits on the issue by the two men don't resolve it.

4. Officially transcribed Warren Commission meeting notes, 1-27-64, in Harold Weisberg, with legal analysis by Jim Lesar, *Whitewash IV* (Frederick, Md.: Weisberg, 1974); Warren Commission Document #751.

5. Larry Hancock interview of FBI Agent James Hosty.

6. Newman, *op. cit.*, p. 352.

7. *Ibid.*, p. 358.

8. *HSCA: Lee Harvey Oswald, the CIA in Mexico City* (the Lopez Report), declassified 1993, p. 128; Newman, *op. cit.*, p. 389.

9. CIA 104-10098-10093, 10-31-63, declassified 6-20-96, "Dispatch: AMWORLD - Safehouse."

10. Peter Dale Scott, *Deep Politics III*, http://history-matters.com/pds/dp3.htm.

11. *Ibid.*

12. David Atlee Phillips, *The Night Watch* (New York: Atheneum, 1977), pp. 11, 114, 116, 123, 126.

13. Newman, *op. cit.*

14. Newman, *op. cit.*, p. 354.

15. Anthony Summers, *Not In Your Lifetime* (New York: Marlowe & Co., 1998), pp. 276, 277.

16. Newman, *op. cit.*, p. 356.

17. Newman, *op. cit.*, p. 369.

18. *Washington Post* 3-17-96

19. Gaeton Fonzi, *The Last Investigation* (New York: Thunder's Mouth, 1994), p. 295.

20. *HSCA: Lee Harvey Oswald, the CIA in Mexico City* (the Lopez Report), declassified 1993, pp. 91, 107.

21. Scott, *Deep Politics III*.

22. Jefferson Morley, "What Jane Roman Said," *Washington Post* (http://mcadams.posc.mu.edu/morley1.htm), 2003.

23. *Ibid.*

24. *Ibid.*

25. Interviews with Mike Cain about his upcoming book on Richard Cain.

26. Charles Rappleye and Ed Becker, *All American Mafioso* (New York: Barricade, 1995), p. 178.

27. Interviews with Mike Cain about his upcoming book on Richard Cain.

28. Scott, *Deep Politics III*.

29. CIA memo for Director of Security, subject: Cain, Richard Scully, 12-19-69, declassified 1992.

30. CIA memo for Chief, Western Hemisphere Division, 1-10-74, declassified 1994.

31. HSCA 180-10144-10405, declassified 8-23-95.

32. 9-25-63 CIA memo about 9-12-63 CIA call about Cain and the DRE.

33. CIA memo for Director of Security, subject: Cain, Richard Scully, 12-19-69, declassified 1992.

34. CIA memo 9-23-63, 1993.08.02.15:28:19:750028, declassified 8-2-93.

35. Scott, *Deep Politics III*.

36. *Ibid.*

37. CIA record number 104-10125-10239, "Mr. Phillips will arrive", 10/4/63, declassified 8/11/93; CIA record number 104-10100-10134, "Arrival of David Phillips C/Cuba Ops for Consultation," 10/4/63, declassified 3/7/94.

38. Paul Hoch, "Echoes of a Conspiracy," 7-22-88.

39. 10-27-91 and 12-9-91 phone interviews with Naval Intelligence surveillance source.

40. *Ibid.*

41. *Ibid.*

42. *Ibid.*

43. Anthony Summers, *Conspiracy* (New York: Paragon House, 1989), pp. 335-338.

44. 10-27-91 and 12-9-91 phone interviews with Naval Intelligence surveillance source.

45. Paul Hoch, "Echoes of a Conspiracy," 7-22-88.

46. 10-27-91 and 12-9-91 phone interviews with Naval Intelligence surveillance source.

47. Phone interview with high Florida law-enforcement source 12-10-96.

48. Paul Hoch, "Echoes of a Conspiracy," 7-22-88.

49. 10-27-91 and 12-9-91 phone interviews with Naval Intelligence surveillance source.

Chapter Forty-Seven: Fall 1963: Rosselli, Robert Kennedy, and Ruby

1. Bradley Ayers, *The War that Never Was* (Canoga Park, Calif.: Major Books, 1979), pp. 16, 21, 29.

2. Foreign Relations of the United States, Volume XI, Department of State, #296.

3. JCS 202-10002-10116, declassified 10-07-97.

4. Ayers, *op. cit.*, pp. 29, 30.

5. *Ibid.*, p. 77.

6. *Ibid.*, pp. 104, 105.

7. *Ibid.*, p. 129.

8. *Ibid.*, p. 183.

9. *Ibid.*, p. 192.

10. *Ibid.*, pp. 196, 197.

11. Warren Hinckle and William Turner, *Deadly Secrets* (New York: Thunder's Mouth, 1992), p. 220.

12. Ayers, *op. cit.*, p. 198.

13. *Ibid.*, pp. 58, 59.

14. *Ibid.*, pp. 38, 45.

15. *Ibid.*, p. 39.

16. *Ibid.*, p. 129.

17. *Ibid.*, p. 139.

18. *Ibid.*, p. 199.

19. Warren Hinckle and William Turner, *The Fish Is Red* (New York: Harper & Row, 1981), p. 217, which cites *Miami Herald* 4-1-77.

20. Hinckle and Turner, *Deadly Secrets*, pp. 241-244; Mike Wales, *Ed Arthur's Glory No More: Underground Operations from Cuba to Watergate* (Westerville, O.: Dakar, 1975), pp. 80-84.

21. John H. Davis, *Mafia Kingfish* (New York: McGraw-Hill, 1989), p. 87.

22. *Ibid.*, pp. 157, 158.

23. William Scott Malone, "The Secret Life of Jack Ruby," *New Times* 1-23-78.

24. *Ibid.*

25. *Ibid.*

26. "A Quick Critique of the *New Times* article of 1/23/78 on *The Secret Life of Jack Ruby*" by Michael Ewing, from the files of the Assassination Archives and Research Center.

27. Peter Dale Scott, *Deep Politics III*, http://history-matters.com/pds/dp3.htm.

28. Malone, *op. cit.*

29. HSCA Vol. IX, p. 191.

30. *Ibid.*, p. 201.

31. Richard D. Mahoney, *Sons & Brothers* (New York: Arcade, 1999), p. 273.

32. Peter R. Whitmey, "The Winnipeg Airport Incidents," *The Fourth Decade*, November 1995.

Chapter Forty-Eight: More Kennedy Pressure on the Godfathers

1. Richard D. Mahoney, *Sons & Brothers* (New York: Arcade, 1999), p. 230.

2. *Ibid.,* p. 393.

3. *Ibid.,* p. 230.

4. *Ibid.,* p. 231.

5. *Ibid.,* p. 233.

6. Ed Reid and Ovid Demaris, *The Green Felt Jungle* (New York: Pocket Books, 1964), p. 192.

7. *Ibid.,* p. 212.

8. Mahoney, *op. cit.,* p. 232.

9. Douglas Valentine, *The Strength of the Wolf: The Secret History of America's War on Drugs* (London, New York: Verso, 2004), pp. 281, 282.

10. They were officially the "Senate Committee on Government Operations, Permanent Subcommittee on Investigations: Organized Crime and Illicit Traffic in Narcotics."

11. Senate Committee on Government Operations, Permanent Subcommittee on Investigations: Organized Crime and Illicit Traffic in Narcotics, Sept./Oct. 1963.

12. *Ibid.*

13. In 1972, Muskie would be the front-runner for the Democratic nomination, until he was the target of illegal dirty tricks by several of Richard Nixon's operatives, who included two of Trafficante's men.

14. Senate Committee on Government Operations, Permanent Subcommittee on Investigations: Organized Crime and Illicit Traffic in Narcotics, Sept./Oct. 1963.

15. *Ibid.*

16. *Ibid.*

17. *Ibid.*

18. *Ibid.*

19. Valentine, *op. cit.,* p. 298.

20. John H. Davis, *Mafia Kingfish* (New York: McGraw-Hill, 1989), p. 170.

21. Phone interview with John Diuguid 9-30-04.

Chapter Forty-Nine: The Godfathers' Plan to Kill the President

1. John H. Davis, *Mafia Kingfish* (New York: McGraw-Hill, 1989), p. 143.

2. *Ibid.,* p. 169.

3. *Playboy,* October 1967, summarized by Edward T. Haslam in *Mary, Ferrie & the Monkey Virus: The Story of an Underground Medical Laboratory: A Non-fiction Work* (Albuquerque: Wordsworth, 1995), p. 11.

4. Davis, *Mafia Kingfish* (McGraw-Hill, 1989), p. 155.

5. Phone interview with high Florida law-enforcement source 12-10-96.

6. Warren Commission Document #87; Davis, *Mafia Kingfish* (McGraw-Hill, 1989), pp. 162.

7. Davis, *Mafia Kingfish* (McGraw-Hill, 1989), pp. 170, 181, 301.

8. CIA memo for Director of Security, subject: Cain, Richard Scully, 12-19-69, declassified 1992.

9. Phone interview with high Florida law-enforcement source 12-10-96.

10. David E. Scheim, *Contract on America: The Mafia Murder of President John F. Kennedy* (New York: Zebra, 1989), pp. 141-142; Warren Commission Hearings Vol. 23, p. 335; Warren Commission Documents Vol. 4, p. 529.

11. Anthony and Robbyn Summers, "The Ghosts of November," *Vanity Fair,* December 1994.

12. Arthur Schlesinger, Jr., *Robert Kennedy and His Times* (New York: Ballantine, 1979), pp. 664, 665.

13. CIA #104-10308-10098, declassified 9-18-98.

14. Andrew St. George, "The Attempt to Assassinate Castro," *Parade* 4-12-64.

15. Howard Kohn, "Execution for the Witnesses," *Rolling Stone* 6-2-77.

16. *Ibid.*

17. *Ibid.*

18. Dr. John Newman MIT presentation 10-1-95 as transcribed by Joseph Backes in "The Eighth Batch, Released 12/20/95."

19. Interview with confidential Kennedy administration official source 3-6-95.

20. CIA 104-10408-10029 8-25-76 CIA memo.

21. CIA 104-10308-10080, memo regarding June 28-29, 1964 AMWORLD meeting, declassified 9-18-98.

22. CIA 104-10308-10092, memo by Henry D. Hecksher, "AMWORLD Meeting in Washington, 7 to 10 November 1963."

23. The Staff and Editors of *Newsday, The Heroin Trail* (New York: Signet, 1974), pp. 114-119.

24. Henrik Krüger, *The Great Heroin Coup* (Boston: South End Press, 1980), pp. 177, 178.

25. CIA Progress Report for February 1965, declassified 1993, from the National Archives courtesy of Dr. John Newman.

26. Bernard Fensterwald, Jr. and Michael Ewing, *Coincidence or Conspiracy?* (New York: Kensington, 1977), p. 512.

27. *Ibid.*

28. CIA Operation Monthly Report for February 11963, declassified 1993, from the National Archives courtesy of Dr. John Newman.

29. CIA 1994.03.08.09:40:46:690007, declassified 3-8-94.

30. CIA 1994.03.08.09:40:46:690007, declassified 3-8-94.

31. Gus Russo, *Live by the Sword* (Baltimore: Bancroft Press, 1978), p. 165.

32. CIA #104-10308-10265, declassified 9-21-98, from the National Archives courtesy of Larry Hancock and Stuart Wexler.

33. CIA memo typed 1-14-64, Operational Progress Report for Chief, Special Affairs Staff from Chief of Station, JMWAVE, declassified 1993, from the National Archives courtesy of Dr. John Newman.

34. CIA 1994.03.08.09:40:46:690007, declassified 3-8-94.

35. *Ibid.*

36. FBI airtel to Director, FBI from SAC, Dallas, 11-29-63, HSCA #1801007810057; Ray and Mary La Fontaine, *Oswald Talked: The New Evidence in the JFK Assassination* (Gretna: Pelican, 1996), pp. 207, 286.

37. HSCA 1801007810066, HSCA 1801007810068, HSCA 1801007810069.

38. *Ibid.*

39. Anthony and Robbyn Summers, "The Ghosts of November," *Vanity Fair*, December 1994.

40. "Davis 222" file, from the Assassination Archives and Research Center.

Part III

Chapter Fifty: Laying the Groundwork for Chicago

1. *Atlanta Journal Constitution* 11-25-66.

2. Dr. Jerry D. Rose, "J. B. Stoner: An Introduction," *The Fourth Decade*, November 1995.

3. FBI Atlanta Field Office file 105-3193, 12-1-63.

4. David Ferrie long-distance phone record, page 16, on file at the Assassination Archives and Research Center.

5. FBI Atlanta Field Office file 105-3193, 12-1-63.

6. FBI teletype 11-27-63, Springfield to Director and Dallas. According to the FBI report, the secretary said Oswald's visit happened in the summer of 1962 or 1961, but the New Orleans TV reference clearly places it in 1963. As several authors have noted, when some FBI interview subjects were later shown the resulting FBI reports, details in the reports were sometimes wrong and the errors almost always slanted away from any suggestion of conspiracy.

7. FBI teletype 11-27-63, Springfield to Director and Dallas.

8. Michael L. Kurtz, *Crime of the Century: The Kennedy Assassination from a Historian's Perspective* (Knoxville: University of Tennessee Press, 1982), cited in Dave Reitzes, "Oswald in New Orleans."

9. The authors would like to gratefully acknowledge the work of Anthony Summers, who first brought the Salinger information to their attention.

10. 11-24-64 FBI memo from Handley to Rosen, released 6-18-94; HSCA 1801006810070, FBI memo 11-25-63, declassified 6-3-93.

11. Seth Kantor, *The Ruby Cover-Up* (New York: Zebra Books, 1978), p. 275.

12. Phone interview with Pierre Salinger 4-10-98; phone interviews with Jim Allison 4-15-98, 4-16-98.

13. Phone interviews with Jim Allison 4-15-98, 4-16-98.

14. *Ibid.*

15. Based on an analysis of all the available information, October 27, 1963 is the most likely date Allison saw Ruby in Chicago. Forty years later, it's not possible to determine the date with exact certainty, so it cannot be ruled out that it was another weekend, like October 6, 1963, when the Chicago Bears played the Baltimore Colts. Also, while both witnesses recall the meeting as being on a Sunday morning, it cannot be ruled out that it might have been the preceding Saturday morning.

16. Phone interviews with Jim Allison 4-15-98, 4-16-98.

17. *Ibid.*

18. *Ibid.*

19. *Ibid.*

20. Phone interview with Pierre Salinger 4-10-98; phone interviews with Jim Allison 4-15-98, 4-16-98.

21. HSCA Vol. IX, p. 1098; Warren Commission Vol. XXV, p.318. The only indication of any Ruby activity was a one-minute call from Ruby's home phone, which could have been made by his roommate or after Ruby returned from Chicago.

22. HSCA 1801006810076, FBI memo 11-25-63, declassified 6-3-93.

23. Robert F. Kennedy, *The Enemy Within* (New York: Popular Library, 1960).

24. *Time* 8-8-77, cited in David E. Scheim, *The Mafia Killed President Kennedy* (New York: SPI Books, 1992), p. 368.

25. Scheim, *The Mafia Killed President Kennedy,* p. 135.

26. *Ibid.,* p. 368; Confidential interview with source close to Richard Cain.

27. Kantor, *The Ruby Cover-Up* (New York: Zebra Books, 1978), p. 62.

28. Warren Commission document #1016.

29. HSCA Vol. IX, pp. 1098, 1099.

30. John H. Davis, *Mafia Kingfish* (New York: McGraw-Hill, 1989), p. 162.

31. HSCA Vol. IX, pp. 1090, 1093; Warren Commission document 1016, p. 4; HSCA Vol. V, pp. 169, 170.

32. HSCA 1801007510310, declassified 6-20-93.

33. HSCA Vol. IX, p. 1098; Warren Commission Vol. .XXV, p. 254.

34. The CIA operations Ruby was tied to include the 1959 CIA–Mafia plots and the fall 1963 CIA–Mafia plots, by virtue of his meetings in Miami with Johnny Rosselli in late September or early October 1963.

35. *New York Times* 10-29-63; *Bartone v. United States,* 375 US 52, decided October 28, 1963, available on Findlaw.com.

36. CIA document, HSCA, Record Number 180-10143-10209, CIA Segregated Collection, Agency File Number 28-43-01, declassified 8-16-95.

37. Dan E. Moldea, *The Hoffa Wars* (New York, SPI, 1993), pp. 118, 141, 151, 163, 164, 170.

38. *Ibid.;* Walter Sheridan, *The Fall and Rise of Jimmy Hoffa* (New York: Saturday Review Press, 1972), pp. 406-408.

39. Dan E. Moldea, *The Hoffa Wars: Teamsters, Rebels, Politicians, and the Mob* (New York, SPI, 1993), pp. 163, 164; David E. Scheim, *The Mafia Killed President Kennedy* (New York: SPI Books, 1992), p. 124.

40. F82-0272/2; Jan 64 cable to CIA Director from (censored).

Chapter Fifty-One: The Cuba Contingency Plan and the Phony Cuban Agent

1. CIA 104-10434-10267 and CIA 104-10434-10283, both declassified 11/18/98.

2. Joseph J. Trento, *The Secret History of the CIA* (Roseville: Prima, 2001), pp. 226, 227.

3. CIA 104-10308-10209, declassified 9-21-98.

4. Interview with Larry Hancock about new David Morales CIA documents 7-2-05.

5. CIA memo declassified 8-16-93, still partially censored.

6. CIA F82-0272/1, 82-1625 (4).

7. F82-0272/2; Jan 64 cable to CIA Director from (censored).

8. CIA F82-0272/1, 82-1625 (4); CIA F82-0272/2; Jan 64 cable to CIA Director from (censored); CIA memo declassified 8-16-93, still partially censored.

9. CIA F82-0278 (the document number is hard to read, and might be F82-02781).

10. David Atlee Phillips, *Secret Wars Diary* (Bethesda, Md.: Stone Trail Press, 1989), p. 166; Richard Helms and William Hood, *A Look Over My Shoulder* (New York: Random House, 2003).

11. Joseph Franco with Richard Hammer, *Hoffa's Man: The Rise and Fall of Jimmy Hoffa as Witnessed by His Strongest Arm* (New York: Prentice Hall, 1987), p. 198.

12. The Mafia's use of Saez would have the desired effect whether a real individual named Miguel Casas Saez made all of the trips CIA documents indicate he made, or just some of them—or if Saez was simply reported to have made them, while he remained in some out-of-the-way locale. There's even a chance that Saez didn't exist at all, but was simply the creation of someone like Rosselli or Trafficante, who planted information about him by feeding it to individuals they knew reported to the CIA.

13. Dick Russell, *The Man Who Knew Too Much* (New York: Carroll & Graf/R. Gallen, 1992), p. 723.

14. CIA "Response to Item Comments on Draft Report" 6-13-76, in the National Archives, from the files of Anna-Marie Kuhns-Walko.

15. CIA 104-10309-1008, declassified 9-4-98.

16. SSCIA #157-10005-10258, declassified 4-25-94.

17. Dick Russell, "JFK and the Cuban Connection," *High Times* March 1996.

18. CIA 104-10434-10267 and CIA 104-10434-10283, both declassified 11/18/98.

19. CIA "Response to Item Comments on Draft Report" 6-13-76, in the National Archives, from the files of Anna-Marie Kuhns-

Walko: "The desk officer, who was charged with responsibility for investigating the President's assassination was not aware of the AMLASH operation, so he was not in a position to assess its possible connection with the assassination at the time."

20. HSCA Vol. V, p. 315.

21. 1967 CIA Inspector General's Report, p. 87.

22. Background report on the travels of Mertz, Bud Fensterwald Mertz files at the Assassination Archives and Research Center.

23. Larry Hancock, *Someone Would Have Talked* (Southlake, Tex.: JFK Lancer, 2003), p. 220.

24. 1967 CIA Inspector General's Report, p. 94.

25. 1967 CIA Inspector General's Report, p. 91.

26. Church Committee Report, Vol. V, p. 87.

27. Evan Thomas, *Robert Kennedy: His Life* (New York: Simon & Schuster, 2000), p. 271.

28. CIA 104-10315-10003, 12-19-60, declassified 1-27-99, provided by Larry Hancock.

29. CIA 104-10309-1008, 9-27-63 memo, declassified 9-4-98, provided by Larry Hancock.

30. CIA 104-10309-1008, 9-27-63 memo, declassified 9-4-98, provided by Larry Hancock.

31. Church Committee Report, Vol. V, p. 74.

32. FBI 104-10419-10021, SAC Miami to FBI Director, 8/7/64, cited by Larry Hancock.

33. Church Committee Report, Vol. V, p. 16.

34. 1967 CIA Inspector General's Report, p. 94.

35. Gus Russo, *Live by the Sword* (Baltimore: Bancroft Press, 1978), p. 237.

36. Army Intelligence memos on the Cuban Officer Training Program prepared by 112th Intelligence Corps Group, San Antonio, Texas, 11-1-63, cited in Larry Hancock, *Someone Would Have Talked* (Southlake, Tex.: JFK Lancer, 2003).

Chapter Fifty-Two: Three Weeks Before Dallas: The Chicago Assassination Attempt

1. CIA memo for Director of Security, subject: Cain, Richard Scully, 12-19-69, declassified 1992.

2. Interviews with Mike Cain about his upcoming book on Richard Cain.

3. HSCA 180-10105-10393, Secret Service memo 3-29-63, declassified 12-1-93.

4. CIA memo for Director of Security, subject: Cain, Richard Scully, 12-19-69, declassified 1992.

5. CIA memo for "Chief, LEOB/SRS" from Sarah K. Hall 12-11-67; CIA memo to Chief, SRS from M. D. Stevens, 10-9-67, declassified 1992.

6. 12-12-67 CIA memo to Director of Security, #272141.

7. Bud Fensterwald, "The Case of Secret Service Agent Abraham W. Bolden," *Computers and Automation* 6-71; HSCA, p. 231; UPI 5-21-64.

8. HSCA 180-10070-10273 interview with Abraham Bolden 1-19-78, declassified 1-5-96.

9. Richard Reeves, *President Kennedy: Profile of Power* (New York: Simon & Schuster, 1993), pp. 385-387.

10. Vincent Michael Palamara, *The Third Alternative* (Pennsylvania: 1993), p. 71.

11. George Black, *The Good Neighbor* (New York: Pantheon, 1988).

12. HSCA 180-10070-10273 interview with Abraham Bolden 1-19-78, declassified 1-5-96.

13. *Ibid.*; HSCA, p. 231.

14. HSCA 180-10070-10273 interview with Abraham Bolden 1-19-78, declassified 1-5-96.

15. Bernard Fensterwald interview of Abraham Bolden 3-29-68; Memo of conversation with Ian Calder, *Nashville Inquirer* 5-25-68, on file at the Assassination Archives and Research Center. At a later time, Bolden recalled one of the names as perhaps being something like Bradley. However, that was at a time during the Garrison investigation when someone named Bradley was being focused on as a suspect, so it's possible his interviewers pressed him for a recall on that particular name.

16. Richard D. Mahoney, *Sons & Brothers* (New York: Arcade, 1999), p. 278.

17. Since an FBI informant had placed Oswald at a Tampa FPCC meeting around this time, as detailed later, that could have linked Oswald to JFK's death as well. Richard Cain's position as chief of the Special Investigations Unit for the Chicago sheriff's office would have allowed him easy access to information about the Tampa FPCC. Law-enforcement—and intelligence—organizations frequently traded information about "subversives" and "subversive groups," as documented by the summer 1963 Dallas newspaper article we cited earlier. For example, New Orleans Police Intelligence (founded by Guy Banister) was in touch with Tampa Police Intelligence about the Fair Play for Cuba Committee, even before Oswald briefly had his phony one-man chapter in New Orleans. Cain could have easily learned about the Tampa FPCC, and made sure names linked to it—and therefore to Gilberto Lopez—would be used as aliases for the assassins. Our research shows that the men named "Gonzales and Rodriguez" who were close to Gilberto Lopez were not involved in the JFK assassination.

18. Phone interview with Gerry Hemming 4-10-96.

19. There are several other possible sources for the FBI's original tip about the four men, based on other FBI investigations going

on at the same time. One individual the FBI was tracking at the time—who may still be alive, so we won't name him here—had links to Cubela, an exile training camp outside New Orleans, and associates of Trafficante and Marcello, and would end "up in a French prison doing an extended sentence for drug smuggling," as noted by Larry Hancock in his book *Someone Would Have Talked* (Southlake, Tex.: JFK Lancer, 2003).

20. Black, *op. cit.*

21. HSCA 180-10070-10273 interview with Abraham Bolden 1-19-78, declassified 1-5-96.

22. HSCA files declassified by the Assassination Records Review Board cited by Vince Palamara in *Deep Politics* magazine, 4-97.

23. HSCA Report, p. 231.

24. FBI Airtel to Director 10-1-74.

25. HSCA 180-10070-10276.

26. Black, *op. cit.*

27. Information provided by Paul Byrne 2-28-97, 4-22-97.

28. Black, *op. cit.*

29. *Chicago Daily News* 12-3-63.

30. HSCA #1801008010154, declassified 10/95.

31. Black, *op. cit.*

32. Information provided by Bill Adams 3-28-97.

33. Warren Commission Document 117.

34. Domestic military surveillance was documented by Senator Sam Ervin in hearings shortly before Watergate, and later by the Senate Church Committee.

35. www.spartacus.schoolnet.co.uk.

36. *Chicago Daily News* 12-3-63.

37. HSCA Report, p. 231.

38. John Birch Society Bulletin, September 1963.

39. Palamara, *op. cit.*, p. 72.

40. This is not to imply that the John Birch Society, as an organization, was involved in JFK's death.

41. Rosselli's Chicago mob, Trafficante's Tampa, and Marcello's territory of Dallas each appears to have had its own local patsy—Vallee, Lopez, and Oswald—for each of the planned attempts to kill JFK. But Vallee may not have been the only patsy the Mafia had slated for Chicago. Before his much publicized leafleting and "fight" in New Orleans, Oswald had tried to join the conservative, anti-Castro Cuban exiles who later attacked him. With that pattern already established by Oswald in the local press in New Orleans, it's not hard to imagine a possible scenario for Chicago. If JFK were killed in Chicago, Thomas Vallee would not be just arrested for having a trunk full of weapons, but a connection could have been made to the pro-Castro Oswald, who would have seemingly deceived the militant right-winger the same way Oswald tried to deceive the anti-Castro group in New Orleans. Plus, Oswald had already been set up to make it appear that he'd tried to deceive Manolo Ray's C-Day group, via Silvia Odio. So, after a Chicago assassination, it might have appeared that ex-Marine pro-Castro Oswald had deceived the far-right ex-Marine Vallee, and gotten Vallee to kill JFK—all as part of a plot inspired by Castro. Coupled with reports of a Cuban agent in the Chicago area, the mob bosses thought they knew exactly how the FBI, CIA, Bobby Kennedy, and the US military—primed for a C-Day invasion—would react.

    JFK's assassination was planned for a Saturday (November 2), so had the attempt not been uncovered on Friday (November 1), it would have been possible to get Oswald or Lopez to Chicago on Friday night after work, or Saturday morning, on some pretext without arousing suspicion. Either could have been told going to Chicago was part of their "mission" to get into Cuba, this time via Canada—which also had flights to Havana—instead of Mexico City, the way Oswald had tried and Lopez would successfully use after the Tampa and Dallas attempts. David Ferrie conveniently flew back to New Orleans from Guatemala on November 1, and, as a pilot, he (or Mertz, who could also fly small aircraft) could have secretly flown anyone into Chicago. In Chicago was Thomas Vallee, the ex-Marine who was the type of far-right activist Oswald had said he was going to Chicago to contact. Shadowy supposed Cuban agent Miguel Casas Saez was also reported to be in Chicago by November 1, the day before JFK's motorcade.

42. Vincent Michael Palamara, *The Third Alternative* (Pennsylvania: 1993), pp. 72, 73, citing HSCA Report, pp. 231-232.

43. HSCA 180-10070-10276, 1-19-78 interview summary for Edward Tucker.

44. FBI Airtel to Director, 10-1-74.

45. John H. Davis, *Mafia Kingfish* (New York: McGraw-Hill, 1989), pp. 167, 168.

46. *Ibid.*, pp. 162.

47. HSCA 180-10070-10273 interview with Abraham Bolden 1-19-78, declassified 1-5-96.

48. Black, *op. cit.*

49. HSCA 180-10070-10273 Interview with Abraham Bolden 1-19-78, declassified 1-5-96.

50. Black, *op. cit.*

51. HSCA Vol. IX, p. 1098; Warren Commission, Vol. XXV, p. 254.

52. HSCA 180-10070-10273 interview with Abraham Bolden 1-19-78, declassified 1-5-96.

53. *Ibid.*

54. One exile group involved in arms deals in Chicago was linked to the Frenchman arrested for the September 1963 Castro assassination plot. Those exiles were not part of C-Day. However, one of the exiles involved in the Chicago arms deals said on the day before JFK's death in Dallas "that his backers would proceed 'as soon as we take care of Kennedy.'" The House Select Committee on Assassinations found that that particular exile "group was backed financially by" an organization whose money "allegedly came from individuals connected to organized crime." Historian Richard Mahoney later found that some of the organization's money came from Johnny Rosselli.

55. *Chicago Daily News* 12-3-63.

56. Black, *op. cit.*

57. FBI memo 12-2-63.

58. FBI Airtel to Director, 10-1-74.

Chapter Fifty-Three: JFK's Chicago Motorcade: Cancelled at the Last Minute

1. *Chicago Daily News* 11-2-63.

2. HSCA Report, p. 231.

3. Vincent Michael Palamara, *The Third Alternative* (Pennsylvania: 1993), p. 73 citing George Black, *The Good Neighbor* (New York: Pantheon, 1988).

4. Palamara, *op. cit.*, pp. 73, 75; Phone interview with Vince Palamara 12-10-96.

5. HSCA 180-10087-10190; HSCA 180-10078-10493 and HSCA 180-10099-10491, cited in JFK Assassination Records Review Board Update presentation by Joseph Backes at the JFK Lancer Conference, November, 1996; HSCA Secret Service interviews cited by Vince Palamara in *Deep Politics* magazine 4-97.

6. HSCA 180-10070-10273 interview with Abraham Bolden 1-19-78, declassified 1-5-96.

7. Black, *op. cit.*

8. HSCA Report, p. 231.

9. HSCA 180-10070-10273 interview with Abraham Bolden 1-19-78, declassified 1-5-96.

10. *Ibid.*

11. Palamara, *op. cit.*, p. 75.

12. Bud Fensterwald interview with Abraham Bolden 3-29-68.

13. One man named Rodriguez was arrested on 10-29-63 and had several narcotics dealing charges in his past; another man who sometimes used the name Rodriguez was really named Angel, and was born in Puerto Rico. Another Rodriguez was arrested on 10-31-63 for having a stolen license plate.

14. Philip H. Melanson, "Dallas Mosaic: The Cops, the Cubans and the Company," *The Third Decade*, Vol. 1 #3, March 1985.

15. Warren Commission Vol. X, p. 60.

16. 12-12-67 CIA memo to Director of Security, #272141.

17. *New York Times* 12-6-67.

18. HSCA #1801008010154, declassified 10/95.

19. HSCA Report, p. 231.

20. HSCA #1801008010154, declassified 10/95, after being originally "referred" and not released on 7-24-93.

21. HSCA Report, p. 231.

22. *Ibid.*

23. *Ibid.*

24. Black, *op. cit.*

25. *Ibid.*

26. FBI 2-5-64 memo FBI 62-109060.

27. Palamara, *op. cit.*, p. 73; Phone interview with Vince Palamara 12-10-96.

28. HSCA 180-10087-10191, cited in JFK Assassination Records Review Board Update presentation by Joseph Backes at the JFK Lancer Conference, November, 1996.

29. HSCA Report, p. 231. We can verify from several interviews with former Justice Department agents that they were often able to recall many details of their actions in 1963 over thirty years later with amazing precision, even without notes or advance preparation. After all, attention to detail is a key part of the work of such agents. The HSCA interviews took place only fifteen years after the Chicago threat.

30. Presidential Secret Service Agent Gerald Behn was head of the White House detail, but was "unable to recall anything about the President's cancellation of his planned appearance on 11/2." Though Behn would have been at the center of preparations for the trip and its sudden cancellation, Behn "did not [even] remember hearing about either the trip or its political purpose" (HSCA 180-10104-10481 & HSCA 180-10105-10305, cited in JFK Assassination Records Review Board Update presentation by Joseph Backes at the JFK Lancer Conference, November 1996).

31. *Chicago Daily News* 12-3-63.

32. How could the story about the four-man team have been kept out of the press, even after JFK's motorcade was cancelled? The CIA's own files confirm that stories related to CIA anti-Castro operations were being suppressed in the fall of 1963. For example, in October 1963 in Florida, an AMTRUNK boat piloted by Cuban exiles ran out of gas. A CIA memo "dispatched" on October 18, 1963 says that the AMTRUNK boat was "picked up by the Coast Guard and" had "to be towed into the town dock" where the boat was greeted by police, newspaper photographers and tourists." The CIA was able to handle the embarrassing incident "through liaison with two local newspapers," and "all photographs showing identifiable team member faces were suppressed and obtained for" the "files" of the Miami CIA station. The memo about the news suppression—kept secret for the next thirty-five years—was sent by David Morales's boss at the Miami CIA station to Desmond FitzGerald, who at that time was supervising AMTRUNK as well as the CIA's side of C-Day, AMWORLD. CIA 104-10309-1008, declassified 9-4-98.

33. FBI 12-9-63 B62-6115-69.

34. For example, the governor of Tennessee was asked by the Secret Service to keep secret an attempt to kill JFK after a speech at Vanderbilt University in May 1963. While JFK waited for a helicopter, a man had approached JFK with a pistol under a sack, but Secret Service agents grabbed him. The Secret Service told the governor: "If you can keep this quiet, we would deeply appreciate it, because every time an assassination attempt is made or anything close to an assassination attempt gets into the media, the number of threats on the President's life triples" (Congressman Bob Clement, cited in "JFK survived assassination attempt 6 months before Dallas," article on file at the Assassination Archives and Research Center, Washington, D.C.).

Chapter Fifty-Four: Laying the Groundwork for Tampa

1. Richard D. Mahoney, *Sons & Brothers* (New York: Arcade, 1999), p. 278.

2. John H. Davis, *Mafia Kingfish* (New York: McGraw-Hill, 1989), p. 168.

3. Dick Russell, *The Man Who Knew Too Much* (New York: Carroll & Graf/R. Gallen, 1992), p. 723.

4. Peter R. Whitmey, "The Winnipeg Airport Incidents," *The Fourth Decade*, November 1995.

5. Larry Hancock, *Someone Would Have Talked* (Southlake, Tex.: JFK Lancer, 2003), p. 167, citing Treasury Dept. memo, McBrein to Albrecht, about "Reopening of Warren Commission."

6. Rory O'Connor, "Oswald Visited Tampa," *Tampa Tribune* 6-24-76; Phone interview with confidential high Florida law-enforcement source 12-10-96; Skip Johnson and Tony Durr, "Ex-Tampan in JFK Plot?," *Tampa Tribune* 9-5-76.

7. Hancock, *Someone Would Have Talked* (JFK Lancer, 2003), p. 167. It's important to note that James Hosty has denied making those statements.

8. *Ibid.*, p. 170.

9. Ian Griggs, "Oswald: A Driving Force," *Deep Politics* April 1997.

10. CIA 104-10400-10130, declassified 10-26-98.

11. CIA 104-10400-10130, declassified 10-26-98.

12. *New York Times* 11-18-63.

13. CIA 104-10400-10130, declassified 10-26-98.

14. CIA memo released 8-16-93, still partially censored.

15. HSCA Report, p. 232.

16. *Ibid.*

17. Dan Christensen, "JFK, King: The Dade County links," *Miami* magazine 12-76.

18. HSCA Report, p. 232; Miami Police Department transcript of 11-9-63 Milteer conversation with William Somersett; Phone interview with confidential high Florida law-enforcement source 12-10-96.

19. Interview with William Somersett transcribed on 11/26/63.

20. *Ibid.*

21. *Ibid.*

22. *Ibid.*

23. *New Orleans Times-Picayune* 5-12-63, 12-6-63, both cited by Jerry P. Shinley and A. J. Weberman.

24. Christensen, *op. cit.*

25. *Ibid.*

26. HSCA Report, p. 232.

27. Christensen, *op. cit.*

28. *Ibid.*

29. *Ibid.*

30. Peter Dale Scott, Paul L. Hoch, and Russell Stetler, eds., *The Assassinations: Dallas and Beyond: A Guide to Cover-Ups and Investigations* (New York: Vintage, 1976), pp. 118-134.

31. Miami Police Department transcript of 11-9-63 Milteer conversation with Somersett.

32. "Who was really responsible for the Kennedy assassination?," *West Side Leader* 4-10-97, provided by Deanie Richards and Gordon Winslow.

33. Warren Commission Exhibit 762, cited in Russell, *op. cit.*, pp. 550, 551.

34. HSCA Report, p. 232; G. Robert Blakey and Richard N. Billings, *The Plot to Kill the President* (New York: Times Books, 1981), p. 9.

35. HSCA Report, p. 232.

36. Vince Palamara article in *Deep Politics* magazine July 1998.

Chapter Fifty-Five: Mid-November 1963: The President Prepares a Message for the Coup Leader

1. Church Committee Report, Vol. V, p. 18.

2. *Ibid.*, Vol. V, p. 20.

3. *Ibid.*, Vol. V, p. 19.

4. CIA AMTRUNK documents and summaries in Russell Holmes work files 4-77.

5. CIA AMTRUNK documents and summaries in Russell Holmes work files 4-25-77; CIA 104-10400-10128.

6. CIA AMTRUNK documents and summaries in Russell Holmes work files 4-77.

7. "James Johnston, former counsel with Church Committee," *Washington Post* 9-27-92.

8. *New York Times* 11-7-63.

9. Interviews with Harry Williams 2-24-92, 4-92, 7-1-92, 11-13-92, 7-24-93, 2-21-95.

10. For example, 105-1126109-19, 3-31-64 FBI report and 6-19-64 FBI Report (Tampa) were sent to Naval Intelligence (ONI).

11. SSCIA 157-10011-10002.

12. Foreign Relations of the United States, Volume XI, Department of State, #375 and #376, 11-12-63.

13. Evan Thomas, *Robert Kennedy: His Life* (New York: Simon & Schuster, 2000), p 449.

14. NLK-78-473, declassified 5-6-80; the only date on the memo is 11-12-63, but the memo is heavily censored, so it's possible that that date is referencing an earlier meeting—or JFK's big 11-12-63 meeting—and this meeting might have been held a few days after that.

15. Interviews with confidential Kennedy administration official source 3-6-95, 3-8-96, 4-18-96.

16. Gus Russo, *Live by the Sword* (Baltimore: Bancroft Press, 1978), p. 303.

17. Edwin O. Guthman and Jeffrey Shulman, eds., *Robert Kennedy: In His Own Words* (Toronto, New York: Bantam, 1988), pp. 375.

18. Ernst Halperin, "Unfair Play for Cuba," review of Haynes Johnson with Manuel Artime and others, *The Bay of Pigs* (New York: Norton, 1964), *New York Review of Books* 7-9-64.

19. Interviews with Harry Williams 2-24-92, 4-92.

20. Church Committee Report, Vol. V, p. 20.

21. *Ibid.*, p. 19; "Chronology of Significant Documents in AMTRUNK File" in Russ Holmes Work File 4-77.

22. Arthur Schlesinger, Jr., *Robert Kennedy and His Times* (New York: Ballantine, 1979), p. 598.

23. Seymour M. Hersh, *The Dark Side of Camelot* (Boston: Little, Brown, 1997).

24. Frank DeBenedictis, "Four Days before Dallas," *Tampa Bay History* Fall/Winter 1994.

25. Seth Kantor, *The Ruby Cover-Up* (New York: Zebra Books, 1992), p. 61.

26. FBI reports 44-24016-288, 44-24016-212, 92-3267-260, as cited in Larry Hancock, *Someone Would Have Talked* (Southlake, Tex.: JFK Lancer, 2003), pp. 168, 171, 173.

27. Charles Rappleye and Ed Becker, *All American Mafioso* (New York: Barricade, 1995), p. 247.

28. Hancock, *op. cit.*, p. 171.

29. HSCA Report, Vol 9, p. 1099.

30. John H. Davis, *Mafia Kingfish* (New York: McGraw-Hill, 1989), p. 155.

31. CIA 104-10434-10283, declassified 11/18/98.

32. Anthony Summers, *Conspiracy* (New York: Paragon House, 1989), p. 275.

33. *Ibid.*, p279; *New York Times* 11-19-63.

34. Church Committee Report, Vol. V, p. 62.

35. Anthony and Robbyn Summers, "The Ghosts of November," *Vanity Fair*, December 1994.

36. Phone interview with high Florida law-enforcement source 12-10-96.

37. Bernard Fensterwald memo, 5-25-68, on file at the Assassination Archives and Research Center.

38. Tim Gratz and Mark Howell, "The Strange Flight of Gilbert Lopez," *Key West Citizen* 11-20-03.

39. Phone interview with Blanche Andrea Leon 3/2/96.

40. FBI Airtel to Dircetor from Miami, declassified 2-16-83.

41. Church Committee Report, Vol. V, p. 62.

42. HSCA Report, pp. 118-121.

43. Church Committee Report, Vol. V, p. 62.

44. Lopez was not able to simply fly to Havana on one of the flights from Miami, because his US passport had expired earlier in the year.

45. Church Committee Report, Vol. V, p. 62.

46. HSCA Report, pp 118-121; CIA 104-10419-10226, declassified 12-2-98.

47. Skip Johnson and Tony Durr, "Ex-Tampan in JFK Plot?" *Tampa Tribune* 9-5-76.

48. Phone interview with confidential high Florida law-enforcement source 12-10-96.

49. Davis, *Mafia Kingfish* (McGraw-Hill, 1989), p. 172.

50. *Dallas Morning News* 6-10-79, cited in Hancock, *op. cit.*, p. 170.

51. Hancock, *op. cit.*, p. 170.

52. HSCA 180-10141-10420, declassified 8-3-95.

53. Army document, from Director of Foreign Intelligence to Office, Secretary of the Army attn: Mr. Joseph Califano, General Counsel; 12-11-63, Califano Papers, Record Number 198-10004-10011, declassified 10-7-97.

54. Interviews with Harry Williams 2-24-92, 11-13-92, 7-24-93.

55. *Tampa Tribune* 11-17-63.

56. "International relations chief Alberto Fowler dies at 58," *New Orleans Times-Picayune* 12-30-87; *U.S. News & World Report* 1-7-63.

57. Statement of Alberto Fowler in the Office of the District Attorney 1-23-67; memos by Harold Weisberg on file at the Assassination Archives and Research Center.

58. *New Orleans Times-Picayune* 11-22-73.

Chapter Fifty-Six: November 18, 1963: The Attempt to Assassinate JFK in Tampa

1. JFK Assassination Records Review Board Final Report, 1998, p.149.

2. "Threats on Kennedy Made Here," *Tampa Tribune* 11-23-63; "Man Held in Threats to JFK," *Miami Herald* 11-24-63—it is bylined "Tampa (UPI)," so it may well have appeared in other newspapers; and, if so, the fact that it reprints just a few sentences from the *Tampa Tribune* article may have caused earlier researchers to overlook it.

3. Frank DeBenedictis, "Four Days before Dallas," *Tampa Bay History* Fall/Winter 1994.

4. FBI Airtel to Director from Miami, declassified 2-16-83.

5. 1967 CIA Inspector General's Report, p. 91, citing 11-19-63 CIA memo; HSCA 180-10074-10394, cited in JFK Assassination Records Review Board Update presentation by Joseph Backes at the JFK Lancer Conference, November 1996.

6. HSCA Secret Service interviews declassified by the Assassinations Records Review Board, cited by Vince Palamara in *Deep Politics* magazine, 4-97.

7. Phone interview with Vince Palamara 12-10-96.

8. Phone interview with J. P. Mullins 12-10-96.

9. Phone interview with confidential high Florida law-enforcement source 12-10-96.

10. Frank DeBenedictis, "Four Days before Dallas," *Tampa Bay History* Fall/Winter 1994.

11. FBI 12-9-63 B62-6115-69; Phone interview with confidential high Florida law-enforcement source 12-10-96.

12. Phone interview with J. P. Mullins 12-10-96.

13. Phone interview with confidential high Florida law-enforcement source 12-10-96.

14. *Tampa Tribune* 11-23-63.

15. *Tampa Tribune* 11-18-63; *St. Petersburg Times* 11-18-63.

16. *Tampa Tribune* 11-23-63.

17. RIF 154-10002-10423, cited by Vince Palamara.

18. Mary Evertz, "John F. Kennedy: The Exhibition," *St. Petersburg Times* 11-11-99.

19. *Ibid.*

20. Article by Vince Palamara, *Deep Politics* magazine 10-96.

21. Evertz, *op. cit.*

22. DeBenedictis, *op. cit.*

23. Evertz, *op. cit.*

24. Phone interview with confidential high Florida law-enforcement source 12-10-96.

25. *Ibid.*

26. These are just some of the many pages of transcripts of phone calls the FBI recorded in Tampa: FBI 124-10249-10282, FBI 124-10249-10287, and FBI 124-10249-10295, all declassified 5-17-94. Contrast with FBI Airtel to Dircetor from Miami, declassified 2-16-83.

27. Interview with ex-Secret Service Agent Abraham Bolden 4-15-98.

28. According to an 11-26-63 interview of Miami police informant William Somersett, Milteer said JFK "could have been killed in Miami"—and this reference to Miami (instead of Tampa) is yet another reason the Tampa attempt stayed secret for so many years. It's not clear if Milteer's use of "Miami" indicates that there was a backup plan to try to kill JFK in Miami— which would have been difficult, since there was no large, public motorcade—or if it means that Milteer wasn't fully informed about the city where the November 18th attempt would occur.

29. Rolando Cubela had not been one of "the twelve" in the Sierra Maestra mountains with Fidel Castro, unlike Raul Castro and Che Guevara.

30. *New York Times* 11-19-63.

31. *Marietta Daily Journal* 11-19-63.

32. *New York Times* 11-19-63.

33. CIA AMTRUNK files (Russ Holmes work file, 4-77.

34. *Miami Herald* 11-24-63.

35. *Kennedy Assassination Records Review Board Final Report*, 1998, p.149.

Chapter Fifty-Seven: November 19–21: Regrouping for Dallas

1. Phone interview with John Diuguid 9-30-04.

2. Charles Rappleye and Ed Becker, *All American Mafioso* (New York: Barricade, 1995), pp. 248, 249.

3. Larry Hancock, *Someone Would Have Talked* (Southlake, Tex.: JFK Lancer, 2003), pp. 105, 106.

4. CIA 104-10406-10212; 124-90033-10039.

5. Warren Hinckle and William Turner, *Deadly Secrets* (New York: Thunder's Mouth, 1992), pp. 130, 196.

6. 6-4-92 interview of Robert Plumlee, apparently by Robert G. Vernon. Plumlee's account appears to have become more detailed over the years, so we tend to focus on those parts of his story that have remained most consistent over the years and those parts for which there is some independent corroboration.

7. "Police Nab 2 ex-convicts with load of stolen guns," *Dallas Morning News* 11-19-63.

8. Ray and Mary La Fontaine, "Oswald's lost cellmate and the gunrunners of Dallas," *Washington Post* 8-7-94.

9. *Ibid.*

10. John H. Davis, *Mafia Kingfish* (New York: McGraw-Hill, 1989), p.173.

11. Statement of Eddie Piper to Dallas Police 2-17-64, Dallas Municipal Archives and Records Center.

12. Bud Fensterwald interview with William Somersett 6-5-68.

13. Interviews with Chauncey Marvin Holt 9-28-91. We did not find Holt's account of being one of the tramps in Dealey Plaza credible, and have included none of it in this book. Holt appeared to be a highly intelligent sociopath, capable of weaving elaborate stories from a few facts. However, the now-deceased Holt did have organized-crime connections with people on the fringes of the JFK plot. Further investigation showed that he appears to have participated in the murders of two Artime associates in the 1970s, and may have learned a few relevant facts from them before their deaths.

14. Church Committee Report, Vol. V, pp 30, 61-63; *House Select Committee on Assassinations Report*, pp. 118-121.

15. Document # 104-10017-10066, 12-5-63 CIA memo, cited by Joe Backes.

16. Memorandum by Bud Fensterwald, submitted to the US Justice Department 7-13-82.

17. *Ibid.*

18. Statements of Michel Roux 3-7-64 and 3-9-64 to French authorities, and FBI report about Roux, contained in the files of Bud Fensterwald at the Assassination Archives and Research Center.

19. Davis, *Mafia Kingfish* (McGraw-Hill, 1989), pp. 175, 176.

20. Richard D. Mahoney, *Sons & Brothers* (New York: Arcade, 1999), p. 287.

21. FBI reports contained in Memorandum by Bernard Fensterwald, submitted to the US Justice Department 7-13-82.

22. Not cited by us previously is an 11-29-63 Secret Service document noted by the HSCA (Vol. 9, p. 1100) about Ruby, titled "Bureau of Narcotics possible involvement in narcotics case."

23. HSCA Vol. IX, p. 1098; Warren Commission Vol. XXV, p. 254.

24. HSCA vol. X, pp. 199-205; Hancock, *op. cit.*

25. Statement of Mr. A. H. Magruder, taken by Det. Frank Meloche and Sgt. Fenner Sedgebeer, 2-23-67.

26. HSCA vol. X, pp. 198-205.

27. John H. Davis, *Mafia Kingfish* (New York: Signet, 1989), pp. 606, 607.

28. Statement of Mr. A. H. Magruder, taken by Det. Frank Meloche and Sgt. Fenner Sedgebeer, 2-23-67.

29. HSCA vol. X, pp. 198-205.

30. Ronald Goldfarb, *Perfect Villains and Imperfect Heroes* (New York: Random House, 1995), pp. 139, 140.

31. Michael R. Beschloss, *The Crisis Years* (New York: Edward Burlingame, 1991), pp. 666, 667.

32. Gus Russo, *Live by the Sword* (Baltimore: Bancroft Press, 1978), p. 272.

33. CIA record number 104-10429-10231.

34. Church Committee Report, Vol. V, p. 19.

35. 1967 CIA Inspector General's Report, p. 91.

36. Church Committee Report, Vol. V, p. 19.

37. Arthur Schlesinger, Jr., *Robert Kennedy and His Times* (New York: Ballantine, 1979), p. 598-600.

38. Warren Commission Vol. VII, p. 475, cited in Lawson to Cornwell and Klein memo 8-15-77 on file at the Assassination Archives and Research Center.

39. *Ibid.*, Vol. IV, p. 163, cited as in note 38.

40. Church Committee Report, Vol. V, p. 19.

41. *Ibid.*

42. William Weston, "The Interrogation of Oswald," *Deep Politics Quarterly* 1-96.

43. Rappleye and Becker, *op. cit.*, p. 248; uncorroborated accounts by Robert Plumlee, James Files, and Chauncey Holt.

44. David E. Scheim, *Contract on America* (New York: Zebra, 1989), p20, 290, 291; William Turner, "The Inquest," *Ramparts* June 1967.

45. Scheim, *Contract on America*, p. 291.

46. G. Robert Blakey and Richard N. Billings, *The Plot to Kill the President* (New York: Times Books, 1981), p. 37; Scheim, *Contract on America*, p. 570.

47. Anthony Summers, *Not In Your Lifetime* (New York: Marlowe & Co., 1998), pp. 459, 460.

48. HSCA Vol. XIII, pp. 37, others; Anthony Summers, *Conspiracy* (New York: McGraw-Hill, 1980), p. 602.

49. Henry Hurt, *Reasonable Doubt* (New York: Henry Holt, 1987), many pages.

Chapter Fifty-Eight: November 22: JFK is Murdered

1. David E. Scheim, *Contract on America* (New York: Zebra, 1989), p. 123; G. Robert Blakey and Richard N. Billings, *The Plot to Kill the President* (New York: Times Books, 1981), p. 314; Anthony Summers, *Conspiracy* (New York: McGraw-Hill, 1980), p. 475.

2. Scheim, *Contract on America*, p. 293.

3. Blakey and Billings, *op. cit.*, p. 313, Summers, *Conspiracy* (McGraw-Hill, 1980), p. 475.

4. Warren Commission Exhibits 1019 and 1020.

5. Scheim, *Contract on America*, p. 295.

6. Summers, *Conspiracy* (McGraw-Hill, 1980), pp. 475, 476.

7. Scheim, *Contract on America*, p. 295.

8. John H. Davis, *Mafia Kingfish* (New York: Signet, 1989), p. 606.

9. Michael Benson, *Who's Who in the JFK Assassination: An A-to-Z Encyclopedia* (New York: Citadel, 1993), pp. 238, 239.

10. Warren Commission Vol. XV, pp. 660, 661

11. Scheim, *Contract on America*, p. 295.

12. Summers, *Conspiracy* (McGraw-Hill, 1980), pp. 87, 88.

13. *Ibid.*; Blakey and Billings, *op. cit.*, p. 362; Henry Hurt, *Reasonable Doubt* (New York: Henry Holt, 1987), pp. 96, 97.

14. Summers, *Conspiracy* (McGraw-Hill, 1980), p. 36; Michael R. Beschloss, *The Crisis Years* (New York: Edward Burlingame, 1991), pp. 670, 671.

15. Hurt, *op. cit.*, pp. 96, 97; Jim Garrison, *On the Trail of the Assassins: My Investigation and Prosecution of the Murder of President Kennedy* (New York: Sheridan Square Press, 1988), pp. 127, 128.

16. Kirkpatrick's brutally honest investigation and evaluation of the Bay of Pigs is detailed in Peter Wyden, *Bay of Pigs* (New York: Touchstone, 1980), pp. 322-324.

17. Blakey and Billings, *op. cit.*, p. 151, Church Committee Report, Vol. V, many passages.

18. Noted muscian Shawn Phillips is the nephew of David Atlee Phillips. Reportedly, shortly before David Phillips died, he told Shawn's father that he had been in Dallas on November 22, 1963. However, he did not confess to any role in the JFK assassination; www.coverthistory.blogspot.com.

19. John H. Davis, *Mafia Kingfish* (New York: Signet, 1989), p. 197.

20. Blakey and Billings, *op. cit.*, p. 199.

21. *Ibid.*, p. 11.

22. Summers, *Conspiracy* (McGraw-Hill, 1980), p. 112.

23. Hurt, *op. cit.*, p. 90; Summers, *Conspiracy* (McGraw-Hill, 1980), p. 106.

24. Scheim, *Contract on America*, p. 297.

25. Summers, *Conspiracy* (McGraw-Hill, 1980), pp. 105-107; Blakey and Billings, *op. cit.*, pp. 21, 363.

26. Blakey and Billings, *op. cit.*, pp. 11, 12.

27. Hurt, *op. cit.*, p. 90; Summers, *Conspiracy* (McGraw-Hill, 1980), p. 107; Josiah Thompson, *Six Seconds in Dallas* (New York: Bernard Geis, 1967), p. 296.

28. Hurt, *op. cit.*, p. 90.

29. Warren Commission Vol. VVIV, p. 201; Hurt, *op. cit.*, p. 117; Thompson, *Six Seconds in Dallas* (New York: Bernard Geis, 1967), pp. 153, 154.

30. Hurt, *op. cit.*, p. 92; Summers, *Conspiracy* (McGraw-Hill, 1980), pp. 73, 74 108, 110; Thompson, *Six Seconds in Dallas* (New York: Bernard Geis, 1967), p. 297.

31. Summers, *Conspiracy* (McGraw-Hill, 1980), pp. 106-108; Hurt, *op. cit.*, p. 91; Thompson, *Six Seconds in Dallas* (New York: Bernard Geis, 1967), p. 234.

32. Hurt, *op. cit.*, p. 90; Scheim, *Contract on America*, p. 361; Garrison, *On the Trail of the Assassins*, p. 361.

33. FBI report 11-25-63; Summers, *Conspiracy* (McGraw-Hill, 1980), p. 478; Scheim, *Contract on America*, p. 297; Garrison, *On the Trail of the Assassins*, p. 245, 246.

34. Summers, *Conspiracy* (McGraw-Hill, 1980), pp. 72, 110; Michael Benson, *Who's Who in the JFK Assassination: An A-to-Z Encyclopedia* (New York: Citadel, 1993), pp. 124, 125, 138, 139.

35. Blakey and Billings, *op. cit.*, p. 13.

36. Hurt, *op. cit.*, pp. 93, 94; Summers, *Conspiracy* (McGraw-Hill, 1980), pp. 74, 75.

37. Summers, *Conspiracy* (McGraw-Hill, 1980), pp. 58, 59.

38. *Ibid.*, p. 61; Thompson, *Six Seconds in Dallas* (New York: Bernard Geis, 1967), pp. 155, 248.

39. HSCA 180-10099-10491, cited in JFK Assassination Records Review Board Update presentation by Joseph Backes at the JFK Lancer Conference, November, 1996.

40. Summers, *Conspiracy* (McGraw-Hill, 1980), p. 37.

41. Article by Vince Palamara in *Deep Politics* magazine 4-97.

42. HSCA 180-10074-10079, cited in JFK Assassination Records Review Board Update presentation by Joseph Backes at the JFK Lancer Conference, November, 1996.

43. Interview with Dave Powers 6-5-91 at the John F. Kennedy Presidential Library; William Novak, *Man of the House: The Life and Political Memoirs of Speaker Tip O'Neill* (New York: Random House, 1987), p. 178; Hurt, *op. cit.*, pp. 14, 67; Summers, *Conspiracy* (McGraw-Hill, 1980), pp. 58, 59; Thompson, *Six Seconds in Dallas* (New York: Bernard Geis, 1967), pp. 44-6, 220-1.

44. Interview with Dave Powers 6-5-91 at the John F. Kennedy Presidential Library; Hurt, *op. cit.*, p. 14; Summers, *Conspiracy* (McGraw-Hill, 1980), 54; Thompson, *Six Seconds in Dallas* (New York: Bernard Geis, 1967), pp. 72-7, 292-5.

45. HSCA 180-100882-10452, cited in JFK Assassination Records Review Board Update presentation by Joseph Backes at the JFK Lancer Conference, November, 1996.

46. Thompson, *Six Seconds in Dallas* (New York: Bernard Geis, 1967), pp. 72-7, 292-5.

47. Interview with Dave Powers 6-5-91 at the John F. Kennedy Presidential Library; Thompson, *Six Seconds in Dallas* (New York: Bernard Geis, 1967), pp. 106-125, 155-7, 165-170; Garrison, *On the Trail of the Assassins*, pp. 41, 43, 233; Blakey and Billings, *op. cit.*, pp. 89, 90; Hurt, *op. cit.*, p. 14; Summers, *Conspiracy* (McGraw-Hill, 1980), p. 53-60; Warren Commission Vol. XVIII, p. 758.

48. Scheim, *Contract on America*, pp. 42, 43; Summers, *Conspiracy* (McGraw-Hill, 1980), p. 80; Thompson, *Six Seconds in Dallas* (New York: Bernard Geis, 1967), pp. 161-3.

49. Scheim, *Contract on America*, p. 140.

50. Harold Feldman, "Fifty-one Witnesses: The Grassy Knoll," *Minority of One* March 1965.

51. Hurt, *op. cit.*, p. 87; Blakey and Billings, *op. cit.*, p. 16; Garrison, *On the Trail of the Assassins*, p. 23; Summers, *Conspiracy* (McGraw-Hill, 1980), pp. 110, 111, 112.

52. Warren Commission Vol. VII, pp. 105, 531; Michael Benson, *Who's Who in the JFK Assassination: An A-to-Z Encyclopedia*

(New York: Citadel, 1993), pp. 474, 475; Hurt, *op. cit.*, p. 110; Scheim, *Contract on America*, pp. 37-44; Blakey and Billings, *op. cit.*, p. 90; Summers, *Conspiracy* (McGraw-Hill, 1980), pp. 81, 82, 536; Thompson, *Six Seconds in Dallas* (New York: Bernard Geis, 1967), pp. 164-5, 247; Michael Canfield and Alan J. Weberman, *Coup d'État in America: The CIA and the Assassination of John F. Kennedy* (New York: Third Press, 1975), pp. 55-7.

53. Benson, *op. cit.*, pp. 192, 193; Scheim, *Contract on America*, pp. 40, 42; Thompson, *Six Seconds in Dallas* (New York: Bernard Geis, 1967), pp. 159-162.

54. Summers, *Conspiracy* (McGraw-Hill, 1980), p. 82.

55. Robert MacNeil, ed., *The Way We Were: 1963, the Year Kennedy Was Shot* (New York: Carroll & Graf, 1988), p. 195.

56. Warren Commsion document #385.

57. Thompson, *Six Seconds in Dallas* (New York: Bernard Geis, 1967), pp. 304-311, 314, 315; Craig later said the man may have been black.

58. Hurt, *op. cit.*, p. 110.

59. Garrison, *On the Trail of the Assassins*, p. 339.

60. Dan Wise and Marietta Maxfield, *The Day Kennedy Died* (San Antonio: Naylor, 1964); Garrison, *On the Trail of the Assassins*, pp. 233-4.

61. Scheim, *Contract on America*, p. 67; Thompson, *Six Seconds in Dallas* (New York: Bernard Geis, 1967), pp. 173-5, 186, 247; Summers, *Conspiracy* (McGraw-Hill, 1980), pp. 476, 477.

62. Hurt, *op. cit.*, p. 17; Jim Garrison, *A Heritage of Stone* (New York: Putnam, 1970), p. 95.

63. William Turner presentation abstract, COPA Conference 10-94.

64. William Manchester, The Death of a President, November 20-November 25, 1963 (New York: Harper & Row, 1967), chronology on inside front covers; Hurt, *op. cit.*, p. 14; Thompson, *Six Seconds in Dallas* (New York: Bernard Geis, 1967), pp. 51-62.

65. Hurt, *op. cit.*, p. 84.

66. FBI report 11-25-63.

67. Hurt, *op. cit.*, p. 17; Summers, *Conspiracy* (McGraw-Hill, 1980), p. 83.

68. Summers, *Conspiracy* (McGraw-Hill, 1980), pp. 115, 602.

69. Blakey and Billings, *op. cit.*, p. 18.

70. Garrison, *On the Trail of the Assassins*, pp. 336, 337.

71. Summers, *Conspiracy* (McGraw-Hill, 1980), p. 115.

72. Garrison, *On the Trail of the Assassins*, p. 339.

73. Hurt, *op. cit.*, pp. 163, 164.

Chapter Fifty-Nine: RFK's Suspicions and C-Day is Put on Hold

1. Interview of Martino's friend Fred Claassen by Earl Golz, 1978, on file at the Assassination Archives and Research Center.

2. David Atlee Phillips, *The Night Watch* (New York: Atheneum, 1977), p. 12.

3. Article by Dennis Ford, *Third Decade* 11-92.

4. As noted in a previous chapter, Ruby had $7,000 on him that day, and said later he was carrying a pistol on November 22 (if asked by authorities, he could have claimed he had the pistol for protection because he was carrying so much cash). So Ruby would have been able to come up with a credible scenario if he had an opportunity to shoot Oswald on November 22, either when Oswald was "fleeing" from the Book Depository or if Ruby had encountered a pistol-toting Oswald in the Oak Cliff neighborhood (Ruby could have claimed Oswald attempted to rob him).

5. Rosselli's role as a producer was uncredited on the film, but is confirmed by court documents—see Charles Rappleye and Ed Becker, *All American Mafioso* (New York: Barricade, 1995), pp. 120, 121.

6. Anthony Summers, *Conspiracy* (New York: McGraw-Hill, 1980), pp. 109, 114.

7. Summers, *Conspiracy* (McGraw-Hill, 1980), p. 115.

8. Warren Commission Vol. VI, pp. 438-444; William Turner presentation abstract, COPA Conference 10-94.

9. Summers, *Conspiracy* (McGraw-Hill, 1980), pp. 114, 117, 118, 124.

10. Summers, *Conspiracy* (McGraw-Hill, 1980), p. 115.

11. Larry Harris, "The Other Murder," *Dateline Dallas* 11-22-63.

12. David E. Scheim, *Contract on America* (New York: Zebra, 1989), pp. 37, 56; Summers, *Conspiracy* (McGraw-Hill, 1980), pp. 116-126; Jim Garrison, *On the Trail of the Assassins: My Investigation and Prosecution of the Murder of President Kennedy* (New York: Sheridan Square Press, 1988), pp. 375-380.

13. Anthony Summers, *Conspiracy* (New York: Paragon House, 1989), p. 557; Michael Benson, *Who's Who in the JFK Assassination: An A-to-Z Encyclopedia* (New York: Citadel, 1993), pp. 36, 37, 146.

14. "The Other Murder" by Larry Harris, *Dateline Dallas*, 11-22-63.

15. The following quotes are from Larry Harris, "The Other Murder," *Dateline Dallas* 11-22-63: The lineups regarding Oswald and the Tippit slaying have been described as "a travesty. In the first two, the disheveled and bruised Oswald was paraded before witnesses (including Markham) accompanied by two detectives and a jail clerk who were neatly attired in slacks and dress shirts." The next day's lineup, viewed by Tippit witness (William) Scoggins, "was even more outrageous: Oswald, two teenagers, and a Hispanic man." The key witness regarding Oswald and the Tippit slaying was Helen Markham. Researcher Larry Harris notes that while "publicly the Warren Report called 'Markham's . . . testimony reliable,'" in private memos, the Warren staff said "This witness is very unsure of herself on most points." Warren staff attorney Joseph Ball "complained that her account was 'full of mistakes' and 'utterly unreliable,'" and "several years later Ball derided Markham publicly during a debate, called her an 'utter screwball.'" Warren attorney Wesley Liebeler "dismissed her story as 'contradictory' and 'worthless.'" Another key witness for the Warren Commission regarding Oswald and the Tippit slaying was William Scoggins. "But an FBI report reveals that two days later, when FBI agents showed him a photograph of Oswald, Scoggins told them he couldn't be sure the person he observed on Nov. 22 was 'actually identical with Oswald.'"

16. Anthony Summers, *Not In Your Lifetime* (New York: Marlowe & Co., 1998), p. 75.

17. Henry Hurt, *Reasonable Doubt* (New York: Henry Holt, 1987), p. 17; Summers, *Conspiracy* (McGraw-Hill, 1980), pp. 83, 84; Tippit chronology by Larry Harris.

18. Article by William Turner in *Ramparts* magazine, 1-68.

19. Hurt, *op. cit.,* pp. 17, 18; Summers, *Conspiracy* (McGraw-Hill, 1980), p. 126; Article by Dennis Ford, *Third Decade,* 11-92.

20. G. Robert Blakey and Richard N. Billings, *The Plot to Kill the President* (New York: Times Books, 1981), p. 19; Garrison, *On the Trail of the Assassins,* pp. 95-117; Hurt, *op. cit.,* p. 18.

21. Blakey and Billings, *op. cit.,* p. 316; Garrison, *On the Trail of the Assassins,* p. 361; Summers, *Conspiracy* (McGraw-Hill, 1980), p. 497.

22. Summers, *Conspiracy* (McGraw-Hill, 1980), p. 246.

23. *Ibid.,* p. 231.

24. Garrison, *On the Trail of the Assassins,* pp. 145, 146.

25. Hurt, *op. cit.,* pp. 61-7.

26. Scheim, *Contract on America,* p. 158; Blakey and Billings, *op. cit.,* p. 315; Summers, *Conspiracy* (McGraw-Hill, 1980), p. 134.

27. David S. Lifton, *Best Evidence: Disguise and Deception in the Assassination of John F. Kennedy* (New York: Carroll & Graf, 1988), p. 91; Hurt, *op. cit.,* pp. 15, 70; Josiah Thompson, *Six Seconds in Dallas* (New York: Bernard Geis, 1967), pp. 207-212, 228, 229.

28. Phone interview with John Diuguid 9-30-04; Scheim, *Contract on America,* p. 80, Blakey and Billings, *op. cit.,* p. 246.

29. *Ibid.,* all three references.

30. John H. Davis, *Mafia Kingfish* (New York: Signet, 1989), pp. 198, 199.

31. *Ibid.,* p. 199.

32. 1967 CIA Inspector General's Report, p. 93a.

33. Church Committee Report, Vol. V, p. 101.

34. Interviews with Harry Williams 2-24-92, 4-92, 7-1-92, 11-13-92, 7-24-93, 2-21-95; John McCone's desk calendar for 11-22-63, on file at the National Archives.

35. Richard D. Mahoney, *Sons & Brothers* (New York: Arcade, 1999), p. 294.

36. *Ibid.;* also John McCone's desk calendar for 11-22-63, on file at the National Archives.

37. Mahoney, *op. cit.,* p. 294.

38. Arthur Schlesinger, Jr., *Robert Kennedy and His Times* (New York: Ballantine, 1979), p. 664.

39. John McCone's desk calendar for 11-22-63, on file at the National Archives.

40. James P. Hosty, Jr., *Assignment: Oswald* (New York: Arcade Publishing, 1996), p. 219, cited in Peter Dale Scott, *Deep Politics III,* http://history-matters.com/pds/dp3.htm.

41. Hosty, *op. cit.,* p. 219.

42. *U.S. News & World Report* 3-15-93.

43. Scheim, *Contract on America,* p. 217; Blakey and Billings, *op. cit.,* 144; Summers, *Conspiracy* (McGraw-Hill, 1980), pp. 433, 434.

44. Phone interview with J. P. Mullins 12-10-96.

45. FBI Airtel to Director, 10-1-74.

46. Jack Newfield, "I want Kennedy killed," *Penthouse* 5-92; Summers, *Conspiracy* (McGraw-Hill, 1980), p. 500; Walter Sheridan, *The Fall and Rise of Jimmy Hoffa* (New York: Saturday Review Press, 1972), p. 300.

47. Bernard Fensterwald, Jr. and Michael Ewing, *Coincidence or Conspiracy?* (New York: Kensington, 1977), pp. 359-63.

48. Haynes Johnson, "One Day's Events Shattered America's Hopes and Certainties," *Washington Post* 11-20-83.

49. Mahoney, *op. cit.*, pp. 294, 295.

50. Interviews with Harry Williams 2-24-92, 4-92, 7-1-92.

51. *New Orleans Times-Picayune*, 11-22-73.

52. Statement of Alberto Flower in the Office of the District Attorney 1-23-67; Peter Dale Scott, *Crime and Cover-Up* (Santa Barbara, Calif.: Open Archive Press, 1993), pp. 16, 17.

53. Interviews with Harry Williams 2-24-92, 4-92, 7-1-92.

54. Minute-by-minute transcript, NBC News, 11-22-63.

55. Frank Ragano and Selwyn Raab, *Mob Lawyer* (New York: Scribners, 1994), pp. 147, 148.

56. Hurt, *op. cit.*, pp. 18, 19; Garrison, *On the Trail of the Assassins*, p. 206.

57. Fensterwald and Ewing, *op. cit.*, pp. 322-3.

58. Navarre and Simms Memorandum of June 1, 1967, cited by A. J. Weberman.

59. Blakey and Billings, *op. cit.*, p. 166.

60. FBI report 11-25-63, 94-448-12.

61. HSCA Vol. X, pp. 113, 114.

62. Summers, *Conspiracy* (McGraw-Hill, 1980), pp. 497, 506.

63. Peter Dale Scott, *Deep Politics and the Death of JFK* (Berkeley: University of California Press, 1993). pp. 131-135.

64. Travis Kirk, cited by A. J. Weberman.

65. Peter Dale Scott, *Deep Politics and the Death of JFK* (Berkeley: University of California Press, 1993), p. 329.

66. Scheim, *Contract on America*, p. 62; Blakey and Billings, *op. cit.*, pp. 46, 397; Summers, *Conspiracy* (McGraw-Hill, 1980), p. 483; HSCA Vol. X, p. 113.

67. Mahoney, *op. cit.*, p. 273.

68. Scheim, *Contract on America*, p. 159; Blakey and Billings, *op. cit.*, p. 317; Summers, *Conspiracy* (McGraw-Hill, 1980), p. 480.

69. Scheim, *Contract on America*, pp. 533, 534; Garrison, *On the Trail of the Assassins*, pp. 193, 194; Blakey and Billings, *op. cit.*, p. 318.

70. Garrison, *On the Trail of the Assassins*, p. 193.

71. Blakey and Billings, *op. cit.*, p. 318; Summers, *Conspiracy* (McGraw-Hill, 1980), p. 480.

72. Scheim, *Contract on America*, p. 160; Blakey and Billings, *op. cit.*, p. 318.

73. Scheim, *Contract on America*, pp. 163, 164, 166; Garrison, *On the Trail of the Assassins*, p. 325, 326.

74. FBI memo by T. N. Goble 4-2-64, cited by Paul Hoch, EOC vol. 10 #2 7-22-88.

75. William Manchester, *The Death of a President* (New York: Harper & Row, 1967), chronology on inside front covers; Anthony Summers, *Conspiracy* (New York: McGraw-Hill, 1980); Garrison, *On the Trail of the Assassins*.

76. Filmed interview with FBI Special Agent James Sibert by William Law, presented at 2002 JFK Lancer Conference in Dallas.

77. Lifton, *Best Evidence*, many passages.

78. Interview with Dave Powers 6-5-91 at the John F. Kennedy Presidential Library; Interview with confidential Kennedy C-Day aide source 3-17-92.

79. Lifton, *Best Evidence*, many passages.

80. Phone interview with confidential Kennedy C-Day aide 3-17-92; phone interview with confidential Kennedy Foreign Policy Advisor source 4-18-96.

81. *Warren Commission Hearings*, Volume 22, page 96.

82. Dr. George Burkley's Oral History at the JFK Presidential Library.

83. HSCA document #002071, p. 2, cited by Kathleen Cunningham, COPA abstracts 10-94.

84. Gus Russo, *Live by the Sword* (Baltimore: Bancroft Press, 1978), p. 325.

85. Interview with confidential Kennedy C-Day aide source 3-17-92.

86. Interview with Dean Rusk 3-5-92; interview with ex-FBI Agent Courtney Evans; Harry Williams interview 4-92; "official account" reference withheld to protect source confidentiality, but will be released upon source's death.

87. Author's interview with confidential Kennedy C-Day aide 3-17-92; the source made reference to Jack Anderson's 1988 TV special about the JFK assassination and said while it had details wrong (including any suggestion that Castro was involved in JFK's death), he believed its basic premise—that JFK was killed by mobsters involved in the CIA–Mafia plots, with help from one or more Cuban exiles—was true. The mobsters the special focused on were Rosselli, Trafficante, and Marcello.

88. Hurt, *op. cit.*, p. 49.

89. Alexander M. Haig, Jr., *Inner Circles* (New York: Warner Books, 1992), p. 108.

90. Department of the Army document dated 9-14-63 provided by the State Department, in SSCIA record number 157-10005-10372 dated 3-27-76, declassified 2-18-94.

91. Haig, *op. cit.*, pp. 113, 114.

92. Joseph A. Califano, Jr., *The Triumph & Tragedy of Lyndon Johnson: The White House Years* (New York: Simon & Schuster, 1991), pp. 13, 14.

Chapter Sixty: Another Mob Hit in Dallas Devastates Bobby

1. Richard D. Mahoney, *Sons & Brothers* (New York: Arcade, 1999), p. 417.

2. Bernard Fensterwald, "The Case of Secret Service Agent Abraham W. Bolden," *Computers and Automation* 6-71.

3. "Threats on Kennedy Made Here," *Tampa Tribune* 11-23-63.

4. "Man Held in Threats to JFK," *Miami Herald* 11-24-63.

5. Evan Thomas, *The Very Best Men* (New York: Simon & Schuster, 1995), pp. 307, 308.

6. Anthony Summers, *Conspiracy* (New York: McGraw-Hill, 1980), p. 417.

7. Michael R. Beschloss, *Taking Charge: The Johnson White House Tapes, 1963-64* (New York: Simon & Schuster, 1997), p. 22.

8. Peter Dale Scott, *Deep Politics III,* http://history-matters.com/pds/dp3.htm.

9. Gus Russo, *Live by the Sword* (Baltimore: Bancroft Press, 1978), p. 566.

10. CIA #104-10429-10231, 11-24-64.

11. "James Johnston, former counsel with Church Committee," *Washington Post,* 9-27-92.

12. Evan Thomas, *Robert Kennedy: His Life* (New York: Simon & Schuster, 2000), p. 279.

13. [a] Virgil Bailey phone interviews with Gary Shaw 4-26-80, 4-28-80; [b] additional information from the files of Bud Fensterwald.

14. Ibid. [a]; Ibid. [b]; Jean-Pierre Charbonneau, *The Canadian Connection* (Ottawa: Optimum, 1976) pp. 47, 262.

15. Virgil Bailey phone interview with Gary Shaw 4-28-80.

16. Mertz was an experienced professional only doing the hit for the money, so if he could have sent another man to Dallas in his place, he certainly would have done that.

17. Anthony Summers, *Conspiracy* (New York: Paragon House, 1989), p. 311.

18. Garrison, *On the Trail of the Assassins,* 215.

19. FBI 44-24016-275; C. Ray Hall Warren Commission Exhibit 3; FBI DL 44-1639; all cited by A. J. Weberman.

20. G. Robert Blakey and Richard N. Billings, *The Plot to Kill the President* (New York: Times Books, 1981), p. 319.

21. David E. Scheim, *Contract on America* (New York: Zebra, 1989), 159, 168; Blakey and Billings, *op. cit.,* p. 319.

22. Blakey and Billings, *op. cit.,* p. 320.

23. *Ibid.;* Scheim, *Contract on America,* p. 169.

24. Scheim, *Contract on America,* p. 174-8.

25. Warren Commission Document #205; Church Committee Report, Vol. V, pp. 30, 61-63; Skip Johnson and Tony Durr, "Ex-Tampan in JFK Plot?," *Tampa Tribune* 9-5-76.

26. CIA F82-0272/1, 82-1625 (4); F82-0272/2; Jan 64 cable to CIA Director from (censored); HSCA Report, p. 117; Summers, *Conspiracy* (New York: McGraw-Hill, 1980), p. 444.

27. Michael Benson, *Who's Who in the JFK Assassination: An A-to-Z Encyclopedia* (New York: Citadel, 1993), p. 401.

28. Gus Russo, *Live by the Sword* (Baltimore: Bancroft Press, 1978), p. 498.

29. "'We never thought it would come to this,' Harris attorney says," CNN, 2-13-03.

30. John H. Davis, *Mafia Kingfish* (New York: Signet, 1989), p. 225.

31. Dick Russell, *The Man Who Knew Too Much* (New York: Carroll & Graf/R. Gallen, 1992), p. 551.

32. *Ibid.*

33. Scheim, *Contract on America,* pp. 148, 180, 181; Summers, *Conspiracy* (McGraw-Hill, 1980), p. 483.

34. Blakey and Billings, *op. cit.,* pp. 320-322; Summers, *Conspiracy* (McGraw-Hill, 1980), pp. 483, 490-492; Garrison, *On the Trail of the Assassins,* p. 202.

35. Scheim, *Contract on America,* pp. 155, 172, 173, 179; Blakey and Billings, *op. cit.,* p. 320; Seth Kantor, *The Ruby Cover-Up* (New York: Zebra Books, 1978), p. 64.

36. Scheim, *Contract on America,* p. 179; Blakey and Billings, *op. cit.,* p. 320; Summers, *Conspiracy* (McGraw-Hill, 1980), p. 65.

37. Summers, *Conspiracy* (McGraw-Hill, 1980), p. 604.

38. Anthony and Robbyn Summers, "The Ghosts of November," *Vanity Fair,* December 1994.

39. Blakey and Billings, *op. cit.,* p. 320; Scheim, *Contract on America,* p. 183; Henry Hurt, *Reasonable Doubt* (New York: Henry Holt, 1987), p. 19.

40. Scheim, *Contract on America,* pp. 155, 182; Blakey and Billings, *op. cit.,* p. 320; Summers, *Conspiracy* (McGraw-Hill, 1980), p. 484.

41. Blakey and Billings, *op. cit.,* pp. 321-3; Summers, *Conspiracy* (McGraw-Hill, 1980), pp. 484, 486, 487.

42. Blakey and Billings, *op. cit.,* p. 320; Scheim, *Contract on America,* pp. 182, 183.

43. Blakey and Billings, *op. cit.*, pp. 320, 321, 330; Summers, *Conspiracy* (McGraw-Hill, 1980), pp. 137, 484, 485.

44. Police inteview with William Somersett transcribed on 11-26-63.

45. Blakey and Billings, *op. cit.*, p. 324; Summers, *Conspiracy* (McGraw-Hill, 1980), p. 483; John H. Davis, *Mafia Kingfish* (New York: Signet, 1989), p. 603.

46. Hurt, *op. cit.*, p. 19; Blakey and Billings, *op. cit.*, pp. 22, 321.

47. Davis, *Mafia Kingfish* (Signet, 1989), p. 603.

48. Blakey and Billings, *op. cit.*, pp. 321, 324.

49. Peter Dale Scott, *Deep Politics and the Death of JFK* (Berkeley: University of California Press, 1993), p. 154.

50. Scheim, *Contract on America*, p. 149.

51. Evan Thomas, *Robert Kennedy: His Life* (New York: Simon & Schuster, 2000), p. 281.

52. 11-24-64 FBI memo from Handley to Rosen, released 6-18-94.

53. Evan Thomas, *Robert Kennedy*, pp. 282, 283.

54. John Davis presentation, 1993 ASK Conference.

Chapter Sixty-One: The Legacy of Secrecy

1. HSCA Vol X, pp. 105-136; Anthony Summers, *Conspiracy* (New York: Paragon House, 1989), John H. Davis, *Mafia Kingfish* (New York: McGraw-Hill, 1989), and David E. Scheim, *Contract on America* (New York: Zebra, 1989), all many passages.

2. HSCA Vol X, pp. 199-205; new documents and testimony cited by Larry Hancock in *Someone Would have Talked* (Southlake, Tex.: JFK Lancer, 2005, advance draft).

3. Warren Commission Vol. XIV, pp. 471, 596, 597; Carl Sifakis, *The Mafia Encyclopedia* (New York: Facts On File, 1987), pp. 103, 104; Scheim, *Contract on America*, many passages.

4. Warren Commission documents #561, #657, 662, and many FBI reports about John Martino; Anthony Summers, *Conspiracy* (New York: McGraw-Hill, 1980), pp. 447, 448, 594; Alexander M. Haig, Jr., *Inner Circles* (New York: Warner Books, 1992), p 115; Gus Russo, *Live by the Sword* (Baltimore: Bancroft Press, 1978), p. 341; Many Warren Commission documents cited in *Crime and Cover-up, Deep Politics,* and *Deep Politics III* by Peter Dale Scott; Joseph A. Califano, Jr., *The Triumph & Tragedy of Lyndon Johnson* (New York: Simon & Schuster, 1991), p. 295; HSCA Vol. XI, pp. 438-441.

5. Anthony and Robbyn Summers, "The Ghosts of November," *Vanity Fair,* December 1994.

6. *Ibid.*; Michael R. Beschloss, *Taking Charge* (New York: Simon & Schuster, 1997), p. 67.

7. Phone interview with confidential Naval Intelligence investigator source 10-27-91; HSCA Vol. XI, pp. 542-551.

8. Foreign Relations of the United States, Volume XI, Department of State, #384, 12-3-63.

9. Interview with Kennedy Administration official 3-6-95.

10. Interviews with Harry Williams 2-24-92, 4-92, 7-1-92.

11. Church Committee Report, Vol. V, p. 31.

12. David Corn, *Blond Ghost* (New York: Simon & Schuster, 1994), pp. 110, 433; CIA Record #104-10076-10252 dated 12-10-63.

13. See Chapter 12 for many examples of the large level of US support Artime received throughout 1964 and into 1965. In early 1964, the monthly intelligence budget for what was left of AMWORLD was $9,000, according to CIA 104-10308-10083.

14. Martin Ebon, *Che: Making of a Legend* (New York: New American Library, 1969), p. 52.

15. Carlos Franqui, *Family Portrait with Fidel: A Memoir* (New York: Random House, 1984), pp. 218, 219.

16. Joseph A. Califano, Jr., *Inside* (New York: PublicAffairs, 2004). pp. 126, 127; Interviews with Harry Williams 2-24-92, 4-92, 7-1-92. Alexander Butterfield began working with Haig and Califano about the Cuban exile troops around this time, per Summers and Summers, "The Ghosts of November," *Vanity Fair,* December 1994.

17. Handwritten notes on file at the Assassination Archives and Research Center titled "Official level: 2nd bay of pigs," courtesy of Jim Lesar.

18. Arthur Schlesinger, Jr., *Robert Kennedy and His Times* (New York: Ballantine, 1979), p. 780.

19. See 1964 AMWORLD files, including CIA 104-10308-10080, 104-10308-10084, 104-10308-10098, and many others; See also Menoyo, Ray, and Artime CIA files for 1964 and FBI reports from early 1964 about their groups working together.

20. Dorothy J. Samuels and James A. Goodman, "How Justice Shielded the CIA," *Inquiry* 10-18-78, cited by Peter Dale Scott in *Drugs, Contras and the CIA: Government Policies and the Cocaine Economy. An Analysis of Media and Government Response to the Gary Webb Stories in the San Jose Mercury News (1996-2000);* Scott also cites US Cong., House, Committee on Government Operations, Justice Department Handling of Cases Involving Classified Data and Claims of National Security. 96th Cong., 1st Sess.; H. Rept. No. 96-280 (Washington: GPO, 1979).

21. HSCA vol. X, p. 59; CIA document from HSCA, Record Number 180-10141-10419.

22. RIF 104-10241-10065.

23. CIA cable March 17, 1963 cited in HSCA Vol. X, pg. 78; CIA Document dated 3-19-64, Document ID #1993.07.31.12:25:16:530059, declassified 7-31-93.

24. CIA document; 4-25-77, Record Number 104-10400-10123, Russ Holmes Work File, Subject: AMTRUNK Operation, declassified 10-26-98.

25. Tad Szulc, *Fidel: A Critical Portrait* (New York: Morrow, 1986), p. 599.

26. Jorge G. Castañeda, *Compañero: The Life and Death of Che Guevara* (New York: Knopf, 1997), p. 275, 1997.

27. CIA document, HSCA, Record Number 180-10143-10209, CIA Segregated Collection, Agency File Number 28-43-01, declassified 8-16-95; Enrique G. Encinosa, *Cuba: The Unfinished Revolution* (Austin: Eakin, 1988), p. 196.

28. Szulc, *Fidel*, p. 603.

29. HSCA Vol. X, p. 184.

30. Felix I. Rodriguez and John Weisman, *Shadow Warrior* (New York: Simon and Schuster, 1989), p. 133.

31. Castañeda, *op. cit.,* pp. 279, 296, 316-318; Daniel James, *Che Guevara: A Biography* (New York: Stein and Day, 1969), p. 154.

32. Castañeda, *op. cit.,* pp. 317, 1997.

33. James, *op. cit.,* pp. 154, 155.

34. Richard Goodwin, *Remembering America: A Voice from the Sixties* (Boston: Little, Brown, 1988), pp. 205, 206; James, *op. cit.,* p. 284 (and others); Castañeda, *op. cit.*

35. Rodriguez and Weisman, *op. cit.,* p. 171. Gaeton Fonzi, *The Last Investigation* (New York: Thunder's Mouth, 1994), pp. 373, 376, 389.

36. James, *op. cit.,* p. 285.

37. Interviews with Harry Williams 2-24-92, 4-92, 7-1-92.

38. Several accounts can be found in Michael Benson, *Who's Who in the JFK Assassination* (New York: Citadel, 1993) and Scheim, *Contract on America*. While there have been many "mysterious death" lists about the JFK assassination over the years, the most credible and relevant accounts are those involving mobsters, mob associates, or those whose testimony threatened mobsters.

39. Interview with ex-Secret Service Agent Abraham Bolden 4-15-98.

40. John Kidner, *Crimaldi, Contract Killer: A True Story* (Washington: Acropolis, 1976), pp. 203-297; Carl Sifakis, *The Mafia Encyclopedia* (New York: Facts On File, 1987), pp. 30, 52, 78, 103, 104, 124, 139, 281, 349.

41. Interview with ex-Secret Service Agent Abraham Bolden 4-15-98; House Select Committee on Assassinations Report 231, 232, 636; *New York Times* 12-6-67; Abraham Bolden file at the Assassination Archives and Research Center.

42. The Staff and Editors of *Newsday, The Heroin Trail* (New York: Signet, 1974), p. 115.

43. Letter from Martin Waldron (no relation to author) of the *New York Times* to the New Orleans Police Dept., 11-21-66; a copy was given to District Attorney Jim Garrison and later wound up in the files of the Assassination Archives and Research Center.

44. Scheim, *Contract on America*; Seth Kantor, *The Ruby Cover-Up* (New York: Zebra Books, 1978).

45. Davis, *Mafia Kingfish,* pp. 346, 348-355; Scheim, *Contract on America,* pp. 319-331.

46. Handwritten notes of Richard E. Sprague's interview with Haynes Johnson at the Madison Hotel, Washington, D.C., dated 1-12-73 on file at the Assassination Archives and Research Center; William Turner interview with Harry Williams 11-28-73. In addition to the beneficial actions of Haig, Califano, and Butterfield in Watergate, the authors feel that James McCord has not received enough credit for exposing the crimes of Watergate. As he notes on the McCord family Web site (mccordfamilyassn.com/endpage.htm), "The top news stories of 1973 were these two stories: who planned Watergate and who carried out the Watergate cover-up and only James McCord first disclosed that information to the public."

47. After leaving the CIA, Harvey's last job had been as an editor at a firm slated to publish Bradley Ayers's book about his work with the CIA, where he encountered Johnny Rosselli. In July 1976, Johnny Rosselli disappeared in Florida, a short time after he had met with Trafficante. His body was discovered, dismembered, floating in an oil drum, several days later.

48. Fonzi, *op. cit.,* several passages; (Nicoletti) *Miami Herald* 4-1-77; Benson, *op. cit.,* several passages.

49. FBI DL 183A-1f035-Sub L 3.6.86, cited by A. J. Weberman.

50. FBI Dallas 175-109 3.3.89, cited by A. J. Weberman.

51. FBI 124-10253-10112, cited by A. J. Weberman.

52. CR 137A-5467-69, 6-9-88, cited in Brad O'Leary and L. E. Seymour, *Triangle of Death: The Shocking Truth About the Role of South Vietnam and the French Mafia in the Assassination of JFK* (Nashville: WND Books, 2003).

53. Article by Jack Newfield, *New York Post,* 1-14-92.

54. "Truth or Fiction?," *St. Petersburg Times* 4-18-94.

55. Jack Newfield, "I want Kennedy killed," *Penthouse* 5-92.

56. Researcher A. J. Weberman found that a CIA handbook from November 1974 said that documents with "RYBAT . . . sensitivity" should be placed "in an envelope sealed with black tape" and if there are many documents, "the desk officer may blacktape the entire dossier." Such files "will be handled as restricted dossiers." "RYBAT" was one of the code designations that was supposed to be placed on the CIA's AMWORLD documents. It's not hard to image thousands of such dossiers related to C-Day, all of them withheld from most government investigating committees.

INDEX

NOTE: All dates without a year are from the year 1963 (May 28 means May 28, 1963).

ACKNOWLEDGMENTS

Most people usually don't read Acknowledgments, so to give you an incentive, we've included one new revelation about the assassination and Senator Arlen Specter in the following pages. That way, you'll also get to read about some of the many people who've made this book a reality.

We benefited not only from Paul Hoch's decades of research, but also from his friendship and assistance over the years. His encyclopedic knowledge about areas ranging from the Odio Incident to Naval Intelligence documents was of tremendous help, and his guidance was invaluable.

William Turner's work and life have been an inspiration in many ways. As an FBI veteran, he had the courage to stand up to J. Edgar Hoover in the early 1960s, at a time when most of America's most powerful politicians were afraid to do so. He not only wrote the first book on US covert actions against Cuba, but knew from the start that those actions had somehow impacted JFK's assassination. Turner was the first investigator to interview Harry Williams, and he generously shared his notes with us, allowing us to hit the ground running and learn far more than we ever expected.

Gary Shaw was tenacious in pursuing Freedom of Information lawsuits to obtain JFK documents in the 1980s, and was always ready to share his vast knowledge. His work in the areas of Michel Victor Mertz, QJWIN, and the Frenchman deported from Dallas was especially helpful.

Larry Hancock continues to do groundbreaking research in the areas of David Morales, John Martino, and CIA anti-Castro operations like Operation Forty and AMWORLD. He also puts on the annual JFK-Lancer Conference in Dallas, along with Debra Conway, which brings together a wide variety of experts and researchers. Debra's nonprofit JFK-Lancer Web site acts as a valuable resource for obtaining the latest information and research. Among the new generation of researchers is Stuart Wexler, who—along with Larry—provided us with some of the most recently released AMWORLD documents.

Dr. John Newman was the first person to uncover the code name AMWORLD, in the early 1990s, when I first described to him the plan that Harry Williams had outlined. Dr. Newman's unique background as both a history professor and a retired Army major with military-intelligence experience, gave him insights into the arcane world of CIA documents that we benefited from greatly.

Mike Cain has spent many years researching the life of his half-brother, Richard Cain, and helped us gain a better understanding of Richard and his associates in the Chicago Mafia. Mike, a mild-mannered computer programmer, couldn't be more different from Richard, and we look forward to his upcoming book about his fascinating sibling.

Gordon Winslow is a recognized expert in the field of Cuban exiles and their covert operations, especially Rolando Masferrer. Always quick to share information, Gordon's excellent Spanish was very helpful when we interviewed Antonio Veciana about his meeting with Oswald.

Vince Palamara has made a specialty of researching JFK's Secret Service agents, and we are grateful to him for putting us in touch with Abraham Bolden. French journalist Stephane Risset was able to obtain information from Jean Souetre—and about Michel Victor Mertz—that was very important. In England, we were ably assisted by Paul Byrne and his associates such as Ian Griggs.

Many experts in the field have been just as gracious in person as their books are informative, and the following were especially important to us. Gaeton Fonzi's work as a Senate and Congressional investigator uncovered crucial information about David Atlee Phillips and David Morales. One can only imagine what he must have felt like in the 1970s when one witness after another—Prio, De Mohrenschildt, Artime—died before he could fully interview them. Also pursuing potentially dangerous investigations in those days, when Trafficante and Marcello were still in power, was Dan Moldea, the nation's top expert on Jimmy Hoffa. Likewise, Anthony Summers, now aided by Robbyn Summers, was investigating Guy Banister and David Ferrie in New Orleans when Carlos Marcello still ruled. John H. Davis had the guts to write a full-length biography of Carlos Marcello when Marcello was still alive. Those authors, and many more, were willing to dig into places others feared to tread, and we benefited hugely from their efforts. Mary Ferrell was another fearless researcher, whose absence is sorely missed.

Much research doesn't involve things like interviewing an aspiring assassin on a dark waterfront or driving an airport hit man to the airport (more about those experiences in our next book), but instead involves digging through hundreds of books and hundreds of thousands of documents. Jim Lesar at the Assassination Archives and Research Center has carried on the work of Bud Fensterwald, both in providing an incredible research facility and in being one of the country's top Freedom of Information attorneys. The Center is a repository for the work of earlier investigators, and by going through all of their public files, we were able to build upon the private research of many of the top experts in the field.

The only place with more JFK documents is probably the National Archives, just outside Washington. Steve Tilly and his staff have always been very helpful, and an increasing number of key documents—especially about the Coup Plans prepared by Cyrus Vance and others—are viewable on their Web site. Not nearly as large, but more focused on covert operations, is the National Security Archive at Georgetown University. Their targeted collections especially relevant for this book include the Bay of Pigs, the Cuban Missile Crisis, the CIA's 1954 Guatemala coup, and US actions against Chile and Nicaragua (which involved several C-Day veterans). Many documents are available at the National Archives and other research facilities due to the efforts of the JFK Assassination Records Review Board, and its director, Jeremy Gunn. They found and declassified many crucial document troves, ranging from AMWORLD files to collections focusing on the Joint Chiefs and Joseph Califano. Many in the media were also helpful in the efforts to get more documents declassified, such as Evan Thomas, whose books on the CIA and Bobby Kennedy we found very useful.

Also helpful in our research was the John F. Kennedy Presidential Library and its longtime director, Dave Powers. As we mentioned in the Introduction, Powers vividly described the shots from the grassy knoll, which he said were also witnessed by Kenneth O'Donnell, another JFK aide in the limo with him. Since they were in the limo directly behind JFK's, they had a tragically perfect view as the events unfolded. Five years after JFK's death, Powers and O'Donnell told Tip O'Neill—later Speaker of the House—what they saw. As recounted in O'Neill's autobiography, when he asked O'Donnell why he didn't tell the Warren Commission what he saw, O'Donnell said he "told the FBI . . . but they said it couldn't have happened that way . . . so I testified the way they wanted me to."

In O'Donnell's Warren Commission testimony on May 18, 1964, he said the shots came "from the right rear"—the direction of the Book Deposi-tory—but qualifies it a bit by saying that "in part is reconstruction" and "would be my best judgement." Powers was apparently more problematic for the Commission. Powers, one of JFK's closest aides, did not actually testify to the Warren Commission. Instead, his remarks are represented by an affi-davit. Even in the affidavit, while saying his first "impression was that the shots came from the right and overhead," Powers added that "I also had a fleeting impression that the noise appeared to come from the front in the area of the triple overpass" (the grassy knoll). Powers made it clear in our inter-view that he was sure at least two of the shots came from the front.

Powers indicated to us that the FBI, possibly Hoover himself, had pres-sured O'Donnell to testify as he did. As far as his own statement was con-cerned, Powers said something like "the Warren Commission was handed this theory on a platter, and anything that didn't conform with it, they just didn't take." Powers said that when he tried to tell his story, one of the Warren people kept interrupting him. Perhaps that's why Powers is repre-sented only by an affidavit, not by full testimony like O'Donnell.

In Warren Commission Volume VII, Powers's affidavit bears his typeset name, but gives no indication of which Warren Commission counsel might have taken his statement. With the help of the National Archives staff, we were able to get a copy of Powers's hand-signed statement for the first time. Surprisingly, it bears another signature as well—Arlen Specter, the father of the single (magic) bullet theory.

We did not get the affidavit with Specter's name until February 5, 1999, and Powers had passed away a year earlier. Specter conducted the interroga-tion of O'Donnell the same day Powers gave his affidavit. It's unclear if Powers felt pressured and was interrupted by Specter, or if Powers had ear-lier talked to someone else higher in authority. Thom had the impression that Powers had indicated that the pressure had come from someone on the level or Warren or Ford, but Thom wasn't sure.

When the story of what Powers and O'Donnell really saw started to break on June 15, 1975, *Chicago Tribune* reporter Bob Wiedrich said "the FBI warned O'Donnell and Powers that" if they said what they really saw, it "could lead to an international incident." So, "for the good of the country and global tranquility, the FBI is alleged to have told the two aides, it would be better if they made no mention of their suspicions to the Warren Com-mission." O'Donnell denied the published story at the time, so it remained mostly forgotten. Still, one has to wonder what would have happened to

Specter's single-bullet theory if Powers and Donnell hadn't gone along with whoever got them to change their testimony.

Many more researchers helped us make sense of what Powers and other Kennedy associates told us. Peter Dale Scott has specialized in unraveling the complexities of covert operations, Cuban exiles, and organized crime. Gus Russo was able to get many CIA veterans to give him their version of events. Walt Brown's *Deep Politics Quarterly* was always a fountain of valuable information, as was Jerry Rose's *The Fourth Decade*. A. J. Weberman's quest for documents, which he shares on the Web, was invaluable. Tampa residents Frank DeBenedictis and Chris Barrows helped us with the Tampa side of the investigation. Carlos in Atlanta gave us many insights into Cuban heritage, language, and what it was like in Bay of Pigs era Miami.

This book couldn't exist without the folks at Carroll & Graf and their parent company, Avalon Publishing, especially Charlie Winton. His interest and support over the years have been extraordinary, and it seemed fated that he would be the one to finally publish this book. It was a massive effort to which many in the company contributed, especially publisher Will Balliett, Mike Walters, Vince Kunkemueller, Gayle Hart, Maria Fernandez, Denise Silva, Sabrina Young, Karen Auerbach, and Linda Kosarian. I learned a lot from my excellent editor, Walter Bode; and copyeditor Phil Gaskill was indispensable, not only for the text of the book, but in helping compile the extensive endnotes as well.

Susan Barrows, Louise Hartmann, and Barbara Winton all put up with a great deal for a long time, and we are very grateful. This book wouldn't be possible without the love and support of my father, Clyde Waldron, and both of our families, who have been extremely understanding over the years. Jim Steranko's interest and ideas were a steady source of encouragement. There are too many supportive friends to acknowledge, but these three are no longer with us to thank in person: Owen, Rip, and Tom.

The following people all helped in one way or another: Abraham Bolden, Jake Shepard, David Scheim, Senator Gary Hart, Gerald Hemming, the Colorado School of Mines Alumni Association, Nigel Turner, Pierre Salinger, Jim Allison, Ronald Goldfarb, Tom Kennelly, Marvin Loewy, John Diuguid, Richard Goodwin, Antonio Veciana, Carlos Bringuier, George Michael Evica, Carl Hiaasen, Carol Hewitt, Alan Rogers, Lisa Pease, Jim Olivier, Michael Griffin, Doug Smith, and Chris Crane. Those whose work we found especially helpful include: Michael Beschloss, Dr. Cyril Wecht, David Corn, Harold Weisberg, David Lifton, Josiah Thompson, Ed Becker, Charles Rappleye, Warren Hinckle, Dick Russell, Michael Benson, Bradley Ayers, Rex Bradford, and Jerry P. Shinley.

Finally, thanks are due to Forrest J. Ackerman, Stan Lee, and Ray Bradbury for their encouragement and inspiration over the years.

Lamar Waldron
Thom Hartmann
October 14, 2005

Just because we're grateful to someone or have extensively cited their work, it doesn't necessarily mean that we agree with certain conclusions they may have expressed in the past or hold now.